African American National Biography

African American National Biography

SECOND EDITION

HENRY LOUIS GATES JR.

EVELYN BROOKS HIGGINBOTHAM

Editors in Chief

VOLUME 4: DICKSON, AMANDA AMERICA – GAYE, MARVIN

OXFORD
UNIVERSITY PRESS

OXFORD
UNIVERSITY PRESS

Oxford University Press is a department of the University of Oxford.
It furthers the University's objective of excellence in research, scholarship,
and education by publishing worldwide.

Oxford New York
Auckland Cape Town Dar es Salaam Hong Kong Karachi
Kuala Lumpur Madrid Melbourne Mexico City Nairobi
New Delhi Shanghai Taipei Toronto

With offices in
Argentina Austria Brazil Chile Czech Republic France Greece
Guatemala Hungary Italy Japan Poland Portugal Singapore
South Korea Switzerland Thailand Turkey Ukraine Vietnam

Published in the United States of America by
Oxford University Press
198 Madison Avenue, New York, NY 10016

Library of Congress Cataloging-in-Publication Data
African American national biography / editors in chief Henry Louis Gates Jr., Evelyn Brooks Higginbotham. – 2nd ed.
p. cm.
Includes bibliographical references and index.
ISBN 978-0-19-999036-8 (volume 1; hdbk.); ISBN 978-0-19-999037-5 (volume 2; hdbk.); ISBN 978-0-19-999038-2 (volume 3; hdbk.); ISBN 978-0-19-999039-9 (volume 4; hdbk.); ISBN 978-0-19-999040-5 (volume 5; hdbk.); ISBN 978-0-19-999041-2 (volume 6; hdbk.); ISBN 978-0-19-999042-9 (volume 7; hdbk.); ISBN 978-0-19-999043-6 (volume 8; hdbk.); ISBN 978-0-19-999044-3 (volume 9; hdbk.); ISBN 978-0-19-999045-0 (volume 10; hdbk.); ISBN 978-0-19-999046-7 (volume 11; hdbk.); ISBN 978-0-19-999047-4 (volume 12; hdbk.); ISBN 978-0-19-992077-8 (12-volume set; hdbk.)
1. African Americans – Biography – Encyclopedias. 2. African Americans – History – Encyclopedias. I. Gates, Henry Louis. II. Higginbotham, Evelyn Brooks, 1945-
E185.96.A4466 2012
920'.009296073 – dc23
[B]
2011043281

1 3 5 7 9 8 6 4 2
Printed in the United States of America
on acid-free paper

African American National Biography

CONTINUED

Dickson, Amanda America (20 Nov. 1849–11 June 1893), slave and later a wealthy black woman, was born in Hancock County, Georgia, the daughter of Julia Frances Lewis Dickson, a slave, and David Dickson, a wealthy, white Georgian planter, businessman, and slave owner. Amanda America Dickson's birth resulted from the rape of thirteen-year-old Julia Dickson by David Dickson, the forty-year-old son of the slave owner Elizabeth Sholars Dickson. After she was weaned, Amanda was taken from her mother and placed in the home of her white owner and grandmother, Elizabeth Sholars Dickson. Julia, on the other hand, remained in living quarters outside the Dickson house. Until her white grandmother's death in 1864, Amanda lived with her in the same bedroom where she spent most of her time "studying her books and doing whatever she was told to do" (Leslie, *Woman of Color*, 42). According to the Dickson family's African American oral history, tutors were frequently brought to the house to teach Amanda.

Much of what is known about the relationship between Amanda and her father is passed down orally from her great-granddaughter Kate Dickson McCoy-Lee. McCoy-Lee suggested that Amanda was never considered by her white father as a slave or even as black. According to McCoy-Lee, David Dickson often pampered and spoiled his daughter. Amanda learned to play the piano, dress impeccably, and behave like a lady in every sense. In the Dickson's household, Amanda "learned the skills and manners appropriate to the family's class" (*Woman of Color*, 44). Oddly, some white Dickson family members offered a different portrayal of Amanda's position in the white Dickson family circle. David Dickson's nephews reported that Amanda carried out tasks normally performed by servants such as "sweeping the floor." Some have speculated that white family members regarded her as they would a "pet," as something "to love and spoil" (*Woman of Color*, 43).

Though Amanda lived within the standards of white privilege and learned the manners and behaviors of a "lady," neither her white father nor her grandmother freed her. Under state law, slave owners could manumit their property, but only if they immediately relocated them beyond the state's borders. Perhaps their reluctance to see Amanda leave their plantation home explains the Dickson's refusal to emancipate her. Some years later, David Dickson commented that he thought it was his duty to care for his daughter.

In 1864 Amanda's white grandmother died, which left David Dickson in charge of Amanda. Julia, still in the role of housekeeper, was brought into the Dickson's house to live and help with Amanda. Because of Amanda's position as David Dickson's daughter, it was common for slaves on the plantation, including her father and slave mother Julia, to call her "Miss Amanda" or "Miss Mandy." It is not known how Julia responded to Amanda being called "Miss Mandy or being raised in the white Dickson's house. In 1866 David Dickson arranged the marriage of his daughter, now freed by the Thirteenth Amendment, to his white first cousin Charles Eubanks. Because Georgia law prohibited marriages between blacks and whites, the couple married in Boston. The marriage produced two sons, Julian Henry Dickson (1866–1937) and Charles

Amanda America Dickson in a photograph provided by her great-granddaughter, Joan Jackson. (Austin/Thompson Collection.)

Green Dickson (1870–c. 1910). In 1870 Dickson's marriage abruptly ended when she returned to her father's home with her two sons declaring, "I want to live with you, Pappie" (*Woman of Color*, 64). The cause of the break up is unclear, although one source speculated that Amanda refused to be controlled by her white husband (Leslie, *Southern Women*, 80). There is, however, no record of a formal divorce. Six years later, at the age of twenty-seven, Amanda Dickson left her sons with her father to attend the Normal School of Atlanta University. According to Julia Frances Dickson, Amanda remained there until 1878, and then she returned to her father's house in Hancock County.

In 1885 David Dickson died at the age of seventy-six. In his will, he left the majority of his estate to his daughter and her sons, making her "the richest colored woman in the United States" (*Woman of Color*, 107). Because Amanda Dickson had been a slave, her father's relatives contested the will. They lost a lower court decision and then appealed to the Georgia Supreme Court. In September 1886, while waiting for the court's decision, Dickson took control of her business affairs and moved to a large expensive house in Augusta's elite white community. In June 1887, the state Supreme Court finally ruled in her favor, declaring that "the rights of each race are controlled and governed by the same enactments or principles of law, that is to say that whatever rights and privileges belonged to a bastard white child belonged to a mixed-race child as well" (*Woman of Color*, 102).

In October 1887, Amanda Dickson's younger son, Charles Green Dickson, married Kate Holsey of Augusta, Georgia, the daughter of Harriet and Bishop Lucius Henry Holsey of the African Methodist Episcopal (AME) Church. By 1900 Kate had divorced Charles Dickson for squandering his inheritance on horse racing and women, both black and white. After the divorce, Charles moved to Stockton, California, where he passed for white and was known as Fred V. Carlyle. He died in Stockton in 1912 at the age of forty.

On 14 July 1892 Amanda Dickson married light-skinned Nathan Toomer of Perry, Georgia. Toomer was wealthy and educated and later became the father of the Harlem Renaissance writer JEAN TOOMER.

In 1893 Amanda traveled to Baltimore to witness the trial of her son Charles Dickson, who had attempted to kidnap Mamie Toomer, his stepsister, with whom he had become infatuated. Following the hearing, Amanda returned to Augusta on 7 June 1893, but during the trip she became ill after her private railroad car was disconnected from the train and left on a side track in the sweltering summer sun. A few days later, Amanda America died at her Augusta home a victim of complications from heat exhaustion.

After Amanda's death, Julia Dickson, continued to live in Sparta, where she died some time after 7 January 1914.

FURTHER READING

Leslie, Kent Anderson. "Amanda America Dickson: An Elite Mulatto Lady in Nineteenth-Century Georgia," in *Southern Women: Histories and Identities* (1992).

Leslie, Kent Anderson. *Woman of Color, Daughter of Privilege: Amanda America Dickson, 1849–1893* (1995).

LYNETTE D. MYLES

Dickson, Moses (5 Apr. 1824–28 Nov. 1901), African Methodist Episcopal (AME) minister, activist, and Freemason, was born in Cincinnati, Ohio, to Robert and Hannah Dickson. Little is known of his youth. His Virginia-born parents died before he reached adulthood, though he was able to attend school for a time and learned barbering. Accounts of Dickson's early adulthood blend myth and revolutionary promise; the root of most such accounts appears to be anonymous reports included in late-nineteenth-century black Masonic and neo-Masonic ritual books that were either written or influenced heavily by Dickson. These reports claim that Dickson found work aboard a steamer in his late teens, traveled across the South, saw the horrors of slavery, and began raising a hidden army of slaves awaiting his call to revolt. The army supposedly grew as Dickson interacted with free blacks in the Midwest, which he reportedly traversed between 1844 and 1846. By the 1850s, there were supposedly several thousand "Knights of Liberty," but, on the verge of beginning the revolution, Dickson supposedly foresaw the Civil War and decided to hold back.

Dickson married Mary Elisabeth Peters Butcher, a young widow and the daughter of a German stone-cutter and a free black woman with ties to the wealthy Choteau family, on 5 October 1848 in Galena, Illinois. The young couple settled in St. Louis the following year and had a daughter in December of 1860, Mamie Augusta (who would later marry Harry Halyard Hayden—about whom little is known—and, c.1890 presumably after Hayden's death, the Canadian-born carpenter James Robinson), soon after. In St. Louis, Dickson seems to have continued barbering and community activism centering on education, economic uplift, and underground abolitionism. He subscribed to *Frederick Douglass's Paper* in the mid-1850s, and began a long association with the African Methodist Episcopal Church. Biographers who would later chronicle his life for Masonic publications claim he saw action as a Union soldier in the Civil War, but proof of such has not yet been found. He was in St. Louis in 1862, and wrote the *AME Christian Recorder*, a long report on St. Paul's Chapel Sunday School (of which he was secretary) that was published on 3 May 1862. The *Recorder* named him a handful of times over the next few years, reported that he was named a district deputy in the neo-Masonic Independent Grand Tabernacles of Bands of Love and Charity (a rank he shared with the Boston black abolitionist John S. Rock), and printed two of his letters in 1866.

He soon grew into a figure of national import within the church; when he visited Philadelphia in 1868, he was invited to speak at Mother Bethel AME Church. He was ordained a deacon at the August 1868 meeting of the Missouri Annual Conference of the African Methodist Episcopal Church. He was quite active in the church, attended its conventions, and helped formulate their governing rules, and among his activities disseminated copies of the church's paper, the *Christian Recorder*, to colleagues in Missouri. By the next year he had established Carondelet (outside of St. Louis) as his base. There he led a drive to complete an impressive new church—one that was destroyed by arson only a month after it opened; he then led the rebuilding process. His "circuit" gradually grew and later included charges in Hannibal and St. Joseph, though he maintained close ties to the St. Louis area. In 1870 he helped organize the first national AME camp meeting, and he continued to be a key representative of the Midwest in the AME Church until his death.

His community activism—at the local, state, and national levels—continued too. Beginning in 1864 Dickson was a regular at the Missouri Republican Convention, and he was deeply supportive of the Radical Republican agenda. He also worked on a national level with figures ranging from the abolitionist George T. Downing to the editor and activist Philip Bell in the fights for the ratification of the Fifteenth Amendment and broader civil rights. He was an early supporter of Missouri's Lincoln Institute (later Lincoln University) and helped raise money for Wilberforce University, served as an elector-at-large for Ulysses S. Grant in 1872, was active in fights for black suffrage, was a leader among the state's black Freemasons, and distinguished himself in combating racial prejudice within the Masonic fraternity. He also founded the Knights and Daughters of Tabor and the Heroines of Jericho, two neo-Masonic organizations, wrote and published the rituals for both, and shepherded both their growth and their engagement with the community. Both organizations remain active at the beginning of the twenty-first century.

Dickson's combination of religious, political, and community ties placed him in a powerful position among Missouri's (and especially St. Louis's) black community, and so he was the logical choice to chair the Refugee Board, one of the central groups that provided aid to the massive number of Exodusters who passed through St. Louis in the late 1870s. In 1892 Dickson again took on a major leadership role—this time working with Missourians from James Milton Turner to John Boyer Vashon in a statewide push for "Lamentation Day," held on 31 May 1892 to commemorate blacks who were victims of racial violence. Dickson died at his St. Louis home, and funeral services were massive; they included, among other tributes, memorial services by the Heroines of Jericho that were chaired by Dickson's friend, the slave narrative author LUCY DELANEY.

A major figure at the state and local levels Dickson remains understudied, though his combination of religious, political, and Masonic activism make him an important figure in the second half of the nineteenth century.

FURTHER READING

Several of Dickson's letters appeared in the *Christian Recorder*.

Dickson, Moses. *Manual of the International Order of Twelve of Knights and Daughters of Tabor* (1891).

O'Brien, William Patrick. "Moses Dickson." *Dictionary of Missouri Biography*, eds. Lawrence O. Christensen, et. al. (1999).

Pipkin, J. J. "Rev. Moses Dickson," in *The Story of a Rising Race* (1902).

ERIC GARDNER

Diddley, Bo (20 Dec. 1928–2 June 2008), guitarist, songwriter, and musical innovator, was born Otha Ellas Bates in McComb, Mississippi, the only child of Ethel Wilson, a sharecropper in her teens, and Eugene Bates. He was raised with a number of other children by Ethel's first cousin, Gussie McDaniel. When McDaniel's husband died in 1934, the family moved to Chicago as part of the Great Migration, and the young boy's surname was changed to McDaniel to allow him to enter the public school system. There, he received the name Bo Diddley,an appellation whose origin has been variously explained by an array of stories. (Diddley himself claims not to know the origin, and downplays a possible connection to the diddley bow—a single string attached to a wall or house frame and played with a bottleneck slide or nail—stating that he never played one.) Diddley showed an aptitude for music early on; he studied the violin from the age of eight until he was fifteen under a classical instructor, O. W. Frederick, at the Ebenezer Missionary Baptist Church. He also took up drums, and he received his first guitar on his twelfth birthday. Owing to his large hands, he was not able to treat the fretboard delicately and came to approach the instrument something like a drum set, driving material forward by virtue of rhythm rather than melody. He began his first band, a trio named the Hipsters and later the Langley Alley Cats, after he dropped out of high school, and he supported his musical endeavors by working in a grocery store and a picture frame factory, in addition to being an elevator operator.

Bo Diddley tunes his guitar at a concert near Bronson, Florida, 18 February 2006. (AP Images.)

Songwriting came early and easily to Diddley, who wrote his first piece, "I Don't Want No Lyin' Woman," at age sixteen. In an effort to counteract the noise in the venues where he performed, Diddley built an amplifier by hand. He intuitively understood from the start that his style would conjoin volume and rhythm, and therefore, early on, he enlisted the assistance of a neighbor, Jerome Green, on maracas to underscore the beat. Together with Green, the harmonica player "Billy Boy" Arnold, and others, Diddley established a reputation in the local clubs of Chicago.

The sound they produced proved to be unique, for Diddley amalgamated a body of musical practices that originated in the rhythms of the church, the percussive speech patterns of the street, and the "shout mode" that harked back to drum-playing traditions in Africa. He combined that rhythmic approach along with a declamatory style in his vocals that prefigured rap. Acutely aware of his innovations, Diddley routinely objected to efforts to label this sound or to single out its influences: "Guys kind of piss me off trying to name what I'm doing, and you know, they don't want to accept what I tell them, so they want to use their own thing so they can title it. But I do know what it is, and a lot of times I tell people I don't, I just play it. But I know" (*Chess*, CH3-19502, 1990, 7). No matter what the source or the name of his musical style, Diddley etched a singular path by making his band stress rhythm over melody, and he frequently employed repetitious, often childlike words, drawn from street games or from the verbal one-upmanship associated with signifying, words used more for their sound than their sense. Diddley developed a "shave-and-a-haircut—two bits" sequence of rhythmic accents that audiences indelibly associate with his music. In 1946, he married Ethel Mac Smith and they had two children before the marriage ended in divorce. In order to break into the record business in 1955, Diddley, still performing under the name Ellas McDaniel, made a demonstration record of two songs: "Uncle John" and "I'm a Man." He took them to several local companies, including the black-owned Vee Jay Records, that turned him down. He then turned to Chess Records, owned by Leonard and Phil Chess. Established in 1947, the label initially made its mark with blues, recording such titans of the genre as MUDDY WATERS, HOWLIN' WOLF, and LITTLE WALTER JACOBS. The Chess brothers were on the lookout for artists who could sell to a broad, not necessarily racially segregated audience. They were about to succeed with CHUCK BERRY, and they heard in McDaniel something that could be as marketable.

Inadvertently, while performing "Uncle John," the group proclaimed, "Bo Diddley." At first, Leonard Chess worried that this name might defame blacks. When he was assured it would not, the title of the track became "Bo Diddley," and a career was launched. Both sides of the single took off, and within weeks they occupied the number one and two spots on the *Billboard* jukebox charts as well as rising on the *Billboard* list of what disk jockeys were playing. These songs clearly appealed to both black and white listeners, and therefore, in the parlance of the music business, they "crossed over."

A string of successful singles followed, including "You Don't Love Me" (1955), "Mona" (1957), and "You Can't Judge a Book by the Cover" (1962). Diddley consolidated his success with a riveting stage presence. His homemade square-shaped guitar and boosted amplification captivated audiences, as did the manner in which his behavior mirrored the sexual braggadocio of his lyrics. He strutted across the stage like the legendary bluesman CHARLEY PATTON, playing his guitar with his teeth, behind his back, over his head, and between his legs. He further upped the ante by adding, on more than one occasion, a female second guitarist, giving her such names as Lady Bo and the Duchess.

However, despite the galvanizing nature of his material and performance, Diddley's rise to the top of the charts was brief. With the appearance of the Beatles in the United States in 1964, many black artists associated with early rock and roll fell out of favor or were treated condescendingly as objects of nostalgia. Diddley continued to record for the Chess label until 1974, yet few of his albums or singles achieved commercial success.

Lamentably, Diddley found himself not only toppled from the charts but also convinced that he never received his due financial reward, either from Chess Records or from the companies that subsequently owned their recordings. He was relegated to Oldies venues for much of the 1970s, 1980s, and early 1990s, even though countless musicians and writers applauded his material and credited its influence upon rock and roll. Some of his songs became part of the permanent repertoire of American popular music, but the concrete rewards for that achievement were few.

Slowly, the tide turned. Tributes on the part of younger musicians led to renewed media exposure. Diddley appeared in the EDDIE MURPHY film comedy *Trading Places* (1983) and in a 1989 Nike commercial with the sports figure BO JACKSON. Honorific organizations across the musical spectrum honored him. Diddley was inducted into the Rock and Roll Hall of Fame in 1987, and received the *Guitar Player* magazine Lifetime Achievement Award in 1990 and the Pioneer Award from the Rhythm and Blues Foundation in 1996. He accepted a lifetime achievement award at the 1998 Grammy Awards and was inducted into the Grammy Hall of Fame.

But awards do not pay the bills, and Diddley continued to perform into his seventies to keep his legacy alive. The influence and magnitude of that achievement cannot be underestimated. He codified a rhythm that has become an indelible feature of American vernacular music. His guitar style can be heard in genres as broad as rock and roll and heavy metal, and his use of technology to augment the impact of his material set in motion popular music's long-standing attachment to volume. Diddley's musical influence is clearly seen in the careers of such performers as Elvis Presley, Buddy Holly, and the Rolling Stones. Furthermore, his playful and yet sophisticated use of language and his declamatory delivery have made him one of the forefathers of rap. In 2007 Bo Diddley suffered a stroke while touring. In August the same year he suffered a heart attack. Ten months later, Diddley died from heart failure in his home in Archer, Florida.

FURTHER READING

Cohodas, Nadine. *Spinning Blues into Gold: The Chess Brothers and the Legendary Chess Records* (2000).

Palmer, Robert. *Rock and Roll: An Unruly History* (1995).

White, George R. *Bo Diddley: Living Legend* (1998).

DISCOGRAPHY

The Chess Box (CH3-19502).

Obituary: *New York Times*, 3 June 2008

DAVID SANJEK

Diggs, Charles Coles, Jr. (2 Dec. 1922–24 Aug. 1998), United States Congressman, was born in Detroit, Michigan, to Charles Diggs Sr., a mortician, and Mamie Ethel Jones Diggs, a homemaker. As the product of a middle-class family, he learned politics at the knee of his father. Charles Sr. owned a mortuary, an insurance company, and an ambulance company. More importantly, Charles Sr. was very active politically, eventually serving in the Michigan State Senate. Detroit was also a major destination for African Americans escaping the South during the Great Migration, and thousands relocated to Detroit in the search for jobs and security. The combination of his father and the tectonic shifts taking place in Detroit seemed to have prompted the younger Diggs to excel academically. He graduated from Miller High School in 1940 and briefly attended the University of Michigan. He transferred, however, to Fisk University after a couple of years. While he was at Fisk, the world around him was changing as the United States became a participant in World War II. He served in the Army-Air Forces from early 1943 to the summer of 1945, eventually reaching the rank of second lieutenant in 1944. Following his service in segregated units in Alabama, Diggs returned to Detroit, where he attended the Wayne College of Mortuary Science. He graduated in 1946 and began work at his father's mortuary business. Diggs had six children during his lifetime and was married four times.

Charles C. Diggs Jr. Democratic representative from Detroit, 15 November 1972. (Library of Congress/Congressional Portrait Collection.)

Fresh out of the service and school, Diggs took an avid interest in public affairs by conducting a local radio program devoted to public issues. Another major reason for the program was to defend against allegations that his father was corrupt. It was alleged that the elder Diggs had accepted bribes while in office. The scandal destroyed the elder Diggs's career and resulted in his serving time in prison until 1950. Even though his father won office after his release, the legislature's decision to refuse him entry prompted the younger Diggs to run for the seat. He won and served for three years, 1951–1954. However, the lure of life in the state capital was not enough to keep Diggs content for long.

In 1954, Diggs ran for and won a seat in the United States House of Representatives for the predominantly African American 13th district in Detroit. In doing so, Diggs defeated an entrenched Democratic congressman. Diggs was the first African American elected to the Congress from the state of Michigan and just one of three in Congress at that time. Once in office, Diggs, like most African American politicians of the day, was interested in securing civil rights for all Americans. He served on the Veteran's Affairs committee and the Committee on Interior and Insular Affairs. He took a strong interest in human rights beyond the shores of America, as evidenced by his service on the Foreign Affairs committee. Arguably, his most important political interest was protecting African Americans from the searing experience of racism and Jim Crow. He supported the prosecution of those responsible for the lynching and murder of teenager Emmett Till in Mississippi. Diggs, however, earned particular praise for traveling to Mississippi (his father's birthplace) to attend the trial, and for highlighting that the indignities of segregation applied even to him, a member of the U.S. House. Diggs pushed for both civil rights and voting rights legislation, notably in the 1957 Civil Rights Act. Also he became a leading opponent of the apartheid regime in South Africa.

Diggs was not only a fervent supporter of African Americans but also a skilled operator in the halls of Congress. He learned from his mentors, Adam Clayton Powell Jr. of New York and William Dawson of Illinois, the importance of seniority and committee memberships. Diggs played a pivotal role in developing the Democratic Select Committee in 1969 to bring unity and collective purpose to African American members of Congress. The very next year the Congressional Black Caucus was founded, with Diggs as its first chair. Ultimately the CBC became one of the most prominent and powerful voting blocs in Congress, but had only a handful of members at its founding. He also chaired the House Subcommittee on Africa and the District of Columbia Committee. Diggs's criticism of the retrenchment of civil rights under President Richard Nixon earned him a place on Nixon's infamous "enemies list."

Diggs's career ended in controversy, however. In 1978, he was charged with accepting kickbacks from staff members. He was convicted in October 1978 of falsifying public documents and mail fraud. He always claimed he was innocent, but the damage was done. His career was never the same, and he gave up his committee chairmanships. Subsequently, Diggs was censured by the House, a less serious punishment than expulsion. He vacated his seat on 3 June 1980 after twenty-five years in office. Returning to his roots, Diggs went back into the mortuary business and tried to get elected to the Maryland legislature but lost. Congressman Charles Coles Diggs Jr. died on 24 August 1998 in Washington, DC, from a stroke.

FURTHER READING

U.S. Congress, House, Committee on House Administration of The U.S. House of Representatives. *Black Americans in Congress, 1870–2007* (2008).

Obituary: *Washington Post*, 26 Aug. 1998.

DARYL A. CARTER

Diggs, Ellen Irene (13 Apr. 1906–14 Mar. 1998), anthropologist, educator, sociologist, was born Ellen Irene Diggs in Monmouth, Illinois, to Henry Charles Diggs and Alice Scott. Her working-class parents lived in a community of about ten thousand, about two hundred of whom were black. They supported their precocious child, one of five, who read voraciously and achieved the highest grade average in her school. Recognizing her ability, the Monmouth Chamber of Commerce awarded her a scholarship to attend Monmouth College in Monmouth, Illinois. In 1924 she transferred to the University of Minnesota, which offered a far larger number of courses, where she majored in sociology and minored in psychology. She received an AB degree in 1928 and then attended Atlanta University, a premier institution for the education of African Americans founded in 1865 and located in Atlanta, Georgia. The institution began to offer graduate degrees in 1929 and in 1933, under the direction of W. E. B. DuBois, Diggs received an M.A. in Sociology, the first offered by the university. The sociology department had an applied focus and offered courses that evaluated "the American Negro Problem" including: "Karl Marx and the Negro," "Research in Social Problems," and "Seminar in Sociological Problems." Diggs's thesis was titled "A Study of Delinquency Among Negro Girls in Atlanta."

After graduation Diggs was employed at Atlanta University as DuBois's secretary and research assistant from 1932 to 1942. Among other duties Diggs provided considerable research support for many of his works, including *Black Reconstruction* (1935), *Black Folk: Then and Now* (1939), and *Dusk of Dawn* (1940). Some critical sources suggest that she and DuBois cofounded *Phylon: A Review of Race and Culture*, with DuBois serving as editor in chief. However, it is unclear whether Diggs was an official cofounder of the distinguished journal as the first issue of *Phylon*, published in 1940, does not note her contributions. A 1943 issue officially noted Diggs for the first time on its editorial page as the journal's circulation manager. However, as DuBois's secretary and research assistant, and as a distinguished graduate of Atlanta University's sociology department, it is likely that Diggs significantly contributed to the founding of this eminent journal.

Beginning in 1942 Diggs embarked on the first of many travels outside of the United States to study and analyze the histories and cultures of African peoples throughout the Diaspora. She attended the University of Havana, where she studied Spanish and in February 1943 she was awarded a maintenance fellowship from the Institute of International

Education to continue her studies from 1943–1944 in the field of anthropology. In 1944 Diggs received her doctorate in anthropology from the University of Havana. She was the first African American woman to earn a Ph.D. in that field and the first to do so at her institution. Following CAROLINE STEWART BOND DAY, who completed a master of arts, she was the second woman to receive a graduate degree in anthropology. Diggs's doctoral research focused on the survival of West African customs in Cuba.

Diggs joined the faculty of Morgan State University in 1947. During her tenure there she published numerous articles and reviews on race and culture in the United States and Latin America. Many of them appeared in *Phylon*, *Crisis*, and the *Journal of Negro History*. Diggs's mainstream publishing opportunities were limited by a resistance to traditional anthropological scholarship conducted by African American women. However, Diggs skillfully employed scholarly reviews as a critical medium through which to challenge anthropological, historical, and sociological scholarship that perpetuated African and African American stereotypes. In addition, these reviews and articles were a medium for Diggs to assert her own theories regarding race and culture.

In 1951 Diggs's research interests moved outside the African diaspora and she participated in the New York University Israel Workshop. She traveled throughout Israel and studied its culture, government, and other social institutions. In 1953 she published an article titled "Israel" in *Phylon* describing the rapid cultural changes in Israel during the early 1950s caused by the effect of mass immigration following establishment of the State of Israel in 1948. She theorized that a distinctive Israeli culture would emerge from the diverse ethnic populations. As in her research on West African customs in Cuba, Diggs remained concerned with analyzing complex cultural change.

She retired from Morgan State College in 1976 but continued to be involved in foreign research projects in Cuba and remained active in numerous academic associations, including the American Anthropological Association and the Society for Applied Anthropologists. In 1983 Diggs published her best-known work, *Black Chronology: From 4000 B.C. to the Abolition of the Slave Trade*. Edited by Charles T. Davis and HENRY LOUIS GATES JR. *Black Chronology* is a singular achievement in chronicling African and African American histories and dispelling long held myths about African and African American history and culture. Diggs is among a number of African American female and male pioneers in American anthropology. ZORA NEALE HURSTON is perhaps best known, but Diggs's body of work illustrates a long-standing commitment to rigorous anthropological scholarship that addressed both broad and specific themes concerning race, culture, and history in the African diaspora and beyond.

FURTHER READING

Bolles, A. Lynn. "Ellen Irene Diggs: Coming of Age in Atlanta, Havana and Baltimore," in *African American Pioneers in Anthropology*, eds. Ira E. Harrison and Faye V. Harrison (1999).

Bolles, A. Lynn. "Seeking the Ancestors: Forging a Black Feminist Tradition in Anthropology," in *Black Feminist Anthropology: Theory, Politics, Praxis, and Poetics*, ed. Irma McClaurin (2001).

JENNIFER L. FREEMAN MARSHALL

Dihigo, Martin (25 May 1905–22 May 1971), baseball player, was born in Matanzas, Cuba. Little is known about his parents or his early life. Dihigo's professional baseball career began in 1922 with the Havana Reds when he was just seventeen years old. The following year he made his first trip to the United States to play in the inaugural season of the Eastern Colored League. He was signed by Alejandro Pompez, owner of the Cuban Stars, one of six teams in the new league. Playing initially as a middle infielder, at second base and shortstop, he was immediately recognized by his peers for his skill, ability, and grace on the field. He developed quickly as a hitter. Dihigo returned to the United States each summer to play Negro League baseball. He remained with the Cuban Stars through the 1927 season. In 1926 he led the Eastern Colored League in home runs while posting a .421 average, and he opened the 1927 season in spectacular fashion, driving in nine runs with two grand slams and one solo home run during an opening day contest against the Hilldales. He finished the season hitting .370 and tied for the league home run title.

During this period Dihigo was returning home to Cuba each winter. Playing in Havana he hit .413 during the winter of 1926–1927 and .415 the following winter. Dihigo left the Eastern Colored League in 1928 to play with the independent Homestead Grays. In 1929 he was traded to the Philadelphia Hilldales of the American Negro League. By this time Dihigo had become one of the biggest names in black baseball and earned a team high salary of four hundred dollars per month; this put him in the top 10 percent of player salaries in the Negro Leagues during this period. He finished the 1928 season second in the league in home runs with a .386 batting average. In 1930 Dihigo returned to the Cuban Stars and hit .393 for the season.

It was during the 1930s that Dihigo began making more appearances as a pitcher. In 1931 with the Hilldales his pitching record was 6-1. After leaving the Hilldales, Dihigo appeared briefly with the Baltimore Black Sox in 1931, after which he spent three seasons in the Venezuelan League. Salaries in Latin America were generally higher than in the United States for black players during this period. His pitching in the Venezuela League was outstanding. In 1932 he pitched a no-hitter, and in 1933 he compiled a record of 6-0 with a 0.15 ERA.

Dihigo returned to the United States in 1935 as player-manager for the Negro National League's New York Cubans. That season he received the most votes of any outfielder in the balloting for the annual East-West All-Star game. Illustrating his versatility he played center field and pitched during the contest. That season, with a .372 average and a 7-3 pitching record, he led his team to the second-half title in the Negro National League. Dihigo was the winning pitcher in game one and game four of the championship series, but the Cubans lost the series to the Pittsburgh Crawfords, four games to three.

That winter Dihigo returned to Cuba as player-manager of the Santa Clara team. At age thirty he posted an 11-2 pitching record and won the batting title with a .358 average, and his team won the Cuban League championship. The potent talent in Cuba and other Latin American countries made his numbers all the more impressive. Dihigo returned to the United States with the New York Cubans for the 1936 season. In 1937 he played in the Dominican Republic with Aquilas Cibaenas, recording a 6-4 pitching record and a team-leading .351 batting average.

In 1938 Dihigo went to Mexico to play and he made his presence felt immediately in the Mexican League. In September 1938 Dihigo pitched the first no-hitter in Mexican League history. He ended the 1938 season leading the league in hitting (.387) and in pitching (18-2, 0.90 ERA). Dihigo played in Mexico through the 1944 season. Well into his thirties, he continued to be a dominant player. In 1942 he led the league with 211 strikeouts and a 2.53 ERA. In 1943 he again led the league in strikeouts (134). He finished his Mexican League career with a lifetime pitching record of 119-57. In Cuba he finished with a lifetime record of 115-60. In 1945 Dihigo returned to the United States for his final season of professional baseball. Although he only hit .204 for the season with a 1-2 pitching record, he was selected to pitch in the 1945 Negro League East-West All-Star game.

Dihigo was a national hero in Cuba. After retiring from baseball he was involved in radio play-by-play broadcasting. After Fidel Castro came to power he appointed Dihigo minister of sports in Cuba, a position Dihigo held until his death in Cienfuegos, Cuba.

During the course of his career Dihigo played every position on the field and played it well. Because of his command and proficiency at each position, many historians consider him the best all-around baseball player in the early twentieth century. Dihigo is also remembered fondly in every country where he played. He has been called the most versatile man ever to play baseball. In his homeland of Cuba he was known as "El Maestro," while in Mexico he was called "El Immortal." His career accomplishments earned his election to three halls of fame: the Cuban Baseball Hall of Fame in 1951, the Mexican Sports Hall of Fame in 1964, and the National Baseball Hall of Fame in Cooperstown, New York, in 1977.

FURTHER READING

Holway, John. *Blackball Stars* (1988).

Riley, Jim. *The Biographical Encyclopedia of the Negro Baseball Leagues* (1994).

This entry is taken from the *American National Biography* and is published here with the permission of the American Council of Learned Societies.

TODD BOLTON

Dill, Augustus Granville (1882–9 Mar. 1956), sociologist, business manager of *The Crisis*, curator, and musician, was born Augustus Granville Dill in Portsmouth, Ohio, to John Jackson and Elizabeth Stratton Dill. Having finished his secondary schooling at the age of seventeen, Dill briefly taught in Portsmouth before attending Atlanta University, where he earned his B.A. in 1906. Dill's extracurricular interests included playing the piano for the university choir and serving on the debating team. He earned a second B.A. at Harvard University in 1908 and an M.A. from Atlanta University on his return to Atlanta in the same year. There he was mentored by W. E. B. DuBois, whose post as associate professor of sociology Dill assumed when DuBois left Atlanta in 1910.

In 1913 DuBois persuaded Dill to move to New York and assume the responsibilities of business manager and editorial assistant of *The Crisis*. Although Dill had no professional training for such a position, he diligently contributed to the magazine's success. In his autobiographical *Dusk of Dawn*, DuBois acknowledges that Dill "gave to the work his utmost devotion and to him was due much of its phenomenal business success" (226). By 1919 the circulation of *The Crisis* had reached 104,000.

In 1920 Dill, DuBois, and Jessie Fauset published *Brownies' Book*, a culturally affirming magazine for

African American children, intended in part as a reaction to the negative portrayal of black people in D. W. Griffith's popular film, *Birth of a Nation* (1915). Although well produced *Brownies' Book* was financially unsuccessful and closed after two years of publication.

DuBois and Dill collaborated on other projects, including four books: *The College-Bred Negro* (1911), *The Common School and the Negro American* (1912), *The Negro American Artisan* (1912), and *Morals and Manners among Negro Americans* (1915). While working on *The Crisis* and *Brownies' Book*, Dill joined the Intercollegiate Liberal League, a group that fostered debate of contemporary political issues among college students. He urged the members of the league to consider how racial discrimination and intimidation at the polls were contributing to the ongoing disenfranchisement of African Americans. At the league's meeting at Harvard in 1921, Dill is quoted in the *New York Times* as dismissing as "foolish" any "talk about industrial or political democracy so long as you ignore the 12,000,000 Negroes in the United States."

While living in New York, Dill enthusiastically immersed himself in the arts. His talent as a pianist and organist enabled him to accompany noteworthy performers in concert. Dill also participated in cultural events at the 135th Street Library, a well-known meeting place for the artists, writers, and intellectuals of the Harlem Renaissance. In August 1921 Dill organized an important exhibition of art works by black artists at this venue. There Dill was sometimes seen as an eccentric figure. After a lecture by Carl Van Doren, for example, Dill curled up on the speaker's table to ask questions. Such outrageous behavior, along with his taste for fine clothing and his ever-present chrysanthemum buttonhole, was excused as dandyism. In 1928, however, Dill was arrested for engaging in homosexual sex in a subway bathroom, a venue commonly used by closeted men. The public exposure from the incident led DuBois to fire Dill from *The Crisis* and brought an end to the pair's longtime collaboration.

Subsequently Dill was unable to secure steady employment. He supported himself in New York by playing piano and organ (he once accompanied the singer Roland Hays in performance) and by running a bookstore. In 1952 he went to live with his sister, Mary Dill Broadus, in Louisville, Kentucky, with whom he was living when he died. Dill contributed most significantly to African American intellectual culture through his academic collaborations with DuBois and through his editorial work on *The Crisis*. His obituary in the *New York Times* acknowledged his important input to the NAACP through his management of its journal. In addition, he encouraged and enabled a celebration of African American identity and artistic expression and has become a symbol of gay culture during the Harlem Renaissance.

FURTHER READING

Chauncey, George. *Gay New York: Gender, Urban Culture, and the Making of the Gay Male World, 1890–1940* (1994).

Logan, Rayford W., and Michael R. Winston, eds. *Dictionary of American Negro Biography* (1982).

Schwarz, A. B. Christa. *Gay Voices of the Harlem Renaissance* (2003).

Wright, Earl. "The Atlanta Sociological Laboratory 1896–1924: A Historical Account of the First American School of Sociology," *Western Journal of Black Studies* (Fall 2002).

DENNIS GOUWS

Dinkins, David N. (10 July 1927–), mayor of New York City, was born David Norman Dinkins in Trenton, New Jersey, the first of two children of William H. Dinkins, a barbershop owner and real estate agent, and Sally (maiden name unknown), a domestic worker and manicurist. David's parents divorced when he was six years old, and he lived briefly with his mother after she moved to Harlem, New York, although he soon returned to Trenton to live with his father and stepmother, Lottie Dinkins (maiden name Hartgell), a high school English teacher.

After graduating from high school in Trenton, Dinkins became one of the first African Americans to serve in the U.S. Marine Corps, and he graduated magna cum laude in 1950 from Howard University, where he majored in mathematics. He graduated from Brooklyn Law School in 1956 and practiced law in New York City until 1975. Dinkins and his wife, Joyce Burroughs, whom he married in 1953, have two children.

Dinkins became involved in politics through his wife, the daughter of a Democratic ward leader in Harlem. He served one term in the New York state assembly, two years as president of the New York City Board of Elections, and ten years as the city clerk. When his close friend Percy Sutton resigned as Manhattan borough president in 1977, he encouraged Dinkins to try for the position. After three unsuccessful attempts, Dinkins was elected borough president in 1985. A quiet, unassuming politician throughout his long and generally undistinguished public career, he managed, even as Manhattan borough president, to remain largely invisible to New York City voters.

David Dinkins, former New York City mayor, speaks at the Children's Health Fund's 20th Anniversary Gala, 30 May 2007. (AP Images.)

Known as a stolid and courtly gentleman, but certainly not a dynamic or forceful leader, the sixty-two-year-old Dinkins surprised the political experts with his decision to challenge the incumbent mayor Edward Koch in 1989. The deterioration of race relations in New York City during the Koch years had accelerated during Koch's third term, and the local black press called for the election of the city's first black mayor. The racial unease plaguing the city intensified in the months preceding the August 1989 primary election, and Koch's responses to racially charged incidents seemed increasingly inadequate to many African Americans. Dinkins spoke about the need for racial rapprochement and promised to be a healer; he won the primary election with 50.8 percent of the vote to Koch's 42 percent. In the general election that followed, the Republicans fielded a strong candidate in Rudolph Giuliani, a well-known federal prosecutor who had indicted a long list of Mafia dons, crooked politicians, and corporate embezzlers. Giuliani conducted an aggressive campaign, promising New Yorkers a tough law-and-order administration, while Dinkins continued to emphasize his ability to bring the city together, to calm the roiling racial seas that seemed to be pounding the city from all sides. On 7 November 1989 a slender majority of the New York City electorate provided Dinkins with a 47,000-vote victory margin out of 1.9 million votes cast.

New York City's finances had been balanced over a precipice for decades, and Koch left his successor no shortage of worrisome dilemmas. The city's first black mayor inherited a billion-dollar deficit, with even greater fiscal problems on the horizon, as contracts would soon expire for 360,000 municipal employees. City officials counted 75,000 homeless in New York City, only 35,000 of whom found shelter nightly, and the city needed 250,000 more housing units. Schools, social agencies, and the health-care system lacked adequate resources. The closing of bridges, highways, and streets, as well as the frequent explosion of water mains, gave the impression that New York City's aged infrastructure was collapsing. Throughout his administration, Dinkins had to grapple with the intractable problem of how to balance the city's budget, satisfy the business community's demand for fiscal responsibility, and still find the resources to offer the costly social programs that much of his constituency and his own liberal beliefs demanded—all at a time when the federal government had reduced its largess to cities and the nation's economy remained mired in recession.

While struggling from year to year to manage the city's nettlesome financial problems, Dinkins also had to respond to a series of violent incidents that threatened to undermine the racial comity he had promised to nurture. On 18 January 1990, just seventeen days after Dinkins assumed office, an altercation between a Haitian American resident of the Flatbush section of Brooklyn and the Korean American owners of a neighborhood grocery store heightened racial tensions in the city. African Americans, led by AL SHARPTON, initiated a boycott of the store that lasted nearly a year and, as violence between blacks and Asians increased in Flatbush, critics accused Dinkins of being insensitive to the Asian immigrants.

The following year, three days of rioting erupted in the Crown Heights section of Brooklyn after a car driven by a Hasidic Jew accidentally struck and killed a black girl and seriously injured her brother. In retribution, an angry gang of black youths murdered a rabbinical student. The mayor tried unsuccessfully to mediate between African Americans and Hasidim in Crown Heights. Jewish leaders excoriated Dinkins for what they saw as his lack of impartiality, while African Americans praised him for what they considered his restraint.

More criticism came over the mayor's handling of yet another racial disturbance, a clash between police and Dominican immigrants in the upper Manhattan neighborhood of Washington Heights. Despite Dinkins's frequent attempts to cool angry passions, five days of rioting followed in Washington Heights. In the aftermath of the disturbance, the Policemen's Benevolent Association charged that the mayor had proved too tolerant of rioters and had expressed excessive criticisms of the police.

In 1993 Rudolph Giuliani easily secured the Republican nomination for mayor and launched an aggressive campaign that hammered constantly at a single theme—in four years, Dinkins had repeatedly demonstrated his inability to manage the myriad affairs of the complex city. Giuliani characterized the Dinkins administration as ineffective and wasteful, and the mayor himself as inept and unresponsive to whites, Latinos, and Asians. The result of such mismanagement, charged the former prosecutor, was evident in the deterioration of the quality of life in New York City, and no more so than in the escalating crime rate that had become a major focus of editorial comment in the press.

Dinkins ardently defended his record in city hall, attributing persistent economic problems to forces outside mayoral control. If racial tensions had risen nearly to the boiling point, Dinkins asserted, his administration had kept the lid on. New York City, he argued, had experienced no massive outbreak comparable to the riots in Los Angeles in 1992, following the announcement that Los Angeles police officers had been exonerated in the beating of RODNEY KING. Dinkins lost the vote for reelection by a narrow margin, receiving 48.3 percent of the vote to Giuliani's 50.7 percent, and thus became the first black mayor of a major U.S. city to relinquish the office after just one term.

Dinkins's mayoralty produced an ambiguous legacy. Because of New York City's preeminence among the nation's urban places, his election constituted a landmark in U.S. politics. Unlike successful black candidates in other large cities with black electoral majorities, Dinkins triumphed in 1989 in a city where blacks composed just 25 percent of the population. The *New York Times* recognized Dinkins's achievement, calling his election "a political coming of age" for African Americans (2 Jan. 1990). The lack of success of his reelection campaign in 1993 resulted from a perception that a courtly and cautious man had failed to effectively manage the city's affairs. His failure to solve New York's fiscal woes bespoke the difficulties facing a host of black mayors who arrived in city halls at a precarious time of urban retrenchment, suburban expansion, and dwindling resources. Yet by 1992 Dinkins had brought the city from massive deficits to a budget surplus and his community-policing programs resulted in a steady decrease in crime. However, his failure to convince voters of his ability to deal fairly and evenhandedly with all ethnic groups and races in New York City proved to be a serious shortcoming, in part because of the intense scrutiny inevitably applied to black mayors when issues of race relations arise.

Life after city hall included a professorship in public affairs at Columbia University and a weekly radio show, *Dialogue with Dinkins*, which allowed the former mayor to engage wtih New Yorkers. These positions also provided a platform for Dinkins to comment on the actions of his successor. Acrimony between Dinkins and Giuliani intensified when the latter publicly apologized in 1998 on behalf of the city for its response to the disturbances in Crown Heights. The relationship worsened a year later when Dinkins, angered by the police shooting of the West African immigrant Amadou Diallo, was among the protesters arrested for trespassing at police headquarters. A model of grace and courtliness, Dinkins remained willing to intervene when his conscience demanded it.

FURTHER READING

Biles, Roger. "Mayor David Dinkins and the Politics of Race in New York City," in *African-American Mayors: Race, Politics, and the American City*, eds. David R. Colburn and Jeffrey S. Adler (2001).

Siegel, Fred. *The Future Once Happened Here: New York, D.C., L.A., and the Fate of America's Big Cities* (1997).

ROGER BILES

Dinkins, Lottie Lee (1906–12 Dec. 1980), English and drama teacher, poet, and civil rights leader, was born in Trenton, New Jersey. Her father was a headwaiter in a hotel and her mother a homemaker. Lottie was the youngest of three children. Her parents sacrificed immensely to send her to Howard University, the university that her mother considered the best and most prestigious of colleges.

Dinkins entered Howard University in September 1925 and earned a bachelor of arts degree in education in June 1929. Her first choice for a career was journalism, but administrators at Howard discouraged her in this. Instead, Dinkins's first job after graduation was teaching at Leland College in Baton Rouge, Louisiana. After four years there, she returned to Trenton. She met and married William Harvey Dinkins, the father of Mayor DAVID N. DINKINS (the first African American mayor of New York City, 1989–1993). William Dinkins was a real estate broker and barbershop owner. Her husband worked for years to establish a successful business, and she dedicated her time to teaching and acting as a political and social advocate for minorities.

Dinkins was not pleased with the segregation in the public schools in Trenton. With the NAACP, she helped spearhead efforts to place local African American children into better schools. As a teacher at the new Lincoln School built in 1923 for blacks in Trenton, Dinkins fought to gain equal access to public swimming pools and for the same education given to the white students. A 1939 New Jersey legislative report revealed that white students were taught in more modern facilities, while minority students were not given even the minimum requirements. Books were substandard, and gym and shop equipment rarely existed at all. In those rare instances in which white and black students did share a school building, they nevertheless were taught in separate classrooms and used separate entrances, bathrooms, and playgrounds.

Despite the unequal treatment they were forced to endure, Dinkins encouraged her stepchildren to excel in education. When David Dinkins returned from the U.S. Marines at the end of the summer of 1952, he felt that it was too late to apply for admittance to Howard University for the fall semester. His stepmother encouraged him to apply; through her contacts she made it possible for her stepson to enroll immediately. David Dinkins graduated in 1956 with a degree in mathematics and then completed a law degree at Brooklyn College.

Lottie Dinkins later studied at Columbia (New York) and Rutgers University (New Jersey). In later years, Dinkins continued her education, selecting New York University to complete a masters program in dramatic art.

Dinkins's educational advocacy extended beyond her family. She is listed as a founding member of the Central New Jersey chapter of the Links, Inc., founded in 1946 to focus on the civic, cultural, and educational needs of African Americans. The group successfully organized prominent women to assist their communities, increasing membership and newly formed chapters throughout the United States. The Central New Jersey chapter, organized in May 1949, provided Dinkins with another venue to explore and discuss issues that created barriers for African Americans. Her involvement in the organization led her to take on the role of national vice president, recognizing that the collective efforts of a few could make a difference in the lives of many disadvantaged individuals. Dinkins imparted the need for advancement through education as a mother, social leader, and civil rights champion during an era when African Americans were seeking their place in the expanding yet segregated American society.

Dinkins retired from forty years of public service (1933–1973) in the Trenton Public Schools. Her untiring dedication to the students made her the recipient of the Trenton High School yearbook dedication. The *Spectator*, the high school newspaper, honored Dinkins as a creative teacher and the prime organizer of the student government at Trenton High School. She performed in numerous plays and coauthored a musical drama, *Unfinished Revolution*, dedicated to Trenton's Bicentennial Celebration. Her poems, "To a Brown Baby" and "Tree on a Hill," were favorites remembered by her family.

In 1978 Dinkins was honored by the Mercer County, New Jersey, chapter of the National Conference of Christian and Jews and the Trenton chapter of the NAACP. Her dedication to community service led her to serve on the board of trustees at Trenton Junior College-School of Industrial Arts; she also held memberships in the American Association of University Women, the NAACP, the Council of Human Relations, the Central YMCA, and she was a former president of the local Epsilon Epsilon Omega chapter of Alpha Kappa Alpha sorority. One of Dinkins's students, U.S. District Judge A. LEON HIGGINBOTHAM praised her for encouraging him to strive and to become a success. Lottie Lee Dinkins, an innovative educator lived most of her life in Trenton, yet her efforts to improve conditions for all African Americans were significant nationwide. Lottie Lee Dinkins was among the five-member delegation (supported by the NAACP) that forced the New Jersey Supreme Court decision to provide better educational services for the black students of Trenton. By 1944 the case was decided in favor of minority students allowing them to attend previously all-white public schools.

FURTHER READING

Hornsby, Alton. *Chronology of African-American History from 1942 to the Present* (1997).

CONSTANCE B. WILLIAMS

Dinwiddie Quartet (1898–1904), a four-member vocal group composed of Sterling C. Rex (first tenor), James Mantell Thomas (second bass),

J. Clarence Meredith (second tenor), and Harry B. Cruder (first bass, and in some references, his last name is spelled as Cryer).

At the end of the ninteenth century, the music that represented the pain and peril of slavery and the Civil War began to change toward celebrated sounds of jubilant spiritual music. By the early twentieth century, the era of blackened face minstrels, of black and white men portraying stereotyped images of African Americans as buffoons, neared its end in theater. Between the years of 1898–1904, the Dinwiddie Quartet sang as a group, locally first, under the management of Charles B. Cheshire at John Dix Industrial School in Dinwiddie, Virginia. They soon would follow the parade of quartets from schools like Fisk University and Tuskegee Institute, singing gospels and spirituals in cities throughout America's north and south. The spiritual jubilant songs of the Dinwiddie Quartet gained following as they traveled and performed for blacks and whites in Virginia, Maryland, Washington, D.C., Philadelphia, and New York.

Earlier on, their singing venues allowed the Dinwiddie Quartet to earn money to help fund their schooling at the John Dix Industrial School. Although members of the group did not graduate from the school, Dinwiddie Quartet recorded six songs for the Victor Talking Machine Company (Victor). In New York City in 1902, the Dinwiddie Quartet would be one of the first groups to record four-part harmony, a cappella style, for Victor.

The sound of their tenor and bass voices on each recording is lively and cheery. Victor produced the quartet's recordings in what was considered a monograph recording. Monograph recordings were songs or instrumentals recorded around certain categories, such as male quartets, religious songs, or Native American songs. These monograph recordings provided information about each group and also the significance of each song on the album. The quartet's six songs were under the theme coon [Negro], genuine jubilee and camp meeting shouts. The term *coon* was replaced by the term *Negro* in some of the literature about the group. *Coon shouts* was, at that time, the norm for black vocal groups and the term appeared in titles of lyrics, minstrel, and vaudeville acts, as well as theatrical show tunes. Many African Americans disapproved of the use of the term, but tolerated it because the songs provided a music genre and style that was enjoyed by many during that time.

Under the Victor Talking Machine Company label, the quartet's name was changed to the Dinwiddie Colored Quartet. The Dinwiddie Quartet recorded a total of six disc recordings. Most of the songs were in the tradition of call-and-response. Titles of the songs were: "Down on the Old Camp Ground," "Poor Mourner," and "Steal Away," which the quartet recorded in New York City on 29 October 1902. Below is the first stanza of "Down on the Old Camp Ground":

There's a jubilee,
There's a jubilee,
There's a jubilee.
Way down on the old campground.

The group repeats the chorus again and Rex delivers the next lyrics in tenor voice:

The little white cart came a-rollin' down,

Then the chorus responds in homophonic chorale sound:

Way down on the old campground.

The song continues in this manner with four more stanzas of folklore lyrics.

On 31 October 1902, the quartet returned to Victor to record "My Way Is Cloudy," which was not found on the monograph recording, "Gabriel's Trumpet," and "We'll Anchor Bye and Bye."

The Dinwiddie Quartet, in 1901, now under the management of J. A. Porter, joined the Smart Set Company and thus sang in Bob Cole's all black musical theater productions. The Smart Set Company, a black acting company, performed musical comedy shows regularly throughout most urban northern cities. The quartet performed in Cole's productions with performers like Ernest Hogan and Billy McClain. The Dinwiddie Quartet entertained the audience by performing songs between the skits. The quartet became part of the vaudeville circuit, performing on an average three shows a day.

Bob Cole and Billy Johnson's production of *A Trip to Coontown* was directed, produced, and performed by African Americans in 1898, and was enjoyed by both black and white audiences. In the 1902 production of *A Trip to Coontown*, the Dinwiddie Quartet performed the spiritual song "Palms" at the Empire Theater in New Jersey. In another Cole and Johnson show, *Southern Enchantment*, which was performed in Philadelphia, at the National Theater on 27 October 1902, the quartet sang "Palms" and "Come out Dinah on the Green." The reviews for both shows were favorable and audiences enjoyed the quartet's arrangement of both songs.

The Dinwiddie Quartet broke up in 1904, shortly after they appeared in Cole and Johnson's show. It is not known what caused the split of the

Dinwiddie Quartet two years after they recorded for Victor. Perhaps the group members choose to simply move on with their lives and careers, such as Rex and Thomas (second bass) did. In 1908, Rex performed in BERT WILLIAMS's and GEORGE W. WALKER's *Bandana Land* at the Majestic Theater. In another Williams play, Rex and Thomas played lieutenants in the 1909, opera/comedy, *Mr. Lode of Koal* that played in Chicago and New York. Rex, Thomas, and also Clarence Redd, another singer in the show, sang one of the songs from the show, "Bygone Days in Dixie." In the New York show, J. E. Lightfoot (lead singer of the Right Quartet) would also join the chorus. Although Rex and Thomas continued to be part of the black vaudeville circuit, they did not always perform in the same shows. Thomas eventually went on to sing with the Right Quintet, who recorded on Columbia's label in 1915. Regrettably, not much is known, after the break up, of the other two members Clarence Meredith, second tenor, nor first bass Harry B. Cruder.

The Dinwiddie Quartet went on to other endeavors but their recordings provide a reminder of how uplifting their harmonic voices were. The integrity of the group's singing is as notable today as it was in 1902. The Dinwiddie Quartet opened the doors for all African American vocal groups that sing and record music since that time. After their split up, the quartet may not have accomplished the same fame as their recordings and earlier performances in the black theater circuit, but they left a legacy of six songs to be enjoyed by future generations.

FURTHER READING

Brooks, Tim. *Lost Sounds: Blacks and the Birth of the Recording Industry 1890–1919* (2004).

Sampson, Henry T. *The Ghost Walks: A Chronological History of Blacks in Show Business 1865–1910* (1988).

Tawa, Nicholas E. *The Way to Tin Pan Alley: American Popular Song, 1866–1910* (1990).

DISCOGRAPHY

The Earliest Negro Vocal Quartets, 1894–1928 (Document Records, 1991).

AISHA PEÑA

Dismukes, William "Dizzy" (15 Mar. 1890–30 June 1961), Negro League baseball player and manager, was born in Birmingham, Alabama. Little information is available about his upbringing or early years. It appears he attended college, though where exactly he did so is not clear.

Dismukes's long baseball career as a pitcher appears to have begun with the East St. Louis Imperials in 1908. He went on to play with a number of minor teams over the next few years: the Indianapolis ABCs (1909); the St. Louis Giants (1912); the Philadelphia Giants (1913); and the Brooklyn Royal Giants (1914). That year, he ended the season on the mound in an ultimately unsuccessful playoff series against RUBE FOSTER's storied Chicago American Giants.

After the 1914 season, Dismukes returned to the ABCs, which had recently been bought by C. I. TAYLOR. Taylor's team would go on to achieve a status in Negro League baseball rivaled only by Foster's American Giants. Stats from Dismukes's early career have been lost (or were never kept), but during his first season with the ABCs he rang up a 19–5 record. He was widely known as a master of the submarine pitch, essentially a sidearm pitch that is released so near the ground that the pitcher's hand turns nearly palm-up. The submarine pitch causes the ball to take an unpredictable path and has long been a bane of hitters. Dismukes also excelled at learning the tendency of rival hitters and repositioning his defensive players accordingly. Dismukes's second turn with the ABCs was nearly as successful as the first, and he posted a 17–6 record. As in the previous season, he ended the year in a championship set against the American Giants, albeit with a different team.

During World War I, Dismukes enlisted with the 803rd Pioneer Infantry. In Nantes, France, he played with the unit baseball team, and led them to a championship. He returned to the States and took up a managerial position with the Dayton Marcos, but a year later he was back on the mound with the ABCs. His record that season was a league-leading 11–6. Dismukes remained with the ABCs until 1922, the year of C. I. Taylor's death. After that, Dismukes jumped from team to team: the Birmingham Black Barons, Memphis Red Sox, and St. Louis Stars. He returned to the ABCs for a brief time in 1924 in the role of on-field manager.

It was as a manager that Dismukes would spend the next phase of his career. When Rube Foster died in 1930, Dismukes took over as head of the American Giants. Over the next few years, he moved again from team to team. The year 1932 found him with the Detroit Wolves. Six years later, he was in the dugout with the Birmingham Black Barons. Six years after that, he was with Memphis. In 1941 he was hired by the Kansas City Monarchs, where he soon became personnel director. In 1945 he helped the team acquire JACKIE ROBINSON. Dismukes remained in the Monarchs home office until 1952. As a manager he was known as both a sound strategist and a fine baseball mind, traits that had served him well during his years on the mound. He was especially skilled with developing young players, and helped many of them successfully transition to professional play. In 1953 he was hired as a scout by the famed Major League Baseball squad the New York Yankees. He later filled the same position with the Chicago White Sox. He retired in 1956, having been one of baseball's early stars and pioneers.

Dismukes died in 1961, in Campbell, Ohio.

FURTHER READING

Peterson, Robert. *Only the Ball Was White: A History of Legendary Black Players and All-Black Professional Teams* (1992).

Riley, James A. *The Biographical Encyclopedia of the Negro Baseball Leagues* (1994).

JASON PHILIP MILLER

Dixon, Big Willie James (1 July 1915–29 Jan. 1992), blues musician, composer, and arranger, was born in Vicksburg, Mississippi, to Daisy McKenzie and, putatively, her husband Charlie Dixon. Willie was one of seven surviving children (out of fourteen). It is likely that Anderson "A. D." Bell, whom Willie Dixon called his stepfather, was actually his biological father, as records show that Daisy and Charlie Dixon finalized divorce proceedings in 1913. As a youth Dixon worked in his mother's restaurant as well as spending time in Vicksburg's barrel houses and juke joints. Along with his mother's interest in reading and writing poetry, contact with blues legends such as CHARLEY PATTON and EURREAL WILFORD "LITTLE BROTHER" MONTGOMERY led Dixon to begin writing songs of his own.

The search for work and his own wanderlust put Dixon on the road at a young age. Arrested while traveling as a hobo through Clarksdale, Mississippi, and sentenced to thirty days on the Charles Allen Prison Farm, Dixon escaped to Memphis, Tennessee, on the back of a mule. Freight trains carried him north until he reached his sister in Chicago in 1929. Between 1926 and 1936 Dixon found his way to New York City, Ohio, Florida, and numerous hobo jungles throughout the South. He even shipped out to Hawaii, mistakenly boarding a vessel bound for the islands while he was cleaning ships.

Despite these adventures, it was back in Vicksburg that Dixon's career as a musician and songwriter began to take shape. When in Mississippi, he sold song lyrics to country and western musicians and sang bass with the Union Jubilee Singers, a gospel quartet. This group's popularity brought singing engagements around Mississippi and led to regular appearances on WQBC radio, doing weekly live broadcasts from the station's Vicksburg studios.

Always large for his age, as Dixon matured he approached three hundred pounds and began training seriously as a boxer. Fighting under the name James Dixon, he won the 1936 Illinois Golden Gloves in the heavyweight division. However, Dixon's professional boxing career was put on hold when he drew a suspension for brawling outside the ring. Soon afterward, the musician Leonard "Baby Doo" Caston persuaded Dixon to focus his energies on music full-time.

With Caston's help, Dixon left boxing behind. Not only did Caston make Dixon's first bass from an oil can and a strand of wire, he also introduced Dixon to people in the music business. When the musicians' union recording ban of 1936–1937 was lifted, Dixon played bass at his first recording session with Caston and a vocal group called the Bumping Boys. In 1939 Caston and Dixon returned to the studio as members of the Five Breezes, cutting eight tracks that were released on Bluebird, RCA's "race record" label. (Race records were those produced or marketed with African American consumers in mind.)

The association with Caston and the other members of the Five Breezes established Dixon on the Chicago music scene. He moved about town, selling song sheets or printed copies of his version of the folk rhyme "The Signifying Monkey." He became a fixture at the many music clubs on Maxwell Street and also played at Martin's Corner on the city's West Side. However, Dixon's run of good fortune came to an abrupt end when the United States entered World War II following the Japanese attack on Pearl Harbor in December 1941. In 1942, he was literally pulled off the stage and arrested as a draft resister. Refusing military service, he was, like BAYARD RUSTIN and other conscientious objectors, imprisoned and became entangled in a lengthy court battle. In his memoir, *I Am the Blues*, Dixon stated, "I wasn't going to fight nobody.... I told them I didn't feel I had to go because of the conditions that existed among my people" (54). He served ten months for resisting the draft, and was released in 1944.

After the war Dixon and Caston reunited, forming a vocal trio along with Ollie Crawford. Calling themselves the Big Three (after Churchill, Roosevelt, and Stalin), the group had a run of hit records in the mid-1940s, including "The Signifying Monkey." White audiences embraced the Big Three's swing-oriented pop sound, and the group toured extensively throughout the Midwest. Even as the trio enjoyed their success, Dixon tired of the traveling and the musical direction the group was taking. In order to spend more time with his wife, Marie, and their eleven children, he began hiring himself out to Chicago studios when his touring schedule allowed.

During the late 1940s Chicago experienced a blues renaissance, as raw, down-home sounds were electrified in small clubs and bars on the South Side. As this music found the ears of black audiences in Chicago and around the country, a number of independent record producers sought to cash in, including Leonard and Phil Chess. Late in 1948, after watching Dixon perform in late-night jam sessions on Forty-seventh Street, Leonard Chess offered the bass player studio work for an upcoming session with the bluesman ROBERT NIGHTHAWK. This began a relationship between Dixon and Chess that was, if nothing else, extremely productive for the former and very profitable for the later. Using Dixon's feel for the music as their guide, the Chess brothers, who were minor players in the race record market in the late 1940s, became hit makers in short order.

Throughout the 1950s and 1960s Dixon wrote, arranged, and played the music that made Chess Studios an assembly line of hits that topped both the blues chart and the R&B (rhythm and blues) charts. Artists such as MUDDY WATERS, HOWLIN' WOLF, and LITTLE WALTER JACOBS drew from Dixon's extensive songbook, recording tunes such as "Hoochie Coochie Man," "Little Red Rooster," "Back Door Man Spoonful," "You Shook Me," and "Wang Dang Doodle." While at Chess, Dixon became a contributor to the foundation of rock and roll, playing bass and doing studio work in sessions with CHUCK BERRY and BO DIDDLEY. Dixon also served as an A&R (artist and repertoire) man, finding new talent for the Chess brothers. He was instrumental in ushering into the Chess empire the next wave of hit makers, including OTIS RUSH and BUDDY GUY. Working through his own Yambo label, Dixon also promoted the recording careers of KOKO TAYLOR, Lucky Peterson, and the Five Blind Boys of Mississippi.

Dixon toured overseas during the late 1950s and early 1960s, helping to awaken interest in the blues on an international scale. By playing in Europe and Great Britain, as well as at American folk festivals, he contributed to the so-called blues revival and witnessed his songs pass to a new generation of musicians. British acts including the Rolling Stones, Led Zeppelin, and Eric Clapton, as well as American rockers such as the Grateful Dead and The Doors, had hits with his songs. However, these musical transfers were not without complications. After Leonard Chess's death in 1969, Dixon took legal action to regain the rights to his songs from Arc Music, the Chesses' publishing company. In 1977 he reached an out-of-court settlement, after which the rights were transferred to his Ghana Publishing Company. Soon afterward Dixon filed a successful suit for copyright violation against Led Zeppelin for their recording of "Whole Lotta Love."

As a statesman and steward of the blues, Dixon continued to perform and record in his later years. He was honored with numerous awards and citations, including the Blues Ink Lifetime Achievement Award and the W. C. HANDY Award. Despite health complications due to diabetes, Dixon worked to establish the Chicago public schools "Blues in the Schools" program and the Blues Heaven Foundation, a nonprofit organization dedicated to assisting older blues performers and providing scholarships to young musicians. He died in Burbank, California.

FURTHER READING

Dixon, Willie, with Don Snowden. *I Am the Blues: The Willie Dixon Story* (1989).

Flanagan, Bill. "Willie Dixon," in *Written in My Soul: Rock's Greatest Song Writers Talk about Their Music* (1986).

Wynn, Ron. "Blues Perspective," *Living Blues* 103 (May–June 1992).

Obituary: *Chicago Tribune*, 30 Jan. 1992.

MICHAEL A. ANTONUCCI

Dixon, Dean (10 Jan. 1915–4 Nov. 1976), orchestra conductor, was born Charles Dean Dixon in New York City, the son of Henry Charles Dixon, a lawyer and hotel porter, and McClara Dean Ralston. Both of Dixon's parents were West Indian—his mother was born in Barbados and his father in Jamaica. Because more than two decades elapsed before his parents secured their U.S. passports, according to Dixon, "[T]here is a lot of legal questioning as to whether I am an American or whether I only have an American passport. Both [of] my parents were Commonwealth citizens when I was born" (Dunbar, 189–190).

Before he had reached the age of four Dixon was learning to play on a fifteen-dollar pawnshop violin. Though his mother had no musical training she was able to recognize talent. Such was evidenced for her when she saw young Dean holding two sticks in violin position. An avid concertgoer, particularly to New York City's Carnegie Hall, she generally carried her son along, and she taught him to read music almost before he learned the alphabet.

Dixon began taking three lessons a week, with monitored daily practice of four to five hours, and before long he was performing at church and lodge

Dean Dixon, American conductor, 17 September 1941. (Library of Congress/Carl Van Vechten, photographer.)

concerts. When Dixon was thirteen, his instructor suggested that his lessons be discontinued, believing that a career in classical music was unrealistic for an African American. Both Dixon and his mother ignored the advice, although Mrs. Dixon began to consider a medical career for her son, planning for Dixon to offer private lessons on the piano and violin to defray the cost of his medical study.

As Dixon approached his graduation from DeWitt Clinton High School in 1932, the head of the music department convinced Mrs. Dixon that her son should pursue a career in music and exerted his influence to secure Dixon's acceptance into the Institute of Musical Art (the Juilliard School). Dixon was admitted on the basis of a violin audition and pursued a violin degree for the first half year; he then began following the music pedagogy course of study. In 1932 Dixon organized the Dean Dixon Symphony Orchestra, with one violin and one piano, using a pencil for a baton. They rehearsed at the Harlem Young Men's Christian Association, and within a short period of time the number of musicians reached seventy. Dixon received a B.S. degree from Juilliard in 1936 and an M.A. from Columbia University Teachers College in 1939, while concurrently studying conducting on a graduate fellowship at Juilliard under Albert Stoessel.

Dixon conducted his first professional orchestra concert in 1938 at Town Hall with the League of Music Lovers Chamber Orchestra. In 1939 he and several of the city's finest instrumentalists formed the New York Chamber Orchestra.

Though struggling financially, Dixon and the Dean Dixon Symphony Orchestra were prospering artistically and hit a run of good fortune in the late 1930s, when a women's group began offering them a subsidy. Having come to the attention of First Lady Eleanor Roosevelt, the orchestra presented a concert at Heckscher Theater in May 1941. In attendance was the NBC music director Samuel Chotzinoff, who was so impressed that he contracted Dixon to lead the famed Arturo Toscanini's NBC Symphony Orchestra for two concerts. Other important engagements followed: performances with the New York Philharmonic Orchestra (1942), the Philadelphia Orchestra (1943), and the Boston Symphony (1944, "Coloured American Night"). In 1944 Dixon also organized the American Youth Orchestra. Dixon merited a chapter in David Ewen's book *Dictators of the Baton* when it was reissued and enlarged in 1948. The same year Dixon received Columbia University's Alice M. Ditson Award of one thousand dollars "for outstanding contributions to American Music" and was designated "Outstanding Conductor of the Year," by Columbia. Yet between 1944, when he last conducted the Boston Symphony, and 1949, no invitations came from any established organization. When in 1949 he received an invitation from the Radio Symphony of the French National Radio, he accepted, beginning a "self-imposed" exile from the United States. Later, Dixon remarked, "I felt like I was on a sinking ship and if I'd stayed here, I'd drown."

Before leaving the country Dixon distinguished himself with several orchestral innovations. His programs for children four years and older, in which he sat the children among the instrumentalists to be fascinated by both sight and sound, created quite a bit of excitement. His "Symphony at Midnight" concerts given at a reduced price for those who could not attend the regularly scheduled performances also were quite popular. Most innovative for the late 1930s and early 1940s was the "blindfold test" technique, in which musicians auditioning for Dixon's orchestra displayed their skills for the maestro while his back was turned.

When he worked with various training ensembles, including the Works Progress Administration and the National Youth Administration Orchestra in the late 1930s, Dixon consistently changed the seating arrangements, often placing string players among woodwinds and brasses among strings, a method that helped his players listen better and learn the complete score.

By 1952 Dixon had become America's most active musical ambassador abroad. The American press reported that during the 1951–1952 season, Dixon led thirty-two concerts in nine different European countries. In 1953 he became the resident conductor of the Göteburg (Sweden) Symphony, in which position he remained until 1960. His next major appointment was with the Hesse Radio Symphony Orchestra in Frankfurt, Germany (1961–1974). During this tenure he was also principal conductor of the Sydney Symphony Orchestra in Australia (1964–1967). He frequently received guest conducting invitations from other organizations, including symphony and radio orchestras in Amsterdam, Athens, Belgrade, Berlin, Copenhagen, Leipzig, Mexico City, Rome, Stockholm, Tokyo, and Zurich, among many other stops.

Dixon's first substantial American conducting invitation came in 1970. After twenty-one years abroad he returned to conduct the New York Philharmonic in three park concerts and enjoyed guest stints with the Pittsburgh Symphony at Temple University's Ambler Festival and with the Saint Louis Symphony at the Mississippi River Festival. A 1971 conducting tour, sponsored by the Schlitz Brewing Company, included the Kansas City, Minnesota, Milwaukee, and Detroit symphony orchestras, while a 1972 tour included appearances with the National, Chicago, and San Francisco symphony orchestras.

Having recently retired as musical director of the Frankfurt Radio Orchestra, Dixon was called back to the Sydney Symphony Orchestra in 1975, first for a two-week season, then for a twenty-four-concert tour of Australia, during which he also conducted the Melbourne Symphony Orchestra. After only nine concerts, however, Dixon returned to his home in Switzerland to undergo open-heart surgery. He continued his guest conducting activities in early 1976, but he died later in the year in Zug, Switzerland.

News of Dixon's death appeared in the press worldwide. Ronald Smothers captioned his entry for the *New York Times* (5 Nov. 1976), "Dean Dixon, 61, Dies, Conductor in Exile/First Black to Lead Philharmonic/Left the U.S. in 1949 to Build His Reputation in Europe." During the course of his life Dixon had three wives: Vivian Rivkin, an American Caucasian whom he married in 1947; Mary Mandelin, a Finnish woman reared in France whom he married in 1954; and Roswitha "Ritha" Blume, a German whom he married in 1973. He had two daughters.

FURTHER READING

Berg, Beatrice. "Dixon: Maestro Abroad, Stranger at Home," *New York Times*, 19 July 1970.

Dunbar, Ernest, ed. *The Black Expatriates: A Study of American Negroes in Exile* (1968).

Handy, D. Antoinette. *Black Conductors* (1995).

Trudeau, Noah Andre. "When the Door Didn't Open: A Cool Classicist and a Soldier for Social Equality," *High Fidelity* 35 (May 1985).

This entry is taken from the *American National Biography* and is published here with the permission of the American Council of Learned Societies.

ANTOINETTE HANDY

Dixon, George (29 July 1870–5 Jan. 1908), boxer, was born in Halifax, Nova Scotia, Canada, but was brought by his parents to Boston when he was eight years old. There he attended school and, in 1884, began working for Elmer Chickering, a photographer who specialized in making portraits of boxers. While on a job Dixon saw boxing matches at the Boston Music Hall and decided to pursue a boxing career. After a few amateur bouts he attracted the attention of Tom O'Rourke, a former boxer who taught Dixon and managed him throughout most of his career.

Dixon became a professional boxer in 1888, and by the end of the year he was well known in the Boston area due to a thrilling series of fights with a local hero, Hank Brennan. Weighing less than 100 pounds Dixon proved to be an extremely clever boxer, good at defense and capable of landing hard punches with both fists. In 1889 he grew into the featherweight division, the weight limit at that time being 116 pounds. He made rapid progress and ended the year by making his first New York City ring appearance, in which he scored a two-round knockout of the highly regarded Eugene Hornbacker.

On 7 February 1890 Dixon boxed Cal McCarthy in Boston for the American featherweight title. The fight, which started after midnight and ended nearly five hours and seventy-eight rounds later, was called a draw because both men had fought themselves to exhaustion. O'Rourke then launched his man on a campaign to become world feather weight champion, taking him to England, where he knocked out a British contender, Nunc Wallace. After returning to the United States Dixon scored a forty-round knockout of contender Johnny Murphy. On 31 March 1891 in New York he knocked out McCarthy in twenty-two rounds; in July in San Francisco he won a five-round knockout over contender Abe Willis, the Australian champion; and finally on 27 June 1892 in Brooklyn, he knocked out the British champion Fred Johnson in fourteen rounds. These victories gained worldwide featherweight championship recognition for Dixon.

During this era of boxing the champion was allowed to set the weight limit at which his title would be defended. Because Dixon's fighting weight at the time was only between 114 and 116 pounds, he initially set the limit below 120 pounds, but the limit was increased as he added weight. His first defense, in New Orleans on 6 September 1892, was against the noted amateur Jack Skelly, at 116 pounds, with Dixon winning by a knockout in eight rounds. This bout was significant in two respects: it was the first boxing match held in New Orleans before a racially mixed audience, and it was part of a series of championship fights leading to the world heavyweight title match between John L. Sullivan and James John Corbett. In 1893 in Brooklyn, New York, Dixon made two successful defenses at 120 pounds, against Eddie Pierce and Solly Smith, knocking out his opponents in three and seven rounds, respectively.

Dixon had reached the zenith of his career; he had lost only twice, once by a disqualification early in his career, and once on a four-round decision to the Englishman Billy Plimmer in 1893 in a nontitle fight. He seemed almost unbeatable in the ring, but his personal affairs were another story. He often drank heavily, gambled his money away on horseracing, and even bought racehorses that were mortgaged and then lost when he could not keep up the payments. In addition to his genuine ring battles he made theatrical tours, taking on all comers.

First married at age fifteen, Dixon later married O'Rourke's sister. Dixon was brown-skinned, hence his popular name of "Little Chocolate," and claimed to be one-fourth black and three-fourths white. During his theatrical tours he was forced to take lodgings at "colored" boardinghouses apart from his wife, who stayed in "white" hotels with his manager.

In 1894 and 1895 Dixon fought two epic nontitle battles with the famous Australian fighter Young Griffo, who outweighed him by many pounds. Both fights were called draws, the first in twenty rounds in Boston, 29 June 1894, and the second in Brooklyn in twenty-five rounds, 19 January 1895. On 27 August 1895 he again successfully defended the featherweight title, at 128 pounds, against Johnny Griffin in Boston over twenty-five rounds. In the next two years he fought several important nontitle fights, including another with Young Griffo, three with Frank Erne, and another with Griffin.

Dixon lost the featherweight title by decision to Solly Smith at San Francisco on 4 October 1897, in twenty-five rounds. Smith soon lost the title to Dave Sullivan, and Dixon defeated Sullivan by disqualification in ten rounds on 11 November 1898 to regain it. In 1899 he won nine of ten fights against dangerous opponents, including seven title defenses. On 9 January 1900 he made his last title defense and was knocked out in eight rounds by Terry McGovern in New York.

Dixon continued to fight until 1906, but he lost most of his remaining battles. At times he showed traces of his former boxing brilliance, but he was no longer a title contender. He went to Great Britain and boxed there for more than two years to stay active. O'Rourke refused to continue handling his affairs, and his second wife left him. After returning to the United States he suffered a crushing two-round knockout in Philadelphia by Tommy Murphy and finally retired after a few more inconsequential fights. Dixon was then penniless and had no means of supporting himself. He lived on the charity of others, drank heavily, and eventually died in New York City of acute alcoholism.

For many years George Dixon was the standard against which featherweight champions were measured, and he was long considered to be the greatest fighter of all time at that weight. He was elected to the International Boxing Hall of Fame in 1990.

FURTHER READING

Fleischer, Nathaniel S. *Black Dynamite*, vol. 3, *The Three Colored Aces, George Dixon, Joe Gans, and Joe Walcott* (1938).

Obituary: *Philadelphia Item*, 7 Jan. 1908.

This entry is taken from the *American National Biography* and is published here with the permission of the American Council of Learned Societies.

LUCKETT V. DAVIS

Dixon, Julian Carey (8 Aug. 1934–8 Dec. 2000), congressman, lawyer, and activist, was born in Washington, D.C., the son of a postal worker. He attended the District of Columbia public schools in his middle-class black neighborhood until he was eleven, at which time he and his mother moved to Los Angeles. Raised to have a strong sense of loyalty, Dixon would remain committed to both Washington and Los Angeles throughout his life.

After graduating from Los Angeles's Dorsey High School, Dixon served in the army. He continued his education after his military service, receiving his B.S. from Los Angeles State College (later California State University in Los Angeles) in 1962 and going on to obtain his LLB from Southwestern University in Los Angeles in 1967. Dixon practiced law from 1967 to 1973, concomitantly serving as an aide to the California state senator MERVYN DYMALLY. It was while he was working in this capacity that Dixon decided to begin his own elective career, running in 1972 for the state assembly seat vacated by YVONNE BRATHWAITE BURKE, who was running for the U.S. House of Representatives. Dixon won the election easily.

In the state assembly, Dixon became head of the Democratic caucus, forging powerful allegiances with the politicians Howard Berman and Henry Waxman, who would remain his longtime friends and allies, and who would themselves become congressmen.

In 1978, when Burke gave up her seat in the House to pursue other political ambitions, Dixon entered the race to replace her. The Democratic primary that year was a hot contest, but Dixon ran a compelling campaign against his opponents, a state senator and a Los Angeles councilman. Dixon emerged triumphant.

His victory was particularly notable because California's Thirty-second Congressional District, which Dixon represented in Congress, was one of the most racially and economically diverse districts in the country. Stretching across the west side of Los Angeles, the district was home to an unusual mixture of white, black, Asian, and Hispanic constituents throughout Dixon's tenure. Perhaps because of his constituency, Dixon developed a reputation as a black congressman who did not focus only on "black politics." Still, he was a champion of civil rights. In 1983 Dixon was selected chair of the Congressional Black Caucus (CBC), a position he held for the two-year duration of the Ninety-Eighth Congress, and he served as president of the Congressional Black Caucus Foundation. Dixon wrote the first economic sanctions law against South Africa and once got arrested for participating in an anti-apartheid protest at the South African embassy. He was also a solid supporter of civil rights for women and gays.

Within Congress, Dixon was renowned as a bridge builder, someone who was able to work effectively with both Republicans and Democrats, who did not browbeat or harangue. His colleagues called him soft-spoken, kind, and trustworthy. This disposition led *Congressional Quarterly's Politics in America* to name Dixon one of twelve "Unsung Heroes in Congress." Moreover, for these qualities Dixon was rewarded with senior positions of a particularly sensitive and potentially explosive nature. For more than a decade he chaired the House Committee on Standards of Official Conduct. In 1984 Dixon became the first African American to chair the Standing Committee on Rules for the Democratic National Convention, and he was a long-standing member of the House Appropriations Committee.

Dixon received extended national attention in 1989, when, as the House ethics committee chairman, he led the investigation into then-speaker Jim Wright's book sales. Wright, a fellow Democrat, had come under scrutiny for selling copies of a vanity-press book that his critics thought violated congressional earnings limits. Dixon presided over all sixty-nine counts of rules violations against Wright, managing to gain a reputation for being judicious and fair-minded in a highly charged situation that ultimately resulted in Wright's resignation from the House. He also received attention during that time for not seeking attention; he turned down countless requests to hold television interviews and press conferences, preferring to do his job rather than showcase himself.

Dixon was an unusually private man among elected officials, shielding personal inquiry from the media at every turn. He kept out of the public eye his first wife, Felicia Bragg, and their son, Cary Gordon Dixon. When he married his second wife, Bettye Lee, a board member of Duty Free Shoppers Inc., he continued his practice of reticence. Consequently, little about his personal life is publicly known.

Dixon used much of his political energies on the needs of his home district. In 1992 after the Los Angeles riots, he lobbied extensively for economic support to rebuild the bruised parts of the city. For decades Dixon led the charge in Congress to fund mass transit in Los Angeles. Recognizing that Southern California, with its rapidly growing population, needed an alternative to automobiles in order to maintain both economic growth and a healthy quality of life, he championed not only the development of a Los Angeles subway but also the reorganization of bus services and operating systems in the region.

Dixon also tried to serve his native Washington, as a fourteen-year member of the House Appropriations Subcommittee on the District of Columbia. In that role he struggled to win the city more money; in 1991, when the city was in its most dire straits, he successfully lobbied for an extra $100 million appropriation. Initially a supporter of the D.C. mayor MARION S. BARRY JR., Dixon became increasingly frustrated with what he perceived as waste and inefficiency within the District government. By 1995 Dixon was lambasting city officials for their poor financial management, accusing them in a D.C. Subcommittee meeting of acting in bad faith with Congress.

Dixon proved to be extraordinarily popular with his constituents, winning most of his reelection bids with more than 75 percent of the vote. In his last election, a month before his death from a heart attack, he received an overwhelming 84 percent of the vote.

After his death, Dixon received dozens of eulogies from his colleagues in the House of Representatives. Many of these remembered Dixon for his low-key demeanor, as well as his willingness to serve on committees considered difficult or unglamorous. Though Dixon was unabashedly liberal, his diplomatic skills allowed him to forge cross-partisan coalitions that his colleagues had trouble forming in his absence.

FURTHER READING

Obituary: *Los Angeles Times*, 9 Dec. 2000.

SUSAN J. MCWILLIAMS

Dixon, Melvin (29 May 1950–26 Oct. 1992), poet, novelist, translator, literary critic, and professor, was born in Stamford, Connecticut. Dixon's parents had moved from the South to settle in west Stamford, as part of the broader Great Migration to the North, where Handy, Dixon's father, a sharecropper from Pee Dee, North Carolina, started a new professional life as a contractor and a house painter, and Jessie, his mother, from Irmo, South Carolina, became a nurse. Indeed, Stamford's social and cultural milieu—namely, the interface of the North and South—would later shape Dixon's creative enterprise. Dixon went on to receive his B.A. from Wesleyan University in 1971 and his M.A. in 1973 and Ph.D. in 1975 from Brown University. Dixon emerged as a literary figure with the publication of *Change of Territory* (1983), his first collection of poems. In *Change*, as in much of Dixon's early work, the idea of geography figures prominently. Narratives of the Great Migration and his own transatlantic journeys (particularly to Senegal and France) helped inform his worldview, for easy to discern is the unique way such encounters—in and through physical space—supply Dixon figures for apprehending erotic, mnemonic, antecedent, and spiritual worlds; furthermore, these encounters provide occasions for shifts in poetic meter and language. For instance, in the poem "Tour Guide: La Maison des Esclaves," Dixon uses his visit to the Gorée Island in Senegal—a barracoon on the Atlantic coast where slaves were temporarily held prior to being shipped off to the New World—as an occasion to imagine the past through a concrete encounter between a Senegalese tour guide and the Western tourists. The physical and the imaginary collide in Dixon's poems, offering a complicated appraisal of the relationship between Africa and its diaspora. Unlike his immediate predecessors in the Black Arts Movement, Dixon eschews easy romanticization of Africa. Of the tour guide, for example, Dixon writes:

> The rooms are empty until he speaks.
> His guttural French is a hawking trader.
> His quick Wolof a restless warrior.
> His slow, impeccable syllables
> a gentleman trader. He tells
> in their own language
> what they have done. ("Tour Guide," 31)

Whether the Gorée Island, or Dakar, Port-au-Prince, Pee Dee, Manhattan, or Paris, each place affords the poet a life-world to inhabit and imaginatively refract thereafter. Indeed, it was travel, says Dixon, that propelled him to write poetry in the first place:

> When I went to West Africa for the first time in 1974, I found it an experience that totally wiped out all of my preconceptions about Africa, about America, about Europe. I was faced with this void, and the only way I could gather my impressions was to try to convey some of that tension and some of that joy of discovery in poetry. (de Romanet, 85)

The preoccupation with geography and place continues in *Ride Out the Wilderness: Geography and Identity in Afro-American Literature* (1987), a work of literary criticism. Dixon illustrates persuasively how African American writers use "language to create alternative landscapes where black culture and identity can flourish apart from any marginal, prescribed 'place'" (p. 2). Dixon considers the works of JEAN TOOMER, ZORA NEALE HURSTON, AMIRI BARAKA (LeRoi Jones), JAMES BALDWIN, GAYL JONES, and TONI MORRISON, among others, to show the ways language and place allow for the performance and realization of African American identities. "The wilderness, the underground, and the mountaintop," for example, argues Dixon, "are broad geographic metaphors for the search, discovery, and achievement of self" (*Ride Out the Wilderness*, 4–5).

For sure, Dixon's own critical and interpretive work gives us particular access into his imaginative work, notably his first novel, *Trouble the Water* (1989). Jordan, a black professor previously living in an all-white college town in the North, returns home to North Carolina after a significant absence. The return south reconnects him to a communal, spiritual world. The Great Pee Dee River, the majestic Appalachians, the mysterious woods of the Yadkin Valley, and the rich vernacular lend themselves to discoveries both intimate and allegorical.

While the theme of sexuality was latent in Dixon's early work, it receives pointed attention later in his career. Dixon's intellectual coming-of-age in the 1980s coincides with a larger flowering of black gay art—which included notable figures such as ESSEX HEMPHILL, MARLON RIGGS, JOSEPH FAIRCHILD BEAM, and Assoto Saint, all of whom also died of AIDS-related illnesses, and all of whom, in their short-lived careers, plumbed erotic worlds with great candor and insight. *Vanishing Rooms* (1991), Dixon's second novel, foregrounds gay life and desire, as it takes up the disparate worlds of New York City in the mid-1970s. In this elegiac novel, Dixon weaves together the various narrative positions to tell a story of same-sex desire, interracial love, intragender friendships, loss, and violence, while attuned to the undersides and possibilities of New York City.

Love's Instruments (1995) offers Dixon's most sustained deliberation (though not exclusively) on death and dying, a deliberation that finds wry emphasis in the volume's posthumous publication. In many of the poems, Dixon figures himself as a double mourner: on the one hand, he grieves for his partner, Richard Horovitz, who died of an AIDS-related illness fifteen months before Dixon, and other friends lost to the epidemic; and, on the other hand, he mourns his own imminent death. In several poems Dixon appropriates various elegiac modes from black America to apprehend such aggregating and compounded loss. Most notably, Dixon appropriates the Negro spirituals—which provide the poet a history and an elegiac context—in order to write AIDS elegies. But unlike the spirituals, Dixon's poems offer no otherworldly solace or advice. In a poem titled "One by One," for example, which borrows the refrain "many thousand gone" from a spiritual, he arrives at an elegy laced with a stark, sorrowful realism.

Dixon was also an accomplished translator of works in French. In 1983 he translated Geneviève Fabre's *Drumbeats, Masks, and Metaphor: Contemporary Afro-American Theatre*; and, in 1991, he translated Léopold Sédar Senghor's *Collected Poetry*, the first complete English translation of one of the pioneers of negritude and postcolonial Africa. Of translation as an enterprise, Dixon observed: "I realized that translation for me is a way of getting into the meat of language, it's like getting into the clay: you're actually down there getting dirty, and you're shaping, re-shaping something" (de Romanet, 95).

In addition to helping reshape the contours for how we "practice Diaspora," Dixon, in his short life, charted his own distinct imaginary world, a world that deserves serious contemplation. As his friend and mentee, the poet ELIZABETH ALEXANDER, writes of Dixon: "I would characterize him as most essentially possessing fierce elegance, the fiercest, not a decorative elegance but rather a distilled and streamlined way of being and presenting. Or, in the vernacular, Melvin was *fierce*" (*Love's Instruments*, 6).

FURTHER READING

Alexander, Elizabeth. "Introduction," in *Love's Instruments*, by Melvin Dixon (1995).

Alexander, Elizabeth. "Memory, Community, Voice," *Callaloo* (Spring 1994).

de Romanet, Jerome. "A Conversation with Melvin Dixon," *Callaloo* (2000).

Dixon, Melvin. *Ride Out the Wilderness: Geography and Identity in Afro-American Literature* (1987).

Hoyrd, Andre. "Melvin Dixon (1950–1992)," in *Contemporary African American Novelists: A Bio-Bibliographical Critical Sourcebook*, ed. Emmanuel S. Nelson (1999).

McBride, Dwight, and Justin Joyce. "Introduction," in *A Melvin Dixon Critical Reader* (2006).

Pinson, Hermine D. "Geography and Identity in Melvin Dixon's *Change of Territory*," *MELUS* (Spring 1996).

DAGMAWI WOUBSHET

Dixon, Sheila (27 Dec. 1953–), politician, was born Sheila Ann Dixon in Baltimore, Maryland, one of three children of Phillip Sr. and Winona Adelaide Dixon. Her father was a car salesman, and her mother was a teacher's aide and community activist; both of her parents were active members of the African Methodist Episcopal church. Dixon grew up in the solidly middle-class Ashburton neighborhood of West Baltimore and attended city public schools. At an early age she had been imbued by her parents with the ideals of public service. Upon graduating from Northwestern High School, a select, all-girls school, she enrolled at Towson University in suburban Baltimore, where she earned a Bachelor of Arts degree in Elementary Education in 1976. Dixon went to work in her hometown first as a kindergarten teacher at Stuart Hill Elementary and then as an adult education instructor with the Head Start Program. Meanwhile, she attended Johns Hopkins University, where she earned a Master of Science degree in Educational Management in 1985. Though she was employed for seventeen years as an international trade specialist with the Maryland Department of Business and Economic Development, her ascent into the realm of politics began in 1986, when she was elected to the Baltimore City State Central Committee to represent the 40th legislative district. The following year, Dixon was elected to the Baltimore City Council as the 4th Council district representative. After twelve years as a district representative, Dixon announced her bid for Baltimore City Council president, a position she won with 83 percent of the vote in 1999. During her tenure as the first African American council president in Baltimore, she created a commission to address HIV/AIDS in Baltimore and pushed for laws that would remove lead from drinking water at city schools, limit alcohol and tobacco advertisements in city neighborhoods, and prohibit race-based traffic stops by police officers. Dixon served on the Baltimore City Council for twenty years.

As City Council president, Dixon was second in line for the mayoralty. On 17 January 2007 the former mayor Martin O'Malley was sworn in as governor of Maryland, and Dixon was officially sworn into office the next day, making her the first female mayor of the city. During the remaining term of her predecessor, Dixon oversaw the enactment of a public smoking ban and a redoubling of efforts to revitalize the city and public housing. Dixon decided to enter the race to hold her appointed position as mayor and won the Democratic primary in September 2007 with 63 percent of the vote over her challenger, Councilman Keiffer J. Mitchell Jr., the grandson of civil rights leader Clarence Mitchell. She moved into the general election with the support of Governor O'Malley, the AFL-CIO, the former NAACP president and Democratic congressional representative Kweisi Mfume, the United Auto Workers, and others. Unsurprisingly given the overwhelmingly Democratic city, Dixon won the mayoral seat in November 2007 with 87.7 percent of the vote over her Republican opponent, Elbert Henderson. Dixon inherited a city known as the "homicide capital of the U.S.," with a murder rate seven times that of the national average and six times the average for New York; however, under her administration this rate was brought down to a twenty-year low. Furthermore, she instituted changes within the city's Fire Department that saved the city $7 million annually in overtime pay, at the same time attaining a 44 percent reduction in fire deaths by educating residents on safety. She also increased recycling services by 53 percent and joined the Mayors Against Illegal Guns Coalition.

Dixon served one year in office before suspicions that had been raised in 2006 about her ethics regarding financial matters resurfaced. On 18 June 2008 investigators from the Office of the State Prosecutor presented the mayor with a warrant to seize and search her residence in southwest Baltimore. Investigations took place into gifts she had received, misappropriated funds, bribery, and preferences given to associates for city contracts, and five of her aides were subpoenaed.

The court trial to address corruption under the Dixon administration began on 9 November 2009. She was convicted on 1 December on one count of fraudulent misappropriation related to the use of $500 in retail gift cards intended for distribution to needy families, and acquitted on two counts of felony theft and one of misconduct. On 6 January 2010, Dixon announced her resignation as the mayor of Baltimore effective 4 February 2010. As part of her plea agreement, Dixon was barred from seeking a new trial, made subject to four years of unsupervised probation during which time she could not run for a city or state office, instructed to perform five hundred hours of community service, and required to donate $45,000 to the Bea Gaddy Foundation, an organization for the homeless. In exchange she was allowed to keep her $84,000 annual pension, an arrangement that has drawn sharp rebuke from her critics. During her tenure Dixon has been described as tough, arrogant, and sometimes confrontational (in an incident in 1991, she waved her shoe in the air and yelled to white members of the Baltimore City Council, "You've been running things for the last 20 years. Now the shoe is on the other foot"). Nevertheless, Dixon was admired by many in the city of Baltimore, who embraced her as one of their own.

In 1988 Dixon married Thomas E. Hampton, a certified public accountant and certified public examiner employed by the District of Columbia Department of Insurance, Securities and Banking, with whom she had two children, Jasmine and Joshua; the couple divorced in 2006, the same year Hampton was confirmed as the District of Columbia Commissioner of Insurance, Securities, and Banking. She is also the aunt of the professional basketball players Juan Dixon and Jermaine Dixon. Dixon has a black belt in karate.

FURTHER READING

Bykowickz, Julie, and Annie Linskey. "Dixon Convicted of Embezzlement," *Baltimore Sun*, 1 Dec. 2009.

Fritze, John. "City Mayoral Race Begins to Take Shape." *Baltimore Sun*, 9 Nov. 2006.

Urbina, Ian. "Mayor Agrees to Step Down in Baltimore Theft Case," *New York Times*, 6 Jan. 2010.

SAFIYA DALILAH HOSKINS

D.M.C. *See* McDaniels, Darryl.

Dobbs, Mattiwilda (11 July 1925–), opera singer, was born in Atlanta, Georgia, the fifth of six daughters of John Wesley Dobbs, an activist for black equality often called the "Unofficial Mayor of Auburn Avenue," and Irene Dobbs. When she was six years old, Dobbs performed her first solos, many of which were heard in Atlanta's First Congregational Church. Dobbs's parents bought a piano soon after they were married, and she learned to play when she was seven years old.

Education was important in the Dobbs household. Dobbs graduated from high school in 1942 and then attended Spelman College, where she majored in music and studied under the voice teachers Willis Laurence James and Naomi Maise. Dobbs graduated from Spelman in 1946 as valedictorian of her class. Dobbs augmented her bachelor's degree by earning a master's degree in Spanish at Columbia Teachers College.

After college, Dobbs quickly began to build her career, traveling to New York City to work with Lotte Leonard, a teacher from Germany. Dobbs also took instruction at New York's Mannes College of Music to improve her singing skills and knowledge of opera. She was granted scholarships that allowed her to attend the Opera Workshop at Berkshire Music Center at Tanglewood (in Massachusetts), and she also won the Marian Anderson Award. A $3,000 fellowship from the John Hay Whitney Foundation enabled her to travel to Europe to study with Pierre Bernac for two years. Despite an injury to her ankle, she won first prize at the Geneva Conservatory, outperforming hundreds of competitors from all over the world with her unmatched coloratura soprano. She was then invited to an audition for La Scala and was eventually offered the opportunity to sing in this renowned European opera house. In 1953 she became the first African American to sing at La Scala. Dobbs also worked with Lola Rodriques de Aragon in Spain during this time. Dobbs found that the more inclusive and tolerant culture in Europe made it easier for African Americans to excel in the arts. Dobbs also performed in Amsterdam with the Netherlands Opera and was seen in Paris, London, Vienna, and Milan. While living in Spain, Dobbs married Luis Rodriguez. The couple had only been married a little over a year when Rodriguez died in 1954 from liver complications.

Sol Hurok eventually took Dobbs back to the United States where she debuted in the role of Zerbinetta in Richard Strauss's *Ariadne auf Naxos*. Having performed and perfected this role overseas, she received favorable reviews in New York. Following a subsequent tour of Australia and other locations throughout the world, Dobbs was offered an audition with the Metropolitan Opera in 1955 and was given the role of Gilda in Verdi's *Rigoletto* in 1956. Dobbs was the first African American female to have a regular commitment and contract with the Metropolitan Opera, having followed Marian Anderson and Robert McFerrin as the first African Americans to perform in the coveted hall. Dobbs's agreement with the Met lasted through eight seasons, and she participated in more than 29 performances, playing six different roles.

Although Dobbs was breaking racial barriers in the Metropolitan Opera House, segregation remained legal in the South. In 1957 Dobbs was prohibited by Georgia state law from marrying her second husband, a white Swede named Bengt Janzon, in her hometown of Atlanta. Instead, the couple married in New York City. Refusing to sing for segregated audiences, she was unable to perform in Atlanta until 1962.

Other noteworthy performances included Dobbs's 1954 role in Rimsky-Korsakov's *The Golden Cockerel* at the Royal Opera House, Covent Garden, in London, England, in front of Queen Elizabeth II, Prince Philip, and the visiting King Gustave and Queen Louise of Sweden. She desegregated the San Francisco Opera Company during a performance there in 1955. Dobbs also showcased her talents at Scotland's Edinburgh Festival, Ireland's Wexford Festival, and at Perth in Australia. In 1978 Dobbs had the opportunity to sing in front of President Jimmy Carter during the Congressional Gold Medal ceremony for Anderson. In 1983 Dobbs received the JAMES WELDON JOHNSON Award in Fine Arts from the National Association for the Advancement of Colored People.

After retiring from performing in the 1970s, Dobbs taught at Howard University for 14 years, where she served as a professor of voice. Dobbs also sat as a member of the National Endowment for the Arts Solo Recital Panel. Some of her recordings were released by the Columbia, Angel, and Deutsche Grammophon labels, including *Arias and Songs* in 2000. After a long and illustrious career, she retired in Arlington, Virginia.

FURTHER READING

Pomerantz, Gary M. *Where Peachtree Meets Sweet Auburn: The Saga of Two Families and the Making of Atlanta* (1996).

TIFFANI MURRAY

Doby, Larry (13 Dec. 1923–18 June 2003), baseball player and Hall of Famer, was born Lawrence Eugene Doby in Camden, South Carolina, the only child of David Doby and Etta Brooks. Abandoned by his father and left behind by his mother, who went north to look for a better life, he lived with his maternal grandmother and was known as Bubba Brooks for ten years. After his grandmother suffered a mental breakdown, he went to live with an Aunt Alice and Uncle James in 1934, at about which time he reclaimed his given name. Larry later remembered the four years that he spent with aunt and uncle, from 1934 to 1938, as the happiest of his young life.

At age fifteen, summoned by his mother, Doby arrived in Paterson, New Jersey, where he set the high school athletic world on fire with sparkling performances in baseball, football, basketball, and track. Like MONTE IRVIN, he adopted an alias—Larry Walker—to preserve his amateur status while playing professional baseball for the Newark Eagles in the Negro League. Admitted to Long Island University on a basketball scholarship, he stayed briefly before transferring to Virginia Union. His college career was cut short when he joined the U.S. Navy in 1943.

Upon his return to civilian life Doby reunited with Monte Irvin on the championship Newark Eagles, for whom he played second base opposite Irvin at shortstop. This dynamic duo arguably constituted the best hitting keystone combination in baseball history. Before entering major league baseball Doby led the Negro National League with a whopping .458 batting average, fourteen home runs, sixteen doubles, thirty-six runs, and thirty-five RBIs in only forty-two games. Cleveland Indians owner Bill Veeck was watching. This courageous maverick had wanted to integrate baseball in 1942 with the purchase of the hapless Philadelphia Phillies but was thwarted by Commissioner Kennesaw Mountain Landis.

Doby's marriage in August 1946 to Helen Curvy, the first black employee hired by New Jersey Bell Telephone, provided him with a vital anchor during the turbulent times to come. They would have five children together. In 1947, "the year that all hell broke loose," in the apposite words of the broadcaster Red Barber, baseball's racial landscape changed dramatically. Branch Rickey had beaten Bill Veeck to the punch with the historic signing of JACKIE ROBINSON. Eleven weeks later, on 5 July, after learning that Doby did not smoke, swear, or drink (not even coffee), Veeck signed him to a contract, making him the first African American in the American League. Unlike the parsimonious Rickey, who stole Robinson and other stars from the Negro Leagues, Veeck paid owner Effa Manley $15,000 for the right to sign Doby. In a move that he later regretted, the Cleveland owner refused Manley's offer of Monte Irvin's services as well. In his last game as a Newark Eagle, on 4 July, the youthful Doby hit a home run.

A wily father figure, Veeck advised Doby not to argue with umpires and opposing players and to avoid white women. When he entered the Indians' locker room for the very first time, several players refused to shake his hand. Former Yankee star Joe "Flash" Gordon broke the ice by playing catch with the newcomer. In his debut Doby struck out, and the young slugger was converted into an outfielder. One day he misjudged a fly ball with the bases loaded, resulting in a bruise (the ball hit Doby in the head), loss of face, and the loss of the game. Answering a challenge posed by Coach Bill McKechnie, Doby hit a home run the very next day to win a game. McKechnie joined the player-manager Lou Boudreau, catcher Jim Hegan,pitcher Bob

Lemon, and veteran second baseman Joe Gordon to help the first African American play in the junior circuit. Later, others tried to befriend Doby, but he withdrew into silence. He experienced verbal abuse. Opponents spit in his face, and vile epithets followed him everywhere. Franklin Lewis, a *Cleveland Press* reporter, would later describe Doby as "controversial, gifted, morose, sullen and on occasion downright surly." What Lewis failed to articulate was that silence served as Doby's defense against an openly hostile world.

Doby's first season resulted in five hits in thirty-two plate appearances; not the stuff of legends. However, in 1948, his first full year in the majors, Doby hit .301 with fourteen home runs and sixty-six RBIs, the start of a distinguished thirteen-year career with the Indians and, briefly, the White Sox and Tigers. Doby powered the Indians to a World Series win in 1948; belting a home run in game four and hitting .318 over the six-game series.

Overshadowed by such peers as Jackie Robinson, Willie Mays, Mickey Mantle, and Duke Snider, Doby did not enjoy the benefit of larger market venues. Yet he too could—and did—hit tape-measure home runs: a 470-foot clout to dead center in Yankee Stadium and a 500-foot blast at Griffith Stadium in Washington. Statistically his best year was 1950 when "Larruping Larry" (in the announcer Mel Allen's rubric) hit .326 and led the American League with 32 home runs and 126 RBIs. When he finally hung up his spikes, Doby had amassed 253 round trippers and a .283 lifetime batting average. A complete player, and the pride of Paterson, New Jersey (where 10,000 came out to greet him following the 1948 World Series), Doby could hit with power, run, field, and throw. Indeed, the graceful and mercurial outfielder once held a record for consecutive errorless play that spanned more than two seasons.

As a player, Doby also made history in 1957. According to his biographer, Joseph Moore, one incident merits consideration as a turning point in baseball history. During a game played on 13 June of that year, the Yankee pitcher Art Ditmar aimed a ball at Doby's head. Dusted, Doby charged the mound and sent a solid left to the pitcher's jaw. Never before had a black player thrown the first punch at a white player in a baseball brawl. The *Washington Post* writer Shirley Povich hailed the incident as a milestone, one that signaled the full acceptance of blacks into baseball.

In 1978 Bill Veeck again tapped Doby to serve as trailblazer, this time by appointing him manager of the Chicago White Sox. Despite his historic role in breaking barriers, it is evident that Doby lacked the fiery temperament of either Paul Robeson or Jackie Robinson. More like the even-tempered Irvin, he avoided confrontations, and seemed content with his loner status.

Often linked in the great chain of baseball and social history, Doby and Robinson invite different reactions. The poet and activist Amiri Baraka preferred Doby as "an authentic Negro." Buck O'Neil, the great Negro Leagues player and manager and Major League coach, said of Larry Doby, Jackie Robinson, and Satchel Paige, "I loved Jackie as a person; I love Satchel as a friend, and I love Larry as a son" (Moore, 172). After his release from managerial duties Larry Doby left baseball in 1979. He moved into pro basketball, serving as director of community relations for the New Jersey Nets. Doby was honored at long last by the Baseball Hall of Fame in 1998.

FURTHER READING

Moore, Joseph T. *Pride against Prejudice: The Biography of Larry Doby* (1988).

Overmyer, James. *Queen of the Negro Leagues: Effa Manley and the Newark Eagles* (1998).

Peterson Robert. *Only the Ball Was White: A History of Legendary Black Players and All-Black Professional Teams* (1970).

Obituary: *New York Times*, 19 June 2003.

JOSEPH DORINSON

Dockery, Sam (8 Sept. 1929–), jazz pianist, was born Samuel Dockery Jr. in Lawnside, New Jersey, the eldest son of Mavis Reddick and Samuel Dockery Sr. His mother was a homemaker and church pianist, and his father was a construction worker and the minister of the Church of God in Christ in Atlantic City. Sam Dockery grew up on Cherry Street in Camden, New Jersey, with eight siblings, including bassist Wayne Dockery and drummer Lemuel "Doc" Dockery. Dockery attended Camden public schools and graduated from Camden High School. All through his teen years Sam Dockery studied the piano informally, learning from his mother and listening to jazz and classical recordings. He was especially influenced by the recordings of the pianist Bud Powell, which he heard on the radio. Dockery also attended shows featuring nationally known big bands at the grand Stanley Theater on Broadway and Market streets. A local Camden pianist, Earl Stark, was an early mentor and introduced the young Dockery to harmonies that were crucial for playing jazz. During the 1940s a lot of jazz could be heard up and down Kaighn Avenue in Camden.

> They had one joint where we'd listen in on musicians playing, and they'd play all day.... Used to be a piano player named Earl Stark. He was from the swing era naturally when I was a teenager and he had fast hands and he played two handed piano. He played tempos fast. And he knew all the tunes. Good standards. I sat under him many a night. I'd say, 'what chord is that?' He showed me a 13th chord (Interview with Suzanne Cloud Tapper, 27 Nov. 2000).

By the age of twenty-five Sam Dockery was the house pianist at Music City in Philadelphia, Pennsylvania, a combination music store and performance space on Chestnut Street. Owned by the jazz drummer Ellis Tollin, Music City became a full-blown jazz club on Tuesday nights, when it featured such notables as ROY ELDRIDGE, MILES DAVIS, Gerry Mulligan, and a fifteen-piece band. Dockery's name quickly became known around town and he was sought out by the saxophonist JIMMY HEATH to play in his band, which featured the bassist Buster Williams and the drummer Specs Wright. In 1954 Dockery was hired to play a summer tour with the Buddy Rich big band. He returned to his Music City gig the next year, where, on 31 May 1955, Sam Dockery played in what would become one of the most famous recording sessions in jazz history—the last record session of the trumpeter CLIFFORD BROWN. According to Nick Catalano's book *Clifford Brown: The Life and Art of the Legendary Jazz Trumpeter* published in 2001, this session, immortalized on the Columbia Jazz Masterpieces recording *The Beginning and the End* in 1952, Sam Dockery was on piano, Ziggy Vines and Billy Root on saxophones, Ace Tisone on bass, and Ellis Tollin on drums. (Although many sources say this session took place the following year in June, Catalano's research irrefutably establishes the May 1955 date.) At this time, the style of bebop was acquiring new characteristics, becoming blusier with darker and rougher tone colors, and a hard-driving pulse with consistent swinging. It was called hard bop and the musicians who specialized in this new style mostly hailed from Philadelphia and Detroit.

In 1956 the drummer ART BLAKEY and the pianist HORACE SILVER, whose collaboration had created the legendary quintet the Jazz Messengers with the trumpeter Kenny Dorham and the tenor saxophonist HANK MOBLEY, parted ways and Sam Dockery replaced Silver as the pianist. Art Blakey and the Jazz Messengers would become a major force in hard bop and serve as an incubator for up-and-coming jazz musicians for the next thirty years. In December 1956 the recording *Hard Bop* by Art Blakey and the Jazz Messengers was released on Columbia Records featuring Bill Hardman on trumpet, Jackie McClean on alto sax, Spanky Debrest on bass, Art Blakey on drums, and Sam Dockery on piano. In 1957 Art Blakey led a plethora of sessions for eight different record labels, mostly with Sam Dockery on piano: *Ritual* (Columbia Records, 1957); *Hard Bop Academy* (Affinity, 1957); *Mirage* (Savoy, 1957); *Selections from Lerner and Lowe* (Bluebird, 1957), *Tough!* (Cadet, 1957); *Cu Bop* (Jubilee, 1957); *Art Blakey and the Jazz Messengers Live* (Calliope, 1957); *Hard Drive* (Bethlehem, 1957).

From late 1957 to 1958 Dockery toured with the guitarist TINY GRIMES, a distinguished member of the pianist ART TATUM's trio in the early 1940s, and in 1959 through the early 1960s Dockery became the house pianist for one of Philadelphia's most famed jazz nightclubs—The Showboat. The nightclub was at Broad and Lombard and featured some of the most luminous names in jazz: Benny Golson, LEE MORGAN, SONNY STITT, Gloria Lynne, Miles Davis, and JOHN COLTRANE. In 1964 Dockery recorded for the Pacific Jazz label the album *People*, with the drummer ROY HAYNES, the alto saxophonist Frank Strozier, and the bassist Larry Ridley.

Throughout the late 1960s and 1970s Dockery stayed close to home, playing in bands led by the tenor saxophonist Jimmy Oliver, one of the most influential players in Philadelphia jazz history, the singer EVELYN SIMMS, and many other music notables who came into town. In the late 1970s Dockery went back to school and received his bachelor of music from the University of the Arts in Philadelphia in 1988, becoming an instructor at the school as well. Sam Dockery continued to play jazz in Philadelphia, where he joined the Legends of Jazz big band at the Clef Club and played at a number of other jazz venues, such as Ortlieb's JazzHaus, and at many jazz festivals, such as the Cape May Jazz Fest. Dockery can also be heard on *Live at Ortlieb's* on the Dreambox jazz label, which he recorded in 2000. In December 2006 Dockery appeared with the Mellon Bank Community Jazz Award winner BUTCH BALLARD at a concert in southern New Jersey. Sam Dockery never married and had no children. According to the jazz journalist Alex Henderson, Dockery was a "very hard-swinging, straight-ahead player" who should have been recorded more. "In a perfect world, any pianist of his caliber would have a huge catalog."

FURTHER READING

Catalano, Nick. *Clifford Brown: The Life and Art of the Legendary Trumpeter* (2001).

Gioia, Ted. *The History of Jazz* (1997).

Henderson, Alex. "Sam Dockery Bio," Artist Direct. Available at http://www.artistdirect.com/nad/music/card/0,,424026,00.html.

Tapper, Suzanne Cloud. *Children of the Earle Theater: The Philadelphia Jazz Community and the Jazz Aesthetic*. Ph.D. diss., University of Pennsylvania, 2003.

SUZANNE CLOUD

Doclas, Nicholas (c. 1718–1816), freed slave and successful landowner, was either born in Natchitoches, Louisiana, in the very earliest days of the French colony, or he arrived there as an enslaved young adult. Because his name, Doclas (sometimes spelled Docla) is not French, it is presumed to have an African origin.

Doclas was baptized into the Catholic Church as an adult slave of the white French Derbanne family on 26 September 1737. Three days later, he married Judith, another slave owned by the family. Little is known of Doclas's years as a slave, although he probably served the Derbannes in many capacities. When the Spanish acquired Louisiana from France in 1763, the Derbannes's prominence in trade and local government disappeared with their connections to colonial authorities, so they switched to agriculture. Nicholas probably worked in the tobacco fields for which the area was famous. The Derbannes eventually rewarded Doclas's service by giving him his freedom. There is no information about when or under what circumstances he was liberated, but in the Natchitoches Parish Catholic Church tax rolls of 1790, he was noted as a free black owning no slaves. Doclas must have been quite elderly by then, and the Derbannes family probably considered his most productive years behind him. This was not the case, however. In the 1793 Catholic Church tax roll he owned no land and thus was not liable for taxation. But he was certainly working a plot of land, for on 24 August 1794 he bought an enslaved man, Joseph, and by 1795 he was recorded as owning two slaves. On 21 February 1799 he bought Jacques, a black Senegalese man, for $800, and on 26 September 1803 he bought another enslaved African, Baptiste, aged sixteen, for $875.

In 1802 Nicholas bought a piece of land south of Natchitoches on the Cane River, near another free black, MARIE-THÉRÈSE COINCOIN. The site was already partially cleared, and Nicholas was soon running a profitable plantation. The 1809 baptismal records of the Catholic church, mention eight slaves owned by him: Augustin, Dominique, Baptiste, Zenon, Reine, Marie, Mago, and Susanne. However, by the 1810 Census he owned only five slaves. Perhaps some were sold, or died. There is no record of how Doclas viewed or treated his slaves. It is not certain whether Doclas was born in Africa, though based on his date of birth it is likely he would have come from the Senegambia region of West Africa. It is possible that Doclas would have felt some empathy for the young African men that he bought—one of whom was from Senegal—since he had been in that situation so many years before.

During the early years of the nineteenth century, many free blacks were granted or bought, but then lost, agricultural land. This could either be because they failed to repay loans for which their land was surety, or because after Louisiana became American in 1803 they failed to make a valid legal case that the Spanish grants they were given were rightfully theirs. Doclas won a land grant case over a white man, Louis Tomassino, from whom he had bought the land, but his second wife—Marianne, whom he had married not long before (what happened to Judith is not known)—lost a similar case. Doclas was obviously familiar with his legal rights, and he was able to pay for legal representation.

He finally sold his land on 22 April 1816, at a very advanced age, and his death from fever is recorded in the parish records in the following July. His widow, Marianne, died in 1827.

Although Doclas spent most of his life as a slave in a remote community in Louisiana, when the opportunity came for him to gain his freedom, he re-created himself as a landowner and successful agriculturalist. At the time of his emancipation, he was one of very few people of African descent in the area who had their freedom, and his careful management of his affairs made him a role model for many free people who followed him.

FURTHER READING

Surviving records pertaining to Doclas can be found in the Natchitoches Parish Courthouse, Natchitoches, and at the Cammie G. Henry Research Center, Northwestern State University, Natchitoches.

FIONA J. L. HANDLEY

Doctor Daddy-O (1 Apr. 1911–13 Dec. 1993), an early New Orleans radio show host, who made his name in rhythm and blues, but devoted most of his life to gospel, was born Vernon Winslow in Dayton,

Ohio, the son of Harry and Lenora Winslow; his father was the foreman at a sign company, while his mother stayed home raising seven children. Four brothers and two sisters were all born in Ohio; their father was born in Indiana around 1886, and their mother in Kentucky around 1888.

By 1930, his father was gone, probably deceased, and Lenora Winslow was raising her family in Chicago, Illinois. The oldest sons, Wendell and Vernon, were the primary breadwinners, working as a porter for a retail store and a messenger at the office of an oil company, respectively. Somehow, carrying this responsibility at the age of nineteen, Winslow was able to attend Morehouse College in Atlanta, then complete his bachelor's degree in Design at the University of Chicago and Chicago Art Institute, and earn a master's degree in Education from Tulane University. A member of Alpha Phi Alpha fraternity, Winslow moved to New Orleans via Atlanta in 1936 to fill a vacancy teaching art at Dillard University.

Winslow prepared the illustrations in *Country Life Stories* (1938) "for the teaching of Negro children in rural communities of the South." In 1939 he resigned as art instructor at Dillard—although he would return to the campus years later—to enter the Bauhaus School of Design in Chicago, also teaching art at Hull-House (*Opportunity: The Journal of Negro Life*, 1939, Vol. 17, p. 257).

Winslow was assistant director of the South Side Community Art Center in Chicago, a Works Progress Administration facility he helped to open, which was sponsored by more than sixty South Side citizens and organizations. The chair of the Philosophy Department at Howard University, Alain Locke, assisted in the planning, characterizing 1930s paintings initially displayed as "a vigorous, intimate and original documentation of Negro life" (Mullen, Bill, *Popular Fronts: Chicago and African-American Cultural Politics, 1935–1946*, 1999, p. 84). Winslow's *Barber Shop* was displayed in one of the first exhibitions focused on black labor, amid the personal and political struggles of the Great Depression.

Winslow's October 1941 article in *The Crisis*, "Why Not a Negro Art Center?" offered clues to his future career, rejoicing in a one-hour radio program featuring Marian Anderson, Eddie (Rochester) Anderson, Canada Lee, Louis Armstrong, and Duke Ellington, while recounting the dedication of the South Side Community Art Center in Chicago the previous May by Eleanor Roosevelt. He referred to Dillard University, "young as it is," having become synonymous with a well-developed Arts Festival.

In February 1941, Winslow wrote "Negro Art and the Depression," for *Opportunity*, the magazine of the National Urban League. Within the next two years, Winslow returned to Dillard, and his designs were accepted by Harmony Musical Instrument Company to decorate the faces of ukeleles being distributed to service men in the army, navy, and marine corps (*The Crisis*, Mar. 1943, p. 69). He served as visiting faculty of Atlanta University's summer school in 1946.

His radio career began when he called to compliment an announcer at WJBW on his knowledge of jazz. A year later, he wrote to local radio stations seeking work as an announcer, to which one station responded that black programming would not be on air for some years. He got an interview with WJMR in 1947, apparently taken for "white" because of his olive skin, northern accent, and relatively straight hair. The station manager, Stanley Ray, eventually asked "By the way, are you a nigger?" Winslow firmly replied that he was a "Negro." He was offered a job teaching a series of four or five men classified as "white" to "sound black" on a show called "Jam, Jive and Gumbo."

A college-educated northern man, he had to hang out at bars, particularly the Dew Drop, to pick up local slang, literally writing it down in a notebook. Winslow gave the announcer trainees the rhyming name Poppa Stoppa (local slang for a condom), wrote their lines, fed them phrases—and was fired after reading a few of his own scripts on the air, when the announcer left the studio. (An announcer named Clarence Hayman seems to have been one of the better known to use "Poppa Stoppa.")

In 1949 the Fitzgerald Advertising agency hired him to tap into the newly studied market potential of the African American population. Putting together the name "Doctor Daddy-O" by which he became famous, he took *Jivin' with Jax* on the air on 29 May, at station WWEZ, sponsored by the Jackson Brewing Company, maker of Jax Beer. The beer company also paid for his weekly column, "Boogie Beat Jive," in the *Louisiana Weekly*. Still, he had to take the freight elevator to get to the broadcast studio, located in the New Orleans Hotel—it was another fifteen years or more before people with dark complexions could freely ride in the same elevator with "white folks."

Nelson George and many historians of New Orleans music credit Doctor Daddy-O with bringing rhythm and blues to stations that had mostly played swing jazz. Giving a lot of play to Roy Brown's "Good Rockin' Tonight" in 1947 helped make it a national hit the following year, opening space for Fats Domino, Little Richard, and many others to follow. Art Neville, one of the five Neville Brothers who formed the Hawketts, remembered that Doctor Daddy-O "was an educated cat; he tutored me in Spanish" (Neville, *The Brothers*, 2001, p. 63).

White supremacists darkly hinted that letting a black man on the radio to influence white teenagers would incite citywide race riots, but *Our World* magazine, published by JOHN PRESTON DAVIS, reported in 1951: "With records and 'mod' chatter, Dr. Daddy-O has bettered race relations in the Crescent City" (Bertrand, Michael T., *Race, Rock and Elvis*, 2000, p. 169). Rhythm and blues emerged in the late 1940s as a term for what previously had been called "race music." Jax eventually franchised the "Doctor Daddy-O" name (which the company owned) to announcers in Houston, Baton Rouge, and other cities in Louisiana and Texas. Cesta Ayres used the name at KTHT in Texas, and George Buck Jr. at WJNO radio in West Palm Beach, Florida, (*Billboard*, 26 Mar. 1955, p. 141).

During the 1950s, Winslow had a third job as sales manager for the Pontchartrain Park subdivision, and selling burial plots in Keystone Life Memorial Park. He told researchers preparing *The Human Side of Urban Renewal* (Millspaugh and Breckenfeld, 1960, p. 153) that holding several jobs is "the Negro's answer to his desire to get ahead."

Vernon Winslow backed away from rhythm and blues to concentrate on playing gospel music at WMRY. Winslow's show, *Glory Road* on WYDL, was reported by *Jet* on 5 June 1969 to be in its twentieth year. Winslow was also recognized in *Billboard* as a key deejay promoting gospel music, along with Irene Johnson in Mobile, Alabama (16 Aug. 1969, S-18). People who knew him at Dillard recalled that he had a love for the music of Sister Rosetta Tharpe and Mahalia Jackson. He was still known as "Doctor Daddy-O" while working as gospel programmer at station WBOK in his last decades.

A member of Central Congregational United Church of Christ, and the American Federation of Television and Radio Artists, Winslow retired from Dillard in 1989. He died from complications of pneumonia at Lafon Nursing Home of the Holy Family, New Orleans. He was survived by a son, Vernon Winslow Jr., a daughter, Leslye Higgins, four brothers, Wendell, Harold, Eugene, and Alfred, two sisters, Blanche Perkins and Elizabeth Wheeler, and two grandchildren. There appears to be no published reference identifying his wife.

FURTHER READING

Berry, Jason, Johathan Foose, and Tad Jones. *Up from the Cradle of Jazz: New Orleans Music since World War II* (2009).

Coleman, Rick. *Blue Monday: Fats Domino and the Lost Dawn of Rock 'n' Roll* (2007).

George, Nelson. *The Death of Rhythm & Blues* (2003).

Jackson, Joyce Marie. "The Changing Nature of Gospel Music: A Southern Case Study." *African American Review* 29, no. 2 (Summer 1995).

Obituary: New Orleans *Times Picayune*, 15 Dec. 1993.

CHARLES ROSENBERG

Doctor Jack (c. 1780–1860), root doctor and physician, first appears in the historical record in the early 1830s as a slave in Maury County, Tennessee. At the time he was owned by William H. Macon, who hired him out to practice medicine in six counties in the middle Tennessee frontier. Doctor Jack seems to have begun his general practice throughout Tennessee in the 1820s, though he may well have attended to the medical needs of his fellow slaves and others in the community for several years before. Like CESAR and other slave physicians in early America, Doctor Jack probably gained a knowledge of traditional African folk remedies using roots and herbs from other slaves, though he may also have learned of various cures from Native Americans or European settlers in the region. In the late 1820s one of his patients expressed the view that the "world would be peopled a great deal sooner, & mankind would enjoy a great deal more health and strength" if the growing dependence on manufactured drugs was abandoned in favor of the roots and herbs that "nature has wisely (and graciously) formed," and which Doctor Jack dispensed (Schweninger, 68). Interviews of former southern slaves in the 1930s and the memoirs of black "granny" midwives such as ONNIE LEE LOGAN and MARGARET C. SMITH reveal that traditional herbal remedies remained a central part of African American medical practices not only in the nineteenth century but also well into the twentieth.

Although Doctor Jack was allowed to keep only a portion of the payments for his services, he enjoyed greater freedom of movement than did many slaves in the 1820s. Given the general concern among many slaveholders that African American root doctors might use their skills to poison whites, he began traveling with letters of testimonial from former patients when making house calls. These testimonials indicate that he cared for both slaves and whites and that he cured a variety of complaints, among them the "bloody flux" (dysentery) and other gastrointestinal complaints, backaches, and inflamed joints. In one typical testimonial, a husband related that his wife had been bedridden with "great misery in the back and loins, together with a numbedness [*sic*] in her thighs" for five months and that she had grown progressively worse despite being attended by several white doctors, among them one reputed to be the best in the county. Yet within a few days of being attended by Doctor Jack, who treated her with various roots, the woman made an immediate recovery, returned to the "ordinary business of life," and soon came to enjoy "as good health as she has done for several years" (Schweninger, 72). Other patients had suffered from various ailments for as many as ten years before being cured by Doctor Jack's herbs.

In 1831 the Tennessee General Assembly threatened Doctor Jack's freedom to travel and practice medicine when it passed a law forbidding slaves to practice medicine. The new requirement was part of a general effort by southern legislatures to tighten control over slaves in the wake of the Nat Turner rebellion in Virginia that same year. While most whites in Tennessee agreed in general with the need for such restrictions, more than 120 white citizens in six counties petitioned their legislature in 1831 to exempt Doctor Jack from this proscription "in the firm belief that" his continuation as a practicing doctor would advance the "public good." The petitioners, who included several physicians, may have disparagingly referred to the fifty-year-old Jack as a "boy" but were otherwise unstinting in their praise of him, stating:

> Though he may be a slave ... his character for honesty and fair correct deportment, is fair and not often excelled by many who profess to possess more than he does.... In his profession ... he has practiced with great & unparalleled success for many years (Schweninger, 70).

While the legislature did not exempt Doctor Jack, he continued his practice for several years, protected from the letter of the law by his owner and his many prominent white patients.

In August 1843, however, when William Macon moved from Maury County to Fayette County, bringing Doctor Jack with him, several of their new white neighbors demanded that Jack cease practicing medicine. A far larger group of more than one hundred whites, many of whom had known the doctor for over two decades, responded by again petitioning the state legislature to allow him to continue his practice. The petitioners sought to allay any fears Fayette County citizens may have had about Doctor Jack's "character," describing him as "humble, unobtrusive, peaceable, and quiet; and in his morals altogether irreproachable" (Schweninger, 76). That same month a group of sixty white women sent a similar petition, praising Doctor Jack's medical skills, "especially in obstinate cases of long standing," and demanding that "the people ought not to be denied the privilege of commanding his services" (Schweninger, 76). This latter petition is all the more remarkable in that it is one of the few examples in the antebellum South in which a group of women petitioned a legislature for any reason.

Like other skilled slaves in the upper South, Doctor Jack appears to have eventually earned enough money to purchase his own freedom. By 1853 he was living in Nashville and appears in that city's business directory simply as "Jack, Root Doctor." He died in Nashville in 1860 and was buried in the black section of the city cemetery as "Jack Macon, known as 'Dr. Jack.'"

FURTHER READING

Numbers, Ronald L., and Todd L. Savitt. *Science and Medicine in the Old South* (1989).

Schweninger, Loren. "Doctor Jack: A Slave Physician on the Tennessee Frontier," in *Trial and Triumph: Essays in Tennessee's African American History*, ed. Carroll Van West (2002).

STEVEN J. NIVEN

Dodd, Joseph Eldridge (1907–Nov. 1945), landscape and figure painter, was born in Wood County, near Parkersburg, West Virginia, to Charles T. Dodd and Senora Tibbs Dodd. Dodd attended local schools and began studying art by correspondence. In 1925 he attended the West Virginia Colored Institute (later West Virginia State College) in Institute, West Virginia. He graduated second in his class and was student body president. In 1929 he received a scholarship to study at the National Academy of Design in New York.

In 1932 Dodd returned to West Virginia and worked as an art professor at Bluefield State College in Bluefield, West Virginia. Dodd was a practicing artist during the years that he taught. He taught numerous classes, showcasing his many talents. He taught introduction to art classes for public school teachers not aspiring to be practicing artists but who wished to have some art background. The range of Dodd's teaching—he taught everything from the essentials of lettering to art appreciation—is quite astounding. In order to teach the various classes, he had to be proficient in each and every medium.

Considered by his students to be a demanding but fair teacher, Dodd in 1937 was voted favorite teacher by the Bluefield State College student body. During his time at Bluefield, Dodd rented a room on Park Street, an upscale neighborhood that was home to a number of the city's prominent African Americans.

In 1939 he painted *Bluefield, View from My Room,* an oil-on-canvas work that uses rich colors and depicts the town and surrounding foliage. The painting is now owned by West Virginia University's West Virginia Historical Art Collection in Morgantown, West Virginia, which also holds seven other paintings by Dodd. In one untitled painting, an athletic man sits on a stool holding a pole. His musculature is highlighted and studied with various angles. In *Laurel Pass* three naked men are posed on jagged rocks. The man on the highest point holds a tattered red and blue flag, while the two other men are posed semi-reclining in exhaustion or pain. Each figure's musculature is highlighted with chiaroscuro and different shades of color.

In the fall of that year, Dodd took a leave of absence from Bluefield State College and began graduate study at Yale University. He won numerous awards and remained at Yale until 1942, when he was drafted into military service. In 1945 Dodd returned to Bluefield from the South Pacific in deteriorating health. He died from coronary hearth disease in November 1945, while resting against the wall that he painted in his signature work, *Bluefield, View from My Room.*

The West Virginia Historical Art Collection owns several works by Dodd. His landscapes, nude studies, and other figure drawings are in private collections in Parkersburg, West Virginia, and Columbus, Ohio.

FURTHER READING

Archer, Bill. "Visions of the Ideal" (forthcoming).
Cuthbert, John A. *Early Art and Artists in West Virginia* (2000).

KIMBERLY L. MALINOWSKI

Dodds, Baby (24 Dec. 1898–14 Feb. 1959), jazz drummer, was born Warren Dodds in New Orleans, Louisiana, the son of Warren Dodds. His father played quills (a type of musical pipe made from reeds), his mother (name unknown) played the melodeon, his sisters were accomplished on both organ and harmonica, and his older brother JOHNNY DODDS became an outstanding jazz clarinetist. Named for his father, Warren Dodds at an early age became "Baby," an appellation he carried for life. As a child he was given a tin flute, but he never mastered it and eventually gave it to Johnny. His father thought drums were too noisy, but Dodds nevertheless constructed a primitive set out of tin cans in which he punched holes; he used discarded chair rungs as his sticks. Finally, at age seventeen, he obtained a rope bass drum and a snare drum. He rounded out his first set of real drums with others he picked up at pawnshops. Lacking formal lessons, he was basically self-taught.

To trace Dodds's subsequent career is to mention virtually every major personality in the rise of New Orleans jazz. His first paying jobs came in 1912 at small New Orleans clubs. Dodds also played street parades with Frankie Dusen's and BUNK JOHNSON's bands and occasionally sat in with ARMAND PIRON's group. For several years he periodically performed with his childhood friend Willie Hightower's American Stars, sometimes playing for ice cream. His initial inspiration on drums was Mack Murray, who also performed in both the popular street parades and the John Robichaux band. But influences were everywhere: an early teacher was "Rabbit" from MA RAINEY's band, and the drummer Walter Grundy taught him to read music. He admired the drummers Henry Zeno, Henry Martin, Tubby Hall, Louis Cottrell, Roy Palmer, and Dave Perkins.

OSCAR "PAPA" CELSTIN hired Dodds briefly in 1917 for roadhouse work, including at the 101 Ranch in New Orleans, a popular venue for aspiring musicians. As jazz spread in popularity, the bassist GEORGE "POPS" FOSTER got him jobs on riverboats plying the Mississippi. There he played with LOUIS ARMSTRONG in a group led by FATE MARABLE called the Jaz-E-Saz Band. Photographs dated 1918 or so show Dodds on board the SS *Capitol* and the SS *Sydney*, both of which were run by the St. Louis–based Streckfus family, pioneers of the floating dance hall. At this time Dodds was already noted for having a great smile and an utterly reliable beat, two of his most memorable traits.

Although classified as a drummer, Dodds was also accomplished on washboard, a novelty instrument popular in the 1920s. He mastered the use of cowbells, wood blocks, tom-toms, and other crowd pleasers, sometimes being accused of overexuberance. Additionally, to the ears of some listeners, he tended to overuse the bass drum. Yet others credit him as the first to extract the full potential of this percussion instrument.

In 1921, while playing on the riverboat *St. Paul*, KING OLIVER asked Dodds to accompany him to San Francisco as drummer with Oliver's famous Creole Jazz Band. While there, he also played with KID ORY. During this period Dodds made yearly visits to Chicago either with Oliver and Armstrong or on his own. In 1924 he returned to Chicago with LIL HARDIN ARMSTRONG. Once there he also played with FREDDIE KEPPARD, Willie Hightower, and his brother Johnny. He in fact stayed with his brother off and on until 1940, when Johnny died. The two did not always get on smoothly because Baby drank and Johnny did not.

As his reputation spread Dodds in 1926 played in the Hugh Swift Band at the Evergreen Golf Club, which included doing some radio broadcasts and playing concerts featuring semiclassical pieces, not jazz. The year 1927 found him with the Charlie Elgar Band in Chicago. Popular white bandleaders such as Paul Whiteman and Guy Lombardo were impressed with Dodds, both for his skills and the sheer number of songs he knew. A high point in Dodds's career occurred in 1927, when Louis Armstrong formed his Hot Seven Band, with Armstrong on trumpet, Lil Hardin on piano, Johnny Dodds on clarinet, Kid Ory on trombone, and JOHNNY ST. CYR on banjo (these first-named also constituted the equally famous Hot Five), along with Pete Briggs on tuba and Baby Dodds on drums. This association burnished his reputation.

During the Depression Dodds played a variety of Chicago clubs. By the early 1940s, his fame well established, Dodds recorded and played with many different groups. He performed with Bunk Johnson, JELLY ROLL MORTON, Jimmie Noone, SIDNEY BECHET, Mezz Mezzrow (including a trip to France in 1948), Art Hodes, MIFF MOLE, Bob Wilber, and Lee Collins. Dodds also led several groups of his own during this period.

Dodds was the first of the influential drum stylists, and he revolutionized the drumming of his time. In contrast to many of his contemporaries, he was light-handed, yet he seldom used brushes. Actually, Dodds was more of a percussionist than a drummer. He thought in terms of tonal colors and how to mix them. He correctly realized that drums and cymbals were pitched and needed tuning and that they had a wide range of tonal variations. They could fit harmonic as well as rhythmic patterns. Unfortunately, there exists little recorded evidence of Dodds's genius. On most of his early recordings he is virtually inaudible; but he may not have been playing anything other than wood blocks, since early audio technology could not accommodate the sound of actual drums.

Louis Armstrong encouraged Dodds to play an even four beats instead of emphasizing the second and fourth, which was more characteristic of the time. The result lightened the pounding drum sound immeasurably. Dodds also developed breaks, brief drum solos that fill the gap at the end of another instrument's solo. This eventually led to the drum solo, which has become so much a part of jazz since then. He attempted to play behind soloists—to whom he was always attentive—not overpower them. His playing has been recognized for its subtle nuances. As his later recordings attest, his drumming provided the pulsating rhythmic undercurrent that exemplified jazz.

Dodds was married at least twice (his second wife's name was Ruth). He died in Chicago after a series of strokes, starting in 1949, that gradually incapacitated him.

FURTHER READING

Hodes, Art, and Chadwick Hansen, eds. *Selections from the Gutter* (1977).

Shapiro, Nat, and Nat Hentoff, eds. *The Jazz Makers* (1957).

DISCOGRAPHY

Baby Dodds: Talking and Drum Solos.

This entry is taken from the *American National Biography* and is published here with the permission of the American Council of Learned Societies.

WILLIAM H. YOUNG

Dodds, Johnny (12 Apr. 1892–8 Aug. 1940), jazz clarinetist, was born John M. Dodds in Waverly, Louisiana, the son of Warren Dodds, a farm worker, warehouse employee, and handyman, and Josephene (maiden name unknown). Raised in New Orleans from 1901, at age seventeen Dodds was given a clarinet by his father, an amateur musician who sang religious songs with the family and played a variety of instruments. A high school graduate, Dodds studied clarinet with the legendary Creole master LORENZO TIO JR. and the bandsman Charlie McCurdy. He also began paying serious attention to SIDNEY BECHET, who though five years his junior was already a skilled jazz improviser. In 1911 the bassist POPS FOSTER heard Dodds practicing clarinet while on a lunch break from his job at a rice mill; impressed with his abilities, Foster brought him to the attention of KID ORY. Dodds sat in with the trombonist's band at the Globe Hall and was hired immediately for his first professional job in neighboring Gretna. During this time Dodds also took jobs with Jack Carey's and other marching bands.

In 1917 Dodds traveled to Chicago with Billy and Mary Mack's Merrymakers. He then played from May to September 1918 on the Streckfus line riverboat SS *Sidney* with FATE MARABLE's twelve-piece band, whose personnel included LOUIS ARMSTRONG, the banjoist JOHNNY ST. CYR, Foster, and Dodds's younger brother, the drummer (Warren) BABY DODDS. On his return to New Orleans Dodds rejoined Ory in 1919, and in January 1920 he returned to Chicago to join KING OLIVER's new band. In June 1921 Oliver began an extended engagement at the Pergola Dance Pavilion in San Francisco, leaving in September for a series of ballroom and theater engagements in Los Angeles and other West Coast cities. Back in Chicago in the spring, Oliver's Creole Jazz Band began its historic residency at the Lincoln Gardens in mid-June, and in late August its ranks were strengthened by the addition of Armstrong, completing the personnel of the first great jazz band in history. However, after recording thirty-seven performances from April until December 1923 (most of them featuring Dodds), in early 1924 dissensions resulted in the band's partial breakup. The Dodds brothers, the trombonist HONORE DUTREY, and the bassist BILL JOHNSON, along with the cornetist FREDDIE KEPPARD and the pianist Charlie Alexander, left the Gardens to work at Bert Kelly's Stables, a regular club job for Dodds through New Year's Day 1930.

From 1925 until 1929 Dodds enjoyed his most prolific period of recording, appearing not only on the classic Armstrong Hot Five and Hot Seven series with Ory, Lil Hardin Armstrong, St. Cyr, and Baby Dodds but also on dates with JELLY ROLL MORTON and others, including many recorded under his own leadership. Throughout the 1930s Dodds continued to lead small groups, usually with Dominique, Baby Dodds, and the pianist Leo Montgomery, at such clubs as the Three Deuces, the New Stables, and the Hotel Hayes. On 18 May 1937 the Dodds quartet appeared in concert at the Congress Hotel opposite ROY ELDRIDGE's swing band, ZUTTY SINGLETON's sextet, and the Bob Crosby orchestra at a benefit for the pneumonia-stricken pianist Joe Sullivan. In January 1938, eight and a half years after his last recording session, Dodds made his first and only visit to New York to record with LIL ARMSTRONG and members of JOHN KIRBY's sextet, but in May 1939, while leading a sextet at the Hotel Hayes, he suffered a stroke, his second in a year and one that left him unable to play for many months. Despite dental problems, as well, he then worked occasionally with his quartet, now under Baby Dodds's contractual leadership, at the 9750 Club (Jan.–Mar. 1940). In June, equipped with full dentures, he recorded two titles for Decca's *New Orleans Jazz* album, and from mid-July he played at 5400 Broadway. After suffering a third stroke, he died in Chicago.

In direct contrast to his highly emotional, expressive musical persona, Dodds was a serious and sober man who disapproved of his younger brother's wild and carefree lifestyle. On stage he always conducted himself in a professional manner, and he expected the same of his bandsmen. Similarly, as a family man, while earning top salaries in the 1920s, he started to invest in real estate, ultimately acquiring clear title to a three-story apartment building, as well as maintaining a financial interest in his older brother's taxicab company and garage. Even after the onset of his physical problems, he supported his wife and three children on the income from his investments.

Although his playing was integral to the artistic success of the records he made with Oliver, Armstrong, and Morton, most of Dodds's own more fully realized performances are on the 1926–1929 dates issued under his own name or such sobriquets as the New Orleans Wanderers, New Orleans Bootblacks, Chicago Footwarmers, and the Beale Street Washboard Band. He worked exceedingly well with Armstrong, yet he usually played at his best in the company of less commanding cornetists such as GEORGE MITCHELL, Natty Dominique, and Herb Morand. As Bechet had done earlier, Dodds developed a strong lead style by the mid-1920s, and although he never lost his skill at ensemble counterpoint, by the late 1920s he was clearly the major force in the front line.

Dodds's reputation as the best blues and stomp clarinetist in jazz history is not unfounded. Throughout his career he played with an inventiveness, rhythmic drive, technical assurance, and variety of timbral expression that many critics feel was surpassed only by Bechet on soprano sax. Frequently he would play with a warm intimacy in the broad, dark, lower recesses of his range and then, with bold, darting lines, either leap or gradually ascend to a raw, almost savage, visceral intensity in his searing upper register. By no means though was this a formulaic pattern; his performances are valued for their unpredictability as much as for their consistency. Like Bechet he favored a hot, throbbing vibrato and a free-flowing, almost rubato phrasing, but because his sound was personal and part of an age forgotten by the later 1930s, his later years were spent in comparative obscurity. Dodds's greatest period of influence occurred following the New Orleans Revival of the mid-1940s, when hundreds of young white clarinetists attempted to duplicate his tone and feeling.

Johnny Dodds was perhaps the most uncommercial, aesthetically pure jazz clarinetist of all time. Well into the swing era, when big bands prevailed, Dodds still played the same informal, heartfelt small-band jazz that he had played in the 1920s, his slashing, blues-drenched sound soaring above his surroundings, untouched by the changes in the world around him.

FURTHER READING

Chilton, John. *Sidney Bechet: The Wizard of Jazz* (1987).
Collier, James Lincoln. *Louis Armstrong: An American Genius* (1983).
Dodds, Baby, and Larry Gara. *The Baby Dodds Story* (1959).
Foster, Pops, and Tom Stoddard. *The Autobiography of Pops Foster* (1971).

DISCOGRAPHY

Johnny Dodds: Blue Clarinet Stomp (RCA, 1990).
Johnny Dodds: South Side Chicago Jazz (MCA, 1990).
Johnny Dodds: 1926–1928 (JSP, 1990).
Rust, Brian. *Jazz Records, 1897–1942*, 5th ed. (1982).

This entry is taken from the *American National Biography* and is published here with the permission of the American Council of Learned Societies.

JACK SOHMER

Dodson, Howard, Jr. (1 June 1939–), historian, lecturer, and administrator, was born in Chester, Pennsylvania, the eldest of four children and the only son of Lou Bird Jones Dodson, a dry-cleaning plant worker, and Howard Dodson Sr., a construction worker. During his childhood he was active in the Bethany Baptist Church, the Cub Scouts, and the Boy Scouts. With the encouragement of his parents and teachers, he did well academically throughout his time in the Chester Public Schools.

After completing high school in 1957, Dodson attended West Chester State College, graduating in 1961 with a degree in social studies and English. He then enrolled in a master's program in history and political science at Villanova University, graduating in 1964. Dodson went on to join the Peace Corps as a volunteer in Ecuador, South America, where he spent two years before continuing with the organization as a deputy director of recruiting and director of minority and specialized recruiting.

In the wake of DR. MARTIN LUTHER KING JR.'s assassination in 1968, Dodson sought to better understand the social and historical roots of the unrest of the day by reading and studying black classics in history and literature. He elected to engage in this independent study in San Juan, Puerto Rico, where he spent a year. In 1969 he entered the doctoral program in black history and race relations at the University of California at Berkeley, but left the program without a degree in 1974. In 1970 he married Jualynne White, a sociologist. They had two children, a son and a daughter, before divorcing.

From 1974 to 1979 Dodson was the executive director of the Institute of the Black World, a research institute in Atlanta, Georgia, that sought to eradicate discrimination and to promote black self-determination as well as social and political equality for blacks. He also lectured part-time at Emory University. From October 1979 to January 1982 he was a consultant to the chairman of the National Endowment of the Humanities. He served as the administrative director of the "Black Studies Curriculum Development Project," of the Institute of the Black World in Washington, D.C., a project to study and make recommendations concerning undergraduate courses in black studies.

In 1984 Dodson was appointed to the position of chief curator at the Schomburg Center for Research in Black Culture. The Schomburg Center had been a cultural gathering place as well as a library for many years, and Dodson expanded this tradition by offering a wide array of public programs including plays, lecture series, and exhibitions. Under his leadership the already substantial collections of the Schomburg Center increased fourfold. Dodson. Dodson instituted Schomburg's scholars-in-residence program to provide six- and twelve-month fellowships for scholars whose research was largely based on the Schomburg's collections. This program also enabled the scholars to share their research with one another and with the Schomburg staff.

Dodson also directed successful capital campaigns and construction projects that made possible the LANGSTON HUGHES auditorium, new exhibition halls, and the Moving Image and Recorded Sound Division. A later renovation project made possible a new lobby, new reading room for the General Research and Reference division, and more space for the scholars-in-residence program. Dodson also curated several exhibitions at the

Schomburg Center, including Lest We Forget: The Triumph over Slavery, Black New Yorkers/ Black New York: 400 Years of African American History, and Invoking the Spirit: Worship Traditions in the African World.

Dodson was a frequent speaker at cultural events and educational institutions and was a sought-after consultant to black museums, black colleges, and black studies programs. He also served on the boards of directors of a number of organizations, including the Apollo Theater Foundation and the Upper Manhattan Empowerment Zone. He was a leader in developing a memorial for the site of the African Burial Ground in lower Manhattan. When human bones of slaves and others of African descent were discovered at a federal construction site in 1991, Dodson saw the importance of preserving the site. Originally called the "Negro Burial Ground," the cemetery was used as a burial ground in the seventeenth and eighteenth centuries, when as many as 15,000 Africans were buried there. In order to keep the burial ground in the public consciousness—and to prevent the area from being covered by other kinds of construction—Dodson and others supported the creation of a memorial on the site.

In 2001 Dodson became the Institute of Museum and Library Services' African American Migration Experience Project director. The components of this project included an exhibition, a Web site making essays, books, manuscripts, and illustrations electronically accessible, and *In Motion: The African-American Migration Experience*, a National Geographic publication.

Through both his position as the chief of the Schomburg Center and his work as a scholar and lecturer, Dodson played a major role in promoting the collection, dissemination, and preservation of resources documenting the culture and history of peoples of African descent. Through his aggressive educational and cultural initiatives, Dodson raised the profile of the center to that of one known throughout the world as the most comprehensive research institution of its kind.

FURTHER READING

"Howard Dodson, Jr.," *Contemporary Black Biography*, vol. 52 (2006).

Smith, Jessie Carey. *Notable Black American* Men (1999).

Wadler, Joyce. "Public Lives: Pursuer of the Paper Trail on Malcolm X Boulevard," *New York Times*, 14 Mar. 2002.

LISA FINDER

Dolphy, Eric (20 June 1928–29 June 1964), jazz musician, was born Eric Allan Dolphy Jr, in Los Angeles, California, the son of Eric Dolphy Sr. and Sadie Gillings. He showed a strong interest in music during his preschool years and began playing clarinet in the first grade. He participated in musical activities throughout his grade school years, and he studied privately with Lloyd Reese, a well-known Los Angeles music teacher who also taught the jazz musicians Buddy Collette, DEXTER GORDON, and CHARLES MINGUS. After graduating from high school Dolphy enrolled in music classes at Los Angeles City College. By this time he also was playing alto saxophone with local bands, and he made his first recordings with a big band led by the drummer Roy Porter. After serving in the army during the early 1950s he returned to Los Angeles and reentered the music profession. Early in 1958 his friend Buddy Collette recommended him to the drummer Chico Hamilton, who needed a woodwind player. Dolphy moved from local to national prominence in jazz, playing flute, clarinet, bass clarinet, and alto sax in Hamilton's quintet. (He is heard on Hamilton's album *Gongs East*, Dec. 1958.) The group at the time was well known for playing a type of gentle bebop popularly known as "cool" jazz, although Dolphy's style leaned toward the more exuberant in that idiom.

At the end of 1959 Hamilton's quintet broke up, and Dolphy soon began working and recording with Mingus in New York City, appearing with him prominently on the album *Charles Mingus Presents Charles Mingus* (20 Oct. 1960). Mingus's groups played an energetic, almost chaotic brand of jazz, combining elements of bop, DUKE ELLINGTON's music, and basic classical techniques in a style much better suited to Dolphy's taste than that of Hamilton's quintet. During his tenure with Mingus, Dolphy recorded with other players and made his first recordings as a leader, most notably on the album *Out There* (15 Aug. 1960). After a year he left Mingus's group and recorded some highly regarded and historically important albums with other leaders, including ORNETTE COLEMAN's *Free Jazz* (21 Dec. 1960), Oliver Nelson's *The Blues and the Abstract Truth* (23 Feb. 1961), and GEORGE RUSSELL's *Ezz-Thetic* (8 May 1961). He also participated in some of the composer Gunther Schuller's concerts and recordings of third-stream music, which attempted, sometimes successfully, to blend jazz and European-style classical music.

Intermittently from 1961 until 1963 Dolphy wrote arrangements for and played with the saxophonist

John Coltrane appearing on *Spiritual* (1 Nov. 1961) and on concert recordings made in Europe (Nov. and Dec. 1961). Coltrane at the time was the most prominent avant-garde player in jazz, so Dolphy's association with him was professionally as well as musically important. During the same period he also rejoined Mingus's group for short stays and led groups of his own. He took part in a short European tour with Mingus in April 1964 and remained on the continent to perform on his own. On 27 June he began a nightclub engagement in Berlin, but he was too sick to complete the first night's performance. Two days later he died of a heart attack, possibly triggered by a diabetic condition. His body was flown to Los Angeles for burial.

Dolphy had a solid musical background in bebop, the jazz style that Dizzy Gillespie, Charlie Parker, and others had developed in the 1940s. Indeed, Dolphy's style of improvisation held many similarities to Parker's. But he went beyond the bebop idiom's norms of harmony, melody, and tone quality and became a leading figure in the "free jazz" or "action jazz" idiom. This stylistic evolution was aesthetically rewarding but economically costly. Free jazz, then and later, was the least understood and least liked of jazz styles, and he often went without playing jobs. For a time he supported himself mainly by private teaching. He found steadier work and more sympathetic audiences in Europe than in the United States.

Like Coltrane, Dolphy had a thorough command of his instruments and of both the bebop and the post-bebop jazz styles. In the early 1960s the music that Dolphy and Coltrane created was often attacked by the jazz audience and press. When a widely read critic labeled their music "nonsense," "nihilistic exercises," "anti-jazz," and "gobbledegook," the two men felt compelled to defend their music in print. In their published interview Dolphy explained that some of what he played on flute imitated birdcalls, including the nonstandard pitches that birdcalls contain. He believed his music to be inspiring and moving, and he wished that critics would ask the performers about the music before writing uninformed reviews that could hurt the musicians economically.

Dolphy dedicated himself untiringly to developing his forceful personal style and to mastering several instruments, principally alto saxophone, flute, and bass clarinet. He remains the principal bass clarinetist in jazz history. His unaccompanied bass clarinet solo, "God Bless the Child" (8 Sept. 1961), recorded in Copenhagen, is a landmark. His album *Iron Man* (July 1963), on which he mainly plays alto saxophone, is a prime example of his mature playing. In some of the album's pieces he creates melodies with wide leaps, sudden changes of direction, and rapid flurries of notes; these freely ranging, angular melodies have little obvious connection with the harmonies of the themes. Yet on the ballads his command of the traditional harmonic vocabulary of jazz is clear and idiomatically consistent.

FURTHER READING

Gordon, Robert. *Jazz West Coast: The Los Angeles Jazz Scene of the 1950s* (1986).

Horricks, Raymond. *The Importance of Being Eric Dolphy* (1988).

Litweiler, John. *The Freedom Principle: Jazz after 1958* (1984).

Reichardt, Uwe. *Like a Human Voice: The Eric Dolphy Discography* (1986).

Schroedl, Blake, and Jeff Schroedl. *The Eric Dolphy Collection* (2003).

Simosko, Vladimir, and Barry Tepperman. *Eric Dolphy, a Musical Biography and Discography* (1974).

Obituary: *Down Beat*, 13 Aug. 1964.

This entry is taken from the *American National Biography* and is published here with the permission of the American Council of Learned Societies.

THE ANB EDITORS

Domingo, Wilfred Adolphus (26 Nov. 1889–14 Feb. 1968), socialist, journalist, and Jamaican nationalist, was born in Kingston, Jamaica. He was orphaned at an early age and raised by his uncle, Adolphus Grant, and was trained as a tailor. In Jamaica, he joined Sandy Cox's National Club, a pioneering nationalist organization, and became a leader along with Marcus Garvey. In 1910 Domingo moved to Boston, where he attended night school in preparation for medical school. In 1912 he instead moved to New York, where he became a successful importer of Caribbean food. When Garvey settled in New York in 1916, Domingo introduced him to local black political leaders. He became the first editor of the *Negro World* in 1917, the paper associated with Garvey's Universal Negro Improvement Association, a Pan-African nationalist organization. At the same time, Domingo—along with other "New Negro" radicals, including Chandler Owen, A. Philip Randolph, and Richard Benjamin Moore—became increasingly active in the Harlem Socialist Party (SP). In general the

American SP ignored the oppression of black people, at worst supporting segregation and at best arguing that blacks were subject to only class, and not race, oppression. However, the Harlem branch uniquely attempted to work out a socialist program to deal with black oppression, thanks in part to the work of the pioneer black socialist HUBERT HENRY HARRISON (who had left the SP by the time Domingo joined).

Domingo, like many radicals from the British Caribbean, opposed the World War both as a socialist internationalist and as an opponent of British imperialism. Domingo's socialist politics increasingly put him at odds with Garvey, and in 1919, Garvey fired him. He quickly became associated with Owen and Randolph's *Messenger*, and in 1920 he also helped Moore edit the short-lived, anti-Garvey *Emancipator*. At the same time he was a leading member of the radical black nationalist African Blood Brotherhood (ABB), organized by Moore, Grace Campbell, and CYRIL VALENTINE BRIGGS. Unlike other members of the New York ABB, however, Domingo did not join the Communist Party. In fact, in 1919 he criticized the precursor to the Communist Party for not paying enough attention to racial oppression.

In the mid-1920s Domingo withdrew from active political life, focusing instead on his business. He did, however, contribute a chapter to ALAIN LEROY LOCKE's anthology *The New Negro* (1925) on West Indians in the United States in which he articulated his perspective on the role of black immigrants on black politics, arguing: "The outstanding contribution of West Indians to American Negro life is the insistent assertion of their manhood in an environment that demands too much servility and unprotesting acquiescence from men of African blood." In 1923, when the *Messenger* attacked Garvey for his Caribbean background, Domingo broke with the *Messenger*, not out of sympathy with Garvey but to protest the paper's increasingly anti–West Indian bias, among other disagreements.

In the 1930s Domingo became active in Caribbean politics. He helped form the Jamaica Progressive League in New York in 1936, which advocated self-rule; it soon merged with Norman Manley's Jamaican nationalist People's Nationalist Party. In 1937–1938 he toured Jamaica, and in the late 1930s he contributed to the *Jamaican Labour Weekly*, Jamaica's first labor paper. With Moore he helped organize the West Indian National Committee in 1941, which, while supporting the British in World War II, sought Caribbean self-determination. In 1941 Manley invited Domingo to visit Jamaica for six months to help organize there. Even before touching shore Domingo was arrested by British authorities under the auspices of wartime emergency powers. Despite the fact that, unlike during World War I, Domingo clearly supported the British, he was held for twenty months in a Jamaican detention center without being charged. Liberals—including the American Civil Liberties Union—radicals, and nationalists took up his case, and in February 1943 the British released him. However, it was not until 1947 that the U.S. government would allow Domingo—who had never become a U.S. citizen—to again enter the country. In the 1950s he broke with his comrades in both the United States and in Jamaica and opposed the short-lived West Indian Federation. In the late 1950s he wrote two pamphlets on this subject, *The British West Indian Federation: A Critique* (1956) and *Federation: Jamaica's Folly* (1958). Some sources report that he was married to a classical pianist, but all details of this alleged relationship, including the woman's name, are a mystery. In 1964 Domingo suffered a stroke and four years later died in New York City.

FURTHER READING

Allen, Ernest, Jr. "The New Negro: Explorations in Identity and Social Consciousness, 1910–1922," in *1915: The Cultural Moment*, eds. Adele Heller and Lois Rudnick (1991).

Hart, Richard. *Towards Decolonisation: Political, Labour and Economic Development in Jamaica, 1938–1945* (1999).

James, Winston. *Holding Aloft the Banner of Ethiopia: Caribbean Radicalism in Early Twentieth-Century America* (1998).

Samuels, Wilfred D. *Five Afro-Caribbean Voices in American Culture, 1917–1929* (1977).

Turner, Joyce Moore. "Richard B. Moore and His Works," in *Richard B. Moore, Caribbean Militant in Harlem: Collected Writings 1920–1972*, eds. W. Burghardt Turner and Joyce Moore Turner (1988).

J. A. ZUMOFF

Domino, Fats (26 Feb. 1928–), rock and roll musician, was born Antoine Domino in Crescent City, New Orleans, one of nine children. His first language was French, and he was born into a musical family. His father was a well-known violinist, and Antoine was taught to play the piano by his brother-in-law, Harrison Verret, who was twenty years his senior. His first performance took place when he was ten years old, and he dropped out of school at fourteen to work in a factory so that he could play in nightclubs. When he was nineteen years old he married Rosemary Hall, with whom he would go on to raise eight children. Among his early influences were the boogie-woogie innovator Albert Ammons and the jazz pianist Fats Waller.

Domino joined the Dave Bartholomew band in the 1940s, and in 1949 he signed to the Imperial Records label and made his first independent recording, engineered by Cosimo Matassa. Matassa, the engineer and owner of J&M and Cosimo recording studios in New Orleans, is considered fundamental to the development of New Orleans rhythm and blues and rock and roll during the 1950s and 60s. One of the eight songs to come out of this session was "The Fat Man," considered by some to be the first rock and roll record and the record from which Domino derived his stage name, "Fats." The song was based on an old barrelhouse standard, "Junker's Blues," and displayed an abundance of local influences, ranging from the ensemble playing of black funeral bands (Domino was accompanied on this song by drums, string bass, guitar, and saxophone), the syncopated "second line" rhythms of Mardi Gras parades (these accompany the "first line" rhythm in a New Orleans Mardi Gras parade, in a call and response format), boogie-woogie piano style, and the country blues of the Mississippi Delta. The song was a huge hit and ultimately sold a million copies.

The team that produced "The Fat Man," from the musicians to the engineer to Domino's co-writer Bartholomew, would go on to be behind almost every one of Fats Domino's hits over the course of the next twenty years. Domino would also become known as by far the most successful exponent of the style of "jump blues" developed in New Orleans and southern Louisiana. Another performer with a similar style, Roy Byrd, who went by the stage name "Professor Longhair," was also popular, although his impact and influence has been more closely associated with New Orleans, in contrast to Domino's national reputation.

Domino's next big hit came in 1952 with "Goin' Home," the first of his nine number 1 hits on the rhythm and blues charts. His singing style evolved from the high-pitched whoops of the "Fat Man" to a deeper voice that emphasized his Louisiana accent. A key point in his career came in 1954 when he performed as part of the well-known disc jockey Alan Freed's "Moondog Jubilee of Stars under the Stars." The concert took place at Ebbets Field in Brooklyn, New York, and Domino shared a bill with important artists such as Muddy Waters and the influential vocal group the Orioles.

Though Domino's record sales (typically between 500,000 and a million) indicated that his appeal went well beyond a strictly black audience, it was not until 1955 and his hit "Ain't That a Shame" that Domino would be widely regarded as a "cross-over" performer. Still, the version recorded that same year by Pat Boone far outsold Fats Domino's recording, and went to number 1 on the pop charts. This pattern of a white performer benefiting from Domino's song-writing talents was repeated in 1957 when his hit "I'm Walkin'" was used to launch the career of the teenage sensation Ricky Nelson. Domino did, however, receive songwriting royalties, and an article in *Time* magazine that same year credited him with being the most important performer in rock and roll, outside of Elvis Presley.

Domino himself was widely regarded as an artist whose success was due in no small part to his ability to craft different elements of his musical style to suit a broader—that is to say, white—audience. The lyrics of "The Fat Man," for example, originally referred to drug abuse, but Domino edited them to give the song greater commercial appeal. Meanwhile his public image was regarded as being safe and unthreatening.

Domino's biggest hit was "Blueberry Hill," released in 1956. The slow rhythm and safe double entendre—"I found my thrill on blueberry hill"—proved immensely popular. The song, as well as a number of other Domino recordings, would go on to become pop culture clichés, evoking the innocence with which the decade was associated in television series such as *Happy Days*. It would also make him one of the most popular performers of the decade. Other big hits included "I'm in Love Again" (1956), "Blue Monday" (1956), "Whole Lotta Loving" (1958), "Be My Guest" (1959), "Walking to New Orleans" (1960), "My Girl Josephine" (1960), and "Let the Four Winds Blow" (1961).

Fats Domino sold more records (65 million) than any other rock and roll performer in the 1950s, other than Elvis Presley. Between 1950 and 1963 he had songs in the rhythm and blues singles chart fifty-nine times, and in the pop music Top Forty thirty-seven times. He also performed in several rock and roll films, including *The Girl Can't Help It* (1956), *Jamboree* (1957), and *The Big Beat* (1957).

The hits stopped coming in 1963 after Fats Domino left Imperial Records for ABC-Paramount. He also recorded for Mercury and Reprise labels during the 1960s. His last big hit was, ironically, a song written by John Lennon and Paul McCartney to emulate his style, "Lady Madonna" (1968). He backed it up by releasing a moderately successful album titled *Fats Is Back* and became a staple of the "oldies" circuit.

Fats Domino was inducted into the Rock and Roll Hall of Fame in 1986. In 1987 he received a Lifetime Achievement Award at the Twenty-Ninth Annual Grammy Awards, where he was celebrated for his role in building the bridge between rhythm and blues and rock and roll. During this same period he became a permanent resident of New Orleans, living in a mansion in the Ninth Ward. In 2005, as Hurricane Katrina approached, Domino refused to evacuate, because of the poor health of his wife, Rosemary. After the hurricane he was believed dead until his daughter, the gospel singer Karen Domino White, identified him in a photograph broadcast on CNN. In 2006 he recorded an album, *Alive and Kickin'*. Proceeds from the album are donated to the Tipitina's Foundation, a charity organized to preserve the musical heritage of New Orleans. On January 12, 2007, New Orleans mayor, RAY NAGIN declared "Fats Domino Day in New Orleans." On that day he also received a Lifetime Achievement Award from *Offbeat* magazine.

FURTHER READING

Broven, John. *Rhythm and Blues in New Orleans* (1983).
Coleman, Rick. *Blue Monday: Fats Domino and the Lost Dawn of Rock and Roll* (2006).
Palmer, Robert. *Rock and Roll: An Unruly History* (1995).

WILLIAM DEJONG-LAMBERT

Donaldson, Jeff (15 Dec. 1932–29 Feb. 2004), visual artist, art historian, and art critic, was the youngest child born to Frank Donaldson and Clementine Richardson Donaldson of Pine Bluff, Arkansas. When Jeff Donaldson was four years old his father died. To support the family Clementine Donaldson worked as a grammar school principal and high school principal. Donaldson received his early education in Pine Bluff, where he studied art with John Miller Howard, a professor at Arkansas AM&N College (later the University of Arkansas at Pine Bluff). After earning a B.A. in Studio Art from Arkansas AM&N in 1954, he returned to Chicago, where he had moved as a teenager with his family, and took courses at the School of the Art Institute of Chicago. Donaldson went on to study photography, color and design, and printmaking at the Illinois Institute of Technology, where he earned an M.S. in Art Education and Administration in 1963.

In 1967 Donaldson began work on his doctorate at Northwestern University. There he studied African art history and extensively researched African American cultural history; he also was significantly influenced by his mentor, the New York–based artist Romare Bearden. That same year Donaldson founded the Visual Artists Workshop of the Organization for Black American Culture (OBAC) in Chicago, a group that he helped form. At the workshop the artists decided to make a collective statement in honor of black heroes by creating the *Wall of Respect*, an outdoor mural on a tavern in South Side Chicago. This mural of fifty famous African American scholars, musicians, actors, statesmen, athletes, authors, and religious figures inspired artists in hundreds of cities across America to create their own Walls of Respect, but in Chicago the building displaying the original has been razed.

The following year, 1968, Donaldson and the artist Wadsworth Jarrell founded the African Commune of Bad Relevant Artists, or AfricCobra, a collective of nine black artists from Chicago's South Side neighborhoods. AfricCobra pioneered the development and analysis of a Pan-African aesthetic relevant to African American communities, especially those who lived in Chicago's housing projects. In his essay "The Role We Want for Black Art," published in the *College Board Review* in 1969, Donaldson articulated the artistic and intellectual agenda that he worked diligently throughout the rest of his life to fulfill: his goals were to institute the inclusion of African and African American artists in art history courses at colleges and universities and to create art for the sake of African American people as opposed to for the sake of art itself.

In 1970 Donaldson received a Ph.D. from Northwestern University and became chair of the art department in the College of Fine Arts at Howard University, a position he held until 1976. As chair he revised the department's curriculum to include African and African American art history as nationally accredited major fields of study. At this time Donaldson served as director of the art gallery at Howard and curated faculty exhibitions that distinguished the art department as a major repository of African American art. In 1970 Donaldson also organized CONFABA, the Conference on the Functional Aspects of Black Art, to discuss the development of a black aesthetic.

In February 1974 Donaldson served as the executive director for Howard University's North American Zonal Festival held at Howard University. Along with the actor OSSIE DAVIS, Donaldson organized the interdisciplinary festival at which he and Davis selected participants from among two thousand artists for the Second World Black and

African Festival of Arts and Culture (FESTAC). From 1974 to 1977 Donaldson and Davis co-chaired the committee for the North American participants in FESTAC, an arduous task that involved raising more than a million dollars to promote the festival and pay for participants' travel expenses. In 1977, after many delays and financial difficulties, FESTAC was held in Lagos, Nigeria.

From 11 December 1981 to 8 January 1982 the retrospective exhibition Jeff Donaldson, 1961–1981, was displayed at Howard University's art gallery. In 1985 Donaldson became the associate dean of Howard's College of Fine Arts. He participated in the group exhibition Art in Washington and Its Afro-American Presence: 1940 to 1970 in Washington, D.C. Also in 1985, he served as guest curator with Dr. Robert L. Douglas of Ohio University and the University of Louisville for the traveling exhibition Beyond 1984: Contemporary Perspectives on American Art at the Trisolini Gallery of Ohio University (1985). In addition to being guest curator for the exhibition, Donaldson contributed three mixed-media works.

In 1990 Donaldson was promoted to dean of the College of Fine Arts at Howard University. In 1996 his essay "Africobra and TransAtlantic Connections" was published in the exhibition catalog *Seven Stories about Modern Art in Africa*. In 1998, the year he retired, Donaldson was guest editor for a special issue of the *International Review of African American Art* on "The Art of Political Struggle and Cultural Revolution of the 1960s and 70s." He was one of eight African American artists who displayed works with eight African artists in the exhibition Transatlantic Dialogue shown in 2000 at the National Museum of African Art in Washington, D.C. Three years later he contributed to the exhibition catalog *Ethiopian Passages: Contemporary Art from the Diaspora*. Donaldson died from prostate cancer in Washington, D.C., in 2004.

Donaldson's art, scholarship, teaching, and research articulated an Afrocentric aesthetic that synthesized colorful images, musical rhythms, and symmetrical designs. In addition to preserving and promoting African American art and cultural expression, Donaldson contributed illustrations and frontispieces to works of African American literature. Through words and images he preserved and promoted African American art and cultural expression. Donaldson was committed to reversing the devastating social, political, and psychological effects of racism. Donaldson's art, scholarship, teaching, and research articulated a trans-African aesthetic that synthesized colorful images, musical rhythms, and symmetrical designs.

FURTHER READING

Bullock, Starmanda. *Jeff Donaldson, 1964–1981* (1981).

Gaither, Edmund B. "Jeff Donaldson: The Mind behind the Cultural Revolution," *International Review of African American Art* 18.1 (2001).

Harris, Michael D. "Dedication to Jeff Donaldson," *International Review of African American Art* 19.3 (2004).

Obituary: *Washington Post*, 7 Mar. 2004.

KIMBERLY M. CURTIS

Donegan, Dorothy (6 Apr. 1922–19 May 1998), jazz pianist and entertainer, was born in Chicago, Illinois, the older of two children (she had a brother, Leone), of Donazell Donegan and Ella Day Donegan. Donegan's father was a cook on the Chicago, Burlington, and Quincy Railroad, and her mother supplemented the family income by letting out rooms. Dorothy's musical virtuosity revealed itself when she was eight, when she began playing a neighbor's piano for the first time. Recognizing her daughter's talent, her mother arranged for piano lessons and soon Donegan was playing at local churches and, by the time she was fourteen, for tips in local South Side spots. She continued formal music studies at DuSable High School with Walter Henri Dyett, who taught other future notables, including the singer DINAH WASHINGTON and the saxophonist Johnny Griffin.

In 1939, at age seventeen, Donegan was booked to play at Costello's Grill, a downtown club hitherto reserved for whites. She continued her studies with the renowned conductor Rudolph Ganz at the prestigious Chicago Musical College, and in 1943 she became the first African American female to concertize at Chicago's Orchestra Hall, in a program consisting of works by Grieg and Rachmaninoff, as well as a number of jazz pieces. Not only did Donegan receive a favorable review in the *Chicago Tribune* but she also caught the ear of the great jazz pianist ART TATUM, who offered her some jazz instruction.

Though Donegan had enjoyed some early success, she soon ran into the barriers familiar to black female musicians. She aspired to play European classical music with a symphony orchestra, but as she told the reviewer Stephen Holden years later, "There were racial barriers in that field. And I guess there still are" (*New York Times*, 9 Oct. 1981). Jazz paid her bills. For her recording debut in 1942 for

Bluebird Records, she recorded two sets of piano solos. The boogie-woogie was issued, the classical pieces were rejected. By now word had gotten out about the young woman with tremendous technique and she was offered a part, along with CAB CALLOWAY and Sophie Tucker, in a Hollywood movie called *Sensations of 1945*, in which she played a jazz duet with the pianist Gene Rodgers. Donegan seemed poised for a wider audience. She appeared on Broadway in a revue called *Star Time* but the show was a flop, as was *Almost Faithful*, a play she performed in as an actress in 1947. But if the shows fizzled, Donegan's piano act sizzled. One of a number of African American women pianists, including HAZEL SCOTT, Rose Murphy, and MARY LOU WILLIAMS, who were the toast of European royalty and Manhattan socialites, Donegan was a favorite in the boites and supper clubs of habitués like Tallulah Bankhead and Ava Gardner and the Duke and Duchess of Windsor.

Donegan returned to Los Angeles, and in 1948 she married the nightclub owner John McClane. During that lively post-war era she appeared in many clubs, headlining at the first all-black show at Hollywood's famous Tom Breneman Café in 1949. She had a son, John T. McClane, in 1954, divorced McClane in 1959, and found steady work in New York at the elegant Embers Club and in Chicago's London House. She soon remarried, to Walter Eady, and had another son, Donovan, in 1965. After that marriage ended in divorce in 1974, Donegan began frequent tours of Europe. She married and divorced once more, to William Miles. In the 1980s Donegan commented that she finally realized that artists like herself who were so devoted to their art should not marry.

Donegan's love of the classical repertoire never waned. Her longtime drummer Ray Mosca once commented that she was really a classicist. She continued to take master classes at UCLA and the University of Maryland and occasionally performed in formal concerts, as in 1976 when she played a Grieg concerto with the New Orleans Philharmonic at Tulane University. Like others, notably the classically trained pianist Hazel Scott, her closest rival, Donegan became known for "swinging" the classics. But she had her own special tricks at the piano as well. Dressed in elaborate sequined gowns and headdresses she shimmied and shake-danced, told risqué jokes, and performed devastating vocal impressions of singers. Not surprisingly, some jazz lovers were put off by the hectic vaudevillian element in her act. The writer Whitney Balliett, while admiring Donegan's extravagant musical gifts, bemoaned what he termed her penchant for *gallimaufry*—the hodgepodge of musical snippets and clowning she sandwiched between her often-brilliant renditions of standards. The formidable jazz pianist Mary Lou Williams snapped that Donegan played too many notes, but Donegan's response—"Some can, some can't. You don't play enough."—made clear her artistic priorities. To her, jazz was about entertaining, yet she was capable of a blissful, even brilliant, transcendence in her playing, with a ferociously brilliant attack. Still, her potential standing as one of the greats of jazz piano suffered. The jazz authority Frank Driggs decried the "very showbiz stuff [she threw in] for the squares" (liner notes, *Women in Jazz: Pianists*, Stash Records). The *New York Times*' longtime jazz critic John S. Wilson, reviewing a 1971 performance, commented, "Her reputation as a lounge entertainer has virtually buried the fact that she is potentially the greatest jazz pianist playing today." A reader will look in vain for mention of Dorothy Donegan in many of the standard jazz texts. A spotty recording output did not help. Reportedly, the masters from a cluster of recordings made in the 1940s and 1950s for labels including Decca and Continental vanished and her output in the 1960s and 1970s was slim. Still there are a number of excellent recordings, including some live dates on cruise ships from the 1980s, showing Donegan at her most impressive. Certainly she was an artistic conundrum, a pianist who alienated some with her extra-musical "entertainment" and thrilled many others with her art. Suffering from diabetes and cancer, Dorothy Donegan continued to perform until the fall of 1997, when she withdrew and died the following spring in her Los Angeles home. A 1980 *New York Times* tribute by John S. Wilson marveled at her "almost subliminal sense of swing." Make that her *sublime* sense of swing.

FURTHER READING

Balliett, Whitney. "Wonder Woman," in *American Musicians II: 71 Portraits in Jazz* (1986, 1996).

Dahl, Linda. *Stormy Weather* (1994).

Gourse, Leslie. *Madame Jazz, Contemporary Women Instrumentalists* (1995).

Handy, D. Antoinette. *Black Women in American Bands and Orchestras* (1999).

Obituary: New York Times, 22 May 1998.

LINDA DAHL

Doner, Sam (12 Mar. 1907–14 Nov. 1997), one of about 635 African American males involved in the Tuskegee Study of Untreated Syphilis (TSUS), was the son of Wiley West and Mae Burke, born in Tuskegee, Macon County, Alabama. His parents put him up for adoption at an early age, and Sam's adoptive parents raised him. Sam had at least one sibling, Willie Doner. A lifelong resident of Macon County, Doner attended Cooper Chapel African Methodist Episcopal Zion Church most of his life. His favorite adult pastime was serving there as a deacon, until he became too ill to attend services. Local churches served as recruiting centers for the Tuskegee study. Doner worked as a school bus driver and a farmer and owned over ten acres of land. He married Emily Chambliss. Though there were no children born to that union, they adopted a son, Willie M. Doner. After his wife died, Doner developed a relationship with Mary Cox and fathered two children, Roger and Gwendolyn Cox.

Conducted by the U.S. Public Health Service, the TSUS studied the effects of late syphilis in black males in and around Macon County, Alabama. Most participants were poor, uneducated sharecroppers who did not know that they had syphilis, or even what syphilis was. The men were told they were being treated for "bad blood," a term that covered a multitude of medical and psychological problems. TSUS was a forty-year experiment during which the men were studied (but not treated) from 1932 to 1972 for the effects of syphilis on the "Negro male," spawned by the general belief that syphilis progressed differently in blacks than in whites. TSUS only ended after the study was exposed through an Associated Press story on 26 July 1972, and some of the remaining survivors decided to sue. The attorney FRED D. GRAY filed suit in federal court on behalf of the seventy-one survivors in 1972, but the case never went to trial. Instead, the Justice Department settled out of court with Gray and his clients. The government agreed to give each survivor and his heirs $37,000 and free medical and health care and offered $15,000 to the families of the control group. There was also a U.S. Senate subcommittee investigation, headed by Senator Edward Kennedy nearly twenty-five years later, and a Department of Heath, Education, and Welfare probe that resulted in legislation designed to prevent such an experiment from happening again. It also required the signing of an informed consent form for participants in clinical trials.

The Tuskegee Syphilis Study Legacy Committee formed in 1996. A year later, on 16 May 1997, President Bill Clinton offered a public apology on behalf of the United States during a meeting with the eight survivors and their families: Fred Simmons, CHARLIE WESLEY POLLARD, ERNEST HENDON, Frederick Moss, George Key, Carter Howard, HERMAN SHAW, and Sam Doner. Two years later the National Center for Bioethics in Research and Health Care was established at Tuskegee University. The Alabama State House of Representatives issued its own apology in 2002.

Sam Doner died at a nursing home in Tuskegee, Alabama, at ninety years of age, a mere six months after the apology. His cause of death is not listed as syphilis, but rather myocardial infarct (heart attack), hypertension (high blood pressure), and diabetes, all complications of syphilis.

FURTHER READING

Gray, Fred. "The Tuskegee Syphilis Study," in *Bus Ride to Justice, Changing the System by the System. The Life and Works of Fred Gray* (1995).

Jones, James H. *Bad Blood: The Tuskegee Syphilis Experiment* (1993).

Reverby, Susan M., ed. *Tuskegee's Truths: Rethinking the Tuskegee Syphilis Study* (2000).

KAREN SUTTON

Donnell, Clyde Henry (4 Aug. 1890–10 Oct. 1971), physician, was born in Greensboro, North Carolina, the son of Smith Donnell, a real estate developer, and Lula Ingold. Donnell was raised in Greensboro, where he attended the public schools for African Americans and the high school operated by North Carolina Agricultural and Technical University. He received an AB in 1911 from Howard University and an M.D. in 1915 from Harvard University. While at Harvard he studied under Milton J. Rosenau, the world-renowned scientist in preventive medicine and founder of the world's first school of public health, at Harvard in 1909. Since few hospitals would accept African Americans as interns at the time of Donnell's medical school graduation, he rotated as a fellow and observer at Boston City Hospital, Massachusetts General Hospital, and the Children's Hospital from 1915 to 1916. Donnell's subsequent career was devoted to African American health education, insurance, and banking.

African American insurance companies, intended to provide financial protection against sickness and aid at the time of death, were organized in the American South in the mid-nineteenth century. White insurance companies actively competed for African American business during the mid-to-late nineteenth century. In 1881, however, Frederick L. Hoffman, statistician for the Prudential Insurance Company, published a study arguing that "excessive mortality among this element [African American] of the population [is such] that unless the company adopted a restrictive course, it would soon find itself in difficulty because of inordinate losses experienced on this class of policy-holders" (Hoffman, 137). Fearing greater exposure to risk, as a result white insurance companies reduced the size of policies they were willing to write for African Americans and significantly increased the premiums. One of the effects of the new policy was to promote the growth of black-owned insurance companies. In October 1898 the North Carolina Mutual Life Insurance Company was formed in Durham—later to become the largest African American–owned financial institution in the United States. By 1920 the company had approximately $33 million of insurance in force.

During its formative years the company noted an exceptionally poor mortality experience. Throughout the 1920s N.C. Mutual paid more in death benefits than anticipated. In 1920 whites died at the rate of 12.4 per 1,000 population; African Americans at 18.7 per 1,000. In some urban areas the African American death rate was close to twice that for whites. Tuberculosis was the principal cause of this excess mortality, a fact generally attributed to differences in socioeconomic and sanitary conditions. Tuberculosis accounted for 11 percent of all African American deaths in the United States in 1930 (Weare, 125). N.C. Mutual ascertained that to sustain itself it needed not only to select healthier customers but also to improve African American health in general.

Donnell received a North Carolina medical license in 1916, moving from Boston to Greensboro in 1917. He met in Durham and married in 1919 Martha Merrick, youngest daughter of JOHN MERRICK, one of the founders of N.C. Mutual. They had no children. Another founder was Dr. AARON M. MOORE, Durham's first African American physician. Donnell became associated in a general medical practice with Moore. Their office shared a building with N.C. Mutual. To help address the problem of death and disability among the company's customers, Donnell was hired by N.C. Mutual in 1917; Moore and Donnell created the company's Life Extension Department.

Donnell became the company's medical director following Moore's death in 1923. He hired black physicians to replace white physicians to conduct field examinations of prospective policyholders. This represented a conscious effort to build the clinical practices of black physicians. Complex cases or prospective purchasers of large policies were referred to Donnell for a definitive examination. Donnell hired another African American physician, Roscoe Brown, a former employee of the U.S. Public Health Service, as his assistant. Donnell used the second floor of the Durham company's home office both for his private practice and for company work, and every day he saw a large number of patients, including company employees. Donnell had a special interest in tuberculosis as well as in the therapeutic use of ultraviolet light. His Life Extension Department conducted lecture tours, showed films, and distributed health promotion bulletins from state and federal health departments along with a variety of its own pamphlets. Sales agents also distributed health education materials. Health hints were provided to policyholders, medical information was given to field agents, and continuing education was provided to field physicians.

There was, however, no clear decline in mortality among the company's policyholders following the establishment of the Life Extension Department. The company's financial status did not significantly improve until it hired ASA SPAULDING, the United States' first African American actuary. Combining Donnell's medical knowledge with Spaulding's actuarial training, the company instituted significant underwriting reforms and insurance practices particularly suited to the health status of southern African Americans. These significantly contributed to the company's profitability. Changes in the economic and social status of African Americans in this period make it difficult to identify a particular benefit from the Life Extension Department, although it clearly served the company as a valuable marketing tool.

Donnell was deeply committed to continuing medical education for African American physicians, who maintained their own structure of local, state, and national medical associations—similar to the better-known all-white societies. Donnell was founder in 1918 and primary mover in Durham's Academy of Medicine, Pharmacy and Dentistry. He was secretary-treasurer of the Old North State Medical Society for thirty-two years. He was also active in the National Medical Association, serving as journal business manager and secretary-treasurer from 1924 to 1928. Donnell was also chairman of the board of trustees of Durham's Lincoln Hospital, a 150-bed African American facility.

Donnell is remembered as an ebullient, gregarious, generous, and outgoing "people person." Acquaintances recall him as being "full of fun," always ready with a joke, and fond of socializing. He enjoyed walking in Durham's African American neighborhoods and chatting with tradesmen. Donnell rose in N.C. Mutual to become vice president and a member of the board of directors. N.C. Mutual was closely tied to Durham's African American–owned Mechanics and Farmers Bank. At the time of his death in Durham, Donnell was chairman of the bank's board of directors.

His life's work illustrates the efforts of African Americans to improve their health through public health education and the continuing medical education of physicians. In Donnell's case these efforts were undertaken for altruistic reasons as well as for the economic benefits to the insurance company and his fellow African American physicians.

FURTHER READING

Hoffman, Frederick L. *History of the Prudential Insurance Company of America* (1900).

Weare, W. B. *Black Business in the New South: A Social History of the North Carolina Mutual Life Insurance Company* (1973).

Obituary: *New York Times*, 11 Oct. 1971.

This entry is taken from the *American National Biography* and is published here with the permission of the American Council of Learned Societies.

EDWARD C. HALPERIN

Doram, Dennis (1796–Oct. 1869), farmer and businessman, was born at Indian Queen Tavern in Danville, Kentucky. Doram was a son of Lydia Barbee, a free black woman, who had been a slave of the Revolutionary War General Thomas Barbee. According to family tradition, Barbee was Doram's father and that of his siblings. Lydia and her six children were the first people mentioned in Barbee's will, which freed her and provided for the emancipation and education of the children.

When Boyle County, Kentucky, was formed in 1842 Doram was already a leading figure in the community and, by 1850, was considered "the wealthiest member of his race" in the county (Brown, 427). His business concerns included the local Caldwell School for Women and a rope factory, in addition to his growing and selling hemp. The county's 1850 tax list shows Doram as the owner of 215 acres along Dix River, three town lots in Danville, ten horses and/or mares, ten cattle, "a pleasure carriage or barouche," and a buggy. His property was valued at $8,875. In 1860 he had 300 acres, four town lots, eight horses, thirty cattle, thirty hogs over six months old, one "jennie" (a female donkey), one bull, and one slave.

Doram married Diademia Taylor, a former slave, on 15 February 1830. When he died, his will provided a town lot in Danville, a horse, and bed to each of his twelve children. Doram's financial and educational assistance to his children allowed them to become successful citizens. His son Gibeon J. was a "rope spinner" and later the builder and operator of a Danville grocery. Also sometimes known as George, Gibeon and his brother John/Joshua B.—identified in contemporary Boyle County records as "prominent colored men of this place"—were delegates to the 1871 Republican State Convention. Joshua was a Union army veteran of the Civil War.

An apparent slave cemetery was located at the site of Barbee's home in 2003. The preserved home and grounds are operated as the Old Crow Inn Winery in Danville.

Portraits of Dennis and Diademia Doram—painted by the artist Patrick Henry Davenport in 1839—were found ripped and covered with layers of dust and dirt in a Boyle County barn in 1995. They were subsequently purchased by the Kentucky Historical Society in 2000. The works, the only known nineteenth-century portraits of an African American couple in Kentucky and the only known portraits of African Americans painted by Davenport, were repaired and conserved for the society at a cost of $15,000. They are on permanent display in the society's museum at the Thomas D. Clark Center for Kentucky History in Frankfort.

FURTHER READING

Some of the information for this article was gathered from the 1850 and 1860 U.S. censuses of Boyle County, Kentucky.

Brown, Richard C. "The Free Blacks of Boyle County, Kentucky, 1850–1860: A Research Note," *Register of the Kentucky Historical Society* 87.4 (Autumn 1989).

Brown, Katherine Tandy. "Something to Crow About: Danville's Old Crow Inn Offers Hospitality and Then Some," *The Lane Report* (June 2003).

TOM STEPHENS

Dorman, Isaiah (?–26 June 1876), frontiersman and interpreter, was known as "Teat," or the Wasicun Sapa (Black White Man), among the Sioux of Dakota Territory. Nothing is known of his life before he entered the territory as a young man around 1850. He is thought to have been an escaped slave who fled to the wilderness to avoid capture. Sioux tribal history records his presence in their midst from that date. He became known to white settlers in 1865, by which time he had become fluent in the Sioux dialect. About this time he married a Sioux woman and built a log cabin near Fort Rice, in Dakota Territory, not far from present-day Bismarck, North Dakota. For a while he earned a living cutting wood for the fort and for a trading firm, Durfee and Peck.

In November 1865 Dorman was hired by the U.S. Army to carry the mail between Fort Rice and Fort Wadsworth, some 180 miles away. Dorman's hard work and reliability earned him the respect of army officials, and he was often called on to perform other jobs as well at Fort Rice, for an average monthly salary of sixty dollars, a considerable sum at the time. In 1871 Dorman served for several months as guide and interpreter for the survey crew of the proposed Northern Pacific Railroad, and in October of that year he was appointed post interpreter at Fort Rice, at a salary of seventy-five dollars per month. According to official army records, Dorman was an asset to the post. His language skills, coupled with a natural ability to mediate differences, helped avoid potential conflict at the post between white settlers and Indians. Dorman's ease in handling the Sioux was also attributed to the large stores of smoking and chewing tobacco that he always kept on hand and willingly shared.

Although the situation at Fort Rice was relatively stable, conflict with Sioux elsewhere in the territory was escalating by the mid-1870s. This was largely a consequence of a dramatic increase in the white population, caused by both the building of the Northern Pacific Railroad and the discovery of gold in the Black Hills in August 1875, which quickly drew thousands of prospectors to the region. The man responsible for the Black Hills gold rush was the U.S. Army general George A. Custer, who had made his discovery while leading a military expedition to the territory.

In May 1876 Custer was ordered to lead the Seventh Cavalry against hostile Sioux settled farther west, along the Little Bighorn River in what is now southern Montana. Dorman's reputation as an outstanding civilian employee of the army was widespread, and he was the natural choice of Custer as interpreter for the expedition. He assumed his new duties on 15 May, again at the salary of seventy-five dollars a month.

On 25 June 1876 Custer's forces assembled some fifteen miles east of the Little Bighorn, at a landmark known to the Indians as the Crow's Nest. There Custer divided his command, and Dorman, along with most of the other civilian employees, was assigned to Major Marcus A. Reno's battalion of three companies. Reno's battalion crossed the Little Bighorn, and the next day they attempted an attack on the Sioux but were driven back to the west bank of the river. In the course of the fighting Dorman was fatally shot in the chest with a rifle by an Indian marksman. An army burial detail that recovered his body a few days later reported that he had been stripped and mutilated.

No records show Dorman to have fathered any children, and he apparently left no survivors, including his wife, since his back pay of $102.50 was never claimed.

FURTHER READING

Campbell, Edward G. "Saving the Custer Muster Rolls," *Military Affairs* 10.2 (Summer 1946).

McConnell, Roland C. "Isaiah Dorman and the Custer Expedition," *Journal of Negro History* 33 (July 1948).

This entry is taken from the *American National Biography* and is published here with the permission of the American Council of Learned Societies.

ANN T. KEENE

Dorr, David F. (1827 or 1828–1872), author, runaway slave, traveler, and public speaker, was born a slave in 1827 or 1828 in New Orleans. No information is available about his parents except that they were presumably of mixed-racial heritage because Dorr referred to himself as a "quadroon" and was light enough to pass for white. His owner was Cornelius Fellowes, a lawyer, with whom Dorr traveled around Europe and the Near East from 1851 to 1854. Fellowes promised to manumit Dorr upon their return to the United States but reneged on his promise, at which time Dorr escaped to Cleveland. There he decided to publish an account of his travels based upon the diary he had kept. In 1858 his book *A Colored Man Round the World* was privately printed and attracted enough attention to be reviewed in a number of important Cleveland newspapers.

A Colored Man Round the World is the only antebellum African American travel narrative about a journey through the Near East, and that too as a slave. More importantly, the book breaks with the literary and ideological conventions that separated Anglo and African American writing. Unlike most escaped slaves, who wrote under the aegis of white abolitionists and began writing by offering accounts of harsh living under slavery and of their attempts to escape, Dorr chose instead to write a travel narrative without any note of authentication, introduction, or preface from a white person.

Dorr's subversion and deliberate confusion of racial categories was evident to his contemporary reviewers. The reviewer for the *Cleveland Plain Dealer* wrote, for instance, "The author is a Quadroon but would readily pass any where as a white man (and an excellent white man, too,) but he is still not ashamed to call himself 'A Colored Man Round the World.'" Antebellum African American travel writers like William Nesbit wrote about different African or Caribbean countries as potential sites of emigration, while others, like WILLIAM WELLS BROWN, described their experiences of the relative absence of racism in Europe. Dorr, however, wrote within the genre of the Anglo-American travel narrative, in which travel abroad was a mark of leisure and culture. Even though he was a slave during his travels, he projects himself as a leisured gentleman who can mock his uncouth owner, Cornelius Fellowes, through the lens of class, scoffing, for instance, at Fellowes's lack of judgment when the latter threw down some coins for beggars, who then proceeded to surround and hound him. Simultaneously, however, by dedicating his book to his slave mother and by invoking racial pride by linking his ancestry with ancient Egyptian civilization, Dorr clearly demarcated solidarity with African Americans.

Although Dorr did not publish any other work during his lifetime, he became reasonably well known in Cleveland. While he made his living as a clerk, he was probably known on the lecture circuit because notice of his May 1860 talk on ballet girls and quadroon ladies appeared in all three major Cleveland newspapers. On 26 August 1862 Dorr enlisted as a private in the Seventh Ohio Volunteer Infantry and served till he was wounded in his jaw and shoulder at the battle of Ringgold in Georgia. He was discharged on 15 August 1864 in Cleveland. Because he was disfigured and unable to perform any labor, he was pensioned in 1865. In 1871 Dorr moved back to New Orleans, where a year later he died.

Dorr remained in relative obscurity until a 1999 republication of his unusual work occasioned critical attention. Dorr will be remembered as a writer whose work questions the conventions of African American writing and challenges us to think about the variegated forms that protest writing can take.

FURTHER READING

Dorr, David F. *A Colored Man Round the World*, ed. Malini Johar Schueller (1999).

Fuad, Sha'ban. *Islam and Arabs in Early American Thought* (1991).

Pettinger, Alasdair. "'At Least One Negro Everywhere': African American Travel Writing," in *Beyond the Borders: American Literature and Post-colonial Theory*, ed. Deborah L. Madsen (2003).

Schueller, Malini Johar. "Performing Whiteness, Performing Blackness: Dorr's Cultural Capital and the Critique of Slavery," *Criticism* 41.2 (1999).

Stowe, William W. *Going Abroad: European Travel in Nineteenth-Century American Culture* (1994).

MALINI JOHAR SCHUELLER

Dorsett, Tony (7 Apr. 1954–), football player, was born Anthony Drew Dorsett in the steel mill town of Aliquippa, Pennsylvania, one of seven children of Wes Dorsett, a mill worker, and Myrtle Dorsett. As a child Tony was timid and respectful, a sharp contrast to his older brothers who were wilder and often in trouble. His parents were determined that their youngest son not follow the same path. Wes did hard, dangerous work to provide for the family and looked forward to a future in which his children would not have to do the same. All of the Dorsett siblings had excelled in sports, particularly football, and Tony felt pressure to follow suit. Although he was frail physically and a bit frightened by the game, he began playing football in junior high and displayed the rare speed that his brothers also exhibited.

As part of a school busing plan initiated to remedy segregated housing patterns, Tony attended Hopewell High School in a nearby town rather than Aliquippa High. His hometown school was troubled and its graduates often went straight to work in the mills. Although Tony was in the racial minority at Hopewell he considered the school a blessing. "Had I gone to Aliquippa High, I might have ended up a hoodlum like some of my friends," he later recalled (Dorsett and Frommer, 11).

At Hopewell he came under the influence of the teacher and coach "Butch" Ross, who saw Tony as both a prodigy and a challenge. His retiring nature and small size, barely 150 pounds, made him an unlikely choice to be a football star. Nevertheless Ross motivated him to display more passion and to use his impressive speed to its fullest advantage as a running back.

Many large college programs actively recruited him, and for a time it seemed likely that Penn State, known for its excellent football program, would be his choice. Instead Tony announced that he would attend the University of Pittsburgh, whose team was so bad that the school was considering disbanding its football program altogether. Despite its having won only one game in 1972, the school's proximity to his family and an energetic new coach, Johnny Majors, were appealing to Dorsett. When practices for the 1973 season began, teammates looked in disbelief at the 157-pound freshman who was supposed to lead the team to glory. Dorsett responded by using his exceptional speed to make one big play after another in practice. When the season began, the bottom-ranked Pitt squad began upsetting powerful opponents. Dorsett was named All-American as a freshman, running for 1,686 yards as Pitt posted a respectable 6-5-1 record. They improved to 7-4 in 1974 and to 8-4 in 1975. He capped his remarkable college career with the Heisman Trophy after the 1976 season, and his record of 6,082 career rushing yards stood for twenty-two years.

Celebrity made Dorsett uncomfortable, and he likened his life at Pitt to being in a fishbowl. His success on the field emboldened him off it, and entering the National Football League as a highly paid rookie on one of the best teams, the Dallas Cowboys, exposed his immaturity. He quickly spent a large part of his $1.6 million rookie contract and struggled to adjust to the overt racism and expectations that he "mind his place" in Texas. Aliquippa was working-class and diverse, whereas Dallas was affluent and segregated. He bristled under the racial tension prevalent in the South at the time and got a reputation among the fans and media as a terse, fast-living playboy. The Cowboys were celebrities, and Dorsett did not shy away from excesses.

Such social tensions, however, did nothing to hamper his performance on the field. From his rookie year in 1977 until 1985 Dorsett rushed for more than one thousand yards every year, excepting the strike-shortened 1982 season. The Cowboys won the Super Bowl in his second season, 1978, and his personal awards and accolades were numerous. He was a regular at the NFL Pro Bowl, won several league rushing titles, and set an unbreakable record in 1982 by running for a ninety-nine-yard touchdown.

Career success did not protect Dorsett from difficulties in his personal life. In 1973, during his first season at Pitt, Dorsett had fathered a child, Anthony Jr., out of wedlock. His NFL lifestyle strained his relationship with his son. In 1981 he married Julie Ann, but they divorced three years later. He and four other Cowboys players—all African Americans—were subjected to a highly publicized drug investigation in 1983. Dorsett was ultimately exonerated, but less than a year later the IRS sued him for $400,000 in back taxes. Numerous investments failed, leaving him with little from the millions he earned.

Although the period from 1980 to 1985 was difficult for Dorsett off the field, he continued to be a star on it. But in 1987 the Cowboys acquired another Heisman Trophy winner, Herschel Walker, to take over at running back, a move that infuriated Dorsett. He demanded a trade and was sent to the Denver Broncos in 1988 at age thirty-four. In Denver he surpassed the career rushing yardage total of the legendary Jim Brown. After twelve excellent professional seasons, a knee injury forced him to retire in 1989. He was voted into the Pro Football Hall of Fame in 1994, his first year of eligibility.

Following his retirement Dorsett appeared in several feature films and television series. His son Anthony Jr. enjoyed a successful NFL career in his own right, playing for the Tennessee Titans and Oakland Raiders franchises from 1996 to 2003.

Tony Dorsett made the transition from a small, shy kid to a larger-than-life talent and personality. He left the University of Pittsburgh as college football's all-time leading rusher and followed with a twelve-year NFL career that ensures his place in history as one of the game's great runners. He experienced life in Texas at the tail end of the era of overt racism and segregation, and many times he handled such pressures imperfectly. As the city of Dallas changed over time, so did Dorsett.

FURTHER READING

Dorsett, Tony, and Harvey Frommer. *Running Tough: Memoirs of a Football Maverick* (1980).

EDWARD M. BURMILA

Dorsette, Cornelius Nathaniel (c. 1852–7 Dec. 1897), physician, was born into slavery at Eden in Davidson County, North Carolina, the son of David Dorsette and Lucinda (maiden name unknown). Two months after his birth he was separated from his mother. After Emancipation he lived with his grandmother on a small farm and attended school in Thomasville, North Carolina.

Dorsette attended Hampton Institute in Virginia, graduating in 1878. A white Hampton Institute trustee, Dr. Vosburgh, offered Dorsette a job in Syracuse, New York. Dorsette became Vosburgh's driver and handyman. Encouraged by his employer to become a doctor Dorsette studied

Latin to prepare for medical school and enrolled at Syracuse University College of Medicine but soon quit as a result of ill health, fatigue, and a lack of sufficient funds for tuition. After his health was restored and Vosburgh offered to pay his expenses, Dorsette applied to the medical department of the University of the City of New York. He was refused because he was black; however, the University of Buffalo department of medicine did accept him, and Dorsette went on to receive his M.D. in 1882.

Eager to establish himself professionally and to reimburse Vosburgh (which he did in full by 1884), Dorsette practiced in a variety of positions during the next two years. He was assistant physician of the Wayne County, New York, almshouse and insane asylum and conducted a part-time general practice in Lyons, New York. He also worked in the mental ward at the Lyons hospital.

Wanting more opportunities than were available in New York, Dorsette contacted his college friend Booker T. Washington, who convinced him to move to Alabama. "In all the South, I know of no place that would afford a better opening for you than Montgomery," wrote Washington in 1883, assuring Dorsette that there were not yet any black doctors in the city, which in 1880 was 59 percent African American. Observing that a black doctor in Atlanta then earned two thousand dollars annually, Washington stated, "Don't see why one can't do as well in Montgomery. There are some good progressive col[ored] people in Montgomery whom I know you could depend on." Washington also emphasized that a white minister, Robert Charles Bedford, was "very anxious for you to locate here" and promised to introduce him to Montgomery's white and black ministers to establish a clientele. Noting that Tuskegee was only forty miles northeast of Montgomery, a two-hour train ride away, Washington promised, "I could give you an introduction that would go a good ways." Offering to assist Dorsette whenever needed, Washington invited him to Tuskegee Institute's commencement because "it would be a good opportunity to get advertised."

Dorsette visited Montgomery and decided to stay. In 1884 he passed the six-day state medical examination and became Alabama's first licensed black physician. At the National Educational Association meeting that summer, Washington spoke of Dorsette's accomplishments, commenting that "when his white brother physicians found out … that he had brains enough to pass a better examination, as one of them said, than many of the whites had passed, they gave him a hearty welcome." Montgomery's white physicians offered Dorsette assistance in setting up his practice and also agreed to consult on cases.

Dorsette told Washington that although the white town leaders accepted him, Montgomery's blacks were hostile toward him. Initially suspicious and distrustful, the African American community gradually approached Dorsette for health care. During his early days in Montgomery, Dorsette often drove into the surrounding countryside to deliver babies and treat patients. He claimed that he was an "idol" to the "country folk." He also traveled to Tuskegee as Washington's personal physician and to care for his family, faculty, and students. When a smallpox epidemic threatened central Alabama's public health, Dorsette was praised for using his knowledge of vaccines, much of it previously unavailable in Alabama, to protect the populace.

Despite his successes Dorsette encountered racial violence. White residents accused him of having a "big head" and threatened him. He wrote Washington on 17 April 1888, "I have been on the go day & night and have not been molested though have met some of the bullies after mid night." The situation worsened, and three days later he commented, "I see signs of an undercurrent of sentiment that I dont [*sic*] like and while I hope for the best yet I dare not trust them. However I am here & here to stay unless removed by death. I trust the God that cares for a sparrow will care for me."

Feeling wronged, Dorsette longed for quiet, claiming he was tired of "this cussed nonsense." He vowed, "I have never flinched nor do I intend to even if death stars [*sic*] me in the face." Believing that opening a business would convince his harassers that he could not be intimidated to leave, he told Washington, "I am now determined to open a Drugstore if I only have one bottle on the shelves." Although he lacked money to finance a business, in 1888 he asked Washington for assistance because "I am more and more convinced that my only safety & stability depends upon my owning something visible and that denotes permanency."

By May 1888 Dorsette had opened a drugstore underneath his office, proving that he intended to remain in the community. Located on a prominent corner of Dexter Avenue near the state capitol, the three-story brick Dorsette building contained professional offices and an auditorium. Harassers ceased their threats toward Dorsette, and he recruited professional blacks to work in Montgomery. Physicians, a dentist, a pharmacist, and a lawyer rented office space, and the

Montgomery Argus, a black weekly newspaper, was edited in the building. He also helped physicians prepare for the state medical examination.

Establishing the Hale Infirmary, the state's first black hospital, was Dorsette's most significant accomplishment. In 1884 or 1885 he had married Sarah Hale, the daughter of James Hale, Montgomery's wealthiest and most influential black resident. Dorsette emphasized to James Hale the great need for an infirmary to treat black patients. Most black Alabamians, he explained, lacked access to quality health-care professionals. Hale donated land for Dorsette's infirmary, which operated in Montgomery from 1890 to 1958.

Washington praised Dorsette for his "wonderful success" and often cited him as an example of what blacks could accomplish. Congratulating him for breaking racial barriers and for having the "largest practice of any colored physician in the country," Washington considered Dorsette a medical missionary to the African American community. As Washington's "closest ally" in Montgomery, Dorsette supported Tuskegee Institute financially, offered to consult with the governor on the school's behalf, provided medical assistance, and served as a member of the school's board of trustees from 1883 to 1897. He gave the students oysters for Christmas dinner and a "large school bell." Dorsette introduced speakers at the annual Tuskegee Conference. He was pleased when Washington hired his sister, Cornelia, as a spelling teacher.

Dorsette helped organize the National Medical Association for black physicians and served as the group's first president. He was active in the state Republican Party, acting as a delegate to the Republican National Convention, and especially studied legislation affecting education and health care. A member of "secret orders," he was captain of the Capital City Guards, the Colored Battalion of the National Guard. Dorsette advised black residents how to handle racial threats and violence. In autumn 1895 he acted as assistant commissioner of the Negro Building at the Atlanta Cotton States and International Exposition, organizing the Alabama exhibits.

Dorsette and his first wife, Sarah Hale, had no children, and she died within a year of their marriage. He married Lula Harper in 1886; they had two daughters and lived near his professional building on Union Street. Dorsette suffered chronic illnesses. In 1892 he confided to Washington that he was "having trouble with my head" and worried about his health. Despite the damp, cold weather Dorsette went hunting on Thanksgiving Day 1897 and developed pneumonia. He died shortly thereafter.

FURTHER READING

Dorsette's letters to Booker T. Washington are in Washington's papers at the Library of Congress and Tuskegee University.

Cobb, William Montague. "Cornelius Nathaniel Dorsette, M.D., 1852–1897," *Journal of the National Medical Association* 52 (Nov. 1960).

Morais, Herbert M. *The History of the Afro-American in Medicine* (1976).

This entry is taken from the *American National Biography* and is published here with the permission of the American Council of Learned Societies.

ELIZABETH D. SCHAFER

Dorsey, Basil (1810?–15 Feb. 1872), self-emancipated slave and teamster, was born in Libertytown, in Frederick County, Maryland. The best evidence suggests that his father and mother, like Dorsey, were slaves of Sabrett (sometimes known as Sabrick) Sollers, though Sollers himself is several times mentioned as Dorsey's father. He had three brothers, Charles, William, and Thomas. Dorsey contended that his grandfather was from England and that he was, by rights, a free man. His escape from slavery is remarkably well documented for a case where no written narrative was produced.

Dorsey married Louisa, who may also have been a slave of Sollers, although several sources claim she was a free woman. She may have been manumitted by her second owner, Richard Coale. The couple had three children, the first of whom was Eliza, born 4 November 1834.

Dorsey was to have been freed upon the death of his owner. But when Sabrick Sollers died on 17 July 1834, the settlement of the estate provided for the sale of eighteen of the twenty-three Sollers slaves. Sollers's son Thomas acquired Dorsey for $300 and offered him his freedom for $350. Dorsey appealed to Richard Coale to be his bondsman for that amount but when the price was raised by Sollers to $500, Coale encouraged Dorsey to take his freedom, which he did, according to one account, on 14 May 1836. Louisa, who gave birth to their second child, John Richard, four days later, stayed behind in Maryland.

With his three brothers, Charles, William, and Thomas, Basil Dorsey traveled through Pennsylvania by way of Gettysburg, Harrisburg, and Reading, to Philadelphia. There the prominent African American abolitionist ROBERT PURVIS offered assistance. Thomas Dorsey stayed in Philadelphia while the other brothers were provided haven on Purvis's farm in Byberry (now Bensalem) near Bristol in Bucks County. Basil continued working on the Purvis estate, while William and Charles settled at neighboring farms.

In July 1837 slave hunters hired by Thomas Sollers tracked Dorsey to the farm, seized him, and with the aid of a local constable jailed him in Bristol. News of Dorsey's capture reached Purvis who hired a well-known trial lawyer, David Paul Brown, to defend him in court. William and Charles escaped with help from Purvis's brother Joseph, who took them to New Jersey. Purvis, who had arranged housing for Louisa and the children in Philadelphia, brought them to the courtroom in Doylestown, Pennsylvania, where Dorsey awaited trial. In the meantime, Purvis had organized local blacks to assist Dorsey should the judge rule in favor of the claimant. Sollers tried to settle the case by again offering to sell Dorsey his freedom, now at the cost of $800, which Purvis agreed to provide. When the price was raised to $1000 Dorsey, infuriated, exclaimed, "No more offers if the decision goes against me. I will cut my throat in the Court House; I will not go back to slavery" (Smedley, 359–360). Judge John Fox ordered Dorsey to be released on the technicality that the prosecutor was unable to prove that slavery was the law in Maryland. After the verdict, Purvis and the local black abolitionists prevented another attempt to recapture Dorsey, and he was moved to New York City.

In New York he was introduced to the abolitionist Joshua Leavitt, editor of the antislavery journal *Evangelist*, and DAVID RUGGLES, secretary of the New York Vigilance Committee. Leavitt set Dorsey on a course to Northampton, Massachusetts, where Col. Samuel Parsons drove him to Leavitt's father and brothers in Charlemont, Massachusetts. While living at the home of Roger Hooker Leavitt, records show that Dorsey paid 50 cents for his membership in the Massachusetts Anti-Slavery Society.

A third child, Charles Robert, was born to Basil and Louisa on 29 August 1838. Two months later on 7 November 1838, Louisa died and was buried in the Leavitt town cemetery. In 1844, Dorsey moved with his family to the village later known as Florence, Massachusetts, three miles northwest of Northampton. The Northampton Association of Education and Industry (NAEI) had been established there in 1842 as a community of abolitionists and radical reformers of the stripe of William Lloyd Garrison. It was Garrison's brother-in-law, George W. Benson, a founder of the NAEI, who hired Dorsey as the teamster for the Bensonville Manufacturing Company. SOJOURNER TRUTH and DAVID RUGGLES were members of the Association and FREDERICK DOUGLASS visited on several occasions. In 1849 Dorsey purchased Lot #12 of Bensonville Village Lots and built his first house—now on the National Register of Historical Places. In 1850, along with Dorsey, as many as thirty-five African Americans lived on what later became known as Nonotuck Street. Bensonville, as Florence was then known, with a population of around 600, was just under 10 percent African American as of the 1850 federal census. Dorsey, age 40, is listed with his second wife, Cynthia, age 19, their first child Louisa, age four months, and two children from Dorsey's first marriage, Charles and John.

On 22 October 1850 one month after passage of the Fugitive Slave Act, Dorsey, with nine other self-proclaimed fugitives from slavery, published a call for local residents to come to their aid and resist any effort to return them to the South. Local citizens were concerned that Dorsey was at risk in his travels as a teamster and raised $150 to purchase his freedom, which was effected in May 1851, fifteen years after his escape. Bensonville was renamed Florence in 1852. Bensonville Manufacturing became Greenville Manufacturing after George W. Benson's departure but Dorsey remained as head teamster under its president, J. P. Williston, a Northampton abolitionist.

A biographical sketch published in the *Hampshire Gazette* of 2 April 1867 describes an incident that occurred when Dorsey accompanied Roger Hooker Leavitt on a train trip to Albany. Passengers demanded the conductor move Dorsey to the black section. Dorsey refused and "divesting himself of his hat and coat threatened to pitch through the window any man who should molest him."

Basil Dorsey died in Florence on 15 February 1872.

FURTHER READING

Blockson, Charles L. *African American in Pennsylvania: Above Ground and Underground: An Illustrated Guide* (2001).

Hampshire Gazette (Northampton, Massachusetts), 2 April 1867.

Magill, Edward H. "The Underground Railroad," *Friends Intelligencer* 55 (1898).

Smedley, R. C. *History of the Underground Railroad in Chester County* (1883).

STEVE STRIMER

Dorsey, Decatur (1839–10 July 1891), soldier and Civil War Medal of Honor recipient, was born a slave in Howard County, Maryland. Little is known of his early life, but according to an 1867 slave compensation claim, Edward Rider Jr., of Baltimore, Maryland, bought Decatur Dorsey from the state of Maryland in June 1861. Following his purchase by Rider, Dorsey's status as slave or freedman is not clear from surviving records, but it seems likely he ran away from his master sometime between 1861 and 22 March 1864, when he enlisted as a private in Company B, Thirty-ninth United States Colored Troops (USCT). On his enlistment papers he describes himself as a free laborer. He stood six feet tall, with black eyes and hair, and was twenty-five years old at the time of enlistment.

Military life in the Thirty-ninth USCT agreed with Dorsey. A private in March, he was promoted to corporal by July 1864 and became the regiment's designated color sergeant (flag bearer). Duty as a regiment's color bearer was one of the highest honors an enlisted soldier could achieve during the American Civil War. At some point in his early life Dorsey learned to read and write, which might explain his rapid promotion through the ranks. Following a brief period of organization and training, the Thirty-ninth USCT was ordered to Virginia to participate in the siege of Petersburg, in June and July 1864.

On 30 July Federal forces hatched a plan to explode a mine laden with tons of explosives under Confederate fortifications defending Petersburg. As part of the Ninth Corps, Fourth Division, First Brigade, the Thirty-ninth USCT was ordered to support white troops who were to advance into the salient created when the mine exploded beneath Confederate soldiers. Things did not go as planned; Confederate soldiers quickly recovered from their initial shock after the explosion, shored up the massive hole in their lines, and stopped the Federal advance. The Thirty-ninth and nearly a dozen other USCT regiments were ordered into the deadly mine in an unfortunate attempt to move the Federal attack forward. Despite intense fire and heavy casualties, Decatur Dorsey led the regiment's charge on Confederate lines and managed to plant the regimental flag on the enemy's works. He held the flag there for several minutes while attempting to rally the Thirty-ninth, but the Confederate fire was too heavy, and the Thirty-ninth was forced back with heavy losses. Dorsey used his flag to rally the badly battered regiment, as many of its white officers were killed or wounded in the attack. Nearly a quarter of all black soldiers who charged the Confederate works at what became known as the "Battle of the Crater" were killed, wounded, or captured.

Some months later, while the regiment was stationed in Wilmington, North Carolina, the commanding officer of the Thirty-ninth USCT, Colonel Ozora P. Stearns, recognized Dorsey's bravery at the Battle of the Crater by taking the unprecedented step of writing the Department of North Carolina Headquarters recommending that Dorsey be promoted to the rank of a commissioned officer. In the curt reply from headquarters, Colonel Stearns was admonished that army policy called for the commission of only whites as officers in the USCT.

Nevertheless, for his actions at the Crater, Decatur Dorsey received the Medal of Honor on 7 November 1865. He was one of only sixteen African American soldiers to receive the Medal of Honor during the Civil War and the only African American to receive one for heroism at the Battle of the Crater. In January 1865 Dorsey was promoted to first sergeant in the Thirty-ninth USCT. For the next few months he continued to serve with distinction in military operations around Petersburg and Richmond. As a member of the Thirty-ninth USCT, Dorsey also took part in the Battle of Hatchers Run, Virginia, on 28 and 29 October 1864; the capture of Fort Fisher, North Carolina, on 15 January 1865; and the capture of Wilmington, North Carolina on 22 February 1865. But the long months in the trenches before Petersburg began to take their toll on his health. In the early fall of 1865 First Sergeant Dorsey would be in and out of hospitals for recurring bouts of malaria and typhoid fever, as well as rheumatism. On 4 December 1865, Dorsey mustered out of the military service with the rest of his regiment and returned to Baltimore.

One month later, on 4 January 1866, he married Mannie Christie, a Baltimore laundress and seamstress who was six years his junior and was also literate (both Decatur and Mannie signed their marriage certificate). The ceremony was held at Saint James Episcopal Church of Baltimore. The couple eventually settled in Hoboken, New Jersey. Mannie continued to find work as a laundress and seamstress, but Decatur was never regularly employed because of chronic rheumatism in his right shoulder and both legs. It appears the couple's major source of income was an invalid pension awarded to Decatur for his Civil War service. On 10 July 1891 Decatur Dorsey died in Hoboken of heart disease and was buried at Flower Hill Cemetery in nearby North Bergen, New Jersey. Mannie survived on a widow's pension until her death on 11 March 1897. They had no children.

FURTHER READING

Gladstone, William. *Men of Color* (1993).

Quarles, Benjamin. *The Negro in the Civil War* (1989).

Records of the Adjutant General's Office, 1780's–1917: Compiled Military Service Records; Decatur Dorsey, Civil War, 1861–1865 (Record Group 94). National Archives and Records Administration Building, Washington, D.C.

Records of the Adjutant General's Office, 1780's–1917: Records and Pension Office, Correspondence (Medal of Honor File), File R&P 517565 (Record Group 94). National Archives and Records Administration Building, Washington, D.C.

Records of the Department of Veterans Affairs: Records of the Pension Office; Pension Certificate Number #342969 (Record Group 15). National Archives and Records Administration Building, Washington, D.C.

Trudeau, Noah. *Like Men of War* (2002).

Wilson, Joseph T. *The Black Phalanx: African American Soldiers in the War of Independence, the War of 1812, and the Civil War* (1994).

MICHAEL F. KNIGHT

Dorsey, James Arthur (9 Mar. 1890–7 Feb. 1978), athlete and physical director, was born in Allegheny City, Pennsylvania, one of eight children of Allen Dorsey, a shipping clerk, and Mary C. Sparksman. Allegheny City was later incorporated as part of Pittsburgh's north side. The five Dorsey brothers would all earn reputations as accomplished athletes in Pittsburgh's sporting community in the early twentieth century.

As a child Dorsey showed an interest in sports while watching students play basketball in the basement gym of the Pittsburgh Theological Seminary. After the death of his father in 1905, he went to work to help support his family. The following year, while working as a janitor on a north side estate, he secretly opened the estate gymnasium for pickup basketball games and soon organized a team with practices held on Sundays. Two of the players who attended were the future Homestead Grays baseball legends Cum Posey and Sellers Hall. Around 1910 Dorsey began coaching a full basketball team, the Monticello Athletic Association, while employed as a janitor at Washington Park, a recreation center in Pittsburgh's Hill District. In 1911 the Monticellos played Howard University in what was billed as the black basketball championship. After defeating Howard, the Monticellos enjoyed the prestige and reputation as the best African American basketball team in the nation. Dorsey played center on the team while Cum Posey, the future manager and owner of the Homestead Grays, played guard and was regarded as one of the best black basketball players in the country. Dorsey also played football and was a fullback on the Collins Tigers and later the Delaney Rifles, teams that regularly competed against black colleges such as Lincoln, Wilberforce, and Storer College at the annual Thanksgiving Day game in Pittsburgh's Exposition Park.

Between 1915 and 1916 Dorsey pursued a degree in physical education at the University of Pittsburgh, and in 1915 he became physical director at Washington. In 1917 he accepted a position as coach and assistant physical director at the Virginia Theological Seminary and College in Lynchburg, Virginia. Dorsey served as assistant football coach and trainer and had the opportunity to continue his education. Returning to Pittsburgh in 1918, he worked at Carnegie Steel's Homestead Works plant and in March of that year he married Zerbie E. Turfley. The couple had nine children.

Shortly after his marriage Dorsey joined the Army National War Work Council. The Army National War Work Council was started in 1917 and affiliated with the YMCA and YWCA programs and other charities to help the war effort as the United States entered into World War I. Dorsey was part of the YMCA work council and performed recreation director duties in Alabama and South Carolina. Dorsey was assigned to the Air Nitrates Corporation in Muscle Shoals, Alabama, where he served as recreation director. In September 1918 he transferred to Camp Jackson, South Carolina, where he worked as the physical secretary of YMCA headquarters until April 1919. These opportunities gave Dorsey experience and insight into the potential value of the services that recreation centers could offer to the public. Upon leaving South Carolina, he returned to Pittsburgh as acting physical director at Washington Park. In 1922 he moved on to the new Crawford Recreation Center (Bath House). Some in the black press, such as the *Pittsburgh Courier*, ran numerous editorials about the situation. John T. Clark, a *Courier* writer and secretary of the Pittsburgh Urban League, wrote to Margaret Gray, head of the city's recreation department, protesting the appearance of segregation at the Crawford and Washington Park centers. Clark felt that Dorsey's transfer from Washington Park, an integrated facility, to Crawford, a new facility the recreation department planned to designate as black only, signaled an effort by the city's authorities to segregate the recreation department. Evidence for this change was the "Negroes Only" signs posted by Margaret Gray at the Crawford Bath House pool. Dorsey resigned from Crawford in 1923 and took the post at the Centre Avenue YMCA the same year.

Opened in September 1923 with a standing-room-only ribbon cutting and located across the street from the black weekly paper the *Pittsburgh Courier*, the Centre Avenue YMCA became that organization's main facility for African Americans in the city. Dorsey had a familiarity with the YMCA, since its old location was near his childhood home and his father-in-law, Dr. G. G. Turfley, was a treasurer of the branch. Dorsey, also a contributor to the building fund, had the experience and reputation that the new facility needed to ensure the success of its programs. To that end he worked at the new facility, which featured an indoor pool, gymnasium, and housing units, for two years.

With the segregation controversy over, the signs were removed from the Crawford pool after Dorsey left and Margaret Gray was replaced as director of recreation in 1925. Dorsey returned to the Crawford Bath House and supported the establishment of a youth baseball team that won the city recreation league championship in 1926. For fifteen years he directed the Crawford facility and oversaw the youth baseball team as it moved under new ownership to professional status and stardom as the Pittsburgh Crawfords. In 1940 Dorsey accepted an appointment as physical director of the Ammon Recreation Center in the Hill District, which had become a predominantly African American neighborhood.

From 1940 to 1950 Dorsey developed programs at Ammon, such as drama classes, basketball, soccer, softball, tennis, swimming, football, various children's games, tournaments, concerts, fairs, and other activities, that helped prepare community residents for wartime and that provided services for returning disabled veterans in need of health care and physical therapy. Dorsey also placed a great emphasis on the physical well-being of future generations, commenting in 1943, "Nothing in Pittsburgh should be of greater importance than the welfare of its people, especially its children" (*Pittsburgh Courier*, 2). To that end, he ensured that Ammon had one of the most diversified programs of all the city's recreation centers. Its indoor gymnasium, outdoor pool, baseball field, and auditorium provided ample space for Dorsey's programs to flourish. Returning to Washington Park in 1950, he helped organize a reunion in 1954 to acknowledge the central role the playground had played in the lives of many Hill District residents since 1900. After the city decided to demolish the entire lower Hill District to make way for the Pittsburgh Renaissance, a development project that included a new civic arena, many current and former neighborhood residents gathered on 24 April 1954 to share their Washington Park stories.

Retiring in 1960, Dorsey could look back on a career that put him at the center of African American sport and the recreation movement in Pittsburgh. From the playgrounds and gyms of the 1910s, the Negro Baseball Leagues of the 1920s and 1930s, and the expansion of recreation centers throughout the Hill District, Dorsey was a part of it all. At a time when there were only a few African American physical directors in the country, Dorsey was the dean of directors in Pittsburgh.

FURTHER READING

The Dorsey-Turfley Family Papers are housed in the Library & Archives of the Senator John Heinz History Center.

"Ammon Center in Forefront of City Recreation Plans," *Pittsburgh Courier*, 24 July 1943.

Black, Samuel W. *James A. Dorsey and the Support of Black Sport in Pittsburgh* (2004).

Ruck, Rob. *Sandlot Seasons: Sport in Black Pittsburgh* (1993).

SAMUEL W. BLACK

Dorsey, John Henry (28 Jan. 1874–30 June 1926), Roman Catholic priest, was born in Baltimore, Maryland, the son of Daniel Dorsey and Emmaline Snowden. He was baptized at St. Francis Xavier Church in Baltimore, the oldest black Catholic parish in the United States. As a young boy Dorsey was encouraged to study for the priesthood by Father John Slattery, SSJ, the superior of the Mill Hill Fathers (later the Josephites), who was interested in encouraging religious vocations among African Americans. In 1888 Dorsey was sent to St. Thomas College, a minor seminary in St. Paul, Minnesota. In 1889 he entered Mill Hill Seminary, Epiphany Apostolic College, in Baltimore. Four years later he enrolled at St. Joseph Seminary, at that time a residence for the Josephite seminarians taking courses at nearby St. Mary's Seminary.

On 21 June 1902 Dorsey was ordained a priest in the Baltimore cathedral by James Cardinal Gibbons. He sang his first Mass the following day at St. Francis Xavier Church in Baltimore. He was the sixth African American to be ordained a Catholic priest following the ordination of JAMES AUGUSTINE HEALY in 1854. He was the second black priest to be educated and ordained in the United States. In many places black priests still faced either outright hostility or subtle resistance. Slattery, the preacher at Dorsey's first mass, delivered a forthright and somewhat angry sermon calling for the ordination of more black priests and denouncing the racism within the American Catholic Church. Within the year Slattery had resigned his position and a few years later left the priesthood and the Catholic Church.

Dorsey was a powerful and impressive preacher. He became an immediate success with black Catholics in both the South and the North as he was sent on a preaching tour to black congregations immediately following his ordination. He was described as "projecting an air of authority." Dorsey's popularity among African Americans was seen as proof that an increase in the number of black priests would greatly increase the number of black converts to Catholicism. Following his first tour of preaching missions, he was given a position in 1903 at the St. Joseph Catechetical College in Montgomery, Alabama. He stayed there a year and a half and was then assigned to the black parish in Pine Bluff, Arkansas. In the spring of 1905 he was made pastor.

Dorsey was the first black priest to become a pastor of a parish in the South. Almost immediately he met with hostility and suspicion from the local white pastor, a former Confederate army officer, and even from some of the black sisters in the school who would have preferred a white priest. Charges were leveled against him concerning the administration of the parish and misconduct with one of the women whom he had converted. None of these charges was proved. In fact many in the parish signed a petition in support of their pastor. Notwithstanding, the bishop of Little Rock, John B. Morris, requested the superior of the Josephites to remove Father Dorsey. In 1907 the superior of the Josephites was forced to comply.

From 1909 to 1917 Dorsey was part of a team of three priests who traveled throughout the South preaching mainly to African American Catholics. Here Father Dorsey was eminently successful. He was equally popular with many black Protestant listeners to whom he explained the teachings of Catholicism. He was also instrumental in the formation of the Knights of Peter Claver, an African American Catholic fraternal organization. He along with three other Josephite priests and three black Catholic laymen established the organization in 1909 in Mobile, Alabama. He served as national chaplain for fourteen years.

Despite his success and achievements, Dorsey faced relentless criticism and hostility because of his race. He was caricatured in the anti-Catholic southern press as a black ape wearing a stole and listening to the confessions of a young white woman. Weariness, racial prejudice, and loneliness contributed to his becoming overweight and sickly, and to his becoming an alcoholic. Eventually, his poor health forced him to retire from the preaching circuit. In 1918 he was assigned to St. Monica's Church, a small black parish in south Baltimore.

At this time the newly elected superior general of the Josephites, Louis B. Pastorelli, officially introduced a policy of no longer accepting black candidates for the priesthood into their seminary. The policy was adopted as a result of the many difficulties experienced by the black clergy up to this point and the many complaints against black priests by some southern bishops and whites. Aware of the new policy Father Dorsey supported those black Catholics in Baltimore who publicly challenged the Josephites on their exclusion policies in the African American press. These actions further alienated him from the leaders of the Josephite society. John Henry Dorsey died in Baltimore after a long illness resulting from blows to his head inflicted by an irate father—a former convict—angered by the disciplinary action taken by Dorsey against his daughter in the parish school.

John Henry Dorsey's experience as one of the first black Catholic priests in the United States is a testament to the hardships and tribulations faced by African American priests in the early twentieth century. The clerical hierarchy had little sympathy for their suffering and did little to cultivate a black Catholic priesthood. In 1920 the Holy See opened a seminary in Mississippi run by members of the Society of the Divine Word for the training of African American men for the priesthood. A century after Dorsey was ordained a black bishop, WILTON D. GREGORY would become president of the U.S. Conference of Catholic Bishops and lead the church in ways that Dorsey could have only dreamed.

FURTHER READING

Brown, Joseph A., S.J. *To Stand on the Rock: Meditation on Black Catholic Identity* (1998).

Foley, Albert, S.J. *God's Men of Color: The Colored Catholic Priests of the United States, 1854–1954* (1955).

Ochs, Stephen. *Desegregating the Altar: The Josephites and the Struggle for Black Priests, 1871–1960* (1990)

Ochs, Stephen. "The Ordeal of the Black Priest," *U.S. Catholic Historian* 5 (1986).

This entry is taken from the *American National Biography* and is published here with the permission of the American Council of Learned Societies.

CYPRIAN DAVIS

Dorsey, Thomas Andrew (1 July 1899–23 Jan. 1993), blues performer, gospel singer, and composer, was born in Villa Rica, Georgia, the son of Thomas Madison Dorsey, a preacher, and Etta Plant Spencer. Dorsey's mother, whose first husband had died, owned approximately fifty acres of farmland. Dorsey lived in somewhat trying circumstances as his parents moved first to Atlanta and Forsyth, Georgia, and then back to Villa Rica during the first four years of his life. In Villa Rica the Dorsey family settled into a rural lifestyle supported by marginal farming that was slightly mitigated by his father's pastoral duties.

Though economically pressed, Dorsey's parents found enough money to purchase an organ, and it was on this instrument that their young son began to play music at around six years of age. Dorsey was exposed not only to the religious music that pervaded his home but also to the secular music—especially the emerging blues tradition—that encompassed the music universe of a young black American growing up in rural Georgia in the early twentieth century. His experience with secular music came through his friends as well as his uncle Phil Plant, who picked the guitar and wandered across southern Georgia as a bard. His mother's brother-in-law Corrie M. Hindsman, a more respectable member of the local black establishment, gave Thomas a rudimentary formal music education, including singing out of the shape-note hymnals and learning some of the antebellum spirituals.

In 1908 the family moved to Atlanta after Dorsey's parents finally tired of the lack of opportunities available to black Americans living in rural Georgia. Both worked at a variety of menial jobs while the elder Dorsey occasionally also worked as a guest preacher. Atlanta's higher cost of living meant

Thomas Dorsey at the piano with his band, the Wandering Syncopators Orchestra, in 1923. (AP Images.)

a decline in social and economic status, however, and young Thomas dropped out of school after the fourth grade. He slowly became part of the commercial music scene that revolved around Decatur Street and the Eighty-one Theater in particular. By his midteens Dorsey was regularly working as a pianist at the clubs and at local Saturday night stomps, house parties, and dances sponsored by organizations such as the Odd Fellows. For three years, between the summers of 1916 and 1919, Dorsey shuttled between Atlanta and Chicago in search of more lucrative and steady musical employment. He was principally a blues pianist who occasionally performed with small combos that played jazz, and well into the early 1920s Dorsey was still struggling to survive on his meager earnings from music. Although he attended the 1921 National Baptist Convention in Chicago (his Uncle Joshua invited his nephew to accompany him) and after the convention became music director of Chicago's New Hope Baptist Church, Dorsey remained committed to the secular world. He was in a good position to cash in on this music when the blues records of Bessie Smith, Alberta Hunter, and Ma Rainey gained popularity in the mid-1920s. For several years he served as Rainey's pianist and arranger, touring the country playing tent shows and vaudeville stages. In 1928 he teamed with Tampa Red, and they soon had a hit with "It's Tight Like That"; until 1932 the duo earned a steady living playing on stage and recording for the Vocalion label. Dorsey also worked as a music demonstrator in Chicago music stores from 1928 on and as an arranger and session organizer for Brunswick and Vocalion records.

Dorsey's personal life had changed in August 1925 when he married Nettie Harper, who had recently arrived in Chicago from Philadelphia. He was given to occasional bouts with depression, and his marriage helped to stabilize him. When these periods descended upon him he turned not only to Nettie but also to his own religious upbringing. As early as 1922 Dorsey began publishing sacred songs in addition to blues. His 1926 composition "If You See My Savior, Tell Him That You Saw Me," came during one of his depressive periods and is perhaps the first "gospel blues" piece ever published. Dorsey pioneered this genre by combining sacred lyrics with the harmonic structure and form of the popular blues songs. In 1928 Dorsey met and mentored the seventeen-year-old Mahalia Jackson, one of the first singers he knew who was able to combine the emotional feeling of blues with the sentiments of his new gospel songs.

Almost exactly seven years after their marriage, Nettie died in childbirth, followed within a day by their infant son, their only child. Dorsey fell into deep melancholy that lasted for months. He finally started to climb out of his depression by writing "Take My Hand, Precious Lord," and from that point until his own death Dorsey devoted his life to gospel performing, composing, and organizations. During the decade after his wife's death, Dorsey worked tirelessly to promote gospel music, first in Chicago and then across the United States.

As early as a year before Nettie's passing Dorsey had been turning more and more of his attention to the sacred music realm. He founded and helped to direct the first gospel choir at Chicago's Ebenezer Baptist Church in late 1931. One year later Dorsey, along with the gospel singer Sallie Martin, was instrumental in establishing the National Convention of Gospel Choirs and Choruses, formed in response to the steadily growing number of gospel choruses. These proved to be popular, though controversial, innovations within the African American church. The old-line, more conservative mainstream church members proved resistant to change; they protested the showmanship that accompanied these groups' programs and were appalled by the clapping, highly syncopated rhythms, choreographed movement, and overt emotionalism that Dorsey instilled in the gospel choruses with which he worked. While sometimes troubled by criticism, Dorsey was undeterred. His final major contribution during this early period was to open the Thomas A. Dorsey Gospel Songs Music Publishing Company. This fledgling company sold thousands of copies of early gospel songs for ten cents apiece, disseminating them mainly at local churches and the early annual meetings of the National Convention of Gospel Choirs and Choruses.

Dorsey worked tirelessly over the next two decades in service to the growth of gospel blues and the organizations that he helped found. He traveled across the country teaching workshops, leading choruses, and occasionally singing, all the while retaining his Chicago base. He published scores of sacred songs during this period, including "There'll Be Peace in the Valley" (1938), "Hide Me in Thy Bosom" (1939), "Ev'ry Day Will Be Sunday By and By" (1946), and "I'm Climbing Up the Rough Side of the Mountain" (1951). In 1940 he married Kathryn Mosley, with whom he had two children, and in the 1960s and 1970s he served as an assistant pastor at the Pilgrim Church.

Slowed by age and the desire to stay closer to his Chicago home, Dorsey became less prolific over the last four decades of his life, composing fewer than twenty songs. Throughout his life Dorsey remained proud of his work in blues and of his guidance of Mahalia Jackson early in a career that eventually touched millions of Americans, black and white. By the late 1950s the pop singers Pat Boone and Elvis Presley had underscored Dorsey's impact on modern gospel music through their influential recordings of "Peace in the Valley" and other Dorsey-inspired compositions. The 1982 documentary film *Say Amen, Somebody* pays warm tribute to Dorsey and other gospel pioneers. During the final years of his life Dorsey became recognized as the patriarch of the gospel blues movement, which he lived to see from its inception to its widespread acceptance. After several years of severely diminished health, he died in Chicago.

FURTHER READING

Dixon, Robert M. W., and John Godrich. *Blues and Gospel Records, 1902–1943* (1982).

Harris, Michael. *The Rise of Gospel Blues—The Music of Thomas Andrew Dorsey in the Urban Church* (1992).

Obituary: *New York Times*, 25 Jan. 1993.

This entry is taken from the *American National Biography* and is published here with the permission of the American Council of Learned Societies.

KIP LORNELL

Douglas, Aaron (26 May 1899–2 Feb. 1979), artist and educator, was born in Topeka, Kansas, the son of Aaron Douglas Sr., a baker from Tennessee, and Elizabeth (maiden name unknown), an amateur artist from Alabama. Aaron had several brothers and sisters, but he was unique in his family in his singular drive to pursue higher education. He attended segregated elementary schools and then an integrated high school. Topeka had a strong and progressive black community, and Aaron was fortunate to grow up in a city where education and social uplift were stressed through organizations such as the Black Topeka Foundation. He was an avid reader and immersed himself in the great writers, including Dumas, Shakespeare, and Emerson. His parents were able to feed and clothe him but could offer him no other help with higher education. When he needed money to pursue a college degree, he traveled via rail to Detroit, where he worked as a laborer in several jobs, including building automobiles. It was hard work, but it increased his desire to attend college.

Upon his return to Topeka, Douglas decided to attend the University of Nebraska and arrived ten days into the term with no transcripts in hand. This was the first in a series of steps he made to educate himself and improve his artistic skills. The chairman of Nebraska's art department realized Douglas's potential and agreed to accept him on the condition that his transcripts would follow. At Nebraska, Douglas discovered the writings of W. E. B. DuBois and found inspiration in them. By 1921 he was a constant reader of *Crisis* magazine, and later, *Opportunity*, and he began to seriously consider the nation's racial situation. Douglas graduated from Nebraska with a BFA in 1922 and accepted a teaching position at Lincoln High School in Kansas City, Missouri, where he was one of only two black faculty members. In 1925, after seeing a special issue of *Survey Graphic* magazine, which focused on Harlem and featured a portrait of the black actor Roland Hayes on its cover, Douglas decided to quit his job and pursue his dream of working as a full-time artist. Hoping for wider artistic opportunities and contact with a larger black community, Douglas moved to Harlem in 1925. While he was full of dreams, Douglas had very few connections in New York.

Only days after his arrival, the *Crisis* editor W. E. B. DuBois hired him to work in the magazine's mail room and to help illustrate the magazine. DuBois, who had been editing *Crisis* for fourteen years, was struggling against the competition, *Opportunity* magazine, published by the National Urban League. Needing a stronger visual message, DuBois turned to Douglas, commissioning bold covers, prints, and drawings to accompany essays, stories, and editorials expressing DuBois's vision of what African Americans should know about the world around them, and what causes they should support. In 1927 Douglas was made art director at *Crisis*. When Douglas had started work at *Crisis*, he had also been hired by James Weldon Johnson to illustrate for *Opportunity* magazine. Douglas soon found himself in the unique, and pleasant, position of having two major publications vying for his talents. Through his *Crisis* connections, Douglas met the Bavarian artist Winold Reiss, who offered him a scholarship to study with him in his New York atelier, where Douglas immersed himself in the study of black life. Douglas was soon noticed by other patrons, and he quickly became one of the most sought-after illustrators of the Harlem Renaissance, receiving commissions to illustrate magazines and book covers as well as to execute a number of private

Song of the Towers, the fourth panel in the *Aspects of Negro Life* mural series by painter and graphic artist Aaron Douglas, 1934. (Schomburg Center.)

commissions and public murals. From his earliest Harlem paintings and prints, Douglas developed a strong commitment to establishing an African American identity tied to an African past, a history and identification encouraged by both DuBois and ALAIN LOCKE. Douglas was drawn to African art even while he knew very little about it. As one of the key visual spokesmen for what became known as the Harlem Renaissance, Douglas used the art of the Ivory Coast, Ethiopia, and Egypt to establish a firm connection between African Americans and African culture. As he wrote to his future wife, Alta Sawyer, in 1925:

> We are possessed, you know, with the idea that it is necessary to be white, to be beautiful. Nine times out of ten it is just the reverse. It takes lots of training or a tremendous effort to down the

idea that thin lips and a straight nose is the apogee of beauty. But once free you can look back with a sigh of relief and wonder how anyone could be so deluded (Kirschke, 61).

Douglas married Alta in 1926. Over the years the couple's Harlem home became a central meeting place for the artists and writers of the Harlem Renaissance. Meanwhile, Douglas's illustrations, full of race pride and African heritage, had wide distribution and were seen across the country, in libraries, schools, social clubs, beauty parlors, and homes. He also provided artwork for other magazines, including *Theatre Arts Monthly*, as well as for numerous books. Douglas produced covers and interior illustrations for some of the Harlem Renaissance's most significant literary achievements, including Alain Locke's *New Negro*, WALLACE THURMAN's *The Blacker the Berry*, Paul Morand's *Black Magic*, James Weldon Johnson's *God's Trombones*, COUNTÉE CULLEN's *Caroling Dusk*, and CLAUDE MCKAY's *Banjo*, and several works by LANGSTON HUGHES. Douglas was moved by the artistic milieu in which he worked, especially the literature of the time, written by his friends, which, along with his own work, described black life. Douglas's work articulated the black experience in Harlem in the 1920s and 1930s, including the tremendous output of visual arts and music, and the effects of discrimination and the Depression. Douglas offered a unique visual style, which combined elements of American and European modernism, including cubism, orphism, precisionism, and art deco patterning, with a strong Pan-Africanist vision. His linoleum cuts, pen and ink drawings, oils, gouaches, and frescos forged a distinct combination of modernist elements.

In 1928 Douglas and GWENDOLYN BENNETT became the first African American artists to receive a fellowship to study at the Barnes Foundation in Merion, Pennsylvania. Douglas's one-year fellowship was followed, in 1931, by a year of study in Paris at the Academie Scandinave, where he met the African American painters HENRY OSSAWA TANNER and PALMER HAYDEN.

In addition to his work as an illustrator, Douglas was a painter, particularly of portraits. He was interested in murals and received several mural commissions, including a mural at the Harlem branch of the YMCA, the College Inn in Chicago, and Bennett College in South Carolina. His most innovative project—created for Cravath Hall Library at Fisk University in Nashville, Tennessee, in 1930—was a massive cycle of murals celebrating philosophy, drama, music, poetry, and science, as well as African and African American culture. Restoration of these murals in 2003 revealed orphist-like geometric circles and abstract papyrus-topped columns, as well as four murals that had been covered for decades. One mural depicts Africans left behind as their family members and friends are taken away, never to be seen again. The mural cycle chronicles the history of blacks from Africa and slavery, to their triumphant release from servitude through education. Ambitious in its Pan-Africanist vision the mural includes elements drawn from Egypt, West Africa, and the Congo. In the 1960s Douglas entirely repainted the Fisk murals with a much brighter, bolder palette. In 1934 Douglas completed *Aspects of Negro Life*, four large mural panels sponsored by the WPA for the Countée Cullen Library at 135th Street (now the Schomburg Center for Research in Black Culture). Like the Fisk murals, these panels illustrate life in Africa before enslavement, through the years of slavery, emancipation, and into the African American present. Douglas offered hope even in the Depression, through creativity, music, and culture.

The Fisk mural commission led to Douglas's return to the university in 1937, where he established the university's first art department, remaining as chair of the department for over thirty years, until his retirement in 1966. In 1944, after years of part-time graduate work, he earned his M.A. from Columbia University Teacher's College. He taught and worked as an artist well into his seventies and considered his work as an educator at Fisk to be his greatest accomplishment. Douglas, whose work influenced countless artists with its unique vision of African American identity linked to a Pan-Africanist vision, died in Nashville in 1979.

FURTHER READING

Douglas's papers are held in the Fisk University Special Collections, Nashville, Tennessee, and at the Schomburg Center for Research in Black Culture of the New York Public Library.

Kirschke, Amy Helene. *Aaron Douglas: Art, Race and the Harlem Renaissance* (1995).

Obituary: *New York Times*, 22 Feb. 1979.

AMY HELENE KIRSCHKE

Douglas, H. Ford (1831–11 Nov. 1865), abolitionist and military officer, was born in Virginia, the son of a white man, William Douglas, and a slave, Mary (surname unknown). The initial in his name stood for Hezekiah. Sometime after his fifteenth birthday, he escaped from slavery and settled in Cleveland, Ohio, where he worked as a barber. Self-educated, he became an active member of the antislavery movement and the Ohio free black community in the 1850s. He served as the Cleveland agent for the *Voice of the Fugitive*, a black newspaper published in Canada that was devoted to the "immediate and unconditional abolition" of slavery.

Douglas became a leader in the black state convention movement of Ohio. He supported William Lloyd Garrison's position that the U.S. Constitution was a proslavery document that recognized the slave trade, approved slavery, and provided for the recapture of fugitive slaves. Unlike those abolitionists who sought to uproot slavery through moral suasion or political activity, Douglas advocated African American emigration, along with Edward Wilmot Blyden, Martin R. Delany, and David Walker. He soon gained a reputation as an eloquent orator and at age twenty-two was appointed one of the vice presidents of the 1853 Ohio State Convention of Colored Freemen in Columbus. Achieving prominence at the 1854 National Emigration Convention in Cleveland, Douglas delivered a brilliant defense of emigration. He argued that African Americans could not wait indefinitely for change in the United States after two hundred years of oppression and little improvement in their status. While Douglas knew that African Americans would never achieve equality as long as slavery continued, he believed that this system was destined to last for a long time. Under these circumstances, he refused to proclaim allegiance and loyalty to the United States.

After the 1854 National Emigration Convention, Douglas moved to Chicago, where he became a proprietor of the Provincial Freeman, a black newspaper published in Canada. He also became active in the Illinois black state convention movement. At the 1856 meeting in Alton, he chaired the Committee on Declaration of Sentiment, which denounced the racial prejudice that African Americans encountered in their "native land." Remaining in Chicago for only a few years, Douglas soon moved to British-controlled Canada West (now Ontario), where he believed black people could give their allegiance to a government that protected them. He described the United States as a country that robbed, kidnapped, plundered, raped, and murdered black people "with the cant of liberty, democracy and Christianity upon her lips."

Douglas married Statira Steele in October 1857; they had one child. In 1858 Douglas returned to Chicago. The emigrationist movement, which had once considered Canada the ideal destination, turned its attention to Africa and Haiti. Douglas, however, became interested in Central America and signed up as an agent for Francis P. Blair Jr.'s Central American Land Company. Blair, a congressman from Missouri, advocated settling free blacks in Central or South America. With assistance from the U.S. government, Blair argued, African Americans could lead comfortable and prosperous lives in an area free of slavery. Blair proposed Honduras as a suitable location that could also assist the United States in its competition with Great Britain for control of trade in Central America. Because of the area's climate, Blair argued that whites could not settle the region but that blacks would thrive there. Blair's proposal made little progress, however, especially because the Guatemalan government, which controlled the territory of Honduras, opposed the scheme.

In May 1860 Douglas made his first visit to New England at the invitation of Parker Pillsbury, a Garrisonian whom Douglas had met during a lecture tour through the Midwest. Douglas was soon much in demand as an abolitionist speaker. Newspaper accounts of his 4 July 1860 address to an antislavery rally in Framingham, Massachusetts, describe him as having "a physique so noble and a presence so attractive as to charm and interest the listener at once." In that speech, Douglas criticized the United States for not measuring up to the standard of a great nation because it supported slavery. He argued that on the slavery question there was not much difference between Stephen A. Douglas and Abraham Lincoln.

Douglas lectured widely throughout New England during the latter part of 1860 as a traveling agent for the Massachusetts Antislavery Society. With growing praise for John Brown (1800–1859) and his raid on the federal arsenal at Harpers Ferry, Virginia, Douglas increasingly favored the use of violence to end slavery. He remained in New England through January 1861, when he returned to Chicago as an agent for James Redpath's Haitian Emigration Bureau. His duties involved recruiting prospective emigrants, informing them about Haiti, and describing the facilities offered by the Haitian government.

With the outbreak of the Civil War, Douglas traveled to Kansas, where he encouraged slaves from Missouri to escape to freedom. He later passed for white and joined Company G of the Ninety-fifth Regiment Illinois Infantry Volunteers in July 1862, in Belvidere, Illinois. Six months later, Douglas, who was overjoyed at Lincoln's freeing the slaves, wrote Frederick Douglass about the Emancipation Proclamation and his role in the war. He encouraged Douglass to support the war by recruiting and commanding a black regiment to prove that black men deserved equality. Once the Union army officially enlisted black troops, Douglas requested a transfer to a black unit. Brigadier General John P. Hawkins, Commander of the South, assigned him to the Tenth Louisiana Regiment of African Descent (Corps d'Afrique) in June 1863. While stationed with the Corps d'Afrique in Mississippi, Douglas contracted malaria and returned home to Chicago to recover. He rejoined the military in July 1864 and recruited an independent battery of light artillery, of which he became captain. Douglas was one of fewer than thirty black commissioned officers in the Union army and was probably the only black combat captain during the Civil War.

Douglas left the service in July 1865, still suffering from malaria. He tried unsuccessfully to operate a restaurant in Atchison, Kansas, but died there four months after his discharge. Although not as well known as Frederick Douglass, H. Ford Douglas was a popular and effective antislavery speaker. As was true of Douglass, his complexion and physical features made clear to audiences the ravages of slavery. Contrary to Douglass, however, he advocated emigration on the grounds that African Americans would never achieve their full potential in the United States until the nation abolished slavery.

FURTHER READING

Materials relating to Douglas's military career are in the records of the Adjutant General's Office, 1780s–1917, in the National Archives, Washington, D.C., Record Group 94 and Pension File 191423.

Harris, Robert L., Jr. "H. Ford Douglas: Afro-American Antislavery Emigrationist," *Journal of Negro History* 62.3 (July 1977), 217–234.

Ripley, C. Peter, ed. *The Black Abolitionist Papers 1830–1865* (5 vols., 1985–1992).

This entry is taken from the *American National Biography* and is published here with the permission of the American Council of Learned Societies.

ROBERT L. HARRIS

Douglas, Louis (14 May 1889–19 May 1939), dancer, choreographer, actor, and impresario, was born Winston Louis Douglas in Philadelphia, Pennsylvania, the son of Frederick Douglas (no relation to the veteran antislavery campaigner FREDERICK DOUGLASS, although Louis's name is sometimes found spelled in the latter way). Frederick Douglas was a music hall or vaudeville performer whose specialty was juggling with plates; young Louis started life on the boards handing plates to his father, ad-libbing when the act went wrong and the plates tumbled. His mother, a devout Catholic, ensured his formal education at a missionary school and hoped he would become a missionary to Africa; instead Douglas traveled across the Atlantic at an early age as a member of the Georgia Pickaninnies, one of many vaudeville troupes that featured young black performers while drawing heavily on racial stereotypes. The troupe arrived in Ireland in 1903 and started a European tour that would last until 1912. But Douglas left the troupe soon after its arrival, and from 1904 he traveled with the mezzo-soprano Belle Davis as one of her Pick Chicks—"tiny negro boys of astonishing suppleness and comic power" ('Exbl.-', *Der Artist*, Nr. 997, 1904, unpaginated). This European circuit served as Douglas's apprenticeship in show business. Around 1908 Belle Davis and Louis Douglas parted company. Perhaps Douglas had grown too tall to play a child dancing companion to Davis; perhaps he wanted to get away on his own. What is certain is that in 1926 he told reporters in Berlin that he had seen the opportunities in theatrical management during his time in England in 1903.

Douglas crossed and recrossed Europe, playing the leading theaters in major cities both as a solo act and with partners. Now boldly headlined as "the American King of Dancers" he was always well reviewed and his success in St. Petersburg was such that he returned every year until prevented by war. For two decades black dancers had been a staple in the theatrical diet of Europeans, who knew what to expect from "Nigger Dance" and "American Song & Dance" billed to appear at their local theaters. Despite the somewhat jaded nature of many such acts, Douglas performed to considerable acclaim during the 1910s, and he frequently appeared in London stage productions, such as *Honi Soit* (1910), *Pick-a-Dilly* (1914), and *Cheerio* and *Any Old Thing* (both 1917). The outbreak of war in August 1914 restricted Douglas's career. From a base probably in Britain Douglas toured Scandinavia. Whatever else he was doing in 1918 and 1919 Louis Douglas met, courted, and married Marion Abigail Cook, daughter of the leading African American theatrical personalities WILL MARION COOK and ABBIE MITCHELL. Cook was twenty-one and Douglas thirty when they married in the British east coast fishing port of Grimsby on 15 August 1919. The registrar recorded his name as Lewis. Douglas and his partner Sonny Jones, the dancer and ragtime pianist, were still touring the British Isles as "The Syncopated Black Faced Comedians" when, on 21 May 1920, Douglas's daughter Abbie Louise Douglas, who would later be known as Marion Douglas and Maranantha Quick, was born in North Marylebone, England.

In 1923 the Douglases and Jones toured South America with a typical French revue titled "Parisys," which starred La Mistinguette, the legendary French music hall star and revue artist. From there Douglas returned to the United States to act briefly in his father-in-law's *Negro Nuances*, alongside Abbie Mitchell, Lucille Handy (daughter of W. C. HANDY), FLOURNOY E. MILLER, and Aubrey Lyles. By April 1924 Douglas was back in Paris and continuing his career in French revues, but he also had a guest appearance in "a real-Colored midnight show in Paris—*Midnight Shuffle Along*" (Chicago *Defender*, 8 Feb. 1924).

A year later the white backer Caroline Dudley Reagan employed Douglas as assistant director for the sensational *Revue Nègre*, in which he also served as interpreter, organizer, choreographer, dancer, actor, and singer. The composer and pianist Spencer Williams wrote for the show, and CLAUDE HOPKINS's seven-piece orchestra included SIDNEY BECHET, whose first experience of Europe had been with Will Marion Cook's orchestra in London in 1919. JOSEPHINE BAKER's electric presence in this revue made her the talk of Paris. Baker, Douglas, and the orchestra were also successful in Berlin, where in 1926 he organized *Black People*, his first all-black revue, later followed by *Black and White*, *Black Follies* or *Negro Follies*, *Louisiana* or *Darktown Frolics*, *Black Birds*, and *The Black Flowers* or *Liza*. For *Black People*, Douglas seems to have taken some material from the *Chocolate Kiddies* show, which had brought SAM WOODING and his orchestra to Europe in 1925, with music by Spencer Williams. In fact Douglas offered employment to the top black entertainers and musicians available in Europe, and the revue had two jazz bands, one of which was directed by Bechet. Over the next years Douglas toured widely with his revues, from Copenhagen to Cairo.

Douglas was at the height of his career and in 1931 took part in his second film, *Niemandsland* (*No Man's Land*). But this time he had the principal acting role in an avant-garde, pacifist movie. Four soldiers—a German, a Briton, a Frenchman, and a Russian—are shown before the war, in Berlin, London, Paris, and the Jewish region of Poland/Russia. The second part has them sheltering together from the indiscriminately murderous shells and grenades in no man's land. The carpenter, sculptor, mechanic, and Jew are joined by a soldier of France's colonial army—Louis Douglas, playing an international entertainer who becomes the mediator and interpreter, able to speak all the languages, after a fashion. Above all he is a sensible human being with no single national loyalty that conflicts with the German, British, French, or Jewish points of view. An island of international tolerance in no man's land is created by the neutral yet cosmopolitan black, and finally the five walk off together in a vision of peace and international understanding. The Nazis found the film extremely unpalatable, and it was immediately banned after the party's ascension to political power in 1933. Recognition must be given to Louis Douglas, alongside PAUL ROBESON, as a pioneer serious actor whose role, despite stereotyping, was a brilliant performance in a movie that presented blacks as individuals.

Douglas was based in Paris between 1932 and 1938, where he was employed by the Casino de Paris for its annual revues, but he also guested with visiting black ensembles such as the *Harlem Black Birds 1936*. Douglas embarked upon another tour of Europe in 1937, which ended in disaster in Italy. His wife Marion became ill, the troupe broke up in Naples, and Douglas was left with large debts, prompting his father-in-law to appeal for help, as Douglas was unable to raise the required sum himself. In a letter to ALAIN LOCKE, the editor of *The New Negro*, Cook spoke of Douglas's poor health and mental breakdowns and asked Locke to use his influence in order to obtain an advance from the U.S. government to finance Douglas's repatriation to the States. In 1937 Douglas returned to New York, where he appeared at the Apollo in the ANDY RAZAF–Eubie Blake *Tan Manhattan* show, and in the same theater's *Tan Town Topics*; with the band of JAMES P. JOHNSON, Douglas and Johnson also collaborated on *The Policy Kings*, which Douglas directed and which opened at the Nora Bayes Theatre on 29 December 1938. A few months later, shortly after his fiftieth birthday, Louis Douglas died in New York.

FURTHER READING

Goldfarb, David A. "Marion Douglas," in *Black Women in America: An Historical Encyclopedia*, ed. Darlene Clark Hine (1993).

Lotz, Rainer E. *Black People—Entertainers of African Descent in Europe and Germany* (1997).

RAINER E. LOTZ

Douglas, Robert L. (4 Nov. 1882–16 July 1979), professional basketball player and team owner, was born in St. Kitts, British West Indies. No information is available concerning Douglas's parents or his early education. He observed his first basketball game shortly after arriving in New York City in 1902. In around 1919 Douglas and some friends organized the Spartan Field Club, which offered black New York City youths the opportunity to participate in amateur cricket, soccer, track, and basketball. Coach Douglas's basketball team, the Spartan Braves, were successful, and at times he joined them on the court.

In 1922 Douglas ran into problems with the Metropolitan Basketball Association, an amateur organization, over the status of a couple of his players. Because of this controversy Douglas organized the New York Renaissance, a professional basketball team. He approached the owner of the Renaissance Ballroom in Harlem, agreeing to use the name "Renaissance" in return for practice and playing space. The name was soon shortened to the Rens. Three of the members, Leon Monde, Hilton Slocum, and Frank Forbes, had played for Douglas as Spartan Braves. The Rens played the first game of their twenty-six-year existence on 3 November 1923. In that game they defeated the Collegiate Five, a white team, 28-22. The Rens finished their first season with a record of 15-8.

The Renaissance team was the first full-salaried black professional basketball team. Before it was common practice Douglas required contracts from his players. Steeped in a West Indian immigrant culture that emphasized economic self-sufficiency, Douglas displayed an astute business sense. Though he lacked a high school or college education, he worked hard and persevered to become a winning coach and top businessman in the 1920s and 1930s.

By the late 1920s the Rens were playing as many as 150 games each year. They played any and all teams—amateur and professional—including clubs, Young Men's Christian Associations, and colleges. Douglas booked his team for games as much as one year in advance, requiring a guarantee plus expenses for their appearance.

In the 1930s the Rens became a barnstorming team, traveling the Midwest and the South to play opposing teams. On the road, the players faced constant racism and discrimination, and they had difficulty finding hotels and restaurants that would house or serve them. Because of this the Rens traveled in a custom-designed team bus called the "Blue Goose," in which they often slept and ate their meals out of brown bags. Douglas believed that touring enhanced the image of his team and also helped to improve the quality of the game itself among blacks. He encouraged the growth of southern black teams by arranging games between them and his Rens. The Renaissance team traveled four months out of the year, usually playing seven or eight games per week.

Before many of the rule changes in the mid-1930s, players were required to face a jump ball after every basket. Games were low scoring and poorly officiated. Nonetheless Douglas insisted that his players be disciplined and work as a team. Initially, due to slippery ballroom floors, the Rens developed a system of fast breaks made up of passing. Rather than dribbling the ball down the court, the ball passed from player to player and ended up in the basket. This style of play quickly became a Rens trait.

In the 1932–1933 season the Rens won 88 consecutive games and had an overall 127-7 record. They were one of the few teams to consistently beat the Original Celtics, the top white team of the era, though it was the Original Celtics who ended the Rens's winning streak of 1932–1933. The Rens won 100 or more games over fourteen straight seasons. So popular were Douglas's Rens that they drew up to 15,000 spectators, both black and white, per game even during the mid-Depression.

In 1939 in Chicago the Rens won the first World Professional Championship Basketball title. After claiming victories against the New York Yankees and the Harlem Globetrotters, the Rens went on to defeat the Oshkosh All-Stars, a white team, by a score of 34-25. During World War II Douglas was forced to curtail the number of games his team played owing to gas rationing. Many of his players traveled to Washington, D.C., on the weekends and played as the Washington Bears. After the war ended Douglas gathered his team back together and resumed normal play.

The New York Rens moved to Ohio and became the Dayton Rens in 1948, the first black team to join the National Basketball League. They served as a replacement for the Detroit Vagabonds, an all-white team. The financially troubled Dayton Rens had a 16-43 season, playing their last game ever against the Denver Nuggets in Rockford, Illinois, on 21 March 1949.

Over twenty-six years, the Rens's record stood at 2,318 wins and 381 losses. According to ARTHUR ASHE, the Rens "were the first black team to win a world professional title in any sport and led the way for the post–World War II surge of blacks who eventually dominated the sport [basketball] at every level" (50).

In 1963 the 1932–1933 Renaissance team was inducted into the Naismith Basketball Hall of Fame. Members of this team included CLARENCE "FATS" JENKINS, James "Pappy" Ricks, Eyre "Bruiser" Saitch, John Holt, Bill Yancey, TARZAN COOPER, and "Wee" Willie Smith. Douglas, later referred to as the "father of black basketball," was elected to the Hall of Fame as a contributor in 1971, the first black individual to be so honored. In 1975 the Robert L. Douglas Basketball League, the summer professional league in New York, was named for him. Douglas served as the first president of the New York Pioneer Athletic Club and until 1973 managed the Renaissance Ballroom in Harlem. He was married twice, although little information is available. Sadie (maiden name unknown) died, and Douglas was married to Cora Dismond (date unknown). He never had any children. Douglas was the oldest living member of the basketball Hall of Fame when he died in New York City at the age of ninety-six.

FURTHER READING

Ashe, Arthur. *Hard Road to Glory: A History of the African American Athlete, 1919–1945* (1988).

Chalk, Ocania. *Pioneers of Black Sport* (1975).

Dickey, Glenn. *The History of Professional Basketball since 1896* (1982).

Obituary: *New York Times*, 17 July 1979.

This entry is taken from the *American National Biography* and is published here with the permission of the American Council of Learned Societies.

SUSAN J. RAYL

Douglass, Anna Murray (c.1813–4 Aug. 1882) wife of FREDERICK DOUGLASS, antislavery activist, and Underground Railroad agent, was born free as Anna Murray in Denton, Caroline County, Maryland, the eighth child of Bambarra and Mary Murray, both slaves, who were freed one month prior to Anna's birth. When Anna Murray was seventeen years old, she traveled to Baltimore to work as a domestic servant, first for the Montell family, and two years later for the Wells family. Despite her own illiteracy, she became involved in a community known as the East Baltimore Improvement Society, which provided intellectual and social opportunities for the city's free black population.

In 1825 Frederick Augustus Washington Bailey (Douglass), a slave, was hired out to work as a house servant and then as a caulker in Baltimore's shipyards. He remained in Baltimore until 1838, during which time Murray and Bailey became acquainted, probably through the Improvement Society. Although details of their courtship are not known, Murray agreed to assist Bailey with his escape plans; after this escape was successfully carried out, the couple planned to marry. To fund his journey north, she gave him her life savings—money earned from nine years of domestic service—and sold her featherbed to add to the sum she had given him. After one failed escape attempt, early in September 1838 Bailey succeeded in reaching New York. According to a brief memoir written by Anna Murray Douglass's daughter ROSETTA DOUGLASS SPRAGUE, Bailey escaped wearing the sailor's clothing that Murray had made for him.

As soon as Murray heard from Bailey that he had arrived at a safe house in New York City, she traveled to meet him. They were married in New York on 15 September 1838 by the abolitionist leader the Reverend JAMES WILLIAM CHARLES PENNINGTON, also a fugitive slave from Maryland. The couple then traveled to New Bedford, Massachusetts, where they found a small home that they furnished with Murray's possessions. At this time, Frederick Bailey assumed the surname Douglass. Frederick and Anna Douglass struggled to make ends meet, Anna taking in laundry and Douglass working as an unskilled laborer. In June 1839 the couple's first child, Rosetta, was born. Their first son, Lewis Henry, who became sergeant major of the famed Fifty-fourth Massachusetts Regiment during the Civil War, was born in October 1840.

The year 1841 proved to be a turning point in their lives. After an antislavery speech in New Bedford, Frederick was discovered by the white abolitionist leaders William Lloyd Garrison and Wendell Phillips, which led to his employment as a paid lecturer for the Massachusetts Anti-Slavery Society (MASS). To be closer to Boston and the offices of the MASS, the Douglass family moved to Lynn, Massachusetts, while Mrs. Douglass was pregnant with their third child, Frederick Jr., who was born in 1842. While the family lived in Lynn, Douglass's husband traveled extensively for the MASS and the American Anti-Slavery Society, leaving Anna at home to support and care for their family much of the time. Because the household could not be supported on her husband's salary alone, Douglass took in piecework as a shoe binder. From time to time, white women affiliated with the Boston Female Anti-Slavery Society contributed money to the upkeep of the Douglass family and household, as they did to a number of other needy antislavery agents.

Women's roles in the abolitionist movement focused on fund-raising. White and black women hosted fairs, bazaars, and other entertainments to raise money to keep agents in the field. Douglass participated in the abolitionist women's activities, although the extent of her involvement is unclear. It is known that she was a member of a committee of women in charge of refreshments for at least one of the annual antislavery fairs held in Boston. Her daughter Rosetta stated that her mother was a member of the Lynn Ladies' Anti-Slavery Society, and was a regular at its weekly sewing circle. Although the activities of this group have not been detailed, women's antislavery groups typically produced items to be sold at antislavery bazaars, sewed clothing for fugitive slaves, and read aloud from antislavery newspapers as they worked. During the years in Lynn, Douglass regularly contributed a portion of her meager earnings to the antislavery cause.

In October 1844 Douglass gave birth to the couple's fourth child, Charles Remond. The next year, publication of the *Narrative of the Life of Frederick Douglass*, caused her to fear that her husband's outspokenness would endanger him and his family. Late in 1845 he departed for Europe, remaining there for more than a year, leaving Douglass in charge of the family once more. Upon his return in the early months of 1847, Douglass's husband planned to move the family to Rochester, New York, so that he could begin publication of *North Star*, an antislavery newspaper. The move was difficult for Douglass, who had to leave a community where she had established ties and friends. In Rochester, she did not participate in the antislavery movement as much as she had in Lynn, probably because there were fewer opportunities to do so. She was notably more reticent and reserved than she had been in years past, perhaps owing in part to her ill health. The exact nature of her indisposition is not known, although by 1860 it is evident that she was suffering from symptoms that appear to be neurological.

Douglass's activities in Rochester focused on her home and family. The Douglass homestead was also a station on the Underground Railroad, and she did everything possible, including providing food and bedding, to make the fugitives comfortable at her home. Since her husband continued to travel for long periods, she was in charge of the station in his absence. According to one source, she cared for over four hundred slaves on their journey to freedom in Canada. The Douglass home was also a gathering place for traveling abolitionists and antislavery activists in the Rochester area for whom Douglass served as hostess.

As a couple, Anna and Frederick Douglass experienced their greatest closeness while living in New Bedford. With the move to Lynn and the rise in her husband's career in the abolitionist movement, his work and traveling schedule drove them apart. The move to Rochester further separated them, as her husband's need for educated conversation and companionship drew him into relationships with well-educated white female abolitionists. Despite her husband's urgings, Anna never fulfilled his wishes that she become literate. Although Rosetta Douglass affirmed that her mother had some reading ability and managed the household accounts brilliantly, she remained functionally illiterate. The most important of her husband's relationships was with Julia Griffiths, an Englishwoman who lived with the Douglass family for three years, and with the German journalist Ottilie Assing, who spent many summers at the Douglass home. Both women claimed that they maintained good relationships with Anna Douglass, but visitors and others in the abolitionist community disapprovingly noted the tension and mounting disharmony in the Douglass home.

In March 1860 the death of the fifth and youngest Douglass child, Annie, came as a devastating blow to both parents. Frederick Jr., however, helped recruit black troops for the Union war effort during the Civil War, while Charles served in the Fifth Massachusetts Cavalry. Around this time, Douglass's illness had progressed alarmingly, causing her to be enfeebled often. A devastating fire started by an unknown arsonist destroyed their Rochester home in 1872, prompting her husband to move the family to Washington, D.C. Five years later, the family moved to Cedar Hill, a large home on a sizable tract of land on the Anacostia River. On 9 July 1882 Anna Douglass suffered a stroke that completely paralyzed her left side. A month later, she died at Cedar Hill.

FURTHER READING

McFeeley, William S. *Frederick Douglass* (1991).

Smith, Jessie Carney. "Anna Murray Douglass," in *Notable Black American Women* (1992).

Yee, Shirley. *Black Women Abolitionists: A Study in Activism, 1828–1860* (1992).

JUDITH E. HARPER

Douglass, Frederick (Feb. 1818–20 Feb. 1895), abolitionist, civil rights activist, and reform journalist, was born Frederick Augustus Washington Bailey near Easton, Maryland, the son of Harriet Bailey, a slave, and an unidentified white man. Although a slave, he spent the first six years of his life in the cabin of his maternal grandparents, with only a few stolen nighttime visits by his mother. His real introduction to bondage came in 1824, when he was brought to the nearby wheat plantation of Colonel Edward Lloyd. Two years later he was sent to Baltimore to labor in the household of Hugh and Sophia Auld, where he remained for the next seven years. In spite of laws against slave literacy, Frederick secretly taught himself to read and write. He began studying discarded newspapers and learned of the growing national debate over slavery. And he attended local free black churches and found the sight of black men reading and speaking in public a moving experience. At about age thirteen he bought a popular rhetoric text and carefully worked through the exercises, mastering the preferred public speaking style of the time.

Literacy and a growing social consciousness made Frederick into an unruly bondsman. In 1833, after being taken by master Thomas Auld to a plantation near St. Michael's, Maryland, he organized a secret school for slaves, but it was discovered and broken up by a mob of local whites. To discipline Frederick, Auld hired him out to a local farmer who had a reputation as a "slave breaker." Instead he became increasingly defiant and refused to allow himself to be whipped. Hired out to another local farmer, he again organized a secret school for slaves. Before long, he and his pupils had plotted to escape to the free state of Pennsylvania, but this too was discovered. Expecting further trouble from Frederick, Auld returned him to Baltimore in 1836 and hired him out to a local shipyard to learn the caulking trade. Taking advantage of the relative liberty afforded by the city, Frederick joined a self-improvement society of free black caulkers that regularly debated the major social and intellectual questions of the day.

After an unsuccessful attempt to buy his freedom, Frederick escaped from slavery in September 1838. Dressed as a sailor and carrying the free papers of a black seaman he had met on the streets of Baltimore, he traveled by train and steamboat to New York. There he married Anna Murray [Douglass], a free black domestic servant from Baltimore who had encouraged his escape. They soon settled in the seaport of New Bedford, Massachusetts, where Frederick found employment as a caulker and outfitter for whaling ships, and began a family; two

Frederick Douglass, slave, abolitionist, civil rights activist, newspaper editor and writer. (Library of Congress.)

daughters and three sons were born to the union in a little more than a decade. At the urging of a local black abolitionist, he adopted the surname Douglass to disguise his background and confuse slave catchers. He also joined the local African Methodist Episcopal Zion Church and became an active lay leader and exhorter. Soon after arriving in New Bedford, Frederick Douglass was drawn to the emerging antislavery movement. He began to read the *Liberator*, a leading abolitionist journal edited by William Lloyd Garrison, and to attend antislavery meetings in local black churches, occasionally speaking out about his slave experiences. His remarks at an August 1841 convention of the Massachusetts Anti-Slavery Society on Nantucket Island brought him to the attention of Garrison and other leading white abolitionists. Society officials, impressed by Douglass's eloquence and imposing presence, hired him as a lecturing agent. Over the next two years, during which time he moved his family to Lynn, Massachusetts, he made hundreds of speeches for the society before antislavery audiences throughout New England and New York State. In 1843 he joined other leading abolitionist speakers on the One Hundred Conventions tour, which sought to strengthen abolitionist sentiment in upstate New York, Ohio, Indiana, and western Pennsylvania. His oratorical skills brought him increasing recognition and respect within the movement. But antislavery lecturing was a hazardous business. Douglass and his colleagues were often subjected to verbal assaults, barrages of rotten eggs and vegetables, and mob violence. And, as a fugitive slave, his growing visibility placed him in constant danger of recapture. He had to conceal or gloss over certain details in his life story, including names, dates, and locations, to avoid jeopardizing his newfound freedom.

Douglass's growing sophistication as a speaker brought other difficulties in the mid-1840s. At first, his speeches were simple accounts of his life in bondage. But as he matured as an antislavery lecturer, he increasingly sought to provide a critical analysis of both slavery and northern racial prejudice. His eloquence and keen mind even led some to question whether he had ever been a slave. As Douglass's skills—combined with his circumspection—prompted critics to question his credibility, some white abolitionists feared that his effectiveness on the platform might be lost. They advised him to speak more haltingly and to hew to his earlier simple tale. One white colleague thought it "better to have a *little* of the plantation" in his speech (McFeely, 95).

Douglass bristled under such paternalistic tutelage. An answer was to publish an autobiography providing full details of his life that he had withheld. Although some friends argued against that course, fearing for his safety, Douglass sat down in the winter of 1844–1845 and wrote the story of his life. The result was the *Narrative of the Life of Frederick Douglass, Written by Himself* (1845). The brief autobiography, which ran only to 144 pages, put his platform tale into print and reached a broad American and European audience. It sold more than thirty thousand copies in the United States and Britain within five years and was translated into French, German, and Dutch. Along with his public lectures, "the *Narrative* made Frederick Douglass the most famous black person in the world" (David W. Blight, ed., *Narrative of the Life of Frederick Douglass* [1993], 16).

Although the *Narrative* enhanced Douglass's popularity and credibility, it increased the threat to his liberty. He was still a fugitive slave—but now one with a best-selling autobiography. Antislavery colleagues advised Douglass to travel to Britain to elude slave catchers, also hoping that his celebrity would mobilize British abolitionists to bring international pressure against American slavery. He sailed in August 1845 and remained abroad twenty months, lecturing to wildly enthusiastic audiences in England, Scotland, and Ireland. Douglass broadened his reform perspective, grew in confidence, and became increasingly self-reliant during this time. English antislavery friends eventually raised the funds necessary to purchase his freedom from the Aulds and permit his return home. They also collected monies to allow him to begin his own antislavery newspaper in the United States. In December 1847 Douglass moved his family to Rochester in the "burned-over district," a center of reform activity in upstate New York. There he launched the weekly reform journal *North Star*, which promoted abolitionism, African American rights, temperance, women's rights, and a host of related reforms. Like his later journalistic ventures, it was well written and carefully edited and carried Douglass's message to an international audience. While it served as a personal declaration of independence, it initiated an ever-widening rift between Douglass and his Garrisonian colleagues, who sensed that they were losing control of his immense talent.

Douglass's movement away from Garrisonian doctrine on antislavery strategy also signaled his growing independence. Unlike Garrison, who viewed moral suasionist appeals to individual conscience as the only appropriate tactic, Douglass was increasingly persuaded of the efficacy of politics and violence for ending bondage. He attended the Free Soil Convention in Buffalo in 1848 and endorsed its platform calling for a prohibition on the extension of slavery. In 1851 he merged the *North Star* with the *Liberty Party Paper* to form *Frederick Douglass' Paper*, which openly endorsed political abolitionism. This brought a final breach with the Garrisonians, who subjected him to a torrent of public attacks, including scandalous charges about his personal behavior. Nevertheless, Douglass endorsed the nascent Republican Party and its moderate antislavery platform in the elections of 1856 and 1860. At the same time, he increasingly explored the possibilities of abolitionist violence. As early as 1849 Douglass endorsed slave violence, telling a Boston audience that he would welcome news that the slaves had revolted and "were engaged in spreading death and devastation" throughout the South (Quarles, *Allies for Freedom* [1974], 67). After passage of the Fugitive Slave Act of 1850, which put the federal government in the business of capturing and returning runaway slaves, he publicly urged resistance to the law, with violence if necessary. And he became active in the Underground Railroad, hiding numerous fugitives in his Rochester home and helping them on the way to Canada West (now Ontario). Douglass's growing attraction to violence is evident in his 1852 novella, *The Heroic Slave*, generally considered to be the first piece of African American fiction, which glorified the leader of a bloody slave revolt. Later in the decade Douglass became involved in the planning for John Brown's 1859 raid at Harpers Ferry, Virginia, and secretly helped raise funds for the venture, although he thought it ill conceived. When the raid failed, he fled to Canada East (now Quebec), then on to England, fearing arrest on the charge of being Brown's accomplice. He returned home in 1860, disillusioned about African American prospects in the United States and planning to visit Haiti in order to explore the feasibility of black settlement there.

The coming of the Civil War revived Douglass's hopes. From the beginning of the conflict, he pressed President Abraham Lincoln to make emancipation a war goal and to allow black enlistment in the Union army. After Lincoln issued his Emancipation Proclamation in January 1863, Douglass spoke widely in support of the measure. Believing that military service might allow black men to demonstrate their patriotism and manhood, winning greater equality as well as helping to end slavery, he recruited for the Massachusetts Fifty-fourth Infantry, one of the first African American regiments organized in the North. His stirring editorial "Men of Color, to Arms" was often reprinted in Northern newspapers and became a recruiting poster. Nevertheless, Douglass was disgusted by the government's failure to keep its recruiting promises and met with Lincoln to protest discrimination against black troops. Before long, the War Department offered him a commission to enlist and organize African American regiments among the slaves fleeing to Union lines in the lower Mississippi Valley. He stopped publication of *Douglass' Monthly*, which he had begun in 1859, and waited. But the commission never came, and Douglass, refusing to go South without it, continued to lecture and recruit in the North. As the war wound toward a conclusion in 1864–1865, he worked to shape public memory of the war and the character of the peace. He reminded audiences that the conflict had been fought to abolish slavery; it would only be successful, he argued, if the former slaves were granted equal citizenship rights with other Americans.

The end of the war and the Thirteenth Amendment outlawing slavery posed a crisis for Douglass. After a quarter of a century as the preeminent black abolitionist, he wondered if his career was at an end. But he soon recognized that important work remained to be done. In an 1865 speech to the American Anti-Slavery Society, many of whose white members were calling to disband the society, he forcefully argued that "the work of Abolitionists is not done" and would not be until blacks had equal citizenship rights with other Americans. Although he vigorously supported the Fourteenth Amendment and other civil rights statutes, he believed that a meaningful Reconstruction required two essential elements: keeping the old leadership elite from returning to power in the South, and giving the freedmen the vote. Putting the ballot in the hands of black men, he argued, would prove the key to uplifting and protecting African American rights. When President Andrew Johnson refused to endorse these principles in an 1866 meeting with Douglass, the race leader became one of his most vocal critics. He lobbied hard for passage of the Fifteenth Amendment, even at the cost of a breach with many friends who opposed the measure unless it also granted women the vote.

The 1870s were a "time of troubles" in Douglass's life. An 1872 fire destroyed his Rochester home and the files of his lengthy journalistic endeavors. He moved his family to Washington, D.C., where two years earlier he had purchased the *New National Era*. Through careful editorial guidance, he attempted to shape the weekly into a mouthpiece for the race. But persistent financial troubles forced him to stop publication of the paper in 1874. That same year Douglass was named president of the Freedman's Savings Bank, a federally chartered savings and lending institution created to assist the economic development of former slaves. He soon found that the bank was in severe financial distress; it was forced to declare bankruptcy in a matter of months. These two failed ventures cost Douglass thousands of dollars and some public respect. Other black leaders increasingly criticized his alleged moderation on key race questions, his devotion to American individualism (most clearly seen in his oft-repeated lecture, "Self-Made Men"), and his unswerving loyalty to the Republican Party. They openly attacked his failure to criticize the party's abandonment of the Reconstruction experiment in 1877.

The end of Reconstruction dashed Douglass's hopes for a meaningful emancipation. Even so, he never abandoned the fight for African American rights. And he still regarded the Republican Party as the likeliest vehicle for black advancement. A skilled practitioner at "waving the bloody shirt"—linking Democrats with slavery and the Confederacy—he campaigned widely for Republican candidates during the 1870s and 1880s. Partisanship brought rewards. President Rutherford B. Hayes appointed Douglass as the U.S. marshal for the District of Columbia (1877–1881), and President James A. Garfield named him the district's recorder of deeds (1881–1886). These offices made him financially secure. But changing family circumstances unsettled his personal life. His wife, Anna, died in 1882. Two years later he married Helen Pitts, his white former secretary. This racially mixed marriage stirred controversy among blacks and whites alike; nevertheless, it failed to limit Douglass's influence.

Douglass was not lulled into complacency by partisan politics. He pressed Republicans as forcefully as ever on issues of concern to the African American community, while continuing to campaign for party candidates. President Benjamin Harrison rewarded him with an appointment as U.S. minister to Haiti (1889–1891). In this capacity he became an unwitting agent of American expansionism in the Caribbean, unsuccessfully attempting to negotiate special shipping concessions for American business interests and the lease of land for a naval base at Môle St. Nicholas. He eventually resigned his post and returned home in disgust.

Douglass continued to claim the mantle of race leader in the 1890s. He denounced the wave of disfranchisement and segregation measures spreading across the South. He threw much of his energy into the emerging campaign against racial violence. Between 1892 and 1894 he delivered "Lessons of the Hour"—a speech attacking the dramatic increase in black lynchings—to dozens of audiences across the nation. He personally appealed to Harrison for an antilynching law and used his position as the only African American official at the 1893 World's Columbian Exposition to bring the issue before an international audience. He had just returned from another lecture tour when he died at his Washington home.

The most influential African American of the nineteenth century, Douglass made a career of agitating the American conscience. He spoke and wrote on behalf of a variety of reform causes: women's rights, temperance, peace, land reform, free public education, and the abolition of capital punishment. But he devoted the bulk of his time, immense talent, and boundless energy to ending slavery and gaining equal rights for African Americans. These were the central concerns of his long reform career. Douglass understood that the struggle for emancipation and equality demanded forceful, persistent, and unyielding agitation. And he recognized that African Americans must play a conspicuous role in that struggle. Less than a month before his death, when a young black man solicited his advice to an African American just starting out in the world, Douglass replied without hesitation: "Agitate! Agitate! Agitate!" (Joseph W. Holley, *You Can't Build a Chimney from the Top* [1948], 23).

FURTHER READING

Personal papers, including letters, manuscript speeches, and the like, are in the Frederick Douglass Collection at the Library of Congress.

Douglass, Frederick. *Life and Times of Frederick Douglass* (1881; rev. ed., 1892).

Douglass, Frederick. *My Bondage and My Freedom* (1855).

Douglass, Frederick. *Narrative of the Life of Frederick Douglass, Written by Himself* (1845).

The Frederick Douglass Papers: Speeches, Debates, and Interviews, ed. John W. Blassingame (5 vols., 1979–1992).

Life and Writings of Frederick Douglass, ed. Philip S. Foner (5 vols., 1950–1975).

Andrews, William L., ed. *Critical Essays on Frederick Douglass* (1991).

Blight, David W. *Frederick Douglass' Civil War: Keeping Faith in Jubilee* (1989).

Martin, Waldo E., Jr. *The Mind of Frederick Douglass* (1984).

McFeely, William S. *Frederick Douglass* (1991).

Preston, Dickson J. *Young Frederick Douglass: The Maryland Years* (1980).

Quarles, Benjamin. *Frederick Douglass* (1948).

Voss, Frederick S. *Majestic in His Wrath: A Pictorial Life of Frederick Douglass* (1995).

Walker, Peter F. *Moral Choices: Memory, Desire, and Imagination in Nineteenth-century American Abolition* (1978).

This entry is taken from the *American National Biography* and is published here with the permission of the American Council of Learned Societies.

ROY E. FINKENBINE

Douglass, Grace Bustill (1782–1842), activist, was born in Philadelphia, Pennsylvania, to Cyrus Bustill and Elizabeth Morey. Her mother was of mixed race, part English and part Native American (Delaware). Her father, already fifty years old at the time of her birth, was a baker who had purchased his own freedom and had built a thriving business that included supplying American troops in the Revolution, winning him the endorsement of George Washington. A Quaker in practice (though not a formal member), he was also active in both aiding his fellow free blacks in Philadelphia—he was an early member of the Free African Society—and fighting against slavery. When Bustill retired in 1803 to set up a school for black children in his home, Grace took over his shop at 56 Arch Street and opened a millinery business. Three years later she married Robert Douglass, a free African American from Saint Kitts who had become a successful hairdresser and perfumer. They quickly had six children: Elizabeth, William Penn, Charles, James, Robert Jr., and Sarah Mapps. Though they had economic security and were clearly among Philadelphia's African American elite, the Douglass family struggled against racism in organized religion, public and private education, and daily life.

The Douglasses were married in the Episcopal faith, yet Grace continued to attend Quaker meetings. The strand of racism that ran through many Friends proved too much for Robert to take, however, and he eventually helped found the First African Presbyterian Church, of which he was a deacon. He and his sons attended First African; Grace and her daughters generally attended Quaker services, though Grace seems to have been directly cautioned against applying for membership because of her race. Still, she practiced Quaker ways throughout her life, and, though the family grew affluent, she adopted a style of domestic economy with the conscious goal of having extra funds to aid the less fortunate. (One of her extant letters—to Reverend John Gloucester—talks of how "if Christ lived a self-denying life, [I, too,] might deny myself, take up the cross, and follow him" [qtd. in Sterling, 104].) She also developed abiding friendships with more open-minded Friends such as Lucretia Mott and the Grimké sisters; she was one of the interracial party of guests at the wedding of Theodore Weld and Angelina Grimké in 1838.

Educated by her parents, Douglass had come to value learning greatly and even sent elder daughter Elizabeth to a private school, from which she was promptly dismissed when white parents complained. Rather than give up, though, Douglass worked with the prominent black Philadelphian James Forten to set up a school specifically for African American children. Elizabeth and her siblings were educated there; Sarah Mapps Douglass took over the school in 1827 and built it into a model for African American schools. Near the end of her life, in 1841, Grace Douglass was one of the founding members and the first treasurer of Philadelphia's Gilbert Lyceum, an educational outlet for free blacks.

In part because of these experiences and in part because of her background, Douglass exhibited early an intense commitment to social justice and especially to abolition. She was a driving force behind several women's efforts to fight slavery—especially through the Female Anti-Slavery Society, which she helped found (with, among others, her daughter Sarah) in 1833. When the first national women's antislavery convention was held in 1837, she was a vice president. She was also active in conventions in 1838 (during which a mob burned down Philadelphia Hall in an attempt to intimidate the activists) and 1839. Throughout this period she was a staunch early defender of the white abolitionist William Lloyd Garrison.

Her children, though, seem to have been her greatest joy; however, for all of the happiness they seem to have brought her, there was also sorrow. Elizabeth, William, and Charles all preceded her in death. Robert Douglass Jr., who became not only an active abolitionist but also a fine painter and one of the first African American daguerreotypists (his image of the bandleader Francis Johnson is one of the few known), flirted with colonization and spent time in Haiti. While he was in the States, though he was an active fighter for his race, he was also consistently saddened by the limitations racism placed on him. James eventually took over his father's business, and while this certainly allowed continued affluence, it was also a reminder that he was in one of the few fields open to the "best men" of the race. Sarah Mapps worked tirelessly beside her mother but suffered racism as well, from those who should have been first to fight such—her abolitionist and Quaker brethren. Grace Bustill Douglass's influence and memory went beyond her children to succeeding generations of both Bustills and Douglasses, including the writer and activist Gertrude E. H. Bustill Mossell.

Although these later figures are better known, Douglass was an important early fighter for social justice and struggled for African American rights and women's rights throughout her life.

FURTHER READING

A handful of primary texts on or by Douglass are available in the Bustill-Mossell Family Papers at the University of Pennsylvania and in the Records of

the Female Anti-Slavery Society at the Historical Society of Pennsylvania in Philadelphia, as well as the *Black Abolitionist Papers*.
Sterling, Dorothy, ed. *We Are Your Sisters: Black Women in the Nineteenth Century* (1984).
Winch, Julie, ed. *The Elite of Our People: Joseph Willson's Sketches of Black Upper-Class Life in Antebellum Philadelphia* (2000).

ERIC GARDNER

Douglass, Joseph Henry (3 July 1871–1935), a renowned violin soloist, was born in Washington, DC to Charles Remond Douglass, a U.S. government clerk, and Mary Elizabeth Murphy Douglass.

Joseph Douglas was one of the first black instrumentalists to have a successful career as a concert artist. He was a grandson of FREDERICK DOUGLASS, who in addition to being a renowned abolitionist and civil rights advocate, was an accomplished amateur violinist. Joseph's father, Charles, also played the instrument. Frederick Douglass, who enjoyed playing duets with Joseph, was highly supportive of his grandson's musical ambitions, and helped to launch his career.

While still a teenager, Joseph played in an all-black chamber orchestra based in Washington DC, which his grandfather had a hand in organizing and for which he served as president. The orchestra was conducted by WILL MARION COOK, a brilliant young European-trained violinist who later became a pioneer of black musical theater. The orchestra made a couple of brief tours of the East Coast before disbanding.

Douglass was accepted at the New England Conservatory of Music in 1889. After graduating from the famous school, he landed a position as a violin instructor at Howard University in Washington, DC. He also taught privately, and counted among his pupils JAMES REESE EUROPE, who became a highly influential New York band leader and recording artist, and Clarence Cameron White, whose acclaim as a violin soloist and composer eclipsed even Douglass.

Douglass first achieved national recognition when he performed at the World's Columbian Exposition, held in Chicago in 1893 to celebrate the 400th anniversary of Christopher Columbus's arrival in the New World. Douglass, Will Marion Cook, the baritone HARRY T. BURLEIGH, and the poet Paul Laurence Dunbar took part in a well-reviewed program of music and poetry as part of an otherwise controversial "Colored Folks Day" at the fair. Douglass performed "a violin fantasie from 'Trovatore,'" according to the *Chicago Tribune* (Abbott and Seroff, p. 283).

A concert company known as Edith Pond's Midnight Stars formed from the talent that had gathered in Chicago during the exposition, including Douglass, the highly regarded soprano Rachel Walker, and the popular "dramatic reader" Ednorah Nahar. The company, which was later renamed the Ednorah Nahar Concert Company, toured the Midwest, but disbanded in December 1893, following several disappointing programs.

Douglass toured extensively for the next three decades. He often performed as a soloist accompanied by his wife, Fannie Howard Douglass, on piano, but sometimes he was part of larger programs along with other leading black musicians and singers such as Carl Diton, a European-trained pianist and composer who was the first black concert pianist to make a transcontinental tour of the United States, and the coloratura soprano Anita Patti Brown, "our globe-trotting prima donna" according to the *Chicago Defender* (Southern, p. 262). He performed for both black and white audiences in a variety of venues, but appeared most often in black churches and educational institutions. He is credited with being the first African American concert artist to make transcontinental tours.

Douglass appeared on several occasions with—or at least on the same program as—the renowned soprano SISSIERETTA JONES, known as the "Black Patti" in reference to the Italian opera star Adelina Patti. Jones was the most famous African American singer of the late nineteenth and early twentieth centuries. A series of programs organized by the impresario (and Jones's manager) Major J. B. Pond to promote Jones's career became known as forums for the best black talent of the time. On 27 September 1893, one month after "Colored Folks Day," Jones appeared at the World's Columbian Exposition in the Assembly Hall at the Columbian Exposition Woman's Building in a program also featuring Douglass. Jones and Douglass also appeared at the "Grand Military Concert" sponsored by the U.S. Marine Band in Washington to commemorate the presidential inauguration of Grover Cleveland.

Douglass appeared at Carnegie Hall in the 1910s. He also recorded for the Victor Talking Machine Company in 1914, though the recordings were never released. Douglass served as a conductor from time to time. He appeared twice at the White House, performing for both President William McKinley and President William Howard Taft.

Joseph Douglass carved out a career as a performer of art music at a time when white audiences were not highly receptive to black classical musicians. His famous name was certainly a draw, but his success appears to be principally an outcome of his enormous talent, drive that kept him touring year in and year out under often grueling conditions, and a keen understanding of how to appeal to both black and white audiences.

FURTHER READING

Abbott, Lynn, and Doug Seroff. *Ragged but Right, Black Traveling Shows, "Coon Songs," and the Dark Pathway to Blues and Jazz* (2007).

Southern, Eileen. *The Music of Black Americans: A History* (1971).

DAVID K. BRADFORD

Douglass, Lewis Henry (9 Oct. 1840–19 Sept. 1908), Civil War soldier, reformer, and businessman, was the second of five children of the abolitionist leader and orator FREDERICK DOUGLASS (1818–1895) and ANNA MURRAY DOUGLASS (1813–1882). Lewis, born in New Bedford, Massachusetts, where his father settled shortly after his flight from slavery, proved the most successful of the Douglass children and the one his father most relied upon in later years. After the family moved to Rochester, New York, the eight-year-old Lewis and his siblings became beneficiaries of his father's successful efforts to desegregate the city's public schools—a tradition that Lewis maintained as an adult when he lived in the District of Columbia. As soon as he was old enough, he helped his father with the publication of his antislavery newspapers and after his father fled Federal authorities in the wake of John Brown's 1859 raid at Harpers Ferry, the nineteen-year-old Lewis managed his father's business affairs.

Little else is known of his activities before 1863, although Douglass's obituary (*Washington Bee*, 26 Sept. 1908) stated that he taught school in New Jersey when Gov. John A. Andrew issued his call for volunteers for the 54th Massachusetts Regiment, the best-known of the Civil War's black regiments. He enlisted on 25 March 1863—his brother Charles Remond Douglass (1844–1920) joined the unit on 18 April, but soon transferred to the 5th Massachusetts Cavalry—and became the regimental sergeant major on 23 April. He participated in the 18 July 1863 assault on Battery Wagner, just outside of Charleston, South Carolina, in which the regiment's gallantry ended the Northern debate over black recruitment. Two days later, Douglass wrote to his parents describing his actions and the heroics of his comrades leading up to the famous attack, which his father published in the August issue of *Douglass' Monthly*. "Our men fought like tigers; one sergeant killed five men by shooting and bayoneting." His description of the 18 July attack swelled with pride but also relayed the tragic news that the 54th lost "in killed, wounded and missing in the assault, three hundred of our men. The splendid 54th is cut to pieces." In the vanguard of the charge, he had his sword sheath shot off his belt. Although Douglass survived the battle, he sent his parents what he thought might be his last letter: "If I die tonight I will not die a coward." He saw no other action and on 10 May 1864 received a medical discharge.

Along with his father and other prominent African American leaders, Lewis Douglass attended the January 1866 black national convention that met in Washington, DC, to formulate goals for Reconstruction. Speaking for all African Americans, Douglass, GEORGE T. DOWNING, JOHN F. COOK JR., and several other black leaders addressed Congress on 17 January, asserting that the legislature should extend the right to vote "on the idea that there can be of right no privileged class before the law in a republican government." (unidentified newspaper clipping, Douglass papers). At the same time, Douglass, his father, Downing, and others representing the convention met with President Andrew Johnson. After the delegation expressed the convention's unwavering principle that blacks must receive the right to vote, Johnson rebuked them with the warning that a race war would result from such a move. He then advised Douglass and his associates to colonize themselves as the solution to the nation's racial problems. The committee, including Douglass and his father, issued a public letter declaring that Johnson's views were "entirely unsound, and prejudicial to the highest interests of our race, as well as our country at large.... Peace between the races is not to be secured by degrading one race and exalting another" (*Christian Recorder*, 17 Feb. 1866).

Later that year, Douglass and his brother Frederick Jr. (1842–1892) moved to Denver, Colorado, where they solicited assistance from former associates of their father who had become members of the city's black elite. Lewis opened a laundry and when it failed he set up a lunch room with a loan arranged by WILLIAM J. HARDIN. Douglass earned enough to repay most (or all) of the loan, but he soon closed that business as well. By the fall of 1867, Douglass had joined with Lorenzo M. Bowman, a former slave, and Jeremiah Lee to establish the Red, White and Blue Mining and Reducing Company. Bowman had first discovered silver in Georgetown, about sixty miles from Denver, and many blacks in the area bought land with the hope of establishing silver mines. Douglass and his associates formed a joint stock company, intending to sell stock only to other blacks (in Denver and throughout the country) and printed a call for support in the black press. "Here is a field for enterprising colored men, with some means to operate. Here is plenty of mining property in the hands of colored men, and of the best kind." He hoped to see the mountainsides "covered with furnaces owned by colored men" (*Christian Recorder*, 21 Dec. 1867). While in Denver, Douglass and his brother also worked with his father's former antislavery colleague HENRY O. WAGONER to gain black suffrage in the territory and to end school segregation (not achieved until 1873). Black territorial leaders clearly understood the benefit of having the sons of Frederick Douglass in the vanguard of their struggle for civil rights. Lewis Douglass and the other leaders advised the territory's white establishment that African Americans would not support statehood without the guaranteed right to vote. But the move failed, as did the mining venture, and Douglass sought work as a typographer in Denver. In 1868, he found his way back to the District of Columbia where he would spend the rest of his life.

The next year, Douglass married Helen Amelia Loguen (1843–?), the daughter of JERMAIN WESLEY LOGUEN, the former slave, African Methodist Episcopal Zion bishop, and Syracuse, New York, abolitionist; the couple had no children. An experienced printer, Douglass found work as a typographer in the Government Printing Office. He then applied for membership in the Columbia Typographical Union, causing a national furor. While many Union members supported Douglass's application, the group refused to approve it, falsely asserting that he had previously worked as a "rat" worker (scab) in Denver (*Cincinnati Daily Gazette*, 2 June 1869). His membership application then came before the National Typographical Union, which also refused to render a decision, claiming that membership was a local matter. The union's prejudicial conduct went far toward explaining why blacks struggled so desperately to achieve financial stability. The incident also enraged Douglass's father who could not tolerate the insult to a man who had "stood on the walls of Fort Wagner with Colonel Shaw." The senior Douglass well understood the "iron hand of Negro hate before, but the case of this young man gave it deeper entrance into my soul than ever before" (McFeely, *Frederick Douglass*, p. 271). Having refused to admit Douglass, the union took great pride in announcing that it had admitted a "Miss Mary C. Green," a white woman who also worked in the Government Printing Office, into the union as a compositor (*Albany Evening Journal*, 20 Sept. 1870). Douglass eventually was admitted in 1870—which propelled him into labor organization work—but the case exposed the depth of racial prejudice in the labor movement.

Douglass then went to work in the office of his father's last newspaper, the *New National Era*, with his brother Charles, George T. Downing, and the former minister and abolitionist J. SELLA MARTIN. Douglass assumed many duties in the paper's office and before it closed in 1874 he had taken over full editorial responsibility. Although he never went back to the newspaper business, Douglass remained an active figure in the black press, attending conventions of black editors and publishers. During the 1870s, he served as deputy U.S. Marshall for the District of Columbia under his father and also in the District legislature, where he promoted public schools. He remained a member of the District's black National Guard unit until the army disbanded it in 1891, organized local support for the 1875 Civil Rights Act, and planned annual emancipation celebrations. He attended black Civil War soldiers' conventions and the black national conventions of the 1880s. During the late 1890s, he emerged as a powerful anti-imperialist spokesman, denouncing President McKinley's Philippine adventure as "hypocrisy of the most sickening kind." He lamented in the press that "wherever this government controls, injustice to dark races prevails" (Gatewood, *Black Americans*, p. 212).

Douglass and his father had suffered severe financial losses with the collapse of the Freedman's Savings Bank in 1874, but he nevertheless branched out into banking, becoming an officer in the Capital Savings Bank—which operated until 1902—and in the 1880s attained success as a real estate agent and developer. Perhaps his most successful ventures were the "Striver's Row" housing units near the current Shaw area of the District and Highland Beach in Anne Arundel County, Maryland, a summer resort community for well-to-do black Washingtonians.

The elder Douglass's death in 1895 only intensified strains on the family that had begun with his marriage to Helen Pitts (1837–1903) in 1884. No one on either side of the family ever accepted the patriarch's marriage to the white woman. Even RICHARD T. GREENER, who assisted Douglass with publication of the *New National Era*, explained that the Pitts-Douglass marriage fulfilled the maxim that "reason ceases when love begins" (Martin, *Mind of Frederick Douglass*, p. 99). Despite denials in the press by Lewis and his brother Charles, the Douglass children virtually went to war with their step-mother over settlement of the estate, with Helen Douglass unsuccessfully pressing her claim for $10,000 through the local courts, to the U.S. Supreme Court, which declined to hear the case.

Despite finding a much-delayed level of financial success, Douglass never overcame the intensified racial prejudice that gripped the nation's capital. A few months before his death in 1908, and much to his dismay, he found that the Treasury Department lunchroom refused to serve African Americans. He spent his final days suffering from a prolonged but unspecified illness and died at his home attended by his wife and a niece, Kathryn Crummell.

FURTHER READING

Berwanger, Eugene H. "Reconstruction on the Frontier: The Equal Rights Struggle in Colorado, 1865–1867," *Pacific Historical Review* 44 (Aug. 1975): 313–329.

Douglass, Frederick. Frederick Douglass Papers at the Library of Congress. "American Memory" online at http://memory.loc.gov/ammem/doughtml.

Gatewood, Willard B., Jr. *Black Americans and the White Man's Burden, 1898–1903* (1975).

Martin, Waldo E., Jr. *The Mind of Frederick Douglass* (1984).

Matison, Samuel Eliot. "The Labor Movement and the Negro during Reconstruction," *Journal of Negro History* 33 (Oct. 1948): 426–468.

McFeely, William S. *Frederick Douglass* (1991).

Moore, Jacqueline M. *Leading the Race: The Transformation of the Black Elite in the Nation's Capital, 1880–1920* (1999).

DONALD YACOVONE

Douglass, Sarah Mapps (9 Sept. 1806–8 Sept. 1882), abolitionist and educator, was born in Philadelphia, Pennsylvania, the daughter of Robert Douglass Sr., a prosperous hairdresser from the island of St. Kitts, and Grace Bustill, a milliner. Her mother was the daughter of Cyrus Bustill, a prominent member of Philadelphia's African American community. Raised as a Quaker by her mother, Douglass was alienated by the blatant racial prejudice of many white Quakers. Although she adopted Quaker dress and enjoyed the friendship of Quaker antislavery advocates like Lucretia Mott, she was highly critical of the sect.

Sarah Mapps Douglass, educator, organizational leader, and abolitionist. (Library of Congress/Austin and Thompson Collection.)

In 1819 GRACE BUSTILL DOUGLASS and the philanthropist James Forten Sr. established a school for black children, where "their children might be better taught than ... in any of the schools ... open to [their] people." Sarah Douglass was educated there, taught for a while in New York City, and then returned to take over the school.

In 1833 Douglass joined an interracial group of female abolitionists in establishing the Philadelphia Female Anti-Slavery Society. For almost four decades, she served the organization in many capacities. Also active in the antislavery movement at the national level, she attended the 1837 Anti-Slavery Convention of American Women in New York City. The following year, when the convention met at Philadelphia's ill-fated Pennsylvania Hall, which in 1838 was burned by an anti-abolitionist mob, she was elected treasurer. She was also a delegate at the third and final women's antislavery convention in 1839.

Douglass repeatedly stressed the need for African American women to educate themselves. In 1831 she helped organize the Female Literary Association of Philadelphia, a society whose members met regularly for "mental feasts," and on the eve of the Civil War she founded the Sarah M. Douglass Literary Circle.

Throughout the 1830s Douglass wrote poetry and prose under the pseudonyms "Sophanisba" and

"Ella." Her writings—on the blessings of religion, the prospect of divine retribution for the sin of slavery, the evils of prejudice, and the plight of the slave—were published in various antislavery journals, including the *Liberator*, the *Colored American*, the *Genius of Universal Emancipation*, and the *National Enquirer and Constitutional Advocate of Universal Liberty*. During the 1830s and 1840s Douglass was beset by financial problems. Her school never operated at a profit, and in 1838, deciding she could no longer accept the financial backing of her parents, she asked the Female Anti-Slavery Society to take over the school. The experiment proved unsatisfactory, however, and in 1840 she resumed direct control of the school, giving up a guaranteed salary for assistance in paying the rent. In 1852, now reconciled with the Quakers, she closed her school and accepted an appointment to supervise the Girls' Preparatory Department of the Quaker-sponsored Institute for Colored Youth. From 1853 to 1877 she served as principal of the department.

For more than forty years Douglass enjoyed a close friendship with the abolitionists Sarah Grimké and Angelina Weld Grimké. After an uneasy start, the relationship between the daughters of a slaveholding family and the African American teacher deepened into one of great mutual respect. Sarah Grimké, fourteen years Douglass's senior, eventually became her confidante. After her mother's death in 1842 left Douglass as an unpaid housekeeper to her father and brothers, Grimké sympathized with her: "Worn in body & spirit with the duties of thy school, labor awaits thee at home & when it is done there is none to throw around thee the arms of love."

In 1854 Douglass received an offer of marriage from the Reverend William Douglass, a widower with nine children and the minister of Philadelphia's prestigious St. Thomas's African Episcopal Church. Grimké considered him eminently worthy of her friend. He was a man of education, and his remarks about her age and spinster status were only proof of his lively sense of humor. As for Douglass's apprehensions about the physical aspects of married life, the unmarried Grimké assured her, "Time will familiarize you with the idea." The couple was married in 1855. The marriage proved an unhappy one. On her husband's death in 1861, Douglass wrote of her years "in that School of bitter discipline, the old Parsonage of St. Thomas," but she acknowledged that William Douglass had not been without his merits.

In one respect, marriage gave Douglass a new freedom. A cause she had long championed was the education of women on health issues. Before her marriage, she had taken courses at the Female Medical College of Pennsylvania. In 1855 she enrolled in the Pennsylvania Medical University and in 1858 embarked on a career as a lecturer, confronting topics that would have been considered unseemly for an unmarried woman to address. Her illustrated lectures to female audiences in New York City and Philadelphia drew praise for being both informative and "chaste."

Through the 1860s and 1870s Douglass continued her work of reform, lecturing, raising money for the southern freedmen and -women, helping to establish a home for elderly and indigent black Philadelphians, and teaching at the Institute for Colored Youth. She died in Philadelphia.

As a teacher, a lecturer, an abolitionist, a reformer, and a tireless advocate of women's education, Sarah Mapps Douglass made her influence felt in many ways. Her emphasis on education and self-improvement helped shape the lives of the many hundreds of black children she taught in a career in the classroom that lasted more than a half-century, while her pointed and persistent criticism of northern racism reminded her white colleagues in the abolitionist movement that their agenda must include more than the emancipation of the slaves.

FURTHER READING

A number of letters to and from Douglass are in the Weld-Grimké Papers at the University of Michigan and the Antislavery Manuscripts at the Boston Public Library. Douglass's role in the antislavery movement is documented in the records of the Philadelphia Female Anti-Slavery Society at the Historical Society of Pennsylvania and in the published proceedings of the three national women's antislavery conventions held between 1837 and 1839.

Barnes, Gilbert H., and Dwight L. Dumond, eds. *Letters of Theodore Dwight Weld, Angelina Grimké, and Sarah Grimké, 1822–1844* (2 vols., 1934).

Sterling, Dorothy, ed. *We Are Your Sisters: Black Women in the Nineteenth Century* (1984).

Winch, Julie. *Philadelphia's Black Elite: Activism, Accommodation, and the Struggle for Autonomy, 1787–1848* (1988).

This entry is taken from the *American National Biography* and is published here with the permission of the American Council of Learned Societies.

JULIE WINCH

Dove, Rita Frances (28 Aug. 1952–), writer, was born in Akron, Ohio, the second of four children of Ray A. Dove, the first black scientist in the tire industry, and Elvira Elizabeth Hord. Rita, who attended public school, read voraciously and began writing plays and stories while in elementary school. Selected as one of the most outstanding high school graduates in the nation, she visited the White House as a Presidential Scholar in 1970, after which she enrolled at Miami University in Oxford, Ohio, graduating summa cum laude with a B.A. in English in 1973.

She spent the next year as a Fulbright Scholar at the University of Tübingen in West Germany. Although Dove's presence drew attention from the locals—"Most Germans don't consider it impolite to stare, so they simply gawked at me or even pointed" (Taleb-Khyar, 350)—the German language had a lasting impact on her work. "German," Dove explained, "has influenced the way I write: I have tried to re-create in poems the feeling I had when I first began to speak the language—that wonderful sensation of being held hostage by a sentence until the verb comes along at the end" (Steffen, 168).

Upon her return to the United States, Dove began graduate study at the prestigious Writers' Workshop at the University of Iowa, earning an MFA in 1977. While in Iowa, Rita met the German writer Fred Viebahn. The couple married in 1979 and had one daughter. In 1981 Dove began teaching creative writing at Arizona State University in Tempe, where she remained until 1989, when she became Professor of English at the University of Virginia in Charlottesville. Almost immediately, Dove began to win grants and fellowships, including a National Endowment for the Humanities (NEH) award that allowed her to serve as a writer in residence at the Tuskegee Institute in 1982. In the late 1970s Dove's poems appeared in a number of magazines and anthologies, and she published several chapbooks, including *Ten Poems* (1977) and *The Only Dark Spot in the Sky* (1980). Dove's first book of poetry, *Yellow House on the Corner* (1980), treats both private, everyday events—a first kiss, family dinners—and the historical events of slavery. Referring to her second collection of poems, *Museum* (1983), Dove revealed, "One of my goals with that book was to reveal the underside of history, and to represent this underside in discrete moments" (Taleb-Khyar, 356).

Dove explored these themes further in her next poetry collection, *Thomas and Beulah* (1986), based on the lives of her maternal grandparents. Consisting of two parts—the first written from Thomas's point of view, the second from Beulah's—the poems cleverly undercut the idea of a single historical narrative by offering alternative versions of the same events. In preparing the book, Dove interviewed her mother, read transcripts of Works Progress Administration interviews, studied the history of black migration, and listened to blues recordings. "What fascinates me," Dove explained, "is the individual caught in the web of history" (Taleb-Khyar, 356). Critics agreed, and *Thomas and Beulah* earned a Pulitzer Prize in 1987.

Dove's other publications include the poetry collections *Grace Notes* (1989), *Selected Poems* (1993), *Mother Love* (1995), *Evening Primrose* (1998), and *On the Bus with Rosa Parks* (1999); a collection of short stories, *Fifth Sunday* (1985); a novel, *Through the Ivory Gate* (1992); and a play, *The Darker Face of the Earth* (1994), which employs elements of Greek tragedy in a story set on an antebellum slave plantation in South Carolina.

In 1993 Dove became the youngest person and the third African American appointed Poet Laureate Consultant in Poetry at the Library of Congress, a position she held through 1995. As Poet Laureate, Dove organized lectures and conferences, poetry and jazz evenings, and brought local Washington, D.C., students and Crow Indian children to the Library of Congress to read their poetry and be recorded for the National Archives. She presided over high-profile cultural events, including the 1994 commemoration of the two-hundredth anniversary of the U.S. Capitol, and the unprecedented gathering of Nobel laureates for the Cultural Olympiad in Atlanta, Georgia, in 1995. "I'm hoping that by the end," Dove told reporters, "people will think of a poet laureate as someone who's out there with her sleeves rolled up, not sitting in an ivory tower."

Ever since Dove began singing and playing cello in elementary school, music has been the companion of and inspiration for her poetry. As she explained:

> My youth was filled with musical language: the acid drawl of an uncle spinning out a joke; the call-and-response of the AME church; jump rope ditties and BESSIE SMITH on the phonograph; the clear ecstasy of Bach and the sweet sadness of BILLIE HOLIDAY. Buoyed by this living cushion of sound, I began to write (*Essence*, 1995).

In the 1990s Dove produced several major musical collaborations, beginning with *Umoja—Each One of Us Counts*, commissioned by the 1996 Atlanta Olympic Summer Games. Her other large-scale productions include *Singin' Sepia* (1996), *Grace Notes* (1997), and *The Pleasure's in Walking Through* (1998), a collaboration with John Williams.

Writers, like musicians, Dove reminded her students, must study and practice. Dove has always revised incessantly, putting her poems through as a many as fifty or sixty drafts. In the years before she had family and public obligations, she wrote for up to eight hours each day. For Dove, writing combines serendipity and puzzle solving, and her working methods encourage detours and tangents. "When I'm working on poems, I'm reading all the time," she revealed, "I just go to the bookshelf almost like a sleepwalker" (Taleb-Khyar, 363). She also relies on notebooks she has filled over the years with fragments of language: snippets of conversations, words, ideas, images, even grocery and "to do" lists.

While she is interested in character and plot, Dove is generally more interested in the way stories are told than in the stories themselves. As a child, Dove challenged herself to write novels composed of words from school spelling lists; later, she found the same thrill in crossword puzzles. "I think my puzzle fetish has something to do with the way poems are constructed. Words start to reverberate by virtue of their proximity to one another. That's a spatial thing as well as a temporal one" (Steffen, 169). When it comes time to put a draft away, Dove uses an intuitive filing system that eschews organization by subject, date, or title. Instead, she files by color, by how a poem "feels" to her.

Coming of age after the peak of the Black Arts Movement, Dove subscribes to a less polarized, more inclusive, approach to writing and to race than poets one or two decades her senior, such as Amiri Baraka, June Jordan, Audre Lorde, and Nikki Giovanni.

> When I was growing up, I did not think in terms of black art or white art or any kind of art; I just wanted to be a writer. On the other hand, when I became culturally aware ... it was exciting to recognize heretofore secret aspects of my experience—the syncopation of jazz, the verbal one-upsmanship of signifying or the dozens—not only to acknowledge their legitimacy, but to see them transformed into art (Steffen, 169).

Dove found herself less beholden to the collective, and more interested in the individual, her intimate relationships, and daily life. "I could do nothing else but describe the world I knew—a world where there was both jazz and opera; gray suits and blue jeans, iambic pentameter and the dozens, Shakespeare and [James] Baldwin" (*Essence*, 1995).

In addition to more than a dozen honorary doctorates, Dove has been honored with many awards, including the Duke Ellington Lifetime Achievement Award, the Charles Frankel Prize awarded by the NEH, the Heinz Award in the Arts, the Academy of American Poets' Lavan Younger Poet Award, and fellowships from the Mellon and Rockefeller Foundations. She has served on the advisory or editorial boards of the Associated Writing Programs, the MacDowell Colony, the Thomas Jefferson Center for Freedom of Expression, *Callaloo*, and *Ploughshares*, and her media appearances have included interviews on all major television networks, collaborations with public television, and a visit to *Sesame Street*. She has served on juries for the Walt Whitman Award of the Academy of American Poets, the National Book Award, the Ruth Lilly Prize, and the Pulitzer Prize. From 2004 to 2006 Dove served as Poet Laureate to the Commonwealth of Virginia.

The power of language to transform and alter perception is at the heart of Dove's literary enterprise. "Poetry at its best..." she holds, "nudges the body awake. Poetry resonates and transforms by injecting us with the palpable pleasure of language: Words impress their contours on the tongue, and we breathe with the heartbeat and silences of the line tugging against the sentence as it wraps its sense around the instinctual axis" (*Ploughshares*, spring 1990).

FURTHER READING

Harrington, Walt. "A Narrow World Made Wide," *Washington Post Magazine*, 7 May 1995.

Rubin, Stan Sanvel, and Earl G. Ingersoll. "A Conversation with Rita Dove," *Black American Literature Forum* (Autumn 1986).

Steffen, Therese. *Crossing Color: Transcultural Space and Place in Rita Dove's Poetry, Fiction, and Drama* (2001).

Taleb-Khyar, Mohamed B. "An Interview with Maryse Conde and Rita Dove," *Callaloo* (Spring 1991).

LISA E. RIVO

Dove, Ulysses (17 Jan. 1947–11 June 1996), choreographer and dancer, was bought up in Columbia, South Carolina, the eldest of three children born to Ulysses and Ruth Lee (Smith) Dove. Dove showed considerable interest in dance as a child, often creating performances for his family. When he began college at Howard University in Washington, D.C., in 1964, however, he enrolled as a premedical student to please his family, rather than study dance. In 1967 Dove decided to pursue dance more seriously and transferred to the University of Wisconsin at Milwaukee to study with Xenia Chilistwa of the Kirov Ballet. He later received a dance fellowship at Bennington College, from which he graduated with a B.A. in Dance in 1970. During his college years he studied with Judith Dunn, Mary Hinkson, and Carolyn Tate.

After graduation Dove moved to New York City and danced with several companies, including those of Mary Anthony, Pearl Lang, José Limón, and Anna Sokolow. During this same period he received a scholarship to study with Merce Cunningham and performed with his dance company from 1970 to 1973. After the period with Cunningham, Dove became a member (and eventually a principal dancer) of the ALVIN AILEY American Dance Theater from 1973 to 1980. It was with the Alvin Ailey company that Dove began his work as a choreographer. His first dance was *I See the Moon ... and the Moon Sees Me* in 1979. He maintained strong ties to the Ailey company throughout the rest of his life and career, and the company long kept several of Dove's pieces in its repertoire.

In 1980 Dove shifted his focus from dancing to choreography. He relocated to Europe and served as the assistant director of the Groupe de Recherche Choreographique de l'Opéra de Paris from 1980 to 1983, and then from 1983 to 1996 he worked as a freelance choreographer in both the United States and Europe. Notable companies for whom he composed dances include Alvin Ailey American Dance Theater, American Ballet Theatre, Les Ballets Jazz de Montreal, Ballet France de Nancy, the Basel Ballet, Cullberg Ballet of Sweden, New York City Ballet, Dayton Contemporary Dance Company, and the Swedish National Ballet. He was also the choreographer for the Robert Wilson and Philip Glass opera, *the CIVILwarS*.

Dove's choreography is known for its energy, intimacy, and athleticism. Ironically, his reputation as a choreographer blossomed in Europe before he was recognized in the United States. Several of his pieces, including *Episodes*, which won a Bessie Award, were created as a reaction to the AIDS crisis. Among his other well-known pieces are *Bad Blood* (1984), *Vespers* (1986), *Urban Folk Dance* (1990), *Serious Pleasures* (1992), *Dancing on the Front Porch of Heaven* (1993), *Red Angels* (1994), and *Twilight* (1996).

Dove won the National Choreography Project Award in 1985, the Monarch Award for choreography in 1988, and a New York Dance and Performance Award (or "Bessie") for *Episodes* in 1990. The 1995 PBS documentary about his work, *Dance in America: Two by Dove* (which consisted of *Vespers* and *Dancing on the Front Porch of Heaven*, performed by the Alvin Ailey American Dance Theater and later by the Royal Swedish Ballet), received an Emmy Award.

Ulysses Dove died of AIDS in June 1996 in New York City within a week of what would have been the first full evening of his choreography in his lifetime. Because Dove was a freelance choreographer, never having had a company of his own, there had never been a full evening devoted exclusively to his work. A gala titled "For the Love of Dove" had been planned by the Actor's Fund as a celebration of his work during the period in which his health deteriorated. This event was performed at New York's Lincoln Center the week following his death, serving as a memorial rather than a celebration. The chairwoman and host of the event was Princess Christina of Sweden, and several of Broadway's greatest stars (including GREGORY HINES) came out to pay tribute to Dove's memory.

Dove's works continue to be performed in the repertoire of many major dance companies, and his choreography and trademark style remain a powerful force in modern dance and continue to influence choreographers and dancers to this day.

FURTHER RE.ADING

The Dance Collection of the New York Public Library maintains several materials relating to Ulysses Dove, including several videotapes of his works, oral histories, and a clippings file.

Barton, Peter. *Staying Power: Performing Artists Talk about Their Lives* (1980).

"'For the Love of Dove,' and It Was." *New York Times*, 19 June 1996.

Obituaries: *New York Times*, 12 June 1996; *Washington Times*, 14 June 1996.

MERON LANGSNER

Dowden, Leonard E. (1921–17 July 1945), World War II soldier and Distinguished Service Cross recipient, was born in Louisiana, probably New Orleans. Little is known about Dowden's life and family background except that, according to army enlistment records, he achieved a grammar school education.

Leonard Dowden enlisted in the U.S. Army on 27 October 1942 and after completing boot camp training at an unknown locale, was eventually assigned to the 368th Infantry Regiment of the 93rd Infantry Division. The 93rd Division was one of just two divisions in the army to which African Americans were assigned. The first black army division to be activated in World War II, the 93rd was formed in the spring of 1942 and first trained at Fort Huachuca, Arizona. The 93rd Division would subsequently undergo further training in Louisiana in 1943, where perhaps Dowden joined his regiment, and later in California. Finally, in January 1944, with the war dragging on and political pressure mounting to allow African American troops to serve in combat operations, the 93rd Division was sent for duty in the Pacific.

The service of African American men during World War II such as 93rd Division soldiers Dowden, ISAAC SERMON, and ROTHCHILD WEBB, is an oft-overlooked but important story. Discriminated against at almost every turn, this pioneer combat unit, consisting entirely of African American enlisted personnel and with over 60 percent of its officers being men of color, gained its first combat training on Guadalcanal and subsequently entered combat in late March 1944 at Bougainville in the Northern Solomons–New Guinea island chain. With no prior combat experience and but little training in jungle fighting, the 93rd Division's first combat patrols were not considered effective. Those who believed that African American soldiers were inferior to whites, both within the army's command and out, seized on these early deficiencies of the 93rd and widely publicized their criticism. Though the division would see further action, and its men soon became experienced veterans, its reputation was damaged, and the unit was unfairly tainted for the duration of the war. To this day, the contributions made by the men of the 93rd Division are largely forgotten, usually overshadowed by the performance of the 92nd Division, the only other African American army division, in the European theater.

As with most of his life, the details of Leonard Dowden's army career are also lacking. However, the fact that he rose to the rank of staff sergeant by April 1945 tells us that he was a skilled soldier and a leader of men. Though he was small in stature (he measured but five feet seven inches in height and weighed less than 150 pounds), Sergeant Dowden's role as a noncommissioned officer in I Company of the 368th Infantry Regiment was important; experienced sergeants were, and still are, the backbone of the army's command hierarchy. To the privates and corporals that he commanded, Dowden was likely not just a man of authority and experience, but also a trainer, a motivator, perhaps even a father figure at times. He would subsequently demonstrate his leadership skills to the highest level just as the war was coming to an end in July 1945. On 17 July Staff Sergeant Leonard Dowden and Company I, about thirty-five men strong, were on patrol on Jolo Island, located in the Sulu Archipelago, and tasked with mopping up Japanese resistance on the island. They subsequently encountered a force of 100 Japanese soldiers, and a fierce firefight erupted. Dowden moved his men close to the Japanese position, and then crawled forward alone to assault an enemy machine gun position. Wounded in the chest during his advance, Dowden continued onward, ordering one of his men who came to his aid to stay under cover, and was soon thereafter shot and killed just ten yards from the Japanese position while rising up to throw a hand grenade. Subsequently nominated for a posthumous award for valor, Leonard Dowden was awarded the army's second highest medal, the Distinguished Service Cross (DSC), on 20 December 1945.

Staff Sergeant Leonard Dowden was one of just nine African American soldiers awarded the DSC during World War II, only three of which were awarded to black soldiers serving in the Pacific. Dowden was also the only soldier of the 93rd Division to earn this high award. Though largely forgotten in the years after the war, Dowden's name came to the fore briefly in the 1990s when the army began to examine its awards and decorations practices in regard to African Americans during World War II, and specifically, why no black soldiers were awarded the Medal of Honor, the United States' highest award for valor. A detailed report, commissioned by the army, issued by a team of scholars at Shaw University in Raleigh, North Carolina, documented Dowden's exploits and included him among their list of ten men recommended as candidates for consideration as possible Medal of Honor recipients. Unfortunately, Dowden's name was among the three whose names, including ROBERT PEAGLER and JACK THOMAS, that were subsequently dropped from Medal of Honor consideration. It is unknown for certain why Leonard Dowden was dropped from consideration. Perhaps it was felt that his deeds of valor fell just short of the necessary requirements, but unfair perceptions surrounding the reputation of the 93rd Infantry Division cannot but also be considered.

FURTHER READING

Converse, Elliot V., Daniel K. Gibran, John A. Cash, Robert K. Griffith, and Richard H. Kohn. *The Exclusion of Black Soldiers from the Medal of Honor in World War II* (2008).

Jefferson, Robert F. *Fighting for Hope: African American Troops of the 93rd Infantry Division in World War II and Postwar America* (2008).

GLENN ALLEN KNOBLOCK

Downing, George Thomas (30 Dec. 1819–21 July 1903), abolitionist, businessman, and civil rights advocate, was born in New York City, the son of Thomas Downing, a restaurant owner, and Rebecca West. His father's Oyster House was a gathering place for New York's aristocracy and politicians. Young Downing attended Charles Smith's school on Orange Street and, with the future black abolitionists J. McCune Smith, Henry Highland Garnet, Alexander Crummell, and Charles Reason and Patrick Reason, the African School on Mulberry Street. He completed his schooling privately and in his mid-teens was active in two literary societies.

Before he was twenty Downing participated in the Underground Railroad and worked with his father to lobby the New York legislature for equal suffrage. In 1841 both were delegates to the initial convention of the American Reform Board of Disenfranchised Commissioners, one of many organizations formed by African American men to fight for the elective franchise in New York. That same year George Downing married Serena Leanora de Grasse, the daughter of a German mother and a father from India. She attended Clinton Seminary in Clinton, New York, and spent vacations at the home of a classmate, the daughter of the white political abolitionist Gerrit Smith; it was here that Downing courted her.

Downing started his own restaurant in 1842 in New York. In the summer of 1846 he opened a branch of his father's restaurant in Newport, Rhode Island; four years later he began a catering business in Providence. He set down roots in Newport in 1855 when he built the Sea Girt House, a luxurious summer resort for whites only. Although he traveled extensively, lived in Providence and Boston before the Civil War, and managed the House of Representatives dining room in Washington, D.C., during and after the Civil War Newport was his home.

Outside of his real estate, catering, and restaurant interests, Downing devoted himself to activism. An early abolitionist, he participated in several rescues of fugitive slaves, including the famous cases of James Hamlet and Anthony Burns. He zealously asserted the right of black children to equal education and was a member of the first board of trustees of the New York Society for the Promotion of Education among Colored Children, founded in 1847. In 1857 he began and financed a successful nine-year campaign to integrate the schools of Rhode Island's three major cities, Providence, Newport, and Bristol. Downing expressed reservations about a manual labor school proposal by Frederick Douglass, in part because it was racially exclusive.

His opposition to efforts by the largely white American Colonization Society to persuade blacks to migrate to Liberia was both persistent and passionate. He believed blacks should stay and fight for their freedom. When Henry Highland Garnet formed a parallel black African Civilization Society to encourage emigration, Downing led a bitter fight to neutralize its efforts, using parliamentary maneuvers, personal attacks, and threats of violence in the conventions of 1859, 1860, and 1864.

In 1860, over the protests of Boston officials, Downing and a handful of black leaders held a large meeting honoring the first anniversary of John Brown's death. The Civil War raised the question of enlisting black troops; before recruiting, Downing secured from the Massachusetts governor John A. Andrew a pledge that there would be equality of treatment "in every particular" for black soldiers. During and after the war he supported Senator Charles Sumner's attempts to advance civil rights and was instrumental in removing the color ban from the gallery of the U.S. Senate.

In a well-publicized 1866 interview of a dozen black leaders with President Andrew Johnson, Downing told the president that they had come as "friends, meeting a friend.... We are in a passage to equality before the law." He asked for legislation to enforce the Thirteenth Amendment and for the right to vote. To do less, he said, "will be a disregard of our just rights." Johnson's reply was long, rambling, and negative, but over the next decade the Fourteenth and Fifteenth amendments and the 1875 Civil Rights Act gave a fleeting taste of victory.

While Downing never lost his fervor for equal rights, he maintained his interest in economic affairs. His real estate holdings in 1856–1857 were valued at $6,800. Shortly after the war, he tried without success to create "a great mercantile house" in New York and "establish business relations" with the South. He was a key figure in organizing the Colored National Labor Union in 1869 and served as the first convention's temporary chair and the union's initial vice president. Downing condemned the racial intransigence of the white National Labor Union and urged freedmen to seek loans, not donations, from northern capitalists to underwrite their business efforts.

His ties to the Republican Party began to loosen as early as 1869, when he told the Colored National Labor Union convention that the party deserved "respect and support," but it "should have been more consistent, more positive" in confronting the race's "enemies." He predicted that after the ratification of the Fifteenth Amendment the party's "adhesive element" would dissipate and new issues such as labor would emerge. His 1873 attack on Rhode Island Republicans for blocking the repeal of a law against racial intermarriage—he believed that race blending would eradicate barriers and once wrote, "The world has no such beauties as are the product of the Africo-American with other races in America"—provoked charges of apostasy from both races.

Downing's support for the 1879 Exodusters challenged Frederick Douglass and chastised the Republican president Rutherford B. Hayes for a failed southern policy. The Kansas migrants from Louisiana and Mississippi were victims of southern oppression, he affirmed, because the South "is not ready to accept … equality before the law for all men." The next decade saw Downing firmly in the Democratic camp. He favored Grover Cleveland for president in 1884 and, with Democratic support, tried three times without success to win a Rhode Island legislative seat, an effort that nevertheless weakened "the blind adhesion of the colored people to one party." When Senator William Sprague was elected governor in 1887, he recognized Downing's support by appointing him to the state prison commission and to an ad hoc committee of leading citizens.

Downing retired from business in the early 1880s, financially secure and recognized as "one of the institutions of Newport." He devoted his time to his dogs and his collections of memorabilia. He told a friend in 1899 that his writing aimed "to force the inevitable on prejudiced Americans." Downing died at home in Newport. The *Boston Globe* called him "the foremost colored man in the country" and praised his efforts on behalf of liberty, adding, in an editorial, "Narrowness was never safe where George T. Downing was present."

FURTHER READING

Bartlett, Irving H. *From Slave to Citizen: The Story of the Negro in Rhode Island* (1954).

Freeman, Rhoda G. *The Free Negro in New York City in the Era before the Civil War* (1994).

Hewitt, John H. "Mr. [Thomas] Downing and His Oyster House: The Life and Good Works of an African-American Entrepreneur," *New York History* 74 (1993).

Quarles, Benjamin. *Black Abolitionists* (1969).

Obituaries: *New York Times*, 22 July 1903; *Cleveland Gazette*, 1 Aug. 1903; *Boston Globe*, 22 and 23 July 1903.

This entry is taken from the *American National Biography* and is published here with the permission of the American Council of Learned Societies.

LESLIE H. FISHEL

Downing, Henry Francis (1846?–19 Feb. 1928), diplomat, editor, and author, was born in Manhattan to Henry and Nancy (Collins) Downing. His family operated an oyster business and restaurant, and his uncle was GEORGE THOMAS DOWNING, a Rhode Island businessman and civil rights leader. Nothing is known of Henry Downing's education before he entered the U.S. Navy at age eighteen.

Serving from 1864 through 1865 he worked on three vessels, the *North Carolina*, *Pawtuxet*, and *Winooski*. Afterward he traveled widely, spending three years in Liberia, where his cousin, Hilary Johnson, later became president (1884–1892). In Liberia, Downing worked as secretary to the Liberian secretary of state. Upon his return to New York he reenlisted in the navy, serving from 1872 to 1875 on the *Hartford* in the Pacific.

After his discharge Downing again returned to New York City and married Isadora (maiden name unknown) on 8 July 1876. They had at least two children. During the 1880s Downing became a prominent black Democrat. Rewarding his support, President Grover Cleveland appointed Downing the consul to Luanda, Angola, a Portuguese colony. Arriving in Luanda in September 1887, he worked to promote U.S. trade but financial difficulties caused him to resign less than a year later.

Back in New York he continued in politics. During the first years of the 1890s, Downing edited a weekly newspaper that attempted to advance the Democratic Party's cause among African Americans in Brooklyn. Through the summer of 1892 he remained prominent among black Democrats; his favor with former president Cleveland persisted, and he attended a Negro National Democratic Committee meeting held in support of Cleveland's reelection. Downing hoped black support for the Democrats in the North would convince southern Democrats of the expediency of promoting better relations with African Americans.

His allegiance to the Democratic Party, however, was troubled. Attending the National Democratic Convention in June 1892, he proposed adoption of a plank pledging to end racial violence in the South, but the plank was rejected. He broke publicly with the party in September after learning its National Committee sought to use a pamphlet on "Negro domination" as a campaign document.

By 1894 Downing's first marriage had ended, and on 30 June of that year he married Margarita Doyle, a white woman of Irish descent. In 1895 they moved to London, where they lived for twenty-two years. In 1900 Downing spoke at the Pan-African Conference in London. Of his presentation the London *Times* reported: "The Hon. H. F. Downing said the black race had no intention to comply with the wish of those who desired that they should remain slaves in perpetuity. They did not seek freedom by force of arms; they would win it by deserving it" (26 July 1900). During the conference Downing toured Fulham Palace with W. E. B. DuBois and others, and at the conference's conclusion he was appointed with Samuel Coleridge-Taylor to the Executive Committee of what was hoped would be the permanent Pan-African Committee.

By 1902 Downing was managing director of New Cotton Fields, Ltd., a firm intending to relocate African American families experienced in cotton growing to properties in West Africa. To that end, Downing asked Booker T. Washington to recommend an expert capable of locating West African lands suitable for cotton plants, but Washington's reply is unknown. With or without the help of the "Wizard of Tuskegee," Downing's business ventures began to fail: in September 1904 his name appeared in the London *Times* among the bankruptcy adjudications.

Later in the decade Downing proved a gadfly to Booker T. Washington's efforts to use U.S. interest in Liberia to help that nation resist English and French aggression. In 1908, for instance, Washington wrote to Liberian vice president James Jenkins Dossen, "This man Downing is a deadly enemy to Liberia.... I am only making this statement in order to emphasize the necessity of watching this man" (Booker T. Washington Papers, vol. 9, 631). In addition, Downing was probably DuBois's source for much of the material on England published in early issues of *The Crisis* (Green, 215).

In London Downing also began his career as an author, publishing a handful of plays in 1913. In 1914 he wrote at least three more plays, including *A New Coon in Town: A Farcical Comedy Made in England* and *Voodoo: A Drama in Four Acts. Voodoo* depicts a failed Maroon revolt in Barbados running parallel with England's "Glorious Revolution" of 1688. Downing collaborated with his wife in writing *Placing Paul's Play: A Miniature Comedy* as well as other, unpublished plays. He arranged to have several of his plays performed at London's Royal Court Theatre, but the productions were cancelled when the Royal Court closed during World War I.

In 1913 he also wrote an apparently incompletely published serial novel for Duse Mohammed Ali's *The African Times and Orient Review*, the journal for which Marcus Garvey worked during 1913 and 1914. Shortly before Downing left London in 1917, the Neale Publishing Company released his *The American Cavalryman: A Liberian Romance*, which depicts African Americans, American Liberians, and Africans in a plot involving kidnapping and racial misrecognition.

Settling in Harlem around 1917 Downing continued to write about Liberia, authoring *A Short History of Liberia, 1816–1908* (c. 1922) and *Liberia and Her People* (1925). In 1920 the Quality Amusement Corporation agreed to produce his final play, *The Racial Tangle*. Having lived his last years on a pension, Downing died at Harlem Hospital of nephritis and arteriosclerosis in the same month that the black filmmaker Oscar Micheaux released *Thirty Years Later*, an adaptation of *The Racial Tangle*. In 1930 Micheaux would base his film *A Daughter of the Congo* on Downing's *The American Cavalryman*.

Although Downing was well known in certain circles during his life, associating with prominent figures and writing prolifically, he has not attracted significant scholarly attention. Scholarship on Downing has been made difficult because his papers were apparently lost during his 1917 move from London to New York City.

FURTHER READING

Most of Downing's books and plays are housed at the Schomburg Center for Research in Black Culture in New York City. Additional materials are in the National Archives, the Booker T. Washington Papers at the Library of Congress, and the Grover Cleveland Papers (published by the Library of Congress in 1958).

Contee, Clarence G. "Downing, Henry F[rancis]," in *Dictionary of American Negro Biography*, eds. Rayford W. Logan and Michael R. Winston (1982).

Green, Jeffrey. *Black Edwardians: Black People in Britain, 1901–1914* (1998).

Peterson, Bernard L. *Early Black American Playwrights and Dramatic Writers: A Biographic Directory and Catalog of Plays, Films, and Broadcasting Scripts* (1990).

Rodgers, Lawrence R. "Downing, Henry F.," in *The Concise Oxford Companion to African American Literature*, eds. William L. Andrews, Frances Smith Foster, and Trudier Harris (2001).

Obituary: *New York Times*, 21 Feb. 1928.

BRIAN R. ROBERTS

Doyle, Henry Eman (15 Mar. 1910–2 Mar. 1985), attorney, judge, poet, and activist, was one of ten children born to Albert, a laborer, and Mary Burleson Doyle, a laundress, in a four room house in Austin,

Henry Doyle, seated at a desk at the University of Texas, 1947. (Library of Congress/Visual Materials from the National Association for the Advancement of Colored People Records.)

Texas. In 1928 Doyle graduated Salutatorian from Anderson High School and magna cum laude from Samuel Huston College (later Huston-Tillotson College) in 1933. After college he taught in the Austin public school system and later took graduate courses at Columbia University.

On 4 March 1947 the Texas State University for Negroes (later Texas Southern University) was established to keep Heman Sweatt, a black applicant, from entering law school at the University of Texas (UT). This new school offered something unavailable to blacks in Texas, the opportunity to attend law school in their own state. On 22 September 1947 Doyle was the first student to register at the new law school. This would be the first of many firsts for Doyle. When Dean Ozie Johnson met the first two students, Heaullan (Hulan) Lott and Henry Doyle, he admired their fortitude to enroll in the school and remain despite efforts to intimidate them.

The makeshift facility had two classrooms and a separate library in the basement. The students asked to hold classes in the basement library because it gave them immediate access to the books. These library classes and the makeshift facilities—far from equal to those at UT—were viewed by the public as evidence of the new school's inadequacies and resulted in it being called the "basement law school."

Doyle knew the advantage of attending the segregated law school was the student-to-teacher ratio. His class had two students to one professor, versus fifty to sixty students in the UT classes. As a result he had to be familiar with every case every day; with only two students, there was a good chance he would be called upon. Doyle later noted, "It was the one time I benefited from segregation" (Mouton, 3–4).

After 1 September 1948, at which time the law school moved to Houston, Doyle was the only student to continue. In November 1949 he passed the Texas bar examination and became the first student of the law school to receive a license to practice law in Texas. In May 1950 he became the law school's first graduate or as he fondly stated, "I graduated number 1 in my class" (Mouton, 3–4). After graduating, Doyle opened a law practice with Francis Williams; the partnership lasted fifteen years. In 1952 the firm defended Johnny Morris, a black man accused of killing a white Houston bus driver. Doyle and Morris argued the case before an all-white jury and managed to spare their client the death penalty. This highly publicized criminal case boosted Doyle's practice. A turning point in Doyle's career occurred when he became legal counsel for the Houston branch of the NAACP. On 27 August 1953 the catalyst for a series of civil rights suits occurred when Matthew Plummer, a black attorney, sought service in the Harris County Criminal Courthouse cafeteria and was told the cafeteria did not and would not serve "colored people." His suit resulted in the integration of the cafeteria.

In 1962 Doyle was involved in two other major suits to integrate the county-owned Sylvan Beach in LaPorte and the Houston Independent School District. While these cases put Doyle in the spotlight, they also caused many judges to dislike him. Doyle became a renowned civil rights attorney during the twenty-seven years he practiced law.

In 1976 Doyle ran unsuccessfully for judge of the domestic relations court. In 1977 he was appointed to the Houston Municipal Court Number 6. On 1 December 1978 he became the first black to be appointed to a Texas appellate court with multi-county constituency, when he was selected as an associate justice of the First Court of Civil Appeals in Houston after the court added three new judges positions and initially filled the new seats by appointment. At the end of those terms, the new judges had to run for re-election. Doyle won re-election in 1980 and retired from the bench on 31 December 1984. He died three months after his retirement, and was survived by his wife, Verndya, and son, Vernon. Judge Henry Doyle's many successes made him a true trailblazer in Texas legal history.

FURTHER READING

Manley, Brent. "Judge Has Come Long Way: Career Started in a Basement," *Houston Post*, 5 Feb. 1984.

Mouton, Virgie. "In Honor of Henry E. Doyle First Graduate of Texas Southern University Law School Class of 1950," *The Solicitor: Thurgood Marshall School of Law, Texas Southern University* (1997): 3–4.

Pace, Clint. "UT Negro Law School Enrolls First Student in State History," *Austin American*, 22 Sept. 1947.

"State Negro Law School Registers First Student," *Texas Bar Journal* 10.9 (Oct. 1947): 423.

"Texas Negro Law School Graduate Gets License," *Texas Bar Journal* 13.1 (Jan. 1950): 17.

DECARLOUS SPEARMAN

Doyle, Sam (1906–1985), folk artist, was born Samuel Doyle on St. Helena Island, the Gullah Islands, South Carolina, one of nine children of Thomas Sr. and Sue Ladsen Doyle, farmers on the Wallace plantation of mostly freed slaves. Doyle attended the Penn School, which was one of the country's first vocational and agricultural schools created by the Freedmen's Associations of Philadelphia to educate freed slaves on St. Helena's Island. He studied literature and carpentry through the ninth grade, but was recognized for his drawing skills. A teacher encouraged him to travel to New York, where he could better nurture his talent with the growing opportunities available to African American artists; however, owing to financial constraints Doyle chose to remain on the island. He dropped out of the Penn School following the ninth grade and found a job as a store clerk. He later took on work as a porter in a wholesale store, where he worked for twenty years. During that time he married Maude Brown and had three children, two girls and one boy. Maude operated a small café out of a building adjacent to their house.

Maude Doyle and her children eventually moved to New York City in 1944, but again Doyle chose to remain on the island in the small cottage he had built in 1940. After his family moved, Doyle took a job as a laundry worker on the Parris Island Marine Corps base. He held this job for sixteen years before retiring in the late 1960s.

Upon retirement Doyle turned the former café into a studio, which he used only during inclement weather, preferring to pursue his passion for drawing and painting outdoors. His primary materials were enamel house paint, roofing tin, and large wooden panels. Rather than making preliminary sketches for his works, Doyle created his compositions in process. His paintings were rich and colorful portraits of island residents, sports and music celebrities, and depictions of heavily African-influenced Gullah culture, including superstitious beliefs and religious practices that slaves brought with them from West Africa during the Triangle Trade. One of his favorite portraits was of Dr. Buzzard, a Vodou doctor and the island's wealthiest African American resident. He also painted his grandmother, Lucinda Ladsen, who was the island's first African American midwife. In addition to his grandmother, he painted St. Helena's other African American "firsts," including the owner of a passenger ship, the bus driver, the postman, the policeman, and the undertaker. As a deeply devout Christian, Doyle balanced his secular work with paintings of Christian themes, such as the Annunciation and the Crucifixion.

Starting in the early 1970s, Doyle experimented with sculpture. He used tree trunks and limbs, driftwood, and lumber to create serpents, fowl, and other animals. He usually painted his sculptures either dark brown or tarred and feathered them. Superstition's strong presence in Gullah culture as well as the manner in which Doyle placed his sculptures around his property led historians of both Doyle's work and the island's community to conclude that his sculptures did not function solely as art objects for Doyle, but also as fetishes to protect him, his art, and home from evil spirits.

Doyle's home and yard operated as gallery and museum space. His work did not receive national attention until only a few years before his death, most likely because of the landmark group exhibition Black American Folk Art of the 20th Century at the Corcoran Gallery of Art in Washington, D.C., which traveled across the United States in 1983. Prior to the Corcoran exhibit, Doyle's work was on view at the Gibbs Museum of Art in Charleston, South Carolina, from November 1982 to January 1983. The Pat Hearn Gallery in New York and the Janet Fleisher Gallery in Philadelphia mounted posthumous exhibits of his work in 1986 and 1999, respectively.

FURTHER READING

Bailey, Cornelia, and Christena Bledsoe. *God, Dr. Buzzard, and the Bolito Man: A Saltwater Geechee Talks about Life on Sapelo Island* (2000).

Perry, Regina. "Sam Doyle: St. Helena Island's Native Son: Regina Perry Looks at One of America's Leading Masters of Southern Folk Art," *Raw Vision* 23 (Summer 1998).

Spriggs, Lynne E. *Local Heroes: Paintings and Sculpture by Sam Doyle* (2000).

CRYSTAL AM NELSON

Dozier, Lamont Herbert (16 June 1941–), songwriter, music producer and performer, was born in Detroit, Michigan. Information about his parents is largely unknown. As a young child he rehearsed with a local Baptist church's gospel choir and listened to his aunt play classical music on the family piano. His interest in music developed in the late 1940s and early 1950s as he heard popular singers such as NAT KING COLE, Frank Sinatra, and Tony Bennett through his father's record collection. Later he started his own collection of singles by singers such as JOHNNY MATHIS and vocal and doo-wop groups that included Frankie Lymon and the Teenagers and the Spaniels. Though he was a self-taught musician, he was writing his own lyrics by the age of eleven and music by the age of twelve, and at the age of thirteen he formed the musical group the Romeos.

In 1957 the Romeos released the single "Moments to Remember You By," with "Fine Fine Baby," a rhythm and blues single, on the reverse side, on Detroit's small Fox record label, which was later picked up by the ATCO label. In 1959, after the Romeos disbanded, Dozier joined the doo-wop group the Voice Masters, who released a couple of singles for Detroit's fledgling Anna Records, founded by Gwen Gordy, the sister of Detroit's Motown Records label founder BERRY GORDY JR. and named after their sister Anna. Dozier's breakthrough as a solo artist came with the novelty song "Popeye the Sailor Man," issued on Anna in 1960 and recorded under the pseudonym Lamont Anthony. However, in response to the objections of King Features, who owned the rights to the cartoon strongman, the song was recut as "Benny the Skinny Man" and reissued. In 1961 Dozier released "Just to Be Loved" on Check-Mate, a subsidiary of Chicago's legendary Chess Records label run by Berry Gordy's former partner Billy Davis.

By 1962 Dozier was attracted to the burgeoning Motown label by Berry Gordy, who was interested in the multitalented singer and songwriter. The same year Gordy released Dozier's "Dearest One" under the label's Mel-O-Dy subsidiary, Dozier's first and only single under his own name as a solo recording artist for Motown. However, "Dearest One" is perhaps most significant for marking the first appearance of what became Motown's most successful writing and production team, Holland-Dozier-Holland (as the trio is best known), composed of Dozier and Eddie Holland and Brian Holland, two singer-songwriter brothers.

According to the rock critic Dave Marsh in *The Heart of Rock and Soul: The 1001 Greatest Singles Ever Made* (1999): "As Motown's (and arguably the world's) premier production team, Holland-Dozier-Holland have as much right to be considered artists as anybody in the history of rock and soul. Their records had an essential coherence that went beyond the specific acts with which they worked" (496). The deep gospel influence of Dozier's early church choir experiences, especially the prominent rhythm of the tambourine, and the lush strings gleaned from his aunt's classical piano came to define the Motown signature sound (or "the sound of young America" as advertised by the label) and dominate the popular music charts during the early and mid-1960s. According to Eddie Holland in his liner notes for *The Complete Motown Singles: 1959–1967*, "Lamont was usually the guy who'd start things at the piano" (vol. *1966*, 6). Between 1963 and 1967 Holland-Dozier-Holland was responsible for more than fifty of Motown's—and rock and soul's—most memorable songs, especially for the Four Tops, who recorded, among others, "It's the Same Old Song" (1965), "I Can't Help Myself (Sugar Pie Honey Bunch)" (1965), and "Reach Out I'll Be There" (1966); and for the Supremes, who scored historic hits with "Baby Love" (1964), "Where Did Our Love Go" (1964), and "Stop! In the Name of Love" (1965). Holland-Dozier-Holland also contributed hits to most of Motown's leading artists, including Martha and the Vandellas' "Heat Wave" (1963) and "Nowhere to Run" (1965), Marvin Gaye's "Can I Get a Witness" (1963) and "How Sweet It Is" (1965), and the Miracles' "Mickey's Monkey" (1963).

However, in 1967, amid a myriad of lawsuits over royalties and workload, Dozier and the Hollands left Motown to form the Invictus and Hot Wax record labels. Their music during this period was nearly as successful as their most important Motown work and includes producing and writing Freda Payne's anti–Vietnam War anthem "Bring the Boys Home" (1970) and the Chairmen of the Board's hit "Give Me Just a Little More Time" (1970). Following the collapse of the Invictus label in 1972, Dozier once again pursued a solo career. He moved to California and with the major label ABC-Dunhill recorded and released his debut album *Out Here on My Own* (1973), which included the hits "Trying to Hold on to My Woman" and "Fish Ain't Bitin." Ironically considering he had been in music since the 1950s, the album scored him a Billboard Magazine Best New Artist Award. His solo career continued in the 1970s and early 1980s with recordings for a string of major labels, including Warner Bros., which released the hit "Going Back to My Roots" (1977). In 1980 he moved to Europe with his wife, Barbara Ullman Dozier, and their two children; while overseas he wrote songs for the vocalist Alison Moyet, including her top ten hit "Invisible" (1984), the British group Simply Red's hit "You've Got It" (1989), and "Hung Up on Your Love" and "Run" for the guitar legend Eric Clapton's 1985 album *August*. Dozier and Phil Collins collaborated in 1988 on the song "Two Hearts" for the soundtrack to the movie *Buster*, which earned the duo a Grammy Award and an Oscar nomination.

Dozier was elected to the Songwriters Hall of Fame in 1988 and the Rock and Roll Hall of Fame in 1990. In 1991 Dozier again signed with a major label, Atlantic Records, for the album *Inside Seduction*, but record company politics soon disillusioned him. Following the release's poor sales, Dozier and his wife, Barbara, started their own record company, and Dozier released *An American Original* (2002), featuring reinterpretations of the songs that made him a songwriting legend. The album, originally released only over the Internet and later renamed *Reflections of … Lamont Dozier* (2004) with bonus tracks, was nominated for a Grammy Award for Best Traditional R&B Vocal Album.

FURTHER READING

George, Nelson. *Where Did Our Love Go? The Rise and Fall of the Motown Sound* (2007).

Marsh, Dave. *The Heart of Rock and Soul: The 1001 Greatest Singles Ever Made* (1999).

DISCOGRAPHY

The Complete Motown Singles: 1959–1967, 7 vols. (2005–2007).

STEVE FEFFER

Dr. Dre (18 Feb. 1965–), hip-hop artist, disc jockey, and record executive, was born André Romel Young in Los Angeles, California, the son of Verna Griffin and Theodore Young. Both of his parents were semi-professional musicians. They divorced shortly after André's birth; Griffin attended college and then worked for an aircraft company. She raised André and his younger brother, Tyree, in Compton, California; she would later marry Warren Griffin Jr. and they would have a son, Warren "Warren G" Griffin III. As a child Young acquired the nickname Dr. Dre because of his great admiration for the basketball player JULIUS ('Dr. J") ERVING. Dre demonstrated a fascination with music, a passion his mother encouraged by buying him equipment and designing costumes for his performances.

In his teens Dre developed a reputation as a skilled disc jockey, quickly graduating from performing at neighborhood parties to Los Angeles–area nightclubs, including Eve's After Dark in Compton. When Dre was seventeen, the owner of Eve's, Alonzo "Lonzo" Williams, recruited Dre, DJ Yella, and Cli-N-Tel to form the musical core of the World Class Wreckin' Cru. The group recorded in a bare production studio connected to the Eve's complex and released a series of regional hits that reflected Southern California's distinct, electro funk–influenced variation on hip-hop. Dre and Yella were eventually hired to be disc jockeys for the Los Angeles radio station KDAY, notable for being the first radio station to offer an all-day, all-hip-hop format, beginning in 1983.

Despite their quick success, Dre and Yella were dissatisfied with the direction of the Wreckin' Cru sound, which had grown softer and wispier over time. Dre spent his free time in the studio at Eve's, developing a raucous, sample-based style of hip hop that reflected his appreciation for the expansive sound of 1970s funk artists like Zapp and GEORGE CLINTON and the scatological wit of comedians like RICHARD PRYOR and Rudy Ray Moore. In 1986 Dre befriended ICE CUBE, a talented local rapper who shared Dre's sense of humor—Dre helped script one of Ice Cube's early rap routines, in which Cube performed a parody of Run-DMC's "My Adidas" called "My Penis." The pair shared a common hope to push hip-hop to rougher, raunchier, and more confrontational extremes. They began writing raps for Ruthless Records, a local label founded by a former drug dealer named Eric "Eazy-E" Wright. When one of Ruthless Records' acts refused to record a Dre and Cube composition, Eazy-E agreed to record it himself. The single, "Boyz N the Hood," became a regional hit. Dre, Cube, Eazy-E, and Yella—along with MC Ren and Arabian Prince, whose tenure with the group was brief—decided to form their own group, N.W.A., or Niggaz With Attitude. It was not a difficult decision for Dre and Yella to leave the Wreckin' Cru; though their last recordings for

Williams would result in hit singles, they were never compensated.

N.W.A.'s debut album, *Straight Outta Compton* (1988), was one of the grimmest recordings of any genre of the 1980s, laying down the foundation for a subgenre of hip-hop that would come to be known as "gangsta rap." The controversial album became a hit despite little radio airplay. The FBI issued N.W.A. a letter of warning after the success of their single "Fuck the Police." Ice Cube departed the group in 1989 amid financial disagreements. Dre refined his production techniques by working on the D.O.C.'s *Nobody Can Do It Better* (1989) and Above the Law's *Livin' Like Hustlers* (1990). N.W.A.'s final two releases, the *100 Miles and Runnin'* EP (1990) and *Efil4zaggin* (1991), featured denser, more sophisticated arrangements as well. Despite N.W.A.'s success—*Efil4zaggin* debuted at number 2 on the pop charts, achieving platinum status two weeks later with virtually no national radio airplay—Dre was at the center of many controversies. In 1991 he assaulted Dee Barnes, the host of a televised rap program. Later that year Dre left the group to found a new label, Death Row Records, with his bodyguard, an ex-football player and gang-member named Marlon "Suge" Knight. While nobody has ever confirmed this, oft-circulated rumors suggest that Knight resorted to violence to procure Dre's contract from Ruthless Records.

In 1992 Dre released his debut solo single, "Deep Cover." It featured a cameo verse from the rapper SNOOP DOGGY DOGG, whom Dre met through his stepbrother, Warren G. Dre's full-length solo debut, the Grammy Award–winning *The Chronic* (1992), is often seen as one of hip-hop's sonic paradigm shifts. The album's breezy sound and apolitical, laidback attitude belied the tense backdrop of a Los Angeles still recovering from the RODNEY KING riots. *The Chronic*, along with Snoop's debut album, *Doggystyle* (1993), made the pair bona fide pop stars and popularized Southern California's bass-heavy, 1970s-funk–influenced "G-Funk" sound. But controversy dogged Death Row Records, as Snoop faced murder charges (he would be acquitted), the rapper TUPAC ("2Pac") SHAKUR grew increasingly unstable, and the label's violent imagery was scrutinized by watchdog organizations. Dre began to reconsider the trajectory of his life and career. On 26 March 1995 Eazy-E died of complications related to AIDS; his death affected Dre deeply, as the two had never reconciled following the dissolution of N.W.A. That year Dre married his longtime girlfriend Nicole Threatt, another decision that inspired Dre to leave his hard-living ways behind. In 1996 Dre split from Knight and founded Aftermath Records, a partnership with Interscope Records. He oversaw two albums, *Dr. Dre Presents ... The Aftermath* (1996) and *Nas, Foxy Brown, AZ, and Nature Present The Firm: The Album* (1997). Though both achieved platinum status, neither found critical favor.

In 1998 Dre signed Marshall "Eminem" Mathers, a white rapper from Detroit, to Aftermath. Dre's endorsement of the controversial Eminem facilitated the breakthrough success of the latter's major label debut, *The Slim Shady LP* (1999). Later that year Dre released his long-awaited second solo album, *Dr. Dre 2001* (1999). His production style had evolved yet again. Instead of 1970s funk samples, the two albums featured strident piano and string melodies atop live drumming and original bass lines. This new, organic approach earned Dre a Grammy Award for Producer of the Year in 2000. In 2002 Dre and Eminem—both of whom were now high-ranking executives at Interscope Records—coproduced the debut album from the Queens rapper 50 Cent, *Get Rich or Die Tryin'* (2003).

FURTHER READING

Bogdanov, Vladimir, ed. *The All Music Guide to Hip-Hop: The Definitive Guide to Rap and Hip-Hop* (2003).

Light, Alan, ed. *The Vibe History of Hip Hop* (1999).

HUA HSU

Drake, St. Clair, Jr. (2 Jan. 1911–15 June 1990), anthropologist, was born John Gibbs St. Clair Drake Jr. in Suffolk, Virginia, the son of John Gibbs St. Clair Drake Sr., a Baptist pastor, and Bessie Lee Bowles. By the time Drake was four years old his father had moved the family twice, once to Harrisonburg, Virginia, and then to Pittsburgh, Pennsylvania.

The family lived in a racially mixed neighborhood in Pittsburgh, where Drake grew to feel at ease with whites. His strict Baptist upbringing gave him a deep understanding of religious organizations. His father also taught him to work with tools and to become an expert in woodworking, a skill Drake later employed in his field research.

A trip to the West Indies in 1922 with his father led to major changes in Drake's life. The Reverend Drake had tried to instill in his son a deep respect for the British Empire, but the sight of the poverty in the Caribbean led the Reverend to abandon his support of racial integration and convert to MARCUS GARVEY'S ideas in favor of racial separation and a return to an African homeland for the black diaspora. He quit his pastorship and went to work as an itinerant organizer for Garvey. The young Drake was to trace his interest in anthropology to this trip with his father.

While his father worked for Garvey as an organizer and was constantly away from home on trips, Drake and his mother moved to Staunton, Virginia. In contrast to his Pittsburgh experiences, Drake encountered the caste system in full force in Virginia. These experiences led him to an appreciation of the radical African American poets of his day, particularly LANGSTON HUGHES, COUNTÉE CULLEN, and CLAUDE MCKAY. They also led him to combine action with study.

After graduating with honors from Hampton Institute in Hampton, Virginia, in 1931, Drake worked with the Society of Friends on their "Peace Caravans." These caravans worked for racial harmony and civil rights. Once again Drake met with whites in a common cause as an equal. He continued to work with the Quakers while teaching at one of their boarding schools. For a time he considered becoming a member of the Society of Friends; however, the realization that there was still prejudice in such a liberal group kept him from converting to the religion.

Drake decided to study anthropology in an effort to better understand the roots of human behavior. After teaching high school at the Christianburg Institute in Cambria, Virginia, from 1932 to 1935, he became a research assistant at Dillard University in New Orleans. There he combined his field research with action, joining the Tenant Farmers Union and the Farmers Union in Adams County, Mississippi. By his own accounts in "Reflections on Anthropology and the Black Experience," these periodic forays into activism nearly cost him his life. On one occassion, he and fellow workers barely escaped a lynch mob. Drake recounts another incident where he was badly beaten and left unconscious.

After a year at Columbia University in 1936, Drake entered the University of Chicago in 1937 on a Rosenwald Fellowship. There he met the sociologist Horace Clayton and joined his research under the auspices of the Public Works Progress Administration (WPA), specializing in the African American church and the urban black population. This work became the basis for his contributions to *Black Metropolis* (1946), which he jointly authored with Horace B. Cayton. Drake married the sociologist Elizabeth Dewy Johns in 1942; they had two children.

During World War II, Drake became actively involved in the struggle of African Americans for equality. He concentrated his efforts on the conflict in northern war industries and housing. He worked with various African American organizations for which he gathered hard data, joined in work actions, and served on various war boards concerned with presenting African American grievances to the federal government. While gathering data for *Black Metropolis*, Drake worked in a war plant and experienced inequality firsthand. Drake grew bitter at his fellow citizens who so enthusiastically fought fascism abroad but were unwilling to combat it in the United States. In response to these experiences Drake joined the merchant marine, in which he believed he would not encounter the same prejudice and segregation that he might have in the U.S. armed forces.

Following his discharge from the service, Drake completed his Ph.D. in Anthropology at the University of Chicago in 1946 and accepted a position teaching at Roosevelt College that same year. Drake worked extensively in Africa, teaching in both Liberia and Ghana. In 1961 he developed a training program for Peace Corps volunteers in Africa. Over the years he was a personal adviser to many African leaders, including Kwame Nkrumah in Ghana and various high officials in Nigeria. However, as military rule steadily replaced civilian rule in the 1960s, Drake left Africa, refusing to work with dictators.

A prolific scholar, Drake focused his writing on racial concerns such as the problem of inequality, the plight of the urban poor, religion, race relations, and the relationship of African Americans to Africa. His major works include *Race Relations in a Time of Rapid Social Change* (1966), *Our Urban Poor: Promises to Keep and Miles to Go* (1967), and *The Redemption of Africa and Black Religion* (1970). He edited numerous journals and books and brought intellectuals together to discuss the issues of the day and propose actions to meet these problems.

In 1969 Drake moved to Stanford University, where he established the Center for Afro-American Studies, an African American studies department that became a model for other universities. Drake refused to bow to the demand of radicals who wanted the department to be a center exclusively for black students, where others interested in African and African American history would not be welcome. He refused to teach Afrocentric notions that saw Africans as the center of all civilizations and the inventors of all wisdom. He resisted the efforts of black militants outside and inside academia—STOKELY CARMICHAEL, James Turner at

Cornell, Felix Okoye, and others—who believed that a person's skin color accredited or discredited him or her as an expert in African and African American studies. Drake insisted on establishing his center on solid academic grounds.

Throughout his life, Drake showed personal integrity in working to achieve his goals of equality and respect for African Americans and their accomplishments. He founded the American Society for African Culture and the American Negro Leadership Conference on Africa in the early 1960s. He was never afraid to risk his life in pursuit of his goals. Drake died at his home in Palo Alto, California.

FURTHER READING

Some of Drake's manuscripts are in the collection of the Schomburg Center for Research in Black Culture of the New York Public Library.

Romero, Patrick W. *In Black America, 1968: The Year of Awakening* (1969).

Uya, Okon Edet. *Black Brotherhood: Afro-Americans and Africa* (1971).

Washington, Joseph R., Jr. *Jews in Black Perspective* (1984).

Obituary: *New York Times*, 21 June 1990.

This entry is taken from the *American National Biography* and is published here with the permission of the American Council of Learned Societies.

FRANK A. SALAMONE

Dranes, Arizona (4 Apr. 1894–27 July 1963), gospel singer and pianist, was according to her death certificate born Arizona Juanita Dranes in Dallas, Texas, to Cora Jones and an "Unknown Dranes." Some writers have suggested—based on Dranes's middle name—that she was of Mexican and African American descent. Dranes was raised in a neighborhood famous for its barrelhouse piano players called State Thomas, not far from "Deep Ellum." Blind from birth, Dranes mastered the piano and all the instrumental styles—for example ragtime, stride, and boogie—then popular in that African American community.

Dranes was affiliated with the Church of God in-Christ (COGIC), the Memphis-based church founded in 1907 by Bishop Charles Mason that was to become the country's largest black Pentecostal denomination. Within the COGIC Dranes became a local celebrity for matching the highly polyrhythmic, often a cappella, sanctified singing with the raucous barrelhouse piano playing found in the region's jook joints and other secular venues. Her singing and piano playing became so popular in the Dallas–Ft. Worth area that Dranes came to the-attention of Chicago's Okeh Phonograph Company. She was apparently invited to Chicago on the strength of an audition and a recommendation from a local COGIC Elder: "Since she is deprived of her natural sight, the Lord has given her a Spiritual sight, that all the churches enjoy that sweet melody made from the Instrument. She loyal and obedient. Our prayers ascend for her" (Shaw, nd). Some writers have maintained that it was the pianist Richard M. Jones who auditioned Dranes in Fort Worth in early 1926.

Dranes recorded six songs at this session, playing piano on all six sides and singing on four of them: "In That Day," "It's All Right Now," "John Said He Saw a Number," and "My Soul Is a Witness for the Lord." On the latter two, Jones and the blues singer Sara Martin (who by this time was already an Okeh recording artist and popular stage performer) sang background in a call-and-response mode typical of COGIC group singing. "The template Dranes created with six tracks in one day came to be called 'the gospel beat'; it is still played against a polyrhythm of handclaps in black church services today" (Corcoran 2003, 14). The records sold well and on the strength of their popularity Dranes toured widely playing COGIC churches and revivals.

The music educator Adrian York described Dranes's style:

> She defined the essential elements of the gospel piano style: The left hand plays the bass, the middle register supports and harmonizes the melody and the upper end adds fills and countermelodies. The harmony is straight from the Protestant hymnals, diatonic with diminished chords, but with an added blues influence; the rhythm can be straight or swung with much use of syncopation (231).

The gospel scholar Horace Boyer described Dranes's use of the piano as a "rhythm section." "[T]he left hand assumes the role of the bass guitar—playing single notes or octaves *on* and *between* the beats—and the drum, by attacking the keys in a *percussive* rather than legato manner. The right hand takes the part of the guitar, playing chords on and after the beat with intermittent 'licks' of two or three single tones, followed immediately by chords" (32).

Dranes returned to the studio in November of 1926 and recorded four songs backed by the Reverend F. W. McGee and the Texas Jubilee Singers: "I'm Glad My Lord Saved Me," "Lamb's Blood Has Washed Me Clean," "I'm Going Home on the Morning Train," and "Bye and Bye We're

Going to See the King." The last of these became a gospel favorite and was covered by BLIND WILLIE JOHNSON, Blind Mamie Forehand, and the white country trio the Carter Family, among others.

In May 1927 Dranes accompanied the Reverend McGee on his first recording, the powerful "Lion of the Tribe of Judah" and most likely was the pianist on Jessie May Hill's three recordings (one of which was released as the flipside of McGee's song). Dranes is generally credited with introducing McGee to Okeh.

"Arizona Dranes and Choir" was the label billing on the records released from Dranes's last recording session as leader. Six songs were recorded accompanied by unknown female singers and on four songs an unknown mandolin player. Two of these songs remained unreleased until well after Dranes's death. Dranes is also thought to be the pianist on the Texas Jubilee Singers's Columbia session in Dallas in December 1928, and possibly on Laura Henton's record made by Columbia during the same Dallas fieldtrip. It has also been suggested that she played piano and sang with the Reverend Joe Lenley on his December 1929 Columbia session in Dallas.

Based on the one known photograph of Dranes (from the *Dallas Observer*) she was a large woman. She was apparently also sickly—canceling several scheduled recording sessions owing to illness. Soon after Dranes's last Okeh session, the recording industry went into a significant decline with the coming of the Great Depression. Dranes continued to work the COGIC circuit, often opening for COGIC founder Bishop Charles Mason.

Dranes is known to have worked in Memphis (headquarters of the COGIC), the Birmingham/Bessemer area of Alabama (where she was received with excitement by both blacks and whites), St. Louis (where her performances had a profound influence on the singing and guitar playing of the gospel great Sister ROSETTA THARPE), and in Oklahoma City (where she helped build McGee's church and musical ministry). Dranes's last known public concert was in Cincinnati in 1947.

In 1948 Dranes moved to South Central Los Angeles. During the last fifteen years of her life Dranes played occasionally at the Emmanuel Church of God in Christ founded by her former Ft. Worth associate, the Reverend Samuel Crouch (great-uncle of the gospel singer ANDRAE CROUCH). At the age of sixty-nine Dranes died of cerebral arteriosclerosis in Long Beach, California, and is buried in Paradise Memorial Park in Santa Fe Springs. No obituaries or tributes were published at the time of her death.

Dranes's influence on COGIC (and therefore all African American Pentecostal) music is substantial. In addition to Tharpe and McGee, Dranes's sound had an admitted effect on that of other singers including Ernestine W. Washington and the celebrated ROBERTA MARTIN. Just as COGIC music played an essential role in the amalgamation of denominational and black secular music that gave birth to African American gospel, Dranes's influence as a primary progenitor of the COGIC musical style spreads far beyond the COGIC world.

Dranes was recording her new sanctified sound when the "father of gospel music," THOMAS A. DORSEY, was still performing as the pianist Georgia Tom in blues and hokum bands. Dorsey, a Baptist, admitted to attending sanctified meetings in Chicago (where Dranes often performed) to learn his style. Boyer stated "the most famous of the blind singers was Sister Arizona Dranes; her thin but intense soprano influenced many later singers, and her piano style was a model for that of the first gospel songs recorded by Dorsey" (256). Timothy Kalil explained that Dorsey's primary contribution to the Dranes piano style was to make it "swing," adding the "improvisational quality of 1920s jazz and blues" (178). The Dranes/Dorsey piano style was to become the standard for all forms of African American gospel music.

Dranes was also one of the first to employ the "vamp" on record. The vamp is "a device [that] relies upon repetition with minor variations to emphasize and then reemphasize a particular point" (Lornell 1995, 146)—a device also found in African American linguistic behavior, oral culture, and secular music.

Arizona Dranes, gospel music pioneer and one of its first stars, has been largely forgotten. She receives only brief mention in most monographs on the history of gospel music and her name does not appear at all in the official COGIC history. Much in contemporary American culture came out of the black church; Arizona Dranes played a significant role in this process of transculturation.

FURTHER READING

Information about Dranes and her music is located in the *Arizona Dranes Collection*, Archives of African American Music and Culture, Indiana University.

Boyer, Horace Clarence. "Black Gospel Music," in *The New Grove Dictionary of American Music* (1986).

Boyer, Horace Clarence. "Contemporary Gospel," in *The Black Perspective in Music* (1979).

Corcoran, Michael. "Holly Roller: Arizona Dranes," *Blues & Rhythm* (2003).

Kalil, Timothy Michael. "Thomas A. Dorsey and the Development and Diffusion of Traditional Gospel Music," in *Perspectives on American Music, 1900–1950*, ed. Michael Saffle (2000).

Lornell, Kip. *"Happy in the Service of the Lord": African-American Sacred Vocal Harmony Quartets in Memphis* (1995).

Shaw, Malcolm. *Arizona Dranes, 1926–1928* (Liner notes to Herwin LP 210).

York, Adrian. "Keyboard Techniques," in *The Cambridge Companion to Blues and Gospel Music*, ed. Allan Moore (2003).

DISCOGRAPHY

Dixon, Robert M. W., John Godrich, and Howard W. Rye. *Blues and Gospel Records, 1890–1943* (1997).

FRED J. HAY

Drew, Charles Richard (3 June 1904–1 Apr. 1950), blood plasma scientist, surgeon, and teacher, was born in Washington, D.C., the son of Richard Thomas Drew, a carpet-layer, and Nora Rosella Burrell. Drew adored his hard-working parents and was determined from an early age to emulate them. Drew's parents surrounded their children with the many opportunities available in Washington's growing middle-class black community: excellent segregated schools, solid church and social affiliations, and their own strong example. Drew's father was the sole black member of his union and served as its financial secretary.

Charles Drew, the African American surgeon who became the first director of the American Red Cross blood bank. During World War II, Drew helped establish blood banks to serve the Allies in Europe. (AP Images.)

Drew graduated from Paul Laurence Dunbar High School in 1922 and received a medal for best all-around athletic performance; he also won a scholarship to Amherst College. At Amherst he was a star in football and track, earning honorable mention as an All-American halfback in the eastern division, receiving the Howard Hill Mossman Trophy for bringing the greatest athletic honor to Amherst during his four years there, and taking a national high hurdles championship. A painful brush with discrimination displayed Drew's lifelong response to it: after Drew was denied the captaincy of the football team because he was black, he ended the controversy by quietly refusing to dispute the choice of a white player. His approach to racial prejudice, as he explained in a letter years later, was to knock down "at least one or two bricks" of the "rather high-walled prison of the 'Negro problem' by virtue of some worthwhile contribution" (Love, 175). Throughout his life Drew, whether as a pioneer or as a team leader, helped others scale barriers so they too could serve society. While recuperating from a leg injury, Drew decided to pursue a career in medicine. He worked for two years as an athletic director and biology and chemistry instructor at Morgan College (now Morgan State University), a black college in Baltimore, Maryland, to earn money for medical school. There were few openings for black medical students at this time, but Drew was finally admitted to McGill University Medical School in Montreal, Canada. Despite severe financial constraints, he graduated in 1933 with an MDCM (doctor of medicine and master of surgery) degree, second in his class of 137. He was vice president of Alpha Omega Alpha, the medical honor society, and won both the annual prize in neuroanatomy and the J. Francis Williams Prize in Medicine on the basis of a competitive examination. Drew completed a year of internship and a year of residency in internal medicine at Montreal General Hospital. He hoped to pursue training as a surgery resident at a prestigious U.S. medical institution, but almost no clinical opportunities were available to African American doctors at this time. Drew decided to return to Washington, taking a job as an instructor in pathology at Howard University Medical School during 1935–1936.

Howard's medical school was then being transformed from a mostly white-run institution to a black-led one, through the efforts of NUMA P. G. ADAMS, dean of the medical school, and the charismatic MORDECAI JOHNSON, Howard's first black president. Adams nominated Drew to receive a two-year fellowship at Columbia University's medical school.

No black resident had ever been trained at Presbyterian Hospital when Drew arrived at Columbia in the fall of 1938, but Drew so impressed Allen O. Whipple, director of the surgical residency program, that he received this training unofficially, regularly making rounds with Whipple. In the meantime, Drew pursued a doctor of science degree in medicine, doing extensive research on blood-banking, a field still in its infancy, under the guidance of John Scudder, who was engaged in studies relating to fluid balance, blood chemistry, and blood transfusion. With Scudder, Drew set up Presbyterian Hospital's first blood bank. After two years he produced his doctoral thesis, "Banked Blood: A Study in Blood Preservation" (1940), which pulled together existing scientific research on the subject. He became the first African American to receive the doctor of science degree, in 1940. In 1939 Drew had married Minnie Lenore Robbins, a home economics professor at Spelman College. They had four children.

Drew returned to Howard in 1940 as an assistant professor in surgery. In September of that year, however, he was called back to New York City to serve as medical director of the Blood for Britain Project, a hastily organized operation to prepare and ship liquid plasma to wounded British soldiers. He confronted the challenge of separating liquid plasma from whole blood on a much larger scale than it had ever been done before and shipping it overseas in a way that would ensure its stability and sterility. His success in this led to his being chosen in early 1941 to serve as medical director of a three-month American Red Cross pilot project involving the mass production of dried plasma. Once again Drew acted swiftly and effectively, aware that the model he was helping to create would be critical to a successful national blood collection program. Red Cross historians agree that Drew's work in this pilot program and the technical expertise he amassed were pivotal to the national blood collection program, a major life-saving factor during the war.

Soon after being certified as a diplomate of the American Board of Surgery, Drew returned to Howard in April 1941. In October he took over as chairman of Howard's Department of Surgery and became chief surgeon at Freedmen's Hospital, commencing what he viewed as his real life's work, the building of Howard's surgical residency program and the training of a team of top-notch black surgeons.

In December 1941 the United States entered the war, and the American Red Cross expanded its national blood collection program. It announced that it would exclude black donors, and then, in response to widespread protest, it adopted a policy of segregating the blood of black donors. Drew spoke out against this policy, pointing out that there was no medical or scientific reason to segregate blood supplies by race. (The Red Cross officially ended its segregation of blood in 1950.) His stance catapulted him into the national limelight: the irony of his being a blood expert and potentially facing exclusion or segregation himself was dramatized by both the black and white press and highlighted when he received the National Association for the Advancement of Colored People's Spingarn Medal in 1944.

A demanding yet unusually caring teacher, Drew stayed in touch with his students long after they left Howard. Between 1941 and 1950 he trained more than half the black surgeons certified by the American Board of Surgery (eight in all), and fourteen more surgeons certified after 1950 received part of their training from him. In 1942 he became the first black surgeon appointed an examiner for the American Board of Surgery. Other responsibilities and honors followed: in 1943 he was appointed a member of the American-Soviet Committee on Science, and in 1946 he was elected vice president of the American-Soviet Medical Society. From 1944 to 1946 he served as chief of staff, and from 1946 to 1948 as medical director of Freedmen's Hospital. In 1946 he was named a fellow of the U.S. chapter of the International College of Surgeons; in 1949 he was appointed surgical consultant to the surgeon general and was sent to Europe to inspect military medical facilities.

Throughout this period Drew was struggling to open doors for his young black residents, who still were barred from practicing at most white medical institutions as well as from joining the American Medical Association (AMA) and the American College of Surgeons (ACOG). Throughout the 1940s he waged a relentless campaign through letters and political contacts to try to open up the AMA and the ACOG to black physicians; he himself joined neither.

While driving to a medical conference in Alabama, Drew died as the result of an auto accident in North Carolina. His traumatic, untimely death sparked a false rumor that grew into a historical legend during the civil rights movement era, alleging that Drew bled to death because he was turned away from a whites-only hospital. Drew's well-publicized protest of the segregated blood policy, combined with the hospital's refusals of many black patients during the era of segregation, undoubtedly laid the foundation for the legend that dramatized the medical deprivation Drew spent his life battling. Drew was a great American man of medicine by any measure; his extraordinary personality was best summed up by one of his oldest friends, Ben Davis: "I can never forget him: his extraordinary nobleness of character, his honesty, his integrity and fearlessness" (David Hepburn, *Our World* [July 1950]: 28).

FURTHER READING

The Charles R. Drew Papers are located in the Moorland-Spingarn Research Center of Howard University.

Love, Spencie. *One Blood: The Death and Resurrection of Charles R. Drew* (1996).

Wynes, Charles E. *Charles Richard Drew: The Man and the Myth* (1988).

Yancey, Asa, Sr. "U.S. Postage Stamp in Honor of Charles R. Drew, M.D., MDSc.," *Journal of the National Medical Association* 74, no. 6 (1982): 561–565.

Obituaries: *Journal of the National Medical Association* 42, no. 4 (July 1950): 239–246; *The Crisis* (Oct. 1951): 501–507, 555.

This entry is taken from the *American National Biography* and is published here with the permission of the American Council of Learned Societies.

SPENCIE LOVE

Drew, Howard Porter (28 June 1890–19 Feb. 1957), track and field athlete, was born in Lexington, Virginia, the son of David Henry Drew and May E. Mackey. At age twenty-one, after working for several years in a railroad depot, he entered high school in Springfield, Massachusetts. By the time Drew entered high school he ranked high among the nation's best sprinters. In 1910 and 1911 he won both the 100- and 220-yard dashes at the junior Amateur Athletic Union (AAU) track and field championships. Drew's best times as a junior were 10.0 seconds for 100 yards and 21.8 seconds for 220 yards.

In 1912 Drew competed in the senior AAU track and field championships and captured the 100-yard dash in ten seconds flat. In the 1912 U.S. Olympic trials the Springfield High School sophomore defeated the nation's top collegiate sprinter, Ralph Craig of the University of Michigan, in the one-hundred meters. After winning two qualifying heats of the one hundred meters in the 1912 Olympics at Stockholm, Sweden, Drew pulled a muscle in the semifinal and was unable to compete in the final, won by Craig.

Although never achieving Olympic success, Drew enjoyed an outstanding track career, winning national championships and setting world records at several distances from 50 to 220 yards. After the 1912 Olympic Games he set indoor world records of 5.4 seconds for 50 yards, 6.4 seconds for 60 yards, 7.2 seconds for 70 yards, and 10.2 seconds for 100 meters. In 1913 Drew defended his AAU senior title in the 100-yard dash and won the 220-yard dash as well. That same year he set world records of 7.6 seconds for 75 yards, 9.2 seconds for 90 yards, 11.6 seconds for 120 yards, 12.8 seconds for 130 yards, and 21.2 seconds for 220 yards. In 1914 he equaled the world record of 9.6 seconds in the 100-yard dash.

In addition to his track successes Drew graduated from Springfield High School in 1913 and married Ethel Hawkins; they had two children. He then attended Lincoln University in Pennsylvania for one year before transferring to the University of Southern California (USC) in Los Angeles, where he graduated in 1916. At USC he competed on the track team, served as the assistant manager of athletics, and edited sports for the college newspaper. In 1916 Drew entered Drake University in Des Moines, Iowa, and in 1920 he graduated with a law degree. That same year, at the age of thirty, Drew attempted but failed to qualify for the U.S. Olympic team.

A member of the Connecticut and Ohio bar associations, Drew became the first African American to become the assistant clerk of the city court of Hartford, Connecticut, in 1943. He died in West Haven, Connecticut, after a protracted illness.

Drew was the first of a long line of African American sprinters to earn the title of "world's fastest human." His performances astounded sportswriters and led Michael Murphy, the track coach of the U.S. Olympic Team and the University of Pennsylvania, to comment that he had never "seen any sprinter with such wonderful leg action, his legs fly back and forth just like pistons." Murphy, as well as other track and field coaches, thought that Drew might have had the quickest start of any sprinter of that time. Charles Paddock, the 1920 Olympic gold medalist in the 100 meters, remembered Drew as being "the smoothest piece of running machinery the world had ever seen." His record of 9.6 seconds in the 100-yard dash stood until 1929, when Eddie Tolan lowered it to 9.5 seconds. His record of 21.2 seconds in the 220-yard dash stood until 1921, when Paddock lowered it to 20.8 seconds.

FURTHER READING

Ashe, Arthur. *A Hard Road to Glory: A History of the African-American Athlete, 1619–1918* (1988).
Menke, Frank G.*The Encyclopedia of Sports*, 4th rev. ed. (1969).
Obituary: *New York Times*, 22 Feb. 1957.

This entry is taken from the *American National Biography* and is published here with the permission of the American Council of Learned Societies.

ADAM R. HORNBUCKLE

Drew, Timothy. *See* Ali, Noble Drew.

Drewry, Elizabeth Simpson (1893–24 Sept. 1979), educator and the first African American woman elected to the West Virginia State Legislature, was born in Motley, Virginia, the eldest of eleven children of Katherine Douglass, a housewife, and H. Grant Simpson, a barber. The Simpsons were among the first wave of blacks to move north during the Great Migration. Hoping to take advantage of the growing coal mining industry, the family settled in Elkhorn, a small coal mining town in McDowell County in southern West Virginia. They were a part of the expanding black middle class of the late nineteenth and early twentieth centuries that adhered to a philosophy of personal advancement and racial uplift. With an increase in the number of blacks working in the coal mines in West Virginia came an increase in black businesses and other professions. Grant Simpson was the owner of a barbershop that catered to both blacks and whites. Although this was unusual at the time, he was regarded as a man in good standing among coal company operators and he was the personal barber of John Lincoln, general manger of the Crozer, Upland, and Page Coal & Coke Companies in Elkhorn.

Little is known about Drewry's childhood. However, she was educated in McDowell County and received normal school training. Before she was twenty years old, Drewry had become a wife and a mother. She married William Drewery in 1906—for unknown reasons, she made a distinction in the spelling of their last name—and their daughter, Lucille, was born in 1908. Both she and her husband were public school teachers. Scant information is available concerning Drewry's husband, but he was an itinerant teacher and elementary school principal, and was regarded as an early pioneer of black education in McDowell County. For reasons unclear, he eventually moved to Chicago, where he remained until his death in 1950. Silent about her marriage and despite the odds against her, Drewry supported herself and her daughter through teaching and renting rooms in her home to boarders.

Although a normal school education was legally sufficient to teach elementary school, Drewry went on to enroll at Bluefield Collegiate Institute and graduated in 1934 with a B.S. in Elementary Education. She was a hardworking, self-sufficient woman who loved teaching and regarded it as a special opportunity to mold and shape the minds and boost the confidence of black children.

Drewry soon became dissatisfied with the plight of teachers and working people. She identified three sources of conflict that resulted in the demands of African Americans going virtually unheard: conservatism in the American intellectual community, America's economic objectives, and America's political procedures, none of which, according to Drewry, adequately addressed the needs of blacks. She decided to run for political office to push for needed change.

Drewry first campaigned for and won a seat on the city council of Clark in 1923. Later, when she moved to Northfork, she eventually held a seat on the Northfork town council. Like most blacks during the early twentieth century, Drewry was a strong supporter of the Republican Party. By the end of World War II and after the "party of Lincoln" had begun to lose its broad appeal among African Americans, she was one of a number of blacks who became disillusioned. Switching to the Democratic Party, she chose to wage her own fight against inequity by running for the West Virginia House of Delegates in 1946 and again in 1948. She lost both times, but the results of the 1948 primary were highly controversial. The primary had been marked by a bitter fight between pro-labor candidates endorsed by the United Mine Workers Union (UMW) and the anti-union candidates. In the final vote, Drewry, who was also pro-labor, won fifth place on the general election ticket. However, the sixth-place candidate demanded a recount that credited him with thirty-two votes more than

Drewry in the final outcome. Outraged, she petitioned the McDowell County Court, alleging fraud and misconduct. *The Welch Daily News* revealed that district authorities had explained that official district tabulators had mistakenly recorded the thirty-two votes in Drewry's favor when transferring figures from the poll tally sheet to the official tally sheet. As a result, both the County and Circuit Courts refused to hear her case.

By the 1950 election, Drewry was better prepared. Canvassing from door-to-door and with the support of a black constituency, the NAACP, and the UMW, Drewry won the election and made history by becoming the first African American woman elected to the West Virginia State Legislature. News of her victory was featured in both the *Chicago Defender* and *Ebony* magazine. She never lost another election.

During the early weeks of her victory, Drewry was approached in the capitol building by I. J. K. Wells, State Superintendent of Negro Education. She revealed to House leaders that Wells had given her a handwritten note, offering her $1,000 or a trip to Europe if she would help to pass controversial Bill #105, known as the "Fire Boss Bill." Strongly supported by coal operators, but opposed by the UMW, the measure would allow mine foremen to conduct safety inspections in the state's coal mines. The UMW preferred that union members or outside agents serve as inspectors. Although it had been a long-standing practice, a State Supreme Court decision in December 1950 held that it was illegal for such inspections to be conducted by mine foremen.

Drewry immediately turned the note over to the appropriate authorities. Another McDowell County delegate supported her charge, claiming that he too had been offered $1,000 for a vote favorable to coal operators. Although Wells denied the charges, Drewry stood her ground, and the incident got significant attention from both the black and mainstream media.

The House of Delegates formed a special committee to investigate the charges. After extensive interrogations of eighteen subpoenaed witnesses, the committee concluded that the entire matter was a misunderstanding and ruled that Wells was not guilty. Wells maintained that the charges had been unfounded, were nothing more than a case of dirty politics. He also accused Drewry of having been coerced into making the accusation against him by House leaders. However, Drewry's record of unimpeachable honesty kept her in good standing with her constituents. With continued support from the miners in McDowell County, Drewry was reelected to the House for eight consecutive terms, in spite of the fact that her opponents were consistently white men.

Pledging to support working people, Drewry actively advocated on the behalf of teachers, wage workers, and women. As a member of the House of Delegates, she supported legislation to prevent age discrimination in hiring, crusaded for silicosis (black lung) compensation benefits, and fought for higher pay and increased retirement benefits for teachers. Drewry's 1955 argument that—since they were taxpayers and voters—there was no reason why women should not also be allowed to serve as jurors resulted in women being granted the right to serve on juries throughout the state. She also vigorously supported the Fair Employment Practices Bill, pushing for laws to bar racial discrimination in employment.

Although little has been documented about the history of black women in West Virginia, Elizabeth Drewry was one of many black women in the state who, as Patricia Hill Collins stated in her book *Black Feminist Thought*, established a tradition of activism based on either a struggle for group survival or institutional change. In 1966 a stroke forced Drewry to relinquish her seat in the House. After spending some time in rehabilitation, she returned to her home in Northfork but continued to decline in health and died in 1979.

FURTHER READING

Elizabeth Drewry's papers are housed in the Eastern Regional Coal Archives, Craft Memorial Library in Bluefield, West Virginia.

Collins, Patricia Hill. *Black Feminist Thought: Knowledge Consciousness and the Politics of Empowerment* (1991).

Eller, Ronald D. *Miners, Millhands, and Mountaineers: Industrialization of the Appalachian South, 1880–1930* (1982).

Trotter, Joe William, Jr. *Coal, Class, and Color: Blacks in Southern West Virginia, 1915–32* (1990).

Weiss, Nancy J. *Farewell to the Party of Lincoln: Black Politics in the Age of FDR* (1983).

Williams, John Alexander. *West Virginia, A History* (2001).

M. LOIS LUCAS

Drexler, Clyde A. (22 June 1962–), professional basketball player, was born in New Orleans, Louisiana, the son of Eunice Drexler Scott and James Drexler.

Clyde Drexler scores during the NCAA play-off between Houston and Louisville in Albuquerque, New Mexico, 3 April 1983. (AP Images.)

Eunice left James when Clyde was three years old and moved to Houston, Texas. There, Eunice met her second husband, Manuel Scott. Eunice and Manuel worked at Rice Food Market in South Park. They were married for thirteen years. Drexler completed high school at Ross Sterling High School in Houston, Texas, graduating in 1980. In ninth grade Clyde was five foot eight and just an average basketball player. Clyde has said he was much more focused on academics and working at the family restaurant, run by his uncle, Thomas Prevost. Going into tenth grade Clyde had grown to six foot two and finally began to dunk the basketball. Drexler made the varsity basketball team as a senior in high school and soon received tremendous attention from college recruiters. During a Christmas tournament in 1979 he scored thirty-four points and grabbed twenty-seven rebounds against Sharpstown High School. The University of Houston recruited Drexler, and he started his college career as a basketball player in 1980; he majored in finance. Drexler played as a forward in college and led the team to the NCAA Final Four twice, both in 1982 and 1983. While at college Drexler received his nickname, "The Glide," for his seemingly effortless play and athleticism on the court. The nickname followed him throughout his basketball career. In his junior season with the University of Houston, Drexler averaged 15.9 points, 8.8 rebounds, and 3.8 assists while shooting over 50 percent from the floor. Drexel teamed with the future National Basketball Association (NBA) greats Hakeem Olajuwon and Larry Micheaux while at the University of Houston. Drexler left the University of Houston in 1983 to enter the NBA draft. Drexler was selected in the first round as the fourteenth overall pick in the 1983 NBA draft by the Portland Trail Blazers.

In his rookie year, 1983–1984, Drexler did not make a tremendous impact, nor did he make the All-Rookie Team. Drexler averaged 7.7 points per game as a rookie and saw only 17 minutes of playing time per game playing as a shooting guard for the Trail Blazers. In his second season, 1984–1985, his scoring jumped to 17.2 points per game. By Drexler's third year, 1985–1986, he had become an NBA All-Star, averaging 18.5 points and ranking third in the NBA in steals and tenth in assists. Over the next several years Drexler continued to bring his game to new levels. During the 1988–89 season Drexler's scoring average was 27.2 points, which was a Portland record; he was voted Portland's most valuable player by his teammates. In 1988 Drexler also married his wife, Gaynell Floyd, on 30 December. He has four children: Erica, Austin, Elise, and Adam (the last three with Gaynell).

During the 1991–92 season, Drexler earned All-NBA First Team and made the United States Olympic Basketball team. As Drexler's game improved, he led the Trail Blazers to two NBA championship series, one in 1990 and the other in 1992. However, Drexler was not able to win an NBA championship with the Trail Blazers. In 1995 Drexler requested to be traded to a NBA championship-contending team, and his request was granted. Drexler joined the Houston Rockets midseason and was reunited with his college teammate Hakeem Olajuwon. In 1995 the Rockets won the NBA championship, sweeping the Orlando Magic for the title. This was Drexler's third NBA finals appearance.

Drexler received many accolades over his career; he was a ten-time NBA All-Star (1986, 1988–1994, 1996, 1997). He made All-NBA First Team (1992), he made All-NBA Second Team (1988, 1991), he made All-NBA Third Team (1990,

1995), and he was an Olympic Gold Medalist (1992). Drexler was named one of the 50 Greatest Players in NBA History in 1996. In 1998 Drexler retired and took over head coaching duties at his alma mater, the University of Houston, where he coached for two years (1998–2000). Drexler ended his memorable NBA career joining OSCAR ROBERTSON and John Havlicek as the only players in NBA history to top 20,000 points, 6,000 rebounds, and 3,000 assists. In 2001 Drexler was inducted into the Oregon Sports Hall of Fame as well as the Naismith Memorial Basketball Hall of Fame in 2004. Considered one of the game's all-time greatest guards, Drexler currently ranks 22nd in NBA history with 22,195 career points and ninth with 2,207 career steals.

Drexler is the subject of the book *Clyde Drexler: Clyde the Glide*, by Kerry Eggers. He also wrote the introduction to the children's book *Shrews Can't Hoop* (1995).

FURTHER READING

Drexler, C., and Eggers, K. *Clyde Drexler: Clyde the Glide* (2004).

Moran, M. "N.C.A.A. Final Matches Ball-Control against Power." *The New York Times*, 4 Apr. 1983.

SHEENA C. HOWARD

Driskell, David (7 June 1931–), artist, art historian, curator, and educator, was born David Clyde Driskell in Eatonton, Georgia, the youngest of four children and the only son of George W. Driskell, a Baptist minister, and Mary L. Clyde Driskell. When Driskell was five years old, his family moved to Polkville, North Carolina, a community located in the Appalachian Mountains. He attended Rutherford County public schools and graduated from Grahamtown High School in 1949. He began his matriculation at Howard University in 1950 where he joined the Reserve Officers' Training Corps. He married Thelma G. DeLoatch on 9 January 1952, and had two daughters. In 1953 he began studying at the Skowhegan School of Painting and Sculpture, located in Skowhegan, Maine. After he graduated from Howard with a B.A. in Art in 1955 Driskell was commissioned a second lieutenant in the U.S. Army, later being promoted to first lieutenant. Driskell began his career as an educator in 1955 when he accepted a position as assistant professor of art at Talladega College. As early as 1956, Driskell began exhibiting his artwork, which included paintings, collages, prints, drawings, and sculptures. He remained in the Army Reserves until 1965. In 1962, he received a master of fine arts degree from Catholic University of America, and in 1964 completed postgraduate work at the Netherlands Institute for the History of Art in The Hague. After leaving Talladega in 1962, he became an associate professor of art at his alma mater, Howard University, from 1962 to 1966, and then professor of art and chair of the Department of Art at Fisk University from 1966 to 1977. At Fisk, Driskell founded the Aaron Douglass Gallery in honor of the Harlem Renaissance artist and former chair of the Art Department. He then became chair of the department of art at the University of Maryland, College Park in 1977 as well as professor of art in that department. In 1981 he received the Distinguished Alumni Award in Art from Howard University.

Driskell was recognized as a national and international authority on African American art, has curated more than forty African American art exhibitions, published articles in various periodicals, and written books for various exhibitions including *Two Centuries of Black American Art* (1976), *Hidden Heritage: Afro-American Art 1800–1950* (1985), *Contemporary Visual Expressions* (1987), *Harlem Renaissance: Art of Black America* (1987). In addition, Driskell is the author of *The Other Side of Color: African American Art in the Collection of Camille O. and William H. Cosby, Jr.* (1991), which is a result of Driskell's dual roles as cultural adviser and curator of the Cosby Collection of Fine Arts since 1977. In 1995 Driskill wrote the exhibition book for *African American Visual Aesthetics: A Postmodernist View*. Driskell also selected the works of African American artists that were used on the set of the television series *The Cosby Show*. He was named Distinguished Professor in Art at the University of Maryland in 1995. In 1995 President William J. Clinton and First Lady Hillary Clinton asked Driskell to select an African American artwork for the White House. His choice, Henry Tanner's painting *Sand Dunes at Sunset: Atlantic City* was installed there on 29 October 1996. Also in 1996, at the DeForest Chapel at Talladega College, sixty-five stained glass windows that Driskell created were installed. That same year he was awarded both the National Art Education Association's Annual Award and the Distinguished Alumni Award in Art from the Catholic University of America. Two years later, *Narratives of African American Art and Identity: The David C. Driskell Collection* was published for the traveling exhibit that began at the University of Maryland, College Park, in October 1998 and was displayed at museums in Maine, California, and Georgia, before ending in New Jersey in 2001. The exhibition contained one hundred pieces from Driskell's eminent collection of nineteenth- and twentieth-century African American art that he began acquiring in 1954. In 1997 he won the President's Medal from the University of Maryland, College Park. Driskell was appointed professor emeritus in 1998, the same year the University of Maryland created the David C. Driskell Center for the Study of the Visual Arts and Culture of African Americans and the African Diaspora in recognition of his contributions to society as artist, scholar, educator, and collector. He also has served as visiting professor of art at Bowdoin College, the University of Michigan, Queens College, and Obafemi Awolowo University in Nigeria. In December of 2000 Driskell was awarded the National Humanities Medal, which was presented to him by President Clinton.

Driskell served as a member of advisory boards and committees as well as a member of boards of directors, governors, or trustees for a variety of organizations such as the Association of International Art Critics, Maine College of Art; Colby College Museum; WETA-TV's African American Art Program; Bronx Museum of Art; Lincoln University; American Federation of the Arts; Amistad Research Center; the Skowhegan School of Painting and Sculpture; College Art Association of America; Duke Ellington School of Arts; and National Endowment for the Arts. Driskell was a member of the Smithsonian's African American Museum Initiative, and he served as the chair of the commission for the Smithsonian's National Museum of African Art. He eventually became president of the Clara Elizabeth Jackson Carter Foundation.

His work has been exhibited at the American Academy of Arts and Letters, the Baltimore Museum of Art, Bomani Gallery, Corcoran Gallery of Art, Midtown Payson Galleries, Smithsonian Institution, Studio Museum of Harlem, Southern University, the White House, as well as at many other galleries and institutions. Among Driskell's additional accolades are honorary doctorates from at least nine colleges and universities. He also received citations from a variety of museums, cities, counties, and states.

FURTHER READING

McGee, Julie L. *David C. Driskell: Artist and Scholar* (2006).

Smith, Jessie Carney, ed. "David C. Driskell," in *Notable Black American Men* (1999).

LINDA M. CARTER

Drumgoold, Kate (Aug. 1858–after 1900), author and teacher, was born into slavery near Petersburg, Virginia. According to her narrative, which remains the source of most of her biographical information, Drumgoold lived with her mother and sisters until her mother was sold south in 1861. Cared for by her mistress Bettie House—whom she referred to as her "white mother"—for three years, Drumgoold was reunited with her real mother near the end of the Civil War. In 1865 the family moved to Brooklyn, New York, where they joined the Reverend David Moore's Washington Avenue Baptist Church. Drumgoold, already working as a domestic, was baptized in 1866. Through the church, she gained basic literacy skills, and through work with a kind boardinghouse keeper, Lydia A. Pousland, as well as summer work in Saratoga Springs, she attained some level of economic security. Still, her domestic work was repeatedly interrupted by illness, and she felt a growing desire for further education.

After recovering from an extended bout with smallpox, Drumgoold moved to Washington, D.C., in 1875 to attend Wayland Seminary, which she was able to attend through the financial support of her Washington Avenue Church. After almost four years at Wayland, she began teaching in rural Virginia and West Virginia. Apart from what seems to have been a brief return to Brooklyn in about 1880, she continued teaching until at least 1888—some of it in Harpers Ferry and some in Hinton, West Virginia—though her teaching was sometimes interrupted by illness. She gave a public speech—probably tied to black education—in Talcott, West Virginia, in 1888; some members in her audience reportedly encouraged her to consider writing her autobiography.

Drumgoold moved back to Brooklyn in October of 1895, probably in large part because of family ties. She mentioned having siblings living in the Brooklyn area, and her mother continued to live in there until her death on 28 February 1898.

Drumgoold wrote *A Slave Girl's Story* between 1896 and 1898 and self-published it, probably with aid from friends, in 1898. Undoubtedly, some of Drumgoold's reasons for writing her narrative were economic; the narrative thus repeatedly praises Drumgoold's various white employers. Like many of the slave narratives of the 1890s, it offers a message of racial uplift, faith, and education. At times it is fairly unfocused, and so has received only limited attention from critics, most of whom concentrate on the separation and reunification of Drumgoold's family and Drumgoold's representations of her birth mother and her "white mother." Nonetheless, her story offers a rare portrait of a former slave who moved between the highly urbanized environment of New York City and the rural South. Drumgoold seems to have turned again to domestic work during this period; however, she is listed in the 1900 federal census of Brooklyn as a teacher; she lived in the same building as her widowed, elder sister Ella S. Rodwell, who worked as a laundress and domestic. She seems to have attended the Hanson Place Methodist Episcopal Church during this period, but no record has surfaced of Drumgoold after 1900. Neither she nor her sister Ella appeared in the 1910 or 1920 census.

FURTHER READING

Drumgoold, Kate. *A Slave Girl's Story* (1898).
Andrews, William L., ed. *Six Women's Slave Narratives* (1988).
Fleischner, Jennifer. *Mastering Slavery: Memory, Family, and Identity in Women's Slave Narratives* (1996).
Gwin, Minrose C. *Black and White Women of the Old South: The Peculiar Sisterhood in American Literature* (1985).

ERIC GARDNER

Dryden, Charles Walter (16 Sept. 1920–24 June 2008), member of the famed Tuskegee Airmen, was born in the Bronx, New York City, the son of Charles Levy Tucker Dryden, a World War I veteran and teacher, and Violet Adina Buckley, also a teacher. Dryden was raised in a loving, disciplined home among a large extended family. He was taught, he wrote in his 1997 autobiography, to "love and serve God, obey your parents, be loyal to your family, and get a good education"—in that order (7). But what Dryden most wanted to do, from a very early age, was fly.

As a two-year-old, Dryden tore strips of paper, threw them in the air, and shouted "Air'pwane! Air'pwane!" He built meticulously detailed model airplanes and read aviation pulp magazines as a youth. Like others of his generation he idolized Charles Lindbergh and the other aviation heroes of the 1920s and 1930s. "Everyone on the block," Dryden later wrote, "knew about the crazy Black kid who wanted to fly" (Dryden, 10). Fortunately, he was unaware at the time that careers as pilots with the U.S. Army Air Corps and all major American airlines were unavailable to African Americans.

After graduating from Peter Stuyvesant High School in Manhattan, Dryden enrolled in the City College of New York's School of Mechanical Engineering. Dryden was one of two African Americans accepted into the school's Civilian Pilot Training Program (CPT) in 1940, and earned his civilian pilot's license later that year. He immediately attempted to enlist in the U.S. Army Air Corps as a pilot cadet, but a recruiting sergeant told him flatly, "The United States Army is not training any Colored pilots, so I can't give you an application" (Dryden, 22). When an intensive lobbying effort on the part of civil rights organizations, black newspapers, and historically black colleges forced the Army Air Corps to create an experimental program to train pilots for an African American flying squadron, Dryden re-applied for aviation training, and this time was accepted.

In August 1941 Dryden and ten others entered the class of 42-D at Tuskegee, Alabama, the site of the Air Corps' training facility for African American pilots. One class of thirteen cadets, among them Capt. BENJAMIN O. DAVIS JR., a West Point graduate, had preceded them. Dryden's class of cadets began their primary flight training at Moton Field, a basic facility operated under contract for the Air Corps by Tuskegee Institute, and lived on the institute's campus. Of the original eleven cadets in 42-D only Dryden, Sidney P. Brooks, and Clarence C. Jamison graduated from basic and advanced training at the nearby Tuskegee Army Air Field in April 1942. They were commissioned second lieutenants in the 99th Fighter Squadron. In 1943 Dryden married Irma "Pete" Cameron, a nurse at Tuskegee Army Air Field; they would have three children before divorcing in 1975.

Having trained competent black pilots, the Army Air Corps clearly had no idea what to do with them. By August 1942 the 99th had its full complement of pilots, but the leaders of the Air Corps left them with little to do other than to practice their combat skills against one another in the skies over Alabama. The 99th would not deploy for overseas combat until April 1943. The squadron, now under the command of Col. Benjamin O. Davis Jr., joined the war in the North African theater, and on 9 June 1943 Dryden, along with five other pilots of the 99th, encountered the *Luftwaffe* for the first time at the island of Pantelleria off the coast of Sicily. (Dryden flew a P-40 he had named "A-Train" after the popular DUKE ELLINGTON song, "Take the A-Train.") "Up until that very moment I had harbored a fear deep within myself," Dryden wrote (126). The pilots of the 99th did not shoot down any German planes on that day, but they did acquit themselves well. Dryden was relieved to learn that he could overcome "my fear of possibly turning yellow and turning tail at the first sign of the enemy." The pilots of the 99th had the hopes of millions of black Americans flying with them. What Dryden and his comrades truly feared was letting them down.

Tuskegee Army Flying School continued to graduate pilots, and the Air Corps began to form an all-black fighter group. In addition to the 99th, the Air Corps created the 100th, 301st, and 302nd Fighter Squadrons (which collectively made up the 332nd Fighter Group), and the 477th Medium Bombardment Group, an all-black B-25 outfit. In September 1943 Dryden and four other veterans of the 99th, now stationed in Italy, learned that they would join Col. Davis at Selfridge Field in Michigan to train the pilots of the 332nd in aerial combat tactics. Dryden would fight his most important wartime battles on American soil.

Col. William L. Boyd, commanding officer of Selfridge Field, had declared Lufberry Hall, the base's officers club, off-limits to African American officers—in defiance of army regulations extending to officers of all races the rights of full membership to such facilities. Officers of the 477th and 332nd—some of whom, like Dryden, were combat veterans—attempted to use the facility and were threatened with court-martial. Rather than trying the officers, however, Boyd closed the club. Major General Frank O'D. Hunter, commanding general of the First Army Air Force, told the men at Selfridge that they were not ready to fly airplanes in combat and could not expect to be treated as whites' equals for 200 years (172). Dryden's unit, by now suffering severe morale problems, soon transferred to what Dryden called "Godforsaken Walterboro Army Air Base in the piney woods of South Carolina." Walterboro's base commander ensured the pilots that they would be expected to abide by local customs of racial segregation.

Dryden reached his breaking point when he saw German prisoners of war entering the "whites only" side of the base facilities, while black officers and enlisted men were cordoned off into their own sections. He responded to the humiliation by "buzzing" the air base and the town of Walterboro. On a sleepy Sunday morning Dryden led a training flight through the town of Walterboro and past the base tower "on the deck doing 250 knots" (at extremely low altitude, traveling close to 300 miles per hour). The effect on the townspeople of Walterboro was predictable, and Dryden was court-martialed. His initial sentence was dismissal from the service, but the sentence was overturned on appeal. Dryden was finally suspended from promotion eligibility, fined, and restricted to base for three months, but he was allowed to continue his career in the Army Air Corps.

That career, somewhat to Dryden's surprise, survived the end of World War II. He was assigned as an executive officer to commanding officer Col. Benjamin O. Davis Jr. at Lockbourne Air Base near Columbus, Ohio, from February 1946 to June 1949. Lockbourne was a nearly all-black facility; the men stationed there formed what was by all accounts an unusually tight camaraderie, and the African American community of Columbus proved hospitable to them. Under Davis's leadership, moreover, the pilots of Lockbourne proved that they could compete with the very best in the Air Force, winning the service's first "Top Gun" gunnery competition in 1949. In 1948, however, President Harry Truman's Executive Order No. 9981 desegregated the armed services, and the men of Lockbourne were eventually scattered to the four winds. Dryden relished the opportunity to prove himself in what was now supposed to be a colorblind Air Force, but made no secret of his bittersweet feelings upon leaving the base he called "Camelot."

Dryden remained in the Air Force until 1962; he retired as a lieutenant colonel. He married Marymal (maiden name unknown) Dryden in 1977. In the mid-1970s, Dryden joined Tuskegee Airmen, Inc. (TAI), a non-profit organization of Tuskegee veterans, and became an indefatigable public speaker. Dryden and other members of TAI raised money for college scholarships, introduced young African Americans to careers in aviation, and preserved the historical legacy of the Tuskegee Airmen. Dryden personally educated thousands of Americans about the conditions he and his comrades had faced while serving their country in World War II, leaving audiences and readers with the questions, "Who was my worst enemy, really? Was it the fascist abroad or the racist at home?" His life an illustration of the contradictions of America, Dryden died in 2008 at the age of 87.

FURTHER READING

An oral history interview with Dryden is housed in the archives of the National Park Service's Tuskegee Airmen Oral History Project, in Tuskegee, Alabama.

Dryden, Charles W. *A-Train: Memoirs of a Tuskegee Airman* (1997).

Scott, Lawrence P., and William Womack Sr. *Double V: The Civil Rights Struggle of the Tuskegee Airmen* (1992).

Obituary: *Los Angeles Times*, 25 July 2008.

J. TODD MOYE

DuBois, Nina Yolande (21 Oct. 1900–Mar. 1961) school teacher, was born in Great Barrington, Massachusetts, the second child and only daughter of the intellectual, activist, and editor, W. E. B. DuBois, and Nina Gomer DuBois. She was born at the home of her father's uncle, James Burghardt, while her already famous father was on his way home from the first Pan-African Conference in London.

Nina Yolande DuBois spent her infant years in Atlanta, where her father was a professor at Atlanta University, and her parents came to loathe the city for the pervasive and virulent racism taking an unprecedented grip on daily life. During the 1906 Atlanta Riot, in which whites destroyed black property and killed several African Americans, her father rushed home from New York. W. E. B DuBois sat with a shotgun on the steps of South Hall, where the family lived, protecting Yolande and her mother.

Nina Yolande DuBois in a June 1927 photo. (University of Massachusetts, Amherst.)

In 1911, mother and daughter joined her father in New York, where W. E. B. DuBois had accepted a position the previous year as director of publicity and research, and editor of the magazine, *The Crisis*, for the National Association for the Advancement of Colored People. In 1914 she was sent, on her father's initiative, to the Bedales School in Hampshire, England, an experimental coeducational country boarding school with a college preparatory curriculum. The British Labour Party leader Ramsay McDonald gave Yolande a recommendation to the school, where his own sons were enrolled. The young DuBois did not respond well to the school, academically or socially, despite her father's exhortations; her mother wrote, "I presume, though she wouldn't acknowledge it, that she's beginning to feel she's colored" (in Lewis, 1993, p. 458).

Graduated in 1920 from Girls' High School in Brooklyn, she missed the senior class prom, due to a vote of 43–11 by the senior class to restrict the event to "white girls," thereby excluding DuBois and three classmates. Entering her father's alma mater, Fisk University, she was elected president of the Decagynian Society, a female students' club. Fellow students observed that she was "like glue" with Jimmie Lunceford, the Fisk bandleader and athletic star with letters in baseball, football, basketball, and track, later an accomplished jazz band conductor. Her father discouraged the match, observing "Nothing is more disheartening and idiotic than to see two human beings without cultivated tastes, without trained abilities and without power to earn a living, locking themselves together and trying to live on love" (in Lewis, 2001, p. 108).

The two saw little of each other after leaving Fisk, but meeting DuBois and her daughter backstage at Baltimore's Royal Theater many years later, Lunceford tearfully observed that the girl fingering the keys of his saxophone "should have been mine" (in Lewis, 2001, p. 107). "Lunceford was Yolande's enduring passion" concludes Lewis, "the man about whom she would spend much of her life dreaming, wondering how different things could have been if they had married" (2001, p. 107). In 1924 she graduated from Fisk with an A.B. in Fine Arts.

DuBois was married 10 April 1928 to Countée P. Cullen, already a promising poet, published in *The Crisis*, at Salem Methodist Episcopal Church, where Cullen's foster father was pastor. The wedding was a huge social event, attended by 1500 guests in formal dress. The couple had known each other since 1923. After first meeting DuBois, Cullen wrote to a friend "she is not beautiful but one is drawn to her by some indefinable magnetism of refinement and soulful honesty" (Perry, p. 9). The couple spent most of the next two years in Paris, France, where DuBois divorced him in 1930, after he confessed to a sexual attraction for men.

Returning to the United States, DuBois began teaching art and English at Frederick Douglass High School in Baltimore. In September 1931, she married Arnett Williams, who had enrolled in a night school at Douglass after dropping out of Lincoln University in Pennsylvania. W. E. B. DuBois insisted that Williams return to Lincoln, providing funds to pay for his tuition. In October 1932, Nina gave birth to a daughter, Yolande DuBois Williams, nicknamed "Baby DuBois." With her new husband at Lincoln, DuBois moved in with her mother in New York (her father was teaching in Atlanta), beginning classes at Columbia University Teachers College, where she earned her masters degree.

In 1935, the Williamses reunited in Baltimore. Although her husband had graduated from Lincoln, and found work in the midst of the Depression, he drank a lot and physically abused his wife. In January 1936, Virginia Alexander, the DuBois family's physician, and her sister-in-law, the attorney SADIE TANNER MOSSELL ALEXANDER, intervened to convince Nina to leave her husband and divorce him. She did so. For the next three years, "Baby DuBois" lived with her grandmother Nina Gomer DuBois in New York, then with both her grandparents in Atlanta.

Nina Yolande DuBois continued to teach in Baltimore, but was troubled by her overweight condition and frequent illnesses. In 1939, W. E. B. DuBois and his wife moved to Baltimore, hiring the architect C. J. White to design a house on Montebello Terrace in Morgan Park. The neighborhood had been designed as a haven for middle-class African Americans, in an era of rigidly segregated housing. His daughter soon joined them. Years later, DuBois Williams recalled that "Granma made the whole thing work. Mama was the child, which I wasn't" (Wolters, Raymond. *DuBois and His Rivals*, p. 244). Shortly after Nina Gomer DuBois died in 1950, her husband sold the house and married Shirley Graham, moving to New York.

DuBois's teaching career in the Baltimore public schools lasted until her sudden death in 1961. She taught English and social studies, particularly history, and directed the drama club at Dunbar High School. Both Douglass and Dunbar were segregated schools, specifically for students considered to be "colored." A former student, Edmonia Yates, recalled DuBois as a ninth grade social studies teacher at Dunbar who enjoyed telling stories about her famous father. (Chalkley, Tom, "Circle Unbroken," *Baltimore City Paper*, 18 June 2003). Nina DuBois may well have been, as the historian David Levering Lewis described her, "outstandingly ordinary—a kind, plain woman of modest intellectual endowment" (*When Harlem Was in Vogue*, p. 201). But life in the shadow of as powerful and driven a man as her father cannot have been easy. Like other children of famous parents, the burden of expectations that were hard to meet undoubtedly took its toll.

Nina DuBois became a grandmother in 1957, with the birth of Arthur Edward McFarlane II, named after her daughter's husband. She died of a coronary attack in Baltimore as her father was preparing to move to Ghana.

FURTHER READING:

Lewis, David Levering. *W.E.B. DuBois: Biography of a Race, 1868–1919* (1993).

Lewis, David Levering. *W.E.B. DuBois: The Fight for Equality and the American Century, 1919–1963* (2001).

Perry, Margaret. *A Bio-Bibliography of Countée P. Cullen, 1903–1946* (1971).

CHARLES ROSENBERG

DuBois, Shirley Lola Graham (11 Nov. 1896–27 Mar. 1977), author, composer, playwright, and activist, was born Shirley Lola Graham in Evansville, Indiana, the daughter of David A. Graham, a minister in the African Methodist Episcopal Church, and Etta Bell Graham, a homemaker. Graham's father had read many novels to his daughter, including *Uncle Tom's Cabin, Les Misérables, Ben-Hur*, and *Quo Vadis?*, influencing her to become a voracious reader. His storytelling and commitment to intellectual pursuits strongly influenced Graham's literary development.

Young Graham's early education began in New Orleans, where her exposure to classic literature put her at an advantage over many of her classmates. When she was eight or nine years old, her family moved to Nashville, Tennessee, where she earned her first income writing for the local newspaper. In 1912 she attended Tenth Street High School in Clarksville, Tennessee, where she distinguished

Shirley Graham DuBois, 18 July 1946. In 1932, she became the first African American woman to write and produce an all-black opera, *Tom-Tom: An Epic of Music and the Negro.* (Library of Congress/Carl Van Vechten, photographer.)

herself as the class poet, and won an essay contest with a paper titled "BOOKER T. WASHINGTON." Her father's constant relocations resulted in the family's move to Spokane, Washington, where she graduated with honors from Lewis and Clark High School in 1915. In 1921 she married her first husband, Shadrach McCants, who worked for a newspaper and was also a tailor who owned a clothing store. They had two sons, Robert and David Graham, born in 1923 and 1925, respectively. However, the couple later divorced with the decree rendered in Portland, Oregon, in 1927. Graham began to compose songs, musical plays, and operas while at the Sorbonne in Paris, France, in 1929 where she studied music composition. In 1930, Graham returned to the United States and taught music at Morgan College in Baltimore, Maryland, for two years. She then entered Oberlin College in Ohio to complete her bachelor's degree. In 1932 she composed *Tom-Tom* for a school production at Oberlin College, which later developed into a highly acclaimed opera dramatizing the history of African Americans, set in Africa in the beginning, and ending in Harlem. In 1934, Graham earned a bachelor's degree in music from Oberlin and a M.A. in Music History in 1935. From 1935 to 1936, Graham taught music and arts at Agricultural and Industrial State College in Nashville. She won a Julius Rosenwald Fellowship in 1938 for creative writing and spent two years at the Yale School of Drama, where she wrote a three-act play, *Dust to Earth*. She also wrote other short plays that were produced by the Gilpin Players in Cleveland, Ohio, including *Coal Dust* (1938) and *I Gotta Home* (1939). During the same period she wrote a radio play, *Track Thirteen*, that was produced in 1940.

In addition to her teaching and writing, she served as supervisor of the Negro Unit of the Chicago Federal Theater from 1936 to 1938. During World War II, she was USO Director at Fort Huachuca in Arizona, and later became the NAACP's national field secretary and founding editor of *Freedomways* magazine, where she remained until 1963. Graham is also remembered for her marriage to W. E. B. DUBOIS. She met him when she was only thirteen years old after her father invited him to Colorado Springs, Colorado, to deliver a lecture; he was in his early fifties. As a young woman, she had admired his writings and faithfully tracked his career through the NAACP's magazine *The Crisis*, which he edited. While at Oberlin, Graham sent a draft of her thesis, "Survival of Africanisms in Modern Music," to W. E. B. for suggestions and comments and he returned it with favorable remarks. Through this medium, W. E. B. became Graham's literary mentor for various writing projects and their professional relationship blossomed into love. Shortly after the death of his first wife, the fifty-four-year-old Graham and eighty-four-year-old DuBois were married without publicity on 14 February 1951. The union was immediately complicated by her husband's indictment on 9 February 1951, from charges related to his peace activism and support for Communism. The federal government branded him as an agent of an unnamed foreign power—presumably the Soviet Union—and had him arrested. Upon his release, the two began traveling extensively and raising funds to support her husband's cause.

DuBois and her husband received considerable criticism for their involvement with the Communist Party during the 1950s, spurring their travel to Western and Eastern Europe, the Soviet Union, and China. The experience dramatically changed Shirley DuBois's political consciousness, and in 1962 she and her husband joined the Communist Party and moved to Accra, Ghana, on invitation from President Kwame Nkrumah. DuBois resigned her position as editor of *Freedomways* to accompany her husband and assist him in completing his epic writing project, the *Encyclopedia Africana*.

After her husband's death in 1963 at the age of ninety-five, DuBois wrote two books about her husband. She remained in Ghana, writing and sorting out details for many of his unfinished projects. In 1967, when Nkrumah was ousted from the presidency, DuBois was forced to leave Ghana and took up residence in Cairo for a few years. In 1971 she attempted to move to New York, but the Justice Department denied her a visa, claiming that she had been associated with more than thirty organizations on the U.S. attorney general's list of subversive groups. The government eventually relented and allowed her to visit the United States for two months. Stateless, she ended up in Beijing, China, where after several years she lost her battle with breast cancer and died in 1977 at the age of sixty-nine. Her influence was great even in China, where officials held a memorial service on 2 April 1977 at the Papaoshan Cemetery for Revolutionaries. DuBois was a controversial figure, yet she represented an important advocate for civil rights and employed her skills as an author, playwright, and composer to fight racial discrimination. DuBois was a prolific writer as well. She not only composed numerous plays and songs but also a number of popularized biographies including: *Dr. George Washington Carver Scientist* with George D. Lipscomb and Elton C. Fax (1944); *Paul Robeson Citizen of the World* [juvenile literature] (1946); *There Was Once a Slave: The Heroic Story of Frederick Douglass* (1947); *Your Most Humble Servant: The Story of Benjamin Banneker* (1949); *The Story of Phillis Wheatley* [juvenile literature] (1949); *The Story of Pocahontas* (1953); *Jean Baptiste Pointe Du Sable: Founder of Chicago* [juvenile literature] (1953); *Booker T. Washington: Educator of Hand, Head, and Heart* (1955); *His Day Is Marching On: A Memoir of W. E. B. DuBois* (1971); *Gamel Abdul Nasser, Son of Nile* (1974); *Julius K. Nyerere: Teacher of Africa in* (1975); and *The Zulu Heart* (1978).

FURTHER READING

DuBois, Shirley Graham. *DuBois: A Pictorial Biography* (1978).

DuBois, Shirley Graham. *His Day Is Marching On: A Memoir of W. E. B. DuBois* (1971).

Golus, Carrie. "Shirley Graham DuBois," *Contemporary Black Biography*, vol. 21 (1999).

Horne, Gerald. *Race Woman: The Lives of Shirley Graham DuBois* (2000)

VERNITTA BROTHERS TUCKER

DuBois, W. E. B. (23 Feb. 1868–27 Aug. 1963), scholar, writer, editor, and civil rights pioneer, was born William Edward Burghardt DuBois in Great Barrington, Massachusetts, the son of Mary Silvina Burghardt, a domestic worker, and Alfred DuBois, a barber and itinerant laborer. In later life DuBois made a close study of his family origins, weaving them rhetorically and conceptually—if not always accurately—into almost everything he wrote. Born in Haiti and descended from mixed race Bahamian slaves, Alfred DuBois enlisted during the Civil War as a private in a New York regiment of the Union army but appears to have deserted shortly afterward. He also deserted the family less than two years after his son's birth, leaving him to be reared by his mother and the extended Burghardt kin. Long resident in New England, the Burghardts descended from a freedman of Dutch slave origin who had fought briefly in the American Revolution. Under the care of his mother and her relatives, young Will DuBois spent his entire childhood in that small western Massachusetts town, where probably fewer than two-score of the four thousand inhabitants were African American. He received a classical, college preparatory education in Great Barrington's racially integrated high school, from whence, in June 1884, he became the first African American graduate. A precocious youth, DuBois not only excelled in his high school studies but also contributed numerous articles to two regional newspapers, the Springfield *Republican* and the black-owned New York *Globe*, then edited by T. THOMAS FORTUNE. In 1888 DuBois enrolled at Harvard as a junior. He received a B.A. cum laude, in 1890, an M.A. in 1891, and a Ph.D. in 1895. DuBois was strongly influenced by the new historical work of the German-trained Albert Bushnell Hart and the philosophical lectures of William James, both of whom became friends and professional mentors. Other intellectual influences came with his studies and travels between 1892 and 1894 in Germany, where he was enrolled at the Friedrich-Wilhelm III Universität (then commonly referred to as the University of Berlin but renamed the Humboldt University after World War II). Because of the expiration of the Slater Fund fellowship that supported

W. E. B. DuBois, 31 May 1919. DuBois was the first African American to earn a doctoral degree from Harvard University. Throughout his life he served as one of black America's leading intellectual voices. (Library of Congress/Cornelius M. Battey, photographer.)

his stay in Germany, DuBois could not meet the residency requirements that would have enabled him formally to stand for the degree in economics, despite his completion of the required doctoral thesis (on the history of southern U.S. agriculture) during his tenure. Returning to the United States in the summer of 1894, DuBois taught classics and modern languages for two years at Wilberforce University in Ohio. While there, he met Nina Gomer, a student at the college, whom he married in 1896 at her home in Cedar Rapids, Iowa. The couple had two children. By the end of his first year at Wilberforce, DuBois had completed his Harvard doctoral thesis, "The Suppression of the African Slave Trade to the United States of America, 1638–1870," which was published in 1896 as the inaugural volume of the Harvard Historical Studies series.

In high school DuBois came under the influence of and received mentorship from the principal, Frank Hosmer, who encouraged his extensive reading and solicited scholarship aid from local worthies that enabled DuBois to enroll at Fisk University in September 1885, six months after his mother's death. One of the best of the southern colleges for newly freed slaves founded after the Civil War, Fisk offered a continuation of his classical education and the strong influence of teachers who were heirs to New England and Western Reserve (Ohio) abolitionism. It also offered the northern-reared DuBois an introduction to southern American racism and African American culture. His later writings and thought were strongly marked, for example, by his experiences teaching school in the hills of eastern Tennessee during the summers of 1886 and 1887.

Although he had written his Berlin thesis in economic history, received his Harvard doctorate in history, and taught languages and literature at Wilberforce, DuBois made some of his most important early intellectual contributions to the emerging field of sociology. In 1896 he was invited by the University of Pennsylvania to conduct a study of the Seventh Ward in Philadelphia. There, after an estimated 835 hours of door-to-door interviews in 2,500 households, DuBois completed the monumental study, *The Philadelphia Negro* (1899). The Philadelphia study was both highly empirical and hortatory, a combination that prefigured much of the politically engaged scholarship that DuBois pursued in the years that followed and that reflected the two main strands of his intellectual engagement during this formative period: the scientific study of the so-called Negro Problem and the appropriate political responses to it. While completing his fieldwork in Philadelphia, DuBois delivered to the Academy of Political and Social Science in November 1896 an address, "The Study of the Negro Problem," a methodological manifesto on the purposes and appropriate methods for scholarly examination of the condition of black people. In March 1897, addressing the newly founded American Negro Academy in Washington, D.C., he outlined for his black intellectual colleagues, in "The Conservation of the Races," both a historical sociology and theory of race as a concept and a call to action in defense of African American culture and identity. During the following July and August he undertook for the U.S. Bureau of Labor the first of several studies of southern African American households, which was published as a bureau bulletin the following year under the title *The Negroes of Farmville, Virginia: A Social Study*. During that same summer, *Atlantic Monthly* published the essay "The Strivings of the Negro People," a slightly revised version of which later opened *The Souls of Black Folk* (1903).

Together these works frame DuBois's evolving conceptualization of, methodological approach to, and political values and commitments regarding the problem of race in America. His conceptions were historical and global, his methodology empirical and intuitive, his values and commitments involving both mobilization of an elite vanguard to address the issues of racism and the conscious cultivation of the values to be drawn from African American folk culture.

After the completion of the Philadelphia study in December 1897, DuBois began the first of two long tenures at Atlanta University, where he taught sociology and directed empirical studies—modeled loosely on his Philadelphia and Farmville work—of the social and economic conditions and cultural and institutional lives of southern African Americans. During this first tenure at Atlanta he also wrote two more books, *The Souls of Black Folk*, a collection of poignant essays on race, labor, and culture, and *John Brown* (1909), an impassioned interpretation of the life and martyrdom of the militant abolitionist. He also edited two short-lived magazines, *Moon* (1905–1906) and *Horizon* (1907–1910), which represented his earliest efforts to establish journals of intellectual and political opinion for a black readership.

With the publication of *Souls of Black Folk*, DuBois emerged as the most prominent spokesperson for the opposition to BOOKER T. WASHINGTON's policy of political conservatism and racial accommodation. Ironically, DuBois had kept a prudent distance from Washington's opponents and had made few overt statements in opposition to the so-called Wizard of Tuskegee. In fact, his career had involved a number of near-misses whereby he himself might have ended up teaching at Tuskegee. Having applied to Washington for a job shortly after returning from Berlin, he had to decline Tuskegee's superior monetary offer because he had already accepted a position at Wilberforce. On a number of other occasions Washington—sometimes prodded by Albert Bushnell Hart—sought to recruit DuBois to join him at Tuskegee, a courtship he continued at least until the summer of 1903, when DuBois taught summer school at Tuskegee. Early in his career, moreover, DuBois's views bore a superficial similarity to Washington's. In fact, he had praised Washington's 1895 "Atlanta Compromise" speech, which proposed to southern white elites a compromise wherein blacks would forswear political and civil rights in exchange for economic opportunities. Like many elite blacks at the time, DuBois was not averse to some form of franchise restriction, so long as it was based on educational qualifications and applied equally to white and black. DuBois had been charged with overseeing the African American Council's efforts to encourage black economic enterprise and worked with Washington's partisans in that effort. By his own account his overt rupture with Washington was sparked by the growing evidence of a conspiracy, emanating from Tuskegee, to dictate speech and opinion in all of black America and to crush any opposition to Washington's leadership. After the collapse of efforts to compromise their differences through a series of meetings in 1904, DuBois joined WILLIAM MONROE TROTTER and other Washington opponents to form the Niagara Movement, an organization militantly advocating full civil and political rights for African Americans.

Although it enjoyed some success in articulating an alternative vision of how black Americans should respond to the growing segregation and racial violence of the early twentieth century, the Niagara Movement was fatally hampered by lack of funds and the overt and covert opposition of Washington and his allies. Indeed, the vision and program of the movement were fully realized only with the founding of a new biracial organization, the National Association for the Advancement of Colored People (NAACP). The NAACP grew out of the agitation and a 1909 conference called to protest the deteriorating status of and escalating violence against black Americans. Racial rioting in August 1908 in Springfield, Illinois, the home of Abraham Lincoln, sparked widespread protest among blacks and liberal whites appalled at the apparent spread of southern violence and lynch law into northern cities. Although its officers made some initial efforts to maintain a détente with Booker T. Washington, the NAACP represented a clear opposition to his policy of accommodation and political quietism. It launched legal suits, legislative lobbying, and propaganda campaigns that embodied uncompromising, militant attacks on lynching, Jim Crow, and disfranchisement. In 1910 DuBois left Atlanta to join the NAACP as an officer, its only black board member, and to edit its monthly magazine, *The Crisis*.

As editor of *The Crisis* DuBois finally established the journal of opinion that had so long eluded him, one that could serve as a platform from which to reach a larger audience among African Americans and one that united the multiple strands of his life's work. In its monthly issues he rallied black support for NAACP policies and programs and excoriated white opposition to equal rights. But he also opened the journal to discussions of diverse subjects related to race relations and black cultural and social life, from black religion to new poetic works. The journal's cover displayed a rich visual imagery embodying the sheer diversity and breadth of the black presence in America. Thus the journal constituted, simultaneously, a forum for multiple expressions of and the coherent representation and enactment of black intellectual and cultural life. A mirror for and to black America, it inspired a black intelligentsia and its public.

From his vantage as an officer of the NAACP, DuBois also furthered another compelling intellectual and political interest, Pan-Africanism. He had attended the first conference on the global condition of peoples of African descent in London in 1900. Six other gatherings followed between 1911 and 1945, including the First Universal Races Congress in London in 1911, and Pan-African congresses held in Paris in 1919; London, Brussels, and Paris in 1921; London and Lisbon in 1923; New York City in 1927; and in Manchester, England, in 1945. Each conference focused in some fashion on the fate of African colonies in the postwar world, but the political agendas of the earliest meetings were often compromised by the ideological and political entanglements of the elite delegates chosen to represent the African colonies. The Jamaican black nationalist MARCUS GARVEY enjoyed greater success in mobilizing a mass base for his version of Pan-Africanism and posed a substantial ideological and political challenge to DuBois. Deeply suspicious of Garvey's extravagance and flamboyance, DuBois condemned his scheme to collect funds from African Americans to establish a shipping line that would aid their "return" to Africa, his militant advocacy of racial separatism, and his seeming alliance with the Ku Klux Klan. Although he played no role in the efforts to have Garvey jailed and eventually deported for mail fraud, DuBois was not sorry to see him go. (In 1945, however, DuBois joined Garvey's widow, AMY JACQUES GARVEY, and GEORGE PADMORE to sponsor the Manchester Pan-African conference that demanded African independence. DuBois cochaired the opening session of the conference with Garvey's first wife, AMY ASHWOOD GARVEY.)

The rupture in world history that was World War I and the vast social and political transformations of the decade that followed were reflected in DuBois's thought and program in other ways as well. During the war he had written "Close Ranks," a controversial editorial in *The Crisis* (July 1918), which urged African Americans to set aside their grievances for the moment and concentrate their energies on the war effort. In fact, DuBois and the NAACP fought for officer training and equal treatment for black troops throughout the war, led a silent protest march down Fifth Avenue in 1917 against racism, and in 1919 launched an investigation into charges of discrimination against black troops in Europe. Meanwhile, the unprecedented scope and brutality of the war itself stimulated changes in DuBois's evolving analyses of racial issues and phenomena. *Darkwater: Voices within the Veil* (1920) reflects many of these themes, including the role of African colonization and the fundamental role of the international recruitment and subjugation of labor in causing the war and in shaping its aftermath. His visit to Liberia in 1923 and the Soviet Union in 1926, his subsequent study of Marxism, his growing awareness of Freud, and the challenges posed by the Great Depression all brought him to question the NAACP's largely legalistic and propagandistic approach to fighting racism. In the early 1930s DuBois opened the pages of *The Crisis* to wide-ranging discussions of the utility of Marxian thought and of racially based economic cooperatives and other institutions in the fight against race prejudice. This led to increasing antagonism between him and his colleagues at the NAACP, especially the executive director WALTER WHITE, and to his resignation in June 1934.

DuBois accepted an appointment as chair of the sociology department at Atlanta University, where he had already been teaching as a visiting professor during the winter of 1934. There he founded and edited a new scholarly journal, *Phylon*, from 1940 to 1944. There, too, he published his most important historical work, *Black Reconstruction in America: An Essay toward a History of the Part Which Black Folk Played in the Attempt to Reconstruct Democracy in America, 1860–1880* (1935), and *Dusk of Dawn: An Essay toward an Autobiography of a Race Concept* (1940), his most engaging and poignant autobiographical essay since *Souls of Black Folk*. During this period DuBois continued to be an active lecturer and an interlocutor with young scholars and activists; he also deepened his studies of Marxism and traveled abroad. He sought unsuccessfully to enlist the aid of the Phelps-Stokes Fund in launching his long-dreamed-of project to prepare an encyclopedia of black peoples in Africa and the diaspora. By 1944, however, DuBois had lost an invaluable supporter and friend with the death of JOHN HOPE, the president of Atlanta University, leaving him vulnerable to dismissal following sharp disagreements with Hope's successor.

Far from acceding to a peaceful retirement, however, in 1944 DuBois (now seventy-six years old) accepted an invitation to return to the NAACP to serve in the newly created post of director of special research. Although the organization was still under the staff direction of DuBois's former antagonist, Walter White, the 1930s Depression and World War II had induced some modifications in the programs and tactics of the NAACP, perhaps in response to challenges raised by DuBois and other younger critics. It had begun to address the problems of labor as well as legal discrimination, and even the court strategy was becoming much more aggressive and economically targeted. In hiring DuBois, the board appears to have anticipated that other shifts in its approach would be necessary in the coming postwar era. Clearly it was DuBois's understanding that his return portended continued study of and agitation around the implications of the coming postwar settlement as it might affect black peoples in Africa and the diaspora, and that claims for the representation of African and African American interests in that settlement were to be pressed. He represented the NAACP in 1945 as a consultant to the U.S. delegation at the founding conference of the United Nations in San Francisco. In 1947 he prepared and presented to that organization *An Appeal to the World*, a ninety-four-page, militant protest against American racism as an international violation of human rights. During this period and in support of these activities he wrote two more books, *Color and Democracy: Colonies and Peace* (1945) and *The World and Africa: An Inquiry into the Part Which Africa Has Played in World History* (1947), each of which addressed some aspect of European and American responsibilities for justice in the colonial world.

As ever, DuBois learned from and was responsive to the events and developments of his time. Conflicts with the U.S. delegation to the United Nations (which included Eleanor Roosevelt, who was also a member of the NAACP board) and disillusionment with the evolving role of America as a postwar world power reinforced his growing radicalism and refusal to be confined to a safe domestic agenda. He became a supporter of the leftist Southern Negro Youth Congress at a time of rising hysteria about Communism and the onset of the cold war. In 1948 he was an active supporter of the Progressive Party and Henry Wallace's presidential bid. All of this put him at odds with Walter White and the NAACP board, who were drawn increasingly into collusion with the Harry S. Truman administration and into fierce opposition to any leftist associations. In 1948, after an inconclusive argument over assigning responsibility for a leak to the *New York Times* of a DuBois memorandum critical of the organization and its policies, he was forced out of the NAACP for a second time.

After leaving the NAACP, DuBois joined the Council on African Affairs, where he chaired the Africa Aid Committee and was active in supporting the early struggle of the African National Congress of South Africa against apartheid. The council had been organized in London in the late 1930s by MAX YERGAN and PAUL ROBESON to push decolonization and to educate the general public about that issue. In the postwar period it, too, became tainted by charges of Communist domination and lost many former supporters (including Yergan and RALPH BUNCHE); it dissolved altogether in 1955. Having linked the causes of decolonialization and antiracism to the fate of peace in a nuclear-armed world, DuBois helped organize the Cultural and Scientific Conference for World Peace in March 1949, was active in organizing its meetings in Paris and Mexico City later that year, and attended its Moscow conference that August. Subsequently this group founded the Peace Information Center in 1950, and DuBois was chosen to chair its Advisory Council. The center endorsed and promoted the Stockholm Peace Appeal, which called for banning atomic weapons, declaring their use a crime against humanity and demanding international controls. During this year DuBois, who actively opposed the Korean War and Truman's foreign policy more generally, accepted the nomination of New York's Progressive Party to run for the U.S. Senate on the platform "Peace and Civil Rights." Although he lost, his vote total ran considerably ahead of the other candidates on the Progressive ticket.

During the campaign, on 25 August 1950, the officers of the Peace Information Center were directed to register as "agents of a foreign principal" under terms of the Foreign Agents Registration Act of 1938. Their distribution of the Stockholm Appeal, alleged to be a Soviet-inspired manifesto, was the grounds for these charges, although the so-called foreign principal was never specifically identified in the subsequent indictment. Although the center disbanded on 12 October 1950, indictments against its officers, including DuBois, were handed down on 9 February 1951. DuBois's lawyers won a crucial postponement of the trial until the following 18 November 1951, by which time national and international opposition to the trial had been mobilized. Given the good fortune of a weak case and a fair judge, DuBois and his colleagues were acquitted. Meanwhile, following the death of his wife, Nina, in July 1950, DuBois married Shirley Graham, the daughter of an old friend, in 1951. Although the union bore no children, David, SHIRLEY LOLA GRAHAM DUBOIS's son from an earlier marriage, took DuBois's surname.

After the trial, DuBois continued to be active in the American Peace Crusade and received the International Peace Prize from the World Council of Peace in 1953. With Shirley, a militant leftist activist in her own right, he was drawn more deeply into leftist and Communist Party intellectual and social circles during the 1950s. He was an unrepentant supporter of and apologist for Joseph Stalin, arguing that though Stalin's methods might have been cruel, they were necessitated by unprincipled and implacable opposition from the West and by U.S. efforts to undermine the regime. He was also convinced that American news reports about Stalin and the Soviet bloc were unreliable at best and sheer propaganda or falsehoods at worst. His views do not appear to have been altered by the Soviets' own exposure and condemnation of Stalin after 1956.

From February 1952 to 1958 both W. E. B. and Shirley were denied passports to travel abroad. Thus he could not accept the many invitations to speak abroad or participate in international affairs, including most notably the 1957 independence celebrations of Ghana, the first of the newly independent African nations. When these restrictions were lifted in 1958, the couple traveled to the Soviet Union, Eastern Europe, and China. While in Moscow, DuBois was warmly received by Nikita Khrushchev, whom he strongly urged to promote the study of African civilization in Russia, a proposal that eventually led to the establishment in 1962 of the Institute for the Study of Africa. While there, he also received the Lenin Peace Prize.

But continued cold war tensions and their potential impact on his ability to travel and remain active in the future led DuBois to look favorably on an invitation in May 1961 from Kwame Nkrumah and the Ghana Academy of Sciences to move to Ghana and undertake direction of the preparation of an "Encyclopedia Africana," a project much like one he had long contemplated. Indeed, his passport had been rescinded again after his return from China (travel to that country was barred at the time), and it was only restored after intense lobbying by the Ghanaian government. Before leaving the United States for Ghana on 7 October 1961, DuBois officially joined the American Communist Party, declaring in his 1 October 1961 letter of application that it and socialism were the only viable hope for black liberation and world peace. His desire to travel and work freely also prompted his decision two years later to become a citizen of Ghana.

In some sense these actions brought full circle some of the key issues that had animated DuBois's life. Having organized his life's work around the comprehensive, empirically grounded study of what had once been called the Negro Problem, he ended his years laboring on an interdisciplinary and global publication that might have been the culmination and symbol of that ambition: to document the experience and historical contributions of African peoples in the world. Having witnessed the formal détente among European powers by which the African continent was colonized in the late nineteenth century, he lived to taste the fruits of the struggle to decolonize it in the late twentieth century and to become a citizen of the first new African nation. Having posed at the end of the nineteenth century the problem of black identity in the diaspora, he appeared to resolve the question in his own life by returning to Africa. Undoubtedly the most important modern African American intellectual, DuBois virtually invented modern African American letters and gave form to the consciousness animating the work of practically all other modern African American intellectuals to follow. He authored seventeen books, including five novels; founded and edited four different journals; and pursued two full-time careers: scholar and political organizer. But more than that, he reshaped how the experience of America and African America could be understood; he made us know both the complexity of who black Americans have been and are, and why it matters; and he left Americans—black and white—a legacy of intellectual tools, a language with which they might analyze their present and imagine a future.

From late 1961 to 1963 DuBois lived a full life in Accra, the Ghanaian capital, working on the encyclopedia, taking long drives in the afternoon, and entertaining its political elite and the small colony of African Americans during the evenings at the comfortable home the government had provided him. DuBois died the day before his American compatriots assembled for the March on Washington for Jobs and Freedom. It was a conjunction more than rich with historical symbolism. It was the beginning of the end of the era of segregation that had shaped so much of DuBois's life, but it was also the beginning of a new era when "the Negro Problem" could not be confined to separable terrains of the political, economic, domestic, or international, or to simple solutions such as integration or separatism, rights or consciousness. The life and work of DuBois had anticipated this necessary synthesis of diverse terrains and solutions. On 29 August 1963 DuBois was interred in a state funeral outside Castle Osu, formerly a holding pen for the slave cargoes bound for America.

FURTHER READING

DuBois's papers are at the University of Massachusetts, Amherst, and are also available on microfilm.

DuBois, W. E. B. *The Complete Published Works of W. E. B. DuBois*, comp. and ed. Herbert Aptheker (1982).

Horne, Gerald. *Black and Red: W. E. B. DuBois and the Afro-American Response to the Cold War, 1944–1963* (1986).

Lewis, David Levering. *W. E. B. DuBois: Biography of a Race, 1868–1919* (1993).

Lewis, David Levering. *W. E. B. DuBois: The Fight for Equality and the American Century, 1919–1963* (2000).

Marable, Manning. *W. E. B. DuBois: Black Radical Democrat* (1986).

Rampersad, Arnold. *The Art and Imagination of W. E. B. DuBois* (1976).

Obituary: *New York Times*, 28 Aug. 1963.

This entry is taken from the *American National Biography* and is published here with the permission of the American Council of Learned Societies.

THOMAS C. HOLT

Du Sable, Jean Baptiste Pointe (1745?–28 Aug. 1818), explorer and merchant, was born in San Marc, Haiti, the son of a slave woman (name unknown) and Dandonneau (first name unknown), scion of a prominent French Canadian family active in the North American fur trade. Surviving historical journals record the name of Jean Baptiste Pointe du Sable (Pointe au Sable by some accounts), a Haitian of mixed-race ancestry, as the first permanent settler of Chicago. In her 1856 memoir of frontier life in the emerging Northwest Territory, Juliette Kinzie, the wife of the fur trader John Kinzie, makes note of the fact that "the first white man who settled here was a Negro." Several of the voyageurs and commercial men who regularly traversed the shores of southern Lake Michigan in the last decade of the eighteenth century kept accurate records of their encounters in journals and ledger books. One such entry describes du Sable as a "large man; a trader, and pretty wealthy."

Du Sable's pathway to economic reward in the emerging West began in Haiti many years earlier. Because of his race, du Sable was excluded from direct political participation but enjoyed the same basic rights as freedmen and thus was allowed social intercourse with the French settlers. There is no historical rendering of du Sable's activities prior to his departure from Santo Domingo. In general, though, his occupation seems to have been that of a trader. Accordingly, du Sable sailed from Haiti to pursue the dream of greater economic reward in a foreign land aboard the sloop *Susanne*. He arrived in New Orleans in 1764. Less than a year later du Sable completed a historic six-hundred-mile journey up the Mississippi River in the company of Jacques Clamorgan, a successful explorer and merchant who went on to become one of the first judges of the Court of Common Pleas in St. Louis. Du Sable's association with a man of Clamorgan's stature indicates that he was welcomed into a higher social class than one might normally expect of a man born to a slave woman in those times. There seems to have been less social rigidity in the western frontier, thus allowing du Sable to engage in commerce with the white settlers.

Du Sable staked a claim to eight hundred acres of farmland in Peoria and tended this property for several years until he made the decision to relocate to northeast Illinois in the land the Potawatomi tribe called "Eschecagou" (Chicago: literal translation, "land of the wild onions"). There du Sable founded the region's first commercial enterprise, a trading post on the marshy north bank of the Chicago River overlooking Lake Michigan. Juliette Kinzie's memoir provides some additional details of du Sable's holdings during this period. In addition to his "mansion" (measuring 22×40 feet), du Sable owned two barns, a horse mill, bakehouse, dairy, workshop, henhouse, and smokehouse. The inventory of farm equipment indicates that du Sable was harvesting wheat and cutting hay. To run such a busy trading operation and farming enterprise required that du Sable employ skilled labor. Undoubtedly many of his "employees" were Potawatomie Indians.

Du Sable cultivated a good relationship with the native peoples. For a time he lived among the indigenous tribe and took Catherine, the daughter of the Potawatomie chief Pokagon, as his common-law wife. The marriage was formalized at Cahokia in 1788, but the union had been sanctioned by Indian tribal customs years earlier. The couple had two children. The flourishing frontier outpost along the Chicago River was disrupted by the arrival of Charles-Michel Mouet de Langlade, a

French nobleman and commercial trader, in 1778. De Langlade, whom midwestern historians consider to be the "father of Wisconsin," drove du Sable and his family from the region in order to claim the local trade and because of his racial enmity. Du Sable abandoned his claim and moved his family farther east. He took up residence in Michigan City, Indiana, but hostilities between the American colonists and the British government resulted in du Sable's arrest in August 1779. British regulars garrisoned at Fort Michilimackinac (Mackinac Island, Michigan) descended on du Sable's cabin adjacent to the River Chemin and removed him to their military encampment at Port Huron, north of Detroit.

Du Sable and his family were detained by the British for the duration of the American Revolution, a five-year period ending in approximately 1784. A report submitted by Lieutenant Thomas Bennett describes the circumstances of du Sable's arrest and subsequent confinement. "Corporal Tascon, who commanded the party, very prudently prevented the Indians from burning his home, or doing him any injury. The Negro, since his encampment, has in every respect behaved in a manner becoming to a man in his situation and his many friends who give him a good character." Du Sable fully cooperated with his captors and signaled his willingness to take charge of the Port Huron trading post after reports filtered back to Lieutenant Governor Patrick Sinclair that du Sable's predecessor, a Frenchman named Francois Brevecour, had badly mistreated the Indians. The "Pinery," as the British outpost and commissary was known, was maintained by du Sable until 1784, when historians believe that he returned to Illinois to reclaim his vacated properties following the cessation of war.

The Great Lakes region was fast becoming an important hub of commerce; much of the trade came from the Spanish settlements west of the Mississippi River. Thus, du Sable built and maintained a successful trading post at the mouth of the Chicago River. Historians differ on the precise year du Sable started his business. However, journal accounts maintained by Hugh Heward, a Detroit commission agent, establish the presence of du Sable in Chicago on 10 May 1790. During this period du Sable supplied his customers with pork, bread, and flour in return for durable goods and cash. He lived in peace with the Indians, and the white traders passing through the region commented favorably on his character and business acumen.

These early observations describe the region's first settler as an honest man, fond of drink but well educated by contemporary standards. When du Sable sailed to Mackinac with his Indian companions in 1796, the British soldiers greeted him with a cannon salute as a token of esteem. It was a remarkable gesture indicative of his reputation and good character up and down the Great Lakes.

In May of 1800 Jean Baptiste du Sable disposed of his property for reasons not entirely clear. With certainty we can say that Chicago's first settler completed Chicago's first real estate transaction of any consequence when he sold the trading post to Jean La Lime, a French Canadian trapper from St. Joseph, for the sum of six thousand livres. The sale was witnessed by John Kinzie of Niles, Michigan (who in turn would purchase the estate from La Lime four years later in 1804), and was duly recorded in Detroit, the seat of government for the territory of Illinois.

We can only speculate about du Sable's motivations for wanting to leave Chicago. Perhaps his decision to vacate the region at this historic juncture had something to do with the arrival of the eastern settlers who were already pouring into this desolate marshland previously populated only by American Indians and wild animals. Fort Dearborn was erected in April 1803 to protect the interests of the white settlers from the native peoples. This frontier outpost would soon evolve into the city of Chicago.

Du Sable briefly returned to his farmland in Peoria and remained there for little more than a decade. It is believed that Catherine died in Peoria prior to June 1813, when du Sable retired to St. Charles, Missouri. In his declining years du Sable took great precautions to ensure that he could live out the remainder of his life in comfort. He deeded his home in St. Charles to a granddaughter, Eulalie Baroda Denais, in return for her assurance that she would care for him and provide him with a proper burial in the local Catholic cemetery. Whether du Sable achieved these modest aims is less certain, but village records from St. Charles suggest that the venerable pioneer encountered serious financial setbacks late in life and was imprisoned as a debtor in September 1814. Du Sable died at his daughter's residence. No information is available concerning his financial condition at this time.

For many years afterward there was a self-conscious tendency on the part of Chicago chroniclers to deny Jean Baptiste Pointe du Sable credit for his role in the development of Chicago as the commercial hub of midwestern commerce. The fact of du Sable's race disturbed the nineteenth-century writers who touted the accomplishments of Chicago's original settlers in any number of civic boosterism tomes to appear during that era. His questionable lineage, his friendship with the American Indians, and his dealings with the English army during a time of war cast du Sable in an unfavorable light for many years. Not until 1935 and the opening of du Sable High School in Chicago was any significant honor accorded this man. In 1961 MARGARET BURROUGHS founded the du Sable Museum of African American History on the city's South Side. Her museum remains a shrine to his memory.

FURTHER READING

What little we know of Jean Baptiste Pointe du Sable is gleaned from surviving journal accounts, most notably the *Journal of a Voyage Made by Mr. Hugh Heward to the Illinois Country*. A copy of the original manuscript is in the reference library of the Chicago Historical Society. See also the manuscript collection of the Wisconsin State Historical Society for materials covering the early settlement of Illinois Territory.

Cortesi, Lawrence. *Jean du Sable: Father of Chicago* (1972).

Quaife, Milo M. *Checagou: From Indian Wigwam to Modern City* (1933).

Sawyers, June Skinner. *Chicago Portraits: Biographies of 250 Famous Chicagoans* (1991).

This entry is taken from the *American National Biography* and is published here with the permission of the American Council of Learned Societies.

RICHARD C. LINDBERG

Dubois, Silvia (1788?–1889), backwoods legend, was born on Sourland Mountain, New Jersey, the daughter of Cuffy Baird, a Revolutionary War fifer who may have seen action at the battles of Trenton (1776) and Princeton (1777), and Dorcas Compton. Although they had different masters, both of Dubois's parents were slaves. Dubois may in part have inherited her own ferocious desire for freedom from her mother, who tried repeatedly but unsuccessfully to buy her own freedom. Dubois was owned by Dominicus (Minna) Dubois, a strict yet accommodating master much more congenial to Silvia than was his wife, who beat Silvia badly. Aside from Dubois's memories of moving as a young girl to the village of Flagtown and as a teenager to Great Bend, Pennsylvania, where her master kept a tavern, little biographical information exists about her childhood.

An imposing physical presence, the adult Dubois stood approximately 5'10" 'in height and usually weighed more than 200 pounds. Renowned for her strength, endurance, and industry Dubois epitomized a self-reliance and fearlessness that made her a local celebrity. She learned at an early age, for example, to pilot the ferry at Great Bend that ran across the Susquehanna and had the reputation of running the boat better than any man on the river. Possessing cunning commensurate to her strength, Dubois regularly stole customers from one of the ferry captains and, characteristically, took delight in the success of such confidence games. She inspired both awe and terror among her community, children in particular fearing that Dubois would—as she told them—kidnap and swallow them whole. Famed as well for her fighting (with men and women alike), dancing, drinking, and swearing, Dubois brooked no opposition to her appetite for freedom; to her, bondage and restraint were "akin to death" (Larison, 45).

The turning point of Dubois's life—and the root of her legend—was the battle with her mistress that led to her freedom. Dubois's apparent chief offense against her mistress was impertinence, but her mistress's wrath was such that it found expression through a variety of whips, sticks, and impromptu cudgels. As a result Dubois's body was permanently scarred from lashings, and the side of her skull bore a deep depression from a blow from a fire-shovel. From girlhood on, Dubois nursed plans to avenge herself on her mistress, and an opportunity arose, probably in 1807 or 1808, when Minna was away from Great Bend because of grand-jury duty in Wilkes-Barre. Struck by her mistress for failing to scrub the barroom floor with exactitude, Silvia Dubois retaliated by landing what she remembered as a "hell of a blow" that knocked her mistress against a door and nearly killed her (Larison, 65). When the patrons of the bar rallied to the mistress's defense, Dubois wielded her fists at the crowd, cowing the group by threatening to thrash each and every one of them.

Having made her battle with her mistress into a dramatic public spectacle, Dubois quickly left Great Bend for Chenang Point (Chenango, New York) but, acknowledging the authority her master still held over her, returned to Minna when he summoned her. Instead of punishing her, Minna offered Dubois her freedom, apparently recognizing the dangerously irreparable gulf between slave and mistress. He wrote her a pass, and with her year-and-a-half-old child she set out the next morning for Flagtown, where she expected to find her mother. The journey to New Jersey was frequently harrowing. Alone except for her tiny child, Dubois had to pass through the Beech Woods, which was full of panthers and wildcats. She had little to eat and nowhere fitting to sleep. Yet when one white man accosted her and demanded to know to whom she belonged, a defiant Dubois quelled her accuser by showing him her fist and asserting she belonged only to God.

When Dubois reached Flagtown she learned that her mother had moved to New Brunswick, where Silvia found her and worked for several years. Subsequently, she worked for a family in Princeton and took care of her maternal grandfather on Sourland Mountain; upon his death Dubois inherited his property, Put's Tavern, where she dwelled until it was burned down. When her second house burned down sometime before 1883, she went to spend the last years of her life back on Sourland Mountain with her daughter Elizabeth. Dubois had six children, but her biography provides no information about the paternity of the offspring or, for that matter, her marital status.

Complicating any attempt to reconstruct Dubois's life is the fact that the primary source of information about her, C. W. Larison's *Silvia Dubois (Now 116 Yers Old) A Biografy of the Slav who Whipt Her Mistres and Gand Her Fredom* (1883), is problematic in many ways. The book is not so much a biography as it is a colloquy, a written dialogue, between Larison and Dubois. In fashioning the interview, however, the white male Larison (variously, a schoolmaster, physician, writer, and professor) significantly shaped and arguably distorted the representation of Dubois. His claim, for example, that Dubois was 116 years old at the time of the interview has been persuasively challenged by the Dubois editor Jared C. Lobdell, who suggests that she was actually about twenty years younger than that. Generally the reader of the text is unsure of the authenticity of the speaking voice of Dubois, although even Larison noted his subject's vernacular eloquence. Moreover, Larison, a zealous advocate of spelling reform, printed the Dubois book in his own idiosyncratic phonetic alphabet; Larison intended the book to be as much a classroom exercise in his orthographic system as a testimony to the power and resourcefulness of a singular nineteenth-century African American woman.

Although Dubois resisted attributing historical significance to her life, her narrative helps chronicle the peculiarities of northern slavery. The narrative also stands as a record of her mockery of nineteenth-century stereotypes of the obedient, docile slave and the pure, submissive woman. Dubois's bold, hyperbolic life makes her as much a figure of American folklore as American history.

FURTHER READING

Larison, C. W. *Silvia Dubois, a Biografy of the Slave Who Whipt Her Mistres and Gand Her Freedom*, ed. Jared C. Lobdell (1988).

Weiss, Harry B. *Country Doctor: Cornelius Wilson Larison of Ringoes, Hunterdon County, New Jersey, 1837–1910; Physician, Farmer, Educator, Author, Editor, Publisher and Exponent of Phonetic Spelling* (1953).

MICHAEL BERTHOLD

Dubuclet, Antoine (1810–18 Dec. 1887), politician, was born in Iberville Parish, Louisiana, the son of Antoine Dubuclet Sr., a plantation owner, and Rosie Belly. The Dubuclets were members of the *gens de couleur libre*, the class of free blacks permitted certain social and legal rights not typically accorded blacks in the antebellum South. Dubuclet's father owned slaves and a share of a plantation. After his father's death in 1828, Dubuclet remained on the plantation, while his mother and siblings moved to New Orleans. He learned the family business and prospered, owning more than one hundred slaves and an estate valued in 1864 at $94,700. Such substantial holdings made Dubuclet the wealthiest of Louisiana's free blacks and more successful than many white planters.

Dubuclet's fortunes suffered during the Civil War, a time of economic chaos in Louisiana. The demise of slavery meant the end of ready and inexpensive labor, a blow to the plantation economy. The sugar industry, a major source of Dubuclet's wealth, was nearly ruined. Production on his plantation fell dramatically and never returned to prewar levels.

The war also brought social change. The state constitutional convention of 1864 rejected universal male suffrage and ignored President Abraham Lincoln's request that wealthy free blacks be allowed to vote. Black opposition to the new constitution coalesced immediately, and blacks and whites formed numerous political organizations dedicated to black civil rights. In late 1865 Dubuclet served on the central committee of the Republican Party, the party that supported many of the objectives of the black organizations. Dissatisfaction at the national level with southern postwar politics resulted in the Reconstruction Act of 1867, which allowed black males at least twenty-one years old to vote. Approximately half the delegates to the state constitutional convention of 1867–1868 were black. The convention produced a constitution that ended the repressive black codes and included a bill of rights, thus marking a new era in Louisiana politics.

Dubuclet did not serve as a delegate to the constitutional convention, but his rise to political prominence indicates that he supported the new constitution and held the confidence of blacks and moderate whites. He received the Republican Party's nomination for state treasurer on 14 January 1868, but he opposed an attempt to nominate a black governor, siding with moderates who argued that such a move would precipitate violence. The final ticket included the carpetbagger Henry C. Warmoth for governor and the former slave OSCAR J. DUNN for lieutenant governor. Black support for the Republican ticket ensured its victory, and in the elections held on 16–17 April 1868, Louisiana voters ratified the new constitution and elected the Republicans to office. On 29 June 1868 Dubuclet took office as state treasurer.

As state treasurer, Dubuclet managed a financial system near collapse. Wartime devastation, property confiscation, title disputes, and the transition from slavery to free labor had ruined Louisiana's economy. Taxes during the wartime years were in arrears, and assessed taxable property value had declined by nearly 50 percent, from $470 million to $250 million. Instead of cutting spending in response to the loss of revenue, the state government increased expenditures, and Louisiana was bankrupt. Dubuclet recommended reduced appropriations and reform of the state's methods of revenue collection, but the legislature ignored him. One practice he objected to was that of accepting warrants for tax payments. Short on cash, the state issued warrants to pay for its legislators. To give these warrants value, the state took them in lieu of cash for payment of taxes. Warrants fluctuated in value, were often altered, and complicated bookkeeping. The legislature again ignored his suggestions, and Dubuclet turned his attention from reform to management of the treasury.

Along with economic decline and legislative irresponsibility, corruption too assailed Louisiana's financial health, reaching the highest public offices and draining the state of badly needed funds. Dubuclet resisted the temptation to enrich himself and opposed corruption. In 1869 a state commission consisting of Dubuclet, Governor Warmoth, and two state legislators was formed to sell bonds for levee repair. When the other commission members decided to retain a portion of the bond sales for themselves, Dubuclet protested. In Dubuclet's absence the other commission members voted to pocket some of the funds despite the treasurer's objections. Dubuclet learned of their deception and initiated court proceedings, which earned him the praise of the conservative press in New Orleans.

Dubuclet was reelected to a four-year term of office in 1870 by the considerable margin of 25,000 votes. The political and social turmoil of Reconstruction worsened during the new decade, and despite Dubuclet's capable management, the state's finances remained a shambles. He supported an 1874 fiscal reform measure offered by house member THEOPHILE T. ALLAIN. The measure passed the legislature, but the final appropriations bill for that year rendered Allain's efforts futile. Angered by the failure of reform, several prominent black politicians, including Dubuclet, issued an "Address of the Colored Men to the People of Louisiana," which was distributed as an extra in the *Louisianian* on 8 October 1874 and reprinted in other newspapers. The statement denounced the charge that black political participation was ruining the state and argued that black politicians were being intentionally excluded from Republican Party operations. Although Dubuclet's annual reports as treasurer remained silent on reform issues, his signature on the document illustrates his support for the reform movement and his concern over the role of blacks in Louisiana government.

Dubuclet's ability earned him respect from unusual quarters. When militant whites seized the statehouse in September 1874, placing their own men in state offices, they allowed Dubuclet to continue his work unmolested and apologized to him when he was mistakenly refused entry into his office. The coup failed after five days. Later that year voters again returned Dubuclet to office, but this term was marred by political conflict. In 1876 a house committee controlled by Democrats accused him of stealing $200,000. The charge was politically motivated, and Dubuclet was exonerated. An investigation of the treasurer's office in 1878 revealed only minor technical irregularities, and both Democrats and Republicans agreed that Dubuclet had faithfully discharged his duties. He did not seek reelection in 1878.

Dubuclet married twice. During the 1830s he wed Claire Pollard; they had nine children before she died in 1852. In the 1860s he married Mary Ann Walsh; they had three children. After retiring from office in 1879, Dubuclet returned to Iberville Parish, where he lived with Felicite Roy. He sold his plantation to his son Francois and lived on a small homestead. Financial difficulties reduced the value of his property to $1,130. He died in Iberville Parish.

FURTHER READING

Vincent, Charles. "Aspects of the Family and Public Life of Antoine Dubuclet: Louisiana's Black State Treasurer," *Journal of Negro History* 66 (Spring 1981).

Vincent, Charles. *Black Legislators in Louisiana during Reconstruction* (1976).

Obituary: *New Orleans Daily Picayune*, 21 Dec. 1887.

THOMAS CLARKIN

Dudley, Edward Richard (11 Mar. 1911–8 Feb. 2005), diplomat, was born in South Boston, Virginia, the son of Edward and Nellie Dudley. Dudley spent most of his early years in Virginia and then went on to earn his B.S. from Johnson C. Smith University in Charlotte, North Carolina. His original plans for a career as a dentist went unfulfilled, however, and during the harshest years of the Great Depression, Dudley took up a variety of jobs, including as a public school teacher and as a real estate salesman. He eventually ended up in New York City, where for a short time he was able to gain employment with the Works Progress Administration's federal theater project. Dudley returned to school and earned his law degree from St. John's University in 1941. He had become active in New York Democratic Party politics, and his hard work resulted in his appointment as New York State assistant attorney general in 1942.

In 1943 Dudley left his position with the state attorney general's office to take the post of assistant special counsel to the NAACP Legal Defense and Education Fund. Here he worked under the supervision of THURGOOD MARSHALL, assisting in the preparation of numerous lawsuits filed on behalf of African American voters and civil rights activists in the South. Dudley's work in New York and with the NAACP did not go unnoticed by the administration of President Harry S. Truman. In 1945 Dudley was named legal counsel to the governor of the U.S. Virgin Islands.

After a brief return to work with the NAACP in 1947, Dudley was again approached by the Truman administration in 1948. This time, however, the offer was to become the next U.S. minister to Liberia. Election-year politics partially explained Dudley's selection for the post. The president expected a tough battle for reelection in 1948, and courting the African American vote by appointing a proven civil rights activist to a high-profile diplomatic position was a smart strategic move. Also playing a role in the naming of Dudley as U.S. minister was Liberia's long history as part of the so-called Negro circuit. This phrase referred to the U.S. Department of State's practice of appointing African American diplomats to an extremely circumscribed circuit of "black" posts: Liberia, Haiti, and Madagascar were the three most popular destinations. For these appointees, their diplomatic careers became a dreary cycle of moving from one of these posts to the other with little or no opportunity for career advancement. No African American had ever attained the position of U.S. ambassador.

Like many other Americans in 1948, Dudley was not optimistic about Truman's chances for reelection and so went to Liberia for what he believed would be a fairly short stay. Nevertheless Dudley tackled his job with his usual professionalism and energy. Liberia was a nation of increasing importance to the United States, not only for its economic value (natural rubber was a major crop) but also as a strategic window on Africa from which America could keep a wary eye on the crumbling European colonial empires on the continent and on any possible Communist influences. Dudley fought for and secured substantially increased U.S. foreign aid for Liberia. He also established a strong working relationship with the Liberian president William V. S. Tubman. This was not always an easy task, for Tubman was a virtual dictator of his country and did not appreciate anything that smacked of U.S. interference with his regime. Dudley adopted a pragmatic approach to his dealing with Tubman; because there was no organized or realistic opposition to Tubman and because the Liberian leader was a staunch anticommunist, it seemed advisable to work with him rather than against him. In recognition of Liberia's growing importance to the United States, Dudley also successfully lobbied for improvements to the American mission in Monrovia, including new buildings, new equipment, and more and better staff.

In addition to his official duties as U.S. minister, Dudley also committed himself to improving and increasing the African American profile in America's diplomatic corps. As a longtime member of the NAACP, Dudley was well aware of the Department of State's reputation as one of the most segregated federal agencies and of the NAACP's consistent criticisms of that reputation. He witnessed the results firsthand upon his arrival in Liberia: a corps of dedicated, competent African American diplomats condemned to the Negro circuit with their careers stagnating.

Quietly but persistently Dudley began working with a small group of supportive officials in the Department of State to break the cycle. Progress was slow, but Dudley was assisted in his efforts to seek wider career opportunities by growing international criticism of America's race problem. As the United States thrust itself forward during the cold war as the leader of the free world, the contradiction between that role and the reality of a segregated America came into sharp focus. Friends and foes alike decried the U.S. hypocrisy that called for freedom and justice around the globe but denied millions of its own citizens even the most basic civil and human rights.

One answer to these criticisms was the appointment of African Americans to higher-profile positions overseas. Dudley sensed the opportunity and quickly moved to take advantage. In the next few years, Dudley's persistence resulted in new assignments in Paris, Lisbon, Copenhagen, New Delhi, London, and Rome for the African American diplomats and staff who had been in Liberia. Although most African American diplomats continued to be assigned to African nations in the decades that followed, the Negro circuit was finally broken during Dudley's tenure in Liberia.

In early 1949 Dudley received word that the U.S. mission in Liberia was to be raised to embassy status and that he would be promoted to the position of U.S. ambassador. For the first time an African American would serve in the highest office obtainable by a U.S. diplomatic representative. Black newspapers and magazines took note of the important change with several feature articles. The decision on the part of the U.S. government to raise the status of the mission in Liberia was based on both international and domestic considerations. Liberia had become more and more important to the United States, and raising the mission to embassy status would show this. In addition it would also signal to the people of Africa that America took the continent and its issues seriously. Yet there was also a domestic side to the decision. Naming Dudley as a U.S. ambassador would both dampen African American criticisms of what they routinely referred to as the "lily-white club" of the Department of State and also thank the African American voters for their crucial support in the very close 1948 election.

Dudley saw his promotion as another opportunity to push for greater career options for African American diplomats. He immediately began pressing the case for naming black ambassadors to other, higher-profile nations. Beyond some desultory discussion in the Department of State, however, Dudley's pleas went unheeded. It was not until 1959 that an African American served as U.S. ambassador to a nation other than Liberia, when John Howard Morrow was named ambassador to Guinea. And it was not until 1961 that an African American was appointed as U.S. ambassador to a nation outside of Africa, this occurring when Clifton Reginald Wharton Sr. was selected for the post in Norway.

With the election of the Republican Dwight D. Eisenhower as president in 1952, Dudley tendered his resignation. There was some discussion about other assignments, but Dudley wished to return to his work with the NAACP, and his family yearned to return to the United States after nearly five years in Liberia. He immediately took up the directorship of the NAACP's Freedom Fund, which is designed to raise money for scholarships and recognition of landmarks in African American history. In 1955 he rejoined the New York City legal system when he became a judge in the city's domestic relations court. The election of John F. Kennedy in 1960 brought Dudley back into the diplomatic fold, albeit only briefly, when he served as a consultant on the new president's Africa task force. There were also some inconclusive discussions about his appointment as U.S. ambassador to Nigeria. New York politics, however, exerted a greater pull, and in 1962 he served as the first African American chairman of the New York County Democratic Committee. In 1965 he was elected as a justice to the New York State Supreme Court. He served in that capacity until his retirement in 1985. He died at age ninety-three of prostate cancer.

FURTHER READING

The primary sources of information on Edward R. Dudley and his career are his personal papers, which are held at the Amistad Research Center, Tulane University, New Orleans, Louisiana, and an oral interview that was done in 1995 and is now on deposit at the Foreign Affairs Oral History Program, Lauinger Library, Georgetown University, Washington, D.C.

Krenn, Michael L. *Black Diplomacy: African Americans and the State Department, 1945–1969* (1999).

Miller, Jake C. *The Black Presence in American Foreign Affairs* (1978).

MICHAEL L. KRENN

Dudley, Sherman Houston (1873–29 Feb. 1940), vaudeville entertainer and theatrical entrepreneur, was born in Dallas, Texas. The names of his parents are unknown. Though in later interviews Dudley frequently changed the story of how he broke into show business, his earliest stage work was most likely in Texas and Louisiana as part of a medicine show. This job, in which he played music and told jokes to draw a crowd to the pitchman and his wares, was an appropriate beginning for a man who always sought to be the center of attention. Dudley eventually became an artist and businessman who, as demonstrated by both his actions and writings, was passionately concerned with cultivating the rights and strengthening the dignity of African American performers during an era when what it meant to be a black entertainer was greatly in flux.

Dudley's apprenticeship in the professional theatrical world took place during the last decade of the nineteenth century, and as a young man he worked with many of the most influential and recognized black performers of minstrelsy and vaudeville. He formed the Dudley Georgia Minstrels in 1897 to perform around Texas, and his first real touring show was with P. T. Wright's Nashville Students during the 1898 season. Even in this early show, he was described in newspaper articles as not only one of the top comedians but also as a writer of humorous sketches. Throughout his career Dudley performed only in comedies and always in blackface, an expected practice for vaudevillians of the day. He apparently met his first wife while part of WILL MARION COOK's Clorindy company. Alberta Ormes-Dudley, a talented actress herself, toured with her husband throughout the first decade of the twentieth century and frequently acted opposite him. In 1900 Dudley worked with veteran minstrel BILLY KERSANDS in the ill-fated *King Rastus* and later reteamed with Kersands in 1902 as part of Richards and Pringle's Georgia Minstrels. He stayed with the show for two years, acting, writing, and stage managing. Reviews singled him out for his energetic wit and comic timing.

His break into stardom occurred in 1904, when he signed up with the Smart Set Company to replace the recently deceased Tom McIntosh as the show's headliner. His three shows with the Smart Set became his theatrical legacy and gave him both the industry contacts and financial security to embark on the next phase of his career. He also developed his signature routine at this time, which became synonymous with his name and was demanded of him by audiences around the country. The routine was called "Dudley and His Mule," and it was worked into the narratives of each of his Smart Set shows. Dudley would stroll onstage with a live mule, which, dressed in a pair of overalls, would amble around the stage while his human sidekick commented on his bad behavior. In a June 1932 article for *The Crisis* magazine, Dudley commented, "I had to follow the mule not the mule to follow me. My cues came from him. And I had to answer mighty quick. I talked to the mule about what he did and the audience thought he was doing what I had taught him" (203).

The typical Smart Set show consisted of a thin plot that was little more than an excuse to showcase female dancers, ragtime music, and zany comedy. In *The Black Politician*, Dudley made a hit of the humorous ditty "Come after Breakfast, Bring 'Long Your Lunch, and Leave before Supper." The next production was titled *His Honor the Barber*, in which Dudley played Raspberry Snow, a small-town barber whose ambition in life is to shave the president. When he is about to get his chance, the whole affair is revealed to have been a dream. *Dr. Beans from Boston* debuted in 1912 and ran intermittently for several years. Dudley's character, Gymnasium Butts, masqueraded as the eponymous doctor in order to scam a southern town's drugstore. Even as *Dr. Beans* was touring, Dudley embarked on the next phase of his lengthy career, that of theater owner and circuit manager.

For black entertainers the first two decades of the twentieth century were marked by a new economic freedom coupled with both increased mobility and visibility, which in turn brought new forms of prejudice. Most U.S. theaters at the time were organized within large white-owned chains called circuits. These immensely powerful and lucrative enterprises dictated which vaudeville and variety acts performed within the chain of theaters, and in exchange the performers were guaranteed regular employment. African Americans were frequently limited to a single act on an evening's bill, and the houses were normally segregated. Dudley—who in 1906 wrote a letter praising Chicago's black-owned Pekin Theatre—saw an opportunity as both a savvy businessman and a conscientious African American to create a separate circuit exclusively presenting black acts and catering to black audiences. He bought his first theater in Washington, D.C., in 1912 and named it after himself. By 1914 the Dudley Circuit had become a conglomeration of nineteen theaters in the East, South, and Midwest. As an owner and promoter, Dudley was known for his fair dealings and his willingness to cultivate young talent. In 1916 he joined with two white promoters to create the Southern Consolidated Circuit (SCC). The SCC's chain of more than twenty-five theaters allowed hundreds of black performers to work steadily for an entire season.

Two major events occurred at the beginning of the 1920s that changed how the African American entertainment business was run, and Dudley was at the center of both. Noting the profitability of the SCC, a group of white theater managers revived the near-defunct Theatre Owners' Booking Association (TOBA) in 1920 to compete with the SCC for the same performers and over similar routes throughout the circuit. The feud between the organizations was short lived, however, because the next year the SCC was absorbed into its rival. Dudley was briefly left off of the board of directors but was reinstated in January 1922. TOBA (which performers said was an acronym for "Tough on Black Asses") quickly began booking the talent into segregated houses and squeezing extra performances out of its acts. The Colored Actors' Union (CAU), the voice of entertainers in the industry, was founded shortly after this merger. Always the joiner, Dudley was one of the charter members of the organization and was its first treasurer. He noted this contradictory position in several of his frequent letters to the black press and confessed that he was attempting to balance the interests of both owners and performers. He also continued to produce specific shows that toured in TOBA houses, like *Bamville Follies* in 1926 and *Ebony Follies* in 1928.

In 1924 Dudley was married a second time, to Desdemona B. Dudley, a former employee. Her background is a mystery. In 1926 he sought a divorce on the grounds of infidelity, but before the case could go to trial, she was killed by the man named in the suit as her alleged lover.

Dudley also became an early black entrepreneur in the budding movie industry. Much like his advancements in the theatrical world, his ability to work with white businesspeople supported his more altruistic ideas of aiding African American artists. Dudley had always been a vocal advocate of "race pictures," films that featured African American performers and were intended for black audiences. In 1927 he assumed the presidency of the financially struggling Colored Players Film Corporation, which until that time had been run by a group of white Philadelphians. The company produced the silent film *The Scar of Shame*, starring Lucia Lynn Moses and Lawrence Chenault, in 1929 and then quietly folded. At the same time, Dudley's theaters were hit hard by the economic effects of the Depression, and by 1930 he had sold off much of his interest in the chain.

Dudley had lived in the Washington, D.C., area since the early days of the Dudley Circuit, and in the last decade of his life he continued working with the CAU and breeding racehorses on his Oxen Hill farm. Starting in the mid-1930s he co-produced variety shows with his son Sherman H. Dudley Jr. One of Dudley's obituaries noted that his son, following in his father's footsteps, was working on opening a show at the Apollo Theater in Harlem, New York (*Baltimore Afro-American*, 16 Mar. 1940).

FURTHER READING

Hill, Anthony D. *Pages from the Harlem Renaissance: A Chronicle of Performance* (1996).

Sampson, Henry T. *Blacks in Blackface: A Source Book on Early Black Musical Shows* (1980).

KEVIN BYRNE

Duke, Bill (14 Feb. 1943–), actor, writer, and director, was born in Poughkeepsie, New York, to William Henry Duke Sr., a machinist, and Ethel Louise Duke, a domestic worker who later became a practical nurse. He had one sister. As a child Duke was tall and big for his age. Introverted by nature, he preferred to write about his feelings rather than talk about them with other kids. Duke's parents, neither of whom finished elementary school, emphasized to him the importance of education. During his school years he developed an interest in writing poetry. When his high school English teacher caught him writing poetry in a textbook during class, she confiscated the book and secretly submitted Duke's poems to the National Poetry Contest. Duke's work won first place.

Duke's parents hoped that he would go into medicine or teaching, and after earning an associate of arts from Dutchess Community College in 1963 he enrolled in an undergraduate program at Boston University. However, a speech and drama class he took there fueled his interest in acting. His parents worried that the odds were against him as a black man in film or television, but he was determined to succeed and entered wholeheartedly into dramatic training. His mentor at Boston University was Lloyd Richards, one of the first African American television directors. After he graduated in 1966 (the first member of his family to graduate from college), Duke earned a master of fine arts in acting and directing in 1968 from New York University's Tisch School of the Arts and an MFA in directing in 1971 from the American Film Institute, where his student film *The Hero* attracted considerable attention. In 1969 he made his New York stage debut as Leroi Jones in *Slave Ship* at the Brooklyn Academy of Music. His Off-Broadway acting debut came in 1970 with the Negro Ensemble Company in Douglas Turner Ward's *Day of Absence*. The following year he first acted on Broadway in MELVIN VAN PEEBLES's *Ain't Supposed to Die a Natural Death*. He directed more than thirty Off-Broadway plays, including GARRETT MORRIS's *The Secret Place* (1972).

After moving to Los Angeles in the early 1970s, Duke found work as an actor, teacher, writer, and director. He was active at the Mark Taper Forum and the L.A. Actors Theater, and he broke into television work as a guest star on a show called *Santiago's Ark*. Guest-starring roles on better-known series followed, including *Kojak* (1976), *Starsky and Hutch* (1978), and *Charlie's Angels* (1978). In 1976 he played Abdullah in the high-profile motion picture comedy *Car Wash*, directed by Michael Schultz. His career in directing for television began in 1979, after he received his second MFA, from the American Film Institute, with episodes of the popular weekly drama *Knots Landing*.

In the early 1980s Duke helmed episodes of *Falcon Crest* (1982) and remained busy as an actor as well, appearing in the film *American Gigolo* (1980) and in two television series, leading the cast as a regular in *Palmerstown, U.S.A.* (1980) and guest starring on *Benson* (1981). Though *Palmerstown, U.S.A.* (created by the *Roots* author ALEX HALEY) was short-lived, Duke regarded his portrayal of Luther Freeman, a father and community leader, as perhaps his favorite among all the roles because of its multilayered emotional complexity.

In 1983 Duke survived a near-fatal airplane crash. His career continued to accelerate as he directed episodes of *Hill Street Blues* (1983), *Cagney & Lacey* (1983–1984), *Spenser: For Hire* (1985), *Matlock* (1986), and *Miami Vice* (1988), among many others. In 1985 he worked for PBS and directed his first feature film, *The Killing Floor*, for the *American Playhouse* series. The film was shown at the Cannes and the Sundance Film Festivals that year (it was awarded the Special Jury Prize at the latter). In 1989 he made another film, *The Meeting*, for *American Playhouse*. The made-for-television movie, in which Duke also performed, was a fictionalized account of a meeting between Dr. MARTIN LUTHER KING JR. and MALCOLM X in the 1960s. The same year, Duke directed an Emmy-nominated made-for-television adaptation of LORRAINE HANSBERRY's *A Raisin in the Sun*. As he had done throughout his career he continued to direct and act simultaneously, starring in big-budget action films such as *Commando* (1985) and *Predator* (1987) opposite Arnold Schwarzenegger, and *Action Jackson* with Carl Weathers.

In the 1990s Duke directed episodes of many television series, including *The Outsiders* (1990), *New York Undercover* (1994), and *America's Dream* (1996). But it was in feature films that he achieved his greatest success as a director. His debut came with *A Rage in Harlem* in 1991, an adaptation of the classic CHESTER HIMES detective novel, followed by his first collaboration with the actor LAURENCE FISHBURNE, the narcotics drama *Deep Cover* (1992). *The Cemetery Club* (1993) was followed by the comedy *Sister Act 2: Back in the Habit* (1993), and the period gangster film *Hoodlum* (1997), again with Fishburne. He continued acting at this time, and appeared in feature films such as *Bird on a Wire* (1990) and *Menace II Society* (1993). In 1999 Duke starred in *Payback* and *Fever*, and had an uncredited but critically acclaimed role as a DEA agent opposite Terence Stamp in Steven Soderbergh's *The Limey*.

After 2000 Duke directed episodes of *City of Angels* (2000), PBS's *American Experience* (2003), and Michael Mann's *Robbery Homicide Division* (2003), among others. He remained busy as an actor as well, appearing in the feature films *Exit Wounds* (2001), *Red Dragon* (2002), and *X-Men: The Last Stand* (2006), and the TV series *Fastlane* (2002–2003), *Karen Sisco* (2003–2004), *Battlestar Galactica* (2006), and *Lost* (2006).

In the mid-1980s Duke founded his own production company, Yagya Productions (later Duke Media). Through it Duke produced many of his own films as well as the work of others; he also mentored and offered apprenticeships to young African American actors and directors.

Duke was also socially committed, and supported and advocated for the Willow Opportunity Center, an organization in the Bronx that provided the homeless with training and life skills, and Educating Young Minds, a non-profit learning center in Los Angeles that offered tutoring and other academic instruction to underprivileged children.

Duke continued his commitment to learning by serving as the Time Warner Endowed Chair in the department of radio, television, and film at Howard University from 1998 to 2001. He was appointed in 2001 to the serve on the National Endowment for the Humanities by former President Bill Clinton and selected in 2004 to the California Film Commission Board by California Governor Arnold Schwarzenegger. Duke was elected to the Board of Trustees of the American Film Institute in 2000.

FURTHER READING

Brown, Keith Michael. *Sacred Bond: Black Men and Their Mothers* (2000).

Donaldson, Melvin. *Black Directors in Hollywood* (2003).

Moon, Spencer. *Reel Black Talk* (1997).

DAVID BORSVOLD

Dukes, Hazel (17 Mar. 1932–), politician and civil rights activist, was born in Montgomery, Alabama to Edward, a Pullman porter, and Alice Dukes; she was an only child. Growing up in the segregated South, Dukes found out early on the importance of fighting for one's rights. She credits her father with this lesson alongside the strong influence of grandparents on both sides of the family and the thriving black community to which she belonged. A prominent member of the NAACP, she first became involved with the organization when she was a student at the Alabama State Teacher's College, where she also got her associates degree in 1950. Her education continued in 1955 when she moved to New York with her parents and began attending Nassau Community College while working at a local department store. Interested in business administration, she soon found herself working as a public servant and community organizer, although she would not get her degree in the field until 1978.

In the early 1960s Dukes became active in the NAACP's Great Neck–Manhasset–Port Washington–Roslyn branch on Long Island, New York, where she served in a variety of capacities including regional secretary, membership coordinator, and later president. At the same time, Dukes was making inroads into local politics. She started as a committeewoman in Nassau County on Long Island, and later became the vice chairman of the Nassau County Democratic Committee. Moreover she was often on the frontlines of local civil rights activities. In an era when social justice organizations like the Congress of Racial Equality (CORE) and the NAACP worked closely together, Dukes walked the picket line at a local duck farm to protest the treatment of black migrant workers. During the late 1960s she also helped lead a group of activists who sought to integrate a local Long Island apartment complex.

Hazel Dukes, the president of the New York State NAACP, speaks at a conference, 1990. (AP Images.)

Dukes's rise to power in the NAACP belies the reality of the sexual discrimination that was deeply ingrained in the civil rights movement of the 1950s and 1960s. Women's leadership was a fact of life in the early days of the organization's history, and women like Ida B. Wells Barnett and Rosa Parks (both members of the organization) played a tremendous role in the struggle for civil rights. Nevertheless, for the most part women occupied a second-class status within the NAACP because of what many consider to be the patriarchal traditions of the black church and out of the need for black male leaders to assert their masculinity in a culture dedicated to denying black manhood. Dukes herself once complained of the standoffish attitude some of her male colleagues exhibited toward her. Even when she served as president of the national organization from 1990 until

1992, she was often ignored and policy decisions were made in her absence.

A long-standing Democrat, Dukes was also a member of the Democratic National Committee from New York from 1975 to 1993 and served as a New York delegate to the Democratic National Convention in 1976 and 1980. In 1978 she also became president of the New York State Conference of NAACP branches. Moreover her foray into politics brought her a series of political appointments. In 1989, for example, Dukes was nominated to the state university board of trustees by then New York governor Mario Cuomo. One year later, she was appointed by then New York mayor David Dinkins as president of New York City's Off-Track Betting agency (OTB) under his administration. The first black woman to head the organization, Dukes was routinely the object of both controversy and criticism. Critics claimed that the organization under Dukes's leadership was marked by corruption and cronyism. Dukes, however, countered that she had implemented $7.6 million a year in cost savings and had plans to increase the city's portion of the OTB's revenues. Controversy found Dukes again in 1997 when she pleaded guilty to embezzling $13,000 from an OTB employee with leukemia who had trusted Dukes with her finances. Dukes admitted that she had not kept adequate records of her purchases on behalf of the employee and was pleading guilty in order to get on with her life. As a result of these events she was asked to voluntarily resign from the NAACP board; she refused. In December of that same year Dukes was ousted. She also resigned her post on the board of trustees at the State University of New York after then New York State attorney general Dennis Vacco ruled that by admitting guilt in the case, she had violated her oath of office.

Despite her political ups and downs, Dukes remained a steadfast champion of the local and national NAACP organizations. "I lead by example," Dukes once told *The New York Amsterdam News*. "If I work hard and focus on the national program priorities, then the local branch volunteers are encouraged to work hard, as well," she continued. "We cannot rest on our laurels, however, because freedom is under fire from many fronts. We must and we will go forward with renewed energy and dedication to the task of protecting civil rights in our quest for equal justice under the law" (25 July, 2002). Yet Dukes's leadership of the New York State Conference was also controversial. In 2005, for example, she rescinded the election of officers in Ossining, New York, and put the chapter in receivership, ostensibly because of the group's support of the death row prisoner and journalist MUMIA ABU-JAMAL.

Dukes also took on such diverse issues as the alleged undercounting of minorities by Nielsens Media Research rating system, the fight for smaller class sizes in the New York public schools, and better wages for security guards. While she often lamented the African American community's failure to bring along a new generation of leaders, she remained committed to ferreting out and dismantling the more subtle forms of discrimination occurring in society. Dukes was a senior member of the NAACP's National Board of Directors and also served on the Black Leadership Council on AIDS, and was a member of several civic organizations including the-League of Women Voters. Dukes also served as the project coordinator and clergy consultant for the Community Health Alliance of Harlem, where she worked in the areas of health care, public policy, and diversity.

FURTHER READING

Daniels, Dawn, Marie Sandy, and Candace Sandy. *Souls of My Sisters* (2000).

Giamo, Benedict, and Jeffrey Grunberg. *Beyond Homelessness: Frames of Reference* (1992).

ELEANOR BRANCH

Dumas, Charles "Charley" Everett (12 Feb. 1937–4 Jan. 2004), Olympic high jump champion, teacher, and track coach, was born in Tulsa, Oklahoma, one of six children of Monroe Dumas and Nancy Dumas. His family moved to Los Angeles in 1941, when Dumas was four years old. Beginning high jumping with "the best performance ... in his physical education class" in eighth grade (Hornbuckle, 83), Dumas specialized in the event. He shared second place in the city championship in his freshman year at Centennial High School and placed fourth in the state meet. In 1955 at eighteen years of age, he jumped six feet ten and one-quarter inches (2.089m).

In 1955, during his senior year in high school, Dumas set a national interscholastic record of six feet nine and three-eighths inches (2.07m). Shortly after graduating, he shared the national Amateur Athletic Union (AAU) championship with the defending high school champion, Ernie Shelton. Since Dumas had already graduated from high school, his state meet record of six feet ten and one-quarter inches (2.089m) was not considered a national high-school record. He ranked first or second in U.S. high jump ratings from 1955 to 1960 and was AAU champion from 1956 to 1959.

At six feet, two inches and 178 pounds, the nineteen-year-old Dumas was the first man to officially jump seven feet, which he accomplished in 1956 at the Olympic Trials (seven feet and five-eighths inches, or 2.15m) in Los Angeles. Advised by the high-jump official to set the bar slightly above seven feet, since "once the mental barrier was gone ... a dozen guys will do it next week" (Hornbuckle, 83), his jump sent a shock wave through the track and field world. The 34,000 spectators in the Los Angeles Coliseum gave him a standing ovation in "a moment comparable to ... breaking the four-minute mile barrier" (Hornbuckle, 83), a mark set barely two years earlier. The front page of the *New York Times* announced the feat.

In the 1956 Olympics in Melbourne, Australia, Dumas was the favorite, and he won the high-jump gold medal at six feet, eleven and one quarter inches (2.12m) on his third try. At the time, Dumas was still nineteen years old, and he found himself in a tough competition again Australian national high jump champion, Charles "Chilla" Porter of Brisbane. Besting the previous Olympic record by three inches (8cm), Dumas noted, "winning the gold medal was very satisfying, but to be the first man to jump seven feet ... was the magic moment" (Hornbuckle, 83). He dominated the high jump for the rest of the 1950s, until he was eclipsed by John Thomas; it would take thirty-three years before Javier Sotomayor of Cuba raised the record to eight feet in 1989.

In 1956 Dumas entered Compton Junior College and in early 1957 transferred to the University of Southern California in Los Angeles. With "very smooth technique" (Lawson, 179), "he used a surprisingly slow run, but had a tremendous lift" (Quercentani, 171). Rarely jumping in practice, he was a pioneer in using stretching to prepare for the high jump (Hornbuckle, 84). According to his USC coach Jess Mortensen, his "body [was] as loose as a sack of ashes" (ibid.). He was also an excellent 120-yard hurdler and helped the USC Trojans win the National Collegiate Athletic Association (NCAA) championship in 1958 as a three-time varsity letter winner from 1958 to 1960.

In the 1958 and 1959 USA vs. USSR meets, Dumas was beaten by two Russian jumpers, including the future 1960 Olympic champion, Robert Shavlakadze. In 1958 he jumped 6 feet 10 ½ inches (2.10m) in Japan and in 1959 he won the Pan American games high-jump gold medal with a jump of the same height, a meet record. In the 1960 U.S. Olympic trials at Stanford University, he placed third behind world record–setting John Thomas and Joe Faust. Despite a knee injury, Dumas finished sixth in the 1960 Rome Olympics, behind two Russians, Shavlakadze and Valery Brumel, as well as U.S. teammate Thomas, in whose shadow Dumas would continue to jump after the Russians' startling upset of the record-holder in Rome.

Dumas graduated from USC in 1961. Though he had initially retired from jumping after the 1960 Olympic Games, he made a comeback four years later at age twenty-seven and was still able to clear 7 feet ¼ inches (2.14m) for the Southern California Striders track club in 1964. Still a national competitor, he was ranked sixth in the United States. After five national high-jump titles and an Olympic medal, the same knee injury ended his jumping career. In later years, he rejected the idea of jumping as an athelete in masters' competition (over age 35) for fear of injury, despite feeling he could clear six feet, six inches.

Dumas worked as a teacher, coach, and administrator at several schools in the Los Angeles Unified School district for nearly forty years following his graduation from college. He also earned a master's degree in school management and administration from UCLA. Dumas was inducted into the National Track and Field Hall of Fame in 1990 and the USC Athletic Hall of Fame in 1997. He died of cancer in 2004 in Inglewood, California.

Married to Gloria Dumas, he was survived by his son, Kyle, and daughter, Keasha. Though others had previously jumped seven feet unofficially, Charles Dumas was the first man and African American to shatter a major physical and psychological barrier in international track and field.

FURTHER READING

Danzig, Allison. "Coast High Jumper First to Top 7 Feet," *New York Times* (30 June 1956).

Hornbuckle, Adam R. "Charles Dumas," in *African-American Sports Greats* (1995).

Lawson, Gerald, MD. "Charles Dumas," in *World Record Breakers in Track and Field Athletics* (1997).

Quercetani, Roberto L. "Jumps-High Jump," in *Athletics: A History of Modern Track and Field Athletics, 1860–2000* (2000).

Snyder, Don. "Dumas Sets Sights on 7 Feet," *Los Angeles Times* (March 1956).

Obituaries: *New York Times*, 17 Janurary 2004; *Los Angeles Times*, 5 June 2004.

RICHARD SOBEL

Dumas, François Ernest (1837–26 Mar. 1901), businessman, Civil War veteran, and Reconstruction politician, was the son of the influential Creole New Orleanian Joseph Dumas, one of the owners of the Dumas Brothers French Quarter clothiers, a firm that specialized in imported French cloth and luxury apparel. Joseph Dumas invested his share of the firm's profits in real estate and accumulated a considerable fortune in property holdings and slaves. In 1860 African American Louisianans like François and Joseph Dumas constituted the wealthiest population of free blacks in the United States.

Joseph Dumas's import business necessitated that the Dumas family sojourn frequently in France, and it was there that François, was born, raised, and educated. François arrived in New Orleans shortly before the Civil War to manage the family business. He married Marguerite Victoria Victor, and the couple had five children, three girls and two boys. By 1860 he had become one of the ten wealthiest free blacks in the South with property holdings valued at $250,000. By 1868 he and his brother P. A. Dumas had expanded the business to two locations and changed the name to F. E. Dumas & Brother Clothiers

François was said to be a distant cousin of Alexandre Dumas, the legendary French novelist of African descent whose dedication to republican ideals François clearly shared. Following Alexandre Dumas's example (he had played an active role in the 1830 and 1848 French Revolutions and helped procure arms in Italy for the unificationist Giuseppe Garibaldi), François Dumas embraced the Unionist cause. In France he "imbibed his Republicanism and principles of the equality of men" (Hirsch and Logsdon, 228). He conceived of the struggle against slavery and racial oppression in the South as another chapter in "the great universal fight of the oppressed of all colors and nations" (Houzeau, 75). In Civil War and Reconstruction Louisiana he became an active agent of liberation and democracy and, though he did not achieve Alexandre Dumas's fame, his accomplishments were nonetheless substantial.

In New Orleans Dumas joined his father's highly politicized circle of community activists. The men had banded together to resist an increasingly harsh slave regime that deprived them of citizenship, denied them free movement, relegated them to a debased condition, and imposed upon them restrictive manumission and exclusion laws that curtailed the size and mobility of their community. They had channeled some of their discontent into a number of philanthropic activities including the founding of a school for destitute orphans of color and a Catholic convent of free women of color dedicated to missionary work among the city's slaves and free black indigents.

The Dumas family's philanthropy stemmed from a Latin European religious ethic that attached high moral value to good works, viewed slavery as an unnatural human condition, and considered a master's manumission of his slave an act of benevolence that would win God's favor. Together with the revolutionary currents sweeping the Atlantic world, this religious ethic shaped François Dumas's dealings with the slaves he inherited from his father. He treated them, it was reported, "as freemen, and ... he would not sell them at any price, because he would not give them a master" (*Tribune*, 2 July 1867). By the 1850s, legal emancipation was scarcely an option. In 1852 Louisiana state law required emancipated slaves to leave the United States within twelve months and in 1857 slave emancipations were entirely prohibited. Indeed, in 1859 the legislature admonished free persons of African descent like Dumas "to choose their own masters and become slaves for life" (Bell, 87).

With the coming of the Civil War Dumas and his allies envisioned a new era when the nation would propagate republicanism around the world so that "our brothers in every country can profit from this divine gift" (*L'Union*, 1862). When Union forces occupied the city in May 1862 they offered their services to General Benjamin F. Butler and assured him that "their people could not have any other feelings except those of perfect loyalty to the Federal cause" (Desdunes, 119). The men impressed Butler and near the end of the summer he finally agreed to their enlistment.

Within two weeks of the general's call to arms, African Creole soldiers filled a thousand-man regiment. Butler appointed Dumas a captain of the first regiment but quickly promoted him to the rank of major of the second African American regiment. The promotion made Dumas the Civil War's highest ranking African American combat officer. In 1863 Butler paid tribute to Dumas: "He is a man who would be worth a quarter of a million, in reasonably good times. He speaks three languages besides his own, reckoning French and English as his own.... He had more capability as Major, than I had as Major-General, I am quite sure, if knowledge of affairs, and every thing that goes to make up a man, is any test" (Houzeau, 74; Blassingame, 39).

As a newly commissioned officer Dumas disregarded the military's restriction against slave recruits, instead freeing and arming his bondsmen at his own expense in the tradition of the Haitian Revolution's free black slaveholders. He was reported to have called them together and asked them if they were willing to "break the bonds of their fellow men" (Bell, 233). When they said yes, he organized them into a company.

In September 1862, Dumas's brother, P. A. Dumas, invited eight Union officers, both black and white, to his home for an evening's entertainment. A white officer, John W. De Forest, related his impressions:

> Our entertainer is a man of about thirty who looks like a West Indian; his brother [François Dumas] has the complexion of an Italian and features which remind one of the first Napoleon. Both of them, although natives of New Orleans, have spent a great part of their lives in Paris, and speak good French, but nothing else. They did not differ in air and manners from the young Frenchmen whom I used to know abroad. One of the three [African American] officers present, of this mixed blood, was an extremely blond youth with curly yellow locks. Madame Dumas, about twenty years old, with regular features, handsome dark eyes, wavy black hair and a pale but healthy color, looks like a Jewess of southern Europe.... Then there were two girl-cousins of sixteen, lately from convent schools in Paris, two jolly little brunettes with slim figures and lively French manners (De Forest, 47–48).

In 1863 Major Dumas commanded several Union companies of black soldiers stationed at Ship Island in the Gulf of Mexico. As they advanced upon the coastal town of Pascagoula, Mississippi, a company of Confederate cavalrymen attacked. Dumas's troops retreated to the waterfront toward the cover of a Union gunboat. As they approached the vessel, white Union crewmen opened fire on them instead of firing on their Confederate pursuers. The vengeful attack stemmed from an incident in which a black sentry had killed some white soldiers at their Ship Island outpost. Major Dumas wheeled his men around and repulsed the Confederate attack, thereby rescuing the trapped soldiers. Dumas and three of his junior officers were singled out for special commendation. The men, their commander reported, "were constantly in the thickest of the fight, and by their unflinching bravery, and admirable handling of their commands, contributed to the success of the attack, and reflected great honor upon the flag under and for which they so nobly struggled" (Bell, 239).

The heroism of Dumas and his fellow officers notwithstanding, the Union commander who replaced Butler in 1862 had began a purge of black officers from the military in a concession to Louisiana's white conservatives. Under constant pressure Dumas finally resigned in disgust in the fall of 1863. By mid-1864 most of the seventy-five black officers commissioned by Butler had been replaced by white officers.

Dumas rejoined his allies in the political struggle in a campaign centered at two African Creole newspapers, *L'Union* (1862–1864) and its successor the *Tribune* (1864–1870). The newspapers condemned slavery; insisted that military service entitled black soldiers to political equality; compelled the president and the Congress to take up the issue of black voting rights even before the end of the war; and urged the Federal government to divide confiscated plantations into ten-acre plots to be distributed to displaced black families insisting that the former slaves "are entitled by a paramount right to the possession of the soil they have so long cultivated" (*Tribune*, 10 Sep. 1864).

In 1868 Dumas's *Tribune* faction engineered his Republican nomination for governor but even before the balloting began the party's dominant white conservatives had locked up a victory for their own candidate, Henry Clay Warmoth. Dumas rejected Warmoth's offer of the nomination for lieutenant governor. His misgivings were well placed. In 1871 Oscar J. Dunn, Warmoth's black lieutenant governor, wrote that Warmoth was the party's "first Ku Klux Governor" (Bell, 277).

In 1869 Dumas declined President Ulysses S. Grant's offer of the ambassadorship to Liberia. In Louisiana, despite his superior education and his proven talents as a businessman, community leader, and distinguished Civil War veteran, Dumas held only one office during Reconstruction, when he was appointed as engineer in 1871 on a federal project to rebuild levees on the Mississippi river.

FURTHER READING

Information related to Dumas is scattered and fragmentary. The most useful sources are Marcus B. Christian, "A Black History of Louisiana," typescript, Earl K. Long Library, University of New Orleans (n.d.).

Bell, Caryn Cossé. *Revolution, Romanticism, and the Afro-Creole Protest Tradition in Louisiana, 1718–1868* (1997).

Blassingame, John W. *Black New Orleans, 1860–1880* (1973).

De Forest, John William. *A Volunteer's Adventures: A Union Captain's Record of the Civil War*, ed. James H. Croushore (1996).

Desdunes, Rodolphe Lucien. *Our People and Our History*, ed. and trans. Sister Dorothea Olga McCants (1973).

Hirsch, Arnold R., and Joseph Logsdon, eds. *Creole New Orleans: Race and Americanization* (1992).

Houzeau, Jean-Charles. *My Passage at the New Orleans "Tribune": A Memoir of the Civil War Era*, ed. David C. Rankin and trans. Gerard F. Denault (1984).

Schweninger, Loren. *Black Property Owners in the South, 1790–1915* (1997).

CARYN COSSÉ BELL

Dumas, Henry (20 July 1934–23 May 1968), author, poet, educator, and civil rights activist, was born in Sweet Home, Arkansas, and with his family migrated to Harlem, New York, in 1944. After graduating from Commerce High School in 1953, Dumas studied briefly at the City College of New York prior to entering the U.S. Air Force in 1953, in which he served four years, including tours in San Antonio, Texas, and the Middle East. In 1955, while still enlisted, Dumas married Loreta Ponton. Upon completing his armed services commitment in 1957, he entered Rutgers University, but his tenure was short, and he did not receive a degree. In 1958 he and his wife started a family, which comprised two sons, David, born in 1958, and Michael, born in 1962.

From 1963 to 1964 Dumas worked at IBM, and it was at this time that his concern for civil rights began to take shape. Like many other African American writers, Dumas was affected by the turbulent political times and the civil rights movement of the 1960s and became an integral part of the Black Arts Movement, not only as a poet but also as a political activist. He supported the ideologies of the Black Power movement and was heavily influenced by the blues and jazz. In 1966 he teamed up with the African American jazz musician SUN RA, with whom he recorded *The Ark and The Ankh*, a compilation of conversations between the two artists on the important issues of the day, including MALCOLM X, the Black Arts Movement, and the state of black Americans.

Dumas began his teaching career in 1967 at Hiram College in Hiram, Ohio, where he edited several publications, including the *Hiram Poetry Review*. Shortly thereafter he relocated to Southern Illinois University, and as part of the U.S. government's War on Poverty's program Experiment in Higher Education, he directed the language workshops and worked with other poets and academics as a teacher and literary mentor. It was within this academic environment that Dumas first came into contact and formed an alliance with someone who would become the most important proponent of his work, Eugene Redmond. With Redmond and Sherman Fowler, Dumas contributed his poetry and literary philosophies to the establishment of the Black River Writers Press, located in East St. Louis, Illinois.

On 23 May 1968, after concluding a rehearsal with Sun Ra and his Arkestra in Harlem, Dumas was misidentified by a New York Transit police officer, who shot and killed him in the 125th Street subway station in the neighborhood of his youth. Not much more is known about the incident, but the loss of Dumas was felt within the hearts of young black scholars and artists alike. Because of Redmond's service as the executor of his estate as well as an editor of his work, Dumas had a stellar posthumous literary career, with most of his work published by the press he helped get off the ground, Black River Writers.

The first of the posthumous publications, *The Ark of Bones*, is a collection of short stories that appeared in 1970 and was followed that same year by *Poetry for My People*. *The Ark* makes personal connections between Dumas's African ancestors, the Middle Passage, and his childhood home in Arkansas and is in keeping with the dialect of the streets, while *Poetry*, which was republished in 1974 as *Play Ebony: Play Ivory*, is a collection of heartfelt poems about nature, humanity's place in it, and the importance of respecting and connecting to land, earth, animals, and other people. These two volumes introduced a young generation of poets, writers, and musicians to the spirit of nature and Afrocentricity that Dumas was able to capture. In 1976 Dumas's title *Jonoah and the Green Stone* was released. Although it was not a completed manuscript and is his only novel, with the editorial guidance and experience of Redmond, the publication found an audience and was well received. In 1979 *Rope of Wind and Other Stories*, which was reviewed as Dumas's reflections on folk music, was published, and a decade later *Knees of a Natural Man: The Selected Poetry of Henry Dumas* was released. Celebrating his life and the twentieth anniversary of his death, 1988 marked the rejuvenation of Dumas, and he quickly gained a following of young writers who highly anticipated and praised the 1989 title *Goodbye, Sweetwater*. TONI MORRISON, who, along with Redmond, championed his work, agreed with most who have reviewed Dumas that his literary production was not only extensive over a short period of time but also of a quality not usually seen in writers of his age.

In 2003 *Echo Tree: The Collected Short Fiction of Henry Dumas* was published. The book memorializes his sons, both of whom committed suicide, in 1987 and 1994, respectively; MARGARET WALKER; GWENDOLYN BROOKS, and Raymond R. Patterson. Published as part of the Coffee House Press's Black Arts Movement series, *Echo Tree* includes most of Dumas's best works of short stories, including "The Metagenesis of Sunra," an ode to Sun Ra and His Arkestra, which was so popular that most stores never had more than one copy available, with promises of more on the way.

The work of Henry Dumas permeated not only the literary world but also the music world and the college classroom. His work is a valuable tool in promoting understanding of African Americans during the Black Arts Movement and beyond. Dumas wrote about the black experience from a point of view that is unique both within and outside of his known community ties and had a profound effect on neo-soul music and the spoken word. His style of writing is recognizable in the poetry of TUPAC AMARU SHAKUR, Ursula Rucker, Mos Def, and Jill Scott.

FURTHER READING

Baraka, Amiri, and Larry Neal, eds. *Black Fire: The Seminal Anthology from the Black Arts Movement* (2007).

Black American Literary Forum 22.2 (1988).

Looker, Benjamin. *Point from Which Creation Begins: The Black Artists' Group of St. Louis* (2004).

Rivkin, Julie, and Michael Ryan, eds. *Literary Theory, an Anthology* (2004).

Smethurst, James Edward. *The Black Arts Movement: Literary Nationalism in the 1960s and 1970s* (2005).

Obituary: *East St. Louis Monitor*, 6 June 1968.

ELLESIA A. BLAQUE

Dummett, Clifton O., Sr. (20 May 1919–7 Sept. 2011), periodontist, public health specialist, and educator, was born Clifton Orin Dummett in Georgetown, British Guiana (later Guyana), the youngest of four children of Eglantine Annabella Johnson, a homemaker, and Alexander Adolphus Dummett, a pharmacist and registered dentist. Clifton attended St. Phillips Elementary School from 1924 until 1930 and Queen's College high school from 1930 until 1936, both in Georgetown, British Guiana. His values were strongly influenced by his father, mother, and uncle, Reginald Johnson, an Edinburgh-trained public health physician in Georgetown. "I came from a family that believed in the equality of man. I respected all peoples and demanded similar respect from those with whom I came in contact" (personal communication with the author).

Right after high school, in 1936, Alexander Adolphus Dummett obtained a student visa for his son to study in the United States at Howard University in Washington, D.C. Clifton shipped out of Georgetown, British Guiana, aboard the steamship *Lady Hawkins*, a Canadian National Steamship, and arrived a few days later at Boston, Massachusetts. From there he traveled almost immediately by train to Washington, D.C. He was eager to begin his education and felt he had little time for sightseeing. Clifton arrived in the U.S. capital determined to emulate his father, whom he described as serious, thorough, industrious and totally focused; "I always wanted to be just like him" (personal communication with the author). During his two years at Howard, Clifton Dummett describes himself as "quite a serious and introspective youngster. I devoted all my time and energies to education and study and did rather well at Howard" (personal communication with the author). During an interview at the opening of the exhibit, The Future Is Now! African Americans in Dentistry, at the California African American Museum in 2006, Dummett commented on his long struggle for equal rights: "I never resented the fight [for equal rights]. What I resented was the discrimination. I treated everyone with respect, but at the same time, I demanded it." In 1936, however, Washington, D.C., was a Jim Crow city. Respect and human equality was for white people. This environment must have encouraged the budding dentist to alter his plans. After two years, Dummett departed Washington to attend the Northwestern School of Dentistry in Chicago, joining the second wave of black migration to Chicago in search of better jobs and better lives. There he found life "pleasant" enough that he could tolerate the many "irritating racial incidents" that he encountered (personal communication with the author).

In 1943 Dummett married Lois Maxine Doyle, a physician's daughter from Chicago. Not only his spouse, she was also his publishing partner, editorial associate, and mother of their only child, Clifton Jr. The Dummetts left Chicago in 1943 for the Meharry School of Dentistry in Nashville, Tennessee. Four years later, at twenty-eight, he was named full-time dean, the youngest dental dean in the United States. He brought to Meharry his belief that all Americans should have "adequate health care regardless of race, creed, or color" (personal communication with the author).

Young Dean Dummett was soon tested. Jim Crow, sustained by the U.S. Supreme Court's decision in *Plessey v. Ferguson* (1896), dominated life in Nashville and throughout the South. The Southern Regional Plan was proposed by eleven southern governors in response to the *Gaines* decision of 1938, whereby the U.S. Supreme Court ruled that Lloyd Gaines, an African American from St. Louis, must be either admitted to the Law School of the University of Missouri, or else a School of Law established at Lincoln University, maintained by Missouri for the higher education of African Americans, to which he could be admitted. An attempt to perpetuate racial segregation, the Southern Regional Plan would have allowed the eleven states to contract among themselves for services unavailable in one state but available in already established institutions in another. This would create a means to send blacks students who wanted a medical education but lived in a state with no medical school for blacks to another state that had such a school, for example, Meharry Medical School in Tennessee. Meharry's president, M. Don Clawson, supported the plan, which promised Meharry needed financial support. Dummett, however, disagreed on principle and promptly resigned. He refused to support segregation's continuation and expansion in the health professions in the South or anywhere else. He called on his Meharry colleagues to join the mainstream of professional education and practice at all levels. Separate but equal on the basis of race, creed, class, or economic status, whether in education, health care, or the society at large, was not to be tolerated. Dummett was soundly criticized for his actions by representatives of organized dentistry at all levels.

The Meharry incident seems to have been pivotal in encouraging Dummett to engage in what Martin Luther King Jr., referring to Rosa Parks, called "creative witness." In the late 1940s and early 1950s Dummett began to chronicle the history and role of African Americans in the health care of the United States. In the mid- to late 1940s there were only about three hundred black dental students, mostly at Howard and Meharry, and Dummett pushed for expanded opportunities for African American admission to all American dental schools. By 2000 more than eight hundred African American students were attending dental schools. Regarding this improvement, Dummett remarked that "African American access to dental education in the United States is good, especially when viewed in comparison with what it was like in my early career. I would like to see more African American youngsters involved" (personal communication with the author).

Dummett used his writing skills as creative witness to advocate and keep alive the case for human rights, equality, and justice. He also set examples: he was the first black faculty member at the University of Alabama School of Dentistry, as well as a charter member of the first chapter of Omicron Kappa Upsilon honor society at a primarily African American dental school; he is "the one individual credited with preserving the history of African Americans in dentistry" (Rosemary Fetter, Executive Director, National Museum of Dentistry).

In 2000, with his wife, Lois, Dummett coauthored *NDA II: The Story of America's Second National Dental Association*. This volume probes the history of the first National Dental Association, which began as an organization of exclusively white dentists and evolved into the major African American dental association. In an early publication Dummett laid out his vision for African Americans in dental health:

> Prepare yourselves for the best type of dentistry. Get the best wherever it is available. Then help in the fight to make and keep it the best in our own institutions so that sometime in the not too distant future what we now call our "Negro" institutions will not be Negro institutions, but will be world institutions that have made such outstanding contributions that they too will be regarded as places where the very best in dental knowledge can be obtained (*The Bulletin of the National Dental Association* 5. 2 [1947]).

In 2011 Dummett died in Los Angeles. He was 92.

FURTHER READING

Dummett, Clifton O. *The Growth and Development of the Negro in Dentistry in the U.S.* (1952).

Dummett, Clifton O., and Lois D. Dummett. *Dental Education at Meharry Medical College: Origin and Odyssey* (1992).

Dummett, Clifton O., and Lois D. Dummett. *NDA II: America's Second National Dental Association* (2000).

LOUIS M. ABBEY

Dunbar, Paul Laurence (27 June 1872–9 Feb. 1906), author, was born in Dayton, Ohio, the son of Joshua Dunbar, a plasterer, and Matilda Burton Murphy, a laundry worker. His literary career began at age twelve, when he wrote an Easter poem and recited it in church. He served as editor in chief of his high school's student newspaper and presided over its debating society. While still in school, he contributed

Paul Laurence Dunbar, as shown in the frontispiece to his *Lyrics of Sunshine and Shadow*, 1905. (Library of Congress.)

poems and sketches to the *Dayton Herald* and the *West Side News*, a local paper published by Orville Wright of Kitty Hawk fame, and briefly edited the *Tattler*, a newspaper for blacks that Wright published and printed. He graduated from high school in 1891 with the hope of becoming a lawyer, but, lacking the funds to pursue a college education, he went instead to work as an elevator operator.

Dunbar wrote and submitted poetry and short stories in his spare time. His first break came in 1892, when the Western Association of Writers held its annual meeting in Dayton. One of Dunbar's former teachers arranged to have him deliver the welcoming address, and his rhyming greeting pleased the conventioneers so much that they voted him into the association. One of the attendees, poet James Newton Matthews, wrote an article about Dayton's young black poet that received wide publication in the Midwest, and soon Dunbar was receiving invitations from newspaper editors to submit his poems for publication. Encouraged by this success, he published *Oak and Ivy* (1893), a slender volume of fifty-six poems that sold well, particularly after Dunbar, an excellent public speaker, read selections from the book before evening club and church meetings throughout Ohio and Indiana.

In 1893 Dunbar traveled to Chicago, Illinois, to write an article for the *Herald* about the World's Columbian Exposition. He decided to stay in the Windy City and found employment as a latrine attendant. He eventually obtained a position as clerk to FREDERICK DOUGLASS, who was overseeing the Haitian Pavilion, as well as a temporary assignment from the Chicago *Record* to cover the exposition. After a rousing Douglass speech, the highlight of the exposition's Negro American Day, Dunbar read one of his poems, "The Colored Soldiers," to an appreciative audience of thousands. Sadly, when the exposition closed, Chicago offered Dunbar no better opportunity for full-time employment than his old job as elevator boy, and so he reluctantly returned to Dayton. However, he did so with Douglass's praise ringing in his ears: "One of the sweetest songsters his race has produced and a man of whom I hope great things."

Dunbar's determination to become a great writer was almost derailed by a chance to pursue his old dream of becoming a lawyer. In 1894 a Dayton attorney hired him as a law clerk with the understanding that Dunbar would have the opportunity to study law on the side. However, Dunbar discovered that law no longer enthralled him as it once had; moreover, he found that working and studying left him no time to write, and so he returned to the elevator and his poetry. He soon had enough new poems for a second volume, *Majors and Minors* (1895), which was published privately with the financial backing of H. A. Tobey of Toledo, Ohio. This work contains poems in both standard English ("majors") and black dialect ("minors"), many of which are regarded as among his best. In 1896 William Dean Howells, at the time America's most prominent literary critic, wrote a lengthy and enthusiastic review of *Majors and Minors*'s dialect poems for *Harper's Weekly*, a highly regarded literary magazine with a wide circulation. The review gave Dunbar's career as a poet a tremendous boost. Sales of *Majors and Minors* skyrocketed, and Dunbar, now under the management of Major James Burton Pond's lecture bureau, embarked on a national reading tour. Pond also arranged for Dodd, Mead and Company to publish *Lyrics of Lowly Life* (1896), a republication of ninety-seven poems from Dunbar's first two volumes and eight new poems. Howells, in the introduction to this volume, described Dunbar as "the only man of pure African blood and of American civilization to feel the negro life aesthetically and express it lyrically." The combination of Howells's endorsement and Dunbar's skill soon led the latter to become one of America's most popular writers. After the publication of *Lyrics of Lowly Life*, Dunbar went on a reading tour of England. When he returned to the United States in 1897, he accepted a position as a library assistant at the Library of Congress in Washington, D.C. Meanwhile, several national literary magazines were vying for anything he wrote, and in 1898 Dunbar seemed to have developed the golden touch. *Lippincott's Monthly Magazine* published his first novel, *The Uncalled*, which appeared in book form later that year; *Folks from Dixie*, a collection of twelve short stories that had been published individually in various magazines, also came out in book form; and he collaborated with WILL MARION COOK to write a hit Broadway musical, *Clorindy*. At this time he developed a nagging cough, perhaps the result of an abundance of heavy lifting in the dusty, drafty library combined with skimping on sleep while pursuing deadlines. Partly because of his success and partly because of ill health, he resigned from the library at the end of 1898 to devote himself full time to his writing.

In 1899 Dunbar published two collections of poems, *Lyrics of the Hearthside* and *Poems of Cabin and Field*, and embarked on a third reading tour. However, his health deteriorated so rapidly that the tour was cut short. The official diagnosis was pneumonia, but his doctor suspected that Dunbar was in the early stages of tuberculosis. To help ease the pain in his lungs, he turned to strong drink, which did little more than make him a near-alcoholic. He gave up his much-beloved speaking tours but continued to write at the same breakneck pace. While convalescing in Denver, Colorado, he wrote a western novel, *The Love of Landry* (1900), and published *The Strength of Gideon and Other Stories* (1900), another collection of short stories. He also wrote two plays, neither of which was ever published, as well as some lyrics and sketches. In the last five years of his life, he published two novels, *The Fanatics* (1901) and *The Sport of the Gods* (1901, in *Lippincott*'s; 1902, in book form); two short story collections, *In Old Plantation Days* (1903) and *The Heart of Happy Hollow* (1904); eight collections of poetry, *Candle-Lightin' Time* (1901), *Lyrics of Love and Laughter* (1903), *When Malindy Sings* (1903), *Li'l Gal* (1904), *Chris'mus Is A-comin' and Other Poems* (1905), *Howdy, Honey, Howdy* (1905), *Lyrics of Sunshine and Shadow* (1905), and *Joggin' Erlong* (1906); and collaborated with Cook on another musical, *In Dahomey* (1902).

Dunbar had married writer Alice Ruth Moore (ALICE DUNBAR-NELSON) in 1898; they had no children. In 1902 the couple separated, largely because of Dunbar's drinking, and never reconciled. After the breakup Dunbar lived in Chicago for a while, then in 1903 returned to live with his mother in Dayton, where he died of tuberculosis in 1906.

Dunbar's goal was "to interpret my own people through song and story, and to prove to the many that after all we are more human than African." In so doing, he portrayed the lives of blacks as being filled with joy and humor as well as misery and difficulty. Dunbar is best known for his dialect poems that, intended for a predominantly white audience, often depict slaves as dancing, singing, carefree residents of "Happy Hollow." On the other hand, a great deal of his lesser-known prose work speaks out forcefully against racial injustice, both before and after emancipation, as in "The Lynching of Jube Benson," a powerful short story about the guilt that haunts a white man who once participated in the hanging of an innocent black. Perhaps his two most eloquent expressions of the reality of the black experience in America are "We Wear the Mask," in which he declares, "We wear the mask that grins and lies, ... /We smile, but, O great Christ, our cries /To thee from tortured souls arise," and "Sympathy," wherein he states that "I know why the caged bird sings, ... /It is not a carol of joy or glee, /But a prayer ... that upward to Heaven he flings."

Dunbar was the first black American author to be able to support himself solely as a result of his writing. His success inspired the next generation of black writers, including JAMES WELDON JOHNSON, LANGSTON HUGHES, and CLAUDE MCKAY, to dream of and achieve literary success. Dunbar was celebrated and scrutinized by the national media as a representative of his race. His charm and wit, his grace under pressure, and his ability as a speaker and author did much to give the lie to turn-of-the-century misconceptions about the racial inferiority of blacks.

FURTHER READING

Dunbar's papers are in the archives of the Ohio Historical Society.

Gentry, Tony. *Paul Laurence Dunbar* (1989).

Martin, Jay, and Gossie H. Hudson, eds. *The Paul Laurence Dunbar Reader* (1975).

Williams, Kenny J. *They Also Spoke: An Essay on Negro Literature in America, 1787–1930* (1970).

Obituary: *New York Times*, 10 Feb. 1906.

This entry is taken from the *American National Biography* and is published here with the permission of the American Council of Learned Societies.

CHARLES W. CAREY JR.

Dunbar-Nelson, Alice (19 July 1875–18 Sept. 1935), writer, educator, and activist, was born Alice Ruth Moore in New Orleans to Joseph Moore, a seaman, and Patricia Wright, a former slave and seamstress. Moore completed a teachers' training program at Straight College (now Dillard University) and taught in New Orleans from 1892 to 1896, then in Brooklyn, New York, from 1897 to 1898. Demonstrating a commitment to the education of African American girls and women that would continue throughout her life, Moore helped found the White Rose Home for Girls in Harlem in 1898.

Moore's primary ambition, however, was literary, and she published her first book at the age of twenty, *Violets and Other Tales* (1895), a collection of poetry in a classical lyric style, essays, and finely observed short stories. The publication of Moore's poetry and photograph in a Boston magazine inspired the famed poet PAUL LAURENCE DUNBAR to begin a correspondence with her that led to their marriage in 1898. Her second book, *The Goodness of St. Rocque and Other Stories* (1899), a collection of short stories rooted in New Orleans Creole culture, was published as a companion volume to Dunbar's *Poems of Cabin and Field*, and their marriage was celebrated as a literary union comparable to that of Robert and Elizabeth Barrett Browning. The couple separated, however, in 1902, after less than four tumultuous and sometimes violent years, due in part to Paul's alcoholism. Paul Laurence Dunbar died of tuberculosis four years later. Although the couple never reconciled, Alice Dunbar expressed regret and outrage that his family did not inform her of his last illness, or even his death, which she learned of from a newspaper article.

In the fall of 1902 Alice Dunbar resumed her teaching career at Howard High School in Wilmington, Delaware. As an English and drawing instructor, then head of the English department, Dunbar also served as an administrator and directed several of her own plays at the school. Dunbar also pursued scholarly work at various institutions, including Columbia University and the University of Pennsylvania, ultimately completing an M.A. degree at Cornell University. A portion of her master's thesis on the influence of Milton on Wordsworth was published in the prestigious *Modern Language Notes* in 1909. In 1910 Dunbar secretly married a fellow Howard High School teacher, Henry Arthur Callis, although they soon divorced.

During this busy period of teaching, administration, and study, Dunbar also participated in the burgeoning black women's club movement, through which she delivered lectures on a variety of subjects, most commonly race, women's rights, and education. However, she achieved the most renown when speaking as the widow of Paul Laurence Dunbar. Like her late husband, she struggled with the preference among white audiences for Paul's "dialect" poetry, although she ably performed these works, along with his "pure English poems," which she preferred. Building on her work as a public speaker, Dunbar edited and published *Masterpieces of Negro Eloquence* (1914), a collection of Negro oratory from the pre– and post–Civil War era, designed to celebrate the fiftieth anniversary of the Emancipation Proclamation.

In 1916 Dunbar married Robert J. Nelson, a widower with two children, but maintained her association with her first husband by hyphenating her name. In *The Dunbar Speaker and Entertainer: The Poet and His Song* (1920), Dunbar-Nelson assembled a wider range of African American oratory than in the political speeches of *Masterpieces of Negro Eloquence*, and included a large number of her husband's and her own poetry deemed suitable for performance, along with poetry, fiction, and speeches by JAMES WELDON JOHNSON, CHARLES W. CHESNUTT, and others. Dunbar-Nelson seems to have found her lifelong connection to her first husband both an asset, in furthering her writing and speaking career, and a burden, evidenced by several unsuccessful attempts to publish under a pseudonym.

Dunbar-Nelson's third marriage was satisfying both personally and professionally; as a journalist Nelson was supportive of Dunbar-Nelson's writing and political activities. Dunbar-Nelson combined her literary and political interests through the production and publication of *Mine Eyes Have Seen the Glory* (1918), a play promoting African American involvement in World War I. She also toured the South for the Women's Committee for National Defense on behalf of the war effort and was active in the campaign for women's suffrage. She continued her political activism despite protests from her employers at Howard High, and in 1920 lost her job following an unsanctioned trip to a social justice conference in Ohio.

Relieved of her teaching duties, Dunbar-Nelson devoted herself more fully to political activism, and from 1920 to 1922 enjoyed a close collaboration with her husband through their publication of the liberal black newspaper, the *Wilmington Advocate*. She joined a delegation of black activists to meet with President Warren G. Harding in 1921, worked for passage of the Dyer Anti-Lynching Bill in 1922, and organized black women voters for the Democratic Party in 1924. As a member of the Federation of Colored Women, she cofounded the Industrial School for Colored Girls in Marshalltown, Delaware, and worked as a teacher and parole officer for the school from 1924 to 1928.

Dunbar-Nelson's journalistic and historical writings date from 1902, when she wrote several articles for the *Chicago Daily News*. In 1916 her lengthy historical work "People of Color in Louisiana" was published in *The Journal of Negro History*, and from 1926 to 1930 she was a newspaper columnist for the Pittsburgh *Courier* and the Washington *Eagle*. Many of her columns were syndicated by the Associated Negro Press, and her subjects ranged beyond the usual material considered suitable for women journalists, taking on political and social issues of the day, which she dealt with in a witty and incisive style. By contrast, many of Dunbar-Nelson's literary efforts, including four novels, went unpublished in her lifetime, although the best of them are now collected in a three-volume set, *The Works of Alice Dunbar-Nelson* (1988). Included are previously published and unpublished works of poetry, fiction, essays, and drama, which give evidence of Dunbar-Nelson's wide range of interests, both thematically and formally.

Dunbar-Nelson's exquisitely crafted fiction secures her position as a pioneer of the African American short story. Interestingly, her fiction and poetry, which she considered the most "pure" from a literary point of view, deal only tangentially with the racial issues that so occupied her political and journalistic activities. In these works she focuses instead on issues of gender oppression and psychology, and evidences a frustration in her diary at the lack of interest from mainstream white publishers. The African American press was more receptive to her literary work, and between 1917 and 1928 Dunbar-Nelson published poems in *The Crisis*, *Opportunity*, *Ebony*, and *Topaz*, and other African American journals, enjoying a small heyday as a poet with the advent of the Harlem Renaissance.

In addition to recording her often frustrated literary ambitions, Dunbar-Nelson's diary, begun in 1921, offers a glimpse of her romantic relationships with both men and women, her lifelong worries about finances, and her struggle with traditional women's roles. Even in her mostly amicable relationship with Robert Nelson, Dunbar-Nelson objects to his insistence on her managing both household and professional duties, and she chafes at the regulation of her dress and makeup by male employers. The extant portions of the diary include the years 1921 and 1926–1931, and were published as *Give Us Each Day: The Diary of Alice Dunbar-Nelson* (1984).

In 1932 Robert Nelson received a political appointment to the Pennsylvania Athletic Commission and the couple moved to Philadelphia. Living in prosperity for the first time in her life, Dunbar-Nelson maintained an active social life among the black elite, including such luminaries as James Weldon Johnson, W. E. B. DuBois, Langston Hughes, Georgia Douglas Johnson, and Mary Church Terrell. No longer burdened by financial want, Dunbar-Nelson remained active in the last years of her life as a philanthropist and political activist. She died in Philadelphia of a heart condition.

Alice Dunbar-Nelson's life and work are testament to the diverse talents and activities of educated African American women of the late nineteenth and early twentieth centuries. As a light-skinned woman of mixed African, European, and Native American ancestry, Dunbar-Nelson was acutely sensitive to the resentment of both whites and darker-skinned African Americans, but also occasionally passed for white in order to gain access to the racially segregated world of opera, museums, theater, and bathing spas. In much of her literary work, Dunbar-Nelson focused on nonracial themes, often creating white or racially ambiguous characters, but in her work as an educator, journalist, and activist, Dunbar-Nelson placed herself firmly within African American culture, where her contributions remain vital.

FURTHER READING

Dunbar-Nelson, Alice. *Give Us Each Day: The Diary of Alice Dunbar-Nelson*, ed. Gloria T. Hull (1984).

Hull, Gloria T. *Color, Sex, and Poetry: Three Women Writers of the Harlem Renaissance* (1987).

ALICE KNOX EATON

Duncan, Harry (30 Apr. 1863–27 July 1894), bootblack, barber, porter, actor, singer, and politician, was born William Henry Harrison Duncan in Columbia, Missouri, to former slaves. A close friend, Henry Massey, persuaded him to come to St. Louis, where he was a "sport, a jolly fellow, a swell dresser, a ladies' favorite, but, above all, he was a magnificent singer."

As a member of Massey's Climax Quartet Duncan gained fame for his low, smooth, rich, sure, bass voice. He was also an actor and performed regularly at the London Theatre in St. Louis.

In Clayton, Missouri, west of St. Louis, Duncan was hanged for the murder of an Irish American policeman named James Brady in Charles Starkes's saloon at 715 N. 11th Street. A popular ballad complex ("Duncan and Brady," "Brady and Duncan," "Brady," "King Brady") arose after the murder.

At about 8:30 P.M. on 6 October 1890 a crowd of men, mostly African American, had gathered on the sidewalk outside Starkes's saloon to watch a fist fight between Harry's brother Luther, whose barbershop was next to the saloon, and Bob Henderson. Soon officer John Gaffney arrived, ordered everyone off the street, and threatened to arrest Luther, who protested, "You can go to hell, you can't take me away." When Gaffney grabbed Luther's arm, both Harry and Luther started hitting him. With the crowd's help Gaffney was pushed into the street and knocked out. Regaining consciousness he drew his revolver and fired two shots into the air. They were heard by officers Daniel Maloney, John Connors, and James Brady.

Luther fled into Starkes's saloon, followed by Gaffney, revolver in hand. Someone shouted, "Don't shoot!" Gaffney turned and was struck in the head with a billiard cue stick wielded by Harry. As Gaffney staggered away, Harry grabbed his gun. When officers Maloney and Connors came into the saloon and saw Gaffney, covered in blood, Starkes pointed to Harry and said, "Here is the man who did it." Harry shot at the officers and crouched behind the bar as they returned fire. Brady came in, calling for Harry to surrender. When Harry refused, Brady leaned over the bar and fired a shot. According to some, Harry stood up, shot Brady in the chest, and subsequently surrendered to the other officers, saying, "I've killed one; I'm satisfied."

The African American neighborhood where this occurred, the "Bloody" Third District, was adjacent to the Irish American Kerry Patch. There was intense antipathy between local blacks and Irish. Brady's death at age thirty-one, leaving behind a wife and three small children, caused an uproar among whites and led to street fights characterized as "race war." In song at least, the events were celebrated by blacks.

> Soon's the women heard Brady was dead
> They went straight home and dressed in red.
> Came a-skippin' and toddlin' along,
> 'Cause they's glad old Brady was gone.
> Been on a jolly so long!
> (Dorothy Scarborough, *On the Trail of Negro Folk-Songs* [1925], 86)
> Brady's dead and Gaffney's down,
> We'll get busy in this town,
> Chase the policemen off the beat,
> Chase the white folks off the street.
> (David [1976], 113)

Harry's lead attorney was Walter M. Farmer, an African American who had graduated from the Washington University Law School, St. Louis, in 1889. Farmer argued successfully for a change of venue and Harry was tried in Clayton. He was convicted in November 1892, and sentenced to death. After several postponements he was hanged at the courthouse in Clayton on 27 July 27 1894.

There is considerable doubt that Harry fired the shot that killed Brady. Farmer argued that Brady's pistol, which Harry had fired, was out of ammunition when Brady was shot. He argued further that the path through the body taken by the bullet was not consistent with Harry's and Brady's positions at the time of the shooting. These efforts failed in the face of testimony that Brady had had two pistols and the consideration that Brady was shot in the front while he could have been leaning over the bar.

Duncan maintained his innocence, and Farmer called the trial and hanging "a sin, a shame, and an outrage. If ever an innocent man was hanged, that man was Duncan." Thomas Wallace testified that he had seen Starkes shoot Brady, but he later recanted, saying that his false testimony had been solicited by Duncan. Ben Newman also testified that he had seen Starkes shoot Brady. Two days before his execution and over a month after Starkes died, Duncan claimed to have seen Starkes shoot Brady. A month after the execution Lawler Daley said he too had seen it. Ten years later it was reported that the dying Starkes had confessed to the crime.

The ballad, "Duncan and Brady," probably began circulating shortly after the events described above.

> Duncan, Duncan was a-tendin' the bar
> When in walked Brady with a shinin' star;
> Cried, "Duncan, Duncan, you are under arrest."
> And Duncan shot a hole in Brady's breast.
> Brady fell down on the barroom floor,
> Cried, "Please, Mr. Duncan, don't you shoot no more."
> The women cried, "Oh, ain't it a shame,

He's shot King Brady—gonna shoot him again."
(John and Alan Lomax, *Our Singing Country* [1941], 333–335)

The jocularity of these texts, and the jauntiness of the tunes to which they are sung, may attest to the bitterness with which African Americans regarded Irish Americans in St. Louis in the early 1890s.

FURTHER READING

David, John Russell. *Tragedy in Ragtime: Black Folktales-from St. Louis*. Ph.D. dissertation, St. Louis University (1976). University Microfilms International 7622522.

JOHN GARST

Todd Duncan, baritone opera singer renowned for his role as Porgy in *Porgy and Bess*, 1942. (Library of Congress/New York World-Telegram and the Sun Newspaper Photograph Collection.)

Duncan, Robert Todd (12 Feb. 1903–28 Feb. 1998), baritone, concert and opera singer, and master pedagogue, was born in Danville, Kentucky, to John C. and Letitia C. Duncan. John Duncan was a farmer in Danville and soon moved the family to Indianapolis, where he became a chauffeur and butler. Letitia ("Lettie") Duncan was a well-respected piano teacher and church musician. Unfortunately, the parents experienced marital problems, and Robert, an only child, moved at age seven to Somerset, Kentucky, to be raised by his maternal grandfather, (Robert) Owsley Cooper. Cooper, a skilled brick mason, stone mason, and railroad worker, had a beautiful baritone voice and directed the church choir. Duncan's mother moved to Somerset after her divorce. In 1923 she married John Cambron and returned to Indianapolis.

Music permeated Todd Duncan's life, surrounded as he was by his musical parents and grandfather. Duncan's parents spent many evenings at the piano, which his mother played while his father sang. Duncan also witnessed a steady stream of children coming to the house for piano lessons. When his mother overhead him playing Bach at the piano, she knew he was ready to begin formal training. At age five he began to study piano with his mother, who became his only significant piano teacher. She was a strict and exacting woman with high standards and instilled in her son solid discipline, work ethics, musicianship, and artistry. Her axiom "obey the composer, serve the poet, and make music" pervaded her teaching and became Duncan's precept throughout his career. For a short period of time he also took violin and trumpet lessons.

Duncan attended public schools in Indianapolis and in Somerset. Since there was no high school for blacks in Somerset, he was admitted as a high school student at Simmons University in Louisville. Duncan demonstrated leadership and participated in musical, academic, and athletic programs. He became captain of the basketball team, played tennis, and won awards; he served as the secretary of the YMCA, sang in the Male Glee Club, started and directed a Male Quartette, and played piano in the orchestra. In 1921 he graduated from the academic department and in 1922 from the music department.

After hearing vocalist ROLAND HAYES in concert, his focus shifted from piano to singing. Sara Lee became his first and most significant voice teacher. Lee (born Liebowitz) was a Jewish immigrant on the faculty of the Louisville Conservatory of Music. She defied segregation laws by teaching at Simmons University, where she worked with five young men, including Duncan.

In 1925 Duncan then earned a bachelor's degree in English from Butler College in Indianapolis. While attending Butler he studied music at the Indiana School of Fine Arts. He taught in an Indianapolis public school for a very short time and assisted his mother with the church choir.

Duncan returned to Simmons to teach Latin, English, and music in the Normal Department. He maintained existing ensembles and developed others, while also traveling and performing before royalty.

Sara Lee then advised Duncan to move east, believing it to be more fertile for the discovery and full realization of his talent. He pursued an M.A. in English Literature at Columbia University Teachers College in New York City. Upon completion of his degree in 1931, Duncan joined the faculty of Howard University, in Washington, D.C., as an instructor, and later became the head of Public School Music. Quickly acclimating himself into the musical life of the area, he earned an excellent reputation. He directed church choirs, developed a private voice studio, and continued to perform and tour as a concert artist. On 23 June 1934 Duncan married Nancy Gladys Jackson Tignor, a schoolteacher who sang in church choir and was to become well respected in political circles. He adopted Charles Andrew Tignor Jr., her son from her previous marriage, and had the child's name changed to Charles Tignor Duncan. The younger Duncan would become distinguished in the field of law.

A few weeks after his marriage, Duncan made his professional operatic debut as Alfio in Mascagni's *Cavalleria Rusticana* with the Aeolian Opera Association in New York. The artistically successful production was a financial disaster and unexpectedly closed after opening night. That same year, composer George Gershwin, in search of singers for his opera *Porgy and Bess*, invited Duncan to audition. Duncan initially declined the famed composer's invitation because of a prior commitment to solo in a church concert, but rescheduled to audition at a later time. Gershwin heard Duncan sing only measures of a seventeenth-century Italian aria before asking, "Will you be my Porgy?" Lacking enthusiasm for Gershwin's work, Duncan said, "I don't know, I have to hear your music first." George and Ira Gershwin played and sang through the opera with him; Duncan fell in love with the work. Adopting the stage name "Todd Duncan," he created the role of Porgy in 1935 with overwhelming success. His career catapulted, and he immediately rose to international prominence.

Duncan sang many times in the White House and was featured in *The Sun Never Sets* (1938), the stage musical *Cabin in the Sky* (1940), the movie *Syncopation* (1942), and subsequent productions of *Porgy and Bess*. Since he remained on the faculty of Howard University until 1945, he took many extended leaves of absence to accommodate his performance schedule.

In 1942 Duncan left *Porgy and Bess* to pursue his passion for the concert stage, performing with piano accompanist William Duncan Allen for the next ten years. With a vast repertoire of airs and art songs in Italian, German, and French; songs of foreign origin sung in English; and spirituals, the two toured the United States and traveled extensively around the globe, often singing to record-breaking, capacity-filled, or overflowing concert halls. They experienced particularly enthusiastic audiences in Australia and Central America. Duncan's performances emphasized subtle nuances, and his showmanship brought excitement.

Amid phenomenal audience responses, Duncan encountered many roadblocks. A major recording company reneged on an offer. The Metropolitan Opera Company never invited him to sing, stating that "America just was not ready [for a person of his race]." An unyielding man of principle, Duncan refused to sing in segregated venues. This position caused various places, including the National Theater in Washington, D.C., to reexamine its biases. His wife, frequently traveling with him, shielded him from the impact of many injustices.

In 1945 Duncan made an historic debut with the New York City Opera. He became the first African American featured in a traditionally "white" lead role with a major American opera house, singing Tonio in Leoncavallo's *I Pagliacci*. He created the role of Stephen Kumalo in Weill's *Lost in the Stars* (1950), for which he won the Donaldson Award and the Drama Critics Award for the Best Male Performance in a Musical. In the 1950s he often toured with soprano Camilla Williams, and in 1955 he was featured in the film *Unchained*.

Duncan retired from the concert stage in 1964 and taught in his private studio full-time. From 1979 to 1992 he taught at the Curtis Institute of Music. Initially he commuted to Philadelphia; then students commuted to Washington, D.C. He conducted master classes in various American universities and summer programs. Duncan often said, "I want to die with my boots on." He scheduled students until the day he died. On the morning of 28 February 1998 a student with his accompanist appeared at the door for the scheduled lesson only to learn that Duncan had just passed away.

Porgy was Duncan's most famous performance, but he was faithful to the concert stage, and he emerged as one of the finest interpreters of song. He opened operatic doors for others of his race. His legacy lies not only in his performances but also in his teachings. Duncan's students, who regard him as their most profound teacher, contribute meaningfully and widely to the profession worldwide in universities, private teaching, and school systems and on the concert and opera stages. Duncan has been awarded numerous honorary doctorates and prestigious awards from colleges, universities, and cultural organizations. Major national cultural organizations, including the National Association of Teachers of Singing and the National Opera Association, have established awards bearing his name. Duncan was inducted in the Kentucky Civil Rights Hall of Fame in 2005 and the Kentucky Music Hall of Fame and Museum in 2006.

FURTHER READING

Robert Todd Duncan's Papers are housed in the Eva Jessye Collection, University of Michigan, Ann Arbor.

Jablonski, Edward, and Lawrence D. Stewart. *The Gershwin Years* (1958).

Robinson-Oturu, Gail M. *The Life and Legacy of Todd Duncan: A Biographical Study* (2000).

GAIL ROBINSON-OTURU

Duncan, Thelma Myrtle (14 Oct. 1902–29 July 1987), playwright, writer, and music teacher, was born in St. Louis, Missouri. Precise information about Duncan's parents is unknown, but she was raised in St. Louis by Samuel L. Duncan, a laborer, and Addie Duncan, a homemaker. Duncan's intellect was recognized by Samuel and he made plans to send her to college. On 1 October 1920 Duncan began her studies in music at Howard University, where she studied under the respected theater professor Montgomery Gregory and became a member of the Howard University Players.

Duncan and her peers wrote prolifically under the tutelage of Gregory and produced several plays about the experiences of Africans and African Americans. Like many other African American female artists of this period Duncan used her work to explore issues of race, identity, gender, education, and class. In her one-act play *Sacrifice*, the moral drama centered on the struggles and pressures of Mrs. Payton, a widowed washerwoman who wants her children Ina and Billy to have better lives than she and her deceased husband had. On 7 April 1923 the Howard Players presented another Duncan play, *The Death Dance*, at Howard University's Rankin Memorial Chapel. *The Death Dance* was a one-act play centered around the trial of Kamo, an African villager accused of stealing gold from one of the village elders, and Asumana, a young dancer who dances for the village medicine man to try and save Kamo from a death sentence. Other Duncan plays from this period include *Drifter*, *Jinda*, *Payment*, and *The Scarlet Shawl*.

In 1924 Duncan graduated from Howard University with a degree in music. While well received, her production of *The Death Dance* did not situate Duncan among the ranks of more well-known playwrights of the Harlem Renaissance like ANGELINA WELD GRIMKE, GEORGIA DOUGLAS JOHNSON, or ZORA NEALE HURSTON. In the summer of 1929 Duncan traveled to New Mexico, El Paso, Texas, and Mexico before returning to her family's home in La Junta, Colorado, to continue writing. Duncan was resolute in her commitment to her vocation. In a 1929 letter to Professor Gregory, she wrote, "I shall continually write on something whether it be good or bad."

In 1931 Duncan sold her play *Black Magic* to Row Peterson and Company, a noteworthy accomplishment, as many playwrights, both black and white, had difficulty selling plays during the Depression. To supplement her income as a writer, Duncan taught piano lessons to African American, Spanish, Mexican, and Japanese students. On 21 September 1932 Duncan entered into a brief marriage with Roosevelt Brown, a railroad employee, and settled in Albuquerque, New Mexico. At the same time Duncan changed her preferred genre. In a 23 April 1934 letter to Professor Gregory, she told him of her plans for a novel, tentatively titled *Ham's Children*. Duncan did not provide any details about the novel, and the book was never published. Duncan's career continued to wane.

Duncan was eventually divorced from Brown. She later married a postal worker named John H. ("Bud") Greene and worked for over fifty years as a music teacher. She was also an active member of Delta Sigma Theta, the NAACP, the Postal Workers Women's Auxiliary, the Eureka Matrons Club, the Music Teacher Association of Music Club, the Theater Guild, the Grant Chapel African Methodist Episcopal (AME) Church, and the First United Methodist Church and Choir. After her marriage to Green, Duncan never again published.

FURTHER READING

Letters by Duncan to Professor Thomas Montgomery Gregory are housed in the Thomas Gregory Collection, Moorland-Spingarn Research Center, Howard University Library, Washington, D.C.

Bzowski, Frances Diodato. *American Women Playwrights, 1900–1930: A Checklist* (1992).

Locke, Alain, ed. *Plays in Negro Life: A Source Book of Native American Drama* (1970).

Peterson, Bernard L. *The African American Theatre Directory, 1816–1960: A Comprehensive Guide to Early Black Theatre Organizations, Companies, Theatres, and Performing Groups* (1997).

Richardson, Willis, and May Miller. *The Negro History in Thirteen Plays* (1935).

Wise, Claude Merton, ed. *The Year Book of Short Plays* (1931).

EUNICE ANGELICA WHITMAL

Duncanson, Robert S. (1821?–21 Dec. 1872), painter, was born in Fayette, New York, the son of John Dean Duncanson, a carpenter and handyman, and Lucy Nickles. Robert's grandfather Charles Duncanson was a former slave from Virginia who was emancipated and around 1790 moved north. Perhaps because he was the illegitimate offspring of his master, Charles had been permitted to learn a skilled trade and later to earn his release from bondage. After the death of Charles, the Duncanson family moved west to the boomtown of Monroe, Michigan, on the tip of Lake Erie. There Robert, along with his four brothers, was raised in the family trades of house painting, decorating, and carpentry, a legacy of his grandfather's bondage. At the age of seventeen, after several years of apprenticeship, Robert entered into the painting trade with a partner, John Gamblin, advertising as "Painters and Glaziers."

For unknown reasons the painting partnership disbanded after only a year. Apparently Duncanson was not satisfied pursuing a trade and was determined to embark on a career as an artist. He moved to Cincinnati, the economic and artistic center of the United States west of the Appalachian Mountains and one of the major population centers of the free black population in the United States and a locus of abolitionist activity.

On account of the limited opportunities to learn the art of painting, Duncanson, like many American artists, was forced to teach himself art by painting portraits, copying prints, and sketching from nature. Seeking commissions to sustain his burgeoning artistic career, he became an itinerant painter, traveling regularly between Cincinnati, Detroit, and Monroe. The *Portrait of a Mother and Daughter* (1841) is Duncanson's earliest datable painting. The mannered and labored style of this portrait is typical among limners of this era but demonstrates considerable potential. This painting suggests the style of Duncanson's *Fancy Portrait*, which marked his exhibition debut in 1842. Within two years Duncanson painted his most impressive portrait of this period, *Portrait of William J. Baker* (1844). By the mid-1840s the artist's paintings improved considerably, prompting the *Detroit Daily Advertiser* to declare that "the young artist [paints] portraits ... historical and fancy pieces of great merit" (2 Feb. 1846).

In 1848 Duncanson received his most important commission to date from the abolitionist minister, the Reverend Charles Avery, to paint *Cliff Mine, Lake Superior, 1848*. Duncanson's haunting image of the ravaged cliff resonates with metaphors of the destruction of nature and indicates his awareness of the Hudson River school–style of American landscape painting. This commission launched Duncanson into landscape painting and entrenched the artist in the network of abolitionist patronage that would sustain him throughout his career.

The commission from Avery resulted in Duncanson's emergence as the most significant African American artist of his generation and one of the primary Ohio River Valley landscape painters. In this fertile environment for landscape painting Duncanson's style improved dramatically to the point that in 1851 he created one of the landmark landscape paintings of the era, *Blue Hole, Flood Waters, Little Miami River*. His romantic landscapes emphasized themes of humanity in nature and were indicative of mainstream landscape painting of the era.

In 1853 Duncanson produced his only painting of an explicitly African American subject, *Uncle Tom and Little Eva*, after Harriet Beecher Stowe's novel *Uncle Tom's Cabin* (1852). The moment portrayed in the novel foreshadows Eva's death while she is teaching her slave, Tom, to read the Bible. For Duncanson this scene represented his belief in the potential for salvation from slavery through religious faith.

Duncanson's rise to artistic prominence prompted local arts patrons to sponsor his tour of Europe in 1853. Duncanson was the first African American artist to make the traditional "grand tour" of Europe. His art was enriched by the experience of Europe, which in his own words, "shed a new light over my path" (Spencer letters, 22 Jan. 1854, Newberry Library), as in his painting of ancient Roman ruins, *Time's Temple* (1854). After his return he produced a series of American landscapes, such as *Western Forest* (1857) and *Rainbow* (1859), that culminated in his recognition as "the best landscape painter in the West" (*Daily Cincinnati Gazette*, 30 May 1861).

As a free person of color Duncanson sympathized with his enslaved brethren and actively participated in abolitionist societies and their activities. In addition to receiving abolitionist patronage, on several occasions he donated paintings to support antislavery organizations. Notices of his work often appeared in the antislavery journals of the day, which championed his accomplishments and his contributions to African American society. In 1855 Duncanson collaborated with the African American daguerreotypist JAMES PRESLEY BALL on an antislavery panorama, *Mammoth Pictorial Tour of the United States Comprising Views of the African Slave Trade*, that toured the country.

Duncanson not only actively participated in antislavery activities but many of his paintings also contained a veiled content that expressed the concerns of an African American artist living in the antebellum United States. At the end of the 1850s political concerns of the impending Civil War occupied the artist's thoughts. In response Duncanson created the most ambitious easel painting of his career, *Land of the Lotus Eaters* (1861). Duncanson's vast tropical landscape relates a tale from Homer's *Odyssey* that depicted dark-complexioned natives serving white soldiers. The painting evokes the evils of slavery and prophesies the forthcoming long and bloody civil conflict. Reviews of *Lotus Eaters* proclaimed the painting as Duncanson's masterpiece and noted his ambition to tour the painting in Europe. Exiling himself from the Civil War, the artist escaped in 1863 to Montreal, Canada, where he was eagerly received as a master American painter and "where his color did not prevent his association with other artists and his entrance into good society" (*Daily Cincinnati Gazette*, 24 Nov. 1865). By the time of his departure for England two years later, he had helped spawn the first native Canadian landscape painting school. Duncanson exhibited *Lotus Eaters* in Dublin, Glasgow, and London to great praise, with critics proclaiming him a "master" (*Art Journal*, 1866: 95).

While exhibiting *Lotus Eaters* in England, Duncanson took picturesque tours of the countryside, especially the Scottish Highlands. After his return to Cincinnati in 1867, with the laurels of international acclaim, Duncanson revealed his enchantment with the land and lore of Scotland in a series of landscapes that culminated his career. The last of these, *Ellen's Isle, Loch Katrine* (1871), is considered to be the pinnacle of his aesthetic and technical accomplishments. Inspired by Sir Walter Scott's epic poem *Lady of the Lake*, Duncanson depicted the island home of the Highland princess, Ellen Douglas, isolated on Lake Katrine. FREDERICK DOUGLASS had taken his surname from the Highland lord in Scott's poem, and W. E. B. DUBOIS fondly remembered the poem as the "sort of world we want to create for ourselves in America."

Tragically, at the same time Duncanson achieved his ultimate artistic success, he was suffering from a degenerative mental disorder. In the late 1860s he developed a severe dementia that led to extended periods of artistic inactivity and great difficulty in his personal life. By 1870 his condition had so worsened that it was painfully evident to his patrons and the public. He experienced dramatic swings in temperament and suffered from delusions, hallucinations, and violent outbursts. He had become a spiritualist and was convinced that he was possessed by the spirit of a past artist, a woman, who assisted him in the creation of his paintings such as *Ellen's Isle*. His psychotic behavior became so disruptive in 1872 that he produced little work that year. Somehow he managed to have enough paintings for an exhibition in Detroit that October. While hanging his paintings he suffered a seizure and collapsed, dying shortly thereafter. He had married twice. His first wife was Rebecca Graham, who died sometime before 1850. In around 1855 he married Phoebe (maiden name unknown).

Duncanson's remarkable artistic achievements and international reputation blazed the trail for subsequent African American artists and eased their passage and acceptance into the international cultural community. Shortly after his death Duncanson's work fell into obscurity. This unfortunate fate befell an artist whom the *Daily Cincinnati Gazette* regarded as the most important landscape painter working in the western United States and the key transitional figure in the emergence of the African American artist.

FURTHER READING

Bearden, Romare. *A History of African American Artists: From 1792 to the Present* (1993).

Ketner, Joseph D. *The Emergence of the African American Artist: Robert S. Duncanson, 1821–1872* (1994).

McElroy, Guy, and the Cincinnati Art Museum. *Robert S. Duncanson: A Centennial Exhibition* (1972).

Obituary: *Daily Cincinnati Gazette*, 28 Dec. 1872.

JOSEPH D. KETNER

Dungy, Tony (6 Oct. 1955–), professional football player and NFL coach, was born Anthony Kevin Dungy in Jackson, Michigan, one of four children of Wilbur Dungy, a professor of physiology, and Cleomae, a high school English teacher. Despite his parents' insistence that he focus on academics, Dungy demonstrated an early preference for athletics. At Parkside High School he played on both the football and the basketball squads. Following his graduation in 1973 he enrolled at the University of Minnesota, where as a freshman he played quarterback on the football team. He was also on the basketball team. His football playing was distinguished enough that after graduating in 1977 with a B.A. in Business, he entered the NFL draft as a free agent and was selected by the Pittsburgh Steelers, having been passed over by a number of NFL scouts as too small for the pro game.

In college Dungy had been a standout on offense, but in the NFL he held a reserve spot in the defensive backfield. In 1978 he was named starting safety with the Steelers and played with that team in Super Bowl XIII. In 1979 he was dealt to the San Francisco Forty-niners but remained there only a year before again being traded, this time to the New York Giants. Cut before the beginning of the regular season in 1980, Dungy moved into coaching.

Unlike many prospective NFL head coaches, Dungy's time coaching in the college ranks had been short. He had served just one year, 1980, at his alma mater, the University of Minnesota, as a defensive backs coach. But he was soon courted by the Steelers organization, which hired him as an assistant coach in 1981. In 1982 Dungy married Lauren Harris, and the couple had six children. Two years later, in 1984, Dungy was named the Steelers' defensive coordinator—the first African American to rise to that sideline position in the NFL. Successful coaches in the defensive coordinator spot were frequently considered attractive candidates for head coaching jobs. However, it is possible the league's famous unwillingness to

Tony Dungy, (center), the head coach of the Indianapolis Colts, explains a play during the team's practice, 8 August 2006. Quarterback Peyton Manning (left), guard Jake Scott (right center), and center Jeff Saturday (right) look on. (AP Images.)

embrace African Americans as head coaches was why Dungy remained with the Steelers until 1989, at which time he took a step backward to become the Kansas City Chiefs' defensive backs coach. He left the Chiefs after the 1991–1992 season to take on the defensive coordinator role with the Minnesota Vikings.

Dungy's leap to head coach came in 1996, when he took over what had been an unsuccessful Tampa Bay Buccaneers franchise. Dungy's task was to turn the league's worst team around; a year later, in 1997, the Bucs had their first winning season in nearly fourteen years. Much of their success came on the defensive side of things, where the Bucs, under Dungy, were routinely ranked among the league's best. With redesigned uniforms, a new theme park–like stadium, and a vastly improved defense, the Bucs became one of the NFL's elite teams. In 1999 the Buccaneers won their division; however, after too much regular-season promise and not enough play-off success, Dungy was fired at the end of the 2001 season.

In 2002 Dungy was hired by the Indianapolis Colts, a team known for its high-scoring offensive unit (especially after the addition of the quarterback Peyton Manning) and its poor defense. As had been the case in Tampa Bay, the Colts showed great promise in Dungy's first regular season with the team, but they struggled in the postseason. In 2005 the Colts prompted much talk of a perfect season after winning their first thirteen games, but they were then beaten in the play-offs by the Pittsburgh Steelers. In October of that year Dungy's eighteen-year-old son James, struggling with depression, overdosed on prescription painkillers; in December, James committed suicide in Lutz, Florida.

The opening of the 2006 regular football season saw renewed enthusiasm from Colts fans and hopes that the team might finally make it through the play-offs and into the Super Bowl. The Colts won the American Football Conference (AFC) South Division title before defeating the Kansas City Chiefs, Baltimore Ravens, and longtime AFC rival New England Patriots to reach Super Bowl XLI. Because the AFC Championship Game was scheduled later in the day than that of the National Football Conference (NFC), Dungy officially became the second African American head coach to lead his team to the Super Bowl. His longtime friend and former assistant coach from Tampa Bay, the Chicago Bears' Lovie Smith, earned the distinction of being the first only hours earlier. After a week of intense media attention, much of it focusing on the fact that two black coaches were facing each other in the NFL Championship Game, the heavily favored Colts defeated the Bears 29-17. Dungy was a conservative Christian whose soft-spoken demeanor and seemingly imperturbable sideline posture made him something of an oddity among often hotheaded NFL head coaches. In 2007 he publicly and controversially declared his opposition to gay marriage. With his wife, Dungy participated in several charitable organizations, including the Prison Crusade Ministry, Big Brothers/Big Sisters, and the Boys and Girls Club. He founded Mentors for Life, which aimed to give away tickets to Bucs games to kids and their mentors in Tampa Bay. Besides being the second black head coach to reach the Super Bowl and the first to win one, Dungy was also the first NFL coach to record wins against all thirty-two franchises.

Dungy stepped down as Colts' coach in January 2009.

FURTHER READING

Dungy, Tony, and Nathan Whitaker. *Quiet Strength: The Principles, Practices, and Priorities of a Winning Life* (2007).

Neft, David S. *The Football Encyclopedia: The Complete History of Professional NFL Football, from 1892 to the Present* (1991).

JASON PHILIP MILLER

Dunham, Katherine Mary (22 June 1909–21 May 2006), dancer, choreographer, school founder, and anthropologist, was born in Chicago, Illinois, to Albert Millard Dunham Sr., an African American tailor and amateur jazz musician, and Fanny June Guillaume Taylor, a school administrator of French Canadian, English, Native American, and possibly African ancestry. The Dunhams lived in the predominantly white suburb of Glen Ellyn, Illinois, until Fanny's death when Katherine was four. Forced to sell the family home, Albert Dunham became a traveling salesman and sent Katherine and her older brother, Albert Jr., to live with relatives on the South Side of Chicago, where she was exposed to black vaudeville and blues performances.

Although Albert Sr. reunited the family after he remarried and purchased a dry cleaning store in Joliet, Illinois, he became increasingly unpredictable and violent. Katherine found an outlet in athletics and dance while attending public high school and junior college in Joliet. Hoping to extricate his sister from an unpleasant home situation that included Albert Sr.'s growing sexual interest in his daughter, Albert Jr. convinced nineteen-year-old Katherine to transfer to the University of Chicago, where he was studying philosophy on scholarship.

Dunham relished the independence and freedom she found in Chicago. Money was tight, but she managed to support herself working as a librarian and giving dance lessons. Dunham's ballet teacher, Madame Ludmila Speranzeva, took her to performances by the Isadora Duncan Dance Company and the Ballet Russe, and Albert Jr. introduced her to the theater crowd at the Cube Theater, which he cofounded. Inspired by Chicago's thriving African American intellectual scene, Dunham began hosting salon-style get-togethers, inviting a diverse group of artists, writers, performers, scholars, and social scientists, including the choreographers Mark Turbyfull and Ruth Page, the artist Charles Sebree, the actor Ruth Attaway, Zora Neale Hurston, Benjamin O. Davis Jr., and Alan Lomax. Determined not to be a "polka dot," her term for a token black dancer, Dunham organized her own dance troupes, the first of which disbanded shortly after performing at the 1931 Chicago Beaux Arts Ball. Dunham featured her new troupe, the Negro Dance Group, two years later in a program commissioned by the 1933–1934 Chicago World's Fair.

Katherine Dunham in costume and dance pose, 1946. (AP Images.)

All the while, Dunham had continued studying under Robert Redfield at the University of Chicago in one of the country's most innovative anthropology departments. Dunham's investigation into the role of dance in culture, a field she later called dance anthropology, dovetailed with the university's liberal humanist and interdisciplinary philosophy. Dunham was ahead of her time in seeing the possibilities in cross-pollinating her academic and performance work. With endorsements from Melville Herskovits, head of African Studies at Northwestern University, Charles S. Johnson, and Erich Fromm, Dunham applied successfully for a fieldwork scholarship from the Rosenwald Fund. In May 1935 she left for Jamaica, Martinique, Trinidad, and Haiti on a yearlong trip that proved fundamental to both her scholarly and performing careers.

Dunham wrote *Journey to Accompong* (1946) about her fieldwork in Jamaica, and the rituals of Martinique provided material for many choreographies. But it was Haiti and its African-based rhythms and movements that most affected Dunham. She documented the country's rich tradition of voodoo rituals, drumming, and sacred and secular dancing, and published two books devoted to Haiti, *Dances of Haiti* (1947) and *Island Possessed* (1969). In 1949 she purchased a villa near Port-au-Prince and began spending part of each year there.

Dunham received a B.A. in Anthropology from the University of Chicago in 1936 and immediately continued with graduate work at the University of Chicago and Northwestern University, eventually turning her research into *Dances of Haiti*. Although Dunham shifted focus to her performance career without completing a graduate degree, she remained devoted to anthropology, doing research in each country she visited, and serving as a visiting professor and lecturer at universities and anthropological societies worldwide. In 1938 Dunham was appointed director of the Negro Unit of the Chicago branch of the Federal Theater Project, through which she choreographed dances for *Emperor Jones, Swing Mikado*, and *Run Lil' Chillun* and premiered her ballet *L'Ag'Ya*, based on her Caribbean research. The next year, Dunham was on Broadway in the 1939 labor union musical *Pins and Needles*. While in New York she opened her first revue, *Tropics and Le Jazz Hot: From Haiti to Harlem* at the Windsor Theater to rave reviews. Back in Chicago, Dunham and her troupe spent evenings performing in nightclubs with Duke Ellington and days establishing a repertoire of programs that included "Rara Tonga," "Barrelhouse," and "Woman with a Cigar."

Dunham's revolutionary choreography blended Caribbean, South American, and African styles of movement and folk narrative with modern dance and ballet, leading the way for ALVIN AILEY's American Dance Theater and ARTHUR MITCHELL's Dance Theater of Harlem. By combining her interpretations of a dance lexicon drawn from African and Caribbean sources with a vocabulary of African American social dances such as "Cakewalk," "Ballin' the Jack," and "Strut," Dunham established black dance as an art form for the first time. A serious artist with popular appeal, Dunham created entertainment that was both academic and showbiz friendly, authentic, yet theatrical. In the 1950s European fashion houses even produced "Dunham" and "Caribbean" lines of clothing.

Soon after moving her troupe, now called the Katherine Dunham Dance Company, to New York City, Dunham's career soared to new heights when she starred on Broadway in the 1940 all-black musical *Cabin in the Sky*, which she choreographed with George Balanchine. Over the next twenty years, the Dunham Dance Company performed in sixty-nine countries, and Dunham choreographed one hundred dances and five revues, four of which were performed on Broadway. Dunham shows, including *Tropical Revue, Carib Song*, and *Bal Negre*, featured Caribbean and Latin American numbers, ballets often drawn from folk sources, and medleys of African American spirituals and social and plantation dances.

Between 1941 and 1948 the Dunham dancers toured throughout North America, and, beginning with their triumphant first visit in 1948, the company toured Europe annually, eventually adding North Africa, the Middle East, South America, Australia, and Asia to their schedule. Ever the anthropologist, Dunham "would collect 'something': a cultural expression, a movement, a local musician, or a dancer" in each location (Aschenbrenner, 147). Following *Carnival of Rhythm* (1941), a short film made about the company, Dunham appeared in or choreographed several Hollywood films, including *Star-Spangled Rhythm* (1942), *Stormy Weather* (1943), *Pardon My Sarong* (1942), *Casbah* (1948), and *Mambo* (1954). She also became a television pioneer when, in 1940, her company was the first to perform an hour-long dance broadcast.

In 1941 Dunham married the white Canadian-born theater designer John Pratt, who worked as chief designer of Dunham's shows until his death in 1986. In 1951 the couple adopted Marie Christine Columbier, a four-year old French Martinique girl of mixed ancestry. (Dunham had been married briefly in the early 1930s to Jordis McCoo, a post office worker and part-time dancer.)

In 1945 Dunham opened the Dunham School of Dance and Theater in New York. Within a few years it had become the premier training ground for African American dancers and a host of actors, including BUTTERFLY MCQUEEN, Marlon Brando, and James Dean. Dunham's mission was multifold: "To establish a well-trained ballet group. To develop a technique that will be as important to the white man as the Negro. To attain a status in the dance world that will give to the Negro dance student the courage really to study and a reason to do so. And to take Our dance out of the burlesque—to make of it a more dignified art" (Aschenbrenner, 110). The Dunham Method treated dance as part of a holistic enterprise involving the mind and spirit as well as the body. The school's faculty, which included Lee and Susan Strasberg, taught theater, literature, philosophy, music, and world cultures until it closed in 1955.

Financial pressures and arthritic knees forced Dunham to dissolve her company shortly after choreographing her last Broadway show, *Bambouche*, in 1962. The following year, she became the New York Metropolitan Opera's first black choreographer when she mounted a daring interpretation of *Aïda*, casting black performers as Egyptians before it became fashionable. In 1967, after a year spent choreographing for the National Ballet of Senegal, Dunham opened the Performing Arts Training Center (PATC) in East St. Louis, close to Southern Illinois University, where she taught until 1982. PATC offered classes in humanities, theater, dance, and martial arts, and its curriculum used dance to teach other subjects, such as reading, storytelling, and mathematics. In 1977 Dunham and Pratt opened the Katherine Dunham Dynamic Museum, a public facility that houses Dunham's art collection and materials documenting her career.

Dunham protested injustices throughout her career, particularly by challenging the racial segregation of hotels, restaurants, and rehearsal halls. When, over the objections of the U.S. State Department, she persisted in performing *Southland*, a ballet she choreographed that dramatized a lynching, the FBI mounted a campaign that financially damaged her company. In 1992 at the age of eighty-two, Dunham waged a forty-seven day hunger strike to protest the U.S. government's treatment of Haitian refugees.

In addition to a dozen honorary degrees, Dunham has received numerous awards including the Albert Schweitzer Music Award in 1979, a Kennedy Center Honors Award in 1983, the French Légion d'Honneur, the Southern Cross of Brazil, and several honors from the Haitian government. The author of numerous articles, Dunham published a childhood memoir *A Touch of Innocence* (1959) and a novel *Kasamance* (1967), set in Senegal. In 2000 the Library of Congress received $1 million from the Doris Duke Foundation to collect and preserve materials relating to Dunham's legacy. Although in her later years Dunham was faced with poor health and serious financial problems, she nevertheless remained the subject of retrospectives by dance companies and received attention from universities and art groups. Despite financial difficulties and failing health, she continued to make public appearances and grant interviews. Dunham died in an assisted-living facility in Manhattan on 21 May 2006.

FURTHER READING

Dunham's papers are held at the Southern Illinois University in Carbondale.

Dunham, Katherine. *A Touch of Innocence* (1959).

Aschenbrenner, Joyce. *Katherine Dunham: Dancing a Life* (2002).

Beckford, Katherine. *Dunham: A Biography* (1979).

LISA E. RIVO

Dunjee, Roscoe (21 June 1883–1 Mar. 1965), newspaper publisher and civil rights leader, was born in Harpers Ferry, West Virginia, the son of John William Dunjee, a former slave, and Lydia Ann Dunjee. The elder Dunjee, a Baptist minister, moved his family first to Minnesota and then to Oklahoma Territory in 1892. A library of fifteen hundred volumes was an important part of the family belongings and played a major role in Roscoe's education.

When his father died in 1903, Dunjee was left to care for his mother on their fruit and vegetable farm. He earned extra money by writing stories for local newspapers until he purchased a small printing plant in Oklahoma City in 1913. On 5 November 1914 he printed the first edition of the *Black Dispatch*, a paper targeting the growing black community in Oklahoma City, the state capital. Dunjee was criticized by local black leaders for using the word "Black" in the title of the paper. However, he dismissed such criticism as the opinions of people who were ashamed of their race.

From its inception, the *Black Dispatch* became the voice of the disenfranchised blacks of Oklahoma City. Through his editorials, Dunjee prodded readers to organize and fight for civil rights. In 1915, when Logan County election officials denied blacks the right to vote, Dunjee led the suffrage campaign. He publicized these injustices until the Supreme Court, in *Guinn v. United States*, struck down as unconstitutional Oklahoma's voting laws. This decision gave the fledgling National Association for the Advancement of Colored People its first national victory. Over the next half century, circulation of the *Black Dispatch* would reach a high of twenty-four thousand, with readers in every state and many foreign countries. One of Dunjee's young readers and newspaper carriers in the 1920s was the author RALPH ELLISON, whose father had been killed in an accident. Dunjee became a father figure to Ellison, who credited the publisher with inspiring his belief that civil rights could be obtained under the rule of American law.

In 1930 Dunjee rose to meet another challenge when GEORGE WASHINGTON CARVER, who had given a speech to the Oklahoma Association of Negro Teachers, was refused a ticket for a Pullman sleeping car on the Santa Fe Railroad. The incident spurred a series of attacks on Oklahoma's segregated public transportation laws and soon drew attention to the related problem of housing segregation in Oklahoma City. Dunjee raised money to fight ordinances that prevented blacks from living outside a small, overcrowded section of the city. He also organized mass public meetings to express the community's outrage. Soon, city leaders began to seek his counsel on race-related questions.

Public education was a subject dear to Dunjee's heart, for he recognized that a quality education was the key to economic opportunity for his people. He once asked an audience, "What goes on in a child's mind when he sings 'Sweet Land of Liberty' and at the same time remembers there are libraries in his city or village that he cannot enter and other educational opportunities around him which he dare not attempt to utilize?" Dunjee also fought for equal funding for black schools in Oklahoma and publicly criticized state officials for leaving black schools without adequate funds to maintain buildings and pay teachers.

If a need existed in the black community in Oklahoma City, Dunjee was aware of it. He helped desegregate parks and swimming pools and raise the standard of medical care. Early on, he realized that the battle for civil rights would be won or lost in a courtroom. He had great respect for the law and American justice and pledged to hire the best lawyers he could find to carry on the battle. He personally sought out witnesses and established a defense fund for a young black man, Jess Hollins, sentenced to die for raping a white woman. In 1934 the U.S. Supreme Court used Hollins's case to end the practice of excluding blacks from Oklahoma juries.

Dunjee chartered Oklahoma's first NAACP chapter in 1914 and later became close friends with the NAACP lawyer THURGOOD MARSHALL, who advised him in legal situations and who came to Oklahoma to represent aggrieved blacks in several lawsuits. The most famous case was that of *Ada Lois Sipuel Fisher v. Oklahoma State Board of Regents* (1948). Fisher had been denied admission to the University of Oklahoma (OU) School of Law. Dunjee persuaded Fisher to become the plaintiff in a sweeping lawsuit that attacked the foundations of the segregated system of higher education in many southern states. Fisher had graduated with honors from Langston University and was well qualified for admission to the OU law school. However, in a much-publicized decision, the school's board of regents refused her, citing an antiquated discriminatory law that made it a misdemeanor in Oklahoma for white teachers to teach black students. Dunjee used his newspaper to raise funds to wage the battle. With Marshall as chief counsel, the Fisher case went to the Supreme Court, which ordered the state to provide Fisher a legal education equivalent to that of white Oklahomans. The Oklahoma leadership initially sidestepped this decision by setting up a sham law school in the basement of the state capitol solely for Fisher, who later attended the OU School of Law, graduated, and began a long and distinguished career as an educator and civil rights activist. Ironically, she was appointed in the 1980s as a member of the OU board of regents, the same body that had denied her admission decades earlier.

Where other papers equivocated, the *Black Dispatch* stated resolutely that in all matters of education "segregation is obvious discrimination." In 1948 Dunjee used the plight of GEORGE MCLAURIN to change the way black students were treated. McLaurin was forced by OU administrators to sit in a classroom alcove, where he could see the teacher but the white students could not see him. He also had separate eating and toilet facilities. Once again, Dunjee championed Marshall's legal efforts, which in 1950 resulted in a unanimous Supreme Court decision against OU for violating McLaurin's right to equal access to education. In its decision the court cited the Fourteenth Amendment and Oklahoma's own constitutional provisions for equal educational opportunities for all races.

Dunjee, who never married, died shortly before his eighty-second birthday. At his funeral, Marshall, who later that year became the first black member of the Supreme Court, said, "Roscoe Dunjee gave us inspiration to get the job done. He didn't wait for somebody else. He didn't back down, even when his own people said he was wrong." Although his vision and his brilliance can be clearly seen in the broad strokes of his editorial pen, the magnitude of Dunjee's contributions was not appreciated until years after his death. The extent to which he influenced the course of Oklahoma history and of the struggle for civil rights is immeasurable.

FURTHER READING

Burke, Bob, and Denyvetta Davis. *Ralph Ellison: A Biography* (2002).

Burke, Bob, and Angela Monson. *Roscoe Dunjee: Champion of Civil Rights* (1998).

Miles-LaGrange, Vicki, and Bob Burke. *A Passion for Equality: The Life of Jimmy Stewart* (1999).

BOB BURKE

Dunlap, Mollie Ernestine (2 Sept. 1898–7 July 1977), librarian, was born in Paducah, Kentucky, to Robert H. Dunlap and Emma M. (Donovan) Dunlap. Robert Dunlap, alternately listed in censuses and directories as a laborer and a driver, was Donovan's second husband, and Mollie Dunlap was raised in a large family that eventually included three siblings, four step-siblings, and her maternal grandmother. She attended schools in Paducah until the family moved north to Kalamazoo, Michigan, about 1918. She continued her education—specifically studying English and elementary education—at Wilberforce University, apparently worked at Wilberforce in the early 1920s, and also taught in Kalamazoo, where she is listed with her family in the 1920 Federal Census (p. 6B).

Dunlap accepted a position as a teacher and librarian at Winston-Salem Teachers College in North Carolina in 1925. She returned north to take an AB from Ohio State University in 1928 and, with the aid of a fellowship from the Julius Rosenwald Fund, an AB and an M.A. in library science from the University of Michigan in 1931 and 1932, respectively. She became a member of the American Library Association in 1931, and she continued working at Winston-Salem until 1934. In 1933, the *Journal of Negro Education* published her trail-blazing "Recreational Reading of Negro College Students," an article that marked both the beginnings of her longtime assertions that librarians needed to consider "what people actually read" (p. 448) and the initial rumblings of her lifelong struggle to give black librarians voice. In recognition of her wide-ranging abilities and nascent activism, she was elected Vice President of the North Carolina Negro Library Association at its inaugural April 1934 meeting and arguably set the groundwork for that organization's eventual affiliation with the American Library Association.

Wilberforce invited her to return as its librarian in 1934, and there she turned some of her energies to identifying resources for black studies. Her 1935 *Journal of Negro Education* article on "Special Collections of Negro Literature in the United States" was germinal in bibliographic studies and certainly shaped her later work in helping found the *Negro College Quarterly* in 1944, as well as her efforts—along with Wilberforce professor Anne Williamson—on a large study, "Institutions of Higher Learning among Negroes in the United States of America: A Compendium," which was published in the June 1947 issue of the *Quarterly*.

But Dunlap also continued her fights to place African American librarians fully in dialogue with the American Library Association. As part of the ALA's Special Committee on Racial Discrimination, Dunlap helped write a 1936 resolution calling for "full equality" in "all rooms and halls assigned to the Association for use in connection with ... [its] conference." That resolution was published in the January 1937 *American Libraries*, and Dunlap continued to fight to see it enforced throughout the 1930s.

In 1947, after the state of Ohio made an unsuccessful attempt to take over Wilberforce, which caused the University to split and founded Central State University, Dunlap chose to join the new institution as the library director—probably in part because of the promise offered by the construction of the new Hallie Q. Brown Memorial Library. She maintained a strong relationship with colleagues at Wilberforce, however, and worked with the Wilberforce University chapter of the American Association of University Women to publish *Despite Discrimination: Some Aspects of Negro Life in the United States* in 1949. While the *Negro College Quarterly* was a casualty of the splitting of Wilberforce, Dunlap later aided in founding Central State University's *Journal of Human Relations*. She began one of her most important undertakings, the *Index to Selected Negro Publications Received in the Hallie Q. Brown Library*, in 1950; it is still recognized as a major early bibliographic tool.

Dunlap retired briefly in 1966, but soon returned to Central State to build its black studies collection and archives; she was named the University Archivist in 1968. In 1976, the University of Michigan gave her its Distinguished Alumnus Award. Dunlap died in Ann Arbor, but is buried at Massie's Creek Cemetery in Wilberforce.

ERIC GARDNER

Dunn, Oscar James (1826?–22 Nov. 1871), politician, was born in New Orleans, Louisiana. His family origins are obscure. His mother was apparently a former slave who ran a boardinghouse for white actors and actresses. Dunn took his last name from his stepfather, a stage carpenter. A brother later became the sheriff of Madison Parish. Dunn attended a school for free children, for which his family paid tuition. Apprenticed as a plasterer to a contracting firm, he ran away in December 1841, prompting a five dollar reward notice. Years later, before a congressional committee, Dunn called himself a plasterer by trade. He also worked as a music teacher and as a barber on Mississippi River steamboats. Dunn apparently married, but nothing is known about his wife.

When the Union army occupied New Orleans in 1862, Dunn was among the first blacks to enlist, serving as a captain before he resigned in 1863, reportedly when a promotion he sought went to a white officer. Dunn then turned his energies to former slaves, establishing an employment agency and working with the Freedmen's Bureau to help blacks secure fair contracts for plantation work.

Dunn also entered politics. Already prominent among blacks in the city, he was appointed by military authorities to the board of aldermen. There he helped set an agenda for postwar New Orleans, advocating universal public education and working to improve basic services such as firefighting. In the wake of the bloody July 1866 riot that left many African Americans dead, Major General Philip Sheridan appointed Dunn president of the metropolitan police board. Making the most of such powerful backing, Dunn emerged from turmoil as a capable politician and a strong force in Louisiana's Republican party. The 1868 state convention nominated him as lieutenant governor, and the Republican ticket swept into office in April over the disfranchised Democrats in an election plagued by violence.

The first black lieutenant governor in U.S. history, Dunn struck a moderate tone in his inaugural address: "As to myself and my people we are not seeking social equality; that is a thing no law can govern.... We simply ask to be allowed an equal chance in the race of life; an equal opportunity of supporting our families, of educating our children, and of becoming worthy citizens of this government."

A pioneer among black politicians, Dunn encountered plenty of resistance. During the November 1868 presidential election, for example, African Americans were targeted and killed for trying to vote, and African American leaders, including Dunn, were forced to stay away from home. Asked at a congressional hearing whether he had voted, Dunn replied: "No, sir; I didn't go near any of the polls. In fact I was bothered a great deal by the colored people, many of whom did not understand my rights and powers, and who would come to me for protection which I could not give, and consequently I avoided them as much as possible."

By all accounts Dunn was an effective lieutenant governor. In a city and state notorious for corruption, he maintained a reputation for integrity, refusing a $10,000 bribe in 1870. An eloquent speaker, he used his oratorical and political skills to preside over a contentious state senate. During his term the Republican Party in Louisiana gradually polarized into two factions—one centering on Governor Henry C. Warmoth and the other around federal patronage officials led by Collector of Customs James F. Casey, brother-in-law of President Ulysses S. Grant. At the 1870 party convention the latter group prevailed and elected Dunn as presiding officer over Warmoth. Dunn's credibility as a New Orleans native and a black leader augmented his stature in the customhouse wing, made up mostly of northern whites appointed by Grant. He was elected chairman of the state Republican committee in 1871.

In the spring of 1871 Warmoth briefly left the state to recuperate from an injury. Dunn's temporary assumption of executive control, coupled with several bitter patronage disputes, exacerbated the power struggle. During subsequent months Dunn traveled to Washington to meet with Grant and wrote him twice in the summer of 1871, warning that the situation had deteriorated. In a letter to the *New York Tribune* editor Horace Greeley that same summer, Dunn challenged Greeley's support of Warmoth. "We are engaged in no strife of factions, but the people gravely and earnestly are fighting for their personal and political rights, against the encroachments of impudent and unfaithful public servants."

Dunn's sudden death in New Orleans, while the factional dispute gripped the city, sparked unsubstantiated rumors of poisoning. His absence left a void in the customhouse wing of the party. The choice of his replacement as lieutenant governor—P. B. S. Pinchback, a northern black allied with Warmoth—hastened the Republicans' decline. More importantly, Louisiana blacks lost in Dunn a leader who sought to transcend the patronage politics of Reconstruction and offer a social vision grounded in basic human dignity.

FURTHER READING

Christian, Marcus B. "The Theory of the Poisoning of Oscar J. Dunn," *Phylon*, 6, no. 3 (1945).

Foner, Eric. *Freedom's Lawmakers: A Directory of Black Officeholders during Reconstruction* (1993).

Perkins, A. E. "Oscar James Dunn," *Phylon*, 4, no. 2 (1943).

Taylor, Joe Gray. *Louisiana Reconstructed* (1974).

Warmoth, Henry Clay. *War, Politics and Reconstruction: Stormy Days in Louisiana* (1930).

This entry is taken from the *American National Biography* and is published here with the permission of the American Council of Learned Societies.

AARON M. LISEC

Dunnigan, Alice Allison (27 Apr. 1906–6 May 1983), journalist, was born near Russellville, Kentucky, the daughter of Willie Allison, a sharecropper, and Lena Pittman Allison, who took in laundry. Determined not to work as a domestic, Dunnigan graduated from the Kentucky Normal and Industrial Institute (later Kentucky State University) and became a teacher at a rural school. In 1925 she married Walter Dickinson, a tobacco farmer, but her desire to escape rural isolation and poverty led to their divorce in 1929. She married a childhood friend, Charles Dunnigan, in 1931, and their only child, Robert, was born the following year. Habitually unemployed, her husband soon abandoned the family. Alice Dunnigan left her son with her parents, who raised him while she took a job with the Works Progress Administration (WPA) cleaning public buildings.

As an unpaid fund-raiser for M & F College in Hopkinsville, Kentucky, Dunnigan had written a poem about the school and sent it to the local black newspaper, *Rising Sun*. The editor of the *Kentucky Reporter* saw her work and proposed that she write a column on health, homemaking, and women's issues, "Scribbles from Alice's Scrapbook." No salary was involved, but the column gave her some visibility as a writer. In 1935 she moved to Louisville to become society editor for the *Louisville Leader*.

Her sights set on a career as a reporter, Dunnigan enrolled in 1936 at Tennessee A & I State College, the nearest black college that offered courses in journalism. She also resumed teaching in a high school near Russellville. After the United States entered World War II, she took a civil service typing test in 1942 and got a job with the War Labor Board in Washington, D.C. She enrolled in night school courses in economics and statistics at Howard University and gained a professional-level position at the Office of Price Administration, which she held until the agency was abolished after the war.

While working for the government, Dunnigan also did freelance reporting for the Associated Negro Press (ANP). The Chicago-based ANP compiled and mailed news stories twice each week to African American newspapers across the country. In 1946 she applied to become ANP's Washington correspondent. CLAUDE BARNETT, who directed the news service, doubted that a woman could handle his biggest national assignment, but he gave her a chance to prove herself—at half the salary he had been offering to men. On 1 January 1947 Dunnigan became the chief of ANP's Washington bureau and its sole full-time staff member. As a Washington correspondent, she covered the White House, Congress, and government agencies—the first African American woman to do so—as well as collecting international news from visiting dignitaries and foreign embassies, and interviewing stage and screen celebrities and athletes. She also reported from Israel and the Dominican Republic on trips underwritten by their governments.

After Dunnigan's initial bid for a congressional press pass was rejected, she discovered that the Associated Negro Press had never bothered to endorse her application. As Dunnigan recorded in her autobiography, Claude Bennett explained to her, "For years we have been trying to get a man accredited to the Capitol Galleries and have not succeeded. What makes you think that you—a woman—-can accomplish this feat?" (Dunnigan, 209). To Barnett's astonishment, Dunnigan persisted and in July 1947 was granted formal press accreditation. Race and gender were "twin strikes" against her, she wrote, but of the two she considered her gender the more most difficult barrier.

In 1948 Dunnigan paid her own way to cover one of President Harry S. Truman's campaign train trips to the West Coast. The ANP required that her stories always have a "Negro angle," which proved difficult at many Western stops, when she could see no African Americans in the crowds that greeted the train. She achieved a scoop when she was the only reporter to file a story on Truman's response to a question in which he endorsed a civil rights plank for the Democratic platform. In Cheyenne, Wyoming, a military officer tried to shove her out of the press contingent. Other reporters rushed to her defense, and she was pleased and flattered when President Truman personally visited her compartment on the train to make sure that she was being well treated.

The ANP's limited resources kept Dunnigan's salary below subsistence level, which forced her to take on other part-time jobs. In 1948 she addressed audiences in Kentucky for the Democratic Speakers Bureau, and in 1950 she began working as a clerk-typist at the Washington Navy Yard, while continuing her Washington correspondence.

Dunnigan was in the House press gallery in 1954 when Puerto Rican nationalists fired shots into the chamber and wounded five representatives. She breathlessly called the ANP headquarters in Chicago to report what she had seen. Claude Barnett asked if either of the two African American representatives, WILLIAM DAWSON or ADAM CLAYTON POWELL, had been shot. When she said no, he replied that she had no story.

In 1955 she became the first African American member of the Women's National Press Club, shortly after the all-male National Press Club had accepted LOUIS LAUTIER as its first black member. Dunnigan resented the many years that it had taken the other women journalists to admit a single minority, but in her memoir she called belonging to the club a great advantage because it "opened avenues for many exclusive stories and personal interviews with prominent dignitaries" (Dunnigan, 478). An advocate of the civil rights movement, Dunnigan regularly attended President Dwight D. Eisenhower's press conferences and asked questions about civil rights. Rather than writing as an objective reporter, Dunnigan wove opinion into her articles as a means of promoting civil rights and racial equality. Eisenhower initially fended these questions off by referring Dunnigan to the departments that handled the specific issues. Eventually he stopped calling on her. At John F. Kennedy's first presidential press conference in 1961, he pointedly called on both Dunnigan and ETHEL PAYNE, the other African American reporter long ignored by Eisenhower.

Dunnigan resigned from the ANP in 1961 to join the staff of the President's Commission on Equal Employment Opportunity, at triple the salary she had earned as a journalist. In 1967 she moved to the Council on Youth Opportunity, where she remained until her retirement in 1970. In later years she chronicled her lifelong quest for dignity and self-respect in her autobiography. She died in Washington, D.C., of an intestinal ailment.

FURTHER READING

Dunnigan contributed an oral history to the Schlesinger Library at Harvard, included in Ruth Edmonds Hill, ed., *The Black Women Oral History Project* (1991), vol. 3. Her papers are deposited at Howard University, and many of her letters are in the Claude Barnett papers at the Chicago Historical Society.

Dunnigan, Alice. *A Black Woman's Experience—From Schoolhouse to White House* (1974).

Streitmatter, Roger. *Raising Her Voice: African-American Women Journalists Who Changed History* (1994).

Obituaries: *Washington Post*, 8 May 1983; *Jet*, 23 May 1983.

DONALD A. RITCHIE

Duplex, Edward P. (1830–5 Jan. 1900), entrepreneur, activist, and politician, was born in New Haven, Connecticut, to Prince and Adeline Duplex. His middle name is sometimes given as Park and sometimes as Parker. His paternal grandparents were Prince Duplex, a slave of the Reverend Benjamin Chapman and a War of Independence veteran who later gained his freedom, and Lement Parker. The younger Prince Duplex, who was active in New Haven's first black church, died when his son Edward was a child, and Adeline, who briefly married a second husband surnamed Whiting, reared Edward, his elder brother Elisha C., and his sister Adeline Frances. Both Edward and his brother trained as barbers and moved west in 1852.

Though Elisha and Edward seem to have mined briefly, they both settled in Yuba County, California, in 1855 and returned to barbering. Elisha died of consumption, but Edward established the Metropolitan Shaving Saloon in Marysville and prospered. When Marysville hosted the California State Fair in 1858, he expanded his thriving establishment to a staff of seven barbers to meet fairgoers' demand. In part because his successes in business made him a community leader and in part because he came from a tradition of eastern race activists, Duplex became deeply involved in civil rights efforts among California blacks. He served as a Yuba County delegate to the 1855 California Colored Citizens Convention, and then assumed a leadership position as a state executive committee member at the 1856 convention. He aided efforts to allow black testimony in courts and to gain educational rights for blacks. He was also a Freemason and was involved in the creation of California's first black newspaper, the *Mirror of the Times*. He wrote occasionally about California for *Frederick Douglass's Paper*. Duplex's involvement in the black press was lifelong; he worked as an agent for the San Francisco *Elevator*, befriended the writer Jennie Carter ("Semper Fidelis"), wrote occasionally for both the *Elevator* and *Pacific Appeal*, and supported the press through convention work.

Duplex visited Connecticut briefly in early 1860 and then returned to Yuba County with his mother, a dressmaker. At some point during this period, he married Sophia Elizabeth, who had come to California from New York. The couple had at least five children, though only two survived to adulthood: Edward, who later worked as a barber in Oakland, and Louisa. During the Civil War, Duplex remained at the forefront of Northern California efforts for emancipation and civil rights. He also expanded his business efforts significantly, becoming part owner of the Sweet Vengeance Mine, and served as secretary of the board of trustees of the Rare, Ripe Gold and Silver Mining Company, which was incorporated in 1868 under the company president John H. Gassoway, also a Marysville black barber. He continued to be a community leader in Marysville, especially in the Mt. Olive Baptist Church.

In the mid-1870s Duplex moved to nearby Wheatland, where he founded another barbershop at 415 Main Street, sold his "Eau Lustral Hair Restorative," and later opened a bathhouse. Duplex was recognized as a key citizen of Wheatland—so much so that on 11 April 1888 the town's board of trustees elected him mayor. After completing his term, he returned to his business efforts. He died in Sacramento but is buried in Marysville. Probably the first elected black mayor in the far West, Duplex was also an important early activist and entrepreneur.

FURTHER READING

Beasley, Delilah. *Negro Trail Blazers of California* (1919).

Lapp, Rudolph. *Blacks in Gold Rush California* (1977).

ERIC GARDNER

Duplex, Prince, Jr. (1796–18 Sept. 1832), the son of a Revolutionary War veteran of the same name, was born in Wolcott, Connecticut, and served as the first clerk of the African Ecclesiastical Society in New Haven. Although sparse and sometimes conflicting accounts in published literature have confounded records of the father and son, recently genealogical research in Tompkins County, New York, has clearly identified and distinguished the two from original records.

On 18 July 1756 "Prince, the negro servant child of Samuel Riggs & Abigail his wife" was baptized, according to church records in Derby, Connecticut. Although the word "slave" was not routinely used during that period, he was a servant "for life," valued at £50, and was inherited at Riggs's death by his daughter Abigail, married to a Reverend Mr. Chapman. Duplex enlisted 18 May 1777 in one of the Connecticut regiments commanded by Colonel Sherman and Colonel Giles Russell, formed to fight in the American Revolutionary War. Like most of the thirteen former British colonies, Connecticut had no distinct "colored" regiments in the war of independence.

Mustered as a "free man of color," he may have either already been free, or freed as a reward for enlisting. He served for three years in the army commanded by General George Washington, fighting at Mud Island, Germantown, and Monmouth, and enduring the winter at Valley Forge 1777–1778. Honorably discharged in 1780 at the end of his term of enlistment, he reenlisted in 1782, serving until the end of the war in 1783.

His marriage to Lement Parker, 20 February 1782 in Wolcott, Connecticut, produced seven children who survived infancy; Prince Duplex Jr., the fifth of the seven, was born around 1796. By 1804, Prince Duplex Sr. owned a farm and was listed in tax records. While several of the Duplex children settled as adults in New Haven, their parents moved around 1816, to Danby, New York, where their father died at age seventy-one, on 29 October 1825. Their mother lived until 1847.

Prince Duplex Jr. appears to have worked for four years in the household of Dr. Ensign Hough, in Meriden, Connecticut. Hough owned what was known as "the old tavern." Duplex was selected as the first clerk to serve the African Ecclesiastical Society, founded between 1820 and 1824 in New Haven. Smith Jocelyn, an artisan and member of the Center Congregationalist Church, inspired and supported the organization of the society, observing that among the 624 African Americans counted in New Haven in 1820 (out of a total population of 8,327), only a few belonged to churches where they were "tolerated rather than welcomed," while others "were absolutely without moral and religious instruction and nobody seemed to care." Jocelyn began inviting "prominent African-Americans" to his home for private religious services (Mickens, p. 6).

The majority of New Haven residents, who thought of themselves as "white," did not expect men and women of African descent to be independent, well dressed, or self-respecting. The new society inspired a race consciousness that promoted self-improvement while developing some protection from white hostility. On 25 August 1829, the Western Association of New Haven County officially recognized the church, with an initial membership of four men and seventeen women. All had completed an examination on Congregationalist doctrine, made a formal profession of faith, and entered the covenant, placing them potentially among "the Elect of God." About half (including Duplex) were former members of other churches, the rest "gathered from the world, as fruits of revival," as reported in the 29 August 1829 *Religious Intelligencer*.

Completing a new building the same year on Temple Street, the church grew to over one hundred members. The Temple Street African Congregational Church developed a Sabbath school, a day school, and a temperance society. An evening school for adults was opened for the same reason most early New England schools had been formed: concern that many adults were unable to read the Bible. Initially, the church exemplified the teachings of Reverend Thomas Brainerd, who believed that the church should bring "the practical learning of schools to the people," with an educated clergy to "stimulate friendships among the best of society" while raising the "rude and degraded" to "neatness and good order" (Mickens, p. 7). The church continued through the nineteenth and twentieth centuries, becoming, in the 1960s, the Dixwell Avenue United Church of Christ.

In 1825 Duplex married Adaline L. Francis, a professional seamstress. They had three children, Edward Parker, Elisha, and Adeline Frances. Duplex supported the family working as a steward on the New Haven Steamship Line traversing Long Island Sound to New York City. He died in 1832, eulogized in the *Connecticut Herald* as "an accomplished gentleman."

Vashti Elizabeth Duplex, the first black school teacher in New Haven, is often referenced as the daughter of Prince Duplex. Church records from First Church of Christ in New Haven show that she was the daughter of Prince Duplex Sr., born in 1800, and the sister of Prince Duplex Jr. Nineteenth-century census enumerations confirm her age. She married John Creed. Their son, Cortland Van Rensselaer Creed, was the first American of African descent to receive a medical degree from an Ivy League university (Yale), and was appointed assistant surgeon of the Thirteenth Connecticut Volunteers in 1863. One Creed descendant served in World War I in the Harlem Hellfighters (367th Regiment), and another in World War II, with the Tuskegee Airmen (99th Pursuit Squadron).

FURTHER READING

Mickens, Ronald E., Willie Hobbs Moore, and Elmer Samuel Imes. *Edward Bouchet: The First African-American Doctorate* (2002).

Warner, Robert Austin. *New Haven Negroes: A Social History* (1969).

CHARLES ROSENBERG

Duplex, Prince, Sr. (Feb. 1754–29 Oct. 1825) one of at least 289 people of African descent who enlisted in the Connecticut Line during the American Revolutionary War, was born in Southington, Connecticut, where by the laws of that time he was the property of Samuel Riggs, a status inherited from his mother. He was baptized on 18 July 1756. Historical sketches published in 1875 mention that he had a brother named Peter, whose later life is unknown.

Prince's mother and father were later assigned as servants for Reverend Benjamin Chapman, pastor of Southington Congregational Church, who had married Riggs's daughter Abigail in 1756. When Riggs died in 1770, probate of his property listed "a negro boy Prince £50," who presumably was part of Abigail's share of her father's estate. The young man's parents may be the Peter and Hannah initially bequeathed by Riggs to his wife. The entire family eventually became part of the Chapman household, where the young man's mother was the cook. Later nineteenth-century reminiscences infer that the servants were well fed, lived with some minimum of human comfort, and held Chapman in some degree of esteem.

It is not known whether Duplex was already free when he enlisted in the 8th Connecticut Regiment on 18 May 1777. He appears on the muster roll as a "free man of color," a status that may have been granted on condition of serving as a soldier. He was enrolled in a company initially commanded by Captain Nehemiah Rice, later by Captain Jesse Kimball. The 8th Connecticut, also numbered as the 17th Continental, was commanded until March 1778 by Colonel John Chandler, then by Colonel Giles Russell until his death in October 1779. From 1777 to 1780, Duplex served in several battles of the Pennsylvania Campaign, including the Battle of Brandywine Creek on 11 September 1777. The 8th Connecticut marched in General Alexander McDougall's Brigade, part of the column commanded by General Nathaniel Greene, down Limekiln Road, in the surprise attack on British General Howe's main camp at Germantown on 4 October 1777.

Duplex also fought in the defense of Fort Mifflin at Mud Island (10–15 Nov. 1777), and spent the winter at Valley Forge, Pennsylvania, beginning in December 1777. Although muster rolls show him sick from January to April, he remained among the 346 soldiers in the regiment, and 233 fit for duty, who were still there in June 1778 to march out with Varnum's Brigade, Lee's Division. His next major battle was at Monmouth, on 28 June. General Lee's inexplicable retreat during the battle got him court-martialed and suspended, but the troops endured a great deal of fighting and marching, remaining in good order. Lieutenant Colonel Isaac Sherman took command of the regiment, after Russell's death near the end of 1779; the following year, Duplex was discharged at Morristown, New Jersey, 16 May 1780. A Treasury Office order dated 1 June 1782 shows that he was paid four pounds, six shillings, and one penny for his service.

Duplex married Lement Parker on 20 February 1782, at the Congregational Church in Wolcott, Connecticut, a rural community near Southington that was not fully incorporated as an independent town until 1796. Reverend Alexander Gillett, pastor of the church, presided at the wedding. The same year, Duplex enlisted again, serving until 1783 with regiments guarding Horseneck and Stamford, Connecticut. After the Revolutionary War, Duplex acquired property in Wolcott, owning two and a half acres by 1804. The couple had nine children, two of whom died in infancy. Daughters Sylvia and Vashti, and son Prince Duplex Jr., moved to New Haven, where they were among the founders of Temple Street Church, which later became the Dixwell Avenue Congregational Church.

In 1816, Prince and Lement Duplex, together with their oldest son, George, and two daughters, Arsena and Craty, moved to Danby, New York. They were among the earliest pioneer families to settle in the village, ten miles south of Lake Cayuga, in what became Tioga County. George Duplex acquired a substantial farm, and it appears he may have been providing partial support to his parents. Two years after arriving, Prince Duplex applied for a pension available to "certain persons engaged in the land and naval services of the United States in the Revolutionary War," solemnly swearing that "I have not, nor has any person in trust for me, any property or securities, contracts or debts due me," and that he had not since March 1818 disposed of any property to diminish his net worth so as to qualify for the pension.

Duplex listed property worth $5.44, including two drawing knives, four jack knives, one axe, one hoe, two wooden plates, two iron teaspoons, and one kettle. His occupation at the time was basket maker. He listed debts of $29, consisting of two notes of $10 each, one of $5, and one of $4. Although described as of ordinary health, his wife "had been afflicted with a fever sore for 17 years and has been at much expense in doctoring." He appears on the pension roll for Tioga County, New York, in the 1835 report by the Secretary of War for the middle Atlantic states. As a private soldier in the Revolutionary War, he was allowed $96 a year, paid monthly, commencing 27 April 1818, and up to the time he died received $721.14. A state census in 1825 showed that he owned no real property.

Duplex died at the age of seventy-one, survived by his wife, who lived until 1847; his son George; and six other sons and daughters. His grandson, Edward P. Duplex, son of Prince Duplex Jr. and Adaline L. Francis Duplex, was elected mayor of Wheatland, California, on 11 April 1888. Another grandson, Cortlandt Van Rensselaer Creed, son of John Creed and Vashti Duplex Creed, graduated from Yale Medical College in 1857.

FURTHER READING

Matthews, Harry Bradshaw. "Three African American Revolutionary War Patriots in Central New York." *USCT Civil War Digest* (Sept. 2009).

White, Olive David. *Connecticut's Black Soldiers, 1775–1783* (1973).

CHARLES ROSENBERG

Dupree, Anna Johnson (27 Nov. 1891–19 Feb. 1977), businesswoman, philanthropist, and humanitarian, was born Anna Johnson in Carthage, Texas. She was the first of Lee and Eliza Johnson's six children. Her great-grandfather, a slave owner, was German. Her maternal grandmother, Jane Sims, was part Native American and came to Texas from Kentucky. The family lived in poverty and Anna's grandmother helped pay the bills by working as a cook in a local hotel. The rest of the family, Anna included, worked in the cotton fields of East Texas. When she was thirteen, the family moved from Carthage to Galveston hoping for a better life. Her mother found work as a maid for several prominent Galveston families and Anna assisted her. With a natural creative talent and an eye for pretty things, Anna made her own clothes. Mrs. Zula Kay, a prominent resident of Galveston, noticed her and invited Anna to move to Houston to work for her mother as a domestic which she did in 1911. In addition to her maid duties Anna apprenticed at Ethel Baird's Beauty Shop.

During a visit to Galveston to see her family, Anna met Clarence Dupree. They married in 1914 and settled in Galveston for two years. In 1916 they moved to Houston, where Clarence worked as a porter at the Bender Hotel and then later at the famous "Old Brazos Hotel." In 1917 he left for France to serve in the U.S. Army during World War I. During their separation Dupree worked at the Ladies Beauty Shop on Main Street. During his military service, her husband worked as a mess sergeant in order to earn extra money. He also shined shoes, cut hair, loaned other soldiers money, and served as a French interpreter. He returned to Houston in 1920 with $100,000 wrapped around his waist. This money was used to start a businesses that would fund the couple's future philanthropic projects.

In 1922 Dupree began work at the Bristol Beauty Shop and her reputation as an excellent hairdresser spread to the elite sections of white Houston. Eventually she took a position at a River Oaks Salon and began making house calls to her well-heeled clients. In 1930 a beautician inspector visited her home and informed Dupree that she could no longer do residential work in her clients' private homes. White beauticians, threatened by her success, had formed a protective organization in an effort to confine entrepreneurial black hairdressers to shops. Defiantly, Dupree informed the inspector that she would build her own shop and it would be the best in Houston.

In 1936 Anna's Institution of Health and Beauty became a reality. She installed a Turkish bath and massage tables, and Carlton Pulliam, a graduate of Howard Medical School in Washington, D.C., trained her masseurs. In no time, Dupree's clients included some of Houston's most prominent white socialites. During this time many segregated black businesses lacked city amenities, such as paved roads, and Anna's salon was no exception. Some of her white customers complained about the inconvenience of the unpaved dirt road they had to take to reach her shop. As Marcella Washington noted in a 1 March 1980 *Houston Forward Times* article, Dupree's response was, "Don't holler at me about your car. Am I a white woman? Can I vote? Am I one of God's little angels? I got you pretty, now you get my street fixed." Agitation by devoted white female customers resulted in a paved road.

By 1940 combined savings and profits from the Duprees' jointly owned businesses that included the Pastime Theatre on McKinney Street, Anna's Institution of Health and Beauty, and the El Dorado Center, resulted in a donation of $20,000 toward the construction of an orphanage for black children called the Anna Dupree Cottage of the Negro Child Center. In the mid-1940s the Duprees' donated property in Highland Heights and led a fund drive to build the Eliza Johnson Home for the Aged. Initially it was a facility for elderly blacks, but they eventually opened it to all races. Named after Dupree's mother, the facility opened in 1952. Not only did the couple donate land and money but they also donated their time. They cooked meals, planted a garden, and harvested fresh vegetables. In 1946 the Duprees donated $11,000 to the construction of the first permanent building to the Houston College for Negroes (later Texas Southern University). They also sponsored the first black little league baseball team and raised funds for the state's only Girl Scout camp for black girls. Dupree and her husband were instrumental in getting the Houston millionaire Lamar Fleming to donate land for the South Central YMCA and St. Luke's Episcopal Church.

Dupree's vision for charitable projects was expansive. She formulated plans for a home for unwed girls, a nursery for abandoned babies and cottages for both the mentally ill and the physically handicapped. The proposed facility was to be called "Welcome Acres" and Dupree spoke about it for the duration of her life. Unfortunately this was the only item on Dupree's agenda that was never finished, owing to the sudden death of her husband in 1959 and her own deteriorating health. She moved into the Eliza Johnson Home that she eventually donated to the city of Houston. In 1972 the mayor's office hosted a tribute to celebrate Dupree's eighty-first birthday. Invited guests were all admirers of this remarkable woman and included people from all ages, races, and walks of life. Dupree's final significant contribution came at the time of her death at age eighty-five, when she donated her body to medical science. Her spirit of giving and service to the community was evident to the end.

FURTHER READING

Information related to Dupree is held in the Women's Collection of pamphlets and newspaper clippings about notable Texas women, Texas Woman's University Library, Denton, Texas.

Jones, Yvette. "Seeds of Compassion," *Texas Historian* 37.2 (1976).

Washington, Marcella. "Awakening in Houston: Black Women's Political Movement," *Houston Forward Times*, 1 Mar. 1980.

Winegarten, Ruth. *Black Texas Women* (1996).

Obituary: *Houston Post*, 22 Feb. 1977.

DIANNE DENTICE

Dupuy, Charlotte (1787?–?), slave litigant, was born Charlotte Stanley on the Eastern Shore of Maryland, the daughter of Rachel and George Stanley. Charlotte, commonly known as Lotty, spent her childhood enslaved, along with her mother and two siblings, by Daniel Parker in Dorchester County, Maryland. Whether George Stanley was born a slave is uncertain, but he was free by 1792 when he purchased Rachel and Charlotte's siblings Leah and Jonathan. He immediately manumitted his wife and stipulated the freedom of the two children upon their reaching the legal age. Charlotte, for reasons that are still unclear, remained enslaved in Parker's household until age nine, when she was sold to James Condon for one hundred dollars. Condon was a tradesman who lived nearby with his wife and at least one other slave. Rachel paid her daughter frequent visits, and the Condons may have promised Charlotte eventual freedom. Condon's apprentice later recalled that "I frequently heard Mrs. Condon say, at times when a little provoked with Lotty's conduct that she [Lotty] should not be free so soon as Lotty expected—I have also heard in Condon's family that Lotty was promised her freedom" (Records of the Court). Nevertheless, when Charlotte was about eighteen years old Condon moved her with his family to Lexington, Kentucky, and he made sure to register her as a slave in that state.

After her arrival in Lexington, Charlotte became acquainted with Aaron Dupuy, a slave at Ashland, the estate of then-twenty-nine-year-old Whig political titan, Henry Clay. Charlotte Stanley married Dupuy nearly a year later. Their marriage prompted Condon and Clay, one of the state's largest slaveholders, to agree to Charlotte Dupuy's sale. Clay purchased her for $450 on 12 May 1806. The Dupuys worked as domestic servants in the Clay household—Aaron as Clay's personal body servant and Charlotte as a nursemaid to his children. While at Ashland, Dupuy gave birth to two children, Charles and Mary Ann, and the family apparently remained in Kentucky while Clay—elected to the U.S. House of Representatives in 1810—cultivated his political career in Washington. In 1817 or 1818, Clay, who had become the Speaker of the House almost immediately after his arrival in Congress, moved the Dupuys to the capital to help run his ever more impressive establishment. Upon his appointment as secretary of state in 1824, Clay moved his household to a grand brick townhouse situated adjacent to the White House on the President's Park. Here Dupuy likely interacted with the capital's most seminal political figures—as well as its burgeoning free black population, including former slave ALETHIA TANNER, who operated a grocery stand on the park. Also during her residence in the city, Dupuy paid at least two extended visits to her relatives on Maryland's Eastern Shore.

At the end of his term as secretary of state, Clay rejected an offer of appointment to the U.S. Supreme Court, opting instead to return to his Kentucky estate. Dupuy, perhaps unhappy to leave a city that afforded her independence and proximity to family, resisted the impending return to Clay's plantation. Her defiance took the bold form of a lawsuit against her owner. On 13 February 1829, Robert Beale filed a petition on Dupuy's behalf in the U.S. Circuit Court of the District of Columbia. The suit asserted that she and her children "are entitled to their freedom and who are now held in a state of slavery by one Henry Clay (Secty of State) contrary to law and your petitioners' just rights" (Records of the Court). Dupuy based her claim on the contention that the free status of her mother and grandmother entitled her to her own freedom. She further cited Condon's assurances of emancipation when she reached the age of eighteen, thus rendering her transport to Kentucky and subsequent sale to Clay illegal.

Clay, who was accustomed to political conflict and controversy, insisted that Dupuy acted not on her own accord, but under the influence of political rivals bent on instigating scandal. Outraged, Clay wrote that the suit "has been instigated by motives distinct from the desire to liberating the petitioners, for the purpose of injuring and embarrassing this respondent" (*Clay Papers*, vol. 7, 623). In his correspondence with Clay regarding the suit, Dupuy's former owner James Condon similarly argued that her actions resulted from "some evil disposed person operating upon the mind of Lotty improperly" (*Clay Papers*, vol. 7, 632). Clay further asserted the impossibility of Dupuy's pretensions to freedom, recalling that she never exhibited any inclinations to run away, even when presented with such an opportunity when visiting her relations in Maryland. Condon also corroborated this notion, assuring Clay that while he did at one time promise her manumission, Dupuy "voluntarily relinquished [the possibility of emancipation] by marrying Your Servant Boy Aron [*sic*] and by her own pressing solicitations I sold her to you" (*Clay Papers*, vol. 7, 632).

With Clay and the remainder of her family in Kentucky, Dupuy continued to reside for the duration of the suit in Clay's former President's Park home, now assumed by his successor as secretary of state, Martin Van Buren. The court investigated her allegations for nearly a year, collecting the testimony of witnesses in Maryland and Kentucky. Her other previous owner, Daniel Parker, was deceased at the time of the lawsuit, but several residents of Dorchester County, Maryland, testified that he sold her to Condon as a "slave for life." Based on such testimony, as well as the receipt of manumission of her mother and the bill of sale between Condon and Clay, the court finally rejected Dupuy's claim to freedom in mid-1830. Soon after, Henry Clay demanded Dupuy's return to Lexington, complaining that "her conduct has created insubordination among her relatives here, I think it high time to put a stop to it, which can be best done by her return to duty" (*Clay Papers*, vol. 8, 261). However, Dupuy remained reluctant to leave, further enraging Clay, who ordered her immediate imprisonment and transport to Kentucky. Dupuy was instead carried to New Orleans, arriving "very penitent" in December 1830 (*Clay Papers*, vol. 8, 309). She remained in New Orleans at the home of Clay's daughter in the years that followed, separated from her husband and children. His daughter wrote in 1832 that "I cannot thank my dear Mother enough for having spared Lotty to me, she is the best creature I ever saw and appears to be quite as much attached to the children as she ever was to yours" (*Clay Papers*, vol. 8, 441).

In time, Clay apparently regained his good opinion of Dupuy; on 12 October 1840, a decade after her failed fight for freedom, he emancipated Dupuy and her daughter Mary Ann, noting

Dupuy's dedicated service as a nurse to his children and grandchildren. Her son Charles continued to serve as Clay's personal servant until his own manumission in December 1844. Dupuy's grandson Henry, the child of Mary Ann, was sold by Clay in 1848 under the condition that he would be freed at age twenty-eight. It appears that Clay never emancipated Dupuy's husband, as his family continued to refer to "old Aaron" in their correspondence through late 1850. What became of Charlotte Dupuy and her children following their emancipation remains unknown. In the 1960s Dupuy's home in Washington, D.C., where Clay lived during his tenure as secretary of state, was opened as the Stephen Decatur House Museum. There, the history of Charlotte Dupuy's life and her fight to win her freedom are presented along with the history of the house's other residents, including its original owner Stephen Decatur, who died in a duel, and Clay, Van Buren, five antebellum U.S. congressmen, and a U.S. vice president.

FURTHER READING

Records of *Charlotte Dupuy vs. Henry Clay* are available in the records of the Circuit Court of the District of Columbia for Washington County, National Archives, Washington, D.C.

Seager, Robert, II, ed. *The Papers of Henry Clay*, vol. 7 (1982).

Troutman, Richard L. "The Emancipation of Slaves by Henry Clay," *Journal of Negro History* 40:2 (Apr. 1955).

CARLA JONES

Durham, Eddie (19 Aug. 1906–6 Mar. 1987), jazz musician, composer, and arranger, was born in San Marcos, Texas. The names and occupations of his parents are unknown. Durham's early instruction in music came from an older brother. He started out on banjo but soon switched to guitar and trombone, performing on both instruments throughout his career. The family of six brothers formed the Durham Brothers Orchestra, a professional ensemble that traveled throughout Texas.

Still in his teens Durham married and moved on to a better-paying job with the 101 Ranch Brass Band, a marching band associated with circuses. With this outfit he began to develop his arranging skills. He joined the Dixie Ramblers in 1926, followed by a brief stay with Gene Coy's Happy Aces and then a period with WALTER PAGE's Blue Devils. By 1929 he was a member of BENNIE MOTEN's band in Kansas City.

Convinced that the band could be greatly improved with better personnel, Durham persuaded Moten to hire the trumpeter HOT LIPS PAGE, the vocalist JIMMY RUSHING, and the pianist COUNT BASIE. Early in his tenure with the Moten band, Durham provided most of the arrangements, but with a decline in the band's engagements, he occasionally worked with the newly formed Count Basie band. Following a brief tenure with Basie and about a week with CAB CALLOWAY, he then joined the JIMMIE LUNCEFORD band in early 1935.

Durham was a pioneer in developing the amplified jazz guitar. Around 1937 he attracted the attention of another southwestern guitarist, CHARLIE CHRISTIAN, and although Christian popularized the electrified instrument, Durham had an important influence on his approach.

Durham also introduced the banjoist and ukulele player Floyd Smith to the electric guitar. Christian went on to be featured in Benny Goodman's band, and Smith was sometimes showcased with ANDY KIRK and His Twelve Clouds of Joy. Durham, however, recorded the first jazz solo on amplified guitar (using an aluminum resonator). The recording was Lunceford's "Hittin' the Bottle." Durham was also the first jazz guitarist to use an electric amplifier. Although Lunceford was fascinated with the resonator, Durham had been hired to enlarge the trombone section and to assist with arrangements. Only occasionally did he play the guitar.

The trumpeter SY OLIVER, a Lunceford arranger, designated Durham as "probably our best jazz arranger at the time." When the Kansas City Basie band began enjoying some success in New York City, Durham again joined the group. He contributed "John's Idea," written in honor of John Hammond who had convinced Basie to bring his band east, to one of Basie's early recordings for Decca. Durham also played trombone and did the arrangements for Harry James's first recording under James's own name. He was a member (on electric guitar) of the select Kansas City Six that participated in the now famous Carnegie Hall concert "From Spirituals to Swing" on 23 December 1938. His relationship with the Basie band ended a few months earlier, as Durham had elected to test himself at making a living as an arranger. During this period he arranged for the Artie Shaw, Glenn Miller, Jan Savitt, and Ina Ray Hutton orchestras. He formed his own band in 1940, but with the outbreak of World War II, it became impossible to keep the group going.

Not long after the all-female, all-black jazz band the International Sweethearts of Rhythm left its founding institution (Piney Woods Country Life School) in April 1941, Durham was brought in as musical director. He had gained experience working with female musicians when he arranged for and coached the Hutton band. Durham organized his own all-female band during the same brief period that he was associated with the Sweethearts. He later offered this explanation to the jazz historian Stanley Dance: "That was the only way I could stay out of the army.... So long as I kept the girls' band, I'd be deferred from the army every six months for the duration." He was also obligated to give some service to the USO.

With a decline in the big band business Durham took advantage of other options. He became music director of various tour packages, participated in the 1947 "Cavalcade of Jazz," and led a small combo backing the blues singer WYNONIE HARRIS and the vocalist Larry Darnell. He later led his own quartet on weekends at a Long Island supper club. In the 1970s he worked with a band led by the former Basie tenor saxophonist Buddy Tate. Through the years Durham's compositions (individually and cowritten) included "Moten Swing" (for Benny Moten), "Lunceford Special" (for the Lunceford band), and "Out the Window" and "Topsy" (for the Basie band). Other works in the Durham catalog include "Good Morning Blues" and "Sent for You Yesterday and Here You Come Today." Only the weekend before his death in Brooklyn, Durham appeared at Oberlin College with the Harlem Blues and Jazz Band, a group with which he was associated for ten years.

FURTHER READING

Hoefer, George. "Held Notes: Eddie Durham," *Down Beat* 29:20 (1962).

Obituary: *New York Times*, 7 Mar. 1987.

This entry is taken from the *American National Biography* and is published here with the permission of the American Council of Learned Societies.

ANTOINETTE HANDY

Durham, James (1 May 1762–?), physician, was born a slave in Philadelphia, Pennsylvania. His surname is sometimes spelled Derham. Despite his slave status, he learned basic reading and writing skills from his first owners, whom he described as Christians. Durham also received his medical training from his masters. At that period most American physicians acquired their medical education through the apprenticeship system. Durham began a form of apprenticeship at the age of eight, when he became the slave of John A. Kearsley Jr., a physician who taught him to compound medicines and to perform routine medical procedures. Durham later belonged to other doctors in Philadelphia, at least one of whom was a British sympathizer. This association with a Loyalist master probably explains why Durham later became the property of George West, a surgeon in the British Sixteenth Regiment.

Along with his new master, Durham performed amputations on wounded troops along the Eastern Seaboard. Smallpox and various febrile diseases wreaked havoc among the British troops in the colonies, and Durham and other medics also attempted to save the lives of men stricken with these diseases. In 1781 Spanish forces defeated the British at Pensacola, Florida, and carried Durham with their other spoils of war to Spanish-controlled New Orleans. There Robert Dow, a Scottish physician, purchased Durham.

For the next two years Durham, working under Dow's supervision, practiced medicine in the city's French Quarter. Their patients were probably victims of malaria, yellow fever, influenza, and many other diseases common in eighteenth-century Louisiana. Although Durham had worked closely with the surgeon George West, it appears that he performed little if any surgery on Dow's patients.

Durham later described Dow as a good man, and there seems to have been mutual respect and admiration between slave and master. In April 1783 Dow permitted Durham, described as his faithful servant, to purchase his freedom for 500 pesos. Thereafter the two men enjoyed a close professional relationship for more than twenty years, during most of which Durham lived in New Orleans.

In 1788 Durham returned for about a year to Philadelphia, where he probably searched for family members and acquaintances whom he had not seen since before the Revolutionary War. During this sojourn he met America's foremost physician, Benjamin Rush. Like some of his peers, Rush was an early antislavery activist who wanted to meet talented blacks. At that time abolitionists believed that by publishing accounts of talented blacks and their achievements, they could counter arguments that slavery was justifiable on the grounds that Africans were intellectually inferior to whites. Through Rush's description of Durham, published in the *American Museum* (4 [July–Dec. 1788], 81–82), this former slave became well known in abolitionist circles.

Eighteenth-century Philadelphia was America's most sophisticated city, and Rush was able to introduce Durham to several prominent physicians and members of the Philadelphia College of Physicians and Surgeons. Durham was the first black medical practitioner most of them had encountered; moreover, he was certainly the first black man known to have appeared before an American medical society. Rush and Durham also talked at length about the diseases and medications used in Louisiana. Rush believed Durham was quite knowledgeable about the drugs of that time. He was also impressed with the former slave's fluency in French and Spanish.

In the spring of 1789 Durham was back in New Orleans, where he and Dow resumed their professional relationship. Their patients included some of the city's most prominent residents. It appears that Durham, like some other persons of color in early New Orleans, was not a victim of racial prejudice.

Durham remained in touch with Rush and corresponded with him over a period of sixteen years. In several letters he asked Rush to ship medical supplies to him and Dow, noting that on at least two occasions fire had destroyed their office and medical supplies. Durham, Rush, and Dow were familiar with the same medicines because all had studied under British physicians, and these medications were probably more readily available in Philadelphia than in New Orleans. Occasionally Durham sought advice from Rush regarding certain patients. The two men also exchanged views regarding the treatment of diseases such as yellow fever, which ravaged both Philadelphia and New Orleans during the 1790s.

That Rush respected Durham's expertise was evident when Rush read a paper written by the former slave before a session of the College of Physicians and Surgeons of Philadelphia. This treatise described a method used by Durham to treat "putrid sore throat," or diphtheria. It was one of the earliest medical papers written by an African American and was read before some of America's most respected physicians.

Durham experienced no difficulties with his medical practice in New Orleans until 1801, when Spanish authorities attempted to subject medical practitioners to restrictions not found under British colonial administration. The Spanish commissioners decreed that certain persons be forbidden to practice medicine in New Orleans until they had graduated from a medical school. Among those cited as a physician without the appropriate training was Durham. However, the commissioners agreed that Durham, even though he did not have formal training in medicine, could continue to treat diseases of the throat; apparently other members of his profession saw Durham as something of a specialist in this area.

Evidently Durham abided by this ruling; however, in a letter to Rush in 1802, he mentioned that he and Dow had encountered some cases of cowpox and wanted Rush's opinion regarding the most efficacious treatment. Possibly Durham had assumed some type of apprenticeship with Dow, working independently only when patients were stricken with diphtheria or some other ailment of the throat.

James Durham's correspondence with Rush ended in 1805. A few years earlier Durham had questioned Rush about the possibility of his practicing medicine elsewhere in the United States. When and whether he left New Orleans, however, remains a mystery, as do the date and place of his death.

FURTHER READING

Durham's letters to Rush are in the Benjamin Rush Papers, Manuscript Collection, Historical Society of Pennsylvania, Philadelphia; some appear in *Letters of Benjamin Rush*, ed. Lyman Butterfield, vol. 1 (1950), 497–498. He is mentioned in the Records of the Cabildo, New Orleans Public Library.

Morais, Henry M. *The History of the Afro-American in Medicine* (1976): 8–10.

Plummer, Betty E. "Letters of James Durham to Benjamin Rush," *Journal of Negro History* 65 (1980): 261–269.

Shryock, Richard H. *Medicine and Society in America: 1660–1860* (1960).

BETTY E. PLUMMER

Durham, John Stephens (18 July 1861–16 Oct. 1919), diplomat, lawyer, and journalist, was born in Philadelphia, Pennsylvania, the son of Samuel Durham and Elizabeth Stephens. Two of his uncles, Clayton Durham and Jeremiah Durham, were noted clergymen who helped Bishop RICHARD ALLEN establish the African Methodist Episcopal (AME) Church. Durham, who could almost pass for white, studied in the Philadelphia public schools and graduated from the Institute for Colored Youth in 1876.

For five years after leaving high school Durham taught in Delaware and Pennsylvania. In 1881 he entered Towne Scientific School, a branch of the University of Pennsylvania, from which he earned a bachelor's degree in 1886 and a civil engineering degree in 1888. He held several positions during his college career, including reporter for the *Philadelphia Times*. He excelled as a newspaperman, and his unique abilities eventually led him to the assistant editorship of the *Philadelphia Evening Bulletin*, one of the city's most respected white newspapers, which supported the Republican Party. As a writer, Durham won acclaim for his articles dealing with the socioeconomic problems of blacks and the complexity of international relations.

Active in community matters, Durham endeavored to improve the quality of life for blacks in Philadelphia. For six years (1885–1891) he organized workingmen's clubs and other organizations to help the black community meet the challenges of impoverished urban life. He was an advocate of hard work, temperance, and good citizenship, and he helped secure jobs for blacks in the city's accounting firms, shops, and factories.

Fluent in Spanish and French, Durham aspired to a diplomatic post and asked Secretary of State James G. Blaine to appoint him consul to the Dominican Republic. With the support of Philadelphia's community leaders, Durham received the appointment from President Benjamin Harrison in May 1890.

At the time, the famous former slave, antislavery crusader, and journalist FREDERICK DOUGLASS was minister to the Dominican Republic and Haiti, which share the island of Hispaniola in the Caribbean Sea. Douglass was embroiled in a controversy involving the U.S. Navy's attempts to negotiate a lease at Môle St. Nicolas, a port city on Haiti's northwest coast, for a coaling station. Douglass understood that such a lease might provoke a nationalistic reaction within Haiti and possibly a civil war. When the negotiations failed, he was blamed, prompting him to resign. Durham succeeded Douglass as minister and consul general to Haiti and chargé d'affaires to the Dominican Republic. Despite Haiti's tumultuous political atmosphere, Durham was able to conclude a claims settlement for U.S. citizens who suffered losses and had property and goods seized during some of Haiti's many civil uprisings. Durham's most important diplomatic effort was the agreement he reached with the Dominican dictator Ulises Heureaux in 1892 regarding the Bay of Samaná on the northeast coast. The bay was judged to be the country's best natural harbor, and the U.S. Navy had long had its sights on it. Durham proposed a treaty that granted the United States a ninety-nine-year lease, but the *New York Herald* broke the story before the treaty was signed, setting off a patriotic reaction in Santo Domingo. In face of the opposition, Heureaux retreated and terminated the treaty, but not before the U.S. Congress had appropriated $250,000 for the first payment.

Durham resigned his diplomatic posts when Grover Cleveland became president for the second time in 1893. He returned to Philadelphia, where he was admitted to the bar. Other demands were made on his time, particularly as a speaker. The series of lectures he gave at Hampton and Tuskegee institutes was published in 1897 as *To Teach the Negro History (A Suggestion)*. In the mid-1890s he managed a sugar refinery at San Pedro de Marcorís in the Dominican Republic. In 1897 he married Constance Mackenzie, a schoolteacher. They had no children.

Because of his experience in Haiti, Durham served as assistant attorney with the Spanish Treaty Claims Commission in Cuba from 1902 to 1905, and while there he and J. Martin Miller, a representative of the Navy Department, evaluated the damages caused by the eruptions of Mount Pelée in Martinique. Their findings were published in 1902 as *The Martinique Horror and St. Vincent Calamity*. Durham's personal reminiscences as a diplomat in Haiti appeared that same year in *Lippincott's Monthly Magazine* as a novelette titled "Recollections of Haiti."

From 1905 until his death Durham practiced law in his native Philadelphia, often representing the interests of the United States and European countries in the Caribbean. He died of stomach cancer in London, England, while on a business trip.

FURTHER READING

Durham's diplomatic reports are in the U.S. National Archives in the Despatches from the Ministers of Haiti and the Dominican Republic.

Herrick, Walter R., Jr. *The American Naval Revolution* (1966).

Padgett, James A. "Diplomats to Haiti and Their Diplomacy," *Journal of Negro History* 25 (July 1940): 265–330.

Plummer, Brenda Gayle. *Haiti and the United States: The Psychological Moment* (1992).

This entry is taken from the *American National Biography* and is published here with the permission of the American Council of Learned Societies.

THOMAS M. LEONARD

Durham, Tempie Herndon (c. 1834–?), slave narrator, was born Tempie Herndon in Chatham County, North Carolina. All that is known about her appears in a Federal Writers' Project interview that she gave in Durham, North Carolina, in 1937 when she claimed to be 103 years old. As in many WPA narratives, the interviewer transcribed Durham's speech in a dialect that exaggerates the rhythm and syntax of southern Black English. Although Durham does not name her own parents, she provides quite a lot of information about her owners, "my white fo'ks" (Rawick, 285), as she calls them, George and Betsy Herndon, who ran a large plantation in Chatham County. Their large slave workforce grew corn, cotton, and tobacco, and also raised cattle, sheep, and hogs.

Durham's work routine centered on a large weaving room on the Herndon plantation, where female slaves made blankets and winter clothing. They were sometimes accompanied by the mistress of the house, who like Tempie enjoyed the clacking sound of the loom. Durham also recalled the communal singing of other slaves as they worked in a carding and spinning room, and the skills of Mammy Rachel, who worked in the dyeing room, and "knew every kind of root, bark, leaf an' berry dat made red, blue, green, or whatever color she wanted" (Rawick, 286). In the era before the widespread production of synthetic dyes, such native knowledge was essential to the fledgling southern textile industry. Ironically, when southern textiles expanded in the decades after the Civil War, most mill owners systematically excluded African Americans from their factories in favor of an all-white workforce, even though former black slaves like Durham possessed the relevant skills.

Although Durham was perhaps overeager to provide her interviewer with a positive assessment of slavery and her owners, her narrative reveals the reality of power and powerlessness that existed on antebellum plantations. This is most evident in her recollection of her wedding, probably in the early 1850s, to Exter Durham, a slave on the Snipes Durham plantation, just across the county line in Orange County. The wedding ceremony, held on the front porch of the big house, was a grand affair attended by the entire plantation, black and white, and presided over by George and Betsy Herndon. The bride recalled that she wore a white dress, long white gloves to her elbow, white shoes, and a white veil made by her mistress out of curtains. She stood at the altar with her groom on a "sho nuff linen sheet." After a service performed by the plantation's black preacher, the newly married couple jumped a broomstick, a traditional African American custom, though in this instance performed in part because "Marse George got to have his little fun." The elaborate preparations for Tempie Durham's wedding were not typical of most slave marriages, but they do reflect the efforts of some slaveholders to be seen as genial, paternalistic masters with the best interests of their slaves at heart. The competing slaveholder's impulse of maximizing profits and upholding the sanctity of property rights was also evident in George Herndon's case. Herndon allowed the married couple to stay at the cabin for their wedding night, but required that Exter Durham leave the next day, as "he belonged to Marse Snipes Durham an' he had to go back home." Tempie Durham recalled that Exter "left de next day for his plantation, but he come back every Saturday night an' stay 'twell Sunday night" (Rawick, 288).

Tempie Durham was under no allusions that these weekly visits were partly for the benefit of her master, since "de more chillun a slave had de more dey was worth." As the mother of nine "muley strong and healthy" children before the war, she understood that she "was worth a heap to Marse George" (Rawick, 288). She also recalled that the slaves on the plantation had plenty to eat during the Civil War, but only because their master remained at home and kept them working, looking after the livestock and tending the crops. When freedom came, she was overjoyed, since she could be with Exter all the time, instead of just on weekends. The couple remained on Herndon's plantation for several years, renting the land for a quarter of the profits they made, and eventually saved $300 to purchase their own farm.

Whatever affection Durham may have exhibited for her former owners in her WPA interview may have been partially calculated to appease her white interviewer, but it may also have been a product of genuine appreciation for the white Herndons' provision of furniture, seed corn, and cottonseed after the war. The Durhams' eventual success as small farmers depended, however, on their own labors, and especially on the work of their eleven children—two of whom were born free—who worked in the fields as soon as they could walk. In the context of a life of hard labor, the distinction between slavery and freedom mattered less to Durham than to other former slaves, such as Delia T. Garlic, also interviewed by the WPA in the 1930s, who recalled that "dem days was hell" (Rawick, 129). Tempie Durham recognized, however, that her own experience of slavery was not necessarily typical. "Maybe everybody's Marse and Missis wuzn' as good as Marse George and Miss Betsy" (Rawick, 290).

FURTHER READING

Griffin, Rebecca J. "'Goin' Back over There to See That Girl': Competing Social Spaces in the Lives of the Enslaved in Antebellum North Carolina," *Slavery and Abolition* (Apr. 2004).

Rawick, George P. *The American Slave: A Composite Autobiography, Ser. 2, v. 14, North Carolina Narratives* (1972–1979).

White, Deborah Gray. *Aren't I a Woman: Female Slaves in the Plantation South* (1985).

STEVEN J. NIVEN

Durnford, Andrew (1800–12 July 1859), plantation and slaveowner, physician, was born in New Orleans, Louisiana, the son of Thomas Durnford, an-English immigrant and merchant, and Rosaline Mercier, a free woman of color. Thomas Durnford was a cousin of Colonel Elias Durnford of the Royal Engineers, lieutenant governor of British West Florida. Andrew Durnford, reared by parents who were denied marriage by law, grew up in New Orleans's free colored community with the comforts afforded the family of a successful merchant and speculator. His schooling, like most of his early life, is a matter of conjecture. In his adult years he revealed a working knowledge of written and spoken English and French, the rudiments of elementary arithmetic, and medical procedures. He apparently passed freely between the white community with his father and the free colored community with his mother and her family. For example, John McDonogh, a successful merchant and planter of New Orleans and Baltimore, had business ties with both Durnford and his white father. In 1825 Durnford married fifteen-year-old Marie Charlotte Remy, a free woman of color; they had four children, three of whom lived to adulthood. Thomas Durnford died in 1826, two weeks before his namesake, Thomas McDonogh Durnford, was born. In 1828 Andrew Durnford left New Orleans to build a plantation on lands purchased from McDonogh, where he resided until his death.

St. Rosalie Plantation was established thirty-three miles south of New Orleans on the west bank of the Mississippi River in Plaquemines Parish. Durnford had purchased his estate in three parts over four years, all on credit, from McDonogh. McDonogh also financed Durnford's original purchase of plantation slaves. For seven thousand dollars Durnford purchased seven men, five women, and two children. As the plantation grew from ten front-arpents (frontage on the Mississippi River) in 1828 to fifteen in 1829 and nearly twenty-five by 1832, Durnford directed his slaves in the planting and harvesting of sugarcane. Neighbors processed the St. Rosalie cane into sugar and molasses until machinery was purchased and put into operation. Durnford's first sugar was produced in 1831.

A growing plantation demanded a larger labor force. Durnford scorned the local slave market, believing the prices much too high for the people offered. Bypassing local sellers, he undertook a slave-buying trip to Virginia in 1835. Letters to McDonogh chronicle the rigors of the journey, the bargaining for human beings, and the difficulties of moving a coffle of slaves hundreds of miles from the point of purchase to the plantation. The letters reflect the man who wrote them. The trip was an education for Durnford, who made it in the company of his trusted body servant and slave, Barba. He visited Philadelphia, Pennsylvania, where he sold the sugar that he had brought to market. While in the city Durnford enjoyed the company of Elliott Cresson, the British abolitionist and promoter of the American Colonization Society. The slave-buying journey provided Durnford with two-dozen slaves and an understanding of the slave trade. After 1835 he no longer complained of high prices in his letters to McDonogh, and he purchased slaves in the local market. The business of buying and moving human property was not without risk and cost.

A cliometric study of Durnford's planting career suggests that St. Rosalie was not a profitable business. Like his peers Durnford attached a value to his status of planter and slaveowner that compensated for the failure of his operation to earn as much as the same capital could have earned in alternative enterprises.

Durnford was also a practicing physician who cared for himself, his family and slaves, and the people and slaves in the parish. On one occasion a group of parish residents subscribed $185 to buy him a pair of horses in appreciation of his medical services.

Durnford lived comfortably for his time. He owned seventy-seven slaves and a fully operating sugarcane plantation. He practiced medicine and considered himself a philosopher. He read newspapers and books and corresponded regularly with other intellectuals. He formed and expressed opinions on issues of the day, including slavery, money, social ills, metaphysics, ambition, and power. He was contemptuous of money and money dealers, perhaps because he never mastered the science of money management. He held slavery to be an evil but recognized its value in bringing wealth and social position.

Durnford's planting career and life in general are sketched in letters between him and McDonogh and in Durnford's letters to his son, Thomas, when Thomas was a student at Lafayette College in Easton, Pennsylvania, in the 1840s. Durnford copied his letters to his son into his plantation journal.

In 1844 McDonogh emancipated eighty-five slaves and paid their expenses to Liberia, Africa. Durnford expressed appreciation of the gesture and exchanged letters with some of the freedmen but did not imitate his friend. As he wrote to McDonogh in 1843 Durnford believed that "the total extinction of slavery in these United States will be in future ages to come, a subject which the general government will undertake aided by individual donations &c and a few emancipations now and then from rich and noble minded men. Self interest is too strongly rooted in the bosom of all that breathes the American atmosphere. Self interest is al la mode."

Durnford died at his plantation in Plaquemines Parish. He was a rare antebellum American, a black, slave-owning planter with a medical practice and social contacts in the white community.

FURTHER READING

Durnford's papers reside within the John McDonogh collections at the Tulane University Library and the Louisiana State Museum, both in New Orleans.

"A Black Entrepreneur in Antebellum Louisiana," *Business History Review* 45 (1971).

"Slave Buying in 1835 Virginia as Revealed by Letters of a Louisiana Negro Sugar Planter," *Louisiana History* 11 (1970).

Whitten, David O. *Andrew Durnford: A Black Sugar Planter in Antebellum Louisiana* (1981).

Whitten, David O. "Rural Life along the Mississippi: Plaquemines Parish, Louisiana, 1830–1850," *Agricultural History* 58 (1984).

This entry is taken from the *American National Biography* and is published here with the permission of the American Council of Learned Societies.

DAVID O. WHITTEN

Duse, Mohammed Ali (26 November 1866–25 June 1945), actor, journalist, and Pan-African activist, was born in Alexandria, Egypt, to an Egyptian father and a Sudanese mother. In various documents he called his father, who was an army officer, either "Abbas Mohammed Ali" or "Abdul Salem Ali." Early in his life Duse was separated from his family and forgot any knowledge of Arabic. He claimed to have been brought to England at the age of nine by a French officer with whom his father had studied at a military academy. In 1882 his father was killed by a British naval bombardment in a nationalist uprising at Tel-el-Kebir, and his mother returned to the Sudan bringing Duse's sisters with her. He subsequently lost all communication with his family. During his early theatrical career in London he adopted the non-Arabic name "Duse," maintaining that it derived from the surname of the officer who had brought him to England. The name carried a certain cachet on account of the Italian-born actress Eleanora Duse, who was renowned for her leading roles in stage adaptations of novels by Alexandre Dumas. Despite his indistinct family background, speculation that Duse's parents were African American has not been verified.

In 1885 Duse was engaged as an actor by Wilson Barrett, a leading actor-manager, with whose company he toured England and later the United States and Canada. In 1898 he was contracted by the theater company of Sir Herbert Beerbohm Tree and in 1902 staged his own productions of *Othello* and *The Merchant of Venice*. Between 1909 and 1911 Duse embarked on a career as a journalist and contributed a number of articles to the influential socialist journal *New Age* on topics relating to Egyptian nationalism and Pan-Islamism. In 1911 Duse also participated in the Universal Races Congress in London and published a history of Egypt titled *In the Land of the Pharaohs*. Following this publication Duse was elected to honorary membership of the American Negro Academy and the Negro Society of Historical Research in New York. But the history also led to accusations of plagiarism against Duse that brought an end to his connection with the *New Age*. He subsequently founded his own newspaper, *African Times and Orient Review* (*ATOR*), which provided a lively forum for early Pan-African and Pan-Islamic politics in Britain; *ATOR*'s headquarters in London, at 158 Fleet Street, became the hub of a multifaceted group of organizations related to Egyptian, West African, and Indian nationalisms, as well as the All-India Muslim League, Pan-Islamism, the Khilafat Movement, and black nationalisms in the United States.

There is little information available about Duse's wife, Beatrice Mohammed, except that she was white and British and that he permanently separated from her in 1921. In that year Dusé (now accenting the last letter of his name) left Britain on a business trip to the United States. On behalf of the Inter-Colonial Corporation, which he established in partnership with JOHN EDWARD BRUCE, Dusé aimed to negotiate African American contracts for cocoa to be supplied from West African traders. This scheme, along with subsequent Pan-African business ventures, proved largely unsuccessful. Nonetheless Dusé's reputation as a historian allowed him to make a living by lecturing in the United States, and from 1921 to 1931 he led a peripatetic life as a lecturer, journalist, actor, and radio broadcaster, going to New York, Boston, Washington, Tuskegee, Detroit, Chicago, and Saint Louis.

In New York, Dusé renewed his association with MARCUS GARVEY, who had briefly worked as a messenger boy at *ATOR* before establishing himself as a leading international black activist. Between 1922 and 1924 Dusé headed an African Affairs department for Garvey's Universal Negro Improvement Association (UNIA) and contributed articles to UNIA's newspaper, the *Negro World*. Dusé's self-identification as an Egyptian Muslim and his practice of wearing the fez probably appealed to Garvey, who liked to deploy uniforms and other regalia for their popular appeal. More important, the friends and contacts that Dusé had established in London were invaluable to UNIA, and his presence in the organization during this period may account for the distribution of the *Negro World* in Nigeria, Sierra Leone, and the Gold Coast. But by the time that Garvey was imprisoned in February 1925, Dusé had parted ways with him.

For a short period in 1925 Dusé was secretary of the American Asiatic Association in Detroit. If he was not actually involved in founding the Nation of Islam, his lecturing and other Islamicist activities in Detroit probably helped to establish a political climate congenial to the development of that movement there under Wallace Fard Muhammad. After 1926 Dusé returned to New York and renewed his efforts to establish a trading business between the United States and West Africa, first in partnership with the Gold Coast businessman Winfried Tete-Ansa and later alone. But again his business plans were unsuccessful.

In 1931 Dusé traveled to Nigeria in the company of a white American woman, Gertrude La Page. He lived with her in Lagos, where he managed and edited a local newspaper, the *Comet*. His novel *Ere Roosevelt Came*, which depicts racial politics in the United States, was serialized in the *Comet* from February to October 1934. A thinly fictionalized version of the conflict between Garvey (characterized as "Napoleon Hatbry") and W. E. B. DUBOIS ("Reginald Bologne De Woode") showed Dusé's support for Garvey's program of economic enterprise over DuBois's one of political and cultural advancement. Dusé's autobiography, "Leaves from an Active Life," which was serialized in the *Comet* from 12 June 1937 to 5 March 1938, made no reference to Garvey; this was possibly because of the changing political climate and fear of deportation.

In competition with Nnamdi Azikiwe's *West African Pilot*, sales of the *Comet* gradually declined. Dusé eventually retired as an editor but maintained his role as company director of the newspaper until his death in Lagos on 26 February 1945. Although he had not directly participated in the official Pan-African Congress movement established by DuBois, Dusé played an important role as an international advocate for Pan-Africanism. Although he clearly preferred the economic model of black commercial unification advanced by Garvey, he consciously advocated and actively linked Pan-African ideology with other struggles for democratic change among subjugated peoples in the United States, Africa, and Asia.

FURTHER READING

Duffield, Ian. "The Business Activities of Dusé Mohammed Ali: An Example of the Economic Dimension of Pan-Africanism, 1912–1945," *Journal of the Historical Society of Nigeria* 4 (June 1969): 571–600.

Duffield, Ian. "Dusé Mohammed Ali: His Purpose and His Public," in *The Commonwealth Writer Overseas: Themes of Exile and Expatriation*, ed. Alastair Niven (1976).

Duffield, Ian. *Dusé Mohammed Ali and the Development of Pan-Africanism 1866–1945*. Ph.D. dissertation, University of Edinburgh, 1971.

Hill, Robert, and Carol A. Rudisell, eds. "Biographical Supplement: Dusé Mohammed Ali," in *The Marcus Garvey and Universal Negro Improvement Association Papers* (1983).

Mahmud, Khalil. "Introduction to the Second Edition," in *In the Land of the Pharaohs: A Short History of Egypt*, by Duse Mohamed (1968).

Mohamed, Duse. "Leaves from an Active Life," *The Comet*, 12 June 1937–5 March 1938.

ÍDE CORLEY

Duster, Alfreda Barnett (3 Sept. 1904–2 Apr. 1983), community activist, social service worker, and history conserver, was born Alfreda Marguerita Barnett in Chicago, Illinois. She was the youngest child of Ida B. Wells Barnett, the journalist, suffragist, and anti-lynching crusader, and Ferdinand Barnett, the attorney, civil rights activist, and founder of Chicago's first black newspaper. Along with her three full siblings—Ida, Herman, and Charles Aked—Alfreda had two half-brothers, Albert and Ferdinand Jr., from her father's first marriage. Duster recalled her childhood as happy and both her parents as kind, dedicated people of integrity. She described her father as gentle and quiet, her mother as outspoken and firm. Other activists like Carter G. Woodson, William Monroe Trotter, and Hallie Quinn Brown regularly visited the Barnett home.

The Barnetts lived in a largely middle-class, interracial, sometimes racially tense area on Chicago's South Side. A bright student who handled herself confidently among her white classmates, Alfreda skipped several grades at Stephen Douglas Elementary, then attended Lucy Flower and Wendell Phillips high schools, graduating early from the latter in 1921. Barnett earned a bachelor of philosophy degree in 1924 at the University of Chicago, where the athletic facilities and women's dormitories were whites-only, and where she joined a student club that promoted interracial dialogue.

Although Barnett then spent a year working in her father's law office, she did not pursue her parents' hope that she would become an attorney herself. On 9 July 1925 she wed Benjamin C. Duster Jr., a clerk in Ferdinand Barnett's practice. Benjamin Duster was ten years her senior, a native of Mount Vernon, Indiana, and Herman Barnett's friend and classmate at the University of Illinois. After leaving his clerk position Benjamin Duster worked irregularly as a construction laborer, interior decorator, banquet hall manager, driver's license tester, and civil rights special investigator for the state attorney general. He proved a devoted family man and passionate activist in local Republican politics. Despite their financial struggles, especially during the Depression, Alfreda Duster firmly pursued her aspirations to be a homemaker and to have a large family of six children. She had enjoyed growing up as one of that particular number, and she considered this an ideal family size to seek herself.

In 1931 Ida B. Wells Barnett died, leaving behind forty-seven chapters of typewritten, unfinished autobiography. In 1936 Ferdinand Barnett Sr. passed away, and the Dusters' fifth and last child was born. Four years later the city of Chicago opened the Ida B. Wells public housing project. This event stimulated great curiosity about Wells Barnett even as accurate public information about her had become scarce. Benjamin and Alfreda Duster resolved to edit and publish Wells Barnett's autobiography. Publisher after publisher responded to their inquiries, if at all, with rejections or at best with leads that went nowhere. Meanwhile, as she volunteered with the PTA and other community organizations, Duster resourcefully shepherded the children through a daily routine of after-school play, chores, homework, and educational games meant to foster close family ties and eventually qualify them for college scholarships.

In 1945 Benjamin Duster died after a short illness. Alfreda Duster was left with $52 and five children ages nine to seventeen (and one short of her goal of six). Her sister, Ida Barnett, who already lived with them, took on more child-care responsibilities. Duster found paid employment with the Southside Community Committee (later the Woodlawn Community Services Agency) as a secretary, juvenile delinquency prevention coordinator, academic enrichment worker with the Catalyst for Youth program, and administrator of Camp Illini for urban youth. She also worked as secretary to Democrat Charles Jenkins, one of the few blacks in the Illinois legislature. By the early 1960s each of the five Duster children had finished Wendell Phillips High School as a valedictorian or salutatorian and won college scholarships.

In 1965 Duster retired and soon traveled around Western Europe. She concentrated primarily on editing and publishing her mother's autobiography, a task relegated for many years previous to evenings and weekends. Because a fire in the early 1930s had destroyed most of Wells Barnett's other papers, Duster painstakingly researched and verified her mother's accounts of historic events. Times had changed since the 1940s. The civil rights movement was generating great national interest in black history, even among publishers. The historian John Hope Franklin, senior editor of a proposed "Negro biography" series from the University of Chicago Press, responded positively when Duster showed him the manuscript. In 1970 the press issued *Crusade for Justice: The Autobiography of Ida B. Wells* to excellent reviews from both majority-culture and African American media.

The book won Duster a National Council of Negro Women Award for Literary Excellence and

Outstanding Humanitarian Contributions. Her other awards included Mother of the Year from the PTA (1950 and 1970); the Bootstrap Award, Opportunity Centers of Chicago (1970); Citation for Public Service, University of Chicago Alumni Association (1973); an honor for senior black women community leaders, Harris YMCA (1974); and honorary doctorate of humane letters, Chicago State University (1978). Like her mother, Duster accumulated an impressive club and volunteer service record. Along with the PTA she belonged to the Citizens' School Committee, Chicago Urban Life Center, Chicago International Program, the University of Chicago Women's Board, United Methodist Women, CROP, the Rural Life Association, and the National Federation of Colored Women's Clubs. She was founder of the Alfreda Wells Duster Civic Club, a lifetime member of the NAACP, an honorary member of the Rust College Alumni Association, an officer of the Mid-South Model Cities Area Council, and a service guild president of Woodlawn United Methodist Church.

Duster died at age seventy-eight from a brain hemorrhage. In accord with her wishes her body was donated to science. Her stated priority in life was to build caring, self-respecting community. She successfully raised five children through difficult circumstances, lived long enough to enjoy grandchildren, and aided perhaps three to four thousand other young people. Her thirty years of devoted effort in the end powerfully returned her mother Ida B. Wells Barnett, a moving spirit of black history, to American public consciousness and memory. Alfreda Barnett Duster considered penning her own remarkable life story but never did. Despite this irreparable loss, the positive effects of her abundant care have endured, although their source has sometimes gone unrecognized.

FURTHER READING

The Ida B. Wells Papers, Special Collections Research Center, University of Chicago Library, contain archival materials on Alfreda Duster and her family.

Duster, Michelle. "Alfreda Marguerita Barnett Duster," in *Women Building Chicago 1790–1990*, eds. Rima Lunin Schultz and Adele Hast (2001).

Giddings, Paula. "Alfreda M. Duster," in *Notable Black American Women, Volume One*, ed. Jessie Carney Smith (1992).

Schlesinger Library on the History of Women in America. *Black Women Oral History Project, Volume 52: Interview with Alfreda Duster, March 8 and 9, 1978* (1979).

Wells, Ida B. *Crusade for Justice: The Autobiography of Ida B. Wells*, ed. Alfreda M. Duster (1970).

Obituary: *Chicago Defender*, 4 Apr. 1983.

MARY KRANE DERR

Dutrey, Honore (1894–21 July 1935), trombonist, was born in New Orleans, Louisiana. His parents' names and occupations are unknown, but he was of Creole descent. It is unclear whether, owing to this French-influenced heritage, his given name was properly spelled with an acute accent, Honoré, as some researchers have written it. He was the youngest of four brothers: Pete played violin, Sam (Sr.), clarinet, and Jimmy, drums.

Dutrey's association with the cornetist King Oliver in New Orleans dates at least to 1908, when Oliver joined the Magnolia Band, according to Pops Foster, who was also a member of this six-piece group. Dutrey married in 1909, but details of his family life, including his wife's name and the number of children they had, are unknown. It was perhaps around this time that he began daywork as a bricklayer. He played in the Melrose Brass Band around 1910. He worked with the violinist John Robichaux's Elves of Oberon and with Oliver in 1913, at which time he joined the Silverleaf Orchestra. At some point he joined the band formed in 1914 by Buddy Petit and Jimmie Noone. Also around 1914 the four Dutrey brothers played with Pops Foster on a cruise ship bound for Honduras. Dutrey played with the Silverleaf until 1917, at which time he joined the navy. With Dutrey in the service, his wife moved to Chicago, where he later joined her.

According to John Chilton in *Who's Who of Jazz: Storyville to Swing Street*, Dutrey suffered carbide poisoning while on duty in the torpedo room of a ship. The accident led to respiratory problems and his early death and, naturally, it also restricted his ability to blow the trombone. But making good from bad, he subsequently developed a sparse style that was celebrated for its appropriateness to the role of the trombone in New Orleans jazz, intertwining with and complementing the trumpet and clarinet melodies, without getting in their way.

On leave from the navy and about to be discharged, Dutrey went to Chicago. Surviving photos identify Dutrey and Oliver as members of the clarinetist Lawrence Duhe's White Sox Boosters, a seven-piece band that performed at the ballpark during the World Series of 1919 (the year of the notorious Black Sox scandal). Dutrey joined Oliver's new six-piece band in January 1920 after KID ORY declined Oliver's offer to be the group's trombonist. Each night they performed successively at the Dreamland Cafe and the Pekin Cabaret. Leaving Chicago, the group began an engagement at the Pergola Dance Pavilion in San Francisco in June 1921. With two new members added, Oliver's band also played at the California Theatre. According to the group's drummer BABY DODDS: "At a matinee performance, a smart guy in the audience called out, 'I thought you said those guys were Creoles. Those guys are no Creoles. Those are Niggers!' With great presence of mind, Joe Oliver and Honore Dutrey, who were the only band members who spoke patois, began talking it together very fast. That ended the episode" (Allen, 10). This ugly story, typical of the jazz life, also testifies to Dutrey's Creole and African American heritage.

The group worked sporadically on the West Coast for less than a year, but details are unknown. Dutrey left Oakland and returned to Chicago, followed soon after by Oliver, who rehired Dutrey for a renowned engagement at the Lincoln Gardens in June 1922. Now known as King Oliver's Creole Jazz Band, the group soon brought on a second cornetist, LOUIS ARMSTRONG, and played various jobs away from Lincoln Gardens, including a midwestern tour in spring 1923, but most importantly the Creole Jazz Band made pioneering recordings that year. Dutrey may be heard on several sessions for the Gennett and Okeh labels, although not on Oliver's titles for Columbia. He solos on a portion of "Jazzin' Babies Blues," leads the ensemble at the beginning of "Tears," and presents a composed melody (played successively by clarinet, trombone, and cornet) on "Riverside Blues." The group broke up at the beginning of 1924, and Dutrey briefly joined FREDDIE KEPPARD at Burt Kelly's Stables.

Dutrey led his own band at the Lincoln Gardens until June 1924. Among its personnel were his former colleagues in the Creole Jazz Band, the brothers JOHNNY DODDS and Baby Dodds, with whom he worked with the remainder of the decade, including engagements under Johnny Dodds's name at Kelly's Stables and recordings in 1928–1929. Dutrey also toured with CARROLL DICKERSON and worked in Chicago at the Sunset Cafe with Dickerson around 1926 and with Armstrong's Stompers in 1927, with whom he recorded one title. Intensifying respiratory problems forced him to retire from performance in 1930; nothing is known of his last years. He died in Chicago.

Dutrey's significance lies in his participation in the first substantial body of recordings by an African American jazz band. His contribution helped define "tailgate" trombone, a style of New Orleans jazz playing that involves supplying an inner voice in collective improvisation and takes advantage of the instrument's ability to make slides from note to note. Owing to his shortness of breath and his musical taste, Dutrey's style was not as raucous, crass, or comical as that of many other players. Casual listeners may find it easier to pick out details of that style on later recordings, due to the dramatic improvements in recording fidelity that came after Oliver's sessions of 1923. The single title with Armstrong, "Chicago Breakdown" (1927), and Johnny Dodds's "Bucktown Stomp" (1928) together exemplify Dutrey's characteristically spacious, loping approach to collectively improvised passages, with a strong dose of upward swoops, as at the start of "Chicago Breakdown," where after the piano introduction he enters first. Additionally, on "Bucktown Stomp," before the piano solo he plays a tuneful, slow-paced, moaning blues solo.

FURTHER READING

Allen, Walter C., and Brian Rust. *"King" Oliver*, rev. Laurie Wright (1987).

Charters, Samuel Barclay, IV. *Jazz: New Orleans, 1885–1963* (1963).

This entry is taken from the *American National Biography* and is published here with the permission of the American Council of Learned Societies.

BARRY KERNFELD

Dutton, Charles (30 Jan. 1951–), actor, was born Charles Stanley Dutton in Baltimore, Maryland. When he was a teenager Dutton quit school and joined his peers on the street corners of Baltimore. He earned the nickname "Roc," a shortening of "Rockhead." What started as simple fights between teens throwing rocks at each other turned lethal when Dutton was only seventeen. It was then that he was stabbed eight times. In retaliation he took his attacker's life.

Dutton was sent to prison in 1967, where he gained a passion for reading, due in part to the time he spent in solitary confinement for insubordination. He was released on parole after two years, but returned to jail on a weapons possession charge. His sentence was lengthened when he attacked a prison guard. The turning point during his internment occurred when a fellow inmate stabbed him, severely damaging one of his lungs. Refusing to

Charles Dutton (left) and Theresa Merrit speak with baseball player Hank Aaron about their performance of *Ma Rainey's Black Bottom* at the Cort Theatre in New York City, 26 October 1984. (AP Images.)

retaliate, Dutton avoided lengthening his stay in jail. His interest in acting, which had begun with his involvement with a prison drama club, deepened and he eventually completed a two-year associate's degree from a junior college prior to his release in 1976.

Once out of jail, Dutton completed his college studies at Towson State University in Baltimore. He then took another step in his acting training by enrolling in the Yale School of Drama, where he received a master's degree in acting. During his studies, Dutton learned from the director Lloyd Richards and the playwright AUGUST WILSON, who became his mentor. In 1983 Dutton appeared Off-Broadway in a production of *Richard III*. However, it was *Ma Rainey's Black Bottom*, managed by both Richards and Wilson, that would be Dutton's Broadway acting debut. The production, which had been initially staged at Yale, moved to Broadway in 1984. Dutton's performance as Levee was nominated for a Tony Award for Best Featured Actor in a Play. Dutton and Wilson worked together again in 1990 in the Broadway production of Wilson's *The Piano Lesson*. Again, Dutton was nominated for a Tony Award for Best Actor. Dutton made his way from the stage to film and television in the mid-1980s. His most memorable films include *Secret Window* (2004) with Johnny Depp; *Gothika* (2003) with HALLE BERRY; Robert Altman's *Cookie's Fortune* (1999); SPIKE LEE's *Get on the Bus* (1996); ALLEN and ALBERT HUGHES's *Menace II Society*; and the third installment of the popular science fiction trilogy *Alien3* (1992). In 1989 Dutton married the soap opera star Debbie Morgan. They divorced in 1994. Meanwhile Dutton appeared on such television programs as *Miami Vice*, *Cagney & Lacey*, *Homicide*, and *The L Word*, among others, but it was the FOX Network show *Roc* that put him on the map. *Roc* was unusual in that some of its episodes were performed live. As the title character, Dutton played a man taking the lead in family life and in the community. He won an NAACP Image Award in 1994 for his performance on the show. Dutton also brought August Wilson's work to the screen in the television adaptation of *The Piano Lesson* (1995), for which he was nominated for an Emmy, a Golden Globe, and an Image Award, making him one of the few performers to receive so many award nominations for a single role.

Dutton extended his interest in drama to directing. His debut was the HBO television movie, *First Time Felon* (1997), which starred Omar Epps and Delroy Lindo. He also returned to his hometown of Baltimore to shoot the HBO series *The Corner* in 2000. The dramatic series focused on the residents of a Baltimore neighborhood, paying particular attention to the ways in which the lure of crime and drugs affect a single family. The series won Dutton an Emmy Award for Outstanding Direction for a Miniseries and a Black Reel Award for Best Director. More important, perhaps, it marked Dutton's return to the very same streets that initiated his incredible journey.

TIFFANI MURRAY

Dwight, Ed (9 Nov. 1933–), painter and sculptor, was born on a small farm just outside Kansas City, Kansas, the second of five children of Ed Dwight Sr., a professional baseball player with the Negro League's Kansas City Monarchs, and Georgia Baker, a devout Catholic, who took on the primary care of the children. The family moved into Kansas City when Dwight was ten years old and his mother opened a restaurant. The children worked alongside her. Dwight was a precocious child who displayed his artistic talent from age two, drawing cartoon characters and painting throughout his childhood. He began making signs for his mother's restaurant. When he was fourteen years old, he opened his first lucrative business, a sign shop that served retail establishments and area churches.

Dwight attended Catholic schools and graduated from Bishop Ward High School in 1951, and he joined the air force in 1953. In 1955 he married his first wife, Sue James, and the couple had two children before they divorced in 1959. Dwight had long dreamed of flying jet airplanes and entered the Experimental Test Pilot School on Edwards Air Force Base in California in 1962. After completing the Aerospace Research Pilot Course, he was qualified to be an astronaut. He went on to earn a degree in aeronautical engineering from Arizona State University in 1961. The space program expanded during the John F. Kennedy administration, and the air force was instructed to look for an African American candidate for astronaut training. When Dwight's friend and mentor, the National Urban League's WHITNEY MOORE YOUNG JR., nominated him in 1962, Dwight became the nation's first black astronaut trainee—though NASA never named him to a space mission. In 1966 Dwight resigned from the air force and married his second wife, Barbara Curtis, a career educator. The couple, with two children each from their previous marriages, had a child together and made their home in Denver, Colorado.

Dwight pursued a variety of job opportunities after the military, working as an aviation consultant, a real estate developer, a systems engineer, and a marketing representative for IBM. But he never lost his childhood interest in painting and creative expression. In the mid-1970s, he decided to study art at the Kansas City Art Institute and the University of Denver, where he learned to operate the university's metal casting foundry. He put his painting aside and began to sculpt, selecting bronze as his primary medium. Dwight's first commissioned work was a sculpture of George Brown, Colorado's first black lieutenant governor. The Colorado Centennial Commission gave Dwight his second commission, "Black Frontier Spirit in the American West," a series of thirty bronzes that brought to life the stories of people like Estevan de Dorantes, BILL PICKETT, JIM BECKWOURTH, and other black pioneers, explorers, trappers, farmers, and soldiers, that also brought Dwight widespread acclaim.

In 1977, after he received an MFA from the University of Denver, Dwight set up his studios in Denver and focused his attention on works that spoke to the storied history of African Americans. His large hangar-sized studio also housed an extensive library of publications in African American history that informed his work. In a 2007 telephone interview, Dwight explained, "I am a student of our culture. I didn't understand my blackness until I was in my forties. So I studied everything and I bought all the books I could."

The National Park Service in St. Louis commissioned Dwight in 1979 to create his next major series of bronzes, "Jazz: An American Art Form," tracing the evolution of jazz music from its roots in Africa to twentieth-century jazz superstars such as MILES DAVIS, CHARLIE PARKER, LOUIS ARMSTRONG, ELLA FITZGERALD, and Benny Goodman. Dwight's list of more than ninety-five sculptures and public art projects includes his first binational monument in Detroit, Michigan, and Windsor, Canada, dedicated in 2001 to the International Underground Railroad Movement. In addition he created the African American History Monument on the Capitol grounds in Columbia, South Carolina, statues of

Dr. Martin Luther King Jr. in Denver's City Park (2002) and George Washington Carver in Phoenix, Arizona (2004), the Alex Haley–Kunta Kinte Memorial in Annapolis, Maryland (1999), the Battle Creek, Michigan, Underground Railroad installed in 1993 as the nation's largest monument to the Underground Railroad, and four twenty-five-foot-high bronze sculptures of a guitarist, saxophonist, trumpeter, and female jazz singer, done with nonfigurative abstract faces, uncharacteristic for Dwight, for the Chicago Jazz & Blues Cultural Music District and Sculpture Park, which included central sculptures of music mentor Captain Walter Dyett and the first black mayor of Chicago, Harold Washington (2005). Dwight's commission for the Black Patriots Memorial on the Mall in Washington, D.C., is a $4 million national monument to the more than five thousand freed men and slaves who fought the British in the American Revolution. Its ninety-foot-high design was the largest memorial to African Americans at the time of its creation. Dwight created a statue, *Our Mother of Africa and Divine Son* (1997), and a narrative relief on the wall of the chapel nave in the Our Mother of Africa Chapel at the National Shrine of the Immaculate Conception in Washington, D.C. He had numerous portrait sculptures, including one of baseball legend Hank Aaron in Atlanta (1982), Frederick Douglass in Anacostia, Maryland (1981), and more than six thousand other sculptures. His works were collected by commercial and private collectors and on exhibit in national and international galleries, with some on permanent display at the Smithsonian Institute.

A major controversy occurred in early 2007 when Dwight was contracted by the King Memorial Foundation as lead designer for a memorial statue of Martin Luther King Jr. on the National Mall in D.C. Since Dwight did not work in granite, it was originally understood that he would create the design and hire another sculptor to work with a huge block of granite that would become the centerpiece of the planned $100 million memorial: a thirty-foot high statue of King called *Stone of Hope*. After three years on the project, Dwight was replaced as lead sculptor, without consultation, with a Chinese artist who had worked in granite but had no experience in African American sculpture. His replacement led to a national outcry from other black artists and many African Americans supporting Dwight's retention. Although Dwight walked away from the project, the Foundation made appeals to him to remain associated with the memorial project.

Dwight was recognized as an innovator of the "negative space technique," in which the "holes" or space around and between parts of a sculpture are negative or not there and the area behind the sculpture can be seen through these holes, affecting the way we look at the art work and as one of most prolific and insightful sculptors in America. However, his massive monument proposals have sometimes been met with criticism and controversy. They were seen as too extravagant, too detailed, too overpowering, and too controversial. Such criticism was directed at his African American History Monument in Columbia, South Carolina, which was situated across from a Confederate memorial. In a telephone interview Dwight responded to his critics, "I am different. I don't like putting up works of art that have no context. I tell stories. I don't do statues. I don't want to put a statue on a pedestal with no context, with no engraved information."

In 2007 Dwight was working on an autobiography to be titled *Soaring on the Wings of a Dream*. The memoir would cover his creative journey and the politics of art that he encountered along the way. Asked in the telephone interview what he hoped would be his legacy, Dwight stated, "I really want them to remember me as a really good artist who tried to show what black people did in this country. I want to put black images all around the country, to reconstruct this culture and civilization. I want them to say, 'this guy has changed the landscape of America to allow the inclusion of black folk, and their contribution to American life and to the world.'"

FURTHER READING

Dunbier, Lonnie Pierson, ed. "Ed Dwight Jr.," *The Artists Bluebook: 34,000 North American Artists to March 2005* (2005).

Opitz, Glenn B., ed. "Ed Dwight," *Dictionary of American Sculptors: 18th Century to Present* (1984).

Reynolds, Donald M. "The Meaning of the Sculpture Program in Our Mother of Africa Chapel: Sculptor Ed Dwight," *National Black Catholic Congress Online*. Available at www.nbccongress.org/black-catholics/chapel_facts_01.asp.

J. DEBORAH JOHNSON STERRETT

Dykes, De Witt Sanford, Sr. (16 Aug. 1903–4 Aug. 1991) minister and registered architect, was born in Gadsden, Alabama, the second male and the fifth of six children born to Mary Anna Wade, a homemaker, and the Reverend Henry Sanford Roland

Dykes, a lay minister in the Methodist Church (later the United Methodist Church), a brick mason, and construction contractor.

In the early 1900s the family moved to Newport, Tennessee, which was a racially segregated small town with a semirural atmosphere. Henry Dykes served as a circuit riding minister, conducting services on alternate Sundays at Methodist churches in three communities, including one at Newport, but earned enough to support his family as the head of a construction firm on weekdays until his death in 1945. Henry Dykes taught brick masonry and construction skills to not only his sons but also others. By age fourteen, Dykes had become a master mason; by age seventeen he was a construction supervisor. In his teen years, Dykes aspired to become a registered architect based upon his experience in the construction of buildings. Yet his father advised him that racial prejudice would make it extremely difficult to earn a living and become a successful architect. Dykes decided to get a formal education and become a Christian minister, but he retained his vision of an architectural career.

There was little publicly funded education for African Americans in Newport, but Dykes's mother had ambitions for him to get an advanced education beyond what was available in Newport. Beginning in 1919 Dykes would become an on-campus resident student at four schools financed by the Methodist Church. From grammar school through high school, Dykes studied in the precollege division of Morristown Normal and Industrial College in Morristown, Tennessee, using his skills as a brick mason to earn money for tuition and living expenses. He received a high school diploma in 1926. He then attended two schools in Atlanta, Georgia. First, he enrolled in Clark University (later Clark Atlanta University), earning a B.A. with honors in 1930. Junior- and senior-level students with consistent honor roll status at Clark were allowed simultaneous enrollment at the nearby Gammon Theological Seminary. Thus, Dykes was able to complete the normal seven-year course of study in a mere five years, receiving the bachelor of divinity degree with honors from Gammon in 1931. He won a tuition scholarship for graduate study at Boston University, enrolling there and earning the master of sacred theology degree in 1932.

At the urging of his father, Dykes returned to become a minister in the East Tennessee Annual Conference consisting of African American churches in the western parts of both West Virginia and Virginia and the eastern part of Tennessee. The conference was part of a racially segregated structure called the Central Jurisdiction, which was part of the Methodist Church. His first appointment was in 1932 as pastor of Mount Pleasant Methodist Church in Marion, Virginia.

Dykes's first marriage, to Violet Thomasine Anderson, took place in Bristol, Virginia, on 29 November 1932. Dykes first met Violet when she attended the High School Division of Morristown College. Graduating from Morristown ahead of Dykes, Violet earned a B.A. from Morgan College (later Morgan State University) in 1927. Violet was a talented pianist and served as the choral director for the junior choir at Mount Pleasant Church. Violet and De Witt became the parents of two children: Reida B. Dykes Gardiner, who became a public school librarian in Pontiac, Michigan, and De Witt Sanford Dykes Jr., who became a history professor at Oakland University in Rochester, Michigan. Violet Anderson Dykes died on 19 January 1943 in Chattanooga at age 37 as a result of an infection from failed surgery.

Dykes's successful pastorate in Virginia and his advanced seminary education earned him a position with a larger congregation at Wiley Memorial Methodist Church in Chattanooga, where he began as pastor in 1936. In 1946 Dykes was appointed minister of East Vine Avenue Methodist Church (later Lennon-Seney Methodist) in Knoxville, Tennessee, serving until 1954. In the late 1940s, after moving to Knoxville, a short distance from the family home, Dykes resumed part-time work with the Dykes family construction company in Newport. On 14 December 1950 Dykes married Viola G. Logan in Asheville, North Carolina. Viola Dykes taught special education and later became a principal in the Knoxville public school system.

From 1954 to 1955 Dykes was a regional administrator serving as district superintendent of the twenty-five churches in the Chattanooga District of the East Tennessee Annual Conference. Beginning in 1956 Dykes was recruited to do administrative work for a national office of the Methodist Church. He became a staff member of the General Board of Missions and was assigned to the Section on National Missions, Division of Finance and Field Service. Covering a thirteen-state area in the South, Dykes was the traveling field liaison between the church's national office and local congregations that wanted to build new buildings or additions with financial support from the national church.

Soon Dykes began to design and make architectural drawings for the new church buildings, receiving supervision and final approval for the plans from registered architects in the Philadelphia office of the Methodist Church. He designed seventy-two churches, additions, parsonages, and even a fire hall as part of his Board of Missions work. Independent of the Board of Missions, he designed four non-Methodist churches in Knoxville whose former buildings had been displaced by urban renewal policies. He also designed and performed much of the masonry on his own home in Knoxville.

Retiring from the Board of Missions in 1968, Dykes began reading and studying intensely, aiming to pass the rigorous examinations to become a registered architect. Using his past experience as an architectural designer, he passed an oral examination, which satisfied part of the requirements. Dykes underwent a final three-day examination in 1969 and at age sixty-six became a registered architect, earning State of Tennessee Certificate No. 7209 as of 5 March 1970. He was the first African American to become a registered architect in East Tennessee. Subsequently, he designed three additional churches, some family residences, several publicly funded buildings, a mortuary, and buildings for the 1982 World's Fair in Knoxville. He died at age 87 on 4 August 1991 in Knoxville, Tennessee, of strokes in the brain.

Dykes lived through the early twentieth century—a period of severe race-based restrictions, openly expressed racial hostility, and limited educational and job opportunities for blacks—past the high point of the civil rights movement in the 1960s. He also saw the gradual easing of race-based job restrictions and the shift toward greater opportunities for African Americans in the late twentieth century. The early development of his brick masonry skills and a strong work ethic supplemented his formidable intellect. His lifelong connection to the Methodist Church and his determination to develop and maintain his work skills enabled him to combine his passion for the Christian ministry with his love for construction. He was able to make lasting contributions to not only the congregations he pastored but also the buildings and structures that thousands of Christian worshippers admired and used throughout the southern United States.

FURTHER READING

Smith, Jessie C., ed. "De Witt S. Dykes, Sr.," in *Notable Black American Men* (1999).

Wilson, Dreck, ed. "De Witt Sanford Dykes, Sr.," in *African American Architects* (2004).

DE WITT S. DYKES JR.

Dykes, Eva Beatrice (13 Aug. 1893–29 Oct. 1986), scholar and educator, was born in Washington, D.C., the daughter of James Stanley Dykes and Martha Ann Howard. Eva graduated from M Street High (later PAUL LAURENCE DUNBAR High School) in 1910. As valedictorian of her class, she won a $10 scholarship from Alpha Kappa Alpha Sorority to attend Howard University, where in 1914 she graduated summa cum laude with a B.A. in English. After a year of teaching Latin and English at the now defunct Walden University in Nashville, Tennessee, and for another year elsewhere, she was urged by James Howard, a physician and uncle on her mother's side, to enter Radcliffe College in 1916. Subsequently, she earned a second B.A. in English, magna cum laude, in 1917. Elected Phi Beta Kappa, she received an M.A. in English in 1918 and a Ph.D. in English philology in 1921. Her dissertation was

Eva Beatrice Dykes, scholar. Her pioneering work *The Negro in English Romantic Thought; or, A Study of Sympathy for the Oppressed (1942)* examines references to black people in eighteenth- and early-nineteenth-century English literature to determine whether romantic writers were sympathetic to the plight of blacks. (University of Massachusetts, Amherst.)

titled "Pope and His Influence in America from 1715 to 1850."

From 1921 through 1929—the apex of the New Negro movement—Dykes taught at Dunbar High School and later at Howard University (1929–1944), which she joined initially as associate professor of English. In 1944, following a conversion to the Seventh Day Adventist church, she joined the faculty at Oakwood College, a school of the faith in Huntsville, Alabama. By 1946 she had become head of the Department of English. Although she officially retired in 1968, she remained active with the college until 1975 and continued to live on the grounds until her death.

In 1931 Dykes, along with Otellia Cromwell and Orenzo Dow Turner, brought out *Readings from Negro Authors for High Schools and Colleges*. Over a decade later, she published her landmark work, *The Negro in English Romantic Thought* (1942). Between November 1942 and July 1944 Dykes authored more than a half dozen essays—in journals as varied as *Crusader*, *Journal of Negro History*, and *Negro History Bulletin*—about the poetry of the Civil War, the destiny of blacks in higher education, the fate of black publishers, the triumphs of the black professional, and the persistent tone of American romanticism.

Dykes's pioneering work, *The Negro in English Romantic Thought; or, A Study of Sympathy for the Oppressed*, examines references to the figure of the black in English literature of the eighteenth and early nineteenth centuries. Her goals in the work were to determine whether there was "any sympathetic attitude toward the Negro and second, to find out reasons for this attitude." She asserts in the work that slavery was immoral as well as financially ineffective. In part she subconsciously ventriloquizes an African American voice of racial protest through old British texts. She also notes the painful separation of families under the slave system. Most significantly, Dykes challenges the acceptance by so many romantic writers—including women—of the view that black people are less than human. Dykes traces the origins of slavery to the Elizabethan age, whose own monarch occasionally doubted the moral authority of the doctrine. Pleased to rediscover that the romancer Aphra Behn had praised a "noble chieftain" (*Oroonoko, or the Royal Slave* [1688]), Dykes probably winced to see Lady Mary Wortley Montague write to the countess of Bristol on 10 April 1718, "I know you'll expect I should say something particular of the slaves; and you will imagine me half a Turk when I don't speak of it with the same horror other Christians have done before me. But I cannot forbear applauding the humanity of the Turks to these creatures; they are never ill-used and their slavery is in my opinion no worse than servitude all over the world." So, objectively, Dykes lets the offensiveness of the quotation speak for itself. To readers of a later generation, her analysis of classic romanticism seems somewhat flawed, especially her assumption that the canon of romantic writers was fixed. Indeed, much of what she considered in her middle years to be mainstream romanticism has since been recategorized as neoclassicism. What was for her a rebellious undercurrent of romanticism later resurfaced as the actual mainstream of the romantic movement. Hence, her work reminds the reader that literary history is constantly changing.

Dykes is a missing link in the understanding of black critical traditions. As one of the first black American women (with SADIE T. MOSSELL ALEXANDER in economics at the University of Pennsylvania and GEORGIANA R. SIMPSON in German at the University of Chicago) to earn a Ph.D. in the United States, Dykes was in 1921 only a year older than JEAN TOOMER, a writer of modern fiction, and only nine years the senior of the poet LANGSTON HUGHES. By the age of ninety-three, she had completed a scholarly life of a duration unrivaled by that of nearly any famous African American thinker except W. E. B. DUBOIS. Dykes proposed that the abolition of racial slavery in England and the United States had developed more out of a deeply rooted concept of humanity than out of an insistence on leveling social classes. In retracing the roles of race and gender to the dawn of the twentieth century, she recognized that women had been as central to the mission of abolitionism as they had been to all "great historical movements." In this way Dykes foreshadowed a liberation in American thought from the traditional confines of the very canon about which she wrote. Of special importance is that during the Harlem Renaissance, when men such as ALAIN LOCKE were defining the New Negro, Dykes wrote clearly as a black woman about the interplay between race and literature. The pioneering importance of Dykes merits reconsideration. She revealed that the role of the figure of the black within British consciousness must be understood before the role of blacks in the United States could be reassessed. She complemented scholars who, like the legendary STERLING BROWN in the late 1930s and George E. Kent in the late 1960s to 1970s, documented the literary strategies of others for representing blacks within the American psyche. It was Dykes who traced such images to English origins in the age of exploration. By the time that her own criticism had advanced to abolitionist America, she had come to view women as self-creators of their own history. Dykes could possibly never have perceived that the full development of her reasoning—from the historical recognition of the racial stereotype to the personal disapproval of it—would lead to the disruption of Euro-American values. Although she would publish practically nothing during her last forty years, she paved the way, in her own words, for new inquiries. "The growing consciousness of the inhumanity of slavery which finds its reflection in the literature of the eighteenth century, the rising tide of popular opposition and indignation which reached its crest during the romantic period and was responsible for the abolition of slavery in the British colonies, and the concern for the slave in America—all of these facts bespeak a sincere desire to keep the torch of liberty burning and pass it on undimmed to those who follow." While slaves in the early British writings may have been objects, Dykes's criticism stirred new perceptions of them. Clearly Eva Beatrice Dykes represented the early development of an African American critical voice.

FURTHER READING

Archival material is in the Oakwood College Eva B. Dykes Library, Huntsville, Alabama, which was named in her honor in 1978, as well as in the Moorland-Spingarn Research Center at Howard University.

Bathurst, Dana Brewer. *Eva Dykes: A Star to Show the Way* (1989).

Roses, Lorraine E., and Ruth E. Henderson. *Harlem Renaissance & Beyond: Literary Biographies of 100 Black Women Writers, 1900–1945* (1990).

Williams, DeWitt S. *She Fulfilled the Impossible Dream: The Story of Eva B. Dykes* (1985).

This entry is taken from the *American National Biography* and is published here with the permission of the American Council of Learned Societies.

R. BAXTER MILLER

Dymally, Mervyn (12 May 1926–), politician, was born Mervyn Malcolm Dymally in Cedros, Trinidad, to Hamid Dymally, an Indian businessman, and Andreid Richardson, a black Trinidadian. In Trinidad he attended Cedros Government School, St. Benedict School, and Naparima College, from which he graduated in 1944. Upon graduation Dymally took a job as a reporter for the *Vanguard Weekly*, the newspaper of the local oil workers union.

In 1946 Dymally immigrated to the United States to attend Lincoln University in Jefferson City, Missouri, where he planned to study journalism. Unable to adjust to the environment in Missouri, however, he dropped out after one semester and traveled around the United States in search of work and school. After two years of constant travel and countless jobs Dymally settled in Los Angeles, California, and began attending Los Angeles State College, where he received his B.A. in Education in 1954.

After graduation Dymally began teaching in public schools during the day and working odd jobs at night. He soon became involved in local Democratic politics, joining the Pasadena Democratic Club in the late 1950s. He became treasurer of the California Young Democrats soon after and worked as a field coordinator for John F. Kennedy's 1960 presidential campaign. In 1962 he ran for the state assembly seat that represented South Central Los Angeles and part of Watts and that was then being vacated by Assemblyman AUGUSTUS HAWKINS. During the campaign Dymally, still a political unknown and heavy underdog, distinguished himself when he addressed a crowd of African Americans at the Second Baptist Church in Los Angeles to protest the shooting of seven members of the Nation of Islam by the LAPD. After being introduced by MALCOLM X, Dymally related to the crowd his fear of the majority-white and often viciously racist LAPD and his intention to do something about police brutality if elected. The meeting propelled Dymally to the head of the field, and he won the election in November. The historian Taylor Branch has noted that Dymally himself "trace[s] his miracle victory … to the emotional chemistry" of that address (Branch, *Pillar of Fire: America in the King Years, 1963–65* [1998], 12–13).

From that point forward, politics became Dymally's overriding preoccupation. He nonetheless found time to continue his studies, earning an M.A. in Government from California State University, Sacramento, in 1969 and a Ph.D. in Human Behavior from United States International University, San Diego, in 1978. He also found the time to start a family, marrying Alice Gueno, a school teacher, in December 1968. The couple would have two children.

In 1964, as Dymally was running for a second term in the California House of Representatives, the Supreme Court ruled in the case of *Reynolds v. Sims* that all state and local legislative districts must be apportioned on the basis of population. At that time the vast majority of urban state legislative districts were woefully malapportioned, giving undue influence to rural districts. Urban Los Angeles County, for instance, contained two-fifths of California's population but had only one state senate district. When a district court in 1965 directed the state to reapportion the state legislature based on population, the county's number of state senate seats increased to thirteen. When the new district map was finished, the county's only majority black state senate district covered most of the same territory that Dymally's state assembly district did. In 1966 Dymally ran for the new seat and won, making him California's first black state senator.

Dymally entered the state senate as part of a group of young, reform-minded legislators dubbed the "Young Turks." He quickly emerged as an advocate for women and young people. As chairman of both the Select Committee on Children and Youth and the Joint Committee for Legal Equality of Women, Dymally sponsored and helped to secure passage of the Child Abuse Prevention and Treatment Act, the Early Childhood Education Act, the Child Growth and Development Act, the Dymally-Seroti Child Care Construction Act, the Equal Rights Amendment, and the Community Property for Women Law, among others. Dymally also kept his campaign promise to oppose police brutality. He organized STOP (Stop Terrorizing Our People), an organization to oppose police brutality. Dymally's criticisms of the LAPD brought him into constant conflict with Police Chief William Parker.

In 1974 Dymally scored another first when he became the first African American in the United States to be directly elected lieutenant governor. (George Brown, an African American state senator from Denver, was elected lieutenant governor of Colorado in that same year. Unlike Dymally, who was elected in his own right—in California candidates for lieutenant governor run alone—Brown had run on a ticket with the white gubernatorial candidate Dick Lamm.) As lieutenant governor, a position that automatically made him chairman of the California Commission for Economic Development, Dymally focused on reviving the sluggish sectors of California's economy. One of Dymally's most enduring accomplishments during his time as lieutenant governor, albeit one of the most controversial, was his sponsorship of *The Dilemma of Black Politics*, a 1977 report on the "harassment of black elected officials." Since the mid-1960s Dymally had experienced sustained FBI and LAPD surveillance, three frivolous IRS criminal audits, and more than a dozen investigations by the *Los Angeles Times* and the *Sacramento Bee*. These and similar cases of state and news media harassment of black elected officials were detailed in the report, along with the cases of dozens of other black elected officials.

One year after the report came out, an incident of harassment orchestrated by the California attorney general Evelle Younger cost Dymally the lieutenant governorship. In 1978 Dymally faced the Los Angeles record executive Mike Curb in his bid for reelection. Early in the race Dymally appeared strong, racking up large numbers of endorsements. But only weeks before the general election his campaign was derailed by an illegal attack from the office of Attorney General Younger, who was then running for governor on the Republican ticket. A member of Younger's office leaked false information to KCBS-TV alleging that Dymally and a close associate were about to be indicted by a federal grand jury. Using the leaked information the anchor Bill Stout announced on the 10 October *CBS Evening News*, "There is a state investigator's report saying the U.S. Department of Justice has the evidence for indictments of both Dymally and Hugh Pike, his onetime finance chairman" ("Curb's Charge Stems from Prober's Memo," *Los Angeles Times*, 2 Nov. 1978). Rather than denounce the leak as improper and false, Attorney General Younger corroborated Stout's allegations in his public statements. Dymally's opponent subsequently made Stout's allegations a centerpiece of his campaign. The incumbent lieutenant governor tried desperately to defend himself, daring Curb and Younger to produce evidence of his alleged misdeeds, and filing criminal slander complaints against Curb. The allegations doomed Dymally's reelection campaign. On 7 November, he narrowly lost to Curb. In 1980 a grand jury cleared Dymally of any wrongdoing and the investigation begun by the Younger campaign was ended ("Query Led to False Report on Dymally," *L.A. Times*, 15 Oct. 1980).

After a two-year hiatus Dymally reentered public life in 1980 when he ran for U.S. Congress from the Thirty-first Congressional District, situated in the suburbs south of Los Angeles. Although the district was predominantly white, Dymally won the Democratic primary by targeting black voters, who had provided the ten-term Democratic incumbent Charles Wilson with a strong base of support in several previous elections. Dymally also highlighted his close association with Cesar Chavez of the United Farm Workers Union to secure the district's substantial Hispanic vote. He won the general election in the heavily Democratic district by 64 percent over the Republican challenger Don Grimshaw.

While in Congress, Dymally served as chairman of the House Foreign Affairs Committee, Subcommittee on International Relations, and as chairman of the House Committee on the District of Columbia, Subcommittee on Judiciary and Education. He also served as chairman of the Congressional Black Caucus (CBC) from 1987 to 1988. In the late 1980s Dymally was the driving force behind the CBC's efforts to address the harassment of black elected officials.

After serving six terms in Congress, Dymally retired in 1992. He returned to Los Angeles to serve as honorary consul to the Republic of Benin, run several nonprofit community-service organizations, and teach. In 2002 the still energetic seventy-six-year-old reentered California politics by running for and winning his old state assembly seat from south Los Angeles. Because his colleagues considered him a senior member of the legislature, Dymally in 2003 was elected chairman of the Assembly Democratic Study Group and in 2005 was elected chairman of the Legislative Black Caucus.

FURTHER READING

Mervyn Dymally's papers are housed in the California State University Library, Los Angeles, California.

Clay, William L. *Just Permanent Interests: Black Americans in Congress, 1870–1991* (1992).

Dymally, Mervyn, ed. *The Black Politician: His Struggle for Power* (1971).

Elliot, Jeffrey M., and Mervyn M. Dymally, eds. *Voices of Zaire: Rhetoric or Reality* (1990).

Schultz, Bud, and Ruth Schultz. *The Price of Dissent: Testimonies to Political Repression in America* (2001).

GEORGE DEREK MUSGROVE

Dyson, Michael Eric (23 Oct. 1958–), writer, educator, and preacher, was born in Detroit, Michigan, to Addie Mae Leonard, a teacher's aide. In 1990 Dyson was adopted by the auto worker Everett Dyson when Leonard married him. As a child, Dyson read avidly and enjoyed the Harvard Classics. His intellectual vigor earned him a scholarship to the prestigious Cranbrook Kingswood School in 1972. However, Dyson behaved poorly and was expelled in 1974. He then attended Northwestern High School and graduated in 1976.

Michael Eric Dyson discusses his book titled *Is Bill Cosby Right?* during a public reading on 27 July 2005 in New York City's Bryant Park. (AP Images.)

In 1977, Dyson married his girlfriend, Terrie Dyson, who gave birth to Michael Eric Dyson II a year later. Due to the pressures of being a young couple, Dyson and his wife divorced in 1979. To help focus his life, Dyson became a licensed Baptist preacher in 1979 and ordained minister in 1981 with his pastor Frederick G. Sampson II's assistance. He also received his B.A. at Carson-Newman College in 1982 and his M.A. and Ph.D. at Princeton University in 1991 and 1993. While at Princeton, he married the Reverend Marcia Louise Dyson on 24 June 1992 and they later had two children Mwata and Maisha. After his graduation, Dyson started his career as an educator. From 1993 to 1995 he taught ethics and cultural criticism at Brown University. He then became a professor of communication studies and director of the Institute of African American Research at the University of North Carolina, Chapel Hill. In 1997 he was the visiting distinguished professor of African American studies at Columbia University. Two years later, Dyson accepted the esteemed title of the Ida B. Wells Barnett University Professor at Depaul University. He left this position in 2002 to become the Avalon Foundation Professor at the University of Pennsylvania and stayed until 2007, when he left to teach at Georgetown University.

While teaching, Dyson wrote several books. His first book, *Reflecting Black: African-American Cultural Criticism* (1993), examines politics, sexism, and racism and several famous African Americans such as SPIKE LEE and MICHAEL JORDAN. His next book, *Making Malcolm: The Myth and Meaning of Malcolm X* (1995), discusses the legacy of MALCOLM X and race relations. In addition to being named Notable Book of 1994 by the *New York Times* and the *Philadelphia Inquirer* and selected as one of the outstanding books by *Black Issues Book Review*, the book also garnered acclaim from ANGELA DAVIS, the Reverend JESSE JACKSON, and politician CAROL MOSELEY-BRAUN. Dyson then approached the cultural significance of gangsta rap in *Between God and Gangsta Rap: Bearing Witness to Black Culture* (1996) and examined artists such as NWA and Ice Cube. By linking rap to race and culture, Dyson compiled essays for *Race Rules: Navigating the Color Line* (1996). He returned to exploring notable African Americans in the biographies *I May Not Get There with You: The True Martin Luther King, Jr.* (2000), *Holler If You Hear Me: Searching for Tupac Shakur* (2001), and *Mercy, Mercy Me: The Art, Loves, and Demons of Marvin Gaye* (2004).

Dyson's next collection of essays, *Open Mike: Reflections on Philosophy, Race, Sex, Culture, and Religion* (2002), gives a profound look at some of the major issues in African American society. This same candor is found in *Why I Love Black Women* (2003) and *The Michael Eric Dyson Reader* (2004). Dyson uses some of his personal experiences of black pride in *Pride: The Seven Deadly Sins* (2006). This text foregrounds *Is Bill Cosby Right? Or Has the Black Middle Class Lost Its Mind?* (2006) by studying Cosby's statement that poor blacks should have more pride in their education and employment. The book won the NAACP Image Award for Outstanding Literary Work in 2006 and encouraged discussion of black America.

Dyson reexamined the plight of poor blacks in *Come Hell or High Water: Hurricane Katrina and the Color of Disaster* (2006). After this book, he entered a prolific stage and wrote *Debating Race* (2007), *Know What I Mean? Reflections on Hip Hop* (2007), *April 4, 1968: Martin Luther King's Death and How It Changed America* (2008), *Can You Hear Me Now? The Inspiration, Wisdom, and Insight of Michael Eric Dyson* (2009). These texts represent Dyson's ability to explore history, music, identity, and religion in intriguing ways.

Because of his successful career, Dyson is a popular guest lecturer and commencement speaker. His most controversial speech was at the University of North Carolina, Chapel Hill, on 15 December 1996, in which he quoted rap lyrics, used profanity, and criticized MICHAEL JORDAN. He has also appeared on talk shows and started his radio show *The Michael Eric Dyson Show* on 20 January 2006, which ran until February 2007. The program was restarted on 6 April 2009 and addresses many critical African American issues, including his support for President BARACK OBAMA and Obama's nuanced views on race and politics.

FURTHER READING

Jones, Meta DuEwa. "An Interview with Michael Eric Dyson." *Callaloo* 29 (2006).

Kincheloe, Joe L., and Shirley R Steinberg. *White Reign: Deploying Whiteness in America* (2000).

Nishikawa, Kinohi. "Michael Eric Dyson." In *The Greenwood Encyclopedia of African American Literature* (2005).

DORSIA SMITH SILVA

Eagleson, William Lewis (9 Aug. 1835–22 June 1899), editor and political activist, was born a slave in St. Louis, Missouri. The names of his parents and details about his early life are unknown. He married Elizabeth McKinney in 1865 in St. Louis; they had nine children. As a young man he learned both printing and barbering, trades that he practiced intermittently throughout his life. In the 1870s he settled in Fort Scott, Kansas, and started a newspaper, the *Colored Citizen*. In 1878 he moved the paper to Topeka, Kansas, where there was a burgeoning African American community, and began his public career.

Teaming up with a prominent African Methodist Episcopal (AME) minister, Thomas W. Henderson, Eagleson used the *Colored Citizen* to become a visible figure in Kansas political life. The newspaper itself was oriented chiefly toward increasing the influence of blacks in Republican Party politics. Even before moving to Topeka, Eagleson had initiated an unsuccessful effort to get Henderson nominated for lieutenant governor, and he continued to press for the placement of black Republicans in office in his new home. Following a big Republican victory in the 1878 election, Eagleson intensified his campaign for such positions, including efforts to place Henderson as chaplain and himself as assistant doorkeeper of the Kansas House of Representatives, posts which they both eventually held.

The *Colored Citizen* served as Eagleson's main focus until it ceased publication in 1879. Eagleson then became editor of the *Kansas Herald*—later renamed the *Herald of Kansas* for legal reasons—in which he espoused the Republican line and declared the need for racial unity. In 1880 he helped organize the Colored Men's State Convention as a forum for both racial and partisan concerns, and he was appointed to the State Executive Committee of the convention. He also served on a committee sent to Washington, D.C., to discuss the large-scale immigration of African Americans to Kansas.

For the next several years Eagleson withdrew from public affairs. He held various jobs during this time, including jailer of the city prison, clerk in the post office, and janitor at the library and in the offices of the Santa Fe Railroad. He also took an active part in Topeka social life as a member and officer in a number of fraternal organizations.

Around the middle of the decade, he seems to have shifted from the Republican to the Democratic Party, although there is little evidence to indicate the reason. Then, in 1889, he reemerged as a visible figure in what was his most significant project, the building of the all-black town of Langston City, Oklahoma.

Langston City (later Langston) was one of several efforts to create black townships on newly opened lands in the Oklahoma Territory. Eagleson collaborated with other Kansans in the venture, including Edward McCabe, a former state auditor. As business manager of the Oklahoma Immigration Association based in Topeka, Eagleson was the chief publicist in an effort to recruit settlers to the new lands. Both men harbored dreams of using extensive black settlement to build a base for political power in the territory. Eagleson himself moved to Langston City in 1891, where he edited the *Langston City Herald*, using it to promote settlement. Confronting the racial tensions that sprang from the desire of whites to possess land in Oklahoma, he was threatened with mob violence for his organizational efforts before a September 1891 run on newly opened territory. He himself led an armed group of black settlers into a white camp, laying claim to the land and declaring their intention to hold it by any means necessary. Despite these conflicts, the efforts of Eagleson and his colleagues met with some success. African Americans did acquire land in the region, and Langston City grew fairly rapidly.

Eagleson remained in Langston City until around the end of 1892, editing the *Herald*, holding several local offices, including justice of the peace and city council member, and promoting continued immigration. He also dabbled in partisan politics, placing the *Herald* in the Republican camp, apparently much to the amazement of his Democratic friends. As the town grew, however, the leadership changed, and Eagleson returned to Topeka.

Eagleson remained interested in Oklahoma after his return. Drawing on his experiences there, moreover, he also pursued, ultimately without success, the possibility of starting another all-black town, to be called Sumner City, just outside Topeka. Most of his attention he focused on Kansas politics and, again, on the Democratic Party. He was active in black party organizations and beginning in 1895 was president of the Colored Men's Independent League, an organization formed mainly in opposition to Republican loyalism. In 1896 he supported the successful candidacy of the Populist-Democratic fusion governor John W. Leedy, resulting in his own appointment as messenger to the governor in 1896–1897. Though his health was failing he again supported Leedy during his unsuccessful bid for reelection in 1898.

Eagleson pursued other interests during this time. He tried unsuccessfully to acquire another newspaper in Topeka. In his final year he began a project to create a home for the aged to serve Topeka's black community. He died in Topeka. "A constant thinker for the betterment of his race," as he was described in an obituary, Eagleson was an important contributor to the development of an African American community in the western United States.

FURTHER READING

Cox, Thomas C. *Blacks in Topeka Kansas*, 1865–1915 (1982).

Hamilton, Kenneth Marvin. *Black Towns and Profit* (1991).

Littlefield, Daniel F., Jr., and Lonnie E. Underhill. "Black Dreams and 'Free' Homes: The Oklahoma Territory, 1891–1894," *Phylon* 34 (1973).

Obituary: *Topeka Plaindealer*, 30 June 1899.

This entry is taken from the *American National Biography* and is published here with the permission of the American Council of Learned Societies.

DICKSON D. BRUCE

Earley, Charity Adams (5 Dec. 1917–13 Jan. 2002), commander of the only African American unit of the Women's Army Corps stationed in Europe during World War II, was born Charity Edna Adams, the eldest of four children. She was raised in Columbia, South Carolina, where her father was a minister in the African Episcopal Methodist Church. Her mother was a former teacher.

Adams graduated from Booker T. Washington High School in Columbia as valedictorian of her senior class and then from Wilberforce University in Ohio, one of the top three black colleges in the nation in the 1930s. She majored in Math and Physics and graduated in 1938. After returning to Columbia, where she taught junior high school mathematics for four years, Adams enrolled in the M.A.program for vocational psychology at Ohio State University, pursuing her degree during the summers.

As a member of the military's Advisory Council to the Women's Interests Section (ACWIS), MARY MCLEOD BETHUNE, president of the National Council of Negro Women, had fought for the inclusion of black women in the newly formed Women's Army Auxiliary Corps (WAAC) in 1942. The dean of women at Wilberforce identified Adams as a potential candidate with both the education and the character to become a fine female officer. Intrigued by the possibilities of military service, Adams applied in June 1942 and in July 1942 she became the first of four thousand African American women to join what became the Women's Army Corp (WAC). She was one of thirty-nine black women enrolled in the first officer candidate class at the First WAAC Training Center at Fort Des Moines in Iowa, where she was stationed for two and a half years, achieving the rank of major.

The armed forces were segregated in World War II, and Adams suffered indignities from those racist policies, but she handled them with great fortitude and tenacity. One of these incidents happened at Fort Des Moines when a white colonel upbraided her for visiting the all-white officers' club with a major who had invited her there. She was forced to stand at attention for forty-five minutes while the colonel scolded her for "race mixing" and told her that black people needed to respect separation of the races even if they were officers. Indignant, Adams never entered the officers' club again. Adams also encountered American segregation policies in England, where she commanded the only African American WAC unit to serve overseas, a postal unit stationed in Birmingham and then in France. The American Red Cross, working with the U.S. Army, pressured Adams to move her unit from integrated accommodations to a designated London hotel and sent her equipment to be used at a segregated recreational area. Adams refused the move and the equipment, insisting that her unit continue using its integrated facility, and she persuaded her troops not to change their lodgings. Adams also battled occupational segregation within the army. African Americans were routinely assigned menial service jobs and denied access to office work or skilled jobs. Army labor requisitions for WAC personnel often were for administrative jobs, but these were regularly reserved for white women. In an effort to break down these barriers, Adams was sent to the Pentagon in 1943 along with the African American Major Harriet West, assistant to the WAC leader Oveta Culp Hobby, to increase quotas of black women in motor transport and other jobs. They received nominal support from the Pentagon, but racial discrimination in job assignments remained a problem throughout the war for both male and female African American soldiers.

As a black woman in uniform during the 1940s, Adams was subjected to the tensions confronting all black soldiers on the home front as well. On her first visit home to Columbia in December 1942, she accompanied her father to a meeting of the Columbia chapter of the NAACP, which he headed, to discuss the mistreatment of black soldiers by white military police at nearby Fort Jackson. Upon returning home, they discovered that the Ku Klux Klan had parked a line of cars in front of their house. Adams's father gave the family his shotgun to protect themselves while he went to the home of the NAACP state head, only to find that home similarly surrounded and the family out of town. In her autobiography Adams recounts the tense night that followed, as she kept watch over the hooded Klan members until dawn, when they left.

Adams also describes an incident in 1944 at an Atlanta train station, when she was asked by two white military police to produce identification. Several whites in the segregated waiting room had cast doubt on her status as an army officer. Even though she was with her parents, this was a dangerous encounter for Adams. The previous year a black army nurse in Alabama had been beaten by police and jailed for boarding a bus ahead of white passengers, and three African American WACs stationed at Fort Knox, Kentucky, had been similarly beaten for failing to move from the white area of a Greyhound bus station. Despite the risk, Adams took charge by interrogating the MPs herself and demanding the name of their commanding officer so that she could file a report on them if they did not respect her rank. The MPs saluted and disappeared.

After the war Adams returned to Ohio State and completed her M.A.in 1946, after which she served as a registration officer for the Veteran's Administration in Cleveland, as manager of a music school at the Miller Academy of Fine Arts, and as dean of student personnel services at Tennessee Agricultural and Industrial State College and then at Georgia State College. On 24 August 1949, she married a physician, Stanley Earley Jr. Accompanying him to the University of Zurich, where he was a medical student, she learned German and took courses at the university and at the Jungian Institute of Analytical Psychology. Earley returned to the United States with her husband after he completed his training, and they had two children, a son and a daughter. The family settled in Dayton, Ohio, where she was actively involved in community affairs, serving on boards for social services, education, civic affairs, and corporations.

In 1989 Earley published a memoir of her wartime service, *One Woman's Army*. The courage and leadership Earley displayed in her pioneering role in the U.S. Army earned her an award for distinguished service in 1946 from the National Council of Negro Women and, decades later, a place on the Smithsonian Institution's listing of the most historically important African American women. In 1996 the Smithsonian's National Postal Museum also honored Adams's wartime service. She died in Dayton at the age of eighty-three, having established a permanent place in history for her trailblazing accomplishments in World War II.

FURTHER READING

Earley, Charity Adams. *One Woman's Army: A Black Officer Remembers the WAC* (1989).

Jones, Jacqueline. *Labor of Love, Labor of Sorrow: Black Women, Work, and the Family from Slavery to the Present* (1985).

Meyer, Leisa D. *Creating G.I. Jane: Sexuality and Power in the Women's Army Corps during World War II* (1996).

Putney, Martha. *When the Nation Was in Need: Blacks in the Women's Army Corps during World War II* (1992).

Obituary: *New York Times*, 22 Jan. 2002.

MAUREEN HONEY

Early, Gerald (21 Apr. 1952–), essayist, professor, and cultural critic, was born Gerald Lyn Early in Philadelphia, Pennsylvania, the youngest child of Henry Early and Florence Fernandez Early. Gerald's father died when he was nine months old. His mother, who never finished high school but whose practical wisdom shaped Gerald's character, worked as a school crossing guard and a teacher's aide.

Growing up without a father in a tough Philadelphia neighborhood, Early found a role model in Lloyd Richard King, his fifth- and sixth-grade teacher in an all-black Philadelphia public school. King was a dedicated and inspirational instructor who believed that Early would do great things. During a period when there were few African American male elementary school teachers, King became a father figure and strong influence.

Early's initial inclinations toward literature were fostered by his two older sisters—Rosalind and Lenora, both English majors at Temple University—who brought home books and encouraged him to read. JAMES BALDWIN's *Notes of a Native Son* (1955) was especially important. In the essay "Autobiographical Notes" Baldwin wrote, "I want to be an honest man and a good writer." This supplied Early with what he has publicly described as his creed, his source of inspiration, and a model for his life and work.

After finishing high school in Philadelphia, Early enrolled as an undergraduate at Antioch College in Yellow Springs, Ohio. Told by his teachers that his writing was poor and that he needed remedial help, he became discouraged and left school after only a few weeks of classes. For a year he lived with his sister in San Francisco, worked menial jobs, and tirelessly practiced writing. When he returned to school the next year at the University of Pennsylvania, his composition instructor told him that he was the best writer that he had ever had. "I'll be a lot better than this," Early replied. (Washington University *Record*, Feburary 15, 1996).

Early received a bachelor's degree from the University of Pennsylvania in 1974, a master's degree from Cornell in 1980, and a doctorate from Cornell in 1982, all in English Literature. His Ph.D. dissertation, "A Servant of Servants Shall He Be: Paternalism and Millennialism in American Slavery Literature 1850–1859," used a multidisciplinary approach to reconstruct American thinking about slavery in the decade before the Civil War.

Immediately after completing his Ph.D., Early joined the faculty of Washington University in Saint Louis as an instructor in the Black Studies program. In 1990 he became a full professor of English and of African and African American Studies. He served as director and codirector of the university's American Culture Studies program from 1991 to 1996, director of the African and African American Studies program from 1992 to 1999, and director of the Washington University Center for the Humanities beginning in 2001. Gerald and his wife, Ida, met in 1974 and were married in 1977. They had two daughters, Rosalind Lenora Early and Linnet Kristin Early.

Among his works of cultural and literary criticism, Gerald Early is perhaps best known for *The Culture of Bruising: Essays on Prizefighting, Literature, and Modern American Culture* (1994). This book, a sequel to his *Tuxedo Junction: Essays on American Culture* (1989), firmly established Early as a new force in the field of cultural studies and won a National Book Critics Circle Award for criticism. Characteristic of much of Early's work, *The Culture of Bruising* showed a wide-ranging analysis and eclectic approach, blending personal experience with insights from both highbrow and popular culture. Making original and valuable connections among topics ranging from MALCOLM X to Shirley Temple, from jazz, baseball, boxing, and children's literature to *Moby-Dick*, from the Korean War to the Miss America Pageant, Early displays striking intellectual versatility.

The prose essay, which Early believed is centrally important to the history of African American writing, is his favored literary form. His writing is distinguished by an honest, intellectually searching tone and an accessible style that speaks to both specialists and nonspecialists. He rejected pedantic jargon and wrote simply but passionately. "The business of being a critic," Early believed, "is not to sound smart but to sound necessary, not be obscure but to be so vastly absorbed and awed by the humanness of enlightened discernment that one can only be plain in one's utterance in recognition that nothing is more demanding and nothing can better serve" (*Culture of Bruising*, xvii). Essayists whom Early admired and learned from include C. L. R. JAMES, Paul Gilroy, Van Wyck Brooks, and F. O. Matthiessen.

Within African American letters Gerald Early is a highly respected voice, admired for his vast knowledge, his philosophical integrity, and his openness to dissenting opinions. He was the editor of several volumes of essays, including *This Is Where I Came In: Black America in the 1960s* (2003), *Lure and Loathing: Essays on Race, Identity, and the Ambivalence of Assimilation* (1993), and *Speech and Power* (1993), all of which arose out of Early's expressed desire to explore "inclusive and diverse" viewpoints within African American studies. Unafraid of controversy, Early gave equal forums to Afrocentric, conservative, and radical circles. Not bound to any critical school or any single political outlook, he learned from all and was receptive to the challenges that every perspective offers.

In addition to literary and cultural criticism Early published a well-received volume of poetry and a personal memoir entitled *Daughters: On Family and Fatherhood* (1994), which describes the complex daily challenges of American and African American fatherhood. This book was a semifinalist for a 1995 National Book Critics Circle Award. Early also served as a consultant and commentator for several PBS films, including the Ken Burns documentaries *Baseball* (1994), *Jazz* (2001), and *Unforgivable Blackness: The Rise and Fall of Jack Johnson* (2004), projects that displayed Early's multiple proficiencies and increased his national visibility.

Gerald Early is often described as one of his generation's best interpreters of American culture. By discovering for an ever-larger audience the meaning and power of African American experience, along with its centrality to multiple and broader conceptualizations of American life, he enabled both black and white Americans to discover themselves.

FURTHER READING

Early, Gerald. *Daughters: On Family and Fatherhood* (1994).

Early, Gerald. *The Culture of Bruising: Essays on Prizefighting, Literature, and Modern American Culture* (1994).

Early, Gerald. *Tuxedo Junction: Essays on American Culture* (1989).

PATRICK CHURA

Early, Jordan Winston (17 June 1814–1903), minister, was born a slave in Franklin County, Virginia. His mother died when he was three years old, and he was raised by an elderly woman known as Aunt Milly who cared for the plantation's slave children while their mothers worked. She was a devout Christian, and Early later attributed the fact that he became a "useful and intelligent" man to her influence. Early attended many camp meetings in his boyhood, and he later recalled that he was religiously inclined from an early age. He loved nature and often hunted at night with a favorite uncle.

In 1826 Early moved with the Early family to St. Louis. In his new home, he frequently visited churches and listened closely to the white ministers' sermons. A sermon by a Methodist minister named Barger soon led to his conversion; "My conviction was deep and powerful," he related. In 1828 he was baptized and testified to his belief that he had a religious vocation. He was appointed superintendent of the Sunday school, leading prayer meetings and hymn singing. At age eighteen he was employed on a boat that shipped goods between New Orleans and St. Louis. During Early's spare time, a Presbyterian minister in St. Louis gave him reading lessons, and the mate on the boat on which he was employed taught him how to write. In 1833 he was licensed as an exhorter in the Methodist Episcopal Church. It is probable that he had purchased his freedom by the mid-1830s.

In the mid-1830s WILLIAM PAUL QUINN, a pioneer minister in the African Methodist Episcopal (AME) Church, came to St. Louis, the first minister to evangelize there on behalf of his predominantly black denomination. Early was among the first to switch his affiliation to the new church, and he soon rose in its ministerial ranks, receiving a preaching license in 1836 and ordination as a local deacon in 1838. After at first holding meetings in private homes, Early and others procured a small log cabin for their religious services. The rapid growth of the St. Louis AME congregation forced the members to obtain successively larger buildings for worship, and by 1840 they had bought land and built a substantial brick church. Slave patrollers kept a close watch on black church services in the aftermath of NAT TURNER's 1831 rebellion, but the St. Louis mayor stopped the patrol from interfering with Early's congregation, in large part because Early had earned "much favor and respect" among all of the inhabitants of the city.

While traveling on business over the next thirteen years, Early organized AME churches in Burlington and Dubuque, Iowa; Galena, Illinois; New Orleans; and at least nine locations in Missouri, including the state capital, Jefferson City, all without financial support from his church. Especially in the South, his missionary work was fraught with great danger from the police, patrollers, or slaveholders. Early thus proceeded cautiously, usually organizing churches in private homes. The New Orleans congregation, the first AME congregation in the Deep South since 1822, met "in an obscure room as far back from the streets as possible," with a watch posted to signal an alarm if police approached. Where possible Early's congregations built church edifices; in Galena, for example, Early remembered helping to quarry the stone for the church with his own hands.

In 1843 Early married Louisa Carter in St. Louis; they had eight children, four of whom survived to adulthood. Louisa Early died in 1862.

In 1846 Early was called before a grand jury, presumably in Missouri, and interrogated about the transportation of fugitive slaves on the Underground Railroad. He denied having any knowledge of such an escape network, but on several occasions he did help to purchase a slave's freedom.

About 1853 Early decided to enter the paid ministerial ranks of the AME church. He was assigned as a minister to various small churches in Illinois over the next dozen years. During the Civil War Early was once erroneously arrested as a fugitive slave by a mob of armed men, but he was released upon showing his papers to a magistrate. Early's revivals reached a fever pitch in those years, with hundreds converted and brought into the church. From 1865 to 1881 Early pastored AME churches in Louisville, Kentucky, Nashville, and Memphis. During this time cholera epidemics killed many of his congregation members. He instituted many reforms and improvements in the churches he served, such as installing gas lighting in churches, upgrading the church choir, obtaining an organ and organist, and building up Sunday schools. In 1868 he married Sarah Jane Woodson (SARAH JANE EARLY), an 1856 graduate of Oberlin College and a former instructor of English at Wilberforce University. After their marriage Sarah worked as a schoolteacher and later as a principal. One of Early's colleagues observed that much of his ministerial success was due to the efforts of his talented and hardworking second wife.

In 1881 Early was appointed presiding elder for the AME churches in eastern and middle Tennessee. That same year he was seriously injured after being thrown from a horse, but he recovered. From 1881 to 1886 he pastored churches in Nashville and Columbia, Tennessee, remarking that his ministerial tasks were especially arduous because of the lackadaisical work of younger ministers preceding him. He compared these ministers unfavorably to his own pioneering generation. After two more years as presiding elder, Early retired from the ministry in 1888. Sarah Early, however, continued to provide prominent leadership in church-related activities. With her husband's support, she was superintendent of the Colored Division of the Women's Christian Temperance Union from 1888 to 1892 and a vigorous advocate for the Prohibition Party in Tennessee. Jordan Early's place of death is unknown.

Jordan W. Early was one of the pioneering black ministers who, along with religious leaders like HENRY MCNEAL TURNER, JAMES W. HOOD, and DANIEL ALEXANDER PAYNE, fostered the tremendous growth of the AME church and built it into one of the largest independent black denominations in the United States.

FURTHER READING

Early, Sarah. *Life and Labors of Rev. Jordan W. Early* (1894).

NicKenzie, Ellen Lawson, and Marlene Merrill. *The Three Sarahs: Documents of Antebellum Black College Women* (1984).

This entry is taken from the *American National Biography* and is published here with the permission of the American Council of Learned Societies.

STEPHEN W. ANGELL

Early, Sarah Woodson (15 Nov. 1825–1907) educator and temperance leader, was born in Chillicothe, Ohio, the youngest child of Thomas Woodson, a prosperous farmer and former slave, and Jemimma Riddle, about whom little is known. Descendants of Thomas Woodson, relying on an oral history passed down from the nineteenth century, have long believed that he was the oldest son of Thomas Jefferson and SALLY HEMINGS, a slave of mixed race who served Jefferson's family in the years before he became the third U.S. president. Although DNA analysis has confirmed that Hemings's two youngest sons were fathered by either Jefferson, his brother Randolph Jefferson, or one of Randolph's sons, DNA studies have not established a genetic relationship between Thomas Woodson and any of the Jefferson men.

Around 1830, when Early was five years old, the Woodsons and several other African American families left the Chillicothe area to move to Berlin Crossroads in Milton Township in Jackson County, Ohio, to form an all-black agricultural community. There they established a Methodist church, a Sunday school, and a public school. Early grew up in a devout religious community whose residents believed strongly in mutual aid and self-help.

Three of Early's older brothers became pioneering ministers of the African Methodist Episcopal (AME) Church. Her oldest brother, Lewis Woodson, was the best known among them. He viewed education as the most important element in the struggle to improve the lives of African Americans. Very little is known of Early's childhood. But like her brother Lewis, she entered adulthood embracing her religion and determined to acquire higher education.

In 1850, when Early was twenty-four years old, she attended the Albany Manual Labor Academy, a secondary school in Albany, Ohio. In 1852 she entered Oberlin College in Oberlin, Ohio, the only college at the time that accepted both white and black students. She received the college's literary degree in 1856, the only type of degree available to Oberlin women at that time. Moreover, she was one of the first African American women to be awarded a college degree in the United States.

Early paid her Oberlin tuition with the wages she earned teaching summers in all-black schools in Ohio. Although her father possessed considerable wealth (census data revealed that Thomas Woodson owned $15,000 in real estate during her college years), he apparently did not contribute financially to her college education.

From 1856 until 1866 Early was a teacher and principal in all-black schools in Ohio communities whose African American populations worshipped in AME churches. In 1866 Wilberforce University in Xenia, Ohio, which at the time was affiliated with the AME Church, hired her as Preceptress of English and Latin and Lady Principal and Matron. Early thus became the first African American woman to sit on a college faculty in United States history.

After teaching at Wilberforce for two years, Woodson accepted a position as principal at a girls' school in Hillsboro, North Carolina, sponsored by the federal Freedmen's Bureau. Black and white Northern teachers had been leaving their communities to teach freed people in the South since 1862. Teaching freed people during the post–Civil War Reconstruction era was dangerous, challenging work, as the teachers faced hostility and violence from Southern whites. The living conditions of these teachers were exceptionally poor. Food was scarce and of poor quality, and the teachers' lodgings were crowded and substandard; as a result, many teachers left after only a few weeks.

While living in Hillsboro, Early met Jordan Winston Early, an AME minister. The couple married in 1868, when Early was forty-three years old. They moved to Memphis, Tennessee, when Reverend Early accepted a post at a church located there. By 1869 Early was teaching in a small all-black school in Memphis. In 1872 the Earlys moved to a new church in Nashville, Tennessee. During the next sixteen years, Early taught and was principal at black schools located in Nashville (1872 to 1875; 1880 to 1884), Edgefield (1875 to 1879), and Columbia (1884 to 1885), all Tennessee cities in which Reverend Early was minister of an AME church. After their stay in Columbia, the Earlys returned to Nashville, which became their permanent home.

Unlike the vast majority of nineteenth-century ministers' wives, Early continued to work as an educator and school administrator after her marriage. Despite her busy career, she performed all the traditional religious duties of ministers' wives. She taught and assisted in directing the Sunday school of each congregation, participated in women's fund-raising, led women's prayer meetings, visited the sick and elderly, and aided the poor. In her writings she frequently stressed the rarely acknowledged importance of the active, integral role of African American women in the black churches from the beginning of their history in North America. Early also underscored the critical role of the AME Church's ministers. In 1894 her biography of Reverend Early was published. In addition to detailing Reverend Early's life, it also publicized the role of the African American clergy in the AME Church.

When her husband retired, Early left teaching but remained active in her efforts to improve African American society. She dedicated herself to a cause she was passionate about: temperance reform. From 1888 to 1892 she was superintendent of the Colored Division of the Women's Christian Temperance Union (WCTU). She believed that adherence to temperance principles—the strict avoidance of alcohol and adherence to religion—would foster the elevation of African Americans in American society. As a temperance activist, she traveled thousands of miles to dozens of churches, colleges, and prisons in five southern states. She also lectured at national church conferences. Temperance, she believed, was a vital prerequisite to education and racial uplift. Her fellow women temperance activists also advocated hospital and prison reform as well as "social purity," the term used to signify their stance against prostitution.

In the 1980s historian Ellen N. Lawson rediscovered Early while combing through histories published between eighty and one hundred and twenty years ago. Early's achievements had been recognized in histories of the late nineteenth century and the early years of the twentieth century, but had vanished from biographical literature thereafter.

FURTHER READING

Lawson, Ellen NicKenzie, and Marlene Merrill. *The Three Sarahs: Documents of Antebellum Black College Women*. Studies in Women and Religion (1984).

Thompson, Mia Nwaka, and Adrienne Lash Jones. "Sarah Jane Woodson Early," in *Notable Black American Women, Book II* (1996).

JUDITH E. HARPER

Easley, Annie J. (23 Apr. 1933–25 June 2011), computer scientist and mathematician, was born in Birmingham, Alabama, the youngest child of Samuel Bird Easley and Mary Melvina Hoover. Disdaining the segregated schools in the South, her mother put Annie in parochial school in the fifth grade. Easley's mother encouraged her to succeed by telling her that "you can be anything you want to be, but you have to work at it" (Johnson, 4). Easley went on to become valedictorian of her high school class. She then attended the School of Pharmacy at Xavier University in New Orleans, Louisiana, for two years and worked as a substitute teacher in Jefferson County, Alabama, before marrying and moving to Cleveland, Ohio. In Birmingham, as soon as Easley turned twenty-one, she attempted to vote. State law, however, required her to pass a literacy test and pay a poll tax. She would later describe the test giver looking at her application and saying only, "You went to Xavier University. Two dollars." After that she began helping others prepare for the voting test in Birmingham and in Cleveland (Johnson, 20).

In 1954, Easley and her husband moved to Cleveland, where she learned about a pair of twin sisters who worked at the National Advisory Committee for Aeronautics (NACA) Lewis Flight Propulsion Laboratory as computers (mathematicians). Easley applied for a position and was quickly hired in the Computer Services Division to do mathematical computation for the scientists and engineers. Easley was the only African American female working in her department at the time. NACA had one African American man working in engineering and two African American women in another group. By the late 1970s Easley had moved to the Energy Directorate, and in the 1980s she moved to Launch Vehicles. By 1958 NASA had emerged out of NACA, and Easley was assigned to the Flight Software Section at the Lewis Research Center in Cleveland, Ohio. There she worked on many software programs, including those that helped in the launching of the nation's early rocket systems and another that measured solar wind. A number of these programs were still in use at the beginning of the early twenty-first century. Easley also studied the life use of storage batteries that powered electric utility vehicles and the efficiency of energy conversion systems.

While at NASA, Easley received a B.S. in Mathematics from Cleveland State University in 1977. She also became a member of the Speakers Bureau, a tutor, and a college recruiter for the Lewis Research Center Lab. In 1989 she retired after thirty-four years with NASA and became involved with the Cleveland ski council, an umbrella organization of two dozen or more ski clubs in the greater Cleveland area. She served as president of the council for three years. One of her greatest satisfactions in life, however, was tutoring young people between the ages of eighteen and twenty-one who had dropped out of school but who had decided to complete their educations. When she spoke to eighth graders, she would tell them, "Your parents can go back to school. There's no limit. You can always keep learning" (Johnson, 42). She died in 2011.

FURTHER READING

Johnson, Sandra. Annie J. Easley NASA Oral History. Cleveland, Ohio, 21 Aug. 2001. Available at www.jsc.nasa.gov/history/oral_histories/NASA_HQ/Herstory/EasleyAJ/easleyaj.pdf.

Proffitt, Pamela. *Notable Women Scientists* (1999).

Spangenburg, Ray, and Kit Moser. *African Americans in Science, Math & Invention* (2003).

JAMANE YEAGER

Eason, Willie Claude (26 June 1921–16 June 2005), pioneer "sacred steel" guitarist and gospel singer, was born in the Lickskillet community of Schley County, Georgia, the tenth of the fifteen children of Henry Eason and Addie Eason, sharecroppers. The Easons moved to Philadelphia, Pennsylvania, when Willie was less than a year old. His mother withdrew him from high school in January 1939 to enable him to travel with Bishop J. R. Lockley and the Gospel Feast Party, a troupe of Pentecostal musicians and ministers that conducted tent revivals and worship services from New York to Florida.

Eason began to play the steel guitar around 1937. He was influenced by two steel guitarists: his brother Troman, who was sixteen years his senior, and Walter Johnson. Troman Eason took lessons from a Hawaiian musician, remembered by Eason and other family members only as "Jack," whom he heard play the steel guitar over live radio broadcasts in Philadelphia. Although it has not been established for certain, Troman's teacher was most likely Jack Kahauolopua (sometimes spelled Kahanalopua), who was an instructor at the Hawaiian Conservatory of Music at 709 Chestnut Street. Troman became proficient on the instrument and formed a trio that performed professionally. He played in the conventional "Hawaiian" manner popular during the period: sweet, legato melodies frequently rendered in two-part harmony. Walter Johnson played the acoustic steel guitar for gospel music programs at churches in the Philadelphia area and on live radio broadcasts with the Reverend F. D. Edwards. Willie Eason recalled Johnson's technique as consisting of voicelike melodies played on the treble strings and supported by rhythmic strums and bass lines.

Drawing from the techniques of his older brother and Walter Johnson, Willie Eason created an idiosyncratic manner of playing and soon began to perform for worship services at the House of God, Keith Dominion Holiness-Pentecostal church that his extended family attended in Philadelphia. He played slurred passages, often executed on a single string, to imitate closely the ornamented singing that he heard in church. A powerful, engaging singer, Eason often used the steel guitar to echo phrases he sung or to complete phrases from which he intentionally omitted words. His steel guitar technique was very well suited to the spirited services of the House of God, and combined with his moving voice it made for a musical force that aided congregants in becoming infused with the Holy Spirit.

Eason began to establish his national reputation when he traveled with Bishop Lockley's Gospel Feast Party in 1939. Lockley's troupe, with its full complement of accomplished musicians playing professional-grade instruments, created a sensation among the largely poor—and in the South, often rural—blacks who attended the revivals and worship services at which they performed, and Eason and his "talking guitar" were often at the center of attention. But Lockley did not compensate young Eason monetarily. After just one winter season with the Gospel Feast Party, Eason struck out on his own to perform street-corner music ministries for tips and to play for revivals and church worship services, for which he received offerings from the congregations. As he traveled throughout the East, drawing large crowds on street corners and moving people at revivals and worship services to shout and dance in spiritual ecstasy, Eason inspired many to take up the steel guitar.

Among those he influenced very early in his career were Henry Nelson and Lorenzo Harrison, both of Ocala, Florida, who probably saw Eason for the first time in 1939. Both Nelson and Harrison became important steel guitarists who for decades played at large church gatherings throughout the United States—Nelson in the House of God, Keith Dominion and Harrison in the related Church of the Living God, Jewell Dominion. Eason married Henry Nelson's older sister Alyce in 1941. They had five children and were divorced in 1953. In 1956 he married Jeannette Davis of Lake Mary, Florida; the couple had eight children, adopted three, and raised twenty foster children.

Eason's renown increased as he made seven 78-rpm records for popular black gospel labels from 1946 to 1951. Over the years he inspired dozens, if not hundreds, within the House of God, Keith Dominion and the Church of the Living God, Jewell Dominion to play the electric steel guitar for worship services, and he achieved status as a living legend among many congregants and musicians. The steel guitar eventually became the dominant musical instrument in both organizations, a characteristic unique among African American churches. The steel guitar tradition of the House of God, Keith Dominion and the Church of the Living God, Jewell Dominion remained virtually unknown to the general public for more than fifty years until several tradition bearers, including Eason, began to make recordings and perform for public concerts in the 1990s. Enthusiastically received by fans of American music, critics, and scholars, the music became known as "sacred steel," a phrase taken from the title of the first album of the music produced by the Florida Folklife Program and licensed to Arhoolie Records.

In 1987 Eason retired to Saint Petersburg, Florida, where he lived until his death in 2005. In 1995 the Florida Department of State honored him with the Florida Folk Heritage Award for his lifetime contributions to African American sacred steel guitar music.

FURTHER READING

Heilbut, Anthony. *The Gospel Sound: Good News and Bad Times* (1971).

Ruymar, Lorene. *The Hawaiian Steel Guitar and Its Great Hawaiian Musicians* (1996).

Stone, Robert L. "Make a Joyful Noise: A Brief History of the House of God Church and the Sacred Steel Musical Tradition," *Living Blues* 176 (2005).

Obituary: *Saint Petersburg (Florida) Times*, 18 June 2005.

DISCOGRAPHY

Hays, Cedric J., and Robert Laughton. *Gospel Records, 1943–1969: A Black Music Discography* (2 vols., 1992–1993).

ROBERT L. STONE

Easton, Hosea (1798–6 July 1837), minister, author, and abolitionist, was born in North Bridgewater (later Brockton), Massachusetts, to James, a successful businessman, and Sarah Dunbar Easton. Easton's *Treatise on the Intellectual Character, and Civil and Political Condition of the Colored People of the U. States* (1837) was the nation's first systematic study of racism and stands with David Walker's *Appeal* (1829) as among the most important writings by African Americans during the early nineteenth century. The seven children of the Easton family blended African, American Indian, and white ancestry. Thus, the concept of "race," as whites began to redefine it in the early nineteenth century, possessed little meaning to the Eastons. Indeed, one of Hosea Easton's brothers married into North Bridgewater's most distinguished white family.

James Easton had been a much-respected businessman in the greater Boston area (and a Revolutionary War veteran) and viewed his ironworks as a training ground for future black leaders. By the 1820s he had established a manual labor school—allied to his business—to ensure that African American boys would receive the training they needed to gain a career and succeed. But before the close of the 1820s the future that Easton envisioned slipped from his grasp as racial prejudice grew. After a decade of success and the investment of "many thousands of dollars," an explosive growth of racism compelled the school's closure—and even drove the family from their once-integrated church. As Hosea Easton bitterly recalled the incidents and his father's subsequent death, "It fell, and with it fell the hearts of several of its undertakers in despair, and their bodies into their graves" (Price and Stewart, *To Heal the Scourge*, 110–111).

During the late 1820s Hosea Easton began preparing for the ministry and by 1828 he had moved his wife Louisa, whom he married on 14 January 1827, and two children to Boston where he assumed the pulpit of the West Centre Street Church. Before long, he opened the church to meetings of the "Female Benevolent and Intelligence Society" (*Liberator*, 12 Mar. 1831). During the same period Easton and his brother Joshua helped organize the Boston General Colored Association, an early antislavery society that counted David Walker as its most famous member. Hosea Easton also became a founder of the Black National Convention movement and allied himself with the white abolitionists William Lloyd Garrison, Arthur Tappan, and Simeon S. Jocelyn to establish a manual labor college in New Haven, Connecticut, an idea that promised to revive James Easton's plans. Easton agreed to raise an astonishing ten thousand dollars from the African American community to match an equal amount pledged by Garrison and his colleagues, but New Haven whites ruined the proposal with riots and mayhem.

In 1834, African Methodist Episcopal (AME) Zion bishop Christopher Rush ordained Easton as a deacon and elder and assigned him to the pulpit of a Hartford, Connecticut, AME Zion church that shared facilities with the Congregationalist Talcott Street Church. Again Easton sought to advance the principles of uplift and began raising funds to establish a black high school. But that same year race riots in Hartford destroyed Easton's new efforts. Perhaps even more disappointing, fire swept through the new Colored Methodist Episcopal Zion Church building that Easton had erected for his congregation. Racially charged incidents continued and between 1834 and 1836 at least three Hartford mobs had attacked Easton, members of his congregation, or their church. A black person could hardly walk the city streets without stones raining down on them or cries of "nigger! nigger!" (Price and Stewart, *To Heal the Scourge*, 22).

In response Easton directed his anger and disappointment into an astonishing pamphlet. His 1837 *Treatise* situated slavery and racism within a context of evangelical morality and biological imperatives. Directing his commentary to whites, Easton reminded them of the biblical pronouncement that "God hath made of one blood all nations of men" (Price and Stewart, *To Heal the Scourge*, 67). In an arresting analogy, he explained that the "same species of flowers is variegated with innumerable colors; and yet the species is the same.... So it is with the human species" (Dain, 179). Easton believed he had found the key to the plight of African Americans and sought to convince whites that slavery and racial prejudice were diseases that created in its victims all the attributes that whites so despised. In a novel theory of biological environmentalism, Easton asserted that the evils of slavery and prejudice created, even in the mother's womb, a people so degraded "that they sustain the same relation to the ourang outang, that the whites do to them.... The slave system is an unnatural cause, and has produced its unnatural effects, as displayed in the deformity of two and a half millions of beings" (Price and Stewart, *To Heal the Scourge*, 85–86, 87). Yet the insidious effects of slavery and prejudice, he assured his white readers, would be quickly reversed once they halted their scourge of evil. To Easton, the problem rested wholly with the conduct of whites, not anything innate to blacks. Indeed, he asserted, blacks were Americans in every sense of the word and would, like his own father, flourish when whites removed the conditions that crippled them.

Easton hardly understated the destructive effect of racism and his analysis depended upon convincing whites of its ubiquitous nature: "It seems to possess a kind of omnipresence. It follows its victims in every avenue of life" (Price and Stewart, *To Heal the Scourge*, 105). The pamphlet's anger and disappointment, however, were tempered to some degree by Easton's refusal to abandon black self-uplift—despite the frequent setbacks—as well as his confidence that he had discovered the pivot upon which the future of African Americans would turn. His ministerial colleague JEHIEL C. BEMAN saw the Hartford clergyman just before his untimely death only two months after appearance of the *Treatise*. He described Easton as calm and said that "his soul was filled with unutterable glory." We cannot know how calm or resigned Easton felt at the end, but Beman's assessment that "His vision was clear" could not have been more accurate (*Liberator*, 14 July 1837).

FURTHER READING

Dain, Bruce. *A Hideous Monster of the Mind: American Race Theory in the Early Republic* (2002).

Nell, William C. *Colored Patriots of the American Revolution* (1855).

Price, George R., and James Brewer Stewart. *To Heal the Scourge of Prejudice: The Life and Writings of Hosea Easton* (1999).

Price, George R., and James Brewer Stewart. "The Roberts Case, the Easton Family, and the Dynamics of the Abolitionist Movement in Massachusetts, 1776–1870," *Massachusetts Historical Review* 4 (2002).

Swift, David E. *Black Prophets of Justice: Activist Clergy Before the Civil War* (1989).

DONALD YACOVONE

Easton, William Edgar (19 Mar. 1861–10 Jan. 1936), playwright, journalist, and political activist, was born in New York City to Charles F. Easton, a barber, and Marie Antoinette Leggett-Easton. Ancestors on his father's side participated in the Revolutionary War: his great-grandfather was a captain of Indian scouts, and James Easton, his great-uncle, drew the fortification plans for Breeds Hill (Bunker Hill) (*Crisis* 37 [1930]: 276). Ancestors of his mother, a Louisiana native, had fought in Haiti's war of independence. By 1870 the family had moved to Saint Louis, Missouri, where Easton's mother died, after which his father relocated the family to New Bedford, Massachusetts. At thirteen Easton was "entrusted ... to the care of a Catholic priest" by his godmother, a Baroness de Hoffman (Beasley, 258). Easton initially attended the Seminary de Trois-Rivières, Canada, but he left after "students objected to his presence on the grounds of race" (Bruce, 28); he then attended the La Salle Academy of Providence, Rhode Island, and the College of the Congregation de Saint Croix.

In 1883 Easton moved to Texas to teach, marrying in 1888, and between 1890 and 1897 he and his wife, Mary, a Texas native, became the parents of three daughters and one son. He became active in the state Republican Party, which was dominated by African Americans. During the 1880s he served as an elected commissioner of Fort Bend County, secretary of the Republican executive committee, and chairman of the county executive committee in Austin. In the 1890s Easton was appointed clerk of the customhouse in Galveston under the most prominent Republican in Texas, NORRIS WRIGHT CUNEY. According to the 1890 census Easton was the editor of a newspaper, probably the *Texas Blade*. As a newspaperman he has been described as a "fearless advocate and defender" of his race (Beasley, 258). A Roman Catholic, Easton took his advocacy of black Americans to the Black Catholic Congress in Philadelphia in 1892, where as a delegate he argued that black Catholics should establish schools and academies for their children, an undertaking that he believed should take precedence over building churches. In particular he advocated the establishment of a Catholic college in Texas.

Easton's first excursion into playwriting, *Dessalines, a Dramatic Tale: A Single Chapter from Haiti's History* (1893), was also designed to champion African Americans. The published play contained an essay by Norris Wright Cuney and a speech on Haiti by FREDERICK DOUGLASS. In his preface Easton addressed the depiction of blacks on the contemporary stage, bitterly objecting to their caricature as figures of "buffoonery" and bristling at the commonplace portrayal of Othello as a black man who had "sadly metamorphosed" into a "victim of a very mild case of sunburn." Although fair-skinned enough to pass for white, Easton created black characters who were nothing if not proud of their color, and who bore no resemblance to the clownish and tepid black figures of the nineteenth-century American theater. Anticipating a negative reception by white audiences to his departure from racial stereotypes, Easton wrote, "Ye Gods, protect the black proteans from the weight of popular white disapproval." The titular character, loosely based on the Haitian black revolutionary Jean-Jaques Dessalines, becomes in Easton's hands a heroic figure advocating freedom and liberty for the people of colonial Haiti. Sometimes imitating Shakespearean characters and dramatic techniques, Easton enlarges historical events and persons to celebrate his race's heritage. The play was performed in New York and Pennsylvania, and years later in Boston at the Allied Arts Centre, where on 15 May 1930 it was directed by MAUD CUNEY-HARE, the daughter of Norris Wright Cuney.

Easton also proposed forming a traveling concert group for the purpose of portraying black Americans positively on the stage. In 1894 no less a figure than PAUL LAURENCE DUNBAR was enlisted as a member of that troupe; Dunbar even wrote special poetry for the tour and prepared the role of Dessalines as part of the troupe's repertoire. The project never came to fruition, however, due to a lack of funds.

In July 1901 Easton moved his family to Los Angeles as a result of the inhospitable atmosphere in Texas for both Republicans and blacks in the late 1890s. There he held a variety of civic administrative positions and was finally appointed Custodian of the State Offices in Los Angeles, later securing that post under a new civil service system by registering the highest exam score. He was instrumental in opening to black workers the custodial positions at government offices and was also influential in the enactment of an ordinance that prohibited businesses from refusing to serve customers on the basis of race. Sometime after 1910 Easton joined the Progressive Party, which was made up of Republicans disaffected by the growing conservative character of their party. He wrote his second play, *Christophe: A Tragedy in Praise of Imperial Haiti*, which is similar to *Dessalines* in language, style, and subject matter; it was performed in New York and Los Angeles and published in 1911. In addition to his publishing career and his political activities, Easton was appointed to the National Bureau of Speakers for the War Department, a speaker's bureau supporting the American participation in World War I. In that capacity Easton repeatedly made a stout defense of the war—in which his son was a participant—arguing that full democratic participation for blacks at home would follow their support for the war abroad. Easton died in Los Angeles at the age of seventy-four.

FURTHER READING

Bass, Charlotta A. *Forty Years: Memoirs from the Pages of a Newspaper* (1960).

Beasley, Delilah Leontium. *The Negro Trail-Blazers of California* (1919).

Bruce, Dickson D. *Black American Writing from the Nadir: The Evolution of a Literary Tradition, 1877–1915* (1989).

Davis, Cyprian. *The History of Black Catholics in the United States* (1990).

Flamming, Douglas. *Bound for Freedom: Black Los Angeles in Jim Crow America* (2005).

Obituary: *Los Angeles Times*, 15 Jan. 1936.

R. J. FEHRENBACH

Eaton, Hubert A. (2 Dec. 1916–4 Sept. 1991), physician and civil rights activist, was born Hubert Arthur Eaton in Fayetteville, North Carolina, the son of Estelle Atley Jones and Chester Arthur Easton, a Winston-Salem, North Carolina, physician. Eaton attended segregated elementary and secondary schools in Winston-Salem, where he and his two sisters, Hazelle and Lucille, grew up. Following his graduation from Winston-Salem Atkins High School he attended Johnson C. Smith University from 1933 to 1936 on a tennis scholarship after winning the 1933 national junior championship of the all-black American Tennis Association. Eaton then earned a masters degree in zoology from the University of Michigan, after which he entered the university's medical school in 1938, one of fewer than fifty African Americans to attend predominantly white American medical schools.

Following his graduation from medical school in 1942 Eaton returned to North Carolina and began a one-year internship at the Kate B. Reynolds Hospital in Winston-Salem. While all the interns at Reynolds were black, the hospital's only resident was white. Eaton complained to the white superintendent about the exclusion of African Americans from specialty training, which was available to whites. The superintendent told Eaton that "there can be no colored resident doctors until we have an adequate number of colored nurses to staff the hospital," because the hospital "cannot permit colored resident doctors to give orders to our white nurses" (Eaton, 19). Despite this discrimination Eaton completed his residency in 1943 and went into practice with his father-in-law, Dr. Foster Burnett, in Wilmington, eventually establishing the Burnett-Eaton Clinic for the city's black residents. He practiced in the city until his death in 1991.

In addition to his medical practice Eaton was a civil rights pioneer. He and his wife, Celeste Burnett Eaton, had two children, Hubert Jr. and Carolyn, and, in an attempt to improve their academic opportunities, in 1950 Eaton and another physician sued the New Hanover County (North Carolina) board of education to get more money allocated for black schools. Eaton later explained that they were in the best position to file a lawsuit because "as doctors who did not depend on referrals from white practitioners, our income was fairly reprisal-proof" (Eaton, 43). Their lawsuit called for the equalization of school facilities for blacks and whites, not desegregation, and in 1952 the court ruled that the county had to equalize the schools' funding; two years later New Hanover County opened a new high school for the county's black students.

In 1952 Eaton ran for a seat on the county school board. That year there were only 1,800 registered black voters in the county, which had a black population of 23,000. The first African American to seek a seat on New Hanover County's board of education since 1900, Eaton garnered 4,784 votes, losing by a mere 252. His success both in registering and attracting voters did not go unnoticed. Nine months after the election, county officials staggered the terms of school board members to make it more difficult for minority candidates to win election. The new electoral system went into effect in 1954 when Eaton again failed to win a seat on the school board. He unsuccessfully campaigned for the position again in 1956 and 1958.

An exceptional athlete—Eaton was a four-time national doubles champion of the American Tennis Association (ATA) and a member of the North Carolina Tennis Hall of Fame—he was also concerned with the lack of recreation facilities open to African Americans. Excluded from the public tennis facilities in his hometown, he built a court at his home, which he regularly opened to the city's black children. After seeing the young Althea Gibson play at the ATA championships in 1946 he invited the future U.S. and Wimbledon champion to live with his family while he served as her mentor and coach. In the 1950s Eaton began successful protests to integrate Wilmington's public recreational facilities and his crusade for equal access to recreation amenities culminated in 1968 when the city's YMCA admitted its first black member.

Eaton's civil rights activities also extended to the medical world. In 1954 he applied for staff privileges at Wilmington's James Walker Memorial Hospital, which had twenty-five beds for black patients but did not allow black physicians to use its facilities. His request went unanswered, so the next year, joined by two of his colleagues, Eaton again sought access to the hospital, and was again denied. In response the three men filed suit against the hospital in 1956, claiming that as both state-licensed physicians and taxpayers, their Fifth and Fourteenth Amendment rights had been violated. In 1958 *Eaton v. James Walker Memorial Hospital* was dismissed by a federal judge who held that "the act of discrimination did not constitute state action." Again denied hospital privileges in 1960 the three physicians brought another suit, this time joined by two of their patients. In 1964 the circuit court found that James Walker Memorial Hospital could not discriminate against black patients or physicians. The other two physicians were granted courtesy privileges, but Eaton was again denied an appointment. "The successful denial of hospital staff privileges to me was clearly vindictive, but it was meaningless and of no personal consequence," recalled Eaton, "[but] the victory in this lawsuit established a firm legal precedent against the arbitrary denial of hospital privileges to black physicians" (Eaton, 60). Eaton never practiced at Walker Memorial; in 1965 both it and the (all-black) Wilmington Community Hospital were closed and the New Hanover Memorial Hospital was opened. Eaton joined the staff at New Hanover without difficulty.

By the 1960s Eaton had emerged as a full-blown soldier in the civil rights movement and was viewed by white leaders as a spokesman for Wilmington's African American community. In 1962 he met with Wilmington's mayor to discuss the desegregation of the city's public library, which was then carried out with little difficulty. The following year Eaton served as vice chairman of a biracial committee to facilitate a peaceful desegregation of the city's businesses. He also continued his fight for the county's black school children as almost ten years after the U.S. Supreme Court's decision in *Brown v. Board of Education* (1954), the county had still failed to integrate its schools. In 1964 he successfully filed a complaint in U.S. District Court on behalf of his daughter to desegregate the county's schools. Eaton's involvement with school desegregation in North Carolina came full circle in 1981, when he was elected chairman of the University of North Carolina at Wilmington's board of trustees, becoming the first African American to head a predominantly white university in the state.

FURTHER READING

Eaton's papers are held at the University of North Carolina at Wilmington.

Eaton, Hubert A. *Every Man Should Try* (1984).

Morais, Herbert M. *The History of the Afro-American in Medicine* (1978).

Ward, Thomas J., Jr. *Black Physicians in the Jim Crow South* (2003).

THOMAS J. WARD JR.

Eckstine, Billy (8 July 1914–8 Mar. 1993), vocalist and bandleader known as "Mr. B," was born William Clarence Eckstein in Pittsburgh, Pennsylvania, the son of William Eckstein, a chauffeur, and Charlotte (maiden name unknown), a seamstress. He changed the spelling of his name as a young adult, at the suggestion of a nightclub owner who thought his name looked too Jewish. Eckstine had no extensive formal musical education while he was growing up, but his mother was always singing hymns and popular songs, and he sang at local social events and for a short time in the Episcopal choir in Pittsburgh. Around age sixteen he moved to Washington, D.C., and lived with his sister Maxine while finishing high school.

In 1933, on a dare, he sang at an amateur show at the Howard Theater in Washington, D.C., and won first prize. In his last year of high school, much to his parents' dismay, Eckstine worked at the Howard Theater, singing while the chorus girls danced. His parents had their hearts set on all of their children going to college. Eckstine, undecided between singing and football, won a scholarship in 1934 to study physical education at Howard University but quit after a year, after breaking his collarbone. Returning to Pittsburgh, he sang in local clubs and then made his way to Chicago, where, while singing in the DeLisa Club, he was heard by EARL HINES, who asked Eckstine to join his band. Eckstine was Hines's principal vocalist from 1939 through 1943.

At that time, record producers insisted that black musicians stick to the blues. They were unwilling to let a black singer record popular songs, ostensibly because it was impossible to understand their drawl. Hines insisted, however, that Eckstine not be replaced, and he even offered to pay for the arrangements if the producers could not understand the words. Eckstine had impeccable diction. His recording of "Skylark" (1942) outsold Bing Crosby's, and this success opened the way for him to sing ballads. Not that Eckstine was unable to sing blues tunes; his "Jelly, Jelly," written in twelve minutes at the end of a recording session in 1940, became a national hit and ensured the popularity of the new Earl Hines Orchestra even before "Skylark."

It was Eckstine who encouraged Hines to take on CHARLIE PARKER, DIZZY GILLESPIE, and SARAH VAUGHAN, thereby becoming the first major big band to showcase the newly emerging bop style. In the spring of 1944 Eckstine started his own big band, a modern swing band so committed to bebop that his vocals regularly took second place to the instrumentalists. Having learned to play trumpet while on tour with Hines's band, Eckstine played trumpet and trombone alongside the bebop greats he employed at various times, including the saxophonists Parker, Eugene Ammons, Lucky Thompson, and DEXTER GORDON; the trumpeters

Gillespie, Fats Navarro, Kenny Dorham, and Miles Davis; the bassist Oscar Pettiford; drummer Art Blakey; the pianist Clyde Hart; the singer Vaughan; and the arrangers Tad Dameron and Budd Johnson. Unfortunately for his orchestra, the general public did not share Eckstine's love of bop. That worked against them, as did the record ban imposed by a musicians' strike, and the orchestra was disbanded in 1947.

Even before his band folded, Eckstine had been making solo recordings to support it. He had two million-copy sellers in 1945: "A Cottage for Sale" and a revival of Russ Columbo's "Prisoner of Love." In 1947 he was one of the first artists to sign with the newly established MGM Records and thereupon embarked on a highly successful singing career. The high, straightforward voice and style that Eckstine had used with Hines evolved into a deep, liquid baritone with persistent vibrato. In addition, he was outstandingly handsome and had a great deal of charm. His revivals of "Everything I Have Is Yours" (1947), "Blue Moon" (1948), and "Caravan" (1949) were immediate hits, and in 1949–1950 he was widely considered the country's most popular vocalist. His piano accompanist, Robert "Bobby" Tucker, said that Eckstine's ballads and popular songs "seduced the nation" in the 1940s and 1950s. However, as his longtime friend, the composer Quincy Jones, with whom he recorded *Billy Eckstine and Quincy Jones at Basin Street East* (1961), maintained, Eckstine, although perfect for the part, was never promoted as a sex symbol because he was a black man. Eckstine's other recordings include "Blowin' the Blues Away" (1944), "Opus X" (1944), "I Apologize" (1951), and the albums *Billy Eckstine's Imagination* (1958) and *Basie/Eckstine Inc.* (1959).

Earlier, while touring with Hines's band, Eckstine had had to endure numerous difficulties and indignities as a result of racial discrimination, especially in the South. It was not unusual for band members to have to sleep on the bus, and if a restaurant did not have a separate entrance for blacks the white bus driver was sent inside to bring back food for the rest of the band. By 1948, however, as a major recording star, Eckstine had it written into his contracts that he was to be treated as a guest at the hotels where he sang, and everybody was to be admitted to his performances. He became a supporter of the civil rights movement and joined in the 1965 March from Selma to Montgomery.

Eckstine's duet with Sarah Vaughan, "Passing Strangers," was a minor hit in 1957, and it reached number seventeen on the charts in 1969, but recording contracts began to dwindle in the 1960s—blamed on fading popularity for his mannerisms and exaggerated vibrato—and so he concentrated instead on live appearances. He toured with Duke Ellington and Maynard Ferguson in 1966 and briefly signed with Motown in 1967. Eckstine settled in Las Vegas but performed all over, appearing at the Newport Jazz Festival in New York City in the 1970s, at the Grand Finale in New York in 1980, and at Rick's Cafe American in Chicago in 1982. He regularly crossed the ocean, often singing on tour ships, but he recorded only intermittently.

Eckstine's first marriage, to June (maiden name unknown), ended in divorce, and in 1953 he married the model and actress Carol Drake. Of their seven children, five became involved in music. Fulfilling his parents' wish that all their children receive an education, Eckstine earned a B.A. from Shaw University in Raleigh, North Carolina, in 1974 and later began work on a master's degree. He and his second wife were divorced in 1978.

By the time of his death in Pittsburgh, Eckstine had achieved many firsts. His band of the 1940s became the first true bebop big band. His singing of ballads after he went solo in 1947 helped to define the role of the solo jazz vocalist (singing independent of an orchestra) and thereby paved the way for the next generation of jazz soloists who used piano or trio accompaniment. Finally, his refusal to accept the status quo contributed to expanded opportunities for black musicians.

FURTHER READING

Southern, Eileen. "Conversation with William Clarence (Billy) Eckstine: 'Mr. B' of Ballad and Bop," *Black Perspective in Music* 7.2 (1979) and 8.1 (1980).

Travis, Dempsey J. *An Autobiography of Black Jazz* (1983).

DISCOGRAPHY

Brown, Denis. *Billy Eckstine: A Discography* (2000).

This entry is taken from the *American National Biography* and is published here with the permission of the American Council of Learned Societies.

PAULA CONLON

Edelin, Kenneth Carlton (31 Mar. 1939–), physician and advocate of reproductive rights, was born in Washington, D.C., the son of Ruby Goodwin and Benedict F. Edelin. After finishing eighth grade in the segregated Washington school system, he enrolled at the Stockbridge School, a now-defunct progressive private boarding school in western Massachusetts, from which he graduated in 1957.

Edelin earned a B.A. at Columbia University in 1961 and returned to Stockbridge for two years to teach science and mathematics. He then entered Meharry Medical College in Nashville, Tennessee, where in 1964 he helped found the Student National Medical Association. As a medical student, Edelin assisted in treating a seventeen-year-old girl with a massive uterine infection caused by an improperly performed, illegal abortion. The girl's death inspired him to become an advocate of safe and legal abortions.

Edelin earned his M.D. from Meharry in 1967, the year in which he married Ramona Hoage. The couple, who had two children, later divorced.

Edelin then spent four years—including his medical internship year—in the air force at Wright-Patterson AFB, Ohio, and in Great Britain. In 1971 he entered the obstetrics residency program at Boston City Hospital (BCH). Abortions were then legal under Massachusetts law, but because an extensive review was required before each procedure, Edelin was distressed by the delays he faced. In 1973, however, the U.S. Supreme Court's landmark *Roe v Wade* decision voided all state laws regulating abortion, thus making legal abortions more readily available.

In October 1973, while serving as chief obstetric resident at BCH (the first African American to hold that position), Edelin was confronted with a black teenage girl whose mother had brought her to the hospital for an abortion. After estimating that the girl had been pregnant for at most twenty-two weeks, Edelin attempted an abortion by injection of a saline solution. When he found that a saline abortion was not possible in this case, Edelin consulted with the attending obstetrician who agreed that Edelin should proceed with a hysterotomy (a procedure in which an incision is made in the abdomen and the fetus removed through it). A more junior resident who witnessed the operation later claimed that the fetus was viable and that Edelin deliberately allowed it to die by first removing the placenta and leaving the fetus to asphyxiate in the amniotic fluid.

Abortion opponents seized the opportunity provided by the incident and a related case to urge Suffolk County District Attorney Garrett H. Byrne to press charges against Edelin. Because the abortion itself was legal, Byrne charged Edelin with manslaughter. The charge led to Edelin's immediate suspension without prejudice from the hospital staff. To the dismay of many in the Boston medical community, on 15 February 1975, Edelin was convicted and given a one-year suspended sentence. This occurred shortly after the 1974 school integration ruling by U.S. District Court Judge W. Arthur Garrity Jr. that led to the notorious struggles over busing in Boston. There remains some question as to whether opposition to abortion and opposition to forced school integration were conflated in the minds of Edelin's accusers. The 23 March 1975 *Newsweek* reported that one juror claimed that another had said during deliberation, "The nigger is guilty as sin" (23).

The conviction was overturned in December 1976, but the case remained a point of contention for opponents of legal abortion. In June 1981, a play based in the trial, "As to the Meaning of Words," by Mark Eichman, opened in New York City.

In 1978 Edelin remarried, to Barbara Evans, with whom he had another two children. In the same year he was named chair of obstetrics and gynecology at the Boston University School of Medicine and director of the obstetrics and gynecology residency program at Boston City Hospital. In 1988 he was at the center of another, unrelated, dispute. Midwives at BCH accused Edelin of needlessly restricting their right to practice at the hospital. This controversy led Edelin to resign from BCH on 30 June 1989.

Edelin was chairman of the board of the Planned Parenthood Federation of America (PPFA) from 1989 to 1992, and PPFA established an award in his name to honor those who work to support reproductive rights. When Senator Edward Kennedy received the Edelin Award he praised Edelin as "one of the great heroes in our cause, a profile in courage whose name today is a symbol of the importance of persevering in a cause we know is right" (Boston Healing Landscape Project website, www.bmc.org/pediatrics/special/bhlp/pages/about/bios/edelin.htm). A member of the American College of Obstetrics and Gynecology, Edelin chaired its Committee on Health Care for Underserved Women. He served on the board of the NAACP Legal Defense and Education Fund in the first decade of the twenty-first century

From 1996 to 1998 Edelin sat on the Boston Public Health Commission and was Managing Director of the Roxbury Comprehensive Community Health Center. In the first decade of the twenty-first century Edelin was Associate Dean for Students and Minority Affairs at Boston University (BU) School of Medicine. As director of the BU Early Medical

School Selection Program for more than decade prior to his retirement, Edelin succeeded in recruiting an increased number of minority students to the BU School of Medicine.

Still active in his sixties, Edelin was on the board of directors of OneUnited Bank (the first Internet bank controlled by African Americans), the Alan Guttmacher Institute, and the NAACP. Other affiliations included the standards committee of the National Abortion Federation and the Committee on Ethics of the Massachusetts Medical Society. Edelin's honors include membership in Alpha Omega Alpha, the medical honor society. He has been listed in *Who's Who in America*, *Who's Who among Black Americans*, and *Who's Who in the World*, and has received the Good Guy Award from the National Women's Political Caucus and the Lifetime Achievement Award from the National Medical Association. He was named one of America's leading black doctors by *Black Enterprise* magazine and received more than two million dollars in grant support for programs designed to increase the number of under-represented minority physicians in America.

Edelin, always a controversial figure because of his association with the early years of legalized abortion, never hid from controversy. In 2003 he spoke out against both the so-called partial birth abortion bill and plans to invade Iraq. At the same time Edelin said openly that he supported the right of doctors to refuse to perform abortions if it is against their personal moral beliefs. As chair of NARAL Pro-Choice America, Edelin published an open letter to Secretary of State COLIN POWELL on behalf of "African-American Men for Women's Rights" and read it at the March for Women's Rights in April 2004. Besides his work in reproductive rights, Edelin wrote or cowrote many publications dealing with teen pregnancy prevention and drug abuse during pregnancy. He retired from Boston University in June 2006.

FURTHER READING

Nolen, William A. *The Baby in the Bottle: An Investigative Review of the Edelin Case and its Larger Meanings for the Controversy over Abortion Reform* (1978).

Pence, Gregory. *Classic Cases in Medical Ethics* (2000).

EDWARD T. MORMAN

Edelin, Ramona Hoage (4 Sept. 1945–), scholar, activist, and philosopher, was born Ramona Hoage in Los Angeles, California, the only child of George Hoage and A. Annette Lewis Hoage. Edelin's commitment to education started with the influences of her mother and maternal grandfather, both of whom were university professors. ALETHIA ANNETTE LEWIS HOAGE PHINAZEE served as dean of the school of library science at North Carolina Central University in Durham, North Carolina (1970–1983), and has herself been celebrated for her contributions to the field of library science.

The young Hoage got an auspicious start to her own education at the progressive and innovative Oglethorpe Laboratory School at Atlanta University. The campus school's teaching philosophy was geared toward the intellectual advancement of inner-city youth. During Edelin's childhood, the Hoages lived in college towns near South Carolina State and Atlanta and Southern Illinois Universities. In 1963 Ramona graduated from high school in Stockbridge, Massachusetts.

In 1967 Edelin graduated magna cum laude from Fisk University in Nashville, Tennessee, with an AB in Philosophy. The oldest university in Nashville and the first historic black college to obtain a charter for the academic honor society Phi Beta Kappa, into which Edelin was inducted, Fisk had been established in 1866 with the mission of educating newly freed slaves. Other distinguished graduates of Fisk included W. E. B. DUBOIS and President Clinton's secretary of energy HAZEL R. O'LEARY.

Ramona Hoage married KENNETH CARLTON EDELIN, a graduate of Meharry Medical College, in 1967. They had two children: a son, Kenneth Jr., and a daughter, Kimberly. While her husband was stationed in Norwich, England, with the air force, Edelin studied at the University of East Anglia and received her master's degree in Philosophy in 1969.

By 1970 Edelin had returned to the United States. She spent the next few years teaching at various Boston-area institutions. She completed her Ph.D. in 1981 at Boston University. Her dissertation, titled "The Philosophical Foundations and Implications of William Edward Burghardt DuBois' Social Ethic," was an assertion that the social programs and political platforms DuBois promoted were the practical application of his espoused philosophical theory that through democracy, the individual's ability to contribute to community, will come social equality for that individual and their people.

Edelin was a vital contributor to each academic department she was affiliated with: lecturer in logic for the University of Maryland's European Division (1970–1971); full-time instructor in the philosophy department at Emerson College (1971–1972); founder and chair of the Department of African American Studies at Northeastern University (1972–1977); and visiting professor in the Department of Afro-American Studies at Brandeis University (1974–1975). She served on many committees and was affiliated with a number of professional organizations, including the American Philosophical Association, the American Philosophical Association Committee on Blacks, and the Center for African and African American Studies at Atlanta University, and was cofounder of the Boston Area Black Studies Consortium.

In 1977 Edelin joined the National Urban Coalition (NUC) to establish projects to open up opportunities for inner-city youth through education and economic advancement. The NUC, founded in 1967, was an avenue for positive change in response to the race riots that had plagued American cities throughout the decade. Edelin started as executive assistant to President Carl Holman in 1977, then became director of operations in 1979, vice president of operations in 1982, and finally chief executive officer in 1988. She served as president and CEO until 1998. She was instrumental in the establishment of the award-winning program of Say Yes to a Youngster's Future, an early intervention in mathematics, science, and technology for girls and families of color. The goal of the program was to stimulate students' interest in math and science through Saturday sessions with children and their families during which hands-on activities, field trips, and practical demonstrations were conducted by specially trained teachers. The program expanded from a pilot program in ten schools to forty public elementary schools across the country. In 1988 Edelin participated in a meeting of black leaders chaired by the Reverend JESSE L. JACKSON SR., where the term "African American" gained popularity over "Negro" or "black" to refer to American citizens of African ancestry.

In 1991 Edelin joined the board of directors of the Congressional Black Caucus Foundation (CBCF), which was established in 1976 as a nonpartisan, nonprofit public policy research and educational institute based in Washington, D.C. In 1997 Edelin went on to serve as the organization's Executive Director and continured in that position unitl 2003. According to the CBCF mission statement (*About CBCF*, 1 Apr. 2005), the foundation was created to "broaden and elevate the influence of African Americans in the political, legislative and public policy arenas." Examples included the With Ownership Wealth Initiative, designed to increase minority family and student homeownership; the Leadership Institute for Public Service, a series of scholarship, internship, and fellowship opportunities directed toward grooming future leaders of the black community; the many CBCF's public health information dissemination Web sites; and the Support African Globalization, which through conferences and partnerships established connections between African Americans and the African world community addressing critical issues in education, energy, security, health, trade investment, and economic development. Edelin also took an interest in political committees, accepting election to the board of directors of the CBCF in 1991 and chairing a National Political Congress of Black Women commission in 1992.

Edelin served as vice president of Policy and Outreach for the Corporation for Enterprise Development (CFED) from September 2003 to August 2004. CFED was formed to help low-income families build assets that would allow them to reach their homeownership, educational, and entrepreneurial goals. Under Edelin's tenure, the Savings for Education, Entrepreneurship, and Down Payment (SEED) Policy and Practice Initiative was launched; the Senate passed the Savings for Working Families Act; and *Hidden in Plain Sight: A Look at the $335 Billion Federal Asset-Building Budget* was published.

A champion of causes for African Americans, as well as other disadvantaged people, Edelin received many awards and appointments. She was one of *Ebony*'s Women to Watch in 1982 and 100 Most Influential Black Americans from 1993 to 1999. She was appointed by President Clinton to the President's Board of Advisors on Historically Black Colleges and Universities in 1994. She received the prestigious Lamplighter Award for Leadership in 2003, and she was a member-at-large for the Black Leadership Forum.

FURTHER READING

Edein, Ramona Hoage. "The Philosophical Foundations and Implications of William Edward Burghardt DuBois' Social Ethic," Boston University Graduate School doctoral thesis (1981).

"Ramona Hoage Edelin," in *Contemporary Black Biography*, Thomson Gale, vol. 19 (1988).

Smith, Jessie Carney, ed. *Notable Black American Women* (1992).

JOLIE A. JACKSON-WILLET

Edelman, Marian Wright (6 June 1939–), civil rights attorney and founder of the Children's Defense Fund, was born Marian Wright in Bennettsville, South Carolina, to Arthur Jerome Wright, a Baptist minister, and Maggie Leola Bowen, an active churchwoman. Both parents were community activists who took in relatives and others who could no longer care for themselves, eventually founding a home for the aged that continued to be run by family members in the early twenty-first century. The Wrights also built a playground for black children denied access to white recreational facilities, and nurtured in their own children a sense of responsibility and community service. As soon as Marian and her siblings were old enough to drive, they continued the family tradition of delivering food and coal to the poor, elderly, and sick. Arthur Wright also encouraged his children to read about and to revere influential African Americans like MARY MCLEOD BETHUNE and MARIAN ANDERSON (for whom Marian Wright was named).

Marian Wright experienced racial injustice from an early age, despite the efforts of her parents and other elders to protect their children from the harshest excesses of segregation. Maggie Wright was choir director, organist, and coordinator of church and community youth activities and could not always be with her children; thus neighbors and parishioners often looked after the Wright children. Such communal parenting provided Edelman with a series of strong black female role models. These women, she later wrote, became "lanterns" for her childhood and adult life.

In 1956, two years after her father's death, Wright entered Spelman College in Atlanta, Georgia. There she met several people who became influential mentors, including the historian Howard Zinn, the educator and civil rights advocate BENJAMIN MAYS, and MARTIN LUTHER KING JR. At Spelman, she continued the deep religious commitment of her childhood. Her diaries from that time record her prayers, asking God to "help me do the right thing and to be sincere and honest," to "teach us to seek after truth relentlessly, and to yearn for the betterment of mankind by endless sacrifice" (Edelman, 61, 64). This centrality of faith to her daily life persisted throughout Wright's

Marian Wright Edelman, an attorney for the NAACP legal defense fund who became known as the "children's crusader," testifying before the Senate Labor Subcommittee about the anti-poverty program in Washington, D.C., 15 March 1967. (AP Images.)

career. She later identified her life's work as a desire to emulate her mentors in "seeking to serve God and a cause bigger than ourselves" (Edelman, 53).

During her junior year she received a Charles Merrill scholarship that provided a year of European study and travel to Paris, Geneva, and several Eastern Bloc nations. That experience, she wrote in her diary, changed her life. "I could never return home to the segregated South and constraining Spelman College in the same way" (Edelman, 43). Marian Wright was not alone. Inspired by the February 1960 sit-in protests at segregated North Carolina lunch counters, thousands of young black southerners began to actively resist Jim Crow. That spring Wright was arrested with other Atlanta students during a sit-in, and she helped develop a student document, "An Appeal for Human Rights," that was published in both the white-owned *Atlanta Constitution* and the *Atlanta Daily World*, a publication produced by, and primarily read by, African Americans. At Easter, she joined several hundred students, primarily from the South, at a gathering in Raleigh, North Carolina, initiated by ELLA BAKER of the Southern Christian Leadership Conference. That meeting resulted in Wright's participation in the Student Nonviolent Coordinating Committee (SNCC).

In May 1960 Wright graduated from Spelman as class valedictorian and entered Yale University Law School that fall. Having abandoned her earlier plans of studying Russian literature or preparing for the foreign service, she now determined that mastering the law would best prepare her for assisting the black freedom struggle. While at Yale, Wright continued her civil rights commitment through the Northern Students' Movement, a support group for SNCC, and by visiting civil rights workers in Mississippi. During the summer of 1962, she traveled to the Ivory Coast under the Crossroads Africa student cultural exchange program founded by JAMES H. ROBINSON. After graduating from Yale in 1963, Wright spent one year preparing to become a civil rights attorney by working for the NAACP Legal Defense and Educational Fund in New York.

In 1964 Wright moved south to direct the LDF's activities in Jackson, Mississippi. She arrived during "freedom summer," a major voter-registration campaign that helped her forge relationships with ROBERT P. MOSES, FANNIE LOU HAMER, MAE BERTHA CARTER, UNITA BLACKWELL, and other civil rights leaders. Wright remained in Jackson for four years and became the first black woman admitted to the Mississippi bar. She also successfully supported continued federal funding for the Child Development Group of Mississippi (CDGM), one of the nation's largest Head Start programs. CDGM, founded as part of President Lyndon Johnson's War on Poverty, was strongly opposed by conservatives in Mississippi and the state's all-white congressional delegation, who viewed the organization as too radical. To the extent that CDGM wanted to end poverty and inequality for all Mississippians, it *was* radical, indeed, revolutionary. Wright also filed and won a school integration lawsuit that began the process of fully desegregating Mississippi schools. As a result of her civil rights practice and work for the poor in Mississippi, Wright testified before the U.S. Senate in 1967 about hunger and poverty in the state. Prompted by Wright's compelling testimony, Senator Robert Kennedy visited Mississippi to examine her assertions of extreme economic deprivation. Wright guided Kennedy on this fact-finding trip, which resulted in immediate federal relief and, later on, in expansions of the federal food stamp program. Wright also encouraged Martin Luther King Jr. to launch the Poor People's Campaign, to dramatize the problems of poverty in America, and later served as an attorney for that effort following King's assassination in April 1968. That July, Wright married Peter Edelman, a prominent aide to Senator Kennedy. The couple had three sons, Joshua, Jonah, and Ezra.

Edelman moved to Washington in 1968 and continued her civil rights and antipoverty work through a Field Foundation grant that enabled her to found the Washington Research Project (WRP), a public-interest law firm that lobbied for child and family well-being, and for expanding Head Start and other anti-poverty programs. Three years later she moved with her husband to Boston, where she directed the Harvard Center for Law and Education from 1971 to 1973. In 1973 the WRP became the parent organization for the Children's Defense Fund (CDF), whose mission has been to "Leave No Child Behind." Under Edelman's presidency, the CDF has promoted a "healthy start," a "head start," a "fair start," a "safe start," and a "moral start" for all children. By tackling children's welfare, health care, and employment issues, as well as teenage pregnancy and adoption, the CDF became the nation's largest and most successful child advocacy organization. It has several local and state affiliates in many states. At its retreat center on a farm once owned by the *Roots* author ALEX HALEY in Clinton, Tennessee, the CDF focuses on Edelman's vision of transforming America by building a movement for children. CDF programs draw on the methods and lessons of the civil rights movement, for example, in the freedom school trainers program, which exposes young people to civil rights veterans and history. Those selected by the CDF to teach young adults are called Ella Baker Trainers, in honor of her role as a mentor for thousands of young activists like Marian Wright, Bob Moses, and STOKELY CARMICHAEL. The CDF's annual Samuel DeWitt Proctor Institute also reflects Edelman's roots in the black church through its workshops, worship, singing, and inspirational preaching and teaching.

Edelman's tenacious defense of children's rights has earned her respect, opportunity, and honors. From 1976 to 1987 she chaired the Spelman College trustee board, becoming the first woman to hold that post. From 1971 to 1977 she served as a member of the Yale University Corporation, the first woman elected by alumni to this position. She has received numerous awards and honors, including the nation's highest civilian award, the Presidential Medal of Freedom, in 2000, a MacArthur Foundation Fellowship in 1985, the AFL-CIO Humanitarian Award in 1989, and honorary degrees from more than thirty colleges and universities. She has also been praised for several books on child advocacy and child rearing, including *Families in Peril: An Agenda for Social Change* (1987), *Stand for Children* (1998), and *Hold My Hand: Prayers for Building a Movement to Leave No Child Behind* (2001).

Edelman's close friendship with her fellow Yale Law School graduate and CDF activist, Hillary Rodham Clinton, led to speculation that the CDF might wield considerable influence in the White House, when Clinton's husband, Bill Clinton, was elected president in 1992. However, in 1996 Edelman opposed President Clinton for supporting welfare reform legislation that she believed would worsen child poverty. Edelman also criticized Clinton's successor, George W. Bush, who appropriated the CDF's "leave no child behind" motto as a campaign slogan but showed little interest in backing up such rhetoric with meaningful legislation. Responding to President Bush's State of the Union address in 2002, Edelman stated:

> For the annual cost of what the President has already approved in tax cuts to the top one percent of taxpayers, we could pay for child care, Head Start, and health care for all of the children who still need it—as proposed in-the comprehensive Act to Leave No Child Behind. ("Statement by the Children's Defense Fund," 30-Jan.-2002, http://www.childrens-defense.org/statement_stateofunion.php)

In 1996 CDF provided the grass roots constituency for the Bipartisan Hatch–Kennedy bill creating the State Children's Health Insurance Program (S-CHIP). Partly funded by tobacco taxes, S-CHIP provided health coverage to more than 6 million children by 2006.

FURTHER READING

Edelman, Marian Wright. *Lanterns: A Memoir of Mentors* (1999).

Greenberg, Jack. *Crusaders in the Courts: How a Dedicated Band of Lawyers Fought for the Civil Rights Revolution* (1994).

ROSETTA E. ROSS

Edmonds, Helen (3 Dec. 1911–9 May 1995), educator, scholar, and activist, was born Helen Gray Edmonds in Lawrenceville, Virginia, the eldest of four children of John Edmonds, a plasterer and bricklayer, and Ann Williams Edmonds. Her parents inspired and instilled the importance of higher education in Edmonds and her siblings. Edmonds said of her parents that had they been knowledgeable about French history, they would have quoted Napoleon's famous quip, "There are no Alps," a metaphor for the many challenges the family faced living in the Jim Crow South. Edmonds was educated at St. Paul's Elementary and High schools located on the campus of St. Paul's College in Lawrenceville, Virginia. She earned her AB degree in History from Morgan State College in 1933. In 1938 Edmonds received her M.A.in History and in 1946 her Ph.D. in History from Ohio State University. She completed postdoctoral research at the University of Heidelberg in Germany from 1954 to 1955, specializing in modern European history.

Edmonds began her teaching career at the Virginia Theological Seminary and College in Lynchburg, Virginia. For the next five years, she taught history and English at her alma mater, St. Paul's College. In the spring of 1941 the president and founder of North Carolina College (later North Carolina Central University [NCCU] and formerly North Carolina College for Negroes, the first publicly supported liberal arts college in the South) JAMES EDWARD SHEPARD recruited her to join the faculty. Edmonds remained at NCCU for more than three decades, retiring in 1977. During her tenure at NCCU, Edmonds served in a number of roles—professor of history, Drama Club adviser, Department of History chair, Arts and Sciences Graduate School Dean, interim committee member for the administration, university board of trustees member, and author of North Carolina Central University's *Truth and Service Ceremony*. She also held visiting professor and lecturer positions at more than one hundred institutions of higher education in the United States, Europe, the Middle East, and Africa, including Portland State University, University of Rochester, Virginia State University, Ohio State University, MIT, Harvard, Radcliffe College, University of Stockholm, Free University of Berlin, University of Liberia, and the University of Monrovia. After her retirement, she was appointed distinguished professor of History, served on the NCCU board of trustees, was appointed trustee emeritus when her term expired, and provided mentorship to the founder's successors.

Edmonds's lifelong commitment to education was rooted in her earlier education. She was particularly grateful to her high school, college, and graduate school history teachers, including her godfathers, Walter P. Steptoe, Clinton Everett, and Homer C. Hockett. All three influenced her passion for contemplating the challenges of Western civilization and enabled her to imagine a world of complete equilibrium, one of harmony and equality. She often spoke of a "special sense of obligation" toward her students and noted that she frequently learned as much from young people as she taught them (Gardner). She viewed higher education as an endeavor through which to resolve incongruities between what is taught and what is practiced, an effort to achieve logic and consistency between speech and action, a desire for truth and convictions not compromised by human conveniences. She labored by precept and example to develop "responsible leadership and responsible action" in her students (*Gardner Award*). She sought to "restore interpersonal relationships," challenging her students to step outside of a modernized society and the complexities of rapid social change and "reassess those values which they deem eternal" (*Gardner Award*). She was confident that higher education could "reclaim its liberating mission, enabling students to have applicable curricular experiences and become transformative agents of social change" (*Gardner Award*).

A substantial part of her career as an educator was spent in the South. Edmonds recalled in receiving an award for her service in 1975 that one of her professors remarked, as she received the terminal degree "Stay in this area of the nation. You have too much education to take back to the South" (*Gardner Award*). Edmonds acknowledged that she had chosen to attend Ohio State in order to achieve a level of special training that was denied to her in the South. However, she never forgot her southern roots, and all southern youth remained her primary concern.

Edmonds served on the Council of Graduate Schools of the United States, the Danforth Foundation, the Southern Fellowships Fund, and the Southern Association of Colleges and Schools. She also served on the boards of trustees at St. Paul's College, Voorhees College, and Washington Technical Institute. She was the recipient of honorary degrees from eight institutions of higher learning, including Morgan State University, Shaw College at Detroit, St. Paul's College, North Carolina Central University, Ohio State University, Duke University, Virginia Union, and MacMurray College. Her work in the academy led to her receiving the 1975 O. Max Gardner Award, the University of North Carolina System's highest faculty honor, for the "greatest contribution to the welfare of the human race." She also received the William Hugh McEniry Award for Excellence in Teaching from the North Carolina Association of Colleges and Universities "in recognition of principles of dedication and commitment to the education and advancement of the state." In 1977 North Carolina Central established the Helen G. Edmonds Graduate Colloquium of History.

Her scholarship and activism were an extension of her educational philosophy and praxis. Edmonds's publications include numerous articles in professional journals and two books: *The Negro in Fusion Politics in North Carolina, 1894–1901* (1951 and reprinted in 1973) and *Black Faces in High Places: Negroes in Government* (1971). Edmonds's *The Negro in Fusion Politics* drew on her doctoral thesis, a pathbreaking work on North Carolina politics in the last decade of the nineteenth century. Edmonds dismissed the contemporary claims of white supremacists that black voting and officeholding during the era of Republican and Populist ascendancy in the 1890s was tantamount to "negro domination." She also noted that black North Carolinians' allies in the Populist Party and white Republicans were no more committed to social equality with African Americans than were the Democrats, and painted a vivid picture of the fraud, violence, and intimidation of black voters that led to disenfranchisement of North Carolina blacks in 1900. From its publication in the early 1950s, Edmonds's book remained a basic starting point for all scholars interested in the racial politics of the 1890s South.

An ardent Republican Party activist, Edmonds was involved in many political endeavors. She seconded the nomination of President Eisenhower for reelection in 1956. During his presidency, she served as a special emissary in Liberia and as an alternate delegate to the General Assembly of the United Nations. She also chaired the U.S. delegation to the Third Committee of the General Assembly. Edmonds was appointed by President Richard Nixon to serve on the National Advisory Council of the Peace Corps and the National Advisory Council to Education Professional Development of HEW-USOE. She served in various roles for the U.S. Department of State, the U.S. Department of Defense, and on the board of directors for the International Women's Year Conference in Mexico City. President Nixon recognized her with three citations for her governmental service. On her tours of Europe and Africa, representing the Department of State, she was a champion of civil rights issues and applauded the United States for its continual—"though with periodic interruptions"—struggles to realize "the inalienable rights of life, liberty and the pursuit of happiness" for all people (*Gardner Award*).

Edmonds was also active in a wide array of civic and women's voluntary organizations. From 1970 to 1974 she served as the fifth National President of Links, Inc., a black women's educational and service organization that grew to 140 chapters in thirty-four states and the District of Columbia under her tenure. Her initiative, which represented an important collective, civic link of support for "forty one predominantly Negro church-related and privately-endowed colleges and universities throughout the South," addressed the philanthropic crossroads of higher education "guided by the sincere belief that a mind is a terrible thing to waste" (*Gardner Award*). The grant-in-aid program that she developed resulted in the United Negro College Fund becoming a focus for the Links, as well as another extension of her commitment to black education. The Links recognized Edmonds for her outstanding volunteerism with National and International Trends and Services and established an award in her honor, the Helen G. Edmonds International Trends and Services Award. She was also active with the Delta Sigma Theta Sorority, 100 Black Women, the National Council of Negro Women, Inc., the United Negro College Fund, the National Association for the Advancement of Colored People Legal Defense Fund, the Robert Moton Memorial Institute, and the United Research and Development Corporation. She was awarded the Mary Church Terrell Award by Delta Sigma Theta Sorority, Inc., in 1994.

Edmonds died following a brief illness at Duke University Medical Center in Durham, North Carolina.

FURTHER READING

"Dr. Helen Edmonds Honored by American Historical Association," *Durham Morning Herald*, 19 Jan. 1989.

"Historian Receives National Award," *Durham Sun*, 10 Sept. 1982.

Oliver Max Gardner Award. University of North Carolina System, Wilson Library General Administration, Chapel Hill (1975).

"Retired NCCU Historian Receives Scholar Award," *News and Observer*, 19 Jan. 1989.

BLANCHE RADFORD CURRY

Edmonds, S. Randolph (30 Apr. 1900–28 Mar. 1983), playwright and educator, was born Sheppard Randolph Edmonds in Lawrenceville, Virginia, one of the nine children of George Washington Edmonds and Frances Fisherman, sharecroppers and former slaves. His mother had been moved from New Orleans to a nearby plantation around Petersburg, Virginia, during the Civil War. She died when Randolph was twelve. Like many other black children, Edmonds attended school for only a short part of the year—in his case five months—and worked the rest on nearby plantations. He went on to attend St. Paul's Normal and Industrial School (later St. Paul's College), the local high school in Lawrenceville, and worked during the summers of 1918–1920 as a waiter in New York City, where he first attended the theater. In 1921 he graduated as valedictorian, with prizes in both English and history. The director of academics at St. Paul's, J. Alvin Russell, encouraged him to attend his alma mater, Oberlin College.

At Oberlin on scholarship, Edmonds and other black students organized a literary group called the Dunbar Forum. Interested at first in writing poetry, short stories, and essays, he soon began to write plays. He was impressed with the philosophy of Frederick H. Koch, a drama professor at the University of North Carolina at Chapel Hill, who believed that plays should be based on the experiences of the people who would form their audiences. Edmonds interrupted his studies at Oberlin, taking a year off to earn money by scrubbing floors, waiting tables, cutting hair, and working other odd jobs. He graduated from Oberlin in 1926 with a B.A. in English, having seen his own first full-length play, *Rocky Roads*, successfully staged by the Dunbar Players. The Dunbar Players staged three of his short plays during 1927, thus inspiring what would be a lifelong interest in college dramatics.

Edmonds became an instructor in English and drama at Morgan State College in Baltimore, Maryland, and studied Shakespearean drama, playwriting, and play production at Columbia University during the summers from 1927 through 1930. At Morgan he not only organized the Morgan Dramatic Club but also formed, in 1930, the Negro Intercollegiate Drama Association. The Morgan Players won critical acclaim from New York critics after their 10 May 1929 performance of Paul Green's *The Man Who Died at Twelve O'Clock*, placing fourth out of a field of twenty in the Seventh Annual Little Theatre Tournament.

Edmonds received his M.A. from Columbia in 1931. That same year he married Irene Colbert, who was the great-granddaughter of the nineteenth-century abolitionist orator HENRY HIGHLAND GARNET. They had two children, Henriette Highland Garnet and S. Randolph Jr. In 1932 the Morgan Players again took the stage in New York for their presentation of Edmonds's folk play *Bad Man* on NBC radio. Folk plays made use of the materials of everyday African American life that the cultural critic ALAIN LOCKE had seen, at the opening of the Harlem Renaissance, as the untapped wealth of the "New Negro" worthy of development. On sabbatical from Morgan in 1934–1935 Edmonds studied drama at Yale University on a fellowship from the Rockefeller Foundation. Upon his return he accepted an invitation from Dillard University to organize and head the speech and theater department there. He left behind at Morgan the first department of drama in any black school. In 1938 his study of theater in Dublin and London on a Rosenwald Fellowship allowed him to complete *Land of Cotton*, a full-length social drama he had begun at Yale. It also renewed his interest in fantasy, a dramatic mode his earliest plays had exhibited.

In the twelve years Edmonds taught at Dillard his plays met with growing success in their performance by the Dillard University Players. In the 1930s the United States saw a burgeoning of educational theater and Edmonds played a key role in that growth. In 1936 he organized black colleges throughout the South and Southwest into the Southern Association of Dramatic and Speech Arts. The interscholastic theater organization he created for Louisiana high school drama groups joined the Louisiana Interscholastic Athletic and Literary Association. But Edmonds was not only a promoter of dramatic organizations at black colleges; he was also a prolific playwright who championed the use of African American materials in his plays. He wrote several essays and articles in the *Messenger*, *Opportunity*, *Phylon*, *Crisis*, and *Arts Quarterly* to argue the significance of educational theater. Edmonds recognized three necessities for the development of black American theater: playwrights, trained and gifted guidance, and an audience.

Edmonds addressed these needs not only in his own plays but also in two anthologies of his work, *Shades and Shadows* (1930) and *Six Plays for Negro Theatre* (1934). Though he intended the plays in the first collection only to be read, not performed, Edmonds explained in the preface of the second collection that he intended it specifically "for Negro Little Theatres, where there has been for many years a great need for plays of Negro life written by Negroes." The 1934 *Six Plays for Negro Theatre* are so-called folk plays, written in the dialect fashionable at the time and based on subject matter drawn from the lives of common people. *Old Man Pete*, for example, explores the adjustment problems faced by many rural southerners who came to the urban North during the Great Migration. In another play, *Nat Turner*, Edmonds portrays the leader of the 1831 armed slave revolt as a religious visionary motivated by humanitarian concerns. A third collection of Edmonds's work, *The Land of Cotton and Other Plays*, was published in 1943. While most of Edmonds's plays make heavy use of melodrama, they also demonstrate the playwright's interest in teaching black history. As such, his plays were performed in black colleges and universities throughout the South.

In 1942 Edmonds and James E. Gayle established in New Orleans the Crescent Concerts Company, considered the first concert company owned and controlled by blacks. Although short-lived due to continual problems gaining the necessary approval of entertainers from city officials, the company brought to the stage such artists as the singer and actor PAUL ROBESON, the concert pianist PHILIPPA DUKE SCHUYLER, the opera singer MARIAN ANDERSON, and the singer ANNE BROWN, who was the original Bess in Gershwin's *Porgy and Bess*.

S. Randolph Edmonds retired in 1970, recognized as a pioneer in the black theater movement who brought the daily lives of his largely African American audiences to the stage. Among the honors he received before his death perhaps the most significant was the commemoration of the Randolph Edmonds Players Guild at his alma mater.

FURTHER READING

Abramson, Doris. *Negro Playwrights in the American Theatre, 1925–1959* (1969).

Hatch, James V., ed. *Black Theater, U. S. A.: Forty-five Plays by Black Americans, 1847–1974* (1974).

Koch, Frederick N. "Drama in the South," *Carolina Playbook* (June 1940).

MARY ANNE BOELCSKEVY

Edmondson, William (1874–7 Feb. 1951), sculptor, was born in Davidson County, Tennessee, the eldest of Orange and Jane Brown Edmondson's five children. His parents were freed slaves working as field laborers. Edmondson worked for a living from an early age: he recounted boyhood memories of laboring in the corn fields of the former Compton plantation. As he got older, urban railways and housing encroached on this rural landscape three miles from Nashville, signaling economic changes and prompting many black families to resettle in the city. Edmondson's family joined this migration in 1890, a year after his father died.

His first Nashville job was for a sewer works. Later he worked for the railroads, until a leg injury in 1907 led Edmondson to take less strenuous janitorial work at the all-white Woman's Hospital. He worked in various jobs there until the hospital ceased operations. It was 1931 and Edmondson was in his mid-50s. That year, he made his first handcrafted works in stone. He would never again work for an employer.

Although his niece remembered Edmondson as a versatile "tinkerer" who experimented with hobbies from gardening to shoemaking, there seems to be no precedent for his sculptures. Edmondson explained his shift to art as a moment of divine inspiration, although his descriptions of the spiritual encounter would vary. Still, he spoke consistently about his faith, referring to an ongoing dialogue about art with his "heavenly daddy."

As he embraced the risks of artistic pursuit, the property Edmondson owned on 14th Avenue South provided security and a base. A smaller structure on the lot served as a studio. The yard separating this work space from his home was a place to sculpt outside or arrange finished sculptures. Edmondson filled the yard with sculpture, all made from limestone blocks of various sizes and types. There were tombstones and birdbaths, which were practical and appealing to Edmondson's mostly black neighbors. There were also monumental works of art without any specific function. The yard was semipublic, with some sculptures visible to passersby on the street—a situation that ultimately led to the art world's "discovery" of his work.

In 1935, Professor Sidney Hirsch went on a short stroll from his home near Vanderbilt University, and chanced upon Edmondson's yard. Impressed by the work, he made Edmondson's acquaintance. Through Hirsch, Nashville collectors Alfred and Elizabeth Starr came to know Edmondson's work, and with the Starr's introduction, photographer Louise Dahl-Wolfe approached Edmondson to shoot his studio, yard, and sculptures. In 1937, after Dahl-Wolfe's employer, *Harper's Bazaar*, rejected her proposal to publish the Edmondson portfolio, she took the photos to Alfred Barr, director of the Museum of Modern Art (MoMA) in New York. Within months, Barr and his colleagues Thomas Mabry and Dorothy Miller opened an exhibit that made Edmondson the first African American artist with a solo show at America's preeminent museum for new art.

Twelve sculptures were selected by MoMA to represent Edmondson's work. Like all his sculptures, they were carved from discarded pieces of limestone, remnants of buildings and sidewalks. Working without professional tools, Edmondson had recycled and molded each stone into a simple form. With a limited range of marks and representational details, the figures conveyed a sense of fullness, gesture, vitality, and personality. Each one was distinct, whether a bird, an angel, or a woman wearing a petticoat.

As a preeminent art institution, MoMA's embrace of Edmondson had positive repercussions for a time. In 1938, Barr included Edmondson in an exhibit curated in Paris. Coverage of the MoMA show in Art Digest and Art News prompted the New Deal Works Progress Administration (WPA) art program to hire Edmondson between 1939 and 1941. Ultimately, this attention was not sustained. Edmondson's show had been one of a number that MoMA opened in the 1930s seeking to connect modern artists with principles of so-called primitive art, and exemplified in African American folk art and works by the mentally ill. Highly trained white artists might work in this "primitive" manner and be considered modernists.

But given his lack of training, expressed religiosity, and folksy manner, Edmondson faced condescension instead of acceptance. Thus, the *New York Times* embraced the "courage and directness" of the sculptures, while dismissing Edmondson himself as "simple, almost illiterate" and a "modern primitive" (*New York Times*, 9 Oct. 1937). Gradually, the international art world paid less attention to Edmondson. His art career would never bring him the sustaining economic rewards the initial acclaim might have promised.

For black art intellectuals, demonstrating equality with white peers in the modernist mainstream, or countering stereotypical depictions were the major concerns of this time (Lowery Stokes Sims in *Modernist Impulse*, p. 35). So like other self-taught artists Edmondson wasn't immediately accepted within the more elite ranks of the black arts world. Yet Edmondson continued to sculpt, stating he was unconcerned with whether the world embraced or appreciated his creations. Eventually, African Americans in the arts did embrace Edmondson. In Harlem, Edmondson was included in ALAIN LOCKE's "American Negro Art" exhibit in 1942, and in Nashville he was part of JAMES WELDON JOHNSON's "Festival of Arts" exhibit of 1948.

That year, progressive physical ailments brought an end to Edmondson's sculpting. In 1951, Edmondson's death in Nashville drew national press attention for the first time since his MoMA debut. While alive, Edmondson inspired collaborations with photographers who came to his yard and studio, including Edward Weston and Cosuelo Kanaga. He also influenced the African American painter JACOB LAWRENCE. Since the 1960s, retrospective exhibitions have prompted serious reappraisals of Edmondson's importance to art history and art making. Since Edmondson's passing, categories separating black art, folk art, American art, outsider art, African art, and primitive art have shifted. Edmondson was ultimately marginalized by old and narrow definitions.

In contrast, Edmondson's dedication to making art was generous. Recycling cast-off materials from his urban environment, he applied ordinary tools like hammers and chisels to stone. Working "stingily," as he ironically put it, he subtracted carefully to create poised and emotive figures his community would recognize and value. With resourcefulness and wit Edmondson transformed the limited means of his calling into a potent body of work.

FURTHER READING

William Edmonson's archives are at the Cheekwood Museum of Art, Nashville and at the Tennessee State Museum, Nashville.

Fuller, Edmund L. *Visions in Stone: the Sculpture of William Edmondson* (1973).

Helfenstein, Josef, Roxanne Stanulis, and Bill Traylor. *William Edmondson and the Modernist Impulse* (2004).

Thompson, Robert Farris, Bobby L. Lovett, Rusty Freeman, Judith McWillie, Grey Gundaker, and Lowery Stokes Sims. *The Art of William Edmondson* (1999).

Obituary: *New York Times*, 10 February 1951.

TODD PALMER

Edwards, Ballard Trent (1829–27 May 1881), Virginia state legislator, brick mason, plasterer, contractor, and educator, was born free in Manchester (later South Richmond), Chesterfield County, Virginia, the son of Edward Bradbury Edwards Jr. and Mary Trent Edwards. Edwards's family, of black, white, and American Indian ancestry, had been free landowners since the early 1700s. His father was a carpenter and his mother a teacher. Edwards was taught to read and write at an early age by his mother and learned the construction trades from his father. In 1850 Edwards married Sara Ann Coy, also a teacher, and together they had thirteen children.

Throughout his life Edwards was a prominent member of the historic First Baptist Church in South Richmond, which was established by free blacks as the African Baptist Church of Manchester in 1821. Edwards's family was among the founding members of the church, which his father served for twenty-six years as the first clerk. Edwards was elected as the second clerk in the history of the church at the age of seventeen and continued in this office for thirty-four years, along with his service as superintendent and teacher of the Sunday school, deacon, and choir member. Edwards's wife was a leading soprano in the church choir for over fifty years. Descendants of the Edwards family continued to hold membership in this venerable institution for nearly 200 years. The family emphasized education and service to the community, and Edwards was reared amid a level of freedom rarely found among blacks in the pre-Civil War era. As a young adult he became a successful brick mason who was highly respected in his community for his dependability and the quality of his workmanship. In keeping with his family tradition of property ownership, Edwards purchased eight lots in Manchester between 1867 and 1872 at a total cost of $665. He also opened an account with the Freedman's Bank in 1871.

Edwards was widely known as a man of compassion who was always willing to lend a helping hand to those in need. After the Civil War his family continued its service to the community when Edwards and his wife, at their own expense, opened and operated the Ballard School, where they taught hundreds of freed slaves to read and write, and the useful trade of bricklaying. He was the unanimous choice of the Republican Party as candidate to represent his district in the state legislature upon Virginia's readmission to the Union and easily won a seat in the Virginia House of Delegates in October 1869, without serious opposition. He served as a state legislator from 1870 to 1871, when he represented the counties of Chesterfield and Powhatan and the town of Manchester. During his tenure, he was appointed to the Committee on Manufactures and Mechanic Arts, in recognition of his skills in the building trades. His first act upon taking his seat in the legislature was to introduce a bill to ban segregation in public transit conveyances in the commonwealth. He also successfully crusaded for a free bridge over the James River connecting Manchester and Richmond, finding it deplorable that citizens should be required to pay a toll over the one existing bridge. This resulted in the construction of the 9th Street bridge in 1873, which continued to serve the citizens of Richmond for 100 years until it was demolished in 1973 and replaced. One of the most enduring of Edwards's accomplishments as a legislator was the role he is credited in playing in the preservation of the venerable Virginia State Capitol building. Designed by Thomas Jefferson in 1785 and completed in 1788, the building was in deplorable condition by 1870. He called for the repair of the building, and on 17 February 1870 introduced the following resolution:

> Whereas, the appearance of the capitol … is such as a great and proud state should be ashamed of: (Be it) resolved that the committee on public property enquire into the expediency of the general assembly making an appropriation … for the painting or otherwise improving the appearance of the building.

Two months later, the crowded third-floor courtroom of the capitol collapsed into the House of Delegates chamber, killing sixty-three people and injuring several hundred more. Following the capitol disaster, a cry went up across the state to tear down the historic landmark, and a bill was introduced to demolish the structure and erect an entirely new building. Edwards opposed this measure, and, according to the historian Robert W. Waitt Jr., he made an impassioned speech urging the legislators to spare and rehabilitate the landmark, pointing out that the building could be remodeled and restored for less than the cost of a new capitol. The capitol was spared and was ultimately rescued from dilapidation by appropriations allocated in 1904.

Edwards's public service did not end when he left the state legislature. For ten years he held the offices of Justice of the Peace in Manchester and Overseer of the Poor for Chesterfield County. Edwards was also active in fraternal life. He was a charter member of Hobson Lodge No. 23, F&M, and he built the first Masonic hall for the lodge. In 1871 he served as first worshipful master of his lodge and was later selected as Grand Master for the State of Virginia. Throughout his remaining years Edwards devoted his life to his extensive church work and the training of young blacks in the construction trades. He died at the age of fifty-two and was buried along with his wife in the segregated Mount Olivet portion of Maury Cemetery in Richmond.

Though a resolution introduced in the Virginia House of Delegates in 2001 to honor Ballard Trent Edwards with a bust or plaque to be placed in the chamber failed due to challenges from those who disputed his role in saving the capitol from destruction, his contributions to his state and to his people cannot be questioned. Only a short street in South Richmond, Edwards Street, and a bookmark issued by the Virginia House of Delegates exist to commemorate the man who was one of the most influential black political and inspirational leaders in Virginia during Reconstruction.

FURTHER READING

Foner, Eric. *Freedom's Lawmakers: A Directory of Black Officeholders During Reconstruction* (1996).

Jackson, Luther P. *Negro Officeholders in Virginia, 1865–1895* (1945).

Ransome, W. L. *History of the First Baptist Church and Some of Her Pastors* (1935).

Smith, Laverne Byrd. *A Comprehensive History of First Baptist Church, South Richmond, 1821–1993* (1999).

Waitt, Robert W., Jr. "Ballard Trent Edwards: Our Forgotten Statesman," *Richmond Literature and History Quarterly* 1.4 (1970).

ANDREE LAYTON ROAF

Edwards, Bernard (31 Oct. 1952–18 Apr. 1996), bass guitarist and music producer, was born in Greenville, North Carolina, and spent his formative years in Brooklyn, New York.

As an aspiring musician fresh out of high school at the beginning of the 1970s, Edwards's acquaintance with NILE RODGERS, another young New York guitarist, proved invaluable to his developing career. In 1970 the two formed the jazz, rock fusion Big Apple Band (not to be confused with Walter Murphy and the Big Apple Band) and later an all black rock band (first dubbed The Boys and later in a 1976 incarnation Allah and the Knife Wielding Punks). Although they were not the first black rockers (Jimi Hendrix, black Irishman Phil Lynott, and the protopunk Detroit band Death preceded them), Edwards and Rodgers faced a persistent bitter reality: as black men their foray into rock was not warmly received by record labels.

As performers in the 1970s and early 1980s, Edwards and Rodgers were a decade premature in breaking racial barriers, which would not fall until Michael Jackson integrated the new global phenomenon of MTV in 1983.

Undaunted by initial negative reactions to their foray into rock by the music industry, Edwards and company channeled their energies into carving something unique out of the traditional rhythms of R&B and funk that were expected of them by record companies. Along with drummer Tony Thompson, they enlisted singers Norma Jean Wright and Alfa Anderson to create the disco group Chic in New York in the summer of 1977.

The small Buddha label released the band's demo single *Dance, Dance, Dance (Yowsah, Yowsah, Yowsah)* that same year. Capitalizing on the early popularity of the disc, Atlantic quickly signed the band, rereleasing *Dance, Dance, Dance* to top ten success. Chic hurriedly composed a full eponymous album in 1978 and enjoyed a moderate hit with the song *Everybody Dance*. At the departure of Wright, who was replaced by Luci Martin, the group released *C'est Chic* in 1978. *Le Freak*, the album's first single, spent five weeks on the top of the charts and sold six million copies, making it the best-selling single in Atlantic Records' history. This was a very rare feat for a disco song—and remarkable given Atlantic's roster of artists, which included CHARLES MINGUS, JOHN COLTRANE, RAY CHARLES, ARETHA FRANKLIN, and Led Zeppelin.

The band's third album, *Risqué*, released in 1979, also went platinum, but it was released at the cusp of a dying era. The hedonistic days of disco were fleeting, yet the group's second number-one-selling single, *Good Times*, carried Edwards and Rodgers beyond the marked epoch of the discothèque, and allowed them to fulfill their dream of a new music genre by vaulting their musical influence well into the future.

Part of Chic's legacy is indebted to the fact that beneath its fluid, disco rhythms lay the foundation of serious song craft. *Good Times* was more than just a song; it was the epitaph and epitome of an era. With its cast-aside, all-troubles chorus, at first glance it's a mere party anthem, as redolent of disco as cocaine and sequined pants. Only at closer inspection does the politicized, double entendre of the lyric become apparent:

A rumor has it that it's getting late
Time marches on, you just can't wait
The clock keeps turning, why hesitate
You silly fool, you can't change your fate

At the song's 1979 release the United States was undergoing an economic recession. Indeed, as Nile Rodgers later recalled, Edwards and company turned to classic Depression era songs, which enlisted happiness in the face of despair, such as Milton Ager's *Happy Days Are Here Again*, and Al Jolson's *About a Quarter to Nine*, to draw a cheeky, yet evocative parallel between the Depression and the monetary crisis of the day ("The Pop 100: The Seventies," *Rolling Stone*, 7 Dec. 2000).

The most distinguishing feature of *Good Times* is Edwards's infectious bass line. If the birth and demise of an explosive cultural trend can be pinpointed to a moment, 1979 marks the year disco began to relinquish the pop culture crown to rap. Edwards and Rodgers, as the driving force behind Chic, were integral to this changing of the guard.

In a seminal pop culture year, rappers The Sugar Hill Gang released *Rapper's Delight*, which opened with Bernard Edwards's distinctive *Good Times* bass line. *Rapper's Delight* became the first rap song to go gold, peaking at number 36 on the U.S. pop charts and number 4 on American R&B charts. Yet The Sugar Hill Gang were merely the first in a countless list of musicians to either sample Edwards's signature bass beat outright or nod to it in the marginally altered bass progression of their own recordings. Edwards's rhythmic "walk" shapes Blondie's *Rapture* (1981), Queen's *Another One Bites the Dust* (1980), and Grand Master Flash and the Furious Five's *The Adventure of Grand Master Flash on the Wheels of Steel* (1981). *Good Times* ranks number 224 on *Rolling Stone's* list of the 500 Greatest Songs of All Time, and with a little help from Edwards, *Rapper's Delight* made number 248 on the same list.

If 1979 was the year disco died, for Edwards and Rodgers, theirs was a gilded swan song. In addition to propelling their own band to the heights of success, they made their first notable foray into production for other artists with the Sister Sledge hit *We Are Family*. This victory opened the door for production work with Diana Ross in 1980 on the smash singles *Upside Down* and *I'm Coming Out*. The duo also produced Deborah Harry's debut solo album *Koo Koo* in 1981. Another Edwards/Rodgers-produced Sister Sledge number, *He's the Greatest Dancer*, and Ross's *I'm Coming Out* would also be heavily sampled in rap.

The Chic albums *Real People* and *Believer*, released in 1980 and 1983, respectively, were not met with the same reception in sales or chart positioning as previous recordings by the band, and both Edwards and Rodgers embarked on bigger projects as producers. Indeed, it would be as writers and producers that the musical innovations of Edwards and his partner would go on to form the backbone of the new music form of rap. Edwards and Rodgers's success in producing white artists also made it more plausible for black producers to work with mainstream and white pop and rock acts. Together they produced the soundtrack for the 1982 film *Dinner for One*, and throughout the 1980s, Bernard Edwards produced songs for a range of artists including Kenny Loggins, Gladys Knight, Jody Watley, and Robert Palmer, who garnered Edwards's most notable success as a producer with the 1986 U.S. Hot 100 number one single *Addicted to Love*. Enlisted by Rodgers who was acting as producer, Edwards also played bass on Madonna's 1984 debut album, *Like a Virgin*.

Edwards's 1983 solo album *Glad to Be Here* was released without fanfare. Still thirsting for new challenges and creative outlets, Edwards joined the pop super group Power Station in 1984, along with Chic drummer Tony Thompson, guitarists John Taylor and Andy Taylor of Duran Duran, and English vocalist Robert Palmer. The group enjoyed success with the 1985 hit singles *Some Like It Hot* and *Get It On*, a remake of Marc Bolan's 1971 glam rock hit.

In 1992 Edwards reformed Chic with Rodgers and two new singers, releasing the album *Chic-ism* to mixed reviews for Warner Bros. In 1996 Rodgers was invited to Japan to be honored for his work as a producer. He called upon Edwards, guitarist Slash of Guns N' Roses, Duran Duran's Simon LeBon, the English soul singer Steve Winwood, and Sister Sledge to join him there for the performance of a career retrospective. Edwards succumbed to pneumonia in a Tokyo hotel room during the tour. He had just finished work on a new Power Station album and had been finalizing plans to tour with that group.

Edwards was survived by six children from his marriage to first wife Alexis: Bernard Jr., Portia, Michael, Mark, David, and Leah. Bernard "Focus" Edwards Jr. has produced songs for Beyoncé and Busta Rhymes.

In 2005 Chic was inducted into the Dance Music Hall of Fame. Their song, *Good Times*, was also inducted, as were Edwards and Rodgers as producers. Chic was nominated for induction into the Rock and Roll Hall of Fame in 2003, 2006, 2007, and 2008, but has yet to be officially inducted. Edwards, who played a Music Man StingRay guitar, employing his forefinger and thumb like a pick, was one of the most respected and imitated bass guitar players in popular music history. His iconic status among bass players is summarized well by John Taylor of Duran Duran: "There was tremendous power and energy in both [The Sex Pistols and Chic]. Chic had tremendous energy and power but with refinement and sophistication. It was around the time I started playing bass. ... To that point I'd had no interest in the instrument ... Bernard Edwards from Chic became the new model for me" (Malins, *Duran Duran Notorious*, 2004, p. 23).

FURTHER READING

Easlea, Daryl. *Everybody Dance: Chic and the Politics of Disco* (2004).

Stuart, Clayton. *Nile Rodgers and Bernard Edwards: Funk and Disco Grooves* (2008).

Obituaries: *Jet* 13 May 1996, vol. 89, no. 26, 60; *Village Voice*, 7 May 1996.

CAMILLE A. COLLINS

Edwards, Donna (28 June 1958–), U.S. congresswoman, was born Donna F. Edwards in Yanceyville, North Carolina, one of six children of John Edwards, an officer in the Air Force, and Mary Edwards who cared for the children. Edwards grew up in a military family and moved often, traveling throughout the United States and around the world. When she

Donna Edwards, Congresswoman, in an official photo.

was a child she had aspirations of becoming president of the United States. Edwards was a teenager when her oldest brother, John, enlisted in the Air Force during the height of the war in Vietnam. When she graduated from high school she was presented with the opportunity to enroll in the first class to admit females at the Air Force Academy; however, she chose instead to pursue an undergraduate education at Wake Forest University in North Carolina, where she was one of six African American women in her freshman class. In 1980 Edwards earned a Bachelor of Arts degree in English and Spanish from Wake Forest; she married a classmate and moved to Silver Spring, Maryland, to work for Lockheed Corporation at Goddard Space Flight Center in Greenbelt, Maryland. As part of the Spacelab program, she was a systems engineer, performing tests and assisting to translate projects. In 1986, after the Space Shuttle Challenger disaster that claimed the lives of crew members including Ronald McNair, the second African American in space, Edwards decided to attend the Franklin Pierce Law Center in New Hampshire. In 1989 she earned a juris doctorate from Franklin Pierce, moved to Fort Washington, Maryland, and began work as a DC Superior Court Judge clerk. Edwards now focused on legal matters of public interest.

In 1995 Edwards cofounded the National Network to End Domestic Violence, a coalition of state organizations with over two thousand member organizations providing advocacy, research, fund-raising, legal support, and programs for battered women. She joined the nonprofit organization Public Citizen as a lobbyist and later became executive director for the Center for a New Democracy. In 2000 Edwards was appointed executive director of the Arca Foundation, an organization for social equality and justice through public policy. Having served the public on issues that affected both local and national policy as an activist and lawyer, Edwards decided to run for political office and in 2006 entered the Maryland Democratic Primary against the seven-term congressional incumbent Albert Wynn. Edwards was liberal by comparison to Wynn, who had been dubbed conservative by many Democrats for supporting the 2002 Iraq War Resolution and for supporting the 2005 Bankruptcy Bill, which would make it difficult for debtors to file bankruptcy. She was endorsed in the 2006 primary by the *Washington Post* on 30 August. On 12 September 2006, Edwards lost the election, garnering 46.4 percent of the vote compared to the 49.7 percent won by Wynn. In 2008 Edwards again challenged Wynn. She confronted Wynn for his acceptance of corporate donations. Wynn in turn reminded Edwards of her own participation in corporate endeavors as the executive director of Arca Foundation, with money in gas and oil. On 12 February 2008, Edwards won the congressional seat with 60 percent of the vote compared to only 35 percent gained by Wynn. Wynn announced his retirement from office after the primary election votes had been cast; this earned Edwards the Democratic nomination in a special election to serve out the last six months of his term beginning 17 June 2008. After being endorsed with near unanimity by local Democratic Party officials, Edwards won the special election in June by 81 percent of the vote against the Republican candidate, Peter James, and the Libertarian candidate, Thibeaux Lincecum. In November 2008, Edwards won her first full-term office with 85 percent of the vote and the designation as the first African American woman to represent Maryland in the United States Congress.

On 27 April 2009 Edwards was one of several U.S. lawmakers—including representatives John Lewis of Georgia and Lynn Woosley of California—arrested outside of the Sudan embassy in Washington, D.C., in a protest against genocide in Darfur. Edwards's congressional committee assignments have included the Committee on Science and Technology; subcommittees on Space and Aeronautics and Technology and Innovation; the Committee on Transportation and Infrastructure, subcommittees on Economic Development; Public Buildings and Emergency Management; Highways and Transit; and Water Resources and Environment.

In 1989 Edwards became the mother of a son, Jared.

FURTHER READING

Helderman, Rosalind S., and William Wan, M.D. "Challenger Edwards Wins Stunning Victory over Long-Time Incumbent Wynn." *Washington Post*, 13 Feb. 2008.

Labbe'-Dubose, Theola, and John Wagner. "More Than 100 Arrested in Series of Protests." *Washington Post*, 28 Apr. 2009.

SAFIYA DALILAH HOSKINS

Edwards, Gaston Alonzo (12 Apr. 1879–5 Oct. 1943), architect, teacher, and education administrator, was born in Belvoir, Chatham County, North Carolina, one of six children of William Gaston Snipes, a white farmer, and Mary Foushee Edwards, a black homemaker and farm worker. Some uncertainty exists as to Edwards's precise year of birth, with contradictory U.S. Census records allowing for a birth date sometime between 1874 and 1879. Census records show that his parents were legally registered as living side by side on different land parcels, because interracial marriage was illegal in North Carolina during this time. Edwards's earliest education was given at home and at local schools, and he worked during the evenings as a barber and a farmhand to help support the family.

Edwards earned enough money to attend Agricultural & Mechanical College for the Colored Race (now known as North Carolina A&T State University) at Greensboro in 1896. After amassing sufficient funds to attend graduate classes, he was accepted at Cornell University in Ithaca, New York, in 1899 to take "short-term courses," which were offered in the summer and winter terms. Edwards attended classes from 1899 through 1908, after which he returned to North Carolina to begin work as a practicing architect. He concurrently accepted a position at the Raleigh Institute for the Colored Deaf, Dumb, and Blind, where he created an industrial arts program.

Edwards was hired in 1908 by Shaw University in Raleigh, North Carolina, to teach natural science and building trade classes. He advanced to the position of supervisor of the industrial department while continuing to work as a professional architect, at the same time earning the first Master of Science degree awarded by his alma mater in Greensboro on 27 May 1909.

Although many of the buildings Edwards designed were created for organizations outside his home state, such as the American Baptist Home Mission Society in New York City, he also designed community and many university structures in North Carolina. These included the Leonard Medical School Hospital on the Shaw University campus in 1910 (known today as Tyler Hall) and the Masonic Temple Building located nearby at 427 South Blount Street in Raleigh in 1907. The temple originally served as home to the Widow's Son Lodge No. 4 and the Excelsior Lodge No. 21 of the Free and Accepted Masons.

During his tenure at Shaw University, Edwards met Catherine Ruth Norris, a music student, and the couple married on 1 September 1909. They subsequently had five children, one of whom, daughter Hazel, went on to marry noted photojournalist Alex Rivera. In 1912 Edwards was appointed by North Carolina governor Coleman Livingston Blease to serve as a delegate to the Negro National Education Congress, which had first been organized in 1909. The Congress focused on promoting secondary and industrial schools, rather than higher education, for African Americans.

North Carolina instituted licensure requirements for architects in 1915. The process included an examination, issuance of a license, and registration requirements for all architects practicing in the state. Edwards passed the required exam and was issued a license on 22 July 1915, becoming the only black architect on the state rolls. His business card read, "Never build without a plan, consult G. A. Edwards—the only Negro licensed to do business in North Carolina."

Upon Edwards's appointment to the presidency of Kittrell College in 1917, he and his family moved to Vance County, North Carolina. First established in 1886 and primarily funded by the African Methodist Episcopal Conference of North Carolina, Maryland, and Virginia, Kittrell had yet to develop a formal industrial arts program. Edwards oversaw the physical development of the college, which included the construction of numerous buildings on 216 acres of land. When he arrived, the school was conducting elementary and high school classes, but by the end of his tenure, its coursework and two-year degree programs were recognized as college-level instruction. On 23 May 1920 Edwards was given an honorary Master of Arts degree by Allen University of Columbia, South Carolina.

Edwards opened a full-time architecture practice in Durham in 1929, but his timing was poor. Because of the encroachment of the Great Depression, Edwards was subsequently forced to accept a position in Durham as principal of Lyon Park Elementary School, later moving to a similar position at Whitted School in the same city. Concurrent with both jobs, he worked as a part-time architect designing residential houses. Even though Edwards's practice did receive commissions, his daughter, Hazel Ruth Edwards, reported that he was often consulted but rarely listed as the architect of record because of legal discrimination against black professionals.

Edwards participated in Durham community affairs and served on boards of the Banker's Fire Insurance Company, Southern Fidelity Insurance Company, and the Mechanics & Farmers Bank. He served actively on the Durham Committee of Negro Affairs, whose members established the strongest and most effective black voting rights organization in the pre-Civil Rights era South and played a leading role in challenging segregation and racism throughout North Carolina.

Edwards died of a heart attack in his family home in Durham.

FURTHER READING

Caldwell, A. B. *History of the American Negro and His Institutions* (1917 and 1921).

Camp, Norman C. "Kittrell College Systems Approach," *Community and Junior College Journal* vol. 44, no. 7, 1074, pp. 16–17.

Wilson, Dreck Spurlock, ed. "Gaston Alonzo Edwards," in *African-American Architects: A Biographical Dictionary* (2004).

DAVID BORSVOLD

Edwards, Harry (22 Nov. 1942–), sociologist, civil rights activist, and author, was born in East St. Louis, Illinois, the eldest son of Adelaide Cruise, a homemaker, and Harry Edwards, a factory worker. Growing up in the poor, predominantly black neighborhood of Southend, Edwards and his seven brothers and sisters suffered from inadequate housing, malnutrition, and absentee parents. On two separate occasions, his mother left the family without warning, and his father spent more time at work at the chemical and defense plant that were his two main places of employment and at a local saloon than he did at home. Edwards attended two segregated elementary schools, Denverside and Dunbar, alongside illiterate adults who wanted to learn how to read. Many of his teachers remembered the 1917 race riots in East St. Louis, and they were the first to instill in him the importance of learning African American history. In 1954, the same year as the U.S. Supreme Court's decision in *Brown v. Board of Education*, Edwards attended Hughes-Quinn Junior High School and became involved in organized sports. After graduating and establishing himself as a star athlete, Edwards attended the newly integrated East St. Louis High School and competed in football, basketball, and track and field as a discus thrower. During his time at East St. Louis, Edwards witnessed little positive interaction between black and white students, though he did notice that the black students often fell victim to institutionalized racism and violence.

Following his graduation from East St. Louis, Edwards moved to California and enrolled in Fresno City College. He promptly joined the college's track team and within the year had set new school, conference, state, and national junior college records in the discus throw. He accepted an athletic scholarship from San Jose State College (later San Jose University), nicknamed Speed City because of the high number of Olympic athletes it produced. Fewer than sixty African Americans attended the college in 1960, and its fraternities, sororities, and housing complexes completely excluded blacks. As a sociology major, Edwards received a Woodrow Wilson Fellowship and attended graduate school at Cornell University in Ithaca, New York, in the fall of 1964. On Sunday mornings, Edwards would take a bus to New York City to hear MALCOLM X speak. The assassination of Malcolm X and the Watts riots of 1965 had a profound effect on Edwards and forced him to reevaluate his life. In 1966 he returned to California to serve as a researcher for the Santa Clara County Economic Opportunity Commission, and he started a position as a half-time instructor in sociology at San Jose State.

One year later Edwards and a student named Ken Noel approached the administration of SJSC with a series of complaints about the treatment of black students on campus and in the city of San Jose. Their petition demanded that the college integrate all fraternities, sororities, housing facilities, and organizations and make a better effort to recruit minority students. Calling his organization the United Black Students Association (UBSA), Edwards threatened to create a boycott among SJSC's and Texas-El Paso's football players in order to prevent the playing of SJSC's opening football game in the event the college failed to meet his demands. The administration of SJSC eventually agreed to meet the conditions of UBSA but not before it had canceled the game, fearing violence among white and black spectators. Following the SJSC protest movement, Edwards became a national civil rights figure. Between 1967 and 1970 he delivered speeches on more than two hundred college campuses, and SJSC had to move the classes taught by Edwards to a larger auditorium to accommodate student enrollment. The FBI began conducting surveillance on Edwards and placed his name on its "Rabble Rousers Index," a catalog of individuals deemed to be racial agitators or militants.

Edwards gained fame for his decision in October 1967 to lead a movement that proposed a boycott of black athletes of the 1968 Olympic Games in Mexico City. His new organization, the Olympic Project for Human Rights (OPHR), drafted a resolution stating that the U.S. government regarded African Americans as second-class citizens. The OPHR had four goals: to protest the violation of human rights in the United States, to show how the United States exploited black athletes and used them as propaganda tools, to forge a sense of political responsibility among African American students, and to spread awareness in the black community about the social and economic pitfalls of organized sports for black athletes. A number of prominent black athletes and activists supported the boycott movement. The UCLA basketball star Lew Alcindor, who later changed his name to Kareem Abdul-Jabbar, and the Boston Celtics great Bill Russell spoke on behalf of the OPHR, and Martin Luther King Jr., Louis Lomax, and CORE director Floyd McKissick held a press conference to voice their support for Edwards. The sports establishment, which included team owners, writers, organizers, coaches, and players, responded with their own campaign to discredit Edwards. African American star athletes like the sprinter Jesse Owens and the baseball player Jackie Robinson also spoke out against the boycott, believing that disrupting the Olympics was the wrong form of protest. Despite its partial failure, the movement did make a splash in Mexico City, when on 16 October 1968 the black sprinters Tommie Smith and John Carlos raised their black-gloved fists in a salute of black power on the victory podium following the 200-meter dash. The International Olympic Committee president Avery Brundage responded by banning Smith and Carlos from the Olympic Village and from amateur sports competition from that point on.

After the Olympic boycott movement, Edwards remained a prominent black activist. He returned to Cornell in 1968 to pursue a doctorate in sociology and published two books during the 1968–1969 academic year, *Revolt of the Black Athlete* (1969) and *Black Students* (1970). In 1970 he married the activist Sandra Boze and accepted a position to teach in the sociology department at the University of California at Berkeley. Between 1971 and 1972 Edwards organized the first section on the sociology of sport for the American Sociological Association, and in 1973 Dorsey Press published his book *Sociology of Sport*. A leading authority on sport and sociology, Edwards published articles in *The Black Scholar*, *Intellectual Digest*, and *Psychology Today*. In 1987 the commissioner of baseball Peter Ueberroth hired Edwards to help Major League Baseball promote the hiring of more minorities as managers, general managers, and administrators. He served as a consultant to the San Francisco 49ers football team and Golden State Warriors basketball team and continued to give public lectures across the country.

FURTHER READING

Edwards, Harry. *The Struggle That Must Be: An Autobiography* (1980).

Bass, Amy. *Not the Triumph but the Struggle: The 1968 Olympics and the Making of the Black Athlete* (2002).

Hartmann, Douglas. *Race, Culture, and the Revolt of the Black Athlete: The 1968 Olympic Protests and Their Aftermath* (2003).

ERIC ALLEN HALL

Edwards, Harry Thomas (3 Nov. 1940–), federal judge, was born in New York City. Raised by his mother, Arline Ross, a psychiatric social worker, and his father, George F. Edwards, an accountant and state legislator, Edwards enjoyed a very close relationship with his maternal grandfather, a tax attorney, and two uncles who also were lawyers. His decision to attend law school after graduating with a B.S. degree from Cornell University in 1962 was due to his admiration of his grandfather and encouragement from his two uncles.

Harry Thomas Edwards, Chief Justice of the United States Court of Appeals, delivering the commencement address at Washington and Lee's Law School graduation, 8 May 2004. (AP Images.)

In 1962 Edwards entered the University of Michigan Law School, where he achieved a stellar academic record. He served as an editor of the *Michigan Law Review*, was selected for membership in the Order of the Coif, a legal honor society reserved for the top 5 percent of students, and received American Jurisprudence Awards for outstanding performance in labor law and administrative law. As a result of this record, Edwards earned a J.D. degree with distinction in 1965.

Edwards began his professional career as an associate attorney with the Chicago firm of Seyfarth, Shaw, Fairweather, and Geraldson, where he practiced law in the labor department from 1965 to 1970. Leaving the firm in 1970 to begin a teaching career at the University of Michigan Law School, he served as an associate professor of law from 1970 to 1973, and later as professor of law from 1973 to 1975. From January to June 1974 he was a visiting professor at the Free University of Brussels, participating in the Program for International Legal Cooperation. In 1975 Edwards began teaching at Harvard, where in 1976 he became only the third African American awarded tenure at Harvard Law School. While at Harvard, Edwards taught labor law, collective bargaining and labor arbitration, and negotiation and labor-relations law in the public sector. In 1977 Edwards rejoined the law faculty at the University of Michigan Law School. During his time at the university, Edwards also served as a member and then chair of the board of directors of AMTRAK, the largest passenger railroad company in the United States.

In 1980 President Jimmy Carter appointed Edwards to the U.S. Court of Appeals for the District of Columbia, the most influential federal appeals court in the nation. Since joining the bench, Edwards wrote hundreds of notable opinions, including decisions involving issues such as labor and employment, antitrust, administrative, tax, constitutional, civil rights, and criminal law. In his twenty-two years on the bench, Edwards developed a reputation for meticulous and thorough preparation for oral argument, as well as superbly crafted, tightly organized, and carefully annotated opinions.

In December 1982 Edwards was recognized by the *American Lawyer* as an Outstanding Performer in the legal profession for his judicial opinions in the area of labor law, and he continued to write important opinions in labor law in the 1990s. One such opinion was *Association of Flight Attendants, AFL CIO v. USAir, Inc.* (1994), where the court was faced with the question of whether flight attendants employed by an airline that had been purchased by USAir were subject to the airline's collective-bargaining agreement with its own flight attendants. In his opinion, Edwards held that USAir's collective bargaining agreement did not apply to the new flight attendants because a "mere change in union representative had no effect on the status quo applicable to shuttle flight attendants." Thus the newly acquired flight attendants were able to adhere to the terms of their premerger collective bargaining agreement.

Edwards has been recognized for a series of articles regarding legal teaching and scholarship. In "The Growing Disjunction between Legal Education and the Legal Profession," in *Michigan Law Review*, vol. 91 (1) (1992), he argues that law schools are failing to educate students adequately by overemphasizing abstract theory at the expense of practical scholarship and pedagogy and that law firms are failing to ensure that lawyers practice law in an ethical manner. The article sparked a national debate among legal scholars and practitioners on the proper method of legal teaching and reform in law schools and law firms. Another of his articles, "The Effects of Collegiality on Judicial Decision Making," in *Pennsylvania Law Review*, vol. 151 (2003), explains how appellate judges decide cases. Edwards specifically refutes the common claim that the personal ideologies and political leanings of the judges on the District of Columbia Circuit are deciding factors in the ultimate holdings of the court. Despite his judicial duties, Edwards has also continued to influence students by teaching on a part-time basis at a number of law schools, including Harvard, Michigan, Pennsylvania, Georgetown, Duke, and New York University. Over the course of his teaching and judicial career, Edwards has found time to coauthor four critically acclaimed books: *Labor Relations Law in the Public Sector* (3d edition 1985), *The Lawyer as a Negotiator* (1977), *Collective Bargaining and Labor Arbitration* (1979), and *Higher Education and the Law* (1979, annual supplements 1980–1983). He has also published numerous articles and pamphlets concerning issues in labor law, equal-employment opportunity, labor arbitration, higher education, alternative-dispute resolution, federalism, judicial process and administration, and comparative law.

Edwards became chief judge of the District of Columbia Circuit in 1994. During his seven-year stint as chief judge, he directed numerous automation initiatives at the court of appeals, oversaw a complete reorganization of the clerk's office and legal division, implemented case management programs that helped to reduce the court's case backlog and disposition times, and successfully pursued congressional support for the construction of an annex to the courthouse building. He also established programs to enhance communications with the lawyers who practice before the court, and received high praise from members of the bench, bar, and press for fostering collegial relations among the members of the ideologically divided court. In 2000–2001 Edwards presided over the court's hearings in *United States v. Microsoft*, the largest antitrust case in U.S. history. In this case, the court reviewed the legal conclusions regarding three alleged antitrust violations and the resulting remedial order imposed on Microsoft by the United States District Court for the District of Columbia. Edwards participated in the court's *per curiam* opinion that affirmed in part and reversed in part the district court's judgment that Microsoft violated section 2 of the Sherman Act.

In July 1996 the *American Lawyer* and the *Washington Legal Times* published personal profiles of Edwards, applauding his efforts in managing the District of Columbia Circuit as chief judge and in helping to bring collegiality to the court. Edwards stepped down from his position as chief judge in July 2001.

Edwards has served on numerous boards, including the board of directors of the National Institute for Dispute Resolution, the executive committee of the Order of the Coif, the executive committee of the Association of American Law Schools, and the National Academy of Arbitrators (as vice president). His numerous awards include the Society of American Law Teachers Award, recognizing distinguished contributions to teaching and public service; the Whitney North Seymour Medal, presented by the American Arbitration Association for outstanding contributions; the 2001 Judicial Honoree Award presented by the Bar Association of the District of Columbia, recognizing significant contributions in the field of law; and eleven honorary J.D. degrees. He was a member of the American Law Institute, the American Judicature Society, and the American Bar Foundation. Edwards served as a teacher/mentor at the Unique Learning Center in Washington, D.C., a volunteer program established to assist disadvantaged inner-city youth. Married to Pamela Carrington-Edwards in 2000, Edwards has two children from a previous marriage to Ila Hayes Edwards.

Edwards begins his seminal article in the *Michigan Law Review* on legal education with a quotation from Felix Frankfurter, the former associate judge on the U.S. Supreme Court: "In the last analysis, the law is what the lawyers are," but this could also aptly apply to Edwards's professional career, for in the last analysis, the laws made by Edwards are what he is and what his life represents—a shining example of professionalism.

FURTHER READING

Edwards's papers have not been archived. Personal profiles of Edwards can be found in the July 1996 editions of the *American Lawyer* and *The Washington Legal Times*.

F. MICHAEL HIGGINBOTHAM

Edwards, Honeyboy (28 June 1915–29 Aug. 2011), blues singer and guitarist, was born David Edwards in Shaw, Mississippi, the eldest of the four children of Henry Edwards and Pearl Phillips, sharecroppers. Henry had five children from a previous marriage, and after his first wife died, he married Pearl, who helped raise his two daughters while his three sons lived in Vicksburg. David's older half-sister, Lessie, started calling him "Honey" and "Honeyboy" when he was taking his first steps as a toddler, and the name stuck.

Sharecropping was a difficult way of life, offering little more than bare subsistence and perpetual debt. In the rainy winter of 1927 the Mississippi River broke through the levees and flooded much of the Delta, as recounted in the famous blues "High Water Everywhere" by CHARLEY PATTON. No crops were planted that year, and families were moved to higher ground to live in boxcars and eat in mess halls. Clothes were donated from around the nation, and food and care were administered by the Red Cross. Honey's mother was pregnant and remained behind in a hotel in Shaw. She became ill, and both she and the baby died. The next year, Honey's older sister Lessie died of pneumonia. A few years later, his other older sister, Blanche, was murdered by her husband. Honey left school at age twelve.

Honey's father had twice remarried by 1929, when the family moved to the Wildwood Plantation in Greenwood, and there was a record cotton crop that year. Henry Edwards managed some real profit for a change, and he bought Honey a suit and, more significantly, a guitar. Henry played guitar and violin himself, and he encouraged Honey to learn standard guitar tuning in addition to the open tunings popular in the Delta, so that he could accompany other musicians, and he taught Honey to play such traditional songs as "STAGOLEE" and "John Henry." After his sister Blanche bought a phonograph, Honey spent 1928 and 1929 soaking in the new and exciting sound of BLIND LEMON JEFFERSON.

Honey met the blues singer and guitarist Tommy McClennan on the Wildwood Plantation when McClennan came to play at a dance. In addition TOMMY JOHNSON had moved to the area to pick cotton and Honey went to hear him sing and play guitar. Johnson was an accomplished guitarist, and Honey learned a lot by watching him. He also first met Rice Miller (SONNY BOY WILLIAMSON II) in 1929 and was impressed by his harmonica playing.

But the Depression followed soon after, and conditions got much worse in the Delta. Honey's family just managed to scrape by, hunting and foraging for food. Times were rough and Honey witnessed the injustice heaped upon black people by whites, as well as violence within the black community itself. He spent a lot of time with Tommy McClennan and the singer and guitarist Robert Petway, learning some of the duo's repertoire, including "Catfish Blues." He was also exposed to the influential bluesman Kokomo Arnold, as well as to RUBIN LACY, whose "Hambone and Gravy Blues" was popular on the jukeboxes.

In 1931 Honey was sixteen and had no taste for toiling in the fields. He started hoboing on freight trains and had enough ability as a singer and guitar player to get by playing on the street. He had to be careful so the railroad police and local sheriffs would not charge him with trespassing or vagrancy, though he was once caught and put on a county farm for two months.

Thanks in no small part to his frequent exposure to bluesmen passing through the region, Edwards developed considerable skill at an early age. In 1932 BIG JOE WILLIAMS came to the area, and Edwards became smitten with his driving blues and custom nine-string guitar. Williams took a liking to the seventeen-year-old and offered to teach him. The pair played together and hoboed on freight trains, Williams womanizing and drinking heavily but teaching Edwards how to take care of himself and providing him the wherewithal to stay out of the fields. Typically, they would go into a town and find a spot on a street corner to sing and play for dimes and nickels. On Saturdays many people would come into town for groceries after working all week in the fields. Playing all afternoon near the grocery store the two musicians would end the day at a juke joint or fish fry in the country or a barrel house or brothel in the city.

Edwards traveled throughout the Delta and frequently went to New Orleans. Along the way he learned to roll dice, a skill that provided him with as much money as his music did. Determined to stay out of the fields Edwards now had three ways of getting by: music, gambling, and the charity of the female admirers he met in his travels.

Honeyboy was adept at many different musical styles. With the knowledge his father had passed on, he could play traditional tunes in ensembles similar to the Memphis Jug Band as well as the solo Delta styles, including slide guitar. In his travels he met just about every bluesman of note. In 1935 he connected with the harmonica player BIG WALTER HORTON, whom he met in Memphis. The young men pooled their talents and their earnings. Edwards met Charlie Patton, SON HOUSE, WILLIE BROWN, and HOWLIN' WOLF and took it all in. In 1937 he met ROBERT JOHNSON, who though heavily influenced by Son House, Kokomo Arnold, and Skip James had ushered in a newer, more modern type of blues. Johnson had recorded songs like "Terraplane Blues" that were enjoying popularity throughout the region. In addition Johnson was dating Edwards's cousin, Willie Mae Powell, who was immortalized in the classic "Love in Vain."

Edwards continued his travels and hustling throughout the South and often performed with harmonica players, including Little Walter Jacobs. He met and played with Elmore James and Robert Nighthawk and knew the great barrelhouse pianists, Sunnyland Slim and Memphis Slim. In 1942 the folklorist Alan Lomax recorded Honeyboy Edwards for the Library of Congress. He recorded seventeen songs in ninety minutes, including "Stagolee," "Just a Spoonful," and "Worried Life Blues," until the session was interrupted by a violent storm. Edwards was paid twenty dollars, the most money he had ever made at one time. Though not highly original, this collection of songs displays Edwards's versatility and proficiency as a guitarist, singer, and harmonica player.

In 1945 Honeyboy and the harmonica player Little Walter Jacobs went to Chicago and played at the famous open air market on Maxwell Street. Chicago was booming, and Maxwell Street was a busy bazaar where many bluesmen played beside the vendors. The club scene was beginning to explode, and by the late 1940s and through the early 1960s Chicago had the most active blues market in the country. Artists such as Muddy Waters, Howlin' Wolf, Elmore James, Little Walter, and Sonny Boy Williamson II were big stars there, playing their electric blues for the thousands of migrants from the Delta. Little Walter stayed in Chicago, but Honeyboy continued to St. Louis, Helena, and Memphis.

In 1947 Honey met his future wife Bessie in Helena, Arkansas. They were inseparable and traveled the South together from Texas to Florida, then north to Memphis and back again, as Edwards gambled and played to make money. They married in 1952, and their son David was born that year.

Edwards recorded four songs for Artist Records in Houston in 1951. Two songs, "Build Myself a Cave" and "Who May Your Regular Be" were issued that year. The former was originally sung by Willie Love over the air on KFFA's famous *King Biscuit Time* radio show. Edwards heard it and was the first to record it. The second song was Edwards's original composition. The Artist label was owned by Miss Lola Anne Collum, who had had earlier success with Lightnin' Hopkins, and she teamed Edwards with the pianist "Thunder" Smith for these recordings. Collum traveled with Edwards to help get his records on jukeboxes and help him find gigs. He later regretted leaving her label for no good reason other than his need to keep moving on. Edwards claimed he later went to Chicago to audition for Chess Records but was passed over because his slide guitar playing was too similar to that of Muddy Waters's. Edwards also claimed he had recorded the Robert Johnson song "Sweet Home Chicago" for Sam Phillips's Sun Records label in Memphis but for some reason Phillips released it under the name of the singer and pianist Albert Joiner. Edwards also recorded for Don Robey's Peacock label, but was not open to artistic direction and later admitted that his cantankerous attitude undermined his own interests.

After drifting so long throughout the South, Edwards and his wife moved to Chicago in 1956 at the urging of his siblings, who had already settled there. Edwards fell in once more with his old partner Walter Horton and also filled in with Elmore James, Junior Wells, and Magic Sam. Chicago was still booming, and musicians could find work every day of the week.

After the birth of his daughter Betty Jean, Edwards played less, got a full-time job, and enjoyed being close to his extended family. He became reacquainted with Tommy McLennan, but the latter died of alcoholism in 1962. Little Walter, too, had substance abuse problems that ruined his career, and he died after a fight in 1968 at the age of thirty-eight.

By the 1960s—and with the emergence of soul music—blues music was losing its popularity among African Americans. At the same time, however, blues music was becoming increasingly popular among white American and European audiences. Edwards was invited to play in Vienna and flew to Europe for the first time in 1968. When he returned he lost his job as a security guard and went back to playing his guitar full time. In 1969 he played on the "Fleetwood Mac in Chicago" album, in a session set up at Chess studios by Willie Dixon.

Edwards's wife died in 1972, and he never remarried. He traveled around the world, playing and singing his blues in clubs, concert halls, and festivals. Too busy with travel and work, he never focused on song writing or recording and it may be that his true mastery lies in his prodigious and accurate memory, which made him a living encyclopedia of the blues throughout much of the twentieth century. He died in Chicago at the age of 96.

FURTHER READING

Edwards, David. "Honeyboy," in *The World Don't Owe Me Nothing*, as told to Janis Morrison and Michael Robert Frank (1997).

Palmer, Robert. *Deep Blues* (1981).

DISCOGRAPHY

Delta Bluesman (Earwig 4922CD).

Leadbitter, Mike, and Neil Slaven. *Blues Records 1943–1966* (1968).

MARK S. MAULUCCI

Edwards, James (6 Mar. 1918–4 Jan. 1970), radio, stage, and screen actor, was born in Muncie, Indiana, and raised in Hammond and, later, Anderson, Indiana. He was the eldest of nine children born to James Valley Edwards, a laborer, and Anna M. Johnson, a domestic (she would earn a degree in theology in 1949). He graduated from Anderson High School, and after a brief career as a prizefighter, earned a bachelor's degree in psychology from Knoxville College in Tennessee in 1938. He was employed for a time in the department of industrial personnel at the Calumet Steel Mill and also worked for two years as a district representative for the War Production Board.

Edwards either enlisted or was drafted (his service records were later lost in a fire) in the U.S. Army sometime around 1944, starting as a private in the all-black 92nd Infantry Division of the 370th Infantry Regiment. Commissioned as a 2nd lieutenant, he was later 1st lieutenant and assigned to the Signal Corps. While still on active duty he was severely injured in a car accident. His recovery was long, and he endured a number of surgeries required to rebuild his face and vocal cords. To bolster his patient's confidence as his scars healed, a doctor suggested that he enroll in nearby Northwestern University, where he took classes in speech and drama and appeared in University Theatre productions of *Death Takes a Holiday*, *The Little Foxes*, and *The Petrified Forest*.

By 1948, after taking roles in a number of small theater productions around Chicago, Edwards earned a part in the touring company of the Broadway production of the Arnaud d'Usseau and James Gow play *Deep Are the Roots*, a social drama about a postwar southern family. Edwards portrayed Brett Charles, a black soldier who returns to his roots after having served as a decorated army officer. The play, with themes of race and interracial love, earned positive reviews for its honest exploration of postwar America's changing social landscape.

With the accolades received for his performance in *Deep Are the Roots*, Edwards made his move to film, first appearing in a nonspeaking role in *Manhandled* (1949). Following this he appeared as the boxer Luther Hawkins in the 1949 film noir *The Set-Up*. It would be his appearance that same year in the Stanley Kramer production of *Home of the Brave*, however, that would establish Edwards's position in the history of African Americans in film.

The film script for *Home of the Brave* was based on the Arthur Laurents's stage play, which dealt with anti-Semitism; in the motion picture, this theme was changed to racial prejudice. Edwards portrayed the character Peter Moss, a black soldier on duty in the Pacific who succumbs psychologically to the toll of bigotry. He is the only black soldier in his squad, which also includes a white soldier whose hatred of blacks is blatant. After surviving a brutal enemy attack that takes the life of his friend, Finchy Moss, Moss finds that he cannot walk. Though he shows no apparent wounds, he must be carried to the aid station; his paralysis is psychosomatic. Moss's story is told in flashback to the army psychiatrist assigned to rehabilitate him and to convince Moss that he need not be ashamed for being glad that though his friend was killed, he is still alive. The doctor proposes to "cure" Moss of his sensitivity to being "different" and therefore release him from the detrimental effect that racism has had upon his psyche.

Though made on a low budget, *Home of the Brave*, with its taboo subject matter, exerted a strong effect upon postwar audiences of all colors. The film received nearly universal praise from the black and mainstream press and would become the most talked-about film of 1949. *Home of the Brave* was the first Hollywood production to address, in striking fashion, America's urgent need to confront what was then called "the Negro problem."

Edwards appeared in other films that explored America's race problems, such as *Bright Victory* (1951), where a blinded soldier rejects Edwards's character's friendship after learning he is black, and *Night of the Quarter Moon* (1959). Edwards played a soldier or sailor in many feature films and television shows as well, including the emotionally riveting Korean War film classic *The Steel Helmet* (1951), *The Caine Mutiny* (1954), *Men at War* (1957), *Battle Hymn* (1957), *Blood and Steel* (1959), *Pork Chop Hill* (1959), and the television shows *Navy Log*

(1955), the *TV Reader's Digest* production of "Mr. Pak Takes Over" (1955), and the *Zane Grey Theatre* production of "Mission" (1959). In 1970 he was cast as a sergeant who is assigned as a personal aide to General George Patton in the 1970 motion picture *Patton*, a picture he would not live to see released.

A popular figure throughout his career, Edwards was a busy professional whose activities included performances on local and national radio programs and stints as a director and producer of stage plays. He was also a screenwriter who developed film scripts for Universal-International in the mid 1950s. In 1958 he received a credit for his conception of the story for the *Westinghouse Desilu Playhouse* production of the teleplay "Silent Thunder" (1958).

Edwards militantly refused to accept any acting role that he considered demeaning. His postwar portrayals of characters with intellect, aspiration, and insight were a counterstatement to depictions of black people as grinning comics and mindless servants, and his performances helped change commonly-held misconceptions about African American life and culture. Edwards's success as an actor—indeed, his very appearance in film and on television—ushered in new hope for postwar African Americans buoyed by the civil rights gains of the war years.

FURTHER READING

Bogel, Donald. *Bright Boulevards, Bold Dreams: The Story of Black Hollywood* (2005).

MacDonald, J. Fred. *Blacks and White TV: African Americans in Television Since 1948* (1992).

Obituaries: *New York Times* and *Los Angeles Sentinel*, 8 Jan. 1970.

PAMALA S. DEANE

Edwards, Jodie "Butterbeans" (19 July 1898?–28 Oct. 1967), comedian, was born Jodie Edwards in Marietta, Georgia. Little is known about his early life, including his exact birth date, which has been listed as both 1898 and 1895. It is believed that Edwards began performing professionally in carnivals at age twelve with the Moss Brothers Carnival doing minstrel routines.

In 1915 Edwards met Susie Hawthorne, who later became his wife, while they were both working for the *Smart Set* variety show, which was run by MA RAINEY and performed out of a tent. In 1916 the pair left the show and set off on their own, originally as a dance act. Soon they added comic banter in between their dances. In 1917 they left *Smart Set* for good and went off on their own as a musical comedy team.

In May 1917 Edwards and Hawthorne were married on stage as a publicity stunt in either Philadelphia, Pennsylvania, or Greenville, South Carolina (or perhaps in both places or several places). Though they originally "married" as a show business stunt, they either "really" married at some point or simply counted an onstage marriage as a real one. At any rate, they remained by all accounts a loving couple (despite making their living from sometimes hostile onstage bickering) until Susie's death on 7 December 1963.

Their mock-bickering routine, later expanded and perfected, was originally gleaned from an earlier couple. In 1917 they joined "Stringbeans and Sweetie Mae," a popular husband and wife comedy duo. Mel Watkins claims that Edwards and Hawthorne, now calling themselves "Butterbeans and Susie," appropriated the routine of Stringbeans and Sweetie Mae upon the death of Butler "Stringbeans" May (or Budd "Stringbeans" LeMay) a few months after the two couples started performing together. Many sources report that the mock-married-couple-argument routine, which Butterbeans and Susie made famous, later became the basis of the famous routine of George Burns and Gracie Allen, who became household names through their comic bickering. According to Lynne Abbot, a St. Louis theater manager named Charles Turpin suggested that Edwards call himself "Butterbeans." Part of usurping Stringbeans's act meant wearing overly tight and somewhat ridiculous-looking suits that contrasted with the more fashionable dresses worn by Susie.

Butterbeans and Susie's act consisted of singing, dancing, and joke telling. They were quite popular from the 1920s through the 1940s, continuing even into the 1960s, when, after Susie's death, their daughter played her role for a time. According to historian Mel Watkins, "They usually began their act with a duet. Then, after she [Susie] sang a blues tune, they might join in a duet or begin the comic patter.... Humorous send-ups of marital squabbles were also a part of their act, and they would often punctuate their song and dance routines with snappy quips and lighthearted signifying" (Watkins, 376). Butterbeans would conclude with a dance called "The Heebie Jeebies" or "The Itch," which was a big success with audiences. Watkins cites James Cross (who is known to have played "Stump" in the act of Stump and Stumpy) describing the "Heebie Jeebies/Itch" dance as such: "He

[Edwards] kept his hands in his pockets and looked like he was itching to death, and when he took his hands out of his pockets and started to scratch all around the beat, the audience flipped" (Watkins, 377).

During the 1920s the couple had a successful recording career, working for "race record" labels such as Okeh Records. They made many "hokum blues" records, slow tempo recordings in which they would signify at each other, trading insults and banter. These good-natured and mildly entertaining tunes seem to have been thought of as a little corny. Some of these records were full of sexual innuendo. One of their songs, "I Want a Hot Dog for My Roll," with its highly suggestive lyrics, was famously not released by their record label. (It would later be made available, however, on their *Complete Recorded Works.*)

Despite their risqué lyrics and worldly comic routines, Jodie and Susie Edwards were a religious couple who gave generously to Pilgrim Baptist Church in Chicago. Indeed, they were rather comfortable financially, thanks to prudent spending and to long years of hard work on the Theater Owners Booking Association (TOBA) circuit. In later years they lived in a large house at 3322 South Calumet Avenue in Chicago. The doors of the house were open to performers from the old days who may have fallen on hard times or whose shtick had fallen out of fashion, such as Lincoln Perry (STEPIN FETCHIT). Perry, a close friend of the Edwardses, claimed that their door was always open to him when he was down on his luck in later years, and that he knew he could always get a meal at their home. Also, the Edwardses are said to have discovered and promoted the comedian MOMS MABLEY.

Jodie "Butterbeans" Edwards died as he walked on stage at the Dorchester Inn in Harvey, Illinois. His funeral was said to have been attended by Mabley, Perry, REDD FOXX, and LOUIS ARMSTRONG.

FURTHER READING

Hoekstra, Dave. "'Butter and Sue' Set the Stage in Bronzeville: Vaudeville's Couple," *Chicago Sun-Times*, 26 Mar. 2006.

Peterson, Bernard L. *Profiles of African American Stage Performers and Theater People, 1816–1960* (2001).

Watkins, Mel. *On the Real Side: Laughing, Lying, and Signifying—The Underground Tradition of African American Humor That Transformed American Culture, From Slavery to Richard Pryor* (1994).

PAUL DEVLIN

Edwards, Lena (17 Sept. 1900–3 Dec. 1986), physician and activist, was born Lena Frances Edwards in Washington, D.C., the youngest of three children of Thomas Edwards, a professor of dentistry at Howard University, and Marie Coakley. Dissuaded from becoming a dentist by her father, the young Lena instead set her heart on a medical career. She graduated from Dunbar High School as valedictorian in 1918 and enrolled at Howard University. Her plans were nearly derailed when she fell victim to Spanish influenza during the deadly epidemic of 1918. Edwards managed to sufficiently recover to quickly resume her studies. The experience of narrowly escaping the "purple death" may have influenced Edwards to cram as much as possible into every hour of every day remaining to her. She took summer classes at the University of Pennsylvania and earned a bachelor's of science from Howard in June 1921 after only three years of study. Accepted into Howard University Medical School she rushed through the program and graduated in June 1924. On the day after graduation Edwards married her classmate Keith Madison but, unusually for the era, elected to keep her maiden name professionally. In July 1925 Edwards and her husband moved to the Lafayette section of Jersey City, New Jersey, to take over the practice of a retiring physician. Lafayette was primarily a neighborhood of immigrant factory workers, particularly Poles, Czechs, Germans, and Italians. For reasons of modesty immigrant women preferred to consult female health professionals and Edwards developed a thriving practice. The decision to leave Washington, D.C., for New Jersey was also motivated by a desire on the part of Edwards and Madison to find integrated parochial schools for their children. Edwards delivered their first child, a daughter, in September 1925 and subsequently gave birth to one more daughter and four sons. The Edwards-Madison marriage failed in 1947. The couple never obtained a divorce, presumably because of religious objections, but also never lived together again. Edwards became a single mother.

The 1920s and 1930s were marked by widespread efforts to upgrade obstetrical practice, eliminate midwives, and move childbirth to the hospital. In keeping with this trend, in 1931 Edwards became an assistant attending physician at the new Margaret Hague Maternity Hospital, where she was the only black female doctor on staff. The hospital administration refused to promote Edwards to resident physician until April 1945, apparently for reasons of racism, thereby blocking her from the training necessary for professional advancement. She only earned a promotion through her persistent demands and the fact that many male doctors had been called up for service in World War II. In 1946, following the completion of eighteen months of residency training, Edwards remained on the staff of Margaret Hague but also joined the staff of Jersey City Medical Center as a physician with full privileges.

Edwards held traditional medical beliefs, perhaps in some part because her largely immigrant patients remained faithful to them. Although anesthesia had become commonplace in childbirth by the 1890s, Edwards promoted natural childbirth in the belief that anesthesia was bad for the baby. Anesthesia was known to occasionally cause problems during normal labor and delivery by decreasing uterine contractions, protracting labor, and causing breathing difficulties in newborns. Still, Edwards's stance marked her practice as old-fashioned. Additionally, as a Catholic, she refused to perform sterilizations or therapeutic abortions. The routine sterilization of black women, particularly in the South, in the service of eugenics or as surgical practice for medical residents, was well known in the black community and may have added to Edwards's determination not to participate in these procedures.

In 1948 Edwards became certified as a Diplomate of the Board in Gynecology and Obstetrics after traveling to Washington, D.C., where she was forced to use the service entrance at her hotel to take her examinations. The board honor made little difference to the administration at Margaret Hague. Racism continued to bedevil Edwards at the hospital, where she was the only certified obstetrician in Hudson County without full privileges. A blunt, outspoken woman never noted for her tact, Edwards threatened a political scandal over the matter and received a promotion. Problems with the administration continued in the early 1950s, when Edwards successfully protested the segregation of white and black patients at the hospital. After delivering an estimated five thousand babies Edwards left New Jersey in 1954 to follow in her father's footsteps by teaching at Howard University.

A lifelong Catholic, Edwards constantly pushed the church hierarchy to be more welcoming toward African Americans. She belonged to the all-black Christ the King Church in Jersey City and joined the Catholic Interracial Council. In 1950 Edwards took her devotion to the poor and needy a step further by becoming a member of the Third Order of St. Francis, for whom she took vows of poverty and simplicity.

Edwards wanted to volunteer for missionary work before age robbed her of the chance to do so. She left Howard University in 1961 to become the only doctor at the remote St. Joseph's Mission, near Hereford, Texas. The clinic had been built for migrant farm worker families of Mexican ancestry and Edwards lived in the small cinder-block building for ten months before moving into a house in the nearby town. Unlike many black women of her class who attempted to uplift people of minority races to the standards of middle-class white women, Edwards deliberately made it a point to accept the culture of racially and economically disadvantaged people. She did not attempt to change the Mexican workers but instead operated within their culture. She established a training program in the clinic for young women from the labor camp to prepare them for hospital jobs as practical nurses or nurses' aides. Since many of the migrants were more comfortable seeking aid from midwives, Edwards established a training center for midwives at the clinic to counteract infant mortality in the camp. Many of the funds that supported the maternity clinic came from the fees paid by the ranchers' wives that Edwards treated at the county hospital and from the office visits of non-Mexicans.

In 1960 she used her own money to build a modern maternity hospital, Our Lady of Guadalupe, to serve the labor camp. Long hours took their toll, however, and Edwards suffered a heart attack in 1964 shortly before receiving the Presidential Medal of Freedom. Edwards left Texas in July 1965. After volunteering with New Jersey's Head Start program for pre-school children and joining her daughter's medical practice, Edwards retired from medicine in 1970. She died in Jersey City.

FURTHER READING

Holmes, Linda Janet. "The Life of Lena Edwards," *New Jersey Medicine* (May 1988).

LuSane, Cheryl Day. *Past and Promise: Lives of New Jersey Women* (1990).

Scally, Sister M. Anthony. *Medicine, Motherhood, and Mercy: The Story of a Black Woman Doctor* (1979).

Obituary: *New York Times*, 10 Jan. 1987.

CARYN E. NEUMANN

Edwards, Mel (4 May 1937–), visual artist and educator, was born Melvin Eugene Edwards Jr., in Houston, Texas, the eldest of four children of Thelmarie Felton Edwards and Melvin Eugene

Edwards Sr. His father was a brilliant and gifted man who worked as a waiter, laborer in the oil industry, photographer, and a professional scout for the Boy Scouts of America. His mother, a seamstress, from whom Edwards learned to sew, was also athletically and artistically talented. His grandmother was a quilter, whose patternmaking and use of color influenced Edwards. Woodcarving was passed down on his father's side, and one of his maternal ancestors was a blacksmith brought to America from West Africa. Both his father and George Gilbert, a family friend that Edwards considered an uncle, were interested in art and they nurtured Edwards. His father built his first easel. Edwards Sr. also passed on a love of music, especially jazz, to his son. Both his parents conveyed their love of reading and learning to him. The family's *National Geographic* magazines prompted his early interest in Africa and adventure.

In pursuit of economic opportunity, the family moved to McNair, Texas, when Edwards was five years old; when he was seven, the family relocated to Dayton, Ohio. Edwards began drawing at an early age, making sophisticated, life-like figures. In Dayton, he studied the exhibited works at the Dayton Art Institute and other venues. Edwards's family moved back to Texas when he was twelve. At Houston's Phillis Wheatley High School, one of his teachers, Ethel Ladner, furthered Edwards's study of the relationships between music and art. James Thomas, who taught drawing and architecture, emphasized precision, structure, and the relationship between human beings and their environment. Edwards became acquainted with the artist John Biggers, who taught at Texas Southern University. Edwards and his classmate, Joe Louis Johnson, were selected to take art classes at Houston's Museum of Fine Arts in 1953. Edwards became committed to realizing his goal of making his living as an artist.

After graduating from high school in 1955 Edwards moved to California, where he joined the naval reserve and lived with an aunt and uncle. From 1955 to 1960 Edwards studied art at the Los Angeles City College, the University of Southern California (USC), and the Los Angeles Institute of Art (later the Otis Art Institute of Parsons School of Design), where the painter Charles White taught and where Edwards studied sculpture with Renzo Fenci. In 1959 Edwards first exhibited his paintings at the All City Exhibition in Barnsdall Park in Los Angeles and he participated in community exhibitions with the Seekers, an African American artist collective. Edwards played on the USC football team and credited his study of diagrammed plays with helping him to understand composition, space, and movement with greater insight. While in school and during the summers he worked at the post office, at Los Angeles City and Cedars of Lebanon hospitals, on the Houston waterfront, and in the warehouse district. All of this experience offered him material for his drawings.

In 1960 Edwards married the painter Karen Hamre, with whom he would have three daughters. Edwards supported his family by working with Tony Hill, an African American USC alumnus. Hill owned a factory where he produced decorative ceramics, along with other arts-related enterprises. On his lunch hour, Edwards often visited a nearby printmaking workshop, where he met artists Leon Golub, Richard Hunt, and Louise Nevelson, among others. He sought the company of other artists to learn from the creative problems they worked to solve. It was also in this year that Edwards became more deeply involved with sculpture. He created works in wood and plaster, and began taking welding courses at USC with George Baker.

In 1963, in response to sociopolitical conditions in the United States and human rights struggles worldwide, Edwards began his best known body of work, *Lynch Fragments*. He has dedicated more than forty years to this highly acclaimed series of organically welded steel wall sculptures that comment on power, human sacrifice, and the terrible knottiness of living.

The year 1965 was an auspicious one for Edwards. He earned a BFA from USC and had his first solo exhibition at the Santa Barbara Museum of Art. He received the Los Angeles Contemporary Art Council Award and participated in three other exhibitions including one in Chicago. He joined the faculty of the Chouinard Art School. In 1966 Edwards moved to New York and established a studio there. Two years later he and Hamre divorced.

Edwards' solo exhibitions included groundbreaking shows at the Whitney Museum of American Art (1970), the Studio Museum of Harlem (1978), the New Jersey State Museum (1981), the Sculpture Center Gallery in New York (1982), those at colleges and universities across the United States, and at leading art venues around the world.

In 1971, and 1984, he received a National Endowment for the Arts Fellowship for Visual Arts. In 1972 Edwards joined the faculty at Rutgers University, where he was instrumental in the development of the innovative visual arts program at the

Mason Gross School of the Creative and Performing Arts. He began his *Rocker* series that year. These kinetic works represent the intersection of childhood memories and African sculptural aesthetics. Edwards was awarded a John Simon Guggenheim Memorial Foundation Award in 1975, the year he married avant-garde poet and performance artist JAYNE CORTEZ. He would produce artwork for many of her jazz-influenced, incantatory books and albums.

In 1988 he won a Fulbright Fellowship to Zimbabwe. In 1993 Edwards won the grand prize of the Fuji-Sankei Biennial in Japan, and in 1995 his work was included in the Cairo Biennial. His work has been included in the collections of the Metropolitan Museum, the Museum of Modern Art, the Brooklyn Museum, the Bronx Museum, the Studio Museum in Harlem, the Art Institute of Chicago, and the LA County Museum of Art. His significant public commissions include *Confirmation*, installed in the Federal Plaza in Jamaica, New York.

In his extensive travels throughout Africa, the Caribbean, Europe, and Asia, Edwards met with master sculptors and artisans, learning from and incorporating into his own work their aesthetics, approaches, and interpretations of abstractions. Edwards's commitment to abstraction, sacred geometry, and his use of chain, barbed wire, and implements of labor have allowed him to meld the political, philosophical, spiritual, and architectural. Through this convergence, he has offered his vision of the souls of black folk.

FURTHER READING

Igoe, Lynn, with James Igoe. *250 Years of Afro-American Art: An Annotated Bibliography* (1981).

Neuberger Museum of Art. *Melvin Edwards Sculpture: A Thirty-Year Retrospective 1963–1993*.

Patton, Sharon F. *African-American Art* (1998).

Powell, Richard J. *Black Art: A Cultural History* (1997).

MONIFA LOVE ASANTE

Edwards, Stoney (24 Dec. 1929–5 Apr. 1997), country musician, was born Frenchy Edwards near Seminole, Oklahoma, the fourth of seven children born to Bub Edwards, a farmer, and his wife Red, a music teacher.

Stoney Edwards was named Frenchy after a local bootlegger, and received his better-known nickname as an adult. His father was of African American and Irish descent and his mother of Native American heritage. His parents had abandoned their children by the time Edwards was a teenager, and so the future country singer was compelled to serve in the role of caretaker for his three younger siblings. He never attended school and did not learn to read or write.

Because of his mixed-race background, Edwards experienced frequent discrimination during his early years growing up in rural Depression-era Oklahoma, and found that playing country music offered one avenue to social acceptance. His first exposure to the genre involved listening to his bootlegger uncles perform string band music and Jimmie Rodgers songs; Edwards later heard Bob Wills's music and *Grand Ole Opry* broadcasts on the radio. Edwards loved country music, and he soon began to perform it locally and to compose his own country songs. "I wrote songs because I didn't know nothing else to sing," he told the music journalist Peter Guralnick. "I got tired of 'Old Joe Clark' and church hymns and the few Bob Wills songs I got off the radio—those were the only songs I knew all the way through. So I *had* to write, I had to make up my own" (Guralnick, 269).

At one point during his teenage years Edwards earned a living by washing dishes in Oklahoma City, where he was temporarily reunited with his father. In the early 1950s Edwards moved to Oakland, California, where he lived with an uncle and worked as a janitor, a trucker, and a cowboy. In 1954 Edwards married, and he and his wife, Rosemary, moved to Richmond, California, and started raising a family. They would eventually have three children together. For the next decade and a half, Edwards was employed as a laborer (as a machinist, construction worker, and crane operator), performing music occasionally. In 1968 a work-related accident resulted in near-fatal carbon dioxide poisoning which left Edwards mentally and physically debilitated and unable to work as a laborer. His wife prevented the state from committing him to an institution.

As he recuperated Edwards turned to music, composing songs and performing frequently. He joined a rhythm and blues band, then quit that band to play country music. In 1970, while appearing at a benefit concert in Oakland for recent stroke-victim Bob Wills, Edwards was "discovered" by a local lawyer, Ray Sweeney, who encouraged Edwards to make a demo. He did so, and shortly thereafter, Capitol Records, recognizing his singing and songwriting talents and noting CHARLEY PRIDE's emergence as a major country music star, signed Edwards to a recording contract. Less polished and more "honky tonk"-sounding as a singer than Pride, Edwards's recordings never reached the highest positions on the country music singles charts, as Pride's many hits regularly did. Nonetheless, two of Edwards's singles rose into the country music Top 20: "She's My Rock" (highest position #20, 1972) and "Mississippi You're On My Mind" (#20, 1975). Ten of Edwards's other Capitol singles charted within the country music Top 100. While he did not compose his two biggest hits, Edwards did write several of the songs that would constitute his most enduring recordings, including his first hit, "A Two Dollar Toy" (# 68, 1971), and three non-charting album tracks, "The Fishin' Song" (1973), "Pickin' Wildflowers," and "Head Bootlegger Man" (both 1976). In 1975 Edwards released the single "Blackbird (Hold Your Head High)" (#41, 1975). Written for Edwards by Chip Taylor, the song generated controversy for its use of the word "nigger," though the lyric re-appropriated the slur as part of a positive message about being true to oneself. All told Edwards recorded five albums for Capitol: *Stoney Edwards* (1971), *Down Home in the Country* (1972), *She's My Rock* (1973), *Mississippi You're On My Mind* (1975), and *Blackbird* (1976).

At the end of his stint with Capitol Records, Edwards and Rosemary moved to San Antonio, Texas. By 1978 he had signed with the JMI label, for which he recorded the #60 country hit "If I Had to Do It All Over Again." He and Rosemary soon divorced, and in the early 1980s he returned to Oklahoma, now married to his second wife, Cindy. In 1981 *No Way to Drown a Memory*, an album on the Music America label, featured the two last charting singles of Edwards's career, though both were only minor country hits. Throughout the 1980s Edwards experienced bad luck and poor health. In 1984 he lost the lower part of his right leg after accidentally shooting himself during a game of quickdraw. In 1986 Edwards recorded, for the Ragged but Right label, his final album, *Just for Old Time's Sake*, which featured a band made up of several major country musicians, including Johnny Gimble, Ralph Mooney, and Ray Benson. By 1989 Edwards was suffering from diabetes and the next year from lung cancer. In 1996 Edwards was diagnosed with stomach cancer, and he passed away the following year. In recognition of Edwards's unique achievement as one of the most talented and popular country performers, the Razor & Tie label in 1998 released a CD compilation entitled *The Best of Stoney Edwards: Poor Folks Stick Together*.

Edwards was one of several African American musicians to achieve national recognition as a performer of country music (the others being DeFord Bailey, Ray Charles, Charley Pride, Big Al Downing, O. B. McClinton, and Cleve Francis). While Pride achieved the most sustained success in crossing country music's "color-line," Edwards's contributions to country music have increasingly been recognized by scholars and fans. Critics, for instance, have lauded his authentic hard country voice. For example, John Morthland acknowledged that Edwards sang "in a grainy, stray-cat voice rich in both vibrato and a proud Texas-Oklahoma twang" (CD liner notes). Critics also praised the high quality of Edwards's idiosyncratic songs. Guralnick, for instance, called Edwards "a great writer.... [H]is writing can be compared favorably to that of two heroes of his, Merle Haggard and Lefty Frizzell" (273). Morthland pointed out that, while Edwards may have emulated his heroes in his music, he also possessed a distinctiveness not previously heard in country music: "Stoney was a stylistic follower of Lefty Frizzell and Merle Haggard, but he [was] ... arguably the only modern black country artist whose blackness did come through in his music."

FURTHER READING

Guralnick, Peter. *Lost Highway: Journeys & Arrivals of American Musicians* (1982).

Morthland, John. CD Liner Notes. *The Best of Stoney Edwards: Poor Folks Stick Together* (1998).

TED OLSON

Edwards, Tommy (15 Oct. 1922–23 Oct. 1969), singer, songwriter, and pianist, was born Thomas Jefferson Edwards Jr. in Henrico County, Virginia, one of six children of Thomas J. Edwards Sr., an educational administrator, and Buena Vista Edwards. His death certificate and family histories indicate that biographies giving him a birth date of February 1922 are incorrect. Also a Henrico County native, Edwards's father was a Hampton Institute graduate who taught wheelwrighting at Tuskegee Institute before being appointed supervisor of the black schools of Macon County, Alabama, by Dr. Booker T. Washington. The senior Edwards returned to Virginia in 1914 to become president of the Negro Reformatory Association and superintendent of the Virginia Manual Labor Training School for Colored Boys. In a home replete with two pianos, Tommy's parents instilled a love of music in their children, and Tommy's special talents became readily apparent at a young age. By high school he performed in his own weekly musical broadcast program on local radio station WRNL. He also formed a trio with his sister Harriet and brother Nathan that performed weekly at the same station (*Baltimore Afro-American,* 12 Aug. 1950).

After graduating from Virginia Randolph High School, Edwards began touring clubs in the Northeast and Midwest. As a young singer and pianist he played some of the most prestigious clubs in New York and Chicago. By age twenty-two Edwards had written scores of tunes and was signed to Decca records (*Billboard Music Yearbook*, 1944, p. 299). Edwards's versatility as a singer, songwriter, and pianist belied his years. He gained notoriety for the hit "That Chick's Too Young to Fry," cowritten with Jimmy Hilliard and recorded by Louis Jordan in around 1946. The best-selling song was on the soundtrack for the black movie *Reet, Petite, and Gone* (Gunter, p. 4).

By 1947 Edwards was performing and recording in the Tommy Edwards Trio for Tops Records (*Billboard,* 11 Oct. 1947). He signed with National Records in 1949. During this time Edwards continued to compose songs and record demonstration records (demos) using other artists to perform the songs. To save money he decided to sing on the demos himself—a fortuitous move. While making the rounds of record companies in 1950 to pitch his song "All Over Again," Edwards stopped by MGM Records. The executives were enamored with not only the tune, but Edwards's voice as well. MGM quickly signed Edwards to an exclusive deal and had him record "All Over Again" and several other songs within weeks (*Chicago Daily Defender,* 16 July 1959). At a time when many black artists were relegated to rhythm and blues labels or divisions, MGM, headed by progressive-minded Frank Walker, embraced and signed black artists who performed popular music. Walker had previously worked as an executive at Columbia and Victor Records, and is credited with providing early recording opportunities to Marian Anderson and Bessie Smith. Edwards and Billy Eckstine became featured performers for MGM (*Norfolk Journal and Guide,* 2 May 1953).

In 1951 Edwards recorded a song that proved pivotal in his career. His version of "It's All in the Game" reached No. 18 on the Billboard singles chart. The song's melody was originally the instrumental "Melody in A Major" written in 1912 by Charles G. Dawes, a financier who later served as vice president of the United States under Calvin Coolidge, and was a corecipient of the 1925 Nobel Peace Prize. In 1951 Carl Sigman composed the lyrics and called it "It's All in the Game." Other notable performers who also covered the song were Nat King Cole, Dinah Shore, Louis Armstrong, The Four Tops, and Elton John. Several Edwards singles entered the charts from 1951 to 1954, including "All Over Again," "My Concerto," and "Please Mr. Sun." Edwards's recording career slowed during the mid-1950s; however, in 1958 MGM had Edwards reprise his hit "It's All in the Game" with a new upbeat arrangement. The newer version skyrocketed to No. 1 on the Billboard chart and remained there for six weeks. It also soared on several European charts and reportedly stayed on the Billboard Hot 100 chart for nineteen weeks. The single sold over 3.5 million records and earned Edwards a gold record. As a result of this single's success, he appeared on *The Ed Sullivan Show, Your Hit Parade,* and *The Dick Clark Show* during 1958 and 1959. During the early 1960s Edwards continued to display his versatility by releasing albums of covers of Hawaiian and country music tunes, among others. In all, he released over a dozen albums and had at least ten singles in the Top 50. One of his last chart entries appears to have been the 1966 release "I Cried, I Cried" for the Musicor label (*Billboard,* 22 Oct. 1966, p. 37).

Edwards died of a brain aneurysm at age forty-seven in his Henrico County home. The inclusion of his 1958 version of "It's All in the Game" in virtually every major compilation of the most popular songs of the twentieth century solidifies his legacy as one of the era's greatest songwriting balladeers.

FURTHER READING

Gunter, Don. "Back in the Game: Research for the *Dictionary of Virginia Biography* Renews Interest in Virginia-Born Singer-Songwriter Tommy Edwards." *Broadside: The Magazine of the Library of Virginia* (Summer 2008): 2–5.

"Richmond Composer Now a Top Recording Favorite." *Baltimore Afro-American,* 12 Aug. 1950.

Obituaries: *Richmond Times-Dispatch,* 24 October 1969; *The Washington Post,* 25 October 1969.

ELVATRICE PARKER BELSCHES

Egypt, Ophelia Settle (20 Feb. 1903–25 May 1984), sociologist, social worker, writer, and teacher, was born Ophelia Settle in Red River County, Texas, one of seven children of Sarah Garth, who died when Settle was four years old, and Green Wilson Settle, a teacher and later principal at the Deaf, Dumb, and Blind Institute in Raft, Oklahoma. The emphasis the Settle family placed upon education influenced Settle's aspiration to become a teacher. She graduated from Howard University with an AB in English in 1925 and taught at the Orange County Training School in Chapel Hill, North Carolina, for a year. She then completed a master's degree in Sociology in 1928 at the University of Pennsylvania.

In 1929 Settle embarked on a journey that culminated in the project that became her lifelong passion. CHARLES SPURGEON JOHNSON, then director of the newly formed Department of Social Science at Fisk University, hired Settle as the first staff member. Johnson had studied at the University of Chicago under Robert Parks, who believed in the sanctity of the unmediated personal story as opposed to oral history, which, Parks and Johnson argued, was almost always mediated when transcribed into a written culture. Both Johnson and Settle embraced the doctrine of first-person accounts, and Settle soon traveled to West Tennessee to conduct studies of families in the state. In the midst of the study, Settle became enthralled by reminisces of octogenarians about their childhood days in slavery. The stories reminded her of those told by her grandparents, who had been slaves. Forgiving her failure to conduct the family studies, Johnson urged her to record the slave stories before that history disappeared with the deaths of the former slaves.

Settle, who recalled interviewing more than one hundred respondents, began drafting her manuscript about the lives of these former slaves, "Raggedy Thorns: The Slaves' View of Slavery, the Civil War, and Freedom," in the early 1930s. With assistance from Johnson, she attempted to have the manuscript published as early as 1942 but met resistance from male publishers uninterested in the work of a woman, a resistance that continued throughout her lifetime. Of the original interviews, the only extant versions are those in the unpublished "Raggedy Thorns" and in *Unwritten History of Slavery: Autobiographical Accounts of Negro Ex-Slaves* (1975), her compendium of verbatim transcripts of thirty-seven interviews. The latter was originally mimeographed and produced under the auspices of the American Psychological Association as a result of Johnson and Settle's desire to make the interviews available for study by sociologists and historians.

Settle's project was likely the progenitor for the Works Progress Administration's Federal Writer's Project Slave Narratives, more generally known as the WPA Slave Narratives. One of Johnson's graduate students, LAWRENCE D. REDDICK, worked with Johnson at the same time that Settle was conducting and recording her interviews. Reddick was credited with having originally proposed to the Federal Writers' Project the plan to interview former slaves. Settle's passion for the "ex-slave material," as she called it, was also evident in another project, *Raggedy Thorns*, an album of slave sorrow songs on which she narrated her respondents' stories before each selection.

In 1933 Settle left Fisk and began her career as a social worker in St. Louis. Two years later she was offered the directorship of the Social Service Department at Flint Goodrich Hospital (now part of Dillard University) in New Orleans. During her tenure there, she completed course work at the Medical Social Work Department of the Washington University of St. Louis Hospital to fulfill field training requirements for a medical social worker. She spent five years at Flint Goodrich. In 1939 she returned to Howard University to work with E. FRANKLIN FRAZIER and INABEL LINDSAY in the university's Division of Social Work, which was soon formed into the Department of Social Work. Just as Settle had helped establish, staff, and organize the nascent Department of Social Science at Fisk University with Johnson, she again developed, taught, and supervised the Howard medical social work curriculum. In 1940 Settle married Ivory Lester Egypt, a native of Washington, D.C.; they had one son.

As assistant professor in Howard's School of Social Work, Ophelia Egypt was criticized by a student for distancing herself from the people on whom she focused her research by remaining in academia. As a result Egypt took a leave of absence from Howard to work at the Juvenile Court of the District of Columbia, where she came face-to-face with persons in need.

Egypt's public service continued when she left Howard and the juvenile court to direct the IONIA R. WHIPPER Home for unmarried black mothers in Washington, D.C. Later in 1954 she took a position with Planned Parenthood in the District of Columbia. Her work with impoverished young women at the Whipper Home had fueled her desire to prevent future generations of young black women from choosing the difficult path of pregnancy without marriage. Her grassroots work with families in three large public housing projects in Southeast Washington earned her community recognition. In 1981 the Parkland Planned Parenthood Center was renamed the Ophelia Egypt Clinic, and 15 October 1981 was declared Ophelia Egypt Day.

The largest collection of her surviving correspondence, housed at Howard University's Moorland Spingarn Research Center, consists of letters between Egypt and her lifelong friend Ruth Lewis Hall, an artist and a Quaker whom Egypt met in 1927. During the 1970s Egypt and Hall compiled several decades of their correspondence into the manuscript "A Sheltering Tree: Letters of Two Women." Their intention was to publish the manuscript, but they were not successful. Progressive in her later years, Egypt was emphatic in her belief that overpopulation was a form of pollution. Her solution to the problem in society at large was a call for knowledgeable use of birth control and individual responsibility for the condition of the world. Egypt voiced her concerns during the 1960s and 1970s in several venues, including a 1960 *Washington Afro-American* article "Population 'Explosion' Stirs Housing, Other Problems" and a 1967 speech for Planned Parenthood, "Family Planning." She dedicated much of her writing and energy toward constructive social criticism. Egypt was also committed to the education of youth. In 1974 she published the children's biography *James Weldon Johnson*. Her admiration for Johnson and his life story inspired her choice. As a result of her participation in the workshop, Egypt decided to publish a children's book using the material from "Raggedy Thorns." Drum and Spear, the only publisher to consider the project, wanted Egypt to fictionalize the stories. She refused, and the book was never written.

During her active life Egypt never wavered from her commitment to bring the stories of formerly enslaved children to the forefront. Although she finally relinquished efforts to have "Raggedy Thorns" published, she remained committed to exposing young people in the District of Columbia to the stories. She was adamant in her belief that modern-day youth could learn something valuable about life and struggle from the actual lives of children who had been enslaved. Egypt died in Washington, D.C.

FURTHER READING

The Egypt collection at the Moorland Spingarn Research Center Manuscript Division, Howard University, Washington, D.C., includes her manuscript, correspondence, and personal memorabilia and Elinor Sinnette's "Transcript of an Oral Memoir of-Mrs. Ophelia Settle Egypt: Sociologist, Social Worker, Educator, and Writer" (1981–1982). Additional correspondence is in the Ruth Lewis Hall Collection at the Moorland Spingarn Research Center; in the Glenn Carrington Collection at the Schomburg Center for Research and Black Culture, New York City; and in the Special Collections Library, Rare Books and Manuscripts, at Pennsylvania State University.

Camper, Joyce A. A. "Ophelia Settle Egypt's 'Raggedy Thorns: The Slaves' View of Slavery, the Civil War, and Freedom': An Archival Study," M.A. thesis, Howard University, 2004.

JOYCE A. A. CAMPER

Eikerenkoetter, Frederick J. *See* Reverend Ike.

Elaw, Zilpha (c. 1790–?), evangelist and writer, was born near Philadelphia, Pennsylvania, to parents whose names remain unknown. In 1802, when Zilpha was twelve, her mother died during the birth of her twenty-second child, leaving Zilpha's father to raise the three children who had survived infancy. Unable to support the family, her father sent her older brother to their grandparents' farm far from Philadelphia and consigned Zilpha to a local Quaker couple, Pierson and Rebecca Mitchel. Within eighteen months Zilpha's father died. Zilpha felt fortunate to stay with the Mitchels for the next six years, until she reached the age of eighteen.

Zilpha had enjoyed a close relationship with her father and was deeply grieved by his passing. The emotional turmoil associated with his death led her to a deeper contemplation of the state of her soul, though she felt that she had no religious instruction or direction to guide her through this period. Zilpha felt spiritually adrift between the public religious expressions she had witnessed as a young girl and the Quaker tradition where religious devotion was "performed in the secret silence of the mind" (Elaw, 54). Concerned about what she felt to be her increasingly impious behavior among the Mitchel children, Zilpha began to experience dreams and visions in which God or the archangel Gabriel warned her of her sinful ways and pressed her to repent before a promised cataclysmic end, when repentance would no longer be possible. When she was still a teenager, these dreams of damnation and her concerns about her feelings of guilt and sin led her to seek affiliation with the Methodists.

Conversion among the Methodists was a gradual process that Zilpha later compared to the dawning of the morning. That she marks her process in this way distinguishes her autobiography, *Memoirs of the Life, Religious Experience, Ministerial Travels, and Labours of Mrs. Elaw, An American Female of*

Colour (1846), from many others in the spiritual autobiography genre, such as Sojourner Truth and Jarena Lee, in which the authors emphasize a single event or a miraculous series of distinctive incidents that worked an immediate and permanent change in the writer. Elaw, conversely, provides a model of slow but sure development over her adolescence and early adulthood.

In another vision Jesus appeared to Elaw as she wrote in her dairy and assured her that her sins had been forgiven. In 1808, at eighteen years of age, she "united [herself] in the fellowship of the saints with the militant church of Jesus on earth" (Elaw, 57), joining a local Methodist society. Conversion, study, church membership, baptism, and the new right to participate in Holy Communion transformed Zilpha's life. She gained a new self-confidence that she had not possessed before her revelation. The society became her family, God became her father, and Jesus became her brother and friend.

The spiritual reverie she enjoyed changed when she married Joseph Elaw in 1810. Joseph was not a born-again Christian. Zilpha's experience in this incompatible union served as the subject for one of the more powerful expositions in her narrative. She warns Christian women against marrying unbelieving men, suggesting that they would be more content to be drowned by a millstone hung about their necks for disobeying God's law. Pride, arrogance, and the independence of young women drove them to make marital choices without parental regulation, guardianship, and government, she argued. In her view, women ought to be subordinate to fathers and, upon marriage, to husbands. The "carnal courtship" was not marriage but fornication, and it promised to deceive and destroy the woman's spirit.

Elaw supported her opinion with scripture but, more convincingly, underpinned her discussion by describing the discord she suffered within her marriage. Joseph objected to Zilpha's zealous and public religious practice and pressed her to take in amusements that he enjoyed, like music and dancing in nearby Philadelphia. Although the temptation to lose herself in these amusements was great, she held fast to her convictions.

In 1811 the Elaws relocated to Burlington, New Jersey, where their daughter was born and where Joseph could ply his trade as a fuller until embargos during the War of 1812 prevented shipping exports. Elaw also attended her first camp meeting in New Jersey. Camp meetings, referred to in the subtitle of her narrative, were open-air religious revivals, often attended by hundreds of worshipers who traveled great distances to participate. These events were popular among the Methodists and provided extraordinary opportunities for women and African Americans to engage in preaching and religious leadership outside the monitored and regulated site of the church.

As Elaw described the meetings, the campgrounds often had segregated living spaces but integrated worship spaces. Consequently, after experiencing another sanctifying vision, Elaw involuntarily began to pray and preach publicly and gained a reputation for her evangelical power. At one camp meeting, she developed the desire to engage in a household ministry among families in her community, and she was endorsed in this enterprise by local Burlington clergy. Elaw maintained this "special calling" despite a chilly reception by some local black Methodist parishioners and the vigorous protests of her husband, who feared that she would be ridiculed.

Throughout her period of household ministry, Elaw struggled with a call to preach to a broader audience, with her divine mission at odds with her sense of feminine propriety. She continued to have dreams about a greater call, but she found little support for this vision as well. All thought of preaching ended for a time when her husband died on 27 January 1823. To support herself and her daughter, Elaw established a school, but closed it two years later, yielding to the call to preach. She placed her daughter with relatives and began to preach, for a while joining with Jarena Lee. Elaw's itinerant ministry took her through the mid-Atlantic and northeastern United States and even below the Mason-Dixon line in 1828 to Maryland and Virginia, preaching to blacks and whites, men and women, believers and nonbelievers. She remarked that she became a "prodigy" to those who heard and saw her. The confluence of her race, gender, and spiritual enthusiasm presented a singular spectacle to many whose fascination with her rendered them susceptible to her persuasive style and rhetoric.

In 1840 Elaw sailed to London, England, to preach and evangelize. She met with success there, but she continued to battle those who were not receptive to women preachers. Her narrative suggests that she intended to return to America in 1845, but no record of her return or activity in the United States exists after the publication of her narrative in 1846.

A notable feature of Elaw's narrative is the regularity with which she attributes her success to the combination of her race, gender, and salvation. Her narrative is modeled after Saint Paul's struggles and salvation, as detailed in his letters to the Christian churches in the New Testament. Taken as a whole, Elaw's narrative characterizes her race and gender as socially constructed "thorns" or burdens that, like Paul, she must endure. These "burdens" were the elements that rendered her a prodigy, or phenomenon to those who heard her preach. The confluence of her race, gender, and spiritual power were, in her understanding, elements of grace with which she had been blessed to do God's work.

Like many women active in preaching activities in the nineteenth century, Elaw traveled, spoke in an impassioned and inspired manner on the Bible, and wrote a narrative of her religious development as a guide to others, especially women, who might follow her path. She did not carry any official designation as a minister or preacher, but was recognized for her powerful and effective evangelism as an itinerant religious leader. As one of the earliest black women to claim the right to preach publicly, Elaw was a key figure in establishing the tradition of African American women religious leaders. This tradition continued throughout the nineteenth century in the work of such notable evangelists as JULIA FOOTE and AMANDA SMITH, and it laid the groundwork for the acceptance of such women as PAULI MURRAY and Bishop BARBARA HARRIS in ministerial roles in the late twentieth century.

FURTHER READING

Elaw, Zilpha. *Memoirs of the Life, Religious Experience, Ministerial Travels, and Labours of Mrs. Elaw, An American Female of Colour; Together with Some Account of the Great Religious Revivals in America* (1846).

Andrews, William L., ed. *Sisters of the Spirit: Three Black Women's Autobiographies of the Nineteenth Century* (1986).

MARTHA L. WHARTON

Elder, Alfonso (26 Feb. 1898–7 Aug. 1974), educator, was born in Sandersville, Georgia, the son of Thomas J. Elder, an educator, and Lillian Phinizy. Thomas Elder founded and served as principal of Sandersville Industrial School (later Thomas J. Elder High and Industrial School) for fifty-three years; his wife served as his assistant. Alfonso's early education was at his father's school.

Elder earned an AB from Atlanta University in 1921, from which he graduated magna cum laude. A fellowship from the General Education Board helped him earn his M.S. from Teachers College at Columbia University in 1924, and he went on to graduate work at the University of Chicago in the summers of 1930 and 1931 and studied at Cambridge University in England. Elder earned an Ed.D. from Teachers College in 1938.

Elder began his teaching career at Bennett College in Greensboro, North Carolina, where he taught mathematics from 1921 to 1922. The following year he taught at Elizabeth City State College in eastern North Carolina. He then moved to Durham State Normal School (later North Carolina Central University) in 1923 as an education professor. He served as dean of the college of arts and sciences at the school—which in 1927 changed its name to North Carolina College for Negroes (NCC)—from 1924 to1943. All of his teaching appointments were at historically black institutions.

In 1931 Elder married Louise Holmes, a graduate of Atlanta University. In Durham, North Carolina, she worked as a librarian at Hillside High School, and while the Elders were at Atlanta University, she served as circulation librarian there. The couple had no children. From 1943 to 1947 Elder headed the department of education at Atlanta University, where he was also in charge of teacher training throughout the Atlanta university system.

After the death of NCC founder and president JAMES E. SHEPARD in 1947, Elder returned to North Carolina to become the second president of NCC (known as North Carolina College at Durham from 1947 to 1969), serving from 1948 to 1963. Elder's accomplishments as president were numerous. While he was president NCC became a member of the Southern Association of Colleges and Schools. In 1950 the NCC law school earned accreditation from the American Bar Association. Enrollment increased from 950 in 1947 to 2,498 in 1962–1963. The school's annual budget grew from $627,238 to $2,873,434 during the same period. The faculty rose to two hundred, and during his presidency faculty salaries tripled. The number of campus buildings nearly doubled, from twenty-one to thirty-eight. Before his retirement Elder successfully lobbied the North Carolina State Assembly to spend $4 million for construction of six new buildings, including a student union (later named for him), a cafeteria, and two dormitories. During the 1960–1961 academic year Elder instituted a program to elevate student performance by creating an honors program and two reading programs. In 1962–1963 the National Council on Accreditation of Teacher Education accredited NCC's teacher education program.

As president of North Carolina College during the turbulent early years of the modern civil rights movement, Elder advocated integrated educational facilities and equal access to quality education for all students. In 1951 the U.S. Supreme Court affirmed the U.S. Court of Appeals's decision in *McKissick et al. v. Carmichael et al.*, requiring the law school at the University of North Carolina in Chapel Hill (UNC) to admit African Americans. Seeking to limit the effect of this decision and delay integration, white education and government officials sought to expand graduate programs offered at black colleges. They proposed that NCC establish a Ph.D. program in education, but Elder saw through their ruse and opposed the plan. When it became clear that UNC would force NCC to establish the program, Elder fought to gain as much funding as possible for NCC's graduate and undergraduate programs. He succeeded in gaining $300,000 in additional operating funds and $1.8 million for capital improvements, thus presiding over the expansion of the graduate program. NCC's Ph.D. program in education was the first doctoral program at any of the historically black colleges in the United States. Fittingly it was during Elder's tenure that NCC awarded its first doctorate, in 1955 to Walter M. Brown. The school awarded four more Ph.Ds in education before the program was disbanded during the early 1960s. By the end of 1961 NCC had awarded 738 M.A. and M.S. degrees, 136 MEd degrees in elementary education, 111 M.A. degrees in public health, 192 M.A. degrees in library science, and 80 law degrees. Most of these were awarded during Elder's tenure.

While white professors from UNC and Duke University had taught most of NCC's graduate classes during the 1940s, and white deans had presided over the graduate programs, by the late 1950s Elder asserted NCC's control over its own graduate programs. NCC professors and deans took over most of the responsibility for the graduate classes. In 1957 Elder appointed NCC English professor Richard K. Barksdale the first full-time dean of the graduate school. Barksdale replaced William W. Pierson, dean of UNC's Graduate School, who had been the acting dean of NCC's Graduate School.

Elder continued to believe that NCC's Ph.D. program in education was a drain on the school's resources and a means to delay the integration of the state's university system. He asserted that NCC needed to concentrate on strengthening the school's undergraduate and master's level graduate programs. In 1961, as the sole African American member of Governor Terry Sanford's North Carolina Commission on Education Beyond the High School, Elder recommended the termination of the Ph.D. program, and in 1962 he got his wish. White officials had decided that with the threat of massive integration behind them, only historically white universities would award Ph.Ds.

While Elder's commitment to integrated and quality education convinced him to call for the termination of NCC's Ph.D. program, it also impelled him to speak out against segregation. He insisted that the Governor's Commission take a strong stand against racial segregation in higher education, but despite his entreaties the commission remained silent. In 1962 Elder implored UNC to hire black professors—it had none at the time—as well as to admit black students, but UNC did not hire its first black professor until 1966.

During the early 1960s Elder consistently spoke out for racial equality and supported the right of his students and faculty, many of whom were active in the civil rights movement, to participate in sit-ins and picketing to protest against segregated public facilities. He permitted students to miss curfew for protest-related activities. He kept dining halls open after hours to accommodate students who were involved in protests. Elder ignored state officials when they pressured him to bar students from participating in sit-ins and picketing off-campus. Elder stood up for his students' right to protest racial injustice. In 1962 he protested inequitable pay scales for faculty at black and white undergraduate colleges in the state system. A faculty member described Elder's leadership style as "quiet, confident, dignified, warm, able, efficient, and generally courageous" (Thorpe, 32).

Elder regularly participated in civic and community organizations. He served on the board of directors of the Mutual Savings and Loan Association, the Human Relations Committee of Durham, the Governor's Committee on Education Beyond the High School, Durham's Committee of 100, was a member of St. Titus Episcopal Church in Durham, and was a trustee of Lincoln Hospital. In 1950, when hospitals were segregated, he helped lead the campaign for a hospital bond issue, which gave significant funding to Durham's black Lincoln Hospital.

Elder retired from the presidency of NCC in 1963, when he was named President Emeritus.

After retiring he continued to live in Durham until his death from heart failure at age seventy-six.

FURTHER READING

A small collection of Alfonso Elder's papers may be found in the Vertical Files, Reference Department, James E. Shepard Memorial Library, North Carolina Central University, Durham, North Carolina.

Gershenhorn, Jerry. "The Ruse, Rise, and Demise of North Carolina College's Doctoral Program in Education, 1951–1962," *North Carolina Historical Review* 82 (Apr. 2005): 156–192.

Thorpe, Earl E. *A Concise History of North Carolina Central University* (1984).

Obituary: *Durham Morning Herald*, 10 Aug. 1974.

JERRY GERSHENHORN

Elder, Larry (27 Apr. 1952–), radio personality and conservative pundit, was born Laurence Allen Elder, the middle of three sons of Randolph Elder, who owned a local café, and Viola Elder. The family called the Pico-Union neighborhood of Los Angeles home, and it was in Los Angeles that the young Elder attended school. Both his father and mother placed a heavy emphasis on education and hard work. Elder's father had scrimped and saved and faced years of prejudice before being able to open his own business. Elder's mother urged her son to pursue a life of education. Elder took their lessons to heart, graduating from Crenshaw High in 1970 near the top of his class and matriculating to Brown University. He graduated with a B.S. in Political Science in 1974. He continued his education at the University of Michigan Law School, from which he earned the J.D. in 1977.

Following graduation, Elder removed to Cleveland, where he landed a job as an attorney with the law firm of Squire, Sanders, and Dempsey. He found the legal profession not entirely to his liking, however, and in 1980 struck out on his own to found Laurence A. Elder and Associates, which helped other lawyers to locate jobs. Meanwhile, he decided to undertake a career as a writer or opinion-maker. His self-described political leanings were libertarian, though like most other libertarians, he largely held orthodox conservative views with slightly less interest in reactionary social policies. He opposed the federal income tax, was against the government's so-called war on drugs, and believed that liberals and the Democratic Party had been poisonous to African Americans and their interests. He associated with the arch-conservative commentator Dennis Prager and was a frequent guest on Prager's talk-radio program. In time, Elder was able to land a job with a PBS affiliate in Cleveland and was eventually given his own opinion program. For the next six years he built his reputation as a sharp, counterintuitive, and often-controversial thinker. His PBS show eventually migrated to the local Fox affiliate, and there Elder remained until 1994. In that year, he relocated to Los Angeles and was hired by KABC to host his own political talk-radio program.

From that seat, Elder continued his assault on what he perceived to be the Democratic Party's crimes against blacks. At least in theory, he supported the idea of reparations to freed slaves, but his rejection of reparations to their descendants rendered his position moot. He insisted that affirmative action had been a disaster and had prevented the African American community from achieving its potential. He believed that some redress for the harms of the past were necessary, but felt that private civic organizations like the NAACP were more than sufficient to carry them out. In 1997 a boycott by a small but vocal organization, the Talking Drum Community Forum, managed to convince KABC to reduce Elder's airtime, but outrage from his loyal listeners soon caused the station to reverse course. In 1998 Elder spoke at the Libertarian Party national convention, though his record of supporting Republican Party presidential candidates remained unbroken.

An African American with such conservative social views was something of a rarity, and so Elder's reputation grew outside the Los Angeles market. In 2001 he began to appear as the "judge" in the syndicated *Moral Court* program, but the show was canceled shortly thereafter. In 2004 a syndicated television version of his show was produced, but it too was soon canceled due to poor ratings. Elder also penned a syndicated opinion column that was carried in some of the most prominent conservative organs, both online and print, including *Investor's Business Daily* and Townhall.com, among numerous others. Beginning in 2002 Elder's radio program went national with the ABC Radio Network. However, following a change in ownership at the network in 2007, Elder's program was canceled, and Mark Levin took over the spot. Elder's show returned to KABC, where he remained until 2008, at which point he gave it up in favor of an online podcast version of the broadcast. In 2010, however, he returned to KABC, where he continued to lambaste Democrats, progressives, and the policies and administration of President Barack Obama.

FURTHER READING

Dawson, Michael C. *Black Visions: The Roots of Contemporary African-American Political Ideologies* (2001).

Walters, Ronald W. *White Nationalism, Black Interests: Conservative Public Policy and the Black Community* (2003).

JASON PHILIP MILLER

Elder, Robert Lee (14 July 1934–), professional golfer, was born in Dallas, Texas, the youngest of eight children of Charles, a truck driver, and Almeta Elder. Charles died in World War II, and Almeta just a few weeks later, leaving Lee to be raised by his older sister Sadie. In 1943 he started shagging golf balls and caddying at Tennison Golf Course, trying to earn money to help his family. The club professional at Tennison allowed caddies to play the holes not visible from the clubhouse, and by age twelve, Elder was a regular player and hustler on the course, including hustling and caddying for the legendary hustler, gambler, and golfer Titanic Thompson (Alvin C. Thomas). In 1949 Elder left Dallas to live with an aunt in Los Angeles, California, mainly to have more opportunities to play golf since blacks were restricted from most courses in Dallas.

Elder continued caddying and hustling in California, but he also worked to improve his game. In 1951 he played in the United Golf Association (UGA) Negro National Open at the Seneca Golf Club in Cleveland, Ohio, losing to the boxer-turned-golfer Joe Louis in the final round. Elder's play caught the eye of the professional golfer Teddy Rhodes, who took Elder in and coached him for three years. Through the 1950s Elder made a living playing in West Coast tours and hustling. In 1959 the army drafted him, and Elder went to Fort Lewis, Washington, where his commanding officer placed Elder on "golf duty." Elder spent two years in Washington and placed second in the all-service golf tournament in 1960.

After his service Elder returned to Los Angeles and became a regular on the UGA Tour. He won five consecutive Negro National Opens, from 1963 until 1967. During the 1966 season he won eighteen of the twenty-two tournaments he entered. On 18 July 1966 he married Rose Lorraine Harper, who began managing his career under the auspices of Elder & Associates, Inc. The couple divorced in 1995.

Though Elder was eligible to try for the Professional Golfer's Association (PGA) Tour in 1961 when the PGA removed the "Caucasian-only" clause from its constitution, he did not have enough money to pay for Qualifying School until 1967. Out of a field of 104, Elder placed in the top twenty and earned his tour card. He set a PGA record by making the cut in his first nine tournaments. He put the tour and world on notice when he battled (but lost to) Jack Nicklaus in a playoff round at the August 1968 American Golf Classic in Akron, Ohio. Maxwell Stanford, the UGA president, said, "Elder did more for Negro golf in 45 minutes than everybody else put together had done in 45 years" (Kennedy, 179). Elder also faced the indignity that many in golf still harbored towards blacks. At the 1967 Monsanto Open, for example, Elder and other black players were not allowed in the clubhouse and were forced to dress in the parking lot.

Early in his PGA career, Elder established himself as a consistent golfer, though a tour victory proved elusive. In 1971 Gary Player invited Elder to play in South Africa. When Elder and Player teed off in front of 5,000 spectators, it was the first integrated sporting event in South Africa. Elder spent three weeks playing in Africa, during which time he won the Nigerian Open. In 1972 the U.S. State Department named Elder the Goodwill Ambassador to Africa. At the 1974 Monsanto Open in Pensacola, Florida, Elder finally won his first PGA Tour event. He staged a comeback over Peter Oosterhuis in the final round to force a playoff, winning on the fourth playoff hole.

Elder's victory turned him into an instant celebrity and he became the first black golfer to receive an invitation to the PGA Masters Invitational in Augusta, Georgia. His life turned into a media circus as Washington, D.C., police had to direct traffic in front of his home and he received many threats, mostly racial in nature. Elder was quite nervous when the tournament finally started in April 1975, fifty-one weeks after his victory at Monsanto Open. Though his opening tee shot was a long drive down the center of the fairway, he struggled with his game and missed the cut by four strokes. Elder commented that everyone at the club, especially the black staff members, were accommodating. Elder played in five more Masters, with his best finish a tie for seventeenth in 1979.

Elder played nine more years on the PGA Tour, posting three more victories. In 1976 he won the Houston Open, and in 1978 he won the Greater Milwaukee Open and the American Express

Westchester Classic. In 1979 he became the first African American to make the U.S. Ryder Cup team when he finished thirteenth in earnings on the 1978–1979 Tour. Elder regularly protested racist policies and situations in the PGA, such as country clubs hosting tournaments while excluding blacks from membership. He also boycotted some tournaments because the galleries were openly hostile to black golfers.

In 1984 Elder moved to the Senior Tour, where, in over fifteen years, he had eight victories to push his career earnings over $2 million dollars. On 14 March 1999 Elder woke up for the final round of the Toshiba Senior Classic with double vision. A nerve had locked up in his eye, a condition that handicapped his game.

Off the course, Elder was an advocate for underprivileged and minority children. In 1974 he established the Lee Elder Scholarship Fund. In 1999 he established the Live the Dream Foundation, another scholarship fund, and his efforts to encourage the disadvantaged to attend college earned Elder induction into the National Collegiate Athletic Association Hall of Fame, though he never attended college. Elder also devoted much effort to promoting golf for minorities. In 1997 Elder started two programs, with the help of his wife Sharon, whom he married in 1995, to promote and grow the game of golf among minorities and in urban areas. The Lee Elder National Junior Golf Foundation and Tour offered free golf clinics in ten cities, and the Lee Elder National Youth Program was a summer program that provided clubs and instructions to young golfers in inner cities. On the twenty-fifth anniversary of his breaking the color barrier at the Masters, Elder lamented that there were fewer blacks on the tour in 2000 than when he played. Elder's career as a consistent competitor served as an example to not only minority golfers, who can look to Elder as proof that golfers from all backgrounds can be successful, but also all golfers on how to be a consummate pro on and off the course.

FURTHER READING

Altman, Linda Jacobs, and Jeffrey E. Blackman. *Lee Elder: The Daring Dream* (1976).

Kennedy, John H. *A Course of Their Own: A History of African American Golfers* (2000).

McDaniel, Pete. *Uneven Lies: The Heroic Story of African Americans in Golf* (2000).

Sinnette, Calvin H. *Forbidden Fairways* (1998).

MICHAEL C. MILLER

Elders, M. Joycelyn (13 Aug. 1933–), physician, scientist, professor, public health official, and first African American surgeon general of the United States, was born Minnie Lee Jones in the small town of Schaal, Arkansas, the oldest of eight children of Curtis Jones, a sharecropper, and Haller Reed Jones. As a child, Jones performed the hard labor demanded of Arkansas farmers and their families, and she often led her younger siblings in their work on the small cotton farm. The family home was an unpainted three-room shack with no indoor plumbing or electricity, and there was no hospital or physician for miles around. Jones watched her mother give birth seven times without medical assistance; the only memory she has of a visit to a physician was when her father took a gravely ill younger brother twelve miles by mule to the nearest doctor.

Haller Jones was determined that her children would have more prosperous futures and instilled the importance of education in all of her children, sending them to school during the winter and constantly drilling them on reading skills during the summer months. Minnie Jones excelled at the small segregated Howard County Training School in Schaal, graduating as valedictorian at the age of fifteen. At the graduation ceremony a representative from the Philander Smith Methodist College in Little Rock awarded her a full scholarship. She almost was unable to accept, as transportation to Little Rock was too expensive and she was too valuable as a work leader in the fields. But the family managed with help from extended family and neighbors, and Jones began her college career in the fall of 1948.

At Philander Smith, Jones decided to pursue a career in science, hoping to work in a laboratory after college. Then, at an event arranged by her sorority, Delta Sigma Theta, she met DR. EDITH IRBY JONES, the first African American medical student at the University of Arkansas. After hearing Edith Jones speak about her experiences there, she felt focused and inspired; Minnie Jones determined that she, too, would go to medical school and become a doctor. At about the same time, perhaps to demonstrate her newfound independence, she began to go by the name of Joycelyn, the middle name she had adopted during childhood.

Joycelyn Jones married a fellow student, Cornelius Reynolds, after graduation, and the couple moved to Milwaukee, Wisconsin, where Reynolds had secured employment. In Milwaukee, she worked as a nurse's aide at the veterans' hospital, where she learned of the Women's Medical Specialist Corps. The WMSC was a program in which the army trained college graduates as physical therapists and made them commissioned officers eligible for the GI Bill. Jones and Reynolds parted amicably in May of 1953, and Jones remained in the army for three years. She left when she had served enough time to pay for medical school at what is now the University of Arkansas for Medical Sciences, where she was the second black woman student to attend, after Edith Irby Jones.

In 1960, the same year she graduated from medical school, Jones met and married Oliver Elders, a high school basketball coach. She then completed an internship in pediatrics at the University of Minnesota and returned to the University of Arkansas for a residency in pediatrics with an emphasis on pediatric surgery. Elders came through at the top of her class and was named chief resident in her third year. Along the way, she had two children: Eric in 1963 and Kevin in 1965. After her year as chief resident, Elders decided on a career in academic medicine, serving simultaneously as a junior faculty member and completing a master's degree in Biochemistry. Elders ascended the professional ladder, achieving a full professorship and board certification in pediatric endocrinology in 1976. In all, Elders worked as a professor and practitioner of pediatric endocrinology for nearly twenty-five years and became especially renowned for authoring more than one hundred published papers and for her expert and compassionate treatment of young patients with diabetes, growth problems, and sexual disorders.

In 1987 Elders was appointed by then Arkansas Governor Bill Clinton to the position of director of the Arkansas Department of Health. She initially accepted with some misgivings about leaving her academic post, but she quickly became passionate about her new position. While in office, Elders and her team helped effect an impressive increase in the state health budget. They introduced a program to provide breast cancer screenings and provisions for funding around-the-clock in-home care for elderly and terminally ill patients, and they instituted programs to expand access to HIV testing and counseling services. Her policy initiatives for children resulted in a nearly 25 percent rise in immunizations and a tenfold increase in the number of early childhood screenings in the state. As director, Elders served on several presidential commissions on public health under President George H. W. Bush, and she was elected president of the Association of State and Territorial Health officers.

Elders was especially committed to lowering the teen pregnancy rate in Arkansas, at the time the second highest in the nation. In order to reduce the catastrophic public health consequences of such a high teen pregnancy rate, Elders and her team worked toward implementing a comprehensive health curriculum in the public schools, in which sex education would be a central topic. This would prove to be one of the most controversial acts of her administration, but Elders never backed down under pressure from her critics; she often commented that she felt she was in a unique position to help those in poor rural communities, having been raised in one, and that she would therefore not abandon the course she believed was right.

As director of the health department, Elders also worked toward establishing comprehensive health clinics in public schools. Because so many poor and rural communities in Arkansas lacked adequate health-care facilities, Elders and her staff reasoned that this would be the best way to expand access to preventive care measures, such as dental screenings and vaccinations. At the discretion of the local school board, these clinics could also be authorized to provide reproductive health counseling services and distribute condoms. Although the service was explicitly available only to students who had obtained their parents' permission, it touched off a heated national debate over the relative merits and dangers of distributing condoms in public schools, and Elders's policies became a regular target of critics nationwide.

In July 1993 Bill Clinton, by then president of the United States, appointed Elders to the position of surgeon general of the Public Health Services, and the U.S. Senate confirmed the appointment in September of the same year. Elders was the first African American and second woman appointed to this post, and during her tenure she served on a number of influential health policy committees and spoke widely on matters of public health. After only fifteen months as surgeon general, however, Elders was forced to resign over a public remark she had made at a United Nations World AIDS Day event. Following her presentation on school health clinics, a reporter asked her if she believed there should be any discussion of masturbation in high school health curricula. Elders responded, "I think it is part of human sexuality, and perhaps it should be taught."

Two weeks later, amid a barrage of press coverage, Elders tendered her resignation and moved back to Little Rock. She returned to her academic post at the University of Arkansas Children's Hospital and a full schedule of public-speaking engagements, writing, and community and church involvement. Elders retired from her academic position in 1998, accepting an emeritus appointment. Since then she has lectured and published on those issues to which she has always been passionately dedicated: adequate health care for the poor, the importance of preventative health care, and the need for sex education in public schools.

FURTHER READING

Dr. M. Joycelyn Elders's personal papers are held privately in a storage facility in Little Rock, Arkansas.

Elders, Joycelyn, and David Chanoff. *Joycelyn Elders, M.D.: From Sharecropper's Daughter to Surgeon General of the United States of America* (1996).

DEBORAH I. LEVINE

Eldridge, Elleanor (26 Mar. 1785–1865?), businesswoman, was born in Warwick, Rhode Island, the last of seven daughters of Robin Eldridge, son of African slaves and a Revolutionary War veteran, and Hannah Prophet, a Native American and African American woman. Elleanor Eldridge was a skilled worker and businesswoman and at one point was the wealthiest African American in Providence, Rhode Island. Almost everything known about her is derived from a memoir produced by a collaboration between Eldridge and a white amanuensis, Frances Harriet Whipple. Whipple, who was related to one of Eldridge's former employers, Captain Benjamin Greene, wrote and published the *Memoirs of Elleanor Eldridge* (1838) to raise funds for Eldridge after she had been defrauded by two white men. The text ran into several printings (between 1838 and 1845) and a second edition that brought Eldridge much-needed funds after losing a lawsuit against the two men who had stolen property from her. While some parts of the text—including the melodramatic description of Eldridge's grandfather's kidnapping from Africa and various botanical details—display the amanuensis's imagination novelized, Whipple corroborated most of the facts laid out in the work.

After her mother died when she was ten years old, Eldridge began work as a domestic in the home of Joseph and Elleanor Baker in Warwick. Eldridge most likely had little, if any, formal education since the first "African" school for children did not open in neighboring Providence until 1819. Many of the details about Eldridge's early years reflect the importance she attached to her own working history. For instance, she negotiated a weekly wage of twenty-five cents when she went to work at age ten; she earned recognition for her cheeses, winning awards for their "premium" quality, became an "expert" at ornamental weaving, and excelled at whitewashing, papering, and painting (Green and Eldridge, 33). At a time when black workingwomen were seen as "drudges" or degraded slave women, the single most positive image of a black workingwoman from the early nineteenth century is the frontispiece portrait of Eldridge with wallpaper brush in hand in the *Memoirs*. The 1803 election of Eldridge's older brother George as "governor of the colored election," an annual election held among otherwise disenfranchised free blacks, suggests that the Eldridge family had some standing in the black community. The *Memoirs'* ample inventory of Eldridge's entrepreneurial initiatives and working collaborations with her sisters, mostly in domestic manufactures like soaps, offers a picture of an energetic young woman who supported herself, helped her family, and settled her father's estate after his death in 1812. To obtain necessary letters, Eldridge traveled 180 miles to Adams, Massachusetts. Whipple's appeal to a white, middle-class, female audience is evident in her account of Eldridge's romantic life. After overcoming her subject's initial reluctance, Whipple offered a highly novelized account of Eldridge's romance with her cousin Christopher, a sailor who died at sea, as a way of explaining her unmarried status. While this account raises as many questions as it answers, the fact that Eldridge chose to report a hardworking aunt's assertion that "marriage is a waste of time" suggests that she remained an independent female entrepreneur by choice, not merely by accident (Green and Eldridge, 100). Whipple—herself a middle-class workingwoman—may have assumed that tragic romantic literary conventions, rather than willing spinsterhood, would better appeal to her presumed audience.

After depicting Eldridge as an attractive and hardworking young woman, Whipple took up the task of describing in great but convoluted detail the facts of the fraud and lawsuit that had placed Eldridge in financial need. In this aspect, later research suggests that Whipple or Eldridge shaped the facts of the story, perhaps to heighten Eldridge's status as a deserving "victim." While court records vary slightly from the published account, the substance of events remains true. Eldridge, who bought land, built, and rented out houses as a source of income, fell afoul of two creditors who colluded with a town official to place a lien and auction off one of Eldridge's houses worth $4,300 for $1,500. Tax records show the proceeds paid off a mortgage and the principle on a small loan for $376, not $240 as cited in the *Memoirs*, and also suggests that Eldridge may have known beforehand of this plan, contrary to the text's claims. Eldridge lost a suit she filed for trespass before the court of common pleas in January 1837, after which the purchaser of the property agreed to let her buy it back for much more than she had originally paid for it, $2,700. It remains unclear what motivated these men's successful con; perhaps Eldridge's ownership of valuable property and the industry and prosperity it symbolized were viewed as a threat to the racial status quo, or perhaps, as Whipple suggests, these men felt entitled to take the property of a "colored woman" simply because they could do so more or less with impunity (Green and Eldridge, 91). More important, the fraud and Eldridge's subsequent legal loss motivated her employers to champion their former employee and to publicly chastise the town officials involved. It is no small testament to her standing among her employers and townspeople who bought the *Memoirs* that Eldridge was able to raise large sums of cash and buy back her property in the middle of the economic panic of 1837.

The *Memoirs* is a remarkable text about a remarkable woman, offering a celebratory depiction of an industrious, black workingwoman that contradicts negative popular understandings of black workingwomen's subordinate status. Whipple's strong emphasis on Eldridge's successful careers and exemplary character provided Eldridge with a framework that complements, rather than completely rejects, her dissent from the dominant middle-class notions of womanhood. It also affirms a tradition of unlettered black women—ELIZABETH FREEMAN (Mumm Bett) in Massachusetts and SOJOURNER TRUTH in New York—who forged successful careers and marshaled their legal and social acumen to overcome racial prejudice. It is not entirely clear when or where Eldridge died, but she was reported to have passed away at age eighty.

FURTHER READING

Cottrol, Robert J. *The Afro-Yankees: Providences Black Community in the Antebellum Era* (1982).

Green, Frances H. [Whipple], and Elleanor Eldridge. *Memoirs of Elleanor Eldridge* (1838) and *Elleanor's Second Book* (1839), Documenting the American South, http://docsouth.unc.edu/neh/eldridge/menu.html.

O'Dowd, Sarah C. *A Rhode Island Original: Frances Harriet Whipple Green McDougall* (2004)

XIOMARA SANTAMARINA

Eldridge, Roy (30 Jan. 1911–26 Feb. 1989), musician, was born David Roy Eldridge in Pittsburgh, Pennsylvania, the younger son of Alexander Eldridge, a contractor, and Blanche Oakes Eldridge, who ran a local restaurant. Eldridge was playing drums at the age of six and, finding that he could play anything he could hear, subsequently taught himself trumpet, flugelhorn, and piano. He dropped out of David B. Oliver High School at age fifteen and joined his saxophone-playing brother Joe's band as a drummer.

After briefly fronting his own local band in 1927 Eldridge played trumpet in carnival and theater circuit bands before moving to the Chocolate Dandies, Hot Chocolates, the Dixie Stompers, the Night Hawk Syncopaters, the Midnite Ramblers, and the variously named bands led by DON REDMAN. By the time he arrived in New York in 1930, first with Cecil Scott and then ELMER SNOWDEN's band, he had developed a remarkable trumpet style that imperfectly fused two elements.

Perhaps the most competitive of jazzmen, addicted to after-hours "cutting" contests with every famous trumpeter he met, Eldridge could play higher and more "on the rim of chaos" than anyone else of his generation. Whitney Balliett wrote that his fingers released notes "the way a dog shakes off water." Contrarily, Eldridge, who idolized the saxophone players COLEMAN HAWKINS, Benny Carter, and LESTER YOUNG, could remove the hard edges, saying he liked to "play nice saxophone on the trumpet."

Later called by DIZZY GILLESPIE "the Messiah of our generation" and by jazz critics the link between LOUIS ARMSTRONG's hot jazz and Gillespie's nervous bebop, Eldridge confessed to being influenced by Armstrong in 1932: "He taught me how to tell a story." Eldridge was with the Teddy Hill orchestra in 1935; the next year he joined FLETCHER HENDERSON's orchestra as lead trumpeter and occasional singer, then formed an eight-piece band with his brother as saxophonist-arranger and began a lengthy recording career. He married in 1937 Viola Lee Fong, a hostess at the Savoy Ballroom; they would have one child and remain married for the rest of their lives, Eldridge dying three weeks after his wife. In 1939 Eldridge, who had quit music for a

Roy Eldridge, posing with Ella Fitzgerald at the airport in Hamburg, West Germany, after arriving for a tour of Germany with other famous jazz musicians, 15 February 1954. (AP Images.)

year because of its emotional demands and according to some accounts because of racism and low pay, was playing "mild dance music" at the Arcadia Ballroom on New York's Broadway. By 1940 he was at Minton's in Harlem, where he encouraged the young drummer Kenny ("Klook") Clarke to play the top cymbal, "superimposing rhythms with his left hand." Clarke, in time the preeminent drummer of the bebop era, said that "with Roy I got everything I'd been trying to do together." Gillespie, arguably the founder of bop, was there too, listening and soaking up everything Eldridge did.

All the bands mentioned above were entirely African American. But in the later 1930s the strict color line in popular music was sometimes breached—Billie Holiday singing with the Artie Shaw band, Henderson writing arrangements for Benny Goodman's orchestra, for which the vibraphonist Lionel Hampton was a "special attraction." In April 1941 Eldridge joined Gene Krupa's orchestra as a "featured soloist." After the trumpeter Shorty Sherock left, Eldridge became one of the first African Americans to play regularly with a "white" band.

During Eldridge's two years with the Krupa band, he proved to be a brilliant soloist and an engaging singer, combining with the young Anita O'Day on several of the Swing Era's most memorable duets. He later said, "I would sit in my dressing room and run over in my mind what I was going to do. But when I got out there I didn't try and make the B-flat or whatever I was thinking of, because I'd go right into a void where there was no memory—nothing but me … riding up on that stage at the Paramount Theatre with the Krupa band scared me to death. I'd shake like a leaf, and you could hear it. Then this light would surround me." It was especially on the Pacific Coast that

Eldridge encountered a racism he could not handle. When the Krupa band played the Hollywood Palladium, Eldridge was not permitted to stay with the others and had to find lodgings in the "colored" section beyond downtown Los Angeles. Under such pressure, in the midst of one of his most famous solos, "Rocking Chair," Eldridge ran offstage and vomited. He took to carrying a gun. After Krupa was jailed for a drug offense, Eldridge led the band until it broke up.

Although Krupa was supportive and Shaw, Eldridge's next white leader (Oct. 1944–Sept. 1945), even more so, racism continued to oppress Eldridge. Yet his reputation skyrocketed. His signature tune "Little Jazz" (a nickname laid on the barely five-foot-tall Eldridge by DUKE ELLINGTON's reed player Toby Hardwick) was recorded with Shaw. He won the *Metronome* magazine poll as top trumpeter in 1944 and 1946, was *Esquire* magazine's top trumpeter in 1945, and was named America's top trumpeter in the 1946 *Down Beat* magazine poll. (Eldridge was later named to the *Down Beat* Hall of Fame.)

After leaving Shaw, Eldridge had his own band again (1946–1948). Ensconced at New York's Three Deuces while Gillespie was at the Onyx, he engaged Gillespie in after-hours contests that became legendary. When the Krupa band re-formed in 1949, he joined it for several months, leaving to join the first of Norman Granz's yearly Jazz at the Philharmonic tours.

Eldridge's last stint with a white band came in 1950, when he joined the Goodman band for a European tour. In Paris the band performed to great acclaim; he later said he had felt no racial prejudice there or anywhere else on the continent. He made a number of recordings, singing in English and French. (When the recordings were re-released thirty years later, they caused a revival of interest in Eldridge.)

Back in the United States at Birdland in New York (1951), Eldridge told the jazz writer Leonard Feather he would never join a white band again: "Man, when you're on the stage, you're great, but as soon as you come off, you're nothing. It's not worth the glory, not worth the money, not worth anything. Never again!"

Subsequently Eldridge led the group that accompanied ELLA FITZGERALD's international concert appearances from 1963 to 1965 and in 1966 spent a year with COUNT BASIE's orchestra, which was still playing swinging jazz. He frequently returned to Europe and appeared at various jazz festivals in the United States, including a miniature festival for President Jimmy Carter on the White House south lawn. From 1969 to 1979, when he gave up playing in public, he led a small swing band at Jimmy Ryan's on West Fifty-fourth Street in New York. In 1980 he suffered the first of several strokes. There followed many concerts in his honor. Suffering from emphysema, Eldridge, a giant of jazz blessed and tortured by extreme sensitivity, died in Valley Stream, New York.

FURTHER READING

Collier, James Lincoln. *The Making of Jazz* (1978).
Gillespie, Dizzy. *To Be or Not … to Bop* (1979).
Shapiro, Nat, and Nat Hentoff. *Hear Me Talkin' to Ya: The Story of Jazz as Told by the Men Who Made It* (1955).
Obituary: *New York Times*, 28 Feb. 1989.

This entry is taken from the *American National Biography* and is published here with the permission of the American Council of Learned Societies.

JAMES ROSS MOORE

Elizabeth (1766–11 June 1866), former slave, and itinerant Methodist minister, was born in Maryland and apparently never used a surname. Elizabeth did not relate the names of her parents or her siblings in the memoir she dictated at one hundred years of age. She did, however, reveal that her parents belonged to a Methodist Society and she recalled that every Sabbath morning from the time she was five until she was eleven years old her father read the Bible aloud to her and the rest of their family. At the age of eleven she was separated from her family when her owner sold her or her services to another plantation twenty or more miles away. Elizabeth ignored her overseer's instructions and visited her mother and family. Inconsolable over the separation from her family, her mother advised Elizabeth that she had "nobody in the wide world to look to but God" (*Elizabeth*, 4). She recalled that those words echoed in her head again and again: "none but God in the wide world." Upon returning to her owner's farm, "I found the overseer was displeased at me for going without his liberty. He tied me with a rope, and gave me some stripes, of which I carried the marks for weeks" (*Elizabeth*, 3). For six months she fell into deep depression until she experienced a prolonged religious crisis that resulted in greater faith and courage to endure her enslavement. Elizabeth's memoir is largely silent on her experiences in slavery and mentions no names and few locations or dates of events, dwelling mostly on her religious faith and experiences as a self-appointed itinerant minister. She did, however, reveal that at some point she was sold to a Presbyterian who did not fully believe in slavery and gave Elizabeth her freedom when she turned thirty. Sometime thereafter, she held her first religious meeting in the home of a "poor widow" in Baltimore. Other black women attended, which raised opposition in the community and attempts to halt Elizabeth's services. After some discussions with church elders, a male representative attended her meetings and for several years she was able to continue her "ministry."

Elizabeth's services increasing attracted local attention and larger crowds, including some local whites who had heard of Elizabeth's powerful sermons:

> At one of the meetings, a vast number of the white inhabitants of the place, and many colored people, attended—many no doubt front curiosity to hear what the old colored woman had to say. One, a great scripturian, fixed himself behind the door with pen and ink, in order to take down the discourse in short-hand; but the Almighty Being anointed me with such a portion of his Spirit, that he cast away his paper and pen, and heard the discourse with patience, and was much affected, for the Lord wrought powerfully on his heart. After meeting, he came forward and offered me his hand, with solemnity on his countenance, and handed me something to pay for my conveyance home (*Elizabeth*, 10).

Her fame spread and she held subsequent meetings in Maryland and in Virginia. Her sermons included condemnations of slavery, and it wasn't long before these attracted the attention of authorities who threatened to imprison her. What resulted from her antislavery sermons, she did not reveal. Elizabeth then traveled widely and for four years lived in Michigan, where she established a school for black students. She also traveled to Canada, holding well-attended services and often participating in Quaker meetings in her travels, perhaps mostly in Philadelphia where she died. During her last days in the summer of 1866, she found a Quaker willing to record her story and captured her last words and painful demise. "Through months of bodily anguish," her caregiver and amanuensis noted, "occasioned by gangrenous sores upon one of her feet, which extended from the toes to the knee, destroying in its terrible course all the flesh, leaving the bone bare and black," she continued to profess her unyielding faith. Her memoir, *A Colored Minister of the Gospel, Born in Slavery*, published by Philadelphia Quakers twenty-three years after Elizabeth's death, certainly speaks to the Quaker notion of the inner light. Moreover its equalitarian message and defense of a woman's right to speak and preach comported well with Quaker thinking and practice. Once, in Virginia, after delivering a sermon that included a condemnation of slavery, whites confronted her and demanded to know by what authority she spoke (if she was an ordained minister). She responded "if the Lord had ordained me, I needed nothing better" (*Elizabeth*, 10–11).

FURTHER READING

Elizabeth. *Elizabeth, A Colored Minister of the Gospel, Born in Slavery* (1889). Available from http://docsouth.unc.edu/neh/eliza2/eliza2.html.

Elizabeth. "Memoir of Old Elizabeth A Coloured Woman," in *Six Women's Slave Narratives*, ed. Henry Louis Gates Jr. (1988).

REGINA V. JONES

Ellington, Arthur "Yank" (1914–?), lynching survivor and litigant, was born in Noxubee County, Mississippi, to parents whose names are unknown. Nothing is known of his early life, but around 1932 he married a woman named Kate, with whom he had two children. They moved a few miles south of Noxubee, to Scooba in Kemper County, where he began working as a farm laborer for Raymond Stuart, a prominent white planter. Ellington's new home county, known since Reconstruction as "Bloody Kemper" because of its reputation for racial violence, had witnessed fourteen lynchings between 1883 and 1930, all of them of African Americans. Indeed, whites in Kemper lynched blacks at twice the rate of other counties in Mississippi, the state with the nation's worst record for lynching.

On 30 March 1934 Ellington nearly became the fifteenth black man lynched in Bloody Kemper, following the discovery of his employer's dead body. Raymond Stuart had died as a result of wounds inflicted the previous evening by someone wielding an axe or similar implement. Although no material evidence linked Ellington to the murder, Kemper County Deputy Sheriff Cliff Dial and a posse of white men came to his home a few hours later, and forcibly took him to the Stuart farmhouse. There twenty or more armed white men confronted Ellington and demanded that he confess to Stuart's murder. When he proclaimed his innocence, insisting that he had been at home in bed with his wife at the time of the alleged murder, Dial led the mob in twice hanging him by a rope to the limb of a tree. When Ellington continued to protest his innocence, his attackers tied him to a tree and whipped him repeatedly before allowing him to return home. Two days later, Dial and another deputy returned to Ellington's home, arrested him, and drove him to a jail in Meridian in nearby Lauderdale County. Ostensibly, this was to protect Ellington from being mobbed again by angry whites in Kemper County, although Stuart had been equally well known in Meridian. Dial's concern for his prisoner's procedural rights and safety did not, however, preclude him from repeatedly whipping Ellington on the journey from Scooba to Meridian, nor from threatening to continue to whip him until he confessed to Stuart's murder. By the end of the journey, which took a circuitous route through Alabama, perhaps to extend the torture, Ellington had confessed.

Ellington's confession on 1 April 1934 led to the arrest of two other black men, Ed Brown, one of Stuart's tenants, and Henry Shields, one of his neighbors. Both of these men were taken to the Meridian jail, where Dial and several prison guards forced them to strip, laid them over chairs, and whipped them across their backs with a buckled leather strap. Again, Dial warned the prisoners that the beatings would continue until they confessed to Stuart's murder in precisely the manner he demanded. When they finally did so, the deputy warned the defendants that they would receive similar punishments if they later retracted their confessions. Despite this threat, all three men retracted their initial confessions at the trial that followed only four days later, on the grounds that they had been forcibly coerced. Far from denying these beatings, several of the officers admitted in court to having assaulted the prisoners, arguing that (in Dial's view) the whipping of Ellington was "not too much for a negro" (cited in Higginbotham, 162). When the prosecuting attorney (and future U.S. Senator) John Stennis asked Ellington whether he was afraid of his jailers, the prisoner, whose neck was still visibly scarred by rope burns, replied, "Yes, sir. I am afraid of all white people" (cited in Cortner, 25). Although each of the defendants presented strong alibis for their whereabouts on the evening of the murder and despite clear evidence that their initial confessions had been coerced, an all-white jury found the three accused black men guilty of murdering Raymond Stuart. On 6 April 1934, exactly a week after Stuart's body had been found, Judge J. I. Sturdivant sentenced Yank Ellington, Ed Brown, and Henry Shields to death. They were to be hanged five weeks later, on 11 May 1934.

Unlike the similar case of the SCOTTSBORO BOYS in Alabama, which became an international *cause célèbre* in 1931, the fate of Ellington, Brown, and Shields provoked little response outside northeastern Mississippi. The extreme poverty of the three men also made an appeal of their sentence unlikely, but one of their court-appointed attorneys, State Senator John Clark, became convinced during their trial that their original confessions had been extracted through torture. In a move that ended his career in Mississippi politics, Clark appealed the convictions to the state's supreme court on the grounds that such obviously coerced confessions were unreliable and constitutionally invalid. Clark lost the appeal, but persuaded two Mississippi supreme court judges to issue vigorous dissents, thus making possible a fresh appeal to the U.S. Supreme Court. In a unanimous decision in 1936, the nation's highest court overturned the convictions and death sentences as a violation of the defendants' rights to due process under the Fourteenth Amendment of the U.S. Constitution. Chief Justice Charles Hughes's opinion in *Brown v. Mississippi* was scathing about the forced confessions and lack of procedural rights given Ellington and the other defendants. The "rack and torture chamber," Hughes concluded, "may not be substituted for the witness stand" (cited in Higginbotham, 163).

The Supreme Court's ruling prevented the state of Mississippi from carrying out its planned execution of the three men, but it left open the possibility that they could be retried in Kemper County, again by an all-white jury. Fearing that they would again face a death sentence, Brown and Shields accepted a plea bargain negotiated between Stennis and their attorney, Earl Brewer. Brown agreed to serve a further seven and a half years in jail, and Shields a further five years, in addition to the two years they had already served. Believing that there was no evidence whatsoever that might convict Yank Ellington, Brewer advised the youngest of the defendants to reject the plea bargain. Ellington, who may well have understood Mississippi "justice" better than did former governor Brewer, accepted the plea bargain, fearing that he might never leave the jail alive unless he did so. Ellington was finally released in May 1937, as was Shields two years later, and Brown in late 1941. It is uncertain what happened to them after that point, although earlier, Ellington had made his determination to leave the state that had placed such a low value on his rights as a human being quite clear.

For nearly six decades *Brown v. Mississippi* remained the guiding principle in criminal cases involving coerced confessions, and was central to the broad liberalization of defendants' rights in the American legal system after World War II.

FURTHER READING

Cortner, Richard C. *A "Scottsboro" Case in Mississippi: The Supreme Court and Brown v. Mississippi* (1986).

Higginbotham, A. Leon. *Shades of Freedom: Racial Politics and Presumptions of the American Legal Process* (1996).

STEVEN J. NIVEN

Ellington, Duke (29 Apr. 1899–24 May 1974), jazz musician and composer, was born Edward Kennedy Ellington in Washington, D.C., the son of James Edward Ellington, a butler, waiter, and later printmaker, and Daisy Kennedy. The Ellingtons were middle-class people who struggled at times to make ends meet. Ellington's mother was particularly attached to him; in her eyes he could do no wrong. They belonged to Washington's black elite, who put much stock in racial pride. Ellington developed a strong sense of his own worth and a belief in his destiny, which at times shaded over into egocentricity. Because of this attitude, and his almost royal bearing, his schoolmates early named him "Duke."

Ellington's interest in music was slow to develop. He was given piano lessons as a boy but soon dropped them. He was finally awakened to music at about fourteen when he heard a pianist named Harvey Brooks, who was not much older than he. Brooks, he later said, "was swinging, and he had a tremendous left hand, and when I got home I had a real yearning to play."

He did not take formal piano lessons, however, but picked the brains of local pianists, some of whom were excellent. He was always looking for shortcuts, ways of getting effects without much arduous practicing. As a consequence, it was a long time before he became proficient at the stride style basic to popular piano playing of the time.

As he improved, Ellington discovered that playing for his friends at parties was a route to popularity. He began to rehearse with some other youngsters, among them the saxophonist Otto TOBY HARDWICK and the trumpeter ARTIE WHETSOL. Eventually a New Jersey drummer, SONNY GREER, joined the group. By age sixteen or seventeen Ellington was playing occasional professional jobs with these and other young musicians. The music they played was not jazz, which still was not widely known, but rags and ordinary popular songs. Ellington was not yet committed to music. He was also studying commercial art, for which he showed an aptitude. However, he never graduated from high school, and in 1918 he married Edna Thompson; the following spring their son, Mercer, was born. Although later Ellington lived with several different women, he never divorced his wife.

He now had a family to support and was perforce drawn into the music business, one of the few areas in which blacks could earn good incomes and achieve a species of fame. Increasingly he was working with a group composed of Whetsol, Greer, and Hardwick under the nominal leadership of the Baltimore banjoist ELMER SNOWDEN. This was the nucleus of later Ellington bands. In 1923 the group ventured to New York and landed a job at a well-known Harlem cabaret, Barron's Exclusive Club. The club had a clientele of intellectuals and the social elite, some of them white, and the band was not playing jazz, but "under conversation music." Ellington was handsome and already a commanding figure, and the others were polite, middle-class youths. They were well liked, and in 1923 they were asked to open at the Hollywood, a new club in the Broadway theater district, soon renamed the Kentucky Club.

As blacks, they were expected to play the new hot music, now growing in popularity. Like many other young musicians, they were struggling to catch its elusive rhythms, and they reached out for a jazz specialist, the trumpeter James BUBBER MILEY, who had developed a style based on the plunger mute work of a New Orleanian, KING OLIVER. Miley not only used the plunger for *wah-wah* effects but also employed throat tones to produce a growl. He was a hot, driving player and set the style for the band. Somewhat later, SIDNEY BECHET, perhaps the finest improviser in jazz at the time, had a brief but influential stay with the band.

Through the next several years the band worked off and on at the Kentucky Club, recording with increasing frequency. Then, early in 1924, the group fired Snowden for withholding money, and Ellington was chosen to take over. Very quickly he began to mold the band to his tastes. He was aided by an association with Irving Mills, a song publisher and show business entrepreneur with gangland connections. Mills needed an orchestra to record his company's songs; Ellington needed both

Duke Ellington, photographed by Gordon Parks Sr., at the Hurricane Club in New York, 1943. (Library of Congress.)

connections and guidance through the show business maze. His contract with Mills gave Ellington control of the orchestra.

As a composer, Ellington showed a penchant for breaking rules: if he were told that a major seventh must rise to the tonic, he would devise a piece in which it descended. His still-developing method of composition was to bring to rehearsal—or even to the recording studio—scraps and pieces of musical ideas, which he would try in various ways until he got an effect he liked. Members of the band would offer suggestions, add counterlines, and work out harmonies among themselves. It was very much a cooperative effort, and frequently the music was never written down. Although in time Ellington worked more with pencil and paper, this improvisational system remained basic to his composing.

Beginning with a group of records made in November 1926, the group found its voice: the music from this session has the distinctive Ellington sound. The first important record was "East St. Louis Toodle-Oo" (1926), a smoky piece featuring Bubber Miley growling over a minor theme. Most important of all was "Black and Tan Fantasy" (1927), another slow piece featuring Miley in a minor key. It ends with a quotation from Chopin's "Funeral March." In part because of this touch, "Black and Tan Fantasy" was admired by influential critics such as R. D. Darrell, who saw it as a harbinger of a more sophisticated, composed jazz. Increasingly thereafter, Ellington was seen by critics writing in intellectual and music journals as a major American composer.

Then, in December 1927 the group was hired as the house band at the Cotton Club, rapidly becoming the country's best-known cabaret. It was decided, for commercial purposes, to feature a "jungle sound," built around the growling of Miley and the trombonist JOE "Tricky Sam" NANTON. About this time Ellington added musicians who would fundamentally shape the band's sound: the clarinetist BARNEY BIGARD, a well-trained New Orleanian with a liquid tone; the saxophonist JOHNNY HODGES, who possessed a flowing, honeyed sound and quickly became the premier altoist in jazz; and COOTIE WILLIAMS, who replaced the wayward Miley and soon became a master of the plunger mute. These and other instrumentalists each had a distinctive sound and gave Ellington a rich "tonal palette," which he worked with increasing mastery.

Through the 1920s and 1930s Ellington created a group of masterpieces characterized by short, sparkling melodies, relentless contrasts of color and mood, and much more dissonant harmony than was usual in popular music. Among the best known of these are "Mood Indigo" (1930) and "Creole Love Call" (1927), two simple but very effective mood pieces; "Rockin' in Rhythm" (1930), a driving uptempo piece made up of sharply contrasting melodies; and "Daybreak Express" (1933), an uncanny imitation of train sounds. These pieces alone won Ellington a major position in jazz history, but they are only examples of scores of brilliant works.

By now he had come into his own as a songwriter. During the 1930s he created many standards, like "Prelude to a Kiss" (1938), "Sophisticated Lady" (1932), and "Solitude" (1934). This songwriting was critically important, for, leaving aside musical considerations, Ellington's ASCAP royalties were in later years crucial in his keeping the band going.

It must be admitted, however, that Ellington borrowed extensively in producing these tunes. "Creole Love Call" and "Mood Indigo," although credited to Ellington, were written by others. Various of his musicians contributed to "Sophisticated Lady," "Black and Tan Fantasy," and many more. Though it is not always easy to know how much others contributed to a given work, it was Ellington's arranging and orchestrating of the melodies that lifted pieces like "Creole Love Call" above the mundane.

By 1931, through broadcasts from the Cotton Club and his recordings, Ellington had become a major figure in popular music. In that year the band left the club and for the remainder of its existence played the usual mix of one-nighters, theater dates, and longer stays in nightclubs and hotel ballrooms. The singer IVIE ANDERSON, who would work with the organization for more than a decade and remains the vocalist most closely associated with Ellington, joined him at this time.

In 1933 the band made a brief visit to London and the Continent. British critics convinced Ellington that he was more than just a dance-band leader. He had already written one longer, more "symphonic" piece, "Creole Rhapsody" (1931). He now set about writing more. The most important of these was "Black, Brown, and Beige," which was given its premiere at Carnegie Hall in 1943. The opening was a significant event in American music: a black composer writing "serious" music using themes taken from black culture.

Classical critics did not much like the piece. The problem, as always with Ellington's extended work, was that, lacking training, he was unable to unify the smaller themes and musical ideas he produced. Ellington, although temporarily discouraged, continued to write extended pieces, which combined jazz elements with devices meant to reflect classical music.

Additionally, beginning in 1936, Ellington recorded with small groups drawn from the band. These recordings, such as Johnny Hodges's "Jeep's Blues" (1938) and REX STEWART's "Subtle Slough," contain a great deal of his finest work. Yet most critics would say that his finest work of the time was a series of concertos featuring various instrumentalists, including "Echoes of Harlem" (1935) for Cootie Williams and "Clarinet Lament" (1936) for Barney Bigard.

In 1939 the character of the band began to change when the bassist JIMMY BLANTON, who was enormously influential during a career cut short by death, and the tenor saxophonist BEN WEBSTER were added. Ellington had never had a major tenor soloist at his disposal, and Webster's rich, guttural utterances were a new voice for him to work with. Also arriving in 1939 was BILLY STRAYHORN, a young composer who had more formal training than Ellington. Until Strayhorn's death in 1967, a substantial part of the Ellington oeuvre was actually written in collaboration with Strayhorn, although it is difficult to tease apart their individual contributions. In 1940 Ellington switched from Columbia to Victor. The so-called Victor band of 1940 to 1942, when a union dispute temporarily ended recording in the United States, is considered by many jazz critics to be one of the great moments in jazz. "Take the 'A' Train," written by Strayhorn, is a simple, indeed basic, piece, which gets its effect from contrapuntal lines and the interplay of the band's voices. "Cotton Tail" (1940) is a reworking of "I've Got Rhythm" that outshines the original melody and is famous for a powerful Webster solo and a sinuous, winding chorus for the saxophones. "Harlem Air Shaft" (1940) is a classic Ellington program piece meant to suggest the life in a Harlem apartment building and is filled with shifts and contrasts that produce a sense of rich disorder. "Main Stem" (1942) is another hard-driving piece, offering incredible musical variety within a tiny space. Perhaps the most highly regarded recording from this period is "Ko-Ko" (1940). Originally written as part of an extended work, it is based on a blues in E-flat minor and is built up of the layering of increasingly dissonant and contrasting lines.

By the late 1940s, it was felt by many jazz writers that the band had deteriorated. The swing band movement, which had swept up the Ellington group in the mid-1930s, had collapsed, and musical tastes were changing. A number of the old hands left, taking with them much of Ellington's tonal palette, and while excellent newcomers replaced them, few equaled the originals. Through the late 1940s and into the 1950s there were constant changes of personnel, shifts from one record company to the next, and a dwindling demand for the orchestra. Henceforth Ellington would need his song royalties to support what was now a very expensive organization. In 1956 Ellington was asked to play the closing Saturday night concert at the recently established Newport Jazz Festival. At one point in the evening he brought the tenor saxophonist Paul Gonsalves forward to play twenty-seven choruses of the blues over a rhythm section. The crowd was wildly enthusiastic; the event got much media attention, and Ellington's star began to rise again.

Through the late 1950s and 1960s Ellington continued to create memorable pieces, many of them contributed by Strayhorn, particularly the haunting "Blood Count" (1967). Also of value were a series of collaborations with Ellington by major jazz soloists from outside the band, including LOUIS ARMSTRONG, COLEMAN HAWKINS, and JOHN COLTRANE. Other fine works were

Strayhorn's "UMMG," featuring DIZZY GILLESPIE; "Paris Blues" (1960), a variation on the blues done for a movie by that name; and an album tribute to Strayhorn issued as ... *And His Mother Called Him Bill* (1967).

But by this time Ellington's main concerns were his extended works, which eventually totaled some three dozen. Many of these were dashed off to meet deadlines, or even pulled together in rehearsal, and are of slight value. Almost all suffer from the besetting flaw in Ellington's longer works, his inability to make unified wholes of what are often brilliant smaller pieces.

Although some critics insist that much of this work is of value, it was not well reviewed outside the jazz press when it appeared. Among the most successful are "The Deep South Suite" (1946), "Harlem (A Tone Parallel to Harlem)," first recorded in 1951, and "The Far East Suite" in collaboration with Strayhorn and recorded in 1966.

To Ellington, the most important of these works were the three "Sacred Concerts," created in the last years of his life. They consist of collections of vocal and instrumental pieces of various sorts, usually tied loosely together by a religious theme. Although these works contain fine moments and have their admirers, they do not, on the whole, succeed. Duke Ellington's legacy is the short jazz works, most of them written between 1926 and 1942: the jungle pieces, like "Black and Tan Fantasy"; the concertos, like "Echoes of Harlem"; the mood pieces, such as "Mood Indigo"; the harmonically complex works, like "Ko-Ko"; and the hard swingers, such as "Cotton Tail." This work has a rich tonal palette. It uses carefully chosen sounds by his soloists; endless contrast not only of sound but also of mood, mode, key; the use of forms unusual in popular music, like the four-plus-ten bar segment in "Echoes of Harlem"; and deftly handled dissonance, often built around very close internal harmonies. Although Ellington was not a jazz improviser in a class with Armstrong or CHARLIE PARKER, his body of work is far larger than theirs, more varied and richer, and is second to none in jazz. Ellington died in New York City.

FURTHER READING

Many Ellington papers and artifacts are housed in the Duke Ellington Collection, National Museum of American History, Smithsonian Institution. Additional materials are lodged in the Duke Ellington Oral History Project at Yale, the Schomburg Center for Research in Black Culture of the New York Public Library, and the Institute for Jazz Studies at Rutgers University.

Ellington, Edward Kennedy. *Music Is My Mistress* (1973).

Collier, James Lincoln. *Duke Ellington* (1987).

Dance, Stanley. *The World of Duke Ellington* (1970).

Ellington, Mercer, with Stanley Dance. *Duke Ellington in Person* (1978).

Jewell, Derek. *Duke: A Portrait of Duke Ellington* (1977).

Ulanov, Barry. *Duke Ellington* (1946).

DISCOGRAPHY

Aasland, Benny. *The "Wax Works" of Duke Ellington* (1979–).

Bakker, Dick M. *Duke Ellington on Microgroove* (1972–).

Massagli, Luciano, Liborio Pusateri, and Giovanni M. Volonté. *Duke Ellington's Story on Records* (1967–).

This entry is taken from the *American National Biography* and is published here with the permission of the American Council of Learned Societies.

JAMES LINCOLN COLLIER

Ellington, Mercedes (9 Feb. 1939–), dancer, choreographer, and teacher, was the only child born to Ruth V. Silas and Mercer K. Ellington. Ellington's parents divorced less than a year after her birth. Her mother remarried the Philadelphia obstetrician and gynecologist James A. Batts, but Mercedes was raised in New York by her mother's parents, Louise and Alfred Silas. Mercedes had two half brothers, Edward and Paul, both of whom were musicians.

Ellington's family was involved in the arts for two generations. Her grandfather was the legendary jazz great DUKE ELLINGTON. Her father, Mercer Ellington, was an arranger, composer, and trumpeter who toured, arranged, and performed with the Duke Ellington Orchestra off and on from 1940 through 1965 and eventually took over operation of the orchestra when Duke Ellington died in 1974.

Ellington took dance lessons from an early age and attended Our Lady of Lourdes School in Harlem. She had public dance classes at her elementary school and private sessions with twin sisters Marian and Marjorie Facey, who maintained a studio in Carnegie Hall. The sisters were trained in the Anna Pavlova technique of dance. Ellington continued her dance classes at St. Walburga's Academy and then studied on a scholarship at the Metropolitan Opera Ballet School. She then did advanced studies in dance and choreography at

Juilliard, graduating with a degree in modern and classical dance in 1960.

Ellington entered show business in 1963, after auditioning and winning a spot as one of the June Taylor Dancers. A well-qualified candidate for the dance troupe, Ellington had been sent to the audition with the support of the NAACP and the Urban League in an effort to break the color barrier against hiring blacks in the entertainment industry, notably television. She made television history when she was named to the dance troupe. The June Taylor Dancers, with Ellington as a member, were a featured act for three summers at the Jones' Beach Marine Theater in Florida. The group was also featured on television's *Jackie Gleason Show*, a popular Saturday evening network program in the 1960s. The dancers were famous for their chorus line dance routine. Ellington remained with the dance troupe for seven years.

Ellington debuted as a performer with the New York City Opera in 1977 and taught tap dancing for the Alvin Ailey American Dance Center. She soon branched out to Broadway, working as both a choreographer and a performer in musicals such as *No, No, Nanette* (1971–1973), *The Night That Made America Famous* (1975), *Together on Broadway* (1977), *The Grand Tour* (1979), *Happy New Year* (1980), and *Sophisticated Ladies* (1981–1983). *Sophisticated Ladies* was a family affair; the musical, based on the music of her grandfather, Duke Ellington, was conducted by Ellington's father. Ellington served as assistant choreographer and was also a featured dancer.

With a resurgence in the popularity of her grandfather's music in the 1970s and 80s, Ellington began to choreograph dance routines to the music he made famous. Ellington and Maurice Hines were the artistic directors of the BalleTap, USA, which incorporated into DancEllington, Inc., from 1984 through 1992. The company, which made its debut in New York with the noted dancer CARMEN DE LAVALLADE as guest artist in December 1984, featured modern tap and dance professionals including both Hines and Ellington.

Ellington continued to perform. She made her Carnegie Hall debut in 1999 and her Metropolitan Opera House debut in 2002. She also appeared in *The Algonquin Hotel: Talk of the Town* at the Bank Street Theater in New York City during 2005 and 2006.

Ellington was the recipient of numerous awards and honors. She was given the Woman of the Year award by the Pajama Program and the Boys' Towns of Italy, Inc., in recognition of her work encouraging dance education for children. Her theater awards included the Black Theater Alliance Award for *Play On!* (based on William Shakespeare's *Twelfth Night*) at the Goodman Theater in Chicago in 1998, the Garland Award for the choreography in *Play On!* at the Pasadena Playhouse in 1999, and a nomination for the Helen Hayes Award from the Washington Theater Award Society in 2001 for outstanding choreography in *Play On!* at the Arena Stage in Washington, D.C. She also earned a Barrymore Award nomination in 2006 for her choreography for *Dreamgirls* performed at the Prince Music Theater in Philadelphia.

Ellington also served on the boards of numerous foundations, including Career Transition for Dancers, American Tap Dance Foundation, New Jersey Tap Ensemble, Governors for the Friar's Club, and the nominating committee for the Tony awards. Her choreography on the plays *Juba*, *Sophisticated Ladies*, and *Play On!* is in the permanent collection of the Lincoln Center Performing Arts Library. She also served as president of the Duke Ellington Foundation, an organization that sought to establish the reputation of the musician as both a writer and painter and that granted scholarships to promote the arts. Additionally, she was involved in SOS New Orleans Jazz Heritage, a fund-raising foundation that helped working musicians to purchase new instruments to replace those destroyed in hurricane Katrina in 2005.

FURTHER READING

Green, Stanley, and Kay. *Broadway Musicals: Show by Show* (1990).

Olmstead, Andrea. *Juilliard: A History*, Music in American Life Series (2002).

Woll, Allen. *Black Musical Theater—From Coontown to Dreamgirls* (1989).

PAMELA LEE GRAY

Elliott, Missy (1 July 1971–), recording artist, producer, and actress, was born Melissa Elliott in Portsmouth, Virginia, to Ronnie Elliot, a U.S. Marine, and Patricia Elliott, who worked for a power company. She was an only child, and the family—owing to Ronnie's service—was frequently on the move. That family life was often difficult and traumatic. Elliott's father was physically abusive, both to Elliott and to her mother. On one occasion, he threatened his daughter and wife with a firearm. Elliott has also spoken openly of her sexual abuse by a cousin. Since 2003 Elliot has been prominent

Missy Elliot, performing during a concert at the Palais X-tra in Zurich, Switzerland, 26 September 2006. (AP Images.)

in speaking out against domestic violence, as a national spokesperson for the Break the Cycle campaign. When Elliott was fourteen, her mother packed up her belongings and fled with her daughter in tow.

At a very young age, Elliott set her sights on a career in music and entertainment. In school, she recalled that she was something of a show-off and class clown. Around 1990 she formed a singing group called Sista and, along with her friend and collaborator Timbaland, relocated to New York to sign with the small Swing Mob label. An album was eventually produced; Swing Mob ran into financial trouble and collapsed before it could be released. Elliott was left without a contract and facing the prospect of starting over.

Her break came a few years later, when, in 1996, she again teamed with Timbaland, this time to write and produce tracks for Aaliyah's double-platinum *One in a Million* album. Elliott also contributed vocals to many of the album's tracks. Such success served to bring her to the attention of the broader recording industry, and that same year Elliott signed with Elektra Records and was allowed to create her own label. Timbaland served as her producer.

A year later, in 1997, Elliott's first solo effort, *Supa Dupa Fly*, made its appearance. The album—propelled up the charts by its hit single "The Rain"—went platinum and garnered for Elliott a Grammy nomination for Best Rap Album. The release of 1999's *Da Real World* saw a continuation of her early success, as did 2001's *Miss E … So Addictive*. *Da Real World* sold three million copies worldwide, while *Miss E … So Addictive* spawned the enormous hip-hop hits "Get Ur Freak On" and "One Minute Man," reaching number two on Billboard's Top 200. Meantime, such was Elliott's celebrity that she began appearing in television advertisements and shows and in motion pictures. She made her initial foray into television with a 1997 broadcast of the situation comedy *Family Matters* and in various other programs, "reality series," and otherwise. In 2001 she appeared on the silver screen in the comedic *Pootie Tang* and followed this up with several other spots—including *Just for Kicks* (2005)—though usually playing herself.

Back in the studio, Elliott released the old-school inflected *Under Construction* (2002). Selling more than two million copies, the album hit number three on the Billboard 200 and netted Elliott two more Grammy Award nominations, including another for Best Rap Album. *This Is Not a Test* appeared a year later, mainly driven by the label's desire to continue the huge success of *Under Construction*. In 2005 Elliott hosted her own reality television show, *The Road to Stardom with Missy Elliott*.

That same year saw the release of *The Cookbook*, and it was a return to form (and bigger sales) for Elliott after the comparative let-down of *This Is Not a Test*. *The Cookbook* was nominated for five Grammy nominations (Elliott won one for Best Rap Video) and secured for Elliott an American Music Award win for Best Female Hip Hop Artist. Her seventh studio album, *Block Party*, again in collaboration with Timbaland, was due to be released in 2009, but she announced in June 2011 that the album had been delayed as a result of the problems she had faced since 2008 battling Graves disease, an autoimmune disorder that causes hyperthyroidism.

FURTHER READING

Chang, Jeff. *Can't Stop, Won't Stop: A History of the Hip-Hop Generation* (2005).

Rose, Tricia. *Black Noise: Rap Music and Black Culture in Contemporary America* (1994).

JASON MILLER

Elliott, Robert Brown (11 Aug. 1842–9 Aug. 1884), Reconstruction politician and U.S. Congressman, was born probably in Liverpool, England, of West Indian parents whose names are unknown. Elliott's early life is shrouded in mystery, largely because of his own false claims, but apparently he did attend a private school in England (but not Eton as he claimed) and was trained as a typesetter. It is likely also that in 1866 or 1867, while on duty with the Royal Navy, he decided to seek his fortune in America and jumped ship in Boston Harbor, without, however, taking out citizenship papers. All that is known for certain is that by March 1867 Elliott was associate editor of the *South Carolina Leader*, a black-owned Republican newspaper in Charleston. Shortly thereafter he married Grace Lee Rollin, a member of a prominent South Carolina free Negro family. The couple had no children.

During Reconstruction South Carolina's population was 60 percent black, and the state had many highly capable black leaders. Between 1867 and 1877, when state rule was formally restored, Elliott, a politically adept orator, developed into the major black spokesman and politician in South Carolina. He was one of the at least seventy-one black delegates to the 1868 Constitutional Convention, which drafted the most democratic constitution in South Carolina history. At the 1868 state Republican convention he was nominated for lieutenant governor but dropped out of contention after finishing third on the first ballot. That same year, while serving as the only black member of the five-man board of commissioners in Barnwell County, Elliott was elected to the South Carolina House of Representatives, where he became a very powerful player in state government. Almost elected as Speaker (placing second in the balloting), he was made chair of the committee on railroads and was appointed to the committee on privileges and elections, both very influential assignments. As assistant adjutant general of South Carolina, he even was placed in charge of organizing a militia. In 1870 Elliott was elected to the United States House of Representatives, defeating a white opponent in a district with only a slight black majority, and he was reelected by a wide margin two years later. Near the end of his second term he resigned in order to run again for the state house, winning easily. This time he did serve as Speaker from 1874 to 1876, when he was elected state attorney general. The next year, however, he was one of five Republicans removed from office following the Democratic takeover of Congress.

Elliott was even more influential within Republican Party ranks. A delegate to three national conventions (twice leading the delegation), he served as party chair in South Carolina for much of the 1870s and was permanent chair of most state nominating conventions.

In all of his political positions Elliott aligned himself with the Radical Republicans. At the state constitutional convention he led the successful opposition to both a literacy test for voters and a poll tax, as he well understood that they could later be used to keep blacks from voting. Also at the convention, he fought successfully to have invalidated all debts related to the sale of slaves. As a state representative, Elliott lobbied successfully for a bill to ban discrimination in public facilities and on public transportation. As a U.S. congressman, he gained some notoriety for a speech favoring federal suppression of the Ku Klux Klan and for his debate with former Confederate vice president Alexander Stephens over proposed legislation that subsequently became the Civil Rights Act of 1875. Also while in Congress he voted against the bill granting political amnesty to former Confederates. Elliott was nationally known by 1874, when black Bostonians asked him to give the oration at a memorial service for the Radical senator Charles Sumner.

Despite Elliott's well-deserved reputation as a racial militant, his record is not that simple. For example, as a delegate to the 1868 constitutional convention he supported the creation of a public school system and compulsory school attendance but opposed integration. Elliott never seriously interested himself in the plight of rural or urban black workers, and as president of a state labor convention in 1869 he favored a permanent halt to the confiscation of planter land. Even a few of his Democratic critics acknowledged that Elliott's view of the role of the militia was more moderate than that of the white governor Robert Scott, who saw it as an offensive and not a defensive force. In his speeches to black audiences, Elliott often expressed a belief in self-help as the means to political and economic empowerment.

Despite his moderate tendencies, Democrats insisted on seeing Elliott as an irresponsible hater of whites and as a troublemaker. White Carolinians, including some Republican enemies, categorized him as one of the state's major "corruptionists," a common and often unsubstantiated charge leveled against both black and white Radicals during Reconstruction. Although Elliott seems to have resisted small bribes and other minor enticements that some black and white politicians routinely accepted, his political career was not devoid of scandal. At least one financially lucrative deal made while he was on the state's powerful railroad committee was suspect; as assistant adjutant general he charged excessive fees; in addition to Republican Party funds he took state monies for his various lobbying efforts; and he distributed large sums of public as well as private money during election campaigns. Thus, even though a succession of law partnerships failed, Elliott maintained a high lifestyle and owned numerous city lots as well as an elegant three-story house in Columbia. Comparatively, however, the corruption of the white governors Franklin Moses Jr., Daniel Chamberlain, and Robert Scott and U.S. Senator John Patterson was far more blatant, and Elliott, unlike several of his black and white contemporaries, was never indicted for any crime.

Elliott's reputation as a racial militant derived primarily from his successful efforts to increase black political participation, especially in terms of nominations to higher offices. In 1870, for example, as chair of the Republican nominating convention, Elliott made sure that black candidates were selected for three of the four congressional seats, that the candidate for lieutenant governor was black, and that overall blacks had greater influence in the party. These tactics angered white Republicans and Democrats alike, as did Elliott's shifting of allegiances so that his political support became the determining factor in important elections—especially gubernatorial elections. Elliott was not politically invincible, however, nor was he always successful in achieving his own political goals. Perhaps his most devastating defeat occurred in the bitter, three-way fight for the Republican nomination for the U.S. Senate in 1872.

As state chair, Elliott was in charge of the 1876 campaign and, despite the Democrats' widespread use of violence and intimidation, courageously spoke throughout the state. He hoped that his election as attorney general would prove to be a stepping-stone to the governorship, but the ouster of all Republican executive branch officeholders by the re-emergent Democrats in 1877 eliminated that possibility. Believing that the lack of Republican opposition would lead to dissension among Democrats, just as the absence of Democratic challengers had earlier produced divisions among Republicans, in both 1878 and 1880 Elliott, as chair, convinced party leaders not to run a statewide campaign. By 1880, however, Elliott had become greatly discouraged, and in 1881 he led a delegation of black protesters who met with President-elect James Garfield. Asserting that black southerners were "citizens in name and not in fact" and that their rights were being "illegally and wantonly subverted," he appealed for federal help, which was not forthcoming.

Personal problems exacerbated Elliott's dire political outlook. Financial losses forced him to close his law office in 1879. His monthly salary as special inspector of customs in Charleston (a patronage position) was not enough to keep him from having to sell his house in order to pay off his debts. Continuing bouts with malaria and his wife's medical problems made his life even more difficult. A delegate to the Republican National Convention in 1880, Elliott was frustrated further by the defeat of his presidential choice, Secretary of the Treasury John Sherman. After eleven months in New Orleans as special agent of the Treasury, Elliott was fired for criticizing his boss and for supporting a losing political faction. A final law firm failed, and his health worsened. He died penniless in New Orleans of malarial fever.

Elliott was a charismatic and effective political leader who provoked outrage among whites and enthusiasm among blacks. What most outraged his opponents was Elliott's racial pride and his insistence on *demanding*, not asking, for his rights and the rights of black Americans. Persistently calling for the unprecedented expansion of national power in order to guarantee the fruits of Reconstruction while also urging blacks to be more worthy of the freedom they had won, Elliott was a precursor of many twentieth-century black leaders. Yet despite his reputation for political militancy, Elliott was always an ardent party man who believed that a strong Republican Party and Union constituted the best hope for racial equality.

FURTHER READING

Elliott's most important letters can be found in the South Carolina Governors Papers of Franklin Moses Jr., Robert Scott, and Daniel Chamberlain, South Carolina Department of Archives, and in the John Sherman Papers, Library of Congress.

Hine, William C. "Black Politicians in Reconstruction Charleston, South Carolina: A Collective Study," *Journal of Southern History* 49 (1983): 555–84.

Holt, Thomas C. *Black over White: Negro Political Leadership in South Carolina during Reconstruction* (1977).

Lamson, Peggy. *The Glorious Failure: Black Congressman Robert Brown Elliott and Reconstruction in South Carolina* (1973).

Rabinowitz, Howard N. *Race, Ethnicity, and Urbanization: Selected Essays* (1994).

This entry is taken from the *American National Biography* and is published here with the permission of the American Council of Learned Societies.

HOWARD N. RABINOWITZ

Ellis, George Washington (4 May 1875–26 Nov. 1919), lawyer and social scientist, was born in Weston Platt County, Missouri, the son of George

Ellis, a farmer, and Amanda Jane Trace. George Ellis left home after completing elementary school, primarily because Weston Platt County could not provide him with the education or training he desired. He moved to Kansas City, Missouri, where he found greater educational opportunities but increased racial hostilities. As a consequence, he soon moved to Atkinson, Kansas, where he completed high school in 1891. Ellis continued his education at the law school at the University of Kansas, receiving an LLB in 1893. While practicing law Ellis pursued a B.A. at Kansas; it is not known, however, if he completed the requirements for the degree. While at the University of Kansas he was active in Republican politics and debated in Kansas's McKinley Club.

Ellis moved to New York City in 1897, where he took courses at the Gunton Institute of Economics and Sociology. He maintained his affiliation with the Republican Party and, as a result of his status as a speaker for the party and his high scores on a civil services examination, Ellis was appointed to the Census Division of the Department of Interior in the nation's capital. While working in Washington, D.C., Ellis pursued his educational interests, taking courses in philosophy and psychology in the School of Pedagogy at Howard University, and participating in Andrew F. Hilyer's sociological study *Colored Washington* (1901).

Ellis excelled at his position in the census office and came to the attention of President Theodore Roosevelt, who appointed him Secretary of the United States Legation in the Republic of Liberia in 1902. Ellis's ethnographic observations and analyses of tribes in both the coastal regions and the interiors helped shape the Department of State's foreign policies with regard to Liberia, a nation established in part by the descendants of former slaves and free African Americans. Ellis's ethnological work was sympathetic to the Muslim-dominated, Vai-speaking tribes of Liberia, who were among the few sub-Saharan African peoples of this period who had created an orthography. Ellis's investigation of the Vai, *Negro Culture in West Africa*, which was rejected by several publishers over the years, was finally brought out by the Neale Publishing Company in 1914. The book, however, was a commercial failure, and Ellis's publisher only grudgingly agreed to bring out his second book, *Negro Culture*, in 1915. When part of the Neale Publishing Company's bindery was destroyed by fire in 1919, the owner cancelled the contract of publication.

During the same period in which Ellis was attempting to publish his magnum opus, he was selected as a contributing editor of *Journal of Race Development*, a quasi-scholarly periodical edited by Alexandra Chamberlain, the first person to receive a doctorate under the father of American anthropology, Franz Boas. Ellis contributed several pieces to that journal over a period of eight years. In 1917 he was chosen as the assistant corporation counsel of Chicago by the Republican mayor William Hale Thompson, who had strong support among black Chicagoans. One of the leaders in Progressive Party politics, Ellis supported President Theodore Roosevelt's re-election bid in 1912. In 1918 Ellis ran for a judgeship in municipal court, losing by a narrow margin in an election marred by voter fraud.

Ellis was persistent in his efforts to educate Americans on the subject of Africa. In 1917 he wrote a second-rate novel *The Leopard's Claw* about "love and adventure in the West African jungle." His attempts to enlighten scholars and the broader public on West African culture and politics, however, were not confined to print. During his tenure in Liberia, Ellis acquired a large collection of African art that he subsequently loaned to the Smithsonian Institution in Washington, D.C. Ellis's sister, with whom he was close, ultimately donated these artifacts to Fisk University in 1951, more than thirty years after his death.

Despite his numerous achievements, twenty-first-century critics might find his cultural biases objectionable, especially his advocacy of the three C's—civilization, Christianity, and commerce—as the most prudent means of redeeming West Africa. His defense of Christianity—Ellis belonged to the African Methodist Episcopal (AME) church and served as a member of its general financial board during the years 1912 and 1916—was often strident. His romantic racialism that asserted that Africans possessed an inherently superior "spiritual nature" and were loyal, suffering servants may seem anachronistic and is subject to intense debate.

Nevertheless Ellis's paradoxical worldview—which had its origins in Americanist anthropology and sociology, American social Christianity, and the African American Church—was an important synthesis. He was a significant figure who will be remembered for his concrete efforts to "redeem" West Africa and to obliterate the negative stereotypes of West African peoples and their descendants in America.

FURTHER READING

Ellis's papers are located at the Chicago Historical Society, Chicago, Illinois.

Childs, John B. *Leadership, Conflict, and Cooperation in Afro-American Social Thought* (1989).

Williams, Vernon J., Jr. *Rethinking Race* (1996).

VERNON J. WILLIAMS JR.

Ellis, Larry (29 Sept. 1928–4 Nov. 1998), first African American Ivy League head coach, 1984 U.S. Olympic men's track-and-field team head coach, and president of USA Track & Field from 1992 to 1996, was born Lawrence Thomas Ellis in Englewood, New Jersey. With two older sisters, Virginia Robinson and Theresa Brisbane, Ellis grew up in the Bronx in New York City, on a street known for its gangs. His parents, Henry Ellis, a tailor, and Anna Wright Hart, a Macy's saleswoman and a child's nurse, separated during his youth and Ellis worked part-time jobs in order to help make ends meet. Ellis's mother and the late Rev. Edler Hawkins, a Presbyterian minister, were positive influences in his younger years. "Basically, I was a good kid," he explained. "I joined the Boy Scouts. I played ball in the street, touch football (Alfano, *New York Times*, Apr. 1984, section 5, 1). For a part-time job in high school, Ellis delivered milk in the early morning by horse and carriage. Tired of waiting for the bus, one morning he planned to run home. Ellis's morning runs helped prepare him for an athletic career.

At DeWitt Clinton High School, Ellis tried out for the cross-country team, and completed his first recorded mile in five minutes and fifteen seconds. "The coach was ecstatic. I had outrun the older kids." Upon graduating in February 1947, Ellis recalls "I had written in the yearbook that I hoped to have a chance to compete in the Olympics" (Alfano, *New York Times*, Apr. 1984, section 5, 1). Ellis earned a spot on New York University's track team and competed on the collegiate level from 1947 to 1951, eventually becoming an All-American middle distance runner. During his freshman year in 1947 he won the Inter-Collegiate Amateur Athletic Association of America (IC4A) cross-country title. In addition, he won the 1950 Canadian indoor one-thousand-yard title, was second in the 1951 IC4A half-mile, and third in the 1951 NCAA eight-hundred-eighty-meter run. He also placed third in the half-mile at the Amateur Athletic Association Championships in 1951. At NYU his best half-mile was 1 minute 51.3 seconds and his best mile was 4 minutes and 14 seconds. After graduating with a B.A. in Physical Education in 1951, Ellis entered the army artillery, serving seven months in the Korean War until honorably discharged in 1953. On August 30 of that year, he married Shirley Brown Beard. Then a social worker, she later became an elementary school teacher.

Ellis began his teaching career in 1953 at Junior High School number 139 in Manhattan and transferred to Jamaica High School in Queens in 1958 after receiving a master's degree in secondary-school administration from NYU in 1957. During his thirteen years at Jamaica High, Ellis became coach of the cross-country and track-and-field teams; he also developed his administrative career, becoming the dean of boys and assistant principal for summer school. As coach, Ellis built his teams to prominence in New York area high school competition. Ellis's best athlete at Jamaica High was Bob Beamon, who later shattered the world long-jump record at the 1968 Olympics in Mexico City.

Realizing that good coaching jobs were rare for blacks at white institutions, Ellis began to move his career toward administration and considered giving up coaching. But the civil rights movement brought change. In 1969 a friend told Ellis about a possible coaching position at Princeton University. When the position became available the following year, the Princeton administration encouraged Ellis to apply. The university hired Ellis, and thus began his twenty-two-year career as coach of cross-country and indoor and outdoor track and field. Ellis was the first African American Ivy League coach and went on to lead the Princeton Tigers to great success. During Ellis's years as cross-country coach, Princeton tallied a 161–62 record. Before Ellis, Princeton had not won an Ivy League title since 1938 and had never won a cross-country title. Under Ellis's leadership, Princeton won eleven Ivy League titles in track and eight titles in cross-country, making him one of the most successful Ivy League coaches in history. In 1973 Ellis became head coach of the U.S. national track team during the second annual Pacific Conference Games in Canada and served as coach of the victorious 1978 U.S. team in a dual meet against the Soviet Union in Berkeley, California. In 1981 Ellis became the head coach for the U.S. team at the World University Games, and for the 1981–1982 season he was named the Division I, District 2 Indoor Regional Coach of the Year and the Cross Country Regional Co-Coach of the Year. That same year he was also inducted into the NYU Athletics Hall of Fame. In December 1981 Ellis was selected as the head coach for the U.S. Olympic men's track-and-field team for the 1984 games in Los Angeles. In all, American athletes won 83 gold medals, 61 silver medals, and 30 bronze medals at the 1984 Olympics, including CARL LEWIS, who took home four gold medals.

While Ellis was happy about the 1984 outcome in the Olympics, he was disappointed that the Soviet Union boycotted the Games that year: "We need an opportunity to meet our fellow men on a common ground and break down some of these barriers ... We can have a common understanding of what we're doing and an appreciation for each other that will defuse some of the myths that we have about other people" (Alfano, *New York Times*, Apr. 1984, section 5, 1). In 1992 Ellis retired from Princeton and served as president of USA Track & Field from 1992 to 1996. Ellis received a heart transplant at Mt. Sinai Medical Center in Manhattan on 9 June 1995, after waiting twelve weeks for an appropriate donor. He was honored with the 1995 Fred Lebow Special Achievement Award on 3 February 1996 at the Metropolitan Athletics Congress and two years later coached the U.S. track team at the World Cup in Johannesburg, South Africa. Just two months later, he unexpectedly died of a pulmonary embolism. He left behind his wife, Shirley (who died in February 2007), their four children, Lesley Smalls, Robin Williams, Joanne Glenn, and Lawrence Ellis Jr., and a sister Ginger Robinson. On 2 December 1999 Ellis was posthumously inducted into the United States Track & Field Hall of Fame in Los Angeles, and in 1999 Princeton honored him with the Marvin Bressler Award. Ellis described the legacy he would leave when he said, "Winning is incidental; teaching is what is important ... I win in terms of the preparation and development of an individual" (Conning, *California Track and Running News*, Oct. 2002).

FURTHER READING

Alfano, Peter. "A Lifetime of Running Toward the Olympics," *New York Times*, 22 Apr. 1984.

Conning, Keith. "The Conning Tower," *California Track and Running News* (24 Oct. 2002).

Obituary: *New York Times*, 6 Nov. 1988.

RICHARD SOBEL

Ellison, John Malcus (2 Feb. 1889–25 Oct. 1979), minister, author, and educator, was born near Burgess in Northumberland County, Virginia, to Robert, a fisherman, and Maggie Ellison, a homemaker. Coming from an impoverished background, he received a rudimentary education and had to work at age fourteen as a farm laborer earning seven dollars per month. His first stroke of good fortune occurred in 1906 when he entered the Virginia Normal and Industrial Institute (later Virginia State College and still later Virginia State University) in Ettrick, Virginia. Getting into Virginia Union University in Richmond was not so easy; there was initial skepticism on the part of its president, Dr. George Rice Hovey, who saw no academic promise in the young man. In 1909 Hovey reluctantly admitted Ellison to the Wayland Academy (as Virginia Union's high school program was then called), and he then went on to the collegiate undergraduate program, graduating in 1917 with a B.A. in Sociology.

Ellison entered the Baptist ministry and taught school for a while in his native Northumberland County, becoming principal of Northern Neck Industrial Academy (1917–1918) and founder and principal of Northumberland County High School (1918–1926), all while pastoring at Shiloh Baptist Church (1917–1926). Ellison matriculated with an MArt in Theology from Oberlin College in 1927 and a Ph.D. in Christian Education and Sociology from Drew University in 1933. In 1927 Ellison joined the faculty of Virginia State College, becoming its first official campus minister, and taught sociology and ethics. In 1934 he accepted a similar position at Virginia Union, gaining acclaim for his preaching, research, and pedagogical abilities.

In 1941 the Virginia Union president William John Clark retired and Ellison overcame a strong field of candidates, including CHARLES SPURGEON JOHNSON, Miles Washington Connor, GORDON BLAINE HANCOCK, and Robert Prentiss Daniel, to become the first African American, as well as the first alumnus, to direct that institution as president. Prior to his appointment he endured an anonymous, virulent smear campaign, which attempted to use his rural background and economically disadvantaged origins to his detriment. The tactic was openly decried by the board of trustees, which voted him in as president on 1 June 1941. Shortly thereafter he renewed acquaintance with his erstwhile detractor, former president Hovey, who admitted to having grossly underestimated his former student's abilities. At Dr. Hovey's funeral in 1943 it was Ellison who, in accordance with Hovey's request, delivered the eulogy.

Ellison's administration at Virginia Union (1941–1955) was the most significant in the venerable history of that historically black college. He modernized and transformed the physical campus, maintained the reputation for academic excellence that had made Virginia Union one of the premier historically black colleges of the early and mid-twentieth century, and guided the institution through war, when its survival was jeopardized by declining enrollment and escalating expenses. By the end of his tenure of office, enrollment had rebounded to unprecedented levels. He was certainly the guiding force in the establishment of the university's internationally renowned graduate school of theology (later the Samuel Dewitt Proctor School of Theology), and it was primarily through his tireless diplomatic and fund-raising efforts that the Belgian pavilion at the 1939 New York World's Fair was transported piecemeal to a permanent home on the Virginia Union campus. The structure, known as the Belgian Friendship Building, was designated a historical landmark and contains artistic treasures: bas-relief friezes by Arthur Dupagne, Oscar Jespers, and Henry Puvrez, and the overall architectural design of Henry Van de Velde, one of the leaders of the art nouveau movement. Virginia Union's gymnasium, Barco-Stevens Hall, was home to many celebrated athletic events.

Though Dr. Ellison was not himself active in the civil rights movement, his encouragement and support made Virginia Union the significant hub for civil rights activity in Virginia that it was throughout the 1950s and 1960s. Many of his protégés and others who graduated during his presidency became effective leaders in the movement (WYATT TEE WALKER, WALTER FAUNTROY, SAMUEL DEWITT PROCTOR, and J. Rupert Picott) or broke new ground for African Americans (Governor DOUGLAS WILDER, Vice Admiral SAMUEL GRAVELY, John Merchant, and Dr. Jean Louise Harris). Because of Dr. Ellison's involvement in educating African students at Virginia Union, the John M. Ellison Hospital in Owerri, Nigeria, was established in his honor.

Retiring from the presidency in 1955, Dr. Ellison became pastor at Saint Stephen's Baptist Church in Caroline County and the first chancellor of Virginia Union University—a post that he held for the remainder of his life. In 1965 he edited *A Century of Service to Education and Religion (An Account of the History of Virginia Union University, 1865–1965)* for the centennial issue of the *Virginia Union Bulletin*, and in 1940 he helped prepare a Hamitic edition of the King James Version of the Bible. Ellison authored *The Negro Church in Rural Virginia* (with C. Horace Hamilton, 1930), *Negro Organizations and Leadership in Rural Virginia* (1933), *Negro Life in Rural Virginia, 1864–1934* (with W. E. Garnett, 1934), *The Art of Friendship* (1943), *Tensions and Destiny* (1953), *They Who Preach* (1956), *They Sang through the Crisis* (1961), *Trilogy on Adventurous Living* (1962), *The Personal Quality of Preaching and the Preacher's Message from the Psalms* (196?), and *The Abiding Influences of a Faithful Minister: A Profile of the Life and Ministry of the Reverend Levi Reese Ball* (undated). He was working on a history of Virginia Union University at the time of his death in Richmond.

Ellison was married three times, first to Mabel McWilliams and then, upon her death, to Ophelia Gray, who also predeceased him. His marriage to Elizabeth Balfour lasted forty-six years. The couple reared six children.

FURTHER READING

The papers and correspondence of Dr. John Malcus Ellison are located in the Archives of the L. Douglas Wilder Library at Virginia Union University, Richmond, Virginia.

Gavins, Raymond. *The Perils and Prospects of Southern Black Leadership: Gordon Blaine Hancock, 1884–1970* (1977).

Pooles, Tina. *Black College Presidents after Brown* (2005).

Toppin, Edgar. *Loyal Sons and Daughters: Virginia State University, 1882 to 1992* (1992).

RAYMOND PIERRE HYLTON

Ellison, Keith M. (4 Aug. 1963–), congressman and the first Muslim to serve in the U.S. Congress, was born Keith Maurice Ellison in Detroit, Michigan, the third of five sons of Clida Ellison, a social worker, and Leonard Ellison, a psychiatrist. The Ellison family was upwardly mobile, part of the rising black professional class of the post–World War II era, which sought to increase African American participation in the nation's civic life. His parents and his grandfather were active in the civil rights movement. Ellison graduated from the University of Detroit Jesuit High School and Academy in 1981. There he got his first taste of politics, participating in student government. In addition, Ellison was active in sports. Following his graduation, he enrolled at Wayne State University in Detroit, Michigan. Ellison's time in college was transformational, as he dispensed with the Roman Catholicism of his youth and converted to Islam. This choice reflected the disenchantment of many urban African Americans since the 1960s with Christianity. Ellison received his B.A. in economics

Keith M. Ellison, United States Congressman, speaking at the Clean Energy Jobs Forum in Richfield, Minnesota, on 8 September 2010.

in 1987 and began searching for a place to study law. In 1987, Ellison moved to Minneapolis, where he enrolled in the University of Minnesota Law School. Three years later, in 1990, he received his law degree. After matriculating at the University of Detroit, he married Kim Ellison, with whom he had four children: Amirah, Isaiah, Jeremiah, and Elijah.

In 1990, as a newly minted attorney, Ellison entered private practice in Minneapolis. For sixteen years, Ellison was a trial attorney engaged in work on civil rights law, employment law, and criminal defense law. Like many politicians, Ellison was active—throughout his adult life—in public service. Ellison conducted a public affairs radio show and assisted Minneapolis youth as a track coach. Further, Ellison was active in defending poor people with pro bono legal work. Despite his legal work, pro bono service, and civic commitment, Ellison wanted something more. In 2002 Ellison announced his candidacy for a seat in the Minnesota House of Representatives. In November of that year, Ellison was elected to represent the 58B House District. His religion was a factor, but only due to his past association with the Nation of Islam and the 1996 Million Man March, whose Minnesota contingent he had helped to organize. However, the liberal tendencies of his district, along with sizable populations of African Americans and Somalis, helped pave Ellison's path to electoral victory.

Ellison's two terms in the Minnesota House revolved around domestic issues such as reforming governmental operations and the judicial system; defending children from the effects of chemicals; increasing the minimum wage for lower income workers; and promoting legislation to deliver ex-offenders their voting rights. By 2006, Ellison saw the opportunity to take his inclusive message about politics, the people, and progressive governance to a national audience. When Congressman Martin Olav Sabo announced his retirement from the U.S. House, Ellison jumped into the race for the 5th Congressional District seat of Minnesota. In a crowded field of ten candidates, Ellison successfully won the Democratic-Farmer-Labor nomination. Although the seat was a DFL stronghold, Ellison faced a fierce general election in November. Despite allegations that he was a militant Muslim, he nonetheless defeated his three opponents with 56 percent of the vote. The district's liberal constituency responded favorably to Ellison, in part, because of his strong opposition to the war in Iraq. In November 2006, Keith Ellison took his seat in Congress as its first Muslim member and first African American elected to Congress from the state of Minnesota.

In Congress, Ellison has served on the Financial Services and Foreign Affairs Committees. His political platform has largely been an expansion of what he had sought in the Minnesota House: inclusiveness, civil rights, human rights, defendant and ex-prisoner rights, progressive environmentalism, and the interests of the working poor. A reliable vote for progressive causes in Congress, he has proven popular among his Democratic colleagues. Ellison, however, has been the subject of controversy as forces in the Republican Party and various media figures took exception to his election, his faith, even his choice of using the Koran (once owned by Thomas Jefferson) to take the oath of office. Virginia Congressman Virgil Goode told his constituents that there would be more Muslims in Congress if immigration reform wasn't accomplished to stop them. In addition, his support for the Million Man March of 1995, led by LOUIS FARRAKHAN, caused some people to question his judgment. Ellison's written support of Farrakhan's message of racial uplift, self-sufficiency, and pride during his law school years has attracted opposition over the years despite his condemnation of Farrakhan's positions, such as militancy and separatism. In fact, Ellison is a Sunni Muslim, not a member of the Nation of Islam.

Ellison has been an active member in Congress during his two terms. He has urged a refocusing of the war against terrorism and promoting peace abroad. Most urgently, Ellison has advocated for a complete withdrawal from Iraq. He has been at the forefront of reforming a financial system that resulted in the long economic recession that began in 2008.

In 2008 Congressman Ellison endorsed and campaigned for U.S. Senator BARACK OBAMA (D-IL) for president. His endorsement of Obama, who is exactly two years older than Ellison, reflected their shared values and commitments as part of the post–civil rights generation. This generational shift among younger African Americans toward a new style of politics based on inclusiveness, hope, and pragmatism, underpinned much of Obama's early black support. Many older black members of Congress and city mayors initially endorsed Obama's Democratic primary opponent, Senator Hillary Clinton (D-NY). During his well-received speech in Cairo, Egypt, in 2009, President Obama cited Ellison's congressional oath on the Koran as evidence of growing American tolerance of Islam, and of the contribution of Muslim Americans to American life.

FURTHER READING

Gillespie, Andra. *Whose Black Politics? Cases in Post-Racial Black Leadership* (2010).

U.S. Congress, House, Committee on House Administration of The U.S. House of Representatives. *Black Americans in Congress, 1870–2007* (2008).

DARYL A. CARTER

Ellison, Ralph Waldo (1 Mar. 1913?–16 Apr. 1994), novelist and essayist, was born in Oklahoma City, Oklahoma, the oldest of two sons of Lewis Ellison, a former soldier who sold coal and ice to homes and businesses, and Ida Milsaps Ellison. (Starting around 1940 Ellison gave his year of birth as 1914; however, the evidence is strong that he was born in 1913.) His life changed for the worse with his father's untimely death in 1916, an event that left the family poor. In fact, young Ralph would live in two worlds. He experienced poverty at home with his brother, Herbert (who had been just six weeks old when Lewis died), and his mother, who worked mainly as a maid. At the same time, he had an intimate association with the powerful, wealthy black family in one of whose houses he had been born. At the Frederick Douglass School in Oklahoma City he was a fair student, but he shone as a musician after he learned to play the trumpet. Graduating from Frederick Douglass High School in 1932, he worked as a janitor before entering Tuskegee Institute in Alabama in 1933. There his core academic interest was music, and his major ambition was to be a classical composer—although he was also fond of jazz and the blues. In Oklahoma City, which was second only to Kansas City as a hotbed of jazz west of Chicago, he had heard several fine musicians, including LESTER YOUNG, Oran HOT LIPS PAGE, COUNT BASIE, and LOUIS ARMSTRONG. The revolutionary jazz guitarist CHARLIE CHRISTIAN and the famed blues singer JIMMY RUSHING both grew up in Ellison's Oklahoma City. However, classical music was emphasized at school. At Tuskegee, studying under WILLIAM LEVI DAWSON and other skilled musicians, Ellison became student leader of the school orchestra. Nevertheless, he found himself attracted increasingly to literature, especially after reading modern British novels and, even more influentially, T. S. Eliot's landmark modernist poem, *The Waste Land*.

In 1936, after his junior year, Ellison traveled to New York City hoping to earn enough money as a waiter to pay for his senior year. Ellison never returned to Tuskegee as a student. Settling in Manhattan, he dropped his plan to become a composer and briefly studied sculpture. Working as an office receptionist and then in a paint factory, he also found himself inspired, in the midst of the Great Depression, by radical socialist politics and communism itself. He became a friend of LANGSTON HUGHES, who later introduced him to RICHARD WRIGHT, then relatively unknown. Encouraged by Wright, whose modernist poetry he admired, Ellison continued to read intensively in modern literature, literary and cultural theory, philosophy, and art. His favorite writers were Herman Melville and Fyodor Dostoyevsky from the nineteenth century and, in his own time, Eliot, Ernest Hemingway, and André Malraux (the French radical author of the novels *Man's Fate* and *Man's Hope*). These men, joined by the philosopher and writer Kenneth Burke as well as Mark Twain and William Faulkner, became Ellison's literary pantheon. (Ellison never expressed deep admiration for any black writer except—for a while—Wright. He liked and was indebted to Langston Hughes personally but soon dismissed his work as shallow.)

In 1937, as editor of the radical magazine *New Challenge*, Wright surprised Ellison with a request for a book review. The result was Ellison's first published essay. Next, Wright asked Ellison to try his hand at a short story. The story, "Hymie's Bull," was not published in Ellison's lifetime, but he was on his way as an author. A trying fall and winter (1937–1938) in Dayton, Ohio, following the death of his mother in nearby Cincinnati, only toughened Ellison's determination to write. In 1938 he secured a coveted place (through Wright) on the Federal Writers' Project in New York, where he conducted research into and wrote about black New York history over the next four years. That year he married the black actress and singer (and communist) Rose Poindexter.

Slowly Ellison became known in radical literary circles with reviews and essays in magazines such as *New Masses*, the main leftist literary outlet. When he became managing editor (1942–1943) of a new radical magazine, *Negro Quarterly*, the lofty intellectual and yet radical tone he helped to set brought him more favorable attention. About this time Ellison came to a fateful decision. He later identified 1942 as the year he turned away from an aesthetic based on radical socialism and the need for political propaganda to one committed to individualism, the tradition of Western literature, and the absolute freedom of the artist to interpret and represent reality.

Facing induction during World War II into the segregated armed forces, Ellison enlisted instead in the merchant marine. This led to wartime visits to Swansea in Wales, to London, and to Rouen, France. During the war he also published several short stories. His most ambitious, "Flying Home" (1944), skillfully combines realism, surrealism, folklore, and implicit political protest. Clearly Ellison was now ready to create fiction on a larger scale. By this time his marriage had fallen apart. He and Rose Poindexter were divorced in 1945. The next year he married Fanny McConnell, a black graduate in drama of the University of Iowa who was then an employee of the National Urban League in Manhattan.

With a Rosenwald Foundation Fellowship (1945–1946) Ellison began work on the novel that would become *Invisible Man*. (One day, on vacation in Vermont, he found himself thinking: "I am an invisible man." Ellison thus had the first line, and the core conceit, of his novel.) In 1947 he published the first chapter—to great praise—in the British magazine *Horizon*. In the following five years Ellison published little more. Instead, he labored to perfect his novel, whose anonymous hero, living bizarrely in an abandoned basement on the edge of Harlem, relates the amazing adventure of his life from his youthful innocence in the South to disillusionment in the North (although his epilogue suggests a growing optimism).

In April 1952 Random House published *Invisible Man*. Many critics hailed it as a remarkable literary debut. However, black communist reviewers excoriated Ellison, mainly because Ellison had obviously modeled the ruthless, totalitarian, and ultimately racist "Brotherhood" of his novel on the Communist Party of the United States. Less angrily, some black reviewers also stressed the caustic depiction of black culture in several places in *Invisible Man*. Selling well for a first novel, the book made the lower rungs of the best-seller list for a few weeks. Then, in January 1953, *Invisible Man* won for Ellison the prestigious National Book Award in fiction. This award transformed Ellison's life and career. Suddenly black colleges and universities, and even a few liberal white institutions, began to invite him to speak and teach. That year he lectured at Harvard and, the following year, taught for a month in Austria at the elite Salzburg Seminar in American Studies.

In 1955 he won the Prix de Rome fellowship to the American Academy in Rome. There he and his wife lived for two years (1955–1957) in a community of classicists, archaeologists, architects, painters, musicians, sculptors, and other writers. While in Rome, Ellison worked hard on an ambitious new novel about a light-skinned black boy who eventually passes for white and becomes a notoriously racist U.S. senator, and the black minister who had reared the boy as his beloved son. He worked on this novel for the rest of his life.

Returning home, Ellison taught (1958–1961) as a part-time instructor at Bard College near New York City. This was followed by a term at the University of Chicago in 1961; two years (1962–1964) as a visiting professor of writing at Rutgers University in New Brunswick, New Jersey; and a year (1964–1965) as a visiting fellow in American Studies at Yale. During this time he published several important essays even as he toiled on his novel. In 1960 he published a short excerpt from his novel in the *Noble Savage*, a magazine that had been cofounded by Saul Bellow, a future Nobel Prize winner and close friend of Ellison's for some time.

Over the years Ellison was involved intellectually and personally with a wide range of major American scholars, critics, and creative writers. These included the philosopher Kenneth Burke, the critic Stanley Edgar Hyman, Bellow himself, the poet and novelist Robert Penn Warren, and the poet Richard Wilbur. Among blacks, his most important friendship for many years was with ALBERT MURRAY, a fellow student at Tuskegee in Ellison's junior year and later a professor of English there. Murray settled with his family in Harlem and published books about African Americans and the national culture. Starting in the 1960s Ellison was devoted to two institutions that honored achievement in the arts. The first was the American Academy and the National Institute of Arts and Letters. (Initially a member of the institute, he was elected later to the inner circle of excellence, the academy.) The other organization was the Century Association in mid-Manhattan, probably the most prestigious private club in the United States dedicated to the arts and literature.

As the years passed and his second novel failed to appear, Ellison's essays and interviews played a crucial role in furthering his reputation as an American intellectual of uncommon brilliance. His collection *Shadow and Act* (1964) reinforced this reputation. In it, Ellison insisted on the complexity of the American experience and the related complexity of black life. The black writer and artist, he insisted, should not be bound by morbid or negative definitions of the black experience but by a highly positive sense that cultural achievements such as the blues, jazz, and black folklore represent the triumph of African Americans over the harsh circumstances of American history—and a triumph of the human spirit in general. The Declaration of Independence, the U.S. Constitution, and the Bill of Rights were sacred documents authenticating the special promise of American and African American culture.

In 1965 a national poll of critics organized by a respected weekly magazine declared *Invisible Man* to be the most distinguished work of American fiction published since 1945. Other formal honors followed. However, the rise of Black Power and the Black Arts Movement about this time led to a backlash among younger, militant blacks against Ellison's ideas. Shunned at times on certain campuses, he was occasionally heckled or even denounced as an "Uncle Tom." Ellison was hurt by these assaults but remained confident about his values and insights. Moreover, the hostility of some younger blacks was offset by a host of honors. In 1966 he was appointed Honorary Consultant in American Letters at the Library of Congress, and the next year he joined the board of directors of the new Kennedy Center for the Performing Arts in Washington, D.C. At a crucial time in the rise of public television, he became a director of the Educational Broadcasting Corporation. In 1969 France made Ellison a Chevalier dans l'Ordre des Artes et Lettres. He also became a trustee of the New School for Social Research (now New School University) in New York and of Bennington College, in Vermont. Also in 1969 he received the highest civilian honor bestowed on a U.S. citizen, the Presidential Medal of Freedom.

From 1970 until 1979, when he reached the age of compulsory retirement, Ellison was Albert Schweitzer Professor of Humanities at New York University. Always interested in art—he and his wife collected African art as well as Western paintings and sculpture—he became a director of the Museum of the City of New York. In addition, he was a trustee of the Rockefeller-inspired Colonial Williamsburg Foundation in Virginia and a member of the Board of Visitors of Wake Forest University in Winston-Salem, North Carolina. He took these two last appointments as proof of important social change in the South, about which Ellison was sentimental because of the South Carolina and Georgia origins of his father and mother, respectively. In 1975 Oklahoma City honored him when he helped open the Ralph Ellison Branch of the city library system. President Ronald Reagan awarded him the National Medal of Arts in 1985.

The following year Ellison published his third book, *Going to the Territory*. Like *Shadow and Act*, this volume collected shorter pieces that reflected his unabated interest in the complex nature of black American and American culture. Vigorous to the end, Ellison died at his home in Manhattan. By this time he had seen his critics of the late 1960s and early 1970s decline in influence even as *Invisible Man* had become established as an American classic in fiction. After his death a succession of volumes have helped keep his reputation alive. These include his *Collected Essays* (1995), *Flying Home and Other Stories* (1996), and the novel *Juneteenth* (1999), all edited by John F. Callahan, who had been a trusted friend of Ellison's as well as a professor of American literature. Ellison's reputation rests on two remarkable books. As a novel of African American life, *Invisible Man* has no clear superior and very few equals to rival its breadth and artistry. With the exception of *The Souls of Black Folk* by W. E. B. DuBois, *Shadow and Act* is probably the most intelligent book-length commentary on the nuances of black American culture ever published.

FURTHER READING

The primary source of information on Ellison is the Ralph Waldo Ellison Papers in the Manuscripts Division of the Library of Congress, Washington, D.C.

Benston, Kimberly. *Speaking for You: The Vision of Ralph Ellison* (1987).

Graham, Maryemma, and Amjitjit Singh, eds. *Conversations with Ralph Ellison* (1995).

Murray, Albert, and John F. Callahan, eds. *Trading Twelves: The Selected Letters of Ralph Ellison and Albert Murray* (2000).

O'Meally, Robert G. *The Craft of Ralph Ellison* (1980).

Rampersad, Arnold. *Ralph Ellison: A Biography* (2007).

Obituary: *New York Times*, 17 Apr. 1994.

ARNOLD RAMPERSAD

Ellison, Stewart (8 Mar. 1832–24 Oct. 1899), city commissioner, entrepreneur, state representative, and prison reformer, was born a slave in Washington, North Carolina. Little information has been found concerning his early life and his parents. But it is agreed that Ellison was apprenticed to a local carpenter at a young age. By 1852 Stewart was working in Raleigh, North Carolina, on commercial construction projects. There is little information on his life during the Civil War. However, after the war he did open a grocery store, continued his work in construction, and became a building contractor, working with the Freedmen's Bureau to erect facilities for the newly freed men and women of Raleigh. Ellison occasionally attended night school, but he was mainly self-educated.

Ellison's political career began in the late 1860s when opportunities for blacks were opened up by Reconstruction. In early October 1866 he attended the State Equal Rights League Convention of Freedmen held in Raleigh, North Carolina. This historic event included many other important figures, including J. H. Harris, the President of the State Equal Rights League who oversaw the Convention of Freedmen, and the keynote speaker for the occasion, JOHN PATTERSON SAMPSON, editor of the *Colored Citizen* in Cincinnati. The Freedmen's Convention served multiple purposes but had two main roles. First, through the Freedmen's Convention, African American leaders reorganized and set forth new political agendas to further the interests of African American communities within the state. Second, the leaders of the convention spoke to the North Carolina state government on behalf of the African American communities they represented. This was important because the state legislature was reluctant to recognize the voices and concerns of people who had so recently been slaves. In the concluding statement of the main document produced by the Freedmen's Convention, thanks are given to the legislature of North Carolina for acknowledging the freedom of African Americans. Trying to push them farther down the path to accepting black citizenship, the concluding statement also requests that the legislature and the state extend the right of suffrage to African Americans.

Ellison was elected to several committees, including the financial building committees. The building committee planned to build a facility that would not only serve as a schoolhouse and town hall but would also provide other services relevant to the political life of African Americans, especially those in Raleigh, a valued site of black political organizing since this was also North Carolina's state capital. Ellison was also nominated vice president of the State Equal Rights League, which convention attendees hoped would serve as an ongoing political forum and advocacy group for former slaves and other African Americans. The Freedmen's Convention was not Ellison's last political activity. In 1868 Ellison was a member of the New Hanover County Board of Assessors and also served as a magistrate. The following year he was elected to the Raleigh Board of Commissioners and served as an alderman for Raleigh's eastern ward. In 1870, 1872, and 1879 he was elected as a representative in the state general assembly. In 1870 Ellison was one of nineteen African Americans elected to the state's general assembly; in 1872 he was one of twelve, and in 1879 he was one of six African Americans elected.

One can certainly mark Ellison's elections as successes for the black population in North Carolina, especially in the eastern region of the state. There were many blacks who took great care to exercise their new opportunities to participate in elections alongside other Republican supporters. But Ellison, like other black officeholders, still faced widespread opposition from those who opposed African American voting and the elections of African Americans to political office. For this reason, on 19 December 1870 Ellison and sixteen other members of the state's general assembly published an address titled "To the Colored People of North Carolina." Using the biblical story of Esther, Mordecai, and Haman, the address warns of the intentions of newly organized white militias to use violence to stop blacks, as well as poor whites, from participating in upcoming elections. The address also noted the strong opposition among former slaveholders to North Carolina Governor William Holden, who had thwarted a similar plot to disfranchise black voters before a previous election. The address urged African Americans to support Holden's efforts to uphold their voting rights and to continue participating in elections.

Ellison's defeat in the 1880 state legislative elections provoked an outcry among black voters who protested this outcome in meetings and through newspapers. Many black North Carolinians concluded that whites in the Republican Party were attempting to quietly remove African Americans from political positions. As fewer and fewer African Americans voted, and as more white Republicans were intimidated into abandoning the party of the Union, Ellison and other similar Reconstruction-era black stalwarts were frequently reduced to accepting patronage positions. Only in black-majority districts were African American politicians still elected; and that, too, would change closer to the end of the nineteenth century—with the widespread disenfranchisement of black citizens.

Ellison began to oversee the North Carolina State Penitentiary. During his four years at this post, Ellison challenged various aspects of the penal system's operations. He protested the beating of prisoners and even proposed a bill that would outlaw whipping them. Unfortunately, the bill did not pass in the state legislature. In 1899, Ellison died in North Carolina, reportedly in poverty. The exact locations of Ellison's death and his grave are unknown.

FURTHER READING

Foner, Eric, ed. *Freedom's Lawmakers: A Directory of Black Officeholders during Reconstruction* (1993).

Kenzer, Robert C. *Enterprising Southerners: Black Economic Success in North Carolina, 1865–1915* (1997).

Nowaczyk, Elaine Joan. "The North Carolina Negro in Politics, 1865–1876," master's thesis, University of North Carolina at Chapel Hill (1957).

Powell, William S. *Dictionary of North Carolina Biography* (1979).

Work, Monroe N., et al. "Some Negro Members of Reconstruction Conventions and Legislatures and of Congress," *Journal of Negro History* (Jan. 1920).

JAMES EDWARD FORD III

Ellison, William (1790–5 Dec. 1861), cotton-gin maker and planter, was born a slave in Fairfield District, South Carolina. His father was probably the planter Robert Ellison or his son William, and his mother was a slave woman whose name is unknown. Originally named April, the biracial child received exceptional treatment. His master apprenticed him to William McCreight, a white cotton-gin maker in Winnsboro. From 1802 to 1816 Ellison worked in McCreight's gin shop, learning the skills of gin making from a master craftsman. During his training, he learned reading, writing, arithmetic, and basic bookkeeping skills. He also became well versed in interracial social skills, as he met scores of planters who came to negotiate with McCreight for gins. These encounters provided him with a valuable network of strategic acquaintances and contacts. Ellison's owner, William Ellison, allowed him to work extra hours and eventually to purchase his freedom on 8 June 1816.

A free man, Ellison moved to the village of Stateburg in the High Hills of Santee in the Sumter District, where he began repairing cotton gins. Sometime between June 1816 and January 1817 he bought and freed his wife, Matilda, and their five-year-old daughter, bringing both to Stateburg. Ellison and his wife subsequently had three sons, all of whom were freeborn.

On 20 June 1820 Ellison appeared at the Sumter District courthouse in Sumterville to petition for a new name. His petition explained that he was a "freed yellow man" who was "endeavoring to preserve a good character and gain a livelihood by honest industry in the trade of Gin making." His ambitions were hampered, he explained, by his slave name. A new name would "greatly advance his interest as a tradesman" and "save him and his children from degradation and contempt which the minds of some do and will attach to the name of April." He asked and was allowed to change his name to William, the name of his former master.

In 1822 Ellison purchased an acre of land in the heart of Stateburg, at the corner of the intersection of the Charleston-Camden and Sumterville-Columbia roads, unquestionably the best business location in the area. On this spot Ellison constructed his gin shop and, along with his sons and grandson, ran it successfully there for decades. From the 1820s until the Civil War, Ellison's shop anchored his economic life. Locals claimed that the Ellison gin was "the best cotton gin" in South Carolina. Whether or not this was the case, it was good enough to allow him to retain his local market, which was growing, and to sell gins to customers from as far away as Mississippi.

From the beginning, the gin shop depended on slave labor. When Ellison's sons were old enough they helped in their father's gin business, but during his early years in Stateburg Ellison hired the time of skilled slaves who belonged to local planters to help him repair gins. By 1820 Ellison had already managed to buy two adult male slaves. In 1830 he owned four men. Each acquisition of a slave brought immediate financial rewards by permitting Ellison to build and repair more gins or accept more general blacksmithing and carpentry work. By 1840 Ellison owned thirty slaves, nine of whom were women. While women could produce children, they could not work in the gin shop. Consequently, in the preceding decade Ellison had purchased 330 acres of agricultural land where all of his slaves could labor. Agriculture and manufacturing meshed effectively. With three arenas for productive work—his gin shop, his fields, and those plantations belonging to his neighbors (where he from time to time hired out his slaves)—Ellison's slave labor force worked at peak efficiency. By 1860 Ellison owned a thriving gin shop, some 900 acres that produced a hundred bales of cotton a year, and sixty-three slaves. His wealth had outdistanced nine out of ten whites in Sumter. He was the largest free black slaveholder outside of Louisiana and probably the richest African American in the South who had begun life as a slave.

Ellison recognized that as a free man of color he depended as much on his standing in the eyes of the established white community as on his skills as a craftsman. Antebellum South Carolina was a slave society in which more than 98 of every 100 blacks were slaves and in which most whites believed all 100 should be. While building the foundation for his business, he just as carefully constructed a reputation for respectability.

Ellison's desire for respectability led to the Church of the Holy Cross, the local Episcopal church. The Stateburg gentry worshiped there and allowed the Ellisons, a handful of other free people of color, and a few slaves to sit in the gallery upstairs. But in August 1824 the Holy Cross vestry resolved "that the free colored man—Wm Ellison, be permitted to place a Bench under the Organ Loft, for the use of himself and Family." No other free family of color was granted the privilege of worshiping on the main floor. Further evidence of Ellison's growing respectability and acceptance came twenty years later when he was permitted to rent a pew in the back of the church.

The gin maker remained alert for other ways to cement his acceptance. In 1828 Ellison appeared in court with W. W. Anderson, the Ellison family's physician, fellow parishioner at Holy Cross, and prominent Stateburg planter, who had agreed to become Ellison's white guardian, as required by state law. In 1838 Ellison bought the Stateburg home of Stephen D. Miller, former governor of South Carolina and father of Mary Boykin Miller Chesnut, the Confederate diarist. The purchase reflected Ellison's economic and social achievement in the two decades since he had become free. In 1849 a visitor to Stateburg confirmed that Ellison was "a man greatly esteemed."

At home Ellison exercised patriarchal control and authority. White scrutiny required that the entire family be above reproach and respectable in every way. He saw that his sons mastered the tools of their trade and the subtle rituals of racial etiquette. All four children married into prominent, light-skinned, African American families of free slaveholders in Charleston, and they all brought their spouses to Stateburg to live in their father's household. Ellison integrated each of his sons into the family economy as gin makers, and they remained economically subordinate to him, apparently sharing their father's belief that solidarity was the best way to confront the family's vulnerability.

When bills in South Carolina's legislature called for the enslavement of the state's free black population, however, the Ellison family's secret behavior demonstrated the limits of their accommodation. In October 1860 one of Ellison's sons sent his children to Philadelphia, Pennsylvania, to enter a private school run by MARGARETTA FORTEN, a prominent free black abolitionist. In December, a month after South Carolina's secession, Ellison himself concluded that the haven he had built in Stateburg was no longer safe, but, although many free African Americans fled from Charleston, Ellison did not leave. He died in Stateburg eight months after the Civil War erupted.

During Ellison's lifetime, freedom held no guarantee for free people of color; their rights depended on the whim of whites. To avoid slipping back into bondage, Ellison adopted the strategy of accommodating to white power. He did all he could—including becoming the master of others—to construct a sanctuary for his family. Despite his history, Ellison never permitted a single slave to duplicate his own experience and gain freedom. Unlike whites, whose liberty was legally secure, Ellison used slaveholding as a central tactic in his drive to secure his family's freedom.

FURTHER READING

Some three dozen letters discovered in 1935 and acquired by the South Caroliniana Library in 1979 allow historians to glimpse the world of free blacks through the eyes of William Ellison and his family.

Berlin, Ira. *Slaves without Masters: The Free Negro in the Antebellum South* (1974).

Koger, Larry. *Black Slaveholders: Free Black Slave Masters in South Carolina, 1790–1860* (1985).

Johnson, Michael P., and James L. Roark. *Black Masters: A Free Family of Color in the Old South* (1984).

Johnson, Michael P., and James L. Roark, eds. *No Chariot Let Down: Charleston's Free People of Color on the Eve of the Civil War* (1984).

This entry is taken from the *American National Biography* and is published here with the permission of the American Council of Learned Societies.

MICHAEL P. JOHNSON

Elzy, Ruby Pearl (20 Feb. 1908–26 June 1943), operatic soprano and actress, was born in Pontotoc, Mississippi, the eldest child of Charlie, a laborer, and Emma Kimp Elzy, a teacher and laundress. As a child, Elzy sang as she helped her mother take care of her three siblings. When Elzy was five, her father left the family, eventually settling in St. Louis, Missouri. Unable to afford instruments and formal vocal training, Elzy was exposed to music by her great-grandmother. Beginning as early as age four, she sang solos in her church choir. Elzy's great-grandmother, who was born a slave, taught her how to sing spirituals, songs that originated with American slaves.

Elzy's passion for singing was obvious to those who knew her. Her mother saw her talent as a gift from God and devoted herself to supporting her daughter while she attended high school, from which she was graduated with honors in 1926. Elzy completed one year of postsecondary studies at Rust College, a college established for blacks in Holly Springs, Mississippi, before meeting Dr. Charles McCracken, a professor of education at Ohio State University in Columbus, Ohio. Dr. McCracken was so impressed with Elzy's talent and ambition that he helped her seek admittance to Ohio State's College of Education, where she planned to study in the music department. In the fall of 1927 Elzy entered Ohio State University as a sophomore. Because Elzy did not have enough money to pay for college, Dr. McCracken helped her secure funding by scheduling concerts at churches and civic organizations. Critics lauded Elzy's interpretation—enhanced by her knowledge of the history American slavery—of the spirituals as exceptional.

After only a few years at Ohio State, Elzy learned to speak Spanish and French, eventually performing in Spanish, French, Italian, and German. Elzy graduated first in her class in the Department of Music at the Ohio State University in 1930 with a bachelor of science in education that qualified her to teach music. Elzy was not interested in teaching, however. She wanted to continue the vocal training she had begun, the training that had developed her voice into a coloratura soprano. Though eager to continue her preparation for a career on stage, Elzy settled for teaching at Rust College when she

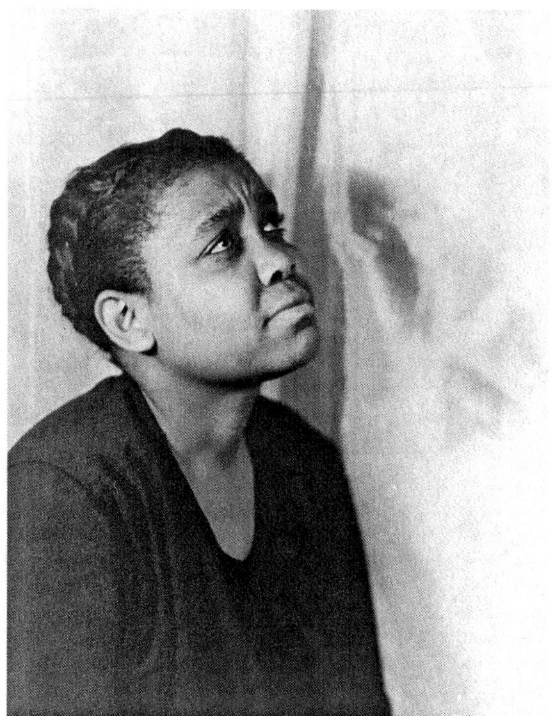

Ruby Elzy, in her role as Bess in *Porgy and Bess*. (Library of Congress/Carl Van Vechten.)

was unable to find funding to further her studies. As fate would have it, Elzy was on the faculty at Rust College for less than a month when Dr. McCracken helped her obtain a Rosenwald Fellowship to attend the Juilliard School in New York. In 1930 Elzy rented a room in Harlem, arriving not long after the Harlem Renaissance had begun in the 1920s.

The 1930s brought Elzy closer to stardom. While looking for a job, she met JOHN ROSAMOND JOHNSON, the brother of the statesman and poet JAMES WELDON JOHNSON. Rosamond hired Elzy to sing in the Rosamond Johnson Chorus. With the chorus she made her debut on Broadway in *Brown Buddies* on 7 October 1930. Upon completion of her first year at Juilliard, Elzy met and fell in love with Gardner Jones Jr., a journalist for the *Afro-American Journal.* The couple married in September of 1931 while Elzy performed in the revue *Fast and Furious* at the New York Theatre. *Fast and Furious* allowed Elzy the opportunity to perform her first solo on Broadway titled "Where's My Happy Ending?" In 1932 Elzy made her debut on national radio in a program on NBC titled *Parade of the States.* Later that same year she graduated from Juilliard with a diploma in voice. Her friendship with Rosamond Johnson also earned her a position as his assistant music director during the filming of *The Emperor Jones* (1933). While working in this position, she was asked to appear in film in the role of Dolly, opposite PAUL ROBESON. Honored with a grant to pursue graduate studies, Elzy earned the Certificate of Maturity and the graduate diploma in voice at Juilliard in 1934. With this accomplishment, she was finally formally trained and prepared for a career as a performer. She joined the Aeolian Opera Company, which was made up of African American performers, founded by Peter Creatore. Though the Aeolian Opera Company quickly folded, Elzy went on to play Serena in *Porgy and Bess* (1935), a production that made the twenty-seven-year-old woman a star. Her performance of George Gershwin's "My Man's Gone Now" is considered a classic. In 1935 Gershwin recorded several of the songs from *Porgy and Bess*, including Elzy's version of "My Man's Gone Now," at CBS. Later she would sing it at Carnegie Hall. Because of her performance in *Porgy and Bess*, Elzy became a co-star on *The Magic Key of RCA*, a radio program on NBC.

Amidst Elzy's triumphs, in 1936 she was forced to accept that her marriage was ending. Devastated, she withdrew from her work but by the following year she had begun to again focus on her career. She recorded five spirituals at Lang-Worth's studios in New York, guest starred on *Deep River*, a program on CBS, and sang at the White House at Eleanor Roosevelt's request. The year 1937 also marked Elzy's debut as a concert singer at Town Hall in Manhattan, New York, for which she received favorable reviews. Elzy accepted roles in several plays, including *Brown Sugar* (1937) (initially titled *Home Sweet Harlem*) and *Run Little Chillun* (1938).

In 1938 Elzy began dating the actor Jack Carr while performing in Merle Armitage's West Coast production of *Porgy and Bess* and in 1940 the couple married. They soon became guardians of Buster (Edward) Elzy, Elzy's nephew. In 1942 Elzy reprised her signature role, the last she would perform, during a national tour of *Porgy and Bess*.

Elzy's unexpected death at the age of thirty-five after minor surgery at Parkside Hospital in Detroit, Michigan, abruptly ended her budding career. She had been in the process of preparing for a role as Aida. She was inducted into the Mississippi Musicians Hall of Fame in 2000 and is remembered as a predecessor of LEONTYNE PRICE and other remarkable opera singers.

FURTHER READING

Weaver, David E. *Black Diva of the Thirties: The Life of Ruby Elzy* (2004).

Obituary: *New York Times*, 28 June 1943.

KAAVONIA HINTON

Emanuel, James (15 Jan. 1921–), poet, critic, and teacher, was born James Andrew Emanuel in Alliance, Nebraska, the fifth of seven children of Cora Ann Mance and Alfred A. Emanuel, a farmer and railroad worker. Emanuel's early years were spent listening to his mother read the Bible, the poetry of PAUL LAURENCE DUNBAR, the *Saturday Evening Post*, and BOOKER T. WASHINGTON's *Up from Slavery*. An avid reader, Emanuel borrowed Western, adventure, and mystery stories from the public library. He also memorized contemporary poems. By junior high school he was writing his own detective stories and poetry. During his young adult years he worked various jobs—elevator operator, baling machine operator, and weighmaster—before being named the class valedictorian and graduating from high school in 1939.

By age twenty Emanuel was working in Washington, D.C., as the confidential secretary to Gen. BENJAMIN O. DAVIS, assistant inspector general of the War Department in the U.S. Army. Eager to support himself financially while attending college, Emanuel joined the army in 1944. He served as a staff sergeant with the 93rd Infantry Division in the Pacific. After serving during World War II, Emanuel enrolled in Howard University in Washington, D.C. He continued to write, publishing several poems in the university's newspaper. He graduated from Howard summa cum laude in 1950 and married Mattie Etha Johnson, whom he met after moving to Chicago, Illinois, where he had begun working as a civilian chief in the pre-induction section of the Army and Air Force Induction Station. The couple had one child, James Jr., who committed suicide in 1983.

While working on a master's degree at Northwestern University in 1952, Emanuel earned a John Hay Whitney Fellowship in English. He published a few of his poems in the campus journal before graduating from Northwestern in 1953 and moving to New York, where he entered a doctoral program at Columbia University. The John Hay Whitney fellowship helped Emanuel finance his last year at Northwestern and his first year at Columbia. While attending Columbia he taught at the Harlem YWCA Business School from 1954 to 1956. In 1957 he began working as an English instructor at the City College of New York. During the late 1950s he published a few poems in *Phylon* and the *New York Times*. He also developed a friendship with LANGSTON HUGHES, who served as the topic of Emanuel's dissertation and as a critical reader of drafts of his poetry. Emanuel's earlier poetry was largely influenced by English poets such as John Keats and William Shakespeare, but his relationship with Hughes and his close readings of Hughes's work altered the direction of his poetry. After earning a Ph.D. in English from Columbia, Emanuel was promoted to assistant professor at City College.

Armed with a keen interest in garnering critical attention for black literature, in 1966 Emanuel developed the first course in black poetry to be offered at City College. He also ran for a position on the Mount Vernon, New York, school board, but he was defeated. He revised and published his dissertation on Hughes in 1967 and co-edited an anthology of black American literature, *Dark Symphony: Negro Literature in America*, in 1968. *Dark Symphony* contains literature by a number of respected writers, such as W. E. B. DUBOIS, PAULE MARSHALL, and Leroi Jones (later AMIRI BARAKA), and of course there are poems by Langston Hughes and Emanuel. During this time Emanuel's scholarly works continued to appear in *Phylon*, *Negro Digest*, and other journals. His first book of poetry, *The Treehouse and Other Poems*, a collection of previously published poems, came out in 1968.

Shortly after *The Treehouse and Other Poems* was published Emanuel traveled to the University of Grenoble, France, where he served as a Fulbright Professor of American Literature from 1968 to 1969. While living in the Alps he began working on poems printed in his 1970 collection, *Panther Man*. The title poem focused on Mark Clark and FRED HAMPTON, Black Panthers murdered by Chicago police officers. The collection also includes a tribute to Langston Hughes.

In 1970 Emanuel was promoted to associate professor of English at City College and began working as general editor of a series of books about black poets published by DUDLEY RANDALL's Broadside Press. In this capacity Emanuel edited five volumes about poets such as PHILLIS WHEATLEY, COUNTÉE CULLEN, and CLAUDE MCKAY. During this time he also worked with MacKinlay Kantor and Lawrence Osgood on *How I Write 2* (1972), a literary analysis of poetry by several poets, including ADDISON

GAYLE, Bernard W. Bell, Haki Madhubuti, SONIA SANCHEZ, and GWENDOLYN BROOKS.

After serving as a visiting professor of American literature at the University of Toulouse, France, from 1971 to 1973, Emanuel was named professor of English at City College in 1973. The following year he divorced his wife, and in 1975 he became the Fulbright Professor of American Literature at the University of Warsaw, Poland, where he taught for a year. Often invited to read his poetry around the world, Emanuel participated in the World Black and African Festival of Arts and Culture in Lagos, Nigeria, in 1977.

Eight years after he published *Panther Man, Black Man Abroad: The Toulouse Poems* (1978) was published. Emanuel went on to publish *A Chisel in the Dark: Poems Selected and New* (1980), *A Poet's Mind* (1983), *The Broken Bowl: New and Uncollected Poems* (1983), *Deadly James and Other Poems* (1987), *The Quagmire Effect* (1988), *Whole Grain: Collected Poems, 1958–1989* (1991), *De la Rage au Coeur* (1992), *Blues in Black and White* (1992), *Reaching for Mumia: 16 Haiku* (1995), and *Jazz from the Haiku King* (1999). Emanuel's poems are in various forms such as sonnet, free verse, and haiku, and some of the themes are love, war, music, youth, black manhood, and social issues.

In 1992 Emanuel created a new poetic genre, jazz-and-blues haiku, that he read when accompanied by musicians. An autobiographical book, *The Force and the Reckoning*, was published in 2001. Two other autobiographical works, "From the Bad Lands to the Capital (1943–44)" and "Snowflakes and Steel: My Life as a Poet, 1971–1980," are housed at Duke University. Emanuel's poems, essays, and book reviews have been included in many anthologies, periodicals, and scholarly journals.

FURTHER READING

Emanuel's works, correspondence, and other documents are at the Library of Congress, Manuscript Division, Washington, D.C. Additional manuscripts and documents are at the Jay B. Hubbell Center for American Literary Historiography at Duke University, Durham, North Carolina.

Baker, Houston A. "Emanuel, James A., Sr.," in *Contemporary Poets*, 7th ed., ed. Thomas Riggs (2001).

KAAVONIA HINTON

Epps, Anna Cherrie (8 July 1930–), medical educator, medical school administrator, researcher, and immunologist, was born Anna Cherrie in New Orleans, Louisiana, the daughter of Dr. Ernest Cherrie Sr., a radiologist who practiced family medicine, and Ann Cherrie, a former schoolteacher who became a full-time homemaker after marriage. Cherrie's brother, Ernest Cherrie Jr., became a physician like his father. In spite of her upbringing in the segregated South, Cherrie and her brother were shielded from the harsh realities of racism. Books, classical music, stimulating conversation, and a parade of accomplished visitors like Andrew Young Sr., father of former congressman, U.N. ambassador, and Atlanta mayor ANDREW YOUNG, and ERNEST NATHAN DUTCH MORIAL, who became the first African American mayor of New Orleans, were fixtures of her privileged environment. Precocious, Cherrie was close to her father, who instilled in her the importance of service to others, a strong work ethic, and a determination to persevere and succeed no matter the odds. Cherrie completed her Catholic school education upon graduating from Xavier University Preparatory High School with honors at the age of fifteen. In 1951, she earned her B.S. in Zoology from Howard University, her father's alma mater.

With a first rate undergraduate academic record and exceptional test scores, Cherrie applied for admission to the Howard University College of Medicine with every intention of following the family tradition and become a physician. Up to this point, she had only experienced encouragement, affirmation, and success in her educational pursuits. When she was denied admission to Howard's medical school, she was devastated. The reasons given for her rejection were astounding. Among the excuses for not admitting her was that, since she was a woman, she could not be as serious as a man about a medical career. Moreover, she was informed, at the age of nineteen, she was too young to master the medical school curriculum and, finally, that granting her admission would deny a male student the opportunity to study medicine and increase his likelihood of being drafted.

Her father's efforts to intervene, using his connections and influence at the medical school, to get the decision reconsidered were fruitless. Undaunted by Howard's decision, she applied to Meharry Medical College, but again was turned down.

Instead of attending medical school as she had planned, Cherrie went to work as a clinical technologist in 1953 at Our Lady of Mercy Hospital in Cincinnati. She returned to New Orleans in 1954 and worked in the clinical laboratory at the

Flint-Goodridge Hospital operated by Dillard University. The supervisor of her lab was Dr. Joseph M. Epps Sr., with whom she had a good professional relationship that developed further over the years. They were married more than a decade later in 1968 and remained wedded until his death in 1984. Anna Epps was recruited by Xavier University to be an instructor and to assist in the expansion of its Department of Medical Technology. During her seven years at Xavier from 1954 to 1961 she became acting chair of the department. As part of a broader civil rights desegregation strategy, she became a test case to challenge the racist policies of taxpayer-supported Louisiana State University. African Americans were denied access to LSU's classes, facilities, services, and overall educational opportunities solely on the basis of race. She was admitted and began taking graduate courses at LSU during the spring semester of 1952 while continuing to work full-time at Xavier.

Epps's dream of becoming a physician diminished, but she remained passionate about furthering her studies in biological science and challenged the discriminatory policies of Loyola University in New Orleans, affiliated with the Catholic Church, that had denied her admission to the graduate school. The board of trustees even weighed in, concurring with the decision that Epps should not be admitted. Nevertheless, two years later in 1957 she began her graduate work and graduated in 1959 with an M.S. in Biological Sciences.

Epps then worked part-time as a researcher in the Department of Medicine at Louisiana State University from 1959 to 1960, investigating areas of proteins, cytology, and radioactive carbon-14. In the summer of 1960 she conducted studies on radioisotopes at Berkeley. Ironically, her first job after completing the M.S. was teaching microbiology at the Howard University College of Medicine. She was interested in immunology and more specifically tropical and infectious diseases and began work on her doctorate at Howard, completing her Ph.D. in 1966 and was elected to Sigma Xi. She continued to teach at Howard until 1969, at which time she received a U.S. Public Health Service (USPHS) Faculty Research Fellowship in the Department of Medicine at Johns Hopkins University School of Medicine. From 1969 to 1971 a second USPHS fellowship allowed Epps to conduct research at Tulane. She served as an associate professor of medicine at Tulane from 1971 until 1980, when she was named the assistant dean of student services at the Tulane Medical Center. She held that position until 1986, when she became the associate dean for student services, and in 1995 she was named interim vice-president for academic affairs. In 1997 Meharry Medical College, which had denied her entry as a medical student almost fifty years earlier, made history when Epps was selected as dean of the school of medicine; thus she became the first African American woman ever to be appointed dean of an American medical school. Subsequently she also assumed the position of senior vice president of academic affairs. In June 2002 Epps stepped down from her dual roles as dean of the school of medicine and senior vice president for academic affairs.

During her nearly three decades at Tulane Medical Center, Epps set the standard for diversity in medical education. She designed, developed, and implemented the Tulane Medical Center's Medical Education Reinforcement and Enrichment Program (MEdREP) to recruit, educate, and retain nontraditional and minority students for careers in health. MEdREP included an eight-week summer program that provided prospective medical students with the tools and skills necessary for them to perform and compete successfully in medical school. Once these students were enrolled in medical school, the program monitored their performance, offered tutoring and assistance with testing, prepared students for licensing and certification requirements, and matched medical students with practicing physicians who served as mentors. Her publication *MEdREP at Tulane: Effectiveness of a Medical Education Reinforcement and Enrichment Program for Minorities in the Health Professions* was the basic text for increasing minority participation in the health professions. Epps was internationally and nationally acclaimed for a second volume, *Medical Education: Responses to a Challenge*, which promoted another of her creative endeavors, the Comprehensive Medical Review Program.

Epps completely transformed the School of Medicine while she was dean of Meharry. From revamping the curriculum and improving student scores on the national qualifying examination, to exceeding the national average annually in student matches to residency programs. After her five-year tenure as dean of the Meharry Medical College School of Medicine, Epps was named as senior advisor to the president and dean emeritus of the school of medicine. In spite of the discrimination she faced from black and white medical institutions, she fulfilled a destiny in an even more expansive way than if she had become a physician, creating opportunities for thousands of aspiring health professionals throughout the country. In recognition of her achievements, Meharry Medical College presented her with a doctorate of letters in 1996. In 2001 she was honored by Howard University with its Alumnus of the Year award and by the Association of American Medical Schools with its History Maker award. Other honors bestowed upon Epps for her leadership in medical education included the National Medical Association's Scroll of Merit and designation as a Leader in American Science. In 2002 she received the coveted Presidential Distinguished Service Award from Meharry Medical College. In 2003 she was honored as the fourth recipient of the Herbert W. Nickens, MD, award for her outstanding contributions to the promotion of justice in medical education and health care.

FURTHER READING

Briton, John. "Anna Cherrie Epps," *Notable Black American Women: Book III* (2002).

Dejoin, Mike. "Doctor Anna Cherrie Epps, Pho. D: Medical Educator and Miracle Worker," *The New Orleans Tribune*, June 1996, 14–15.

Warren, Wini. *Black Women Scientists in the United States* (1999).

PAULETTE COLEMAN

Equiano, Olaudah (1745?–31 Mar. 1797), slave, writer, and abolitionist, was, according to his autobiography, *The Interesting Narrative of the Life of Olaudah Equiano, or Gustavus Vassa, the African*, born in the village of Essaka in Eboe, an unknown location in the Ibo-speaking region of modern Nigeria. Equiano recorded that he was the son of a chief and was also destined for that position. However, at about the age of ten, he was abducted and sold to European slave traders. In his narrative, Equiano recalls the Middle Passage in which "the shrieks of the women, and the groans of the dying, rendered the whole a scene of horror almost inconceivable" (58). Despite falling ill, Equiano survived the voyage and was taken first to Barbados and then to Virginia, where in 1754 he was bought by Michael Pascal, a captain in the Royal Navy. Pascal's first act was to rename the young slave Gustavus Vassa, an ironic reference to the Swedish freedom fighter and later king, Gustavus I Vasa (1496–1560). Documents make it clear that he went by the name of Vassa until the late 1780s.

However, two documents—his baptismal record of 1759 and a muster roll from 1773—call portions of Equiano's autobiographical account into question. Both documents record Equiano's place of birth as South Carolina. Given that Equiano's story after he left Virginia is verifiable historically, but that his preceding narrative is not, some scholars have argued that it is reasonable to conclude that he was indeed born in South Carolina, not Africa, and that the early parts of his *Narrative* were written as rhetorical maneuvers designed to bring attention to the horrors of the slave trade, maneuvers largely "based on oral history and reading, rather than on personal experience" (Carretta, 103). However, it is equally possible that at his baptism and on later occasions Equiano suppressed his African identity and claimed to have been born in South Carolina, only daring, or caring, to tell his real history later in life. Unless further evidence emerges, the truth may never be known. Apart from minor disagreements about dates, which suggest Equiano inflated his age to make the story of his childhood seem more credible, the surviving historical evidence generally supports his autobiographical account from 1755 onward. As a ten-year-old boy Equiano was taken to England and then put aboard Pascal's warship, where he saw action in the French and Indian Wars. Equiano spent much time in London and suffered and recovered from smallpox and gangrene. Shipboard life gave him the opportunity to learn to read, write, and calculate, skills that later enabled him to work toward his own emancipation.

In December 1762 Equiano believed that he had earned his freedom, but in this he was deceived. Pascal swindled Equiano out of both his wages and his prize money, raised from selling captured goods, and sold him to a slave trader bound for Montserrat in the West Indies. There he was bought by Robert King, a Quaker merchant, who employed Equiano as a gauger, a shipboard weights-and-measures officer. In this trusted position Equiano traveled in King's ships throughout the Caribbean and North America. He admired Philadelphia, but was badly beaten by a slave owner in Georgia. After witnessing many scenes of cruelty, Equiano "determined to make every exertion to obtain my freedom, and to return to Old England" (Equiano, 122). He obtained a promise from King that he would be manumitted if he could raise forty pounds (the equivalent of approximately four thousand dollars in 2003), the price King had paid for him. Starting with three pence (approximately two dollars in 2003), he began petty trading and gradually raised the money. After some negotiation, on 11 July 1766 in Monserrat, Equiano's manumission papers were

THE
INTERESTING NARRATIVE
OF
THE LIFE
OF
OLAUDAH EQUIANO,
OR
GUSTAVUS VASSA,
THE AFRICAN.

WRITTEN BY HIMSELF.

Behold, God is my salvation; I will trust, and not be afraid, for the Lord Jehovah is my strength and my song; he also is become my salvation.
And in that day shall ye say, Praise the Lord, call upon his name, declare his doings among the people. Isa. xii. 2. 4.

SEVENTH EDITION ENLARGED.

LONDON:
PRINTED FOR, AND SOLD BY THE AUTHOR.
1793.

PRICE FOUR SHILLINGS.

[*Entered at Stationers' Hall.*]

Olaudah Equiano, prominent black abolitionist who published his autobiography, the first major slave narrative, in 1789. (Schomburg Center for Research in Black Culture, New York Public Library.)

drawn up. "I who had been a slave in the morning, trembling at the will of another, now became my own master, and compleatly free. I thought this was the happiest day I had ever experienced" (137). Equiano had achieved his freedom legally, although it has been argued that by buying his way out of slavery he implicitly acknowledged its legitimacy.

Equiano's first paid employment was as an able-bodied seaman aboard King's ships. On one voyage he safely brought the ship home after the death of the captain. On another occasion he was instrumental in saving the crew after a shipwreck. In July 1767, frustrated at the "impositions on free negroes," especially in Georgia, where an attempt was made to kidnap him, he paid seven guineas (the equivalent of about $750 in 2003) for passage to London. On arrival, he was immediately paid the wages (also seven guineas) from his service in the Royal Navy. Meeting with Pascal he demanded, but was refused, his prize money. Over the winter he learned to play the French horn and, more usefully, how to dress hair.

A year of evening classes depleted his savings, and Equiano returned to sea as a steward. In Turkey he was impressed by Islam, but found Turkish rule in Greece oppressive; in Naples he witnessed an eruption of Vesuvius; in Portugal he observed the workings of the Inquisition; and in Jamaica he was reminded of the horrors of slavery. In May 1773, "roused by the sound of fame," he joined John Phipp's expedition to find a northwest passage to India. The expedition reached only as far as Spitzbergen (Svalbard) in Norway.

On his return to London, Equiano underwent a period of spiritual self-examination. In May 1774 he decided to move to Turkey and embrace Islam. He shipped as a steward aboard a merchantman bound for Smyrna (Izmir), but before sailing, the ship's cook, a former slave called John Annis, was kidnapped and forcibly sent to the Caribbean, a practice that had been declared illegal in 1772 as the result of a campaign by the abolitionist Granville Sharp. After the incident, Equiano approached Sharp for help, and while their attempt to save Annis failed, the event put Equiano in touch with the emerging abolitionist movement in London. A second attempt to reach Turkey was aborted, and Equiano began to see his failure to reach the Islamic country as the work of providence. After much meditation and doubt, on 6 October 1774 he recorded his conversion to Christianity with the words "the Lord was pleased to break in upon my soul with his bright beams of heavenly light" (190).

In 1775 Equiano joined a project to settle a colony on the Mosquito Coast (now Nicaragua). Some have argued that Equiano's official role—buying slaves for the colony—and his self-appointed role as missionary to the Mosquito Indians demonstrate his complicity in both the slave trade and European colonization. By June 1776 however, the colonists' "mode of procedure [became] very irksome" and he left the colony. On the return voyage he was imprisoned by a ship's captain who intended to sell him into slavery at Cartagena, but he made a daring escape and worked his passage back to London. Having "suffered so many impositions," he became "heartily disgusted with the seafaring life" and instead worked as a servant. In 1779 he applied to the Bishop of London to be ordained as a missionary to Africa, but was turned down. In 1784 Equiano returned briefly to sea and visited the newly formed United States where, in Philadelphia, he came into contact with a group of Quakers, led by Anthony Benezet, who had begun to speak out against slavery.

Returning to London in 1786, Equiano was appointed as commissary of stores and provisions to a project to resettle poor black Londoners to a new colony in Sierra Leone, making him the first black civil servant in British history. After complaining about "flagrant abuses," however, he was fired and, as he predicted, the project failed. Equiano then immersed himself in the campaign to abolish the slave trade, writing letters to the newspapers and, in March 1788, petitioning Queen Charlotte.

In May 1789 Equiano published his polemical autobiography, which quickly became a best seller, going through nine British editions in his lifetime. An unauthorized edition was published in New York in 1791. Equiano publicized the book himself, undertaking an extensive lecture tour throughout the British Isles. Financially secure, on 7 April 1792 he married Susanna Cullen of Soham in Cambridgeshire, where they lived and had two daughters, one of whom survived to inherit an estate of £950 (approximately $100,000 in 2003). Equiano died in London in 1797; his place of burial is unknown.

By his own account, Equiano spent fewer than two years visiting regions now in the United States and, while he strongly asserted his African identity, he clearly came to regard England as his home. Yet his position in African American history and culture is important. As the author of the only substantial description of the Middle Passage written from a slave's point of view, Equiano provides an important point of connection between Africa and America. As the author of the first major slave narrative, his rhetorical style was widely emulated by many African American writers recounting their journey up from slavery. And as the first prominent black abolitionist, he offered a model for political activism that has remained relevant into the twenty-first century.

FURTHER READING

Equiano, Olaudah. *The Interesting Narrative and Other Writings*, ed. Vincent Carretta (2003).

Carretta, Vincent. "Olaudah Equiano or Gustavus Vassa? New Light on an Eighteenth-Century Question of Identity," *Slavery and Abolition* 20, no. 3 (1999).

Walvin, James. *An African's Life: The Life and Times of Olaudah Equiano, 1745–1797* (1998)

BRYCCHAN CAREY

Eric B. *See* Barrier, Eric.

Ervin, Booker (31 Oct. 1930–31 Aug. 1970), jazz tenor saxophonist, was born Booker Telleferro Ervin Jr. in Denison, Texas, the son of Booker Ervin, a trombonist who played with the tenor saxophonist Buddy Tate; his mother's name is unknown. Booker played his father's instrument from ages eight to thirteen and then abandoned music. In 1950 he borrowed a tenor saxophone to play in an Army Air Force band, but was discharged in 1952 or 1953 and spent another period away from playing before studying in Boston at the Berklee School of Music in 1953–1954. He returned to Texas and again dropped out of music. From 1955 to 1956 he played with rhythm and blues bands in the Southwest and in Chicago, including a period with Ernie Fields's group. In 1956 he traveled to Dallas and then to Denver, where he played his first jazz jobs but once again became dissatisfied with his playing. He studied mechanical drawing before working for the post office.

Ervin moved east via Pittsburgh late in 1957 and in May 1958 arrived in New York, where his career came into focus, and he became a jazz musician of considerable renown. On the recommendation of the saxophonist Shafi Hadi, Ervin sat in with the bassist CHARLES MINGUS's Jazz Workshop at the Half Note. After some months as a dishwasher, Ervin joined Mingus's reorganized group at this same nightclub in November. He made an immediate splash as Mingus's most distinctive saxophone soloist, as evidenced by his improvisations on recordings such as "Wednesday Night Prayer Meeting" on the album *Blues and Roots* (1959) and "Better Git It in Your Soul" and "Fables of Faubus" on *Mingus Ah Um* (1959).

In the fall of 1959 Ervin left Mingus's band, and over the next half-decade he, like many others, was in and out of Mingus's ever-changing groups. He substituted for the wind player ERIC DOLPHY briefly in late February or early March 1960, and by mid-June he had taken the saxophonist YUSEF LATEEF's place. In July he stayed with Mingus to participate in an alternative festival held at Cliffwalk Manor in Newport, Rhode Island, in protest of the commercialization of the Newport Jazz Festival. He traveled that summer with Mingus to perform in Europe. Ervin married Jane Wilkie; the date is unknown. They had two children.

In addition to his work with Mingus, Ervin led the house band for six months at the Cafe Wha? a coffeehouse in Greenwich Village, and he made his first album as a leader, *The Book Cooks* (1960). For about a year, from 1960 to 1961, he participated in a cooperative group, the Playhouse Four, with the pianist Horace Parlan, the bassist George Tucker, and the drummer Al Harewood. In 1961 they recorded the album *That's It!* under Ervin's name and, with the guitarist GRANT GREEN, the album *Up & Down* under Parlan, but the quartet failed to establish itself and disbanded. During these same years Ervin began playing with the pianist Randy Weston. They performed at the Negro Arts Festival in Lagos, Nigeria, in 1961, and Ervin later figured prominently on Weston's album *Randy!* (1963).

During the first half of 1962 Ervin was again with Mingus. He participated in a United Service Organizations (USO) tour of Greenland in 1963, and he made several brief returns to Mingus's group at the Village Gate in 1963 and at the Five Spot in 1963 and 1964. Most important, as a leader for the Prestige label he made a series of excellent albums, including *Exultation!* and *The Freedom Book* (both 1963), and *The Song Book*, *The Blues Book*, and *The Space Book* (all 1964). The bassist Richard Davis and the drummer Alan Dawson are heard on several of these discs, most often in the company of the pianist Jaki Byard, but unfortunately the quartet never found work together in public. Ervin's hard bop style had fallen out of fashion in the face of the emergence of rock and the temporarily surging popularity of avant-garde jazz.

In October 1964 Ervin moved his family to Copenhagen, Denmark, and from late that year to June 1966 he performed in Scandinavia, France, Germany, Spain, and The Netherlands. With Byard, Dawson, and the bassist Reggie Workman he made two new albums for Prestige in Munich in October 1965, *Settin' the Pace*, featuring Ervin and the tenor saxophonist DEXTER GORDON, and *The Trance*, without Gordon. When opportunities for touring the continental club circuit diminished, Ervin returned to the United States. He continued to make new recordings, but these did not match the albums of 1963 to 1965. He visited Europe again in 1968. He died in New York City of a kidney ailment.

Ervin's playing originated in part in a geographical and stylistic tradition known as the Texas tenor, a label applied to tenor saxophonists such as Herschel Evans, Buddy Tate, ILLINOIS JACQUET, and Arnett Cobb and connoting above all a powerful sound on the instrument and a fluency in southwestern blues melody. Ervin came into jazz a generation later than these men, more because of his late start in music than his age. Reflecting significant changes in taste during this period, he differed from the pioneering Texas tenors in his preference for a hard, steely, unsentimental tone, in his mastery of bebop improvisation at even the most blisteringly fast tempos, and in his having borrowed from JOHN COLTRANE the idea of floating streams of motivic-related ideas against a firm rhythmic underpinning. He also differed from the other Texas tenors in his ability to translate into an instrumental setting the sound of African American gospel preaching, which under the name of soul was just beginning to make its way into jazz and popular music in

1959, when Ervin recorded definitive examples with Mingus.

FURTHER READING

Priestley, Brian. *Mingus: A Critical Biography* (1982).

Obituaries: *New York Times*, 2 Sept. 1970; *Down Beat* 37 (15 Oct. 1970); *Jazz Monthly* 188 (Oct. 1970); *Jazz Journal* 23 (Nov. 1970).

DISCOGRAPHY

Wattiau, George. *Book's Book: A Discography of Booker Ervin* (1987).

This entry is taken from the *American National Biography* and is published here with the permission of the American Council of Learned Societies.

BARRY KERNFELD

Erving, Julius (22 Feb. 1950–), basketball player, was born Julius Winfield Erving III in Hempstead, New York, and raised by a single mother, his father having abandoned the family when Julius was only three years old. Since his family life was difficult to cope with, Julius spent a great deal of time on the streets and playing basketball at the local community courts. Julius received his familiar "Dr. J" moniker during a childhood pickup game; it was a nickname that would stick with him throughout his long and astonishing basketball career. By the time Julius was ten years old, he was playing with a local Salvation Army basketball team. He had already learned how to dunk—albeit on Prospect Elementary's lower baskets—and in just a few short years he was able to dunk the ball on regulation posts.

When Erving was thirteen, his mother remarried, and in 1963 the family relocated to nearby Roosevelt, New York, where Erving attended Roosevelt High School and played for the varsity squad with distinction. His style of play was precise, fluid, and marvelously skilled. His large hands, excellent speed, and above-average leaping ability helped him compensate for his lack of great height. (Erving was six-feet six-inches tall, not a towering height for basketball.) Soon he came to the attention of basketball coaches from colleges and universities across the country. In 1968 he enrolled at the University of Massachusetts, a school that was hardly a basketball powerhouse. Erving, however, was determined not to make basketball his entire life and therefore chose the school he thought offered the best mix of sports and academics. At Massachusetts, Erving led the nation in rebounding and his team with an impressive twenty-six points per game (besting all scorers in forty-six of fifty-two varsity matches), broke the school's freshman scoring and rebounding records, and increased his fame as a slam dunk artist almost without equal. During summer breaks, Erving toured Europe and what was then the Soviet Union with the NCAA All-Star Team.

In those days it was unusual for students to leave school before graduation to join the professional leagues, but Erving did so in 1971, partly because of his family's dire financial straits. Though he played just two varsity seasons, Erving shared or held outright some fourteen school records, including career scoring and rebounding averages. For the 1971–1972 season he signed with the Virginia Squires of the American Basketball Association (ABA) and went on to earn rookie of the year honors by scoring twenty-seven points per game, an average he increased the following year to lead all league scorers. However, the ABA was a fractious and sometimes hapless league. It was common for teams to be short on cash, to be badly mismanaged,

Julius Erving, on the court during an NBA Championship playoff game against the Los Angeles Lakers in Los Angeles, California, 31 May 1983. (AP Images.)

or simply to disband. On top of this, the league was locked in a struggle for limited basketball markets with the National Basketball Association (NBA). After his second season with the Squires (and following a period of nasty legal maneuvers after Erving attempted to join the rival NBA), the cash-strapped team was forced to sell Erving's contract to the New York Nets in 1973. In his first season with New York, Erving led the league in scoring and also led his team to the ABA championship over the Utah Stars, capturing the ABA's most valuable player (MVP) Award for 1974. In 1976 the Nets made it to the finals once again, this time against the Denver Nuggets. Erving's play was brilliant. Despite Denver's superior lineup, Erving again led his team to victory—and in one game he scored forty-eight points. In his five seasons in the ABA, Erving won two championships, three MVP awards, and led his teams in points and rebounds; he was also named an ABA All-Star all five years he was in the league.

By 1976 the ABA was in such a shambles that Erving was at last able to join the rival NBA. Primarily due to his reputation, the NBA agreed to a merger that kept several of the old ABA teams alive. Erving signed with the Philadelphia Seventy-Sixers, the team he played for during the remaining eleven years of his pro career. However, some still questioned his abilities, suggesting that the ABA's relatively weak rosters had given him the illusion of invincibility. Among these detractors was the Celtics' Red Auerbach, who dismissed Erving as too small to effectively play the forward position.

Such suspicions proved invalid. Erving exploded in the 1976 NBA All-Star Game, scoring thirty points, bringing down twelve rebounds, and making four steals. He was named the game's MVP. In 1979 Erving even performed off the court, starring in a motion picture called *The Fish That Saved Pittsburgh*.

Erving was an All-Star each of his eleven years in the NBA. Perhaps his most legendary moment occurred during game four of the 1980 NBA finals, when Erving executed the baseline move that stands as one of professional sports' most amazing and celebrated plays: a gravity-defying right-to-left movement across the backboard past defenders for a sweeping backward scoop and score. He was named league MVP in 1981, led his team to an NBA title in 1983, and averaged twenty points and seven rebounds per game during his career. His rivalry with Boston's star forward Larry Bird became legendary and helped make the NBA one of the country's premier professional sports attractions. During his career Erving scored more than thirty thousand points, a feat matched by only two other players in NBA history: WILT CHAMBERLAIN and KAREEM ABDUL-JABBAR. Erving retired in 1987.

Following his retirement, Erving served as a sports commentator for NBC (1993–1997) and sat on the boards of several corporations. In 1997 he took the position of executive vice president for the Orlando Magic basketball franchise.

Erving's enduring fame and popularity for even casual basketball fans everywhere owes much to his disposition. Many consider the mild-mannered and kindly Erving to be basketball's best ambassador. But it was his spectacular and stunning feats on the court that won him the adoration of basketball fans throughout the world. His astonishing baseline jam during an ABA slam dunk contest in 1976 remains the stuff of legend. There was an array of driving-to-the-hoop moves that delighted fans throughout the course of his long and storied career—especially his patented "tomahawk" slam dunk move. Erving was inducted into the Naismith Memorial Basketball Hall of Fame in 1993.

FURTHER READING

Bell, Marty. *The Legend of Dr. J* (1975).

George, Nelson. *Elevating the Game: Black Men and Basketball* (1992).

JASON PHILIP MILLER

Espy, Michael Alphonso (30 Nov. 1953–), secretary of agriculture in the cabinet of President Bill Clinton; U.S. congressman, and attorney, was born in Yazoo City, Mississippi, the son of Henry Espy and Willie Jean Espy, prominent owners of a chain of funeral homes. A member of New Hope Baptist Church in Jackson, Mississippi, Espy was married to Portia Denise Ballard on 17 April 1999. The couple had three children: Jamillla Morgan, Michael William, and Ian Michael Espy. Upon graduating from Howard University in Washington, D.C., with his B.A. in Law, in 1975 he matriculated at the University of Santa Clara School of Law in Santa Clara, California, where he received his juris doctorate degree in 1978. Espy went on to teach at the prestigious Kennedy School of Government, Harvard University, and Stanford Law School, as well as many other institutions of higher education across the country.

In Mississippi, Espy served in various appointive and elective offices of government. From 1978 to 1980, he served as assistant secretary of state and chief of Mississippi Legal Services. He also acted as assistant secretary of public lands division

Michael Alphonso Espy, leaving U.S. District Court in Washington, D.C., 1 October 1998. (AP Images.)

from 1980 to 1984. After working as a trial lawyer in Mississippi, Espy was elevated to the position of assistant state attorney general in 1984 and served in that capacity until his election to the U.S. Congress in 1986. He was the first African American congressperson from Mississippi since Reconstruction. Representative Espy drafted legislation designed to provide federal government grants and mandates to help improve the economic situation in the Mississippi Delta. This bill was signed into law by President Ronald Reagan and was coined "the Lower Mississippi Delta Development Act." Espy also served as national vice chairman of the Democratic Leadership Council and was a member of the Democratic Party Caucus's whips organization. He served for seven years, from January 1987 until his resignation in 1993. In that latter year he was appointed secretary of agriculture in the cabinet of President Bill Clinton, and served until his resignation in 1994. The context surrounding his ascent and untimely departure from his post continues to baffle many after he was acquitted of charges that he had violated federal gratuities laws by allegedly accepting gifts from various corporations. It was alleged that Espy illegally used his position as agriculture secretary to acquire nearly $35,000 in gifts from corporations—among them including Quaker Oats Company and Tyson Foods Inc. In the wake of an investigation by the independent counsel Donald Smaltz, many observers, including jurors who sat during the trial, came to believe that Espy was unfairly targeted. Jurors who served on the trial, as reported in the *Washington Post*, were quoted as saying that the American people did not want any more of these types of petty, trivial cases and that the trial, at a cost of $17 million, was a travesty. Former government officials inside the U.S. Department of Agriculture and White House had even testified that Espy had done a good job. Ultimately Espy was acquitted of all criminal charges in December of 1998. Despite all this, during his tenure as secretary of agriculture, Espy was instrumental in structuring change in the Department of Agriculture by negotiating agricultural commodity trade treaties and initiating new policies in the national system of inspecting food for food-borne illnesses. After exiting public service, Espy began operating his own law firm, Mike Espy, PLLC, which specialized in, among other matters, public finance, government relations, agribusiness, and international law and complex litigation. He was a member of the Mississippi Bar Association, Magnolia Bar Association, and American Bar Association. Outside of his law practice, he ran AE Agritrade, an agricultural consulting agency that offered consulting services on agricultural issues for food charities, agribusiness companies, and governmental offices. Espy's knowledge and skills were recognized by heads of state and government ministers in places such as Korea, Cuba, China, and Haiti, as well as in countries in South America and Africa. Espy served as a consultant for international charities and assisted in humanitarian outreach projects in more than fifty countries around the world. He also served on the board of directors of a Canadian-based biotechnology company, Toxin Alert, Inc., as well as Farm Foundation, Inc., a think tank that specialized in agricultural issues. He was also affiliated with a number of organizations aimed at charitable giving, economic development, and community service, including the Enterprise Corporation of the Delta, the Hope Community Credit Union, and Feed the Children, Inc. He was often sought after as a lecturer and speaker to conduct presentations on social, political, and economic issues.

FURTHER READING

Espy, Michael. "Reinventing the U.S. Department of Agriculture: 1994 Annual Report of the Secretary of Agriculture" (1 June 1995).

"Final report of the independent counsel in re Alphonso Michael (Mike) Espy," available online at http://www.access.gpo.gov/oic/.

RICHARD T. MIDDLETON IV

Estabrook, Prince (c. 1740–1830), the first black soldier in the American Revolution and slave to Benjamin Estabrook, was born around 1740 in an unknown locale and of unknown parentage. Estabrook was the first known African American soldier to fight in the American Revolution and earned his freedom by serving throughout most of the War of Independence, but he is most famous for his involvement at the inaugural battle of the American Revolution, the Battle of Lexington and Concord, where he is said to have fought beside his master's eldest son, Joseph Estabrook, then only seventeen years old. Little is known of how Prince ended up in the Lexington area, but he had reportedly lived with the Estabrook family since at least 1773.

Estabrook was a part of Captain John Parker's Company in West Lexington, referred to as the Lexington Minutemen, and may have joined the militia as early as 1773. There were about 120 other men, ranging from ages sixteen to sixty-five, in the company; Estabrook was reportedly thirty-four years old at the start of the war and the only black member of the Lexington Minutemen. Estabrook was wounded in the shoulder at the opening battle of the war in Lexington when the British major John Pitcairn marched upon the city on 19 April 1775 at around 4:30 A.M. with just over 600 soldiers. Pitcairn's platoon was actually on its way to Concord but needed to march through Lexington. Upon arriving in Lexington, the British noticed that approximately seventy minutemen, including Estabrook, were lined up on the common. Captain John Parker reportedly told his men not to fire at the British, since the minutemen were so vastly outnumbered, but he also ordered them not to retreat. Though the minutemen were ordered not to shoot, they did not lower their weapons, and when a shot rang out (the shooter remains a mystery), the British charged the Lexington militia. During the fight Estabrook was shot in the shoulder, eight colonists were killed, and fifty-one other members of the company suffered injuries. Later that afternoon, after what was aptly described as a massacre in both colonial and British newspapers on the part of the British, Major John Pitcairn marched his troops onward to Concord, and Captain John Parker's remaining men followed soon after. Because of his injury, Estabrook was unable to take part in the Battle of Concord, but according to Alice Hinkle, he was back in action by June 1775. The Battle of Lexington, later collectively referred to as the Battle of Lexington and Concord, remains significant because it marked the beginning of the American Revolution.

Various sources mistakenly claim that Estabrook, reportedly "one of the best soldiers in Lexington," was killed during this first battle at Lexington and Concord, or even at the Battle of Bunker Hill, but the official ledger listing the names of those who were killed or wounded in the Battle of Lexington and Concord states that Estabrook was wounded and not killed (Fraden, 107). Furthermore, Estabrook could not have been killed during the Battle of Lexington and Concord since in July 1776 he responded to a call for soldiers in northern Massachusetts. In that year Estabrook fought as part of Colonel Jonathan Reed's militia at Fort Ticonderoga, along with POMPEY BLACKMAN, a former slave also from Lexington. Pompey Blackman and Estabrook were the only African American members of this band of seventy-three privates.

Estabrook fought until the war's end in 1783 when, according to Richard Kollen, he returned to Lexington to live with his former owner, Benjamin Estabrook, probably as "a paid laborer" (Kollen, 34). Soon after Benjamin Estabrook died in 1803, Prince moved to Ashby, Massachusetts, where he would live for the rest of his life, with Benjamin Estabrook's youngest son, Nathan. There is some speculation that Prince may have lived in a small house owned by Nathan Estabrook in Ashby along the road to New Ipswich and that he may have had a wife, but public records do not confirm this. Little else is known of Estabrook's life after he moved to Ashby.

Estabrook died of unknown causes in 1830 at the age of ninety and was reportedly buried behind the Ashby Church, identified only as "Prince Estabrook, Negro." However, in 1930 a headstone was placed by the U.S. War Department in the pauper section of Ashby's First Parish Universalist Church Graveyard, the site of both Nathan Estabrook and his wife Sally's graves. The acknowledgement of Prince Estabrook's role in the American Revolutionary War, and the many others like him, by the U.S. War Department stands as proof of the important role that African Americans played in the formation of the United States as an independent nation.

FURTHER READING

Fraden, Dennis Brindell. *Samuel Adams: The Father of American Independence* (1998).

Hinkle, Alice M. *Prince Estabrook: Slave and Soldier* (2001).

Kollen, Richard. *Lexington: From Liberty's Birthplace to Progressive Suburb (Making of America)* (2004).

MARLENE DAUT

Esteban (?–May 1539), explorer, enslaved North African, and the first representative of the so-called Old World to encounter peoples of today's American Southwest, was born in Azamor, Morocco. His career as an explorer began in 1528 with the journey to Florida of Pánfilo de Narváez.

This initial Spanish exploration of Florida ended in disaster. The Narváez expedition included four hundred men sailing on five ships. They departed Havana, Cuba, in April 1528 and reached present-day Tampa Bay on 1 May. There Narváez split his forces, ordering the ships to sail along the coast while he marched inward with three hundred men, searching for a fabled city of gold and its attendant riches. A series of attacks by natives reduced the Spanish forces, but they continued their explorations, reaching Apalachen, principal settlement of the Apalachee people (located near present-day Tallahassee) by July 1528. Overwhelmed by native forces defended by highly skilled bowmen, the Spaniards fled south to the Gulf of Mexico in a vain search for their ships, which had returned to New Spain after a year of unsuccessful attempts to rejoin with Narváez. The Spanish explorers quickly constructed five barges out of palmetto fibers and horsehair and sailed west, mistakenly believing themselves closer to Mexico than to Cuba. For a month and a half, they sailed along the Gulf coast. Fierce storms off the Texas coast sank three of the five barges, but the barge carrying Esteban weathered the storm. In November 1528 the remnants of the Narváez expedition landed on a sandbar near present-day Galveston, Texas, which they named the Island of Ill Fate.

Esteban, Captain Andrés Dorantes (his master), Alvar Núñez Cabeza de Vaca, and thirteen other men managed to survive the winter. When spring approached, the men moved to the mainland. Soon thereafter, an encounter with Karankawa Indians resulted in their enslavement for five years until 1534. Twelve of the Spanish explorers did not survive their captivity. In 1534 the four remaining explorers, Esteban, Andrés Dorantes, Cabeza de Vaca, and Alonso del Castillo Maldonado, escaped from their captors. They traveled inland, where they encountered friendlier Indians, who believed them to be medicine men. The four survivors quickly transformed themselves into "cultural brokers," learning various native languages and folkways to survive. Apparently, Esteban was particularly adept at learning languages, functioning as the group's interpreter and go-between. The four wandered from tribe to tribe throughout modern-day Texas and northern Mexico, presenting themselves as healers and religious figures, the "Sons of the Sun." According to one historian, their healing powers consisted mostly of prayers and theatrics, but included at least one surgery. The journey provided the four survivors with an unparalleled knowledge of native cultures, languages, wealth (or lack thereof), and of the region's topography.

This knowledge was highly prized when the quartet returned to Mexico City in July 1536, after wandering some fifteen thousand miles over the course of eight years. A chance encounter with Spaniards on a slaving expedition in northwestern Mexico ended the group's years of wandering. Dressed Indian-style and traveling with some six hundred native escorts, the four were barely recognizable as nonnatives.

Despite their truthful reports of very little wealth to be found among the northern indigenous tribes, the return of Esteban, Andres de Dorantes, Cabeza de Vaca, and Castillo Maldonado precipitated a flurry of excitement about the "northern mystery," as the Spanish termed the unknown lands to the north of Mexico. Plans for expeditions abounded, but such ventures could only proceed with the permission of the viceroy. And when it came to the possibility of an *otro Mexico*, another discovery with the same potential for wealth as the Aztec Empire, Viceroy Antonio de Mendoza had plans of his own. When the three European survivors refused to head an exploration venture, Mendoza purchased the slave Esteban, planning to send him in search of the Seven Cities of Cíbola, the fabled vast riches enjoyed by northern natives. For the sake of propriety, however, such an expedition could not be headed by a slave. Mendoza recruited a Franciscan friar, Marcos de Niza, to lead the expedition.

Esteban and Fray Marcos set out on their expedition to the north in 1539. By previous arrangement, Esteban ranged several days' journey ahead of the Franciscan. Also by previous agreement, Esteban left crosses of various sizes, which would indicate to Fray Marcos the magnitude of his findings.

Esteban maintained his "Son of the Sun" persona, using his skills as a linguist and a healer to ensure his safe passage through native lands. Indians later reported to members of the 1540 Coronado expedition that Esteban covered his sizable frame with animal pelts and adorned his ankles and arms with bells, feathers, and pieces of turquoise. He soon gathered some three hundred native followers, both men and women, who trusted in his powers as a medicine man and showered him with gifts. He experienced no trouble until he reached the Zuni pueblo of Hawikuh, where, in response to his message that "he was coming to establish peace and heal them," elders warned him not to enter the village. A red and white feathered gourd rattle accompanying Esteban's message apparently angered the chief, who threw it to the ground, saying, "I know these people, for these jingle bells are not the shape of ours. Tell them to turn back at once, or not one of their men will be spared" (Gutiérrez, 39). Disregarding this warning, Esteban proceeded into the pueblo, where he was taken prisoner, and the village authorities tried to discern the reasons behind his arrival. According to one account, Esteban explained that other "children of the sun" would follow him, and then demanded wealth and women. These responses convinced the village elders that Esteban was a witch and a foreign spy, and as such, could not be allowed to live (Gutiérrez, 39–40). Other scholars have speculated that perhaps Esteban interrupted an important religious ceremony, or that the Zuni recognized Esteban as the advance flank of an invading force. If he were eliminated, an invasion or conquest might be avoided. According to Zuni oral tradition, Esteban behaved rudely toward the female members of the pueblo, incurring the wrath of the pueblo's men, who then killed him. Whatever the case, Esteban met his demise at Hawikuh in May 1539.

Noting the increasingly large crosses left for him, Fray Marcos viewed Hawikuh from afar, but with great anticipation. Word of Esteban's fate had reached him, and he was reluctant to journey any closer to the Zuni. So he took a long look at Hawikuh, as the bright sun beat down on its adobe apartments, making them gleam as if golden. Fray Marcos returned to Mexico City and to his benefactor, Viceroy Mendoza, reporting that Esteban's death had not been in vain, for he had found the fabled golden city of Cíbola. Eager to exploit such riches, the viceroy quickly organized another expedition to the north, to be led by Francisco Vásquez de Coronado accompanied by Fray Marcos. When Coronado reached Hawikuh, he found not a city of gold, but a village of mud huts and a people whose only recognizable wealth lay in a few stones of turquoise.

Esteban's appearance in Hawikuh must have made a lasting impression on the Zunis. Legends make Esteban the impetus for Chakwaina, a black ogre kachina, or spirit, who reflects the Pueblo oral tradition regarding the appearance of a black Mexican in their midst who represents both the Pueblo people's fears and the role Esteban played as the harbinger of European conquest.

FURTHER READING

Gutiérrez, Ramón A. *When Jesus Came, the Corn Mothers Went Away: Marriage, Sexuality, and Power in New Mexico, 1500–1846* (1991).

Hammond, George P., and Agapito Rey, eds. *Narratives of the Coronado Expedition, 1540–1542* (1940).

McDonald, Dedra S. "Intimacy and Empire: Indian-African Interaction in Spanish Colonial New Mexico, 1500–1800," in *Confounding the Color Line: The Indian-Black Experience in North America*, ed. James F. Brooks (2002).

Taylor, Quintard. *In Search of the Racial Frontier: African Americans in the American West, 1528–1990* (1998).

Weber, David J. *The Spanish Frontier in North America* (1992).

DEDRA MCDONALD BIRZER

Estes, James F., Sr. (9 Sept. 1919–31 July 1967), lawyer and minister, was born James Frank Estes to Melvoid Estes and Bertha Lee Walker Estes in Jackson, Tennessee. Graduated from Lane College in 1942, Estes captained the football team and married a friend and classmate, Frances D. Berry. Enlisting in the Army the same year, he served on active duty in Europe and was one of the few African Americans accepted to Officer Candidate School. Estes was commissioned a second lieutenant in 1943 for the racially segregated 1317th Engineers General Service Regiment. The 1317th engaged in the Normandy landings on D-Day, as well as the Allied Forces Rhineland Campaign and battle for Central Europe. At his discharge in 1945 Estes remained in the reserves and enrolled at Marquette University in Milwaukee, Wisconsin, which conferred on him an LL.B. degree in 1948. Returning to Tennessee, Estes opened a law office on Beale Street, the economic center of Memphis's black community. In September 1950 he was recalled to active military duty and served for the remainder of the Korean conflict at the army's Transportation Center at Fort Eustis, Virginia. Posted as the Plans and Training Officer, he was a company commander and a key figure in organizing the Transportation Replacement Training Center. He retired from the newly desegregated military with the rank of major.

Estes returned to law practice and is best known for legal work with civil rights cases and bootstrap community development efforts in and around Memphis. An active member of the National Association for the Advancement of Colored People (NAACP), he handled a test of the indefinite language in the 1954 *Brown v. Board of Education* decision by directing an unsuccessful desegregation attempt at Memphis State College (now University of Memphis) in June 1954. In three attempts over successive weeks college administrators refused to admit black students on the grounds that they lacked adequate academic credentials. Because only two months had passed since the Supreme Court's *Brown* decision, the NAACP chapter decided not to file suit. In 1955 Estes addressed arbitrary racial inequalities in Memphis's veterans' affairs services by organizing Veterans Benefit Incorporated as a nonprofit entity. He used it to push publicly for service-bonus payments to veterans, mostly black, imperfectly covered by the GI Bill. A parallel venture, the Security Mortgage Company (never formally incorporated), was to provide a financing institution for black Memphians. Veterans Benefit moved toward becoming a social-support organization and disbanded after congressional passage of improved benefits legislation in 1958, but voter registration had already become an emphasis of Veterans Benefit, which generated anonymous telephone threats for its director.

In 1958 Estes defended apprehended fugitive Burton Dodson in a consequential Fayette County murder case. In open court during jury selection Estes secured admissions from many potential jurors, all of whom were white, that they did not oppose black citizens being registered to vote so that they could serve on juries. With this catalyst, voter registrations in Fayette County and Haywood County, Tennessee's black-majority counties, began immediately. In May 1959 Estes helped incorporate and thereafter served as legal counsel to the grassroots Civic and Welfare League organized in each county. The local power structures responded by blacklisting politically active black citizens, denying them access to services and commodities in an economic attempt to drive registered black voters out of both counties. Estes shepherded each organization through a series of voting-rights complaints and methodically documented the white business boycott of black buyers. When black voters were systematically refused at Fayette County polls on racial grounds during the August 1959 Democratic primary, Estes filed a federal complaint that drew the Federal Bureau of Investigation into an investigation. In January 1960, at the invitation of Student Nonviolent Coordinating Committee organizer Ella Baker, Estes drove Harpman Jameson, John McFerren, and Curry Boyd to Washington, DC, where McFerren and Boyd testified about racial intimidation in West Tennessee before the Volunteer Civil Rights Commission hearings. Unable to curb civic aspirations among their hired help, white landowners began canceling traditional annual labor contracts in December 1960 and evicting tenants and sharecroppers who had registered to vote. When "Tent City," a displaced-persons camp, was pitched on private land outside Somerville, Tennessee, Estes founded and published a weekly newspaper from his law office, the *Times-Herald*, to disseminate accurate news and encourage broader reporting. For the Dodson case and despite two years of legal work, primarily in Fayette County, and with the Justice Department becoming more deeply involved, he reached a point of being unable to sustain his practice on "minimal cash and a generous supply of fresh vegetables from various gardens" (James Estes Jr. interview with author, April 2007). His request for payment on legal fees split the Fayette County Civic and Welfare League in February 1961 over the issue of donated funds being used for administrative operations rather than solely for direct relief.

Estes continued community development advocacy in conjunction with his law practice. In 1965 he helped establish the Arkansas Community College, a private training school across the Mississippi River from Memphis in Crittenden County, Arkansas. The school attempted to provide a street-level venue for teaching basic business and clerical skills among the former sharecroppers flocking to urban Memphis looking for work. The school secured a federal grant as a sponsor for the new Operation Head Start Program, but dissatisfaction among board members resulted in Estes's resignation. Lacking both incorporation and accreditation, the educational venture folded the following year.

Estes also entered the ministry and pastored the Vance Avenue Baptist Church in Memphis. During the 1966 Tennessee gubernatorial campaign he was instrumental in the Ministers' Independent Council for Political Leadership, an urban political action group in Memphis backing Buford Ellington's Democratic candidacy. Despite Ellington's election, Memphis offered few new opportunities for Estes. Late in 1966 he closed his law practice and departed Memphis for New York City, where in mid-1967 he was selected to the pastorate of First Baptist Church in Glen Cove, New York, and as director of the Coney Island Housing Authority. He was unable to assume either position because of a brief illness, which resulted in his unexpected death at age forty-seven.

FURTHER READING

Saunders, Richard L. "James F. Estes: Grassroots Advocate," *West Tennessee Historical Society Papers* 64 (2010).

Obituary: *Tri-State Defender*, 12 August 1967.

RICHARD SAUNDERS

Estes, Simon Lamont (2 Mar. 1938–), opera singer, teacher, and philanthropist, was born in Centerville, Iowa, to Simon Estes, a coal miner and hotel porter, and Ruth Naomi Jeter Estes. The grandson of slaves and one of four children, the younger Estes attended the public schools of Centerville and sang at the local Second Baptist Church. He was a boy soprano in the church's choir and at age 13 won Bill Riley's "Talent Search," a program that had been an Iowa institution for several decades.

From 1957 to 1963 Estes attended the University of Iowa, where one of his music professors, Charles Kellis, "discovered" him. He had entered Iowa as a pre-med student, then studied theology and psychology, before settling on music. Kellis encouraged his young, gifted student, reclassified him as a bass-baritone, and prepared him for further study at the Juilliard School of Music, New York City.

Following one year at Juilliard, from 1964 to 1965, Estes made his professional debut in Berlin. He performed the role of Ramfis in *Aïda* at the Deutsche Opera. He later sang at the Beyreuth, known as the opera house of Richard Wagner, becoming the first African American to perform there in a major role; Estes went on to appear at the La Scala in Milan; Covent Garden in London; and at the Washington (D.C.) Opera.

Estes made his Metropolitan Opera debut in New York in 1982. From then until 1999 he performed in many Met productions, including *Carmen*, *Norma*, *Tannhäuser*, *Die Walküre*, *Parsifal*, *Elektra*, *Aïda*, and *Porgy and Bess*.

His opera career allowed him to work with some of the most respected conductors in the world, including James Levine, Sir Colin Davis, Lorin Maazel, Riccardo Muti, Sir Georg Solti, and Seiji Ozawa. He shared the stage with opera's leading stars, such as Luciano Pavarotti, JESSYE NORMAN, Mirella Freni, Christa Ludwig, and LEONTYNE PRICE.

After 1983 Estes devoted much of his time to philanthropy. He began the Simon Estes Educational Foundation in Tulsa in 1983. As of the early twenty-first century, the foundation had granted over $1 million in college scholarships to deserving students. Estes established scholarship programs at the University of Iowa, Centerville Community College (later Indian Hills Community College), and the Juilliard School of Music.

In 1989 Estes, in collaboration with Rotary International, brought 40 music students from South Africa to Des Moines. The students studied at Des Moines-area high schools and lived in the homes of local families. He also continued to support the Simon Estes Music High School outside Cape Town, South Africa. This school operated for underprivileged students from surrounding black townships.

In 2001 he established the Simon Estes Iowa Educational Foundation, a multiracial group that provided three scholarships per year to disadvantaged Iowa children. He also supported the Leesons West Group, an HIV/AIDS advocacy group founded by his cousin, Bernard Lewis. The foundation brought attention to AIDS, a significant cause of death among African Americans in the late twentieth and early twenty-first centuries.

Estes received a wide array of honors for his contributions to music, education, and aspiring musicians. In 1996 he received the Iowa Award, the highest honor given to Iowans. The Iowa House of Representatives passed a resolution in 2000 to recognize his achievements as a vocalist, musician, and humanitarian. The city of Des Moines named a new performance space in his honor: the Simon Estes Riverfront Amphitheater. He was named the Wendell Miller Distinguished Artist-in-Residence at Iowa State University in 2001 and distinguished professor and artist-in-residence at Wartburg College in Waverly, Iowa, in 2002.

Estes was married to his first wife, Yvonne Baer, for 21 years. Together, they raised three daughters: Jennifer Barbara, Lynne Ashley, and Tiffany Joy. He married Ovida Stong in 2001. They maintained residences in Switzerland, South Africa, and Iowa.

The life of Estes represented one of tremendous success. Born into a poor black family in a nearly all-white society, he overcame great odds. He rose from rural poverty to star on the stages of the world's finest opera houses. He won universal renown as a performer, teacher, role model, and philanthropist.

FURTHER READING

The papers of Cecile Cooper, 1964–1987, documenting the career of her nephew, Simon Estes, are held by the University of Iowa, Iowa Women's Archives.

Estes, Simon, and Mary L. Swanson. *Simon Estes: In His Own Voice: An Autobiography* (1999).

"On Singing Title Role in Metropolitan Opera's Production of *Porgy and Bess*," *New York Times*, 5 Feb. 1985.

MATTHEW A. HAFAR

Estes, Sleepy John (25 Jan. 1904–5 June 1977), blues musician, was born John Adam Estes near Ripley, Tennessee, the son of Daniel Estes and Mille Thornton, sharecroppers, and grew up on his family's farm. (Although some sources claim he was born in 1899, he is thought by most scholars to have been born in 1904.) His nickname, "Sleepy John," derived from a chronic blood pressure disorder that gave him a drowsy appearance and occasionally caused him to pass out. As a child he lost sight in his right eye after being injured during a baseball game. He was raised in dire poverty, and in 1915 his family moved to Brownsville, Tennessee, which would remain his base for the rest of his life, despite frequent trips to Memphis and Chicago. His experiences growing up in a sharecropping family would inform much of his music, providing a consistent theme throughout his career.

By the late 1920s Estes had moved to Memphis, where he began playing blues and jug music on street corners, accompanied by the mandolinist James Rachell ("Yank" Rachell), with whom he would collaborate for the next thirty years. He also associated with his fellow blues musician John Lee Williamson (Sonny Boy Williamson), and Estes later fondly recalled their teenage years in "Easin' Back to Tennessee."

In 1929 a Victor Records talent scout approached Estes and Rachell and encouraged the duo to cut a record. These initial sessions, recorded at Memphis's Peabody Hotel, produced the seminal Estes track "Milk Cow Blues," and the rollicking b-side jug song "What'cha Doin'?" These tracks also included the work of Jab Jones on piano, and this trio began performing in Memphis clubs as the "Three J's Jug Band." Estes's first recordings proved moderately successful, yet the onset of the Depression hampered his ability to continue recording. Returning to his Brownsville home, he did not make another record until 1935. Thus began a signature feature of his career: short bursts of creativity and fame, followed by longer stretches of obscurity and poverty.

When he resumed his recording and performing career in 1935—cutting tracks for the new Chicago-based Decca label—Estes had changed his sound considerably. Gone were the freewheeling jug-band instrumentation and light-hearted lyrics. Instead his Decca recordings displayed more conventional time signatures and included the backing of harmonica player and friend Hammie Nixon. Estes still played upbeat numbers like "Stomp that Thing" to entertain crowds at clubs and dance halls, but his music had generally become starker, reflecting his constant struggle to earn a living. In his lyrics Estes often referred to himself as "poor John," and the subject matter of his songs continued to evolve—from chronicling his difficulties in his relationships with women to broader concerns such as poverty and poor health. Moreover the specter of racism infuses much of his Decca sessions, as he often refers, if obliquely, to the discrimination endured by African Americans in the South.

Estes's work for the Decca label marked his most active period of recording, and during the 1930s he wrote a number of songs that would become staples of his concert repertoire: "Drop Down Mama," "I Ain't Gonna Be Worried No More," "Married Woman Blues," and perhaps his best-known tune, "Someday Baby Blues," which would later be covered by a wide range of artists, including Lightnin' Hopkins, B. B. King, Ray Charles, and Jerry Garcia. After switching to the Bluebird label in 1941 Estes teamed with Charlie Pickett, Lee Brown, and Son Bonds to form the Delta Boys. He subsequently performed both with this group and as a solo performer. However, World War II brought on the rationing of shellac—the essential component of records in this era—which caused the recording industry, and "race" music in general—to grind to a standstill. For the next many years Estes nearly dropped out of the music business altogether, save only for infrequent appearances in Memphis.

In 1950 Estes lost sight in his left eye as well as his right, and he moved back to Brownsville, where he lived in an abandoned sharecropper's shack. In 1948 he married Olie Estes, with whom he had six children. One of his daughters, Virginia, later married Hammie Nixon. Back in Brownsville Estes and his family lived in poverty, something he noted in his song "Rats in My Kitchen."

Estes was largely forgotten until 1962, when the Chicago documentary filmmaker David Blumenthal, researching blues artists for his film *Citizen*

South, learned of Estes's whereabouts from the musician MEMPHIS SLIM. Blumenthal casually mentioned this discovery to executives at Delmark Records, who summoned Estes to Chicago, where to his surprise, Estes discovered that his brother Sam, with whom he had long been out of touch, was working in a shop next to the Delmark offices. With Blumenthal's help Estes booked a string of concerts at Midwestern universities. After recording some preliminary tracks Estes returned to Brownsville and a few weeks later went back to Chicago to record more songs. This time he brought with him Hammie Nixon on harmonica, and the bassist Ed Wilkinson. Along with the pianist Knocky Parker, the group recorded concert dates in Milwaukee, and these sessions were warmly received by critics as the return of Sleepy John Estes.

Estes gained considerable acclaim for his appearance at the 1964 Newport Folk Festival, where he performed with Yank Rachell and Hammie Nixon. He continued to perform throughout the 1960s, capitalizing on the popularity of blues music, especially among college audiences. All of his recordings from the 1930s had gone out of print, but Delmark released several records, including his older work as well as new recordings from his live concerts. In 1969 he cut his last album—his sixth release in a remarkably fruitful decade. Although his health began to decline in the 1970s he continued to perform, booking well-received tours in Europe. After returning once again to Brownsville, Sleepy John Estes died at the age of seventy-seven. Although critics have often noted his limited ability as a guitarist, Estes displayed a gift for expressing his personal troubles in his music, and he is generally regarded as an important, if often overlooked, figure in the history of the blues.

FURTHER READING

Charters, Samuel B. *Sleepy John Estes, 1929–1940* (1964).
Congress, Richard. *Blues Mandolin Man: The Life and Music of Yank Rachell* (2001).

DISCOGRAPHY

The Illustrated Discography of Sleepy John Estes. Available at http://www.wirz.de/music/estesfrm.htm.

BRENTON E. RIFFEL

Etheridge, Louis Cullen, Jr. (4 July 1916 – 31 Jan. 1997), World War II Coast Guard sailor and Bronze Star Medal recipient, was born in Edenton, North Carolina, the eldest son of Louis and Claudie Etheridge (Parton). The Etheridge family lived in their own home in Yeopim, North Carolina, in the 1920s, but later lived with Louis Etheridge Jr.'s grandfather, Abraham Parton, as well as his uncle and aunt, William and Mary Parton. Little is known of Louis Jr.'s early life, but it seems likely that he was related to the pioneering African American captain of the Pea Island Life-Saving Station, Richard Etheridge. Richard Etheridge, along with his all black crew, operated the station, part of the Lifesaving Service (a forerunner of the Coast Guard) on North Carolina's Outer Banks for twenty years and was renowned for his seafaring and lifesaving skills. Louis Etheridge Jr. would later continue the family's high level of service while serving at sea with the Coast Guard during World War II.

Louis Etheridge enlisted in the U.S. Coast Guard, probably in North Carolina, on 25 February 1935 at the age of nineteen. With the Great Depression in full swing in America, it may be speculated that Etheridge joined the Coast Guard in order to find gainful employment. However, the African American tradition of service in the Coast Guard for men from the Carolina coast was also very strong and this, too, may have played a large role in the young Etheridge's decision to serve his country. The details of Louis Etheridge's first year of service are unknown, but by late October 1936 he was assigned to the Coast Guard cutter *Roger B. Taney*, and subsequently the cutter *Campbell* on 24 March 1938. Both these ships were Treasury class combat cutters, the largest and most prestigious of all the ships operated by the Coast Guard.

When Etheridge joined the Coast Guard, that service, like all other branches of America's military, was segregated in nature. Because of this, men of color like Etheridge were restricted to serving as mess attendants (also called officer stewards); their job was to prepare and serve meals to the ship's officers, as well as help maintain their quarters. While this was a subservient role that reflected prevailing social conditions for African Americans ashore, stewards like Etheridge, CHARLES DAVID, and WARREN DEYAMPERT were important to the Coast Guard. Because of the overall small size of the service and the ships it operated (as compared to the U.S. Navy), and because of its tradition of African American service, the Coast Guard was considered, by far, the least racist of all of America's military branches. Indeed, Coast Guard stewards, despite their rating, were usually well trained in the art of seamanship and were valued members of the crew. Further, because many Coast Guard ships had small crews, stewards had frequent contact with their fellow crewmen who were white, and many times messed or even bunked with them. The role of African American crewmen aboard Coast Guard ships would be further enhanced during World War II, when many captains allowed their stewards to serve in gunnery positions during times of battle. Among these men who served with great competence and valor was Louis Etheridge Jr.

Etheridge's lengthy service aboard the cutter *Campbell*, which totaled eleven of his twenty-five years in the service, would make him a legend in the Coast Guard. By 15 July 1941 he was promoted to petty officer third class, and by July 1942 was promoted to petty officer first class. There can be little doubt that Etheridge was a highly valued member of the crew; it is even possible that Etheridge himself proposed to his captain that the ship's stewards be allowed to man a gun position, as happened aboard other Coast Guard and naval ships during the war. From October 1941 through February 1943, Etheridge and the crew of the *Campbell* were employed in the North Atlantic on convoy duty, escorting groups of merchant ships and their important cargoes between Newfoundland, Canada, to points in Iceland and Northern Ireland and back again. This duty was among the most arduous performed by sailors during World War II, who had to simultaneously battle the cold and stormy seas of the northern waters and German U-boats.

On 22 February 1943 the *Campbell* and her crew, along with the Polish destroyer *Burza*, were escorting Convoy ON-166 from Northern Ireland to Canada when the signals of a nearby U-boat were detected. The cutter subsequently hunted and tracked the enemy submarine for over seven hours; among the men manning the *Campbell*'s gun positions was Officer's Steward First Class Louis Etheridge Jr. and the steward-gunners under his command, including Lester Carr, Coy Allen, Cleveland Powell, Earl Phillips, William Fitzpatrick, Arthur Galloway, Johnnie Elliott, James Spence, and Willie Samuel. Together, these men operated the ship's big 3-inch gun battery. As the battle developed, the cutter closed in on the U-boat and dropped several depth charges that damaged the submarine. The U-boat was so close to the cutter that it collided with the *Campbell*, causing great damage. However, the gun crews of the cutter would not let their prey escape, and Etheridge and his men depressed their guns to the maximum and fired down on the U-boat. This heavy fire, along with that from the cutter's smaller 20 mm batteries, caused the German sailors to abandon their boat and end the battle. However, the *Campbell*'s fight was not yet over; badly damaged in the collision with the U-boat and taking on water, the cutter was in danger of sinking. As a precaution, over half of the cutter's complement was transferred to the *Burza*, which subsequently escorted the damaged cutter as it was towed to St. John's, Newfoundland, arriving on 2 March. Among the men that remained aboard the stricken cutter was Louis Etheridge.

For its action in sinking *U-606*, the crew of the *Campbell* was later awarded the Presidential Unit Citation, and some men, Etheridge among them, received individual commendations from the captain. However, the role the ship's African American stewards played in the events were not fully appreciated until many years later. Finally, in February 1952, Louis Etheridge Jr. was awarded the Bronze Star Medal by the commandant of the Coast Guard. While several other Coast Guard stewards were awarded medals for their lifesaving heroics during World War II, Etheridge is the only African American Coastguardsman known to have received a combat award above that of the Purple Heart.

After the sinking of the *U-606*, Louis Etheridge Jr. continued his service with the Coast Guard both during the war and beyond, rising to the highest level possible, that of chief petty officer. Etheridge eventually retired from the service in 1959 and was a resident of Willingboro, New Jersey, at the time of his death. Though little is known about Etheridge's private life, after his retirement he was considered a legendary Coastguardsman and frequently attended steward veterans' reunions in his later years.

FURTHER READING

Knoblock, Glenn A. *African American World War II Casualties and Decorations in the Navy, Coast Guard, and Merchant Marine: A Comprehensive Record* (2009).

GLENN ALLEN KNOBLOCK

Europe, James Reese (22 Feb. 1880–9 May 1919), music administrator, conductor, and composer, was born in Mobile, Alabama, the son of Henry J. Europe, an Internal Revenue Service employee and Baptist minister, and Lorraine Saxon. Following the loss of his position with the Port of Mobile at the end of the Reconstruction, Europe's father moved his family to Washington, D.C., in 1890 to accept

James Reese Europe, regimental bandleader with the Fifteenth "Hellfighters" Infantry Regiment, brought live ragtime, blues, and jazz to Europe during World War I. (National Archives.)

a position with the U.S. Postal Service. Both of Europe's parents were musical, as were some of his siblings. Europe attended the elite M Street High School for blacks and studied violin, piano, and composition with Enrico Hurlei of the U.S. Marine Corps band and with Joseph Douglass, the grandson of FREDERICK DOUGLASS.

Following the death of his father in 1900, Europe moved to New York City. There he became associated with many of the leading figures in black musical theater, which was then emerging from the tradition of nineteenth-century minstrelsy. Over the next six years, Europe established himself as a composer of popular songs and instrumental pieces and as the musical director for a number of major productions, including ERNEST HOGAN's "Memphis Students" (1905), John Larkins's *A Trip to Africa* (1904), Bob Cole and JOHN ROSAMOND JOHNSON's *Shoo-Fly Regiment* (1906–1907) and *Red Moon* (1908–1909), S. H. DUDLEY's *Black Politician* (1907–1908), and BERT WILLIAMS's *Mr. Load of Koal* (1909). During *Red Moon*'s run, he was involved with, but did not marry, a dancer in the company, Bessie Simms, with whom he had a child. In April 1910 Europe became the principal organizer and first president of the Clef Club of New York, the first truly effective black musicians' union and booking agency in the city. So effectual was the club during the years before World War I that, as JAMES WELDON JOHNSON recalls in his memoir *Black Manhattan* (1930), club members held a "monopoly of the business of entertaining private parties and furnishing music for the dance craze which was then beginning to sweep the country." Europe was also appointed conductor of the Clef Club's large orchestra, which he envisioned as a vehicle for presenting the full range of African American musical expression, from spirituals to popular music to concert works. On 27 May 1910 he directed the one-hundred-member orchestra in its first concert at the Manhattan Casino in Harlem. Two years later, on 2 May 1912, Europe brought 125 singers and instrumentalists to Carnegie Hall for an historic "Symphony of Negro Music," featuring compositions by WILL MARION COOK, Harry Burleigh, John Rosamond Johnson, WILLIAM TYERS, Samuel Coleridge-Taylor, and himself. It was the first performance ever given by a black orchestra at the famous "bastion of white musical establishment," and Europe returned to direct concerts there in 1913 and 1914.

In 1913 Europe married Willie Angrom Starke, a widow of some social standing within New York's black community; they had no children. Later that year, he and his fellow Clef Club member FORD DABNEY became the musical directors for the legendary dance team of Vernon Castle and Irene Castle until the end of 1915 when Vernon Castle left to serve in World War I. Irene Castle recalls in her memoir *Castles in the Air* (1958) that they wanted Europe because his was the "most famous of the colored bands" and because he was a "skilled musician and one of the first to take jazz out of the saloons and make it respectable." With the accompaniment of Europe's Society Orchestra, the Castles toured the country, operated a fashionable dance studio and supper club in New York City, and revolutionized American social dancing by promoting and popularizing the formerly objectionable "ragtime" dances, such as the turkey trot and the one-step. The most famous of the Castle dances, the fox-trot, was conceived by Europe and Vernon Castle after an initial suggestion by the composer W. C. HANDY. As a result of his collaboration with the Castles, in the fall of 1913 Europe and his orchestra were offered a recording contract by Victor Records, the first ever offered to a black orchestra. Between December 1913 and October 1914 Europe and his Society Orchestra cut ten sides of dance music for Victor, eight of which were released.

In 1916 Europe enlisted in the Fifteenth Infantry Regiment of the New York National Guard, the first black regiment organized in the state and one of the first mobilized into federal service when the United States entered World War I in 1917. After encountering severe racial hostility while training in South Carolina, the infantry was sent directly to France and assigned to the French army. Europe, who held two assignments, bandmaster of the regiment's outstanding brass band and commander of a machine gun company, served at the front for four months and was the first black American officer to lead troops in combat in the Great War. The entire Fifteenth Regiment, which was given the nickname "Hellfighters," emerged after the Allied victory in November of 1918 as one of the most highly decorated American units of the war. Europe's band, which performed throughout France during the war, was the most celebrated in the American Expeditionary Force and is credited with introducing European audiences to the live sound of orchestrated American ragtime, blues, and a new genre called "jazz."

On 17 February 1919 the regiment and its band were given a triumphant welcome-home parade up Fifth Avenue, and Lieutenant Europe, hailed as America's "jazz king," was signed to a second recording contract; he and the band subsequently embarked upon an extensive national tour. Europe's career ended abruptly and tragically a few months later, however, when during the intermission of one of the band's concerts in Boston, he was fatally stabbed by an emotionally disturbed band member. Following a public funeral in New York City, the first ever for a black American, Europe was buried with military honors in Arlington National Cemetery.

Europe composed no major concert works, but many of his more than one hundred songs, rags, waltzes, and marches exhibit unusual lyricism and rhythmic sophistication. His major contributions, however, derive from his achievements as an organizer of professional musicians, a skilled and imaginative conductor and arranger, and an early and articulate champion of African American music. Through his influence on NOBLE SISSLE, EUBIE BLAKE, and George Gershwin, among others, Europe helped to shape the future of American musical theater. As a pioneer in the creation and diffusion of orchestral jazz, he initiated the line of musical development that led from FLETCHER HENDERSON and Paul Whiteman to DUKE ELLINGTON. Without the expanded opportunities for black musicians and for African American music that Europe helped to inaugurate, much of the development of American music in the 1920s, and indeed since then, would be inconceivable.

FURTHER READING

Badger, Reid. *A Life in Ragtime: A Biography of James Reese Europe* (1995).

Charters, Samuel B., and Leonard Kunstadt. *Jazz: A History of the New York Scene* (1962).

Erenberg, Lewis A. *Steppin' Out: New York Nightlife and the Transformation of American Culture, 1890–1930* (1981).

Kimball, Robert, and William Bolcom. *Reminiscing with Sissle and Blake* (1973).

Riis, Thomas. *Just Before Jazz: Black Musical Theater in New York, 1890–1915* (1989).

Obituaries: *New York Times*, 12 May 1919; *Chicago Defender*, 24 May 1919.

This entry is taken from the *American National Biography* and is published here with the permission of the American Council of Learned Societies.

REID BADGER

Evans, Gloria Yetive Buchanan (25 Dec. 1917–2 Jan. 2004), educator, administrator, and vocalist, was born in Otsego, Michigan, the youngest of six children of Martha Keith, homemaker, of Greenwood, North Carolina, and Edward Lewis Buchanan, paper mill superintendent and inventor, from Edwards, Mississippi. Edward Buchanan, who had a sixth grade education, rose from sweeper to superintendent and then consultant and troubleshooter for the paper industry in the United States and the Caribbean. (Mr. Buchanan is credited with an invention, Paper Pulp Consistency Regulators, which changed the manufacture of paper.) In the early 1920s, after being hired by the John Strange Paper Company, he moved his family to Menasha, Wisconsin, where they were the sole black family in the predominantly Polish and German city. Indeed, there were few if any African Americans in the state north of Milwaukee.

Evans grew up in a home that was very supportive of education for women as well as men. Both her father and mother were very determined that each of their children would seek higher learning. An honor student in high school, Evans received many accolades, among them election to the National Honor Society. Because of her selection to the society, Evans was asked to perform a work she had written. A board member of the society, upon learning that Evans was black, suggested that she submit her work to be presented by another more acceptable member. Not one to be discounted, Evans, a quiet, petite student, fought to present her own work. She went on to win a National Elks Oratorical Contest Scholarship that enabled her to pursue an undergraduate degree at the University of Wisconsin. She majored in speech education and graduated in 1940.

Because of her beautiful contralto voice, Evans performed with the University's Glee Club. She excelled as a student. Through her involvement with the school's newspaper, she developed an interest in mass communication, in which subject she earned a Ph.D. from Northwestern University in 1963.

She married a fellow college professor, Glen Lemoyne Evans, in 1940, but the union lasted only a couple of years. Shortly after the birth of their son, Glenn Leroy in 1942, the couple divorced. Dr. Evans has two granddaughters, Rhiannon Evans and Meredith Evans. Dr. Evans never married again and focused her life on the education of black students.

After one year teaching at Lemoyne-Owen College in Memphis, Tennessee, Evans moved on to Jackson State College in Jackson, Mississippi, in 1942. Her passion for excellence in education caused her to found and serve as director of the school's verse-speaking choir for a number of years. She also served as adviser for *The Blue and White Flash*, the school's newspaper, and *The Jacksonian* yearbook. She also directed the Dunbar Dramatic Guild. As part of the effort to raise Jackson State from college to university status, Dr. Evans structured and gained approval for the school's first major in speech and drama and served as the department's head for over ten years. When the college did become a university in 1974, Dr. Evans's pioneering efforts to restructure the department to a concentration of mass communications led to the development of Jackson State's Department of Mass Communications. Because of her dedication to the program, she became the first Director of Graduate Studies in Mass Communication and an important figure in the achievement of Jackson State's university status.

During the civil rights movement, Evans participated in voter registration efforts in Mississippi, the state activists found to be the most difficult area to organize because of intense white resistance. When given the test for voter eligibility by a registrar, Evans was handed a copy of the Declaration of Independence. However, she immediately realized it had been printed to read right to left to deceive voters with poor literary skills. Thus, the examiner was dismayed when she read it, and was thus qualified and had to be registered. A very subdued, coolheaded person, Evans also challenged Jim Crow with dignity. On one occasion Evans ordered her breakfast at a not yet integrated lunch counter in Jackson. She noticed the waitresses peering at her around a corner as she moved her scrambled eggs about the plate, thus discovering an insect that had been folded into her food. After leisurely finishing her coffee, Evans placed the bug on a napkin next to her plate and, after paying for her breakfast, said "Thank you" with a smile and left.

Affiliated with numerous organizations to include Zeta Phi Eta Professional Speech Fraternity, Alpha Rho National Broadcasting Society, National Association of Educational Broadcasters, Women's Institute for Freedom of the Press, International Society of General Semantics, National Council of Teachers of English, American Association of University Professors, and National Education Association, Dr. Evans was also selected Teacher of the Year and the 1978–1979 issue of the Jacksonian yearbook was dedicated to her for her years of devoted service.

Dr. Evans was committed to the future of the South but more explicitly to the education and lives of the black students who lived and matriculated there. She served as a role model to many youth and adults alike. The civil rights leader MEDGAR EVERS was her student. She was asked to edit one of Dr. MARGARET WALKER's books. With qualifications and accolades that would have gained a faculty position at any number of colleges, she chose to remain at Jackson State University. Dr. Evans explained that she felt like she could really make a difference at Jackson State. She felt rooted there. Upon her 1963 retirement, Dr. Evans was honored as an Extremist for Excellence in Education. She was often visited in retirement by former and current students for counseling and direction.

LORIN NAILS-SMOOTE

Evans, Henry (?–Nov. 1810), preacher, shoemaker, and founder of the world's third oldest African Methodist Episcopal (AME) church, was born in Charles City County, Virginia. Little is known of his parents, upbringing, or eventual marriage.

En route to Charleston in the 1780s Evans arrived in Fayetteville, North Carolina. According to William Capers, a Methodist bishop, Evans stayed in Fayetteville because "the people of his race in that town were wholly given to profanity and lewdness, never hearing preaching of any denomination, and living emphatically without hope and without God in the world." Evans's initial efforts to instruct slaves in the vicinity of Fayetteville met with stout resistance from whites. Fearing that his preaching would incite sedition and insurrection, white officials jailed him. Eventually released, Evans continued his evangelistic efforts at clandestine meetings in the sand hills outside of town.

Evans's persistence paid off. By 1802 the "public morals of the negroes," Capers noted, had affected a "change in the current of public opinion." An ordinance passed by the city of Fayetteville in 1802 did prohibit "nightly meetings of negroes, under the pretence of religious worship." But the same ordinance allowed black preachers to preach to slaves "on every Sunday only, between the rising and setting of the sun" so long as the preacher obtained a "license" from the magistrate (Colin McIver, ed., *Laws of the Town of Fayetteville* [1828], p. 63). Evans obtained his license and continued his efforts to convert fellow blacks. The itinerant evangelist James Jenkins came to Fayetteville in 1802 and, though he found "no white [Methodist] society there," he did find "a small society of colored people, under the care of a colored man by the name of Evans."

From 1803 until Evans's death, the church made inroads into the white community. Initial efforts to attract whites met with little success, but between 1807 and 1810 whites began to pour into the church. Pearce recalled that "twenty came forward at one time and gave him their hands," and the white membership increased to "over one hundred souls." The church's "General Minutes for 1810" confirm Pearce's recollection, counting: "110 whites, 87 colored members." Capers also noted Evans's appeal to whites:

> Evans had … become famous, and the seats were insufficient … there was no longer room for the negroes in the house when Evans preached; and for the accommodation of both classes, the weatherboards were knocked off and sheds were added to the house on either side; the whites occupying the whole of the original building, and the negroes those sheds as a part of the same house.

A sense of Evans's dedication comes from his final address—delivered at a South Carolina Methodist conference shortly before his death—to a group of black parishioners:

> I have come to say my last word to you. It is this: None but Christ. Three times I have had my life in jeopardy for preaching the gospel to you. Three times I have broken the ice on the edge of the water and swum across the Cape Fear to preach the gospel to you. And now, if in my last hour I could trust to that, or to any thing else but Christ crucified, for my salvation, all should be lost, and my soul perish for ever.

Evans died in Fayetteville, and Bishop Capers preached his funeral service, noting that it was attended by "a greater concourse of persons than had been seen on any funeral occasion before." By 1814 the church Evans founded had grown sufficiently large and significant to warrant its hosting the 1814 meeting of the South Carolina Conference. But the hopeful ray of racial harmony would fail. After 1810 the white members' social status and slaveholdings began to increase. By 1835—the year the North Carolina Constitution was amended to prohibit free blacks and mulattoes from voting—racial views had sufficiently hardened to impel the whites to withdraw from Evans's church to form their own congregation.

But a quarter century earlier whites and blacks had sat together at the feet of an African American preacher "so remarkable," according to Capers, "that distinguished visitors hardly felt that they might pass a Sunday in Fayetteville without hearing him preach." Evans's successes came at a time when some southern whites had begun to question racial inequality. The "spirit of '76" underscored the inconsistencies of slavery and libertarian ideology in the decades after the Revolution, and evangelicals questioned the morality of holding fellow believers in bonds. Indeed, the Methodists in 1784 went so far as to pass a "slave rule," forbidding Methodists, upon penalty of expulsion, from holding slaves. Though they ultimately retracted the measure, it represented a flicker of racial equality seldom seen in the antebellum South.

John H. Pearce, a white parishioner in Evans's church, referred to him as "an unlettered man" whose "education was barely sufficient to enable him to read the Bible." Yet Evans's hortatory abilities and his biracial church earned him renown. William Capers called the African American preacher "the father of the Methodist church, white and black, in Fayetteville." In 2001 the General Assembly of North Carolina passed a resolution honoring Evans on the bicentennial of the founding of his church.

FURTHER READING

Some materials pertaining to Evans's church are in the archives of the Evans Metropolitan AME Zion Church in Fayetteville, N.C.

Capers, William. *Autobiography*, reprinted in William M. Wightman, *Life of William Capers* (1859; repr. 1958).

Franklin, John Hope. *The Free Negro in North Carolina, 1790–1860* (1943).

Pearce, John H. "Negro Preacher of Great Power," *Christian Advocate and Journal*, reprinted in *North Carolina Review* (4 Dec. 1910).

This entry is taken from the *American National Biography* and is published here with the permission of the American Council of Learned Societies.

MONTE HAMPTON

Evans, Mari E. (16 July 1923–), writer, was born in Toledo, Ohio. Since the beginning of her career Evans has been reticent about revealing personal information, saying that her work speaks for her. It is known that she attended public schools in Toledo and went to the University of Toledo to study fashion design before taking up writing; it is also known that she is divorced and is the mother of two sons. She has resided for most of her adult life in Indianapolis, Indiana, where she has been actively involved in community organizations including the Fall Creek Parkway YMCA, the Marion County Girls Clubs of America, the Indiana Corrections Code Commission, and the Statewide Committee for Penal Reform.

Two childhood events are significant for Evans. In "My Father's Passage," an essay published in the groundbreaking anthology that she edited, *Black Women Writers (1950–1980)* (1984), she credits her father and LANGSTON HUGHES with influencing her eventual choice of career. She describes how her father displayed a story of hers that had been published in the school newspaper, inscribing it with the date and his own comment, and she notes her identification with Hughes's *Weary Blues* (1926). And in an article published in Indianapolis's *Nuvo* weekly in 2004, Evans relates another memory that may have shaped her resistance to autobiographical confession and her commitment to harnessing writing's defining power. Evans's father would put her on the Toledo–Indianapolis train each summer to visit relatives, and she was required to wear a tag with identifying information and her destination printed on it. She recalls:

> One could go, happily, alone from home to anywhere. But always "tagged." Tagging was deliberate, something adults thought up when they were by themselves: It destroyed the spirit. It required pinning a note conspicuously to the chest of the traveler's outer garment, after which people could peer at the wearer—me, in this instance—and then at the note, and one's whole history was there. For a child comfortable with withholding information, it was agony past description. I clearly understood the limits it placed on me: I was not only figuratively, but actually, prevented exercising any ability I had to be in charge of myself—to think or plan once that note was on me. (*Nuvo*, May 2004)

Evans's entire body of work resists the limitations that tags create, particularly limitations created by race and gender labels that are written by someone else and read by strangers.

In the early 1960s Evans worked as an editor in Indianapolis, and from 1968 to 1973 she wrote, produced, and directed the acclaimed television program *The Black Experience* for Indianapolis WTTV Channel 4. In 1968 she published *Where Is All the Music?*, her first book of poems, many of which were later reprinted in her best-known collection, *I Am a Black Woman* (1970). The literary critic Wallace R. Peppers has noted that Evans's first collection focuses primarily on an individual's emotions and relationships; he also observes that it illustrates her use of first-person narrators, developed characters, creative typography, and colloquial diction. Yet these poems are wrapped into the second collection, which begins with two sections that focus on a romantic relationship and its demise, then broaden out to provide a social and cultural context for that relationship. As the critic David Dorsey writes, the section that follows focuses on "victims of social (dis)order, usually explicitly children. The next section is a series of vignettes: individuals of the Black ghetto. The final and longest 'chapter' is the most overtly political. Its title is programmatic: 'A Black Oneness, A Black Strength'" (177). The collection's title, *I Am a Black Woman*, frames the final section as well as concluding the book, and many of the poems in the collection focus specifically on female speakers and characters even as they address pressing issues for the community as a whole. The relation between *Where Is All the Music?* and *I Am a Black Woman*—the shift in focus from the individual to the collective, while still insisting on the importance of individual experience—shows Evans enacting the process of mental decolonization through art, an idea that she develops in her essays of the late 1960s and the 1970s.

These books earned Evans a series of academic appointments and prestigious fellowships. In 1969 she was writer in residence at Indiana University and Purdue University at Indianapolis. From 1970 to 1978 she was an assistant professor and writer in residence at Indiana University in Bloomington, and from 1972 to 1973 she was a visiting assistant professor at Northwestern University. In 1975 she won a MacDowell Fellowship. In the late 1970s and through the 1980s Evans held visiting appointments at Washington University in Saint Louis, Purdue University, Cornell University's Africana Studies and Research Center, the State University of New York at Albany, the University of Miami, and Spelman College in Atlanta. In 1984 she was a fellow at Yaddo in Saratoga Springs, New York, and in 1997 she was featured on a Ugandan postage stamp.

Although Evans has published two more books of poetry, *Nightstar: 1973–1978* (1981) and *A Dark and Splendid Mass* (1992), she has chosen to focus much of her attention on writing children's books, plays and musicals, and critical works. The critic Robert P. Sedlack suggests that Evans makes "the affirmation of blackness ... her primary concern" (465), and Dorsey has argued that Evans's primary intent is didactic and that "the lesson is integral to the aesthetic experience" (173). Certainly the forms of writing that Evans has prioritized allow her to teach a wide range of readers about the affirmation of black culture and experience. Her children's books are *JD* (1973), *I Look at Me!* (1974), *Rap Stories* (1974), *Singing Black* (1976, 1998), *Jim Flying High* (1979), and *Dear Corinne, Tell Somebody! Love Annie: A Book about Secrets* (1999).

Evans's dramatic works include *River of My Song* (1977), *Portrait of a Man* (1979), *Boochie* (1979), and *Eyes* (1979), but Evans has received little critical attention for her dramatic writing. However, in 2004 the ETA Creative Arts Foundation in Chicago produced *Eyes* to good reviews and strong audience response. Written in 1979 and produced that year at the Richard Allen Cultural Center in New York and in 1982 at the Karamu Theater of the Performing Arts in Cleveland, *Eyes* is a musical adaptation of Zora Neale Hurston's *Their Eyes Were Watching God*. In addition to the important anthology *Black Women Writers (1950–1980)*, Evans's critical works include the Grammy-nominated album notes accompanying *The Long Road to Freedom: An Anthology of Black Music* (2001), a five-CD set produced by Harry Belafonte, and *Clarity as Concept: A Poet's Perspective* (2006).

FURTHER READING

Evans, Mari E. "My Father's Passage," in *Black Women Writers (1950–1980): A Critical Evaluation*, ed. Mari Evans (1983).

Dorsey, David. "The Art of Mari Evans," in *Black Women Writers (1950–1980): A Critical Evaluation*, ed. Mari Evans (1983).

Hoppe, David. "Mari Evans: Lifetime Achievement Award," *Nuvo* (May 2004). http://www.nuvo.net/guides/cva/.

Pettis, Joyce. "Mari Evans," in *African American Poets: Lives, Works, and Sources* (2002).

Sedlack, Robert P. "Mari Evans: Consciousness and Craft," *CLA Journal* 15 (1972): 465–476.

JENNIFER DRAKE

Evans, Matilda Arabella (13 May 1872–17 Nov. 1935), physician, was born in Aiken, South Carolina, the daughter of Anderson Evans and Hariett Corley, occupations unknown. Her improbable achievement of breaking through the hostile racial environment of post-Reconstruction South Carolina to become a physician was due largely to her drive and talent. It was also a tribute to certain outside influences at work in the South of her youth.

In 1868, moved by the current of interracial idealism that was galvanizing so many northern progressives, the Philadelphia Quaker Martha Schofield had established in Aiken a school for colored youth. Although it emphasized industrial skills, the school also offered a sizable infusion of cultural and scientific subjects. Evans won a place at Schofield's school, and her performance was so impressive that it caught the notice of the Quaker benefactress, who encouraged and aided the younger woman to continue on at the preparatory academy of Oberlin College in Ohio. Evans's record there was also noteworthy, and, although she never earned a degree from Oberlin, by 1893 her sights were sufficiently raised that she contemplated a career in medicine. Her patron, Schofield, fully in step with those plans, helped her gain admission and a scholarship at the Woman's Medical College of Philadelphia. In 1867 Rebecca Cole had become the school's first black graduate, and the second, after Rebecca Lee Crumpler, formally trained African American woman physician in the United States.

At the onset of that schooling Evans had the idea of becoming a foreign medical missionary. By her 1898 graduation, however, she had decided that equally valuable work needed to be done among southern blacks, who faced the worst health conditions in the nation. Among urban migrants especially, mortality levels were so high—tuberculosis, for example, killed blacks at a rate three times higher than whites—that in 1896 a Prudential Insurance Company statistician, Frederick L. Hoffman, concluded that blacks were not holding their own in the struggle for survival. The only possible result of their trying to live in freedom, he predicted, would be their wholesale extinction. Aware of this suffering and loss, Evans chose Columbia, the capital of South Carolina, for her life's mission. Only the second woman to practice medicine in the state, Evans quickly became aware that hospitals, of which Columbia had none that admitted African Americans, were her people's most pressing need. Over the next fifteen years she founded and operated three successive institutions—Taylor Lane, Lady Street, and St. Luke's hospitals—all of which doubled as training schools for nurses.

Although she was given moral and limited financial backing from local white doctors, and although she put most of her own resources into her hospitals, none of them lasted more than a few years. The problem was not only money. Black male doctors, seemingly unwilling to accept competition from a woman, resisted and even undermined her work. One went so far as to threaten a malpractice charge against her. Yet Evans and her hospitals endured, in one place or another, until about World War I, when she tried unsuccessfully to volunteer for the army medical corps. In the process she cared for black patients from as far away as North Carolina and Georgia, sometimes fetching them herself and bringing them to her hospital by wagon.

In 1916, as others were beginning to turn their attention to blacks' hospital needs, Evans shifted her emphasis to preventive medicine. Her key venture was the organization of the Negro Health Association, whose aim was to put a black nurse in each South Carolina county. Although the association was short-lived and Evans succeeded in placing only a handful of nurses, she grasped clearly that blacks' health would improve only if education and services were taken directly to their homes. That such a program had to be initiated and sustained by the underserved population itself was a telling comment on the outlook and early record of South Carolina's official health establishment.

In 1930, after raising the five children of her deceased sister and years of private practice, Evans again turned to community needs. As the Depression deepened, the absence of maternity and infancy clinics was a particular problem as federal funding for those areas had just ceased with the lapsing of the Shepherd-Towner Act. Supported by black businessmen, Evans opened a free clinic for women and children. It had begun on a trial basis, but demand proved so great—nearly 50 percent of black children needed medical care—that by 1932 the Evans clinic was running on a regular basis. It was supported by both the Richland County (Columbia) health department and the state board of health, but Evans was clearly its mainstay and the clinic closed shortly after her death in Columbia. However, the Social Security Act, passed in 1935, permitted a resumption of the maternity-infancy work that proved to be Evans's special legacy.

Evans's successes in providing the first hospital and walk-in clinic care to many South Carolina, North Carolina, and Georgia blacks and in awakening them to the need for better health practices were critical in helping them stay alive and (reasonably) well until federal intervention could make those services available on a permanent basis. Those contributions take on even deeper meaning when it is recognized that they went against the grain of one important southern medical pattern. In that era, black physicians of talent (perhaps as many as 40 or 50 percent) moved north. Thus not only did Evans do useful work but she also grappled with a challenge that a large proportion of her talented contemporaries found too onerous even to contemplate.

FURTHER READING

Beardsley, Edward H. *A History of Neglect: Health Care for Blacks and Mill Workers in the Twentieth-Century South* (1987).

Hine, Darlene Clark. "Co-Laborers in the Work of the Lord: Nineteenth-Century Black Women Physicians" in *"Send Us a Lady Physician": Women Doctors in America, 1835–1920*, ed. Ruth J. Abram (1985).

Wells, Susan. *Out of the Dead House: Nineteenth-Century Women Physicians and the Writing of Medicine* (2001).

Obituary: *Palmetto Leader*, 23 Nov. 1935.

E. H. BEARDSLEY

Evans, Melvin Herbert (7 Aug. 1917–27 Nov. 1984), the first black popularly elected governor of the United States Virgin Islands, Delegate to the United States House of Representatives, and ambassador, was born in Christiansted, St. Croix, Virgin Islands, to Charles and Maude (Rogiers) Evans. He attended the Christiansted Public Grammar and Junior High schools and completed his secondary education at the Charlotte Amalie High School in St. Thomas, where he graduated as valedictorian of his class.

At the age of nineteen, Evans moved to Washington, D.C., and studied at Howard University, where he graduated magna cum laude in 1940. In 1944 he received his medical degree with honors from the Howard University Medical School. Evans married Mary Phyllis Anderson, a nurse he met while completing his medical internship at Harlem Hospital in New York City in 1945, and they had four sons together: Melvin Herbert Jr., Robert Rogiers, William Charles, and Cornelius Duncan Evans.

After completing his medical internship, Dr. Evans returned to his native land where he became Physician-in-Charge of the Frederiksted Municipal Hospital. In 1948 Dr. Evans became the Senior Assistant Surgeon in the United States Public Health Service in Washington, D.C. In 1951 he became Assistant Commissioner of Health for the Virgin Islands and Chief Municipal Physician for St. Croix. In 1956 Dr. Evans was a Fellow in Cardiology at the John Hopkins University. A year later he returned to the U.S. Virgin Islands and by 1959 he was Commissioner of Health for the Virgin Islands.

Dr. Evans attended the Wesleyan Church of St. Croix and was a member of the Masonic Order. In his private medical practice, Dr. Evans was a skilled surgeon and cardiologist. During his lengthy medical career, Dr. Evans served in a variety of medical and public health posts at hospitals and institutions in the United States and the Virgin Islands. He served as Chairman of the Board of Trustees of the College of the Virgin Islands, Chairman of the Board of Medical Examiners, President of the Virgin Islands Medical Association, and Chairman of the Governor's Commission on Human Services. In 1967 Evans earned a Master's degree in Public Health from the University of California at Berkeley.

In 1969 President Richard Nixon appointed Dr. Evans as the tenth Civilian Governor of the U.S. Virgin Islands, succeeding Governor Ralph M. Paiewonsky. He was the first black who was a native to the territory to serve in that post. After the U.S. Congress passed the Virgin Islands Elective Governor Act, providing for the election of a governor by the territory's residents, Evans ran as a Republican and was popularly elected to the governor's office on 17 November 1970. On 4 January 1971, Evans became the first elected Governor of the Virgin Islands, serving a four-year term. Governor Evans was instrumental in establishing the Virgin Islands National Guard, the building of the St. Croix Campus of the University of the Virgin Islands, highway construction, and obtaining millions of dollars to fund social programs for the needy.

In January 1979, Evans became the Virgin Islands' first black delegate to the U.S. Congress. As the delegate from a U.S. territory, he had no voting power, yet he remained a strong force in Congress. As a Congressman, Evans served on the Armed Services, Interior and Insular Affairs, and Merchant Marine and Fisheries committees. Evans used his position in Congress to bring awareness to a variety of local issues and concerns. He attempted to make farm credit loans available to local fishing and agricultural industries and succeeded in having the Virgin Islands classified as a state, making the territory eligible to receive full law enforcement funding.

As one of only seventeen blacks serving in the Ninety-Sixth Congress, Evans advocated increased rights for blacks. Evans became the first Republican member of the entirely Democratic Congressional Black Caucus, where he supported efforts to designate a national holiday for Martin Luther King Jr. After the death of labor leader A. Philip Randolph in May 1979, he eulogized the civil rights leader on the House Floor. He strongly opposed a proposed constitutional amendment to eliminate court-ordered busing in public schools. He also joined many of his House colleagues in expressing outrage against apartheid, the South African government's practice of racial segregation. Evans served his party as Republican National Committeeman for the Virgin Islands from 1976 to 1980. On 6 November 1981 President Ronald Reagan nominated Evans to be U.S. Ambassador to the Republic of Trinidad and Tobago, a position he held until his death.

Evans died in St. Croix, Virgin Islands, after suffering a heart attack. He was sixty-seven years old. He was honored by Virgin Islanders on three occasions: the St. Croix Campus of the University of the Virgin Islands was named in his honor and a highway on St. Croix is named the Melvin Evans Highway. Additionally, in 2008 U.S. Virgin Islands Gov. John P. DeJongh proclaimed 7 August 2008 "Governor Melvin H. Evans Day" in the U.S. Virgin Islands, in recognition of his outstanding public service efforts.

FURTHER READING

Radcliffe, Donnie. "Honoring Newcomers to the Black Caucus," *Washington Post*, 6 Feb. 1979.

Ragsdale, Bruce A., and Joel D. Treese. *Black Americans in Congress, 1870–1989* (1990).

Obituary: *New York Times*, 28 November 1984.

ALEXANDER J. CHENAULT

Evans, Minnie Jones (12 Dec. 1892–16 Dec. 1987), visual artist, was born in Long Creek, North Carolina, the only child of Joseph Kelley and Ella Kelley, farmers. Evans was raised primarily by her maternal grandmother, a domestic worker in the Wrightsville Beach resort community. Evans also believed she had roots in the Caribbean, and specifically, Trinidad, which was reported to be the ancestral home of a female slave ancestor who came to the United States via the Charleston seaport. While Evans was in the sixth grade, financial necessity forced her to abandon her studies. She became a sounder, a type of traveling vendor who sold shellfish from the Atlantic Ocean.

As a young girl, Evans had persistent, color-drenched dreams that informed her nascent, creative vision. The spectral revelations continued well into her adulthood, well after her marriage to Julius Caesar Evans at age sixteen. The Evanses had three sons, Elisha, David, and George, and worked as domestics in the Pembroke Park estate of a wealthy family.

Evans did not turn her private visions into art until a Good Friday sometime in the 1920s or 1930s. According to various oral histories and interviews with Evans, she received an imperative message : "Draw or die." Like Sister Gertrude Morgan and many others labeled "outsider" artists, Evans interpreted the communication as a divine intervention or gift from God.

Evans's first known attempt at illustrating her private fantasy world was an array of circles and apparent scribbles. As a newcomer to art, Evans salvaged familiar materials to document her visions: wax crayons, unlined notebook paper, rough-hewn frames, and coast guard stationery.

Evans recounted many of her visions to Nina Howell Starr, a University of Florida graduate photography student, future art dealer, and later a key patron who helped introduced the artist's work to a wider audience. The pair met in 1961 and that same year Evans launched her first show at the Little Gallery in Wilmington, North Carolina. When Howell Starr moved to New York, she began promoting the artist's works and organized Evans's 1966 shows in two New York churches, appropriate settings for Evans's "Revelation"-like visual maps of her dream universe.

Though self-taught, Evans was not totally without exposure to and appreciation of art. Even the poorest African American families in the Depression-era South were known to decorate their homes, schools, and churches with advertising snipped from periodicals and catalogues, children's drawings, and colorful quilts and rugs. Furthermore, the white households in which Evans worked were likely to have displayed art; at least one of her employers, Henry Walters, amassed a significant art collection that became the core of the Walters Art Museum in Baltimore, Maryland.

Lack of formal arts instruction did not hinder Evans's development of a distinct aesthetic style either. Many of her sketches and paintings feature a single face—sometimes with strong, possibly animalistic features—ringed by rainbows of flora or intricate swirls. The botanical subjects of Evans's artwork may be a reflection of her position as gatekeeper at Wilmington's Airlie Gardens, where she monitored the entrance and performed other tasks from the late 1940s until 1974. From her perch in the gate, Evans gave away or sold countless pieces of artwork.

Other pieces transfer her fantastic dreams to canvas, incorporating angels in alabaster gowns, winged horses, and floating eyes in a highly individualized image-language. Evans's visual vocabulary referenced Christian imagery with depictions of Christ's crucifixion and the Lion of Judah.

Starr's advocacy of Evans's talent led to a one-artist exhibition of her work at New York's Whitney Museum of American Art in 1975. Seven years later, her work was part of the Corcoran Gallery of Art's landmark Black Folk Art in America, 1930–1980, exhibit, the first major show to focus exclusively on self-taught African American artists. In 1983 Evans's life and work were featured in a documentary called *The Angel That Stands by Me: Minnie Evans' Paintings*, directed and produced by Irving Saraf and Allie Light.

Increasingly, art critics and historians placed Evans's oeuvre in a transnational context, though Evans herself rarely left her home state of North Carolina. As Regenia Perry noted, Evans's use of color and spiritual motifs have drawn (sometimes controversial) comparisons with art forms from the Caribbean and China. Some scholars suggest that Evans's complex, symbol-heavy landscapes—often featuring celestial bodies and other elements of natural and spiritual landscapes—have much in common with Jainist religious art from Southeast Asia. Artwork by Evans has been included in collections such as the Collection de l'Art Brut in Lausanne, Switzerland, and the American Folk Art Museum in New York.

After Evans's death, a sculpture garden at the Airlie Gardens, where she earned a livelihood and gained inspiration, was named in her honor.

FURTHER READING

Arnett, William, ed. *Souls Grown Deep: Volume 1: African American Vernacular Art of the South. The Tree Gave the Dove a Leaf* (2000).

Kahan, Mitchell. *Heavenly Visions: The Art of Minnie Evans* (1986).

Perry, Regenia. *Free Within Ourselves: African-American Artists in the Collection of the National Museum of American Art* (1992).

CYNTHIA GREENLEE-DONNELL

Evans, Orrin Cromwell (5 Sep. 1902–6 Aug. 1971), reporter and editor, remembered at his death as "a newsman's newsman" (*The Crisis*), was born in Steelton, Pennsylvania, the son of George J. Evans Sr., and Maud Wilson Evans, a music teacher and the first graduate of African descent from Williamsport Teachers College.

There are reports, attributed to unpublished interviews with family members, that his father worked for the Pennsylvania Railroad and passed for "white" to get a better job, even pretending his wife was a maid and putting his son in a back room when friends from work visited. The 1910 census shows George Evans worked as a butler for a private family, records the entire family as "black," and shows the neighborhood as racially mixed. The 1920 census reports that he owned a garage, again lists the entire family as "black," and their neighbors as "white." When *Ebony* covered his grand-daughter Pat Evans's 1964 win in the Miss America Modeling Contest (vol. 19, no. 10, pp. 77, 82), George Evans Sr. appeared as a proud grandfather. He did indeed have a light complexion.

Evans graduated from West Philadelphia High School, then attended Drexel Institute, possibly the Evening College, since Drexel yearbooks do not contain references to him. He worked as city editor of the *Philadelphia Tribune*, a paper focused on the local African American community, for six years. Evans was sharply critical of the "free verse" and "degenerate" material in LANGSTON HUGHES's 1927 book of poetry, *Fine Clothes to the Jew*, which he saw taking "the least desirable characteristics of the race" to "market it as literature and art" (Lamb, Robert. "A Little Yellow Bastard Boy: Paternal Rejection, Filial Insistence, and the Triumph of African American Cultural Aesthetics in Langston Hughes's 'Mulatto.'" *College Literature*, 22 Mar. 2008). In 1929 he was mentioned as feature editor of the *Tribune* in the acknowledgments for assistance that year in preparation of *From Captivity to Fame: or, The Life of George Washington Carver*, written with Raleigh Howard Merritt.

Evans married sometime before 1930; Florence B. Evans was born in the Germantown section of Philadelphia to parents from Virginia, and graduated from Germantown High School and the University of Pennsylvania, devoting most of her working life to teaching kindergarten in Philadelphia public schools. Published accounts mention only one daughter, Hope, who later married Robert Boyd; in 2010 Elizabeth Evans published *Sanakhou*, dedicated to "my father, Orrin C. Evans." No published record links Hope and Elizabeth Evans as the same person.

When Evans was hired around 1930 by the *Philadelphia Record*, he was most likely the first African American to be hired as a general assignment reporter by a major metropolitan daily newspaper—sometimes collectively known as "the white press" for the general absence of either staff from, or coverage of, the growing and systematically segregated communities of dark-complexioned Americans in their circulation areas.

In January 1935, Evans covered Marian Anderson's homecoming concert at Philadelphia's Academy of Music, sandwiched between New York appearances at Town Hall and Carnegie Hall, after two and a half years in Europe. "Prominent Negro civic figures rubbed shoulders with their domestic employers," he wrote. "Marian Anderson, a product of South Philadelphia, who has achieved the pinnacle in the field of art, was relating a chronicle of victory and courage in the sibilant notes that rolled from her lips" (Keiler, Allan. *Marian Anderson: A Singer's Journey*, 2002, p. 163).

In 1942 Evans chronicled the increase in employment of African Americans in the booming war industries of southeastern Pennsylvania. His series on "Negroes in the Army Camps" included a 1944 article, "How One General Solved Bus Problem for Negroes by Deal with Company," which was inserted in the *Congressional Record* on 22 May 1944. According to the article, Brigadier General George Horkan, "within a few days after he took command" at Camp Lee, Virginia, "learned about the intolerable bus service—that Negro soldiers were jammed into inadequate Jim Crow seats, or passed up altogether and forced to walk to and from camp." Recognizing "something had to be done" about inadequate transportation to nearby Petersburg, as the law stood at the time Horkan knew he "couldn't do anything about the State law." Arranging with the Petersburg-Camp Lee bus company for additional buses exclusively for soldiers, he ordered that seating be first-come first-served—an arrangement praised by Evans and soon adopted as an order for all military bases.

In 1947 Evans remained, in the parlance of the time, "the only Negro reporter" on the staff of the Philadelphia *Record*, when a strike by the Newspaper Guild ended with the owner J. David Stern's decision to close the paper. Walking the picket line, Evans got an idea for what became All-Negro Comics, a business in which his partners were Harry Saylor, the *Record*'s editor, and two other veterans of the defunct paper. A forty-eight-page monthly, selling for fifteen cents, the comic book was intended to overcome the way people of African descent are distorted in comics drawn by artists who think of themselves as "white." The star of the comic was "Ace Harlem," a detective. The villains were zoot-suited, jive-talking muggers (equally dark-skinned), but Evans said it was "all in the family," as both the artists and characters were all of the same race (*Time*, 14 July 1947). Only one issue was ever published.

Evans moved on to a career at the Chester, Pennsylvania, *Times*, where he became city editor. In September 1953 he was named foreign and national wire news editor, supervising sixteen reporters, fourteen correspondents, and five photographers, who *Jet* magazine proudly noted were "all white" (vol. 4, no. 20, 24 Sept. 1953, p. 30). In 1958 he chaired the finance committee at the Newspaper Guild's annual convention. In 1962 he returned to metropolitan Philadelphia as a staff member of the *Philadelphia Bulletin*, where he covered city administration and the explosion of the civil rights movement.

Evans was honored at the 62nd annual convention of the NAACP in Minneapolis, Minnesota, July 1971, with a surprise reception by eighteen reporters covering the event; the delegates also voted to create a scholarship in his honor. He died less than a month later, at Mercy-Douglass Hospital in Philadelphia, after suffering the rupture of a major blood vessel. He was survived by his wife, daughter Hope Evans Boyd, a grandson, and his brother and sister. A memorial scholarship fund was established in his memory at Temple University, for minority journalism students.

FURTHER READING

"Ace Harlem to the Rescue." *Time*, 14 July 1947.

Obituaries: *The Crisis*, Nov. 1971; New York Times, 8 Aug. 1971; Philadelphia Inquirer, 30 May 1990.

CHARLES ROSENBERG

Evans, William Leonard, Jr. (18 Nov. 1914–22 May 2007), advertising executive, magazine publisher, and radio network founder, was born in Louisville Kentucky, to W. Leonard Evans Sr., an executive with the Urban League, and Beatrice, an executive with an insurance company. Shortly after his birth, his family moved to suburban Chicago, where he was raised. Evans attended the Chicago public schools, after which he graduated from Wilberforce Academy in Ohio in 1931. It was a family tradition to go to college at Fisk in Nashville, which he did for several years, studying sociology and learning to do research. He then transferred to the University of Illinois, where he received a degree in business in 1935. He also studied law at Chicago's Kent College of Law.

In 1943 Evans married Maudelle, and the couple would go on to have two sons. Evans became interested in researching the black consumer, and after working for such respected publications as *Ebony* magazine as an advertising executive, he started his own advertising agency in the mid 1950s. It was obvious to him that black consumers in the post–World War II era were spending far more on products and services than was commonly believed. Indeed, the scholar Richard S. Kahlenberg has noted that "[I]n 1940, America had 13 million Negro citizens whose purchasing power was $3 billion annually. In 1950, they had only slightly increased their numbers but had quadrupled their buying power" (quoted by Garnett, 11). Black-oriented radio formats were becoming more prevalent in the early 1950s, and Evans believed there was enough of a market to support a radio network. Along with the advertising executives Jack Wyatt and Reggie Schuebel, Evans created the National Negro Network (NNN) in late 1953, and it made its debut on 20 January 1954, having signed up forty radio stations. The network offered its affiliates radio dramas featuring well-known black performers. Among its programs was *The Story of Ruby Valentine*. Set in a Harlem beauty salon, the fifteen-minute daily soap opera starred JUANITA HALL, who had won a Tony Award as Best Supporting Actress for her work on Broadway in *South Pacific*. NNN had several national sponsors, notably Phillip Morris and Pet Milk, and it had plans to provide a variety of entertaining shows, featuring such big names as the bandleader CAB CALLOWAY and the vocalist ETHEL WATERS, as well as news and religious programming. Unfortunately, while *Ruby Valentine* received critical acclaim and the network acquired as many as fifty affiliates at its height, national advertising agencies, the majority of which were white, remained hesitant to support a black network. After a year, NNN ceased operating.

Undaunted, Evans continued to do research on African American consumer buying habits, and consulted for white advertising agencies interested in improving their understanding of the African American market. His next venture was in print journalism, when in 1965 he created Tuesday Publications. He told a reporter for the *New Yorker* in September of that year that he chose the name for two reasons: one was the fact that black weekly newspapers used to be printed and mailed on Tuesday, and the other was a reference to the nursery rhyme, "Monday's child is fair of face, Tuesday's child is full of grace" ("Full of Grace," 42). Always a strong believer in inter-racial dialogue, he hoped his new magazine, a weekly insert in the Sunday newspapers, would dispel some of the lingering racial stereotypes that white people (and white advertisers) held. He told the *New York Times* that one goal of his magazine was to demonstrate yet again that "[A]ll Negroes are not uneducated, and that all of them don't live in rat-infested slums" (Carlson, 54).

Tuesday, which first appeared in September 1965, started out as a supplement in nine major newspapers, including the *New York Journal-American* and the *Los Angeles Herald-Examiner*. It began as a monthly and then moved to a twice-a-month schedule. *Tuesday* was first directed at cities with large black populations, but soon even cities with smaller African American audiences, such as Boston, were receiving the magazine. And by the early 1970s Tuesday had expanded to include a new monthly publication, *Tuesday at Home*. The original was a general interest publication with features on major celebrities like MARIAN ANDERSON and DICK GREGORY, along with articles about newsmakers and issues that affected the black community; the new publication was aimed mainly at the "black home-maker ... encompassing her culture, hopes, interests, and life-style" ("Tuesday at Home to Circulate," 6).

Evans published *Tuesday* for twelve years. Along the way, he received considerable media acclaim, and also won an Alumni Achievement Award from his alma mater, the University of Illinois (Urbana) in 1975.

After his publishing career ended Evans continued to consult and do research. He also did seminars for news professionals in his ongoing effort to combat stereotypes about African Americans. In his nineties, he was still doing research on economic trends in the black community, even after he and Maudelle retired to Tucson, Arizona. Throughout his long career W. Leonard Evans Jr. embodied the belief that capitalism can work for African Americans and that they can become successful in business.

Evans died in Tucson, Arizona from a stroke.

FURTHER READING

Carlson, Walter. "Advertising: Dialogue for Negro and White," *New York Times*, 15 Apr. 1965.

"Full of Grace," *New Yorker* (18 Sept. 1965).

Garnett, Bernard E. "How Soulful Is "Soul" Radio?" *San Francisco Sun Reporter* (Apr. 1970).

Krizmis, Patricia. "Newsmen Told How to Learn About Blacks," *Chicago Tribune*, 22 Oct. 1969.

"Negro Slanted Radio Network," *Variety* (16 Dec. 1953).

"New Net," *Time* (28 Dec. 1953).

"Tuesday at Home to Circulate," *Bay State Banner*, 22 Apr. 1971.

DONNA HALPER

Evanti, Lillian Evans (12 Aug. 1890–7 Dec. 1967), opera and concert vocalist and composer, was born Annie Wilson Lillian Evans in Washington, D.C., the daughter of Dr. William Bruce Evans and Annie D. Brooks. Her antebellum ancestors made their mark in African American history. Evanti's paternal grandfather, HENRY EVANS, was an abolitionist involved in the 1859 Oberlin-Wellington riot. Her great uncle Lewis Sheridan Leary participated in John Brown's raid at Harpers Ferry,

Virginia. Her mother, Annie Evans, was a schoolteacher in Washington D.C. Her father, William Bruce Evans, whose ancestors came to Washington from Oberlin, Ohio, first served as a physician and later became one of the few black school principals in Washington, D.C.

Lillian Evans was a precocious child who sang her first public recital in 1894 at the age of four. The Evans family loved classical music and singing. They purchased a piano and hired a piano teacher to give their daughter lessons. Lillian regularly performed in public at school commencements, church socials, and holiday celebrations. She attended Armstrong Manual Training School, where her father was principal. With her parents as role models, Lillian decided to become a kindergarten teacher and enrolled in a two-year course at Washington's Miners Teachers College (later part of the University of the District of Columbia).

After graduation she taught kindergarten and gave private music lessons to earn tuition money to attend Howard University, from which she graduated in 1917. At Howard, Lillian met her husband, Roy Tibbs, who was her music professor; they married in 1918. Her stage name was derived from combining her maiden name, Evans, with her married name, Tibbs. Critics and fans dubbed her "Madame Evanti." Their only child, Thurlow Evans Tibbs, was born in 1921, after which Evanti continued teaching. By 1924, however, she had realized that her true ambition was to be an opera singer. She went to Paris that year to study music and acting, despite her husband's protests. One of her teachers urged her to audition at the Nice Opera House in Nice, France, and she was hired. In March 1925 she made her opera debut in the title role in Delibes's *Lakmé*, and at the same time made history as the first black female to sing in a European opera house. In 1927 she reprised the same role at the Trianon-Lyrique opera house in Paris. Her homecoming in Washington, D.C., in October 1925 saw her in concert before a crowd of 1,600 at the Lincoln Theater. Evanti sang in Europe during the remainder of the 1920s and the early 1930s.

In 1932 Evanti took the bold step of auditioning for the Metropolitan Opera in New York. At that time no African American had ever performed in an opera on that stage. Unlike Marian Anderson, who had never sung an opera role before her Met debut in 1954, Evanti already claimed mastery of twenty-four operas. Despite her repertoire and formidable musical training, she was rejected by the Met, and rejected again in 1933 and 1946. While the Met rejections were a career setback for Evanti, most of her public performances were well received. In 1932 she gave a critically acclaimed concert at Washington's Belasco Theater. In 1934 she became the first African American singer invited to the White House since 1882, when soprano Mathilda Joyner sang for President Benjamin Harrison. A few months after her White House appearance Evanti contacted Eleanor Roosevelt about starting an opera house or performing arts center in Washington, D.C. She also went to Congress to advocate "an American National Theater and Academy." Evanti's dream came true when the Kennedy Center for the Performing Arts opened in 1971 in Washington, D.C.

Evanti is most remembered for her performance in the role of Violetta in Verdi's *La Traviata* with the National Negro Opera Company (NNOC) at the Watergate in Washington, D.C., on 28 August 1943. Violetta was Evanti's favorite role; she sang it more than fifty times. Evanti is sometimes erroneously credited with founding the NNOC, but Mary Cardwell Dawson was the actual founder. Dawson and Evanti had artistic differences, and Evanti left the company in the summer of 1944.

Evanti also had a career as a songwriter. W. C. Handy's music publishing company published her setting of the Twenty-third Psalm and her other compositions, including "The Mighty Rapture," "Thank You Again and Again," "Speak to Him Thou," and "High Flight." In the 1940s, when Evanti was a goodwill ambassador to Argentina and Brazil for the U.S. State Department, she composed the song "Himno Pan Americano." For the Republican presidential candidate Thomas E. Dewey in 1948, Evanti composed the tune "There's a Better Day A-coming." In 1949 while campaigning for suffrage for the District of Columbia, Evanti wrote the song "Hail to Fair Washington." She later founded her own music publishing house, Columbia Music Bureau. Evanti organized twenty black women singers in the District of Columbia into the Evanti Chorale. The group debuted in Washington on 18 April 1950 with a program featuring American composers.

Lillian Evanti was a compelling role model for the generation of African American female opera singers such as Leontyne Price, Grace Bumbry, and Mattiwilda Dobbs that emerged in the 1960s. Lillian Evanti died in Washington, D.C.

FURTHER READING

Smith, Eric Ledell. "Lillian Evanti: Washington's African-American Diva," *Washington History* 11.1 (Spring/Summer 1999): 24–43.

Obituary: *Washington Post*, 8 Dec. 1967.

ERIC LEDELL SMITH

Eve, Arthur O., Sr. (23 Mar. 1933–), activist and Democratic state legislator from Buffalo, New York, was born in Harlem to Arthur B. Eve (a maintenance worker) and Beatrice Clark Eve (a theater cashier). His parents divorced when he was five or six years old and he moved to Miami, Florida, where he was raised by his mother and grandmother in a housing project. Eve excelled in sports; he ran track and played basketball for the all-black, segregated Dorsey High School. After earning his diploma in 1951, he attended West Virginia State College for three semesters, where he played basketball and studied physical education.

In 1953 Eve headed to Buffalo with two suitcases and $9.45 in his pocket. He planned to earn money—perhaps working in a steel mill—and then return to college in the fall. But the Korean War interrupted his plans, and in May he was drafted into the United States Army. He completed his basic training at Fort Dix and then shipped out to Germany, where in addition to his military duties he played basketball on a previously all-white team throughout Europe. As a point guard, his role was to drive the ball down the court, to make and to execute plays. Eve's leadership skills were immediately recognized and he was quickly elected captain.

After completing his military service, Eve went to New York City. A deeply religious and Christian man, he believed in forgiveness and he forged a close relationship with his father, with whom he had had little contact. In 1955 Eve bumped into Lee Constance Bowles, whom he had known in college, coming out of a subway station. Eve believed that God was responsible for this chance meeting and he and Bowles were married in 1956. Together, they raised their five children: Arthur Jr., Leecia, Eric, and twin boys: Malcolm and Martin.

In 1963 Eve founded a newspaper, *The Buffalo Challenger*, whose mission was not only to keep the public informed of the workings of their democracy, but also to help people improve their lives and advance in their careers. Three years later, Eve was elected to the New York State Assembly, where he served for the next thirty-six years. From his first term forward, Eve established himself as a political leader who put people above politics. He initiated financial aid programs for minority and economically disadvantaged students, including the Educational Opportunity Program (EOP) in 1967 and the Higher Educational Opportunity Program (HEOP) in 1970. In 1979, he was appointed Deputy Speaker and therefore held the highest position of any minority in New York State's elective governmental system at that time. During his tenure, his legislative agenda successfully focused on children, civil rights, economic development and job training, education, health care, housing, and senior citizens. In short, Eve compiled an unparalleled record of victories for the most underserved, voiceless, and disenfranchised.

Eve was also a courageous public servant. In 1971, he was one of the first two leaders, with State University of New York at Buffalo Professor of Law Herman Schwartz, to sit down with the inmates at Attica State Prison to resolve peacefully the conflict between the prisoners, who were calling for badly needed and overdue prison reforms, and the prison authorities. Eve opposed Governor Nelson A. Rockefeller's refusal to go to Attica to meet with him and the other mediators. He understood that the governor's decision to end the negotiations with brutal force would lead to a massacre, as it did.

In legislative circles, Eve was well known for his wonderfully colorful ties depicting children. He wore these artistic ties because he wanted the people with whom he worked not only to understand, but also to see his top priority: children (author interview with Eve, 24 February 2010).

After over three decades of dedicated public service, Eve retired in 2001. Throughout his long and productive career and after, he was the recipient of numerous awards and honors, including an honorary Doctor of Laws degree from the State University of New York in 2003. In 2010 he received the Percy E. Sutton Empire State and Nation Builder Award for public service.

In sum, Eve devoted his life to the well-being of others. He was indefatigable in his belief in economic justice and educational opportunities for all. The laws and bills he penned and sponsored improved the lives of millions of people throughout New York State and serve as an exemplary model of legislative initiatives for the nation.

FURTHER READING

"Icon! Retired Deputy Speaker Arthur O. Eve Receives Highest Honor at Black and Puerto Rican Caucus Gala." *The Challenger News*, 3 March 2010.

Mortimer, Lenina. "Gala Dinner Transcends Media Frenzy." *The Legislative Gazette*, 23 February 2010.
Sullivan, Erin. "Assemblyman of God." *Metroland*, 20 May 1999.

THERESA C. LYNCH

Everett, Francine (3 Apr. 1920–27 May 1999), singer and actor, was born Franceine Everette in Louisburg, North Carolina. Although Everett always gave her birth year as 1920, there is some evidence that she might have been born as early as 1915. Very little is known about her childhood. Everett got her start in show business in the early 1930s, appearing in the musical production *Hummin' Sam* in New York City in 1933 and performing with a nightclub act called the Four Black Cats. Even though she enjoyed some success as a singer, Everett aspired to be an actress as well, and with that in mind she began studying acting and appearing in plays produced by the Federal Theatre Project (FTP). The FTP was an important part of Franklin Roosevelt's Works Progress Administration and had established sixteen theater units around the United States that were staffed by African Americans. Everett joined the Harlem division of the FTP, which was considered to be the best of the sixteen. Her work with this highly principled and inventive troupe left a lasting impact on Everett, who for the rest of her career would turn down roles that she felt stereotyped or in some other way exploited African American performers.

In 1936 Everett met Rex Ingram, the highly regarded stage actor; they were married the same year. When Ingram was invited to Hollywood to play De Lawd in the film version of *The Green Pastures* (1936), Everett moved to California with him. Reportedly displeased with the way African Americans were depicted in the film, she refused to accept a role in the movie. The marriage ended in 1939, and Everett returned to Harlem.

Back in New York, Everett sought out roles in what were then known as "race" pictures, independent movies made for African American audiences and distributed to the fairly large circuit of black theaters around the United States. Her film debut was *Keep Punching* in 1939. This boxing movie was conceived as a vehicle for an actual boxer, Henry Armstrong. Everett had a supporting role as the loyal girlfriend who stands by as the boxer is tempted by money, fame, and a seductress. Race films were made on low budgets and were mostly ignored by the nation's mainstream film critics; the decision to pursue a career only in African American films says a great deal about Everett's integrity, as she could almost certainly have had a more lucrative career in Hollywood. Instead, she had a short-lived career of eight films in eleven years.

Everett's second film was *Paradise in Harlem* (1939), a crime film in which a Shakespearean actor suffers the dual consequences of witnessing a gangland murder and wanting to stage *Othello* for a Harlem audience. The film was directed by Joseph Seiden, a New York producer and director who had substantial experience making motion pictures for the Yiddish theater circuit and here branched out into serving another specialized audience: African Americans who wanted to see more stories featuring black characters.

Everett did not make another feature film for six years. She still worked quite frequently, however, as she appeared in at least fifty "soundies," short films of singers and musicians performing a single song. In 1945 she returned to motion pictures with *Big Timers*. This movie was what the industry referred to as a "two-reeler," a film lasting approximately forty minutes, or the length of two film reels, and shot on a low budget even by the standards of race movies. A love story about a poor woman who pretends to be wealthy to attract a rich boyfriend, *Big Timers* served primarily as a vehicle for comic performer Stepin Fetchit. Everett followed this with another two-reeler, *Tall, Tan, and Terrific* (1946), a crime movie set in a Harlem nightclub and featuring performances by a number of different entertainers, including Mantan Moreland.

Dirty Gertie from Harlem, U.S.A. (1947) teamed Everett with Spencer Williams, the talented actor and director who had been making independent films since 1941. The movie is an uncredited reworking of W. Somerset Maugham's *Miss Sadie Thompson*, which had already been adapted for the screen in 1928 with Gloria Swanson and in 1932 with Joan Crawford; it would be filmed again in 1953 with Rita Hayworth. Gertie is a sexy and provocative woman who flees Harlem for the Caribbean after cheating on her gangster boyfriend.

Unfortunately, the movie did little to boost Everett's career. She had a supporting role in the 1947 film *Ebony Parade*, starring Dorothy Dandridge; the press had long reported rumors of a rivalry between the two but those stories were most likely unfounded. Everett ended her film career with a small, uncredited role in *No Way Out* (1950), a small-budget Hollywood film about the confrontation between a white racist and an

African American doctor, portrayed by SIDNEY POITIER in his screen debut.

Everett retired from acting in 1950 and spent the next thirty five years working in a clerical position in Harlem Hospital. She remained active in the motion picture industry through her membership in the Negro Actors' Guild and through her participation in seminars about African American cinema hosted by the International Agency for Minority Artist Affairs. Everett died in a Bronx, New York, nursing home in 1999.

FURTHER READING

Obituary: *The Independent* (London), 25 June 1999.

RANDALL CLARK

Everett, Percival (22 Dec. 1956–), writer and professor, was born Percival Leonard Everett II, the elder of the two children of Percival Leonard Everett, a dentist, and Dorothy (Stinson) Everett, who assisted her husband in his practice for thirty years. The younger Percival was born on a U.S. Army base in Fort Gordon, Georgia, while his father was assigned a post as a sergeant and communications specialist. Shortly after his birth, the family moved to Columbia, South Carolina, where he spent his childhood, eventually graduating from A. C. Flora High School in 1974.

The climate of Everett's youth was stimulating, nurturing a strong intellect. The senior Everett was part of a long family legacy in the field of medicine (his own father and two brothers were all doctors) and he was also a voracious reader, filling the family home with books. The younger Everett inherited his father's literary inclinations, though he knew as early as the third grade that he did not want to become a doctor.

In 1977 Percival Everett II earned a bachelor of arts in Philosophy from the University of Miami, where he studied the work of twentieth-century philosopher Ludwig Wittgenstein. Everett continued with philosophy at the graduate level at the University of Oregon, although his enchantment waned. His coursework required he write scenes and dialogue in which everyday discourse was used to consider philosophical issues. This ultimately spawned Everett's interest in fiction as a more organic method for considering the topic. He attended Brown University's creative writing program, where he studied with the experimental fiction legend Robert Coover, among others. By the time Everett graduated from the program in 1982, he had completed the manuscript that became his first novel, *Suder*, published in 1983 by Viking Press.

The book, which was both a critical and commercial success, followed the picaresque adventures of Craig Suder, a third-basemen with the Seattle Mariners, as he underperforms as an athlete, husband, and father. In a 1991 essay in *Callaloo: A Journal of African Diaspora Arts & Letters* (a publication Everett began working with in 1989), Everett recounted his involvement with the producer Norman Lear, who optioned the film rights to the book through Embassy Pictures. Though Everett was enlisted to write the screenplay, the producers asked that the title character, who was black, be cast as white or at least aided by a white principal. Everett would not allow the revision and the book was never adapted. His second novel, *Walk Me to the Distance* (1985), was successfully reinterpreted as the television movie *Follow Your Heart* on the ABC network in 1991. However, Lear and Embassy's lack of confidence in a black principal character made a lasting impression on Everett. *Walk Me to the Distance* and Everett's third publication, *Cutting Lisa* (1986), both featured main characters whose race was not explicitly stated.

Everett amassed a prolific list of publishing credentials, authoring fifteen novels, three short story collections, a children's book, and a volume of poetry. His prose included satire, picaresque tales set in the American West, and modern iterations of Greek myths. For example, in *Erasure* (2002), Everett's most commercially successful work after *Suder*, Thelonius "Monk" Ellison, a lonely black academic, finally finds success when he writes a send-up of so-called black fiction—a novella entitled *My Pafology*—under the nom de plume, Stagg R. Leigh.

Two years after *Erasure*, Everett published *A History of African American People (proposed) By Strom Thurmond As Told to Percival Everett and James Kincaid* (2004), a joint effort with the University of Southern California professor James Kincaid. In it, fictional characters with the same names as the two authors are enlisted by the publishing house Simon & Schuster to help Strom Thurmond, the former South Carolina governor, U.S. senator, and avowed segregationist, on a work about African Americans.

Protagonists who are isolated, perhaps even scorned for their erudition, figured prominently in Everett's work. The breadth and polish of his writing earned him continual praise, though he was often cited as somewhat of a cultish literary figure. Seven of his books were published by the St. Paul, Minnesota-based non-profit Graywolf Press. His resistance to publishing books more reflective of profitable marketing trends that ghettoize black writers was both well documented and well respected. However, his work was not anthologized in the *Norton Anthology of African American Literature* (1997) nor in the *Oxford Companion to African American Literature* (1997).

Still, Everett's numerous awards included a D. H. Lawrence Fellowship (1984), a New American Writing Award (1990), an American Academy of Arts and Letters Award for Literature (2003), and the PEN USA 2006 Literary award for his fifteenth novel, *Wounded* (2005).

In addition to his work as a novelist, Everett was also known as an experienced rancher, spending a decade training mules and horses on a farm outside of Los Angeles and working as a ranch hand as a young adult. He was proficient in the visual arts, occasionally showing and selling his paintings. Everett, who became interested in jazz and blues as a teenager, supported himself as an undergraduate by playing guitar in local Miami bands.

Though he once worked as a high school math teacher, his longest career outside of writing was as a university academic. He taught at the University of Kentucky from 1985 to 1988 and the University of Notre Dame from 1988 to 1991. From 1992 to 1998 he was a professor at University of California at Riverside, where he was also chair of the creative writing program. In 1999 he joined the faculty of University of Southern California, where he was chair of the English department and was appointed a distinguished professor of English.

In 2005 Everett married the writer DANZY SENNA. The couple had a son, Henry, born in 2006.

FURTHER READING

Magill, Frank N. *Masterplots II: African-American Literature Series*, vol. 3 (1994).

Matuz, Roger, ed. *Contemporary Literary Criticism: Excerpts from Criticism of the Works of Today's Novelists, Poets, Playwrights, Short Story Writers, Scriptwriters, & Other Creative Writers*, vol, 57 (1990).

Trosky, Susan. *Contemporary Authors: A Bio-Bibliographical Guide to Current Writers in Fiction, General Nonfiction, Poetry, Journalism, Drama, Motion Pictures, Television*, vol. 129 (1990).

DENISE BURRELL-STINSON

Evers, Charles (11 Sept. 1922–), activist and politician, was born James Charles Evers to James Evers, a farmer, and Jessie Wright Evers, a maid, in Decatur, Newton County, Mississippi. In addition to James and his three siblings, Jessie Evers had three children from a previous marriage. The family was poor, like most of their neighbors during the Depression, but was strengthened by a powerful Christian belief in the dignity of every human being. The Evers subscribed to the *Chicago Defender*, a publication that kept the young Evers informed about life outside the segregated South. Charles developed a strong bond with his younger brother, MEDGAR EVERS, and they each vowed to carry on the other's work if something happened to one of them. Charles attended local schools but would complete high school only later in life.

In 1940 Charles Evers enlisted in the U.S. Army and during World War II served in Australia, the Philippines, and New Guinea. He studied law in the Philippines and was discharged from military service in 1945. Like many black veterans, he returned home with a greater desire to actively pursue his rights as a U.S. citizen, having fought for freedom overseas and experienced better treatment in Europe and Japan than in his own country. Evers also took advantage of the GI Bill to go to college, first completing high school at Alcorn State University in Claiborne County, Mississippi. In 1946 Charles and Medgar Evers registered to vote and in the following year were the first two African Americans to cast a ballot in Decatur, Mississippi since Reconstruction. His interest in politics and civil rights led him to join the NAACP in 1948. He earned a B.S. in Social Studies from Alcorn in 1951. While in college he married and then quickly divorced his first wife. In 1951 he married Nannie Laurie, a former student from Alcorn, and moved to Philadelphia, Mississippi.

Evers's work in the NAACP continued after his move to Philadelphia. The Mississippi NAACP appointed him voter registration chairman in 1953, a year before his brother Medgar was hired as state field secretary by the NAACP. In February 1956 Charles Evers started an NAACP chapter in Philadelphia where he also founded and ran the first taxi company owned by an African American and worked for a radio station, becoming one of the first African American disc jockeys in Philadelphia. His constant appeals to his listeners to pay the poll tax and vote led the white establishment to bankrupt him and chase him out of town. He moved to Chicago in 1956 and supported himself by teaching and engaging in running numbers, bootlegging, and petty crime. Evers met MARTIN LUTHER KING JR. in 1957 and helped him expand the Southern Christian Leadership Conference (SCLC). His profitable activities in Chicago funded Medgar Evers's civil rights work until the latter was murdered on 12 June 1963. By then Medgar had been instrumental in registering some 28,000 blacks to vote in Mississippi.

Faithful to his vow, Charles announced at his brother's funeral that he was replacing Medgar as NAACP field secretary. The position was not technically one he could simply assume, but NAACP national executive Secretary, ROY WILKINS, seeking to avoid a public confrontation with Medgar Evers's brother, allowed him to keep the position despite strong reservations. Medgar Evers's widow, the future MYRLIE EVERS-WILLIAMS, also feared that her brother-in-law might undermine the gains of the NAACP and other civil rights groups under her brother's leadership. Charles Evers moved to Jackson, Mississippi in 1963, and later that year he joined King in the famous March on Washington. He developed political connections with attorney general Robert Kennedy, who helped to integrate the federal marshal force in Jackson. From the beginning Evers adopted a militant stance and at times disobeyed orders from Wilkins and other national and state NAACP officials. Wilkins had advised him to use lawsuits as a means to integrate the South. Instead Evers organized marches and sit-ins and supported the Student Nonviolent Coordinating Committee (SNCC). Many of the grass roots activists of SNCC and the Congress of Racial Equality (CORE), however, soon came to be equally concerned by Evers's independent streak, his abrasive personality, and his unwillingness to listen to advice. Evers likewise had a low opinion of many of the youthful activists, whom he dismissed as communists and outside agitators.

Evers played a role in a number of protests and marches in McComb and other Mississippi communities in 1964 and 1965, but figured most prominently in the response to an attempted assassination of George Metcalfe, president of the Natchez NAACP branch, on 27 August 1965. Although a wide range of civil rights groups, including the Southern Christian Leadership Conference, the Mississippi Freedom Democratic Party, and others descended on Natchez, it was Evers who emerged as the main leader of a series of demonstrations against white violence and a boycott of white businesses. By 1 December 1965, Evers and other NAACP officials reached a settlement with Natchez city officials. When Natchez businessmen and officials agreed to hire six African American city policemen, desegregate all public facilities, and hire and promote black workers at a number of local businesses, Evers called off the boycott. Although some of the younger activists in Natchez believed that they had been sidelined by Evers, Henry Lee Moon, public relations director of the NAACP, declared the Natchez demonstrations the most effective use of direct action protests in the South up to that time.

In 1965 Evers moved to Fayette, Mississippi, the Jefferson County seat, a town of about 1,700 people with a black majority. There he opened the Medgar Evers Shopping Center, which featured various stores, a ballroom, a restaurant, and a dance hall. Evers's businesses, which targeted African Americans, facilitated his civil rights work because he did not have to fear economic reprisals from whites. At the time it was common for whites to withdraw their patronage from those of any race who supported the civil rights movement.

Living in a small town did not restrict the scope of Charles Evers's civil rights activities. Though initially critical, in 1966 Evers participated in the second JAMES MEREDITH March Against Fear. In 1962 Meredith had been the first black student to enroll at the University of Mississippi and graduated the following year with a degree in history. On 5 June 1966 he started a solitary March Against Fear from Memphis, Tennessee to Jackson, Mississippi as way to protest segregation in the South. After leaving Memphis he was shot by a white man, and various black civil rights leaders decided to organize and lead the second James Meredith March against Fear in order to fulfill Meredith's initial vision. On 26 June 1966 the marchers completed the 220-mile journey from Memphis to Jackson. Two years later Evers ran for Congress after being prodded by local supporters. He lost the congressional elections but became the first African American ever appointed to the executive committee of the Democratic Party. In 1969 he was elected mayor of Fayette, making him the first African American mayor of a mixed town in Mississippi in one hundred years. At the time Fayette suffered from a high level of unemployment and a lack of skilled workers. Serving as a local mayor was a foothold for Evers to aspire to larger public role.

Evers ran unsuccessfully for governor of Mississippi in 1971 but his campaign encouraged blacks to vote and to enter politics. As a result about fifty African Americans were elected to public office throughout Mississippi in 1971. Evers was selected as a Mississippi delegate and worked as a committeeman during the 1972 Democratic National Convention, where he successfully maneuvered to have Basil Paterson, a black state senator from New York, elected to the position of vice chairman of the Democratic Party. In 1973 Evers divorced his second wife.

In that same year Evers, with the support of B. B. KING, founded the Medgar Evers Homecoming, a three-day event that commemorated the life and work of his brother. Evers's interest in southern and national politics did not hinder his mayoral work. He invited Thompson Industries, Commercial Chemical, and Lavender House to open new plants, which created hundreds of new jobs, and he dedicated a new vocational technical school that trained seventy-five workers in welding, carpentry, electricity, and brick masonry. Evers gave Fayette its first sewage system and built a $65,000 swimming pool and a $6 million dollar healthcare program.

In 1978 Evers ran unsuccessfully for the U.S. Senate. He endorsed the Republican Ronald Reagan for president in 1980 and later advised him not to veto the extension of the Voting Rights Acts (VRA). Reagan renewed the VRA for forty years. Evers was reelected mayor of Fayette until he lost the 1981 election, but was returned to the office in 1985. His connections to the Reagan White House helped smooth the receipt of a $300,000 grant from the Department of Housing and Urban Development for the rehabilitation of low-income homes. On several occasions he was sent to Africa by Reagan. When the country of Senegal, celebrating its centennial, dedicated Jackson Square to the United States, it was Evers who accepted the honor on behalf of the president. In 1988 Evers awarded the Medgar Evers Humanitarian Award to the fiercely anti-communist Jonas Savimbi, the leader of the National Union for the Total Independence of Angola, who had close ties to the South African apartheid regime. In 1989 Evers lost the mayoral race and joined the Republican Party, acting to recruit a number of African Americans to the party. After leaving politics Evers worked as manager of his own radio station, WMPR, in Jackson.

FURTHER READING

Evers, Charles, and Grace Halsell. *Evers* (1971).

Evers, Charles, and Andrew Szanton. *The Charles Evers Story* (1997).

Dittmer, John. *Local People: The Struggle for Civil rights in Mississippi* (1994).

DAVID MICHEL

Evers, Medgar (2 July 1925–12 June 1963), civil rights activist, was born Medgar Wiley Evers in Decatur, Mississippi, the son of James Evers, a sawmill worker, and Jessie Wright, a domestic worker. He was drafted into the U.S. Army in 1943 and served in the invasion of Normandy and the French campaign. After the war ended Evers returned to Mississippi, where he attended Alcorn Agricultural and Mechanical College, a segregated land-grant institution, from which he graduated in 1952 with a bachelor's degree in business administration. While at Alcorn he met a nursing student, Myrlie Beasley (MYRLIE EVERS-WILLIAMS), whom he married in 1951; the couple had three children.

After graduating from Alcorn, Evers spent several years working as a traveling salesman for the Magnolia Mutual Insurance Company, a business founded by, run by, and serving African Americans. His extensive travels through impoverished areas of Mississippi made him aware of the terrible poverty and oppression suffered by many black southerners and led him to become an active volunteer in the Mississippi chapter of the NAACP. His skill and enthusiasm did not pass unnoticed by the organization's leadership, and in 1954, after Evers's application to the University of Mississippi Law School was rejected on racial grounds, he was appointed to the newly created and salaried position of state field secretary for the NAACP, in Jackson. Evers's duties as field secretary were originally bureaucratic—collecting, organizing, and publicizing information about civil rights abuses in Mississippi. However, his anger, aroused by the refusal of southern authorities to enforce the U.S. Supreme Court's landmark 1954 decision against segregation of public institutions, led him to more direct forms of action, sometimes to the dismay of the generally more conservative NAACP leadership. Evers did not shy away from high-profile activities; he helped to investigate the death of EMMETT TILL, a teenager murdered allegedly for having whistled at a white woman, and he served as an adviser to JAMES MEREDITH in his eventually successful quest to enroll as the first black student at the University of Mississippi.

Evers's more aggressive style of leadership became evident in the early 1960s, when he helped to organize the Jackson Movement, an all-out attempt to end segregation in Mississippi's largest and most densely black-populated city. Throughout 1962 and 1963 Jackson's African American residents, under Evers's leadership, struggled for racial justice, focusing on the issues of integration of public schools, parks, and libraries and the hiring of African Americans for municipal offices and on the police force. Evers's tactics, which included mass meetings, peaceful demonstrations, sit-ins, and economic boycotts of segregated businesses and of the state fair, helped to unify Jackson's black community. His energy and diplomacy helped to resolve conflicts and create unity between radical youth groups and the more conservative organizations of middle-class adults and also attracted the participation of some moderate white Jackson residents. However, Evers's actions were perceived as antagonistic by many other white Jacksonians.

Shortly after midnight on 12 June 1963 Evers returned to his home after a Movement meeting and was ambushed in his driveway and shot to death. News of the murder spread rapidly through Jackson's black community, and a riot was narrowly averted. Evers was buried with full military honors at Arlington National Cemetery, and the NAACP honored him posthumously with its 1963 Spingarn Medal.

A Federal Bureau of Investigation probe of Evers's murder led to the arrest of Byron De La Beckwith, a fertilizer salesman, avowed anti-integrationist, and member of a long-established Mississippi family. Beckwith was tried for the crime, but, despite the testimony of several witnesses who claimed that they had heard the accused boast of having shot Evers, he was found not guilty by an all-white jury. A retrial ended in the same verdict. In February 1994, however, a third trial, this time by a racially mixed jury, ended in Beckwith's conviction for Evers's murder and a sentence of life imprisonment.

Although his career as a political activist and organizer was cut short by his death, Medgar Evers became and has remained an important symbol of the civil rights movement. The brutal murder of a nonviolent activist shocked both black and white Americans, helping them to understand the extent to which areas of the Deep South tolerated racial violence. Evers's death was a crucial factor that motivated President John F. Kennedy to ask the U.S. Congress to enact a new and comprehensive civil rights law, an action that committed the federal government to enforcement of policies to promote racial equality throughout the United States. Evers's name has remained alive through the efforts of the NAACP's Medgar Evers Fund, which provides financial assistance for efforts to improve housing, health care, education, and economic opportunity for African Americans. A branch of the City University of New York was named Medgar Evers College in 1969. His widow, Myrlie Evers-Williams, served as chair of the board of the NAACP from 1995 to 1998.

Medgar Evers, the civil rights activist and Mississippi field secretary for the National Association for the Advancement of Colored People, whose murder in Jackson, Mississippi on 12 June 1963 became a rallying symbol of the civil rights movement. (AP Images.)

FURTHER READING

Bailey, Ronald. *Remembering Medgar Evers* (1988).
Evers, Charles. *Evers* (1971).
Evers-Williams, Myrlie, and William Peters. *For Us, the Living* (1967).
Nossiter, Adam. *Of Long Memory: Mississippi and the Murder of Medgar Evers* (1994).
Salter, John R. *Jackson, Mississippi: An American Chronicle of Struggle and Schism* (1979).
Vollers, Maryanne. *Ghosts of Mississippi: The Murder of Medgar Evers, the Trial of Byron de la Beckwith, and the Haunting of the New South* (1995).
Obituary: *New York Times*, 13 June 1963.

NATALIE ZACEK

Evers-Williams, Myrlie (17 Mar. 1933–), civil rights activist, was born Myrlie Beasley in Vicksburg, Mississippi, and was raised, following her parents divorce, by her grandmother Annie McCain Beasley and her aunt, Myrlie Beasley Polk. Both women were schoolteachers who encouraged young Myrlie in her educational pursuits through activities such as singing, public speaking, and piano lessons. Myrlie hoped to major in music in college, but neither of Mississippi's state schools for blacks, Alcorn A&M College or Jackson State, had such a major. In 1950 Myrlie enrolled at Alcorn, intending to study education and music. Only two hours after arriving on campus, however, she met MEDGAR EVERS, an upperclassman and army veteran seven years her senior. He soon proposed, and they were married on 24 December 1951. Following Medgar's graduation and Myrlie's sophomore year, the couple moved to Mound Bayou, Mississippi, where Medgar took a position as an insurance salesman with Magnolia Mutual Insurance, a black-owned company.

Myrlie Evers entered the civil rights movement through Medgar's work as the NAACP state field secretary for Mississippi. This was the beginning of a lifetime of work against segregation and racial violence against blacks. Medgar's appointment came in 1954, the same year as their daughter Reena Denise's birth and a year after the birth of their first child, Darrell Kenyatta. Son James Van Dyke was born in 1960. Myrlie Evers worked full time as a secretary in the NAACP Jackson office and the Everses worked tirelessly on the NAACP's agenda of securing voting rights, coordinating civil rights demonstrations, and desegregating public facilities. The Everses were also deeply involved in the quest to bring the murderers of EMMETT TILL to justice and in the efforts of JAMES MEREDITH in desegregating the University of Mississippi.

Because of their civil rights work and their direct confrontation with the white supremacist power elite, the Evers family lived under the constant threat of violence. The children were trained to take cover

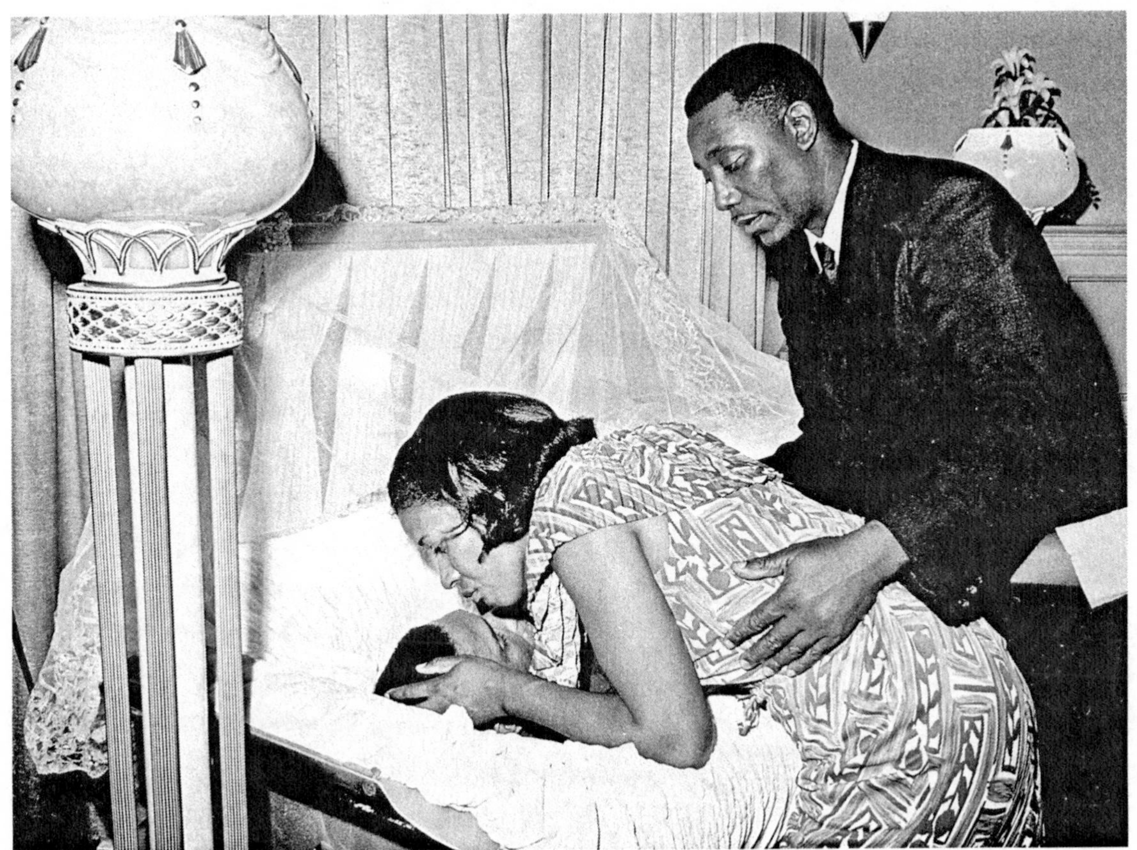

Myrlie Evers-Williams, widow of civil rights activist Medgar Evers, leans down to kiss her late husband's forehead before his casket was opened for public viewing at a funeral home in Jackson, Mississippi, 13 June 1963. (AP Images.)

should gunfire erupt and Myrlie practiced the steps she would take if her husband were shot. In one incident, their home was firebombed while Medgar was away at a meeting, leaving Myrlie to put out the fire while in fear that the arsonists were still nearby. The violence reached its climax for the Evers family on 12 June 1963, when Medgar was killed by a sniper's bullet in front of their home. The Evers children dove for the floor as trained, as Myrlie ran outside and found her husband bleeding from a gunshot wound to the back. Although he was rushed to the hospital and admitted to the emergency room—after hospital officials vacillated on their segregation policy—Medgar Evers died an hour after the shooting.

At the scene of the murder the police retrieved a rifle with the fingerprints of Byron De La Beckwith, an outspoken racist and anti-integrationist. Beckwith was indicted twice but freed by deadlocked, all-white juries. Medgar's murder and the failure of the jury to convict Beckwith were catalysts in Myrlie Evers's quest for justice in the face of racial discrimination. Evers also credits her late husband with raising her racial awareness and pride in her race.

Though he believed Mississippi would be the best place to live were Jim Crow segregation ever abolished, Medgar always thought California would be a good place to raise their children. A year after Medgar's murder and the subsequent trials, Evers and her three children moved to Claremont, California. She cowrote a book about her husband, *For Us, the Living* (1967), and gave speeches for the NAACP. In the book Evers details the tensions and emotions she felt as she grew from a sheltered Mississippi childhood into civil rights activism alongside Medgar in the virulently racist South.

Evers experienced several life changes upon moving to California. She enrolled in Pomona College, graduating with a B.A. in Sociology in 1968. She then served as assistant director of planning and development for the Claremont College system. She also ran for Congress in 1969. Though she lost the race, it was the first time she explicitly stepped out of her murdered husband's shadow, changing her political ticket from "Mrs. Medgar Evers" to "Myrlie Evers." In 1975 Evers married Walter Williams, a longshoreman and union organizer who died of prostate cancer in 1995. In step with her lifetime of activism and achievements, Evers-Williams accomplished two firsts. Los Angeles Mayor THOMAS BRADLEY appointed her to the city's Board of Public Works, making her the first black woman to serve in that capacity. Evers-Williams served on the board from 1988 to 1990, comanaging a million-dollar annual budget. In 1995 Evers-Williams became the first woman to serve as chair of the board of the NAACP. Before leaving the position in 1998, Evers-Williams helped recuperate the organization's image, which was damaged by her predecessors, who left the organization $4 million in debt.

Evers-Williams remained determined to see Beckwith brought to justice. In addition to trips back to Mississippi to track Beckwith's whereabouts, Evers-Williams continued to search for evidence that would spur a new trial. After the Jackson reporter Jerry Mitchell unearthed documents proving the long-suspected collusion between government officials and white supremacists, Evers pressured Mississippi prosecutors to move for a new trial. In 1994, more than thirty years after the assassination, Beckwith was finally convicted of Medgar Evers's murder and sentenced to life in prison, opening the door to the prosecution of other old civil rights cases. In 1996, *Ghosts of Mississippi*, a film directed by Rob Reiner, dramatized the events surrounding the final Beckwith trial. Whoopi Goldberg played Evers-Williams in the film, which centered on prosecutor Bobby DeLaughter's quest to bring Beckwith to trial in 1994.

In 1999 Evers-Williams published an autobiography, *Watch Me Fly: What I Learned on My Way to Becoming the Woman I Was Meant to Be*. She has received seven honorary doctorates and awards from the NAACP, the U.S. Congressional Black Caucus, and the League of Women Voters. In 1988 she established the Medgar Evers Institute, which works to encourage a better understanding of human rights. The Institute's Archive and Justice Center are based in Jackson, Mississippi, while the Oregon State University Medgar Evers Institute Fellowship Center is based in Bend, Oregon.

FURTHER READING

Evers, Mrs. Medgar, with William Peters. *For Us, the Living* (1967).

Evers-Williams, Myrlie, with Melinda Blau. *Watch Me Fly: What I Learned on My Way to Becoming the Woman I Was Meant to Be* (1999).

Hampton, Henry, and Steve Fayer. *Voices of Freedom: An Oral History of the Civil Rights Movement from the 1950s through the 1980s* (1991).

KIMBERLY SPRINGER

Ezra (?–c. Sept. 1777), Ohio frontier settler and slave, was likely born in Africa and brought to the American colonies by slave traders as a young boy. While details about nearly all of his life are speculative at best, Ezra was purchased at Baltimore, Maryland, by Dr. David McMahan in the years before the American Revolution. When Dr. McMahan decided to travel to the Ohio country to claim land for his own in early 1777, he brought along with him his two "Negro slaves," Ezra and Sam (Eckert, 123). Traveling overland from Fort Cumberland on the Braddock Road, the three-man party crossed the Monongahela River and made their way to Wheeling on the Ohio River. Making their way on packhorses loaded with the provisions and supplies needed for homesteading, as well as McMahan's medical gear, the trip was a long and arduous one. While details are lacking, there can be little doubt that Ezra and Sam performed a large share of the work along the way.

The settling of America's first frontier, the Ohio Territory, in the years from 1744 until its establishment as a state in 1803, was an enterprise that was fraught with danger and hardship. The exploration of this wilderness territory required a huge amount of human courage and sacrifice. It was inhabited by sometimes hostile Native American tribes, and encompassed the modern day states of Ohio, Pennsylvania, Kentucky, West Virginia, Indiana, and Illinois. While white men were the primary settlers, they were often accompanied by equally rugged frontier wives and by untold numbers of black men and women, most of whom were slaves.

The settling of the Ohio Territory by African Americans, even if in a secondary role, is an accomplishment that has often been overlooked by historians. The reasons for this may be speculated upon; in many instances, the actions of mere slaves probably were not deemed significant by contemporary chroniclers of frontier events. Later historians may have ignored them for more political reasons; the state of Ohio was a bulwark in the Abolitionist movement, and the idea of slaves settling the Ohio Territory was not consonant with the state's later reputation as a Promised Land for runaway slaves. No matter what the reason, blacks such as Ezra and his fellow slave Sam, as well as others like Rachel Johnson, and Sam, a slave of Richard Elson who died while fighting in a skirmish against English and Indian troops on the Olentangy River in June 1782, all contributed to the taming of Ohio and its growth into a state.

As for Ezra, fate was not so kind to him; captured in an attack by Indian and British forces on Wheeling on 1 September 1777, it is likely that he was made to run the gauntlet, was tortured, and killed soon thereafter by the Indians who held him captive.

FURTHER READING

Eckert, Allan W. *That Dark and Bloody River; Chronicles of the Ohio River Valley* (1995).

GLENN ALLEN KNOBLOCK

Fabio, Sarah Webster (20 Jan. 1928–7 Nov. 1979), poet, critic, and teacher, was born in Nashville, Tennessee. Her father, Thomas Jefferson Webster, was a Pullman porter and her mother, Mayme, raised six children. Sarah Webster entered Spelman College in Atlanta after graduating from Pearl High School at age fifteen. Although she did not earn a degree at Spelman, she transferred to Nashville's Fisk University; she graduated in 1946 at the age of eighteen. Soon after, she married Cyril Leslie Fabio II, who was then enrolled at Nashville's Meharry Medical College as a dental student.

Together the couple had five children. Sarah Fabio enrolled in several colleges as the family traveled throughout the United States and lived abroad, following her husband's military career. It took years of enrollment at various colleges before she completed her master's degree from San Francisco State College (later University) in 1965.

By 1966 Fabio had begun publishing her works with small independent presses. She lectured at Merritt College; at the University of California, Berkeley; and at the California College of Arts and Crafts. She advocated for black studies programs and is credited for promoting black studies at Merritt College around the time of the infamous five-month strike to start black studies programs at San Francisco State College.

Fabio published most of her work at the height of the Black Arts Movement (BAM) during the mid-1960s. The Black Arts Movement, a term first referred to in the works of the scholar Larry Neal, sought to develop an explicit connection between art and politics from the 1960s to the 1970s, particularly in poetry and jazz. In part a reaction to the discrimination faced by black writers trying to publish and teach in mostly white settings, the movement thrived on college campuses and in inner-city neighborhoods, particularly in New York and northern California's Bay Area. Poets such as Amiri Baraka continued to write and perform (performance poetry had mass appeal and could be easily aligned with politics), knowing that their works would not be found in anthologies designed for mainstream classes. Along with others in the movement, Fabio felt that poets had to reflect the spirit of the times in which they wrote. Most of Fabio's works were published through black publishers that emerged in the mid- to late 1960s. In a 1966 article in *Negro Digest* Fabio wrote that language penetrates spirituals, blues, or jazz lyrics and promotes a response to what it means to be oppressed.

Fabio explored the context of language, particularly black English. Although, like many black poets, she was not widely published in mainstream works, she is still considered one of the pioneers of the BAM. The author and activist Askia Toure wrote that black women poets such as Fabio were written out of history. The poet and activist Kalumu ya Salaam particularly credits Fabio as a force in and beyond black studies in the Bay Area. Many of her works highlighted key black figures from Bessie Smith and Duke Ellington to John Coltrane and Sam Cooke.

In a 1971 *New York Times*'s review of June Jordan's novel *His Own Where*, Fabio wrote that it was necessary to violate syntax to get to the meaning of the text. She said that the mind stammers for language, while the heart responds to song, and that music is the bridge to reaching youth. By 1972 Fabio's marriage had ended in divorce, and she went on to teach at Oberlin College in Ohio until 1974. In her most acclaimed recording, *Jujus: Alchemy of the Blues* (1976), Fabio displays exciting presence and grace when reading over the fused jazz beats. Critics noted that Fabio's works were designed for performance and were not meant to be read as text. Fabio's recorded works with musical accompaniments were her trademark. She speaks of her frustration that black literary history was not being represented in mainstream anthologies and argues that this is a result of racism. Fabio's faith that music is a bridge is evident through the accompaniment of her children in her last well-known recorded work, *Together to the Tune of Coltrane's Equinox* (1977). Fabio's children each played critical roles in composition and vocals. While pursuing further graduate work at the University of Wisconsin, Fabio became ill and was diagnosed with colon cancer in 1976. In 1979 she died in Pinole, California, at the age of fifty-one.

In a 2002 *Callaloo* article, the critic Meta Du Ewa Jones noted Fabio's frequent use of familiar conversation and metaphors in her poetry. Indeed, Fabio was an early advocate for the use of black English and was quick to recognize it in the work of others.

FURTHER READING

Fabio, Sarah Webster. "Who Speaks Negro?" *Negro Digest* 16 (Dec. 1966).

Jones, Meta Du Ewa. "Jazz Prosodies: Orality and Textuality," *Callaloo* 25 (2002).

Ward, Jerry W. "Reading South: Poets Mean and Poems Signify," *African American Review* (Spring 1993).

TANITA JASMINE DAWSON

Factor, Pompey (1849–29 Mar. 1928), Black Seminole scout, was born either in Arkansas or in Indian territory west of Arkansas. Nothing is known of his parents or childhood. Sixteen Native Americans won the Medal of Honor for their service in the Indian Wars, as the conflicts between indigenous Native Americans and European settlers and their descendents were known. Four of them, including Factor, a private, were Seminole-Negro Indian Scouts, descendants of the slaves who had found refuge with the Seminoles of Florida during the Seminole Wars of 1817 and 1836 and later migrated to Nacimiento, Mexico, in 1850.

When the Seminoles moved to Texas in 1857, the Black Seminoles remained in Mexico rather than risk being enslaved. They adapted their survival skills to the new region and became invaluable scouts, serving as militia for Mexico against the Comanche and Lipan Apaches. Soon, though, they were sought after by the segregated U.S. Army and its 25th Infantry, a black unit commanded by white officers. In 1870 Major Zenas R. Bliss sent Captain F. W. Perry to Nacimiento to recruit Black Seminoles as scouts. The inducements included pay, rations for the men and their families, and land on which to settle after their time was served. Pay for the privates was $13 a month, the same as a regular army private. Bliss's first detachment of Black Seminole scouts consisted of thirteen men out of a group of 100 who had moved to Fort Duncan from Mexico. In the first group enlisted were John Kibbitt, Joe Dixie, Dindie Factor, Hardie Factor, Adams Fay, Bobby Kibbitt, John Thompson, John Ward, George Washington, and Pompey Factor.

Three years later there were some 180 Black Seminoles in Texas. Initially the scouts devoted their attention to learning the ropes and acquiring their equipment. Bliss was pleased with the first scouts, so he recruited more until they numbered thirty-one in 1871. He also promoted them to regular status, paying private's pay and giving them arms, ammunition, and rations.

In 1872 Col. Wesley Merritt requested that the scouts and their families be transferred to Fort Clark, also in Texas. When Lieutenant John Lapham Bullis took command in 1873 he shared the scouts' field conditions and looked out for their families. Bullis made the scouts into a combat force, and for the next decade they worked with white and black units in the rugged Texas-Mexico border region. They fought Kickapoos and Lipan Apaches at Remilino, Mexico. During the raid against Remolino, Coahuila, the scouts helped to keep the Americans from coming into unwanted contact with Mexican soldiers. They also assisted in making the withdrawal speedy. Pleased by their efforts in Mexico, Colonel Ranald S. Mackenzie used scouts in the punitive expedition to Palo Duro Canyon against the Comanche in 1874 during the Red River War.

On 25 April 1875 a small component of the 24th U.S. Infantry under Bullis's command was pursuing some twenty-five or thirty Comanche who had taken seventy-five stolen horses through Eagle's Nest Crossing near the Pecos River. Bullis and three scouts—Factor, John Ward, and Isaac

Payne—engaged the Indians from about seventy-five yards. The scouts killed three and wounded one in a fourty-five-minute firefight. Once the Comanche recovered from the initial onslaught, they outflanked the small U.S. unit, and the scouts and Bullis broke for their horses. The scouts took off, and then saw that Bullis's horse had bolted. Under fire the scouts returned and took turns carrying Bullis as they withdrew to safety. For their actions Factor, Ward, and Payne received the Medal of Honor.

The scouts had a good reputation with professional military officers. But despite their good work the scouts and their families faced discrimination, racial violence, and government indifference. They waited years for their promised land. The War Department had no land to give them, and the Bureau of Indian Affairs ruled that they were not Indians because they were not on the Seminole rolls, which closed in 1866. To make matters worse, when they left the scouts, they lost their rations. When a Texas sheriff killed Adam Paine in 1877, the second death of a scout within a year and the third within two years, Factor and five other scouts returned to Mexico. In Mexico they fought Indians with the Mexican army under Colonel Pedro Avincular Valdez.

Although Factor received the Medal of Honor and completed honorable service, he received no pension. The War Department said it had no record of his service. Factor was buried in the Brackettville, Texas, Seminole-Negro Indian Scout cemetery.

FURTHER READING

Porter, Kenneth W. "The Seminole Negro-Indian Scouts: 1870–1881," *Southwestern Historical Quarterly* 55.3 (1952).

Mulroy, Kevin. *Freedom on the Border: The Seminole Maroons in Florida, the Indian Territory, Coahuila, and Texas* (1993).

JOHN H. BARNHILL

Fagen, David (1875–1 Dec. 1901?), captain in the Filipino nationalist army, was born in Tampa, Florida. Nothing is known about his parents, including their names, or his early life. In the summer of 1899, just after the United States ended the war with Spain, Fagen was a corporal in the Twenty-fourth Infantry of Company I. He was among the black soldiers of the Twenty-fourth and Twenty-fifth infantries and the Ninth and Tenth cavalries dispatched to the Philippines in the U.S. effort to enforce territorial concessions granted by Spain in a peace treaty signed in February 1899. Emilio Aguinaldo, an ardent Filipino nationalist, led a guerrilla war resisting what he considered the United States' replacement of Spain as colonizer.

Letters written by African American soldiers to newspapers and family members indicate that some of them sympathized with the Filipino cause, and a few even joined its ranks. Fagen's actions in the fall of 1899 mark the beginnings of an extraordinary expression of African American solidarity with Filipino nationalist aspirations for independence. He defected from the U.S. Army, accepted a commission with the Filipino nationalists, and participated in a two-year guerrilla war against the American forces.

Prior to Fagen's defection, his company had clashed with Filipino nationalists in the Nueva Ecija province on the island of Luzon, pushing them out of the towns and into the foothills and mountains on the outskirts of settled areas. According to a U.S. Army report, "Information Slip on David Fagen," he "slipped away and mounted a horse" on 17 November 1899 while his company was preparing to relocate its station to another town. The report states that he was assisted by a nationalist officer who had a horse hidden near the company's barracks. Fagen joined General Urbana Lacuna's forces, which were located at Mount Arayat and in the surrounding area. His immediate commander was José Alejandrino. Fagen is not known to have written a statement detailing the reasons for his defection. Military records note that he had had "continual trouble" with his company's commanding and noncommissioned officers and was often assigned extra work duty as punishment. The tenacity of Fagen's resolve to combat his former compatriots, however, suggests that discipline problems were probably not the sole basis for his decision. In fact, U.S. soldiers who clashed with him recall that in the midst of raging, pitched battles Fagen enjoyed shouting "taunting boasts," some of which had racial overtones. On one occasion he reportedly yelled, "Captain Fagen done got yuh White boys now" (Ganzhorn, 172–173).

Fagen's claim of captaincy was not mere self-indulgence. Indeed, in September 1900 his nationalist commanders promoted him from lieutenant to captain, and from that time until December 1901 (the purported date of his death) he was engaged in a protracted and relentless guerrilla war. The U.S. Army's inability to capture Fagen swiftly earned him a reputation as a shrewd and cunning adversary. John Ganzhorn, a member of General Frederick Funston's elite scouts, recalls violent confrontations with Fagen. Ganzhorn related that in one close encounter Fagen "ambushed two four-mule wagons" (172). After killing all but one of the soldiers, Fagen and his men set the wagons on fire and ambushed another group of American soldiers who were drawn by the smoke.

Perhaps out of embarrassment, American military leaders generated various excuses for their inability to capture Fagen. Remembering an incident when Fagen killed one of his comrades, Ganzhorn wrote, "I've heard Fryburger's cry for me to kill Fagen. God I wanted to! But when I could see to shoot, Fagen was not in sight" (177). General Funston similarly described a battle with Fagen: "In this fight I got a fairly good look at the notorious Fagen at a distance of a hundred yards, but unfortunately had already emptied my carbine" (376).

As time progressed, Fagen's comrades began to buckle under the continuous onslaught of the U.S. Army and an embargo that prevented them from receiving aid and supplies from abroad. Aguinaldo, the charismatic nationalist leader, was eventually captured. Fagen, unwilling to turn himself in, remained in northern Luzon with a small group of nationalist soldiers. General Funston offered a bounty of six hundred dollars for Fagen's head. On 5 December 1901 Anastacio Bartollome arrived at Bongabon, in the Nueva Ecija province, carrying a black man's head that he claimed was Fagen's. However, U.S. military officers who reviewed the report of Fagen's death were not totally convinced and referred to it as a "report of the supposed killing of David Fagen." Historians have pointed out that the question of whether Fagen survived the manhunt should not overshadow the historical significance of his rebellion as an expression of African American militant resistance to American imperialism.

FURTHER READING

Funston, Frederick. *Memories of Two Wars: Cuban and Philippine Experiences* (1912).

Ganzhorn, John W. *I've Killed Men: An Epic of Early Arizona* (1959).

Gatewood, Willard B., Jr. *"Smoked Yankees" and the Struggle for Empire: Letters from Negro Soldiers, 1898–1902* (1971).

Ngozi-Brown, Scot. "African-American Soldiers and Filipinos: Racial Imperialism, Jim Crow and Social Relations," *Journal of Negro History* 82.1 (Winter 1997).

Robinson, Michael C., and Frank N. Schubert. "David Fagen: An Afro-American Rebel in the Philippines, 1899–1901," *Pacific Historical Review* 44 (Feb. 1975).

This entry is taken from the *American National Biography* and is published here with the permission of the American Council of Learned Societies.

SCOT NGOZI-BROWN

Faggs, Mae (10 Apr. 1932–27 Jan. 2000), athlete, Olympic medalist, was born Aeriwentha Mae Faggs in Mays Landing, New Jersey, the second of five children and the only daughter of William and Hepsi Faggs. Her father was a factory worker; her mother was employed in a musical instrument plant making needles, she also worked as a domestic. Faggs was in elementary school when began running track and continued to run as a student at Bayside High School in Bayside, Queens. In 1947, at age fifteen, she became a member of the Police Athletic League (PAL) girl's track team from the 11th Precinct in Bayside, Queens. The same year, Faggs joined the newly formed Amateur Athletic Union (AAU) in Bayside, created for exceptional runners from all over the city by Sergeant John Brennan, who became her coach and mentor. During her tenure with AAU her strength and speed grew, and she entered the 1948 U.S. Olympic trials in Providence, Rhode Island. Faggs competed against such notable athletes as Barbara Jones, Isabelle Daniels, Margaret Davis, and Patricia Monsato to qualify for the U.S. Olympic track team. At age sixteen, she was the youngest member of the U.S. team when she went to the 1948 Olympics and competed at Wembley Stadium in London in the 200-meter dash and the 400-meter relay. Although Faggs did not earn a medal she vowed to emerge a champion during the next world Olympic competition. Meanwhile, in her home state, she won the New York City 220-yard dash at the 1949 AAU national indoor competition, and set the American record at 25.8 seconds. In 1952 in Buffalo, New York, Faggs set an American indoor record for the 100-yard dash; at the British Empire Games in London, England, she was a member of the U.S. National Team that won the 880-yard relay; and, as promised, she returned to compete with the U.S. Olympic Team. At the 1952 Olympics in Helsinki, Finland, Faggs ran first leg, helping her team—Barbara Jones, Catherine Hardy, and Janet Moreau—to win the gold medal for the 400-meter relay competition in a record 45.9 seconds.

In 1952, Faggs left her home and familiar surroundings in New York to move down South, where the fight for civil rights of African Americans was being violently opposed. She had been awarded a scholarship to attend Tennessee State University (TSU), a historically black university in Nashville, where she had been actively recruited by Coach Ed Temple, a professor of sociology at the university who had taken over the team, to join the budding girls track team, the TSU Tigerbelles. She was 5 feet 2 inches tall, spirited and competitive as a member of the Tigerbelles. Faggs encouraged her teammates and, together with Coach Temple, was the impetus behind the nationally recognized Tigerbelles. In 1953, Faggs set another AAU record, this time at the National AAU Women's Championships, for the 100-yard dash; she also ran the 200-meter dash and successfully set a new American record. By the following year, the Tigerbelles had solidified their winning position in the world of track and field, as Faggs maintained her own status as a world-class sprinter. Soon Faggs was friend and mentor to promising young athletes like WILMA RUDOLPH, who had joined the Tigerbelles. At the 1954 National AAU Women's Championships in Harrisburg, Pennsylvania, she was a member of the winning 800-meter relay team and she won first place in the 220-yard run.

The year 1955 brought more success for Faggs. She won the 100-meter dash at the Evening Star Games in Washington, DC. She set records in the 100-meter and 220-yard races at the AAU outdoor nationals in Ponca City, Oklahoma; also, together with the Tigerbelles she set a new U.S. record of 49.1 seconds for the 440-meter relay. Faggs won Olympic Gold for the 100-meter in Chicago, Illinois; and, the silver medal for the 100-meter at the Pan American Games in Mexico City. In Montgomery, Alabama, at the Alabama State Relays, Faggs was victorious in a number of events; she won the 100-yard dash and the 220-yard dash; and, she was a member of the winning 440-yard and 660-yard relay teams. Also, in 1955 she was awarded gold track shoes from Tennessee State University.

The following year, 1956, at the National AAU Women's Championships in Philadelphia, Pennsylvania, she won gold medals in the 100-yard dash and the 220-yard dash; and, together with the Tigerbelles won the 440-yard relay. In Melbourne, Australia, as member of the 1956 U.S. Olympic 400-meter relay team comprised completely of Tigerbelles, including Wilma Rudolph, Faggs took home the bronze medal. In 1956, Faggs fulfilled her athletic scholarship and completed her undergraduate education at TSU; she had won three plaques, twenty-six trophies, and one hundred medals.

Upon departing from her illustrious career at Tennessee State University as a Tigerbelle, Faggs enrolled at the University of Cincinnati, where she earned master's degree in Special Education. She embarked upon a thirty-two-year teaching career, which began at Lockland Wayne High School in Ohio, Lincoln Heights, and included working as an administrator in the Princeton City Schools, eventually leading the Princeton High School girl's track and field team to the 1989 Ohio championship. Faggs retired in 1989. She was a member of Alpha Kappa Alpha Sorority, Inc., the first sorority for African American women.

Faggs married Eddie Starr in 1958; together they had one daughter, Evelyn and a son, Eddie Starr II. At age 67, she died in her home in Woodlawn, Ohio, from cancer. Faggs was the first American woman to compete in three Olympic Games; in total she won eleven AAU titles and was named AAU All-American in 1954, 1955, and 1956. She was elected to the Helms Hall of Fame in 1965. In 1975, Faggs was inducted into the Charlestown, West Virginia, National Track and Field Hall of Fame. She was inducted to the National Track and Field hall of fame in Indianapolis, Indiana, in 1976.

FURTHER READING

Moore, Gina Ruffin. *Cincinnati, Ohio (Black America Series)* (2007).

n.a. "Mae Faggs Sets AAU Dash Record," *Jet Magazine*, 25 June 1953.

Rhoden, William C. "Sports of the Times: The End of a Winding Road," *New York Times*, 9 Nov. 1994.

Obituary: *New York Times*, 11 Feb. 2000.

SAFIYA DALILAH HOSKINS

Fairfax, Jean E. (1920–), civil rights activist, philanthropist, and expert in child education, was born in Cleveland, Ohio, to Dan and Robert Fairfax and Inez Wood Fairfax.

Fairfax inherited a strong belief in the importance of education from her parents, who both earned their college degrees at the turn of the century. She received her bachelor's degree from the University of Michigan in 1941, and completed her master's degree in Comparative Religion at Union Theological Seminary and Columbia University in 1944. Fairfax later attended Harvard University as a Radcliffe visiting scholar, from 1984 to 1986.

Her professional career in education began as dean of women at Kentucky State College from 1942 to 1944, and at Tuskegee Institute from 1944 to 1946. In addition to education, her parents, who were members of the Congregational Church, instilled in her a-strong set of core values that interwove faith with service. "As faithful Christians, we are taught not to separate faith from action," Jean noted. "Back then we talked very much about the need, the obligation that we have as individuals to work for social justice. It was part of my religious upbringing. I have a deep concern about what happens to the community, that is, I don't separate myself from what happens to my people"(*Faith and Family Philanthropy*, 34).

Fairfax served as a program director for the American Friends Service Committee (AFSC), a Quaker organization, for nineteen years. In 1957 she served as the director of the Southern Civil Rights Program for the AFSC, a position she held for eight years. After Freedom Summer 1964, a massive voting rights project organized by a coalition of civil rights organizations that drew scores of student volunteers to the Deep South, Jean traveled to Harmony, Mississippi, with AFSC, where she was instrumental in encouraging African American students to desegregate public schools in Jackson. In 1965 Fairfax began working for the NAACP's Legal Defense Fund (LDF).

In 1985 Fairfax resigned from LDF to devote more time to her philanthropic interests. As a founding member of the Black Women's Community Development Foundation in 1967, she used the organization as a platform to counter studies—such as the controversial 1965 Moynihan Report—that labeled African American families and female-headed single households as pathological. In 1987, while serving as a trustee the Atlanta-based Southern Education Foundation (SEF), Jean and her sister Betty, a high school teacher and guidance counselor, endowed the Dan and Inez Wood Fairfax Memorial Fund with a $125,000 gift to broaden educational opportunities for African American and Latino students, in particular those from low-income familes. That same year the sisters adopted one class of eighth grade students at the Mary McLeod Bethune School in Phoenix, Arizona. Challenging them to complete high school and enroll in a four-year college, Jean and Betty promised to guarantee ninety-two of them $1,000 per year toward their education.

Fairfax maintained a special interest in chronicling and expanding African Americans' involvement in philanthropy. As the author of *Far From Done: The Challenge of Diversifying Philanthropic Leadership*, (1990) and the nonprofit series "Black Philanthropy its Heritage and its Future," in *Cultures of Giving II: How Heritage, Gender, Wealth, and Values Influence Philanthropy* (1995), Fairfax admitted that initially she too believed the myth that "philanthropists were white people with inherited wealth or who made big deals in their investments or in their industrial work, like the Carnegies and the Rockefellers." Rather than live lavishly—and despite their relatively modest incomes—the Fairfaxes donated over $100,000 a year to causes that exemplified their interest in civil rights, social justice, and expanded access to education. Beginning in 1987 the two women created endowments valued at over a million dollars.

As a trustee with the Arizona Community Foundation, Jean Fairfax spearheaded the establishment of a Social Justice Fund to address such issues as educational equity and racial and language discrimination. The Fairfaxes endowed $100,000 to create the Betty H. Fairfax Medallion Scholarship at Kent State University, Betty's alma mater, which provided full scholarships to African American students from Cleveland to pursue careers as teachers in inner cities. Their charitable contributions included the Betty Fairfax Educational Equity at the Arizona Community Foundation and the Betty H. and Jean E. Fairfax Cleveland Foundation to promote the advancement of minority students from community colleges and universities.

Jean Fairfax also worked with Temple University to develop a program called African American Family Reunions and Philanthropy, which encouraged families to use the celebration as an opportunity to discuss philanthropy as a family enterprise. For more than thirty years Jean Fairfax directed civil rights, educational, and philanthropic programs. She also served on a number of boards for various committees and organizations. In 1991 she was the director of Black Presence in Organized Philanthropy, a research project spearheaded by the Association of Black Foundation Executives. She served as a commissioner for the U.S. National Commission for UNESCO, the Central Committee and Programme to Combat Racism of the World Council of Churches, the Planning Committee of the White House Conference on School Lunch Participation, and the National Commission on Secondary Schooling for Hispanics. She was a board member for the Urban Institute, National Public Radio, and Union Theological Seminary, and was a trustee for the Arizona Community Foundation, the Southern Education Fund, the Ruth Mott Fund, the Children's Foundation, the Public Education Fund, and Women and Foundations Corporate Philanthropy.

Throughout her career Fairfax received numerous awards and honors. In 1989 she was the recipient of the Distinguished Grantmaker of the Year Award from the Council on Foundations. She matched the $10,000 prize with $10,000 of her own money and established the Betty Fairfax Fund for Educational Equity at the Arizona Community Foundation in honor of her sister; local residents in turn contributed $150,000. In 1991 Tougaloo College awarded her an honorary doctorate of laws. In 1997 Fairfax received the Lifetime Achievement Award at the First National Conference of Black Philanthropy. In 1998 she received the Leadership for Equity and Diversity Award for Women & Philanthropy. In 2003 Fairfax was awarded the Arizona State University MARTIN LUTHER KING JR. Servant Leaders. In 2000 she and Betty were awarded the President's Social Responsibility Award from Kent State for their lifelong efforts in civil rights and education.

Described as selfless, generous, farsighted, innovative, visionary, and genuinely dedicated to educational and social equity for minorities, Jean Fairfax served the larger communities of Cleveland and Phoenix for over fifty years. Her lifelong support for civil rights and educational causes is keenly felt through her philanthropic activities.

FURTHER READING

Bates, Karen Grigsby. "The Will to Give," *Emerge* 2:2 (Nov. 1990).

Lee, Susan, and Christine Foster. "A How-To-Give Primer," *Forbes* (15 Dec. 1997).

Picker, Lester A. "An African American Family's Experience," in *Faith and Family Philanthropy*, ed. Joseph Foote (2002).

RHONDA D. JONES

Faison, George (21 Dec. 1945–), dancer, choreographer, company director, and educator, was in born Washington, D.C. He graduated from Dunbar High School and then attended Howard University from 1964 to 1966 to study dentistry. During this time, he studied dance with the Capitol Ballet Company and with Carol Tate at Howard. He left school to pursue a dance career after being inspired by a performance of the New York City–based ALVIN AILEY American Dance Theatre. In New York, Faison studied at the School of American Ballet (SAB), where he was taught by ARTHUR MITCHELL, James Truitte, and Elizabeth Hodes.

Early in his New York career, Faison was chosen as Lauren Bacall's dance partner for a television special. In 1967 he became a principal dancer with the Alvin Ailey Dance Company. Faison's most notable performance was in the role of Sinner Man in the company's *Revelations*. He left the Ailey Company after three years and in 1971 founded the George Faison Universal Dance Experience. He created pieces that depicted social problems and highlighted the black experience. Company dancers represented many cultural backgrounds. Faison believed that dance was not just for the elite but for anyone, and his pieces often focused on his belief that there was beauty in ordinary experiences. Faison's interests in music spanned a vast range, including Guiseppe Verdi, MILES DAVIS, Black Sabbath, DIONNE WARWICK, and STEVIE WONDER. *Suite Otis*, set to music by OTIS REDDING, combines traditional and modern dance movements and is one of Faison's best-known choreographed works. In the early 1970s he and his troupe performed around the world, making Faison well known in modern dance. He continued to create pieces, most notably works inspired by MALCOLM X and other contemporary figures and social issues. He also became the favorite choreographer of the Alvin Ailey Dance Company.

Faison's first choreographic experience for a Broadway show was *Don't Bother Me, I Can't Cope* in 1971. The hallmark of his career was the choreography he created for *The Wiz*, the successful all-black musical adaptation of *The Wizard of Oz*. For his work on the show he was the first African American to receive a Tony Award for best choreography in 1975. The Drama Critics recognized Faison for best choreography in a musical the same year. In 1983 he was nominated for a Tony Award for the Radio City Music Hall production of *Porgy and Bess*.

In addition to his dance repertoire and musical theater work, Faison choreographed concerts for many musical artists, including Earth, Wind, and Fire, GLADYS KNIGHT and the Pips, and the Supremes. In 1989 he created and produced the television special "Cosby Salutes Ailey" for the thirtieth anniversary of the Alvin Ailey American Dance Theatre. In 1991 Faison received an Emmy Award for his choreography for the HBO special "The Josephine Baker Story." He also adapted, directed, and choreographed *King* for President Bill Clinton's 1996 inauguration.

Faison founded the American Performing Arts Collaborative (APAC), a not-for-profit organization that develops and presents theatrical, educational, and entertainment events. The collaborative allows University of Massachusetts graduate students to work as interns to receive training in all aspects of the performing arts. In 1997 he founded the Faison Firehouse Theatre in Harlem, a performance and rehearsal facility that helps advance multicultural performing arts productions.

In 2002 Faison was awarded an honorary degree in arts and letters from the University of Massachusetts in Amherst. That same year he re-formed the George Faison Universal Dance Experience, which had been disbanded since the mid-seventies. The group became part of APAC and is housed in the Firehouse Theatre in Harlem.

FURTHER READING

Bembow-Pfalzgraf, Taryn, and Glynis Benbow-Niemier, eds. *International Dictionary of Modern Dance* (1998).

Southgate, Martha. "George Faison, All the Right Moves," *Essence* (Feb. 1991).

BARBARA TOOMER DAVIS

Fakir, Abdul "Duke" (26 Dec. 1935–), singer and member of the Four Tops, was born and raised in the North End neighborhood of Detroit, Michigan. Fakir attended Pershing High School with Levi Stubbs and planned to attend college until they, along with Northern High School students Lawrence Payton and Renaldo "Obie" Benson, formed a singing group, the Four Tops (originally known as the Four Aims) in 1954. The group appeared as a lounge act in Las Vegas and as the opening act or backup singers for Billy Eckstine, Della Reese, and other performers. The Four Tops signed with several record labels before signing with Motown Records in 1963.

Lead singer Stubbs, first tenor Fakir, second tenor Payton, and baritone Benson recorded their first gold record, "Baby I Need Your Loving," in 1964. During the rest of the decade, the Four Tops continued to record mega-hits such as "I Can't Help Myself (Sugar Pie, Honey Bunch)" (1965); "It's the Same Old Song" (1965); "Something about You" (1965); "Reach Out I'll Be There" (1966); "Standing in the Shadows of Love" (1967); and "Bernadette" (1967). After the 1960s, the Four Tops recorded with various record companies and released hits including "Keeper of the Castle" (1972), "Ain't No Woman (Like the One I Got)" (1973), and "When She Was My Girl" (1981). Although the Four Tops recorded hit records less frequently in the 1970s and 1980s, the group remained popular on national and international tour circuits. On 21 December 1988 a delay in taping a television program in England resulted in Fakir, Stubbs, Payton, and Benson missing Pan American World Airways flight 103. The plane left London's Heathrow Airport with a bomb in the luggage compartment and exploded over Lockerbie, Scotland; there were no survivors.

The quartet, inducted into the Rock and Roll Hall of Fame in 1990, was honored with a star on the Hollywood Walk of Fame at 7060 Hollywood Boulevard in 1997. The Four Tops achieved a rare distinction for a vocal group—longevity; for forty-three years, until Payton's death in 1997, there were no personnel changes in the quartet. The Four Tops celebrated fifty years in the music industry in 2004 and received the Grammy Award for Lifetime Achievement in 2009. During the years between the latter two events, Benson and Stubbs died in 2005 and 2008 respectively, leaving Fakir as the only remaining original member of the Four Tops, one of the most popular vocal groups of the twentieth century. Duke Fakir, honoring the Four Tops' legacy, continues to perform the group's rhythm and blues as well as pop classics in concert with three replacement Tops: Theo Peoples, Ronnie McNair, and Lawrence Payton Jr.

FURTHER READING

Dahl, Bill. *Motown: The Golden Years* (2001).

Fong-Torres, Ben. *The Motown Album* (1990).

Maynard, Micheline. "Still Standing; In the Shadows of Motown the Four Tops, with a Change or Two, Celebrate at 50." *New York Times*, 27 July 2004.

Mervis, Scott. "Sole Survivor Abdul 'Duke' Fakir Keeps the Fire Going for the Four Tops." *Pittsburgh Post-Gazette*, 15 Apr. 2010.

LINDA M. CARTER

Falana, Lola (11 Sept. 1942–), dancer and actress, was born Loletha Elaine Falana in Camden, New Jersey, to Bennet and Cleo Falana. Her Cuban father had immigrated to the United States a few years before and was working as a welder, housing the family at the Clement T. Branch Village public housing project in the Centerville section of Camden. A dancer at age three and a singer with the church choir at age five, Falana disregarded her parents' concerns about her future and opted to leave Germantown High School months before graduation to embark on a show business career in New York.

Sleeping in a subway car because she could not afford an apartment, Falana soon landed dancing gigs at Small's Paradise in Harlem and in the singer Dinah Washington's nightclub act. The performer Sammy Davis Jr. recognized Falana's potential and cast her in a feature role in his Broadway musical *Golden Boy* (1964). Their association led to Falana's debut in Las Vegas, where Davis performed most of the year and where his protégée ultimately staked her claim as "The Queen of Las Vegas."

Falana cut her first record, *My Baby*, for Mercury Records in 1965. She also became the first singer that the legendary Lenny Wanoker produced when he came to Warner Bros. in 1966, launching her lively renditions of "Coconut Grove" and "Working in the Coal Mine." Her talents also took her abroad, where she starred in a handful of Italian films, including spaghetti Westerns, and where she was proclaimed a major personality.

Her return to the United States led to several guest appearances on Johnny Carson's *Tonight Show*, solidifying her celebrity status on both sides of the Atlantic. A starring role in the 1975 Broadway musical *Doctor Jazz* earned Falana a Tony Award nomination, with her flair for versatility landing her regular television appearances on the series *Comin' at Cha* with Ben Vereen, *The New Bill Cosby Show*, *Laugh-In*, and several Bob Hope specials. Returning to her musical roots Falana hit Billboard's rhythm and blues charts with her 1975 dance number "There's a Man Out There Somewhere" and signed with ABC to star in four highly acclaimed variety show specials. Her role as spokeswoman for Faberge's Tigress fragrance also was groundbreaking in that she became the first African American woman to endorse a major line of perfume.

The late 1970s heralded Falana's return to the Las Vegas strip, where she sold out shows at the Sands, the Riviera, and the MGM Grand hotels before the Aladdin Hotel made her the highest paid woman in Las Vegas history to that date with a $100,000 weekly salary.

In 1987, following a two-year stint as Charity Blake, a wealthy entertainment mogul on the CBS daytime drama *Capitol*, Falana was stricken with multiple sclerosis, which left her paralyzed and partially blind. Crediting God with her eventual recovery, she returned to Las Vegas in 1989 to perform numerous sold-out shows at the Sands Hotel before undertaking a new, full-time career in 1990 as a Catholic evangelist.

FURTHER READING

"Lola Falana Raises Funds for African Orphans; No Plans for a Showbiz Comeback." *Jet* 102.16 (7 Oct. 2002): 60.

"Lola Falana: Sexy Star Tells Why She Is Giving Up Show Biz to Become a Nun." *Jet* 77.23 (19 Mar. 1990): 56.

ROXANNE Y. SCHWAB

Falconer, Etta Zuber (21 Nov. 1933–19 Sept. 2002), mathematician, educator, college administrator, and mentor to hundreds of black women in science, was born Etta Zuber in Tupelo, Mississippi, the younger of two girls of Walter A. Zuber, a physician, and Zadie L. Montgomery Zuber, a musician. The Zubers were part of a small, black middle class that chose to stay in economically devastated Tupelo during the Depression era. The Zubers' social standing, however, provided little insulation from the closed society that was characteristic of Jim Crow-era Mississippi. Etta attended segregated public schools. She graduated from George Washington High School in 1949 at the age of fifteen and left the security of her home to attend the all-black Fisk University in Nashville, Tennessee. Young Etta had intended to major in chemistry and become a public school teacher. But by her sophomore year, she had decided that she liked mathematics better and switched her major.

Falconer excelled academically and flourished personally at Fisk. She was one of a handful of blacks inducted into the Phi Beta Kappa national honor society and graduated *summa cum laude* in 1953. It was at Fisk that Falconer met Lee Lorch, a white faculty member who would become her lifelong mentor and who would help mold her as person. It was also at Fisk that Falconer met EVELYN BOYD GRANVILLE, a young black female on the faculty in mathematics who had earned a doctorate from Yale University in 1949, becoming the second known African American woman in the United States to earn that degree in Mathematics. For Falconer, Granville was a career role model.

Recognizing Falconer's potential, Lee Lorch encouraged his young student to pursue graduate study in mathematics. Falconer followed Lorch's advice and enrolled in a master's program at the University of Wisconsin. The experience at Wisconsin was unlike any other that she had ever encountered. For Falconer, the shock was in having the opportunity to live and learn with students from places throughout the world—Africa, Thailand, and India. But the joy of that experience was soon replaced by the racial reality of her southern roots and the isolation of being in the white, male-dominated field of mathematics. She was often openly ridiculed by white male classmates who did not take her seriously as a peer or as a student teaching assistant.

After completing the master's degree in 1954, Falconer returned to Mississippi, where she taught mathematics at Okolona Junior College. There she met and married Dolan Falconer, a union that would span thirty-seven years and produce three children. In 1964 the family moved from Mississippi to Illinois after Falconer won a fellowship from the National Science Foundation (NSF) to attend a teacher-training institute. The move seemed to be a good one. Within three years Falconer had been appointed director of the institute and was also accepted into a doctoral program in mathematics at the University of Illinois but wouldn't stay. Her husband had been offered a job as basketball coach at Morris Brown College in Atlanta, Georgia. The family returned to the South in 1965. In need of employment, Falconer sought a position at Spelman College, which was a short distance from the Morris Brown campus.

For Falconer, Spelman held special significance. Her mother had attended this liberal arts college for black women in 1921, which, at the time, had a high school. It was also at Spelman that Falconer would meet Shirley Mathis McBay, a fellow black female mathematician. When Falconer arrived at Spelman, McBay was in the final year of a graduate program at the University of Georgia; she would become the first black at the university to earn a doctoral degree in Mathematics. Inspired perhaps by McBay's lead but certainly encouraged by Albert Manley, Spelman's first black and first male president, Falconer entered the doctoral program at Emory University. In 1969 Falconer would become only the tenth known black woman in the United States to earn the doctorate in pure mathematics, completing research under Trevor Evans on *Quasigroup Identities Invariant Under Isotopy*—a field of algebra. Her first paper, "Isotopy Invariants in Quasigroups," appeared in 1970 in *Transactions*, the journal of the American Mathematical Society.

A research fellowship from the NSF would take Falconer to Norfolk State College for a year in 1971. She published an additional paper, "Isotopes of Some Special Quasigroup Varieties," which appeared in 1971 in *Acta Mathematica*, the journal of the Royal Swedish Academy of Science. But Falconer didn't feel a life of research was for her. She thought she could have greater influence on the field by creating pathways of access for future generations of black women. For Etta Falconer, the notion of establishing a science program for young, African American females was quite simple—she wanted to provide students with a nurturing environment, with mentors and role models because "basically, we were people who went to school with none" (Scriven, 148). Falconer returned to Spelman College.

In 1968 only 28 out of 167 seniors at Spelman were listed as science majors. Faculty in those disciplines argued that the college was not doing enough to encourage student interest. They pointed to the dark, uninviting science building, Tapley Hall; the lack of emphasis on science and health careers; and little recognition of scientists (particularly black women) and their contributions to society in course offerings. Something had to be done.

In 1972 Falconer, McBay, and other science faculty saw an opportunity to strengthen and reinvent the science program. Their efforts came at an especially opportune time. Both the civil rights and women's movements had exposed the under-representation of racial minorities and women in science professions and in college programs. Activists pushed for federal legislation to spark reform. Spelman's classification as an historically black college and as a women's college positioned the institution to take advantage of efforts to improve the participation of underrepresented groups in science. With McBay and Falconer in the lead, faculty in biology, chemistry, and mathematics began by moving to a divisional structure. They believed this strategy would make the college more competitive for funding because faculty would be reviewed as a group with a depth of experience and specialties. Also in 1972 they launched a pre-freshman summer program to recruit and intervene early with students. The summer program was complemented by a health careers program to increase student interest in medicine and related professions, and a dual degree program in engineering, a discipline in which black women were almost nonexistent.

In 1975 Shirley McBay left Spelman to take a position at the NSF. Falconer was appointed chair of the division and continued to work with faculty and the administrations of Donald Stewart, Johnnetta Cole, and Audrey Forbes Manley to execute a plan of growth for the sciences. Under Falconer's thirty-seven year leadership, the growth of the Spelman science program was significant. Chemistry became a full-fledged department in 1977, thus eliminating the need to send Spelman women across the street to the all-male Morehouse College for classes. In 1987 Falconer secured funds from the National Aeronautics and Space Administration (NASA) to establish the Women in Science and Engineering (WISE) Scholars program. Under WISE, the college was able to provide students with critical scholarship dollars and with research experience to increase their competitiveness for acceptance to graduate school. In 1991

Falconer, who had by this time been promoted to associate provost for science programs and policy, worked with the Spelman science faculty to secure a grant from AT&T to establish a program in physics, another area of science in which black women were few.

Grant funding to improve the college's curricular offerings was met with increased student interest. The low enrollments that the science faculty had complained of in the late 1960's were replaced with sizeable increases, from 16 percent of the college's total student enrollment in 1967 to 29 percent in 1977 to 35 percent in 1987. By the late 1990s the science enrollment had grown to account for an average 37 percent of Spelman's nearly 2,000 average student enrollment.

The college's success as one of the top baccalaureate-degree producers of African American females did not go unnoticed. In 1995 the NSF named Spelman a model institution for excellence in undergraduate science and mathematics education, one of only six such named institutions in the country. One year later Spelman completed a $114 million capital campaign, the cornerstone of which included the construction of a 115,000 square foot science facility to support instruction, research and outreach. Spelman named the new facility in Etta Falconer's honor.

The naming of the science facility was one of many honors that recognized Falconer's achievements in increasing the number of African American women scientists, mathematicians, and engineers. The National Association of Mathematicians issued a Distinguished Service and Lifetime Achievement Award (1994). Former colleague, Shirley McBay, who had launched her own organization, Quality Education for Minorities Network (QEM), honored Falconer with the Giants in Science Award (1995). The Association for Women in Mathematics (AWM) presented Falconer with its fifth Louise Hay Award, designed to recognize outstanding achievements in-mathematics education (1995). Falconer's alma mater, the University of Wisconsin at Madison, awarded her an honorary doctorate (1996). And the American Association for the Advancement of Science (AAAS) honored Falconer with its Lifetime Mentor Award (2002).

Falconer retired from Spelman College in May 2002. Four months later she died at Atlanta's Crawford Long Hospital from complications from pancreatic cancer at the age of sixty-eight. Hundreds attended the funeral and spoke eloquently of Falconer's quiet presence and enduring legacy. The influence and effect she had on the lives of hundreds of aspiring black women in the sciences was sure to be felt for generations to come.

FURTHER READING

Information relating to Falconer is held in the Spelman College Archives.

Falconer, Etta Z. "A Story of Success: The Sciences at Spelman College," *SAGE: A Scholarly Journal on Black Women* (Fall 1989).

Association for Women in Mathematics. "Etta Z. Falconer Response on Being Presented the 5th Louise Hay Award" (1995). Available at http://www.awm-math.org/hayaward/1995.html.

Kenschaft, Patricia C. "Black Women in Mathematics in the United States," *American Mathematical Monthly* (Oct. 1981).

Sammons, Vivian Ovelton. *Blacks in Science and Medicine* (1990).

Scriven, Olivia A. *The Politics of Particularlism: HBCUs, Spelman College, and the Struggle to Educate Black Women in Science, 1950–1997*, Ph.D. diss., Georgia Institute of Technology (2006).

Williams, Scott W. "Etta Zuber Falconer," *Black Women in Mathematics*. Available at http://www.math.buffalo.edu/mad/PEEPS/falconner_ettaz.html.

Obituary: *Atlanta Journal and Constitution*, 22 Sept. 2002.

OLIVIA A. SCRIVEN

Farmer, James (12 Jan. 1920–9 July 1999), founder and national director of the Congress of Racial Equality (CORE), civil rights activist, and educator, was born James Leonard Farmer Jr. in Marshall, Texas, the son of James Leonard Farmer (known as "J. Leonard"), a Methodist minister and the son of former slaves, and Pearl Houston Farmer, who had been a teacher. Farmer's father, who earned a doctorate of religion from Boston University, was one of the first blacks in Texas to hold a Ph.D. When Farmer was six months old the family, which included an older sister, moved to Holly Springs, Mississippi, where his father had accepted teaching and administrative posts at Rust College. Able to read, write, and count by the age of four and a half, Farmer was accepted into the first grade. The family soon moved again, as Professor Farmer joined the department of religion and philosophy at Samuel Houston College in Austin, Texas. Farmer's outstanding academic and oratorical skills won him a four-year scholarship, and at the age of fourteen he entered Wiley College in Marshall. He was fortunate in his mentor, the poet Melvin B. Tolson.

James Farmer, director of the Congress of Racial Equality, leaves court after opening trials for sixteen African American leaders arrested in a civil rights demonstration, 3 September 1963. (Library of Congress/U.S. News & World Report Magazine Photograph Collection.)

Farmer was captain of the debating team and president of his fraternity. After his graduation in 1938, he enrolled at Howard University in Washington, D.C., to study for the ministry. Among others, the staff at Howard included Sterling Brown, Ralph Bunche, Carter G. Woodson, Benjamin Mays, and, most notably, Howard Thurman. Poet, philosopher, and preacher, Thurman introduced Farmer to Mohandas K. Gandhi's philosophy on the use of nonviolence to effect social change. At this time Farmer became the part-time student secretary for the Fellowship of Reconciliation (FOR), a Quaker pacifist organization.

During his years at Howard's School of Religion, Farmer focused on the interrelatedness of religion, economics, and race, and he wrote his master's thesis on this theme. As a result of his studies, Farmer decided not to be ordained, as the racial segregation in all denominations was repugnant to him. Close to graduation in 1941 when his father asked him what he then planned to do, he replied, "Destroy segregation." Asked how, Farmer told him it would involve mass mobilization and the use of Gandhi's principles.

Farmer began the grand mission of his life by continuing to work at FOR, first in Chicago, giving antiwar speeches there and in other midwestern cities. In Chicago he used Gandhi's technique for the first time to integrate a coffee shop where Farmer and a friend had been refused service. With added insult, they had been asked to pay one dollar for a nickel doughnut and had had their money thrown to the floor. In May 1942 they returned with a group of twenty-eight others and staged a sit-in that succeeded.

At this time, under the auspices of FOR, Farmer cofounded CORE (Committee of Racial Equality). The acronym came before the name, to indicate its purpose: that racial equality is the core of a just society. In little over a year CORE had chapters in New York, Philadelphia, Detroit, Seattle, and Los Angeles. Its appeal was broad because CORE had always stressed its interracial aspect, mirroring the belief that the "race problem" concerned all Americans, black and white. At its second annual convention in 1944, "Committee" became "Congress," reflecting its rapid growth. Peak membership came in the 1960s when CORE had eighty-two thousand members in 114 chapters. But Farmer described their efforts during the 1940s at integrating housing, banks, amusement parks, and barber shops as "a flea gnawing on the ear of an elephant" (Farmer, 153), for the lack of publicity CORE received.

In 1945 Farmer worked as a union organizer for furniture workers in the South. He also recruited college students for the League for Industrial Democracy, a socialist organization; organized and led strikes for the New York arm of AFSCME (American Federation of State, County, and Municipal Employees); continued to participate in CORE's activities; and became program director for the National Association for the Advancement of Colored People (NAACP), under the leadership of Roy Wilkins. In 1945 Farmer married Winnie Christie; they had no children and divorced the following year. In 1949 he married Lula Peterson; they had two daughters.

In February 1961 Farmer took the helm of CORE, the organization he had founded, as its first national director. "The dream that made our hearts beat since 1942 was in 1960 a reality," Farmer recalled in his autobiography. The Montgomery Bus Boycott of 1956 had been successful, and a lunch counter sit-in, which four students in Greensboro, North Carolina, staged on 1 February 1960, soon became the catalyst for the formation of the national Student Nonviolent Coordinating Committee (SNCC).

In May 1961 Farmer launched the Freedom Rides to the South to end desegregation in interstate transportation and in station waiting rooms. A participant as well as CORE's director, Farmer faced terrifying episodes, and he was in a Louisiana jail on the day of the March on Washington in 1963. The demands for civil rights were answered with bus and church burnings and beatings by mobs and police. The violence escalated into the murders of the CORE members James Chaney, Andrew Goodman, and Michael Schwerner in Mississippi in 1964. Such violence, coming a year after the Birmingham church bombing, in which four young girls died, and the murder of Medgar Evers, motivated civil rights workers to challenge the idea of nonviolence, as well as the large role played by whites within CORE. The preference for more confrontational action undermined Farmer's tenure, and he resigned in 1966.

Farmer then taught at Lincoln University in Pennsylvania and at New York University. In 1968 he ran for a Brooklyn congressional seat but lost to Shirley Chisholm. President Richard Nixon appointed Farmer assistant secretary in the Department of Health, Education, and Welfare in April 1969. "Chaf[ing] in the ponderous bureaucracy and long[ing] for my old role as advocate, critic, activist," Farmer resigned in December 1970. During the 1970s he worked with the Council on Minority Planning and Strategy, a think tank, and with organizations of public employees that made mortgage loans for integrated housing.

In 1985, despite failing eyesight, Farmer completed and published his autobiography, *Lay Bare the Heart*. He then taught history at Mary Washington College in Fredericksburg, Virginia, where he died.

To an enormous degree, James Farmer accomplished the goal he set for himself at the age of twenty-one, to "destroy segregation." His vision and energy challenged the social status quo and eliminated many injustices in American life. As Farmer summed up, "In movement days … the grasping at liberty … ennobled life for this nation" (Farmer, 351).

FURTHER READING

The James Farmer Papers are at the Center for American History at the University of Texas at Austin. Tapes relating to his run for Congress in 1968 are held at the Schomburg Center for Research in Black Culture of the New York Public Library.

Farmer, James. *Lay Bare the Heart* (1985).

Sklansky, Jeff. *James Farmer: Civil Rights Leader* (1992).

Obituaries: *New York Times*, 10 July 1999; *Jet*, 26 July 1999.

This entry is taken from the *American National Biography* and is published here with the permission of the American Council of Learned Societies.

BETTY KAPLAN GUBERT

Farmer, Sharon (10 June 1951–), photojournalist, was born Sharon Camille Farmer in Washington, D.C., the eldest of two children of George Thomas Farmer and Winifred Lancaster Farmer, both public school principals. Farmer's father, who also was a physical education instructor and high school football coach, instilled a love of sports in his daughter. With devoted parents who were heavily involved in their children's lives, the community, and the school system, Farmer grew up taking dance and music lessons and participating in other such cultural activities, such as the D.C. Youth Symphony Orchestra. At Anacostia High School, Farmer wrote for the school's newspaper, which offered her a glimpse into the career that would one day bring her national acclaim. Although Farmer wanted to attend a local college, her parents pushed her to leave her comfort zone. She chose Ohio State University because of its football prowess and well-regarded music department. Initially, Farmer planned to major in music and, eventually, to become a concert bassoonist.

However, one day near the end of her sophomore year, Farmer watched a friend complete an assignment in the darkroom. Witnessing this process of film development led her to change her major and the course of her life. Farmer flourished at Ohio State, a school she both loved for its vast opportunities and took to task when she encountered racial inequality. She wrote articles, took photos, and became managing editor of the school's black publication, *Our Choking Times*. Farmer also became chapter president of her sorority, Delta Sigma Theta, Inc., an organization she remained active in long after college. Also, at Ohio State, she found several African American mentors whom she credited with encouraging the school's small black population to use any prejudice they encountered as a galvanizing, unifying force. This notion of rallying together, getting involved, and working for change, stayed with Farmer through her professional life.

While Farmer's always-supportive parents paid her tuition at Ohio State, she also worked to help pay for her education and living costs. Farmer soon learned she could earn more money taking pictures than she could by grilling burgers part-time on campus. She freelanced for the *Columbus Call and Post*, the local black newspaper, and also took pictures at weddings, meetings, and parties. During her last semester of college, Farmer interned at the Associated Press. Although the international news agency offered her a job in Wisconsin after her graduation in December 1974, Farmer returned to Washington, D.C.

Back home, Farmer did newborn photography through a booking agency and subsequently worked in a camera shop, while freelancing. One of Farmer's friends, a member of the singing group Sweet Honey in the Rock, urged her to work as an independent photographer; the group supported her work, using one of her photographs for its second album's cover. After that, Farmer worked for many other artists in Washington and from 1979 to 1991 freelanced for the *Washington Post*. Farmer would later say that the *Post* assignments became emotionally draining as she grew tired and frustrated with the abundance of negative stories about African Americans. Farmer and other freelancers also had pay disputes with the new management at the *Post*, which prompted a lawsuit by the Newspaper Guild. In the end, the dispute was settled with one freelance photographer being added to the paper's staff, an outcome that left Farmer disappointed and disillusioned with labor unions and again searching for clients as a freelancer.

One of her assignments brought Farmer to Howard University's journalism department newspaper, the *Community News*, where she took photos and reestablished the school's student darkroom. From there, she went on to teach photojournalism at American University and freelanced for clients including the American Association for the Advancement of Science, the Women's Museum, and filmmaker Michelle Parkerson. Her work also appeared in the critically acclaimed book and exhibit *Songs of My People*. From 1988 to 1999 Farmer also maintained a photography studio, where she took headshots and author photos for book jackets.

In late 1992 Bill Clinton, then governor of Arkansas and the Democratic nominee for president, began to assemble a White House staff in the event of his victory in the general election, which was at that point considered likely. Even before her work was reviewed, Clinton's chief photographer, who had admired Farmer's work for years in the *Washington Post*, reached out to her, hoping she would agree to join the president's team when he took office in January 1993. Farmer agreed and went on to chronicle the president's two terms in the Oval Office. In 1999 she was promoted to director of the White House Photography Office, making her the first woman and only the second African American to hold that post.

Documenting presidential meetings with foreign heads of state, the signing of legislation, and the president's daily life and private moments, Farmer said she learned the real workings of government. "I learned if you don't vote you don't have a nickel or a dime," she later said. One encounter that resonated with Farmer was when Clinton met with and apologized to some of the Tuskegee Experiment survivors, men who had contracted syphilis and yet were left untreated by physicians who wanted to study the disease's advance and its ravages. Farmer was also present when the White House acquired *Sand Dunes at Sunset, Atlantic City* by HENRY OSSAWA TANNER: this 1895 painting was the first by an African American painter in this esteemed collection. Farmer's memorable moments also included the Tuskegee Airmen's visit to the White House, Clinton's tearful response to the 1995 assassination of Israeli Prime Minister Yitzhak Rabin, and the announcement of the 1996 plane crash that killed Secretary of Commerce RON BROWN and thirty-four others on an official trade mission in Croatia. The president's trips to Africa also stayed with Farmer, as she later said its nations reminded her most of home and her experiences made her lament the racism America spread around the world.

After the Clinton administration ended, Farmer returned to the Associated Press and worked as a photo assignment editor for three years before reentering politics as the official photographer for the 2004 Democratic presidential ticket of John Kerry and John Edwards. After the Kerry-Edwards campaign team disbanded following President George W. Bush's reelection, Farmer realized that she did not want to return to the office-bound editor's position, for she missed doing what she loved: taking photos. Following her political work in Washington, D.C., Farmer worked in Africa with the Bill and Melinda Gates Foundation, in Jordan with the Global Warming Action Network, and in Houston for the *Essence* Music Festival.

FURTHER READING

Easter, Eric, and Dudley M. Brooks, eds. *Songs of My People* (1992).

OTESA MIDDLETON MILES

Farmer-Paellmann, Deadria (25 Nov. 1965–), slavery reparations activist, is one of six daughters of Wilhemina and James Farmer. She was born and raised in Brooklyn, New York. She received a B.A. in Political Science from Brooklyn College in 1988, a master's degree from George Washington University in 1995, and a law degree from New England School of Law in 1999. New England School of Law was known for the commitment of its students and faculty to social activism. Farmer-Paellmann married a German national, and they had one daughter. Her employment includes acting as executive director of the Restitution Study Group and as an adjunct professor at Southern New England Law School. Her public service interest includes work with the National Coalition of Blacks for Reparations in America.

Farmer-Paellmann's family history sparked an interest in the reparation movement. Family tradition includes memories of her grandfather talking of the family's life in South Carolina, where some of her ancestors labored as enslaved rice farmers. Another formative influence was the protest against the excavation of the slave cemetery in Manhattan, where an estimated twenty-thousand African Americans are buried.

During law school, she authored a paper on reparations. As part of that research, Farmer-Paellmann uncovered archival sources in New York documenting that the parent company of Aetna Insurance insured the lives of slaves and, thus, reduced the risk to individual owners and made slavery a safer business for investors. At her request, Aetna searched its records and turned over some additional evidence of policies on enslaved people, as well as some evidence from a competing company. In 2000 Aetna issued an apology for its role in slavery. Farmer-Paellman told the *New York Times* that "My interest in this is to get these corporations, once they are aware of their own connections, to be our chief lobbyists in Washington for other forms of restitution.... Apologies aren't enough."

In 2000, in the wake of the Aetna apology, California enacted legislation that requires all insurance companies doing business in the state to search their files for records of slave life insurance policies, then to disclose them. Those records, available on the California Insurance Commission Web site, demonstrated that many of the slaves whose lives were insured were involved in particularly dangerous occupations, such as mining and working on railroads. Farmer-Paellmann maintained that she learned through those disclosures that she was related to someone who was insured by the Aetna in South Carolina. Other states followed California's lead in requiring disclosures, leading to boycotts against Aetna and JP Morgan Chase.

In 2002 Farmer-Paellman was lead plaintiff in a series of nine lawsuits filed in federal courts demanding reparations from companies proven to have connections to the institution of slavery. Those companies include Aetna, CSX Corporation, and Fleet Bank. The suits sought payment based on profits made from slavery; they also claimed that the companies had, in more recent times, misrepresented their connections to slavery and, thus, deceived consumers. The implication of the latter complaint is that some people would have boycotted the companies if their relationship to slavery was fully disclosed. The suits asserted that by downplaying their connections, the companies had committed fraud.

The lawsuits were consolidated under the heading *In re African American Slave Descendants Litigation* in the Northern District of Illinois, where they were dismissed without prejudice in 2004, then refiled and again dismissed in 2005. The court explored several arguments for dismissing the suit, including that its filing exceeded the statute of limitations for such a claim, also that the plaintiffs were not linked closely enough to the defendant companies, and that the issue of reparations should be decided by the legislature rather than the courts. The U.S. Court of Appeals for the Seventh Circuit affirmed the dismissal, except that it permitted the suit for consumer fraud to continue.

The dismissal of the lawsuit, which received substantial attention in the press and among legal commentators, was expected by many observers. Among close followers of the suit, the fraud claim appeared to have merit. With the dismissal of *In re African American Slave Descendants* and the dismissal in 2004 of *Alexander v. Oklahoma*, the federal lawsuit for victims of the Tulsa Race Riot of 1921, the strategies of reparations activists seemed to reach a turning point.

Farmer-Paellman stood at the center of reparations activism from 2000 to 2007. Indeed, she was the pioneer of the corporate restitution movement. While testifying for Representative JOHN CONYERS JR.'s H.R. 40 reparations study bill in 2005, she told Congress that her primary motivation for attending law school was to learn how to obtain reparations for slavery.

Her focus began shifting to local action, such as advocating local truth commissions. For example, in North Carolina, the 1898 Wilmington Riot Commission issued a report and apology in May 2006; Brown University established a Steering Committee on Slavery and Justice; in 2007 the legislatures of major slave states, including Virginia and Maryland, issued apologies for slavery and recognized the long-lasting effects of the institution.

One of Farmer-Paellman's trademarks is bringing attention to little-known information about the connections of current businesses to slavery. Her dramatic evidence focused the public's attention on the issue of reparations and will likely continue to do so, as the debate over reparations grows.

FURTHER READING

Farmer-Paellmann, Deadria. Testimony in support of H.R. 40, 6 Apr. 2005.

Groark, Virginia. "Slave Policies," *New York Times*, 3 May 2002.

Lewin, Tamar. "Calls for Slavery Restitution Getting Louder," *New York Times*, 4 June 2001.

Staples, Brent. "How Slavery Fueled Business in the North," *New York Times*, 24 July 2000.

ALFRED L. BROPHY

Farrakhan, Louis Abdul (11 May 1933–), leader of the Nation of Islam, was born Louis Eugene Walcott in the Bronx, New York City, to Sarah Mae Manning, a native of St. Kitts, who worked as a domestic. Farrakhan's biological father was Manning's husband, Percival Clarke, a light-skinned Jamaican cab driver. By the time young Louis was born, however, Manning had left Clarke and was living with Louis Walcott. Manning hoped her baby would be a girl and have a dark complexion like herself and Walcott. Nevertheless, when the child was born male and with a light complexion, she named him Louis and listed Walcott as the father (Magida, 10). Walcott stayed with the family during their move to the Roxbury section of Boston in 1937, but departed shortly thereafter. Raising two young children alone during the Depression was difficult, but Sarah Mae kept her boys from harm and attended to their cultural as well as material needs. At the age of six Louis started violin lessons. He later studied with a Jewish instructor, among others, and became a local prodigy, appearing on the *Ted Mack Amateur Hour* at the age of sixteen. Louis was also an altar boy and choir member at St. Cyprian's Episcopal Church. Next to the church stood Toussaint L'Ouverture Hall, formerly the Boston headquarters for black nationalist MARCUS GARVEY, one of Louis's childhood heroes. Louis was an exceptionally bright student whose academic promise earned him a place at the prestigious Boston Latin School. Not comfortable in those elite surroundings, Louis transferred to the English High School, where black students were still in the minority, but where he could thrive academically and shine as a popular track star.

He had dreams of attending the Juilliard School, but by his teen years Louis's taste in music had broadened to include calypso, and he wondered

Louis Farrakhan, leader of the Nation of Islam, addresses an audience in Chicago during the annual Saviours Day celebration, 25 February 2001. (AP Images.)

if he might not more easily become the next HARRY BELAFONTE than a black Jascha Heifetz. Thus, when the all-black Winston-Salem Teacher's College offered him an athletic scholarship, he left for North Carolina—quite unprepared for the racism and segregation he would encounter. Although there were seven female students for every male student at the college, Louis was in love with Betsy Ross, a young, black Roman Catholic woman back in Roxbury. By the summer following his sophomore year, Betsy was pregnant with the first of their nine children. College had been a disappointment, so instead of returning to campus in September 1953, he married Betsy at St. Cyprian's. For the next few years, Louis supported his family and pursued a career as a calypso entertainer. His melodic voice, suggestive lyrics, provocative dancing, and colorful outfits paid tribute to his West Indian parentage and earned him the stage name "The Charmer."

While touring in Chicago as the feature performer with the Calypso Follies in February 1955, Louis was invited by a friend to attend a meeting of the Nation of Islam (NOI). When Louis arrived at the converted synagogue on Chicago's South Side, he was not impressed by the oratorical ability of ELIJAH MUHAMMAD, the organization's leader, thinking to himself, "This man can't even speak well" (Magida, 31). However, Muhammad's message of black nationalism and his powerful indictment of the white race for a litany of wrongs perpetrated against black people resonated profoundly in Louis's heart and mind. Back in Boston, MALCOLM X, the most dynamic and articulate of Muhammad's ministers, personally oversaw much of Louis's conversion and training. Louis X, as he was then known, rose quickly within the ranks of the Nation of Islam from acolyte to a captain of the Fruit of Islam, a security and fraternal auxiliary. In 1959 Louis X became the minister of Temple No. 11 in Boston, which was located in a building that had formerly been the Boston Rabbinical College. Apparently unaware that the property had changed hands, the city directory listed Louis X as "Rabbi Eugene L. Walcott."

Within five years Louis X had tripled the membership in the Boston mosque to approximately three hundred members, with many more sympathizers and supporters. Like W. D. Fard, the mysterious founder of the NOI who adopted much of the pseudo-Islamic teachings of NOBLE DREW ALI, Louis X propagated the doctrine that their unique form of Islam was the true religion of black people in America, who were, they believed, the lost tribe of Shabazz, and that the "white man" was the devil incarnate (Lincoln, 77–81). Louis X projected the organization's carefully cultivated image of black men who were proud and defiant, well dressed in their trademark bow ties, and able defenders of the black community. To their credit, the NOI was more effective than most rival organizations at rehabilitating criminals, helping drug addicts, and inculcating their particular values, which prohibit drinking, smoking, and extramarital relations. Louis X drew on his artistic talents to aid in recruitment by recording songs such as "A White Man's Heaven Is a Black Man's Hell" and "Look at My Chains," and he wrote two plays: *The Trial*, which literally put the white race on trial for crimes against humanity, and *Orgena* ("A Negro" spelled backward).

In 1964, when Malcolm X informed his protégé that their leader, Elijah Muhammad, had fathered several children with his teenage secretaries, Louis X made it clear that if a conflict should emerge, he would side with Muhammad. When the split occurred that March, an internecine struggle ensued. In December 1964 Louis X published an article in *Muhammad Speaks* declaring Malcolm X a traitor and ominously announced, "The die is set, and Malcolm shall not escape.... Such a man as Malcolm is worthy of death." On 14 February 1965 Malcolm and his family narrowly escaped when their home was bombed; then on 21 February, Malcolm was fatally shot at the Audubon Ballroom in Harlem. Convicted of the murder were three members of the NOI, one of whom was connected to the Newark mosque where Louis X had been the morning of the assassination. Thirty years later, while not admitting to a direct role in the murder, Louis X acknowledged that his rhetoric contributed to a hostile atmosphere.

Three months after the assassination of Malcolm X, Muhammad gave Louis X the name Abdul Farrakhan and appointed him to lead Malcolm's Harlem mosque. Within two years Minister Farrakhan had risen to Malcolm's former position as national spokesman of the NOI. When Elijah Muhammad died of congestive heart failure in 1975, many expected Farrakhan to be named as his successor and were surprised to learn that Muhammad had chosen his fifth son, Wallace (now WARITH) MUHAMMAD to be the next supreme minister. Wallace restructured the NOI in an effort to bring its beliefs and practices in line with the majority of Sunni Muslims throughout the world, a move that required purging the organization of its racial ideology. In October 1976 the NOI was officially dissolved in order to give birth to the World Community of al-Islam, which ultimately became the American Society of Muslims. Farrakhan, who had been transferred to the Chicago headquarters during the reorganization, believed these changes had gone too far, and in September 1977 he called on dissenting ministers and members to join him in restoring the NOI under his leadership.

The resurrection of the Nation of Islam began in a funeral home that Farrakhan purchased in Chicago. From that location he started the newspaper *Final Call* and began to buy properties liquidated by Wallace. In 1986 he purchased Elijah Muhammad's mansion in Hyde Park for $500,000, and in 1988 he acquired the flagship mosque of the NOI in Chicago, which he renamed Mosque Maryam. With a $5 million, interest-free loan from the Libyan leader Mu'ammar Gadhafi in 1985, Farrakhan launched a line of cosmetic products. The NOI also owns farmland and small businesses and broadcasts on several television and radio stations. Though Farrakhan succeeded in rebuilding the NOI, membership in the organization has never exceeded fifty thousand, and he did not come to national attention until the presidential campaign of JESSE JACKSON in 1984. Farrakhan was on the board of directors of Operation PUSH, Jackson's organization, and he traveled with Jackson to Syria that December to secure the release of U.S. Navy lieutenant Robert O. Goodman, an African American airman who had been shot down over Lebanon. Farrakhan received little publicity until Jackson's anti-Semitic reference to New York City as "Hymietown" was reported by the African American journalist Milton Coleman. Farrakhan responded with an oblique threat on Coleman's life and implied the existence of a Jewish conspiracy to perpetuate black subordination. Farrakhan and his spokesman, Khallid Abdul Muhammad, soon found themselves at the center of a firestorm of charges of anti-Semitism, denials, and countercharges.

Farrakhan has referred to Adolf Hitler as "a very great man" (later explaining he meant "wickedly great"), to the Jewish people as the "killer of all the prophets," and to Judaism as a "dirty religion" (Magida, 146–149). Because his remarks range from harsh but legitimate criticisms to ugly stereotyping, different constituencies champion or attack isolated aspects of his persona while ignoring that which does not fit the image they have of him. Farrakhan portrays himself as the paladin of unspoken truth—as with the publication of *The Secret Relationship between Blacks and Jews* (1991)—and his opponents portray themselves as defenders against a rising tide of black anti-Semitism. Farrakhan is aware that his obsession with Jews is unhealthy and easily exploited, but he says, "It's like I'm locked now in a struggle. It's like both of us got a hold on each other, and each of us is filled with electricity. I can't let them go, and they can't let me go" (Gates, 145).

The pinnacle of Farrakhan's influence was reached on 16 October 1995, when he convened the "Million Man March," a mass gathering of black men on the Washington Mall for a day of atonement. The goals of the march were introspective, focusing on accepting personal responsibility and healing the internal wounds of the black family, rather than hurling grievances at the government. The African American community was polarized between those who supported the objectives of the rally and those who would not participate as long as women were excluded and as long as Farrakhan refused to disavow his anti-Semitism. According to some estimates, a million men may indeed have attended. By all accounts the Million Man March far surpassed the size but not the influence of the 1963 March on Washington, and Farrakhan himself had much of the popularity but little of the stature of Dr. MARTIN LUTHER KING JR.; yet, he had undeniably tapped into a deep yearning in the souls of many black folk. In the years following the march, continuing controversy and growing health problems sidelined Farrakhan from mainstream view. On February 25, 2007, Farrakhan gave an address widely held to be his last as leader of the NOI. Farrakhan did, however, continue to make comments on public affairs, and has been very critical of the foreign policies of President BARACK OBAMA, in particular its support for the Libyan rebels who overthrew the Qadaffi regime in 2011.

FURTHER READING

Alexander, Amy, ed. *The Farrakhan Factor* (1998).

Gates, Henry Louis, Jr. "The Charmer," in *Thirteen Ways of Looking at a Black Man* (1997).

Levinsohn, Hamlish Florence. *Looking for Farrakhan* (1997).

Lincoln, C. Eric. *The Black Muslims in America* (1961, rpt. 1973).

Magida, Arthur J. *Prophet of Rage: A Life of Louis Farrakhan and His Nation* (1996).

SHOLOMO B. LEVY

Farrow, William McKnight (13 Apr. 1885–Dec. 1967), painter, graphic artist, printmaker, curator, and educator, was born in Dayton, Ohio. His family later moved to Indianapolis, where he attended high school in 1903 and 1904. While Farrow was in high school, the noted muralist William Edouard Scott recognized his artistic potential and encouraged him to enroll at the School of the Art Institute of Chicago. In 1908 Farrow moved to Chicago to begin classes at the Institute, Scott's alma mater and one of the first U.S. art schools to admit black students.

Farrow studied intermittently at the School of the Art Institute of Chicago from 1908 to 1918, while working for the U.S. Postal Service. When Farrow arrived at the institute, founded as the Chicago Academy of Fine Arts in 1879, it was not yet a world-class art institution. In the early twentieth century, the institute was actively building its collection with European art and quality exhibitions. Separate from these efforts, the Chicago-founded Harmon Foundation supported several institute-affiliated black artists: annually, it presented the William E. Harmon Award for Distinguished Achievement Among Negroes, established in 1914 by Joel E. Spingarn, chairman of the board of the National Association for the Advancement of Colored People (NAACP), and advertised in the *Crisis*, the NAACP's monthly magazine. The Harmon Foundation also sponsored several exhibitions of African American art in major cities, and from 1928 to 1933 it mounted similar group exhibitions that traveled around the United States. In 1917 Farrow participated in a Harmon Foundation-sponsored show in Chicago, which was cosponsored by the Arts and Letters Society of Chicago. A great deal of Farrow's work was displayed in the Harmon Foundation-sponsored exhibits of 1928 to 1933.

Farrow, along with the Chicago artists Charles Dawson, HALE A. WOODRUFF, and Arthur Diggs, also received support from the Art Institute of Chicago. The Institute mounted the Negro in Art Week, one of the first exhibitions to display works done by living black artists. ALAIN LOCKE, who organized this exhibition along with its cosponsors the Chicago Woman's Club and the Art Institute, showcased African American art that met prevailing European art standards of quality and portrayed the emergent New Negro movement. Part of the larger cultural movement variously labeled the Negro Renaissance and the Harlem Renaissance, the New Negro movement was borne by ambitious, black intellectuals, musicians, artists, and performers, and the interest in black creativity. The Chicago Art League, cofounded by Farrow in 1923, embodied the spirit of the times, for it offered classes and exhibition opportunities for local artists. The league organized yearly exhibitions held at the YMCA on Wabash Avenue in Bronzeville.

In 1922, Farrow was hired as an assistant curator at the Art Institute of Chicago and was put in charge of writing labels for displayed art and cataloguing. Eventually he was given oversight of print art, and in 1926 he accepted the position of curator of the Egyptian Collection. He continued to work at the institute until 1945. Farrow's regular column "Art in the Home" appeared in the influential black weekly *Chicago Defender*, and he also wrote essays for the *Crisis* and *Homesteader*.

In 1926 Farrow also accepted a position to teach art at Carl Schurz High School in 1926. While teaching at the high school, Farrow wrote commercial art instruction books including *Easy Steps to Commercial Art* (1931), *Practical Use of Color* (1933), and *Figure*

Drawing and Instruction (1935). In 1948, after the *Pittsburgh Courier* published a profile of his life and work, Farrow was fired from his teaching post. The school's staff had hired Farrow believing he was white and fired him upon learning that he was not.

Farrow's artistic approach was conservative; he-worked in a naturalistic style, founded in the nineteenth-century figural traditions, to render flattering portraits and pleasant landscapes. Farrow, exhibited in New York and Washington, D.C., was well known during his lifetime. His works were on view in the gallery exhibits at Chicago's Southside Community Art Center, part of the Great Depression's Work Progress Administration recovery program that gave work to artists struggling during the Great Depression. The Community Art Center exhibitions influenced a generation of students including William S. Carter, CHARLES WHITE, and the photographer GORDON PARKS, and it was an important gallery space for black artists during the Depression. Farrow's works were featured in exhibitions including the Chicago Art Institute's *The American Negro Expo* in 1940 and a solo show at the New York Public Library in 1940.

Farrow's commercial graphic artwork, most notably the posters he designed for commercial clients, including Pathé phonographs and Kimball pianos, became popular images in poster reproduction. His art is part of the collections at Clark Atlanta University, New York Public Library, and Fort Huachuca (Arizona). His work may be seen in numerous public places including the Steward Community House, Provident Hospital, and Roosevelt High School (all in Chicago). Farrow's portrait of the author and poet PAUL LAURENCE DUNBAR, painted in 1934, hangs in the National Portrait Gallery of the Smithsonian Institution in Washington, D.C.; both Farrow and Dunbar grew up in Dayton, Ohio, and went on to become part of the Harlem Renaissance and New Negro movement.

FURTHER READING

Driskell, David C. *Two Centuries of Black American Art* (1976).

Fine, Elsa Honig. *The Afro-American Artist* (1973).

Kennedy, Elizabeth, ed. *Chicago Modern, 1893–1945: Pursuit of the New* (2004).

Lewis, Samella S. *African American Art and Artists* (1990).

Meyerowitz, Lisa. "The Negro in Art Week: Defining the 'New Negro' Through Art Exhibition," *African American Review* (Spring 1997).

Reynolds, Gary, and Beryl J. Wright. *Against the Odds: African American Artists and the Harmon Foundation* (1989).

Obituary: *Times* (London), 30 Dec. 1927.

PAMELA LEE GRAY

Father Divine (? May 1879–10 Sept. 1965), religious leader and founder of the Peace Mission movement, was born George Baker in Rockville, Maryland, to George Baker Sr., a farmer, and Nancy Smith, a former slave who worked as a domestic with her three daughters before marrying Baker sometime in the 1870s. Nancy, who had been owned by two Catholic masters, exposed her children to the African American spiritual traditions of the Jerusalem Methodist Church in Rockville until she died in 1897.

Following his mother's death, George Baker gravitated to Baltimore, as did thousands of African American in search of a better life. He appears on the census of 1900 as a gardener, and he also found work on the docks, where he witnessed the crime and poverty of the destitute and was moved by a new message of ecstatic salvation emanating from dozens of storefront churches in the city. Baker, a dark, stout man with a high-pitched voice, impressed people with his earnest demeanor. He quickly rose from Sunday school teacher to evangelist. However, it was Baker's message, rather than oratorical skills or charisma, that ultimately distinguished him from any number of itinerant preachers. His message synthesized the teachings of evangelical churches with the "New Thought" ideology of Charles Fillmore and Robert Collier. Essentially a form of positive thinking, proponents of New Thought asserted that correct thinking, which Baker and others interpreted in a religious sense, could empower the believer to improve his or her circumstances. This notion contrasted sharply with the ritualistic or heaven-focused beliefs of many denominations, regardless of their form of worship. Baker's theology could be applied to solving earthly problems of poverty and racism. Indeed, he later referred to his centers as "heavens on earth."

The most striking element of Baker's message, that of his own divinity, gradually emerged after he attended the Azusa Street Revival, which gave birth to the Pentecostal movement in California during the spring of 1906. Baker returned to Baltimore convinced that he had been transformed to serve a higher purpose. The following year Samuel Morris entered Baker's church and proclaimed, "I am the Father Eternal!" (Weisbrot, 19). Morris was cast out by the congregation, who considered his words blasphemous, but Baker was intrigued by Morris's interpretation of 1 Corinthians 3:16, "Know ye not that ye are the temple of God, and the Spirit of God dwelleth in you?"(AV) as establishing the possibility of human divinity. For the next five years the two enjoyed a relationship in which Morris was "Father Jehovia, God in the Fathership degree" and Baker was "the Messenger, God in the Sonship degree" (Watts, 27). Later, John Hickerson, known as "Reverend St. John Divine Bishop," who claimed to speak fluent Hebrew and taught that all black people were descended from Ethiopian Jews, became the third member of their trinity.

In 1912 this divine partnership ended as Hickerson and Baker both began to question whether their own degree of divinity might equal or surpass that claimed by Father Jehovia. Hickerson went north to establish the Church of the Living God in New York City, and Baker went south, preaching in various towns until 1914, when he settled briefly in Valdosta, Georgia. There a group of irate husbands and clergy had Baker indicted on lunacy charges, arguing that claiming to be God and encouraging sexual abstinence even for married women was proof of his insanity. One local paper ridiculed him with the headline "Negro Claims to Be God." He was booked as "John Doe, alias God," indicating that he no longer used the name Baker. But neither on the witness stand nor in interviews did Baker appear to be one of the crazed lunatics that he and his followers were made out to be. The jury found Baker guilty but did not have him committed because he was not a threat to himself or others. Chastened by this experience and by an earlier clash with southern ministers that got him sixty days on a Georgia chain gang, Baker moved in late 1914 to New York City, where he established a religious organization that, for a while at least, kept a relatively low profile.

The prototype for the Peace Missions began in a quiet, middle-class neighborhood in Brooklyn in 1917 and then two years later moved to an affluent white suburb in Sayville, New York, where he was known as "Major Jealous Devine" before settling on the appellation "Father Divine." These missions were experiments in communal living. Residents and visitors entered a world in which race was considered not to exist; even the words "white" and "Negro" were barred from use. Gender distinctions were also treated as suspect, and adherents referred to "those who call themselves women" and "so-called men." Nor were distinctions recognized on the basis of class, title, or office; all identities were subordinate to being a follower of God. On 15 November 1931 Father Divine and ninety-three of his followers were arrested at their Long Island mission for disturbing the peace. The interracial composition of the movement drew the ire of Judge Lewis Smith, who considered race mixing ipso facto a disturbance of the peace. Father Divine, believing that he was being persecuted, refused to pay the five-dollar fine. When the fifty-six-year-old judge suddenly dropped dead three days after imposing a one-year sentence, Father Divine remarked, "I hated to do it." The conviction was later overturned, and the coverage in the black press brought Father Divine to national attention.

During the Depression Father Divine moved his base of operation to Harlem and opened an estimated 160 Peace Missions in the United States, Canada, and Europe. The movement even boasted of a postcard from China addressed to "God, Harlem, USA" that was promptly delivered to Father Divine. While the majority of his followers in New York were black migrants from the South and immigrants from the Caribbean, in other areas of the country, such as California, white membership may have risen as high as 70 percent. A number of Father Divine's wealthy followers contributed land, buildings, and large sums of money to the organization. Where other charities opened soup kitchens for the poor, Father Divine served lavish buffets twice daily, consisting of between fifty and two hundred menu items of the finest fare available. These centers operated on an honor system where the poorest dined for free and others paid as little as ten cents for a meal and two dollars a week for lodging. Critics have argued that Father Divine was merely pandering to the poor, simple, and ignorant, but according to one contemporary academic observer, "Eating is hardly ever advanced as a reason for having come into the movement" (Fauset, 63 n. 10). Father Divine referred to these banquets as "Holy Communions," and in the absence of any formal liturgy for the sect, the meals, songs, and testimonials formed the core of their religious activity.

Father Divine advanced bold political positions, calling for a minimum wage, limits on corporate wealth, the abolition of capital punishment, and the passage of antilynching legislation. He ran his organization through a series of secretaries, mostly women; there were no ministers or clergy other than Father Divine himself. Drinking, smoking, and sexual relations were strictly prohibited, while industry and financial independence were strongly encouraged. By the end of the Depression, the Peace Mission operated scores of businesses, several hotels, a large farming cooperative, a number of mansions, and two newspapers, *New Day* and *Spoken Word*. Yet, the Peace Mission did not pass a collection plate at its meetings, nor did it peddle healing merchandise or accept contributions from nonmembers. Those who lived at a mission center might be expected to donate their earnings to the movement, but Father Divine's propensity to share the wealth seems consistent with his philosophy of prosperity, rather than with the unalloyed avarice of a con artist.

During the 1940s membership in the Peace Mission movement declined rapidly from its height of about 50,000. The end of the Depression diminished Father Divine's appeal and relevance. Moving to his Philadelphia estate in 1942 to avoid a lawsuit, he became separated from his base of support. The death of his first wife, Peninnah, known as "Mother Divine," generated doubt about Father Divine's promise of everlasting life for the faithful. Father Divine's assertion that Peninnah was reincarnated in the form of his second wife, "Sweet Angel," a young, white Canadian whom he married in 1946, cast further suspicion on his omnipotence. He made few public appearances in the 1950s, and rumors of his failing health quickly spread. The man who would be God died of diabetes in 1965, but to a small band of stoic believers, he still exists in spirit.

The acquisition of great wealth and claims of divinity invite comparisons between Father Divine and Daddy Grace, another flamboyant black minister of the period. However, the breadth of Father Divine's poverty programs, the extent of his political activism, and his use of theology to address social conditions suggest that he had more in common with Marcus Garvey as a colorful, complex, and important historical figure.

FURTHER READING

The papers of Father Divine are held by the Peace Mission in Philadelphia, Pennsylvania. Many of the sermons, essays, beliefs, and writings of Father Divine are published in the Peace Mission's two newspapers, *Spoken Word* and *New Day*.

Fauset, Arthur Huff. *Black Gods of the Metropolis* (1971).

Watts, Jill. *God, Harlem U.S.A. The Father Divine Story* (1992).

Weisbrot, Robert. *Father Divine and the Struggle for Racial Equality* (1983).

Obituary: *New York Times*, 11 Sept. 1965.

SHOLOMO B. LEVY

Fats Domino. *See* Domino, Fats.

Fattah, Chaka (21 Nov. 1956–), politician, was born in Philadelphia, Pennsylvania, the son of Sister Falaka Fattah, a community activist and founder of the House of Umoja in West Philadelphia, and Russell Davenport, a U.S. Army sergeant. Chaka Fattah attended various public schools in Philadelphia, including Overbrook High School. Although his high school counselor tried to place him on a manual labor track instead of an academic college one, Fattah insisted on pursuing a college education. He graduated from the Community College of Philadelphia in 1976 and went on to obtain his B.A. from the University of Pennsylvania's Wharton School.

Fattah became the assistant director of the House of Umoja, an institution that his mother had founded to assist troubled African American male teenagers. Using this experience gained at the early age of twenty-one, Fattah later served Philadelphia in various roles, including as special assistant to the director of Housing and Community Development, special assistant to the managing director of the City of Philadelphia, and policy assistant for the Greater Philadelphia Partnership.

In 1982 Fattah became the youngest member of Pennsylvania's House of Representatives. He was twenty-five at the time and held this office through two more terms over the next six years. Fattah served on numerous education committees in the state legislature but did not lose his commitment to his local constituents in the city of Philadelphia. With the purpose of inspiring young African Americans in Philadelphia to pursue a college education, he founded the annual Fattah Conference on Higher Education in 1986. During his tenure as a state representative, Fattah found time to study at Harvard University's Kennedy School of Government, where he completed the Senior Executive Program for State Officials. He received an M.A. in Government Administration from the University of Pennsylvania's Fels School of State and Local Government in 1986. In 1987 he was the architect of the Employment Opportunities

Act that assisted 320,000 of Pennsylvania's welfare recipients in finding jobs.

Fattah was elected to the Pennsylvania state senate in 1988. While a state senator he ran on the liberal Consumer Party ticket for the U.S. House of Representatives but lost to the Democratic nominee, LUCIEN BLACKWELL. The congressional seat had previously been held by WILLIAM H. GRAY III, who went on to become president of the United Negro College Fund (UNCF). Nevertheless Fattah continued serving in the state senate until 1994, when he again declared candidacy for the congressional seat in Pennsylvania's Second District and won on the Democratic ticket.

Congressman Fattah continued his emphasis on college education at the national level. He proposed legislation in May 1998 for a federal program to raise the educational awareness of low-income youths and motivate them to consider attending college. This program, titled GEAR UP (Gaining Awareness and Readiness for Undergraduate Programs), provided approximately two billion dollars in funding to prepare and assist inner-city students to enter college. Over the next two years the High Hopes for College program touted by Fattah provided information to middle school students about college scholarships and loans. This program also included counseling, mentoring, and tutorial services for young students with the purpose of raising their awareness of the opportunities for obtaining a college education. In 2000 President Bill Clinton traveled to Fattah's district to laud the success of the congressman's efforts on these issues.

In Congress, Fattah served on the House Committee on Education, as well as on the powerful House Appropriations Committee, a highly-coveted position because of its influence on budgetary matters. He was also a chair of the Friends of the Caribbean Caucus, as well as a member of the Progressive Caucus, the Congressional Black Caucus (CBC), the Congressional Urban Caucus, and the Democratic Congressional Campaign Committee (DCCC). Soon after his election to the 104th Congress, Fattah exhibited his leadership style by taking on the role of Congressional Black Caucus whip.

Numerous honors, appointments, and accolades were bestowed upon Congressman Fattah. He was awarded honorary doctorates from Saint Paul's College in Lawrenceville, Virginia, the Philadelphia College of Pharmacy and Science, and the Philadelphia College of Textiles and Science. He received the Pennsylvania Public Interest Coalition's State Legislator of the Year award. Because of his interest in education, Fattah was appointed to the Pennsylvania State Board of Education and to the Board of Trustees at the Community College of Philadelphia, Lincoln University, Penn State University, and Temple University. Fattah was the father of three girls and one boy. On 7 April 2001 he married Renée Yvette Chenault, an attorney and a news anchor for a Philadelphia television station.

Though a lawmaker at the federal level of government, Congressman Fattah maintained his commitment to his roots in Philadelphia. He was an outspoken proponent of granting a new trial to MUMIA ABU-JUMAL. In 2003 he formed the CORE Philly Scholarship program, which provided up to three thousand dollars in scholarship funding to any Philadelphia student who graduated from high school and attended college in one of Pennsylvania's state institutions of higher learning.

Chaka Fattah was not the first African American to serve in either chamber of the Pennsylvania legislature or in the U.S. House of Representatives. In fact, he was the fourth African American elected to Congress from his congressional district. When asked how he felt about not being the first, he declared, "That is the last thing we would want to hear now. We hope that time has passed. It would be very unfortunate if we were still celebrating firsts" (Fenno, 116). Instead, Congressman Fattah gained recognition for the strength of his legislative ability in providing for the educational needs of thousands of young African Americans.

FURTHER READING

Chaka Fattah's legislative papers are housed in the Urban Archives of the Samuel Paley Library at Temple University in Philadelphia, Pennsylvania.

Baer, John. "Fattah's a Major Player Now," *Philadelphia Daily News*, 5 Mar. 2001.

Fenno, Richard. *Going Home: Black Representatives and Their Constituents* (2003).

Kalb, Deborah. "Rep. Chaka Fattah," *The Hill*, 25 Oct. 1995.

NATHAN ZOOK

Faulkner, William John (16 Nov. 1891–18 July 1987), folklorist and minister, was born in Society Hill, South Carolina, the son of Laurence Faulkner, a merchant and postmaster, and Hannah Josephine Doby, a midwife. The decade of his birth and earliest development was one of violent repression of blacks across the South, during which the Supreme

Court, in *Plessy v. Ferguson*, propounded its "separate but equal" doctrine. The fact that both parents were enterprising contributed to a sense of security in William despite the brutal reality of night riders and Klansmen roaming the countryside. In addition, religion was a shield against hardship and a source of hope in his life. Raised in a Christian household, by age six he had taken John the Baptist as his hero.

By age nine, with the migration to Society Hill of the former slave and storyteller Simon Brown, Faulkner was exposed to the artistic and spiritual qualities of his slave ancestors. Once a slave in Virginia, Brown took a job at the post office and grocery store run by Faulkner's parents. It was a happy conjunction, for Brown passed on to Faulkner his storytelling gift. That Faulkner's parents did not oppose his grounding in the slave past, relatively rare then in black circles, may have had much to do with the considerable degree to which Brown's tales, rich in Old Testament symbolism, were absorbed by the youngster. The tales that he heard over several years, mostly of a religious nature, affirmed the need to oppose harsh reality with ancestral wit and wisdom. In particular, ironic humor could be used to help digest injustice; that this was an important step in preparing oneself to eradicate it in the future slowly dawned in Faulkner's consciousness.

Faulkner completed grammar and high school at the Mayesville, South Carolina, Educational Institute before attending Springfield Young Men's Christian Association College in Springfield, Massachusetts, from which he received a B.A. in 1914. That year Faulkner accepted a job as secretary of the YMCA in Philadelphia, Pennsylvania, a position he held for three years until 1917, when he accepted a similar post at the YMCA in Atlanta, which he held from 1919 to 1932. Also in 1917 he married Elizabeth Able Cook; they had four children. From 1926 to 1933 he pastored Atlanta's First Congregational Church.

A brilliant student, Faulkner returned to school in his forties to take graduate courses. In 1934 he earned a master's degree in theology at the University of Chicago in 1934, in a decade in which a number of talented young black scholars were in residence there, among them E. Franklin Frazier in sociology, William Allison Davis in anthropology, L. D. Reddick in history, and Horace Cayton in psychiatry. Shortly after receiving his M.A., Faulkner was appointed dean of the chapel at Fisk University in Nashville, Tennessee, and became a leader of the Nashville chapter of the NAACP, for a while serving as its president. During his term he led a struggle for equal salaries for African American public school teachers forced to teach in segregated schools and achieved victory in 1942. In the previous year he had taken additional graduate courses in the social sciences at the University of Pennsylvania.

Faulkner's years at Fisk, from 1935 to 1953, were a time of intellectual growth and excitement. He was often sought after as a speaker and achieved national recognition as a minister when he was invited, in 1948, to give the Easter sermon at New York's Radio City over NBC. Although it would be nearly a quarter of a century before he became known beyond black colleges as a major folklorist and storyteller, perhaps more than at any other time his gift as a storyteller was honed at Fisk. He had an appreciative, particularly sensitive audience there, and that contributed to the iron memory that he developed as storyteller and keeper of the values of his ancestors. The fact that his mandate at Fisk put him in close and continual contact with college students was not unrelated to the student movements that soon began to transform race relations in the South.

In fact, the Student Nonviolent Coordinating Committee, which spearheaded the assault against segregation below the Mason-Dixon Line, had its strongest initial leadership at Fisk in the 1960s for both the sit-ins and the freedom rides. It can be argued that Faulkner helped prepare the spiritual ground for that leadership. Crucial to his identification with the participants in the sit-ins and freedom rides was his ability, cultivated over decades in the chapel as pastor and counselor, to commune with the young.

As pastor at Chicago's Park Manor Congregational Church when the civil rights movement burst on the scene in the 1960s, Faulkner was prepared for the objectives the movement set for itself and for the means by which they were to be achieved. In addition, most of the members of his congregation were either from the South or were the children of southerners. Not only did he see the movement whole, he communicated a sense of the unity of the struggle and its national ramifications. With some of the freedom riders first released from jail in attendance at Park Manor, he identified racial oppression as the continuing tragedy at the heart of the nation. This conviction he conveyed in elevated tones from deep wells of spirituality.

In 1976 Faulkner's stories were finally published as *The Days When the Animals Talked*. Largely

Christian in content, they are also remarkable for the degree to which African spiritual values are concealed in them, the English language acting as a sort of cover. Had African values been expressed openly, brutal repression would have been the response. In fact, Faulkner's tales, invaluable to students of American culture, are best understood when read in conjunction with scholarship on African anthropology and the history of African art. His recordings of his tales reveal his genius as a storyteller and his ability to project disarming humor; to give distinctive voice to slave and master, disguised as "critters"; and to make the spoken word, and therefore the slave sermon, sing.

Faulkner was a minister of uncommon ability and ethical stature whose qualities as a storyteller were no less impressive. While he achieved national recognition among fellow pastors decades before he died, his reputation as a folklorist has grown since his death. Only E. C. L. Adams's *Tales of the Congaree* is comparable in quality to Faulkner's *The Days When the Animals Talked*. Faulkner retired from the ministry at age seventy and thereafter wintered in Miami for many years before suffering a stroke in 1982. He welcomed friends and visitors to a daughter's home in Miami until he died there.

FURTHER READING

The Faulkner papers are housed at the Moorland-Spingarn Collection, Howard University.

Stuckey, Sterling. *Going through the Storm: The Influence of African-American Art in History* (1994).

Stuckey, Sterling. *Slave Culture: Nationalist Theory and the Foundations of Black America* (1987).

Obituary: *Nashville Tennessean*, 20 July 1987.

STERLING STUCKEY

Fauntroy, Walter Edward (6 Feb. 1933–), legislator, pastor, and civil rights activist, was born in Washington, D.C., the son of William Thomas Fauntroy and Ethel Vines Fauntroy. His father worked in the U.S. Patent Office. Upon graduating from Dunbar High School in 1952, Fauntroy entered Virginia Union University in Richmond, Virginia. While there he received strong support and encouragement from his pastor, the Reverend Charles David Foster, and he graduated from Virginia Union in 1955 with a B.A. in History. He received a scholarship to attend Yale University Divinity School, where he earned a bachelor of divinity degree in 1958. In 1959 when his longtime mentor the Reverend Foster died, Fauntroy was named to succeed him as pastor at New Bethel Baptist Church. He married Dorothy Simms on August 3, 1957, and the couple had a son, Marvin Keith, and a daughter, Melissa Alice.

During his college years Fauntroy met and forged a lasting friendship with fellow theological students MARTIN LUTHER KING JR. and WYATT TEE WALKER. They espoused similar ideas for effecting change by nonviolent protest, and in 1960 King and Walker asked Fauntroy to become the SCLC (Southern Christian Leadership Conference) director for Washington, D.C., and their liaison and lobbyist in Congress. He served the SCLC in this capacity for eleven years, when his election to the House of Representatives obliged him to devote himself full-time to his new legislative duties. Even prior to accepting his SCLC post, Fauntroy had initiated nonviolent demonstrations in Washington, enlisting volunteers during the 1960 sit-ins and boycotts. At the height of the civil rights movement Fauntroy was deeply involved in almost every major event, and he established himself as an invaluable contact person between the SCLC and congressional leaders on the one hand, and the White House and federal and state agencies on the other. Acknowledged as being the SCLC's point man in Washington, Fauntroy was assigned by King the challenging task of planning, organizing, and coordinating the SCLC's participation in the March on Washington of 1963, an accomplishment that became one of Fauntroy's most significant contributions to the civil rights cause during the 1960s. Fauntroy also played a key role in directing the-1965 Selma-to-Montgomery March. By then the SCLC had begun to focus on legislative matters, and Fauntroy had advanced closer to the forefront of the organization's leadership. As one of King's inner circle of advisers, Fauntroy lobbied energetically for the passage of the Civil Rights Act of 1964 and for the enactment of the Voting Rights Act of 1965. During the Atlantic City Democratic National Convention of 1964, when the Mississippi Freedom Democratic Party (MFDP) challenged the legitimacy of the "Regular" segregationist delegation, Fauntroy labored tirelessly for the MFDP's recognition by the national Democratic Party. In 1966, in the aftermath of the shooting of JAMES MEREDITH in Mississippi during his March against Fear, it was to Fauntroy that Dr. King turned to coordinate the Mississippi Freedom March on short notice.

Fauntroy's reputation as an effective political operative led to his being named vice chair of the first Washington, D.C., city council, appointed by President Lyndon Johnson; Fauntroy served on the council from 1967 to 1969. Following the assassination of Dr. Martin Luther King Jr., Fauntroy carried out King's final project by coordinating the May–June 1968 Poor Peoples' March in Washington. Thereafter Fauntroy narrowed his focus to more local and legislative issues. Moved undoubtedly by concerns for his city's future after a demoralizing race riot in 1969, he lobbied Richard Nixon's Republican administration to secure home rule for the District of Columbia.

As the 1960s progressed, Fauntroy played a central role in national politics. In 1966 President Johnson appointed him vice chair of the White House conference "To Fulfill These Rights"; he served on the Leadership Council on Civil Rights from 1961 to 1971; and he was director of the Model Inner City Community Organization from 1966 to 1972. In 1970 Fauntroy entered the race for nonvoting representative of the District of Columbia in the House of Representatives; he won both the Democratic primary against CHANNING PHILLIPS and the general election. Despite his nonvoting status, Fauntroy held the title of congressman and in time exerted a significant influence, both visibly and behind the scenes. Fauntroy faced a challenge from the old-line white southern conservative congressional chair of the House District of Columbia Committee, John L. McMillan (a Democrat from South Carolina), who opposed and obstructed any movement toward home rule. Fauntroy, however, was able to rouse sufficient African American opposition to McMillan in his home district to achieve the white Democrat's ouster from Congress. Fauntroy ultimately spearheaded two major pieces of legislation: the Washington, D.C., Home Rule Act of 1975 and the Washington, D.C., Voting Rights Amendment of 1978. However, the second of these measures failed to be adopted as a constitutional amendment by the requisite number of states within seven years, so it never became law.

While in Congress he held the chair for the Subcommittee on International Development, Finance, Trade, and Monetary Policy, which was part of the House Banking, Finance, and Urban Affairs Committee. A founding member of the Congressional Black Caucus, Fauntroy was chosen by his peers to be its chair from 1981 to 1983. His efforts as chair bore fruit in 1983 when Congress passed legislation authorizing Dr. Martin Luther King Jr. Day in January as a federal holiday. In 1979 he was named to the House Select Committee on Assassinations, chairing the Subcommittee on the Assassination of Dr. Martin Luther King Jr.

Reprising his organizational skills once again, in 1983 Fauntroy coordinated the Twentieth Anniversary March on Washington. On 21 November 1984 Fauntroy—along with two colleagues, RANDALL ROBINSON of TransAfrica and MARY FRANCES BERRY of the U.S. Commission on Civil Rights—was arrested at the South African ambassador's residence in Washington while protesting apartheid. Upon their release the three founded the Free South Africa movement. The pressure brought to bear by movement activists is credited with being instrumental in pushing forward the measures for U.S. economic sanctions against South Africa, which Fauntroy helped enact into law in 1986 and which helped to bring about the release of Nelson Mandela in 1990 and the eventual destruction of apartheid.

In 1990 Fauntroy resigned from his congressional seat to run for mayor of Washington, D.C., but he was defeated by SHARON PRATT DIXON KELLY. Upon leaving public office he founded Walter E. Fauntroy & Associates, which specialized in offering consulting services on investments in Africa and within the African American business communities, and he also continued his pastoral duties at New Bethel Baptist Church.

FURTHER READING

Personal and public papers of Walter E. Fauntroy are located at the Gelman Library of George Washington University in Washington, D.C.

Fairclough, Adam. *To Redeem the Soul of America: The Southern Christian Leadership Conference and Dr. Martin Luther King, Jr.* (1987).

Robinson, Randall. *Defending the Spirit: A Black Life in America* (1998).

Swain, Carol M. *Black Faces, Black Interests: The Representation of African Americans in Congress* (1993).

RAYMOND PIERRE HYLTON

Fauset, Arthur Huff (20 Jan. 1899–2 Sept. 1983), folklorist, educator, was born in Flemington, New Jersey, the middle of three children of the Reverend Redmon Fauset, an African Methodist Episcopal (AME) minister who died when Arthur was four, and Bella Huff, a white woman and widow with three children. He was also a half-brother to the author JESSIE REDMON FAUSET, whose mother was Annie Seamon, Rev. Fauset's first wife and mother to seven of their children. Fauset grew up in Philadelphia, Pennsylvania, attending Central High School and then the School of Pedagogy for Men, graduating in 1917. Beginning in 1918 he taught elementary school in the Philadelphia public school system and eventually became principal of the Joseph Singerly School in 1926, a position he held for twenty years. ALAIN LOCKE became Fauset's mentor, encouraging him to pursue higher education and arranging a loan that enabled him to study part time at the University of Pennsylvania while he continued teaching. Fauset also became a protégé of Charlotte Mason, a wealthy and eccentric white patron who contributed financial support to such Harlem Renaissance luminaries as LANGSTON HUGHES, ZORA NEALE HURSTON, AARON DOUGLAS, and Locke. Fauset's essay "American Negro Folk Literature" was included in Locke's groundbreaking 1925 collection, *The New Negro*.

Fauset had discovered anthropology at college and in the summer of 1923 he participated in a six-week field study in Nova Scotia. Fauset's findings were later published as *Folklore from Nova Scotia* (1931). He pursued his study of anthropology when he returned to the University of Pennsylvania for three years. He received all his degrees, B.A. (1921), M.A. (1924), and Ph.D. (1942), from that university. His Ph.D. in Anthropology made him one of the first African American anthropologists. Fauset's early career coincided with the years of the Harlem Renaissance, roughly 1919–1935, when African American arts and letters flourished, and the importance of studying African American culture became paramount for black intellectuals. Fauset's reviews, articles, stories, and essays appeared in African American journals such as *Black Opals*, *Opportunity*, and *Crisis*, as well as in the one and only issue of *Fire!!*, the 1926 arts journal edited by Wallace Thurman. His short story "A Tale of the North Carolina Woods" was published in the January 1922 issue of *Crisis*, and another of his short stories won first prize in the 1926 *Opportunity* contest. Fauset took issue with a basic tenet of Harlem Renaissance civil-rights-through-arts-and-letters thinking in a 1933 *Opportunity* essay, in which he argued that the recognition of African Americans as equal to whites in the arts would not necessarily bring social and economic equality.

A member of the Philadelphia Anthropological Society and the American Folklore Society, as well as a fellow in the American Anthropological Association, Fauset remained primarily interested in folklore, however, and his studies and writings focused on the folklore of Nova Scotia and on African Americans in Philadelphia, the West Indies, and the South. As NATHAN IRVIN HUGGINS observed: "He turned his attention to Negro materials not only because of his racial attachments but because of his fear that the rapidly changing and urbanizing South would soon obliterate this very rich source of the Negro's past" (Huggins, 73). His survey of notable African Americans throughout history in *For Freedom* (1935) included lesser-known figures as well. *Sojourner Truth, God's Faithful Pilgrim* (1938) was republished in 1971, and his 1942 Ph.D. dissertation was the basis for his best-known work, *Black Gods of the Metropolis: Negro Religious Cults of the Urban North* (1944). An examination of the religious cults and religious leaders such as FATHER DIVINE and Prophet F. S. Cherry, the book remains an important study of early-twentieth-century African American urban culture.

In 1935 Fauset married Crystal Dreda Bird. In the November 1938 contest for the Pennsylvania House of Representatives, CRYSTAL BIRD FAUSET became the first African American woman elected to a state legislature. Their marriage ended in 1944, without children. During World War II Fauset enlisted in the U.S. Army but, at the age of forty-two, was too old to serve. He returned to Philadelphia with an honorable discharge. Fauset retired from teaching in the Philadelphia school system in 1946, after over twenty years as a teacher and principal. He continued his research in New York City in the 1950s, eventually making Manhattan his permanent home. In 1969 he collaborated with fellow one-time Philadelphia school principal Nellie Rathbone Bright to write *America: Red, White, Black, Yellow*. Intended for elementary school students, the book surveyed the contributions of minority groups in the making and development of the United States. Fauset remained active until his death, at age eighty-four.

FURTHER READING

Harrison, Ira E., and Faye V. Harrison, eds. *African-American Pioneers in Anthropology* (1999).

Higgins, Nathan Irvin. *Harlem Renaissance* (1973).

Wilson, Sondra Kathryn, ed. *The Crisis Reader* (1999).

MARY ANNE BOELCSKEVY

Fauset, Crystal Bird (27 June 1893–28 Mar. 1965), legislator and activist, was born Crystal Dreda Bird in Princess Anne, Maryland, the daughter of

Benjamin Bird, a high school principal, and Portia E. Lovett. Crystal's father died when she was only four, and her mother took over his principalship of the all-black Princess Anne Academy until her own death in 1900. An orphan by age seven, Crystal remained true to her parents' commitment to education. Ironically, her early loss probably improved the educational opportunities of a child born on Maryland's segregated Eastern Shore. Reared by an aunt in Boston, she attended public school, graduated from the city's Normal School in 1914, and taught for three years. She later earned a B.S. from Columbia University Teacher's College in 1931.

Her personal success notwithstanding, Crystal Bird came to realize that racial inequality was an American, rather than merely a southern, dilemma. In 1918, on the eve of the Great Migration, she began work as a field secretary for the Young Woman's Christian Association, organizing social programs for black women. Traveling throughout the nation, she began to make the connections between race, gender, and class that informed a lifelong crusade for justice.

Although the 1920s witnessed the emergence of a race-conscious "New Negro," Bird developed an enduring faith in interracial cooperation. Beginning in 1927 she worked with the interracial section of the American Friends Service Committee, whose purpose was to articulate to whites the needs and desires of African Americans. She continued this mission six years later, when she helped found Pennsylvania's Swarthmore College Institute of Race Relations.

The misery of the Great Depression convinced Crystal Bird of the need to ground interracial cooperation in political action. The sight of "long, patient bread lines opposite swank Central Park Apartments" persuaded her that the New Deal offered the best hope of change. Resident in Philadelphia since her marriage in 1931 to the high school principal and political columnist ARTHUR HUFF FAUSET (they would have no children), she joined the Democratic Party just as it began to challenge that city's well-entrenched Republican machine. Addressing Democrats in 1935, she lashed out at the "orgy of Republican mismanagement" in Philadelphia's City Hall and pleaded that "living people be given a chance to live."

One year later Fauset made her mark in national politics, serving as director of colored women's activities for the Democratic National Committee. Although many blacks benefited from the New Deal, her work proved no easy task. In the previous election, most African Americans had remained loyal to the party of Abraham Lincoln, and segregated New Deal agencies threatened to keep them in the GOP column. Furthermore, Fauset had to counter the Republican charge that Franklin D. Roosevelt, who had at that time proposed no civil rights legislation, was beholden to southern Democrats. Nonetheless, Fauset reminded northern blacks that they too could wield the ballot to counter the white South. Using the trump card of the First Lady Eleanor Roosevelt, Fauset urged blacks to cast "sentimentality and tradition aside" in support of a "great humanitarian effort."

The 1936 campaign won Fauset plaudits, and two years later she won her party's nomination for a state legislative race. Promising to push for slum clearance, affordable housing, and fair employment legislation, she, along with two white Democrats, easily defeated three Republican candidates.

In the Philadelphia *Afro-American*, Fauset declared her election less a personal victory, than a "recognition of colored womanhood." In one sense that was true: African American women had mobilized throughout the city, boosting black participation as a whole, thereby increasing the Democratic vote. Yet Fauset had won election from West Philadelphia, then an ethnically diverse but predominantly white section of the city. The electoral returns suggest that both whites and blacks had voted the straight Democratic ticket. Community leaders who had recently initiated interracial forums on a variety of issues may also have encouraged white racial tolerance.

As the first black woman elected to a state legislature, Crystal Fauset emerged in the first rank of African American leaders. The *Crisis* magazine, black America's preeminent journal of opinion, heralded her victory on its cover. Likewise, black newspapers followed her speeches avidly, highlighting her appeal that black women actively engage in the making of history.

Yet that same national reputation may have convinced Fauset that she needed a broader stage. After barely a year, she left her Pennsylvania assembly seat to work as a race relations adviser for the state's Works Progress Administration. Then, in October 1941, she was appointed race relations adviser to the Office of Civilian Defense (OCD), a position vital to the coming war effort. Her duties included the coordination of nationwide OCD race programs, publicizing the African American role in the war effort, and promoting black participation in civil defense activities. In pursuing these goals, the writer ROI OTTLEY noted, Fauset displayed "exceeding resiliency under pressure" (*"New World A-Coming": Inside Black America*, 264). As one of only two women in the black cabinet, she now also had the ear of Eleanor Roosevelt, an old friend from the Swarthmore Institute.

The year 1944 proved to be a turning point in Fauset's political and personal life. Going back to electoral politics, she resigned from the OCD to work full time for the Democratic National Committee. However, a tense relationship with the DNC's chairman, Robert E. Hannegan, provoked her to not only resign but also to endorse the Republican Thomas Dewey for president. Fauset attacked the Democratic chairman as "a dictator ... not willing to deal democratically with Negroes." But critics suggested that frustrated ambition explained Fauset's decision. The staunchly Democratic *Chicago Defender* noted, for instance, that Fauset had failed to be appointed recorder of deeds in Washington, D.C. Whatever the reason, her defection prompted one further lifestyle change. Although she and Arthur Fauset had been separated for some time, her husband, a Democrat, filed for divorce a mere two days after she bolted to the GOP.

After World War II, Fauset continued to seek interracial cooperation but focused more on global issues. She helped found the United Nations Council of Philadelphia in 1945, attended the inaugural session of the United Nations in San Francisco, and coordinated programs to promote understanding between whites and people of color. But as African nations gained independence, she became more critical of her own nation's failures with regard to race, protesting in 1957 that a delegation to celebrate Ghana's independence did not include "a woman like myself ... to represent the millions of slave mothers" who had built America.

Fauset died in Philadelphia, just a few short months before the passage of the Voting Rights Act, the zenith of the interracial cause to which she had dedicated her life.

FURTHER READING

Fauset left no consolidated manuscript collection, but much information can be gleaned from the many organizations for which she worked. The Archives of the YWCA (Young Women's Christian Association) in New York City and the Records of the American Friends Service Committee in Philadelphia, Pennsylvania, contain materials pertaining to her early career. The Records of the Office of Civilian Defense, RG 171 of the National Archives, offer a wealth of information on Fauset's OCD activities.

"Mrs. Fauset Fails to Get D.C. Post, Bolts Demos," *Chicago Defender*, 16 Sept. 1944.

"Mrs. Fauset Sees Social Security of Mrs. Roosevelt in White House," *Washington Tribune*, 18 Oct. 1936.

Obituaries: *New York Times*, 30 Mar. 1965; *New York Amsterdam News*, 3 Apr. 1965.

This entry is taken from the *American National Biography* and is published here with the permission of the American Council of Learned Societies.

STEVEN J. NIVEN

Fauset, Jessie Redmon (27 Apr. 1882–30 Apr. 1961), writer, editor, and teacher, was born outside Philadelphia, Pennsylvania, in Camden County, New Jersey, the daughter of Redmon Fauset, an African Methodist Episcopal minister, and Annie Seamon. Fauset was probably the first black woman at Cornell University, where she graduated Phi Beta Kappa with a degree in Classical and Modern Languages in 1905. She taught briefly in Baltimore before accepting a job teaching French and Latin at the famed all-black M Street (later Dunbar) High School in Washington, D.C. While teaching, Fauset completed an M.A. in French at the University of Pennsylvania (1919).

From 1912 to 1929 Fauset contributed numerous articles, reviews, poems, short stories, essays, and translations of French West Indian poems to the *Crisis*, the official publication of the National Association for the Advancement of Colored People. At the urging of its editor, W. E. B. DUBOIS, she moved to New York City to become the literary editor of the *Crisis* from 1919 to 1926. She was instrumental in discovering and publishing most of the best-known writers of the Harlem Renaissance, including LANGSTON HUGHES, CLAUDE MCKAY, JEAN TOOMER, and COUNTÉE CULLEN. In 1920–1921 Fauset also edited a monthly magazine for African American children called *Brownies' Book*. During this period Fauset and her sister made the apartment they shared in Harlem a salon where the black intelligentsia and their allies gathered to discuss art and politics.

Although she exercised substantial influence as a literary mentor, Fauset is best known for her writing. Her poetry appeared in the *Crisis* and was published in numerous anthologies. Her essays and articles run the gamut from Montessori education to international politics to travel essays about her experiences as a delegate to the second Pan-African Congress held in London, Brussels, and Paris in 1921. Her best-known essay, "The Gift of Laughter" (1925), is an analysis of the black comic character in American drama. Fauset is primarily known, however, for her four novels—*There Is Confusion* (1924), *Plum Bun* (1929), *The Chinaberry Tree* (1931), and *Comedy: American Style* (1933)—all novels of manners centering on the careers, courtships, and marriages of the black professional classes, DuBois's so-called talented tenth.

Fauset and her fellow Harlem Renaissance writers WALTER WHITE and NELLA LARSEN, with whom she is frequently compared, were all galvanized into print by the 1922 publication of T. S. Stribling's *Birthright*, a best-selling novel about a mixed race Harvard graduate written by a white man. In a 1932 interview, Fauset remembered how she felt when *Birthright* was published: "Here is an audience waiting to hear the truth about us. Let us who are better qualified to present that truth than any white writer try to do so" (*Southern Workman*, May 1932, 218–219). *There Is Confusion* (1924) was her first attempt to present that truth. DuBois called it "the novel that the Negro intelligentsia have been clamoring for" (*Crisis*, Feb. 1924, 162). It offered some refreshingly positive images of black characters: Joanna Marshall turns the street dances of African American children into a successful stage career; Peter Bye overcomes his bitterness toward the white branch of his family and becomes a surgeon; and Maggie Ellersley, a poor laundress's daughter, establishes her own lucrative chain of beauty shops.

Fauset traveled in Europe and studied French at the Sorbonne and the Alliance Française in Paris in 1925. She left her job as an editor at the *Crisis* in 1926 in order to find employment that would allow her more time for writing. Discrimination made it impossible for her to work in a New York publishing house, so she returned to teaching. From 1927 to 1944 she taught at a Harlem junior high school and DeWitt Clinton High School in New York City.

In 1929 Fauset published her second and best novel, *Plum Bun*, a story about light-skinned Angela Murray, who abandons her darker-complexioned sister to "pass" for white, initially seeking to marry a white man to gain access to power and wealth. Here Fauset turned nursery rhymes and the traditional romance plot to alternative uses, unveiling the complex ways in which racism and sexism make the happy endings such plots promise impossible for black women to achieve. In 1929 Fauset married Herbert E. Harris, an insurance executive. They had no children.

Fauset's third novel, *The Chinaberry Tree* (1931), explores issues of miscegenation, illegitimacy, and "respectability" as they are played out in a small New Jersey town. Only after the white writer Zona Gale agreed to write an introduction to the novel testifying that blacks such as those Fauset depicted—middle-class, hard-working, "respectable" blacks—really existed did the publisher agree to go ahead with the book. Most white publishers and readers preferred black characters that did not challenge stereotypes—primitive, exotic characters displaying uninhibited sexuality in Harlem's slums—to Fauset's portraits of the black professional classes.

Fauset's final novel, *Comedy: American Style* (1933), explores the damage wreaked on the lives of a middle-class black family by the internalized racism of the mother. Olivia Cary's obsession with whiteness leads to the suicide of her dark-complexioned son, the unhappy marriage of her light-skinned daughter to a racist white man, and the emotional and material ruin that follow alienation from their community.

Fauset continued to travel extensively, lecturing on black writers to audiences of various types. She was visiting professor at Hampton Institute in 1949 and taught French and writing at Tuskegee Institute. She died in Philadelphia.

Fauset's literary reputation has experienced some dramatic turns. Initial reviews in both the black and the white press were generally positive. WILLIAM STANLEY BRAITHWAITE, for example, called Fauset "the potential Jane Austen of Negro Literature" (*Opportunity*, Jan. 1934, 50). During the 1960s and 1970s, however, critics of African American literature preferred accounts of poverty and racial protest to Fauset's portrayals of the black elite. Robert Bone, labeling her novels "uniformly sophomoric, trivial, and dull," placed Fauset in the "Rear Guard" of the Harlem Renaissance, contrasting her conservatism with the more politically confrontational texts of younger writers. Feminist critics of the 1980s and 1990s, however, recuperated much of Fauset's work. Fauset's plots—dismissed by earlier critics as melodramatic, sentimental, and marred by coincidence—have been interpreted anew as sites for investigating how class and race complicate the traditional romance plot. Given the structure of American society in the 1920s and 1930s—institutionalized racism and sexism and white control of publishing houses and patronage—Fauset's achievements as an important actor in Harlem literary culture and a theorist of gender, race, and power are particularly noteworthy.

FURTHER READING

Fauset manuscript materials are at the Moorland-Spingarn Research Center at Howard University.

Christian, Barbara. *Black Women Novelists: The Development of a Tradition, 1892–1976* (1980).

McDowell, Deborah. "The Neglected Dimension of Jessie Redmon Fauset," in *Conjuring: Black Women, Fiction, and Literary Theory*, eds. Marjorie Pryse and Hortense Spillers (1985).

Sylvander, Carolyn Wedin. *Jessie Redmon Fauset, Black American Writer* (1981).

Wall, Cheryl. "Jessie Redmon Fauset, 1882–1961," in *Gender of Modernism*, ed. Bonnie Kime Scott (1990).

Watson, Carole McAlpine. *Prologue: The Novels of Black American Women, 1891–1965* (1985).

Obituary: *New York Times*, 3 May 1961.

This entry is taken from the *American National Biography* and is published here with the permission of the American Council of Learned Societies.

ERIN A. SMITH

Fax, Elton (9 Oct. 1909–13 March 1993) artist, writer, illustrator and educator, was born Elton Clay Fax, the son of Mark Oakland and Willie Estele Fax in Baltimore, Maryland. Fax initially matriculated at the historically black institution Claflin University, in Orangeburg, South Carolina, but completed his studies and received a BFA at Syracuse University in Syracuse, New York, in 1931. On 12 March 1929, Fax married the former Grace Elizabeth Turner, and their union produced three children.

In 1934 Fax painted a well-received mural, commissioned by the Public Works of Art Projects (PWAP) at Baltimore's Dunbar High School, depicting the incorporation of southern, black agrarians into the urban, industrial north. Fax's representation of the Great Migration and a pluralistic American workforce was an ideal example of the American Social-Realist art that was supported by Franklin Delano Roosevelt's New Deal projects. Social Realism was a popular style in the 1930s and 1940s which later came to be identified with Communist aesthetics, but was originally perceived to be an appropriate aesthetic statement for the art of the working classes. From 1935 to 1936 Fax was an instructor in art, art history, and history at Claflin University. By the fall of 1936, Fax taught drawing at the Harlem Arts Center in New York City; he continued to work there until 1941, while his salary was paid in part by the Works Progress Administration (WPA). Fax was also instrumental in the selection of the Baltimore Museum of Art as the site for the "Contemporary Negro Artists" exhibition of 1939, organized by Mary Beattie Brady of the William E. Harmon Foundation and philosopher and the cultural critic ALAIN LOCKE.

By 1940 Fax had begun to work as a freelance artist, creating illustrations for magazines and children's books. The latter market would later prove significant to his career. During the 1940s Fax developed a popular weekly cartoon strip titled *Susabelle*, which concentrated upon issues in African American history and appeared in several black newspapers. Fax also began to develop a signature form of presentation described as the "chalk-talk." During his lectures—often about his own travels and interactions—he would create works of art pertaining to the lecture subjects, using spontaneous drawings. In the late 1940s and early 1950s Fax returned to Orangeburg in order to complete a number of significant portrait commissions for prominent, middle-class African Americans in the community.

Fax produced a variety of artistic works demonstrating a range of approaches, generally within the strictures of representational art. His earlier works as a skilled portrait artist are exemplified by such images as his *Portrait of Robert Shaw Wilkinson*, (the second president of South Carolina State College, now South Carolina State University). Fax also painted President Wilkinson's wife's likeness, captured in the portrait, *Marion Birney Wilkinson* (c. 1948, collection of South Carolina State University). The Wilkinsons were both prominent members of South Carolina's black middle-class elite. These elegant, naturalistic portraits demonstrate Fax's firm handling of traditional European and European American aristocratic portraiture. Nonetheless, Fax was perhaps better known for his representations of the poor and disenfranchised. Many of his works were inspired by what he witnessed during a lifetime of international travel. Fax was interested in exposing exploitation: he hoped that his Social-Realist art would encourage audiences to consider the global human condition, and he also wanted to enhance awareness of world poverty and human rights issues.

In 1953 Fax and his family moved to Mexico. During this period (1953–1956) he traveled extensively, visiting Argentina, Bolivia, Uruguay, and various other South and Central American nations. Upon returning to the United States, he was employed from 1957 to 1958 by the City College of New York (now part of the City University of New York) as a teacher of watercolor painting and art history. As a result of his empathetic representations of the poor and disenfranchised in the developing world, Fax was invited to attend the seminal conference of the American Society of African Culture (AMSAC) held in Rome in 1959. Fax's association with AMSAC culminated in a tour of Africa documented in his first publication as both author and illustrator titled, *West African Vignettes*, published by AMSAC in 1960 and subsequently expanded in a new edition in 1963.

The formula of writing and illustrating his international experiences became a successful approach for Fax. In the 1960s and continuing into succeeding decades Fax traveled to various parts of the world, offering his signature "chalk-talks," with the approval of the State Department of the United States. Significantly, Fax was permitted to travel in politically sensitive Third World nations, including Nigeria, northern Sudan, and Ethiopia. Fax also confronted challenging environments in developed countries such as the former Soviet Union during the height of the cold war, often discussing potentially volatile subjects such as the struggle for civil rights in America. Despite the precariously political character of his subject matter, Fax maintained a supportive relationship with government observers of his presentations.

Beginning in the 1970s Fax addressed the creation of publications pertaining to issues of African American history in the United States. Among these, one of his best-known and most popular works is a biography of Marcus Garvey. Fax's work helped to reclaim Garvey from the obscurity to which he was consigned in the 1940s through the 1960s—an obscurity perhaps brought on by the financial scandal and dissolution of his once-powerful organization, the Universal Negro Improvement Association (UNIA). This scandal had culminated in Garvey's imprisonment and eventual deportation from the United States. Fax's illustrated narrative resurrected the positive aspects of UNIA's mission. Along with the efforts of historians and a later generation of black nationalists, Fax's biography of Garvey played an important role in redeeming Garvey's reputation.

The 1970s were a highly productive decade for Fax, who produced a number of books, including *Contemporary Black Leaders* (1970), and *Seventeen Black Artists* (1971). During this era he traveled throughout Asia as a guest of the Soviet Writers' Union in 1971 and again in 1973; in addition to these travels, he completed *Garvey: The Story of A Pioneer Black Nationalist* (1972), *Through Black Eyes: Journeys of a Black Artist in East Africa and Russia*, which he illustrated (1974), and *Black Artists of the New Generation* (1977).

Throughout the 1980s Fax continued to publish and illustrate works, including *Hashar* (1980), a book based on his travels in the Central Asian states of the former USSR in 1978. He also participated in the Bulgarian Writers' Conference in 1977 and in 1982, where he shared the dais with celebrated American authors such as John Cheever and Gore Vidal. Another work that he illustrated himself, *Elyuchin* (1983), was followed by *Soviet People as I Knew Them* (1988). In his 1986 article for the *Black American Literature Forum*, "It's Been a Beautiful but Rugged Journey," Fax discussed his discomfort with American government requests that he report on his observations of potentially dangerous Communist influences in the countries he visited. This did not, however, curtail his travels; his last project, with Glennette Tilley Turner, was creating the illustrations for *Take A Walk in Their Shoes* (1989), a project paying homage to fourteen African Americans who overcame struggle, controversy or difficulty in their lives, to achieve success and transform our global community. After a productive career that spanned almost sixty years, Fax's works remain a compelling testament to his search for the shared humanity of the peoples of the world, which he sought to translate, preserve, and represent in his art and insightful writings.

FURTHER READING

Fax, Elton. *Black Artists of the New Generation* (1977).

Fax, Elton. "It's Been a Beautiful but Rugged Journey," in *Black American Literature Forum* (Autumn 1986).

Bearden, Romare, and Harry Henderson. *A History of African-American Artists 1792–Present* (1993).

York, Jennifer M., editor, *Who's Who Among African Americans*, 16th Edition (2003).

FRANK MARTIN

Fayerweather, Sarah Ann Harris (16 Apr. 1812–16 Nov 1878), antislavery reformer, was born Sarah Ann Harris in Norwich, Connecticut, one of the twelve children of Sallie Prentice Harris and

William Monteflora Harris, a West Indian immigrant. The family attended the Congregational Church in Westminster, a village four miles to the west of Canterbury, and it was there in 1818 that young Harris made a profession of faith and joined the church.

In January 1832 her father purchased a farm and house outside of Canterbury village. That fall, twenty-year-old Harris learned that Prudence Crandall, a young Rhode Island woman with a Quaker background, was beginning a school for girls, and she asked to attend as a day student. She seemed unaware that the presence of an African American student, even one appearing "almost colorless ivory," would be-controversial, but after Harris was accepted, white-parents immediately withdrew their daughters (Brown, 28). Crandall, however, continued her school, advertising in the 2 March 1833 edition of William Lloyd Garrison's abolitionist paper, the *Liberator*, that she would be accepting "young ladies and little misses of color" from several states.

The school became a battleground between the antislavery forces of Garrison and the racist-inspired advocates of the American Colonization Society. Crandall, Harris, and the other students endured near constant threats and harassment: mobs broke their windows, the bodies of dead animals poisoned their well, and they could hardly walk the streets without trouble. On 24 May 1833 Connecticut legislators then passed a bill outlawing the instruction of non-resident blacks. Crandall kept the school open until 9 September 1834, when an arson attempt on the house convinced her that the lives of her pupils were at risk. The state arrested, tried, and eventually convicted Crandall of breaking the state law against instructing non-resident African Americans, although the conviction was later overturned. As the ordeal splashed over the state's newspapers, fewer and fewer residents wanted the odious distinction of imprisoning a woman for teaching, which helped Crandall successfully avoid a long imprisonment. But the school's closure represented a bitter defeat for antislavery forces.

Sarah Harris had been a day student, not a boarder, but as a Canterbury resident, both she and her entire family suffered from the controversy. However, this experience taught Harris the power of antislavery convictions and of friendship, and by 1833 she had begun to reconsider her goal of teaching. She withdrew from classes at Crandall's school and on 28 November 1833 married George Fayerweather III of South Kingston, Rhode Island. She sent a piece of the wedding cake to Helen and William Lloyd Garrison in Boston, a gesture of friendship and thanksgiving for his support of her school.

The couple settled in Canterbury and then moved to New Haven in the 1840s. Fayerweather maintained ties with abolitionists by subscribing to Garrison's the *Liberator*. On occasion, Sarah and George Fayerweather visited the Fayerweather clan in South Kingston, where several of her in-laws were charter members of the local antislavery society. Fayerweather bore six children: Prudence Crandall (1834), Sarah (1835), Isabella (1839), George H. (1842), and Charles (1846). In 1855 the family moved to South Kingston, where her husband began working in the family blacksmith business and the couple joined the Congregational Church.

Well known for her role in integrating Crandall's school, Fayerweather hosted numerous antislavery leaders, whether they were simply passing through, organizing a meeting, or serving as the featured speaker. Several seem to have visited simply to have a private conversation with Sarah Fayerweather. These visitors included the Garrisons, FREDERICK DOUGLASS, WILLIAM WELLS BROWN, and the Hutchinson family singers, the group known for their antislavery song, "Get Off the Tracks, Emancipation's Coming." Assisted by her daughters and sisters-in-law, she supported the antislavery cause by helping with fundraising fairs and by circulating petitions against slavery. Fayerweather also retained her ties with Prudence Crandall throughout the years. After her school closed, Crandall married Rev. Calvin Philleo and moved to Illinois, and Fayerweather and Crandall corresponded, filling their letters with news about children, grandchildren, and progress toward freedom in the South. Fayerweather sent her daughter Isabella to boarding school in New Bedford, Massachusetts, which provided a much larger community of African Americans and antislavery activists. and traveled to antislavery meetings in Boston and New York City. At one such meeting, she met a daughter of Rev. Calvin Philleo, Prudence Crandall's stepdaughter. Philleo reported to a relative that she found Sarah Harris Fayerweather an excellent conversationalist, "very intelligent and ladylike, well informed in every movement relative to the removal of slavery" (Woodward, 10). Fayerweather's enthusiasm for her work continued with her children. Daughter Sarah and son George H. went south during the Civil War to teach the newly freed slaves.

After the war, Fayerweather wrote Garrison: "I praise the name of the Lord that he has prolonged your precious life to see this day. My joy is full" (Woodward, 11). In the postwar period, the Fayerweather family prospered, with Sarah acquiring title to a house and thirty-three acres in Kingston. A widow for nine years, she continued to receive visits from abolitionist friends.

FURTHER READING

The Fayerweather Papers are held at the Special Collections, University of Rhode Island.

"Sarah Harris Fayerweather," in *Homespun Heroines and Other Women of Distinction*, comp. Hallie Q. Brown (1988).

Van Broekhoven, Deborah Bingham. *The Devotion of These Women: Rhode Island in the Antislavery Network* (2002).

Woodward, Carl R. "A Profile in Dedication, Sarah Harris and the Fayerweather Family," *The New England Galaxy* 15 (Summer 1973).

DEBORAH BINGHAM VAN BROEKHOVEN

Fearing, Maria (1838–23 May 1937), domestic servant, teacher, and missionary, was born in Gainesville, Alabama, the daughter of Mary and Jesse Fearing, who were slaves of the planter Overton Winston and his wife Amanda Winston. At a young age Mrs. Winston removed Fearing from the care of her parents and began to train her, alongside her older sister, for work inside the plantation house.

Mrs. Winston, a Presbyterian, taught Fearing Bible stories, hymns, and the Westminster catechism, and she impressed upon Fearing the importance of foreign missions. As a young woman Fearing joined the Winstons' church, a congregation affiliated with the Southern Presbyterian Church in the United States.

After the Civil War Fearing stayed in Gainesville and sought employment as a domestic servant. Motivated by a desire to read the Bible for herself, Fearing gained some measure of literacy through the help of friends. In 1871 a minister told Fearing about Talladega College, a school in Talladega, Alabama, founded by former slaves and supported by the Missionary Association of the Congregational Church. Fearing used her savings to travel to Talladega, where, at the age of thirty-three, she worked to support herself and enrolled in the school's beginners' class. Fearing stayed at Talladega for ten years and completed the ninth grade, at which point she left and taught at a rural school near Anniston, Alabama. Despite her meager salary she saved enough money to buy a home in Anniston and paid the expenses for one of her students to study at Talladega.

After several years of teaching, Fearing returned to Talladega and worked as the assistant matron of the "boarding department." In addition to supervising female students she canned fruits and vegetables and cleaned the school buildings. In 1894 WILLIAM H. SHEPPARD, an African American minister and missionary, spoke at Talladega about his efforts to found a Southern Presbyterian mission in the Belgian Congo. Since Sheppard's white coworker, Samuel N. Lapsley, had died shortly after their work began, Sheppard had returned to the United States to recruit volunteers and raise funds for the American Presbyterian Congo Mission. Sheppard had recently married Lucy Gannt, another Talladega graduate whom Fearing had supervised in the 1880s.

Motivated by her long dormant interest in foreign missions, Fearing at age fifty-six applied to the Presbyterian Executive Committee of Foreign Missions, which turned her down on the grounds that she was too old to send to Africa. The Talladega College faculty wrote the committee on her behalf, and Fearing visited Lapsley's father, a prominent Alabama judge. With Lapsley's encouragement, Fearing offered to pay all of her own expenses for her journey to Africa and her work at the Congo mission. She raised the funds by selling her house to Lapsley and by raising donations. The committee finally relented, and in May 1894 Fearing traveled to Africa with the Sheppards and one other African American volunteer.

Following the long journey across the Atlantic and up the Congo River, Fearing arrived at the church's Luebo mission station, where she would live and work for the next twenty-three years. Fearing helped the other missionaries with various domestic tasks, learned the local dialect, taught Sunday school, and attempted to evangelize the local population.

Fearing began taking orphaned children—many of whom had been kidnapped into slavery—into her care at Luebo. The missionaries called Fearing's home "Pantops," after a Presbyterian school in Virginia. Within several years the Pantops Home housed nearly fifty African children. Fearing trained them in basic domestic skills, introduced them to Western styles of dress and courtship, and also taught them about her Christian faith. The American Presbyterian Congo Mission experienced little evangelistic success in its first decade, but three of the mission's first seven converts were girls under the care of Fearing. Impressed with Fearing's work the Committee of Foreign Missions began gradually to offer her some financial support. Only after several years did she receive the same salary as the other missionaries.

Fearing took a brief furlough to the United States in 1906 to receive medical attention but quickly returned to Luebo. For twelve of her twenty-three years in the Congo, Fearing shared her home with Lillian Thomas, another former Talladega student. Althea Brown Edmiston, another missionary colleague, wrote of Fearing and Thomas that "their friendship, love, and devotion for each other were akin to that of Ruth and Naomi." Fearing was saddened when Thomas married fellow missionary Lucius A. DeYampert, but the two women visited each other daily. In 1917 she accompanied the DeYamperts on a second furlough.

Although she wanted to return to the Congo, the Presbyterian mission board urged Fearing—now almost eighty—to retire. Age, however, might not have been the only issue on the mission board's mind. Race may also have played a role. Though the mission had been interracial since the beginnings in the early 1890s, the Southern Presbyterian Church had gradually reduced its number of black missionaries. Resigned to remaining in Alabama, Fearing lived with the DeYamperts for more than ten years and taught Sunday school at a Presbyterian church in Selma. In 1928, when she was ninety years old, she fell and broke her hip, which enfeebled her for the remainder of her life. After Lillian DeYampert's death in 1929 Fearing remained in the home and helped raise the DeYamperts' two daughters until Lucius DeYampert remarried in 1931. She spent the last six years of her life with one of her nephews.

FURTHER READING

Edmiston, Althea Brown. "Maria Fearing: A Mother to African Girls," in *Glorious Living: Informal Sketches of Seven Women Missionaries of the Presbyterian Church, U. S.*, ed. Sarah Lee Vinson Timmons (1937).

Phipps, William E. *William Sheppard: Congo's African American Livingstone* (2002).

JOHN G. TURNER

Fenty, Adrian (6 Dec. 1970–), politician, was born Adrian Malik Fenty in Washington, D.C., the second-oldest son of Jan and Phillip Fenty. His Italian American mother and Afro-Panamanian father, both avid runners, are owners since 1984 of Fleet Feet, an athletic apparel and shoe store in the multicultural Adams Morgan neighborhood of Washington, D.C. Fenty was raised in Mount Pleasant, a middle-class community in northwest Washington, D.C., along with his older brother Shawn and his younger brother Jess. He attended Macklin Catholic High School and graduated from Woodrow Wilson Senior High School, both in the District of Columbia. Fenty inherited his parent's appreciation for running and participated in high school track and field. Having also adopted their zeal for social and political activism, early on he aspired to a career in law. Desiring a rural experience compared to his familiar urban lifestyle, Fenty declined acceptance at Columbia University in New York and instead enrolled at Oberlin College in Ohio, where in 1992 he earned a Bachelor of Arts in English and Economics. He returned to Washington, D.C., to attend law school at Howard University and earned a Juris Doctorate in 1996.

Fenty gained practical experience in politics as an intern for Senator Howard Metzenbaum (D-OH), Delegate ELEANOR HOLMES NORTON (D-DC), and Representative Joseph P. Kennedy II (D-MA). Subsequently, he became involved in local politics, first as an advisory neighborhood commissioner and later as elected president of the 16th Street Neighborhood Association. For two years, Fenty worked as lead attorney and counsel for the D.C. Council Committee on Education, Libraries, and Recreation. When he decided to run for Ward Four Council, in 2000, he defeated the four-term incumbent Charlene Drew Jarvis, the daughter of the blood plasma and transfusion pioneer CHARLES DREW, by a 57–43 percent margin via an aggressive door-to-door campaign. Fenty was elected for a second term in 2004 after he ran unopposed in both the primary and the general elections.

On 1 June 2005 Fenty announced his campaign for mayor of Washington, D.C. The then-current mayor, Anthony A. Williams, announced that he would not seek reelection and endorsed Council Chair Linda Cropp. Other candidates in the mayoral race included Councilmember Vincent Orange, the businesswoman Marie Johns, and the lobbyist Michael Brown. On 12 September 2006 Fenty made history in the District of Columbia by winning all 142 precincts in the Democratic primary and earning 89 percent of the vote in the general election. In November 2006 Fenty was elected the fifth mayor of the District of Columbia; at age thirty-five, he was also the youngest mayor in the District's history. During his tenure in office his approval ratings

Adrian Fenty, Washington, D.C., mayor, arrives with his wife, Michelle, and daughter, Aerin, as he prepares to vote in the city's 14 Sept. 2010 mayoral primary. (AP Images.)

dropped across a range of issues, which include city schools, creating jobs, and eliminating waste; in contrast, his approval rating for crime reduction increased, primarily owing to votes from white D.C. residents. He has been applauded for attracting new businesses and improving city services but some District residents have questioned his honesty, empathy, and openness because of perceived neglect in the African American compared to the predominantly white neighborhoods and secrecy regarding funds received from the United Arab Emirates for a weeklong trip to Dubai and $11,300 from government entities in China to attend the 2008 Summer Olympics in Beijing.

Fenty is a member of Kappa Alpha Psi fraternity and the Mayors against Illegal Guns Coalition. He participates in triathlons and other races in the District of Columbia and throughout the mid-Atlantic region. In 2008 Fenty publicly endorsed Senator Barack Obama for president of the United States. In 2009 he signed the Religious Freedom and Civil Marriage Equality Act of 2009 to legalize same-sex marriage in Washington, D.C. Fenty's 2010 mayoral campaign broke fund-raising records in the District of Columbia, but he was ultimately unsuccessful in his re-election bid, losing to Vincent C. Gray.

Fenty met his future wife, Michelle Cross, at Howard University Law School in 1994. He was a first-year student; she, British born and of Jamaican descent, was a third-year student and mentor to the former. The couple was married in 1997; together they have twin sons, Matthew and Andrew (2000) and a daughter, Aerin Alexandra (2008).

FURTHER READING

Ifill, Gwen. *The Breakthrough: Politics and Race in the Age of Obama* (2009).

Koncius, Jura. "Campaign Stop: Where Fenty Takes a Break From His Run for Mayor." *Washington Post*, 3 Aug. 2006.

Stewart, Nikkita, and John Cohen, "D.C. Mayor Fenty's Approval Ratings Plummet, Poll Finds." *Washington Post*, 31 January 2010.

SAFIYA DALILAH HOSKINS

Ferebee, Dorothy Boulding (10 Oct. 1898–14 Sept. 1980), physician and social reformer, was born Dorothy Celeste Boulding in Norfolk, Virginia, the daughter of Benjamin Richard Boulding, a superintendent with the railroad mail service, and Florence Cornelia Ruffin, a teacher. She came from a well-established family in which several members were lawyers, but from childhood she wanted to be a physician. When her mother became ill, Ferebee went to live with an aunt in Boston, where she attended secondary school. She graduated from two respected Boston area institutions, Simmons College in 1920 with honors and Tufts University College of Medicine in 1924. Her accomplishments were especially notable because many educational institutions of the time discriminated against women and African Americans. In her class of 137 medical students there were only five women, and, as Ferebee explained, "We women were always the last to get assignments in amphitheaters and clinics. And I? I was the last of the last because not only was I a woman, but a Negro, too." Although Ferebee graduated among the top five students in her medical class, one after another white hospital rejected her application, which required a photograph. Finally Freedmen's Hospital, a black hospital in Washington, D.C., accepted her. In 1927, after she completed her internship, nearby Howard University Medical School hired her as an instructor of obstetrics. She was affiliated with Howard University for most of her professional life, first as an instructor of medical and nursing students and then as medical director of Howard University Health Service from 1949 to 1968. In 1930 she married Claude Thurston Ferebee, a dentist, with whom she had twins, a daughter and a son.

Ferebee settled into a busy life in Washington, D.C., devoting her time to family, teaching, private obstetrical practice, and social reform work. For thirteen years she served as president of the Southeast Settlement House, which she founded in 1929. This center provided day care and recreational opportunities to children. Ferebee had first seen the need for social services for African Americans while performing ambulance duty in the poor black section of the city. The final impetus came when she rescued a nine-year-old boy from the police station. He had been taken in for stealing milk from his neighbor's porch for the younger brother he was watching. Ferebee later explained, "I went down and got him and paid for the milk and right then decided we needed a place for black children of working mothers."

Ferebee's interest in health and welfare for black communities continued throughout her life, but it was her service as medical director of the Alpha Kappa Alpha Mississippi Health Project that led to her national reputation in the field. From 1935 to 1942 she directed a public health program for African Americans in the Mississippi Delta. The project was sponsored by Alpha Kappa Alpha, the oldest black sorority in the United States, founded at Howard University in 1908. For several weeks every summer during the Great Depression, Ferebee led a dozen sorority volunteers in a campaign of medical examinations, vaccinations, and health education. Each summer three thousand to four thousand people attended the clinics, and over the course of the project volunteers immunized fifteen thousand children against smallpox and diphtheria. From 1939 to 1941, during Ferebee's term as head of the sorority, she widely publicized the importance of the health project through numerous public lectures and a CBS radio broadcast.

A poised speaker with political savvy, Ferebee expanded her activities at the national and international levels. She served on the national boards of directors for the YWCA and the Girl Scouts, and from 1971 to 1974 she chaired the District of Columbia's Commission on the Status of Women. One of her proudest moments occurred in 1959, when Simmons College awarded her its first Distinguished Alumna Award. In 1949 she was elected the second president of the National Council of Negro Women, a coalition of organizations representing thousands of black women. In 1951 the U.S. State Department sent her as a delegate to a meeting in Greece of the International Council of Women of the World. Soon after this, the Women's Bureau of the U.S. Department of Labor sent her to Germany to join an international delegation observing the postwar situation of women and children. A decade later, the U.S. State Department and the Peace Corps selected her as a medical consultant; in 1967 she spoke before the World Health Organization Assembly in Geneva, Switzerland. Her international experiences led Ferebee to see herself as part of a global community.

Ferebee was a tireless advocate for human rights and health reform, and her personal life may have suffered in the process. Her husband, who was at one time an instructor at Howard University, grew resentful of her successful career. He even asked her to give up her work, which she would never do willingly. After years of separation, they finally divorced after their daughter died of pneumonia in 1950. Ferebee continued to live in Washington, D.C., until her death there.

FURTHER READING

Ferebee's papers are at the Moorland-Spingarn Research Center at Howard University in Washington, D.C.

Smith, Susan. *Sick and Tired of Being Sick and Tired: Black Women's Health Activism in America, 1890–1950* (1995).

Obituary: *Washington Post*, 16 Sept. 1980.

This entry is taken from the *American National Biography* and is published here with the permission of the American Council of Learned Societies.

SUSAN L. SMITH

Ferebee, London R. (18 Aug. 1849–?), writer, sailor, soldier, teacher, and minister, was one of ten children born in North Carolina to Abel Ferebee, a slave and minister of the African Methodist Episcopal (AME) Zion Church, and Chloe (maiden name unknown), a slave. When London was young his mother was sold, apparently because of her unwillingness to submit to her master and her ability to beat him in a fight. She was sold to a speculator, who offered to sell her to her husband or his master, who had allowed Ferebee to hire himself out to a local farmer so that they both profited from his labor. When she was subsequently bought by one of the two men—it is unclear which—London and two of his siblings were allowed to move with her, though they all remained enslaved.

Once he was old enough to begin laboring, London was immediately set to work on board the ship of Captain E. T. Cowles, and by the age of twelve he had learned to navigate some of the most difficult waters on North Carolina's coast. Because of the boy's nautical abilities Captain Cowles treated him relatively fairly, though Ferebee later recalled that Cowles's wife was not so generous. On 9 August 1861, when Ferebee was only twelve years old, Union forces occupied Roanoke Island, freeing him and the other slaves living there at the time. He immediately headed toward Union lines to seek the protection of the army, only barely outrunning his owner, who tried to take him back into slavery. Ferebee remained with the Union army until he was released on New Year's Day 1863, after which he returned to his family.

His entire family then followed the army to New Bern, North Carolina, where Ferebee immediately enrolled in a newly opened Freedman's Bureau school for black children. They moved again to Roanoke, where Ferebee again enrolled in school, rose quickly to the head of the class, and was soon appointed as an assistant teacher, even though he was still learning to write the alphabet. His enthusiasm for learning was such that he would fill whole notebooks in a single evening of studying and writing. Ferebee's lively intelligence intimidated others in the class, however, even prompting one envious student to stab him. Yet such setbacks did not deter him from continuing his own education and dedicating himself to the education of other freed slaves. In 1866, realizing that his freedom was now assured and that he was free to move anywhere in the country, Ferebee took classes to prepare him for matriculation at Howard University in Washington, D.C., but found that his teacher attended only to his light-skinned students. Undeterred by such discrimination, Ferebee enrolled in the normal college at the Hampton Institute in Virginia and embarked on the teaching career he would continue throughout his life.

Having decided in the late 1860s that he wanted to study law, Ferebee returned to North Carolina and moved to the home of a white judge, C. C. Pool, who agreed to teach him Latin and help him to prepare for a legal career. While teaching to maintain his board, Ferebee began to make connections in the political world and became active in the Republican Party. He ran for election to the North Carolina legislature but was undone by a conspiracy of black and white men, which accused him of forging the school vouchers by which he was paid as a teacher, thereby undermining his respect in the community. According to Ferebee's account the case came to court numerous times, but despite the lack of evidence against him he was found guilty and jailed for twenty-seven days. Pardoned by the governor of North Carolina, he continued to pursue his interest in politics throughout the rest of his life, perhaps until the 1900 disfranchisement campaign, which all but ended black participation in North Carolina politics for several decades. It is unknown when he died.

London Ferebee became a minister in 1877 and was proud of the number of people he had helped to convert. Like many former slaves he spent every effort to improve his own learning and the education of others, and belonged to the post-Emancipation generation of African Americans who were determined to seek the educational opportunities denied to them while enslaved.

FURTHER READING

Ferebee, London R. *A Brief History of the Slave Life of Rev. L. R. Ferebee, and the Battles of Life, and Four Years of His Ministerial Life. Written from Memory. To 1882* (1882).

Cecelski, David S. *The Waterman's Song: Slavery and Freedom in Maritime North Carolina* (2001).

Williams, Heather Andrea. *Self-Taught: African American Education in Slavery and Freedom* (2005).

LAURA MURPHY

Ferguson, Angella Dorothea (15 Feb. 1925–), medical researcher, pediatrician, and hospital administrator, was born in Washington, D.C., to George and Mary Ferguson, occupations unknown. Despite having grown up poor, she decided to become a secretary or an accountant and somehow found enough money to enter Howard University. During her sophomore year, she took a chemistry course that redirected her education and led her to pursue a career in science and medicine. After receiving a B.S. in Chemistry in 1945, she entered the Howard University Medical School and received an M.D. in 1949. Upon completing her internship and residency in pediatrics at Washington's Freedmen's Hospital, which was also Howard's teaching hospital, she opened a private practice as a pediatrician in the nation's capital.

Because Ferguson's practice catered to African American patients, she became interested in determining what constituted normal development in an African American infant. She quickly realized, however, that no reliable answer existed because all of the pediatric studies concerned themselves only with infants of European-American ancestry. This discovery led her to collaborate with Roland Scott, one of her pediatrics colleagues at Howard who had been one of her former professors, in a formal study of early childhood development for African Americans. The study revealed that, in some respects, growing up in poverty, as many African Americans were forced to do in the 1950s, was actually a good thing for an infant's development. For example, the inability of many black parents to purchase such luxuries as playpens and highchairs meant that their children grew up relatively unrestrained, and thus learned to walk and sit up earlier than did white babies.

The study, however, also revealed that that many of the otherwise healthy-appearing babies actually suffered from sickle-cell anemia, a medical condition resulting from a genetic condition common among African and Mediterranean peoples, that has been linked to exposure to malaria, a deadly disease that proliferates in warm climates. The condition causes abnormalities in hemoglobin, the molecule within red blood cells that carries oxygen in the bloodstream. Unlike normal hemoglobin (Hb A), abnormal hemoglobin (Hb S) becomes stacked within the red blood cells in filaments that twist into helical rods. These rods then associate themselves into parallel bundles that distort and elongate the red cells, causing them to become rigid and assume a sickle shape. Because they are deformed, sickle cells deteriorate faster than do normal cells, thus causing anemia and death. To date, no cure has been found for sickle-cell anemia.

Having discovered the prevalence of sickle-cell anemia among African American children, Ferguson next set out to identify the normal development pattern for the disease from the infant to preteen years. She discovered that, between birth and age two, pain and swelling begin to plague the joints, especially the ankles and wrists. From two to six, the abdomen and the internal organs, especially the liver and spleen, begin to swell, the result of which is often the development of a potbelly. From six to twelve, the symptoms recede somewhat, but by age twelve ulcers often begin to develop on the legs. She also discovered what is now known as the "sickle cell crisis," during which damaged red cells clog up a blood vessel, thus causing severe pain, swelling, skin ulcers, and brain damage. Fortunately, Ferguson also discovered that a glass of soda water once a day for children under the age of five decreases the tendency of damaged red cells to clog blood vessels, thus offering some relief from sickle cell crisis. She also discovered that, whenever surgery is performed on a patient with sickle-cell anemia, the symptoms of the condition get significantly worse unless extra oxygen is administered during the procedure.

In addition to her private practice and medical research, Ferguson enjoyed a thirty-eight year career with Howard University as a faculty member and hospital administrator. In 1953 she became an instructor of pediatrics at Howard, and in 1963 she was appointed associate pediatrician at Freedmen's. In 1965 she was named to oversee the construction of the pediatrics wing at Howard University Hospital (HUH), a modern facility that replaced the Freedmen's Hospital. Shortly thereafter, she was named director of programs and facilities of the new hospital and was given oversight over the construction of the entire hospital. Upon completion of HUH in 1975, she was named associate vice president for health affairs. Over the next sixteen years, she oversaw the construction of several more medical facilities at the hospital. In 1991 she retired, having never married, to her home in Washington.

FURTHER READING

Hayden, Robert C. *Eleven African American Doctors* (1992).

Spangenburg, Ray, and Kit Moser. *African Americans in Science, Math, and Invention* (2003).

CHARLES W. CAREY JR.

Ferguson, Clarence Clyde, Jr. (4 Nov. 1924–21 Dec. 1983), law professor, dean, and diplomat, was born in Wilmington, North Carolina, to the Reverend Clarence Clyde Ferguson Sr. and Georgeva Ferguson. After a childhood in Baltimore he served in the U.S. Army from 1942 to 1946, earning a Bronze Star, before attending Ohio State University on a football scholarship. He soon left the football squad to focus on his academic work, completing his AB cum laude in two and a half years. Ferguson earned his LLB cum laude from Harvard Law School in 1951, one of three black members of the class.

After a year as a teaching fellow at Harvard Law School and a year in private practice in New York, Ferguson served as assistant general counsel to the Moreland Act Commission to Investigate Harness Racing. Ferguson married the artist and sculptor Dolores Zimmerman in 1954. After her death in the late 1960s, he raised three daughters alone. From 1954 to 1955 he was assistant United States attorney for the southern district of New York. From 1955 to 1962 he taught at Rutgers University in New Jersey, becoming the first African American law professor to receive tenure there. While at Rutgers he produced two casebooks, *Materials on Trial Presentations* and *Enforcement and Collection of Judgments and Liens*, and authored New Jersey's annotations on Uniform Commercial Code secured transactions. In 1957 he co-authored, with Albert Blaustein, *Desegregation and the Law*. A commercial and critical success, the book combined an appreciation of the Supreme Court's decision in *Brown v. Board of Education* (1954) with a critique of the ruling's "with all deliberate speed" standard.

In the same year Ferguson argued in a speech to the American Bar Association that any use of federal funds that would support segregation was unconstitutional. As general counsel to the Civil Rights Commission from 1961 to 1963, and in law review articles thereafter, he argued for the federal government to use its power to insert and enforce nondiscrimination requirements and to withhold appropriated funds from states that did not end discriminatory practices. From 1963 to 1969 he was dean of Howard Law School. Ferguson was an early advocate of affirmative action. In his article "Civil Rights Legislation 1964: A Study of Constitutional Resources," published in the *Federal Bar Journal*, he wrote that "the emphasis in civil rights is shifting from prohibitory negative measures such as prohibitions against acting out racially discriminatory attitudes, to positive measures requiring affirmative actions designed to assure full opportunity in the society which we now know." In the same period he was among the framers of what became the National Legal Services Program of the Office of Economic Opportunity. In 1964 he organized a major symposium at Howard on international human rights, a subject on which, while at Rutgers in 1956, he had created the first course taught in the United States. He was elected U.S. Expert to the United Nations Sub-Commission on Discrimination in 1965 and was a drafter of the 1967 UNESCO Statement on Race.

It was for his work in diplomacy and human rights that Ferguson gained greatest prominence. His first diplomatic work was in 1952, when he served as a U.S. representative to the Western Hemisphere UNESCO Conference in Cuba. This became a full-time job for six years starting in 1969, when President Richard Nixon named him ambassador at large and special coordinator for Nigeria/Biafra civilian relief. Shuttling among Lagos, New York, the papal secretary of state in Rome, and the International Red Cross in Geneva, Ferguson negotiated the Protocol on Relief to Nigerian Civilian Victims of the Civil War; this and the UNESCO Statement on Race were the two efforts of which he said that he felt most proud. From 1970 to 1972 he was ambassador to Uganda. He was deputy assistant secretary of state for African affairs from 1972 to 1973 and was U.S. ambassador to the U.N. Economic and Social Council from 1973 to 1975. He returned to Harvard Law School in 1975 to teach. In 1978 he was elected president of the American Society of International Law, the first African American to hold the position.

Ferguson viewed international human rights and national civil rights as deeply intertwined, and he fought against injustices as far apart as apartheid in South Africa and terrorism in El Salvador. "It is absolutely certain," he told the TransAfrica Forum in 1983, "that there is no hard line between domestic policy and foreign policy, and you can look the spectrum over. We are what we are, and if we ignore the suffering of black people in Africa it is simply the reflection of how black people are being treated here." In the last years of his life he focused increasingly on the links between human rights and economic development, economic security, and a protected environment. During the week in which he died he circulated a preliminary outline for a human rights program at Harvard Law School.

Ferguson's life was punctuated by personal setbacks, both out of principle and from prejudice and misfortune. At Ohio State he declined a nomination for a Rhodes Scholarship, preferring not to profit from the legacy of the colonialist Cecil Rhodes. As a student at Harvard his grades were just barely too low for him to be made an editor of the *Harvard Law Review*; "this near miss," wrote DERRICK BELL, "in a time when racial discrimination was both legal and widespread, left unanswered questions and lasting bitterness." A lifelong Republican, Ferguson advised senators Clifford Chase of New Jersey and Jacob Javits of New York, as well as New York governor Nelson Rockefeller, but he paid a price for his affiliation. As Bell wrote, "his hope that his government performance would lead to a well-deserved federal court judgeship was doomed when his political party moved swiftly to the right and conservative power brokers intensified their determination to exclude from important appointments even faithful party members of color." According to Walter Leonard, Ferguson was passed over for an appointment to the Federal Court of Appeals for the Third Circuit because he was not the Nixon Administration's "kind of Republican"; this was, wrote Leonard, "one of Clyde's greatest disappointments in life."

In 1977 Ferguson was the second African American professor to receive tenure at Harvard Law School, after Derrick Bell, who believed that Ferguson should have been the first. "While he did much," said Derrick Bell in memoriam, "he was a victim of racial timing, destined never to play out his full potential, or exhibit the full range of his talents. Clyde lived during a time of racial transition when the possibility of equal opportunity brought to blacks who sought it more frustration than fulfillment."

FURTHER READING

C. Clyde Ferguson's papers and a collection of photographs of him are held by the Langdell Library at Harvard Law School.

Bell, Derrick. "A Tragedy of Timing," *Harvard Civil Rights–Civil Liberties Law Review* 19 (1984): 277–280.

C. Clyde Ferguson, 1924–1983: Program of a Memorial Service Held Jan. 19, 1984, at Memorial Church, Harvard University (1984).

Cahn, Jean Camper. "Turn Back Now?" *Harvard Civil Rights–Civil Liberties Law Review* 19 (1984): 281–290.

"Ex-Howard Dean Named Law Society President," *Washington Post*, 29 Apr. 1978.

Leonard, Walter J. "Crossing the Lonesome Valley," *Harvard Civil Rights–Civil Liberties Law Review* 19 (1984): 297–308.

Mitchell, Clarence. "Recollections of C. Clyde Ferguson, Jr.," *Harvard Civil Rights–Civil Liberties Law Review* 19 (1984): 291–296.

"A Tribute to the Memory of Clarence Clyde Ferguson, Jr. (1924–1983)," *Harvard Civil Rights–Civil Liberties Law Review* 19 (1984): 270–276.

Obituary: *Boston Globe*, 22 Dec. 1983.

BENJAMIN LETZLER

Ferguson, David Arthur (8 June 1875–10 Feb. 1935), dentist, dental and medical organizational leader, hospital founder, and author, was born in Portsmouth, Ohio, the oldest of the six children of William B. Ferguson and Cornelia Taylor Ferguson. William Ferguson was a noted educator in Portsmouth, Ohio, in Bowling Green, Kentucky, and at the Christiansburg Industrial Institute in Virginia. David's brother George R. Ferguson, M.D., served as assistant secretary for the National Medical Association (NMA), and his nephew William Ferguson Reid, M.D., was the first African American elected to the Virginia legislature in the twentieth century.

In 1885 William Ferguson moved his family to Bowling Green, Kentucky, where David Ferguson completed grammar school and embarked upon the first of two invaluable dentistry apprenticeships. In 1889 Ferguson began apprenticing for the white dentist Dr. E.T. Barr, for whom he worked until shortly before returning to Portsmouth, Ohio, to enter high school in fall 1892. While in high school he was in charge of the white dentist Dr. Charles P. Dennis's laboratory.

Ferguson graduated from high school in 1896 and enrolled in Howard University's dental college. With his extensive experience and abilities he became an assistant to the dental college demonstrators and several local dentists. In 1897 he married Antoinette V. Carter, and they had two children. Ferguson received his DDS in 1899 and relocated to Richmond, Virginia, where he was granted a temporary license until the dental board could meet in 1900. Ferguson, then more commonly referred to by his first two initials, D.A., passed the dental boards and became the first African American to sit before the Virginia State Board of Dental Examiners.

With few exceptions, organizations representing organized medicine and dentistry at the local, regional, and national levels excluded African Americans from membership in the late nineteenth century. Thus African Americans formed parallel organizations. In 1880 perhaps only a dozen African American dentists had received licenses to practice. By the dawn of the twentieth century, however, their ranks had grown as a direct result of the founding of the dental schools at Howard University and Meharry Medical College in the 1880s. Washington, D.C., was home to the first local medical and dental societies founded by African Americans: the Medico-Chirurgical Society of Washington, D.C., in 1884, and the Washington Society of Colored Dentists of D.C., in 1900.

Several African American physicians had promulgated the need for a national entity to represent themselves, and the National Negro Medical Association of Physicians, Dentists, and Pharmacists (later known as the National Medical Association, or NMA) was founded in 1895, in conjunction with the Cotton States Exposition in Atlanta. In July 1901 the National Association of Colored Dentists was founded in Washington, D.C., spearheaded by Ferguson and Drs. Andrew Gwathney, William Lofton, Charles Fry, D. W. Onley, and Richard Baker, among others. Ferguson was elected president. This organization did not garner sustained support, although it sowed the seeds for future successful organizations. Ferguson became active in the NMA in 1905 and later became chairman of the NMA's highly influential dental section.

In February 1902 Ferguson became a founding member of the Medical and Chirurgical Society of Richmond, Virginia. This organization, founded at the home of Dr. SARAH G. JONES, the first woman of any race to be granted a license by the Virginia State Board of Medical Examiners, included African American physicians, dentists, and pharmacists from Richmond and Manchester. In October 1902 Ferguson and other core members organized the Richmond Hospital Association to establish the Richmond Hospital and Training School for Nurses, which provided a vital continuum of care, because black doctors were generally denied privileges at the white-run hospitals that admitted black patients. Ferguson served as secretary-treasurer of the Richmond Hospital Association and also as an anatomy and physiology instructor at the school.

Ferguson authored several articles on dental practice. He was an early proponent of affiliated dental surgery wards at Howard and Meharry in order to provide graduates experience in this emerging specialty. He lectured and wrote on the importance of high ethical standards and provided numerous workshops on dental procedures at annual medical and dental conventions. In 1907 Ferguson self-published *Souvenir Views: Negro Enterprises and Residences, Richmond, Virginia*, a book containing extraordinarily rare photographs of early black churches, schools, and businesses.

Ferguson was unanimously elected NMA vice president in 1912. The NMA's dental section provided the infrastructure needed to form a tri-state dental society made up of black dentists from Maryland, Virginia, and the District of Columbia. Ferguson proposed the idea in 1912 to the Robert T. Freeman Dental Society (formerly the Washington Society of Colored Dentists of D.C.) and chaired a committee to lead the effort. The Old Dominion State Dental Society was organized in February 1913, paving the way for the Tri-State Dental Association in July 1913, of which Ferguson was president from 1913 to 1918. He was also a founding member of Richmond's Peter B. Ramsey Dental Society in 1917. When the NMA created the office of president-elect, he was unanimously elected in 1917 and made history in 1918 by becoming the first nonphysician to be elected NMA president. During his presidency Ferguson logged more than forty-eight hundred miles visiting constituent societies nationwide to garner support for the NMA. In 1918 the Tri-State Dental Association was reorganized into the Interstate Dental Association to reflect its growing membership.

Ferguson's dedication to excellence permeated every facet of his life. He was a faithful member of Saint Philip's Episcopal Church in Richmond and worked tirelessly in civic organizations. He lobbied for racial inclusiveness in local politics and even ran unsuccessfully for a seat in the Virginia House of Delegates in 1921. He continuously advocated the need for a national organization for black dentists, and in 1932 his work came to fruition with the reorganization of the Interstate Dental Association into the National Dental Association (NDA). In paying homage to its founding father, the NDA members elected Ferguson their first president.

Ferguson died at his home in Richmond at age fifty-nine. In lamenting his passing in the *Journal of the National Medical Association*, the NMA general secretary Walter G. Alexander, M.D., wrote in part, "Without discredit to any, it can be said without fear of contradiction, that no member of the medical profession contributed more to the development of the National Medical Association than D. A. Ferguson."

FURTHER READING

Dummett, Clifton O., and Lois Doyle Dummett. *NDA II: The Story of America's Second National Dental Association* (2000).

Mather, Frank Lincoln, ed. *Who's Who of the Colored Race: A General Biographical Dictionary of Men and Women of African Descent*, vol. 1 (1915).

Webb, Harvey, Jr., and Lloyd Cecil Rhodes. *The Book of Presidents: Leaders of Organized Dentistry* (1977).

Obituaries: *Journal of the National Medical Association* 27.4 (1935); *Richmond Planet* 16 Feb. 1935.

ELVATRICE PARKER BELSCHES

Ferguson, Katy (1774 or 1779–11 July 1854), educator and philanthropist, was born Catherine Williams as her mother, Katy Williams, a slave, was in transit from Virginia to New York City. Nothing is known of her father. When she was only eight years old Katy was separated forever from her mother, who was sold by their master. She later credited her own compassion for children to the pain she suffered at the loss. Katy underwent a conversion experience at the age of fourteen or fifteen and shortly afterward, in 1789, joined New York's Scotch Presbyterian Church (later the Second Presbyterian Church), possibly causing some controversy among the white members of the church, which spatially separated white and black worshippers.

When Katy was sixteen or seventeen she was purchased by a New York woman for $200. The woman's plan was to allow Katy her freedom after six years work in compensation for the payment. However, she agreed to commute the first $100 for eleven months work, and the other $100 was raised by the philanthropist Divie Bethune. Katy married at the age of eighteen, taking her husband's name, Ferguson, and had two children. Both children and her husband, of whom little is known, died young. As a free adult Ferguson supported herself as a cleaner of fine lace and a cakemaker to New York's social elite.

At some time in the late eighteenth or early nineteenth century Ferguson began teaching neighborhood children in her home at 51 Warren Street on Sundays. The Sunday school movement only began in England in the late eighteenth century and initially had little effect on the United States. Ferguson's school was possibly the first Sunday school in New York City and one of the first in the United States. Lewis Tappan, the evangelical abolitionist whose obituary for Ferguson—in part based on an interview with her—is the most important source for her life, does not give a specific date for the founding of Ferguson's school, although he claims that it was the first Sunday school in New York. He described it as beginning with Ferguson's informal instruction of neighborhood children in her home. Around 1814 the school was moved from Ferguson's home to the Murray Hill Presbyterian Church. Ferguson's school is described as integrated and including adults as well as children. She was allied with white New York philanthropists and Sunday school promoters including Bethune and his wife Joanna, Isabella Graham, and the pastor of the Scotch Presbyterian Church, Dr. John M. Mason. Ferguson's ability to instruct the children herself was limited by her own illiteracy. However, she had memorized large portions of the Bible and was able to check the children's reading against her memory. Ministerial students, including Isaac Ferris, later chancellor of New York University, and others visited Ferguson's school to instruct the students in reading and the catechism. Ferguson also took in orphans, black and white. Tappan claimed that she had at one time or another fostered forty-eight children, twenty of them white. She held prayer meetings in her home on Friday nights for forty years, and in her later years on Sunday afternoons as well. Ferguson was concerned about gambling's influence on New York's poor, and she supported missionary efforts in Africa.

Ferguson died of cholera in her home at 74 Thompson Street in New York. After her death, her fame increased as evangelicals and African American writers began to use her life story as inspirational material. The first document giving this heroic narrative of Ferguson's life was Tappan's obituary in the *New York Daily Tribune*. Tappan, whose narrative was based on an interview he had conducted with Ferguson in 1850, referred to her as a "mother in Israel" and a "Christian philanthropist." He portrayed Ferguson as a humble, pious, and loving Christian heroine. Tappan published a slightly revised version of the obituary in the *American Missionary*, which served as the chief source for subsequent biographers. A biography and portrait of Ferguson appeared in Benson J. Lossing's frequently reprinted *Our Countrymen; or Brief Memoirs of Eminent Americans* (first published in 1855), and she was the subject of the American Tract Society's undated four-page pamphlet *Katy Ferguson: Or What a Poor Colored Woman May Do*, which drew heavily from Tappan's obituary. She was included in HALLIE Q. BROWN'S 1927 *Homespun Heroines and Other Women of Distinction*. The Katy Ferguson Home, a privately supported institution that opened in 1920 in New York, was the first American institution for unwed African American mothers. The African American composer and organist Eugene W. Hancock also devoted a musical composition to Ferguson, *Katy Ferguson*.

FURTHER READING

Hartvik, Allen. "Catherine Ferguson: Black Founder of a Sunday School," *Negro History Bulletin* 35 (1972); Reprinted in *Negro History Bulletin* 59 (1996).

Tappan, Lewis. "Catherine Ferguson," *American Missionary* 8:10 (Aug. 1854).

WILLIAM E. BURNS

Ferguson, Lloyd Noel (9 Feb. 1918–), chemist and educator, was born in Oakland, California, to Noel Swithin Ferguson, an insurance office clerk, and Gwendolyn Johnson, who may have been a domestic. When his father lost his job and the family home during the Great Depression, Ferguson was forced to work as a paperboy and as a porter for the Southern Pacific Railroad Company. His need for employment postponed his entrance into college. While in high school Ferguson invented practical household products such as Moth-O (a moth repellent), Presto-O (a silverware cleaner), and Lem-O (a lemonade powder), which he advertised and sold to neighbors. In 1936 he entered the University of California at Berkeley, majoring in chemistry. He graduated with honors in 1940 and was one of nine African Americans awarded bachelor's degrees that year. Although he enjoyed friendly relations with the chemistry faculty (four became Nobel laureates), he was snubbed by student members of Alpha Chi Sigma, a chemists fraternity.

Intending to become an educator, and personally encouraged by the Tuskegee Institute's GEORGE WASHINGTON CARVER, with whom he had corresponded, Ferguson applied and was accepted to do graduate study at the University of California at Berkeley. He was given the job of placing cans of carbon tetrachloride in a cyclotron at the Donner Laboratory and harvesting the radioactive sulfur that resulted. He also worked on a military project that successfully developed a compound that resupplied oxygen in submarines. Ferguson's sensitive work for the government's war effort exempted him from military service. By completing his dissertation, "Absorption Spectra of Some Linear Conjugated Compounds," in 1943, he became the first black student to earn a doctorate in chemistry at Berkeley. The following year he married Charlotte Welch, and they were to have three children.

Ignored by corporate recruiters and forewarned by his graduate adviser that he would not be able to find a job in industry because of his race, Ferguson began teaching as an assistant professor at North Carolina Agricultural and Technical College in 1944. In 1945 he accepted a faculty appointment at Howard University. He remained there for two decades and started the school's doctoral program in chemistry—the first of its kind at a historically black school. In 1965 he was hired to teach at the California State University at Los Angeles (CSULA). Ferguson served terms as chemistry department chairman at both universities and spent sabbaticals in Copenhagen at the Carlsberg Laboratory, with a Guggenheim fellowship, in 1953; and in Zürich at the Swiss Federal Institute of Technology, with a National Science Foundation fellowship, in 1961. With the support of a Ford Foundation grant, he was a visiting professor at the University of Nairobi in Kenya in 1971.

A specialist in organic chemistry and biochemistry, early in his career as a professor Ferguson presented papers and published his research on the chemistry of aroma and taste. Later he focused his research on alicycles and the mechanisms of chemotherapy in relation to naturally occurring organic substances such as steroids and certain antibiotics and vitamins. Ferguson's cancer research sprang from his membership in the National Cancer Institute Chemotherapy Advisory Committee from 1972 to 1975. In the November 1975 issue of the *Journal of Chemical Education*, he published an article titled "Cancer: How Can Chemists Help?" He authored six widely used textbooks: *Electron Structures of Organic Molecules* (1952), *Textbook of Organic Chemistry* (1958), *The Modern Structural Theory of Organic Chemistry*

(1963), *Organic Chemistry: A Science and an Art* (1972), *Highlights of Alicyclic Chemistry* (1973), and *Organic Molecular Structure: A Gateway to Advanced Organic Chemistry* (1975). A colleague once pointed out that, ironically, in the early 1960s—when white students at the University of Mississippi were rioting and protesting against allowing James Meredith, the first black student to enroll—they were unaware that they had been studying chemistry from textbooks written by Ferguson, an African American, and that once a publisher declined to put his photograph on a book jacket for fear of losing sales.

Ferguson was also quite active in professional associations and in efforts to increase the number of African Americans studying science and technology. His work in the American Chemical Society (ACS) would lead to his chairmanship of both the ACS Division of Chemical Education in 1980 and the California Section of ACS. He received numerous invitations by organizations like the National Institutes of Health (NIH), the United Negro College Fund, and the Woodrow Wilson Foundation to serve in various capacities. In the 1960s, as the director of the NIH Minority Biomedical Research Program at CSULA and of the ACS Project SEED (Support of the Educationally and Economically Disadvantaged), Ferguson played a key role in steering blacks and other minorities to careers in the sciences. Additionally, he wrote articles and made oral presentations to high school students and their teachers and counselors to publicize the challenges of and opportunities in scientific careers. He was a fellow of both the American Association for the Advancement of Science and the Chemical Society of London. In 1972 Ferguson co-founded the National Organization for the Professional Advancement of Black Chemists and Chemical Engineers.

He was the recipient of several awards for excellence in teaching, including the California State University and Colleges Trustees Outstanding Professor Award in 1981. He received honorary academic degrees from Howard University in 1970 and Coe College in 1979. Among his recognitions and awards were his inclusion in the CIBA-Geigy Corporation "Exceptional Black Scientists" poster series, mention of his birthday in the ACS "Milestones in Chemistry Calendar," and the 1978 ACS George C. Pimentel Award in Chemical Education.

Ferguson returned to live in the San Francisco Bay area upon retiring from teaching in 1986 but maintained his ties with CSULA as a professor emeritus. In 1995 the annual Lloyd N. Ferguson Distinguished Lecture was established in his honor at CSCLA to bring distinguished scientists to speak at the university. His importance to the development of African Americans and chemistry will forever be marked by the Lloyd Ferguson Young Scientist Award, presented annually by the National Organization for the Professional Advancement of Black Chemists and Chemical Engineers.

FURTHER READING

Hornsby, Alton, Jr., ed. *Who's Who among African Americans* (2004).

Morris, Gabrielle. Interview with Lloyd N. Ferguson, 3 Aug. 1992.

Nagel, M. C. "Lloyd N. Ferguson," in *Notable Black American Scientists*, ed. Kristine Krapp (1999).

Webster, Raymond B. *African American Firsts in Science and Technology* (1999).

ROBERT FIKES JR.

Ferguson, Thomas Jefferson (15 Sept. 1830–30 Mar. 1887), educator, politician, activist, pastor, author, and Masonic leader, was born in Essex County, Virginia, to free parents of mixed white and black ancestry. In 1831 Virginia outlawed the education of free blacks, and many of them migrated to other states, including Ohio. The Act of 1831 may account for the migration of Ferguson's family to Cincinnati, which Ferguson listed as his home when he attended Albany Manual Labor Academy (AMLA) in Albany, Ohio. While it is unclear how Ferguson attained an elementary education, the Albany Manual Labor University records list T. J. Ferguson of Cincinnati as a student in the collegiate department during the 1857–1859 academic year. James Monroe Trotter, veteran of the Fifty-fifth Massachusetts Regiment and musicologist, also attended AMLA. Incorporated as a university in 1853, Albany Manual Labor University (AMLU) offered an integrated education, which accepted students regardless of color or gender. During the antebellum period, besides Oberlin College and Wilberforce University, no other institution in Ohio permitted integrated education. In 1862, however, AMLU closed its doors. Because its replacement in the region Franklin University did not permit the admittance of blacks, a contingent of black men established Albany Enterprise Academy in the town. One of its first soliciting agents who raised funds for the institution was Thomas Jefferson Ferguson.

After graduating from AMLU, Ferguson taught school in many of the rural communities in Ohio and West Virginia. In 1863 he became an agent for the all-black board of Albany Enterprise Academy. Peter H. Clark, an educator and civil rights leader in Cincinnati, was the first president of the board. In addition to Clark, several other notable black men in the region, such as John H. Williams of Chillicothe, Ohio, organized the institution. Clark and the board insisted that the academy be black owned and controlled. Through black ownership the board sustained blacks' educational, political, social, and economic advancement. Whereas Oberlin allowed blacks entrance and Wilberforce educated blacks only, neither was created, owned, and controlled by blacks. Hence, the board could hire whomever they desired and institute a curriculum that would strengthen the position of blacks within the United States. At one time, WILLIAM SANDERS SCARBOROUGH, future president of Wilberforce University, taught at the academy. Scarborough, like his contemporaries, held firm to his belief in the power of education to advance black people. By 1866 Ferguson, like Scarborough, was a teacher at the institution. Eventually Ferguson would become principal and president of the board during his relationship with the institution, one that would last until its closing in 1886, some twenty-three years later.

In 1859 Ferguson purchased land in Albany, where on 9 August 1860 Ferguson married F. R. Cassels, of whom little is known. Ferguson's first wife died on 1 December 1861. Their first son, Ralph Waldo Emerson Ferguson, was born in 1861. R. Waldo Emerson Ferguson published a local paper called *Waldo's Diadem: Literature, Culture and Progress* in Albany from 1883 to 1895. According to the Athens County Court House Records, in 1865 T. J. Ferguson married Margaret B. Taylor. However, records indicate that Ferguson later remarried. In the 1880 census of Albany, Ferguson is married to a woman named Almira, who was born in Virginia; Ferguson was listed as having five children. The entire family is designated as being of mixed black-and-white ancestry. According to the 1885 issue of *Waldo's Diadem*, Ferguson's daughter Luella conducted a school in Middleport, Ohio, where Ferguson had once been a teacher.

During his lifetime Ferguson served as a pioneer in many areas. In 1861 Ferguson founded the Ohio Colored Teachers' Association, and in 1872 he became the first black member of the Albany City Council. He served as president of the Mass Convention of Colored Voters in Athens County in 1879, and in 1880 became the first black to serve on a jury in Athens County. Today a portrait of Ferguson hangs in the Athens County Courthouse. Despite his political activism, which was chronicled by the historian CARTER G. WOODSON, it was Ferguson's work as an educator that had significant effect on the uplift of black people.

Long before the BOOKER T. WASHINGTON and W. E. B. DUBOIS debate of the late nineteenth and early twentieth century regarding the purpose of education for blacks, Ferguson, in his short book *Negro Education: The Hope of the Race* (1866), argued for unlimited access to educational curricula for blacks, particularly Southern blacks. Ferguson contended that education was the means by which blacks would secure personal, political, economic, and social freedom. He advocated that blacks pursue a multidimensional approach to attaining full-citizenship rights. African Americans needed power, and not just political access. Ferguson believed that education prepared people to live as full citizens and to fulfill their destiny in life. Education imparted blacks with dignity and the ability to master their own humanity. Political and educational attainment would advance all African Americans, and Ferguson placed the lion's share of the responsibility specifically on the shoulders of black teachers. Black teachers, he contended, played a central role in the elevation of black people, which moved him to organize the first black teachers' organization in Ohio. He linked the education of blacks not just with the hope of black community but the hope of the country as well.

During his tenure as agent, teacher, principal, and board president, Ferguson raised funds for the institution, taught courses, served as principal and led the board. Consequently, Ferguson through his actions provided the means by which black youth gained the knowledge to prepare to be "teachers or educators of their race or to fill with honor other useful positions in Society" (*Albany Enterprise Academy Catalogue*, 1870). As board president, Ferguson continued the work of Clark, who had organized the Albany Enterprise Academy, through maintaining an educational institution that produced exemplary and competent black teachers, leaders, and professionals of all kinds, in Ohio and elsewhere.

In 1886, after a fire destroyed a good portion of the school, including the dormitory, Albany Enterprise Academy closed. Because of ill health, Ferguson had already retired from the academy. He died on 30 March 1887. In his obituary in the *Athens Messenger*, Ferguson was heralded as a "colored man of exceptional ability" who "possessed unusual gifts as a public speaker" (5). Yet Ferguson was not just a speaker of the word but also a doer. His leadership at the Albany Enterprise Academy provided exemplary schooling for many black youths who became educators, businesspeople, and lawyers. Former students of the academy who went on to distinguish themselves were Olivia Davidson Washington, educator and philanthropist of Tuskegee and Booker T. Washington's second wife; Andrew Jackson Davison, the first black attorney in Athens, Ohio; Edward C. Berry, who owned and operated the Berry Hotel in Athens, Ohio; William H. Holland, Texas politician and educator; and Milton M. Holland, 1872 Howard law graduate and founder of the Alpha Insurance Company in Washington, D.C. Ferguson altered the political, religious, social, and educational efficacy of black Americans whether it was through the classroom, the pulpit, or the courthouse.

FURTHER READING

Ferguson, T. F. *Negro Education: The Hope of the Race* (1866).

African Americans in Southeast Ohio. Available online at http://www.seorf.ohiou.edu/~xx057/.

Jackson, Luther P. *Free Negro Labor and Property Holding in Virginia, 1830–1860* (1942).

Logan, Rayford, W., and Michael R. Winston. *Dictionary of American Negro Biography* (1982).

Ward Randolph, Adah. "Building Upon Cultural Capital: Thomas Jefferson Ferguson and the Albany Enterprise Academy in Southeast Ohio: 1863–1886," *Journal of African American History* (Spring 2002).

Obituary: *Athens Messenger*, 7 Apr. 1887.

ADAH WARD RANDOLPH

Fernandis, Sarah Collins (8 Mar. 1863–11 July 1951), educator, social worker, community activist, and poet, was born in Port Deposit, Maryland, the fourth child of Caleb Alexander and Mary Jane Driver Collins, free African Americans. By 1870 the family was living in Baltimore, where her father worked in a lumberyard and her mother, as did many African American women of the era, worked as a laundress in her home. Collins may have attended a public school, which Baltimore established for African Americans in 1867, or one of numerous private schools that had served Baltimore's black community since the early nineteenth century. She enrolled in the Hampton Institute at age fourteen and graduated in 1882 as salutatorian. At New York University she earned a degree in social work sometime around 1904. She probably chose NYU because African Americans could not enroll in professional schools in the segregated Maryland–Washington, D.C., area.

Collins, like most female Hampton graduates, entered the field of education and in keeping with the school's philosophy worked for the uplift of the entire community. Beginning around 1882 she worked at the Women's Home Missionary Society of Boston, founded in 1880 to financially support teachers in southern schools, and later taught at Hampton and in Philadelphia, North Carolina, Tennessee, Florida, and Baltimore. While teaching in Baltimore, Collins boarded at the home of Rebecca Fernandis, and in 1902 married Fernandis's son, John, a barber who followed the same trade as his father and his Brazilian immigrant grandfather. Since Maryland law prohibited married women from teaching in public schools, Collins and her husband moved to Washington, D.C. Fernandis was hired by Associated Charities, a private national social service agency, to establish its "Colored Department" in a neighborhood so infested with poverty-driven violence that it was called "Bloodfield." It was also fertile ground for her social work and teaching skills. Again in keeping with the Hampton model, Fernandis envisioned a community acting collectively to attack the forces threatening to destroy it. Because her definition of community was broad, she worked with neighborhood residents and with affluent people of both races to organize and operate the Colored Social Settlement House, which opened in October 1902 and was the first such facility for blacks in the nation. The facility offered its residents a variety of services, including a kindergarten, day nursery and library, clubs for children and adults, a food pantry, and sewing and cooking lessons. Ferdinand remained until the time of her enrollment at NYU.

Following graduation from New York University, Fernandis worked in a settlement house in Greenwich, Rhode Island, and in 1913 returned to Baltimore, where she opened a day nursery that offered child-care services and child-rearing lessons for working women. Her vehicle for social change was the Women's Cooperative Civic League (WCCL), Baltimore's first interracial, interfaith group, founded in 1913 by a white socialite and a white physician, and of which Fernandis was elected president. Housing in Baltimore was racially segregated and, under Fernandis's leadership, the WCCL successfully lobbied the sanitation department to provide the same cleaning services in black neighborhoods as it did in white ones. As a result the health department took steps to ensure that milk was sold under sanitary conditions and the city razed an entire residential block where tuberculosis was epidemic and subsequently provided better housing for the displaced residents. Fernandis's group obtained federal funds to build Baltimore's first playground for black children and began a school lunch program, while also successfully petitioning for legislation to require compulsory school attendance. In addition to her employment with the WCCL, Fernandis volunteered with the YMCA, juvenile court, city Welfare Department, and the Children's Aid Society, founded in 1872 in Baltimore to protect and care for the city's indigent and neglected children. She continually preached the gospel of cooperative improvement efforts during visits to community members' homes and at various organizational meetings.

At the onset of World War I Fernandis relocated to Chester, Pennsylvania, where she established a community center for black soldiers. Returning to Baltimore in 1920 she was hired as a social worker in the city's venereal disease clinic, becoming the first black person in the city so employed. In conjunction with the WCCL and a biracial group of health-care professionals, she campaigned for the creation of Henryton State Hospital, Maryland's first residential treatment facility for blacks with tuberculosis. In addition she served as a lecturer for the National League of Women Voters. Fernandis retired from her position with the health department venereal disease clinic in 1933 but continued to work in the WCCL settlement house until 1936. In that year she opened the National Youth Administration Office, a residential job training service for homeless women. Subsequently she volunteered with a variety of agencies and organizations. The author of the lyrics to Hampton's school song, Fernandis also contributed numerous articles to the school's journal, *The Southern Workman*. She was also a prolific poet whose themes frequently echoed her demonstrated commitment to community uplift.

For almost seventy years Fernandis forged alliances across racial and class lines to attack institutionalized practices and policies that degraded African American communities. She placed emphasis on working with those in need of social services and sought to help people to identify and solve their own problems. Her methods were nationally and internationally emulated—social workers from throughout the country and from Oxford, England, and London's East End came to observe and learn from her work—and she was recognized during her lifetime by groups such as the National Conference of Charities and Corrections, the American Institute of Social Service, and the NAACP. Her work is memorialized in Baltimore by a room, named in her honor, at the YMCA. Fernandis died in Baltimore at the age of eighty-eight.

FURTHER READING

Curah, Huguette A. "Sarah Collins Fernandis and Her Hidden Work," in *African American Leadership: An Empowerment Tradition in Social Welfare History* (2001).

Hathaway, Phyllis. "Sara A. Collins Fernandis, 1863–1951 First Negro Social Worker," in *Notable Maryland Women* (1977).

Neverdon-Morton, Cynthia. *Afro-American Women of the South and the Advancement of the Race, 1895–1925* (1989).

Shaw, Stephanie J. *What A Woman Ought To Be and To Do: Black Professional Women Workers during the Jim Crow Era* (1996).

DONNA TYLER HOLLIE

Ferrell, Frank J. (1852–?), activist, inventor, and entrepreneur, was born in Virginia. It is unknown whether he was born free or enslaved. Little information about his early life and education is available. He moved to New York City and in 1873 married Henrietta (maiden name unknown), a New Yorker. The couple had no children. Ferrell reported his occupation as engineer, a term commonly used in this era for machinist, stationary engineer, or boiler tender.

During the 1880s Ferrell joined the Noble Order of the Knights of Labor, the largest labor union in nineteenth-century America. After a major growth spurt in 1885–1886 the organization counted over 600,000 members. The Knights were an inclusive labor organization that enrolled employers and workers, excluding only lawyers, bankers, and liquor peddlers, and unlike most such organizations of the period the Knights accepted African American members. Ferrell belonged to District Assembly 49, a large, politicized union that encompassed the membership in New York City. Ferrell taught economics in a workers' school run by

District Assembly 49 and served as the union's secretary-treasurer. Also active in New York City's Central Labor Union, he was selected for the honorary position of captain of police for its 1884 labor parade.

In October 1886 Ferrell was one of 60 delegates, and the only African American, selected by District Assembly 49 to attend the Knights' annual national convention at Richmond, Virginia, the former capital of the Confederacy. Ferrell and his fellow delegates from New York City were determined to use Richmond as the site to demonstrate the Knights's commitment to a multiracial labor movement. When a Richmond hotel refused to lodge Ferrell, the entire group went to a black boardinghouse. At the opening of the convention Ferrell sat on the stage with Virginia's governor, Fitzhugh Lee, who welcomed the more than 800 delegates, and Grand Master Workman Terence V. Powderly, the Knights's leader. Ferrell's introduction of Powderly was reported in newspapers across America. There was some approval, but considerable disapproval of a black man occupying such a stage as an equal. The New York delegation challenged southern segregation further when it attended a production of *Hamlet* at the Mozart Academy of Music and sat in the whites-only section with Ferrell, a display that prompted another round of commentary in the press. Ferrell became the face of integration for those Knights who wanted to project an image of racial cooperation with black workers.

The labor solidarity espoused by the Knights of Labor did not extend to the Chinese, however, who experienced virulent racism capped by the enactment of the federal Chinese Exclusion Act of 1882, which barred Chinese laborers from entering the United States and denied them naturalization. Ferrell was among a small number of American workers who fought to include Chinese in the labor movement. In 1887 he cooperated with other labor leaders in District Assembly 49 to recruit approximately five hundred Chinese into two of the Knights's local assemblies. The General Executive Board, the Knights's governing body, refused to grant union charters to these locals but eventually allowed the Chinese to join existing locals.

In addition to labor activism Ferrell was involved in electoral politics during the 1880s. In 1883 Ferrell was elected as the first vice president of an association of black New Yorkers who banded together to endorse candidates for public office. Third party efforts, especially for local offices, reached a high point in 1886, as workers formed parties pledged to labor reform. In August 1886, two months prior to gaining national attention during the Knights's national convention, Ferrell became involved in the mayoral campaign to elect Henry George, a nationally known author and advocate of the single tax, an anti-monopoly tax it was hoped would ensure the orderly functioning of the economic marketplace.

The political arm of the Central Labor Union encouraged George to stand for office. Ferrell served on the platform committee of this draft movement and headed the efforts in the eleventh state assembly district, one of the city's twenty-four districts, to set up the new party's apparatus. At the nominating convention held in September, Ferrell, an effective orator, seconded George's nomination. "Our political movement will work a peaceful revolution," proclaimed Ferrell to over four hundred delegates, "a revolution as decisive as that which John Brown preached" (Foner, *History*, 121). George lost the fall 1886 election and the following year saw the United Labor Party defeated in campaigns for statewide office. During the later campaign Ferrell served as vice president of the fledging party, but after the demise of the third party effort he switched his party affiliation to the Republican Party. Ferrell's support of the Republicans resulted in a patronage appointment in 1890 as the chief engineer at the U.S. Post Office building in New York City. In 1894 the "anti-machine" Republican faction selected Ferrell as its candidate in an unsuccessful run for the eleventh state assembly district.

Aside from such commitments to labor and political activities and his job as an engineer, Ferrell was a successful inventor, securing ten U.S. patents between 1884 and 1893. His first patented invention was a "clothes drier," a clothesline with folding arms. In 1890 he received patents for a "steam trap" and an "apparatus for melting snow." Between 1890 and 1893 Ferrell earned patents for seven valves.

Ferrell left the employ of the U.S. Post Office in 1892 to start the Ferrell Manufacturing Company, a steam and gas fitting business. In late 1899 he filed for bankruptcy, listing liabilities of $150,479 against assets of $52,078. At the time he owned three properties, including an eighty-acre farm in Virginia and two Manhattan dwellings. He lost one of his two Manhattan properties in 1900 and the other was foreclosed in 1907. No further mention of Ferrell in the historical record has been located, other than a 1920 obituary note for his wife, Henrietta, who worked eight years as the superintendent of the White Rose Home for young black working women. Ferrell achieved recognition as both an inventor and a labor and political activist during the Gilded Age.

FURTHER READING

Foner, Philip S. *The Black Worker during the Era of the Knights of Labor* (1978).

Foner, Philip S. *History of the Labor Movement of the United States*, vol. 2 (1955).

Foner, Philip S. *Organized Labor and the Black Worker, 1619–1981* (1982).

Kessler, Sidney H. "Organization of Negroes in the Knights of Labor," *Journal of Negro History* 37 (July 1952).

Miner, Claudia. "The 1886 Convention of the Knights of Labor," *Phylon* 44.2 (1983).

PAUL A. FRISCH

Ferrill, London (1789–1854), minister, was born in Hanover, Virginia, to an enslaved woman, and was named after his mother's owner, a British man named Richard Ferrill. Upon Richard Ferrill's death his sister inherited both London and his mother, and when London was eight or nine she separated him from his mother by selling him to a Colonel Samuel Overton for six hundred dollars. Overton eventually freed Ferrill, though the details of his emancipation are not entirely clear.

Ferrill dated his religious conversion to a near-death experience in his childhood, when he nearly drowned. Believing that he would have gone to hell had he died, Ferrill made a covenant with God in the belief that it would change his fate. His baptism at age twenty was an important moment in his life, and he soon felt called to preach. At a time when religious revivals in the South were often integrated, Ferrill's preaching earned praise from both white and black Christians all over Virginia.

After the death of his owner, Ferrill moved to Kentucky, where in 1817 the Trustees of Lexington asked him to serve as a preacher for the local black community. Ferrill consented, as did the congregation of Lexington's African Baptist Church, but his early years of preaching were not without their difficulties. Some men, perhaps jealous of his success, tried to replace him as pastor or created competing churches. Others sought to defame his character. Despite their efforts Ferrill's church gained popularity, was renamed the Elkhorn Baptist Church, a branch of the white First Baptist Church in Lexington, and Ferrill went on to full ordination, able to perform baptisms and other official duties of a minister. By 1833 Ferrill had a large enough congregation and had gathered up enough funds to buy the former white Old Methodist Meeting House, which he renamed the First African Baptist Church. During Ferrill's time as minister the church's congregation grew to over 1,800 members, making it the largest church in Kentucky at the time.

In June of 1833 a cholera outbreak left more than five hundred of Lexington's six thousand residents dead and forced many more to flee the city. All the preachers left, except for Ferrill, who stayed behind to pray for the living and to bury the dead, black and white. Even the death of his own wife in the epidemic did not deter him from coming to the aid of other victims. He decided to forgo marrying another wife so that he could dedicate his life fully to the work of the church. In the years after his wife's death, Ferrill adopted two children, Eleazer Jackson and his own younger sister, Elizabeth Jackson, and they lived together in a house he built in 1839 next to his church.

Ferrill's life story was recorded and published before his death in 1854 by an unknown author in a work titled *Biography of London Ferrill, Pastor of the First Baptist Church of Colored Persons, Lexington, KY*. His death was marked by a grand burial in the Episcopal burial ground. Said to be one of the largest funerals in Lexington history, it is claimed to be second only to Henry Clay's, the famous one-time speaker of the U.S. House, secretary of state, and an early (though wavering) voice for abolition in the American South.

FURTHER READING

Biography of London Ferrill, Pastor of the First Baptist Church of Colored Persons, Lexington, KY (1854).

LAURA MURPHY

Fetchit, Stepin (30 May 1892–19 Nov. 1985), actor, was born Lincoln Theodore Monroe Andrew Perry in Key West, Florida, to immigrant parents that arrived in the United States from the Bahamas just prior to his birth in 1892. His family lived in Key West until Perry was six years old, and then moved to Tampa. According to Fox Studio's biographical information on the actor, Perry lost both of his parents when he was quite young. A well-to-do black woman his mother once worked for took care of him for a time, sending him to Catholic school in Alabama. However, Perry did not take to academics. An inveterate class clown, he eventually ran away from the school and found work in traveling vaudeville and minstrel shows. Although a number of apocryphal stories circulate regarding the

Stepin Fetchit as Gummy in the 1929 movie *Hearts in Dixie*, one of the first all-talkie studio productions to boast a predominantly African American cast. (AP Images.)

origins of Perry's stage name, Stepin Fetchit, the earliest use of this phrase in association with the actor appeared in the early 1920s, when Perry wrote a regular entertainment column for the *Chicago Defender*, a prominent African American newspaper. "Lincoln Perry's Letter" chronicled the activities of the growing black entertainment community in Los Angeles and touted the author's own work as half of a vaudeville act called Step and Fetch It. When his partner left the duo, Perry took the name as his own. As Stepin Fetchit, he appeared in nearly fifty Hollywood films. He continued to write the column into his early years as Stepin Fetchit as well, offering aspiring actors and actresses advice about entering show business.

Stepin Fetchit first appeared on screen in an independently produced film titled *The Mysterious Stranger* (1925). The first of his films with a major Hollywood studio was MGM's *In Old Kentucky* (1927), which featured Fetchit in a small role as a stable boy. In the ensuing years, he appeared in other films, including the 1929 version of *Show Boat*, playing Joe, the same role that celebrated actor Paul Robeson would make famous almost seven years later. In 1929, Fetchit got a major break in Fox's all-black-cast musical *Hearts in Dixie*. He appeared as Gummy, a shiftless, tragicomic black character that would set the standard for the Stepin Fetchit image and performance. Fetchit's trademark bald head, shambling gait, laconic expression, and drawling, garbled speech all made their combined debut in *Hearts in Dixie*.

Stepin Fetchit's appearance as Gummy also signified the beginning of his association with Fox. Fetchit was one of the first black actors to sign a long-term contract with a major film studio; he would ultimately make twenty-four films for Fox. Indeed, part of his myth as an African American screen icon is that in his heyday he was a millionaire once or twice over. This is a myth that Fetchit himself helped to circulate, especially in interviews he granted in the later years of his life. Yet the studio records from his Hollywood days suggest that Fetchit lived his entire film career hand-to-mouth. He had two periods of employment with Fox, one from 1928 until 1929, and a second from 1933 until 1937. The most that Stepin Fetchit was ever paid by Fox was $750 per week. Although this was a handsome sum for a black actor in 1930s America, it would not have made Fetchit a millionaire, and his notorious spendthrift habits kept the actor always waiting for an advance. His patchy work record while not working for Fox eventually landed him in bankruptcy at least twice in his lifetime, once in 1931, and again in 1947. Yet the significance of his relationship with Fox cannot be overlooked.

During this era most black actors could not depend upon steady work with any one production company. They instead had to accept whatever roles they could find, moving from studio to studio. Indeed, this was Fetchit's own experience during his 1929–1933 hiatus from Fox, when he appeared in eight non-Fox films, including *A Tough Winter*, one of the *Our Gang* shorts produced by Hal Roach. The comedian's career is a testament to the mixed blessing that a studio contract could offer. On the one hand, he was at the mercy of the studio, which could drop him at will. On the other, his consistent work and exposure in Fox's films allowed him to develop Stepin Fetchit into an instantly identifiable character that gave him a visibility and notoriety he would enjoy at the height of his career.

Stepin Fetchit was perhaps at his most memorable in the films of John Ford, in which he appeared with the popular actor Will Rogers. The duo appeared in a triad of films for Fox in the mid-1930s, *Judge Priest* (1934), *David Harum* (1934), and *Steamboat Round the Bend* (1935). The films presented a softened and paternalistic vision of American race relations. *Judge Priest*, for instance, opens in a post–Civil War Southern town; Fetchit's character Jeff Poindexter is on trial for chicken-stealing, but is befriended by the town's folksy, lovable Judge Priest (Rogers), who looks after him and takes him fishing. However, Fetchit's idiosyncratic performances in this trio of films also suggest the way his characters could be slyly manipulative of whites.

Nonetheless, Fetchit's glory days were short-lived. During his hiatus from the studio, he had married, fathered a son, and had a highly publicized separation from his wife, who alleged brutality and nonsupport. The actor was bankrupt when he signed with the studio the second time, and he quickly acquired new debts, which included attorneys' fees and judgments against him in various civil court cases for fraud, assault, breach of marriage, and disorderly conduct. Once Fetchit had been re-signed, Fox publicly claimed to be putting his money into a "trust fund," yet the studio actually garnished his check in order to repay loans and advances that had been made on his behalf. The *Chicago Defender*, for which he had once written columns offering thoughtful counsel to entertainers "of the race," criticized him regularly now (as did other black newspapers), publicizing his bankruptcy when he was not working and condemning his scandals and excesses when he was. In his memoir *Amateur Night at the Apollo*, Fetchit's friend, actor, and impresario Ralph Cooper, recalled that one of the actor's ostentatious Cadillacs arrived daily on the Fox set ferrying Fetchit's supply of near beer, "which he drank like water all day long" (Cooper, 126).

When Fetchit stopped work on the set of the Shirley Temple vehicle *The Littlest Rebel* in 1935, claiming medical problems, the studio suspended him. Further, in a move that deeply angered and humiliated Fetchit, Fox replaced him with younger actor Willie Best, who was now capitalizing on Fetchit's fame by billing himself as "Sleep 'n' Eat." Although Fox continued to employ Fetchit through 1937, ostensibly so that he could repay his debts to the studio, toward the end, his brief and isolated appearances in Fox films like *On the Avenue* (1937) reflected his declining fortunes in Hollywood. As the 1930s drew to a close, Fetchit made an appearance alongside fellow comedian W. C. Fields in Hal Roach's *Zenobia* (1939) as a character named Zero. *Zenobia* marked the beginning of his absence from Hollywood films for the next decade and a half.

In the meantime, he made theater appearances, played nightclubs, and performed in a few all-black cast films. Though he reprised his role as Jeff Poindexter in John Ford's period piece *The Sun Shines Bright* (1953) and appeared sporadically after in offbeat movies like *Amazing Grace* (1974) and *Won Ton Ton, the Dog Who Saved Hollywood* (1976), by the 1960s, Stepin Fetchit was a character many decades out of step with the time. As the racial tide in the United States turned, Fetchit tried to turn with it, joining the Nation of Islam. He sharpened the racial content of his iconoclastic stage show, and became associated with boxer MUHAMMAD ALI. In interviews, Fetchit drew parallels between his friendship with Ali and his past friendship with another legendary and outspoken African American boxer, JACK JOHNSON. But such refinements did not shield Fetchit from the harsh criticisms of younger blacks, many of whom were taking part in the civil rights movement and the emerging Black Power movement, and saw him as a racial pariah. He was criticized in a 1968 CBS television documentary hosted by BILL COSBY, *Black History: Lost, Stolen or Strayed*, for perpetuating stereotypical and degrading images of African Americans. Fetchit refuted the charges in media interviews, citing his career as a pioneering effort that made a career the likes of Cosby's possible. Fetchit filed a $3 million lawsuit against CBS for defamation of character, though his case was dismissed in 1974.

A year later, in 1976, Fetchit suffered a severe stroke and was hospitalized with partial paralysis and loss of speech. As a result, he became a resident patient at the Motion Picture Country Home and Hospital in Woodland Hills, California. Fetchit died in 1985 from complications from pneumonia and congestive heart failure.

Fetchit performed with many stars of the classic Hollywood era, including Spencer Tracy, Shirley Temple, Lionel Barrymore, and Alice Faye. His image, though distasteful to most today, was not significantly worse than the roles played by his African American contemporaries in the 1930s. His career and his life provide a sense of the price that African Americans paid to be represented in American popular culture.

FURTHER READING

A partial collection of Stepin Fetchit's papers can be found in the Margaret Herrick Library, Academy of Motion Picture Arts and Sciences, Beverly Hills, California.

Bogle, Donald. *Toms, Coons, Mulattoes, Mammies & Bucks: An Interpretive History of Blacks in American Films* (1996).

Cooper, Ralph. *Amateur Night at the Apollo: Ralph Cooper Presents Five Decades of Great Entertainment* (1990).

Cripps, Thomas. "Stepin Fetchit and the Politics of Performance," in *Beyond the Stars: Stock Characters in American Popular Film*, eds. Paul Loukides and Linda K. Fuller (1990).

Watkins, Mel. *On The Real Side: A History of African American Comedy* (1999).

Watkins, Mel. *Stepin Fetchit: The Life and Times of Lincoln Perry* (2005).

Obituary: "Stepin Fetchit Dead at 83; Comic Actor in Over 40 Films." *Variety*, 27 Nov. 1985.

MIRIAM J. PETTY

Fields, Alonzo (1900–22 Mar. 1994), White House chief butler, was born in Lyles Station, Indiana, an all-black community founded by freed slaves in the 1850s, where his father ran a general store and his mother kept a boarding house. Fields's early love of music was influenced by his father, who directed the only African American brass band in southern Indiana. In 1920 the family moved to Indianapolis, where Fields and his father played together in a YMCA military brass band; Alonzo trained the choir, studied voice, and learned Irish ballads. His dream of becoming a professional singer had to be balanced, however, with his need to make a living, and he again followed in his father's footsteps by running a grocery store. When his business began to decline in 1925, Fields left Indianapolis for Boston, where he enrolled at the New England Conservatory of Music. There he trained at first to be a public school music teacher, before switching to classes focusing on concert work in voice. Around this time, Fields married Edna (maiden name unknown), with whom he had two daughters, Virginia and Dorothy Jean.

As the Great Depression approached, and Fields's funds began to run low, he dropped out of the conservatory—temporarily, he hoped—to train as a butler for Dr. Samuel W. Stratton, the president of the Massachusetts Institute of Technology in Cambridge. Fields hoped that the position would give him a "background of good breeding" that could later help him in a career as a concert singer (Fields, 20). To this end he quickly absorbed a knowledge of fine china, crystal, and furniture, and also became acquainted with men of power and privilege, notably A. L. Lowell, president of Harvard, who talked with him about contemporary race relations; John D. Rockefeller; Thomas Edison; and Lieutenant Frederic Butler, an aide to President Herbert Hoover. When Stratton died in late 1931 Butler offered Fields a position as an assistant butler on the White House staff. Fields had hoped to make his concert debut in Boston in April 1932, but with unemployment reaching record levels, and with a wife and child to feed, he accepted the offer and moved to Washington, D.C., to serve the man who many Americans blamed for the escalating economic crisis.

Fields went on to work at the White House for the next twenty-one years, serving four presidents. He found his first employers, the Hoovers, to be early risers, sticklers for punctuality, routine, and protocol, and somewhat aloof. As an assistant butler Fields learned the details of planning both grand, formal dinners for visiting foreign dignitaries, including Mussolini's foreign minister, and the many less formal teas given by the first lady, which were equally taxing on the staff. Careful not to overtly criticize his employers in his autobiography, Fields does however mention the lengthening unemployment lines, the grievances of protesting "bonus march" veterans on the eve of the 1932 presidential race, and the vibrancy of Hoover's opponent, Franklin Roosevelt, during a White House visit, but does not state his own political preferences in that pivotal election.

Expecting to be replaced by a member of Roosevelt's staff, Fields instead found himself promoted to chief White House butler two weeks after Roosevelt's inauguration. Largely this was because he adapted better than most others in the White House domestic staff to the vastly different entertaining style of the Roosevelts. The new era was established on inauguration day, 4 March 1933, when Eleanor Roosevelt personally began serving the guests, one of whom asked for ice cream before the bouillon was served, and several of whom left the table before the president had finished. The jovial, backslapping Roosevelt appeared not to care, but most of the domestic staff, accustomed to the highly formal Coolidges and Hoovers, resented the changes. Although he regretted that the White House dining experience now more closely resembled a cafeteria than the Waldorf-Astoria, Fields expressed some pleasure that the Roosevelts planned to "throw Old Man Protocol and formality right out the window" (Fields, 48). Among the most radical changes were Eleanor Roosevelt's lifting of President Hoover's ban on women's smoking at formal White House events. Fields notes that the first lady led the way, even if she smoked more as a matter of principle than pleasure. Franklin Roosevelt's lifting of the national prohibition on alcohol also transformed entertaining in the White House, and left Fields with a major dilemma: what to do with the gallons of wine, sherry, applejack, and even sake that flooded into 1600 Pennsylvania Avenue from legions of appreciative, if not always talented, wine manufacturers. His solution was to combine them all in a fairly lethal spiked punch—110 gallons to serve 1,200 guests—the recipe for which he included along with his favorite formal menus in a useful appendix to his memoir. Fields noted wryly that he had expected the demand for his punch to wane once the novelty of the end of Prohibition had worn off, but it never did.

Fields strongly endorsed Eleanor Roosevelt's democratization of White House entertaining by inviting hundreds of guests to afternoon teas, even though these often-chaotic affairs proved highly taxing for him and other members of staff. He also supported the first lady's role in arranging for the contralto MARIAN ANDERSON to sing at the Lincoln Memorial in Washington, D.C., after the Daughters of the American Revolution refused to allow the singer to perform at the city's Constitution Hall. Fields was less impressed, however, by the Roosevelt's continuation of Jim Crow accommodations for their household staff. He noted that the "simple process of eliminating the white help," ended a long-standing White House policy of separate dining rooms for black and white servants, but expressed his "reservations" about the Roosevelt's family home in Hyde Park, New York, where the black staff was excluded from the white help's dining room and was forced to eat in the kitchen (Fields, 42). Fields also noted that, as part of a general cost-cutting exercise, the Roosevelts slashed the salaries of the White House staff by 25 percent. At first Fields earned around ninety dollars per month.

Much of Fields's memoir consists of his recollections of the most famous guests and state occasions during his tenure as White House chief butler. He was greatly impressed by the visit of King George VI and Queen Elizabeth in 1939, though not by the carping and snobbery of their servants. Roosevelt, keen to cultivate relations with Britain on the eve of World War II, took a particular interest in Fields's preparation for the visit, eventually acquiescing to his chief butler's recommendation to upgrade the elegance of the dinnerware and the quality of the food for the state dinner held in June 1939. Fields was also privy to several of the most important decisions of the Roosevelt White House, not least on 7 December 1941, when he observed the president in his study hear the news of the Japanese attack on Pearl Harbor. His recollection of Roosevelt declaiming to himself, "My God! How did it happen? I will go down in disgrace," helps refute those who would later argue that FDR intentionally allowed the attack to happen so as to maneuver a reluctant United States into a world war (Fields, 80).

American entry into World War II greatly increased the tempo of life in the White House, for the domestic staff as well as the policy staff. Fields often found himself assigned to the visiting Winston Churchill, and quickly learned that the key to keeping the British prime minister happy was the one that opened the liquor cabinet: sherry for breakfast; Scotch and soda for lunch; champagne for dinner; and more Scotch in the evening. Roosevelt also assigned Fields to look after Churchill at a secret location in a dry county in Florida, where the butler somehow managed to procure the necessary wines and spirits. He also kept the prime minister's penchant for swimming nude a secret from nearby residents. Fields was less impressed, however, by Madame Chang Kai-shek of nationalist China; Molotov, the Soviet foreign minister; Indian prime minister Jawaharlal Nehru; and Richard Nixon, who complained about the waste of food at a White House function.

After Roosevelt's death in April 1945 Fields continued to serve as chief butler to the new president, Harry S. Truman. Truman was undoubtedly his favorite employer, in part because they shared plain-spoken midwestern values and a love of simple but wholesome food, but also because of the Missourian's "sense of human understanding and appreciation" for the household staff as people, rather than as servants (Fields, 120). Of all the presidents Fields served, Truman was the only one to introduce him to his family; the two men also maintained a warm relationship after Truman chose not to seek a second full term in 1952. Fields served Truman's successor, Dwight Eisenhower, for a few months, but left the White House for good in 1953, to take up a position as a quality controller with the General Services Administration (GSA) in Boston. The move enabled him to be near a clinic where his wife was convalescing from a lengthy illness.

After Fields retired from the GSA in the early 1960s, he published a well-received autobiography, *My 21 Years in the White House* (1961), which drew upon a diary he had kept while in service. In later years he became more openly critical of his early White House experiences than he had been in this memoir, noting the different pay scales for blacks and whites. "The inequality burned me up," he told the Boston *Globe* in a 1992 interview, "but what could you do? At that time you were lucky to have a job; if they laid me off I would have been in the soup kitchen" (cited in obituary). Following the death of his first wife Fields remarried in 1980 to Mayland McLaughlin, with whom he lived in Medford, Massachusetts, until his death at Mount Auburn Hospital in Cambridge.

Though in his two decades in the White House Fields never wielded any significant influence on public policy, he was nevertheless one of the few African Americans to observe at close quarters the decision-making process in the White House during the Depression, World War II, and the onset of the Cold War. That unique vantage point made Fields a compelling contributor to PBS television's American Experience documentaries, *FDR* (1994), *Truman* (1997), and, most notably, to HENRY HAMPTON's *The Great Depression* (1993). In 2002 James Still's "Looking Over the President's Shoulder," a critically acclaimed one-man play based on Fields's life and starring John Henry Redwood, premiered in Rochester, New York.

FURTHER READING

Alonzo Fields's papers are housed at the Harry S. Truman Presidential Library in Independence, Missouri.

Fields, Alonzo. *My 21 Years in the White House* (1961).

Obituary: Boston *Globe*, 23 Mar. 1994.

STEVEN J. NIVEN

Fields, Arabella (31 Jan. 1879–after 1933), singer, dancer, musician, and stage and screen actor, was born in Philadelphia, Pennsylvania. We know nothing of her early life, including her family name at birth. "Fields" was the name of her first husband and the name she retained professionally. We have no information on when he and Bella were married. Fields's career was primarily in Europe. Any earlier career she might have had in the United States would probably have been prior to her marriage; not knowing her maiden name, however, we cannot identify her. Her first husband, James C. Fields, had traveled to Europe in 1894, as a member of the San Francisco Minstrels. Whether Bella was a performing member of this troupe, we do not know, but in January 1896, in Rostow on Don, she resided in Russia on James' passport. Our first sight of her as a performing artist is in an advertisement in 1899 for a performance in Prague: "Mr. James and Miss Bella Fields, Negro Duettists." In Berlin, in February 1902, James Fields applied for a passport for himself and his wife to enter Russia. But in August of that year Bella Fields was back in Hamburg, single, and advertised as "the Black Nightingale," a name that stuck with her throughout her European career, which lasted well into the 1930s. From 1906 she was managed by a German impresario, Engelhardt Albert G. Winter, whom she later married.

Perhaps it was her enterprising second husband who advertised her as alternately an African, Indian, Red Indian, American, South American, Australian, and even a German-African. Bella Fields measured 5'6" and had distinct African features. For the German audiences, she was an exotic sight. A reviewer commented in 1904 that "the audience was particularly interested in the beauty contest, which was won by the Negress, Miss Bella Fields, with 3378 votes. It is quite obvious that the exotic singer owes her victory first of all to her phenomenal voice and less to her exterior" ("Hamburg, Hammonia," *Der Artist* 1030 [1904]). In Berlin, another journalist reported "Quite excellent is la belle Fields, the black nightingale. The impressive Negress has a beautiful alto of quite enormous range: her torch song 'Sweet Marguerite, farewell!' sounded sweet and soft. Her Niggersong sounded highly original, as did the tongue-in-cheek 'Wenn der Auerhahn balzt' ('When the Woodcock Mates'), a little German ditty which she accompanied by excellent yodeling. Miss Fields is a black star of first quality" (Viktor Happrecht, "Berlin, Passage," *Der Artist* 1188 [1907]).

Recognition of her voice led to six recordings by the Anker company in Berlin in 1907. She had great success with German audiences, singing songs by Schubert and others. For her yodeling performances she sometimes dressed as an Alpine girl. But her recorded repertoire consists of Stephen Foster "coon songs," which were also well received by Germans. One published review is especially revealing:

> On top of this month's record list is a vocal phenomenon which remains a mystery to me. I would have classified her straight away as a regular tenor with baritonal coloring, had not

the label informed me that it is actually the contralto of Miss Belle Fields, a colored lady from Philadelphia. I checked the songs again and again. Indeed, especially in the upper falsetto notes, I thought I heard something like a female resemblance. But then again there were the deep tones of the small octave, and then my natural response was again and again: "But it ought to be a male, after all!" ... Then I also remembered the Negro minstrels that were brought to Berlin by Barnum and Bailey in 1900; and I recalled similarities in sound, identical treatment of the vocal parts, of the voice, of the pronunciation. And thus I arrived at the possible conclusion that this female bass was born "down on the Swanee River" and must have dark rather than white skin. But I repeat, this is a guess.... The first song, "Farewell, Marguerite!" is a little bit on the sentimental side, but the crispness of the voice alone saves it from being overly lachrymose. Of course, one is stricken with awe when hearing the Philadelphia diva descend calmly to the low E, and then see her scale limited by the two-line C. And what a thundering resonance in the deep, what a volume at fortissimo in the higher registers. And it should be noted that this singer knows how to produce not only the chest tones but also has quite a nice falsetto register. However, she is not very well versed in the art of shading. Like an organ, she has only three stops, one for fortissimo, one for mezzo-forte, and one for piano; these she used in clearly distinguishable steps, but otherwise she sings with pure voice and she has retained a strong solid sound." (Max Chop, *Phonographische Zeitschrift* 9.7 [1908])

Her records remained popular and were again available after World War I. The last reissue on the Hermophon label occurred in 1928, long after the introduction of the electrical recording process had rendered earlier acoustical recordings technically obsolete; apart from Belle Fields only Enrico Caruso's recordings were kept in catalog. At least one of the titles, Stephen Foster's "Swanee River (Old Folks at Home)" [*sic*] also exists as a Deutsche Bioscope "tone picture," in which a movie film of her was synchronized with a Messter sound recording, possibly making her the first black woman to appear in a sound film.

Fields must have been one of the most widely traveled black artists until the war restricted her movements in Europe. She then took refuge in the Netherlands, where she met other stranded African Americans. On one occasion, in Rotterdam in 1917, the press reported: "Miss Arabella Fields, Philadelphia, Miss Morcashani, Dixie, Miss Olitta, Brooklyn, were voted winners in a contest of soubrettes against their white [Dutch] competitors" (*Nieuwe Rotterdamsche Courant*, 17 May 1917). Her photo, with a caption describing her as "the South-American Caruso," appeared on sheet music published in Amsterdam in 1919.

By 1924 she had returned to Germany. In 1925 in Hamburg, the bandleader SAM WOODING contracted her for a tour of the *Chocolate Kiddies* revue in Scandinavia. In 1926 she joined LOUIS DOUGLAS, touring as a member of *Black People* (sometimes called *Black Follies*), and later with *Louisiana* (sometimes called *Black Flowers*, or *Liza*). Arabella Fields was now past the age of fifty and contemporary programs mention her in the role of "Dinah's Mammy." She also sang spirituals such as "Same Train," "I'll Be Ready" or "Just Before the Battle," as well as comedy numbers. After the tours with Douglas she was engaged by Rex Ingram, a director of the silent film days, for an acting role in his last film, "Baroud" (released also in an American version as "Love in Morocco"). Fields had a remarkable and varied career outside the United States and was applauded first as a singer, then as an actor. The place and year of her death is not known.

FURTHER READING

Lotz, Rainer E. *Black People: Entertainers of African Descent in Europe and Germany* [with audio CD] (1997).

Lotz, Rainer E. "Black Women Recording Pioneers," *The IAJRC Journal* 40.2 (May 2007).

Lotz, Rainer E. *German Ragtime Vol.1: The Sound Documents* (1985)

RAINER E. LOTZ

Fields, Cleo (22 Nov. 1962–), politician and community leader, was born in Baton Rouge, Louisiana, the seventh of ten children. When Cleo was four years old, Isadore, his father, a dockworker, died in an accident while driving home from working a double shift, leaving his mother, Alice, alone to support the family. Unable to pay the rent, the family was evicted. Alice moved the family to a new house and worked days as a hotel maid, and in the evenings she did laundry to make ends meet.

Fields grew up in East Baton Rouge, a community that had been integral in the struggle for civil rights. Fields and his siblings attended McKinley

High School, the first secondary school for African Americans in the historically segregated city. During the years that Fields attended the school, the district remained embroiled in the longest-running desegregation case in U.S. history, which finally culminated in a federal mandate for the district to draw up an adequate desegregation plan in 1980, the year that Fields graduated. Amid this backdrop of struggle Fields became deeply concerned as a young man with his family's financial situation; since the age of fourteen he had worked odd jobs to save money. As a sophomore in college Fields was able to put down ten thousand dollars on a house so that his family could never again be evicted.

Fields majored in mass communications at Southern University in Baton Rouge, with his sights set on marketing. But he soon turned to politics; during his senior year he was elected as a broadly popular and charismatic student government association president. He was also elected that year by his peers in the Louisiana Council of Student Body Presidents to serve as a student member on the Louisiana Board of Regents, the governing board for higher education in the state. He went on to attend Southern University's College of Law and spent his summers clerking for the East Baton Rouge Parish City Prosecutor's office and the Parish Attorney's office. During his final months of law school in 1987, Fields launched his first campaign to become a lawmaker.

Despite his young age of twenty-four, Fields ran a strong campaign for the Louisiana state senate. Using his skills in mass communications he served as his own media consultant, even writing his own radio jingle. His nine brothers and sisters made up his campaign staff. Fields ran an energetic, grassroots campaign as a reformer against an incumbent in his home Fourteenth Senatorial District. Fields won by 227 votes, making him the youngest person in Louisiana's history ever elected to the state senate.

In 1990 Fields ran unsuccessfully to represent Louisiana's Eighth Congressional District, losing by a large margin to the incumbent Republican. Following the 1990 census and an order from the U.S. Justice Department, many states were required to reapportion districts to reflect their minority constituencies. Louisiana's legislature redrew boundaries to create a second "majority-minority" congressional district in the state. This district, as was also the case in the other affected states, was the subject of an extensive legal battle over the next several years. Fields nevertheless took this opportunity to become the second African American from Louisiana to serve in the U.S. Congress in modern times. He was also then the nation's youngest congressman. On 24 August 1991 Fields married his high school sweetheart, Debra Horton Fields. Fields served two terms before the Supreme Court ruled the redrawn district to be unconstitutional in *U.S. v. Hays* (1995).

In late 1994 Fields announced his candidacy for governor of Louisiana, and on 22 January 1995, his first son, Cleo Brandon, was born. Other candidates for the 1995 election were a former governor, the current lieutenant governor, the state treasurer Mary Landrieu, and the state senator Mike Foster. Despite heated competition and dwindling campaign funds, Fields won the runoff seat by a slim nine thousand votes, making him the first African American to reach Louisiana's gubernatorial runoff. As the Democratic candidate pitted against the Republican Foster, Fields found himself battling not only racial overtones in the campaign but also a lack of support from his own party. Foster accepted the endorsement of David Duke, a former Ku Klux Klan leader, while white officeholders offered Fields little more than tepid support. No Democrats from Louisiana's congressional delegation campaigned openly for him, and the prominent Landrieu refused to endorse him. Foster won in a landslide, taking 64 percent of the vote.

In December 1997 Fields made his return to the Louisiana state senate, representing his home Fourteenth District. He was elected in the primary with 75 percent of the vote over five other candidates. At this time his younger brother Wilson was also serving as state senator, which made them the first brothers to serve in the Louisiana senate concurrently. On 28 April 1998, his second son, Christopher Justin, was born. As senator, Fields established the Louisiana Leadership Institute, a nonprofit youth organization that provides programs and services for urban youth. His return to Louisiana politics also made him a leading force in the Democratic Party. He coordinated aggressive grassroots campaigns for various Democrats across the state, spoke out on political and social issues on his weekly statewide call-in radio show, "Cleo Live," and remained involved in the Louisiana Legislative Black Caucus and the Rainbow/ PUSH Coalition. He began private practice as a lawyer in 1998.

In 2000 Fields's reputation was damaged when an FBI surveillance videotape was made public. The tape, used in the prosecution of former governor Edwin Edwards for corruption, showed Fields receiving twenty thousand dollars in cash from

Edwards in a 1997 meeting. Out of office at the time of the taping, Fields was never charged with a crime, although he gave no further explanation of the scene other than to say that the meeting was a mistake and that the cash was returned. The videotape scandal ultimately led to Fields's losing his 2004 campaign for a position on Louisiana's Public Service Commission. Despite numerous setbacks and challenges, Fields remained a formidable figure in Louisiana politics.

FURTHER READING

Thompkins, Gwendolyn. "Cleo Fields Reaching for the Mountaintop after a Rough Climb," *New Orleans Times-Picayune*, 13 Sept. 1995.

Wardlaw, Jack. "Rookie Repls is Ready for Politics D.C.-Style," *New Orleans Times-Picayune*, 16 Nov. 1992.

Weiss, Joanna. "Cleo Fields Emerges as a La. Political Force," *New Orleans Times-Picayune*, 16 Nov. 1998.

KRISTEN L. ROUSE

Fields, Mamie Elizabeth Garvin (13 Aug. 1888–1987), educator and civic activist, was born Mary Elizabeth Garvin in Charleston, South Carolina. Her parents, George Washington Garvin, a carpenter, and Rebecca Mary Logan Bellinger, a seamstress, had seven other children, four of whom died in childhood. As a young girl, Fields was enthralled with learning new ideas, and she began attending Shaw School in her neighborhood when she was just three years old. Her mother's side of the family, particularly the Middleton branch, was regarded as middle class, and many of her relatives were formally educated beyond high school in preparation for professional careers. Fields and her siblings were encouraged by their parents to attend Avery Institute, a private school renowned for the excellent education that it offered middle- and upper-class African American youth. While Herbert, Harriet, and Ruth accepted their parents' prodding, a defiant Mamie refused to be educated at a school where she believed skin color bias favored lighter-skinned black students and often left their darker-skinned counterparts broken emotionally. Instead, Fields decided to accept a full scholarship to Claflin in Orangeburg, South Carolina, which at that time was an elementary-college level institution that, incidentally, her mother had attended. In 1908 Fields graduated from Claflin with the licentiate of instruction and a diploma in domestic science.

Armed with a teaching degree, Fields was determined to become a missionary in an African country, which her parents did not approve of because of the rate at which people on the continent were perishing from yellow fever. Unfortunately, she did not realize her goal of completing the missionary work she envisioned, as yellow fever claimed the life of someone her parents knew had traveled to an African nation, and she was forbidden to make the journey. To overcome her great disappointment, Fields began to strategize, penning a poem that captured her determination to make a difference in the world through education:

> If I cannot give my millions
> And the heathen lands explore,
> I can find the heathen nearer.
> I can find him at my door. (*Lemon Swamp*, 105)

Fields's teaching career began in Pinewood, South Carolina, where she and her sister, Hattie, founded the Pinewood School. Beginning in 1909 Fields worked on Johns Island as a teacher at Humber Wood Elementary and later at Miller Hill as a principal. In 1914 she married Robert Lucas Fields, a bricklayer and high school instructor. Robert and Mamie had three children: Roberta, who died at birth, Robert Jr., and Alfred.

Fields joined the National Association of Colored Women's Clubs (NACWC), the umbrella organization for women interested in the betterment of the African American race through theories of uplift, in 1916. She soon found, however, that while the NACWC was fairly easy to join, becoming a member of one of the local clubs in Charleston was not. Class bias and other forms of elitism kept many hard-working and committed people out of invitation-only social groups, which led Fields, along with Lem(y) Lewis and Viola Ford Turner, to found the Modern Priscilla Club (MPC) in 1926, the same year she began teaching at Society Corner School on James Island. The members of MPC included teachers, housewives, domestic workers, and women in various other careers who were committed to NACWC's motto "Lifting as We Climb." MPC became the organizational model for other Charleston women's associations. At the state level, the South Carolina Federation of Colored Women's Clubs (SCFCWC), dedicated to "carry[ing] on charitable, education, and welfare work among colored children," established and operated the Wilkinson Home, an orphanage for girls in Cayce, South Carolina, where Fields served a considerable amount of time as director (Avery Research Center Archives).

In addition to her role as an educator and active member of MPC, Fields was also twice-elected president of SCFCWC and twice-elected statistician of the NACWC; she garnered many accolades over her lifetime for her work in the Charleston community. In 1971 Fields was named South Carolina's Senior Citizen of the Year; nine years later she was recognized by the City of Charleston with the groundbreaking of a new child care facility in her name, the Mamie Garvin Fields Day Care Center.

Hoping to write a book about her life, Fields began audio recording stories that she was told as a child, as well as events and descriptions of people and places that she encountered throughout her lifetime. With the assistance of her granddaughter, the sociologist Karen Elise Fields, *Lemon Swamp and Other Places: A Carolina Memoir* was published in 1983. Celebrated as a key text in the African American oral history tradition, *Lemon Swamp* is also a salient historical account of the South through the eyes of an African American woman activist from the Gilded Age to the Reagan era.

Fields, an educator and champion of women's and African American uplift, spent most of her life residing at 5 President Place in Charleston, South Carolina. Preceded in death by her husband, Robert (1963), she died there in 1987.

FURTHER READING

Mamie Garvin Fields's papers (1925–1990) are held by the Avery Research Center for African American History and Culture Archive Collection, the College of Charleston, South Carolina.

Fields, Mamie Garvin, with Karen Fields. *Lemon Swamp and Other Places: A Carolina Memoir* (1983).

Drago, Edmund L. *Charleston's Avery Normal Institute: Initiative, Paternalism, and Race Relations* (1990).

Gaines, Kevin K. *Uplifting the Race: Black Leadership, Politics, and Culture in the Twentieth Century* (1996).

Hine, Darlene Clark, and Kathleen Thompson. *A Shining Thread of Hope: The History of Black Women in America* (1998).

MICHELLE D. COMMANDER

Fields, Mary (1832–1914), building foreman and caretaker, U.S. mail coach driver, Montana pioneer, also known as Black Mary or Stagecoach Mary, was born a slave in Hickman County, Tennessee. Information about Fields's parentage and early life remain unconfirmed, although James Franks, whose grandparents knew Fields in the late 1800s in Montana, writes that Fields was the daughter of Suzanna and Buck, slaves of the Dunne family, owners of a Hickman County plantation. The Dunnes sold Buck immediately following Mary's birth. According to Franks, the Dunnes allowed Suzanna to keep her daughter with her in quarters behind the kitchen, and Mary enjoyed a relatively privileged childhood, even becoming friends with the Dunne's daughter Dolly, who was about the same age as Mary. This arrangement, Franks writes, lasted until Suzanna's death forced fourteen-year-old Mary to take over her mother's household duties.

Whether or not Franks's account is accurate, it is certainly likely that Fields remained in slavery until the end of the Civil War. What she did in the years following emancipation has yet to be confirmed. Franks claims that after the war Mary, who could read and write, stayed on at the Dunne's plantation to assist other newly freed slaves. She later became a servant in the home of James Dunne. Later in life, however, Fields recounted stories of her experiences as a maid aboard the steamboat the *Robert E. Lee*, even musing about the events of 30 June 1870, when the *Robert E. Lee* raced Steamboat Bill's *Natchez*. "It was so hot up in the cabins," she told the *Cascade (Montana) Courier* in 1914, "that the passengers were forced to take to the decks." Historians agree that by around 1878 Fields was working as a housekeeper at the Ursuline Convent of the Sacred Heart in Toledo, Ohio, under the protection of the convent's young mother superior, Mother Amadeus. The connection between Fields and Mother Amadeus, who was born Sarah Teresa Dunne, remains cloudy. Franks, who argues that Fields was born on the Dunne plantation, claims that Mother Amadeus was Dolly Dunne, Fields's childhood playmate. Records show, however, that Sarah Teresa Dunne was born, not in Tennessee, in 1832, but in Akron, Ohio, in 1846. If Fields had worked for James Dunne or another Dunne family member, either as a slave or servant, it is possible that she met Sarah Dunne through that connection. It is also possible that Fields, having made her way to Ohio from Tennessee, met and befriended Mother Amadeus while working at the convent in Toledo. Whatever her path to the Ursulines, Fields found a home at the convent for seven years.

In 1884 Mother Amadeus, who would eventually found twelve Indian missions in Montana and several others in Alaska, left Toledo to establish a mission school in the Montana Territory, then home to the Flathead, the Blackfoot, the Gros Ventre, the Assiniboine-Sioux, the Rocky Boy-Cree, the Cheyenne, and the Crow. After six months on a Cheyenne reservation living and teaching with several other Ursuline nuns in a three-room log cabin they had christened St. Labre's mission,

Mother Amadeus was called to St. Peter's Mission, located about thirty-five miles southwest of Great Falls. There she fell gravely ill with pneumonia and sent for Fields. Fields arrived in Montana in 1885 and after nursing Mother Amadeus back to health, stayed on at St Peter's, becoming the mission's resident housekeeper, building foreman, and jack-of-all-trades. In addition to her cooking, laundry, and cleaning duties, Fields maintained the mission's wood cabins and small church, painting, making furniture, and carrying out building repairs. In addition to driving the wagon team and hauling goods and passengers back and forth to the mission, she established and tended a large garden and chicken coops, trading her butter and eggs for lumber and supplies. Fields also became known for her healing skills and an expanding collection of herbs and potions. In December 1891, after living for seven years in the wood cabins of the original mission, Fields moved with the nuns into a newly completed three-story stone convent erected next door. As usual she proved invaluable, taking on most of the heavy lifting and building maintenance during and after the move.

From local Indians Fields learned to tan buckskin, a skill that led to her distinctive manner of dress. After making a buckskin dress for herself Fields fashioned a pair of buckskin pants, which she wore under her dress in the winter months. Topped off with a big buffalo coat, brimmed black hat, and loaded shotgun, Fields bucked gender roles and adapted herself to Montana's cold and rugged terrain. A short, heavy-set woman she further challenged the nun's sense of propriety with her cigar smoking, drinking, and gambling. Despite their reservations, however, and with a few exceptions, the nuns appreciated and protected Fields. Stories of fistfight and gun duels dogged Fields, culminating in a story claiming that she killed, with either a rock or gun, a fellow St. Peter's worker, a white man. While the veracity of these tales remains untested, in the mid-1890s they proved Fields's undoing with the mission, when Bishop John Baptist Brondell, Montana's first Catholic bishop, forced Fields from her job and home after ten years of service. In 1895 Fields moved from the St. Peter's Mission to the nearby town of Cascade. Living on her own for the first time in at least twenty years and separated from the mission's students, nuns, and her friend Mother Amadeus, the move must have been difficult for the sixty-three year old. Though she had been living in Montana for a decade, she had yet to live outside the insular community of St. Peter's. Her new home, the town of Cascade, was a distinct product of its time. Located in the middle of Montana Territory on the Missouri River between Helena and Great Falls, the town was born in 1887 with the arrival of the Montana Central Railroad extension. Within a few years a host of businesses had sprung up. The true development of Montana had begun only a few decades earlier, in the early 1860s, with the discovery of gold. The gold rush had brought immigrants but little government or rule of law aside from miners' courts and vigilance committees. Montana Territory, created in 1864, was not granted statehood until 1889, six years before Fields moved to Cascade. Although a few black fur traders, including EDWARD ROSE and JIM BECKWOURTH, had visited the area on expeditions of the region in the early- and mid-nineteenth century and some African Americans had immigrated to the Montana territory during its gold rush, Montana was home to only a small number of black pioneers and settlers by the late nineteenth century. The 1870 census reported seventy-one blacks living in Helena, with smaller concentrations in six other counties. By the 1880s, Montana had a total black population of 191 black men and 155 black women. With her move to Cascade, Fields became the town's sole African American resident.

Upon her arrival Fields took a room above one of the town's saloons (sources suggests there may have been as many as eleven). With a recommendation from Mother Amadeus, she landed a job with the Wells Fargo Company, driving a mail coach. Though the advent of the railroad had alleviated the need for passenger stagecoaches, coaches were still used for the delivery of mail to areas not serviced by rail. Fields traveled from Cascade to Great Falls to Fort Benton and back, a route which included looping around Mullan Road, the path servicing St. Peter's Mission. On these weekly trips Fields happily visited with her friends at the mission. For the next six years Fields, then in her sixties, rode through Montana's harsh weather and untamed countryside, grounded only by unpassable winter storms. A heavyset, older, black woman, with a pet eagle, holstered guns, and rifle, she was certainly easy to spot on her route, but it was her reputation for drinking, smoking, gambling, swearing, storytelling, and fighting—she was said to have once beat up a man for failing to pay his laundry bill—that carried her fame far beyond mid-Montana. Even Charles "Charlie" Russell, sometimes referred to as the cowboy artist, paid homage to this unusual woman in an 1897 drawing. More than fifty years later the actor Gary Cooper, a native of Dearborn, Montana, wrote a story about Fields, whom he met on a trip to Cascade when he was nine years old. "Born a slave somewhere in Tennessee," Cooper wrote in 1959, "Mary lived to become one of the freest souls ever to draw a breath or a .38" (*Ebony*, Oct. 1959).

In the spring of 1896 Fields bought a small house in Cascade. By the time she retired from driving the mail coach in 1901 she had become a major figure in town. Apparently she received free meals at a local hotel and her birthday (which she approximated from year to year) was treated as a school holiday. An enthusiastic supporter of the Cascade baseball team, she awarded homerun hitters with flower bouquets from her garden. In the last years of her life Fields supported herself by taking in laundry and by selling chickens, eggs, and vegetables from her garden. Mary Fields died at Columbus hospital in Great Falls, Montana. She is buried in a small cemetery on the road between Cascade and St. Peter's Mission.

FURTHER READING

Franks, James. *Mary Fields* (1999).

Shirley, Gayle Corbett. *More Than Petticoats: Remarkable Montana Women* (1995).

LISA E. RIVO

Figgs, Carrie Law Morgan (3 Feb. 1878–14 May 1968), poet and playwright, was born Carrie Law Morgan in Valdosta, Georgia, the eldest of four daughters of Lucinda Linton Morgan and the Reverend James Morgan. Figgs attended grammar school in Valdosta and high school in Palatka, Florida, before graduating from Edward Waters College, an African Methodist Episcopal (AME) Church–affiliated school in Jacksonville, Florida. While scholars have always cited Figgs's work alongside other significant precursive Black Renaissance writers, biographical information about Figgs had been unavailable until basic facts about her life were uncovered in 1997. Still, many of the dates and details surrounding her life remain unknown.

While the exact date of Carrie Morgan's marriage to William M. Figgs, a porter, remains a mystery, she married well before 1914 while she was a resident of Jacksonville and a member of the Mount Zion AME Church. According to the 1914 Jacksonville directory Figgs lived with her husband and three children, Leonard, Cassius, and Gwendolyn, at 1014 Julia Street and taught at the Stanton Grade School. That same year Figgs was an officer in the Most Worshipful Grand Court of Heroines of Jericho, a women's club that began as the African Lodge #459 of Massachusetts based on tenets of freemasonry. Figgs eventually served as the Grand Most Ancient Matron of this organization. While a Mount Zion AME Church member, Figgs also led women's groups, such as the Women's Mite Missionary Society known for "Christian ideals and racial uplift" (Splawn, xix).

Figgs's earliest writing consists of poems about the church as well as her appreciation of Jacksonville as a city with opportunities available to blacks at a time when other southern cities could not boast conditions as hospitable. In 1920 Figgs collected many of these poems, including the resounding "Tribute to the Men of Jacksonville," which distinguishes Jacksonville as a place in which "the Negro has climbed the hill," into her first book of poetry, *Poetic Pearls*, in 1920.

Figgs and her family moved that same year from Jacksonville to Chicago, where she became a member of Bethel AME Church. In 1921 Figgs published her second book of poetry, *Nuggets of Gold*, a collection of nineteen poems, at least one of which mentions her regret at the loss of Florida sunshine in exchange for Chicago's cold weather and whose title poem, "My Nuggets of Gold," celebrates her children. Two other poems in the collection, "Whoa Mule," and "Who's You Talking To," suggest the literary influences of PAUL LAURENCE DUNBAR in their use of black dialect. Figgs excerpts letters of praise for *Poetic Pearls* in the preface to *Nuggets of Gold* and explains with pride how its success inspired her book's publication. A strong alliance with the black conservative ideology of BOOKER T. WASHINGTON is recognizable in both *Poetic Pearls* and *Nuggets of Gold* through Figgs's dogged promotion of temperance, motherhood, thrift, fortitude, and cleanliness.

The Figgs family was still living together in Chicago in 1923—by then her son Leonard was a music teacher and her other son Cassius was a musician—when Figgs self-published her third and last collection, *Select Plays: Santa Claus Land, Jepthah's Daughter, The Prince of Peace, Bachelor's Convention* (1923). The self-published anthology departs from Figgs's usual poetry and, some critics believe, loses focus on the condition of poor African Americans.

While the common thread of Christianity runs through *Santa Claus Land*, a Christmas fantasy written for children, *Jepthah's Daughter*, a biblical tragedy, and *Prince of Peace*, the reenactment of the prophesy of Jesus' conception, *Bachelor's Convention* stands out. A slapstick, feminist comedy in which women make rules and men abide without question, *Bachelor's Convention* harks back to Figgs's roots as a black female teacher working as an agent for social change.

After becoming established in Chicago, Figgs ventured into entrepreneurship, founding and running the successful Commonwealth Real Estate Employment Company from her home. Best known to friends and family as "Mama Figgs," Figgs had a reputation for sharing her advice and wisdom.

Figgs died in her home a little over a month after the assassination of MARTIN LUTHER KING JR. Critics cite Figgs's work as an important step in the evolution of the black experience as well as a noteworthy contribution to African American history of the early twentieth century.

FURTHER READING

Splawn, P. Jane. *Writings of Carrie Williams Clifford and Carrie Law Morgan Figgs* (1997).

Roses, Lorraine Elena. *The Harlem Renaissance and Beyond: Literary Biographies of 100 Black Women Writers, 1900–1950* (1990).

SYLVIA M. DESANTIS

Figures, Michael A. (13 Oct. 1947–13 Sept. 1996), attorney and politician, was born Michael Anthony Figures in Mobile, Alabama, to Coleman and Augusta Mitchell Figures. Coleman Figures, who once cleaned the yards of affluent Mobilians to supplement his income at Mobile's International Paper Company, was an ordained Baptist minister and pastor of the Green Grove Missionary Baptist Church in Mobile. Both mother and father instilled in their children discipline, honesty, and the redemptive values of hard work and education. The youngest of three sons, Michael grew up with a keen sense of social responsibility and believed that the law was a vital tool for achieving social change.

Figures grew up in the segregated South. He graduated from Mobile's Hillsdale High School in 1965. This was just two years after Alabama began its school desegregation process, when Governor George Wallace made his infamous stand against the admission of black students to the University of Alabama. Figures earned a bachelor of arts degree at the historically black Stillman College in Tuscaloosa, Alabama, in 1969. Determined to become a champion for justice, he became one of the first twelve African Americans to enter the University of Alabama School of Law in Tuscaloosa. Figures found law school to be both intellectually stimulating and professionally rewarding. Several of his classmates rose to prominent political offices, including Alabama's governorship. In 1972 he became the first African American to graduate from the university's law school.

Seeking to be a voice for working-class Alabamians, Figures became a litigator with a law firm in Selma, Alabama. He also worked briefly with the Emergency Land Fund in Atlanta, Georgia. In 1975 Figures returned to Mobile and joined one of the great legal minds in the state, Vernon Z. Crawford. Crawford's civil rights achievements included arguing the *Birdie Mae Davis* case in 1963, which led to the desegregation of the Mobile County Public School System. Figures's legal adroitness soon culminated in one of his most memorable battles, the 1975 *Dawes Landfill* case, where his efforts prevented local leaders from building a landfill in a poor rural community in Mobile County.

In 1978, at the age of thirty, Figures became Mobile's first and Alabama's third African American elected to the state senate. During his first term he helped defeat an effort to add a fourth at-large commissioner's seat, arguing that an additional person would dilute the voting strength of the African American community. Figures also played a key role in changing Alabama's property rights laws that discriminated against minority communities. His efforts helped to decelerate the trend of property loss among blacks in the state. Moreover, Figures fought against the application of the death penalty in Alabama, and for reapportionment and greater representation for blacks in Mobile.

In 1982 Figures married Vivian Davis, also from Mobile, and they had three sons. A community activist who eventually succeeded Figures in Alabama's legislature and a graduate in management science from the University of New Haven in Connecticut, Davis helped to shape the rest of Figures's personal and professional life. Davis introduced her husband to Beulah Mae Donald, whose son, Michael Donald, had been lynched in Mobile in 1981 by Klansmen who were enraged because a jury had failed to convict a black man for killing a white policeman in Birmingham. Figures helped to convince a jury to return a seven million dollar judgment that bankrupted the notorious United Klans of America, which had also been responsible for beating Freedom Riders in the early 1960s, for bombing the Sixteenth Street Baptist Church in Birmingham in 1963—killing four children, CAROLE ROBERTSON, DENISE MCNAIR,

Addie Mae Collins, and Cynthia Wesley—and for murdering the civil rights worker Viola Liuzzo in 1965. The *Donald* case, which garnered national attention, became Figures's best-known case and made him one of Alabama's most respected civil rights attorneys.

In 1986 Figures became a charter member of the New South Coalition, a biracial alternative to the state's black caucus, the Alabama Democratic Conference (ADC). The ADC had gained a reputation as Alabama's most influential political organization, second only to the state's National Association for the Advancement of Colored People. The ADC split in 1984 when Figures supported Jesse Jackson for president while other conference leaders endorsed Walter Mondale. Figures eventually served as the New South Coalition's third president. In 1988 he became Jackson's campaign chairman in Alabama.

Perhaps Figures's brightest moment in state politics occurred in 1994 when he carried Governor Jim Folsom's education reform package successfully through the state senate. Although the bill was defeated in the state house of representatives, Figures's success with the senate made him one of the state's most powerful public officials and laid the foundation for another historical moment. A year later he was elected president pro tempore of the senate. Responsible for chairing the senate in the absence of the lieutenant governor, he became an even more prominent dealmaker in the upper chamber. This assignment made him the first African American ever elected to the state senate's number two leadership post and made him Alabama's third-highest official.

Brilliant, articulate, socially committed, savvy, and highly principled, Figures had an adroit political mind that he used to serve the less fortunate. Thus few elected officials matched his political ingenuity. According to Figures, "Fair politics is legitimate and independent points of view that are compromised on both sides until you reach some common ground. Then you can have progress." Figures believed that public office allowed him to accomplish things that he would have been unable to do as a private citizen. He served almost eighteen years as an Alabama state senator. During this time he served on almost every powerful senate committee, including Rules, Judiciary, Finance and Taxation, Economic Expansion and Trade, and Education, along with Tourism and Marketing. His admirers came from both sides of the political aisle, and few doubted that he would soon run for the governor's seat. That political aspiration, however, was cut short by his untimely death in Mobile in 1996 of an intra-cranial brain hemorrhage.

FURTHER READING

Horton, Paulette Davis. *Avenue: The Place, the People, the Memories, 1799–1986* (1991).

TIMOTHY M. BROUGHTON

Fillmore, Charles W. (1864–27 Apr. 1942), soldier, politician, civil servant, and a guiding force in the establishment of the 369th U.S. Infantry Regiment, was born in Springfield, Ohio. Educated in that state, he also studied law in Ohio.

Early in his career Fillmore allied himself with Asa Bushnell, who succeeded William McKinley as governor of Ohio. Following a lynching in Urbana in 1897, Bushnell, then running for reelection as governor, failed to send state troops to protect a black man accused of rape. Bushnell's failure to save the defenseless man outraged African Americans, who believed the governor allowed the lynching, fearing a backlash by white voters if he intervened. At the time of the lynching, Fillmore worked for Bushnell in the office of the secretary of state. He was also a major in the Ninth Ohio Battalion of the Ohio National Guard, then one of four black military units in the United States commanded by African Americans. The Ninth's A Company, composed of Springfield citizens, was dubbed "Bushnell's Guards." When Bushnell was reelected, the Ninth was selected as his personal escort during inauguration ceremonies. After the lynching incident, the fact that guardsmen of color would stand with the governor infuriated other African Americans throughout the state. Much of their ire was taken out on Fillmore, who responded by refusing to march with his men. The gesture was not enough, however, and he resigned from the Ninth Battalion in 1897.

When war broke out with Spain the following year, Fillmore petitioned President McKinley for a commission in the U.S. Army. Only one out of twenty-five hundred officers in the regular army was black; thus it was unsurprising that Fillmore received no commission. However, McKinley did appoint him a lieutenant in the Ninth U.S. Volunteer Infantry (not to be confused with the Ninth Ohio Battalion). The Ninth U.S. Volunteer Infantry was one of three black volunteer regiments the War Department willingly sent to Cuba, believing that blacks, because of their African bloodlines, were immune to tropical diseases. Such mistaken notions also led the army to decline to inoculate the black troops. While serving in the Cuban jungles, Fillmore contracted yellow fever. He survived the virulent disease and took a job after the war in Washington, D.C., with the U.S. Treasury. He later moved to New York City as an operative of the Bureau of Internal Revenue.

When Fillmore arrived in New York, its black citizens had been lobbying the state since before the beginning of the twentieth century for a National Guard regiment of their own. Although New York had fielded African American regiments during the Civil War, getting the state assembly to provide a militia of black citizen soldiers had proved impossible. As Fillmore, a Republican, became more involved in the everyday life of his adopted city and more embroiled in its rough and tumble politics, he took the lead in organizing a regiment of color. In 1911 and again in 1912 he and members of two African American political groups, the Equity Congress and the United Colored Democracy, cajoled white members of the state assembly to introduce bills that called for an all-black regiment—bills that never became law.

Meanwhile, without state blessing, a frustrated Fillmore went ahead and created a provisional regiment on his own with himself as colonel. Many of the city's black business leaders joined him, and he soon had one thousand men in his provisional regiment. In 1912 he used the symbolic date of 12 February, Abraham Lincoln's birthday, to make a clear statement that New York's black community deserved its own regiment and had more than enough men to fill the ranks. Fillmore led a march of six hundred men—lawyers, doctors, merchants, ministers, and even musicians—dressed in somber dark suits with armbands and divided into three battalions of twelve companies down Broadway from Harlem to Union Square. He made the desired impression, and a year later the first-term assemblyman Thomas Kane, whose Twenty-first District included parts of Harlem, introduced Assembly Bill 2100 into the state legislature. Kane's bill directed the adjutant general to "organize and equip a colored battalion of infantry in New York City." His bill passed both houses. On 2 June 1913 Governor William Sulzer signed it into law. An editorial in the *New York Age*, the city's African American newspaper, trumpeted, "We have The Regiment."

But it was not until 1916, when the New York National Guard was called out by President Woodrow Wilson to patrol the border with Mexico, that the Fifteenth New York was officially organized under the governorship of Charles Whitman. It turned out to be a bittersweet moment for Fillmore. He had his regiment but not his colonelcy. Whitman named one of his own political allies as commander, the attorney William Hayward. Fillmore, instead, got a captaincy. After the United States declared war on Germany in 1917, the 15th landed in France as the 369th U.S. Infantry. Fillmore became one of the first African American officers to enter the trenches on the western front. The regiment became known as Harlem's Hell Fighters. Fillmore was cited for bravery in the Champagne sector and received the Croix de Guerre. He later transferred to the 370th Infantry.

After World War I, Fillmore was commissioned a lieutenant colonel. He remained in politics as a Republican and became a leader in Harlem's Nineteenth Assembly District. He worked in the state auditor's office until his retirement in 1933. In 1941 his wife, Jessie, died. Fillmore died in New York in 1942.

FURTHER READING

Black, Lowell Dwight. "The Negro Volunteer Militia Units of the Ohio National Guard, 1870–1954: The Struggle for Military Recognition and Equality in the State of Ohio." Ph.D. diss., Ohio State University, 1976.

Harris, Stephen L. *Harlem's Hell Fighters: The African-American 369th Infantry in World War I* (2003).

Little, Arthur W. *From Harlem to the Rhine* (1936).

Obituary: *New York Age*, 2 May 1942.

STEPHEN L. HARRIS

Finch, William (1 Oct. 1832–Jan. 1911), slave, tailor, and politician, was born in Washington, in Wilkes County, Georgia, to Frances, a slave, and a white man whose surname was Finch. When William was twelve he was sent to live with another Wilkes County native, Judge Garnett Andrews, and in 1847, when he was fifteen, he apprenticed as a tailor. The following year Joseph H. Lumpkin, the chief justice of the Georgia Supreme Court, purchased William and brought him to his home in Athens, where Finch learned to read and write and also began a lifelong commitment to Christianity. Although he later joined the African Methodist Episcopal (AME) Church, it is likely that Finch first converted to the faith of his master, a devout Presbyterian. In 1854 Finch married Laura Wright, with whom he had five children.

Although still legally enslaved the Finch family enjoyed a fairly high degree of autonomy from Lumpkin, who probably allowed William Finch to hire out his time as a tailor. During the Civil War, however, Lumpkin required that Finch serve as a body servant to his son, a Confederate officer. From all accounts Finch enjoyed cordial relations with both Lumpkin and his son, and with Judge Andrews, whom he served in the final years of the war. By that time Finch had saved more than $135 in gold, enough to buy a home for his family in Athens in the summer of 1865. A modest man, he later attributed much of his success in business and politics to the positive influence and encouragement of Chief Justice Lumpkin. Finch's loyalty to his former masters did not extend, however, to loyalty to the cause they served. When Union soldiers of the 144th New York Regiment entered Athens in 1865, Finch presented the army with a Union flag.

Finch threw himself immediately into the business of Reconstruction. In Athens he worked with the Freedmen's Bureau to establish a school and in late 1865 he was elected as the chairman of a four-person delegation from Athens and Clarke County to a meeting of the Equal Rights Association to be held in Augusta, Georgia, in January 1866. At this meeting Finch was elected a vice president of the Equal Rights Association, a forerunner of the Republican Party. His political and business ambitions persuaded Finch to move his family from Athens, first to Augusta in 1866, and then to Atlanta, Georgia's fastest-growing city, in 1868. He arrived $50 in debt, but the influx of thousands of black and white migrants to Atlanta after the Civil War proved lucrative to Finch's tailoring business. By 1870 he was one of the leading black businessmen in Atlanta, owning more than $1,000 in real estate. Finch was also an active clergyman, having been ordained as a minister in the African Methodist Episcopal Church in 1868.

Finch's business success and his prominence in the church and in local Republican politics led him to seek a seat on Atlanta's city council in the elections of 1870. To that end he began to organize a chapter of the Mechanics' and Laborers' Union in Atlanta and in the summer of 1870 was elected chairman of the city's Fourth Ward Republican Club, which in turn duly selected Finch as its candidate for the fall. Probably it did not expect Finch to win election, since no African Americans had ever been elected Alderman in Atlanta. Although blacks in Atlanta had been able to vote since 1868, few had actually done so, in part because of intimidation and violence but also because local whites had altered the electoral rules to make council elections citywide. Since African Americans formed no more than a fifth of Atlanta's population, black candidates needed to win significant support among whites, and few whites were willing to offer it. In October 1870, however, the state's Republican governor ordered a return to Atlanta's traditional method of elections in ten geographically distinct city wards. Blacks formed the majority in both the Third and the Fourth Wards, and formed a sizable minority in the Fifth. In the November elections Finch duly won the Fourth, while George Graham, an unlettered carpenter, won the Third. Only blatant intimidation of black voters by white policemen in the Fifth Ward kept that district in the hands of white Democrats.

Since Democrats held a narrow, six to four, majority on the Atlanta city council, Finch, Graham, and their two white Republican colleagues were generally outvoted on most matters. The Republicans' plans of greatly increased spending on schools and hospitals for both races foundered, even though Finch had strongly advocated the need to build schools in white working class areas as well as in poor black neighborhoods. Finch, however, prided himself on his good relations with whites and secured for himself a place on the committee dealing with the upkeep and repair of city streets. White Democratic aldermen largely ignored Finch's collegial entreaties, and, indeed, in 1871 they even refused to condemn a white policeman who had threatened to arrest Alderman Finch at a session of the mayor's court. On occasion, though, Finch won concessions from the Democratic majority, usually for street repairs in black neighborhoods, by breaking ranks with his fellow Republicans to support Democratic policies. Finch, for example, was the only Republican to support a proposal requiring all men in Atlanta to pay a street tax. Those who failed or were unable to pay—and these disproportionately would be unemployed or underemployed black men—were enlisted as unpaid street repair workers. Alderman Finch's hard line on this matter may have been enough to ensure that the citywide public school system established by the council in 1871 included black schools with black teachers.

On the whole, however, William Finch's conciliatory approach to politics did little to appease his opponents. In August 1871 he was even attacked in a white newspaper for attempting to calm a black crowd who had gathered at the Atlanta courthouse to protest at the trial of a white chain gang guard who had beaten a black prisoner to death. The Atlanta *Sun* declared Finch a villain and a "notorious leader of bad men," who should have left crowd control to the police (cited in Russell and Thornbery, 322). Atlanta's era of biracial politics was to be short-lived. In 1872 Democrats in the Georgia state legislature ordered that Atlanta return to citywide elections. Finch contested the first citywide election as a Republican in 1872, but was defeated. Atlantans would not elect another African American to citywide office until 1953, when RUFUS E. CLEMENT won election to the Atlanta board of education. It was not until 1965, the year of the Voting Rights Act, that another African American, Q. V. Williamson, won election to the Atlanta city council.

Although Finch's party political career ended in 1872, he remained active in civic affairs. Throughout the 1870s he was a forceful advocate for increased public spending on black schools, though not forceful enough to persuade the parsimonious city council to provide adequate resources for black students. He ran again for city council in 1879 and for the state legislature in 1884, but lost both times. His tailoring business continued to prosper, assisted by a clientele that was primarily white and Democratic. Finch's personal life was less happy. Following the death of his first wife, Laura, in 1876, he remarried to Minnie Vason of Madison, Georgia, in 1881. Two years later, however, Finch mourned the death of one of his sons, also named William, who was executed for allegedly killing several soldiers at Fort Still in Arkansas, where he had been working as a barber. William Finch Jr. had apparently shot the soldiers after they had arrested him for attempting to steal a horse. Finch's relations with his fellow black Methodists were also rocky in the late 1870s and early 1880s. Although an elder of Bethel Methodist—one of Atlanta's biggest churches—since 1876, he was reprimanded on several occasions for disorderly conduct and the use of intemperate language. Ill feelings between Finch and Bethel's notoriously autocratic leader, the Reverend WESLEY GAINES, led to Finch's expulsion from the church in 1885.

Although Finch's expulsion from Bethel further weakened his influence in the black community he was to play one final, brief, but significant role in Atlanta politics. In 1886 he successfully persuaded white Atlantans to include blacks on a citywide Committee of Fifty which was to nominate all candidates for the upcoming municipal elections. In a well-received speech that October, Finch spoke of his own lifelong support for Prohibition and promised white business leaders that they could rely on "the better element of the colored people." Finch also reminded whites that he had "fought, bled, and died as a soldier in the Confederate Army," something of an exaggeration of his role as a body servant (Russell and Thornbery, 326). Finch, who was still very much alive, nonetheless struck a chord with his appeal to the Lost Cause: Atlanta's white leaders duly appointed two African Americans to the Committee of Fifty. Ironically, the Reverend Wesley Gaines, Finch's bitter rival, was one of them. The other was a Baptist minister.

When William Finch died in Atlanta, fewer than a thousand blacks were able to vote in that city, the consequence of a wave of white mob violence disfranchisement laws that swept the South in the 1890s and early 1900s.

FURTHER READING

Russell, James M., and Jerry Thornbery. "William Finch of Atlanta: The Black Politician as Civic Leader," in *Southern Black Leaders of the Reconstruction Era*, ed. Howard N. Rabinowitz (1982).

Obituary: Atlanta *Journal*, 11 Jan. 1911.

STEVEN J. NIVEN

Finley, Harold E. (30 Nov. 1905–19 July 1975), protozoologist and microscopist, was born in Palatka, Florida, the son of Lugenia Bryant and Eugene Finley. As a high school student at Central Academy in Palatka, Finley played trumpet for Al Osgood's Hot Five, a local jazz band.

In 1928 he completed a B.S. in Biology at Morehouse College in Atlanta, Georgia, before moving to Madison, Wisconsin, to pursue graduate work in zoology under the direction of Lowell E. Noland. Although he would eventually return to Madison to finish his Ph.D., financial pressures forced Finley to leave the university with his master's in 1929. He married Eva Elizabeth Browning on 30 August that same year. They had two children, Harold Eugene and Eva Kathleen.

Finley's teaching career began in the biology department at West Virginia State College, where he served first as an instructor and later as associate professor. In 1938 he returned to Atlanta as professor and head of the biology department at Morehouse. With his administration's support, he returned to Wisconsin to complete his Ph.D. with

Noland in 1942. In 1947 he was appointed head of the zoology department at Howard University, where he would remain for the rest of his career.

Although Finley's research interest in single-celled organisms (protozoa) was established at Noland's laboratory at the University of Wisconsin, the summers he spent at the Woods Hole Marine Biological Laboratory between 1930 and 1933 in Massachusetts were formative for his future career. The Marine Biological Laboratory was founded in 1888 as an independent research institution that focused on using marine animals as model organisms for investigating biological problems. Many of the most influential biologists of the twentieth century, including more than fifty Nobel laureates, spent time in Woods Hole as students, instructors, or researchers, and the laboratory's summer research institutes became a rite of passage for ambitious American biologists. The opportunity to study at Woods Hole was unusual for a young African American scientist in the 1930s and provided Finley with professional connections that would not have otherwise been available at the historically black colleges and universities where he spent most of his career.

Throughout his career Finley focused on the peritrichs, a group of ciliated protozoa that can live in both freshwater and marine environments. Finley was particularly interested in the genus *Vorticella*, a bell-shaped protozoan that has a retractable stalk. Finley first published on the organism's taxonomy while working with Noland but would remain involved in debates on its classification for the rest of his life. Finley's analysis of the ultrafine structure of the peritrich's stalk, developed using electron microscopy, helped biochemists understand how cells produce and use energy for motion. Noting that peritrichs were often found in polluted environments such as the canals in the Netherlands where Antony von Leeuwenhoek first discovered protozoa in the seventeenth century, Finley believed that they could be used in monitoring bacterial pollution levels. Although Finley died before his prediction materialized, protozoa levels are now commonly used to detect fecal contamination in streams and rivers.

Finley's first wife died in 1954; three years later he married Irene Sealy Pope. In the last two decades of his life, Finley was recognized as an international leader in the study of protozoa. He served as president of both the Society of Protozoologists (1966–1967) and the American Society of Microscopists (1971) and served as a representative of the U.S. National Academy of Sciences to the International Union of Biological Sciences' assemblies in 1967 and 1970. Finley held visiting appointments at an impressive number of institutions, including Indiana University; the Nencki Institute for Experimental Biology in Warsaw, Poland; Chelsea College, London; the Centre de Recherches Hydrobiologiques, Paris; the universities of Utrecht and Leiden, the Netherlands; Charles University, Prague; Bryn Mawr College; Dillard University; Fisk University; the University of Washington; and the Universidade de Brasília, Brazil.

Howard University's department of zoology grew dramatically during Finley's twenty-two years as chair. He oversaw the design and building of a new biology department building (1947–1957), expanded the faculty from five to sixteen full-time members, and obtained graduate-degree granting status for the department. In 1963 two of his students, Nathaniel Boggs and James Oliviere, were the first to receive Ph.D.s in zoology from Howard. A dedicated mentor, Finley supervised the work of forty-four master's students and sixteen doctoral candidates.

Finley never retired and continued his research at Howard University until a month before his death from cancer. Just a few weeks before his death, he was nominated for the President's National Medal of Science.

FURTHER READING

Obituaries: *The Journal of Protozoology* 23 (1976); *Transactions of the American Microscopical Society* 95 (1976).

AUDRA J. WOLFE

Finney, Ernest A. (23 Mar. 1931–), attorney, civil rights activist, state legislator, and Chief Justice of the South Carolina Supreme Court, was born Ernest Adelphous Finney Jr. to Ernest Finney Sr. and Colleen Goodwin on 23 March 1931 in Smithfield, Virginia. Finney's mother died when he was ten years old, leaving his father and aunts to raise him. His father was a longtime educator, who served in various capacities in the Virginia/DC/Maryland area before notably serving as a professor, registrar, and dean of Claflin College (Finney Jr.'s undergraduate alma mater), a private, historically black college in Orangeburg, South Carolina.

During Finney's childhood he knew he wanted to pursue a legal profession. When his father worked as a civil training office for the War Department during World War II, Finney saw how African

American lawyers in the Washington, DC, area were not only influential and respected figures in the community, but also how much they helped to improve the quality of life for the African American community (by the 1940s, African American lawyers were challenging and overturning racial segregation laws in education). Due to his father's constant career advancement, Finney moved often during his childhood. "Finney dealt with the frequent moves by managing change and operating outside his comfort zone" (Lett). This experience would later serve him well.

Finney entered Claflin College in 1949. While he wanted to pursue an academic program that would prepare him for a professional legal education, his father (while not objecting to his career goal) insisted that he pursue a teaching degree as a "fallback" (Lett). This advice proved to be invaluable in relationship to the context of the time. The racial politics during the 1940s and 1950s in South Carolina was not only reflected in the lack of African American lawyers in the state, but also in the difficulty (at the time) for them to make a decent living as a full-time attorney.

During the spring of 1952, Finney earned an A.B. degree in Education from Claflin College with an articulation agreement with South Carolina State College of Law that combined his collegiate senior year with his 1L at the law school. South Carolina State College of Law was at the time newest law school in the state, established in 1948. The South Carolina state legislature had opted to organize a segregated law school rather than desegregate the University of South Carolina School of Law in Columbia. This was due to a 1947 ruling in which John H. Wrighten successfully sued the University of South Carolina College of Law for admission. Although underfunded in comparison to its all-white counterpart, the law school produced fifty lawyers (during its almost twenty-year existence), many of whom would serve as trailblazers in the legal profession and also as catalysts who helped to dismantle racial segregation laws in South Carolina.

Finney graduated from South Carolina State College of Law in 1954. Upon graduating, he accepted a teaching position in Conway and married the former Frances Davenport. By 1960 the Finneys relocated to Sumter, where he established a private practice and took on civil rights litigation. One of his most notable cases was his defense of the "Friendship Nine." The Friendship Nine were a group of college students from Friendship Junior College—a now defunct school in Rock Hill, South Carolina—who were arrested and charged with trespassing while attempting to desegregate a lunch counter on 31 January 1961. The Friendship Nine were among the first sit-in groups who opted to serve jail time rather than paying a fine for their crime. Despite the time spent in jail, this case served as a moral victory for the nonviolent movement. During his early years of private practice, Finney represented close to six thousand people who were involved in some form of civil rights demonstrations in the state.

As Finney's reputation as a civil rights attorney rose, he sought further opportunities in the political arena. After two unsuccessful attempts, Finney was elected to the South Carolina House of Representatives in 1972. His election to the state legislature would make him the first African American to serve on the House Judiciary Committee since Reconstruction. During his tenure in the state legislature, Finney along with other African American state legislators founded the South Carolina Legislative Black Caucus; he served as its chairman from 1973 to 1975. Playing to his ability to operate out of his comfort zone, Finney was able to develop a consensus among his political friends and foes during his tenure in the state legislature. For this, his colleague in the legislature and later on South Carolina Supreme Court Justice, Jean Hoefer Toal, described Finney as a "master of strategy" (Lett).

In 1978 Finney left the state legislature to serve as judge in the 3rd Judicial Circuit. His experience on the bench would lead to an election to the South Carolina State Supreme Court as an associate justice in 1985 and ultimately to chief justice in 1994. Finney would hold this position until he retired in 2000.

Although retired from the bench, Finney served in various capacities of public service. Finney followed in father's footsteps as an educational administrator. During the 2002–2003 academic year, Finney returned to campus of South Carolina State University to serve as the institution's interim president. Into his eighties, Finney continued to work in private practice as the head and founder of the Finney Law Firm (which consists of several associates, notably his sons Jerry Leo and Ernest "Chip" Finney III, who in 2011 was a solicitor for the 3rd Judicial Circuit).

FURTHER READING

Burke, William L., and William C. Hine. "The South Carolina State College Law School: Its Roots,

Creation, and Legacy." In *Matthew J. Perry: The Man, His Times, and His Legacy*, edited by W. Lewis Burke and Belinda F. Gergel, 17–61 (2004).

"Finney Becomes 3rd Circuit Solicitor." *The State*, January 13, 2011. http://www.thestate.com/2011/01/11/1641770/finney-becomes-3rd-circuit-solicitor.html (accessed July 1, 2011).

Glore, Blinzy L. *On a Hilltop High: The Origin and History of Claflin College to 1984* (1997).

Lett, Mark E. "Ernest Finney: From Waiter to State Supreme Court Chief Justice." *The State*, June 5, 2011. http://www.thestate.com/2011/06/05/1847011/12-lives-part-of-a-yearlong-series.html (accessed July 1, 2011).

TRAVIS D. BOYCE AND WINSOME CHUNNU

Fishburne, Laurence (3 July 1961–), film and television actor, producer, director, playwright, and screenwriter, was born in Augusta, Georgia, to Laurence Fishburne II, a corrections officer, and Hattie Fishburne (née Crawford), an educator. Separated by the time Fishburne was born, his parents divorced when he was a young boy, and he moved to Brooklyn, New York, with his mother, where he grew up in a neighborhood riddled by gangs. His father lived nearby, and though never close, they saw each other about once a month, according to Fishburne. Home life with his mother was fractious, but she encouraged Fishburne to perform and, perhaps more important, instilled in him the importance of carrying himself with dignity and pride when dealing with the white world.

At the urging of his godfather, Maurice A. Watson, a professor of oral communications at Brooklyn College who was involved with a semi-professional theater group, the Afro-American Theatre Workshop, Fishburne began auditioning for television and film roles. At the age of ten he made his acting debut when he appeared in the first integrated network soap opera, *One Life to Live*. From 1973 to 1976 he played the role of the son in daytime television's first African American family. During this time Fishburne also made his first film appearance, in *Earl, Cornbread, and Me* (1975).

At the age of fourteen Fishburne won the role of Tyrone "Clean" Miller in Francis Ford Coppola's *Apocalypse Now* (1979) after lying about his age to get the part. He spent a year and a half on location in the Philippines, where, the actor admits, he indulged in increasingly wilder behavior under the influence of actors such as Dennis Hopper and Martin Sheen. Fishburne briefly attended Hollywood High School but soon returned to New York City, where he attended the High School of the Performing Arts in Manhattan. At the age of eighteen Fishburne moved to Los Angeles. As a struggling actor in the early 1980s he was typecast as a criminal or gangster in a series of action films such as *Death Wish II* (1982) and *Quicksilver* (1986) and in dramas such as *Rumble Fish* (1983), *The Cotton Club* (1984), and *The Color Purple* (1985). In an attempt to break out of such stereotypical roles Fishburne took the part of Cowboy Curtis on the popular children's television series *Pee-Wee's Playhouse* (1986–1988).

Fishburne married Hajna O. Moss, also an actor, in 1985. Their son Langston was born in 1987, and their daughter Montana was born in 1991. The couple also adopted Moss's five-year-old nephew. Fishburne and Moss divorced in 1995. In 1991 he began going by his given name, Laurence Fishburne, which he had used interchangeably with Larry Fishburne during his early career. Fishburne landed his first leading role in Carl Franklin's *Deep Cover* (1992). That year he also won the 1992 Tony Award for Best Actor for his performance in the AUGUST WILSON play *Two Trains Running*.

Fishburne was nominated for an Oscar for his sympathetic portrayal of the violent and manipulative IKE TURNER in *What's Love Got to Do with It* in 1993, and he won an Emmy Award for his portrayal of the role Martin in the episode "The Box" in the short-lived television series *Tribeca Stories*. Throughout the 1990s he worked with important directors such as JOHN SINGLETON; Fishburne modeled the strong father character Furious Styles in the film *Boyz 'n the Hood* (1991) on his own father's loving but stern demeanor. In 1995 Fishburne was cast as Othello in the feature film version of the Shakespeare play directed by Oliver Parker. Critics called Fishburne's performance "superb" and "stirring and powerful"; it was the first time in film history that an African American performer had been cast in the role.

Fishburne became most visible in the late 1990s, playing the character Morpheus in *The Matrix* (1999). Fishburne, who married the Cuban American actress Gina Torres on 20 September 2002, went on to star in two additional *Matrix* movies, *The Matrix Reloaded* (2003) and *The Matrix Revolutions* (2003). During this period he also appeared in the action film *Biker Boyz* (2003), as Sergeant Whitey Powers in Clint Eastwood's drama *Mystic River* (2003), as a terrorist in *Five Fingers* (2006), and as a mobster in the cop thriller *Assault on Precinct 13* (2005).

The NAACP awarded Fishburne the Image Award in 1998 for his starring role in the HBO television drama *Miss Evers' Boys* (1997), a film about the Tuskegee Syphilis Experiment, a notorious medical study that used 399 impoverished black men to study the effects of untreated syphilis. The production, for which Fishburne was also executive producer, won five Emmy awards. His continued efforts at directing and producing stem from his belief that "there are lots of black stories, some epic, some intimate, waiting to be told" (*Boston Globe*, 9 June 1993). After that time he served as the executive producer for the film *Hoodlum* (1997) and for the made-for-TV movie adaptation of WALTER MOSLEY's *Always Outnumbered, Always Outunned* (1998), and was producer for *Once in the Life* (2000) and *Five Fingers* (2005).

In addition to his work in film and television Fishburne continued to appear on stage and devote time to pursuits outside of the entertainment industry. He played the part of Henry II in the 1999 Broadway revival of *Lion in Winter*. He wrote, starred, and directed in the play *Riff Raff*, which became the basis of the film *Once in the Life*, which he also wrote and directed. In 1996 Fishburne was selected as an ambassador for the United Nations International Children's Fund (UNICEF). In his capacity as ambassador he visited UNICEF-supported programs for children affected by HIV/AIDS in South Africa and later narrated a "virtual field trip" relating his experience there, lobbied the U.S. government on behalf of UNICEF, and hosted educational events at the United Nations on the Day for the African Child. He was particularly interested in programs that help former child soldiers in Africa and children affected by armed conflict.

A child actor who rose to become a leading man in films that ran the gamut from action to drama, Fishburne was in the vanguard of the increased visibility of African American actors in the film industry in the early twenty-first century. Though he acknowledged the legacy of African American film actors who preceded him, Fishburne emphasized, "I want to be remembered as an actor, not a role model" (*Columbus Dispatch*, 5 Mar. 2000).

FURTHER READING

Bogle, Donald. *Toms, Coons, Mulattoes, Mamies, and Bucks: An Interpretative History of Blacks in American Film* (1994).

Guerrero, Ed. *Framing Blackness: The African American Image in Film* (1993).

Lahr, John. "Escaping the Matrix: Laurence Fishburne on the Streets of Brooklyn, in a Philippine Jungle, and on a Stage of his Own," *New Yorker* (5 Apr. 2004).

LAURA ISABEL SERNA

Fisher, Ada Lois Sipuel (8 Feb. 1924–18 Oct. 1995), civil rights pioneer, lawyer, and educator, was born Ada Louis Sipuel in Chickasha, Oklahoma, the daughter of Travis B. Sipuel, a minister and later bishop of the Church of Christ in God, one of the largest black Pentecostal churches in the United States, and Martha Bell Smith, the child of a former slave. Her parents moved to Chickasaw, Oklahoma, shortly after the Tulsa race riot of 1921. Ada's brother Lemuel had initially planned to challenge the segregationist policies of the University of Oklahoma. After returning from service in World War II, however, he went to Howard University Law School, because he did not want to delay his career with protracted litigation. Ada, who was younger and had been in college during the war, was willing to delay her legal career for the opportunity to challenge segregation. She entered Arkansas A&M College on a scholarship in 1941 but transferred to Oklahoma State College for Negroes (later Langston University) in 1942 and graduated in 1945. In 1944 she married Warren W. Fisher, a longtime family friend and son of a Baptist minister. They had two children.

In 1946 she applied for admission to the University of Oklahoma School of Law, at the time the state's only law school. Following its segregationist policies, the university rejected her application solely on the basis of her race. In an extraordinary meeting, Dr. George L. Cross, the university's president, asserted that but for her race Sipuel would be admitted to the law school. He then willingly put this statement in writing, setting the stage for her lawsuit. Although already married at the time, she sued under her maiden name, and thus the case was known as *Sipuel v. Board of Regents of the University of Oklahoma*.

Two Oklahoma state courts found in favor of the university. THURGOOD MARSHALL, a litigator with the NAACP Legal Defense and Educational Fund, took her case to the U.S. Supreme Court. The Court issued a per curiam decision, summarily reversing the ruling of the Oklahoma courts. The Court relied on the precedent in *Missouri ex rel. Gaines v. Canada* (1938), which had required Missouri to open its only state law school to African Americans, and ordered the University of Oklahoma to admit

Ada Lois Sipuel Fisher files her application, Norman, Oklahoma, 1948. She sits with the dean of admissions, seated left, and, standing left to right, Thurgood Marshall and Amos T. Hall. (Library of Congress/Association for the Advancement of Colored People Records.)

Sipuel to law school. Initially the state tried to circumvent the decision by creating a separate and thoroughly bogus law school for blacks. In the summer of 1949 university officials finally allowed Sipuel to register for classes. She thus became the first African American woman to attend a previously all-white law school in the South.

By the time the law school allowed her to register, the semester had already begun. The law school gave Fisher (as she was now known) a special chair marked "colored" and roped off from the rest of the class. Despite this her classmates and teachers welcomed her and shared notes with her. Students studied with her and helped her catch up on the material she had missed. She was forced to eat in a chained-off and guarded area of the school cafeteria, but she recalled many years later that when the guards were not around "white students would crawl under the chain and eat with me." Adding to these circumstances and the usual difficulties of law school were the pressure of the lawsuit and the desire to succeed for all those who had supported her suit. "I knew the eyes of Oklahoma and the nation were on me," she said later. Moreover, because her lawsuit and tuition were supported by hundreds of small donations, "I owed it to those people to make it"

Fisher graduated from the law school in 1951 and in 1952 began practicing law in her hometown of Chickasha. In 1954 she represented a client before the Oklahoma Supreme Court. In 1957 she joined the faculty at Langston University, where she served as chair of the social sciences department and later as assistant vice president for academic affairs. She later returned to the University of Oklahoma, where in 1968 she earned a master's degree in history. In 1987–1988 she served as assistant vice president for academic affairs and later as director of the Urban Center at Langston University before retiring to become counsel to Automations Research Systems in Virginia. In 1988 the Oklahoma Legislative Black Caucus honored her achievement in pursuing justice in *Sipuel v. Board of Regents of the University of Oklahoma*. On the fortieth anniversary of the U.S. Supreme Court's decision (1974–1975), she served on the Advisory Committee on Civil Rights for the Oklahoma Regents for Higher Education.

Throughout her career Fisher remained active in civil rights organizations, working with the Urban League, the NAACP, and the American Civil Liberties Union. In 1991 the University of Oklahoma awarded her an honorary doctorate of humane letters, and in 1992 Oklahoma governor David Walters appointed her to the Board of Regents of the University of Oklahoma. Fisher noted, "This appointment completes a 45-year cycle." She planned to bring "a new dimension to university policies. Having suffered severely from the bigotry and racial discrimination as a student, I am sensitive to that kind of thing." She died in Oklahoma City.

FURTHER READING

Fisher, Ada Louis Sipuel, with Danney Goble. *A Matter of Black and White: The Autobiography of Ada Lois Sipuel Fisher* (1996).

Kluger, Richard. *Simple Justice: The History of Brown v. Board of Education and Black America's Struggle for Equality* (1976).

Obituary: *Washington Post*, 21 Oct. 1995.

This entry is taken from the *American National Biography* and is published here with the permission of the American Council of Learned Societies.

PAUL FINKELMAN

Fisher, Elijah John (2 Aug. 1858–31 July 1915), was the second youngest of eight sons, and twenty daughters, born to Miles and Charlotte Fisher, who according to the laws of the state of Georgia were the property of Dr. Robert Ridley of La Grange. Miles Fisher, purchased for his carpentry skills, was a lay preacher who named his children for Bible characters; he was generally trusted by Ridley, and able to speak on behalf of the enslaved population on the plantation. Charlotte Fisher's maternal grandfather was a Creek Indian with African blood. Elijah Fisher was "hired out" at age four or five as a companion to the crippled son of Reverend Abner Callaway; according to family recollections, the two boys were blissfully unaware of the caste and color distinctions so important in the lives of their parents. Reverend Callaway baptized Fisher on 19 October 1863.

The family was freed in the summer of 1863, when federal troops arrived at the Ridley plantation. The Fishers continued to work another year for Ridley, then made a down-payment to him on forty-eight acres of their own land. The last payment was made in 1874, but a year later, Miles Fisher died. Although each had an equal inheritance, Fisher's siblings were less interested in farming, and he contracted to buy their shares. During the winter he attended a school conducted by Danny McGee, a literate formerly enslaved man known as "Professor."

In 1876 Fisher had to sell the farm. Two of his older brothers, Miles II and Henry, attacked the pastor of the First Colored Baptist Church for a slighting reference to their father as a "floor preacher," and to save them from prison he had to forfeit his entire crop of corn, cotton, and potatoes, leaving him without means to live or plant the next crop. At the age of nineteen, he found work in the coal mines of Anniston, Alabama, at fifty cents a day. On 25 September 1877, Fisher married FloridaNeely, a copper-colored woman with jet black hair, whose features clearly showed African, Native American, and European ancestry.

The Fishers made their home in La Grange, Georgia, while Fisher worked again in the mines at Anniston, then as a butler to Colonel A. T. Tyler. Eventually, he devoted himself entirely to teaching school, receiving ten cents a month from each child. He was invited to begin teaching at Long Cane, Georgia, but had an accident boarding a train, which severed his left leg above the knee, his second toe on the right foot, and the third finger on his right hand. Despite his injuries, Fisher was ordained a Baptist minister 10 May 1882. Though paid very little money, he was supplied by his congregations with corn, potatoes, chickens, butter, and syrup. The same year the Fisher's second daughter, Shepherd Mattie, was born, joining her older sister Gertrude Lillian. Between 1884 and 1896 the couple gave birth to Elijah John Jr., James Edward, Charlotte E., and MILES MARK FISHER.

Simultaneously responsible for three or more rural churches, Fisher was called in 1883 as pastor to First Baptist Church in Anniston, Alabama, and, with the exception of Mt. Zion in Whitefield Crossing, Georgia (which refused to accept his exit), resigned from his other ministries. Stretched across the state line, Fisher was chosen assistant secretary of the Missionary Baptist Convention of Georgia in 1885, and moderator of the Western Union Association. In October 1889 he was invited to the pulpit of Mt. Olive Baptist Church in Atlanta, where he also entered the divinity department of Atlanta Baptist Seminary, later renamed Morehouse College. He entered as a senior thanks to his excellent entrance exam scores, and graduated in 1890. He served another term as moderator of the Western Union Association 1893–1896. At the Cotton States International Exposition in 1895, Fisher was chosen to be master of ceremonies for Baptist Day.

He moved to Nashville, Tennessee, in 1901, where he served as pastor of Spruce Street Baptist Church until 1903. All three of his daughters graduated from Spelman Seminary in Atlanta; Gertrude Fisher also completed pharmacy school at Meharry Medical College in Nashville. Elijah John Jr. graduated from Kentucky State University in Louisville, James Edward and Miles Mark from Morehouse College in Atlanta.

During the summer of 1902, Fisher spent a vacation at the University of Chicago, where he studied Greek and Hebrew. According to Miles Fisher he was taken aback by "commercialized vice and the licensed saloon cursing the weaker element of his race and marring the splendid record of Negro achievement" (Fisher, p. 90). He received invitations to preach in a number of churches, including Olivet Baptist, the oldest black Baptist church in the city. On 20 October 1902 Olivet extended a call to Fisher, which he accepted.

His first year in Chicago was stormy. The treasurer of Olivet was convicted of embezzling $6,000, apparently beguiled by two men who persuaded him that they could arrange a donation of $15,000 toward the church's debt of $28,000 if the members raised $6,000. Headlines in 1903 blamed the newly arrived Fisher for the church's financial state, calling him "a jack-leg preacher."

Fisher calmly secured financial support, first to continue renting the building, and two years later to repurchase the mortgage. His support was solicited by local candidates for public office; Reverend Fisher made a point of inviting candidates to come see him at the church, rather than going to see them at campaign headquarters. In 1904, he received an honorary Doctor of Laws degree at the commencement exercises of Guadalupe College in Sequin, Texas. By 1905 his church was on a sound footing and his ministry increasingly well respected. In September of that year, Olivet hosted the annual session of the National Baptist Convention, an organization representing two million members.

By 1908 Fisher had inspired a growing array of social programs through the church. That year, the *Chicago Tribune* reported the church was "feeding daily fifty to seventy-five destitute men, women and children, and half of whom are white." A photo from the period shows "Kindergarten children getting their daily milk" through a church program.

By 1911, Olivet had grown from a membership of six hundred to over three thousand. Morehouse College awarded him a Doctor of Divinity degree at its 1912 commencement.

Reverend Fisher was elected chair of the National Baptist Convention's delegation to the World Missionary Conference, held in 1909 in Edinburgh, Scotland. He served as a life member of the executive board and vice president of the National Baptist Convention. He died at home in bed, after several months of illness, with letters from all over the country wishing for his recovery; his sister Sarah observed, "The people are so anxious about him, both white and colored." Florida Fisher remained a church missionary in Chicago, as did their daughter Mattie, and Miles Mark Fisher followed his father into the ministry, serving in 1922 as pastor of Zion Baptist Church in Racine, Wisconsin, and, from 1932 at White Rock Baptist Church in Durham, North Carolina.

FURTHER READING

Fisher, Miles Mark. *The Master's Slave: Elijah John Fisher* (1922).

CHARLES ROSENBERG

Fisher, Gail (18 Aug. 1935–2 Dec. 2000), actress, was born in Orange, New Jersey. She grew up in Potter's Crossing in Edison Township, New Jersey, an area once described as one of the most impoverished rural communities on the East Coast. After her father passed away, when she was two years old, her mother was determined that neither Gail nor her four older siblings would fall prey to the ills that afflicted many in their impecunious surroundings.

For Fisher, one route of escape from her environment was her stunning good looks, an attribute that contributed to her success as a cheerleader and beauty queen. She was crowned Miss Black New Jersey and Miss Press Photographer. Fisher was interested in acting and worked diligently to hone her skills. She often made sacrifices to meet her goals, skipping meals to pay for acting lessons and taking on a variety of jobs that ranged from modeling to working in a factory assembly line. Her brief but lucrative exposure for the black-owned Grace Del Marco fashion model landed her in numerous national magazine advertisements for hair products, soft drinks, cigarettes, and cosmetics where she commanded a near-top-scale (sixty dollars an hour) salary.

In 1960 her determination paid off with an audition that led to a nationally televised commercial for a laundry detergent. The commercial involved spoken lines, the first ever for an African American performer in television advertising. Fisher's success did not lead to increased opportunities in film and television right away; however, she did find some success on Broadway. In 1961 she was an understudy to actress Ruby Dee in the comedy *Purlie Victorious*. Instead she continued to hone her acting skills by studying with renowned acting instructor Lee Strasberg before moving on to the Young Repertory Theater of Lincoln Center and working with directors Elia Kazan and Herbert Blau, who cast her in the role of a young firebrand in the play *Danton's Death*. This play was Fisher's most substantial role to date and one that would transform her career.

Shortly thereafter, Fisher moved to California, where she continued the arduous process of trying to break into film and television. She landed a couple of minor TV roles on *General Hospital* (1963) and *My Three Sons* (1967). Despite these roles, she continued to struggle and support herself by performing odd jobs to make ends meet. One of those jobs was as a secretary for talent manager John Levy. Levy fired her a week before she would have been eligible for unemployment insurance, because she took him at his word when he asked her to "clean out the files" and literally did so by discarding his business records. In spite of the confusion, Levy and Fisher began dating and in January 1965 Fisher gave birth to their daughter, and her second child, Jole. Samara, her eldest, was born in 1960. In March of 1965, the two were married and Levy subsequently became her manager. The following year Jole was born to the union. The name was derived from the first two letters of her father's first and last name.

After Jole was born, Fisher continued to audition and appeared as a guest character on the shows *He and She*, *My Three Sons*, and *Room 222*. Finally, in 1968, she received the opportunity of a lifetime when she was offered the character of Peggy Fair on the CBS show *Mannix*, starring Mike Connors. *Mannix* revolved around the adventures of a private investigator who often had to be extracted from perilous situations by his articulate and shrewd secretary, Peggy Fair. The show had been on the air for a year with teetering ratings before the network decided to overhaul the series. Connors was initially an employee of a high-tech security firm, but the role was changed to a more conventional private detective, one with an office and a secretary. During auditions, the producers had made it clear to all the actresses who responded that the race of the character was neutral.

The role was initially a bit part, but Fisher eventually became a costar in a little more than a season. Unfortunately, her rising popularity did not exempt her from racism behind the scenes. When she started working on the show, she had to wear her own clothes on set because the wardrobe assistant couldn't handle working with black performers; and on the last day of filming of her first season, someone vandalized her dressing room and wrote racial epithets on the walls.

In 1970 she became the first African American woman to win an Emmy Award for best supporting actress in a dramatic series. During her tenure on *Mannix*, Fisher also appeared as a guest on other shows and made-for-TV movies such as *Love American Style* and *Every Man Needs One*.

Mannix remained on the air until 1975. Afterward, Fisher found it difficult to find steady work. She appeared on television sporadically, most notably as a guest character on *Fantasy Island* in 1979 and *The White Shadow* in 1980. During this time Fisher's personal life started to unravel. First, she and Levy divorced and she struggled with substance abuse. Things had gotten so bad that she stopped working and entered into a drug diversion program. Her life seemed to be back on track in 1983 when she appeared on the popular television show *Knight Rider*. In 1987 she starred in the cinema production of *Mankillers*, the only film credit of her career. Her last role was in 1990, in the made-for-television film *Donor*.

On 2 December 2000 Fisher died of kidney failure at a hospital in Los Angeles, California. At the time of her passing Fisher had resided in Beverly Hills and spoke ardently of her accomplishments.

Throughout her career, Fisher remained conscientious about the types of roles she accepted and the images of African Americans on television.

FURTHER READING

Bogle, Donald. *Prime Time Blues* (2002).

Levy, John. *Men, Women, and Girl Singers* (2000).

ARTHUR BANTON

Fisher, Miles Mark (29 Oct. 1899–14 Dec. 1970), minister and historian, was born one of six children to Elijah John Fisher, a Baptist minister, and Florida Neely in Atlanta, Georgia. His father later pastored the Olivet Baptist Church in Chicago, where he had moved his family. The young Fisher grew up in Chicago but was sent to Atlanta to attend Morehouse College where he earned the B.A. in 1918. He was immediately ordained, but worked for the YMCA as camp secretary. Fisher married Ada Virginia Foster, with whom he would have six children.

In 1919 Fisher returned to Chicago to take over the International Baptist Church. One year later he moved to Racine, Wisconsin, to pastor the Zion Baptist Church. In 1921 he published a short biography of Lott Carey, a pioneer black Baptist missionary to West Africa. In 1922 Fisher earned the BD and thus became the first black graduate of Northern Baptist Theological Seminary in Lombard, Illinois. There he researched the history of black foreign missions, displaying an interest in black church history that he would nourish for life. Fisher then earned the M.A. from the University of Chicago in 1922 with a thesis on the history of the Olivet Baptist Church, the oldest black Baptist church in Chicago. In 1922 Fisher moved south and found work as an English instructor at Virginia Union University. That same year he published his first major work, *The Master's Slave*, a biography of his father, who had died in 1915. Fisher's interest in publishing black history must have been nurtured by his Chicago connections. It was in Chicago that Carter G. Woodson had founded the Association for the Study of Negro Life and Culture (ASNLC) in 1915. The following year the ASNLC under Woodson began publishing the quarterly *Journal of Negro History*. Woodson, who earned a Ph.D. in history from Harvard University, was one of the first black trained historians who pushed other blacks to write the history of their own people. In 1921 he released *The History of the Negro Church* which remained for many years the standard work in the field. Following in Woodson's footsteps, Fisher pursued a career as an activist historian, committed to publicizing the accomplishments of the black church and its ministers.

While in Virginia, Fisher pastored several local churches and became the J. B. Hoyt Professor of Church History and New Testament Greek at Richmond Theological Seminary. In 1924 he wrote *Virginia Union University and Some of Her Achievements*, an historical account of a college founded for blacks after Emancipation. In 1933 Fisher accepted the pastorate of the White Rock Baptist Church in Durham, North Carolina. That same year he released *A Short History of the Baptist Denomination*, in which he presented a more extensive discussion of the black Baptist denominations than was then available in existing works. In 1934 Fisher joined the history department of Shaw University, where he remained for two decades as a professor of church history.

While in North Carolina Fisher found time to continue his historical studies at the University of Chicago, where he was awarded the Ph.D. in history in 1948. In 1953 the American Historical Association (AHA) published *Negro Slave Songs in the United States*, a revision of his dissertation, a work that won an award from the AHA. This book treats a theme important to the Harlem Renaissance and argues that black spirituals, which Fisher views as songs of protest, were a unique creation of American slaves, not pale imitations of white songs, as George Pullen Jackson, an outstanding scholar of American folk music, had claimed in *White and Negro Spirituals* (1943). With this last book Fisher won wide acclaim as an historian who offered a fresh interpretation of African American folklore. Fisher also contributed many articles and reviews to scholarly journals. He retired from the pastorate in 1964 and the following year resigned from Shaw. He died in Richmond, Virginia.

FURTHER READING

Murphy, Larry J., Gordon Melton, and Gary L. Ward, eds. *Encyclopedia of African American Religions* (1993).

Obituary: *New York Times*, 19 Dec. 1970.

DAVID MICHEL

Fisher, Rudolph (9 May 1897–26 Dec. 1934), author and physician, was born in Washington, D.C., the son of John Wesley Fisher, a clergyman, and Glendora Williamson. Fisher was raised in Providence, Rhode Island, and in 1919 received his B.A. from Brown University, where he studied both English and biology. Fisher's dual interests, literature and science, were reflected in his achievements at Brown, where he won numerous oratorical contests and was granted departmental honors in biology; the following year he received an M.A. in Biology. In 1920 Fisher returned to Washington to attend Howard University Medical School. He graduated with highest honors in June 1924 and interned at Washington's Freedman's Hospital. Later that year Fisher married Jane Ryder, a local teacher, with whom he had one son.

When Fisher moved to New York in 1925 he made rapid advances in his careers as a doctor and a writer. A bright young physician Fisher became a fellow of the National Research Council at Columbia University's College of Physicians and Surgeons. There he studied bacteriology, pathology, and roentgenology (the use of X-rays) for two years before opening up his own practice and publishing the results of his independent scientific research. Fisher was also an instant success as a fiction writer, publishing four short stories during his first year at Columbia. His story, "The City of Refuge," is an ironic tale that juxtaposed Harlem's promise with its inevitable shortcomings. The story appeared in the prestigious *Atlantic Monthly* (Feb. 1925), a first for a Harlem Renaissance writer, and was included in Edward J. O'Brien's *Best Short Stories of 1925* later that year. From this point onward, Fisher's career as a writer would be characterized by his ability to place his stories in traditionally white, mainstream publications such as the *Atlantic Monthly* and *McClure's*, as well as in black publications such as *Crisis* and *Opportunity*. His stories deal with the conflict between the values of Southern black folk and the demands of Northern urban life as well as the effects of interracial and intraracial prejudice on Harlem's inhabitants.

Fisher's first novel, *The Walls of Jericho* (1928), explores America's equation of white skin with economic opportunity, and the resulting class antagonism in Harlem. Warmly received by black critics because the novel lacked the exotic and erotic sensationalism of many insider exposés of Harlem, *The Walls of Jericho* examines the tensions between the black proletarians, or "rats," and the black middle and upper classes, or "dickties." Although his often comic and ironic dissection of Harlem society skewered upper-class pretensions as well as lower-class ignorance, Fisher nevertheless concluded his novel with a utopian resolution: a truck-driving furniture mover, Joshua "Shine" Jones, overcomes his enmity for a wealthy lawyer, Fred Merrit, who in turn provides him with the opportunity to start his own business.

Following the publication of his novel Fisher pursued various positions that confirmed not only his continued commitment to a dual career in medicine and writing but also his willingness to act as public educator within his community. In 1929 he was appointed superintendent of the International Hospital on Seventh Avenue, a position he held through 1932. In addition he worked as a roentgenologist for the New York Health Department from 1930 to 1934, served on the literature committee of the 135th Street Young Men's Christian Association, and lectured at the 135th Street Branch of the New York Public Library.

Fisher's next novel, *The Conjure-Man Dies: A Mystery Tale of Dark Harlem* (1932), generally recognized as the first black detective novel, is an elaborately plotted work that utilizes flashbacks in order to reconstruct the mystery behind the puzzling murder of a conjurer who later appears alive after the disappearance of the corpse. *The Conjure-Man Dies* allowed Fisher to continue his exploration of Harlem's social climate, while also indulging his interest in science and medicine through his fictional creation, Dr. John Archer. Summoned to examine the murdered corpse, Archer becomes the cerebral assistant to a local police detective, Perry Dart, in the ensuing investigation. Using medical discussions about the properties of blood and scientific debates about determinism, Fisher weaves an eerie tale.

Although he intended *The Conjure-Man Dies* to be the first in a series of Harlem-based detective novels featuring Archer and Dart, Fisher completed only one sequel, *John Archer's Nose*, a novelette published posthumously in January 1935 in *Metropolitan* magazine. Fisher did, however, complete a dramatic treatment of his earlier detective novel, titled *Conjur' Man Dies*, which was staged in 1936 at the Lafayette Theatre in Harlem to mixed reviews.

Rudolph Fisher was killed, ironically, by the intellectual curiosity that fueled his substantial achievements. Exposed to lethal radiation during his work with newly developed X-ray equipment, the multitalented writer known for his acerbic wit was stricken with intestinal cancer and died a tragically early death in New York City. Despite his substantial artistic contributions to the Harlem Renaissance, Rudolph Fisher remained underappreciated by literary scholarship through the end of the twentieth century.

FURTHER READING

Bell, Bernard W. *The Afro-American Novel and Its Tradition* (1987).

Huggins, Nathan Irvin. *Harlem Renaissance* (1971).

Lewis, David Levering. *When Harlem Was in Vogue* (1981).

Obituaries: *New York Times*, 27 Dec. 1934; *New York Age*, 5 Jan. 1935.

This entry is taken from the *American National Biography* and is published here with the permission of the American Council of Learned Societies.

MICHAEL MAIWALD

Fitzbutler, William Henry (1837?– Dec. 1901), the first African American to graduate from the University of Michigan Medical School, civil rights advocate, and journalist, was born in Malden, Essex County, Ontario, the son of a former American slave. His date of birth is uncertain: some sources suggest that he was born on 22 December 1837, while others suggest that he was born on that date in 1842. He was reportedly baptized as William Henry Butler, but in his early twenties he chose not to use his first name and added the prefix "Fitz" to his surname because he found "Butler" too common, and perhaps too servile.

As a youngster Henry attended public schools for blacks in southwestern Ontario. In 1866 he married Sarah Helen McCurdy, the daughter of William H. McCurdy, a prosperous Ontario farmer. The couple initially lived in the predominantly black towns of Amherstburg and New Canaan, Ontario, where Fitzbutler made a living as a teacher in the black schools and also found occasional labor as a tutor, farm laborer, surveyor, and lumberman. He was, however, drawn to the study of science. Some years earlier his older sister Elizabeth had attended Adrian College, a progressive Methodist preparatory school in Adrian, a small town in southeastern Lower Michigan, on a spur of the Underground Railroad. Henry also went to Adrian, spending a year in the college's science department studying biology, chemistry, and geology. Upon his return to Amherstburg he became an apprentice to a white physician, William C. Lundy, an alumnus of Victoria University in Toronto.

Dr. Lundy urged Fitzbutler to pursue a medical career, and he served as Fitzbutler's preceptor when in 1870 Fitzbutler applied and was admitted to the Detroit Medical College in Detroit, Michigan. Sarah Fitzbutler and the couple's two children remained in Ontario when Fitzbutler moved to Detroit. He became the first black student at the Detroit Medical College upon his enrollment in January 1871. Perhaps he encountered race-based prejudice at the college, or perhaps he wished to study at the better-equipped and more widely renowned University of Michigan at Ann Arbor, some thirty-five miles west of Detroit. In any case Fitzbutler moved to Ann Arbor and enrolled in the medical school there in January 1872.

By this time the University of Michigan had some eleven hundred students. Its crusading antislavery president, E. O. Haven, had quietly admitted African American male students in 1868 and initiated other policy changes that led to the widely publicized admission of women students on the same academic terms as men in 1870. Ann Arbor itself had a population of around eleven thousand in 1870, of whom only about a hundred and twenty were black; most of the blacks lived in Lower Town, a segregated black community located north of the Huron River, apart from the University of Michigan campus and the center of Ann Arbor. With his credits from the Detroit Medical College and his experience as an apprentice, in the spring of 1872 Fitzbutler became the first African American to graduate from the University of Michigan Medical School.

Reunited following Henry's graduation, the Fitzbutler family moved to Louisville, Kentucky, where Henry opened his own private medical practice. Although he was socially shunned by white physicians and denied privileges at all of Louisville's hospitals, Fitzbutler's academic credentials and practical experience helped him build a thriving practice among Louisville's large African American community. One incident in 1877 earned him the grudging respect of some in the white medical community. Fitzbutler was among several physicians called to the scene when a sixteen-year-old white girl, Lillian Frivall, was seriously injured after her clothing caught fire in a kitchen accident. While white doctors debated her condition, Fitzbutler began the necessary removal of her clothing and debridement of the wounds. Several white doctors demanded that the girl's father dismiss Fitzbutler because he was black; Mr. Frivall, enraged, dismissed all other physicians, commended Lillian to Fitzbutler's care, and retained Fitzbutler as the family physician permanently thereafter.

Soon after his arrival in Louisville, Fitzbutler emerged as a leader of the African American community, publicly advocating civil rights and social advancement for blacks. In February 1873 he addressed a statewide meeting on the issue of access for black children to Kentucky's public schools and helped spark a movement for education reform that developed over the next decade into a major campaign for reform and equal educational opportunity for African Americans. In Covington in 1874 Fitzbutler led a convention that opposed a state legislative initiative to create a separate school system for blacks. He also ran unsuccessfully several times for the Louisville municipal school board, becoming the first black to seek elective office in Kentucky. In 1883 he participated in the state educational convention held at Frankfort, where he continued to advocate equal access for blacks in the state's public schools.

Fitzbutler's political commitment to racial equality was also expressed in his work as a journalist. In the mid-1870s he provided funding and occasional editing for the *Planet*, a short-lived Louisville newspaper devoted to educational opportunity for blacks. When that paper failed, Fitzbutler launched his own weekly, the *Ohio Falls Express* (1879–1901). Edited and published by Fitzbutler, the paper was aimed at Louisville's growing African American community, which then numbered around fifteen thousand. The *Express* carried national, state, and local news, as well as social, lodge, and church notices specifically about Louisville's black population.

Fitzbutler also encouraged young African Americans to study medicine, and he acted as a preceptor for several young men who sought entry to the few medical schools that admitted black students. Although Louisville had four medical schools in the early 1870s, none admitted African Americans. In 1886 Fitzbutler began to lobby state lawmakers for the establishment of a medical school in Kentucky whose admissions policies would not discriminate on the basis of race or color. He gathered substantial political and financial support, and when in 1888 the state legislature passed a bill permitting the creation of such an institution, Fitzbutler and two other African American physicians, Dr. W. A. Burney of New Albany, Indiana, and Dr. Rufus Conrad of Louisville, immediately opened the Louisville National Medical College.

As its dean and professor of surgery, Fitzbutler oversaw all the college's administrative and teaching activities and also taught courses in surgery, materia medica, and therapeutics. The college's first class—consisting of six students who had entered with advanced standing gained at other institutions—graduated with M.D. degrees in 1889. Initially the college's classes convened in Louisville's United Brothers' Hall, and the 1889 commencement exercises were held in the Center Street Methodist Church. Fitzbutler's successes in fundraising permitted the college to purchase a building on West Green Street (later Liberty Street) that had formerly been home to the Louisville School of Pharmacy. Because black patients were not admitted to Louisville's hospitals, the college acquired two houses next door and opened its Auxiliary Hospital, which treated patients regardless of their race.

Fitzbutler's wife, Sarah McCurdy Fitzbutler, enrolled with the first full class in 1889 and earned her M.D. degree in 1892. Sarah Fitzbutler was appointed superintendent of the hospital, where she also managed a nurses' training program, which was added to the college's work in the mid-1890s. As national standards for medical education were raised, the college kept pace. Its initial three-year curriculum was expanded to four years in 1896. The college also earned a positive assessment in the influential Flexner Report published in 1910, which forced the closure of many smaller medical colleges.

The Fitzbutlers had six children, of whom four became physicians. Henry Fitzbutler died in December 1901 in Louisville. His wife continued to manage the college, the hospital, the nurses' training program, and her husband's private medical practice for another ten years. The Louisville National Medical College closed in 1912, largely because of a lack of assured state funding and because of its policy of providing medical care and training to patients and students who could not pay.

FURTHER READING

A brief biographical card, completed by Henry Fitzbutler on 27 July 1900, is held at the University of Michigan's Bentley Historical Library, in the UM Alumni Association's Necrology File.

Hanawalt, Leslie L. "Henry Fitzbutler: Detroit's First Black Medical Student," *Detroit in Perspective: A Journal of Regional History* 1 (Winter 1973).

Neverdon-Morton, Cynthia. *Afro-American Women of the South and the Advancement of the Race, 1895–1925* (1989).

Scott, Emmett J. *Scott's Official History of the Negro in the World War* (1919).

LAURA M. CALKINS

Fitzgerald, Ella (25 Apr. 1917–15 June 1996), singer and songwriter, was born Ella Jane Fitzgerald in Newport News, Virginia, the only child of William

Fitzgerald, a transfer wagon driver, and Temperance Williams, a laundress and caterer. Fitzgerald never knew her father; her mother married Joseph Da Silva, a Portuguese immigrant, when Fitzgerald was three years old. Following the tide of the Great Migration, the family moved north to Yonkers, New York. Fitzgerald's half-sister, Frances, was born there in 1923.

Fitzgerald's childhood is scantily documented; throughout her life she remained extremely reluctant to grant interviews and to reveal much about her early years in particular. She belonged to Bethany African Methodist Episcopal Church and received her education at various public schools, where she excelled in her studies. At some point she took a few private piano lessons and learned the rudiments of reading music. Singing and dancing were her early loves, and Fitzgerald would show off the latest steps to earn small change on neighborhood street corners and in local clubs. Her mother brought home records by MAMIE SMITH, the Mills Brothers (HARRY and HERBERT MILLS), and the white singing trio the Boswell Sisters. Throughout her career Fitzgerald singled out Connee Boswell, leader of the group and a popular solo artist, as an important early musical influence. After her mother died in 1932, Fitzgerald was allegedly abused by her stepfather and moved to Harlem to live with her mother's sister, Virginia. Like many other children during the Great Depression, she dropped out of school in the struggle for economic survival. She worked running numbers and as a lookout for a local "sporting house," knocking on the door in warning if the police should be nearby. Unfortunately, she must have been caught. Through the family court system, Fitzgerald was sent to Public School 49 in Riverdale-on-Hudson, essentially an orphanage. Thus began a harrowing episode in her life that she never publicly acknowledged.

Ella Fitzgerald sings as Dizzy Gillespie, Ray Brown, Milt Jackson, and Timmie Rosenkrantz watch at Downbeat, New York City, c. September 1947. (© William P. Gottlieb; www.jazzphotos.com.)

Overwhelmed with children—P.S. 49 was the only facility for blacks—Fitzgerald was transferred to the New York State Training School for Girls at Hudson, euphemistically labeled a reform school. In addition to the overcrowded and dilapidated quarters, the girls routinely endured beatings by male staff members. Punishments included shackles and solitary confinement (*New York Times*, 23 June 1996). After her release Fitzgerald joined Harlem's homeless.

In contrast to the singer BILLIE HOLIDAY, for whom similar childhood traumas came to inform her tragic persona, Fitzgerald apparently sought to excise these experiences from her memory. Instead she cultivated a guileless, happy-go-lucky image through her musical repertoire and interviews, one that she perpetuated throughout her life. These traits had an added benefit; they formed a protective insulation that allowed her to negotiate the male-dominated musical culture she soon entered.

The story of Fitzgerald's victory at Apollo Theater's Amateur Night contest on 21 November 1934 has become the stuff of legend. She intended to compete as a dancer, but the presence of the Edwards Sisters, a well-known and glamorously attired dancing team, unnerved her. Instead she sang "Object of My Affection" and "Judy," songs she learned from Boswell's versions.

As her prize, Fitzgerald should have been given a week's engagement at the theater, but she looked so disheveled from living on the streets that the management would not allow it. A second win the following February, this time at the Harlem Opera House, earned her a week-long spot with the TINY BRADSHAW Band. Her real break, however, came that spring with her gradual addition to the CHICK WEBB Orchestra. Already widely admired as a drummer and bandleader, the twenty-seven-year-old Webb craved popular success. His gamble on the young "girl singer" helped turn the band into a lucrative commercial venture that rivaled any such ensemble across the country.

Fitzgerald's career ushered in a new era for popular singers in which they were no longer ancillary performers in big bands, but rather powerful, independent artists. During the early swing era, singers were typically limited to one vocal chorus within a band's arrangement of a given song, and to one or two numbers during a live set. Webb however afforded Fitzgerald an unprecedented amount of the spotlight, and within months of joining the band, she dominated its recorded output. By 1937 she was given equal billing with Webb. Some three months after his death in June 1939 (Webb had battled tuberculosis of the spine), the group was rechristened Ella Fitzgerald and Her Famous Orchestra.

Her talents warranted the high profile. Already exhibiting the vocal ease, perfect intonation, and exuberant swing for which she became admired, Fitzgerald scored her first two hits in 1936: "Sing Me a Swing Song (And Let Me Dance)" and "(If You Can't Sing It) You'll Have to Swing It" (also known as "Mr. Paganini"). However, it was her refashioning of a children's nursery rhyme that made her the most popular singer in America, black or white, at a time when "race music" rarely crossed over into the mainstream. Fitzgerald cowrote "A-Tisket, A-Tasket" (1938) with the arranger Al Feldman, later known as Van Alexander. She authored several other songs over the course of her career and was a member of the American Society of Composers, Authors, and Publishers (ASCAP).

Fitzgerald embarked on a solo career in 1942, but her popularity temporarily waned. Her repertoire had been built on commercial dance band arrangements and "novelty" tunes subject to changing fashion. She was thought of as a pop singer rather than a jazz singer, categories she ultimately transcended.

Fitzgerald had always possessed an uncanny ear, and she began to pick up the new harmonic and rhythmic vocabulary of bebop being developed by musicians such as the saxophonist CHARLIE PARKER and the trumpeter DIZZY GILLESPIE. Scat singing, a kind of wordless vocal improvisation, had been part of Fitzgerald's performances since "You'll Have to Swing It." In that song, scat was considered nothing more than an entertaining gimmick, but Fitzgerald would be among the first singers to emulate the virtuosic bebop solo by "using her voice like a horn," a metaphor common among musicians. In such instances, the song was not a vehicle for storytelling or psychological drama, but rather a springboard that launched her own improvisational flights.

In fact, Fitzgerald counted among the rare musicians who made the stylistic transition from swing to bebop. She toured the South with Gillespie's big band in 1946 and found that jamming nightly with the instrumentalists honed her skills. Around this time, she added three staples to her repertoire that became landmarks of vocal jazz: the wordless "Flying High," "Lady Be Good," and "How High the Moon," the source of the chord changes for Charlie Parker's "Ornithology." Fitzgerald consistently referenced Parker's melody in her performances, making her connection to bebop musically explicit.

Behind the scenes, Fitzgerald had met the bassist Ray Brown, also on the road with Gillespie, and married him the following year. (He was her second husband; her 1941 union with Ben Kornegay was annulled when her manager Moe Gale discovered the groom's criminal past.) The Browns adopted Fitzgerald's nephew, named Ray Jr., but the relationship could not bear their frenetic and often separate touring schedules. They divorced in 1953, yet continued to work together intermittently.

A new phase in Fitzgerald's career began in the 1950s through her association with the impresario Norman Granz, an exceptional promoter of both jazz and racial equality. His *Jazz at the Philharmonic* (JATP) programs brought the music from clubs into concert halls, not only across the United States but also in Europe, Asia, and Australia, creating worldwide recognition for those musicians he presented. Fitzgerald toured with JATP for the first time in 1949, and Granz became her manager in 1953. He liberated her from her longtime recording contract with Decca in 1955 to record for his own new Verve label.

Under Granz's direction she completed a series of groundbreaking "songbooks" dedicated to the work of individual composers and lyricists: Cole Porter (1956), Richard Rodgers and Lorenz Hart (1956), DUKE ELLINGTON (1957), George and Ira Gershwin (1959), and Harold Arlen (1961). With Fitzgerald's performances faithful to the original melodies and with little in the way of embellishment, the songbooks sought to elevate these works from Broadway theater, movie musicals, and dance halls to the status of art song. They further helped Fitzgerald cross over from jazz to general audiences, where she continued to break color barriers in exclusive clubs and other venues.

Granz sold Verve in 1960 but remained Fitzgerald's manager; she moved to the West Coast Capitol label in 1966. Although she attempted to keep up with the pop music of the day, singing songs by the Beatles, among others, she eventually realized that the time for covering other people's compositions was over, and returned to her tried-and-true repertoire.

In the decades that followed, she continued to perform and record as much as her health allowed. Fitzgerald underwent open-heart surgery in 1986. Diabetes led to eyesight and circulatory problems, including the amputation of a toe in 1987 and both legs below the knees in 1993, shortly after she retired from performing. She died in her Beverly Hills home in 1996, the recipient of some thirteen Grammy Awards, eight honorary Ph.Ds, the National Medal for the Arts, and a Kennedy Center award.

FURTHER READING

Ella Fitzgerald's music and business papers are housed at the Library of Congress.

Gourse, Leslie. *The Ella Fitzgerald Companion* (1998).

Nicholson, Stuart. *Ella Fitzgerald: A Biography of the First Lady of Song* (1993; additions 1996).

Pleasants, Henry. *The Great American Popular Singers* (1974).

Obituary: *New York Times*, 16 June 1996.

LARA PELLEGRINELLI

Fitzhugh, Howard Naylor (31 Oct. 1909–26 July 1992), marketing executive and educator, was born in Washington, D.C., to William H. Fitzhugh, a messenger for the Department of Agriculture, and Lillian (maiden name unknown), a counselor at one of the local junior high schools. Both of his parents were involved in the community, his mother in civic affairs and his father through his membership in the Order of the Elks, a fraternal organization whose mission is to cultivate good fellowship and community spirit. In the 1920s, Fitzhugh attended a predominantly black high school, Dunbar High School, during a period of racial segregation in the United States.

Graduating from high school at the age of 16, Fitzhugh distinguished himself with a scholarship to Harvard University, where he was one of only four black students in the entering class. He was not allowed to live in the campus dormitories, but Fitzhugh excelled and graduated with honors in 1931. He was also one of the first black students to be admitted to the Harvard Business School, where he completed his master's in Business Administration and graduated in 1933.

Unlike his white Harvard classmates who were in high demand and received job offers from leading firms, Fitzhugh struggled to find employment. Eventually, he secured a job as an independent salesman for several printing companies with ties to the black community. He also became politically active as a member and organizer of the Washington-based New Negro Alliance, which lobbied the government to compel local employers to hire black employees. In 1939, the Alliance won a Supreme Court case that allowed the organization the right to picket peacefully. According to Fitzhugh, "for a while we picketed stores until they either capitulated or closed."

In 1934, Fitzhugh joined the business faculty at Howard University in Washington, D.C. He spent the next 31 years developing the school's marketing program and Small Business Center. He focused his research on marketing to black consumers and became renowned for developing segmented marketing strategies to reach the black consumer base. Many of these strategies have become standard practice in the industry. He also continued his graduate studies in business, enrolling in classes at Columbia University and American University. He also founded the National Black MBA Association. Fitzhugh also helped found and lead the National Association of Market Developers, a professional organization committed to being a catalyst for positive and progressive change for African Americans. In 1962 he published a U.S. Department of Commerce report on the problems and opportunities confronting blacks in business.

In 1965 Fitzhugh left Howard to join the Pepsi-Cola Company, which was interested in developing the relatively untapped minority market. As vice president of Special Markets, Fitzhugh designed and oversaw the implementation of programs marketing Pepsi products to minority consumers. There were very few black executives during his tenure at Pepsi-Cola, and Fitzhugh remembered his business colleagues applauding his insights and business ideas but added, "... It's hard to remember you're black." In 1968 Fitzhugh introduced his acclaimed educational program, Learn and Earn. Collaborating with the Distributive Education Clubs of America, the program sought to expose high school students to business through practical, hands-on economics seminars.

Fitzhugh left Pepsi-Cola in 1974, though he continued to advise the company on minority marketing in a consulting role. His contribution to the advancement of black business was first recognized in 1975 when Vice President Nelson A. Rockefeller awarded him with a Black Enterprise Achievement Award. In the final stages of his career, Fitzhugh worked as an expert consultant for the U.S. Census Bureau from 1975 to 1981.

Fitzhugh was named the "Dean of Black Business," by *Black Enterprise* magazine in 1974 and received many awards, including an honorary law degree from Howard University, the Distinguished Service Award by Harvard University (1987), and the Heritage Award for lifelong contributions to African American business advancement from the Executive Leadership Council, a distinguished group of black executives. The Pepsi-Cola Company endowed a faculty chair in his name at the Harvard Business School, the Naylor Fitzhugh Professorship in Business Administration, and endowed a fellowship in Fitzhugh's honor to enable students from historically black colleges to attend the school. According to Craig Weatherup, CEO of the Pepsi Bottling Group, "Naylor Fitzhugh's work at Pepsi-Cola has been enormously important in the growth of our company and its people. He had keen insights into people and relationships, which is really what business is all about."

Over the course his lifetime, Fitzhugh faced formidable obstacles yet maintained a hopeful vision for the future of black business leaders. He said:

> An affirmative approach to corporate America calls for optimism as well as realism. It calls for focusing on the half-full glass, rather than the half-empty part—for lighting a candle, rather than cursing in the darkness. There may be occasions when such an affirmative approach seems beyond our reach; however, we should try hard not to let it escape from us when it is within our reach.

Fitzhugh died of cancer in New York in 1992. He was survived by his wife of 54 years, Selma Hare, an educator and psychologist, and by two sons and a daughter.

FURTHER READING

Obituaries: *Black Enterprise*, 1 Oct. 1992; *New York Times*, 29 July 1992.

AYESHA KANJI

Flack, Roberta (10 Feb. 1939–) singer and songwriter, was born in Asheville, North Carolina, to Laron Flack and Irene, whose maiden name is unknown. She was one of four children, three girls and a boy. Both of Flack's parents were musically talented. Her father was a self-taught pianist, and her mother had taken a few formal music lessons, which prepared her for playing piano for the local black Methodist Church. Although, both of Flack's parents were musicians, her first experience with music came through her mother. Flack recalled the experience in an interview with *Ebony*, "I remember insisting that I be allowed to sit on her knee and she let me play the keys. She had a genuine gift for music though she'd only had maybe a couple of lessons" (*Ebony*, 56). She began playing the piano by ear at age four.

When Flack was very young, her family moved to Arlington, Virginia, a suburb of Washington, D.C. In Virginia, her father was employed as a draftsman for the Veterans Administration. Her mother worked as janitor and cook for Wakefield High School. At age nine, Flack took regular piano lessons from Mrs. Blackmon, a woman with an exceptional professional reputation who was also a member of the Flacks' church. Flack soon learned to play the works of such classical composers as Rachmaninoff and Beethoven. Around age twelve, Flack studied classical piano with Hazel Harrison, a prominent African American concert musician. At thirteen, she won second prize in a piano contest for black students in Virginia—for her rendition of the state song, "Carry Me Back to Old Virginny." Flack was overweight and shy as a young girl, but she performed well in school. In fact, she was able to skip several grades, an accomplishment she attributed to her limited social life. In a 1971 *Ebony* interview she said, "I weighed over 200 pounds. All I did was play the piano and eat all day, and I did them at the same time. And study and go to church. That was all I did" (*Ebony*, 56).

Flack graduated from high school at age fifteen, winning a scholarship to Howard University, where she studied music education. She changed her major emphasis of study from instrumental music to vocal music, in part because she was embarrassed after seeing a picture of herself playing a wind instrument in the school band. She said her cheeks were so puffed out, you couldn't tell where she ended and the

Roberta Flack holds the Grammy Award that she won for her record "Killing Me Softly with His Song" at the Grammy Awards in Los Angeles, 4 March 1974. The ballad about the emotional impact of music was named Record of the Year. She also was named best female pop peformer. (AP Images.)

baritone horn started (*Ebony*, 56). As an undergraduate, Flack organized choral groups both at church and at home. She earned extra money directing a choral group of nursing students at Freedmen's Hospital. During her teaching internship, Flack was assigned to Alice Deal Junior High, which was an all-white school where black employees had only served as janitors and cooks in the past. She remembers being pelted with apples when she first began teaching at the school. Flack became the first undergraduate at Howard to give a public recital in vocal literature—including German lieder, Italian ballads, operatic arias, and Negro spirituals.

In 1958, at the age of eighteen, Flack received a B.A. in Music Education. The following year, her father died while she was working on her master's degree. She decided to discontinue her education in order to provide financial assistance to her family. Flack took a job teaching English at a school for African Americans in Farmville, North Carolina. She earned $2,800 per year at Farmville, teaching approximately 2,800 students. She said she earned "a dollar a kid before taxes" (*Current Biography*). Flack taught mostly poor students who often missed school during certain seasons to work in the fields. Many of the students in the higher grades were in their twenties, older than Flack herself. Although she had been hired to teach English literature, she ended up teaching basic grammar to twelfth graders. Her job duties became overwhelming: she was required to teach music, direct the school choir, supervise cheerleaders, and conduct special classes for mentally and physically challenged students. Although she refers to this time as a positive experience, Flack lost forty pounds and nearly had a nervous breakdown.

Over the next several years, Flack taught music at three different junior high schools. Her teaching methods met with disapproval from many of her administrators; they felt that Flack associated too closely with her students. According to Flack, getting close was the only way to get through to her students, especially the unruly ones. In her free time, she played the organ, directed choirs in the churches, and coached voice students for Frederick "Wilkie" Wilkerson, who became her voice teacher. In 1960, after hearing her belt out a popular tune as a joke, Wilkerson advised her to abandon opera and devote herself to popular music, advice she eventually followed.

In 1962, while teaching music in Washington, D.C., Flack began moonlighting as an accompanying pianist for opera singers. Mrs. Blackmon, her former piano teacher, had helped her get a part-time job at the Tivoli Restaurant in the Georgetown section of the city. She would spend more and more of her spare time singing and playing popular songs. Flack also found time for a social life. In 1966 she married Stephen Novosel, a white jazz bassist. However, Novosel's family and Flack's brother opposed their interracial union. When her brother refused to give her away at the wedding, Flack noted that he must have forgotten they had a white grandfather.

In 1967, while she was singing five nights a week at Washington, D.C.'s 1520 Club on K Street, Flack auditioned and was eventually hired to perform at Henry Yaffe's Mr. Henry's Club, an eatery on Capitol Hill. She sang at Sunday brunches for $20 per afternoon. When the school term ended in summer, she quit teaching. When Yaffe opened his Georgetown branch, she began attracting such huge crowds that he built a showcase room for her called "Roberta's." Her enthusiasts included such celebrities as Burt Bacharach, Woody Allen, and Bill Cosby. In 1968 the jazz pianist Les McCann heard Flack and was so taken with her voice that he taped her singing and helped her obtain a contract with Atlantic Records. Her debut album, *First Take*, was released in 1969. In 1970 her second album, *Chapter Two*, sold over one million copies. The same year, an appearance on a Bill Cosby television special brought her national attention. In 1971 her rendition of "The First Time Ever I Saw Your Face," from her first album, was heard on the soundtrack of Clint Eastwood's movie

Play Misty for Me. The song reached the number-one position on popular music charts and made her a household name. During that year, *Down Beat* magazine named Flack the female vocalist of the year, a title ELLA FITZGERALD had held the preceding eighteen years.

The national advance sales of her third album, *Quiet Fire*, totaled one million before its release in 1971. *Stereo Review* recommended it as a recording of special merit and critics agreed. In mid-1972 her fourth album, *Roberta Flack and Donnie Hathaway*, was released to rave reviews. Her popularity escalated to such an extent that the city of Washington celebrated Roberta Flack Human Kindness Day on 22 April 1972. The same year, Flack won a Grammy for her interpretation of "The First Time Ever I Saw Your Face." She also shared the best vocal performance award for a duet with Donnie Hathaway for "Where Is the Love?" Flack performed two concerts with the QUINCY JONES band in Madison Square Garden that year, and she appeared in her own half-hour television special, *The First Time Ever*. Although 1972 was a stunningly successful year in her professional life, it was also the year her marriage to Novosel ended in divorce.

Flack's fifth album, 1973's *Killing Me Softly*, which she also produced, yielded a number-one single of the same title and a Grammy Award for "Best Female Pop Vocals" for the single. Her next album, 1974's *Feel Like Makin' Love*, peaked at number twelve on the album charts and yielded a million-selling single for the album's title track. The credits listed Rubina Flake, a pseudonym of Flack's, as the producer. For the next several years, Flack disappeared from the public eye while she undertook doctoral studies at the University of Massachusetts at Amherst. In 1977 Flack reappeared with a new album, *Blue Lights in the Basement*, an instant hit that reached number eight on the album charts. The album launched another extremely successful single, "The Closer I Get to You," another duet with Hathaway. A few years later, the two joined forces to record a duet album. The collaboration would end in 1979, when Hathaway jumped from the fifteenth floor of a New York hotel to his death. A grief-stricken Flack left the public scene for much of the year. In 1980 *Roberta Flack Featuring Donnie Hathaway* was released, and out of it came two hits, "You are My Heaven" and "Back Together Again."

The following year, Flack recorded an album, *Live and More*, with Peabo Bryson. She remained busy, composing and producing the soundtrack for the 1981 movie *Bustin' Loose*, starring RICHARD PRYOR and CICELY TYSON. She also released a solo effort, 1982's *I'm the One* and a collection of greatest hits, *The Best of Roberta Flack*. In 1983 Flack and Bryson reunited to record *Born to Love*, which yielded the top-twenty hit, "Tonight I Celebrate My Love." Flack had once again found a male singing partner who seemed to perfectly match her style of singing. During the mid-1980s Flack once again disappeared from the music scene. She returned in 1988 to record *Oasis*, a solo album on which four songs were cowritten by the poet MAYA ANGELOU. The album hit number one on the rhythm-and-blues charts. In 1991 Flack hit the studios once again to record *Set the Night to Music*. This album produced yet another top-ten hit with the title track, which was a duet with Maxi Priest. Two years later, Flack coproduced 1994's *Roberta*, a collection of jazz, blues, and pop classics in celebration of her twenty-five years as an Atlantic recording artist. The album earned her a Grammy in the Traditional Pop Vocal category.

In 1996 when the Fugees hit the charts with their rendition of "Killing Me Softly with His Song," Flack was introduced to a new generation of listeners, and she even made a cameo appearance in the video. In early 1997 Flack teamed with folk singer Judy Collins for a series of concerts to benefit the Nina Hyde Center for Breast Cancer Research at Georgetown University and a handful of other breast cancer organizations. These benefits for breast cancer were especially important to Flack, since her mother had died of the disease.

In 2003 Flack was living happily in New York with her much-younger husband, her six Japanese dogs, all Shiba Inu, and several cats. She had just recorded a Christmas album that was selected as one of the top ten holiday buys by the *New York Times*. Flack was also in the process of creating a record label. "The premise of my label will be to let the people own their own work" (Collier, 59). She continued to work hard helping others, sponsoring several children around the world for numerous charities. Flack said it is always important to give.

FURTHER READING

Collier, Aldore. "Roberta Flack," *Jet* (8 Dec. 2003).

"Former D.C. School Teacher Creates a Stir on Soul Scene," *Ebony* (Jan. 1971).

Morse, Charles, and Ann Morse. *Roberta Flack* (1975).

SHARON RENEE MCGEE

Flake, Floyd Harold (30 Jan. 1945–), minister, U.S. Congressman, educator, and business executive, was born in Los Angeles, California, the eighth of thirteen children of Robert Flake Sr., a janitor, and Rosie Lee Johnson. Shortly after Floyd's birth, the family moved into a two-bedroom home in Houston, Texas. The roots of many of Floyd's political beliefs can be traced to his southern upbringing: his family was poor, but proud; racism abounded, but faith and optimism ruled the Flake home.

Floyd's early education took place in segregated, poorly equipped schools, but his teachers were dedicated and took a stern interest in his academic development. One teacher cared enough to make sure that Floyd spent much of his free time involved in youth programs at her African Methodist Episcopal (AME) Church. After graduating from high school Flake entered Wilberforce University, the nation's oldest private African American University, in Ohio. He graduated with a bachelor's degree in 1967, and while working toward his master's—which he received in 1970 from nearby Payne Theological Seminary—he worked as a social worker and as a marketing analyst for the Xerox Corporation. His first academic post was as associate dean of students at Lincoln University in Pennsylvania, which he held from 1970 to 1973.

In 1974 Flake moved to Massachusetts to become director of the MARTIN LUTHER KING JR. Afro-American Center at Boston University. His duties expanded to include serving as a dean and interim chaplain of the university. There he met Margaret Elaine McCollins. The two were married in 1977, had four children, and became ministerial partners. Eventually, they would both earn doctor of ministry degrees from United Theological Seminary; Flake's was awarded in 1994.

Though he had never led a local congregation, in 1976 Flake was persuaded by Bishop Richard Allen Hilderbrand to leave Boston University in order to pastor the Allen AME Church in Queens, New York. By the 1970s Queens had become home to the largest black middle class community in the United States, and the Allen AME Church had 1,400 members when Flake took over. Under his dynamic leadership the church was transformed from an elite sanctuary into an entity deeply involved in social, economic, political, and educational affairs, as such becoming a model of the social gospel made manifest in urban America. Flake argued that "the black church has the potential to be more than just a once a week emotional cathartic experience but, rather, an empowering and liberating force if utilized properly" (Owens, 5).

The creation of the Allen Christian School in 1982 was the first prominent example of Flake's radical approach to old problems. Whereas black ministers in the old-style protest tradition—such as AL SHARPTON, Herbert Daughtry, and CALVIN BUTTS—often inveighed against the failing public schools, Flake was determined to provide a quality education in a safe and clean environment for a fraction of what the city claimed it spent on each pupil. The Allen School grew from the church basement to a new $3.8 million, four-story facility serving over 500 students from preschool through the eighth grade. The church then moved into other areas of concern by creating nearly a dozen corporations (some for profit). The Allen Housing and Development Fund used church and federal money to build a 300-unit senior citizens' complex that also housed drug programs, a health and nutrition center, and other community services. The Allen Housing Corporation functioned as a real estate developer that purchased property, managed commercial businesses, and built over one hundred affordable homes in the vicinity of the church. The Allen Women's Resource Center operated a shelter for battered women with children that offered intervention counseling and legal aid. The Allen Transportation Corporation operated a fleet of coaches that competed favorably with larger bus lines for local business.

On the basis of these accomplishments Flake decided to run for a seat in the U.S. House of Representatives in a special election called in 1986 when Joseph P. Addabbo, a white politician who represented the sixth congressional district for twenty-six years, died in office. Many of Flakes supports believed the election had been stolen from him because Flake defeated the black assemblyman Alton R. Waldon at the polls by 167 votes, but when the absentee ballots—which did not include Flake's name—were counted, Waldon emerged the victor. Energized by this setback (and with the controversial support of Mayor Edward Koch, who campaigned for Flake in the Italian and Jewish areas of the district), Flake won a decisive victory over Waldon a few months later in the regular election.

Flake served in the Congress on the powerful Banking and Financial Services Committee from

1986 to 1997. In many ways he was a maverick, representing a new kind of black politician. Unlike "Yellow Dog" Democrats, who faithfully held the party line, Flake was a "Blue Dog" Democrat, who supported using financial markets and private industry to develop blighted areas and who did not concede the rhetoric of religion and personal responsibility to the Christian right. When some Democrats sounded apocalyptic about the possible effects of Republican control and wailed, "They don't give us a chance, they're taking away our affirmative action, they're taking away our welfare," Flake railed, "I say to you, there was a time when we lived without it, and if they take it away, we can live without it again!" (*New York Times*, 19 Oct. 1997, sec. 6, 60).

Like Kweisi Mfume and William H. Gray III, Flake was a dealmaker and a member of the Democratic Leadership Council (DLC) that produced moderate Democrats such as Bill Clinton. Often his stance put him at odds with the Congressional Black Caucus. He crossed party lines to introduce the American Community Renewal Act, which would have offered educational vouchers to parents who wished to send their children to private or parochial schools. J. C. Watts, the only black Republican in the House, had introduced a similar bill, but Flake was the only Democrat who voted for it. Similarly, Flake was almost alone among Democrats in supporting the capital-gains tax cut. However, his most successful piece of legislation was the Community Development Financial Institutions Act of 1993, which contained a provision called the Bank Enterprise Act that made capital available to black entrepreneurs and those seeking home mortgages. Despite his independent streak Flake won all his reelection contests by wide margins, in part because he was so effective in bringing jobs and money to his constituents. In 1995 he brought home to his district revenue and federal building projects worth $230 million, more than any other downstate representative from New York.

During his tenure in Congress, in 1987, Flake weathered a racial crisis in Howard Beach, Queens, in which four black men were beaten by a white mob and one victim chased to his death. Flake also survived a scurrilous accusation of infidelity and a seventeen-count indictment against him and his wife for income-tax evasion and embezzlement in connection with the senior-citizen home; the presiding judge dismissed the case for insufficient evidence in 1991. In the middle of his term in 1997 Flake gave up his seat in Congress in order to focus more attention on his congregation, which had burgeoned to over ten thousand members and had recently completed construction of a $23 million edifice called the Greater Allen Cathedral. The new name sublimated the church's AME affiliation and allowed it to function as a modern transdenominational "mega church," broadcasting services and other programs on radio and television. By 2004 the church had net assets of over $70 million, and including its many corporations it employed more than six hundred people, making it one of the largest black businesses in the nation and the largest employer in Queens except for John F. Kennedy Airport.

Nevertheless Flake continued to be a shrewd political operator. His fervent belief in charter schools led him to endorse Republicans who also championed the idea, such as Senator Alfonse D'Amato (NY), Governor George Pataki (NY), and Governor Jeb Bush (FL). Flake even embraced George W. Bush as his "home boy" and lauded the president's Faith-Based Initiatives and his No Child Left Behind education program. However, when Flake endorsed the reelection of Rudolph Giuliani, the racially embattled Republican mayor of the city, the city's largest black newspaper, *The Amsterdam News*, editorialized that Flake had "sold out" the black community for the political largesse that he and his church hoped to receive.

The business community and conservative think tanks liked Flake's urbane style, his freethinking, and his appreciation of capitalism at its best. As a result he was invited to serve on such corporate boards of directors as the Fannie Mae Foundation and the Export-Import Bank; he became a senior fellow with the Manhattan Institute for Social and Economic Policy, and an adjunct fellow with the Brookings Institute Center on Urban and Metropolitan Policy; and he became an op-ed columnist for the *New York Post*. From May 2000 to September 2002 Flake served as president of Edison Schools Inc., a national for-profit organization that manages thousands of schools across the nation. In July 2002 he assumed the presidency of his alma mater, Wilberforce University. He is coauthor of two books: *The Way of the Bootstrapper: Nine Action Steps for Achieving Your Dreams* (2000) and *Practical Virtue: Learning to Live With All Our Soul* (2004). Flake managed all of these activities while leading his congregation, making him a modern mix of the conservative Booker

T. Washington and the strident preacher Adam Clayton Powell Jr.

FURTHER READING

Though Flake's personal papers are not yet publicly available, many of the papers covering his congressional career, including speeches, legislation, and voting record can be found at the National Archives and Records Administration in Washington, D.C.

Henderson, Ashyia N., ed. *Contemporary Black Biography* (1998).

Haskins, James. *Distinguished African American Political and Governmental Leaders* (1999).

Owens, Michael Leo. "The Reverend Floyd Flake: African Methodist Episcopal Church Minister for School Choice," in *Religious Leaders and Faith-Based Politics: Ten Profiles*, eds. Jo Renee Formicola and Hubert Morken (2001).

SHOLOMO B. LEVY

Flake, Green (Jan. 1828–20 Oct. 1903), former slave and Mormon pioneer, was born in Anson County, North Carolina. Nothing is known about his family or early childhood. At age ten, Green was given as a wedding gift to James Madison and Agnes Love Flake, wealthy plantation owners in Anson County. In 1841 the Flakes relocated to Kemper County, Mississippi, taking Green and other slaves with them to clear and work the new land. Two years later, the Flakes joined the Church of Jesus Christ of Latter Day Saints, as did several of their slaves, including Green.

The church, commonly known as the Mormon Church, was founded by Joseph Smith, in Fayette Township, New York, in 1830. Many of the group's tenets and practices (they voted in a block, they were antislavery, and they took over land that Missourians did not wish them to have) made them extremely unpopular. Consequently, the members moved frequently to avoid persecution and physical assaults. When the Flakes relocated again, this time to Nauvoo, Illinois, they emancipated all but three of their slaves. Green, given a choice, remained with the family. Described as a large, strong man, he served as a bodyguard to Joseph Smith, with whom he lived for several years. Brigham Young, who succeeded Smith as leader of the church, planned to relocate his flock to a sparsely settled area of the country where they could put their beliefs into practice in safety and without public censure. Utah, not yet admitted to the Union, was chosen as the ideal site, and in 1847 a group was formed to clear a trail through uncharted territory for Young and his followers. Included in this group were three African Americans: Hark Lay, Oscar Crosby, and Green, whose services were volunteered by his owner. This was a physically taxing, labor-intensive undertaking (cutting trees, building roads, and erecting a log house for the Flakes), and their preparations led to the largest religious migration in American history, with more than 180,000 people following, at different intervals, after the advance group. Green, following instructions given by his owner, built a log cabin in preparation for the arrival of the white Flake family in 1848. He and the other members of the advance party also cleared fields, planted crops, and constructed irrigation ditches. He returned to Nauvoo with a wagon in order to transport his owner's family and possessions to the Salt Lake area. Mormon tradition has it that Green drove the wagon on which the ailing Brigham Young rode into the Salt Lake Valley for the first time.

By 1850, James Flake had died, after being thrown by a horse. Subsequently, his widow moved to California, leaving Green in Salt Lake City. He was to work for the church with his labor substituting for the tithes owed by James Flake, as labor in lieu of tithing was a common practice among the Latter Day Saints at that time. Although slavery remained legal in Utah Territory until 1862 when it was abolished by Congress, few slaves lived there. In 1854 Agnes Flake, living in poverty in California, wrote to Brigham Young asking him to sell Green and send her the money for the support of her family. Young, feigning ignorance, responded that he had not seen Green for some time and that he believed him to be in poor health. According to Mormon tradition, Young subsequently emancipated Green. However, in the censuses of 1850 and 1860 Green was listed by name. Since enslaved people were not identified by name in censuses prior to 1870, the census taker must have viewed him as free. Whatever his legal status, he remained in Salt Lake and continued to work for Brigham Young. Flake once remarked, "Most everyone don't want to be a slave and be in bondage to another, because you cannot have even your own thoughts and dreams. You cannot plan for the future when all decisions get made by someone else" (Young, XX). Through hard work Flake transformed his dreams into prosperous reality. In compensation for his service, Brigham Young gave Flake farmland in the Salt Lake Valley, where he grew vegetables and raised cattle, marking them by using a registered brand consisting of his initials with a bar above them. In addition to working on his property, he earned money working for others. The census of 1870 valued his property at $100; by 1881 he was able to purchase twenty additional acres of land for $1,880. Flake also did prospecting, but this venture proved less successful than his other enterprises, and in 1871 he sold his interests to the Elevator Prospecting Company, which had been organized by a group of African American men.

Men of African descent were not able to receive the priesthood of the church, which has a lay priesthood. However, Flake was a devout Mormon. In addition to tithing, he donated money that facilitated the erection of several church buildings, including the temple in Salt Lake City. Flake was noted for his singing ability and his willingness to help his neighbors. It is said that in 1877 he helped to dig the grave of the much revered Brigham Young. In 1897 when the Latter Day Saints celebrated the fiftieth anniversary of the founding of Salt Lake City, Flake was honored for his work in establishing the community. Flake married Martha Crosby, the daughter of Vilate, who was also among the group of original migrants to Salt Lake City in 1847. They had a daughter, Lucinda Vilate (1854), and one son, Abraham (1856); many of their descendants are still residents of Utah and members of the Mormon Church. Following his wife's death on 20 January 1885, Flake relocated to Idaho to live with his son. When he died, he was buried next to his wife in Union Cemetery in Salt Lake City. A monument of blue limestone, which had been designed and partially carved by Flake, adorns their graves. He had directed that the biblical text, John 14:2, "In my Father's house are many mansions" be carved on the tombstone; he said that he wanted his children to be as inspired by the words as he had been.

FURTHER READING

Carter, Kate B. *The Story of the Negro Pioneer* (1965).
Ravage, John W. *Black Pioneers : Images of the Black Experience on the North American Frontier* (1997).
Young, Margaret Blair, and Darius Gray. *Standing on the Promises* (2000).

DONNA TYLER HOLLIE

Flanagan, Minnie (1 Nov. 1901–12 May 1987), political and civil rights activist, was born in Chandler, Henderson County, Texas, in the northeast region of the state, to Ruffin Nealy and Susan Moore Nealy. She moved to Dallas with her family in 1918 and in 1925 married Pat Lee Flanagan, an athletic facility manager at the Dallas Country Club. Flanagan was instrumental in the struggle for political and civil rights in Dallas, Texas, a metropolitan area that believed that it was immune from the civil rights activities of cities in the Deep South.

Flanagan's career as a civil rights activist began in 1937 when she became an executive member of the Progressive Voters League (formerly the Progressive Citizens League), which served as the major African American political organization in Dallas during the 1930s. The all-white primary (in which African Americans were effectively disenfranchised in the Democratic-dominated state by being barred from voting in the party's primary) and financially restrictive poll tax kept many African Americans in Dallas from participating in the political process. Disenfranchisement and disillusionment prevented African Americans from electing leaders who would address issues of poverty, school overcrowding, and high unemployment rates in their community. However by 1936, the white oligarchy in Dallas had begun to take notice of the strength of black electorate. Fueled in part by the Progressive Voters League, the attitude of apathy and inactivity shifted to interest and activity as a record number of African Americans paid their poll taxes and voted in the city's general election.

The increase in African American political participation at the polls continued when Minnie Flanagan, along with fellow Progressive Voters League executive committee member Marzelle Hill, successfully directed the registration of approximately 7,000 voters in an aggressive voter's registration campaign from October 1936 to January 1937. Flanagan and Hill traipsed through neighborhood after neighborhood in their house-to-house canvassing campaigns to register voters. The efforts of the two women were organized and propitious as they created and utilized *Membership and Subscription Cards* and followed a detailed *Captain's Report Blank* to ensure that each individual represented in a voting precinct was contacted and encouraged to pay his or her poll tax before the 31 January deadline. The two women played key roles in the newly organized Progressive Voters League by sponsoring a speaker's bureau and establishing essay contests for students to educate the public on the imperativeness of the ballot and paying poll taxes. Flanagan, Hill, and the Progressive Voters League emerged victorious in the 1937 Dallas city election as they elected an all-white city council that was sympathetic and civically obligated to the needs of the African American population in Dallas.

Flanagan coupled her civic activity with patriotic duty during World War II. She served her country even when the country would not serve her people. She remained active in the Democratic Progressive Voters League for five years after the all-white primary in Texas was overturned by the U.S. Supreme Court decision in *Smith v. Allwright* (1944). The legal victory signaled a positive political shift for African Americans in Texas, but the war abroad served as a constant reminder of the prejudice and discrimination in the country. Flanagan served and supported her country during the war years by volunteering with the Office of Price Administration. She and many other volunteers throughout the country reviewed prices at stores and cafeterias to ensure compliance with the guidelines outlined by the wartime governmental agency. Flanagan was committed to maintaining stable food prices and slowing the country's slide towards inflation.

Flanagan's civil rights activism increased during the latter years of the modern civil rights movement. Between September and October 1956, Attorney General John Ben Shepperd and Smith County District Court Judge Otis Dunagan ordered raids on local NAACP branches and issued a temporary injunction to close down all the branches in Texas. By the late 1950s many conservatives and racists in Texas who did not support integration had grown weary of the successes of desegregation and they began to resist the subtle movement toward egalitarianism. The eight-month injunction and resistance from Citizens' Councils crippled the core leadership in the state and sent the membership into a rapid decline. Flanagan, a relentless activist and public servant was elected president of the Dallas branch of the NAACP in 1959. Instead of presiding over an inactive local branch, she channeled the local organization's energies into crusading against segregated public facilities and accommodations. She supported the local chapter's involvement in sit-ins and public demonstrations at segregated cafeterias and public facilities. The NAACP Youth Council, under the leadership of Juanita Craft, accepted Flanagan's presidential charge and followed the strategies of non-violent protesters across the nation. Youth Council members identified several stores in Dallas where they would initiate sit-ins because of discrimination and segregation. However, at the advent of the Wiley-Bishop sit-ins in 1960, Dallas NAACP members energetically agreed to assist protesters with financial and legal assistance. Flanagan, C. B. Bunkley, and Clarence Laws arranged to provide assistance to the student protesters. During her tenure as the local leader of the NAACP, Roy Wilkins, executive secretary of the national office, traveled to Dallas to speak with African American leaders about sit-in strategies in the city. Unfortunately for Flanagan, her involvement with the director was overshadowed by a more prominent African American male civil rights leader, A. Maceo Smith. Smith, an outstanding longtime activist in the NAACP, would prove instrumental in the peaceful integration of public accommodations and facilities in Dallas. Two decades later, in 1986, Flanagan's commitment and achievement to the NAACP was ceremoniously recognized when she received the NAACP Heritage award.

Minnie Flanagan remained a consummate activist in Dallas civil rights issues until her death.

FURTHER READING

Minnie Flanagan papers are held by the Dallas Historical Society in the Hall of State in Dallas's Fair Park, Dallas, Texas.

Dulaney, W. Marvin. "The Progressive Voters League: A Political Voice for African Americans in Dallas," *Legacies: A History Journal for Dallas and North Central Texas* 3 (Spring 1991).

Gillette, Michael L. "The Rise of the NAACP in Texas," *Southwestern Historical Quarterly* 81 (Apr. 1978).

Sanders, Marc, and Ruthe Winegarten. *The Lives and Times of Black Dallas Women* (2002).

Winegarten, Ruthe. *Black Texas Women: 150 Years of Trial and Triumph* (1995).

YVONNE DAVIS FREAR

Fleetwood, Christian Abraham (21 July 1840–28 Sept. 1914), clerk, editor, Civil War veteran, and recipient of the Medal of Honor, was born to Charles and Anna Marie Fleetwood, free people in Baltimore, Maryland. In 1863 Christian left a lucrative position as a clerk in the Brune shipping and trading empire and joined the Fourth United States Colored Troops as a private. Just over a year later Fleetwood received the Medal of Honor for bravery and coolness under fire at the Battle of New Market Heights (Chaffin's Farm), 29 and 30 September

Christian Fleetwood, in military uniform with his Medal of Honor, c. 1900. (Library of Congress/Daniel Murray Collection.)

1864. He was one of only sixteen African American soldiers to receive the Medal of Honor during the Civil War.

Christian Fleetwood's remarkable story begins in the home of the prominent Baltimore businessman John C. Brune. Fleetwood's father served for a long time as the majordomo in the Brune household, and it was there that Christian received his early education in reading and writing. He was given full access to Brune's extensive library and read widely in classical literature, history, philosophy, contemporary fiction, and world travel. By Fleetwood's own account his education by John Brune was not merely an act of kindness but also an effort to groom him for a position in Brune's sugar-refining business. John Brune invested heavily in sugarcane production in Liberia and felt that Fleetwood's strong intelligence and talent for calculations would serve him well as the Brune company's representative in Africa. Accordingly John Brune financed a trip for Fleetwood to Liberia in 1856. Upon his return to America in 1857 Fleetwood was enrolled by John Brune in the Ashmun Institute of Philadelphia, Pennsylvania (renamed Lincoln University in 1866 in honor of President Lincoln), and three years later he received his college degree. Upon returning to Baltimore in 1860 Fleetwood continued his practical education with a three-year apprenticeship at a local shipping and trading firm conducting business between the Port of Baltimore and Liberia. Despite his duties as clerk and accountant for this firm, Fleetwood still cofounded and edited a weekly newspaper called the *Lyceum Observer* and taught Sunday school at Bethel African Methodist Episcopal Church of Baltimore.

On 1 January 1863 President Lincoln's Emancipation Proclamation took effect. Though often cited as the legal death of the institution of slavery in rebelling states throughout the South, the Emancipation Proclamation was equally important for its call to black soldiers to serve in Negro regiments, designated the United States Colored Troops (USCT) and commanded by white officers. For the first time in the Civil War, African Americans were now afforded an opportunity to strike their own blows toward the end of slavery. Early in spring 1864 Colonel William Birney was authorized to raise a colored infantry regiment in the state of Maryland. Realizing that he would have to look beyond the relatively small pool of freeborn black males in the Baltimore area for recruits, Birney embarked on a series of unusual schemes to fill out the ranks of his new regiment. In one of his first acts as commander of the newly designated Fourth United States Colored Troops, Birney took his new recruits and fellow officers on a raid to the city jail on Baltimore's Pratt Street. Slave owners who feared that their slaves would run away if given the opportunity would work the slaves by day and then have the city jailer lock them up by night. Breaking into the jail, Birney, it is alleged, offered freedom from lockup to any slave who would sign enlistment papers.

In another scheme Birney hired a transport and loaded it with a barrel of rum and a band and sailed it down the Chesapeake, stopping at night at Maryland plantations with large slave populations. Birney's recruiters would pull into shore, drop the plank, and with the band playing entice slaves to enlist in the Fourth USCT. The recruiters were always quick to pull back into the middle of the bay with their new recruits before the slave patrols could interfere. For this stunt the governor of Maryland protested directly to President Lincoln that Birney should be dismissed from the service and his recruiting practices discontinued.

One freeborn African American who answered the call to join the Fourth USCT was Christian Fleetwood. Years later he acknowledged that he could have remained in his isolated, privileged world, sailing for Liberia to take up the position of agent for a powerful trading firm. But Fleetwood was inspired by the new recruits filling the training camps, and he could not resist his chance to contribute to the end of slavery. He enlisted on 11 August 1863, and his education was quickly recognized by the officers of the Fourth USCT. On 19 August 1863 he was promoted from private to sergeant major by Regimental Special Orders Number 17. The regiment was organizing and training at Camp Birney just outside Baltimore, and Fleetwood was put in charge of keeping the regimental books and filing all correspondence and reports due at headquarters. The Fourth USCT was given little time to learn the skills of soldiering; on 25 September the regiment was ordered to Fort Monroe for duty.

In early October, Christian Fleetwood and the Fourth USCT saw their first action while on patrol in Mathews County, Virginia, searching for guerrillas, smugglers, and Confederate coastguards. The regiment first saw major action in the summer of 1864 when it was attached to the Army of the James, Eighteenth Corps, and participated in the campaign against Confederate forces in Petersburg, Virginia, beginning on 15 June 1864. In this initial assault Sergeant Major Fleetwood and the Fourth USCT proved their combat abilities by charging and overrunning Confederate defensive batteries. Ultimately the assault on Petersburg failed to take the city, and the Fourth USCT settled in with other Federal forces to a protracted siege.

On 29 September the Fourth USCT marched north of the James River and was thrown against the Confederate defenses of Richmond at New Market Heights (Chaffin's Farm). The Fourth USCT was one of the leading elements in the initial charge on the Confederate works. Confederate fire was so intense as the Fourth USCT swept up toward their lines that eleven of twelve members of the color guard were cut down within minutes. Seeing the national flag fall, Sergeant Major Fleetwood rushed forward and grabbed the flag to prevent its capture by Confederate soldiers. In January 1865 the Fourth USCT participated in the assault and capture of Fort Fisher and Wilmington, North Carolina. During the occupation of Wilmington, Fleetwood was struck seriously ill with typhoid fever, but perhaps the arrival of his Medal of Honor for bravery under fire in saving the national flag at New Market Heights sped his recovery. His commanding officer thought Fleetwood's exemplary service warranted a promotion to the rank of a commissioned officer, but the War Department refused to consider this recommendation. Christian Fleetwood and the Fourth USCT mustered out of service on 4 May 1866, and by 10 May, Fleetwood had returned to Baltimore.

Perhaps finding that opportunities had passed him by in Baltimore, Fleetwood held a job as a bookkeeper in Columbus, Ohio, until 1867. He moved to Washington, D.C., in that same year and worked as a clerk at the Freedmen's Savings and Trust Company (Freedmen's Bank) and later as a civil servant in the War Department. Christian Fleetwood married Sarah Iridell in Philadelphia on 18 November 1869. Sarah Iridell Fleetwood was a member of the first graduating class of the Freedmen's Hospital Training School, and in 1901 she became superintendent of the Training School for Nurses. The couple had a daughter named Edith, born on 17 May 1885. The Fleetwoods quickly became leading lights in the affluent black middle class of Washington, D.C. At their home they hosted weekly cultural and literary readings that were attended by many of the nationally famous African American socialites, thinkers, and businessmen of the day. Christian Fleetwood also found time to organize black regiments for the Washington, D.C., National Guard, and he was the first instructor of the renowned Washington Colored High School Cadet Corps. Christian Fleetwood died of a heart attack on 28 September 1914.

FURTHER READING

Gladstone, William. *Men of Color* (1993).
Longacre, Edward G. *A Regiment of Slaves: The 4th United States Colored Infantry, 1863–1866* (2003).
Quarles, Benjamin. *The Negro in the Civil War* (1953).
Trudeau, Noah Andre. *Like Men of War: Black Troops in the Civil War, 1862–1865* (1998).
Wilson, Joseph T. *The Black Phalanx: A History of the Negro Soldiers of the United States in the Wars of 1775–1812, 1861–'65* (1887).

MICHAEL FRANK KNIGHT

Fleming, Lethia C. (7 Nov. 1876–22 Sept. 1963), club leader, community activist, and Republican Party organizer, worked through African American women's networks to improve conditions for her race and for women. Born in Tazewell, Virginia, to James Archibald Cousins and Fannie Taylor Cousins, Lethia Henrietta Elizebeth Cousins began her early education in Virginia. She moved to Ironton, Ohio, for her high school education before moving to Morristown, Tennessee, to attend Morristown College. She returned to Virginia for one year to teach and then moved to West Virginia, where she taught for twenty years. During these years she supported temperance and women's suffrage movements.

Cousins's significance as a community leader began with her marriage to a Cleveland lawyer, Thomas Wallace Fleming. Tom Fleming left his native Pennsylvania in 1893 to become a barber in Cleveland, Ohio. As a protégé of HARRY CLAY SMITH, editor of the *Cleveland Gazette*, a race paper that adopted an uncompromising pro-integration position, Fleming studied political behavior. After he passed both the teachers' and bar exams in 1906, he served on the Republican State Executive Committee. He ran unsuccessfully for a city council seat before being elected councilman at large in 1909. Following divorce from his first wife in 1910, he married the thirty-five-year-old Lethia Cousins on 21 February 1912.

Her marriage and her move to Cleveland linked Lethia Fleming to community institutions and to politics. She served on the board of lady managers of the Cleveland Home for Aged Colored People in 1914, chairing the fund-raising committee to build a new facility. As a charter member of the Travelers' Aid Society, Fleming was aware of the dangers for young women coming to the city. Hence she raised $2,500 to purchase the first building for the Phillis Wheatley Association (PWA), and she raised money for furnishings for and later served on the board of the PWA, a temporary shelter for young women founded by JANE EDNA HUNTER in 1913. Fleming's spiritual side led her to study the Baha'i movement, and she served as the first female trustee of Mount Zion Congregational Church and helped to organize the church's Lyceum for debate and discussion of race issues.

As a political wife with no children Lethia Fleming became involved in Republican politics. She helped to mobilize the community in support of her husband's campaign for city council. In 1916 he became the first African American elected to the City Council of Cleveland and represented Ward 11 (Central) until 1929. Lethia Fleming served as the leader of women's activities for the ward during her husband's tenure. She was a supporter of women's suffrage and worked for passage of an amendment to the Constitution. When in 1920, thanks to the Nineteenth Amendment, women gained the right to vote, Fleming received an invitation by the Republican National Committee to become the executive director of the National Association of Republican Colored Women. From her office in Chicago, Fleming applied her skills in Republican politics to mobilizing African American communities to support the presidential campaigns of Warren G. Harding (1920), Herbert Hoover (1928), and Alfred M. Landon (1936). Her efforts won her the office of president of the National Association of Republican Colored Women.

Lethia Fleming's local political leadership rose and fell with that of her husband. In 1929 Tom Fleming was indicted and convicted of unlawful soliciting and corruption in office. While he served time in the Ohio Penitentiary, Lethia Fleming attempted to run for her husband's seat on the council, but she withdrew from the campaign. She also lost her ward leadership position as a result of her husband's political scandal. As a result of Tom Fleming's co-ownership of Starlight Realty and Investment Company, the Flemings held title to nine houses in the Central neighborhood. Lethia Fleming managed these holdings during his absence.

Alone, Lethia Fleming built upon the goodwill that she had earned on her own. She worked as an agent for the Cuyahoga County Child Welfare Board from 1931 to 1951, during which time she increasingly influenced organizations at the state and national levels. As a member of the National Association of Colored Women's Clubs (NACWC), she served as fund-raiser and organizer for the Frederick Douglass Memorial Association and later for the National Negro History Association, both dedicated to preserving the history of the race. As new organizations formed, she joined. A member of the Cleveland branch of the NAACP, Fleming served on the board of the Negro Welfare Association (later the Urban League).

Fleming rose to leadership in both state and regional federations. In 1925 the Ohio Federation joined eleven other states to form the Central Association of Colored Women's Clubs (CACW). She became the seventh president of the Ohio Federation, serving from 1928 to 1933, during which time the state was divided into four districts, and new departments increased to include the Phillis Wheatley Association, Interracial Relations, Peace and Foreign Relations, and others. In 1929 when the CACW met in Kansas City, Missouri, Fleming was elected assistant recording secretary of the CACW. In 1930 she became the CACW assistant secretary. By 1934 she was the CACW corresponding secretary.

In 1935 Fleming was instrumental in bringing the Nineteenth Biennial Convention of the NACWC to her church, Mount Zion Congregational Church. At this convention she became the chairman of the Executive Board of Ohio. Although she continued working with the club movement, she also joined the National Council of Negro Women, founded by MARY MCLEOD BETHUNE in 1935.

This was not the only organization to which she was a devoted member or leader. As a life member of the Improved Benevolent Protective Order of Elks of the World (IBPOEW), Fleming served from 1928 to 1949 as the Daughter Ruler of Glenara Temple #21. Nationally, she served in the Department of Civil Liberties and as the First Grand Commissioner of Education. By 1949 she had risen to the position of Grand Directress of Public Relations of the IBPOEW.

Throughout her life Fleming served community, state, regional, and national organizations dedicated to improving conditions for women and African Americans. Political scandal did not stop her contributions. Her achievements resulted from her singular efforts and organizational abilities. Fleming's final resting place is in an arboretum at Cleveland's Lake View Cemetery alongside her husband, who died in 1948.

FURTHER READING

A collection of manuscripts by Fleming is located in Cleveland at the Western Reserve Historical Society. "My Rise and Persecution" (1932?), a typescript by Thomas W. Fleming, is also available there.

Salem, Dorothy. *To Better Our World: Black Women in Organized Reform, 1890–1920* (1990).

Wesley, Charles H. *The History of the National Association of Colored Women's Clubs: A Legacy of Service* (1984).

DOROTHY C. SALEM

Fleming, Louise "Lulu" Cecelia (28 Jan. 1862–20 June 1899), Congo missionary and physician, was born in Hibernia, Florida, on the Fleming plantation, to slave parents. Her siblings included William and Scipio Fleming, older brothers, and Thomas, Mary, Emma, Anna, and Evan Hawkins, children her mother, Cleo Fleming, bore by her second husband, Clem Hawkins. As the Civil War began, Fleming's father escaped slavery by joining the Thirty-third Colored Regiment of the Union army. He died just as the war was ending, and Lulu, as she was usually called, never knew him.

Fleming credited her mother with her early education, which by 1883 had advanced sufficiently for Fleming to teach in the public schools of Saint Augustine, Florida. She saw her teaching as a ministry, one fruit of her religious conversion at age fifteen. Looking back, she judged that her conversion made her a missionary "like Andrew of old from the very day I found the Lord" (Still, 198).

Fleming was a serious student of scripture. At Bethel Baptist Church in Jacksonville, Florida, she taught the adult Sunday school class, which included her pastor. A visitor who observed her teaching was so impressed that he returned to his Brooklyn congregation and secured support for Fleming to attend Shaw University in Raleigh, North Carolina, an institution supported by the northern American Baptist Home Mission Society.

Fleming attended Shaw in 1884 and 1885, the years-when the American Baptist Missionary Union (ABMU) assumed responsibility from the Livingstone Inland Mission for six mission stations in the Congo. Graduating at the head of her class from Estey Seminary, the women's program at Shaw, Fleming returned to teaching in Florida. The Woman's American Baptist Mission Society of the West, stirred by reports of a great revival in the Congo, sought single women missionaries. Their first recruit was Fleming, who, though supported by the woman's society, was appointed and supervised by the ABMU in Boston.

Fleming arrived at Palabala, lower Congo, in May 1887 and wrote of her amazement at the grandeur of the mountains and the lushness of the Congo Valley. On high ground a dozen miles south of the Congo River and over one hundred miles from the coast, Palabala was a trading and transportation center for those venturing further into the interior. It was also a place of transients, drunkenness, and local rulers hostile to missionaries. Consequently Fleming's students were transients, and authentic conversions were rare. The first converts were men, and because of her school duties, Fleming had few opportunities to make home visits to reach women.

For her first term of four years, Fleming worked as matron and teacher at the station's school with primary responsibility for the nine girls in residence. She savored weekend opportunities to visit area villages and assist with evangelism services. After her first Sunday tour to a nearby town, Fleming reported that the "king" had been pleased by the singing of the schoolgirls and had engaged the missionaries in conversation. Through a translator, Fleming told the king that she was part of his family, "my grandfather and his being of the same country." Reacting with disbelief to Fleming's overture, the king cried, "No, no ... she is a white black woman" (letter from Fleming to ABMU, 23 Mar. 1887, 26 Mar. 1887, 10 Oct. 1887, American Baptist Board of International Ministries Record Group, American Baptist Historical Society).

After one year, Fleming had sufficient skill in Kikongo to speak to her schoolgirls and at preaching services without a translator. In addition to teaching, preaching, and medical work, Fleming was pressed into building a new house. As she explained to the executive committee in Boston, the missionary widow with whom she boarded had so little space that both she and Fleming stored their trunks outdoors.

Fleming emphasized the need for women missionaries to visit homes, since this was often her only opportunity to converse with native women. She rejoiced in 1890 when Nora Gordon, another missionary appointee, joined her in Palabala. Gordon's teaching allowed Fleming to spend half of her day on home visits. She was also assisted by "native helpers" trained in the mission station schools and by the volunteer assistance of her young half-sister Emma Hawkins (1875–1892). Interest in Fleming's work ran high, with contributions in support of her work coming from local women's groups in Raleigh, North Carolina, Plymouth, Massachusetts, and Chatham, New Brunswick, Canada. While her salary came through her sponsoring board, Fleming wrote home to women's groups for help supporting the two young men she sent from the Congo to study at Shaw University and for funds to build a new house in Palabala for her schoolgirls.

Despite mission policy to the contrary, Fleming adopted two Congolese girls. Like other missionaries, she adopted to save a child from forced labor or marriage. Understanding the centrality of family networks to any missionary effort, Fleming pled in vain with the executive committee to appoint Henry M. Stephen, one of the two young men she had sponsored at Shaw, as a missionary to the Congo. The young man, she explained, was the son of a king, the crown prince of Palabala, and would have great influence when he returned home. Both a limited budget and American preferences for homegrown missionaries were likely factors in this decision.

Fleming remained committed to Palabala, even while admitting that she worked in a "less-favored field" and that her preparation had been inadequate. She hoped to extend her service in the Congo to five years—longer than any other missionary's health had lasted. By the end of her fourth year, however, she was in poor health. Prior to her departure for the United States, she managed one more tour of eight nearby towns so she could once more enjoy "breaking to them the Bread of Life and caring for the sick and dying" (Manuscript letter, 10 Jan. 1891, BIM Record Group, American Baptist Historical Society). All this she managed while helpers carried her in a hammock, since by this time she was too weak to travel by other means.

Returning to the states in 1891, Fleming quickly recovered her strength, began medical training at Shaw University and transferred to the Women's Medical College in Philadelphia, graduating in 1893. She completed her M.D. in 1893, becoming the first black female missionary among Baptists. By 1894 she was pressing for a return appointment to the Congo. Citing her poor health, the committee suggested she first visit her mother in Florida.

By 1895 Fleming wondered if she should seek an appointment from another mission. She reminded the committee in Boston that she had delayed three times at its request and that her health was strong enough for her to have completed her medical degree at one of the best programs. Fleming's health was not the only concern. Mission leaders were struggling to find financial support for its missionaries. When Fleming finally understood that this was the reason for the delays, she informed the ABMU executive committee that money was not an issue because Grace Baptist Church of Philadelphia had already committed to her full support.

For her second term in the Congo, Fleming was assigned to Irebu, an interior station farther up the Congo River, where the language was Lingala. There she immediately began her medical work, coping as best she could with a new language, missionary illnesses, and "native wars," during which several school children were kidnapped. Still she managed to keep her focus on "healing the sick and preaching the word" (*Twenty-Sixth Annual Report of the Woman's Baptist Foreign Missionary Society of the East*, 1897, 177).

In 1898 Irebu station was closed for financial reasons, and Fleming relocated to Bolengi. She regretted "most bitterly" the need to close the Irebu station, commenting that the year had been one of "blessed service" that, in addition to her evangelistic and medical work, had included playing the organ at daily chapel services and for three Sunday services. Except on Sundays, she provided clinic and dispensary service each morning, and most afternoons she visited a nearby town to provide medical care and an evangelistic service. In her last year of service at Irebu, Fleming treated 5,475 patients in her dispensary and made "out-calls" to 308 individuals, some requiring multiple visits. Of all these patients, she noted proudly, only six died.

This report for 1898, Fleming noted, would be her last, as she planned "to take up work as the wife of Rev. Mr. James" of the Congo Balolo Mission (CBM). By policy the women's societies only supported single missionaries. If Fleming had planned to marry another ABMU missionary, she might have maintained her connection with the American mission, but the CBM was an English mission society. Marrying Rev. James would have required that Fleming move farther up the Congo River into CBM territory. Her ties with U.S. churches remained. She became ill with sleeping sickness and returned to Philadelphia for treatment. She died while being treated at the Samaritan Hospital. Though only thirty-seven years old, Fleming had been "particularly successful in winning the hearts of the Congo people, putting herself in close touch and sympathy with them." (*Baptist Missionary Magazine*, Aug. 1899, 440). Part of Fleming's contribution was to inspire other young women to mission service. Her legacy also endured in the Congo, where she was remembered and honored into the twenty-first century.

FURTHER READING

The letters exchanged between Fleming and the Executive Committee of the American Baptist Mission Union are in the American Baptist Board of International Ministries Record Group, American Baptist Historical Society, Atlanta, Georgia.

Jacobs, Sylvia M. "Fleming, Louise "Lulu" Cecelia," in *Black Women in America: An Historical Encyclopedia*, vol. 1, eds. Darlene Clark Hine, Elsa Barkley Brown, and Rosalyn Terborg-Penn (1993).

Jennings, Ray. "Lulu Fleming," *American Baptist*, Sept. 1983.

Okewole, Ferron. "'Send Me Too': African American Baptist Women in Early Foreign Missions." *American Baptist Quarterly* 24 (Sept. 2005): 256–263.

Still, William. "Miss Lulu C. Fleming," in *Women of Distinction: Remarkable in Works and Invincible in Character*, ed. Lawson Andrew Scruggs (1893).

DEBORAH BINGHAM VAN BROEKHOVEN

Fletcher, Alphonse, Jr. (19 Dec. 1965–), Wall Street financier, entrepreneur, and philanthropist, was born in New London, Connecticut, the oldest of three sons of Alphonse Fletcher Sr., a technician at General Dynamics and an entrepreneur, and Bettye Fletcher Comer, an elementary school principal and doctor of education. In interviews, Fletcher frequently credited his parents' emphasis on education and discipline as the keys to his success in school and business. In 1987 Fletcher graduated as First Marshal of his class from Harvard College with a bachelor's degree in Applied Mathematics. Having cross-enrolled in the Aerospace Studies Program at the Massachusetts Institute of Technology as part of the U.S. Air Force Reserve Officer Training Corps, he was commissioned in 1987, and served as an officer in the U.S. Air Force Ready Reserve until his honorable discharge in 1997.

The firm of Bear, Stearns & Co., Inc., recruited Fletcher directly out of college, and he joined the staff in 1987 as a trading associate involved in investing the firm's capital, quickly rising to the level of vice president. In 1989 he moved to Kidder, Peabody & Co., a division of the General Electric Company. As a vice president specializing in income arbitration, Fletcher founded and managed one of the company's most profitable teams, again charged with the task of investing the firm's own capital. Prior to leaving Kidder, Peabody in 1991, Fletcher had gained a reputation as one of the company's most successful traders, having organized the strategic transfer of securities between the United States and offshore investors. During this period, Fletcher helped fund his younger brothers' education at Harvard. Fletcher's father died in 1990.

In 1991 Fletcher struck out on his own, founding and serving as chief executive officer of Fletcher Asset Management (FAM). With investments of more than $1 billion in its first fifteen years of operation, FAM—a small but successful firm by Wall Street standards—based its investment strategy on fundamental investment management, corporate finance, quantitative methods, and sustainability screenings.

By 1993 Fletcher had amassed considerable personal wealth, and he made his first foray into large-scale philanthropy, pledging $1 million to the NAACP to bolster its development of programs fostering business leadership among African Americans. In 1994, still shy of the age of thirty, Fletcher donated his holding stock in Fletcher Capital Markets, Inc., an affiliate of FAM, to Harvard University. This gift was worth approximately

$4 million. Several other major gifts to Harvard followed, including funding for the W. E. B. DuBois Institute for African and African American Research, the Division of Applied Sciences, and student scholarships. FAM went public in 1995, and one year later, Fletcher endowed the Alphonse Fletcher University Professorship at Harvard, held until 2001 by Cornel West, the well-known public intellectual and activist and a professor in the Department of African American Studies and the Divinity School. Fletcher's burgeoning reputation as both entrepreneur and philanthropist earned him the Ernst & Young New York City Entrepreneur of the Year Award in 1999, and the Sponsors for Educational Opportunity's Leadership Award in 2002.

In 2004, to commemorate the fiftieth anniversary of the U.S. Supreme Court's *Brown v. Board of Education* ruling, Fletcher announced a $50 million, multi-pronged, multi-year initiative of the Fletcher Foundation, the philanthropic arm of FAM, to support individuals and organizations whose work contributed to improving race relations in American society. Fletcher's mother, Bettye, directed the foundation. At the center of this initiative was the Alphonse Fletcher Sr. Fellowship Program. Modeled on the John Simon Guggenheim Foundation Fellowships and administered through the DuBois Institute at Harvard, the program awarded $50,000 fellowships to writers, artists, and scholars across several disciplines whose work furthered the broad social goals of the *Brown* decision. To do so, the fellows produced scholarly studies, literary works, and artistic performance pieces focusing on the history and effects of racism and discrimination in the United States. Among the forty-four fellows in the first seven classes were the former Black Panther and law professor Kathleen Cleaver, the cultural critic Stanley Crouch, the law professor Anita Hill, who came to national attention during the U.S. Senate confirmation hearings for Clarence Thomas's nomination to the U.S. Supreme Court in 1991, the artists Glenn Ligon and Lorna Simpson, the economist Roland Fryer, the dramatist Anna Deveare Smith, the journalists Brent Staples and Rachel Swarns, the critic Hilton Als, and the poet Elizabeth Alexander.

Fletcher's $50 million gift was one of the largest single gifts in the history of African American philanthropy. Also part of this gift was Fletcher's donation, in conjunction with Microsoft, of Encarta Africana, the CD-ROM encyclopedia of African and African American history and culture, edited by Henry Louis Gates Jr. and the Princeton philosophy professor K. Anthony Appiah, to New York City's 1,100 public schools and to several public schools in Connecticut. In cooperation with Oxford University Press, Fletcher donated copies of *African American Lives* (2004), the biographical dictionary edited by Gates and the Harvard historian Evelyn Brooks Higginbotham, to more than 6,000 public school systems and libraries across the United States. Also in 2004 Fletcher earned a master's degree in Environmental Management from the Yale School of Forestry and Environmental Studies, where he subsequently endowed fellowships for students in the field of environmental justice.

For his unprecedented philanthropic endeavors in the fields of culture and education, Fletcher received the United Negro College Fund's "Extraordinary Black Man Award" in 2004. He won the Harvard Gay and Lesbian Caucus 2005 Civil Rights Award, and the "Candle in the Dark" Award from Morehouse College in 2006. Fletcher was awarded honorary degrees from Connecticut College in 2005, and from the Bank Street College of Education in New York City, Clarkson University in Potsdam, New York, and the State University of New York-Albany in 2006. That year he also endowed the Alphonse Fletcher Professor of Law Chair at the Columbia University School of Law, to support scholarly research on issues such as criminal justice and affirmative action.

Fletcher was active as a board member or trustee of numerous charitable, civic, educational, and arts institutions, including the United Negro College Fund (for which he was chairman of the New York campaign), the New School for Social Research, the Alvin Ailey American Dance Theatre, the Public Theatre/New York Shakespeare Festival, the Studio Museum of Harlem, the American Medical Association, and the National Urban League. In addition to funding numerous educational and cultural initiatives, Fletcher also supported environmental studies and conservation projects.

In 2007, Fletcher and Bay Area venture capitalist Ellen K. Pao married, after meeting as Henry Crown Fellows at the Aspen Institute. They have one daughter.

FURTHER READING

Finer, Jonathan. "Harvard Welcomes Largest Gathering of Black Alumni; University Head Is Applauded in What Is Seen as Sign That Rift Over a 2001 Dispute Is Largely Healed," *Washington Post*, 5 Oct. 2003.

Heller, Zoe. "The Buddy System," *The New Yorker*, 29 Apr. & 6 May 1996.

Rimer, Sara. "$50 Million Gift Aims to Further Legacy of *Brown* Case," *New York Times*, 18 May 2004.

"University Professorship Named for Fletcher: Honors graduate of Harvard Class of 1987," *Harvard University Gazette*, 25 Apr. 1996.

ABBY WOLF

Fletcher, Arthur Allen (22 Dec. 1924–12 Jul. 2005), politician, teacher, and executive director of the United Negro College Fund, was born in Phoenix, Arizona, the son of Cotton Fletcher, a buffalo soldier in the U.S. Ninth and Tenth Cavalry, and Edna Miller Fletcher, a nurse and graduate of Prairie View A&M. Arthur was raised on military bases in the American west and southwest with periods spent in central Los Angeles and Oklahoma City. In 1936 when Fletcher was in the seventh grade in Oklahoma City, he heard Mary McLeod Bethune speak. He was later inspired by the way she had persuaded Eleanor Roosevelt and Secretary of Labor Francis Perkins to convince President Franklin D. Roosevelt of the need for an executive order mandating fair employment practices in federal hiring. (Roosevelt would not implement such a plan, however, until further pressured by Bethune, the NAACP's Walter White, and A. Philip Randolph's planned protest March on Washington on the eve of World War II.) The following year Fletcher's family moved to Ft. Riley, Kansas, where his father was stationed. In nearby Junction City, Fletcher achieved acceptance and his first measure of fame as an all-state athlete and student leader.

Upon graduation from Junction City, Kansas High School in 1943 he went into the U.S. Army and became a military police officer with the "Red Ball Express" of General George Patton's Third Army. Shot through the chest by a German sniper on 21 March 1945 he was evacuated to Fitzsimmons Army Hospital, Denver, Colorado. He eventually recovered, and with the GI Bill and the encouragement of a former coach, Fletcher enrolled at Washburn University in Topeka, majored in political science, and graduated with a B.A. in 1950. There he became a small-college All-American football star and was among the first black collegiate athletes to break the color barrier in the NFL. He was signed in 1950 by the Los Angeles Rams and was later traded to the Baltimore Colts, though ultimately his football career was short-lived.

His career at Washburn, student leadership, and athleticism produced local fame and community connections. Although many African Americans after World War II had switched allegiance to the Democratic Party, or had become Democrats upon migration to northern cities from the Cotton Belt, Fletcher remained loyal to the party of Lincoln; moreover, it was a practical choice, since the Republican Party won most offices in Kansas and held the power in that state. His community connections led to work on behalf of Republican gubernatorial candidate, Fred Hall, elected in the fall of 1954 on a moderate-to-liberal social agenda. Fletcher proved to be an extremely effective campaign operative on Hall's behalf, and was rewarded with a public information position with the state highway department. Hall's political fortunes quickly changed when he pushed for a statewide Fair Employment Practices Commission, a move resisted by conservatives in the Kansas Legislature. Hall's political fortunes, and by extension, his protégé Fletcher's, declined as a result. Fletcher's association with NAACP activists made him even more of a political pariah among Kansas Republicans. A plea for help to a former political patron, now an executive with Aerojet General in California, led to Fletcher's relocation and a less lucrative administrative job with the Aerojet company. The financial hardship was tremendous. In the end, these financial difficulties were a major contributor to the tragic death of his first wife, Mary, in October 1960.

By the early 1960s Fletcher was living in modest circumstances with his five children in one of the poorest neighborhoods in Oakland. Seeing that many in the community were living in even worse circumstances, he began to use his knowledge of politics and government to offer advice, and eventually, leadership. In 1962 he ran unsuccessfully for the California Assembly. For a few years Fletcher worked as a teacher in Berkeley where he met Ayesha Bernyce Hassan. Marrying in 1965, they moved to Pasco, Washington, where Fletcher obtained a community service job as executive director of a War on Poverty community action program called the Higher Horizons Project, initially sponsored by the Lower Columbia Basin YMCA. In November 1967 his efforts to organize a home-owning cooperative among agricultural workers in East Pasco led to his election to the Pasco City Council. A 1968 campaign for the Republican nomination for the office of Lieutenant Governor followed. He won that nomination, a first for an African American in Washington State, but narrowly lost the general election. Fletcher's Republican affiliation, his community organizing success, and support from Washington's new Republican governor, Dan Evans, led to his appointment as Assistant

Secretary of Labor for Wage and Labor Standards under President Richard Nixon's Secretary of Labor, George Schultz. Fletcher's selection was one of the most significant race-related domestic policy appointments of the Vietnam War–era. Fletcher began implementing affirmative action hiring plans on federally funded construction projects in the summer of 1969 with what was known as "The Revised Philadelphia Plan." For Democratic administrations the opposition of white trade unionists, an integral part of the New Deal coalition, had prevented serious efforts at enforcing minority hiring regulations. For Republicans no such problem existed. The Revised Philadelphia Plan mandated hiring minorities in the various trades and crafts on federally funded contracts of $50,000 or more. The policy targeted all-white trade and craft unions that had long resisted African American members, and had the political purpose of dividing two of the Democratic Party's leading constituencies: organized labor and blacks. When federal courts upheld the Revised Philadelphia Plan, Fletcher's office moved swiftly and established similar plans in twenty-six of the nation's major metropolitan areas.

After Fletcher's service in the Labor Department, President Nixon appointed him to the U.S. United Nations Delegation in 1971. He became executive director of the United Negro College Fund in January 1972 and helped establish the Fund's enduring slogan, "A mind is a terrible thing to waste." During the final year of President Gerald Ford's administration, Fletcher served as Deputy Presidential Assistant for Urban Affairs. For the next several years, Fletcher worked as a successful entrepreneur. In 1990 President George H. W. Bush appointed Fletcher to a five-year term on the U.S. Civil Rights Commission where he served three years as chairman.

After Senator Robert Dole's rejected the National Black Republican Council's public appeal to add support of affirmative action to his presidential campaign's platform, Fletcher mounted his own campaign for the 1996 Republican presidential nomination with the slogan "Send 5 to keep AA alive." He often stated that affirmative action was a means of creating economic opportunity for the future, not paying for the past. In his final years Fletcher worked to find an effective way to reach young African American males and instill in them the values he so highly prized—individualism, initiative, and the importance of education. In an era when most African Americans voted Democratic, Fletcher, much like U.S. Senator EDWARD BROOKE and Secretary of Transportation WILLIAM COLEMAN, remained loyal to the party of Lincoln.

FURTHER READING

Axelrod, Alan. *Minority Rights in America* (2002).

Kotlowski, Dean J. *Nixon's Civil Rights: Politics, Principle and Policy* (2001).

Tate, Gayle T., and Lewis A. Randolph, eds. *Dimensions of Black Conservatism in the United States: Made in America* (2002).

Obituary: *Washington Post*, 14 July 2005.

M. A. PETERSON

Fletcher, Barney (c. 1820–1884), African Methodist Episcopal (AME) minister and activist, was born into slavery in Maryland. Nothing is known of his parentage and youth. He gained his freedom, moved west during the Gold Rush, and was living in San Francisco by 1850. Fletcher and a brother (named Charles, George, or Edward in various sources) helped found St. Andrews Church in Sacramento, and Fletcher seems to have moved back and forth between Sacramento and San Francisco and worked at least occasionally as a miner. Some sources report that he earned enough to purchase his wife and children out of slavery. Although no spouse was living with him in 1850, his Virginia-born wife Elizabeth (also listed as Betsy) is named with him in the 1860 census, along with two children, Joseph G. and Mary E.

In addition to his work in Sacramento, Fletcher helped found St. Cyprian's African Methodist Episcopal Church in San Francisco in 1854, which he helped lead for several years, and he worked closely with AME stalwarts like THOMAS M. D. WARD and JAMES H. HUBBARD. Like these men, Fletcher was also deeply active in civil rights efforts in California. He participated in the early state convention movement, served on the financial committee of the San Francisco black newspaper the *Mirror of the Times*, was a Prince Hall Freemason, and was affiliated with the Sacramento Zouaves (a black drill club). He focused especially on efforts to improve education, and he repeatedly joined other community leaders like Jeremiah Burke Sanderson in protesting California's discrimination against black students. He was also a trustee of the Livingston Institute, a failed attempt to create a black secondary school in northern California in the 1860s.

The exact date of Fletcher's ordination remains unclear; he is generally listed in the AME press as a "traveling preacher." Like many black clergymen in the early West, Fletcher practiced long before he was ordained, and he worked a variety of jobs to support his church work—from carpentry to mining. In 1873 the *Christian Recorder* listed both wife and husband as members and worthy contributors to the Union Bethel Church in San Francisco. At this point Fletcher was not the church's minister, although in later years he appears to have temporarily filled the pulpit until the church assigned a new pastor. In September 1875 he was appointed as a messenger for the San Francisco Custom House, and he also worked as a porter for a large San Francisco jeweler and a janitor in San Francisco's City Hall (a position his son Joseph later held). The positions at the custom house and city hall, because they were government appointments, were duly noted as race success stories in the black press.

Fletcher's later life was dominated by his church work and family. Both his son and daughter lived at home until at least 1880, and the family grew with the addition of a godson, Barney Scott, and two wards, Lillie Jackson and Annie Jackson. Although his life is often overlooked outside of California, Fletcher was a key early church figure, and St. Cyprian's was an important ancestor of San Francisco's Bethel AME Church.

FURTHER READING

Beasley, Delilah. *Negro Trail Blazers of California* (1919).
Lapp, Rudolph. *Blacks in Gold Rush California* (1977).
Parker, Elizabeth L., and James Abajian. *Walking Tour of the Black Presence in San Francisco* (1974).

ERIC GARDNER

Fletcher, Benjamin Harrison (13 Apr. 1890–10 July 1949), union activist, was born in Philadelphia, Pennsylvania. The record of Fletcher's early years is sparse, containing no mention of his parents, childhood, or education. As a teenager he evidently secured work at various odd jobs in and around his hometown. He soon drifted into casual work on the waterfront, where he came in contact with a steady stream of radical agitators connected with the Industrial Workers of the World (IWW), or Wobblies. Much of what the Wobblies had to say to the port's unorganized longshoremen appealed to the young Fletcher, particularly their vision of interracial solidarity and worker militancy. So in 1911 he offered his services as a corresponding secretary for a citywide local of the IWW. It was an association that would last a lifetime. Fletcher married and had at least one child, but no details of his family life are available.

Fletcher's life was deeply intertwined with the organizational history of the port's dockworkers, members of Local 8, affiliated with the IWW's Marine Transport Workers Industrial Union. Formed in 1913 following a strike on the city's docks, Local 8 successfully combined revolutionary IWW leadership—of which Fletcher was an important part—with sound organizational principles modeled after the more established American Federation of Labor (AFL) craft unions. This hybrid species of unionism, virtually unknown in the United States, has confounded labor theorists ever since. For some, Local 8 "differed not one whit from a conservative union of the A.F. of L," while others saw Philadelphia's longshoremen as "the vanguard of American labor." In fact the Wobbly union was both. While Local 8 followed many of the AFL's proven organizational methods, including the imposition of high initiation fees and limited membership, it departed from the usual "business union" in several ways, most notably in its racial policies. In addition to enforcing complete and full integration of the workforce, Local 8 mandated rotation in office between white and black union leaders: one month, an African American served as local president with a white vice president; the next month this pattern was reversed. In an industry otherwise known for its practice of racial separatism, Local 8's egalitarianism was a remarkable achievement.

Local 8's progressive racial policies were largely attributable to its indigenous black leadership, particularly Fletcher, whose reputation among his fellow workers was second to none. Jack Lever, a longshoreman who worked alongside Fletcher in the early days, remembered him as simply "one of the best organizers I knew." Articulate and charismatic, Fletcher blossomed into a leading national spokesman for the African American working class. Recognizing his considerable talents, the IWW in 1915 temporarily reassigned Fletcher to Boston, Baltimore, and other North Atlantic cities to organize dockworkers. But his crowning achievement was organizing the port of Philadelphia, where Local 8 almost doubled in size to nearly six thousand members by 1917.

Partly as a consequence of Fletcher's growing following on the docks, he was indicted by the Department of Justice in 1917. Charged with various acts of subversion and disloyalty during wartime, Fletcher was tried along with 165 other IWW leaders in Chicago's federal court amid a growing national hysteria focused on the dangers of "bolshevism" and radicalism. Fletcher, the lone black defendant, did not testify on his own behalf and no questions were asked of him by the prosecution. The case against him rested on several letters that were read at his trial.

Fletcher's real crime, as revealed in a confidential report from the Justice Department, was being "a Negro who had great influence with the colored stevedores ... in building up the Marine Transport Workers Union which at time of indictment had become so strong that it practically controlled all shipping on the Atlantic Coast." In 1918 Fletcher was summarily convicted on four counts, sentenced to ten years in jail, and fined $30,000. Even at his sentencing Fletcher retained his dry sense of humor, reprimanding the judge for "using poor English today. His sentences are too long." On 30 October 1922 he was released from prison under a conditional pardon that he "stay out of trouble," signed by President Warren G. Harding. The next day Fletcher was back on the Philadelphia docks, offering his assistance to the longshoremen who were in the midst of a strike.

The strike that year was crushed. Growing dissension in the ranks of longshoremen led many to join the rival International Longshoremen's Association (ILA), affiliated with the AFL. When the national office of the IWW refused to assist Local 8 in its life-and-death struggle with the ILA, Fletcher marshaled his supporters and together they struck out on their own, forming the Independent Longshoremen's Union in the spring of 1923. It was a painful parting of the ways for Fletcher, and, after a year's absence, he led his integrated membership back into Local 8. Increasing employer and government favoritism for the more conservative ILA placed the Wobblies at a serious disadvantage in the intensifying contest for union loyalty. Following a string of minor skirmishes throughout the port, many of Local 8's key leaders switched allegiance to the ILA in 1925, bringing to a-close the IWW's brief but illustrious history on the-docks.

Fletcher, a man of principle, refused to follow his former comrades into the ILA. His decision was not without its costs, both personal and professional, for it meant that Fletcher's career in the labor movement was effectively over. Indeed, he was not heard from for several years, surfacing briefly in 1931 on the streets of New York City, where he held his listeners "spellbound" for over an hour. "I have heard all the big shots of the labor movement over a period of 25 years from coast to coast," wrote an AFL official who was in the audience, "and it is no exaggeration when I state that this colored man ... is the only one I ever heard who cut right through to the bone of capitalist pretensions ... with a concrete constructive working class union argument." It was to be Fletcher's last known public address. A victim of failing health, he suffered a stroke two years later that all but silenced this gifted orator. Further limited by a heart attack in 1945 he eventually died at his home in Brooklyn—with his membership in the IWW current and paid up.

FURTHER READING

Fletcher's papers are in the Abram Harris Collection, deposited in the Moorland-Spingarn Research Center at Howard University.

Foner, Philip S. "The IWW and the Black Worker," *Journal of Negro History* 55 (Jan. 1970).

Marcus, Irwin. "Benjamin Fletcher: Black Labor Leader," *Negro History Bulletin* 35 (Oct. 1972).

Seraile, William. "Ben Fletcher, I.W.W. Organizer," *Pennsylvania History* 46 (July 1979).

Spero, Sterling D., and Abram L. Harris. *The Black Worker: The Negro and the Labor Movement* (1931).

HOWARD KIMELDORF

Fletcher, Tom (16 May 1873–13 October 1954), entertainer, was born in Portsmouth, Ohio, the son of Luther Fletcher, a steamboat fireman, and Mary Eliza Cox, a cook. A stage performance sometime before 1888 of Harriet Beecher Stowe's *Uncle Tom's Cabin* that featured a cadre of African American actors and in which he played a small part initially inspired Tom Fletcher to pursue a career in entertainment. Later Fletcher became the first black actor to play the role of Uncle Tom.

Fletcher spent more than sixty years on the stage or performing in various venues. As a boy soprano he sang in local talent shows and played in the Portsmouth fife corps. His professional theatrical career began at age fifteen when he appeared with such groups as Howard's Novelty Colored Minstrels, the Old Kentucky show, Ed Winn's minstrel company, and Richard and Pringle's Georgia Minstrels. At the turn of the twentieth century Fletcher launched a new career in vaudeville shows and nightclub performances, frequently performing with Al Bailey in an act known as "Bailey and Fletcher, the Minstrel Boys."

In 1908 Tom Fletcher played a leading role as a singer and dancer in the second edition of the Memphis Students, replacing the ailing founder

Ernest Hogan. The Memphis Students was an ensemble consisting of musicians who were neither students nor from Memphis. They featured the soprano ABBIE MITCHELL and three dancers, Edith Harrison, Esmeralda Statum, and Isola Ringold. Their New York act played Proctor's 125th Street Theater and the Orpheum in Brooklyn with so much success that it was booked for the summer season at Hammerstein's Roof Garden on Broadway. This playing-singing-dancing orchestra was the first to perform syncopated music on a public concert stage, radically departing from the previous dance hall settings or theater orchestra pits. They numbered about twenty, performing predominantly on banjos, mandolins, guitars, saxophones, and drums, along with a violin, a few brass instruments, and a double bass. This historic ensemble paved the way for the acceptance of syncopated song and dance music on the concert stage by the likes of Paul Whiteman and DUKE ELLINGTON nearly a generation later.

In 1919 Fletcher joined the New York Syncopated Orchestra's American tour under WILL MARION COOK's baton and performed in such venues as Orchestra Hall in Chicago, Pabst Theatre in Milwaukee, and Carnegie Hall in Pittsburgh. This unique performing group adopted the term "orchestra" as it was used in its earliest and broadest sense: a group of mixed instruments playing together with more than one instrument on a single part. The fifty players and singers consisted of violins, saxophones, trombones, trumpets, mandolins, banjos, guitars, a bass horn, tympani, and drums, in addition to a male quartet and a soprano soloist. Fletcher was a member of the group for four months, serving as assistant manager, stage manager, leading comedian, and sometimes advance agent. Throughout his career he also entertained the who's who of white America in their homes, hotels, restaurants, and yachts.

No doubt Fletcher is best remembered for his autobiography, *100 Years of the Negro in Show Business*, which gives the only eyewitness account from a black insider of the late nineteenth- and early twentieth-century theatrical players, personalities, and pioneers. His career spanned the rise and fall of minstrelsy, yet he valued its role in the march toward economic equality and social justice.

FURTHER READING

Fletcher, Tom. *100 Years of the Negro in Show Business: The Tom Fletcher Story* (1954).

MARVA GRIFFIN CARTER

Flipper, Henry Ossian (21 Mar. 1856–3 May 1940), soldier and engineer, was born in Thomasville, Georgia, the son of Festus Flipper and Isabelle (maiden name unknown), slaves. During the Civil War and Reconstruction he was educated in American Missionary Association schools and in 1873 gained admission to Atlanta University. That year Flipper also obtained an appointment to the U.S. Military Academy through the auspices of Republican Representative James C. Freeman. He was not the first African American to attend West Point, as Michael Howard and James Webster Smith preceded him in 1870, but neither graduated. Flipper subsequently endured four years of grueling academic instruction and ostracism from white classmates before graduating fiftieth in a class of sixty-four on 14 June 1877. He was commissioned second lieutenant in the all-black Tenth U.S. Cavalry, and the following year recounted his academy experience in an autobiography, *The Colored Cadet at West Point* (1878).

Flipper enjoyed a brief but active military career. He was billeted at various frontier posts, including Forts Elliott, Concho, Davis, and Quitman in Texas, and Fort Sill, Indian Territory (now Oklahoma), and engaged in numerous engineering activities. This regimen included drainage of swamps at Fort Sill, building a wagon road from that post to Gainesville, Texas, and installing telegraph lines from Fort Elliott, Texas, to Camp Supply, Indian Territory. Flipper also distinguished himself in the 1880 war against the Apache Victorio and earned a commendation from Colonel Benjamin H. Grierson. He was then posted as acting commissary of subsistence at Fort Davis in November 1881, when Colonel William R. Shafter accused him of embezzling $3,791.77 in missing commissary funds that were assumed to be stolen. A court-martial cleared Flipper of all charges but found him guilty of "conduct unbecoming an officer and a gentleman," and dismissed him from the service on 30 June 1882. For the rest of his life Flipper professed his innocence and ascribed the end of his military career to racial prejudice.

As a civilian, Flipper remained in the West for nearly half a century and distinguished himself in a variety of mining, engineering, and surveying work. Commencing in 1883, he functioned in northern Mexico as a cartographer for the Banco Minero and as chief engineer for several American mining concerns. Fluent in Spanish, Flipper became an authority on Spanish and Mexican land law, and in 1891 he represented Nogales, Arizona, in an

Henry O. Flipper, the first African American to graduate from the United States Military Academy at West Point in 1877. (Schomburg Center.)

important land grant case. His expertise convinced Justice Department officials to appoint him as a special agent in the court of private claims. In 1882 he published *Mexico Laws, Statutes, etc.*, which was long held as a definitive treatise on the subject.

Flipper returned to northern Mexico in 1901 and spent the next eleven years as resident engineer for a number of American mining companies. In this capacity he befriended Albert Fall, a future U.S. senator from New Mexico, with whom Flipper exchanged extensive correspondence during the Mexican Revolution. When Fall became secretary of the interior in 1921, he appointed Flipper as an assistant working on the commission tasked with locating, constructing, and operating railroads in Alaska. After Fall was implicated in the Teapot Dome scandal of 1923, Flipper left the Interior Department to work for an oil company in Venezuela and compiled another significant work, *Venezuela Laws, Statutes, etc.* (1925). He returned to Atlanta in 1930 to reside with his brother, Bishop Joseph Flipper of the African Methodist Episcopal Church. Flipper died in Atlanta.

Flipper is best remembered as the first African American graduate of West Point and for the controversy surrounding his dismissal. However, his forty-eight-year career as an engineer established him as an important figure in western development. Furthermore, Flipper's impressive linguistic and legal credentials were valuable assets for the growth of mining industries in both the United States and Mexico. His civilian endeavors were all conspicuously marked by the high moral conduct and methodological problem solving imparted to him at West Point. Although he was denied vindication by the military while he was alive, in December 1976 the Department of the Army finally granted him a posthumous honorable discharge and a military reinterment. Furthermore, on 3 May 1977 a bust of Flipper was unveiled at West Point, signifying formal recognition from the institution that had so scorned him. Apparently, he never married.

FURTHER READING

Flipper's military correspondence is in RG 94, Records of the Adjutant General, National Archives. Scattered personal materials are in the Benjamin H. Grierson Papers, Texas Tech University, Lubbock; and the Frank H. Edmund Papers, U.S. Military Academy.

Black, Lowell D. *An Officer and a Gentleman* (1985).

Harris, Theodore D., ed. *Negro Frontiersman: The Western Memoirs of Henry O. Flipper* (1963).

Robinson, Charles M. *The Court-martial of Lieutenant Flipper* (1994).

JOHN C. FREDRIKSEN

Flipper, Joseph Simeon (22 Feb. 1859–10 Oct. 1944), African Methodist Episcopal (AME) bishop and educator, was born in Atlanta, Georgia, the second of five sons of Festus Flipper, an enslaved shoemaker, and Isabella Buckhalter. Flipper's father purchased the freedom of Isabella prior to Flipper's birth. In 1864 Festus and Isabella fled from Atlanta in front of Sherman's army and settled in Macon, Georgia. The Flippers returned to Atlanta as freed people the following year and focused on educating their sons. Flipper attended multiple schools before enrolling in the Storrs School (later Atlanta

University) in 1869; however, he left school after his junior year to become a teacher.

After teaching for several years, Flipper moved to his parents' new home in Thomasville, Georgia. While in Thomasville, he married Amanda Slater on 24 February 1880. He also joined the African Methodist Episcopal Church in 1877 and rapidly rose in the church ranks. He joined the Georgia Conference in 1880 as a pastor and was assigned to serve in Groverville, Georgia. Church regulations allowed pastors to stay in any one parish up to four years, but church leaders recognized Flipper's talent and rapidly promoted him. Within four years he had served in Groverville, Boston Circuit, and Darien Station. Flipper was ordained an elder in 1884 and was assigned to serve in Quitman, Georgia. In 1886 he was called as presiding elder and pastor of the Big Bethel AME Church in Atlanta, which ran the school where he originally began his education.

The AME Church's prohibition on pastors' serving for more than four years in one parish allowed Flipper to preside over many congregations. Wherever Flipper served, he increased his congregation's size and assets and uplifted his race. He raised more money for the Big Bethel Church than had any previous pastor. The AME Church named him a Dollar King at its national convention in 1886 and awarded him a Gold Badge in recognition of his fundraising prowess. Flipper also continued to apply his talents in the education sector. In 1903 the church relieved Flipper of his parish duties and appointed him trustee of Morris Brown College, before electing him president the next year. From 1903 until 1908 he used his expertise to raise necessary funds and increase enrollment at the college.

Flipper continued to pastor different churches around the Atlanta area in the early twentieth century until the delegates of the General Conference of the AME Church, meeting in Norfolk, Virginia, in 1908, elected him one of five new bishops and assigned him to serve in Oklahoma and Arkansas. For the next thirty-six years he also presided over the powerful Georgia, Florida, and South Carolina conferences. Those who knew Flipper characterized him as kind and loving, but he could be extremely combative when he felt attacked.

Bishop Flipper did not hesitate to compromise harmony to achieve specific outcomes. In 1915 a dispute arose over who should be the next secretary of the AME Bishops' Council. Flipper, who had been assistant secretary, sought the position. However, the bishops elected Bishop John Hurst of Baltimore. Flipper took this as a personal and sectional affront, charging northern bishops with conspiring to maintain northern power in the church. While 80 percent of the church's membership resided in the South, more than half of the bishops came from and presided over conferences in northern states. Rather than be humiliated, Flipper walked out of the Bishops' Council meeting in protest but he stayed in town to see how the council reacted. The next day the council said that if Flipper signed a statement acknowledging the council's right to elect whomever it chose, then Bishop Hurst would refuse his appointment and allow Flipper to become secretary. Flipper refused. Apparently, a significant number of the AME bishops felt he was justified in doing so, because this incident, which in part led to some southern discontent, resulted in an increase in the election of southern-born bishops in the years that followed. The event and its consequences also demonstrate the increasing influence that Bishop Flipper wielded within the religion.

Flipper also stirred some waters by once refusing to take the sacrament at an AME Bishops' Council meeting because the wine was passed in individual cups. Flipper explained to the other bishops that the Bible taught him to "take this cup," not "these cups," but his position may have had as much to do with church politics as with religion. At this particular conference, the priest overseeing communion was from the rival African Methodist Episcopal Zion (AME Zion) Church. At this time, several leaders from both denominations sought union of the churches and may have requested the AME Zion priest administer communion. Both denominations recognized the authority of the other to officiate in the ordinances. Flipper's refusal may have been influenced by his stance against integration.

From 1918 to 1932 some leaders in the three major black Episcopal churches, AME, AME Zion, and the Colored Methodist Episcopal Church (CME), made a concerted effort to merge. The smallest denomination, the CME, feared absorption into the AME and dropped out of the proceedings relatively quickly. In 1920 Flipper made a speech supporting merger, yet he continually used his influence to undermine merger proceedings. While he contended that the two sects had uncompromising theological differences, much of his argument against unification focused on the economical inexpediency of the merger. The same AME and AME Zion churches covered approximately the same geographical area. Since neither side was willing to give up any of its bishops, the united church would have thirty bishops leading slightly over a million people, and many areas of the United States would be under the jurisdiction of two bishops: one the former AME bishop and the other the former AME Zion bishop would eventually force a united church to eliminate a number of these duplicated Episcopal districts. Flipper continually pointed out these problems to other bishops and church leaders. Because of Flipper's influence, the merger never occurred.

In the midst of all this Flipper also dealt with several major personal issues. His son Carl Flipper, who had followed him into the ministry, was accused of infidelity in a highly publicized divorce that caused family embarrassment. Flipper himself was accused of immoral conduct in 1921, but the case seemed so outlandish and out of character that the Bishops' Council never investigated it. Flipper's beloved first wife passed away in 1931. The next year he married Susie Erwin, who maintained a strong role in the women's organizations of the church and supported her husband.

In February 1936, upon the death of the previous senior bishop, Flipper became the senior prelate. He held this, the highest position in the AME Church, for the next eight years. As senior bishop Flipper presided over two major changes in the government of the church. He oversaw the creation of a new Episcopal district comprising the Caribbean and South America. He also presided over the conference that decided to retire all bishops over seventy-five years of age at the next quadrennial conference of the church.

To the end of his life, Flipper maintained his focus on the spiritual, educational, and economic uplift of his race. Allen University in Columbia, South Carolina, named its new library the Joseph Simeon Flipper Library after he raised approximately $30,000 for the school, including $9,000 for the library. Speaking at a reception held in his honor for this occasion on 13 March 1943, Flipper, who died a little over a year later, summed up his life and his sixty-four years in the AME Church, stating that whenever he started a project he made sure to see it through. Flipper took ill in early 1944 and died that October in his home in Atlanta, having dedicated his life to church service.

FURTHER READING

Smith, Charles Spencer. *A History of the African Methodist Episcopal Church: Being a Volume Supplemental to a History of the African Methodist Episcopal Church, by Daniel Alexander Payne, D.D., LL.D., Late One of Its Bishops* (1922).

Wright, Richard R., Jr. *The Encyclopedia of the African Methodist Episcopal Church*, 2d ed. (1947).

DONOVAN S. WEIGHT

Flippin, George Albert (8 Feb. 1868–15 May 1929), football player and doctor, was born in Point Isabelle, Ohio, to Charles Flippin, a doctor and a former slave, and Mary Bell Flippin, a white medical worker. The family moved to Kansas briefly before settling in York County, Nebraska, where Flippin received his first education in the area's public schools. By 1891 he had moved to Lincoln and enrolled in the University of Nebraska.

Flippin was an active and popular member of the campus community. He won a university-wide speaking contest and was a member and eventually president of the Palladian Literary Society, the first such organization on campus. He made his biggest mark, though, in athletics. He played four years of football for Nebraska and also competed in track and field contests. Standing at six feet two inches and two hundred pounds, Flippin was a natural at football, and he quickly established himself as the best player at Nebraska, breaking off long runs and usually leading the team in scoring.

He felt accepted on Nebraska's campus but occasionally ran afoul of the color line. In the fall of 1892 the all-white University of Missouri refused to compete against Flippin, but Nebraska held firm and declined to bench its star halfback, causing Missouri to forfeit the game 1-0. That same season, hotels in Colorado and Iowa objected to Flippin's presence in the traveling party, but again Nebraska's team refused to accept separate accommodations and forced the recalcitrant establishments to treat the entire group equally. Flippin himself was not shy about exerting his civil rights. The following year he unsuccessfully sued a sanatorium proprietor who denied him access to a swimming pool. Despite these racial troubles, his teammates stood by him and elected Flippin to the team captaincy—over the objections of the head coach—after the 1894 season.

Financial realities, however, forced Flippin to interrupt his studies. He married Georgia Smith, a black student from the Nebraska Conservatory of Music, in 1893 and quit school to support his family; the couple eventually had two children. He worked a variety of jobs around town before becoming one of the first African Americans to join the Lincoln police force. He soon tired of police work and enrolled at the Chicago College of Physicians and Surgeons (P&S; now the University of Illinois Medical School). An independent institution at the time, P&S fielded a football team, and because of limited rules governing intercollegiate sports, Flippin immediately joined the squad. Still facing financial problems, he was able to secure an athletic scholarship from school administrators. In exchange for free tuition and a yearly stipend of seventy dollars, Flippin agreed to play football only for P&S, which he did for three seasons. He received his medical degree in 1900 but still did not have a B.A. degree, because Nebraska declined to accept transfer credits for an undergraduate degree.

Nevertheless, Flippin began his medical career as an intern at Chicago's Cook County hospital. After one more year in Chicago he moved to Pine Bluff, Arkansas, where he established a medical practice and lived for several years. He returned to Nebraska in about 1903 and settled in Stromsburg in the rural eastern part of the state. With the help of his father he established the private Mawood Hospital, the first such facility in the small town. An accomplished physician, he readily established a successful practice in the nearly all-white city and won admiration for his willingness to make house calls at any hour in any part of the county. His letterhead claimed mastery of "diseases of women and children, chronic diseases, surgery, vibration, x-ray diagnosis, baths, radio vtiant [*sic*], electric light, and modern scientific methods" (Broussard, 7).

Although most local residents respected Flippin and treated him well, occasionally he had to fight against the affects of Jim Crow. For instance in 1912 he forced the state health inspector to acknowledge that there was no color line in state medical law and that black and white doctors were subject to the same and equal standards and regulations. Around the same time he won the state's first civil rights case when he successfully sued a York, Nebraska, café that had refused him service. The court upheld Flippin's rights and awarded him a hundred dollars in damages.

Sometime after returning to Nebraska he divorced his first wife, Georgia, and in about 1910 he married Mertina F. Larson, a white nurse who worked at his hospital. The new couple scandalized some Stromsburg citizens, and one local newspaper harshly attacked Flippin: "We know nothing admirable about him except his nerve. With his Jack Johnson habit of marrying white blood, he is a deteriorating influence in the state, and many people are ashamed that he is a seemingly prominent and influential member of this community" (Broussard, 8). Despite such opposition the couple, who had no children, remained together until Flippin's death, and the Mawood Hospital continued to do a brisk business. Most residents seemed to accept the marriage, and the town later elected Flippin to the Stromsburg board of education. He continued to prize his own studies, too, visiting hospitals around the country and in Europe to learn the latest techniques.

Flippin remained the sole doctor in Stromsburg until he died at the age of sixty-six. His funeral was reportedly the largest in town history, and he was the first African American buried in the Stromsburg cemetery. An athletic and medical pioneer, Flippin is best remembered for his exploits on the gridiron and in 1974 was elected to the University of Nebraska Football Hall of Fame.

FURTHER READING

There is a small collection of George Albert Flippin's personal papers in the Stewart-Flippin Family Collection in the Moorland-Spingarn Research Center at Howard University.

Broussard, Albert S. "George Albert Flippin and Race Relations in a Western Rural Community," *Midwest Review* (1990).

Harding, David. *The Mighty Bugeaters* (1998).

Oschner, David A. "George Flippin Did It His Way," *Nebraska Magazine* (Spring 1999).

Obituary: *Stromsburg (Nebraska) Headlight*, 23 May 1929.

GREGORY TRAVIS BOND

Flood, Curt (18 Jan. 1938–20 Jan. 1997), baseball player and artist, was born Curtis Charles Flood in Houston, Texas, the youngest of six children of Herman and Laura Flood. In 1940 the family moved to Oakland, California. Flood's older brother, Carl, who had trouble with the law from childhood, slipped into a life of crime. Flood, however, began playing midget-league baseball at the age of nine. George Powles coached the team and produced, besides Curt Flood, such players as FRANK ROBINSON, Vada Pinson, JOE MORGAN, and Jesse Gonder. The other factor that kept Flood out of trouble was encountering Jim Chambers, who encouraged his interest and development as an artist at Herbert Hoover High School in Oakland. Flood played baseball throughout his teenage years and became a promising athlete. However, he was small, weighing barely one hundred forty pounds and standing only five feet seven inches tall as a

Curt Flood loosens up his arm during a practice session with the Washington Senators at their winter camp in St. Petersburg, Florida, 19 November 1970. (AP Images.)

senior in high school. Despite his diminutive stature, he was signed by the Cincinnati Reds in 1956 for a salary of four thousand dollars. He received no bonus for signing, but the contract was impressive for a working-class boy who had just graduated from high school. As a minor league player in Tampa, Florida, Flood had to endure the racial taunts and slurs that other black ball players suffered when playing newly integrated baseball in the South. Having grown up on the West Coast, he had never encountered the uncompromising nature of southern segregation, and it was quite a revelation to him. The odds were not in Flood's favor of making it to the major leagues, but he hit .340 in his first year of professional baseball, including twenty-nine home runs. He briefly came up to play with the Reds at the end of the season—Flood was being groomed by the team to be a third baseman—but he had little future in that position with the organization. So, in 1957 Cincinnati traded Flood to the St. Louis Cardinals, who made him a centerfielder, a position he held for them for the next twelve years.

At the time Flood joined the Cardinals, they were geographically the southernmost major league team. Owned by August Busch Jr., who also owned the Anheuser-Busch brewing company, and who was, in many respects, predictably conservative, the team itself exhibited surprisingly liberal tendencies for its day. Minority and white players got along very well, and the team insisted on integrated accommodations for its players during spring training. Under its managers Johnny Keane and Red Schoendienst, the team flourished on the field in the mid-1960s. With stars such as the pitcher Bob Gibson, the third baseman Ken Boyer, the second baseman Julian Javier, the first baseman Bill White, and the outfielder Lou Brock, along with the outstanding play of Flood, who was not only a good hitter but one of the best defensive outfielders of his day, the Cardinals won the World Series in 1964, beating the New York Yankees. Adding the outfielder Roger Maris and the first baseman Orlando Cepeda, they won again in 1967, beating the Boston Red Sox. St. Louis went to the World Series again in 1968, but lost to the Detroit Tigers in seven games. Busch began to break up his championship team in 1968, and the Cardinals did not go the World Series again until 1982.

In October 1969, after a disappointing season for St. Louis, Flood, the catcher Tim McCarver, and the pitcher Byron Browne were traded to the Philadelphia Phillies. Flood was thirty-one years old in 1969, and the Cardinals thought, reasonably enough, that the outfielder's best years were behind him. Flood, shocked and disappointed by the trade and what he took to be the team's cavalier treatment of him, refused to accept it. At first he considered retiring. He had a lucrative business as a portrait artist in St. Louis and many other ties in the city. Moreover, he had heard that Philadelphia was a tough place for a black player to play, though the Phillies offered Flood a salary of ninety thousand dollars, a handsome sum at the time.

After thinking the matter over and talking with his friend Marian Jorgensen, Flood decided to sue Bowie K. Kuhn, Commissioner of Baseball, and the American and National Leagues over baseball's reserve clause, which prevented Flood from being able to negotiate with any team he wished that might desire his services. Flood presented his case to his union, the Players Association, and its new executive director, Marvin Miller, who, though thinking the suit was ill timed and not likely to succeed, supported Flood. His fellow players simply wanted Flood's assurances that he was not challenging the league for racial reasons, which he insisted he was not. The former Supreme Court justice Arthur Goldberg represented Flood.

Flood was not the first player to challenge the reserve clause, which was established in the 1870s and made a player permanently the property of the particular team that possessed his contract; however, he became the most famous. Baseball owners argued that without the reserve clause, their leagues would have no stability, because players would simply move from team to team in order to leverage the highest salary. The history of early baseball actually supported this contention by the owners. However, the main reason for the reserve clause was to control player salaries by not permitting them to offer their services in an open market. The baseball team owners essentially argued that it was a monopoly that could not function successfully unless it completely controlled the freedom of its employees, a position supported by the U.S. Supreme Court, which had exempted professional baseball teams from antitrust laws in 1922.

Flood was facing long odds in his lawsuit. The public was decidedly against him, not feeling great sympathy for a man claiming to be a "slave" and being treated like "a consignment of goods" who was making ninety thousand dollars a year. Most sportswriters were similarly unsympathetic, as were the lower federal courts and the Second Circuit Court of Appeals. Flood lost his case and sat out the 1970 season. While appealing the case to the Supreme Court, he returned to baseball briefly, playing for the Washington Senators, which had made a deal with Philadelphia to get him. But Flood left the Senators after playing only thirteen games. He felt that he no longer had the desire or the ability to play, especially in the face of hostility from the baseball establishment, and he moved to Copenhagen, Denmark, where he spent most of the 1970s. He never played professional baseball again.

On 18 June 1972, the Supreme Court affirmed the Second Circuit's ruling by a vote of 5 to 3. Even though the Court ruled against him, Flood had generated enormous publicity and discussion about the reserve clause. By the end of 1972 baseball owners agreed to salary arbitration, the beginning of the end of the reserve clause. In 1975 the pitchers Andy Messersmith and Dave McNally challenged the reserve clause by working one year without a contract and then declaring themselves free agents. They won their case in labor arbitration, and the age of free agency had arrived.

Flood was right in calling himself "a child of the sixties." There was a strong element of protest and reform in his challenge. Other black athletes of the time, most notably MUHAMMAD ALI, openly defied society's expectations of them and challenged the businesses for which they worked. But Flood's protest transcends race and is more powerfully related to athletes being seen by the public as more than mere performers or machines. Flood argued that athletes were men and women with vital concerns about their well-being and with vital interests that they should be permitted to protect. It must be remembered that all Flood wanted was the right to offer his services to any major league team, the same freedom to move from one job to another that most Americans enjoy.

Flood, who had been a heavy smoker, died of throat cancer at the age of fifty-nine. He was survived by his wife, the actress Judy Pace, and a child by a previous relationship. In 1998 Congress passed the Curt Flood Act, giving Major League Baseball players the same protection under antitrust laws that all other athletes enjoyed.

FURTHER READING

Flood, Curt (with Richard Carter). *The Way It Is* (1971).

Korr, Charles. *The End of Baseball As We Knew It: The Players Union, 1960–1981* (2002).

Miller, Marvin. *A Whole Different Ball Game: The Sport and Business of Baseball* (1991).

Will, George F. *Bunts* (1999).

GERALD EARLY

Flood, Elizabeth Thorn Scott (1828–1867), educator and civic leader, was born Elizabeth Thorn, the daughter of Lydia and Francis Thorn. Flood was raised and educated in New Bedford, Massachusetts. In 1848 she married the mariner Joseph C. Scott and traveled with him to California during the Gold Rush, making the long journey by ship across the Isthmus of Panama. By 1852 the Scotts were living in Placerville, California, where Scott mined for gold until his death. A widow with three young sons, Flood left the rough frontier and moved to Sacramento, a larger town with a sizable black community.

Flood became an education activist after she unsuccessfully attempted to enroll one of her sons in a Sacramento public school. Local school districts, such as Sacramento, had the power to exclude nonwhite children from attending their schools. Furthermore, the state legislature refused to appropriate taxes to fund separate schools for African Americans. Flood was determined to ensure that Sacramento's black community would have access to the same type of high-quality education that she had received in New Bedford. She opened a private school in her home on 29 May 1854, only one week after California's first school for African Americans opened in San Francisco. Flood's fourteen pupils ranged in age from four to twenty-nine. Believing in education equality for all, Flood soon opened enrollment to Native American and Asian students, who were also barred from attending public schools. Despite also paying taxes to fund public schools, each student's family paid a weekly tuition of $1, a sum which covered Flood's salary of $50 per month as well as a few school supplies. In August 1854 the school and its pupils transferred to new facilities in the basement of St. Andrew's African Methodist Episcopal (AME) Church.

In 1855 Flood retired from teaching upon marrying Isaac Flood, a laborer and civil rights activist. Isaac Flood was a member of the California Colored Convention, a statewide group of black leaders who fought for African American civil rights including suffrage, equality in education, and the right to testify in court. Elizabeth and Isaac Flood had a son and a daughter, Lydia Flood Jackson, whose parents' activism influenced her later decision to become a champion of women's rights, suffrage, and equality for African Americans.

Although the Sacramento school closed due to Flood's departure, Jeremiah Sanderson, another transplant from New Bedford, reopened the school a few months later, maintaining an average enrollment of twenty-two students. In 1855 the Sacramento School Board assumed administration of the school and in 1859 began partially funding the school with public money. In 1859–1860 the state legislature finally made provisions to fund segregated schools for African Americans.

By 1856 the Floods had moved to Brooklyn, a community outside Oakland, California. Elizabeth Flood was again dismayed to learn that there were no schools for African American children in the area. She canvassed the black community, garnering support to establish a private school funded by students' families. In 1857 Flood opened the school in her home, making it the first African American institution in Alameda County. Flood was committed to maintaining state educational standards, teaching basic subjects such as reading, writing, and arithmetic, as well as geography, elocution, U.S. history, and general science.

Flood also understood the importance of religious institutions in creating a strong community. In 1858 she convinced several families to join her in founding the Shiloh AME Church, Oakland's first community of worship for African Americans. Church members initially met in each other's homes, but in 1863 the church had grown enough to purchase the abandoned Carpentier School House, a one-room building that had been Oakland's first white public school. The new building served as both the church chapel and the schoolroom where Flood continued to teach until her sudden death at the age of thirty-nine.

Following his wife's death, Isaac Flood successfully petitioned the Oakland School Board to allow African American children to attend the city's public schools, citing the rights guaranteed by the Fourteenth and Fifteenth Amendments of the United States Constitution. In 1872 Lydia Flood was among the first black students to attend Oakland's integrated public schools. In 1880 the state legislature repealed the white-only provisions of school laws, making integrated education the law throughout the state.

Elizabeth Flood paved the way for the public education of African Americans in California. For decades, the two schools that she founded provided the only educational opportunities for African Americans in their communities.

FURTHER READING

Beasley, Delilah L. *The Negro Trail Blazers of California* (1919).

Wagner, Tricia Martineau. *African American Women of the Old West* (2007).

KRYSTAL APPIAH

Flora, William (fl. 1775–1818), war hero and businessman, was born probably in the vicinity of Portsmouth, Virginia, the son of free black parents, whose names are unknown. On the eve of the American Revolution fewer than two thousand free blacks lived in Virginia. The colony's statutes forbade the manumission of slaves except those who exposed an incipient slave uprising. Consequently, William, who was known as "Billy," was probably descended from Africans who arrived in Virginia before 1640, when blacks were treated like indentured servants rather than slaves.

Nothing is known about Flora's life prior to 1775, when he joined Colonel William Woodford's Second Virginia Regiment as a private. He furnished his own musket, suggesting that he had already earned the esteem of his white neighbors, because the colony's statutes also barred free blacks from bearing arms and from serving in the militia. He fought against British and Loyalist forces commanded by Lord Dunmore, Virginia's last royal governor, at the battle of Great Bridge in December 1775. On the morning of the battle Flora was one of several sentinels guarding the narrow bridge over the Elizabeth River, which separated the British and patriot positions, when the British attacked in force. While the other sentinels immediately retreated to the safety of the patriot barricade, Flora fired eight times as he withdrew and, still under enemy fire, removed the plank that afforded access over the barricade. His bravery in combat earned him the approbation of his superiors and a public commendation in the *Virginia Gazette*.

Nothing is known about Flora's activities during the rest of the American Revolution except that he fought at the battle of Yorktown in 1781. The suggestion that he fought against the British for the entire duration of the war is unlikely, since the vast majority of patriot soldiers fought for brief periods and then returned home. In addition, Woodford and virtually the entire Virginia Continental line were taken prisoner in 1780 after the successful British siege of Charleston, South Carolina. It is more likely that Flora left the army in mid-1776, following the departure of Dunmore's forces from Virginia, and returned to arms four years later, when a British force commanded by the traitor Benedict Arnold invaded Tidewater Virginia.

After the British surrender at Yorktown, Flora either began or continued to operate a cartage enterprise based in Portsmouth, hauling agricultural products and freight between the town's wharves and the farms in the surrounding countryside. He also operated a livery stable that rented out riding carriages. In 1784 he purchased two lots in Portsmouth and is believed to have been the first black to own land in that town. For a number of years thereafter he occasionally bought and sold houses and unimproved lots. Exploiting the opportunities made available to him as a consequence of his freedom while conducting himself in such a way as to avoid exciting the jealousies of his white neighbors, he acquired and retained considerable wealth. In 1810 he owned three large wagons, three two-wheeled carriages, and six horses, and when he died he willed two houses and one lot to his heirs. He married a slave woman, but her name and the date of the marriage are unknown. Flora purchased and freed his wife sometime after 1782, at which time Virginia's laws against manumission were liberalized considerably. They had two children.

In 1807, when HMS *Leopard* attacked the USS *Chesapeake*, a wave of anti-British sentiment swept through Virginia and the rest of the United States. Caught up in this patriotic fervor, Flora, armed with his old musket, joined a number of local men who volunteered for service against the British once again. Local authorities courteously rejected their offer. In recognition of his service during the American Revolution, Flora in 1818, along with other Virginia veterans, received a land grant of one hundred acres in the Virginia Military District (now southwestern Ohio). He probably sold the grant to one of the large land companies attempting to settle the area. It is believed he died in 1820 in Portsmouth.

Flora was a hero of the Revolution in Virginia, a prosperous businessman, and a respected member of the Portsmouth community. Although these accomplishments may seem modest, they are significant in that they were achieved by a black man at a time when the vast majority of his white contemporaries regarded people of African descent as lazy and inferior and consequently afforded them second-class citizenship.

FURTHER READING

Davis, Burke. *Black Heroes of the American Revolution* (1976).

Jackson, Luther Porter. "William Flora," in *Virginia Negro Soldiers and Seamen in the Revolutionary War* (1944).

Kaplan, Sidney. *The Black Presence in the Era of the American Revolution 1770–1800* (1973).

Quarles, Benjamin. *The Negro in the American Revolution* (1961).

CHARLES W. CAREY JR.

Florence, Virginia Proctor Powell (1 Oct. 1897–3 Apr. 1991), the first African American woman to complete a professional degree in librarianship, was born in Wilkinsburg, Pennsylvania, the only child of Socrates Edward Powell, a barber, and Caroline Elizabeth Proctor Powell. She spent her early school years in the Wilkinsburg Public school system, but when her mother died either in 1903 or 1904, she moved to Pittsburgh to live with her aunt. Like many children, Powell's love of reading began at an early age, and it probably offered solace from a lonely childhood. Of this time, Powell recalled, "I have always liked books and reading since I was a little girl because I was very much alone" (Lemons, 1). Powell graduated from Pittsburgh's Fifth Avenue High School in 1915 and continued her education at Oberlin College, obtaining a B.A. in English

Literature in 1919. Shortly after graduation she moved to Saint Paul, Minnesota, where she worked as a secretary in the Girl Reserves of the Colored Girls Work, a YWCA club that allowed young women the chance to interact socially, while also stressing the need to learn life skills, social graces, and civic responsibility. Powell enjoyed her work there, which included taking young girls on excursions and reading to them, but she missed her family and Charles Wilbur Florence, a student at the University of Pittsburgh whom she had met during her time at Oberlin.

After a year Powell was back in Pittsburgh, looking for work as a teacher, but she gave up after a few frustrating months when she realized that because of her race there were no opportunities for her. Instead, she worked as a beautician in her aunt's beauty salon. Two years later Charles Florence suggested to Powell that she consider librarianship as a career. She was receptive to the idea and applied to the Carnegie Library School (later part of the University of Pittsburgh). School officials there had reservations about admitting her because of her race, wondering where she would work after graduating. When asked about this, Powell said: "It was on the tip of my tongue to say 'Right here. This is my home.' But I thought, 'I'd better get in before I get out.' So I kept my mouth shut" (Lemons, 1). She was admitted and began her coursework in 1922. The training she received was the same as that afforded her white classmates, except for the practical work classes, which took place at local branch libraries. In these classes Powell's supervisors did not want her to help white library visitors, nor participate directly with the children during storytelling. However, over time, Powell won over supervisors and visitors alike (especially the children), and she enjoyed the classes, acknowledging later that they were her happiest part of library school (Gunn, 155). She completed the rest of the program without incident in 1923.

After graduating, Powell wrote to several libraries, seeking employment. She was hired by the New York Public Library as a librarian assistant and remained there until 1927. Powell then wanted to work in the local school system, so she took and passed the New York high school librarian examination (the first African American to do so) and became a librarian at the integrated Seward Park High School in Brooklyn. She stayed there until the summer of 1931, when she married Charles Florence. They had delayed their marriage for a number of years as they focused on their education and careers. Shortly after her marriage, she accompanied her husband to Jefferson City, Missouri, where he served as president of Lincoln University. In 1938 the couple left so he could take a position in Richmond, Virginia. With no job opportunities there for her, Virginia Florence took and passed another librarian examination, this time for the Washington, D.C., school system, and was hired as a librarian at Cardozo High School, where she remained until illness forced her to retire in 1945. By 1950 Florence's health had returned, and she resumed her career, finding work as a librarian at Maggie L. Walker Senior High School in Richmond. She stayed there until retiring in 1965. Florence remained active during retirement, turning her attention to social causes. On a 1968 Oberlin alumni questionnaire, she wrote: "My husband and I, being Negroes, are especially interested in Civil Rights and better race relations. We work with our church, YWCA, and the Richmond Crusade for Voters toward that end" (*Library Perspectives* 32, 5).

After her husband died in 1974, Florence spent her final years at a convalescent center in Virginia. Although she suffered from debilitating arthritis and was confined to her bed, she still was able to enjoy her favorite pastime—reading. She told an interviewer, "I couldn't play any golf or go dancing, so I'm glad I can read" (Lemons, 1). Florence died in Richmond, but recognition of her career continued. On 2 April 2004 her alma mater, now known as the School of Information Sciences, at the University of Pittsburgh, unveiled a plaque in her honor. The dedication ceremony, attended by Arthur Gunn, retired dean of Clark Atlanta University School of Library and Information Science, and Dr. E. J. Josey, the first black president of the American Library Association, was a testament and fitting tribute to her importance as a pioneer in the field of librarianship.

FURTHER READING

Gunn, Arthur C. "A Black Woman Wants to Be a Professional: The Struggle of Virginia Proctor Powell Florence," *American Libraries* 20 (1989).

Lemons, Teresa. "Librarian Didn't Go by Book," *Richmond Times-Dispatch*, 1 Mar. 1989.

"Virginia Proctor Powell Florence: A Remarkable Oberlin Alumna Librarian," *Library Perspectives* 32 (Spring 2005).

Obituary: *Richmond Times-Dispatch*, 2 May 1991.

LARRY SEAN KINDER

Flowers, Ruth Cave (10 Mar. 1902–1988), educator, was born in Colorado Springs, Colorado, the second daughter of Minnie, a dressmaker, and Edward Cave, a bricklayer. Ruth began her notable career in unpromising circumstances. Her parents were divorced before she was born, and her mother died when Ruth was eleven years old, leaving Ruth and her sister Dorothy in the care of their sixty-year-old grandmother, Minnesota Waters, who was struggling to make her own living in the dying mining town of Cripple Creek. From 1917 to 1924 Flowers, her sister, and her grandmother lived and worked in the small university town of Boulder, Colorado. Within this community marked by segregation and discrimination, Flowers forged her own determination, commitment, and enduring love of the mountains. Waters worked in a local restaurant as a cook and she hired Flowers as a dishwasher, a job she held while attending Boulder High School from September 1917 to June 1920. Flowers never formally graduated from Boulder High School, prevented by a racist principal who, she said, had vowed never to let a Negro student take part in graduation ceremonies. She did have the necessary credits to be admitted to the University of Colorado in the fall of 1920. In college, Ruth took in washing and ironing, which along with general housework were the jobs available to black women at the time. For men, she said, "there was no work; no work for Negro men at all" (Flowers interview).

In 1924 Flowers became one of the first African American woman to graduate from the University of Colorado, earning a degree in Romance languages. However, discrimination prevented her from finding a position in the West, and she was forced to leave Boulder for the segregated South to find a teaching job. She taught French and Latin at Claflin College in South Carolina from 1924 until 1928, returning to Boulder in 1929 or 1930 to care for her grandmother and get an M.A. in French and Education from the University of Colorado. She then moved to Washington, D.C., and taught at Dunbar High School from 1931 to 1945. Her grandmother died in 1943, but she kept her Boulder house, returning to it when she could. She attended Robert F. Terrell Law School at night and received her law degree in 1945. In 1937 she married a fellow law student, Harold Flowers, with whom she later practiced law and had a son. They were divorced in 1949 and Ruth Flowers went on to complete work on a Ph.D. in Foreign Languages and Literatures from Catholic University of America in Washington in 1951. From 1951 to 1959 Flowers was associate professor of Spanish at North Carolina College in Durham. In 1959 she and her son Harold returned to Boulder to live, and she was hired as the head of the foreign languages department at Fairview High School, a position that she held until her retirement in 1967. She was awarded Harvard University's Teacher of the Year Award in 1969 and Bicentennial Mother of Achievement for the state of Colorado in 1975.

In her retirement she tutored reading in a Boulder elementary school, gave talks throughout the school system on African American culture, and delivered public addresses and interviews about her memories of the black community in Boulder. The community that she remembered was dissolved by the coming of World War II, when most residents left for better jobs on the West Coast. Flowers's clear-eyed recollections are the fullest account that exists of the earlier period. She brought her best skills as a teacher to her thorough and unsparing description of the social and economic prejudice that existed in Boulder at that time. She described a small but vital community that, in the face of housing and employment discrimination and restricted public access, forged its own amusements with music groups, ice cream socials, and hikes in the nearby mountains. As Flowers said, "The mountains were free and we loved them." She aimed to raise public consciousness about race relations and, as she wryly put it, "I feel a duty to let people know their fair city is not always as fair as they believe it to be" (Flowers interview). She died in Boulder at the age of seventy-seven.

FURTHER READING

An extensive oral history interview with Flowers is held by the Carnegie Library of Boulder. Parts of the interview were edited by Sue Armitage for the article "The Mountains Were Free and We Loved Them," which appeared in the anthology edited by Quintard Taylor and Shirley Ann Wilson Moore, *African American Women Confront the West* (2002).

SUSAN ARMITAGE

Flowers, Tiger (5 Aug. 1895–16 Nov. 1927), world middleweight boxer, was born Theodore Flowers in Camilla, Georgia, the son of Aaron Flowers, a railroad porter, and Lula Dawson. When he was a small child his family moved to Brunswick, Georgia, where he completed six school grades and afterward held various jobs. In 1915 he married Willie Mae Spellars, and in 1917 they moved to Philadelphia, Pennsylvania, where he worked as a subway laborer, later taking a job in the navy yard when World War I began. While in Philadelphia he received his first instruction in boxing.

After the war ended, Flowers returned to Georgia and, against the wishes of his parents, began to box professionally. He won a few fights in the Savannah-Brunswick area, and rumors of his boxing ability reached Walk Miller, the owner of a gymnasium in Atlanta. Miller contacted Flowers and became his manager, and the two men established a close friendship. Fighting only on all-black programs in the South, Flowers won consistently until he was knocked out by PANAMA JOE GANS, a good middleweight, in Atlanta in late 1921.

Flowers's record in 1922 and 1923 was erratic. Taken out of the South for the first time by Miller, Flowers won twenty-six fights, including two victories over Gans. However, his chin proved to be fragile when exposed to the blows of heavy punchers. He was knocked out four times, by black light heavyweights Lee Anderson, KID NORFOLK, and Jamaica Kid and veteran heavyweight SAM LANGFORD. Fighting in Mexico, he met white opponents for the first time.

In 1924 Flowers won thirty-three of his thirty-five fights, including rematches against Jamaica Kid and Anderson. The turning point in his career came in a close nontitle fight with the reigning middleweight champion, Harry Greb, in Fremont, Ohio, on 21 August, in which no official decision was given. Although reporters at ringside adjudged Greb the winner, Miller immediately mounted an effective propaganda campaign for his fighter, persistently claiming that Flowers actually had the better of the Greb fight, and succeeded in attracting attention to his man. On 9 December Flowers knocked out the former middleweight champion Johnny Wilson in New York City and thus established himself as a leading contender.

On 16 January 1925 Flowers suffered a devastating knockout at the hands of the future light heavyweight champion Jack Delaney in New York. Miller complained vociferously that Delaney had fought with metal objects in his gloves to give his punches greater force. In a rematch on 26 February, Delaney again scored a knockout and then removed his gloves in the ring to show that nothing was concealed. Despite these setbacks Flowers won twenty-five of twenty-nine fights in 1925, including victories over such highly rated middleweights as Jock Malone, Lou Bogash, and Ted Moore. On 23 December he lost a scandalously unfair decision to the former light heavyweight champion Mike McTigue in New York City. According to the noted boxing historian Nat Fleischer, who witnessed the fight, Flowers won nearly every round. The Flowers–McTigue bout occurred as part of a charity program, and the judges on this occasion were businessmen who evidently did not know how to fairly assess the outcome of a boxing contest. Despite his spotty record, Flowers was then matched with Greb for the middleweight title, probably in part because of his convincing performance against McTigue and partly because of the effectiveness of Miller's claims that Flowers had once beaten Greb in a nontitle fight. Flowers and Greb met in New York on 26 February 1926, and Flowers won the decision after a close fight. They fought again for the middleweight title in New York on 19 August 1926, and Flowers again won the decision, although many spectators thought that Greb deserved the decision. On 3 December 1926 Flowers's short reign as middleweight champion ended when he lost a ten-round title fight to the former welterweight champion Mickey Walker in Chicago. Like so many of Flowers's major fights, this one was controversial because nearly every newspaper reporter present thought that Flowers deserved to win.

Flowers was a colorful and unorthodox fighter. A pious Christian who was nicknamed "The Georgia Deacon," he read the Bible every day and prayed in his corner before each fight. When called to the center of the ring for the introductions, he would spring from his corner in a cat-like manner, hence the nickname "Tiger." Once the fighting began he constantly threw punches from a left-handed stance. Although he could hit sharply, many of his blows were light taps landed with an open glove. He often overwhelmed his opponents with the number of his blows, which, combined with great speed and elusiveness, usually saved him from suffering serious punishment. His busy, colorful style made him a popular ring attraction and a difficult opponent.

In 1927 Flowers continued to fight successfully, winning fifteen of eighteen fights. He defeated the highly rated light heavyweights Eddie Huffman and Chuck Wiggins and the former welterweight champion Pete Latzo, lost only to Leo Lomski, and boxed two draws with the future light heavyweight champion Maxie Rosenbloom. The last fight of his career occurred on 12 November in New York City; there, a few days afterward, he underwent an operation for removal of scar tissue from around his eyes. He was anesthetized with ether and failed to regain consciousness. Claiming that Flowers had been murdered, Miller had an autopsy performed, but no evidence of foul play was found.

Flowers saved his ring earnings and lived well during his few years of prominence. A friendly, quiet man who was widely liked, he served as a deacon of the Methodist church in Brunswick. His funeral in Atlanta was a large affair. Eulogies by sportswriters praised him, in the condescending manner of the time, as "white, clean white inside," no doubt in recognition of his gentlemanly demeanor.

Flowers was elected to the International Boxing Hall of Fame in 1993. The first African American world middleweight champion, he was also the first black champion of any professional boxing division after JACK JOHNSON lost the heavyweight title to Jess Willard in 1915.

FURTHER READING

Fleischer, Nat. *Black Dynamite: The Story of the Negro in the Prize Ring from 1782 to 1938*, vol. 5: *Sockers in Sepia* (1947).

Obituary: *New York Times*, 17 Nov. 1927.

This entry is taken from the *American National Biography* and is published here with the permission of the American Council of Learned Societies.

LUCKETT V. DAVIS

Floyd, Silas Xavier (2 Oct. 1869–19 Sept. 1923), minister, educator, and author, was born in Augusta, Georgia, to David Floyd, a minister, and Sarah Jane Nickson. He attended Augusta's Ware High School, the only publicly funded African American high school in Georgia. Following his graduation in 1886, Floyd enrolled at Atlanta University and received a bachelor's degree in 1891 and a master's degree three years later. Morris Brown College in Atlanta awarded him an honorary doctorate degree in June 1902. While at Atlanta University, Floyd explored his interests in writing and literature and also took courses in printmaking. During the summer months, he earned additional income teaching in the rural schools of Jones and Forsyth counties. Upon graduation, Floyd returned to Augusta and assumed editorship of the *Augusta Sentinel* newspaper, an organ established by his former Ware High School principal, RICHARD R. WRIGHT SR. In 1892 Floyd joined six other African American editors in founding the Negro Press Association of Georgia.

Although Floyd enjoyed a distinguished career as a journalist and poet, his love of teaching rivaled his passion for writing. He began working in Augusta's public schools as an assistant principal at the Mauge Street School. In 1892 he was appointed principal of the Third Ward School. The following year, he returned to Mauge Street and began a three-year stint as principal. He married Ella James, a former public school teacher and the daughter of Samuel and Nora Drayton of Gloverville, South Carolina, on 6 May in either 1900 or 1901. From 1903 through 1908, he led the First Ward School, and for fifteen years thereafter, Floyd served as the principal of the Gwinnett Street School. Floyd's long service as an educator was intermittently interrupted by his pursuit of the ministry and his missionary work throughout the South. In June 1896, after being ordained as a minister by the acclaimed evangelist CHARLES T. WALKER, Floyd left his teaching post to assume a position as a field secretary for the International Sunday School Convention. When Walker resigned from Augusta's Tabernacle Baptist Church in 1899 and became the pastor of the Mt. Olivet Church in New York City, Floyd took charge of the Augusta congregation. But his zeal for church administration quickly dissipated. Eager to leave the pulpit to devote more time to his writing and to missionary work, Floyd left his post as pastor in 1901 and spent the next three years as a field worker in Georgia and Alabama for the American Baptist Publication Society.

Floyd's travels throughout the region and his numerous publications generated widespread publicity and placed him in constant demand for speaking engagements. In January 1899 Floyd delivered an address titled "National Perils" for the Negro Literary and Historical Society in Atlanta. At the 1901 Atlanta University Conference, "The Negro Common School," organized by W. E. B. DUBOIS, Floyd offered a speech titled "The Importance of the Public Schools." In August 1902 he joined an array of prominent speakers at the Young People's Christian and Educational Congress in Atlanta. Before an audience of twelve thousand, he called upon delegates to adopt aggressive efforts to stem the tide of black men deserting churches. Like most of Floyd's public addresses, his talk in Atlanta railed against moral depravity among African Americans and emphasized a conservative gospel of respectability and personal responsibility. In a series of speeches, Floyd promoted an optimistic outlook on race relations, arguing that the ultimate solution to the perplexing "Negro problem" rested with African Americans and their efforts to cultivate morality, sobriety, industry, and self-respect within their communities.

Floyd explored similar themes in his written work. Following the demise of the *Augusta Sentinel* in 1896, he remained an active journalist. His columns were published regularly in white newspapers across the South. For over a decade, the *Augusta Chronicle*, a white daily, printed Floyd's "Notes Among Colored People," a widely read summation of religious and cultural activities among African Americans. Additionally, Floyd's poetry, short stories, and essays appeared in a number of other venues from the 1890s through 1920, including the *Atlantic Monthly*, *The Independent*, *Lippincotts's Monthly*, *World's Work*, and *Leslie's Weekly*. When J. Max Barber and J. W. E. Bowen established the Atlanta-based journal the *Voice of the Negro* in January 1904, Floyd's column "Wayside" became a permanent fixture of the periodical.

In 1905 the publishers of the *Voice*, Hertel and Jenkins, released *Floyd's Flowers, or Duty and Beauty for Colored Children*, a collection of didactic stories and vignettes. The work, crafted in the mode of Paul Laurence Dunbar, employed Negro dialect and emphasized the virtues of thrift, respectable behavior, and temperance. Despite the book's success and impressive sales, Floyd's work, the language it employed, and the themes it raised drew heated attacks from other black journals such as the *New York Age* and the *Chicago Defender*. Nevertheless, *Floyd's Flowers* was subsequently revised and republished in 1922 as *The New Floyd's Flowers: Short Stories for Colored People Old and Young*. Floyd's other publications included *Life of Charles T. Walker, D. D.* (1902) and *Gospel of Service and Other Sermons* (1902).

In the course of Floyd's many civic activities, he strongly supported the Georgia State Teachers Association, the National Negro Business League, and the annual Tuskegee Negro Conference where he served as the chair of the committee on resolutions. In 1915 Floyd became the secretary of the National Association of Teachers in Colored Schools, and three years later began editing the organization's quarterly magazine, the *National Note-Book*. When plans unfolded to establish a colored YMCA branch in Augusta, Floyd emerged as an enthusiastic supporter and served for many years as secretary and publicist of the association. But when the Augusta educator Lucy Craft Laney and other leaders struggled to establish a local chapter of the NAACP in 1917, they criticized Floyd and his pastor Charles T. Walker for thwarting the civil rights efforts of the organization.

When Floyd died of heart problems at the age of fifty-three, white newspapers in Augusta hailed him as the most influential African American leader in the city. Yet even as the *Augusta Chronicle* praised Floyd's brilliant career as an educator, minister, and writer, an editorial in the paper eulogized him as one who "cherished no illusions as to the respective spheres of each race, knowing that the negro had his place in the community and the white man has his" (*Augusta Chronicle*, 23 Sept. 1923). Upon Floyd's death, his substantial library was bequeathed to Atlanta University. A local school in Augusta bears his name.

FURTHER READING

Caldwell, A. B. *History of the American Negro and His Institutions, Georgia Edition* (1917).
Mather, Frank L. *Who's Who of the Colored Race* (1915).
Richardson, Clement. *The National Cyclopedia of the Colored Race* (1919).

BOBBY J. DONALDSON

Follis, Charles W. (3 Feb. 1879–5 Apr. 1910), football and baseball player, was born in Botentourt County, Virginia, to James Follis, a laborer and farmer, and Catharine Follis, a laundress. By 1888 the family had moved to Wooster, Ohio, and Follis entered that city's integrated public schools. As a junior at Wooster High School in 1899, he helped organize the school's first varsity football team, and his teammates elected him captain. Follis was the squad's best player and led the team to an undefeated season. During the summer he played catcher for the Wooster Athletic Association (WAA) baseball team, and in 1900 he helped the WAA capture the championship of the semipro Ohio Trolley League.

After graduating from high school, Follis entered the college preparatory department of the nearby University of Wooster (later College of Wooster) in the spring of 1901. He immediately joined the university's varsity baseball team as the starting catcher and starred for two years before leaving school.

He did not represent his school on the gridiron but instead played football for the WAA, which participated in the strong but informal semipro leagues of Ohio. In 1901 the mediocre WAA squad played two games against the nearby Shelby Athletic Club, which contended for the mythical state championship.

Follis's play impressed Shelby's manager Frank C. Schiffer, who enticed the "Colored Cyclone," as Follis was known, to play for Shelby in 1902. He remained on the Shelby Athletic Club roster until 1906, and at some point he signed a contract, making him the first known African American professional football player. He indisputably earned a salary in 1904, but it is unclear when he first received regular payment. Regardless, Schiffer also arranged a job for Follis at a local hardware store that allowed him generous time off to practice and play.

Follis won a starting halfback position, and he immediately impressed with his running ability. During his time with Shelby, he often led the team in scoring and recorded numerous long runs. He also won praise for his defensive ability.

He quickly earned his teammates' respect, and they frequently stood up for him when he faced racial slights. Against Marion in 1903, for example, an opposing player attempted to spike Follis, but a Shelby teammate sprang to his defense and pushed the aggressor away.

Another of Follis's teammates in 1902 and 1903 was the future Brooklyn Dodgers general manager Branch Rickey, then a student at Ohio Wesleyan University. Forty years before bringing JACKIE ROBINSON into Major League Baseball, Rickey played alongside the "Colored Cyclone" and admiringly called him a "wonder" (Roberts, 43).

Follis's ability and sportsmanlike attitude also won the respect of some opponents. In Toledo in 1905 the local fans verbally harassed Follis, but the captain of the home team took offense and stopped the game to address the crowd: "Don't call Follis a 'nigger.' He is a gentleman and a clean player and please don't call him that." The crowd applauded the speech, and, according to the *Toledo News-Bee*, "the colored player was not molested during the rest of the game" (27 Nov. 1905, 6).

Such sentiment was not unanimous, however, even in Shelby. After one rigorous practice, Follis accompanied his teammates to a local tavern. The team crowded into the establishment, but the proprietor announced that only white players were welcome. The "Colored Cyclone" silently withdrew, but his teammates stayed behind.

Follis's football career came to an end in 1906. Beset by injuries, he only played a few games for Shelby. His last known appearance was on Thanksgiving Day against Cleveland's Franklin Athletic Club. The game finished in a 0-0 tie, but the "Colored Cyclone" was helped off the field with a leg injury before the contest ended.

During these years he continued to play baseball. He was back in the Ohio Trolley League in 1906 and also played for all-black teams in Cleveland. A few years later he joined Bright's Cuban Giants, a top barnstorming African American squad. After catching a game for the Giants in 1910, he collapsed into a pneumonia-induced coma and soon died. One Ohio newspaper fondly remembered him: "As a football player and as a baseball player he gained the respect of his associates and opponents ... by his clean tactics and gameness" (Roberts, 58).

The exploits and athletic prowess of the "Colored Cyclone" were largely forgotten after his death. During the 1970s, though, researchers and historians resurrected Follis's memory, and he has since gained new fame as the first known black professional football player.

FURTHER READING

"First Black Pro Grid Star Overlooked," *Chicago Defender*, 15 Nov. 1975.

Peterson, Robert. *Pigskin: The Early Years of Pro Football* (1997).

Roberts, Milton. "Charles Follis: First Black Pro Gridder Labored in Obscurity," *Black Sports* (Nov. 1975).

Ross, Charles K. *Outside the Lines* (1999)

Obituary: *Wooster Daily News*, 5 Apr. 1910.

GREGORY BOND

Fontaine, William Thomas (2 Dec. 1909–29 Dec. 1968), a professional philosopher who taught for twenty years at the University of Pennsylvania, was born William Thomas Fontaine in Chester, Pennsylvania, the son of William Charles Fontaine, a steelworker, and Mary Elizabeth Boyer, who went by the name of Ballard, having been raised by her grandparents. His grandmother on his father's side, Cornelia Wilson Fontaine Smith, with whom he grew up, had been a slave. Fontaine went to an exclusively black elementary school, Booker T. Washington, and then to Chester High School. At this time he gave himself a second middle name, Valeria, a Latin name connoting physical and mental strength. At age sixteen he matriculated at Lincoln University in Pennsylvania, and received his B.A. there in 1930, finishing first in his class. While at Lincoln, Fontaine befriended Kwame Nkrumah, the first black leader of Ghana, and Nnamdi Azikiwe, the first black governor-general of Nigeria and, as assistant editor of the school paper, published some of LANGSTON HUGHES's early poetry.

For the next six years Fontaine taught part-time at Lincoln, instructing in a wide variety of courses, mainly in his field of Latin authors, although in 1935–1936 he taught a pioneering course in black history. During this period he was also taking graduate work in philosophy at the University of Pennsylvania, where he received a Ph.D. in 1936, concentrating in the history of Roman thought. His dissertation, "Fortune, Matter and Providence: A Study of Ancius Severinus Boethius and Giordano Bruno," was published in 1939. But his interests were not merely in the history of ideas, for in 1933 he had spent the summer studying at Harvard, where he absorbed the distinctive views in the "conceptual pragmatism" of C. I. Lewis.

In 1936 Fontaine was appointed to a position at Southern University in Scotlandville, Louisiana. Around this time he married Willa Belle Hawkins, a divorcee with two children, Jean and Vivian. By the time he left Southern in 1942, he had become head of the social sciences department, and his time in the Jim Crow South solidified his interests in racial issues. He combined a pragmatic orientation toward different worldviews with a Marxist account of the social locus of knowing. Sensitized to relativism, he struggled throughout the rest of his life to find a firm basis to criticize the racism and segregation of American life. At the time, these concerns appeared in two notable publications. "The Mind and Thought of the Negro of the United States as Revealed in Imaginative Literature, 1876–1940," published in the *Southern University Bulletin* of 1942, surveyed African American literature using a framework derived from the pragmatist George Herbert Mead; "Social Determination in the Writings of American Negro Scholars," published in the *American Journal of Sociology* in 1944, criticized black thinking on race using the work of the sociologist of knowledge Karl Mannheim.

Fontaine spent the summer of 1940 at the University of Chicago, a stronghold of pragmatism and a central gathering place for African American scholars, especially in the social sciences. In the summer of 1941 and in 1942–1943, Fontaine held grants that returned him to the University of Pennsylvania.

In 1943 Fontaine joined the United States Army and was mustered out at the end of 1945. He served at Fort Holabird Signal Depot in Baltimore as an instructor of illiterate black soldiers. There he met Nelson Goodman, who had recently received his Ph.D. in Philosophy under C. I. Lewis at Harvard. Goodman was to become one of the premier professional philosophers of the twentieth century and in 1946 began teaching at Pennsylvania, while Fontaine accepted a position as head of psychology and philosophy at Morgan State College in Baltimore. In 1947–1948 Goodman received a fellowship, and Fontaine was asked to replace him. Fontaine took leave of Morgan, and the offer was repeated the following year. Receiving a tenure-track appointment at Pennsylvania starting in the fall of 1949, Fontaine left Morgan for good. He directed his philosophical attention to the problem of counterfactual conditionals, a series of conundrums that had made Goodman famous in the white philosophical world.

Shortly before he was to begin teaching as an assistant professor, Fontaine was diagnosed with active tuberculosis. Over the next six years at Pennsylvania, he spent three and one-half on medical leave. The administration would gladly have divested itself of Fontaine, but the philosophers resolutely supported him. While the department's faculty could be condescending, the department included women, Jews, and Catholics, and was notable in its commitment to the sincere if patronizing racial liberalism and multiculturalism of its time. After 1955 Fontaine spent a decade in recovery when his disease went into remission. He was tenured in 1958 and promoted to an associate professorship in 1963. For a long time he was one of the very few African Americans teaching in the segregated white academy, and the only black philosopher in the Ivy League.

By the mid-late 1950s his recovery and the burgeoning civil rights movement propelled Fontaine again to take up questions of race. He sought to find a way in which common factual beliefs might be manipulated to change the opposed attitudes at the heart of racial issues. These views were best articulated in two essays, "Segregation and Desegregation in the United States: A Philosophical Analysis," published in *Présence Africaine* in 1956, and "The Means End Relation and Its Significance for Cross-Cultural Ethical Agreement," published in *Philosophy of Science* in 1958.

In the same period, Fontaine studied the movements of nationalism and anticolonialism in Africa that recalled his time at Lincoln with Azikiwe and Nkrumah. His participation in the 1956 International Congress of Negro Writers and Artists in Paris signaled this new line of thinking. A year later this group founded the American Society of African Culture (AMSAC) and affiliated with the Frenchmen who produced the journal *Présence Africaine*. In 1958 Fontaine went to Rome to deliver a paper at another conference of black intellectuals.

He assisted in hosting AMSAC's Annual Conference in Pennsylvania in 1960, and wrote for its short-lived journal, *African Forum*, as well as for *Présence Africaine*. In 1960 he traveled to Africa, the university sending him to attend the installation of his old classmate Azikiwe as governor-general of Nigeria, and two years later he attended the Conference on African Socialism in Senegal as a delegate. At the end of 1966 Fontaine went on medical leave and never returned to the classroom. During this period of illness he completed *Reflections on Segregation, Desegregation, Power, and Morals* (1967). Fontaine died in Philadelphia at the end of 1968. He had been an outstanding lecturer, winning Pennsylvania's only teaching award in 1958, the Ivy Club Lecturer of the Year. His classroom instruction in social philosophy was perhaps his most enduring legacy. In addition to the rarified learning into which he launched his charges, he jolted the more reflective of his comfortable white students into the realization that they lived in a cultural world defined by racial categories that denigrated the abilities of African Americans. In 1969, the University of Pennsylvania established a Fontaine Fellowship program in his honor, and later created a Fontaine Society to embrace most of its programs for minority graduate fellowships.

FURTHER READING

Kuklick, Bruce. *Black Philosopher: William Fontaine and the Worlds of the Negro Scholar* (2008).

Ross, James. "William T. Fontaine, 1909–1968," *Proceedings of the American Philosophical Association* 43 (1969–70).

BRUCE KUKLICK

Foote, Augustus Keith (29 Apr. 1889–16 Apr. 1953), labor activist; vice president of the Stockyards Labor Council, 1917–1921; and secretary-treasurer, Local 651, Amalgamated Meat Cutters and Butcher Workmen of America.

Known publicly as A. K. Foote, Augustus Keith Foote was born in Memphis, Tennessee, the son of Nelson Foote and Alexenia Foote. His father was a porter, born in Mississippi in 1861, who had taught school in Macon at age sixteen. There were a number of Foote families in Macon in the late nineteenth century, mostly working as farm hands, who are probably related. They included an older Augustus, perhaps a cousin; Foote's paternal grandmother was known as Gusta. Alexenia Foote, born in Tennessee in 1866, had a father from Mississippi—there is no record that she worked outside the family home. The family also included sisters Willeta, one year older, and Ophelia, three years younger. By 1900 the family had moved to Chicago, where they lived at 2214 Dearborn Street, in a three-family apartment house, on a block crowded with African American, German American, Irish American, Canadian, and native-born "white" families. Nelson Foote's aunt, Nettie Holmes, and two male roomers, lived with the Footes (Census, 1870, 1880, 1900).

In 1917 Foote lived at 3560 Prairie Avenue in Chicago, with his wife, Gertrude. He was employed by Armour & Co., the largest of the meatpacking plants at the Union Stock Yards. There is little record of when he became a member or officer of Local 651, but the local played a critical role in the effort to organize Chicago's meatpacking industry between 1916 and 1921. The unwieldy AFL craft union structure was ill-suited to organize a mass production industry; the Chicago Federation of Labor spearheaded a local effort, the Stockyards Labor Council, that found ways to incorporate employees of all skills and skill levels.

Local 651 was sometimes known as the "miscellaneous" local. Common laborers, and workers not qualified for any specific craft union, or not normally acceptable to the Amalgamated Meatcutters, were invited to join. With offices at 43rd and State streets, this local established a cooperative grocery store—Foote's wife was one of two women on the board—and sponsored social events for members and their families. Racially mixed, it was a major opening for the African American workers, who at the time were mostly hired for low-skilled jobs in the meat plants. Local 651 participated in forming a Colored Club within the Cook County Labor Party. One of the benefits for workers who at the time were known as "colored" was respect for seniority rights—if oldest in years of service, when a vacancy opened, a colored worker could even move up to be head of work gang. In the absence of a union contract, this was often enforced by spontaneous work stoppages on the shop floor.

"Men who work together in mixed gangs of white and colored workers believe their trade union ought to be organized just like the work gang," Foote observed. Contemporary estimates that six to ten thousand colored workers joined the SLC were only approximate, because most locals were racially mixed. (Sandburg, p. 45). Some "federated" locals, affiliated directly with the AFL, not with any specific union, were organized as "black" locals to make a special appeal to nonunion workers of African descent. These got a mixed response, as some African Americans wanted institutions for "the race," while others suspected they were being offered second-class union membership.

"If you ask me what I think about race prejudice, and whether it's getting better, I'll tell you the one place in this town where I feel safest is over at the yards, with my union button on," Foote observed. "The union is for protection, that's our cry. We put that on our organization wagons and trucks traveling the stockyards district, in signs telling the white and colored men that their interests are identical" (Sandburg, p. 45).

"Whenever you hear any of that race riot stuff, you can be sure it is not going to start around here. Here they are learning that it pays for white and colored men to call each other brother" (Sandburg, p. 46). In 1919 his local presented a petition to President Woodrow Wilson asking him to "see that the representatives of Ireland [then still a British colony] be given a seat at the peace table and be recognized in the formation of the League of Nations," a matter of furious concern to Irish immigrant workers. As W. E. B. DuBois wrote in *The Crisis* that same year, African Americans and Irish immigrants had a history of mutual hostility, but "Let every colored man read this month a history of Ireland. If he does not rise from it bitter with English cruelty and hypocrisy, he is callous indeed" (p. 234).

In fact, the Chicago race riot of 1919, which did so much to destroy the Stockyards Labor Council, did not start in the stockyards. It started on a beach on Lake Michigan, where Eugene Williams, a seventeen-year-old African American swimming from a point between 25th Street and 29th Street had drifted toward a "white's only" beach, and drowned after a rock was thrown at him. Ominous rumors in both "white" and "black" neighborhoods were fanned to a citywide riot by the "athletic clubs" that functioned as the street gangs of the era, such as the Ragen Colts, the Canaryville bunch, and the Hamburg Club.

Foote was quoted in *The Crisis* the following September: "It's only working people who are fighting each other and killing. We are considering a big mass meeting to be held on the south side with representative trades union men of white and colored races discussing what a foolish thing it is for working people to go after each other with guns and knives." Chicago police did not allow such a mass meeting to occur, but racial tensions were much lower among stockyard workers than in the city's population generally.

Foote participated in a meeting 23 June 1920 with the Colored Preachers Conference, along with AFL organizer John Riley and N. S. Wims, international organizer for the Hotel and Restaurant Employees and Bartenders International Union, which Wims reported had removed all obstacles "that have heretofore kept our people from joining the unions" (CIE, *The Mixer and Server*, vol. 29, p. 24). The obstacles Wims referred to were within the "colored" community of Chicago—many ministers, and community institutions such as the YMCA were financially supported by the packing companies, and notably hostile to the "white man's union." Wims summary was prematurely optimistic.

Organizing in Chicago's meatpacking industry collapsed after the failure of a strike in 1921. Employers cynically brought in black strikebreakers, creating years of racial tension. Ironically, with African American employment at around 30 percent for the following ten years, the next organizing effort in the late 1930s became a model for interracial unity. Foote's life during the intervening period has not been recorded. In 1941, at age fifty-two, Foote stated on his draft registration card that he had no employer. He lived at 4853 Prairie Avenue in Chicago, with his wife, Gertrude. He died in Cook County, Illinois, his passing apparently unremarked by the workers who carried forward to victory the cause for which he helped lay the foundation thirty years before.

FURTHER READING

Barrett, James R. *Work and Community in the Jungle: Chicago's Packinghouse Workers, 1894–1922* (1987).

Halpern, Rick. *Down on the Killing Floor: Black and White Workers in Chicago's Packinghouses, 1904–54* (1997).

Sandburg, Carl. *The Chicago Race Riots, July 1919* (1919).

CHARLES ROSENBERG

Foote, Julia A. J. (1823?–22 Nov. 1900), evangelist and writer, was born the fourth child of freed parents in Schenectady, New York. Little is known of her early life except what can be gleaned from her autobiography, *A Brand Plucked from the Fire* (1879). It is known that she had a brother and an elder sister. She never reveals her family surname, nor does she provide her full name in the text.

Julia's mother—unnamed in *Brand*, though deeply influential in Julia's life—was born a slave in New York and suffered under a cruel master and mistress. Though this is a traditional claim in texts grounded in the slave narrative tradition, as popularized by such accounts as those of Frederick Douglass and Sojourner Truth, Foote (to use her married name) provides graphic detail to support her mother's claim of suffering. When Julia's mother refused her master's sexual advances and reported his behavior to her mistress, the master tied and whipped her. Then, he washed her back with salt water and would not permit her to change her clothing for a week. At the end of the week, realizing that she could not remove the clothing because it had stuck fast to her scabs, the mistress tore the fabric from the wounds, thus reopening them. For Julia, this episode exemplified the lack of an effective voice, the powerlessness, and the vulnerability of African American women struggling in servitude. Her father's youth was no less troubled. He had been born free, but was enslaved as a child. Julia's father eventually bought himself, Foote's mother, and her elder sister out of slavery.

Foote's family was religious, though not nearly as attentive to their faith as Julia would become. As a young couple, her parents joined the Methodist Episcopal church after a drowning scare. They professed their faith, but as Julia states, "They were not treated as Christian believers, but as poor lepers" (Andrews, 167). The sort of treatment they received is reflected in an incident that occurred in her parents' church. Normally, African American members of the congregation did not descend from the gallery to take communion until all the white members had been served. On one occasion, however, her mother and a friend, believing the white members were finished, had started for the communion table when two white women approached the table and reproached her mother saying, "Don't you know better than to go to the table when white folks are there?" Foote attributes the comment to the "fruits of slavery." Her mother's customary hesitance to move forward until whites had been served, and the white expectation that their faith needs would be met before the faith needs of African Americans, was, in Foote's estimation, neither Christian nor humane. Nonetheless, her family continued to attend this church.

At ten years of age, denied access to school in Schenectady, Julia was sent to work for the Prime family, who lived in the local countryside. The Primes took an interest in Julia's intellectual and spiritual growth and secured a place for her in the local school. While she was attending this school, her teacher became involved in a sex scandal, murdered the woman who implicated him, and was publicly hanged. These events reinforced for Julia moral codes that became important elements of her faith as she grew.

Chief among these moral principles was honesty and integrity. While Julia served the Primes, another young person in their employ stole some cakes from their storage cellar. Unable to find the cakes, Mrs. Prime accused Julia of stealing and eating them. Julia protested but would not name the real culprit. Mrs. Prime, enraged because she believed Julia was lying, vowed to whip Julia until she told the truth. The next day, Mrs. Prime rode into town and purchased a whip with which she punished Julia. Early the next morning, Julia chopped the rawhide into little pieces, then walked directly back to her mother's home. When the Primes followed, Julia's mother, having herself experienced even harsher unwarranted punishment, spoke up in defense of her daughter's integrity, yet she had to send Julia back to work for the Primes. By recounting this event in her spiritual autobiography, Foote redeems her mother's integrity, defines a free mother's role in regard to her daughter, and marks herself as a woman acting directly on her own behalf.

In 1838, at fifteen, Julia joined the African Methodist Episcopal church. The gift of a Bible at this time heightened her desire to read more fluently. She read her Bible regularly, even when she was injured six months later and lost sight in one eye. As her spiritual knowledge deepened, Foote took great interest in the doctrines of sanctification and holiness. Though the pursuit of spiritual growth required that she disregard her mother's warnings against pursuing sanctification, thought by many to be available only to the elderly and infirm. Foote believed that her faith justified such acts and that she would be blessed, if not forgiven, for taking them.

At age eighteen Julia married George Foote, though he was not as devout a Christian as she. Since the young man was attempting to secure a position in the shipyards in Massachusetts, they moved to Boston, and Julia began a household ministry, visiting and praying with a few neighbors, including some who were on their deathbeds. Her religious work among her neighbors began to attract the attention of George's coworkers, who ridiculed him for having little control over his wife. Enraged by this turn of events, George threatened to send her home or to an asylum if she did not immediately stop her evangelical work. In the end, Julia persisted, and George signed on with a seagoing vessel. He subsequently died at sea, probably in the late 1840s.

Foote's household ministry was not the work she felt she had been called to do, though she hesitated to pursue the broader public ministry she felt was her calling. After a vision induced by a mysterious illness she feared terminal, she agreed to preach publicly, much to the chagrin of her pastor and noted abolitionist JEHIEL C. BEMAN. The Reverend Beman and members of his Boston congregation eventually excommunicated Foote, but Foote took her complaint to the African Methodist Episcopal Zion (AME Zion) Conference for a hearing. Disappointingly, her claim was never heard. Using the language of the *Dred Scott* case, Foote argued that in the denomination, women had no rights to express their faith as they felt called to declare it; moreover, male ministers should be bound to respect this calling in women just as they respected it in men.

In spite of her problems with the denominational hierarchy, Julia Foote's ministry enjoyed great success. She preached through New England, Ohio, Canada, Michigan, and New York but was eventually forced to quit the work because she could no longer speak due to what she characterized as a "throat difficulty." She settled and worked in Cleveland, Ohio, for about a decade until she regained her voice in 1869. When she began to preach again, she associated herself with the Holiness movement then popular in the Midwest.

Foote's narrative, *A Brand Plucked from the Fire*, recounts the story of her journey toward spiritual development and provides a platform from which she revises the past, reaching toward a future of spiritual liberation. Little is known of her activities after 1879, until she became the first woman to be ordained a deacon in the AME Zion Church in 1894. In 1900, shortly before her death, she became the second woman to be named an elder in the denomination.

Foote's autobiography is a testament to human fortitude and religious faith. The debilitating effects of gender discrimination, particularly against women in the clergy, are a central theme of her writing. This well-crafted spiritual autobiography, with its evocation of traditional slave narratives, provides a model for African American women seeking to find their own voices in the generation after the abolition of slavery.

FURTHER READING

Andrews, William L., ed. *Sisters of the Spirit: Three Black Women's Autobiographies of the Nineteenth Century* (1986).

Collier-Thomas, Bettye. *Daughters of Thunder: Black Women Preachers and Their Sermons, 1850–1979* (1997).

Houchins, Sue, ed. *Spiritual Narratives* (1988).

MARTHA L. WHARTON

Forbes, George Washington (14 Aug. 1864–10 Mar. 1927), librarian, journalist, and African Methodist Episcopal lay church leader, was born in Shannon, Mississippi, the son of William and Sarah Forbes, who had been enslaved until freed by the Emancipation Proclamation of 1863, the arrival of the United States Army in Mississippi, and the Thirteenth Amendment to the United States Constitution.

Working at a young age in brickyards and farms, Forbes left the state at the age of fourteen, attended Wilberforce University in Ohio for a time, then moved to Boston in the 1880s. Mr. and Mrs. Mungin of Smith Court, a forgotten couple who assisted many struggling students, assisted him in finding work as a laborer at Memorial Hall in nearby Cambridge, saving money and studying. In 1888 Forbes enrolled at Amherst College in Amherst, Massachusetts, where he was a classmate of Sherman W. Jackson (later principal of M Street High School in Washington, DC), Fannie Baker Grant, Bessie Baker Lewis, and WILLIAM H. LEWIS (an assistant attorney general under President William H. Taft). When Forbes received a bachelor of arts degree in 1892, a young friend he had met in Boston, W. E. B. DUBOIS, attended the commencement exercises.

Returning to Boston, Forbes founded the *Boston Courant*, which went out of business in 1897 for lack of revenue. The same year, he became librarian at the West End Branch of the Boston Public Library, established in 1896 in the old West Church. Forbes became associated through the Boston Literary and Historical Association with WILLIAM MONROE TROTTER, an outspoken critic of BOOKER T. WASHINGTON. Born in Chillicothe, Ohio, Trotter won election as class president at a Boston high school, where he was the only student of African descent, then to Phi Beta Kappa at Harvard, and built a prosperous real estate business. He naturally clashed with the cautious and deferential methods advanced by Booker T. Washington, seeking the best means of advancement for people whose families had until recently been enslaved, many of whom were still illiterate, generally lacking any kind of property or capital.

Forbes's parents had been enslaved, and he himself had little money when he left Mississippi, but his accomplishments also refuted Washington's emphasis on industrial education, and indefinite acceptance of racially segregated second-class citizenship. Forbes married Elizabeth Harley, a stenographer and musician, daughter of H. G. Harley of Kingston, New York, on 29 November 1900. In 1901 Forbes and Trotter created another newspaper, the *Guardian*, with funds provided by Trotter, while Forbes provided his literary skills as coeditor. After the first issue appeared, 9 November 1901, circulation grew within eight months to 2,500. The paper was located, intentionally, in the same building where William Lloyd Garrison had published the *Liberator*, and where Harriet Beecher Stowe's *Uncle Tom's Cabin* had first been printed.

Washington tried to drive the *Guardian* out of business. He encouraged a libel suit by WILLIAM PICKENS, a Yale student who incurred the *Guardian*'s stinging critique for a prize-winning oration on "Misrule in Haiti." The paper denounced Pickens for "surrendering his self-respect, sacrificing his pride, emasculating his manhood, and throwing down his race." A Washington ally, Wilford H. Smith, referred to by contemporaries as a New York Negro lawyer, encouraged Pickens to sue, asserting "By all means Trotter and Forbes must be muzzled" (Avery, Sheldon. *Up from Washington: William Pickens and the Negro Struggle for Equality*, 1989, p. 17). Pickens, wary of being used as a pawn between two competing leaders, eventually dropped charges in exchange for a qualified apology, published by Forbes while Trotter was in jail—sentenced for "disturbing the peace" during an appearance by Washington in Boston.

Washington also arranged funds to create rival newspapers, competing for subscriptions and advertising within Boston's African American community. ROSCOE CONKLING BRUCE suggested that Forbes's employment and income from the public library would be a useful point of attack. "Just one word from the Librarian would in my opinion shut Forbes's mouth" he wrote to Washington. "Trotter can't carry on the paper alone—& no conceivable coadjutor could equal Forbes!" (Ritchie, Donald A., *American Journalists: Getting the Story*, 1997, p. 188).

Forbes resigned from the *Guardian* in 1904. Threats to his job at the library may have been a factor, but he also had disputes with Trotter, who continued to publish until his death in 1918. According to a letter written toDuBois by the attorney CLEMENT G. MORGAN, after Forbes's death, Forbes thought that "Trotter's bumptiousness and egotism, and eagerness for notoriety made a mess of a well-thought-out scheme to nip in the bud Washington's 'one-as-the-hand, separate-as-the-fingers' doctrine, put forth in his Atlanta speech [in 1895], while Trotter claimed that Forbes lacked the boldness, daring, and risk-all-to-win courage for so subtle and cunning a wizard as the Tuskegeean" (Aptheker, Herbert, ed., *The correspondence of W. E. B. DuBois, Volume 1*, 1997, p. 355).

Forbes participated with DuBois in founding the Niagara Movement in 1905, but by 1910 largely withdrew from politics. In his later years, Forbes wrote for the Boston *Transcript*, and worked on a book titled *The Pen and Voice Achievements of the Negro in Poetry and Prose*, which he never completed. Part of one chapter, on Samuel Ringgold Ward and FREDERICK DOUGLASS, appeared in the Springfield *Republican* on 23 February 1913.

Forbes wrote for the *AME Church Review* for several years, including a favorable review of Freeman H. H. Murray's *Emancipation and the Freed in American Sculpture*, published in 1916. In the early 1920s he authored two editorials in the *Review* sharply critical of MARCUS GARVEY's United Negro Improvement Association (UNIA). Forbes pointedly asked just where in Africa Garvey proposed to settle all the American Negroes he advised to move there, denouncing the "vagaries and obsession of an alien who neither from a knowledge of our past history is able to understand our present status nor with the orderly reflection of a logical mind is able to sketch a plan for our future that would win credence anywhere outside of a mad house" (Burkett, Randall K., *Garveyism as a Religious Movement: The Institutionalization of a Black Civil Religion*, 1978, p. 146).

Forbes remained the West End branch librarian until his death. All the Boston papers noted his passing. The *Jewish Daily Forward* published a glowing eulogy, in Yiddish; DuBois published an English translation in *The Crisis*, No. 34, July 1927, under the title "George Forbes of Boston: A Servant of Jew and Gentile." He was remembered as patient and helpful, welcoming with a warm smile both school children and "professional tramps" who found the library a warm, welcoming place. The West End had become a predominantly Jewish immigrant neighborhood, where he was remembered for helping generations of children overcome difficulties and complete their education.

The funeral, from his home on the South End (where most African Americans lived at the time), was noted for the "white" library workers who served as pall bearers. Children who were library regulars took up a collection to buy flowers, and a gift for Mrs. Forbes, which she said she would remember for the rest of her life. In 1956 an anonymous Amherst alumnus established a loan fund in memory of Mr. and Mrs. Forbes, available "to students in economic need without regard to their race, color or creed." Reporting this, the Boston Library publication, *The Question Mark*, noted, "To this day men and women come to the Branch and ask about him."

FURTHER READING

A collection of George Washington Forbes's papers are housed at the Boston Public Library, Boston, Massachusetts.

Amherst College. *Biographical Record of the Alumni of Amherst College, 1871–1896* (1901).

Ferris, William Henry. *The African Abroad; or, His Evolution in Western Civilization: Tracing Its Development under Caucasian Milieu* (1913). Despite the anachronisms in the title, this work offers bold contemporary perspectives on Forbes and many others.

Goldstein, Fanny (Tr.), "Boston's Intelligent Jews Mourn the Death of a Negro," original from the *Jewish Daily Forward*, reprinted in Ahern, Mary Eileen, ed. *Libraries*, Vol. 32, p. 35.

CHARLES ROSENBERG

Force, Nathaniel and Daniel Force (fl. 1688–1731), mariners, were born free in Bermuda, probably to John Force, a cooper, and possibly to Ann. As part of the tiny free black population in the British colony, the Forces were unusual because of their free status, but their maritime occupation, their birthplace, and the uncertainty of their genealogy were not. Most Bermudan men, black and white, were involved in maritime trades. By the mid-seventeenth century the majority of enslaved and free Africans in Bermuda had been born on the island. Nothing specific is known about the brothers' early life.

In 1688 the lieutenant governor of Bermuda, Robert Robinson, claimed that while Nathaniel and Daniel Force had been born free, they had become "slaves to his Majestie during their life time," and he authorized John Welch, master of the ketch *Bachelor* of Boston, to sell the brothers (Massachusetts Archives Collection 9.119, Massachusetts State Archive, Boston). Welch sold the Force brothers to Sarah Fowler, a wine seller. Fowler did not keep the men long but sold Nathaniel to Thomas Clarke in November 1688 and sold Daniel a month later to Benjamin Backway. Perhaps as a woman alone Fowler needed the quick profit such a sale made her. The case ended up in Boston courts after the brothers took matters into their own hands and left the households to which they had been sold. Nathaniel seems to have left earlier than his brother, as Clarke brought a complaint in at the beginning of October 1689, while Backway did not do the same until January 1691.

Daniel Force explained his actions in the warrant against Sarah Fowler Hall and by extension her husband, William Hall, which records some idea of his words to Benjamin Backway before he left. The warrant related that Daniel Force "hath asserted his owne freedome" because "the said Sarah Fowler nor her husband had no right unto" him. He "being borne free in the Island of Barmudos one of the King of England Plantacions, & never forfeited his freedome by breach of any of the Kings lawes, nor was ever accused or sentenced for so doing, Therefore … Backway cannot hold the said Negroe by the said Bill of sale for his life time or any time whatsoever." The warrant continued that Daniel "is departed there fore, the said Backway's service" (Massachusetts Archives Collection, Massachusetts State Archives, 36.301).

Daniel Force's effort to explain himself demonstrates an awareness of the English legal system—had he escaped without explanation, Backway would probably have gone after him. But since he argued that he had been sold illegally, the fault would fall on the ones who sold him. Robinson would not have had much success if he had tried to seize and sell the Force brothers in Bermuda, no matter how corrupt his administration. The Force family had generational standing in Bermuda as free people of African descent, a fact that would have been widely known and recognized in the small colony. But Robinson knew that if he took Nathaniel and Daniel Force out of the community where they were known to be free, the assumption would be that the sale of two black men was legitimate.

The information that survives about the Forces raises more questions than it answers. Daniel Force does not appear in any other colonial records after he asserted his freedom and left Benjamin Backway's household. Nathaniel Force probably returned to Bermuda relatively soon after escaping to Boston. Within a few years he married a woman named Sarah and immigrated to the Bahamas, where there was a small community of free mixed-race individuals and couples. He and Sarah had a girl, Anna, in

1704 and a boy, Joseph, in 1705. Sarah may have been of European descent, as the 1731 census listed her as white and assigned one white child to Nathaniel Force's household. This slippage in racial designations occurred for several families categorized in a 1724 census as "mulatto." Anna and Joseph were not baptized until they were around twenty years old, but why they waited so long is unknown. Most of the other baptisms recorded were infant baptisms, so it does not seem to be the record of a nascent Baptist community practicing adult baptism. The ministers before 1724 may have been unsympathetic, or Joseph and Anna may have been unable to get to a minister. Or perhaps Nathaniel opposed their participation in a ritual he did not think had helped him, or Sarah may have objected.

In Bermuda and the Bahamas in the seventeenth and early eighteenth century, Africans and people of African descent were sometimes baptized as Christians and participated in what remained largely English Christian churches. This potential inclusion is not as insignificant as it might seem. Even though their membership was not equal to that of English church members and while that membership does not mitigate the horrors of slavery, it does show that some people of African descent became members of Christian churches long before the emergence of African American churches in the nineteenth century. It also demonstrates the variety of racial relations in different British colonies at the same point in time. Nathaniel and Daniel Force faced different cultural contexts in Bermuda and in Boston. However, the legal systems of early modern British colonies were similar enough to enable the brothers to define themselves out of slavery by using the law in addition to removing themselves by using their feet.

FURTHER READING

The Bermuda National Archives in Hamilton, Bermuda, holds colonial records relating to the experiences of black Bermudans, and the Massachusetts State Archives, Massachusetts Archives Collection, vols. 9 and 36, holds papers relating to the suits brought after the Force brothers' departures from Boston.

Benes, Peter, and Jane Montague Benes, eds. *Slavery/Antislavery in New England* (2005).

Bernhard, Virginia. *Slaves and Slaveholders in Bermuda, 1616–1782* (1999).

Jarvis, Michael. "Maritime Masters and Seafaring Slaves in Bermuda, 1680–1783," *William and Mary Quarterly* 59.3 (2002): 585–622.

Packwood, Cyril Outerbridge. *Chained on the Rock: Slavery in Bermuda* (1975).

HEATHER MIYANO KOPELSON

Ford, Arnold Josiah (23 Apr. 1877–16 Sept. 1935), rabbi, black nationalist, and emigrationist, was born in Bridgetown, Barbados, the son of Edward Ford and Elizabeth Augusta Braithwaite. Ford asserted that his father's ancestry could be traced to the Yoruba tribe of Nigeria and his mother's to the Mendi tribe of Sierra Leone. According to his family's oral history, their heritage extended back to one of the priestly families of the ancient Israelites, and in Barbados his family maintained customs and traditions that identified them with Judaism (Kobre, 27). His father was a policeman who also had a reputation as a "fiery preacher" at the Wesleyan Methodist Church where Arnold was baptized; it is not known if Edward's teaching espoused traditional Methodist beliefs or if it urged the embrace of Judaism that his son would later advocate.

Ford's parents intended for him to become a musician. They provided him with private tutors who instructed him in several instruments—particularly the harp, violin, and bass. As a young adult, he studied music theory with Edmestone Barnes and in 1899 joined the musical corps of the British Royal Navy, where he served on HMS *Alert*. According to some reports, Ford was stationed on the island of Bermuda, where he secured a position as a clerk at the Court of Federal Assize, and he claimed that before coming to America he was a minister of public works in the Republic of Liberia, where many former slaves and early black nationalists settled.

When Ford arrived in Harlem, New York City, around 1910, he gravitated to its musical centers rather than to political or religious institutions, although within black culture, all three are often interrelated. He was a member of the Clef Club Orchestra, under the direction of James Reese Europe, which first brought jazz to Carnegie Hall in 1912. Other black Jewish musicians, such as Willie "The Lion" Smith, an innovator of stride piano, also congregated at the Clef Club. Shortly after the orchestra's Carnegie Hall engagement, Ford became the director of the New Amsterdam Musical Association. His interest in mysticism, esoteric knowledge, and secret societies is evidenced by his membership in the Scottish Rite Masons, where he served as Master of the Memmon Lodge. It was during this period of activity in Harlem that he married Olive Nurse, probably around 1916, with whom he had two children before they divorced in 1924.

In 1917 MARCUS GARVEY founded the New York chapter of the Universal Negro Improvement Association (UNIA), and within a few years it had become the largest mass movement in African American history. Ford became the musical director of the UNIA choir, while Samuel Valentine was the president and Nancy Paris its lead singer. These three became the core of an active group of black Jews within the UNIA who studied Hebrew, religion, and history and held services at Liberty Hall, the headquarters of the UNIA. As a paid officer, Rabbi Ford, as he was then called, was responsible for orchestrating much of the pageantry of Garvey's highly attractive ceremonies. Ford and Benjamin E. Burrell composed a song called "Ethiopia," which speaks of a halcyon past before slavery and stresses pride in African heritage—two themes that were becoming immensely popular. Ford was thus prominently situated among those Muslim and Christian clergy, including GEORGE MCGUIRE, chaplain general of the UNIA, who were each trying to influence the religious direction of the organization.

Ford's contributions to the UNIA, however, were not limited to musical and religious matters. He and E. L. Gaines wrote the handbook of rules and regulations for the paramilitary Universal African Legion (which was modeled after the Zionist Jewish Legion) and developed guidelines for the Black Cross Nurses. He served on committees, spoke at rallies, and was elected one of the delegates representing the thirty-five thousand members of the New York chapter at the First International Convention of Negro Peoples of the World, held in 1920 at Madison Square Garden. There the governing body adopted the red, black, and green flag as its ensign, and Ford's song "Ethiopia" became the "Universal Ethiopian Anthem," which the UNIA constitution required be sung at every gathering. During that same year Ford published the *Universal Ethiopian Hymnal.*

Ford was a proponent of replacing the term *Negro* with the term *Ethiopian* as a general reference to people of African descent. This allowed the biblical verse "Ethiopia shall soon stretch out her hand to God" (Psalms 68:31) to be interpreted as applying to their efforts, and it became a popular slogan of the organization. At the 1922 convention, Ford opened the proceedings for the session devoted to "The Politics and Future of the West Indian Negro," and he represented the advocates of Judaism on a five-person ad hoc committee formed to investigate "the Future Religion of the Negro."

Following Garvey's arrest for mail fraud in 1923, the UNIA lost much of its internal cohesion. Since Ford and his small band of followers were motivated by principles that were independent of Garvey's charismatic appeal, they were repeatedly approached by government agents and asked to testify against Garvey at trial, which they refused to do. However, in 1925 Ford brought separate lawsuits against Garvey and the UNIA for failing to pay him royalties from the sale of recordings and sheet music, and in 1926 the judge ruled in Ford's favor. No longer musical director, and despite his personal and business differences with the organization, Rabbi Ford maintained a connection with the UNIA and was invited to give the invocation at the annual convention in 1926.

Several black religious leaders were experimenting with Judaism in various degrees between the two world wars. Rabbi Ford formed intermittent partnerships with some of these leaders. He and Valentine started a short-lived congregation called Beth B'nai Israel. Ford then worked with Mordecai Herman and the Moorish Zionist Temple, until they had an altercation over theological and financial issues. Finally, he established Beth B'nai Abraham in Harlem in 1924. A Jewish scholar who visited the congregation described their services as "a mixture of Reform and Orthodox Judaism, but when they practice the old customs they are seriously orthodox" (Kobre, 25). The Harlem chronicler JAMES VANDERZEE photographed the congregation with the Star of David and bold Hebrew lettering identifying their presence on 135th Street and showing Rabbi Ford standing in front of the synagogue with his arms around his string bass and with members of his choir at his side, the women wearing the black dresses and long white head coverings that became their distinctive habit and the men in white turbans.

In 1928 Ford created a business adjunct to the congregation, called the B'nai Abraham Progressive Corporation. Reminiscent of many of Garvey's ventures, this corporation issued one hundred shares of stock and purchased two buildings; it operated a religious and vocational school in one and leased apartments in the other. However, resources dwindled as the Depression became more pronounced, and the corporation went bankrupt in 1930. Once again it seemed that Ford's dream of building a black community with cultural integrity, economic viability, and political virility was dashed, but out of the ashes of this disappointment he mustered the resolve to make a final attempt in Ethiopia. The Ethiopian government had been encouraging black people with skills and education to immigrate to Ethiopia for almost a decade, and Ford knew that there were more than forty thousand indigenous black Jews already in Ethiopia (who called themselves Beta Israel but who were commonly referred to as Falasha). The announced coronation of Haile Selassie in 1930 as the first black ruler of an African nation in modern times raised the hopes of black people all over the world and led Ford to believe that the timing of his Ethiopian colony was providential.

Ford arrived in Ethiopia with a small musical contingent in time to perform during the coronation festivities. They then sustained themselves in Addis Ababa by performing at local hotels and relying on assistance from supporters in the United States who were members of the Aurienoth Club, a civic group of black Jews and black nationalists, and members of the Commandment Keepers Congregation, led by Rabbi W. A. MATTHEW, Ford's most loyal protégé. Mignon Innis arrived with a second delegation in 1931 to work as Ford's private secretary. She soon became Ford's wife, and they had two children in Ethiopia. Mrs. Ford established a school for boys and girls that specialized in English and music. Ford managed to secure eight hundred acres of land on which to begin his colony and approximately one hundred people came to help him develop it. Unbeknown to Ford, the U.S. State Department was monitoring Ford's efforts with irrational alarm, dispatching reports with such headings as "American Negroes in Ethiopia—Inspiration Back of Their Coming Here—'Rabbi' Josiah A. Ford" and instituting discriminatory policies to curtail the travel of black citizens to Ethiopia.

Ford had no intention of leaving Ethiopia, so he drew up a certificate of ordination (*shmecha*) for Rabbi Matthew that was sanctioned by the Ethiopian government, in the hope that this document would give Matthew the necessary credentials to continue the work that Ford had begun in the United States. By 1935 the black Jewish experiment with Ethiopian Zionism was on the verge of collapse. Those who did not leave because of the hard agricultural work joined the stampede of foreign nationals who sensed that war with Italy was imminent and defeat for Ethiopia certain. Ford died in September, it was said, of exhaustion and heartbreak, a few weeks before the Italian invasion. Ford had been the most important catalyst for the spread of Judaism among African Americans. Through his successors, communities of black Jews emerged and survived in several American cities.

FURTHER READING

The papers of Rabbi Ford are held largely in private collections; however, correspondence between Ford and Matthew is contained in the Rabbi Matthew Collection at the Schomburg Center for Research in Black Culture of the New York Public Library, along with other collections relating to Harlem's black Jews. Detailed records of Ford's efforts in Ethiopia are available at the National Archives, State Department Records for Ethiopia.

King, Kenneth J. "Some Notes on Arnold J. Ford and New World Black Attitudes to Ethiopia," in *Black Apostles: Afro-American Clergy Confront the Twentieth Century*, eds. Randall Burkett and Richard Newman (1978).

Kobre, Sidney. "Rabbi Ford," *The Reflex* 4.1 (1929).

Scott, William R. "Rabbi Arnold Ford's Back-to-Ethiopia Movement: A Study of Black Emigration, 1930–1935," *Pan-African Journal* 8.2 (1975).

SHOLOMO B. LEVY

Ford, Barney Launcelot (1822–14 Dec. 1902), Underground Railroad conductor, barber, and businessman, was born in Stafford County, Virginia, the son of a Mr. Darington (given name unknown), a slaveholder and plantation owner, and Phoebe (surname unknown), one of Darington's slaves. Called "Barney" at birth, he adopted the name Barney Launcelot Ford as an adult to please his soon-to-be wife and to provide himself with a "complete" name.

Ford spent the first quarter-century of his life enslaved. His mother is said to have planted the seeds of education in him as a child by secreting him out of camp at night to meet with sympathetic people who taught him the basics of reading and writing. She may have put herself in mortal danger on many occasions by smuggling in a section of newspaper or a Bible page so that he could practice his studies. Upon his mother's death around 1837, Ford was enslaved on a plantation in Kentucky, where from age fifteen to eighteen he took advantage of any chance he had to read and practice the speech of people around him. At the age of eighteen he was sold again and lived on a plantation in Georgia. The mistress of the plantation allowed him to attend school with her own children, swearing her children to secrecy so that Ford would not be punished for pursuing an education. His self-education continued as he spent nearly five years as a slave on paddle-wheel boats along the Mississippi River. Ford always viewed his insatiable quest for education as his ticket out of captivity.

In 1847 Ford, with the aid of white sympathizers, escaped from slavery while serving on a riverboat in Quincy, Illinois. Donning unusual disguises—he once dressed as a white woman—and relying on his ability to mimic various manners of speech, Ford traveled by the Underground Railroad to Chicago, where he achieved his freedom. For the next four years, in gratitude for his escape and in honor of his mother's efforts toward his education, he became a "conductor" on the Underground Railroad, helping slaves travel from Chicago to Canada. During this time he apprenticed himself to a barber and soon found work cutting hair in a Chicago hotel.

In 1849 Ford married Julia Lyoni, whose brother supervised the Chicago section of the Underground Railroad. That year Ford got word of the California gold rush. For two years he waited for the fares to drop so that he and his wife could make the trip west to try to make their fortune in the mines. When the ship that Ford and his wife took to San Francisco stopped in San Juan Bay, Nicaragua, Ford decided to take advantage of gold rush traffic by opening the United States Hotel and Restaurant. After losing the business to a fire three years later, he hired on as a steward on a local steamship. Within eight months he had bought the California Hotel at Virgin Bay, and five months later he sold it for a profit of $4,940. He sailed back to New York City in 1855. After traveling to Chicago, Ford was persuaded by his wife's family to take over his brother-in-law's livery business. The livery was the main connection for the Underground Railroad in that area, and Ford again became deeply involved in helping enslaved people escape to freedom. During this time, Ford began building his contacts, reading everything he could find about abolitionists, and corresponding with people who would later be influential in his political endeavors. He met with John Brown on several occasions and kept abreast of the increasing news about the possibility of war between the states.

In 1859 Ford was again struck by gold fever, although this time his goal was to reach Colorado. He took a circuitous route, avoiding slave states and hiring on as a cook and wrangler on a wagon train that took him to Denver in May 1860. As a rookie miner, Ford made several attempts at establishing claims, always to have someone take them away from him under threat of death. Eventually Ford became a partner in a Denver barber shop. He used this time to make contacts with the foremost citizens of the city and to help other blacks in town learn about their civil rights. His wife joined him in Denver with their young son (they later were to have two daughters) and elicited a promise from Ford that he would stick to the business he knew, that of being a hotelier and restaurant manager.

Beginning with a small barber shop and a "lean-to" lunch counter in 1861, Ford built a real estate empire, despite being constantly beset by the fires that were common to mining towns with wooden buildings. The opening of his People's Restaurant on 16 August 1863 rated notice in the *Rocky Mountain News*. The building included the restaurant on the ground floor, a bar on the second, and a basement with a barber shop and hairdressing salon. Fresh oysters and Havana cigars were two of the impressive attractions of the establishment.

As Ford prospered, he never lost track of the Civil War and what it meant to blacks. He watched local and national legislation vigilantly, always wary that phrases might be slipped into pending bills that would endanger the freedom and civil rights of blacks. Vocally supporting the suffrage of black men, he fought to keep the territory from becoming a state until suffrage was given to all males. In 1865 the voters refused to make Colorado a state, but not over the issue of suffrage of black males; rather they felt it would simply be less expensive to run a territory than a state. Ford was bitterly disappointed by the lack of support from whites, whom he considered his friends. He sold the hotel, leased the building, hired a lawyer to supervise his improved and unimproved real estate holdings, and took his family to Chicago, along with approximately $23,000.

Ford soon began to feel guilty about giving up his fight for black male suffrage in Colorado. So when friends from Denver asked him to go to Washington, D.C., to lobby the president and Congress, Ford gladly went along. Eventually his political connections paid off, and Colorado, although still a territory, granted full male suffrage. Ford immediately decided to return to Denver. There he opened a new restaurant in 1866 and threw himself into bettering segregated black schools. He remained active in local politics while opening yet another restaurant in Cheyenne, Wyoming, along the western railroad terminus. His next endeavor, Ford's House and People's Restaurant in Denver, was built across from the railroad station. Ford was asked to join the local bank as a trustee, and the city's most influential people were soon visiting his wife in the new Ford mansion. He was appointed a member of the Republican Party Central Committee and served as the first black member of a federal grand jury in Colorado. Inequities for blacks continued to occupy Ford's time, and when a new school was needed for the burgeoning city of Denver, he made sure there was no language in the school bond to keep his children and other blacks from attending.

Ford's empire building continued unabated. When he was worth about $250,000, he sold one restaurant in Denver and bought the four-story Sargent Hotel, renaming it Ford's Hotel. Determined to build the best hotel in Denver, in 1872 he spent over $50,000 on his newest treasure, the Inter-Ocean Hotel. When the depression of 1873 hit, Ford sold the Inter-Ocean for a profit of $25,000 and headed to Cheyenne. He built another restaurant and hotel, also named the Inter-Ocean, and drew praise for his operation from East Coast newspapers. For the next twenty years, Ford bought and sold many more properties, staying ahead of hard times but no longer living in lavish style. In 1885, after two years of political fighting, Ford saw the passage of legislation in Colorado prohibiting discrimination in public facilities. He acknowledged that a law would not guarantee lawful actions by all citizens, but he was proud of his part in the fight for equality. Ford came full circle in his life when he bought two barber shops in Denver and returned to his first trade. Later he hired managers to run the shops, while he sat and visited with political cronies and foes alike. Ford died in Denver.

FURTHER READING

Talmadge, Marian, and Iris Gilmore. *Barney Ford: Black Baron* (1973).

This entry is taken from the *American National Biography* and is published here with the permission of the American Council of Learned Societies.

MARIA ELENA RAYMOND

Ford, Harold Eugene, Jr. (11 May 1970–), politician, was born in Memphis, Tennessee, son of HAROLD FORD SR., a U.S. Congressman, and Dorothy Bowles, an employee of the U.S. Department of Agriculture. Harold Jr. was the oldest of five children: brothers Jake, Isaac, and Andrew, and sister Ava. The Ford family was an institution in the Memphis area; schools, churches, roads, and buildings were named after family members. They ran a successful funeral services business and were active in the civil rights movement and the cause of social justice. Besides his father, two of Ford's uncles were also politicians: John, a local councilman, and Emmitt, who succeeded Ford's father as a member of the Tennessee state legislature.

From an early age Ford expressed an interest in politics. In 1979 Ford's family moved to Washington, D.C., where he attended St. Albans School, an exclusive school for boys. In Washington Ford learned how politics worked by accompanying his father to numerous functions. He also participated in reelection campaigns for his father and other family members. After graduating from St. Albans in 1988, he moved to Philadelphia to pursue a degree in American history at the University of Pennsylvania.

After graduating in 1992 Ford became a staff aide to the Senate Budget Committee. During the same year he would lead his father's successful reelection campaign. He also played a role on Bill Clinton's presidential transitional team as an assistant to the Justice and Civil Rights Cluster. In 1993 he took a position as a special assistant to the Economic Development Association at the U.S. Department of Commerce, where he dedicated the majority of his time to policies targeted at improving economic conditions in Los Angeles in the aftermath of the 1992 riots that erupted when four white LAPD officers were caught on tape beating black motorist RODNEY KING. During this time Ford began law school at the University of Michigan. While there, he again ran a successful reelection campaign for his father in 1994.

During his final year of law school in 1996, Harold Ford Sr. opted not to pursue another Congressional term. At age twenty-five, the youngest age at which it was constitutionally possible to do so, Harold Jr. decided he was capable of succeeding his father. In the Democratic primary, Ford faced Steve Cohen, a state senator, and Rufus Jones, a state representative. Ford won the primary with more than 60 percent of the vote. In the general election Ford faced the same candidate, black Republican Rod DeBerry, who he had helped his father easily defeat in the 1994 election. Ford won with more than 80 percent of the vote and at age twenty-six would become the second youngest member of Congress in history.

Ford was well received when he arrived to Washington as a newly minted Congressman; he was elected president of his Congressional class. He was appointed to the House Committee on Education and the Workforce and the House Committee on Government Reform and Oversight. Ford was a vocal advocate for many Democratic policies and a firm supporter of the Clinton Administration; however, he was not as liberal as his father. In fact, Ford came into Congress with a more moderate agenda. He joined the New Democrat Coalition, a centrist group formed in 1997 to further Clinton's progrowth, probusiness policies within the Democratic Party. Ford advocated abandoning some of the party's liberal orthodoxies and even drew the ire of House Democratic Leader Dick Gephardt. Even though Ford's retreat from traditional liberalism worried some, including his father, his more conservative agenda played well among whites in his home district. Unlike his father and uncles, who in their election campaigns reminded black voters of the long history of racial division and white discrimination, Ford Jr. emphasized racial harmony and advocated policies that would appeal to all races in Memphis.

In 2000 Ford served as keynote speaker of the Democratic National Convention, supporting presidential candidate and longtime family friend Vice President Al Gore. Ford campaigned hard for Gore but could not help him secure the electoral votes in his home state of Tennessee, which would have ensured Gore's victory, regardless of the outcome of the disputed vote count in Florida. Displeased with Democratic losses in the 2002 congressional races, Ford launched an unsuccessful campaign for House Democratic leader against the more liberal House minority whip Nancy Pelosi.

In Tennessee, Ford saw a steady rise in his support among whites and Republicans. His centrist positions were translating into higher approval ratings. In 2005 Ford saw an opportunity to launch a campaign for the U.S. Senate from Tennessee. He easily won the Democratic nomination and went on to face Republican Bob Corker in the general election.

Many notable Democrats made campaign appearances for Ford, including former President Bill Clinton and Al Gore. The race remained fairly even with Ford polling well among both white and conservative voters. Late in the campaign the Republican Party aired a controversial commercial depicting Ford, who was unmarried, as a playboy attracted to white women. The commercial was denounced by members of both parties as racist, but the Republicans refused to pull it. In the end Ford lost the contest by less than 3 percent.

In 2007 Ford became a vice chairman and senior policy adviser for Merrill Lynch, the largest retail brokerage in the United States. He also began teaching at Vanderbilt University and remained active in Tennessee politics, serving as an adviser to Governor Phil Bredesen. In 2010, Ford briefly contemplated a run for the U.S. Senate Seat of Kirsten Gillibrand, whom Governor David Paterson had appointed to the seat vacated by Hillary Clinton when she became Barack Obama's Secretary of State in 2009. Despite support from Republican New York City mayor, Michael Bloomberg, Ford was unable to garner much support from the Democratic Party hierarchy in the state, and decided not to run for the Senate.

FURTHER READING

Ford, Harold, Jr. *Harold Ford, Jr. on Answers* (2006).

De la Cruz, Bonna. "The Fords of Memphis: Service and Scandal Define a Dynasty," *The Tennessean*, 31 June 2005.

Milbank, Dana. "Harold Ford Jr. Storms His Father's House," *New York Times*, 25 Oct. 1998.

White, Jack. "Harold Ford Jr. Reaches for the Stars," *Time* (10 Dec. 2002).

MICHAELJULIUS IDANI

Ford, Harold Eugene, Sr. (20 May 1945–), politician, was born in Memphis, Tennessee, the son of Newton Jackson Ford and Victoria Davis. He was the ninth of fifteen children, only twelve of whom survived early childhood. Ford's father led a successful funeral home, N. J. Ford & Sons, and both parents were leading figures in Memphis's African American community. Newton Ford was active in Memphis politics and encouraged Harold and his two older brothers, John and Emmitt, to advance the cause of civil rights.

As a teenager Ford moved to Nashville to pursue an education at Tennessee State University and also to manage the family funeral business. During this time he experienced his first political campaign, working on his father's unsuccessful bid for the Tennessee state legislature. That campaign helped Ford understand the challenges facing African Americans attempting to break into a political structure dominated by whites. After graduating in 1967 he studied in Nashville for another two years, pursuing a degree in mortuary science at John A. Gupton College before returning to Memphis and the family business full time. In 1968 Ford marched with Dr. Martin Luther King Jr. in support of striking sanitation workers a week before King was assassinated in that city. In 1969 Ford married Dorothy Jean Bowles, mother of his three children, Harold Eugene Jr., Jake, and Sir Isaac.

With the lessons learned from his father's campaign, in 1970 Ford launched his own successful campaign for a seat in the Tennessee General Assembly, becoming one of the few black members of the assembly. During his first term he served as majority whip and chaired a special committee investigating the practices of utility companies across the state. His youth and relentless style also made him attractive to the Democratic Party; he would serve as a delegate to the Party's state and national conventions in 1972.

In 1973 Ford saw an opportunity to advance his political career. The Watergate scandal had weakened Republicans across the country and he believed the incumbent Republican Congressman Dan H. Kuykendall was vulnerable. Many political observers in Memphis and across the nation disagreed. Even though redistricting had increased the number of blacks in the district, African Americans only represented 47 percent of the population. Beyond securing virtually all black votes, he would need substantial support from whites. Ford's campaigning focused primarily on African Americans, much to the displeasure of Democratic strategists. In a meeting with Governor Jimmy Carter of Georgia, chairman of the Democratic Party's campaign committee, Ford walked out over disagreements about his strategy of focusing on black votes at the expense of white votes.

Despite reservations and limited support from his party, Ford did have a very crucial supporter: Memphis resident and entertainer Isaac Hayes, who served as one of the campaign's largest financial contributors and fund-raisers. Through a series of benefit shows, cash donations, campaigning, and garnering endorsements, Hayes was critical in making the Ford campaign viable. Two of Ford's brothers also played significant roles in his campaign and the family's political influence: John, a state senator and Memphis city councilman, and Emmitt, who successfully ran for Harold's seat in the state legislature.

The 1974 election was racially charged and extremely close. Most projections showed Kuykendall winning. But on election night a number of uncounted ballot boxes were discovered in heavily black districts. Ford protested and brought evidence before election officials, who included the ballots in the official tally. When the ballots were counted, Ford won the election by a margin of less than eight hundred votes, making him the youngest (at age twenty-nine), and the first African American in the twentieth century to represent Tennessee in Congress. His brothers also won their respective campaigns, making the Fords the most politically influential black family in Tennessee.

As a freshman Congressman, Ford was assigned to the powerful House Ways and Means Committee, where he chaired the Human Services subcommittee. In Memphis, Ford's popularity among black residents strengthened, but his support among whites was tenuous. Many believed his style to be too racially polarizing and confrontational. In Congress, he was popular with his colleagues in the Congressional Black Caucus, but relationships with white congressional members were cooler. In 1976, a year into his term, Ford was criticized for placing a number of campaign contributors on government payrolls. Many Ford supporters contended that such claims were racially motivated. The Justice Department began monitoring Ford under suspicion of corruption.

In 1983 the Ford family received the first major challenge to their dominance of black Memphis politics. Ford served as campaign manager for his brother John's unsuccessful bid for mayor of the city against white conservative incumbent Dick Hackett. Despite the setback, Ford stayed active in local politics while becoming a leading voice for welfare reform in Congress.

In 1987 Ford faced his biggest political challenge: a Justice Department indictment for corruption. He was accused of conspiring to commit fraud and was linked to bribery involving convicted felons. In light of the allegations Ford relinquished his position as subcommittee chair. Ford's first trial in 1990 was sensational and resulted in a hung jury, divided along racial lines. His second trial proved even more controversial, mired with claims of racism and of being politically motivated. In the wake of the 1992 Los Angeles riots as a result of the Rodney King verdict, there were fears that the outcome of Ford's trial could have a similar impact on race relations in Memphis. In 1993 Ford was acquitted of all charges, after which he returned to his position as subcommittee chair.

In 1996 Ford decided that after twenty-two years it was time to retire from Congress. After fighting back the corruption charges and playing a major role in advocating for welfare reform, he believed the time was right to leave; however, he was adamant about a Ford filling his seat. Ford put forward his twenty-five-year-old son, Harold Ford Jr., to succeed him. Memphis' first black mayor, W. W. Herenton, disagreed, citing the junior Ford's lack of experience and the fact he was still a student at Michigan Law School. Despite skepticism, Ford Jr. won the Democratic primary and eventually his father's seat in Congress. Ford Sr. moved from Memphis to homes in Miami and the Hamptons in New York, remaining active in the Democratic Party and working with a lobbying and political consulting firm.

FURTHER READING

Anderson, Jack, and Les Whitten. "Freshman's Financial Affairs Probed," *Washington Post*, 20 Feb. 1976.

Lewis, John, Jr. "New Ford in Congress," *Chicago Defender*, 28 Dec. 1974.

"Mayor's Victory Bruises Memphis' Ford Family," *Washington Post*, 8 Oct. 1983.

Milbank, Dana. "Harold Ford Jr. Storms His Father's House," *New York Times*, 25 Oct. 1998.

MICHAELJULIUS IDANI

Ford, James William (22 Dec. 1893–21 June 1957), labor leader and Communist Party official, was born James William Foursche in Pratt City, Alabama, the son of Lyman Foursche, a steelworker, and Nancy Reynolds, a domestic. Not long after his birth the family began to use a new surname when a white policeman questioning his father insisted that "Foursche" was too difficult to spell and changed the name to Ford. The most traumatic experience of Ford's boyhood was the lynching of his grandfather, a Georgia railroad worker. Ford started work at thirteen, joining his father at the Tennessee Coal, Iron and Railroad Company, where he worked as a water boy, mechanic's helper, and then steam-hammer operator. Nevertheless, he managed to complete high school.

Entering Fisk University at the age of twenty, Ford excelled in his studies and in athletics, but when America entered World War I in 1917 he withdrew from college to serve in France. He was a radio engineer in the Signal Corps and became a noncommissioned officer. He also organized a protest against the bigotry of a white captain; as a result, the officer lost his command. After his discharge in 1919 Ford returned to Fisk and graduated in 1920.

Moving to Chicago, Ford tried to get a federal job using the skills he had learned in the army, but he was rejected, apparently because of race. He played semiprofessional baseball for a time, and then in 1919 got a job as a parcel dispatcher at the post office. He soon joined the postal workers' union and served as its delegate in the Chicago branch of the American Federation of Labor. He also worked with A. PHILIP RANDOLPH during the early years of the Brotherhood of Sleeping Car Porters. At his job Ford became known as a militant, quick to criticize his bosses and even the leaders of his own union. His aggressive style made enemies, and he was dismissed in 1927.

By this time Ford had abandoned his former conviction that blacks could make their way entirely through education and self-improvement. He had become interested in the left wing of the labor movement when white members of the communist-backed Trade Union Educational League (TUEL) supported his accusations of racial discrimination in the Chicago Federation of Labor. He became a member of TUEL, helped organize the American Negro Labor Congress in 1925, and joined the Communist Party in 1926. The following year, attending the Fourth World Congress of the International Labor Union (ILU) in Moscow as a TUEL delegate, he was elected to the congress's executive committee. In 1928 Ford returned to Moscow for the Sixth World Congress of the Communist International, where he served on the party's Negro Commission. He was one of the first to identify the struggles of black Americans with those of colonized people around the world, and he pressed these views at one international conference after another during the late 1920s and early 1930s.

Moving to New York City Ford threw himself into the activities of the party. He helped organize the Trade Union Unity League (an American affiliate of the ILU), and he directed the Negro Departments of both the TUUL and the TUEL. He was arrested in 1929 for leading a protest against the U.S. presence in Haiti, and again in 1932 during the Bonus March. In fall 1932 Ford was nominated by the Communist Party for vice president of the United States. With the presidential nominee, William Z. Foster, he toured the nation's larger cities until he was disabled by a heart attack. The two received 100,000 votes. Resuming political activity in 1933 Ford became head of the Harlem section of the Communist Party and also served on the party's political committee, national committee, and New York State committee.

During the early 1930s Ford was bitterly critical of black leaders, supporting his party's claim that they were "shamelessly aiding the white master class." But like many communists, he became more amenable to cooperation once the party leadership called for a "Popular Front" against fascism in the summer of 1935. For the next several years he worked actively with black organizations like the National Association for the Advancement of Colored People (NAACP), the National Negro Congress, and the Urban League. The new approach was evident during Ford's 1936 campaign for vice president. Running this time with Earl Browder, Ford called for coalitions among all progressive forces and advocated social legislation, relief for the unemployed, aid to farmers, and equal rights for blacks.

Though by 1940 Ford had become the best-known black communist in America, the party itself was suffering from the country's anger over the recent pact between Stalin and Hitler—a pact that party members refused to disavow. When Browder and Ford headed the national ticket again that year, they faced investigations, arrests, and a hostile press. They received fewer than 50,000 votes, less than half their 1936 total. A year later the political winds changed again when Hitler invaded Russia. Ford, like most American communists, threw himself into the war effort. He now criticized other black leaders for launching the "Double V" campaign (aimed at a second victory, over racial injustice); he accused them of "aiding the Axis camp" by diverting attention from the main task of destroying Hitler.

Once the war ended and Soviet-American relations cooled again, Earl Browder was expelled from the party. Ford sided with Browder's critics, blaming his ally of twenty years for leading the party "into the swamp of revisionism." Ford was stripped of his offices but was allowed to stay in the party, and he remained a loyal member for the rest of his life. He was married twice. The name of his first wife, by whom he had three sons, is not known; his second wife was Reva. (Neither her maiden name nor the dates of his two marriages are known.) He died in New York City.

As a loyal communist Ford often changed his political tactics to conform to the dictates of party leadership. But communism also provided Ford with a core of beliefs that allowed him to integrate his commitment to the labor movement, his experience as an African American, and his interest in liberation movements around the world. At his worst, he operated (in the words of one critic) as "the prototype of the pliable Stalinist functionary." At his best he contributed to the country's dialogue on race relations by highlighting the economic and international context of the African American experience.

FURTHER READING

Davis, Benjamin. *Communist Candidate for Vice-President of the United States, James W. Ford* (1936).

Foner, Philip S. *Organized Labor and the Black Worker, 1619–1973* (1974).

Foner, Philips S., and James S. Allen, eds. *American Communism and Black Americans: A Documentary History, 1919–1929* (1987).

Foster, William Z. *History of the Communist Party of the United States* (1952).

Howe, Irving, and Lewis Coser. *The American Communist Party: A Critical History* (1962).

Record, Wilson. *The Negro and the Communist Party* (1951).

Obituaries: *New York Times*, 22 June 1957; *Daily Worker*, 24 June 1957.

SANDRA OPDYCKE

Ford, Justina Laurena Carter (22 Jan. 1871–14 Oct. 1952), physician, was born Justina Laurena Warren in Knoxville, Illinois. Her parents were Melissa Brisco Warren and Pryor Warren; Melissa Warren's first marriage ended with the death of her husband, Ralph Alexander. When Justina was very young, the family moved to nearby Galesburg, Illinois. She was the seventh child in her family. Her mother was a nurse, which may have influenced Justina's early interest in medicine. Ford recalled that as a young girl she was so focused on becoming a doctor that she wove her passion for medicine into all of her activities. She played hospital, tended the ill, and even used her chores, such as dressing chickens, to study anatomy.

In December 1892 Justina Warren married the Fisk-educated Reverend John E. Ford. After her marriage, Justina Ford enrolled in Chicago's Hering Medical College, and graduated in 1899. She and her husband moved to Normal, Alabama, home of the historically black college Alabama A&M, where she directed a hospital. In 1902 the Fords decided to leave Alabama for Denver, Colorado, where John Ford became the minister at Zion Baptist Church. By the beginning of the twentieth century, Denver's racially segregated housing and job patterns had crystallized. In 1900 around 93 percent of the city's African American women employed outside the home worked as domestic servants. African American professional women were very rare. Most of Denver's black population lived in several adjacent neighborhoods, and Warren established her practice in the middle of the city's African American community. These neighborhoods were not entirely African American; immigrants from Europe and Asia, as well as some U.S.-born whites, Asians, and Latinos, established homes in these communities.

In October 1902 Justina Warren received her license to practice medicine, thus becoming the first African American woman physician licensed in Colorado. Most of Colorado's hospitals barred African American physicians. Blacks could not become members of the American Medical Association, nor of the Denver and Colorado medical societies. Warren was ready to confront these challenges, and she later recalled that she "fought like a tiger" against discrimination in all its forms, whether on the basis of gender, race, or class.

When the church transferred the Reverend Ford to Florida in 1907, Justina Ford chose not to accompany him. The couple eventually divorced, and both partners remarried. Justina Ford married Alfred Allen, a local cook, around 1920, but she did not use his last name. Justina Ford had no children.

Ford established a general practice, but she quickly became a skilled and popular gynecologist, obstetrician, and pediatrician. Her patients called her the "baby doctor." As changes in the medical profession pushed an increasing number of women in the United States to deliver their babies in hospitals, Ford still delivered most of her patients' babies in their homes. During most of her career she did not have the option of practicing in Denver's hospitals. Many of her patients preferred home births anyway, complementing Ford's belief that delivering babies at home was natural. Former patients remembered that when Justina Ford presided over a delivery, she often took over the house, directing family members and neighbors on how to help the mother and new child. One woman recalled that during her labor she and Dr. Ford calmly discussed the future opportunities that awaited "this young man" or "this young lady."

Justina Ford's practice extended beyond Denver's African American neighborhoods to poor neighborhoods throughout the city. Word of mouth brought her patients in surrounding counties, including migrant workers in the sugar beet fields. Ford described her patients as "plain white and plain colored," and she learned enough Spanish, Italian, Japanese, and other languages to make her patients feel comfortable. Justina Ford made it clear that her medical care was not determined by a family's ability to pay. One determined family finally paid off their bill when the baby turned thirteen years old. She often accepted payment in kind, including groceries, chickens, and handcrafts such as handwoven textiles.

Ford was a visible member of Denver's African American community. She participated in Zion Baptist Church and was involved in Denver's Phillis Wheatley branch of the Young Women's Christian Association. Ford gained a reputation as a humanitarian and as a champion of the poor. She was concerned that "good medical care is hard for poor people to get, very hard for poor people." Friends recalled that when she encountered needy families, she often quietly arranged to send them food or coal.

In the 1950s some of the racial barriers in medicine began to soften. Several hospitals gave Dr. Ford privileges, although she recalled that some hospitals still did not welcome her. In January 1950 the Denver and Colorado medical societies finally admitted Ford as a full member. The previous year Ford wrote to the Denver Medical Society to petition for admittance, pointedly noting that "it has required patience and fortitude to endure as I have from 1902 to 1949." Denver's Cosmopolitan Club, an early civil rights organization, gave her their Human Relations Award in 1951.

Justina Ford died in Denver, Colorado, in 1952, fifty years after she had launched her career there. Dr. Ford saw patients until two weeks before her death. Throughout her career she had been Colorado's only African American woman physician, and she was among a handful of pioneering African American medical doctors in the state.

FURTHER READING

Justina Ford's Denver office and home from 1911 to 1952 now houses the Black American West Museum and Heritage Center, and it contains some of her professional effects.

Harris, Mark. "The Forty Years of Justina Ford," *Negro Digest* (March 1950).

Lohse, Joyce B. *Justina Ford: Medical Pioneer* (2004).

Pierson, William S. "Dr. Justina Ford: Honored as the First Black Female Physician in Colorado," *Colorado Medicine* (15 Feb. 1989).

MODUPE G. LABODE

Ford, Len (18 Feb. 1926–14 Mar. 1972), football player, was born Leonard Guy Ford Jr. in Washington, D.C., the son of Leonard Guy Ford, a federal government employee. His mother's name is not known. Ford attended public schools in Washington and graduated from Armstrong High School, where as a senior he captained the football, baseball, and basketball teams and earned All-City honors in football in both 1942 and 1943. Ford recalled that his ambition was to play major league baseball, but since segregation prevented him from doing so he instead enrolled at Morgan State University, an all-black school in Baltimore, Maryland. There he played basketball and football, winning all-conference honors as a tackle his one year at Morgan. In 1944 Ford entered the U.S. Navy, where he met people who told him that at 6'5" and over 220 pounds he should play at a higher competitive level.

As he neared his discharge in 1945 Ford wrote to schools in the Big Nine (later Big Ten) Conference regarding a transfer. He chose the University of Michigan, which under the legendary coach Fritz Crisler had the type of successful program Ford sought. He was a fine end who played mainly on defense in 1946 and 1947, making major contributions to the undefeated 1947 team that trounced the University of Southern California in the 1948 Rose Bowl game. The season was marred only when Notre Dame edged out the Wolverines for the top spot in a controversial national poll. Ford did not make any of the most prestigious All-American teams, however, a slight he attributed to racism. Ford's view is understandable but not necessarily correct, for Michigan had two men who rated All-American status, the acclaimed tailback Bob Chappuis and the offensive end Bob Mann, a black athlete who was selected to some of the postseason All-American squads. Other teammates also received national attention. Few blacks then played major college football in the North and none played in the South, and Ford was recognized by his selection to play in the College All-Star game in 1948.

Ford then joined the Los Angeles Dons of the short-lived All-America Football Conference (AAFC), playing end both on offense and defense during the 1948 and 1949 seasons. His speed, strength, and sure hands made him a standout receiver, and he was also known as a crushing blocker. When the league disbanded at the conclusion of the 1949 campaign, Ford was selected by the rival Cleveland Browns in a special dispersal draft. The Browns had been the most successful franchise in the AAFC and were one of a handful of teams from it absorbed by the National Football League (NFL). Already blessed with outstanding receivers, Cleveland coach Paul Brown believed Ford's greatest contribution to Cleveland would be as a defensive specialist. According to Brown's assistant Blanton Collier, Ford "had the speed and hands to be a fine tight end. But he was so devastating on defense that we knew this was his natural spot. Len was very aggressive and had that touch of meanness in him on the field that you find in most of the great defensive players. He certainly was the top defensive end of his time and maybe as good as any who played the game." In 1950 the Browns, who had several black regulars, entered the NFL, which had begun to integrate its personnel only in 1946. Ford's season was ruined, and his career was jeopardized, in a mid-October game against the Chicago Cardinals in which he was elbowed in the face by an opposing blocker and suffered a broken nose, two cheekbone fractures, and the loss of several teeth. Cleveland owner Mickey McBride charged the player with deliberate roughness, but Ford minimized the incident, saying he had forgotten to duck. After having plastic surgery he rehabilitated more quickly than expected. Wearing a specially designed helmet, he rejoined the team in time to play an important role-in the league championship game in which the Browns defeated the Los Angeles Rams.

Between 1951 and 1955 Ford reached his peak, winning All-Pro recognition each season and intercepting two passes in the Browns' 1954 championship victory over the Detroit Lions. As a mature athlete he weighed 265 pounds, and his size and quickness allowed him to dominate opposing players. He zealously shed blockers to keep runners from turning his corner and to harass opposing quarterbacks. Defensive coach Collier even recalled that the Browns, who had been using a standard six-man line, accommodated Ford's prowess as a pass rusher by dropping two men off the line so Ford at end would be positioned closer to the opposing quarterback. By allowing Ford to take a sharper angle when rushing the quarterback, this alignment made him more difficult to block. The Browns thus became one of the first teams to switch to the 4-3 defense that became increasingly popular in the 1950s. Six times the Browns defense led the league in fewest points allowed, and Ford's skill in rushing the passer was instrumental to the team's success.

After Cleveland entered a rebuilding period following the 1957 season, the team sold Ford to the Green Bay Packers, and Ford retired after one season there. With a career total of twenty fumbles recovered he held the league's lifetime record in that category at the time of his retirement, and he won recognition along with the Baltimore Colts' Gino Marchetti as one of the two dominant defensive ends of the 1950s. At Michigan and during his early years in the NFL, Ford also made a contribution as a pioneering black athlete. His task was especially difficult in the NFL, which had barred blacks from competition for nearly a generation prior to 1946, but in Paul Brown he had a coach who looked for talent first.

After his retirement Ford, who made Detroit his home, worked as a recreation director for the city and also sold real estate. He was married to an attorney and had two children, but the couple divorced. Ford died in Detroit. He was posthumously selected to the Professional Football Hall of Fame in 1976.

FURTHER READING

Dawzig, Allison. *The History of American Football* (1956).

Levy, Bill. *Return to Glory: The Story of the Cleveland Browns* (1965).

Roberts, Howard. *The Big Nine: The Story of Football in the Western Conference* (1948).

Obituary: *New York Times*, 15 Mar. 1972.

This entry is taken from the *American National Biography* and is published here with the permission of the American Council of Learned Societies.

LLOYD J. GRAYBAR

Ford, West (1785–20 July 1863), caretaker of the historic Mount Vernon home of President George Washington, was born in Westmoreland County, Virginia, the eldest son of Venus, a house slave owned by George Washington's brother, John Augustine, and his wife, Hannah. Though some reports suggest that Ford was the son of President Washington—and that Venus told her mistress that George Washington was her child's father—historians dispute Ford's paternity, suggesting instead that one of Washington's nephews may have been his father.

From 1785 until 1791 George Washington frequently visited the Bushfield Plantation. As he grew older Ford served during these visits as Washington's personal attendant. Washington took him riding and hunting, and Ford often accompanied him to Christ Church, where he was provided with a private pew. After Washington became president of the United States, his open visits with Ford ceased.

Following the death of their father, John Augustine Washington's sons, Bushrod and Corbin, made a gift of Ford to their mother, Hannah. Ford moved to the Mount Vernon Plantation in 1799 after the death of George Washington. He was trained as a carpenter and taught how to read and write. He also became the first tomb guard of the dead president's grave, setting the precedent for three generations of Fords serving in this position at Mount Vernon. In 1802 Hannah Washington's last will and testament decreed that "the lad called West" was to be set free at the age of twenty-one.

Around the year 1805 West Ford was granted his freedom. To commemorate the occasion, the Washingtons hired an artist to sketch his portrait, which was later given to the Mount Vernon Ladies' Association by a descendant of John Augustine Washington Jr., the last private owner of Mount Vernon.

The Washingtons never claimed Ford as blood kin, but treated him like a privileged servant. Ford lived as a free and educated man during a time in U.S. history when most black Americans remained enslaved and were forced to adhere to the rigid slave codes implemented throughout the South. Ford, by contrast, became the caretaker of Mount Vernon and was able to travel the Virginia countryside on business without a pass.

In 1812 Ford married Priscella Bell, a free woman, and the couple eventually had four children, who were born and raised on the Mount Vernon plantation. They were educated at the plantation school house despite laws which restricted the instruction of blacks. Between 1830 and 1860 southern states continued to pass laws forbidding the manumission of slaves and enacted laws to expel free blacks from their states. West and his family were granted asylum by the Washingtons from these laws.

Ford was given 160 acres of land by the terms of Bushrod Washington's will in 1829. In 1833 Ford sold his land and purchased 214 acres adjacent to it, which he later divided up into four 52¾ acres for his children. After the Civil War his property became a refuge and depot for freed slaves. His original plot of land would later be the site of a suburb of Alexandria, Virginia, known as "Gum Springs," and Ford would become known as "the Father of Gum Springs."

Ford continued to manage Mount Vernon until the estate was sold in 1858 to the Mount Vernon

Ladies' Association. The Association hired Ford to help refurbish the mansion house. Ford was interviewed and his picture was sketched a second time by Benson Lossing, a historian of the day. An article was printed in an 1859 *New Harper's Monthly Magazine* about West Ford and Mount Vernon. Benson Lossing stated: "I found him prepared having on a black satin vest and silk cravat, and his curly gray hair arranged in the best manner." Ford, aware of Lossing's surprise at his formal attire, stated, "Artists make colored folks look bad enough anyhow." Ford wrote his name on the sketch, further verifying his status as an educated person.

In June 1863 an ailing West Ford was brought from his home to the Mount Vernon estate by the Mount Vernon Ladies' Association. Members of the association cared for West Ford until his death.

Ford's body was interred in the tomb on the plantation that had once held the remains of George Washington.

FURTHER READING

Allen-Bryant, Linda. *I Cannot Tell a Lie: The True Story of George Washington's African American Descendants* (2002).

Burton, Judith Saunders. "A History of Gum Springs, Virginia: A Report of a Case Study of Leadership in a Black Enclave," Ph.D. diss., May 1986.

Robinson, Henry. "Who Was West Ford?" *Journal of Negro History* (1981).

Morgan, Philip D. *Slave Counterpoint: Black Culture in the Eighteenth-Century Chesapeake & Lowcountry* (1998).

Weincek, Henry. *An Imperfect God: George Washington, His Slaves, and the Creation of America* (2003).

LINDA ALLEN BRYANT

Fordham, Mary Weston (c. Jan. 1844–4 July 1905), poet and educator, was born Mary Weston in Charleston, South Carolina, to Furman Weston, a millwright, and Louisa Bonneau, a seamstress. Both parents were free African Americans. Furman Weston was the son of Mary Furman (Mary Furman Weston Byrd, who is eulogized in Fordham's collection of poetry) and John Weston. Furman Weston was part of the extended Weston family of free African Americans who owned land in the Charleston area and that included the noted clergyman Samuel Weston, a founder of Claflin University. Fordham's eulogy to Samuel Weston—which contains the figurative phrase "fond parent"—has misled scholars into assuming that he was actually her father. Louisa Bonneau's mother Jeanette Bonneau (also eulogized by Fordham) also owned land as a free African American in antebellum Charleston and was a daughter of Thomas Bonneau, a pioneering black educator. Mary had one sister, Jeanette, who lived much of her life with her.

Given her parents' and her extended family's relative economic comfort and ties to education in early black Charleston, it can be assumed that Mary Weston received significant schooling through tutors. She herself later ran a semiclandestine school for African American children during the Civil War, and she seems to have been threatened with arrest at least once. After the war ended she was hired by the American Missionary Association (AMA), and she won note in the Charleston AMA schools as a skilled teacher. She worked diligently even though her pay was half that of her white colleagues; she so impressed her supervisors that one seems to have begun adding to her monthly salary from his own pocket when the AMA refused to consider more equitable pay. By 1868 Weston had married James H. Fordham, an African American with Scottish ancestry who worked as a store clerk; though they had their first child, Milton, later that year, she was still listed as a teacher as late as the 1870 census.

Over the next decade the Fordham family increased in both size and status. By 1880 they had had four more children—Louisa B. (named for Mary Fordham's mother and born c. 1870), Alice (born c. 1873), James (born c. 1876), and Alphonse Campbell (born Oct. 1878). Mary Fordham's sister Jeannette (sometimes listed as Jane or Jennie), who had attended normal school in Massachusetts in the early 1870s, also lived with the family. Mary Fordham was no longer teaching by 1880, and her husband was employed as a city policeman. That he gained such a position is a testament not only to the scope of the family's place among the black elite of the city but also—at least in part probably—to the lightness of the Fordhams' skin color: they are actually listed as "white" in the 1880 census.

Mary Fordham's collection of poetry, *Magnolia Leaves*, was published in December 1897. Prefaced by Booker T. Washington, it received some notice in the black press, including a brief review in the *Colored American*. Washington's preface was no coincidence. The family probably met him in his travels to visit with Charleston's black elite, though an entrée might have been provided by the Reverend Daniel Alexander Payne, a powerful minister who had trained with Samuel Weston and who is celebrated in a poem in *Magnolia Leaves*. Most of the poems address the concerns that Washington saw as central to African American families and to women specifically: a deep faith, a clear attention to the ideals of domestic ideology, and a commitment to education. The collection praised Washington even more directly with an "Ode to the Atlanta Exposition," which opened with and expanded on Washington's famous instructions to African Americans to "cast down your bucket where you are." Thus it was that Washington gave his "cordial endorsement," trusting that readers would "find as much to praise and admire as have I done."

The collection otherwise generally ignores issues of race. It echoes much of the period's poetry in general approach and form, though it is more technically proficient than most. Some of the poems do begin to offer a unique perspective of a young wife and mother's self-definition—which can be quite interesting because of that wife and mother's place within Charleston's African American elite. Especially suggestive of Fordham's struggles is the number of eulogies; in addition to those noted above, the poems eulogize, among others, the family friend Isabel Peace (who died 7 Feb. 1883), the relatives Rebecca Weston (who died 11 July 1875) and Edward Fordham, and most touchingly Fordham's own child Alphonse, who died at age six.

Magnolia Leaves seems to have been Fordham's only book-length work. Around the time of its publication James Fordham seemed to have retired from the police force. By 1900 the family, still living in the two-story home pictured in the frontispiece of *Magnolia Leaves*, consisted of James, Mary, sister Jeanette (who was teaching in the Charleston schools), daughters Louisa and Alice (also teachers), and son Palmer, who seemed to have been born after Alphonse. Fordham died in Charleston, and her husband seemed to have died within a year or two of her because he was not listed in the 1910 home shared by Jeanette, Louisa, and Alice. Although Fordham will probably never achieve the reputation of a figure like FRANCES ELLEN WATKINS HARPER, her work is illustrative both of the artistic expression of the Washingtonian strand of thought and of the understudied lives of the southern African American elite at the end of the nineteenth century.

FURTHER READING

Govan, Sandra Y. "Mary Weston Fordham," in *Notable Black American Women, Book II*, ed. Jessie Carney Smith (1996).

Pease, Jane H., and William H. Pease. *Ladies, Women, and Wenches: Choice and Constraint in Antebellum Charleston and Boston* (1990).

Obituary: *Charleston News and Courier*, 6 July 1905.

ERIC GARDNER

Foreman, George (10 Jan. 1949–), boxer and businessman, was born George Edward Foreman in Marshall, Texas, the son of J. D. Foreman and Nancy Ree. His father, a railroad employee and a heavy drinker, was absent for much of George's childhood. His mother worked several jobs, including as a waitress, to support George and his six siblings.

As Foreman describes it, his childhood was marked by intense want and hunger and an anger that often exploded into fighting. Even at a young age, he was larger than normal, and he used his intimidating size to bully his peers. He had little love for school, although football in junior high school proved attractive for its violence and aggression. Foreman did not last long in high school, however. By the age of fifteen he was spending most of his time on the streets of Houston, where his mother had moved the family when he was quite young. He turned to a life of petty crime, using his size and strength to mug and rob people on the streets. A close call with the police convinced Foreman to rethink his life's direction, and at about this same time his sister turned his interest toward a new program started under President Lyndon B. Johnson's Great Society, the Job Corps. Designed to provide young people from poverty-stricken areas with education and job training, the program was tailor-made for Foreman, and he later credited it with literally saving his life. Through this program Foreman became acquainted with Houston's boxing scene, and in just a few months he had become an amateur boxer. With a mere eighteen amateur bouts under his belt, Foreman entered the Olympic trials for the U.S. boxing team in 1968. He stormed through the trials and represented the United States at the Olympic Games in Mexico City. After winning his first bout by decision, Foreman knocked out his next three opponents to claim the gold medal. He created a controversy when he circled the ring after his victory waving a small American flag. Political tensions were high at the 1968 games, and two of his fellow African American teammates displayed their displeasure over U.S. racism and the Vietnam War by giving the Black Power salute as they stood with their medals while the American national anthem

George Foreman, former heavyweight champion, made an appearance in the lobby of his Kinshasa Hotel to sign autographs and talk with admirers after his bout with Muhammad Ali, 31 October 1974. (AP Images.)

played. Although Foreman was applauded by some for his patriotism, some African Americans decried what they saw as attempts to curry favor with white America. It would not be the last time Foreman was placed in this uncomfortable position.

Soon after the Olympics, Foreman declared that he was turning professional. Beginning in June 1969 he ran off a string of thirty-seven straight victories, thirty-four of those by knockouts. The opposition was not exactly first-rate, and except for a knockout of the over-the-hill George Chuvalo, most people considered his record deceiving. When he signed to fight Joe Frazier for the heavyweight championship in January 1973, Foreman was a heavy underdog. It took a mere round and a half for him to prove the skeptics wrong. The mammoth Foreman bounced Frazier around the ring like a basketball. After the sixth knockdown, the referee ended the fight, and Foreman became the world champion. Unlike many previous champions, however, Foreman was not able to turn his fame and accomplishments into money outside the ring. His fearsome demeanor and bullying of his opponents did not win him many admirers.

Foreman did not gain any new fans with his first title defense against the horribly overmatched Jose Roman. The champion crushed the challenger in one round and then glowered at the crowd. His next fight, in March 1974, promised to provide more of a challenge as he faced Ken Norton, an awkward and dangerous fighter. Once again crowds were treated to an awesome display of punching power, and Norton was dispatched in the second round. When Muhammad Ali demanded a fight with the seemingly invincible Foreman, many fans wondered whether Ali's famous arrogance was getting the best of him. It appeared to many boxing aficionados that Ali's best years of boxing were behind him, and some genuinely feared for his safety against the destructive Foreman. The two fighters agreed to meet in Kinshasa, Zaire (later the Democratic Republic of the Congo), on 30 October 1974. Once again Foreman played the bad guy, as Ali charmed adoring crowds in Zaire.

When the two met in the ring, spectators were aghast as Ali fell back to the ropes again and again while Foreman delivered tremendous blows. The worst fears of Ali sustaining serious injury seemed justified. In fact Ali was deploying what he later called his "rope-a-dope" strategy, in which he rested on the ropes, let Foreman flail away—hitting mostly Ali's arms and gloves—and waited for the lumbering giant to tire. That is precisely what happened, and by the fifth round Foreman was staggering at Ali, winging wild shots that were met by effective counters from Ali. In the eighth round, completely frustrated and exhausted, Foreman was pummeled to the canvas by a flurry of blows from Ali. The invincible Foreman had been defeated.

Foreman did not return to the ring until 1976. He registered five straight knockout victories, one of them against his old foe Frazier. In March 1977 Foreman was upset when the slick-boxing but soft-punching Jimmy Young humiliated the bigger man to gain a unanimous decision. Foreman later claimed that in his dressing room after the fight he had a religious experience that forced him to reevaluate his life. Shortly thereafter he announced his retirement from professional boxing, settled down in Houston, and became an ordained minister in the Church of the Lord Jesus Christ. He turned his attention and activities to raising his family, preaching the gospel, and building his own church.

In 1987 Foreman began one of the most remarkable returns in the annals of boxing history. Now nearing forty years of age and not having fought for almost a decade, he announced that he was going to renew his boxing career to raise money for his family and his church. In the next three years Foreman defeated nineteen men, all but one by knockout. A largely nondescript group of fighters, those opponents did include the former cruiserweight champion Dwight Qawi. During this time Foreman became a television favorite. The idea of the old warrior stepping back into the ring was part of the allure, but this was a new, friendlier, and funnier Foreman who often poked fun at his weight and age and whose quirks, such as naming many of his ten children after himself, added to his appeal. Beginning in 1990 he stepped up the level of competition, destroying the former heavyweight star Gerry Cooney in two rounds. With a few more knockouts under his belt, Foreman challenged EVANDER HOLYFIELD for the heavyweight championship on 19 April 1991. Foreman lost a unanimous decision to the younger, busier fighter, but the loss did nothing to erode his popularity. Following the Holyfield fight, Foreman fought less often. He scored three more victories in 1991–1993, then dropped a twelve-round decision to the top heavyweight Tommy Morrison in June 1993.

For a time it seemed that Foreman had again retired, but he then accepted a fight against the much younger World Boxing Association and International Boxing Federation champion Michael Moorer in November 1994. For most of ten rounds the crowd watched as Moorer moved in and out, picking his shots, while Foreman seemed too slow and old to do much about it. In the tenth round Moorer made the mistake of standing still for a split second too long. Foreman fired a short but devastating right hand, and Moorer went down for the count. Just two months short of his forty-eighth birthday, Foreman became the oldest man in history to win the heavyweight championship. He fought just one fight in each of the next three years and was eventually stripped of his world titles by both the World Boxing Association and the International Boxing Federation for refusing to fight mandatory contenders.

By the time Foreman lost his titles because of inactivity, he had turned his attention to the venture that made him millions more than he made in the boxing ring. His monumental appetite had been a butt of jokes for many years, and Foreman played on his weight many times in interviews. When a group of businessmen approached him about becoming the spokesperson for a "smokeless" grill, Foreman jumped at the chance. He appeared in magazine and television ads, and infomercials for the George Foreman Grill ran almost nonstop on cable television. He parlayed his role as spokesperson into the ownership of a major share of the company that produced the grills, and annual sales soon reached millions of dollars. In addition Foreman gained prominence as a spokesman for Meineke, a car care company. Several books, from cooking guides to self-help tomes, aided his transformation from one of boxing's most intimidating fighters to a popular, even beloved public figure.

FURTHER READING

Foreman, George, with Joel Engel. *By George: The Autobiography of George Foreman* (1995).

MICHAEL L. KRENN

Forman, James (4 Oct. 1928–10 Jan. 2005), civil rights leader and writer, was born in Chicago to Octavia Allen and Jackson Forman. He lived on a farm with his maternal grandmother in Marshall County, Mississippi, until he was six. Then his mother and stepfather, John Rufus, who worked in the stockyards, took him back to Chicago, where he attended St. Anselm's—a Catholic school—and Betsy Ross Grammar School. As a teenager he discovered that John Rufus was not his biological father, and he met Jackson Forman, then a taxi driver. Graduating from Englewood High School in 1947, Forman studied at Wilson Junior College for one semester before he joined the air force, where he served for four years.

The year after his discharge in 1951, Forman started classes at the University of Southern California. One night when he emerged from the library, two Los Angeles police officers arrested him on suspicion of robbery and took him to jail, where he was beaten and subjected to brutal interrogation. He was then taken to a state mental hospital. His first wife, Mary Sears, whom he had married after returning from service in Okinawa, helped get him transferred to the Veteran's Neuropsychiatric Hospital in Los Angeles. After his release he separated from Sears and moved back to Chicago. In the fall of 1954 he started classes at Roosevelt University in Chicago, where he became student government president, graduating in 1957. He then spent a year as a graduate student in African affairs and government at Boston University.

After DAISY BATES helped nine black students to integrate Central High School in Little Rock in 1957, Forman obtained press credentials from the *Chicago Defender* to cover the start of their second year. By this time, Forman knew he wanted to be a writer. He also knew that he wanted to help build a mass movement for racial change. Influenced by India's

James Forman, the civil rights activist who organized the Student Nonviolent Coordinating Committee, enters Riverside Church in New York, 11 May 1969. (AP Images.)

Gandhi and Ghana's Kwame Nkrumah, he wrote a novel, "The Thin White Line" (unpublished), in which the northern protagonist uses nonviolence to organize a mass movement in the South. Planning to go south himself, in 1959 he took education courses at Chicago Teacher's College to qualify as a teacher; that same year he married Mildred Thompson, who joined him in his civil rights work. After a wave of student sit-ins shook the southern status quo in the spring of 1960, Forman traveled to Fayette County, Tennessee, on behalf of an emergency relief committee formed by the Chicago chapter of the Congress of Racial Equality (CORE). Seeing himself as "pamphleteer and historian of our cause" (Forman, 130), he supplied the African American press with articles on sharecroppers evicted from their homes for trying to register to vote. In Nashville, Tennessee, he participated in nonviolent demonstrations, and in Monroe, North Carolina, he supported the local NAACP Chairman ROBERT WILLIAMS's challenge of a segregated swimming pool.

Forman had begun to envision an organization in which he and others would work full time building a civil rights movement, and he talked that idea over with students active in the Student Nonviolent Coordinating Committee (SNCC). SNCC had been a loose coalition formed by students involved in the sit-in movement. As SNCC made the transition in 1961 into an organization with full-time fieldworkers, Forman became its executive secretary. From this point on, he was closely involved with civil rights movement campaigns across the South. For the next five years, as SNCC's chief operational officer, Forman was responsible for raising and disbursing funds, providing legal help for SNCC staff in jail, getting coverage from the media, meeting with representatives of other civil rights organizations, and collecting affidavits to bring attention to brutality. With his eye on history, Forman insisted that staff turn in detailed field reports; as a result, the SNCC archives contain an unparalleled record of community organizing. JULIAN BOND, who worked closely with him, would later write of Forman, "He molded SNCC's near-anarchic personality into a functioning, if still chaotic, organizational structure" (Forman, xi). Forman was not just working the phones. He spoke at mass meetings and walked picket lines. He faced police brandishing guns and went to jail for demonstrating.

The 1964 Mississippi Summer Project brought increasing pressure on SNCC by what Forman saw as an alliance of liberals and labor activists critical of SNCC's relations with organizations some considered communist. Losing his patience during the 1965 Selma campaign, Forman gave what the SNCC chairman JOHN LEWIS called "one of the angriest, most fiery speeches made by a movement leader up to that point." Urging the White House to bring Alabama Governor George Wallace to heel, Forman offered this threat in a Montgomery church: "I said it today, and I will say it again. If we can't sit at the table of democracy, we'll knock the fucking legs *off*!" (Lewis, 340).

In May 1966, weary of criticism of his role in SNCC, which was torn by internal debates over excluding whites, Forman declined renomination as executive secretary. Increasingly, his attention was drawn to Africa, which he had several opportunities to visit, and he became SNCC's international affairs director in 1967. Frantz Fanon's *Wretched of the Earth* had strengthened his view of African Americans as colonized people and his acceptance of violence as a road to freedom. Never committed to nonviolence except as a tactic, Forman now spoke out in favor of armed self-defense and in 1968 he briefly held the title of minister of foreign affairs for the Black Panthers.

After he resigned from that position, Forman reemerged in the political limelight at the 1969 National Black Economic Development Conference held in Detroit by the Interreligious Foundation for Community Organization. Believing that class as well as race played a role in the oppression of blacks, Forman presented a Black Manifesto calling for a socialist revolution against capitalism. He demanded half a billion dollars from Christian churches and Jewish synagogues as reparations for the exploitation of African Americans in the slave trade. The money would be used to establish black-controlled media outlets, a southern land bank, and other institutions that would empower black people. The Manifesto urged delegates to disrupt churches to bring attention to their demands. On 4 May 1969, the day Forman had set for the disruption to begin, he walked up the aisle of Manhattan's Riverside Church, interrupting the morning communion service, to demand reparations. Many present did not stay to hear him, although later the minister, Dr. Ernest Campbell, expressed sympathy with the Manifesto's goals. Although some churches did donate funds to various institutions in response to the Manifesto, the results disappointed Forman.

By the winter of 1969–1970, SNCC had been disbanded, replaced by the Student National Coordinating Committee, and Forman had lost his position as international affairs director. Already the author of one book, *Sammy Younge, Jr., The First Black College Student to Die in the Black Liberation Movement* (1968), he published *The Political Thought of James Forman* (1970) and *The Making of Black Revolutionaries* (1972). He subsequently earned a master's degree in African and Afro-American History from Cornell University (1983) and was awarded a Ph.D. by the Union of Experimental Colleges and Universities (1985). His master's thesis appeared as a book, *Self-Determination and the African American People* (1984).

In the 1980s and 1990s Forman held a position as legislative assistant to the president of the Metropolitan Washington Central Labor Council (AFL-CIO) and taught at American University in Washington, D.C. Cancer diagnosed in the early 1990s undermined his health, but he continued his political activities, organizing support for District of Columbia statehood, working in Democratic presidential campaigns, and serving as president of the Unemployment and Poverty Action Committee and publisher of the Black America News Service. Among his projects since then was a campaign for District of Columbia statehood. A collection of his writing, *The High Tide of Black Resistance and Other Political and Literary Writings*, appeared in 1994. Forman had two sons with his third wife, Constancia Romilly: James Forman Jr., a lawyer, educator, and writer, and Chaka Forman, an actor. His marriage to Romilly ended in divorce.

When *The Making of Black Revolutionaries* was republished in 1997, Julian Bond wrote in a foreword that without James Forman, "there would have been no SNCC, at least not the one that developed in the early 1960s" (Forman, xiii). Forman's work with SNCC endures not only in the lasting changes it engendered but also in the SNCC field reports and *The Making of Black Revolutionaries*—dramatic records of the movement he helped to build.

FURTHER READING

The Student Nonviolent Coordinating Committee Papers, 1959–1972, are available on microform from UMI. Forman's correspondence is available at the Schomburg Center for Research in Black Culture of the New York Public Library.

Forman, James. *The Making of Black Revolutionaries* (1997).

Carson, Clayborne. *In Struggle: SNCC and the Black Awakening of the 1960s* (1995).

Greenberg, Cheryl Lynn, ed. *A Circle of Trust: Remembering SNCC* (1998).

Lewis, John, with Michael D'Orso. *Walking with the Wind: A Memoir of the Movement* (1998).

CAROL POLSGROVE

Forrest, Jimmy (24 Jan. 1920–26 Aug. 1980), jazz and rhythm and blues tenor saxophonist, was born James Robert Forrest Jr. in St. Louis, Missouri, the son of James Forrest and Eva Dowd, a pianist and church organist. His father's occupation is unknown, but he also played music. Forrest started on alto saxophone and switched to tenor about two years later. His first jobs were local, with his mother's trio and, at age fifteen, with Eddie Johnson and the St. Louis Crackerjacks. While still in high school he played with FATE MARABLE's band during summer vacations, from 1935 to 1937. He was a member of the Jeter-Pillars big band, which included the bassist JIMMY BLANTON.

Leaving home, Forrest joined Don Albert's band early in 1938 for jobs in Houston, Fort Worth, and Dallas, Texas, and a long tour of the South and the eastern seaboard. He left Albert by year's end. After a period of work with lesser-known bands, Forrest was working in Dallas in the summer of 1942 when JAY MCSHANN's tenor saxophonist Bob Mabane was drafted. Forrest worked with McShann briefly before replacing Al Sears in ANDY KIRK's orchestra, with which he remained until 1948. He replaced BEN WEBSTER in DUKE ELLINGTON's band for about nine months in 1949–1950, during which time he performed in the film short *Salute to Duke Ellington* (1950). He returned home to St. Louis three days before the birth of one of his children. His wife's name and the marriage date are unknown; they had five children.

In St. Louis a small group under Forrest's leadership recorded "Night Train" (1951), an expansion of a blues theme from Ellington's "Happy Go Lucky Local." Now a classic tune, far better known than Ellington's original, "Night Train" became a nationwide rhythm and blues hit and the anthem of striptease dancers. It also flung Forrest out of jazz circles and onto the rhythm and blues touring circuit for about six years. Returning to jazz, he worked in small groups with the trumpeter Harry "Sweets" Edison from 1958 to 1963, either man serving as leader; JOE WILLIAMS often sang with them. Forrest's recordings during this period include Edison's album *The Swinger* (1958), three tracks as a member of the arranger Andy Gibson's band on the album *Mainstream Jazz* (1959), Forrest's own *All the Gin Is Gone* (1959), the trombonist Bennie Green's *Hornful of Soul* (1960), and the organist Jack McDuff's *Tough Duff* and *The Honeydripper* (both 1961).

After another stop in St. Louis, Forrest moved to the West Coast in 1966, only to suffer a heart attack that summer. In December he played with the tenor saxophonist EDDIE "LOCKJAW" DAVIS. He worked in the house band at Marty's in New York and then rejoined Edison. A second heart attack in 1969 forced him to retire temporarily to California. By 1972 he was keen to go on the road again. He substituted for Davis in COUNT BASIE's big band on 2 June and replaced Davis in October. He left to lead his own band in December 1972 and exactly one year later began a long stay as the star tenor soloist with Basie. He toured internationally with Basie until October 1977, when he formed a quintet with the trombonist Al Grey, but this new affiliation was repeatedly disrupted by Forrest's poor health. The two men performed in England in March 1980. Shortly after a two-week stand in Florida with Grey, Forrest died of a liver ailment in Grand Rapids, Michigan. In 1978 he had married a second time, to Betty Tardy.

Forrest was never entirely comfortable with the hard-hitting simplicity of "Night Train," although naturally he had no complaints about its financial rewards. Like his fellow players ILLINOIS JACQUET and Eddie Davis, he preferred to balance emotive outbursts with fast and heady improvised jazz melody. In this vein Forrest is heard to advantage on the aforementioned albums and even more so with Basie's band in the film documentary *Last of the Blue Devils* (in a segment from around 1976), in which he almost steals the movie in his brief appearance.

FURTHER READING

Obituaries: *New York Times*, 28 Aug. 1980; *Melody Maker*, 13 Sept. 1980; *Down Beat* 47 (Nov. 1980); *Jazz Journal International* 33 (Dec. 1980).

DISCOGRAPHY

Tarrant, Don. "Jimmy Forrest Discography," *Journal of Jazz Discography*, no. 3 (Mar. 1978) and no. 4 (Jan. 1979).

This entry is taken from the *American National Biography* and is published here with the permission of the American Council of Learned Societies.

BARRY KERNFELD

Forrest, Leon (8 Jan. 1937–6 Nov. 1997), writer, journalist, editor, and educator, was born in Chicago to Adelaide Green Forrest and Leon Forrest. The couple met in Chicago after migrating to the city in the late 1920s. Forrest's parents were from different backgrounds: his mother was a New Orleans Creole and devout Catholic; his father was of mixed racial ancestry, a Southern Baptist from Bolivar County, Mississippi. Despite their differences they married and settled on the city's South Side with Leon Sr.'s grandmother, Katie Forrest, in a middle-class section of Chicago's Black Belt. Leon Sr. supported the family by working as a bartender on the Santa Fe railroad and was often away from home. Exposed to the divergent family and religious backgrounds of his parents—his mother was a communicant at Saint Elizabeth Church, his father sang in the choir as member of the Pilgrim Baptist Church—and having a lifelong engagement with extended family, Forrest grew up observing the complexities and dynamic forces shaping African American life in the United States. He incorporated these perspectives into a body of fiction that he described as being "beyond double consciousness."

Products of the Chicago public school system, Forrest's parents also helped him gain an appreciation for music and literature: his father sang, recorded, and wrote song lyrics, while his mother, who wrote short stories, instilled in her son a love of jazz. Forrest attended Wendell Phillips, an all-black elementary school where he won the American Legion Award for the best male student in his class. Using the home address of one of Leon Sr.'s coworkers as his own, Forrest was able to attend Hyde Park High School, a racially integrated and nationally ranked public high school. Although his overall academic record at Hyde Park was undistinguished, Forrest demonstrated promise as a creative writer. Following his graduation in 1955, Forrest attended Wilson Junior College in Chicago, where he took courses in journalism and playwriting. Forrest's time as a student at Wilson (later Kennedy-King College) was brief.

Following his parents' divorce in 1956 Forrest began taking classes in accounting at Chicago's Roosevelt University while working at 408 Liquors, a liquor store and taproom that his mother had purchased after her marriage to William Harrison Pitts, a South Side accountant and businessman. Forrest's time at Roosevelt was also short; showing little interest or aptitude in accounting, he soon dropped out. Forrest had another short stay in the academy when he enrolled in a playwriting class at the University of Chicago extension program during fall 1960. This ended when he was drafted into the United States Army. Upon his return to civilian life Forrest once again enrolled in extension classes at the University of Chicago. His schedule included a course in creative writing with Professor Perrin Holmes Lowery. As Professor Lowery's student he was encouraged to complete a three-act play, *Theater of the Soul*, which was produced in 1967. It was through Lowery that Forrest was introduced to the critic John G. Calweti, who was on the University of Chicago faculty at the time. Working within this support network Forrest began writing in earnest, studying and reading Faulkner and Joyce. It was during this time that Forrest also resumed his work at the 408 as a bartender and clerk. The situation provided him with foundational material for *Divine Days* (1992). This formative period in Forrest's career as a writer ended in August 1964 when his mother died during a surgical procedure related to her intestinal cancer. Less than a year later Perrin Holmes Lowery was killed in a car wreck while visiting family in Virginia.

While absorbing these losses Forrest continued to hone his craft as a writer. During this time, living in a South Side building at 61st and Dorchester with an assortment of artists, musicians, and intellectuals, Forrest supported himself by working as a reporter and editor at several Chicago community newspapers, writing before and after work. His first piece of published fiction, "That's Your Little Red Wagon," appeared in a 1966 volume of the short-lived literary magazine *Blackbird*. Forrest's journalistic experience earned him an editorial position on the staff of *Muhammad Speaks*, the Nation of Islam's official newspaper. Originally hired in 1969 as an associate editor, Forrest rose to become managing editor and was the newspaper's last non-Muslim editor. Forrest remained at *Muhammad Speaks* until 1973, when his first novel, *There Is a Tree More Ancient than Eden*, was published.

Forrest signed the publishing contract for *There Is a Tree* in October 1971, shortly after the death of his father and his marriage to Marianne Duncan. Toni Morrison, then an editor at Random House, recognized the potential of "Wakefulness," the novel's working title. Morrison's enthusiasm for Forrest's work was also shared by Ralph Ellison and Saul Bellow, both of whom endorsed the novel. During his November 1972 interview with Ellison, published in *Muhammad Speaks*, Forrest presented Ellison with bound galleys of *There Is a Tree*. After reading the novel Ellison wrote, "Forrest has given his considerable energies and talents to the discovery of the literary means and angles of vision necessary to reduce this confounding pluralistic society of ours to eloquent form." This letter of praise became the novel's foreword. When *There Is a Tree* was published in May 1973, Forrest dedicated it to Dr. Allison Davis, the noted social anthropologist and psychologist who was his friend and mentor.

With the publication of *There Is a Tree*, Northwestern University invited Forrest to join its Department of African American Studies. He accepted, and in fall 1973 he began teaching a range of courses in both the African American literary tradition and African American culture, including courses on the family in African American literature and on oral tradition and literature. Through most of the twenty-four years that he spent at Northwestern, Forrest continued his own studies, working with Marvin Mirsky of the University of Chicago from 1977 to 1991. Forrest was named full professor in 1984 and became chair of the department in 1985; he served as chair for nine years. In addition to teaching and overseeing the department's administrative tasks Forrest also served as president of the Society of Midland Authors. He was the first African American to hold this position. Forrest also established the annual Dr. Allison Davis Lecture, giving the inaugural lecture in 1982.

Despite these academic achievements Forrest always considered himself to be first and foremost a writer. While on the faculty of Northwestern he maintained a rigorous writing schedule. In addition to the three novels published after *There Is a Tree—The Bloodworth Orphans* (1977), *Two Wings to Veil My Face* (1984), and *Divine Days* (1992)—Forrest wrote essays, collected in *Relocations of the Spirit* (1994), had a verse play, *Recreation* (1978), produced, and penned the libretto for *Soldier Boy, Soldier* (1982), an opera with music by T. J. ANDERSON. It is, however, Forrest's dynamic, luminous fiction that brought him international recognition and acclaim. Addressing the contradictions and complexities converging in the American cultural and historical landscape, Forrest's novels survey issues of history, geography, and memory in African American life. Forrest's fiction explores this terrain, fully energized by his amplification of African American vernacular forms, such as the blues, the folk sermon, and the language play of the dozens. Examining the urban spaces of Forest County, the imaginary Chicago that serves as the setting for each of his novels, Forrest's fiction interrogates a range of subjects, including family, slavery, faith, interracial sex, and violence.

Ultimately *Divine Days*, a 1,100-page epic novel, stands as Forrest's most noted work. Besides being called the "*War and Peace* of the African American novel" by HENRY LOUIS GATES JR., *Divine Days* holds an exceptional place in literary history because all but eight copies of the novel, except for a handful of review copies, were destroyed in a warehouse fire in 1992. Reissued by W.W. Norton in association with Another Chicago Press in 1993, the work is discussed by critics in terms of Faulkner, Ellison, Melville, and Proust. According to John Calweti, *Divine Days* "'transforms, reinvents and stylizes' many things but certainly one of them is the magnum opus of modern literature, James Joyce's *Ulysses*" (252).

Beyond this and like praise, Forrest's fiction earned him awards and honors, including the Carl Sandburg Award, the Friends of Literature Prize, and the *Chicago Sun-Times* Book of the Year Award. In addition, 16 April 1985 was proclaimed Leon Forrest Day in Chicago by Mayor HAROLD WASHINGTON. Forrest continued writing until prostate cancer claimed his life on 6 November 1997. Forrest's life and work were celebrated in a memorial service on the Northwestern campus by notables such as Toni Morrison, James Allen McPherson, Barbara Fields, and STERLING D. PLUMPP. In 2000 *Meteor in the Madhouse*, Forrest's unfinished fifth novel, was published. The novelist, critic, and fellow South Sider Jeffrey Renard Allen described this series of interrelated novellas as demonstrating the "redemptive possibilities of art," while issuing a call for further investigation of African American literature's "invisible man."

FURTHER READING

Cawelti, John G., ed. *Leon Forrest: Introductions and Interpretations* (1997).

Obituaries: *New York Times*, 10 Nov. 1997; *Chicago Tribune*, 8 Nov. 1997.

MICHAEL ANTONUCCI

Forsythe, Albert E. (25 Feb. 1897–4 May 1986), physician and aviation pioneer, was born in Nassau, Bahamas, one of six children of Horatio A. Forsythe, a civil engineer, and Maude Bynloss. During his childhood, the family lived in Jamaica, West Indies, where Forsythe received his early education. When he arrived in America in 1912 to attend Tuskegee Institute in Alabama, his original intention was to study architecture, but as a student of GEORGE WASHINGTON CARVER, he switched his focus to a career in medicine. After graduating from Tuskegee, he attended McGill University Medical School in Montreal, Canada, and in 1930 he earned his medical degree as Doctor of Public Health. Forsythe performed his postgraduate work at Providence Hospital in Chicago, Seaview Sanatorium in New York, and Douglass Hospital in Philadelphia. He moved to Atlantic City, New Jersey, where he began to concentrate on flying airplanes, a dream he had harbored since childhood.

Forsythe took up flying in 1930 just for the pleasure of it; yet he became a trailblazer in aeronautics and helped open the door for black Americans in the field of aviation. He challenged the racist notion that only white men could train to become pilots and that black men could not be taught how to fly airplanes. Ernest Buehl, who had been a German pilot during World War I and was then a flight instructor at a small airfield in Pennsylvania, agreed to teach Forsythe. Around this time, he became acquainted with CHARLES ALFRED ANDERSON of Bryn Mawr,

Pennsylvania, who had also been tutored by Buehl. Anderson had become certified as a private pilot in 1929, and in 1932 he became the first African American to receive his transport license as a commercial pilot in Pennsylvania. Forsythe earned his private pilot's license in New Jersey.

Forsythe and Anderson devised a three-part plan that came to be known as the "goodwill flights." This was a plan to use long-distance flights as a way to promote interracial harmony and to demonstrate the skill of black pilots. The first flight would go from Atlantic City to Los Angeles and back; the second would go from Philadelphia, Pennsyvania, to Montreal, Canada, and back; and the third would go from Miami, Florida, to the West Indies and South America and back. "The trip," according to Forsythe, "was purposely made to be hazardous and rough, because if it had been an ordinary flight, we wouldn't have attracted attention." A group of black businessmen, members of the Atlantic City Board of Trade, sponsored the flight.

Forsythe and Anderson left from Atlantic City's Bader Field at 3 A.M. on 17 July 1933 in Forsythe's Fairchild 24 monoplane, *The Pride of Atlantic City*, equipped with only a compass, an altimeter, and a Rand McNally road map to chart their course. They had no radio, no lights, nor space for parachutes, and made fifty stops before landing in Los Angeles. The round-trip flight took a total of twelve days. The pair braved severe rain, hail, and strong winds, and their engine overheated over the Mojave Desert and barely made it over the Rockies. Upon their return to the East Coast, they were honored in Newark, New Jersey, by a parade attended by fifteen thousand people. These were the years of the Great Depression in a segregated America, and this achievement for blacks in aviation encouraged their next venture, a flight to Montreal, Canada, four months later in November 1933. The second flight proved just as successful as the first, and set another record, making them the first African American pilots to fly over an international border.

Forsythe and Anderson departed on their third flight on 8 November 1934. This expedition was sponsored by the Interracial Goodwill Aviation Committee of Atlantic City. The pair headed for the Caribbean in a new plane, a Lambert Monocoupe, christened the *Booker T. Washington*. The Caribbean flights were considered the most difficult because of a lack of facilities. In Nassau, for instance, there were no runways or landing fields—only seaplanes had landed there previously. Forsythe's parents were among the honored guests who welcomed the pilots when they arrived in the Bahamas. Their next stops were Kingston, Jamaica; Havana, Cuba; and Trinidad. Strong tailwinds forced them off course, and they crash-landed, seriously damaging the plane and forcing Forsythe and Anderson to cancel the remainder of the trip. Anderson continued to fly and spent the next six decades training aviators. In 1939 he initiated the Civilian Pilot Training Program at Howard University, and for the next fifty-three years was chief civilian flight instructor at Tuskegee Institute in Alabama.

Once Forsythe completed the goodwill flights he returned to New Jersey and continued to practice medicine in Atlantic City for the next seventeen years. In 1945 he married Frances Turner, a nurse. They moved to Newark in 1952, where Forsythe practiced medicine until his retirement in 1977. In 1982 Forsythe received the Pioneer in the Field of Aviation award at the Black Wings exhibition at the Smithsonian Institution's National Air and Space Museum, and in 1985 he was inducted into the Aviation Hall of Fame in Teterboro, New Jersey. As a tribute to his pioneering role in black aviation history, representatives of Negro Airmen International, the Tuskegee Airmen, and the Black Pilots Association were honorary pallbearers at his funeral in 1986.

FURTHER READING

"Aviation," *Opportunity - Journal of Negro Life* (Sept. 1934).

"Four Added to Aviation Hall of Fame," *New Jersey Historical Commission Newsletter* (April 1985).

Gubert, Betty Kaplan, Miriam Sawyer, and Caroline M. Fannin. *Distinguished African Americans in Aviation and Space Science* (2002).

Gunther, Robert. "Winging It: Pioneer Pilot Soared for Civil Rights," *Atlantic City Press* (Mar. 1986).

Hardesty, Von, and Dominick Pisano. *Black Wings: The American Black in Aviation* (1983).

"Negro Doctor-Aviator Gets Public Health Degree from McGill," *Opportunity - Journal of Negro Life* (July 1939).

Reilly, H. V. Pat, "Plane Truth: The History of Aviation in New Jersey," *Yesterday Today in New Jersey* (Aug./Sept. 1993).

Terrell, Stanley E. "Dr. Albert Forsythe, Pioneer Black Aviator," *Newark Star-Ledger* (May 1986).

Washington, Mary J. "A Race Soars Upward," *Opportunity - Journal of Negro Life* (Oct. 1934).

Webber, Harry E. "Dr. Albert Forsythe, Pioneer Black Airman Leaves Great Legacy," *New Jersey Afro-American* (May 1986).

RICHLYN FAYE GODDARD

Fort, Jeff (20 Feb. 1947–), gang and organization founder, criminal, was born Jeff Fort in Aberdeen, Mississippi, to John Lee Fort, a steel mill worker, and a mother about whom little information is available. In 1955 Jeff moved with his parents and ten siblings to the South Side of Chicago and settled down in Woodlawn, a middle-class white neighborhood prior to the influx of blacks migrating from the South, and the backdrop for Woodlawn native LORRAINE HANSBERRY's play, A *Raisin in the Sun.* Jeff's father John Lee Fort had secured employment in a Chicago steel mill. Spurning hostile neighbors and a divided community, Fort, twelve years old and relatively small for his age, organized a group of boys who patrolled Blackstone Street between the corners of 64th and 66th where his family lived, to battle with white and black gangs in the area. In 1960, one year later, Fort founded the Blackstone Rangers together with rival gang leader Eugene "Bull" Hairston after a truce, earning Fort the nickname "Angel" for his smooth resolution of their differences. Now age thirteen, Fort, whose formal education ended in fourth grade, led a band of petty thieves largely made up of young boys from two Illinois juvenile detention centers, dressed in their colors, red, and shouting their slogan, "Stones Run It!"

Jeff Fort, a leader of the Blackstone Rangers street gang in Chicago, stands to testify before the Senate Permanent Investigations sub committee, 9 July 1968. Fort later walked out of the hearing after only giving senators the opportunity to ask his name. (AP Images.)

In 1965 Fort and Hairston came under the tutelage of John Fry, minister of the First Presbyterian Church in Woodlawn. Fry hoped to redirect Fort's energy in a-positive direction and coordinate the Blackstone Rangers into a humanitarian organization. In 1966 Fort and Hairston held a meeting that would bring together twenty-one leaders of Chicago gangs to form "the Main 21." This alliance, now known as Black P. Stone Nation (BPSN) became Chicago's first to establish itself in states outside of Illinois. The P. in the moniker has been said to stand for "Peace," "Power," and "People." In the same year, Hairston was sent to prison on a drug charge, leaving Fort in charge of BPSN's 50,000 members. Hairston was released two years later, but Fort arranged to have one of Hairston's ranking leaders killed, thereby obstructing Hairston from regaining his seat as leader.

The Woodlawn Organization, born out of a movement to save the community and led by Arthur Brazier of the Apostolic Church of God, agreed with Fry that proper guidance and funding could sway the BPSN in a positive and constructive direction. Chicago mayor Richard J. Daley vehemently opposed any such assistance; nevertheless, BPSN was awarded a federal government grant totaling $927,000 to fund a job-training program, instructed by ranking gang members. Soon thereafter a Senate subcommittee began to investigate BPSN for misuse of government funds and summoned Fort to Washington, D.C., for questioning. Fort appeared before the subcommittee as ordered; however, he only stated his name then walked out, never removing the dark sunglasses from his eyes. Fort reveled in the national media attention he and BPSN were receiving. In 1967 the musician and writer OSCAR BROWN JR., also from Woodlawn, helped Fort organize "Opportunity Please Knock," a musical review company with young people from Woodlawn, most of them not BPSN members. The group flew to Los Angeles to perform on the Smothers Brothers television show, feeding the illusion of Fort's genuine efforts to change the direction of BPSN.

In 1969 Fort, by then convicted of contempt of Congress, was invited to the inauguration of President Richard M. Nixon, whose party believed Fort's group to be exemplary of progress in urban areas under organized leadership and government support. Fort sent Mickey Cogwell, head of the Egyptian Cobras, in his place. The same year Fort met with Fred Hampton, chairman of the Black Panther Party's Illinois State Chapter. Hampton hoped to join forces with Fort in Woodlawn to facilitate children's programs and arouse political involvement. After a brief meeting, Hampton was threatened and dismissed by Fort, who was unwilling to share BPSN-controlled territory.

In 1972 Fort was convicted of conspiring to defraud the federal government of nearly one million dollars that was intended for inner city programs and sentenced to serve four years at Leavenworth. In March 1976 Fort was released from prison; he had become a devout Muslim. When refused membership to the Moorish Science Temple in Milwaukee, Wisconsin, due to his gang affiliation and knowledge of his lawlessness, he founded the El Rukn Moorish Science Temple of America in Chicago's South Side. A month later Fort held a BPSN meeting to announce "El Rukn" as the new name of his religious organization and himself as "Imam" or "Chief Malik," the sole leader of the "El Rukn Nation." The El Rukns purchased an old theater and renamed it the "El Rukn Grand Major Temple of America," commonly referred to as "the Fort," which had reinforced steel doors and windows. The organization bought numerous apartment buildings and hotels on Chicago's South Side, formed the "El-Pyramid Maintenance and Management Corporation," even started a security guard business; however, their biggest earnings came from their dealings in narcotics. During Chicago's 1983 mayoral election, an operative for the candidate Jane Byrne paid $10,000 to Fort's El Rukns to campaign on her behalf. Instead they rallied behind Harold Washington, who would win the election and become the first African American Mayor of Chicago. The El Rukns were also instrumental in Jesse Jackson's 1984 presidential campaign in Chicago. Despite Fort's troubled history, politicians sought his aid and favor because of the control and influence he and his organization held in the African American community and among ranking city officials.

In 1983 Fort pled guilty for interstate conspiracy to distribute narcotics after telephone conversations with an Aberdeen, Mississippi, drug dealer were wiretapped by the FBI. Fort fled to Pakistan to avoid imprisonment then later turned himself in. Directing his "generals" from prison, in 1986 Fort sent El Rukn representatives to Libya to meet with Colonel Muammar al-Qaddafi to negotiate asylum from prosecution for El Rukns and $2.5 million in exchange for acts of terrorism committed against the United States. The El Rukns unknowingly purchased an anti-tank missile launcher from an FBI agent and in 1987, Fort was back in court; this time he would be sentenced to eighty years for conspiring with a foreign government to commit terrorist acts against the United States. Because Fort was known to control his troops from within jail as much as on the streets, his sentence at the federal prison in Marion, Illinois, was to be served in solitary confinement. In the same year, Fort was relocated to Cook County Jail in Chicago to await trial for the murder of a local drug dealer who had been killed prior to his incarceration, and was again free to commune with inmates because federal prison restrictions did not apply. In 1988 at the age of forty-one Jeff Fort was convicted and sentenced to another seventy-five years in the Illinois prison system.

FURTHER READING

Fry, John R. *Fire and Blackstone* (1969).

Lemann, Nicholas. *The Promised Land: The Great Black Migration and How It Changed America* (1992).

Royko, Mike. *Boss: Richard J. Daley of Chicago* (1971).

SAFIYA D. HOSKINS

Fort, Syvilla (3 July 1917–8 Nov. 1975), dancer, choreographer, and dance teacher, was born in Seattle, Washington, the daughter of Mildred Dill. Her mother tried to enroll the four-year-old Syvilla in ballet classes, but teachers refused her entrance because they were afraid they would lose clientele by admitting an African American student. Her mother then recruited a group of black children interested in learning dance and hired the advanced white ballet students to teach them. At nine Syvilla had private teachers and was on her way to becoming an African American pioneer in ballet and modern dance.

Sensitive throughout her life to discrimination, Fort passed on what she learned to other black children. As a high school freshman, she taught ballet, tap, and modern dance to as many as sixteen children under the age of thirteen for fifty cents a lesson. In 1935 Fort received a scholarship and became the first black student to attend the Nellie Cornish School of Allied Arts, known for its experimental melding of dance, music, and drama. She was embraced by the city of Seattle for dance and choreography in which she blended modern dance with ballet. In 1938 she requested that John Cage compose a piano piece for a dance, *Bacchanal*. The result was his first prepared piano composition.

Fort graduated from Cornish in 1938, moved to Los Angeles, and was recommended by William Grant Still, the black composer, to Katherine Dunham, the pioneer black concert dancer and teacher of the 1940s.

Fort toured with the all-black Dunham Dance Company as a soloist and joined Dunham in her mission to return the ceremonial meaning to imported dances—in the words of Dunham, "to take *our* dance out of the burlesque." Dunham accomplished this by imbuing modern dance with dance techniques from African American cultural heritage. To classical ballet Dunham added isolated body movements that she discovered in her study of West Indian and African dance. Early productions in which Fort danced were characterized by theatrical lighting and lush costumes and scenery.

Fort was a solo sensation in Los Angeles after performing in the 1942 All-Negro Artists Concert for Russian war relief at the Wilshire-Ebell Theater. The critic Tom Cullen praised Fort as "incredibly graceful, with a beautifully-built body and the ease that comes with complete mastery of technique." Fort conducted research on the mixed folk dance of Native Americans, Mexicans, and African Americans off the Florida and Georgia coasts, then blended techniques to develop her own version of American dancing. She formed her own group of twelve dancers and "insist[ed] upon it remaining a mixed group. I know from the hard struggle I had to go through that this business of racial discrimination must be dragged out into the open and faced squarely."

Fort teamed up with Dunham because together they had a better chance of attaining their larger vision of getting African Americans recognized as performing artists. Fort appeared with the Dunham dancers in the film *Stormy Weather* (1943). The film's success gained the Dunham Dance Company national recognition. In September 1943 Dunham and her company opened to great acclaim at New York's Martin Beck Theatre in a production titled *Tropical Revue*. The dance *Rites de Passage*, based on a fertility ritual, was banned in Boston for sexual content but hailed elsewhere. In 1945 Fort took the position of ballet mistress and supervising director at Dunham's newly established School of Arts and Research in New York City, teaching Dunham's dance technique and the cultural heritage from which it evolved. Included in the curriculum were philosophy, language, speech, and ethnology. Neglect of a knee injury ended Fort's dancing career, and it was as a teacher of adults and children at the Dunham school that she gained recognition.

After the Dunham school closed in 1955 owing to lack of funds, Fort taught at the Lee Strasberg Institute, Columbia University Teachers College, and New York City's Clark Center of Performing Arts. In 1955 with her husband, the tap dancer Buddy Phillips, she opened the Phillips-Fort Studio in the theater district on West Forty-fourth Street, where she introduced her Afro-modern technique. Fort drew on dance techniques from Africa, the West Indies, Haiti, and early American black jazz to create a technique freer than Dunham's with isolated upper-body movements backed by the roll of African drums. Like Dunham, Fort believed in dance as communication and so believed in training the mind as well as the body. If she imported a dance, she strove to provide an explanation of its original meaning.

Fort taught with an encouraging yet firm approach. Her list of students includes Butterfly McQueen, Alvin Ailey, Eartha Kitt, James Earl Jones, and a host of celebrities, including the actors Marlon Brando and Jane Fonda. Harry Belafonte and the government of Guinea later recruited Fort to go to Africa to help establish a dance company. Fort served as choreographer for Langston Hughes's *The Prodigal Son* and composed many other works. After the death of her husband in 1963, Fort continued to run the small Manhattan studio, but her habit of teaching free of charge led to financial difficulties, and she was forced to close the studio. Before this, however, the young filmmaker Ayoka Chenzira captured Fort on film teaching in her studio. In the documentary *Syvilla: They Dance to Her Drum* (1979), Chenzira recognized Fort as the important developmental link between Katherine Dunham and Alvin Ailey.

Nine months before her death from breast cancer, Fort was honored at the Majestic Theater by the Black Theatre Alliance, formed in 1969 to provide central resources to the African American theater community. The event exhibited Fort's contribution to the development of African American modern dance and the success with which the African American community could organize a benefit occasion. Proceeds from the event established the Syvilla Fort Fund to assist nonprofit dance and theater institutions with scholarships, aid a training school founded by Fort, and provide an emergency fund for dancers. Fort died in New York City.

FURTHER READING

Emery, Lynne Fauley. *Black Dance: From 1619 to Today* (1972).

Long, Richard A. *The Black Tradition in American Dance* (1989).

Thorpe, Edward. *Black Dance* (1990).

Obituaries: *Dance News*, Dec. 1975; *New York Times*, 9 Nov. 1975.

This entry is taken from the *American National Biography* and is published here with the permission of the American Council of Learned Societies.

BARBARA L. CICCARELLI

Forte, Ormond Adolphus (17 Dec. 1887–14 Jan. 1959), journalist and local politician, was born to Lillian L. Forte, a seamstress, in Barbados. After attending Harrison College, the multilingual Forte worked for various European firms with interests in Barbados. He arrived in the United States on 10 May 1910 aboard the S.S. *Karona* along with his future mother-in-law, Edwardina Grant, and future wife, Ida. While his initial destination was Xenia, Ohio, Forte soon settled in Cleveland and married Ida Grant later that year. The couple's first child, a daughter named Hilda, was born in late 1911 and was followed by daughters Thelma and Edna and sons Ormond, Jr., and Frederick. Ida returned to Barbados in 1916 to bring Forte's mother Lillian to the United States permanently. Forte became a naturalized U.S. citizen in March of 1920.

In Cleveland, Forte found employment with Daniel Rhodes Hanna, the white publisher of the *Cleveland Leader* and the *Cleveland News* and a man who had grown rich from the iron and coal industries. In hopes of expanding his market in Cleveland's black community, Hanna supported Forte's founding of the *Cleveland Advocate* in 1914. The paper would last for a decade, taking a much more "moderate" (and often conservative) stance on racial issues than the *Cleveland Gazette*, a competing black newspaper. Still, the *Advocate* was a pioneer among the black press in terms of its coverage of World War I; contributing editor Ralph W. Tyler actually went to France with black troops, reported extensively on the war efforts, and helped Forte put together a historic "Soldiers' Edition" of the paper on 14 June 1919. While Forte's editorial stance became a bit more actively anti-segregationist and engaged larger segments of the black community, the paper's sales base was never especially healthy, and the *Advocate* folded in 1924. Forte began a second paper, the weekly *Cleveland Herald*, soon after; however, it similarly lacked a strong financial base and closed in 1927.

Forte's journalist experience, education, and connections within the black community—as well as his often accommodationist politics—led to a series of local and state engagements as well as minor political appointments. He served for several years as a trustee of Wilberforce University, although he received the most public notice not for his fund-raising work but for a nasty and now generally unknown battle with HALLIE Q. BROWN and the National Association of Colored Women over Brown's removal from a chair in Wilberforce's education department in late 1922 and early 1923.

Forte was an Assistant Superintendent for Cleveland in the late 1920s and moved to a clerk's position in the City Garbage Department in the early 1930s—both through Republican political patronage. In 1932, he was charged with soliciting and accepting bribes from various garbage truck drivers. Forte maintained that he was the victim of a "political frame-up"; at the very least, he was a target of the police, who marked the money he received for one of the bribes. He was convicted and given an indeterminate sentence at the Ohio State Penitentiary in June of 1932, and he was paroled in February of 1933. While this scandal effectively removed him from city government, it did not detract significantly from his power within the conservative black community.

He founded the weekly *Cleveland Eagle* in late 1934 and ran the paper until 1938, when he resurrected the *Herald*. He was sole proprietor of the *Herald* until 1950 and then incorporated it under the rubric of the Ohio Daily Enterprise Corporation, of which he was both president and treasurer. Perhaps the *Herald*'s most significant achievement was its 46-page supplement on "Negro Achievement" published on 4 July 1950, which remains a key source on early black Cleveland residents. Forte sold the paper to Carribell Johnson Cook, a Columbus business woman, in late 1953, and evidence suggests that she closed it down in 1954. Throughout these years, Forte also wrote—mainly on news of black Cleveland—for several other black papers including the *Chicago Defender*, the *Pittsburgh Courier*, and the *New York Amsterdam News*. He also continued his community work, including efforts with the Greater Cleveland Hospital Association.

Forte died at Cleveland's Forest City Hospital. While his influence was largely confined to Ohio, he must be recognized as an important figure both in black Cleveland's early twentieth century history and in African American journalism.

FURTHER READING

The Encyclopedia of Cleveland History, online at http://ech.case.edu.

ERIC GARDNER

Forten, James (2 Sept. 1766–4 Mar. 1842), businessman and social reformer, was born in Philadelphia, Pennsylvania, the son of Thomas Forten, a freeborn sailmaker, and Margaret (maiden name unknown). James's parents enrolled him in the African School of abolitionist Anthony Benezet. When James was seven, his father died. Margaret Forten struggled to keep her son in school, but he was eventually forced to leave at age nine and work full time to help support the family. His family remained in Philadelphia throughout the American Revolution, and Forten later recalled being in the crowd outside the Pennsylvania State House when the Declaration of Independence was read to the people for the first time.

In 1781, while serving on a privateer, Forten was captured by the British and spent seven months on the infamous prison ship *Jersey* in New York harbor.

After a voyage to England in 1784 as a merchant seaman, Forten returned to Philadelphia and apprenticed himself to Robert Bridges, a white sailmaker. Bridges taught Forten his trade, loaned him money to buy a house, and eventually sold him the business. Inheriting most of Bridges's customers and establishing a reputation as a master craftsman in his own right, Forten prospered. His profits were invested in real estate, loans at interest, and eventually in bank, canal, and railroad stock.

In 1803 Forten married Martha Beatte, of Darby township, Delaware County, Pennsylvania. She died in 1804, and a year later he married Charlotte Vandine, a Philadelphian of European, African, and Native American descent. They had eight children. The Forten children, MARGARETTA FORTEN, HARRIET FORTEN PURVIS, SARAH FORTEN PURVIS, James, and ROBERT BRIDGES FORTEN—along with Robert's daughter, CHARLOTTE L. FORTEN GRIMKÉ—were all active in the antislavery movement.

Forten's emergence as a leader in Philadelphia's black community coincided with his growing prosperity. Well-read and articulate, he was often called on to draft petitions and to chair meetings. In 1799 he joined other black citizens in petitioning for an end to the slave trade and for legislation to prevent the kidnapping of free people. When Congress refused to consider the petition, Forten wrote to thank the one man, George Thatcher of Massachusetts, who had spoken in its favor. The letter attracted considerable attention.

In 1813, responding to an attempt by the state legislature to restrict the rights of black Pennsylvanians, Forten published *Letters from a Man of Colour*. Attacking the proposed legislation, he cited Pennsylvania's reputation as a haven for the oppressed. He also objected strenuously to a law that would reduce all black people, including "men of property," to the status of felons.

Forten's role in the debate over African repatriation was pivotal. He was initially enthusiastic about the proposal of the African American shipowner PAUL CUFFE SR. to take American free blacks to Britain's colony of Sierra Leone. Forten had no intention of relocating, but he agreed with Cuffe that less fortunate members of the community might benefit from emigrating.

With the formation of the American Colonization Society (ACS) in 1816, Forten moved from support of African resettlement to outspoken opposition. At first, when approached by an officer of the ACS whom he knew to be a dedicated abolitionist, he gave the organization a qualified endorsement. When others in the ACS spoke of the need to deport free blacks to the new colony of Liberia because of their "pernicious" influence on the slaves, however, Forten expressed alarm. The leaders of the ACS repeatedly urged him to set an example by emigrating. They offered him incentives to begin a packet service between the United States and Liberia. Forten was unmoved, and for the rest of his life he remained one of the most vocal critics of the ACS.

Freeborn, Forten was a lifelong opponent of slavery, and he worked with two generations of white abolitionists. He had many contacts with the "gradualists" in the Pennsylvania Abolition Society (PAS). He hired servants recommended by the PAS, sent his four sons to the PAS school, and even took into his home an African prince the society was educating. However, neither he nor any other African American was invited to join the PAS.

The extent of Forten's involvement in the antislavery cause changed with the emergence of the "new school" abolitionists in the early 1830s. William Lloyd Garrison became a close personal friend and often visited the Forten home. Forten advanced him money to begin publishing the *Liberator*. Thereafter he gave advice on sales and distribution and more money to tide Garrison over periodic crises. In 1832, when Garrison was preparing his *Thoughts on African Colonization*, Forten sent him his own collection of material on the ACS. He was elected a vice president of the new American Anti-Slavery Society and helped organize auxiliaries at the state and local levels.

Forten saw the abolition of slavery as one aspect of a moral crusade to transform society. Temperance, education, pacifism, and women's rights all had their place in his vision of America. In 1834 Forten and a group of like-minded black reformers founded the American Moral Reform Society, braving criticism from their own community that they were unrealistic, naive, and lacking in racial pride as they advocated the abandonment of terms of racial identification, promoted a sweeping reform agenda, and vowed to direct their efforts at all Americans, regardless of race.

In the last decade of his life Forten's faith in the power of reform to regenerate society was severely tested. As a wave of racial violence swept the country, he, his family, and the community institutions to which he belonged all came under attack, including mob violence and destruction of property. On several occasions he received death threats because of his opposition to colonization.

The violence was accompanied by an erosion of the civil rights of Pennsylvania's African Americans. In 1832 Forten and his son-in-law, ROBERT PURVIS, protested a move by the state legislature to restrict the mobility of black Pennsylvanians. In 1838 Pennsylvania's constitution was revised. Blacks, regardless of wealth, were barred from voting, while most adult white men were enfranchised. On behalf of his community, Forten brought suit to establish his right to vote. After losing the case, he helped finance the printing of an appeal urging voters to reject the proposed constitution. Nevertheless, the constitution was ratified by a large majority.

In 1841 deteriorating health obliged Forten to curtail his business activities and his reform work. When he died in Philadelphia, the abolitionist press eulogized him, the local papers commented on the many prominent white merchants who attended his funeral, and the *African Repository*, the journal of the ACS, regretted that to the end he did not change his mind about colonization.

FURTHER READING

Forten's letters are in the Paul Cuffe Papers at the New Bedford Free Public Library, New Bedford, Massachusetts; the Antislavery Manuscripts at the Boston Public Library; the Historical Society of Pennsylvania; and the Pennsylvania Abolition Society.

Billington, Ray Allen. "James Forten—Forgotten Abolitionist," *Negro History Bulletin* 13 (Nov. 1949).

Douty, Esther M. *Forten the Sailmaker: Pioneer Champion of Negro Rights* (1968).

Nash, Gary. *Forging Freedom: The Formation of Philadelphia's Black Community, 1720–1840* (1988).

Ripley, C. Peter, ed. *Black Abolitionist Papers, 1830–1865* (1981).

Winch, Julie. *Philadelphia's Black Elite: Activism, Accommodation, and the Struggle for Autonomy* (1988).

This entry is taken from the *American National Biography* and is published here with the permission of the American Council of Learned Societies.

JULIE WINCH

Forten, Margaretta (11 Sept. 1808–14 Jan. 1875), teacher, abolitionist, and women's rights advocate, was born in Philadelphia, Pennsylvania, the daughter of JAMES FORTEN, a sailmaker and social reformer, and Charlotte Vandine, a Philadelphian of European, African, and Indian descent. Named after her paternal grandmother, Margaret Forten, Margaretta Forten was the oldest of eight surviving children, including HARRIET FORTEN PURVIS, SARAH FORTEN PURVIS, ROBERT BRIDGES FORTEN, and James Forten Jr., who were all active in the antislavery movement. James Forten was a highly successful businessman, and his accomplishments offered Forten and her siblings unusual access to education and influence. She received advanced instruction from a private tutor, was a skilled artist, and most likely had reading knowledge of French. Her father's financial largess also gave her social connections and organizational shrewdness that helped her work among black and white reformers for nearly forty years.

In 1833 Forten was one of forty-two women, nine of them black, including her mother, Charlotte, her sisters Sarah and Harriet, GRACE BUSTILL DOUGLASS, and Lucretia Mott, who organized the Philadelphia Female Anti-Slavery Society (PFASS). SARAH MAPPS DOUGLASS joined the organization soon after. Theoretically the PFASS founders were organizational novices. However, after receiving their charge to organize following the first meeting of the all-male American Anti-Slavery Society, the founders wrote a constitution and developed an organizational structure within a matter of days.

PFASS had a defined hierarchy with tasks assigned to each officer and regularly scheduled meetings. Forten and her peers had a clear sense of mission, and though they might not have had direct experience in management outside a family enterprise, they brought a degree of organizational sophistication to the society. Other female abolition societies appeared in eastern cities, including Boston and New York, during this time, but PFASS was notable because of its longevity and extensive record keeping. Forten was part of a group that intentionally sought to leave a documentary history of the organization's work. The women issued annual reports that chronicled PFASS successes and setbacks in the drive to end slavery and improve educational opportunities for the black community. When the group disbanded, its books and publications were deposited with the Historical Society of Pennsylvania for preservation. These women were not content merely to do good works; they acted to leave a record for posterity.

The Philadelphia society also stood out by virtue of its dual mission: the end of slavery and the eradication of prejudice. Racial integration was one of the society's core concepts, and black women held important leadership positions along with their white peers. Forten became the group's first recording secretary, and Mott served as PFASS's first corresponding secretary. Throughout the thirty-seven-year life of the organization, Forten held positions in which she collected and disbursed funds or affected the society's policy on how best to undermine slavery.

As the PFASS treasurer, Forten oversaw the distribution of funds to a local Philadelphia school for black children. She created balance sheets that carefully identified all credits and debits for the society's annual report. In the years when she was not the treasurer, Forten audited the society's books. Her constant involvement with the PFASS financial records implied that she had a knack for numbers. However, beyond her personal skills, one might consider Forten as a conduit for the particular brand of abolition supported by her father. The ability and willingness-to work with sympathetic whites had been a distinguishing characteristic of the Forten family history. But in the 1830s the male Fortens were squeezed out of positions of influence in abolitionist circles as white hostility to blacks led to riots, exclusion from trades, and legal disenfranchisement.

James Forten had been an early supporter of William Lloyd Garrison. As Philadelphia's black community grew to include other ideological positions on the topics of slavery and race, the Forten rhetoric declined in prominence. Margaretta Forten's brothers James Forten Jr. and Robert Forten never attained their father's visibility in the community of white abolitionists, and the family's financial resources declined with the death of James Forten in 1842. Margaretta Forten was the family member with the most consistent history of participation in abolition. Another indication of her skill in protecting the family's interests came from her father's will. She was one of three persons assigned to oversee the distribution of her father's estate. Her brothers were full-fledged adults when their father died, James Jr. was thirty-one and Robert was twenty-nine, but the responsibility of executing the will rested with Margaretta, her mother, and a son-in-law.

Forten's adroit problem-solving abilities were critical to the survival of her family. She nurtured her niece CHARLOTTE FORTEN GRIMKÉ, negotiated a pension for her brother Robert's widow, and went to court to salvage the property of her sister Sarah Forten Purvis after her husband died. Forten ran a private school from the family home starting in 1850. The school was a source of income and another way to pass along the educational and social values of the Fortens. A statistical report on Philadelphia's black population noted that Forten's school had ten students and that some of the young scholars boarded at the Forten home.

Forten remained a member of PFASS through the best and worst years of the antislavery movement. She was among the conventioneers in 1838, when a mob burned Pennsylvania Hall, a meeting site for which she and her fellow abolitionists had raised funds. She chose not to re-direct her organizational talents when the issue of women's rights caused dissent in the 1840s, nor did she fade from participation when faced with racism from white abolitionists.

Forten forged a career in abolition that stretched the gender and racial boundaries of the period. However, she was much like most women of her generation. She was not a public figure, although black and white abolitionists knew of her work and social connections. Some of the black women who later spoke on the antislavery lecture circuit or who were openly critical of black-white relations were not unfamiliar to Forten, but these were younger women—like MARY SHADD CARY, FRANCES WATKINS HARPER, and SARAH PARKER REMOND—who focused their reform energies on direct communication with the public. Forten's life was notable because she represented a measure of interracial cooperation and optimism that vanished as the abolition movement matured and splintered. A separate women's rights agenda, while important, was not a dominant theme for her work. She died in Philadelphia.

FURTHER READING

Horton, James Oliver. *Free People of Color* (1993).

Nash, Gary B. *Forging Freedom* (1988).

Winch, Julie. *A Gentleman of Color* (2002).

ALFREDA S. JAMES

Forten, Robert Bridges (12 May 1813–25 Apr. 1864), abolitionist, businessman, and Civil War soldier, was born in Philadelphia, Pennsylvania, the fifth of nine children of James Forten, a sailmaker and Revolutionary War veteran, and Charlotte Vandine. He was named for the white craftsman who befriended his father and gave him his start in business. Of his siblings, Margaretta Forten, Harriet Forten Purvis, Sarah Forten Purvis, James Forten Jr., and William Forten became active in the antislavery movement. Robert Forten received his early education at a school his parents and other affluent black Philadelphians established because of the failure of the city's board of education to provide adequate schooling for their children. Eventually Robert and his brothers transferred to the Pennsylvania Abolition Society's Clarkson School, although they may also have studied with the private tutors their parents hired to teach their sisters at home.

Growing up, Forten developed a wide range of intellectual interests. Congressman William D. "Pig Iron" Kelley, a childhood friend, remembered him as an accomplished musician and a talented artist. Another friend, the African Methodist Episcopal (AME) bishop Daniel Alexander Payne, recalled Forten as "a more than ordinary mathematician, and ... gifted with a poetical vein" (Payne, 51). By the time he was in his mid-teens, Forten's formal education ended and he began working in his father's sail loft. Like so many of the members of his extended family, he soon became active in the antislavery cause. He made his debut as a public speaker in 1834, addressing the Philadelphia Female Anti-Slavery Society—of which his mother and sisters were founding members—on the role of women as social reformers.

On 18 October 1836 Forten married Mary Virginia Wood, a native of Hertford, North Carolina, who had been living in Philadelphia for several years. She was a member of the Female Anti-Slavery Society, and it was probably through his own involvement in abolition that Forten met her. The young couple began their married life in Forten's parents' home, where their daughter Charlotte Forten Grimké was born on 17 August 1837. By the time their son was born in 1839 they had purchased a home of their own.

Marriage and a family did not diminish the time and energy Forten devoted to the struggle to end slavery. He continued to speak and write on the need for immediate abolition. As for civil rights, in 1838 he joined other members of the African American community in trying to prevent ratification of the proposed new Pennsylvania state constitution, which categorically barred black men from voting.

In 1840 Forten suffered a devastating double tragedy. On 11 May, just a few days short of his first birthday, Forten's son died. As Forten wrote in reply to a letter of condolence, he knew he must soon face another loss, for his wife was suffering from tuberculosis. She died just two months after her son. After Mary's funeral, Forten moved back in with his parents, and his mother and elder sister assumed the responsibility of raising his daughter.

Work of various kinds offered some solace. As a member of the Philadelphia Vigilance Committee, Forten helped coordinate aid for the hundreds of fugitive slaves who flocked to the city every year. With his father's retirement in 1841, Forten became more involved in the day-to-day running of the sail loft. He also pursued his love of astronomy, teaching the subject at the school Payne opened and constructing his own telescope, which was accepted for exhibition at Philadelphia's Franklin Institute.

Forten clearly found antislavery work and intellectual endeavors more rewarding than trying to keep the family business afloat. The racial climate the younger Fortens had to grapple with by the late 1830s was far more hostile than the one their father had known when he was starting out in business four decades earlier. In addition to growing racism, they had to reckon with the shock waves running through the entire business community as a result of the panic of 1837. Like many firms, James Forten and Sons was left holding worthless notes as customers defaulted.

The firm barely survived the death of its founder James Forten in 1842. Creditors apprehensive about its stability hastened to call in their debts, even as Robert Forten and his elder brother James

Forten Jr. pressed those indebted to them for payment. Robert loaned his own money to the firm, and the family sold real estate in an effort to stave off the inevitable. Bankruptcy overtook the brothers in the spring of 1844. James promptly fled the state, leaving Robert to salvage what he could. Eventually he negotiated a sale of the firm's remaining assets to two of its employees.

Forten regained a measure of financial stability in 1845 through an advantageous second marriage to Mary Hanscome, a wealthy young widow from South Carolina. Her first husband, Joseph Hanscome, had been the son of a Charleston-area planter and a free woman of color. When Joseph Hanscome received his inheritance from his father, he purchased his own plantation, which he operated with slave labor. After his death in 1838, his widow sold the plantation and its slaves and moved to Philadelphia with her late husband's brother and his family. The move was apparently prompted not by unease over the South's "peculiar institution" but by frustration over the increasingly circumscribed status of free people of color in South Carolina.

The alliance of an ardent abolitionist and a woman who had knowingly profited from owning slaves was an unlikely one, but it gave Forten and his daughter financial security. Mary Hanscome Forten's money paid for a forty-acre farm in Warminster, Bucks County, not far from Philadelphia. The 1850 census records a household of seven—Robert and Mary Forten, their two sons, Forten's daughter Charlotte, one of Forten's younger brothers, and a servant—and a modestly successful farming operation producing a variety of crops for the Philadelphia market.

From his rural retreat Forten maintained his involvement in antislavery activities. He wrote antislavery verse for the *National Anti-Slavery Standard*, the *Pennsylvania Freeman*, and other abolitionist periodicals. He publicly condemned what he perceived as the proslavery stance of mainstream American churches. He also differed with FREDERICK DOUGLASS over the nature of the U.S. Constitution, arguing that it was fundamentally proslavery. In the wake of the Compromise of 1850, though, the two men sank their differences and joined in organizing the short-lived American League of Colored Laborers to promote black economic self-sufficiency.

Financial difficulties again overtook Forten in the mid-1850s, possibly because he was a better poet and abolitionist than he was a farmer. Mary decided that the farm, which belonged to her and not to Robert, must be sold so the family could move and start over. Charlotte Forten, at school in Salem, Massachusetts, confided in her journal her hope that her father and stepmother would settle in New England. They did not. The Fortens relocated to London, Ontario.

Forten did no better in Canada than he had in the United States, and in 1858 the family moved again, this time to England. They made their home in London's Kentish Town, and Forten found work as a commercial agent for a large stationery firm. In 1860 tragedy again overtook the family when the Fortens' thirteen-year-old son died of typhus.

His exile in England did not mean that Forten had abandoned his antislavery work. Soon after his arrival he joined the London Emancipation Committee. He also followed as closely as he could events in the United States, keeping in touch with friends and family there as political wrangling over slavery gave way to secession and then to war. Finally, when he learned that President Abraham Lincoln had authorized the enlistment of black troops, Forten decided he could watch from the sidelines no longer. He must return home and serve in the army. His friends were appalled, but his mind was made up.

On 2 March 1864 Forten was mustered into Company A of the Forty-third Regiment, U.S. Colored Troops, to serve for three years or the duration. He was rapidly promoted to sergeant major and sent to Maryland as a recruiter. He reportedly persuaded many African Americans in that critically important border state to enlist, but as his friends had feared, army life took a toll on his health. Ordered back to Philadelphia's Camp William Penn, he caught a cold while drilling his men in the rain. He struggled on until he was so sick that he was forced to ask for a few days' leave. He returned to his mother's home, where he succumbed to typhoid. His funeral was notable for being the first in Philadelphia's history in which an African American soldier was laid to rest with full military honors.

FURTHER READING

Payne, Daniel Alexander. *Recollections of Seventy Years* (1888; repr. 1968).

Stevenson, Brenda, ed. *The Journals of Charlotte Forten Grimké* (1988).

Winch, Julie. *A Gentleman of Color: The Life of James Forten* (2002).

JULIE WINCH

Fortune, Amos (1710?–17 Nov. 1801), tanner and bookbinder, was born in Africa and brought to the colonies as a slave while very young. Nothing is known of Fortune's parentage, birth, or early years. It is thought that he arrived in America around 1725, but little is known of his life in the colonies prior to the mid-1700s. Ichabod Richardson of Woburn, Massachusetts, purchased Fortune around 1740, kept him as a slave apprentice, and taught him the art of tanning. In December 1763 Richardson drafted a "freedom paper" granting Fortune's freedom but died without signing it. Fortune remained a slave of the Richardson family until 1770, when a valid article of manumission signed by Ichabod's sister-in-law, Hannah, secured his freedom.

Remaining in Woburn for several years, Fortune purchased a small homestead from Isaac Johnson in 1774 and continued to run the Richardsons' tannery. During his Woburn years, Fortune married twice. He purchased the freedom of his first wife, Lydia Somerset, from Josiah Bowers on 23 June 1778, but the marriage was short-lived, ending with Lydia's death after only a few months. The couple had no children. In November 1779 he purchased and married another slave, Vilot, from James Baldwin. VILOT FORTUNE survived her husband, but they had no children.

The most significant period of Fortune's life as a free man began in 1781, when he and Vilot moved to the town of Jaffrey, New Hampshire, and established a home and a tannery on land set aside for the town's minister. There Fortune revealed his compassionate nature by taking in a young woman named Celyndia May. Although Fortune's will refers to Celyndia as his "adopted daughter," leading some to conclude that she was Vilot's child from a previous relationship, other sources argue that Fortune brought her into the family after moving to Jaffrey. For many years his tannery was located on the property belonging to Parson Laban Ainsworth, but Fortune relocated his operations after purchasing twenty-five acres, on which he also built a house and a barn. In 1789 he indentured two apprentices to remain competitive with a second tannery in Jaffrey. That same year he again showed his kindness by taking in another young woman, Polly Burdoo. Fortune remained in Jaffrey until his death there.

Fortune learned to read, write, and perform basic arithmetic, all skills attested to in his personal papers. He was a full member of the First Congregational Church of Woburn and the First Church of Christ in Jaffrey, as well as a subscriber to a newspaper and a charter member of the Jaffrey Social Library. His skill as a bookbinder is evident from a 1795 contract with the Jaffrey Social Library, which commissioned him to provide new leather bindings for its books. The fact that customers came from throughout New England to purchase his leather is evidence of his tanning expertise.

By all indications Fortune was a hard-working, sober individual. With its feather bed, writing desk, Windsor chair, six house chairs, and looking glass, his home likewise demonstrated his prosperity. His wardrobe, which included a greatcoat, a striped waistcoat, a black velvet jacket and breeches, a silver watch, and one pair of silver shoe buckles, showed that he enjoyed some of life's finery. Affirming his valuation of religion and education, his will provided funds for the church and "School house No. eight." His dedication to the cost of freedom is proven in the prices he paid to establish his family. Fortune's name has been kept alive through the publication of *Amos Fortune: Free Man*, a children's book by Elizabeth Yates, but he deserves to be remembered for achieving what few African Americans of his day could: he established and ran a successful business during America's most oppressive period for African Americans. As the epitaph on his tombstone attests, "He purchased liberty, professed Christianity, lived reputably, & died hopefully."

FURTHER READING

A collection of Fortune's personal papers, including his will, his estate inventory, and the signed and unsigned articles of manumission, is at the Jaffrey Public Library in Jaffrey, New Hampshire.

Magoun, F. Alexander. *Amos Fortune's Choice: The Story of a Negro Slave's Struggle for Self-Fulfillment* (1964).

Williams, Ralph C. *The Story of Amos Fortune*, reproduced in *History of Jaffrey (Middle Monadnock) New Hampshire: An Average Country Town in the Heart of New England*, Albert Annett and Alice E. Lehtinen (1937), vol. 3 (1971).

Yates, Elizabeth. *Amos Fortune: Free Man* (1950).

This entry is taken from the *American National Biography* and is published here with the permission of the American Council of Learned Societies.

JEFFRY D. SCHANTZ

Fortune, T. Thomas (3 Oct. 1856–2 June 1928), journalist and activist, was born Timothy Thomas in Marianna, Florida, the third of five children, to

Emanuel and Sara Jane, slaves of Ely P. Moore. After emancipation his family took the name Fortune from that of an Irish planter, Thomas Fortune, whom Emanuel believed to be his father. Emanuel was elected to the Florida House of Representatives in 1868, where he served for three years until he was forced to leave Marianna as the reign of terror that drove black office holders from power swept through Florida. Before his family joined him in Jacksonville, they lived in Tallahassee, where the young Fortune worked as a page in the state senate. During his four sessions there, Fortune developed a distrust of black and white politicians from both political parties. Though he spent only a few years at primary schools run by the Freedmen's Bureau, he acquired what he called "the book learning fever," which prepared him for his later literary activities. Fortune's mother died in 1868, and his father, who worked as a carpenter, made wise investments in real estate that allowed him to provide for his children while remaining active in politics until his death in 1897. Fortune got his start in publishing as a printer's devil for the *Jacksonville Daily Union*. When the paper changed hands, Fortune found work at the post office until Congressman J. W. Purman secured a position for him as a special inspector of customs in Delaware. However, Fortune believed that his true calling was to be found in the law, and in 1874 he enrolled at Howard University in Washington, D.C. Fortune had been largely self-educated, yet the polish of his prose outshone that of many of his credentialed peers. Thus, when the bank in which he had placed his savings for college collapsed, Fortune was able find work at a black newspaper, the *People's Advocate*, which earned him enough money during the day to study law at night.

Though Fortune never lost his interest in legal matters, he left Howard University to teach briefly in Florida before going to New York City in 1881 with his bride, Carrie C. Smiley. Of their five children, only Jessica and Frederick lived to adulthood. Fortune's first publishing job in New York was as a compositor for a white religious paper, the *Weekly Witness*. From there he worked as an editor for a black paper that began as the *Rumor* and became the *New York Globe* (1881–1884), the *New York Freeman* (1884–1887), of which he was the sole proprietor, and finally the *New York Age* in 1887, where he was both editor and co-owner. The power struggles, financial reorganizations, and management turnovers that led to so many name changes illustrate the constant battle to survive that Fortune waged during those years. He wrote over three hundred articles during his fifty-year career, but it was the editorials that he wrote between 1881 and 1907 that established his prominence during a bleak period for African American leadership between the decline of FREDERICK DOUGLASS and the rise of BOOKER T. WASHINGTON.

In the decades after the Civil War, the black press had grown from a few dozen antislavery organs to as many as five hundred papers; most were short-lived, weekly newsletters that espoused the positions of the Republican Party, to which the black electorate had been loyal. During an era famous for its "yellow journalism," Fortune attempted to run a truly independent and nonpartisan paper that was national in scope, original in content, and taken note of by the larger white media. He was a fiery critic, a witty satirist, and an astute analyst. As president and chairman of the executive council of the Afro-American Press Association during much of the 1890s, Fortune fought to raise the standards of his profession.

Booker T. Washington recognized Fortune's exceptional talent and hired him to ghostwrite *A Negro for a New Century* (1899) and *The Negro in Business* (1907); Fortune also wrote speeches for Washington and edited large sections of Washington's first autobiography, *The Story of My Life and Work* (1900). When Fortune finished working on the autobiography and noticed how little mention Washington had given to his service, he returned the manuscript with a note that read, "I write in great sorrow and with wounded pride because I have tried to do so much to sustain you and your work and am grieved and pained to find it amounts to so little in the summing up" (Thornbrough, 209). Fortune remained loyal to Washington because he largely agreed with Washington's education and economic policies, though he advocated more militant positions on civil rights than Washington was willing to endorse publicly. Nonetheless, Fortune often defended Washington against his most strident critics, explaining that Washington was a "conservative" while he himself was a "radical." At times Washington seemed to be sincere in trying to help Fortune, as in 1903 when he secured a special assignment for Fortune to study conditions in the Pacific for Theodore Roosevelt's administration. At other times Washington used his financial leverage to manipulate the *Age* as he had other Negro papers.

In January 1890 Fortune assembled in Chicago over one hundred delegates from across the country for the purpose of establishing the National Afro-American League to address African American political concerns. Thirty years before ALAIN LOCKE announced the birth of the "New Negro," Fortune wrote an article in the *Age* to mark

> the death-knell of the shuffling, cringing creature in black who for two centuries and a half had given the right of way to white men, and proclaiming in no uncertain voice that a new man in black, a freeman every inch, standing erect and undaunted, an American from head to foot, had taken the place of the miserable creature. What does he look like? He looks like a man! He bears no resemblance to a slave, or a coward, or an ignoramus (New York Age, 21 Dec. 1889).

The league failed to attract sufficient popular or financial support to survive beyond 1894, but its spirit and much of its platform was adopted by the Niagara Movement (1905) led by W. E. B. DUBOIS and the NAACP (1909). Fortune did not join either of these organizations because of his qualified loyalty to Booker T. Washington, his personal animosity toward their leaders, and his conflicting view of how legal arguments should be framed. He did, however, hold the presidency of the rival National Afro-American Council from 1902 to 1904 before it, too, became defunct.

A leading advocate of women's rights, Fortune was present at the founding convention of the Federation of Afro-American Women in 1895, successfully urging the adoption of the appellation "Afro-American" rather than the more common "Negro" or "Colored." He also did much to advance the careers of journalists VICTORIA EARLE MATTHEWS and IDA B. WELLS BARNETT, who both worked at the *Age* at various times. Nor was Fortune afraid to take controversial positions within the black community: he condemned racism in the North as strongly as he did in the South; he supported the right of "manly retaliation," even though he did not advocate violence; and when Frederick Douglass was roundly criticized in 1884 for marrying Helen Pitts, a white woman, Fortune was one of the few black leaders to come to his defense. Similarly, Fortune found himself at odds with Bishop HENRY MCNEAL TURNER, who urged immigration to Africa; he clashed with EDWARD BLYDEN and ALEXANDER CRUMMELL, whose strand of black nationalism would have excluded people of mixed race, arguing instead that such distinctions would worsen racial conditions by creating a "color line in a color line"; and he railed against the creation of an educated Negro aristocracy of the kind implied by DuBois's "Talented Tenth," warning that his race did not need another "swaggering pedagogue or a cranky homiletician."

In 1884 Fortune published *Black and White: Land, Labor, and Politics*, a scholarly treatise influenced by the writings of Karl Marx, in which Fortune called for a class alliance that would transcend race. This was followed by a historical work, *The Negro in Politics* (1885), and a volume of poetry, *Dreams of Life* (1905).

The dissolution of his marriage, his chronic financial woes, and increased drinking caused Fortune to suffer a mental breakdown in 1907. Though he managed to recover his health over the next several years, he lost control of the *Age* and with it an independent platform from which to express his ideas. He eked out a living as a freelance writer with several African American and white papers until 1923 when MARCUS GARVEY, who had recently been convicted of mail fraud, asked Fortune to become editor of the *Negro World*, even though he was not a member of the UNIA. Fortune held this post until he died of heart disease in 1928, having established a well-founded reputation as the dean of the African American press and providing a model of intellectual rigor and journalistic integrity.

FURTHER READING

A small collection of Fortune's papers and issues of his newspapers are available at the Schomburg Center for Research in Black Culture of the New York Public Library. His lengthy correspondence with Booker T. Washington is located in the Booker T. Washington Collection at the Library of Congress.

Thornbrough, Emma Lou. *T. Thomas Fortune: Militant Journalist* (1972).

SHOLOMO B. LEVY

Fortune, Vilot (c. 1729–13 Sept. 1802), wife of AMOS FORTUNE, was of unknown origin, but it is likely that she was forcibly enslaved and transported from Africa to the New World while young. Few details regarding Vilot's life are known. However, surviving evidence provides an accurate portrayal of her life and what it meant to be a free woman of color in northern New England in the late eighteenth century. Vilot is first documented on 9 November 1779, when she was sold by James Baldwin of Woburn, Massachusetts, to a free black, Amos Fortune, for the sum of fifty pounds. Described as "a Negro Woman ... being now my property," Vilot was fifty years old and had served as a domestic slave for the Baldwin family (Lambert, 38).

Vilot's purchaser Amos Fortune had been enslaved until he was manumitted in 1770 and had previously been married to Lydia Somerset, whom he had also purchased. However, Somerset died three months after their marriage. Amos Fortune's marriages to both women are examples of how African Americans were assimilated into New England society. Just like whites who wished to marry, Fortune was required by Massachusetts laws dating back to Puritan times to publish his intent to marry. Though Amos was following white marital traditions and laws, there were also factors of a more personal nature. That he desired love and companionship cannot be doubted. However, he also had practical matters to consider. By the time he purchased Vilot, he was at the advanced age of sixty-nine. He practiced the arduous profession of a tanner and was surely interested in a woman who could help him maintain a self-sufficient homestead. In addition child care was possibly an issue. Fortune's previous wife Lydia came to him a widow with three daughters. After Lydia's death, Amos and Vilot may have had to provide for them.

The day after her purchase, Vilot married Amos Fortune. The question of her legal status as a slave after her marriage is an interesting one. There is no record indicating that Amos Fortune ever formally freed Vilot. The example of their life together, however, makes it evident that "Vilot my beloved wife" was morally and practically a free woman the moment she became Amos Fortune's wife (Lambert, 50). In a sense, her status as a married woman was much like that of her white counterparts in a time when most legal rights were held by the husband.

Following their marriage, the Fortunes lived in Woburn on Amos's half-acre homestead. While enslaved, Vilot's work as a kitchen domestic certainly made her proficient at the traditional duties performed by all wives of the working class at this time, such as cooking, sewing, cleaning, and tending to domestic animals. Now her work was much more meaningful as a (at least de facto) free woman. Some insight into Vilot's activities may be gleaned from an inventory of Amos Fortune's estate taken after his death. Among the items listed are a cow, a heifer, and a mare, numerous farm tools, currying tools Amos used in his tannery, and "household furniture" including "one cheese press ... one cheese tub ... one meat barrel ... one meat tub ... three pails ... one churn ... one wash tub ... one beer and one pickle tub ... one foot wheel and one woolen wheel" (Lambert, 52). All of these latter items, as was customary, were used by the woman of the household. It is also likely that Vilot was of considerable help in Amos's tannery. Years younger than Amos, she probably helped in the arduous tasks of grinding tree bark into the powder needed for the tanning process or helped scrape hair off animal hides. That Vilot performed all these tasks and more is almost a certainty. Life during and after the American Revolution was tough, and economic times were hard. For an aged African American couple to successfully survive required a tremendous amount of hard work and mutual support.

Upon moving to Jaffrey, New Hampshire, in 1781, Vilot and Amos started life anew. After arriving they were "warned out," asked to leave town for fear they might end up in financial difficulties and rely on the town for welfare support. The warning was "standard" in most towns, and often ignored. The warning out process was typical in New England towns and was applied to most strangers no matter what their color. While a racial bias was present in many locales, this was not the case for the Fortunes, and they soon became established as some of Jaffrey's hardest working citizens. Once again Amos Fortune's activities are well known. He became a successful tanner, a church member, and a founder of the Social Library.

The Fortunes had no children of their own, but several children came to live with them for varying amounts of time, and Vilot was instrumental in their care. One of these children was Polly Burdoo, the daughter of Moses and Lois Burdoo, another free black family in Jaffrey. When Moses Burdoo died, the-Fortunes took in Polly until her death in 1793. Much more mysterious is Amos Fortune's adopted daughter Celyndia. She does not seem to have been with Vilot and Amos when they arrived in Jaffrey but appeared in 1785, when she was treated by the town physician. Celyndia may have been the child of Amos Fortune's first wife, and possibly she came to live with the Fortunes once they were established in Jaffrey. Between 1790 and 1796 Amos took in two apprentices, and Vilot would have cared for them as well. The first apprentice was a young black man, Simon Peter. Three years later a white boy, Charles Toothaker, came as an apprentice. In addition to learning the trade of a tanner, both boys were provided with "sufficient meat, drink, apparel, lodging, nursing and washing fitting for such," while Toothaker was also taught how to read, write, and "cipher" (Lambert, 40–42). The image of an aged black couple caring for and schooling young men in the early years of the republic exemplifies the more racially tolerant post–Revolutionary War era. Equally important, the Fortunes illustrate how northern blacks created African American communities across New England in the late eighteenth century and early nineteenth century.

Amos Fortune died on 17 November 1801 at the age of ninety-one. Vilot died at the age of seventy-three. The gravestone that marks her final resting place along with that of Amos occupies a prominent spot in the Old Burial Ground behind the Jaffrey Meetinghouse. Vilot's inscription reads in part, "By sale the slave of Amos Fortune, by marriage his wife, by her fidelity his friend."

FURTHER READING

The extant documents relating to Vilot and Amos Fortune are in a special collection at the Jaffrey Public Library. Vilot's name is spelled in a variety of ways, as was common in those days. The spelling used here is in both Vilot's bill of sale to Amos Fortune and in Amos's 1801 will. The Magoun and Yates works below are fictionalized biographies that offer credible accounts of what the Fortunes' lives may have been like.

Greene, Lorenzo Johnston. *The Negro in Colonial New England 1620–1776* (1942).

Lambert, Peter. *Amos Fortune: The Man and His Legacy* (2000).

Magoun, F. Alexander. *Amos Fortune's Choice* (1964).

Yates, Elizabeth. *Amos Fortune, Free Man* (1950).

GLENN ALLEN KNOBLOCK

Fort-Whiteman, Lovett (1894–Jan. 1939), a leading black Communist leader in the 1920s, was born in Texas. He attended the Tuskegee Institute in Alabama and also claimed to have been kicked out of the City College of New York for radicalism. In the late teens he was active in organized left-wing politics, including the Industrial Workers of the World (IWW) and the Harlem Socialist Party (SP). While the IWW fought for the rights of all workers, including racial and national minorities, the SP was color-blind and refused to champion the rights of blacks specifically, and instead argued that blacks were subject to class, but not-race, oppression. A core of Harlem Socialists, however—including RICHARD BENJAMIN MOORE, OTTO HUISWOUD, CYRIL VALENTINE BRIGGS, A. PHILIP RANDOLPH, CHANDLER OWEN, and Grace Campbell—were active in the "New Negro" movement of black radicalism and attempted to combine the struggles for socialism and black freedom. By the start of the 1920s, Fort-Whiteman was also a member, although not a charter member, of the African Blood Brotherhood (ABB), a radical black nationalist organization founded by Briggs. Many of the Harlem Socialists, especially those from the Caribbean, were upset with the rightward drift of the SP leadership nationally and, energized by the Russian (Bolshevik) Revolution, joined the ABB. During this period Fort-Whiteman was also involved in acting and writing. In addition, he was the drama critic for Randolph and Owen's notable magazine the *Messenger;* in its first issue, in November 1917, he demanded that white-owned theaters in Harlem put on performances by black writers.

By the early 1920s Fort-Whiteman and other leading New York members of the ABB joined the Communist Party (CP). They did so less because of the particular record of the CP on the "Negro question"—since the party, like its Socialist predecessors, largely ignored black oppression—but more because of the anticolonial struggle of the Bolsheviks. Unlike many early black Communist leaders, Fort-Whiteman was born in the United States, not in the Caribbean. In 1924 he was a delegate (under the pseudonym James Jackson) to the Fifth Congress of the Communist International (Comintern); there he argued that the CP had not paid enough attention to the oppression of black Americans. After the congress he stayed in Moscow for several months for training by the Comintern, probably the first black American to receive such training. In the autumn of 1925 he returned to the United States and became the head of the American Negro Labor Congress (ANLC) along with Moore. According to reports of the founding ANLC convention in Chicago, Fort-Whiteman affected a Russian style of dress and invited a Russian ballet to entertain the delegates. In the mid-1920s Fort-Whiteman was the preeminent black Communist leader and spokesman. Also, he arranged for other black Communists to study in Moscow. He was the national organizer of the ANLC until 1927, when he was replaced by Moore amid criticisms of "sectarianism" and lack of influence among American blacks.

During the late twenties Fort-Whiteman was a supporter of the Lovestone faction within the Communist Party, one of two incessantly battling groupings within the Party. To some degree this is due to his friendship with Jay Lovestone's ally Robert Minor, a white Texan who paid attention to the party's work among blacks. In April 1928 Fort-Whiteman joined the editorial staff of the U.S.

Communist Party's newspaper, the *Daily Worker*, and that same year ran for New York comptroller. By the time of the election, however, he was in Moscow as a delegate to the Sixth Congress of the Comintern. At that Congress Stalin and his allies unveiled the new perspective of "self-determination" for American blacks in the South—that is, for a separate black nation. With little exception, black American Communists, including Fort-Whiteman, were resistant to this idea, since they viewed it as a retreat from the struggle for full rights for blacks. This resistance, as well as his support to Lovestone, whom Stalin was soon to depose as the leader of the CP, damaged his authority within the Party and the Comintern.

Fort-Whiteman never returned to the United States after the congress. Initially, according to the scholar Mark Solomon, he taught political science at the Cercerin Institute near Moscow and lectured on the "Negro question" throughout Russia. He also married a Russian woman; details of their marriage are not known, however. The last years of Fort-Whiteman's life are largely obscure. According to recent researchers in the archives in the Comintern, Fort-Whiteman fell afoul of the Comintern leadership in 1935, was subsequently accused of "Trotskyism"—a catchall charge that Stalin regularly used against his enemies—and, in July 1937, was sentenced to five years of internal exile for "anti-Soviet agitation." A year later he was resentenced to hard labor and died in January 1939, according to a death certificate found in the Comintern archives.

FURTHER READING

Haywood, Harry. *Black Bolshevik: Autobiography of an Afro-American Communist* (1978).

Klehr, Harvey, John Earl Haynes, and Kyrill M. Anderson. *The Soviet World of American Communism* (1998).

Solomon, Mark. *The Cry Was Unity: Communists and African Americans, 1917–1936* (1998).

J. A. ZUMOFF

Foster, Autherine Lucy (5 Oct. 1929–), the first African American to attend the University of Alabama, was born Autherine Juanita Lucy, in Shiloh, Alabama, to Milton Cornelius Lucy and Minnie Hosea Lucy, tenant farmers. The youngest of ten children, she attended public schools in Shiloh and then Linden Academy during her high school years. She graduated in 1947 and spent her undergraduate years at Miles College, in Fairfield, Alabama, where she received a bachelor of arts in English in 1952.

For graduate school, Lucy chose the University of Alabama for its academic reputation and because, as a public university, they had no right to reject her. She was nevertheless rejected, twice; the university claimed that registration for the first semester had already ended. With the help of NAACP attorneys Thurgood Marshall, Constance Baker Motley, and Arthur Shores, Lucy sued, along with Polly Ann Myers Hudson, to gain admission. The University of Alabama was then instructed by Federal Judge Harlan Grooms that it could not reject students based on race according to the U.S. Supreme Court. In response, the university rejected Hudson based on her "conduct and marital action," (Hine) meaning she had become pregnant while unmarried, but notified Autherine Lucy of her acceptance on the eve of registration; however, she would be denied dormitory space and barred from dining halls on campus.

On 3 February 1956 Lucy registered as a graduate student in library science and began classes. That night over 1,000 students marched on the home of university president Oliver Cromwell Carmichael to protest her admission, singing "Dixie" and shouting "Keep 'Bama White!" Another group burned a cross on the front lawn of dean William Adams's home, and a cross was burned at the main quadrangle of the campus. On Monday, Lucy faced a mob gathered around Smith Hall, chanting "Hey, hey, ho, ho, where did Autherine go!" during the class lecture. At the end of the class she was escorted by the dean of women, Sarah L. Healy, and Jefferson Bennett out a back door to a waiting car. After spotting them the mob began to throw eggs and rocks as the administrators sped to her next class. Upon their arrival, Lucy ran out of the car and into the back of the building, where she was pelted with rocks and eggs. After class she was not permitted to leave because the mob had laid siege to the building, a siege that lasted for three hours. Lucy was then escorted back to Birmingham by state police.

That evening the board of trustees sent a telegram to Lucy and notified her of her suspension for her own safety and the safety of other students until further notice on 6 February. The student legislature issued a reprimand for the board's actions and asked the university officials to take a strong moral stand against mob rule. Other students signed a petition to have her reinstated.

Her lawyers, Shores and Marshall, then filed contempt charges in federal court against the trustees.

Included in the charges were the president of the University of Alabama, whom Shores and Marshall cited for suspending Lucy and for conspiring with the mob, as well as the dean of women, for barring her from the dining halls and dormitories, and four other men, for participating in the riots. Marshall later withdrew the conspiracy charge on the grounds that it could not be substantiated.

During the case Lucy had been accused by the university of being a tool of the NAACP and of being paid for her actions in an effort to integrate the University of Alabama. Federal Judge H. Hobart Grooms ordered that the suspension be lifted, but also said that university officials had acted in good faith in protecting Lucy. The University of Alabama board of trustees reacted angrily to the charges and accused Autherine Lucy of "making such baseless, outrageous and unfounded charges of misconduct on the part of the university officials" (Philips), and expelled her permanently from the University of Alabama.

Following her expulsion on 2 March 1956 Autherine Lucy left Alabama for New York, where she was the guest of Thurgood Marshall and his wife. There she was treated for fatigue and nervous tension. Meanwhile, the Alabama state House of Representatives issued a subpoena for Lucy to testify before a committee on whether the NAACP was controlled by communists. This action was denounced by Thurgood Marshall as "a move to harass and intimidate Miss Lucy" (Durdin). The four men who had been named in the contempt-of-court suit then filed damage suits against Lucy totaling $4,000,000. Reaction continued in the Alabama state legislature with the introduction of several bills that would have required that all future applicants produce fitness references from three graduates, and that state funds be cut off from Tuskegee Institute and from the scholarship fund to send black students outside the state should any African American gain admittance to any white college in Alabama. The state senate also passed a resolution calling for federal money to resettle blacks in the South to other parts of the country.

Despite being offered admittance to other schools, including a scholarship from the University of Copenhagen, Lucy chose to marry Reverend Hugh L. Foster, who she met as an undergraduate at Miles College, in April 1956. The couple moved to Texas, where they had four children. There Lucy Foster worked as a substitute teacher for seventeen years until her family moved back to Alabama in 1974.

In 1988 two professors from the University of Alabama invited Lucy back to the school to speak of her experiences in 1956. She was asked if she would ever re-enroll, and following her speech faculty members were able to have her expulsion overturned. Lucy Foster then enrolled in the master's program and in 1992 she received her master of arts degree in Elementary Education along with her daughter Grazia, who received a bachelor's degree in Corporate Finance.

FURTHER READING

Durdin, Tillman. "Miss Lucy Flies Here for a Rest," *New York Times*, 2 Mar. 1956.

"First in Alabama," *Time* (13 Feb. 1956).

Hine, Darlene Clark, ed. "Foster, Autherine Juanita Lucy," in *Black Women in America. An Historical Encyclopedia* (1993).

Phillips, Wayne. "University Ousts Miss Lucy Because of Her Charges," *New York Times*, 2 Mar. 1956.

"Round Two in Alabama," *Time* (12 March 1956).

HOPE HAZARD GAMBOA

Foster, Pops (18 May 1892–30 Oct. 1969), musician, was born George Murphy Foster on a plantation near McCall, Louisiana, the son of Charles Foster, a butler, and Annie (maiden name unknown), a seamstress of mixed African American and Cherokee ancestry. As a boy he attended a Catholic elementary school and played the cello in plantation bands led by his father and uncle. His brother Willie excelled at the banjo and also became a professional musician. When Foster was ten his family moved to New Orleans, where he soon switched from the cello to the double bass. He enrolled at New Orleans University, a secondary school for blacks. Foster did not complete his secondary education, however, because he was heavily involved in the exciting, working-class black musical scene in New Orleans that was giving birth to jazz. He played in pickup groups at lawn parties and fish fries, and he soon gained paid work with the Rozelle Orchestra and in bands led by Frankie Dusen, Kid Ory, Manuel Perez, Freddie Keppard, and John Robichaux. He also worked with such jazz pioneers as the cornetists Bunk Johnson and Joe Oliver. Foster's posthumous autobiography, *Pops Foster: The Autobiography of a New Orleans Jazzman* (1971), is a uniquely colorful account of the vice and street life surrounding early New Orleans jazz. He married his first wife, Bertha (maiden name unknown), in 1912, but they were soon estranged and obtained a divorce in the 1920s.

Pops Foster, a New Orleans jazz musician, plays in New York City, c. February 1947. (© William P. Gottlieb; www.jazzphotos.com.)

They had no children. In 1918 Foster found work on the Streckfus family's Mississippi riverboats, playing in FATE MARABLE's "colored" band for cruises between New Orleans and St. Louis.

Around this time, New Orleans jazz musicians began to travel nationally to exploit the music's growing popularity. In 1921 Foster began the first of two residencies with the Charlie Creath Band in St. Louis, and the following year he traveled with Kid Ory to Los Angeles, where he may have taken part in the first purely instrumental recordings by a black jazz band: "Ory's Creole Trumbone" and "Society Blues" by Spike's Seven Pods of Pepper. In the late 1920s Foster toured the nation with a few groups, and in 1929 he moved to New York and joined the LUIS RUSSELL Orchestra, a popular ensemble that eventually became LOUIS ARMSTRONG's backup band. Also in 1929 he made some of the first interracial jazz recordings with a white band, the Mound City Blue Blowers. Now living in Harlem, Foster married Annie Alma Gayle in 1936; they had no children.

In the 1930s Foster became widely known in the jazz community as the most rhythmically spirited double bassist, the "swinging" equivalent of his fellow New Orleans musicians Armstrong and SIDNEY BECHET. Foster's largely self-taught technique featured the application of strong pressure on the fingerboard with the left hand, as well as bowing, pizzicato, and string "slapping" with the right hand, which sounded sharply and resonated for many seconds—an effect that one analyst, the bassist and teacher Bertram Turetzky, called "attack and decay." He also experimented with an aluminum instrument and other effects to amplify the bass sound in large dance halls. Foster usually filled each bar of music with "walking" (swinging notes that guided the entire ensemble rhythmically), and many critics consider him the musician most responsible for the double bass's supplanting the tuba as the jazz band's harmonic foundation. His recordings with the Luis Russell Orchestra, from 1929 to 1934, and with Sidney Bechet, in 1945, display his style. Dozens of young jazz bassists, including MILT HINTON, JIMMY BLANTON, and OSCAR PETTIFORD, eagerly emulated his style. Foster played at various times with most of the major jazz talents of the 1930s, including DUKE ELLINGTON, FLETCHER HENDERSON, FATS WALLER, JELLY ROLL MORTON, and Benny Goodman, while remaining with the Armstrong-Russell orchestra throughout the decade.

During World War II, as the orchestra was forced to limit its touring, Foster primarily worked as a New York subway employee and as a porter. He benefited from the growing popularity of early New Orleans, or Dixieland, jazz, though, and became a fixture in the jazz clubs of midtown Manhattan, playing in various pickup groups and participating in many recordings. Foster played with Bechet and the veteran pianist JAMES P. JOHNSON, and on the radio program *This Is Jazz* in 1947–1948. In 1948, 1952, and 1955 he made tours of Europe with the Mezz Mezzrow, JIMMY ARCHEY, and Sam Price bands. In 1956 Foster moved to San Francisco, a center of Dixieland activity, and played with EARL HINES's Small Band into the early 1960s. He continued to perform with other groups around the nation and toured Europe again in 1966 with the New Orleans All Stars. Despite increasing health problems, Foster remained an active player, and he was able to dictate his autobiography to Tom Stoddard up to the time of his death in San Francisco.

Foster was one of the best-loved and most respected jazz musicians of his generation. His extraordinary sixty-year career was among the longest in jazz history. A quiet and modest man, his powerful and enthusiastic bass playing nevertheless set a high standard for emerging masters of the instrument in the 1920s and 1930s. Foster's longevity and versatility also helped to ensure that despite the advent of radically new jazz styles after 1940, the early New Orleans sound would remain popular with audiences around the world.

FURTHER READING

Foster, Pops, and Tom Stoddard. *The Autobiography of Pops Foster: New Orleans Jazz Man* (1971; rev. ed. 2005).

Kernfeld, Barry, ed. *The New Grove Dictionary of Jazz* (1988).

Obituary: *New York Times*, 1 Nov. 1969.

This entry is taken from the *American National Biography* and is published here with the permission of the American Council of Learned Societies.

BURTON W. PERETTI

Foster, Robert Wayne "Bob" (15 Dec. 1938–), boxer, was born in Albuquerque, New Mexico. Little is known of Foster's life before he began boxing. Foster himself admitted that he got into numerous fights as a child and a high school student and was once taken to court for fracturing the skull of another young man with one punch. With few options open to him and a close scrape with the law motivating him, Foster signed up for the U.S. Air Force in 1957, shortly after graduating from high school.

Foster's tremendous punching power soon became evident to his air force commanders during informal inter- and intra-unit boxing matches, and they put him on the service's boxing team. For four years Foster traveled with the team all over the United States and the world. He engaged in well over one hundred fights, losing only three. In 1960 he won the light heavyweight title at the Pan-American Games. The victory seemed to assure Foster a spot on the American Olympic boxing team, but the light heavyweight spot on the squad went to another up-and-coming fighter, Cassius Clay, who won the gold medal that year. After finishing his last year in the air force, Foster in 1961 decided to box professionally.

Foster fought his first professional fight in March 1961, and with this start he reeled off nine straight victories, five of them by knockout. In his tenth fight he was matched against Doug Jones, who was then campaigning as a heavyweight. It was the first of Foster's several fights with heavyweights and soon proved to be a questionable career move. As he found in the Jones fight, his devastating punching power as a light heavyweight did not carry over into his fights against heavier men. At 6'3" Foster normally boxed at a weight of 175 pounds. Jones, a small heavyweight, fought at 190 pounds or more. Jones wore Foster down and knocked him out in the eighth round. Foster rebounded with two quick knockouts in his next fights but then took another questionable career move. In October 1963 he traveled to Lima, Peru, to take on the tough light heavyweight Mauro Mina in his home country. Foster later complained that the fight was fixed with bizarre refereeing and even more bizarre timekeeping that led to some rounds being less than two minutes and others nearly five. Whatever irregularities there might have been, Mina was given the decision. Foster did not lose another fight to a light heavyweight until 1978.

For nearly four years Foster worked his way through any and all opponents in the light heavyweight division. He fought twenty times from late 1963 through late 1967. Fighting in his normal weight class, he was a terror. Of his eighteen victories against light heavyweights, sixteen were by knockout. His only two losses were against heavyweights. These heavyweights, Ernie Terrell and Zora Folley, were not pushovers; both were solid heavyweight contenders when they met Foster. Terrell knocked Foster out in seven rounds; Folley took a unanimous decision. Despite these two losses, Foster's decisive victories over most of the light heavyweight competition earned him a title shot with the legendary Nigerian fighter Dick Tiger in May 1968. In four short but brutal rounds Foster accomplished what no other boxer did: he stopped Tiger by a knockout.

During the next six years Foster established himself as one of the most destructive and dominant light heavyweight champions boxing had seen. He fought twenty-four times and won twenty-one bouts, eighteen by knockout. He suffered only two defeats, both by knockout and both again at the hands of heavyweights. These two heavyweight fighters were immortals: JOE FRAZIER (who knocked Foster out in two rounds) and MUHAMMAD ALI (who took Foster out in eight rounds). Foster successfully defended his light heavyweight title fourteen times, which established a record for consecutive defenses in the division.

After his loss to Ali in 1972, Foster defended his crown three more times. The first two fights were against the white South African fighter Pierre Fourie. In the first bout in August 1973 Foster seemed unable to mount his usual furious attack and settled for a unanimous decision. The second fight in December 1973 was historic. Foster, a black man, agreed to meet Fourie in Johannesburg, South Africa. It was the first time in the history of the apartheid regime that a white fighter and a black fighter faced each other. Foster became a symbol of hope to the millions of black South Africans who lived in the strictly segregated African nation, and his second consecutive decision victory over Fourie sparked numerous celebrations throughout their communities.

Foster, however, was no longer the fearsome fighter he once had been. After thirteen years of tough fights, Foster's reflexes had slowed and his vaunted punching power had waned. In June 1974 he made the final defense of his title, fighting to an ugly and controversial draw with Jorge Victory Ahumada. Even Foster later admitted that he believed Ahumada won the fight. Foster announced in 1974 that he was retiring while he was still champion. As with so many other champions, however, the lure of the ring proved too strong, and Foster returned to fighting in 1975. He quickly dispatched five no-name opponents but then suffered an embarrassing knockout in early 1978 against the virtually unknown Mustafa Wassaja, who was fighting in just his tenth bout. Two months later Bob Hazelton (whom Foster had knocked out just the year before) ended Foster's career with a two-round knockout.

Following the Hazelton bout, Foster quit boxing for good. He returned to the job he began after his first retirement, working as a law enforcement officer in his hometown of Albuquerque. He eventually became a deputy sheriff, and after his retirement from the police force he continued to work as a security guard at the city courthouse. He supplemented his income with numerous personal appearances and became involved in the burgeoning autograph industry. In 1990 Foster was inducted into the International Boxing Hall of Fame. More than a decade later the *Ring* magazine named Foster the fifth greatest light heavyweight champion of all time.

FURTHER READING

Ashe, Arthur R., Jr. *A Hard Road to Glory: A History of the African-American Athlete since 1946* (1988).

"Bob Foster." *Ring* (Sept. 2002).

Cozzone, Chris. "'I Was Cocky ... but Damn, I was-Good!': The Bob Foster Story." Available online-at http://www.newmexicoboxing.com/history_newmexico_boxing/bobfoster.html.

MICHAEL L. KRENN

Foster, Rube (17 Sept. 1879–9 Dec. 1930), baseball player, manager, and entrepreneur, was born Andrew Foster in Calvert, Texas, the fifth child of Sarah (maiden name unknown) and the Reverend Andrew Foster, presiding elder of the Methodist Episcopal Church of Calvert. Growing up in a post-Reconstruction world of strictly enforced racial segregation backed by white terrorist violence, Andrew attended the segregated school in Calvert. As a boy Andrew had a knack for baseball, the most popular sport in America at the time. His father, a devout churchman, tried to discourage him from playing, but young Andrew persisted and even organized a team while he was still in grade school. Indeed, Andrew was so drawn to the game that he quit school after the eighth grade to pursue baseball as a career.

Foster started pitching for the Waco Yellow Jackets, becoming a star pitcher by the time he was eighteen. By 1902 he had a reputation for being a tough pitcher, with a fastball, curve, and screwball. That year he joined the Chicago Union Giants (most all-black teams at this time called themselves the Giants) and reputedly won fifty-one games, including a victory over the great white professional pitcher Rube Waddell, which is how Foster earned his nickname. As records for barnstorming black players were poorly kept, it is difficult to know exactly how many games Foster actually won. By this time Foster was officially part of the itinerant, rough-and-tumble world of the professional African American baseball player, a world not unlike that of the black professional prizefighter. Boxing was, like baseball, intensely popular at this time.

Baseball in post–Civil War America was still developing and did not entirely resemble the modern game. By the 1880s, however, three strikes equaled a strikeout, four balls were a walk, leather gloves were regularly used, and pitchers could throw overhand. By 1889 something like today's Major League Baseball existed, with two leagues: the National League, founded in 1876, and the American Association, founded in 1882. The American League, which replaced the American Association, came into existence under the leadership of Ban Johnson in 1901. There were several other professional leagues, as well as a good number of barnstorming teams that traveled around challenging various local nines. Amateur baseball could be found everywhere in America, from company teams to college teams. Though some local teams, such as the Florence (Massachusetts) Eagles with their first baseman LUTHER ASKIN, were occasionally and quietly integrated shortly after the Civil War, amateur baseball was officially segregated in 1867. By 1887 there were approximately twenty black players on professional teams. But on 14 July 1887 the Chicago White Stockings player-manager Cap Anson demanded that the opposing club from Newark not play its two black players, GEORGE STOVEY and MOSES FLEETWOOD WALKER. This was the beginning of the gentleman's agreement that was to keep African Americans, indeed, all black- or dark-skinned men, from playing in any of the established professional leagues until 1945, when the Brooklyn Dodgers signed JACKIE ROBINSON. There were teams that tried to get around the custom by saying that a player was Hispanic or Indian, but this rarely worked and, in any case, any dark-skinned Hispanic or Indian who was as dark as the average African American was not allowed to play professional baseball on the same field as whites. Since many black men had a passion as strong as whites for playing this game as professionals, they were forced to form their own teams and eventually their own leagues.

By the turn of the century, black teams were barnstorming units. They traveled around the country playing other teams, sometimes white, sometimes black. There were many disadvantages to this in selling black baseball to the public. First, players jumped from team to team during the season, willing to leave one team for another if they could get more money. Roster instability made it impossible for managers and team owners to rely on the players through a season. The second disadvantage was that teams were unable to claim the loyalty of fans in a particular location or to have a structured season of competition. The only answer to this confusion and disorganization was to form a league, but this was virtually impossible, although it was a dream of many of the early organizers of black baseball. The dreamers included, most notably, SOL WHITE, whose 1907 book *The History of Colored Base Ball* is one of the most important accounts of black baseball before the formation of leagues.

Foster pitched for the Cuban X-Giants and the Philadelphia Giants. He also played in Cuba, a popular location for black ballplayers during the winter months. In 1907 Foster returned to Chicago to become the manager of the Chicago Leland Giants, establishing himself as a first-rate manager and transforming the Leland Giants into one of the most skilled black teams in the country. In 1911 Foster formed a partnership with John M. Schorling, the son-in-law of Charles Comiskey, owner of the Chicago White Sox. The team that Foster put together, the Chicago American Giants, became one of the powerhouse teams in black baseball history. Foster still pitched occasionally, but he concentrated on managing and general managing, and, although he was stern with his men, he was highly successful at putting together teams and getting the most out of his players. As a manager Foster was a master of "little ball": bunting, the hit-and-run, the steal, the sacrifice. Of course, this was before the age of the home run, and most teams tended to play this way, but Foster's team did it better than most.

Foster's problems with the booking agent Nat Strong regarding scheduling games in the East and his interest in stopping bidding wars for top players eventually led him to form his own league in 1920. The first Negro League was formed in February 1920 at the YMCA in Kansas City and was made up of the Chicago American Giants, the Chicago Giants, the Detroit Stars, the St. Louis Giants, the Kansas City Monarchs, the Taylor ABCs, and the Cuban Stars. Foster became both the president and the treasurer of the league, and he continued to manage the Chicago American Giants as well. All of the Negro League owners were black except J. L. Wilkinson, who owned the Kansas City Monarchs and had previously owned the All-Nations, a team composed of African Americans, Mexicans, Indians, and whites. In 1923 Foster helped to form the Eastern Colored League, ensuring that the Negro Leagues would have the same structure as Major League Baseball. In 1924 the Negro World Series was introduced. With the league undercapitalized, still faced with having to play a great number of barnstorming games, and still facing booking obstacles, it was remarkable that Foster was able to establish a league and make it work. He thus became not just one of the greatest baseball men around, but also one of the most important black entrepreneurs in history.

Foster's autocratic rule created friction and enemies, and eventually he was forced to resign in 1925. He was also suffering from deteriorating mental health, partly induced by overwork, and by September 1926 he was in a state mental asylum in Kankakee, Illinois, where he died in 1930. Foster's body lay in state for several days before his burial in Chicago, the city in which he had achieved his greatest fame.

Foster was not only one of the greatest figures in black baseball but also one of the most important men involved in professional baseball in the United States. Few men have been involved in as many facets of the game. Although records are incomplete, Foster was certainly one of the great pitchers of his era. He was also one of the great managers of the game, introducing sophisticated tactics and strategies. Foster recognized talent and knew how to motivate players and teach them how to play. His men played hard and they played to win at a time when black ballplayers and teams were often employed to clown around and degrade themselves in minstrel-type routines, particularly for white fans. In organizing the league, Foster was also one of the game's great general managers. He was flamboyant, competitive, a "race man," and a dreamer. Foster was elected to the National Baseball Hall of Fame in 1981.

FURTHER READING

Cottrell, Robert Charles. *The Best Pitcher in Baseball: The Life of Rube Foster, Negro League Giant* (2001).

Peterson, Ralph. *Only the Ball Was White: A History of Legendary Black Players and All-Black Professional Teams* (1970).

Ribowsky, Mark. *A Complete History of the Negro Leagues, 1884–1955* (1995).

Riley, James A. *The Biographical Encyclopedia of the Negro Baseball Leagues* (1994).

Rogosin, Donn. *Invisible Men: Life in Baseball's Negro Leagues* (1983).

Rust, Art. *Get That Nigger off the Field* (1976).

GERALD EARLY

Foster, William Hendrick (12 June 1904–16 Sept. 1978), baseball player and college dean, was born in Calvert, Texas, the son of Andrew Foster Sr., a United Methodist minister, and Sarah Lewis. At a young age Foster, his mother, and his sister Geneva joined relatives in Rodney, Mississippi. Foster attended nearby Alcorn College's lab school until 1917, at which time he developed an interest in playing baseball like his older half-brother ANDREW RUBE FOSTER, who founded the Negro National League in 1920. Disregarding his brother's advice to complete his education, Willie Foster made a youthful decision and joined the Memphis Red Sox in 1923, owned by his uncle Robert "Bubbles" Lewis.

To Rube's surprise the young pitcher defeated Foster's Chicago American Giants during a 1923 exhibition game in Memphis. Exercising his powers as league president, Rube demanded that Lewis allow Willie, as he was known, to split the next two seasons between the American Giants and the Red Sox. The American Giants had won pennants in 1920, 1921, and 1922, before the ascendancy of the Kansas City Monarchs. The American Giants needed an excellent left-handed pitcher to challenge the powerful Monarch hitters Hurley McNair, Oscar "Heavy" Johnson, Dobie Moore, and BULLET ROGAN. The 6'1" Foster, who became known for his pinpoint control, hard-breaking slider, and sidearm curve that dropped like Niagara Falls, filled the requirement as the Giants' new ace.

In the winter of 1924–1925 the Negro National League was incorporated by Rube Foster and the attorney Elisha Scott. Rube made Willie Foster plurality owner of the league with a 40 percent share, while the remaining shares were divided between Rube (20 percent), Monarchs owner J. L. Wilkinson (20 percent), and investors Russell Thompson (15 percent) and Walter Farmer (5 percent). Although the largest shareholder, Willie Foster did not play an active role in the league's operation, leaving administrative decisions to Rube.

Foster had perhaps his finest season in 1926, winning twenty-nine games and leading the Giants to the league playoffs against the Kansas City Monarchs. The Monarchs had won the league championship the past two years and were favored to maintain their dominance in the best-of-nine game format. On the final day of the series, with the Monarchs leading four games to three, Foster pitched both games of the decisive doubleheader. He shut out the Monarchs in both games, 1–0 and 5–0, to help the American Giants earn the Negro National League title. He then pitched three complete games in the World Series against the Bacharach Giants of the Eastern Colored League to earn the American Giants their first black world series championship. Foster compiled an outstanding 1.27 ERA in the ten-game series.

In 1927 the American Giants repeated as pennant winners and again faced the Bacharach Giants in the Negro League World Series. Foster won the opening game 6–2 but lost the fifth game, called because of darkness after the sixth inning, and lost the eighth game behind four fielding errors. He came back in the ninth and deciding game to win, 11–4, for the Giants' second Series championship.

After the 1929 season Foster played in a two-game series against an American League all-star team led by the future major leaguer Hank Greenberg and Art "The Great" Shires, who hit .312 that season. In the series Foster struck out Shires three times in the first game and twice in the second. Foster lost the first game but won the second, giving up no runs and no hits over eight innings and striking out nine major leaguers in the process. The Detroit Tigers second baseman Charles Gehringer later testified, "If I could paint you white I could get $150,000 for you right now." In seven recorded games against major league opponents Foster won six. He also won eleven out of twenty-one head-to-head encounters with the legendary SATCHEL PAIGE.

In July 1930 Foster was named player-manager of the Chicago American Giants, succeeding Jim Brown. The next season he bounced between the Homestead Grays and the Kansas City Monarchs. In 1932 Foster returned to the Giants, which had joined the Negro Southern League, and guided them to another pennant. The following season the American Giants joined the reorganized Negro National League and won yet another pennant behind Foster's brilliant pitching. That year Chicago hosted the inaugural Negro League East-West All-Star game at Comiskey Park. The starting lineups were determined by the fans; with 40,637 votes Foster received the highest total. He relished the honor by pitching the only complete game in all-star history. Foster gave up seven hits and two earned runs to capture the victory. He faced a star-studded lineup that included the future Hall of Famers JAMES "COOL PAPA" BELL, OSCAR CHARLESTON, JOSH GIBSON, and WILLIAM "JUDY" JOHNSON, as well as other greats like BIZ MACKEY, Jud Wilson, and Dick Lundy. Foster made his second and final all-star appearance in 1934, receiving a then-record 48,957 votes from the fans. In 1938 Foster closed out his sixteen-year career, pitching again for the Memphis Red Sox. He retired as the all-time Negro League leader in wins with 137, having lost only 62.

In 1933 Foster earned a degree in agriculture education from Alcorn College (later Alcorn State University) in Lorman, Mississippi. In 1960 he became dean of men and a coach at the college. In 1968 Foster married Audrey M. Davis; they had no children. He later sold insurance and managed the Harlem Globetrotters basketball team. He died in Lorman.

FURTHER READING

Holway, John. "Historically Speaking: Bill Foster," in *Black Sports* (1974).

Lester, Larry. "Bill Foster," in *The Ballplayers*, ed. Mike Shatzkin et al. (1990).

LARRY LESTER

Fowler, Bud (16 Mar. 1858–26 Feb. 1913), baseball player, was born John Jackson in Fort Plain, New York, the son of John W. Jackson, a barber, and Mary Lansing. By 1860 the family had moved to nearby Cooperstown, where Fowler grew up and, for reasons unknown, began calling himself John W. Fowler. Sol White, Fowler's contemporary and a pioneer historian of black baseball, claimed that Fowler began his playing career in 1869 with the black Mutuals of Washington, D.C. In 1872 he joined the New Castle, Pennsylvania, club, thereby becoming "the first colored ball player of note playing on a white [professional] team." Though a staple of baseball folklore, White's unsubstantiated claim seems implausible given Fowler's age (fourteen).

Fowler's first documented appearance as a player is with a white team in Chelsea, Massachusetts, in April 1878. After pitching Chelsea to a 2–1 win over the National League champion Boston in an exhibition game, he signed with the Live Oaks of Lynn, Massachusetts, a member of the International Association. On 17 May he became the first African American to play in a professional baseball league. Released after two more games, Fowler for the next five years played as the lone black player on several independent and semipro teams in the United States and Canada, his tenure typically abbreviated by the racism of teammates and spectators. In 1881 he signed with Guelph, Ontario, but he was soon released because, as the *Guelph Herald* explained, "some of the Maple Leafs are ill-natured enough to object to the colored pitcher."

Fowler resurfaced in organized professional baseball in 1884 with Stillwater, Minnesota, of the Northwestern League. He batted .320 and advanced the next season to Keokuk, Iowa. Unable to pitch because of arm problems, the versatile Fowler played several infield and outfield positions, chiefly second base. When the Western League disbanded in July he considered becoming the player-manager of the black Orions of Philadelphia, but he decided instead to continue in white professional baseball despite mounting racial antipathy. In August he signed with Pueblo of the Colorado League, but he was "disengaged" after five games because "his skin [was] against him." In 1886, batting .309 with pennant-winning Topeka, Kansas, he was proclaimed the "best second baseman in the Western League."

The next season Fowler joined Binghamton, New York, in the International League. A .350 batting average as the cleanup hitter and more than twenty stolen bases in thirty-four games demonstrated an ability to excel at the highest level of minor league baseball, but he could not escape racism on the field or among the press. An opposing player admitted that pitchers deliberately tried to hit him (and the other six blacks in the league) when he was at bat, and he played second base "with the lower part of his legs encased in wooden guards" because, "about every player that came down to second base on a steal had it in for him and would, if possible, throw the spikes into him." (Frank Grant, Buffalo's black second baseman, also wore wooden guards; it is unclear which player first used them, but their example prompted all catchers to adopt "shin guards.") Racial animosity from his teammates led to Fowler's release on 30 June, just two weeks before league owners on 14 July agreed to stop signing blacks.

After playing briefly for Montpelier, Vermont, in the Northeastern League Fowler considered entering the growing world of black baseball that emerged in the mid-1880s in response to the spread of racial segregation. He weighed the choices of joining one of the premier black clubs, the Cuban Giants or the New York Gothams, or of forming his own team to barnstorm through the South and far West, but he opted instead to continue his odyssey through the minor leagues. In 1888 he played with clubs in Crawfordsville and Terre Haute, Indiana, in the Central Interstate League, Santa Fe in the New Mexico Territory, and a barnstorming team that traveled from California to Texas. He spent 1889 with Greenville of the Michigan State League, and in 1890 he played with Galesburg, Illinois, of the Central Interstate League, and Sterling, Illinois, and Burlington, Iowa, in the Illinois-Iowa League. In 1891 he joined a racially mixed independent club in Findlay, Ohio, returned to the minors in 1892 with Lincoln and Kearney of the Nebraska State League, and rejoined Findlay in 1893–1894.

Aided by two white businessmen Fowler secured sponsorship in 1895 for a black team from the Page Woven Wire Fence Company of Adrian, Michigan, and from an unnamed bicycle manufacturer in Massachusetts. Based in Adrian and led by Fowler as player-manager, the Page Fence Giants traveled by custom-made railroad car throughout six midwestern states, announcing their arrival by riding into town on bicycles. The Giants enjoyed great success against independent and minor league teams, but for reasons unknown, Fowler bolted the team on 15 July and joined Lansing of the Michigan State League. He rejoined the Findlay club in 1896, remaining until 1899, when his white teammates drew the color line. To continue in professional ball and counter white racism he returned to black baseball. In 1899 he founded the All-American Black Tourists, who for two years combined baseball with burlesque. Arriving in town the Tourists paraded down the main street in formal dress suits with swallowtail coats, opera hats, and silk umbrellas. "By the request of any club," Fowler announced, "we will play the game in these suits." In 1901 he organized the Smoky City Giants of Pittsburgh, and in 1904 he managed the Kansas City Stars. Fowler's efforts to establish a Negro professional baseball league in 1904–1905 failed for want of adequate financial support, and his baseball career came to an end.

Fowler's career mirrored the experiences of blacks in the development of professional baseball after the Civil War. Partly because of the financial instability of franchises and leagues, but primarily because of racism, he played on at least seventeen different teams in at least nine different leagues and took the field in twenty-two states and Canada. The first black in organized professional baseball, he played longer (ten years) and in more games (465) than any other African American in the nineteenth century. He was almost always the lone black on an otherwise white team.

A superb athlete who conducted running and walking exhibitions during the off-season, Fowler began his baseball career as a pitcher and catcher, but his versatility led to his playing other positions, frequently more than one position in a game. He consistently batted above .300, possessed great speed as a base runner, and was an intelligent and exciting fielder. An itinerant ballplayer who supported himself by barbering during and after the playing season, Fowler saw his dream of reaching the major leagues thwarted by institutionalized racism. In 1885 *Sporting Life* declared: "He is one of the best general players in the country.... With his splendid abilities he would long ago have been on some good club had his color been white instead of black. Those who know say there is no better second baseman in the country; he is besides a good batter and a fine base-runner." Called by Sol White "the celebrated promoter of colored ball clubs, and the sage of base ball," Fowler died of pernicious anemia at a sister's home in Frankfort, New York.

FURTHER READING

Davids, L. Robert. "Bud Fowler," in *Nineteenth Century Stars*, eds. Robert L. Tiemann and Mark Rucker (1989).

Tholkes, Bob. "Bud Fowler, Black Pioneer, and the 1884 Stillwaters," *SABR Journal* 15 (1986).

This entry is taken from the *American National Biography* and is published here with the permission of the American Council of Learned Societies.

LARRY R. GERLACH

Fox, John (14 May 1917–26 Dec. 1944), soldier, was born John Robert Fox in Lebanon, Ohio, the son of well-educated, middle-class parents. Fox was the first of three children. His father passed away while Fox was a teenager. While still in his teens, he grew to admire the military and dreamed of a career in the armed forces. Most interested in math and science, he planned to attend college. Although Fox's grades were excellent, he was rejected by several universities before being accepted by the all-black Wilberforce University in Wilberforce, Ohio, where he participated in the Reserve Officer Training Corps for four years and graduated in June 1940 with a degree in biology.

Fox joined the U.S. Army in February 1941, completing Officer Candidate School at Fort Benning, Georgia, where he specialized in rifle and heavy weapons tactics. He then entered the ranks of the 366th Infantry Regiment of the Ninety-second Infantry Division stationed at Fort Devens, Massachusetts.

Fox's life changed quickly after Fort Devens. The Ninety-second Infantry Division, a segregated unit, trained at four separate installations across the nation: Fort McClellan, Alabama, Camp Atterbury, Indiana, Camp Breckenridge, Kentucky, and Camp Robinson, Arkansas. Fox trained at Camp Atterbury. Approximately twelve thousand men served in the division. All of the enlisted personnel were black, and most were from the South. The division, which included two hundred white officers (all senior officers were white) and six hundred black officers, left for Italy in October 1943.

The division was mustered into General Mark Clark's Fifth Army in August 1944 and saw immediate combat. These black soldiers fought against a veteran German army in Italy. The Ninety-second had poor equipment and training, and the typical enlisted man held only a fourth grade education due to discriminatory educational practices. Predictably the Ninety-second Infantry Division suffered a casualty rate of almost 25 percent from August 1944 until the final German surrender in Italy on 2 May 1945.

Fox had served nearly fourteen months in Italy by late December 1944, when he was assigned as a forward observer for the 598th Field Artillery Battalion stationed two miles southwest of Sommocolonia, Italy. Accompanied by Lieutenant Herbert Jenkins and fifty-three other soldiers, Fox and his platoon were practicing close order maneuvers between artillery and ground troops. The detachment stopped on Christmas night 1944 in a tower in this village to rest for the following day's mission. That night German troops, disguised as friendly Italian partisans, slipped into the town.

Daylight found Sommocolonia besieged by several hundred Austrian soldiers, disguised Germans, and Italian Fascists, mostly from the vaunted Austro-German Mittenwald Battalion. Lieutenants Fox and Jenkins's platoon was vastly outnumbered. Jenkins immediately called for support, but it could not penetrate the German lines. As the assault closed in on the tower, Fox called for artillery fire on coordinates only sixty yards from his own position along with a smokescreen to cover the withdrawal of the Allied troops whose rescue attempts had failed. Fox then called for an artillery bombardment directly on his own position. The artillery command questioned his order, but Fox continually demanded an artillery barrage directly on his position. Several platoon members, including Fox and Jenkins, were killed. Fox's orders and the actions of the platoon resulted in the deaths of about one hundred enemy soldiers and delayed the German assault so an Allied counterattack could be organized.

As with many acts of heroism committed in the fog of battle, controversy surrounded Fox and the other soldiers killed by the artillery fire. Subsequent investigations by Lieutenant Jefferson Jordan of the Ninety-second Infantry Division suggested that Fox was killed by friendly fire from American dive-bombers. No official record of a call for aerial bombing can be found, however. Whatever the details, nothing can diminish the sacrifice or bravery of Fox, Jenkins, and the other Americans who perished that day.

For his actions in Italy, Fox was posthumously awarded the Medal of Honor, the nation's highest award for military service, on 17 January 1997 by President Bill Clinton.

FURTHER READING

Gibran, Daniel K. *The Ninety-second Infantry Division and the Italian Campaign in World War II* (2001).

Hargrove, Hondon B. *Buffalo Soldiers in Italy: Black Americans in World War II* (1985).

Motley, Mary Penick, ed. and comp. *The Invisible Soldier: The Experience of the Black Soldier in World War II* (1987).

JEFFERY OTHELE MAHAN

Fox, Lillian Thomas (1866–29 Aug. 1917), elocutionist, journalist, and civic leader, was born in Chicago to the Reverend Byrd Parker, pastor of the Quinn African Methodist Episcopal (AME) Church, and Jane Janette Thomas. Her mother was one of the first black teachers in the Indianapolis public school system; she and Lillian's younger brother Charles T. Thomas died of tuberculosis in 1894.

In her youth Lillian worked at various jobs, including as a stenographer in Louisville, Kentucky. She moved to Indianapolis in 1886 and studied with Madame Hattie Prunk at the Indiana-Boston School of Elocution and at the Indianapolis Institute for Young Ladies. It was during this time that she developed her skills in dramatic reading and dialect. In 1888 she supported herself as a seamstress in her home. In 1891 she was one of the first Indianapolis blacks to take the civil service exam for a clerkship.

Also in 1891 Lillian accepted the position of assistant correspondence editor at the *Freeman*, an important black Indianapolis newspaper. It was through her work at the *Freeman* that she first achieved national recognition as a journalist. The *Freeman* became a lifelong admirer of hers, writing that she was "an original thinker and one who dare[d] to flout the dogma or philosophy be it ever so popular which [did] not consist with [her] cardinal principles of justice and right." The *Freeman* also praised her as "a very versatile and graceful speaker."

In 1893 Lillian married James E. Fox, a prosperous merchant tailor originally from Jamaica. James Fox relocated his business to Indianapolis, and soon after her marriage Lillian Thomas resigned from the *Freeman*. She believed that a women's true sphere of influence was the home. Although curtailing her journalistic career during her marriage, Lillian maintained an active involvement in church activities, especially as a speaker and organizer. She was also frequently asked to speak at black women's clubs. In 1895 Fox was invited to speak at the Atlanta Congress of Colored Women, along with other notable black women activists such as FANNIE BARRIER WILLIAMS and MARGARET MURRAY WASHINGTON. Black women from twenty-five states and Washington, D.C., attended the congress and resolved to continue the formation of women's and children's clubs as part of their work for the "advancement of social purity, home improvement, and child culture" (Wesley, 35).

Although she gained national prominence as a speaker, Fox was not immune to the harsh segregation enforced by the Jim Crow laws. During her travels a conductor on the Southern Railroad ordered her to leave the first-class coach and go to the smoking car, which had seating for blacks. Fox refused to move, and the conductor stopped the train and threw her baggage onto the tracks. While Fox hurried off the train to retrieve her luggage, the conductor restarted the train, intending to strand her by the tracks at 12:50 A.M. Fortunately several passengers demanded that the conductor stop the train and let her back on, but she was forced to sit in the smoking car. After this event Fox filed a lawsuit against the Southern Railroad, the outcome of which is not known.

After her husband's death in 1898 Fox again became available for journalistic employment, and in 1900 she accepted a position as a correspondent for the *Indianapolis News*, becoming the first black journalist to be hired to write a column for a white Indianapolis newspaper. Her Saturday column, titled "Notes of Colored People," listed meetings and events of black organizations in the area. Fox also wrote articles about local African Americans and about national black conventions and gatherings. Although the *Indianapolis News* did not allow Fox to write under a byline, the black press identified the columns as hers by her distinctive style.

Fox continued to write for the *Indianapolis News* for fourteen years. During this period she continued her work for black churches and women's clubs and went on numerous speaking tours in the Midwest and South for various political and religious organizations. She also spoke at conventions of the Afro-American Council, the Negro Business League, and the Anti-Lynching League. In 1903 Fox attended the convention of the National Association of Colored Women's Clubs (NACW) and became enthusiastic to create a local club that would be a member of the national organization. Later in 1903 she founded the Women's Improvement Club of Indianapolis and East Chicago. She was elected the first president of the new club, which from the beginning was made up of some of the most socially prominent black women in the city. The Women's Improvement Club was instrumental in the efforts to eradicate tuberculosis among blacks and to provide facilities for the care of individuals afflicted with the disease.

In 1904 Fox sent out a statewide call for black club women to meet at Bethel AME Church to form the Indiana Federation of Colored Women's Clubs. She was president of the pro tempore organizing body, and then until her death she was an honorary president of the Federation. In 1910 she spoke at the NACW in Louisville, Kentucky, along with such other prominent black women activists as IDA WELLS-BARNETT.

In 1914 Fox left the *Indianapolis News* because of ill health and failing eyesight and was the first black reporter in Indianapolis to receive an indefinite paid leave of absence. By that time she had increased the space allotted for her column to three-fourths of a page and had paved the way for other blacks to write similar columns at other white Indianapolis newspapers.

Lillian Fox was ill for the last three years of her life and curtailed her speaking and club activities. She died in 1917, and the Indiana State Federation of Colored Women's Clubs erected a marker on her grave. She is remembered as a pioneering black journalist and speaker, one whose concern with what was "just and right" sustained her many political and welfare activities in the black Indianapolis community.

FURTHER READING

The archives of the *Freeman* (1891–1893) and the *Indianapolis News* (1900–1914) containing the writings of Lillian Thomas Fox are held by the Indiana University Libraries, Bloomington.

Ferguson, Earline R. "Lillian Thomas Fox: Indianapolis Journalist and Community Leader," *Black History News and Notes* (May 1987).

Hine, Darlene Clark. *When the Truth Is Told: A History of Black Women's Culture and Community in Indiana, 1875–1950* (1981).

Wesley, Charles H. *The History of the National Association of Colored Women's Clubs: A Legacy of Service* (1984)

Obituary: *Indianapolis News*, 29 Aug. 1917.

EUGENIE P. ALMEIDA

Foxx, Jamie (13 Dec. 1967–), singer, musician, actor, and comedian, was born Eric Morlon Bishop in Terrell, Texas, to Shaheed Abdullah, a stockbroker, and Louise Annette Dixon. His mother had difficulty caring for him after her marriage broke up and so allowed her adoptive parents, Mark and Esther Talley, to adopt young Jamie when he was just seven months old. When Foxx was three years old his grandmother insisted he begin piano lessons, thus sparking Foxx's lifelong passion for music. His grandparents were avid churchgoers and encouraged Foxx's involvement in the church. As a teen Foxx became the director of the church choir and music programs. At Terrell High School he formed his own rhythm and blues band and played quarterback on the football team, meriting attention from the Dallas press.

Foxx earned a music scholarship to the United States International University in San Diego (later the Allian International University) from 1986 to 1988. Though he attended Juilliard and studied classic piano, Foxx left school without earning his degree and instead got a job selling shoes. One night at an open-mic club, the Comedy Store, his friends dared him to take the stage and do some impressions. The audience reception was so positive that it sent Foxx down a new career path, and in 1989 he went to Los Angeles to try his hand at stand-up comedy.

Foxx performed in numerous open-mic comedy clubs throughout Los Angeles, but early on noticed that the club's DJs more often called women to the stage before the men. So he changed his name to the androgynous Jamie to improve his chances of being selected to perform. He added the name Foxx as a tribute to his favorite comedian, REDD FOXX. His strategy worked and he was regularly called to the stage to perform, most often to standing ovations. In 1991, when he was twenty-two, Foxx won the Oakland Comedy Competition and that same year auditioned for and was chosen to join the cast of the Fox network's variety show *In Living Color* (1991–1994), where he created the character Wanda, one of the ugliest women in the world. Foxx's Wanda was an instant hit with both critics and the audience. The following year, Foxx was cast in a recurring role as Crazy George in the comedy show *Roc*, and appeared in six episodes. Foxx had his first movie role in 1992, when he appeared in the film *Toys*, starring Robin Williams. In 1993 Foxx was approached by HBO to create a one-man show, resulting in his own HBO special, *Jamie Foxx: Straight From the Foxxhole*.

Meanwhile Foxx also worked on various music projects. In 1994 he released his first R&B album, *Peep This*. The following year his daughter, Corrine, was born. Almost ten years later, in 2005, he released his second R&B album, *Unpredictable*, which was a popular success. Foxx also wrote and performed numerous songs for film and television soundtracks.

In 1996 Foxx created and produced his own show, *The Jamie Foxx Show* (1996–2001), on the WB network, in which he played an ambitious young actor who works in his relatives' hotel. Though the series was never a huge success, it generated a loyal following and earned Foxx his first major award: an NAACP Image Award in 1997 for Outstanding Actor. His exposure on the series also led him to be cast in several comedy films, including *The Truth About Cats and Dogs* (1996), *The Great White Hype* (1996), *Booty Call* (1997), in which Foxx received star billing, *The Player's Club* (1998), and *Held Up* (1999). Though the films were not box-office successes, they afforded Foxx tremendous public exposure.

Foxx's first dramatic role came when the director Oliver Stone cast him as a young quarterback who becomes an instant phenomenon in *Any Given Sunday* (1999). In 2001 the director Michael Mann cast Foxx in the role of Drew Bundini Brown, MUHAMMAD ALI's cornerman and assistant trainer, in the critically acclaimed film *Ali*. In 2003 Foxx starred with Sylvester Stallone in the drama *Shade*, but it wasn't until the following year that he achieved his greatest success by starring in three feature films: *Breakin' all the Rules*, *Collateral*, and *Ray*.

Foxx's performance as RAY CHARLES in *Ray* earned him numerous awards, including the 2005 Oscar for Best Actor in a Leading Role. To prepare for the role, Foxx attended classes at the Braille Institute. And though he lip-synced the film's vocals, Foxx did play the piano for the movie's many musical numbers. Foxx was only the second male actor in the history of the Academy Awards to receive two Oscar nominations for two different movies in the same year; he had been nominated for the Oscar for Best Supporting Actor for *Collateral* as well. For his portrayal of Charles, Foxx earned his second NAACP Image Award for Outstanding Actor; the NSFC (National Society of Film Critics) Award for Best Actor; and the Screen Actors Guild Award for Outstanding Lead Actor. He also won two Golden Satellite Awards in 2005 for Best Actor in a Motion Picture for *Ray* and in a Motion Picture Made for Television for *Redemption: The Stan Tookie Williams Story*. At the 2005 Golden Globe Awards, Foxx was nominated in three categories—Best Actor in a TV Film for *Redemption: The Stan Tookie Williams Story*; Best Supporting Actor for *Collateral*; and Best Actor for *Ray*—and won for *Ray*.

Following his performance in *Ray*, Foxx starred as detective Rico Tubbs in the film version of the 1980s television show *Miami Vice* (2006) and as Curtis Taylor Jr. in the musical *Dreamgirls* (2006), performing musical numbers onscreen and on the film's soundtrack.

FURTHER READING

Collier, Aldore. "The Thrills and Tears of the Ray Charles Story," *Ebony* 60.1 (2004): 96.

Lynch, Jason, et al. "Jamie Foxx: What You Need to Know," *People* 63.6 (2005).

Samuels, Allison. "Crazy like a Foxx," *Newsweek* 138.26 (2004).

DEBBIE CLARE OLSON

Foxx, Redd (9 Dec. 1922–11 Nov. 1991), comedian, was born John Elroy Sanford in St. Louis, Missouri, the son of Fred Sanford, an electrician, and Mary Carson, a radio preacher and domestic worker. He spent his early childhood in St. Louis. After his father deserted the home in 1926, he and his mother moved to Chicago, where she worked for the vice president of the Chicago White Sox baseball team. While attending DuSable High School, he and two friends formed a washtub band, the Bon Bons. In 1939 the trio hopped a freight train to New York, where they met with sporadic success. Although they performed mostly on street corners and in subway stations, they occasionally appeared at the Apollo Theater and on the *Major Bowes Amateur Hour*.

Friends nicknamed Sanford "Chicago Red" because of his red hair. He then added the surname Foxx in admiration of the baseball star Jimmie Foxx. He devised a distinctive spelling of the name he would be known by for the rest of his life: Redd Foxx.

In the mid-1940s Foxx married Eleanor Killebrew; they divorced in 1951. He was married three more times, in 1955 to Betty Jean Harris (divorced in 1974); in the mid-1970s to Yun Chi Chong (divorced in the late 1980s); and in 1991 to Kahoe Cho. He had no children.

In 1942 Foxx got his first regular job as a solo entertainer at Gamby's, a nightclub in Baltimore. He returned to New York in 1945 with a unique, polished act. Two years later he teamed with SLAPPY WHITE and saw his salary rise from $5 to $450 a week. In 1952 DINAH WASHINGTON invited the duo to open for her in California. Foxx and White split up soon after that, but Foxx remained on the West Coast at the end of the engagement. Foxx found the club scene in California even more segregated than on the East Coast. Still, he persevered in finding progressively larger venues and contracts, while supplementing his income with

Redd Foxx, c. 1973. Foxx became famous for his role as the raffish junkman Fred Sanford in the NBC comedy series *Sanford and Son*. (AP Images.)

work as a sign-painter. In 1955 Dootsie Williams, the owner of Dooto Records, caught Foxx's act and approached him with the revolutionary idea of recording an album consisting only of stand-up comic material and devoid of novelty songs. Foxx's sexually suggestive material prevented radio stations from broadcasting the albums. Nevertheless, the "party albums," as they would come to be known, were hugely popular in homes across the country. Foxx eventually recorded fifty-four party albums that together sold well over 10 million copies.

Owing to the popularity of the party albums, Foxx's salary and his acceptance at white nightclubs increased. In the early 1960s two famous patrons in these venues advanced Foxx's career. Frank Sinatra heard him perform, settled his Dooto contract, and signed him to LOMA, a subsidiary of the newly formed Reprise label. In 1964 the television host Hugh Downs saw Foxx at a club in San Francisco. Although television producers had been leery of Foxx's blue reputation, Downs booked him as a guest on the *Today* show. Foxx was a smash, and this appearance led to regular spots on talk shows such as *The Tonight Show* and *The Joey Bishop Show*, as well as appearances on television series such as *Mr. Ed*, *Green Acres*, and *The Addams Family*.

Along with his television success, Foxx appeared regularly in Las Vegas throughout the 1960s. In 1968, when ARETHA FRANKLIN failed to appear for an opening-night show, Foxx, the opening act, entertained the crowd for one hour and forty minutes. Bookers from the Hilton International Hotel who saw this performance were impressed enough to offer him a year-long, $960,000 contract.

Foxx broke into motion pictures in 1970, portraying an aging junk dealer in the United Artists release *Cotton Comes to Harlem*. This led directly to his title role in Norman Lear's adaptation of the British comedy *Steptoe and Son*, NBC's new television series *Sanford and Son*. It was an immediate hit. Foxx created the main character, Fred Sanford, named after his late brother. Foxx's portrayal of the irascible junkman who faked heart attacks—crying out "I'm coming, Elizabeth!" with the arrival of each "big one"—elevated him to his highest popularity. During the show's 1972–1977 run, Foxx was nominated for six Emmy Awards. Initially he had some degree of control over the show, but in 1977 he left it because of continual differences of opinion over the writing.

Although Foxx's talent was still bright, his luck was not. *The Redd Foxx Comedy Hour*, which premiered on ABC after Foxx left NBC, ran only for the 1977–1978 season. A revival of the Fred Sanford character, *Sanford* (NBC, 1980–1981), was also short-lived, as was *The Redd Foxx Show* (1986). Throughout this period Foxx continued to entertain crowds in Las Vegas; however, his lavish spending habits caught up with him in 1989, when the Internal Revenue Service forced him to sell off houses and cars to cover back taxes. In 1991 Foxx's luck was finally turning good again with the early success of another situation comedy, CBS's *The Royal Family*, but he died of a heart attack on the set, just weeks into the show's run.

Although Foxx will be remembered mainly for his work on *Sanford and Son*, his most lasting contribution is the invention of the stand-up comedy album. In his party albums he pioneered not only an innovation in record marketing but also freedom of speech in comedy. As a result, the voices of many other comedians were heard more widely in the homes of America.

FURTHER READING

Foxx, Redd. *Redd Foxx B.S.(Before Sanford)*, ed. Joe X. Price (1979).

Watkins, Mel. *On the Real Side: Laughing, Lying, and Signifying—The Underground Tradition of African American Humor that Transformed American Culture from Slavery to Richard Pryor* (1994).

ALEXANDER BATTLES

Foy(e), William Ellis (c.1819–9 November 1893), Freewill Baptist (FWB) minister and the first visionary of the Seventh Day Adventist (SDA) denomination, was born in Augusta, Maine, according to his death certificate. The same document lists his occupation as preacher, but does not mention the names of his parents. Foy's tombstone gives his age as seventy-four years.

Foy's early religious experiences were a devotional breakthrough that played an important role in the founding of the SDA denomination; but his personal history is elusive. According to J. N. Loughborough, a chronicler of the SDA, the Foy recorded as having visions died or disappeared after his 1845 publication, *The Christian Experience of William E. Foy: Together with the Two Visions He Received in the Months of Jan. and Feb. 1842. The Unknown Prophet*, a biography on Foy by Delbert W. Baker, instead argues that Foy later became a Freewill Baptist minister in New England. Baker's book is primarily about Foy's visions, which came before those of Ellen Gould Harmon White, also from Maine, who is recognized as an early Seventh Day Adventist prophetess.

Foy's central role in the founding of the SDA adds to the theory that the denomination has roots in the religious practices of Africa and black Americans. The writer and minister Charles Edward Dudley, Sr. has written several books on this theory, which has, however, proved controversial within the SDA denomination.

Genealogical research indicates that there were families named both Foy and Foye in early nineteenth century Maine; but Douglas A. Hall, compiler of early black Mainers' genealogies, has found no documentation of William Foy's parents, unless they were listed as white. Hall notes that William was the first name of the firstborn of the early white Foys in Maine. A number of black Foys in the Augusta area in the nineteenth century were known to have been farmers, barbers, and restaurant owners. According to his 1845 pamphlet, *Christian Experience*, William E. Foy was accepted into membership of Augusta's Freewill Baptist Church in 1835. In *Maine's Visible Black History* (2006) historian Anthony Douin notes that African Americans named Foye attended this church, a seat for abolitionists. The predominantly white congregation was a church home to many black people of the time, including the lay preacher John Eason.

Foy moved to Boston via Portland, Maine, in the late 1830s, perhaps to study for the ministry. He lived in the Beacon Hill neighborhood, where black thinkers, activists, and writers were fomenting a movement that would end slavery. The other movement that involved Foy was the Millerites, who predicted the Second Advent of Christ. When that Second Coming did not materialize, resulting in the Great Disappointment in 1844, many Millerites helped found the Seventh Day Adventists (SDA). Foy's recorded visions took place in 1842 in two churches in that neighborhood, the second one lasting for twelve hours in front of a black congregation of one thousand people at the Methodist Episcopal May Street Church. The church's minister was the Rev. SAMUEL SNOWDEN (c.1770–1850), who was the first known ordained black minister in Maine.

Foy then went on the public speaking circuit, alternating with earning a living by working with his hands. He returned to Maine, where a young Ellen Harmon (White) heard him speak and where Foy's *Christian Experience* was published in Portland by the Pearson brothers, who soon became Seventh Day Adventists. A few years later, while White was giving a talk about her visions, Foy jumped up and shouted that he had had one like it. He exclaimed, "The baton has passed." Ronald L. Numbers, a biographer of White, has written that the SDA membership believed that God chose her as a replacement for Foy.

In the late 1840s, William Foy/Foye disappears from the recorded history of the SDA and, assuming he is the same person, began a fifty-year career as a Freewill Baptist (FWB) minister, most of it in Maine. Tracking him through the early FWB churches is challenging, because their ministers moved the church records with them. In the 30 June 1847 issue of the *Morning Star*, a William E. Foye's name is included in a long list of supporters of "Protest and Declaration of Sentiment of Freewill Baptist ministers upon the subject of slavery."

Another notice appears in the New Bedford, Massachusetts, *Mercury*, 16 August 1850: "Whereas my wife, Ann A. Foy, has left my bed and board, without just provocation on my part, I therefore forbid all persons harboring or trusting her on my account, as I shall pay no debts of her contracting after this [date]. New Bedford, August 8, 1850 WILLIAM E. FOY."

Ellen White remembered Ann Foy as being very anxious about her husband's speaking in public. Baker reported that Ann had died sometime before 1850. Whatever became of Ann Foy, a William E. Foye married Caroline H. Griffin (c.1823–1856) in Augusta, Maine, on 17 August 1851. To muddy the waters, a Wm. E. Foye is also listed as Caroline Griffin's spouse in the 1850 census.

Foy then appears sporadically in Maine records, appearing in the Downeast section of the state as a "colored evangelist" who organized a church of twenty-five members on Mount Desert Island. He later moved to Plantation number 7 (Sullivan) where he held services in schoolhouses and halls. Robert L. Potter documented Elder Foy's thirty years in Sullivan. Foy conducted several land transactions, built houses, had at least one poem published, and participated in local affairs, and was feted annually, but is not listed as a voter. He married Precentia W. Rose of Portland in 1873. William Foy died in Sullivan, Maine, twenty years later.

Foy may have descendants through his and Caroline's son Or(r)in Foy(e), born c.1853, if he is the Orrin Foy who married Bessie Roberts (c.1878–1920) and lived on Dyer Island, Maine. They had twelve or thirteen children. There are varying simultaneous records on black Orrin Foys, but it is unlikely these were two separate people. The father of the "baker's dozen" died five days after Bessie and their last child died in childbirth, 10 June 1920.

"Rev. William E. Foye" is etched on his tombstone in Sullivan and his seven year-old daughter Laura is buried beside him. Seventh Day Adventist history tours stop at Foy's grave site and list it in their travel guide. Although Foy's history is elusive, there is substantial evidence that the Free Will Baptist elder buried in Sullivan is likely the visionary honored by the SDA as one of their founders.

FURTHER READING

Information on Foy and Foye family genealogy in Maine can be found in the following:

Baker, Delbert W. *The Unknown Prophet* (1987).

Douglas A. Hall, "The Foye Family of Augusta, Maine and sometimes Foy: A Maine African American Family" (August, 2007).

Foy, William E. *The Christian Experience of William E. Foy: Together with the Two Visions He Received in the Months of Jan. and Feb. 1842* (1845).

Numbers, Ronald L. *Prophetess of Health: A Study of Ellen G. White* (1976).

Potter, Robert L. "William Ellis Foy." *Sullivan (Maine) Historical Society's Newsletter* (September 2004).

Price, H. H., and Gerald E. Talbot. *Maine's Visible Black History: The First Chronicle of Its People* (2006).

Stakeman, Randolph A. "Black Census of Maine 1800–1910," unpublished draft (June, 1997), Maine Historical Society, Portland, Maine.

"The Foye Family of Kennebec County, Maine" (February 2, 2002) in Collection 2256, Maine Historical Society, Portland, Maine.

H. H. PRICE

Francis, John Richard (3 Mar. 1856–23 May 1913), surgeon and civic leader, was born in Washington, D.C. As a youth he attended the segregated black schools in the District of Columbia, and in 1868–1872 he attended Howard University's Normal Preparatory and Commercial Departments, whose curricula emphasized vocational training. At age sixteen Francis was sent to the elite Wesleyan Academy in Wilbraham, Massachusetts, where his studies included mathematics, philosophy, and the natural sciences. Returning to Washington, D.C., in 1875, he became an apprentice to Dr. C. C. Cox, a white physician who was head of the District of Columbia's board of health. Under Cox's supervision Francis enrolled in Howard University's medical college, studying there between 1875 and 1877. Francis left in the autumn of 1877 and enrolled at the University of Michigan as an advanced student, and in the spring of 1878 he received a degree in medicine.

Francis returned to Washington, D.C., where he opened a prosperous private medical practice, which was chiefly patronized by Washington's black elite. He was occasionally called upon as a consultant to other physicians, particularly in difficult cases involving obstetrics and gynecology. Many of these consulting experiences involved patients at the Freedman's Hospital, an all-black facility that had been created in 1862 at the corner of Thirteenth and R streets in Washington. The hospital's mission was to care for freed slaves as well as for disabled, elderly, and indigent black patients. After the Civil War it became the teaching hospital affiliated with the Howard University Medical School. Francis increasingly supplemented his lucrative private practice with less remunerative work at the Freedman's Hospital and became a part-time lecturer in obstetrics at the Howard University Medical School.

By the early 1890s Francis was on the permanent medical faculty of the Freedman's Hospital as a demonstrator in obstetrics, and from 1894 to 1895 he served as first assistant surgeon. For a brief period between April and October 1894 he was the hospital's acting surgeon in chief. The U.S. secretary of the interior appointed Francis as assistant surgeon in chief with an annual salary of eighteen hundred dollars. While he held this post Francis launched the hospital's nurses' training program. He resigned in April 1895 to open his own private hospital in Washington, D.C., but he remained on the advisory board of the Freedman's Hospital for many years and continued to take an active interest in the hospital's affairs.

Francis's private hospital and sanatorium was established in 1895 at 2112 Pennsylvania Avenue. At this fashionable address, a number of trained nurses under Francis's direction provided care for all patients regardless of their race. Most patients at the hospital were black women experiencing or recovering from difficult pregnancies. The hospital itself was arranged to permit long-term care, particularly for those recovering from surgery or in need of a rest cure. A 1901 advertisement for Francis's hospital noted that the facility had such modern fixtures as a telephone and round-the-clock staff. In-patients paid between fifteen and fifty dollars a week, and "no insane, contagious, or other objectionable cases" were admitted.

Several well-trained black physicians with credentials from well-respected medical schools had been refused membership in Washington's all-white Medical Society of the District of Columbia. Francis had applied for membership, but like other blacks he was declared eligible for membership and then denied admission by a vote of the membership in 1894. White women physicians who had been seeking admission since 1876 finally ended the ban in 1891; by late 1894 seven white female physicians had been voted in. Working with FURMAN J. SHADD, Francis brought the issue directly to the U.S. Congress, which manages the affairs of the District of Columbia. Shadd and Francis sought the revocation of the society's charter, which had been granted in 1838, unless the society admitted black male physicians. Congress failed to act.

Nonetheless, with his family and political connections and his income from the private hospital, Francis was well placed to emerge as a civic leader in Washington, D.C.'s black community. He served as a trustee of the Washington, D.C., public schools from September 1886 until September 1889, and his wife also served on the board of education for varying periods between 1900 and 1910. She took a special interest in the work of the Industrial Education and Special Instruction schools, in which most black students were enrolled. Through their service on these boards, both developed extensive social and political contacts with such leading Washington black educators at JOHN FRANCIS COOK, Robert and MARY CHURCH TERRELL, FRANCIS L. CARDOZO, and fellow University of Michigan Medical School alumnus and board of education member Oliver Madison Atwood.

Francis was also devoted to classical, as opposed to strictly vocational, higher education for black students. He was a member of the board of trustees of Howard University from 1908 to 1913. In 1909 he sponsored an initiative to appoint W. E. B. DUBOIS to the faculty of Howard University, but the movement foundered because of strong opposition from another trustee, BOOKER T. WASHINGTON, who believed DuBois to be too radical on race relations.

Francis died in Washington, D.C., in 1913 at the age of fifty-seven. He was buried at Woodlawn Cemetery on Benning Road in Washington, D.C. His service to the black public schools of Washington and to higher education for black students was commemorated in 1928 when a new public junior high school building in Washington was named for him.

FURTHER READING

Biographical cards completed by John Richard Francis in 1900 and 1910 are available in the University of Michigan's Bentley Historical Library in the UM Alumni Association's necrology file. The Charles Sumner School Museum and Archives in Washington, D.C., holds the District of Columbia Board of Education records, as well as a vertical file on Francis Junior High School that contains biographical data on Francis himself.

Hilyer, Andrew F. *The Twentieth Century Union League Directory: A Historical, Biographical, and Statistical Study of Colored Washington* (1901).

Johnson, Georgia A. Lewis, ed. *Black Medical Graduates of the University of Michigan (1872–1960 Inclusive) and Selected Black Michigan Physicians* (1994).

Moore, Jacqueline M. *Leading the Race: The Transformation of the Black Elite in the Nation's Capital 1880–1920* (1999).

LAURA M. CALKINS

Francis, Norman C. (20 Mar. 1931–), educator, activist, and lawyer, was born in Lafayette, Louisiana, one of five children. Francis's father, Joseph A. Francis, a barber who owned his own business, was known around town as "Mr. Joe the Barber." Though his father and mother, a homemaker, provided the necessities for their children, they were considered poor for the times. In what could be considered a foreshadowing of Francis's lifelong career path, his parents believed strongly in the benefits and importance of education for their children. They expressed that belief by sending their children to Catholic schools and making sure they kept up with their studies.

Francis attended Saint Paul Catholic High School in Lafayette, Louisiana. He was the class president and valedictorian. After graduating from Saint Paul in 1948, Francis entered Xavier University of New Orleans. In 1952 he earned his B.A degree from Xavier and enrolled in Loyola University Law School in New Orleans. He was the first African American to attend the law school and upon graduating in 1955, Francis would become the first African American to earn a law degree from Loyola. After law school Francis joined the U.S. Army and served as a member of the Third Armored Division from 1955 to 1957. Then he returned to Xavier and began his service there as dean of men. From 1957 to 1968 he held many positions at the university, including assistant to the president in charge of development and executive vice president.

Francis, who would in 2003 become the longest tenured president at any university in the United States, accepted the position of president of Xavier University on 4 April 1968, the day MARTIN LUTHER KING JR. was assassinated. Just before his death, King acknowledged in his famous "I've been to the mountain top" speech that "longevity has its place" (Carson, 365), and this would prove true for Francis. During his tenure he presided over Xavier's tremendous growth and cultivated its national reputation. He expanded and improved the campus by acquiring buildings and spearheading the construction of new ones. Student enrollment and alumni giving increased, and the school's endowment was soon well into the tens of millions of dollars. Francis and Xavier were particularly heralded for Xavier's position as the premier institution for African American students pursuing health professional careers; Xavier led the nation in pharmacy graduates and was first in the nation in placing African American students in medical school.

Francis's high profile position afforded him the opportunity to spread his influence beyond Xavier and to become involved in and affect change in other arenas. In 1972 he helped found Liberty Bank—a black-owned bank in New Orleans—and served as its chairman of the board of directors. He described the bank at its inception as a "new symbol of minorities controlling their own capital. It was a new experience for our customers to see black tellers and black branch managers" (*New York Times*, 20 Sept. 2005). Additionally, Francis was appointed by President Ronald Reagan to the National Commission on Education Excellence. In 1983 that commission produced a groundbreaking report titled "A Nation at Risk," which candidly portrayed the quality of public education in the United States. In 1968 he joined Louisiana's Commission on Human Rights and Responsibilities, one of the many commissions and boards he served on throughout his tenure at Xavier University.

Francis's work did not go unnoticed. In 2004 he added to his decades-long list of honors and awards when he received the James T. Rogers Meritorious Service Award by the Commission on Colleges of the Southern Association of Colleges and Schools, as well as the Council for Advancement and Support of Education's Executive Leadership Award. In 2006 President Bush also presented him with the Presidential Medal of Freedom, the nation's highest civilian honor. In addition to the awards, Francis received more than thirty honorary degrees from universities such as Harvard, Johns Hopkins, and Drexel.

In 2005 Francis and Xavier faced a course-altering event. Hurricane Katrina tore through New Orleans on 29 August 2005. While the hurricane itself produced little structural damage to the university, the surrounding levee breaks and ensuing flooding resulted in at least six feet of water sitting on parts of the campus. Just as in the past, Francis's focus was on rebuilding not only Xavier but also the community in which Xavier existed. The governor of Louisiana appointed him chairman of the Louisiana Recovery Authority (LRA). In this organization Francis focused on many controversial issues surrounding the Louisiana rebuilding effort. When asked whether the efforts to rebuild New Orleans included building it as the

African American city it had been before Hurricane Katrina, he responded:

> That really is our major responsibility in the LRA and the city's commission. We have got to allow everybody an opportunity to come back home; and that's particularly true for African Americans who really built the city, lived in the city, and have every right to come back (Smiley interview).

Almost every part of the Xavier campus was touched by flooding after the hurricane. Because of this, Francis was left with no option but to cancel Xavier's 2005 fall semester, just as most other local university and college presidents across the city did. With his students spread out at universities across the country, he began the task of rebuilding Xavier. Although he faced criticism for laying off faculty in the wake of the hurricane, he insisted the layoffs were necessary to keep Xavier afloat. When asked about the rebuilding effort, Francis said, "I'm not naïve, and I know it's going to be difficult. But we have to keep the faith and believe it can be done" (Mangan, 48).

FURTHER READING

Norman C. Francis's biographical information and portions of his university correspondence are contained in the University Archives housed at the Xavier University Library in New Orleans.

Finney Peter, Jr. "Dr. Francis Keeps Xavier Striding Toward the Future," *Clarion Herald*, 16 July 2003.

Mangan, Katherine S. "At Xavier U. of Louisiana, an 'Indefatigable Fighter,'" *Chronicle of Higher Education*, 10 Feb. 2006.

Smiley, Tavis. Dr. Norman Francis interview, *PBS*, 22 Nov. 2005.

Stacey, Truman. "Black History Month: Norman Francis," *Catholic Herald* (1997).

TWINETTE L. JOHNSON

Francis, William Trevane (26 Apr. 1869–15 July 1929), lawyer and diplomat, was born in Indianapolis, Indiana, the only child of James and Hattie Francis. Almost nothing of Francis's family and childhood is known, except that his father died before Francis was ten years old. In 1888 he moved to St. Paul, Minnesota, then a booming railroad city of about 130,000 with an African American community numbering perhaps 1,500. At age eighteen Francis found work as a messenger in the headquarters of the Northern Pacific Railroad, then became an office boy, a clerk in the legal department, and finally in 1901 chief clerk, probably the highest position attained by any African American in the railroad at that time. The Twin Cities black community considered Francis's position to be a distinguished one and he remained with the railroad for nearly twenty-five years.

From his earliest days in St. Paul, Francis distinguished himself as a singer and performed frequently as a soloist and in ensembles. In musical work at his church, Pilgrim Baptist, he met the Nashville native Nellie Griswold, herself a woman of talent and drive. They married in 1893 and often performed together in productions at Pilgrim and other St. Paul churches.

In 1889 Francis had begun a long friendship with the St. Paul lawyer and civil rights leader Fredrick L. McGhee, and though the two later had differences, mostly over race politics, their careers became entwined. Both were handsome, articulate, and ambitious, but McGhee was six years older and a renowned trial lawyer, so Francis often stood in his shadow. They worked together in various civil rights organizations, especially the National Afro-American Council, with McGhee always in the more prominent role.

Seeking an outlet for his ambitions, Francis obtained a degree in osteopathy from St. Paul in 1901, but never practiced, then enrolled in law school, graduating from St. Paul College of Law (later William Mitchell College of Law) in 1904. He practiced law on the side while continuing to work at the Northern Pacific, where his law degree allowed him to assume greater responsibilities, including representing the company in legal matters around the Midwest.

With a law license Francis stepped forward as a sort of friendly rival to Fredrick McGhee for prime leadership in the St. Paul black community. He had certain advantages: Francis was a Protestant and Republican, like the great majority of black citizens, while McGhee was a Democrat and Catholic. Moreover, in 1903 McGhee had split from BOOKER T. WASHINGTON over-Washington's manipulations of the National Afro-American Congress at its 1902 and 1903 conventions—while Francis remained loyal to Washington, the far more popular position. In this, Francis and McGhee personified the two great competing currents of African American politics of the time.

In 1906 Francis ran as a Republican for St. Paul city assembly, probably the first African American to do so. Though endorsed by the city's major newspaper, the *Pioneer Press*, he finished last in a field of eighteen. Still, the nearly 10,000 votes he received represented ten times or more the number of eligible black voters in the city. He ran for the state legislature in 1916 and lost again. His devoted work for the Republican Party earned him valuable connections with judges, governors, congressmen, and senators, in Minnesota and elsewhere.

When McGhee died suddenly in 1912 Francis took over McGhee's office and left the railroad to practice law full time. In his early forties Francis came into his own. As a lawyer he had a varied practice, taking on cases involving criminal, personal injury, probate, and business law. He represented and helped create several black-owned businesses and assisted Betty and Sam Williams in creating a guardianship for their nephew, the young Roy Wilkins, who later rose to prominence in the civil rights movement. He spoke often on civil rights issues, pointedly but always within the Booker T. Washington tradition, seeking equality of opportunity (if not social equality) and ascribing white resistance to ignorance rather than racism. He protested the screening of D. W. Griffith's 1915 motion picture *Birth of a Nation* and led a successful effort to secure integration of St. Paul's public baths. Francis was one of just a handful of African American attorneys able to make a living in the Twin Cities.

Francis's wife, Nellie, was fully his equal. While he worked at the railroad, she worked at West Publishing, the legal publisher, one of St. Paul's most distinguished companies. She was an outstanding musician and organizer, leading local African American women's clubs, the NAACP, and Urban League, and in agitating for suffrage. She also led the movement for passage of Minnesota's anti-lynching law in 1921. They were an impressive and accomplished couple. They had no children.

Like most members of St. Paul's black middle class, the Francises were homeowners, living for more than twenty years in the integrated Rondo neighborhood. In 1924 they bought a house in a relatively new, all white part of St. Paul, touching off threats, protests, and vandalism, including two cross burnings, openly organized by white residents of the neighborhood. Though their standing in the community and political connections helped the couple weather the storm, they did not remain in the house for long.

As early as 1911 Francis had been lobbying for a federal appointment. He tried first for minister to Haiti under President Taft, a post for which he assembled the endorsements of Minnesota's governor, St. Paul's mayor, and the representative of the Fourth Congressional District (St. Paul). This effort failed, but in 1926–1927, Francis tried again, this time with the endorsement of his former law school classmate, U.S. Senator Thomas Schall of Minnesota, plus Senator William Butler of Massachusetts, Mary McLeod Bethune, and Emmet Scott, among others. President Coolidge subsequently appointed him U.S. minister to Liberia at a crucial moment, the beginning of the Firestone Rubber Co.'s multimillion dollar investment in Liberian rubber plantations.

This fulfillment of Francis's ambition proved catastrophic. Though diligent and respected, Francis did not thrive as a diplomat, and the strong-willed Nellie clashed with important women in the diplomatic social scene. Then disease struck. In June 1929 Francis contracted yellow fever, and after a month of agony he died in Monrovia.

A key figure in the creation of an African American professional class in Minnesota, Francis was also the first black Minnesotan—and still one of the few—to serve as a U.S. ambassador.

FURTHER READING

Heidenreich, Douglas R. "A Citizen of Fine Spirit: William T. Francis," *William Mitchell* (Fall 2000).

PAUL D. NELSON

Frankie. *See* Baker, Frankie.

Franklin, Aretha (26 March 1942–) singer and pianist, was born Aretha Louise Franklin in Memphis, Tennessee, the daughter of the Reverend C. L. Franklin, a prominent Baptist minister, and Barbara Siggers. Franklin was one of five children, including sisters Carolyn and Erma, brother Cecil, and half-brother Vaughn.

Franklin and her family settled in Detroit, Michigan, where her father, after a brief sojourn in Buffalo, New York, took over the New Bethel Baptist Church in 1948. Aretha Franklin was literally raised in the bosom of African American religious tradition and was thus the direct product of one of the most significant institutions in the African American community. As a youth Franklin was intimately exposed to the artistry of the major black gospel performers of the era, including Sam Cooke (then of the Soul Stirrers), Mahalia Jackson, James Cleveland (who at one time during Franklin's youth was the Minister of Music at New Bethel), and Marion Williams and Clara Ward (both of the Clara Ward Singers). Ward was Franklin's most significant gospel influence. Franklin's father also exposed her to the music of jazz performers like pianists such as Dorothy Donegan, Oscar Peterson, and Art Tatum.

Aretha Franklin poses with her "Best Rhythm and Blues Performance, Female" Grammy Award at the Annual Grammy Award presentation in New York on 3 March 1975. The award is for her performance in "Ain't Nothing Like the Real Thing." (AP Images.)

Among the secular performers who profoundly affected Franklin was the rhythm and blues vocalist DINAH WASHINGTON. As a teenager Franklin began to travel with her father as the opening act for his gospel show. It was in Detroit's New Bethel Baptist Church, however, that the fourteen-year-old Franklin made her first recording. The live album was released by Chess Records in 1956, the same label that distributed her father's sermons.

By the age of eighteen Franklin had left Detroit for New York City. Though she was reportedly wooed by Sam Cooke, then an artist for RCA Records, and by BERRY GORDY JR.'s fledgling Motown label, the legendary producer John Hammond signed Franklin to record for Columbia Records. Hammond had been instrumental in the early career of BILLIE HOLIDAY, and it was with vocalists like Holiday, Dinah Washington, and BESSIE SMITH in mind that Hammond helped to craft Franklin's early recordings for the Columbia label. Franklin's initial recordings—*Aretha (with the Ray Bryant Combo)* (1961), *The Electrifying Aretha Franklin* (1962), and *The Tender, the Moving, the Swinging Aretha Franklin* (1962)—were produced by Hammond and Robert Mersey. The albums included "Blue Holiday" and "God Bless the Child." An accomplished pianist, Franklin was also featured as an instrumentalist on some of these albums. During this period Franklin married Ted White, who also became her manager.

Robert Mersey also produced *Laughing on the Outside* (1963) and *Unforgettable—A Tribute to Dinah Washington* (1964). The latter recording featured Franklin's renditions of some of Washington's best-known recordings, including "This Bitter Earth," "Evil Gal Blues," and "What a Difference a Day Makes." Though Franklin was served well by Hammond and Mersey, it was with Johnny Otis that her career finally exhibited some degree of consistency. Franklin never achieved broad, mainstream appeal during her tenure at Columbia Records (1960–1966), but her recordings with Otis, which included *Runnin' Out of Fools* (1964), *Yeah!!! In Person with Her Quartet* (1965), and *Soul Sister* (1966), positioned Franklin as a rhythm and blues artist, as opposed to a jazz or mainstream pop artist.

Franklin signed with Atlantic Records in 1967 and began a fruitful professional relationship with the producer Jerry Wexler. Wexler's first instinct upon signing Franklin was to have her travel to the South and record at the legendary Fame Studios in Muscle Shoals, Alabama. On the evening of 24 January 1967 Franklin and a group of white rockabilly musicians laid down the basic tracks to "I Never Loved a Man (The Way I Love You)" and "Do Right Woman—Do Right Man," songs that changed the face of American pop music and began Franklin's ascent as one of the most influential musical artists in American history. Franklin's first four albums for Atlantic, *I Never Loved a Man the Way I Loved You* (1967), *Aretha Arrives* (1967), *Lady Soul* (1968), and *Aretha Now* (1968), established her as the most important black female vocal artist since Billie Holiday. The recordings contained a litany of hit singles such as "Respect," "Dr. Feelgood," "Baby, I Love You," "Chain of Fools," "(You Make Me Feel Like) A Natural Woman," and "Think" that are synonymous with the best music produced since the advent of the rock-and-roll era in the mid-1950s. It was in this period that Franklin became universally known as the "Queen of Soul." On the strength of "Respect," Franklin earned her first Grammy Award for Best R&B Vocal Performance, Female. She won the award every year between 1967 and 1974, totaling ten Grammy Awards during that time frame. Though Franklin never viewed her version of "Respect" as explicitly political, the passion with which she expressed her desire for respect, literally spelling out the word in the song's memorable break-down, resonated within both the civil rights and burgeoning women's rights movements.

While Franklin still maintained a significant popular following, her subsequent body of work for Atlantic in the early 1970s was less commercial and more reflective of her maturing artistry. Her music during this period also reflected the end of her tumultuous marriage with Ted White, which ended in 1969, most notably in the song "All the King's Horses." This body of work was marked by the number of recordings written by Franklin and her sister Carolyn. Notable among these recordings are *Aretha—Live at the Fillmore West* (1971), *Young, Gifted and Black* (1972), and *Amazing Grace* (1972). Whereas *Live at the Fillmore West* gave witness to Franklin's wide appeal beyond soul music audiences (and provided a once in lifetime performance with RAY CHARLES on "Spirit in the Dark") and *Young, Gifted and Black* represented Franklin's most cogent statements on the political movement for which many believe her music is the soundtrack, *Amazing Grace* represented the most important musical statement of her career. Recorded live at the New Temple Missionary Baptist Church in Los Angeles, nearly fifteen years to the day that she stepped into Fame Studios, *Amazing Grace* reunited Franklin with James Cleveland and the black church traditions that birthed her. Highlights of the recording include a ten-minute version of "Amazing Grace" and a stirring rendition of Clara Ward's "How I Got Over," with the legendary vocalist sitting in the audience.

During the 1970s Franklin had the opportunity to work with well-known black producers like QUINCY JONES and CURTIS MAYFIELD, who produced *Hey Now Hey (The Other Side of the Sky)* in 1973 and *Sparkle* in 1976, respectively. The latter recording featured music written for the film *Sparkle* and featured "Giving Him Something He Can Feel," Franklin's last major hit for the Atlantic label. She married the actor Glynn Turman in 1978 but their marriage ended six years later. Franklin signed with the Arista label in 1980. *Love All the Hurt Away* (1981), her second album for the label, took advantage of her star-turn in the film *The Blues Brothers* (1979), where she appeared as a soul-singing waitress. The project also featured a duet with George Benson on the title track.

In an effort to update her sound, Franklin was paired with the young songwriters and producers LUTHER VANDROSS and Marcus Miller. Both *Jump to It* (1982) and *Get It Right* (1983) were moderate successes, but it wasn't until 1985, when she joined forces with Michael Narada Walden on *Who's Zoomin' Who?* with the song "Freeway of Love" that Franklin matched her commercial success of the late 1960s and early 1970s. Her follow-up recording, *Aretha* (1986), featured a duet with George Michael on the song "I Knew You Were Waiting," which became her first number one pop song since "Respect." In 1987 Franklin was inducted into the Rock and Roll Hall of Fame, becoming the first woman to achieve the honor. During this period she also returned to her gospel roots, recording *One Lord, One Faith, One Baptism* (1988). Franklin continued to record for the Arista label throughout the 1990s, notably pairing with the hip-hop artist Lauryn Hill on the Grammy Award–nominated "A Rose Is Still a Rose" in 1998. She also received a Lifetime Achievement Award from the National Academy of Recording Arts and Sciences (NARAS) in 1994 and in 2005 Franklin was awarded the Presidental Medal of Freedom, America's highest civilian honor. At the 1998 Grammy Awards ceremony, Franklin performed the aria "Nessun dorma" from Puccini's *Turandot*, filling in at the last moment for the famed Italian tenor Luciano Pavarotti, who had taken ill less than an hour before his scheduled performance. Franklin also has the distinction of performing at inaugural celebrations for presidents Jimmy Carter (1977), Bill Clinton (1993), and BARACK OBAMA (2009) at the funeral for MARTIN LUTHER KING JR., where she sang "Amazing Grace."

Aretha Franklin has been one of the most celebrated black female singers ever. In 2003 and 2005 she was again triumphant at the Grammy Awards, winning in both years for Best Traditional R&B Vocal Performance. Her influence continues to be heard in artists like Miki Howard, Whitney Houston, and Mary J. Blige. Franklin's well-known nickname, "Queen of Soul," acknowledges that she has become one of the yardsticks by which black popular music is measured. Late in her career, Franklin's releases were still viewed as an event.

FURTHER READING

Franklin, Aretha, with David Ritz. *Aretha: From These Roots* (1999).

Bego, Mark. *Aretha Franklin: The Queen of Soul* (2001).

Ward, Brian. *Just My Soul Responding: Rhythm and Blues, Black Consciousness, and Race Relations* (1998).

Wexler, Jerry, and David Ritz. *Rhythm and Blues: A Life in American Music* (1993).

MARC ANTHONY NEAL

Franklin, Buck Colbert (6 May 1879–24 Sept. 1960), attorney, freedman, father of the eminent historian JOHN HOPE FRANKLIN, and Tulsa race riot survivor, was born Buck Colbert Franklin in the Chickasaw Nation, Indian Territory, now part of the state of Oklahoma, the son of David Franklin and Millie Colbert. David Franklin raised cattle, horses, and other livestock for sale. He also farmed. Millie Colbert taught school. The seventh of ten children, B.C. went by his initials as an adult to prevent whites from calling him by his first name. His efforts were only partially successful, as many whites called him Ben, assuming that he was named after Ben Franklin. In reality he was named Buck in honor of his paternal grandfather and Colbert to honor his mother's family name.

Franklin's parents were "freedmen," a term used to define the black citizens of the Cherokee, Chickasaw, Choctaw, Creek, and Seminole Nations, known as the Five Civilized Tribes, in Indian Territory. Many Indians of these nations owned slaves, and most freedmen were former slaves or descendants of former slaves. In his autobiography Franklin wrote that his paternal grandfather purchased his and his family's freedom from their Chickasaw Indian owners long before slavery's end. Therefore Franklin's father grew up free. However, other accounts suggest that Franklin's father grew up as a slave and ran away to join the Union army during the Civil War. Franklin's mother was a Choctaw freedman. Franklin wrote that although his maternal grandmother was black and his maternal grandfather was half Choctaw and half black, his mother was not raised as a slave but as an equal member of her extended Choctaw Indian family. Marriage between members of different tribes was common, and after their union David and Millie Franklin lived on and farmed communal land in the Chickasaw Nation. In the late nineteenth century, however, the U.S. federal government began enrolling tribe members to assign citizenship status and to allot them private landholdings. Before her death in 1891, Millie Franklin attempted to ensure that she and her children would be legally recognized as Choctaw Indians, just as she had been raised. Ultimately, however, B.C. and his siblings were enrolled as Choctaw freedmen and allotted only twenty acres apiece.

Growing up in Indian Territory, Franklin experienced and witnessed many of the injustices committed against freedmen and Indians by whites as the federal government began the process of converting Indian Territory into the state of Oklahoma. He decided to become an attorney to help protect the rights of people of color. This determination led him to become the only one of his siblings to get more than an elementary education. Between 1894 and 1896 Franklin attended the Dawes Academy in Berwyn, Indian Territory. Two years later he entered Roger Williams University in Nashville, Tennessee. At Roger Williams, Franklin met his future wife, Mollie Lee Parker, and his lifelong mentor, JOHN HOPE, future president of Atlanta Baptist College (renamed Morehouse College in 1913). After the death of his father in 1900, Franklin followed Hope to Atlanta Baptist College, but he returned to Indian Territory after one year to settle his family's affairs and begin his adult life.

In his first year home Franklin began farming, and he represented his first client before the Dawes Commission, the federal body responsible for enrolling Indians and freedmen and allotting their land. The experience motivated him to take law school courses by correspondence through the Sprague Law School in Detroit, Michigan. In the meantime, he and Parker married in 1903. They had four children. The couple taught school and farmed until Franklin finished his legal training in 1906.

During the next fifteen years Franklin struggled to establish himself as an attorney. In the process he moved his growing family first to Ardmore, Oklahoma, and then to the black town of Rentiesville, Oklahoma. Over the years he successfully represented several freedmen, thus partially fulfilling his mission. However, in this era of Jim Crow, few blacks and almost no whites were willing to risk hiring a black attorney.

Franklin's problems were compounded by his independent spirit. He was a lifelong Jeffersonian Democrat in an era when most blacks were Republicans (Franklin [1997], 169). Franklin's attempts to explain the differences between his politics, which were modeled after Thomas Jefferson's political philosophy, and those of the racist Democrats who disfranchised blacks in Oklahoma fell upon deaf ears. Instead, he was ostracized by blacks in Ardmore, many of whom would not even speak to him on the street. In Rentiesville the situation was even worse. Franklin earned the open hostility of community leaders when he received desirable civic appointments, like town postmaster and justice of the peace, in part due to his Democratic affiliation. His preference for the Methodist Church in a town dominated by Baptists deepened the resentment against him in Rentiesville. Not until the 1930s, when Franklin Roosevelt was president, would he feel vindicated in his position and be called visionary by his peers. Before this moment of absolution, however, Franklin, Mollie, and their children endured many trials. In 1921, after he received threatening letters and the family's horse was shot, Franklin decided to move his family again. This time he chose Tulsa, Oklahoma, and moved to the city ahead of his wife and children to get his legal practice running and to prepare a place for them.

The Franklin family planned to reunite in Tulsa in the summer of 1921, but their reunion was delayed for several years. Within a few months of B.C. Franklin's arrival, the arrest of a young African American man, Dick Rowland, for allegedly attacking a white woman in an elevator sparked the Tulsa race riot. Greenwood, the black section of Tulsa, was burned to the ground, over one hundred people were killed, and thousands of others were displaced. Like most black survivors who did not escape the city, Franklin was arrested and placed in a detention center. When released, he and his law partners immediately began to represent other riot victims against insurance companies that denied their claims and against a city ordinance hurriedly passed after the riot to prevent blacks from rebuilding. These Tulsa riot cases were among the most important legal work of his career and helped him fulfill his mission to help protect the rights of black people.

In 1959, the year before his death, Franklin was honored by the Oklahoma Bar Association and the Tulsa YMCA. In 1968 Tulsa named a new park in his honor.

FURTHER READING

Franklin, Buck Colbert. *My Life and an Era: The Autobiography of Buck Colbert Franklin*, eds. John Hope Franklin and John Whittington Franklin (1997).

Franklin, John Hope. *Mirror to America: The Autobiography of John Hope Franklin* (2005).

MELISSA NICOLE STUCKEY

Franklin, C. L. (22 Jan. 1915–27 July 1984), preacher, was born Clarence LaVaughn Pitman in Sunflower, Mississippi, to Elijah J. Pitman and Willie Ann Pitman, sharecroppers. Elijah served in Europe during World War I, returned to Mississippi briefly, and then departed. Shortly thereafter, Willie Ann married Henry Franklin, a farmer; the family took his name, and Franklin became Clarence's father. As a boy Clarence usually went to school from December to March, which was when he was not needed in the field. His mother took him and his stepsister, Aretha, to St. Peter's Rock Baptist Church, where he sang in the choir, and eventually became lead tenor. His father, religious but not a churchgoer, exposed Clarence to the blues idiom of BLIND LEMON JEFFERSON and other soulful musicians.

At the age of nine or ten Clarence attended a revival meeting and took his first step toward a career in the ministry when he joined the church. In the tradition of many black Baptist congregations in the South, he sat on the mourner's bench with the other initiates, gave a personal testimony (in his case without ecstatic exaltation), and was voted in by acclamation. Full-immersion baptism in a local river soon followed. As a teenager Clarence heard a sermon by Dr. Benjamin J. Perkins about the "doubting" apostle Thomas that prompted him to wonder if he, too, had a calling to preach. He described receiving a sign, a vision like the burning bush encountered by Moses, except that in his vision the walls of his room were ablaze without being consumed. From the flames came a voice saying, "Go and preach the gospel to all the nations" (Franklin, 9). He preached his first sermon at the age of fifteen or sixteen, but there was no congregation in the vicinity that needed a minister, particularly one so young and inexperienced. He became a migrant worker and itinerant preacher, working on farms from Mississippi to Michigan, picking everything from cotton to strawberries, and preaching at camp meetings and receptive congregations along the way. After a few years he returned to Mississippi, where his father, who needed help on his farm, told Clarence, "Now you have got to make up your mind whether you want to preach or plow" (Franklin, 13).

Clarence decided to devote himself to preaching and was ordained the Reverend C. L. Franklin at St. Peter's Rock when he was only seventeen or eighteen years old. However, finding a congregation capable of supporting a minister during the Depression was very difficult. Many of the black churches throughout the South lacked the resources to engage a permanent minister. Hence, gifted black preachers sometimes worked a network of small congregations in order to sustain themselves. Franklin worked as a traveling preacher until he landed a temporary appointment at the County Line Baptist Church, where he learned painful lessons about the politics of church management that equipped him with skills that proved to be as valuable to his future success as his impressive oratorical ability. While visiting a congregation in Shelby during the late 1930s he met his wife, Barbara Siggers, the church pianist. They had four children before her death in 1952.

Intellectually, Franklin demonstrated a passion for the life of the mind that was equal to his concern for the health of the soul. He studied theology at Greenville Industrial College and took a wide range of courses at LeMoyne College (now LeMoyne-Owen College), in Memphis, Tennessee. His scholarly manner distinguished him from many black preachers who had mastered the unique African American sermonic style, but who lacked Franklin's cerebral depth. Yet, unlike many seminary-trained clerics, Franklin's exegesis of scripture retained the fire associated with the black pulpit. In his view, "the-mental can be spiritual, even more spiritual than the emotional" (Franklin, 16). In his version of "The Eagle Stirreth Her Nest," a traditional sermon that preachers had been adapting since the 1920s, Franklin vividly examines a difficult biblical metaphor with power and insight. In "The Twenty-Third Psalm," he breathes new life into a familiar passage by providing historical context while extracting contemporary relevance.

Some scholars have denigrated the oratorical style of Franklin and other black preachers, suggesting that their use of such rhetorical devices as call-and-response, repetition, syncopation, and the distinctive chant called the "hum" or "whoop" is nothing more than histrionics that only appeal to the emotions of uneducated listeners. Recent scholarship has shown, however, that the best black preachers combine these features into an interpretive style that emphasizes a theological relationship between a mighty God and an oppressed people that is particular to African Americans (LaRue, 19). Many aspects of this style are African in origin, and the hum, which Franklin reserved for his peroration, signifies a collective celebration and affirmation of what has been revealed in the sermon, rather than an academic summary of it. Gary Hatch's study of Franklin's homilies shows that he used narratives to "establish a series of relationships that appeal to the intellect and imagination as well as the emotions. These relationships constitute a type of 'poetic' logic in which reasoning is neither inductive nor deductive, but rather analogical" (Hatch, 228).

During his third year at LeMoyne College, Franklin accepted an offer to pastor the Friendship Baptist Church in Buffalo, New York. There he preached to a prosperous congregation while he studied at the University of Buffalo, but he soon found the environment both too cold and too conservative. In 1945 he spoke at the National Baptist Convention in Detroit. Representatives of the New Bethel Baptist Church in Detroit were so impressed that they invited him to lead their congregation. Over the next three decades, he brought that church from its location in a converted bowling alley to a beautifully renovated theater, and the congregation grew to more than two thousand members. He accomplished this by first acquiring a radio broadcast that attracted local listeners, and then in 1953 he signed a recording contract with Chess Records. Until that point Chess had only recruited musicians such as MUDDY WATERS, "BIG" WILLIE DIXON, and CHUCK BERRY. Franklin began touring the country with renowned gospel groups like the Dixie Hummingbirds and the CLARA WARD Gospel Singers. Later he began touring with his own choir, which included his daughter, ARETHA FRANKLIN, who later achieved stardom as the "Queen of Soul." Over the course of his career, he produced seventy-six recordings of sermons and music that have sold millions of copies.

Throughout the 1960s Franklin was active in the civil rights movement. In 1963 he organized a march in Detroit, where his friend, MARTIN LUTHER KING JR., delivered an early version of his renowned "I Have a Dream" speech before it was heard nationally at the March on Washington. Franklin also worked to elect JOHN CONYERS to the U.S. Congress and COLEMAN YOUNG as the first black mayor of Detroit. His life was tragically cut short on 10 June 1979, when he was shot by burglars; he remained in a comatose state for five years before he died. As the quintessential black preacher, Franklin continues to influence, and perhaps even define, later generations of preachers. As Jeff Todd Titon observed, "Every African American preacher either has imitated him or has tried to avoid doing so" (Franklin, ix), and JESSE JACKSON has said that in the world of black ministers, Franklin is regarded as "the Rabbi" of black preaching.

FURTHER READING

Franklin, C. L. *Give Me This Mountain* (1989).

Hatch, Gary Layne. "Logic in the Black Folk Sermon: The Sermons of Rev. C. L. Franklin," *Journal of Black Studies* 26:3 (1996).

LaRue, Cleophus J. *The Heart of Black Preaching* (2000).
Moyd, Olin P. *The Sacred Art: Preaching and Theology in the African American Tradition* (1995).
Obituary: *New York Times*, 28 July 1984.

SHOLOMO B. LEVY

Franklin, Charles Sumner (22 Aug. 1879–25 Aug. 1958), physician, political activist, teacher, and reformer, was born in Charles City County, Virginia, to Alexander and Anna Franklin in a community known as Mattie Hunt near the banks of the Chickahominy River. Charles's father, Alexander Quincy Franklin, earned his living as a schoolteacher and a farmer and served as a representative in the Virginia legislature during the 1889–1890 session and as commissioner of revenue for Charles City County. Charles's mother, Anna Marion Brown, a housewife, was born into one of the oldest free, landowning African American families in Virginia. Charles was the second of nine children in a family of six boys and three girls.

From an early age Charles Sumner Franklin aspired to a career other than farming. He received his early education at Bullfield Academy, a one-room school in the Ruthville community. His maternal uncle, Daniel Webster Brown, was his teacher. At age eighteen Franklin enrolled at Virginia Temperance Industrial Academy in Claremont. He remained there for only a year—realizing that the educational offerings were too limited—and transferred to Virginia Normal and Industrial Institute (Virginia N&I; later Virginia State University) in Ettrick, Virginia.

At Virginia N&I, Franklin was an outstanding student and football star. He took preparatory classes with the goal of becoming a doctor, and in 1901 he received the bachelor of science degree. Shortly thereafter he accepted a position as a schoolteacher at Wayside Elementary School in Charles City County. For the next two years he walked twelve miles each day to and from the schoolhouse. He saved as much of his salary as he could with the intent of enrolling in a medical school.

At the time there were no medical schools in Virginia where blacks could receive training, and the closest facility that would accept African Americans was the Leonard Medical School of Shaw University, located in Raleigh, North Carolina. One of the first four-year medical programs in the United States, Leonard Medical School offered a high-quality education. Students at Leonard studied a broad curriculum that included surgery, gynecology and obstetrics, pathology, anatomy and physiology, gastrointestinal diseases, chemistry, bacteriology, and histology. An important part of Leonard's curriculum was a practicum, in which students were also trained to dispense medications. Around the turn of the twentieth century the majority of Virginia's black doctors received their medical training at Leonard.

In 1902 Franklin wrote to the president Charles Meserve seeking acceptance to Leonard Medical School for the 1903–1904 academic year. In 1903 Franklin took a train from Richmond, Virginia, to Raleigh, North Carolina, to begin his medical school career at Leonard. While in medical school he supplemented his aid from the university by performing menial labor. He graduated with an M.D. degree in 1907, and shortly thereafter he sat for the Virginia Board of Examination and passed. He started a general medical practice in a room in his parents' house in Ruthville, Charles City County, Virginia, making house calls to patients who were unable to travel.

In 1908 Franklin bought a plantation, Cedar Grove, and built an office adjacent to the main house. Cedar Grove was located near the historic James River plantations—Sherwood Forest, former of home of President John Tyler; Poplar Forest, home of Thomas Jefferson's wife; Berkeley Plantation; and Shirley Plantation. Cedar Grove was one of several land acquisitions that Franklin eventually used to help empower the African American community; he bought land along the highways of the county and eventually resold the land in smaller pieces to other African Americans. He believed that businesses could be successful only if located along major roads, but few African Americans had the financial power to acquire such property. He used his earning power to help others acquire desirable land, and he eventually owned more than a thousand choice acres.

In 1910 Franklin married Julia Burnette Brown; they had four sons. Tragedy struck in 1923 when Julia died as a result of complications of childbirth. In 1924 Franklin married Rebecca Bradby, and he later had two daughters with her. Thanks to his aggressive treatments of skin diseases Franklin quickly became one of the most highly regarded doctors in Virginia. He treated black, white, and Native American patients and often received referrals from white physicians at the Medical College of Virginia.

During World War I, Franklin became a member of the selective service draft board. He also was the examining physician and secretary for Charles City County, Virginia, during World War II. He held the distinction of being the only African American examining physician in the state of Virginia. In 1950 he was appointed medical advisor to the selective service by President Harry S. Truman.

Franklin was active in politics and was appointed commissioner of chancery by the Charles City County circuit court. Franklin and his son Harry spent a great deal of time participating in voter registration drives and tutoring local blacks so that they could pass the required literacy test to be able to vote. In 1947 Franklin ran unsuccessfully for the board of supervisors for Charles City County. He lost this election to a white opponent by seventeen votes.

Franklin was involved in a number of professional organizations. He was an active member of the National Medical Association, the professional organization for black physicians, who were denied membership in the American Medical Association because of their race. Franklin also held membership in the Old Dominion Medical Society and the Rappahannock Medical Society and served as the president of both societies. He remained on the executive boards of these organizations until his death. He was also active at Elam Baptist Church, founded by his maternal great-great-great-grandfather in 1810. Franklin was a philanthropist who supported a number of causes, making generous donations to Virginia State University, Virginia Union University, and Elam Baptist Church. He continued to practice medicine and remained active in politics until his death in 1958.

FURTHER READING

Durham, Diana K. "Leonard Medical School: The Making of African American Physicians," *Carolina Peacemaker*, 16 Feb. 2006.

Jackson, Luther Porter. *Negro Office-holders in Virginia, 1865–1895* (1946).

DIANA KRISTINE DURHAM

Franklin, Eleanor Ison (24 Dec. 1929–1 Oct. 1998), professor of physiology, research physiologist, and medical college administrator, was born Eleanor Lutia Ison, the elder of two daughters born in Dublin, Georgia, to Luther Lincoln Ison, a high school teacher, and Rose Mae Oliver Ison, a teacher and accomplished musician. She attended high schools in Tuscumbia, Alabama, and Quitman, Georgia, before moving with her family to Monroe, Georgia, in the 1940s. Franklin graduated from the Carver High School in 1944 as valedictorian of her class.

At the age of fifteen Franklin entered Spelman College, with the intent to become a doctor. However, under the guidance and tutelage of Dr. Helen T. Albro, chair of the Biology Department, and Dr. Barnett F. Smith, professor of biology and Wisconsin graduate, she chose to pursue postgraduate study in endocrinology and physiology at the University of Wisconsin. Franklin, who had played piano and oboe in high school, saw Spelman as an opportunity to pursue her interest in music. Later she stated that enrichment in the arts and humanities at Spelman had provided balance to her career in science.

After graduating magna cum laude from Spelman in 1948 with a bachelor's degree in Biology, Franklin remained at the institution for a year as instructor of biology, leaving in 1949 to pursue graduate study at the University of Wisconsin, where she earned her master's in Zoology in 1951. She returned to her teaching position at Spelman that same year. As a result of her achievements on the faculty, Franklin was named a Rockefeller Foundation General Education Board Fellow to pursue doctoral study; her dissertation research involved investigation of hormonal influence on sperm development.

In 1957, again at the University of Wisconsin, Franklin earned her doctorate in Zoology, with specialization in Endocrinology and Medical Physiology. That same year she was appointed assistant professor in the Department of Physiology and Pharmacology, School of Veterinary Medicine, at Tuskegee Institute (later Tuskegee University). In 1960 she advanced to the rank of associate professor and was named research associate at Tuskegee's George Washington Carver Foundation and appointed to the graduate faculty. While at Tuskegee, Franklin published papers on how growth hormones affect hypophyseal diabetes; papers were also published on the demonstration of pituitary-adrenal mechanisms in response to nonspecific stress.

In 1963, after six years at Tuskegee, Franklin declined an offer to pursue postdoctoral study at Sloan Kettering Memorial Institute in order to accept an appointment to the faculty of the Department of Physiology at the Howard University College of Medicine. This began an exceptional academic tenure at Howard that lasted for more than three decades. In 1965 she married George W. Franklin, a clinical psychologist. She had one stepson, Reginald Keith.

Eleanor Ison Franklin, as she became known after her marriage, achieved the rank of professor of physiology at Howard University in 1971. She was named associate dean of general administration of the College of Medicine in 1970 and associate dean for academic affairs in 1972, becoming the first woman to hold a deanship in the 103-year history of Howard University. Among her accomplishments as associate dean of general administration was the preparation of special project grants that resulted in funding of approximately $2.6 million. She also developed guidelines for an Accelerated Medical Education Program that became the prototype for the six year combined bachelor of science/ doctor of medicine degree program for Howard University. As associate dean for academic affairs Franklin planned and developed curricula to enhance the medical education program; she also developed and implemented effective evaluation procedures for medical students, faculty, courses, and curricula. Under her leadership an Office of Medical Education was established to facilitate faculty development and student academic support systems. Overall, the effect of Franklin's tenure in the two associate dean positions resulted in significant improvements to teaching and learning experiences for medical school students and faculty. In appreciation for her service to Howard University she was awarded citations for Outstanding Contributions to Graduate Education (1975–1976) and Outstanding and Dedicated Service (1980).

In 1980, after ten years in associate deanship positions, Franklin returned to the Department of Physiology and continued her career in teaching and research. From 1980 to 1995 Franklin served as director of the Edward W. Hawthorne Laboratory of Cardiovascular Research and conducted research in the field of cardiovascular physiology. Franklin received research grant awards of more than $2 million from agencies including the Ames Research Center, the National Aeronautics and Space Administration (NASA), the Washington Heart Association, and the National Institutes of Health Research Service Award. Franklin published and presented numerous articles in the field of cardiovascular physiology.

In 1984 Franklin was named co-chair of the Porter Physiology Development Program of the American Physiological Society. As a part of that program she served as visiting lecturer in physiology at Spelman College for a number of years. In addition to the Visiting Lecturer series, Franklin produced a video tape demonstration titled *Cardiovascular Responses to Selected Drugs and Pacing: A Student Participation Demonstration*. This project was also funded by the Porter Development Committee.

While fully engaged as academician and scholar, Franklin maintained several additional endeavors including dedicated service to her alma mater Spelman College. In 1972 she was elected president of the Spelman College National Alumnae Association, a position she held for four years. As president of the Alumnae Association Franklin laid the foundation for incorporation of the organization and initiated the process for election of the first alumna trustee. She also served as National Alumnae Campaign chairperson from 1972 to 1976. In 1973 she was elected and served two terms as the first alumna trustee of Spelman College, a position she held until 1979. Franklin received many awards from Spelman College in recognition of her dedicated service, including a Centennial Citation for extraordinary contributions to the development and strengthening of the National Alumnae Association in 1981 and election to the National Alumnae Association Hall of Fame in 1987.

Franklin was elected and served two terms as faculty trustee on the Howard University board of trustees from 1980 to 1986. As a founding member of the Association of Women in Science, Franklin was the organizer and writer of the first constitution and by-laws for that organization in 1971. She was also an organizer and director of the Women's National Bank of Washington District of Columbia in 1977 (later the Adams National Bank), the first federally chartered bank in the country organized by women. Franklin was a member of the Alpha Kappa Alpha sorority and held positions of leadership at the local and national levels.

In 1987 Franklin was appointed dean of the Howard University School of Continuing Education, a position she held until her retirement in 1997. During this time she continued teaching and research as professor of physiology in the College of Medicine. In recognition of her many outstanding achievements and contributions to Howard University, Franklin was designated "Magnificent Professor" in May 1998. In accepting this award Franklin stated: "It is axiomatic that the only true rewards of an academic career are the successes of one's students" (*The Physiologist*, 438). Later that year, Franklin died in her home in Washington, D.C.

FURTHER READING

A number of the documents used to prepare this biography are from the Eleanor Ison Franklin

Unprocessed Collection, Box 1, Spelman College Archives.

Patterson, Rosalyn Mitchell. "Black Women in the Biological Sciences," *Sage: A Scholarly Journal on Black Women* 6.2 (1989): 8–14.

Obituaries: *Spelman Messenger* 113.2 (1999); *The Physiologist* 41.6 (1998).

ROSALYN MITCHELL PATTERSON

Franklin, John Hope (2 Jan. 1915–25 Mar. 2009) historian, was born in Rentiesville, Oklahoma, the youngest of four children of BUCK COLBERT FRANKLIN, an attorney, and Mollie Parker, an elementary school teacher. He was named after the famed educator JOHN HOPE, who had taught his parents in Atlanta, Georgia. When John's father had been ejected from a courtroom by a judge in Ardmore, Oklahoma, who refused to preside over a case argued by a "nigger," the family moved to Rentiesville, and then Colbert went alone to Tulsa in 1921 to establish his law practice. The family struggled and worried for his safety after reading reports of the bloody race riot that took place in Tulsa that year. Colbert's office was burned down, but within a few years he had reestablished himself to the point where he could send for his family. Young John was an extraordinary student who won the local spelling bee for three consecutive years. Having been taught to read by his mother at age five, he also had begun to imitate his father's habit of reading or writing late into the night, despite the fact that the family had no electricity. As a boy, Franklin developed a love for classical music and used money he earned from a paper route to attend local concerts. His parents declined to go with him, believing acceptance of the theater's Jim Crow seating arrangement to be a concession to segregation. As a teenager, he expected to follow in his father's footsteps and become a lawyer. Business was so slow during the Depression that when Franklin would stop by the office after school, his father would often have time to instruct him in classical Greek history and philosophy. Franklin was the valedictorian of his high school class and chose to attend Fisk University in Tennessee. Despite his tuition scholarship, he was forced to work several jobs to meet his living expenses. He took great satisfaction in remembering that an early English professor, who told him that he would "never be able to command the English language," later served on the committee that awarded him the prestigious Bancroft Prize for an article published in the *Journal of Negro History*. As president of the student body, he led a protest against the lynching of a black man near the campus and sent letters denouncing the practice to the mayor of Nashville and to President Franklin D. Roosevelt.

John Hope Franklin in his office in Washington, D.C., at Howard University, 14 February 1956. (AP Images.)

Academically, Franklin fell under the intellectual spell of Theodore S. Currier, a white, Harvard-trained historian who, over the course of four years, so imbued Franklin with a passion for history that it soon surpassed his interest in the law. After graduating from Fisk magna cum laude in 1935, Franklin was admitted to graduate school in the history department at Harvard University, but his parents, who had lost their home while he was in college, could not afford to send him. Professor Currier borrowed the five hundred dollars Franklin needed to begin his studies.

In many ways Franklin's career mirrors that of his predecessor W. E. B. DUBOIS, who also attended Harvard after graduating from Fisk, except that DuBois was required to enter as an undergraduate before being admitted to the graduate program. Franklin was the first African American from a historically black institution to enter the graduate history program directly; he completed the M.A. in only nine months while working odd jobs to sustain himself. He won fellowships to cover his tuition during the remaining years. While conducting research for his dissertation, Franklin had a chance meeting with DuBois and was crushed by the elder scholar's condescension. The two men would later become respected colleagues, but Franklin often told the story of their first encounter as an example of the importance of humility among what DuBois called the "talented tenth."

Franklin married his Fisk classmate, Aurelia E. Whittington, in 1940; they had one son, John. In 1941 Franklin received his Ph.D. in History, and his dissertation was soon published as *The Free Negro in North Carolina, 1790–1860* (1943). During World War II he was denied a position as a historian with the War Department, even though white applicants with fewer academic credentials were accepted. From 1936 to 1956 he held faculty appointments at several historically black colleges, including Fisk, St. Augustine's College, North Carolina College, and Howard University.

He was living in Washington, D.C., and teaching at Howard while lawyers for the NAACP Legal Defense Fund were preparing to argue the *Brown v. Board of Education* case before the Supreme Court. THURGOOD MARSHALL asked Franklin to lead a group of scholars in documenting the historical portion of their brief. He also collaborated with CARTER G. WOODSON, known as the father of African American history, and scholars such as RAYFORD W. LOGAN, the chairman of Howard's history department, in promoting the work of the Association for the Study of Negro Life and History. His involvement in the civil rights movement, however, was not limited to the relative comfort of libraries. He prepared a program with the British Broadcasting Corporation called *The Briton's Guide to the March on Washington* in 1963, and in 1965 he joined some forty other historians in the Selma to Montgomery March.

Franklin wrote or edited some twenty books and over one hundred articles. His most significant contributions to the study of history are *The Militant South, 1800–1860* (1956) and *Reconstruction after the Civil War* (1961). These books place him in the revisionist vanguard that debunked the prevailing myths of the halcyon years of the Old South and the so-called tragic years of Reconstruction. Franklin replaced such interpretations with accurate descriptions of a brutal and bellicose society that was quick to go to war and to oppress large segments of its population because of racial difference. Franklin's most widely read book, *From Slavery to Freedom*, appeared in 1947 and has become a staple in the teaching of African American history. By 2003 it had gone through eight editions, had sold over 3 million copies, and had been translated into five foreign languages. *Black Leaders of the Twentieth Century* (1981), which he edited with August Meier, remains a highly regarded anthology. More recently, he coauthored with Loren Schweninger the prizewinning book *Runaway Slaves: Rebels on the Plantation* (1999).

In his reflective volume *Race and History* (1989), Franklin pays tribute to GEORGE WASHINGTON WILLIAMS, the nineteenth-century historian who wrote some of the first studies of black life and who, by insisting that he was not a "blind panegyrist of my race" (Franklin, *Race and History*, 44) set the highest professional standards for later historians. Among Williams's followers are Carter Woodson, BENJAMIN QUARLES, and DuBois, whom Franklin considered to be the father of the broader field of African American studies.

Throughout his career, Franklin received offers to become dean and president of academic institutions for much higher pay than he earned as a scholar and teacher. He refused them all, assuming only the chairmanship of history departments. In 1956 he accepted the chairmanship of the all-white, fifty-two-member history department of Brooklyn College. The southern-born historian of the South measured the academic cost of the racism he experienced in New York City in terms of the price it exacted in scholarship, surmising that in the time it took him to find a home in Brooklyn and a bank that would finance a mortgage, he could have written a small book. In 1964 he joined the history department of the University of Chicago, serving from 1967 to 1970 as chairman. Franklin also became the first African American to head a number of professional organizations: the American Studies Association (1967–1968); the Southern Historical Association (1970–1971); the United Chapters of Phi Beta Kappa (1973–1976), presiding during the organization's bicentennial; the Organization of American Historians (1974–1975); and the American Historical Association (1979–1980).

In 1982 Franklin became the James B. Duke Professor of History at Duke University, and in 1985 he joined the Duke Law School, where he served until 1992. He testified in 1987 before the Senate Committee on the Judiciary in opposition to the appointment of Robert Bork to the

Supreme Court. He received numerous honors. In 1995 Duke University established the John Hope Franklin Collection of African and African American Documentation and in 2001 the John Hope Franklin Center for Interdisciplinary and International Studies, along with the John Hope Franklin Humanities Institutes at the Center. In 1995 Franklin won the NAACP's highest honor, the Spingarn Medal, and President Bill Clinton awarded him the Presidential Medal of Freedom in the same year. Clinton also appointed Franklin in 1997 to lead a presidential commission on race. In 2002 Franklin received the Gold Medal of the Academy of Arts and Letters, and he received over two hundred awards and honorary degrees during his distinguished career.

John Franklin lectured throughout the world. In 2001 he collaborated with the South African Archbishop Desmond Tutu in a PBS film, *Tutu and Franklin: A Journey Toward Peace*, in which the two of them counsel an interracial group of students from the United States, Senegal, and South Africa. Franklin, the consummate Renaissance man, remained engaged in numerous scholarly, civic, and horticultural activities. His prominence in orchid culture resulted in two orchids that bear his name: the *Phalaenopsis John Hope Franklin* and the *Brassolaelia Cattleya John Hope Franklin*.

In March of 2009 Franklin died of congestive heart failure in Durham, North Carolina. Franklin continually challenged the color line during his life and great changes occurred during his ninety-four years in part because of his work—Hope was born in the segregated South but he lived to see a black President.

FURTHER READING

Franklin, John Hope. "A Life of Learning," in *Race and History: Selected Essays 1938–1988* (1990).

Franklin, John Hope. *Mirror to America: The Autobiography of John Hope Franklin* (2005).

Gates, Henry Louis, Jr., and Cornel West. "John Hope Franklin," in *The African American Century* (2000).

Meier, August. *Black History and the Historical Profession, 1915–80* (1986).

Thorpe, Earl E. *Black Historians: A Critique* (1971).

Obituary: *New York Times*, 25 Mar. 2009.

SHOLOMO B. LEVY

Franklin, Martha Minerva (29 Oct. 1870–26 Sept. 1968), nursing leader, was born in New Milford, Connecticut, the daughter of Henry J. Franklin, a laborer and a private in the Twenty-ninth Connecticut Volunteer Division during the Civil War, and Mary E. Gauson. Reared in Meriden, Connecticut, during the post–Civil War period, Franklin lived in a town that had few African Americans. She graduated from Meriden Public High School in 1890. In 1895, having chosen nursing as a career, Franklin entered the Women's Hospital Training School for Nurses in Philadelphia. She graduated in December 1897, the only black graduate in the class, and went on to find work as a private-duty nurse in Meriden and thereafter in New Haven, to which she relocated.

Franklin's interest in organizing the National Association of Colored Graduate Nurses (NACGN) was prompted by the difficulties black women often faced. That black women were rarely accepted into schools of nursing motivated the formation of black hospitals and schools of nursing. Although fully qualified, black nurses were denied membership in their state nurses association, the only avenue to the American Nurses Association, thus precluding their membership in the national organization. In addition black nurses received little respect and less pay than did their white counterparts and, as women, faced the inequality all women experienced in American society.

In 1906 Franklin launched a handwritten survey to analyze the status of the black nurse in American society because she believed that many black nurses shared her concerns. She concluded that only through collective action initiated by black nurses would their problems be recognized and gain the national attention that would in time make it possible to practice nursing without racial bias. Armed with this belief and commitment, Franklin sent out 1,500 letters for two years asking black nurses to consider a meeting in the near future.

Adah Belle Samuels Thoms, a black nursing leader and president of the Lincoln Hospital School of Nursing Alumnae Association, invited Franklin and interested nurses to hold their first meeting in New York as guests of the association. Thoms was an immediate supporter of Franklin and the NACGN. On 25–27 August 1908 fifty-two nurses attended the first meeting of the NACGN in New York. Franklin's leadership and organizational skills emerged as she presided over the meetings.

Franklin's goals became the goals of the association: she wished to advance the standards and best interests of trained nurses, break down discrimination in the nursing profession, and develop leadership within the ranks of black nurses. Franklin believed that an organized group would gain the attention, cooperation, and support of nursing leaders. She was elected president of the NACGN by acclamation. At the 1908 meeting the National Medical Association (NMA), the black physicians association whose convention was in New York at the same time, lent its enthusiastic support to the NACGN.

Franklin worked toward building the newly founded organization. In 1909 the NACGN met in Boston, Massachusetts, where it acquired a strong source of support from Mary Eliza Mahoney, America's first black registered nurse. Franklin, Thoms, and Mahoney developed a professional bond of mutual respect and friendship; they were the pillars and major supporters of the NACGN, and in 1976 they were posthumously admitted to the Nursing Hall of Fame.

The NACGN grew to 2,000 members during World War I and to more than 12,000 by 1940, with members from nearly every state. As the organization grew, a national registry was established to assist black nurses in securing positions. The NACGN gained community and national support systems by organizing local citizens committees in New York and an advisory council on the national level. The NMA helped the organization greatly by allowing and encouraging it to publish all of its news and announcements in the *Journal of the National Medical Association* until the NACGN obtained its own journal, the *National News Bulletin*, in 1928.

Franklin was light-complected, and as she rose to national prominence she was sometimes mistakenly characterized by nursing leaders as a white nurse who had befriended colored nurses.

In about 1920 Franklin relocated to New York City, completed a postgraduate course at Lincoln Hospital in the Bronx, and became a registered nurse in New York State. She worked in the New York City public school system as a school nurse. Committed to continuing her education, at fifty-eight years of age she was admitted to Teachers College, Columbia University, and during 1928–1930 she was enrolled in the Department of Practical Arts (later the Department of Nursing Education).

Franklin returned to New Haven, Connecticut, to retire. She resided with her sister Florence. Franklin attended the Dixwell Congregational Church of Christ in Connecticut regularly until advancing age precluded her weekly attendance.

FURTHER READING

Staupers, Mabel K. *No Time for Prejudice: The Story of the Integration of Negroes in Nursing in the United States* (1961).

Stewart, Isabel, and Annie Austin. *A History of Nursing: From Ancient to Modern Times, a World View*, 5th ed. (1962).

Thoms, Adah B. *Pathfinders: A History of the Progress of Colored Graduate Nurses* (1929).

This entry is taken from the *American National Biography* and is published here with the permission of the American Council of Learned Societies.

ALTHEA T. DAVIS

Franklin, Shirley (10 May 1945–), politician, was born Shirley Clarke in Philadelphia, Pennsylvania, the daughter of Eugene Haywood Clarke, an attorney, and Ruth Lyons White. Clarke graduated from the Philadelphia High School for Girls in 1963, a historic and highly competitive institution. Clarke had early aspirations of becoming a dancer. Despite her lack of participation in high school student government, upon graduating, Clarke became active in the civil rights movement as an undergraduate at Howard University in Washington, D.C. In 1968 Clarke earned a Bachelor of Arts degree in Sociology from Howard, then, returned to her hometown to attend the University of Pennsylvania. She graduated from Penn in 1969 with a Master of Arts degree in Sociology.

In 1972, Clarke married the entertainment attorney David McCoy Franklin; together the couple settled in Atlanta, Georgia. The couple, who divorced in 1986, had three daughters; Kai Ayanna, Cabral (Candice) Holsey, and Kali Jamilla. Shirley Franklin was introduced to politics in 1973 by her politically active husband, who was prominent in the election of Maynard Jackson, the first black mayor of Atlanta. Franklin made her foray into the realm of politics, in 1978, as Atlanta's commissioner of cultural affairs, appointed during Jackson's second term in office. In 1982 she assumed the role of chief administrative officer and city manager in the administration of the civil rights leader and former United Nations ambassador Mayor Andrew Young. Franklin governed daily operations of Atlanta, a $1 billion budget, and over eight thousand employees; she was the first woman in the United States to hold such a position in city government. In less than ten years, she supervised the development of Atlanta's Hartsfield-Jackson International Airport and the construction of over fourteen thousand new housing units, a new city hall, and court buildings. Jackson returned for a third term in 1990 and appointed Franklin as executive officer for operations. In 1991 Franklin became the top-ranking woman on the Atlanta Committee for the Olympic Games; in 1996 she served the committee as senior vice president for external affairs and assisted in the development of Centennial Olympic Park.

In 1997 Franklin entered the private sector as CEO and founder of Shirley Clarke Franklin & Associates; a consulting firm for strategic planning, community and public affairs. She was appointed one of three members on the transition team for the newly elected governor, Roy Barnes, in 1998. In addition, Franklin had become a majority partner of Urban Environmental Solutions, LLC, and vice chair of the Georgia Regional Transportation Authority. In 2000, she issued her formal announcement to run for mayor of the City of Atlanta. Wearing her signature platinum blonde cropped hairdo, Franklin was recognized by voters as having an outgoing personality and earthy approach to campaigning; yet she still came across as an educated, articulate, and experienced candidate. Even more, she was noted for her frankness and accessibility during her campaign. In her first run for an elective office, in 2001 Franklin triumphed at the polls, and was elected the 58th mayor of Atlanta. She was the first African American female to hold that position. She won over 50 percent of the vote, leading the next candidate in a crowded field by 13 points. Franklin ran a pop-culture infused campaign and pledged to address environmental issues that were financially taxing to the city. Franklin had both raised and spent over $3 million in her campaign, more than any previous Atlanta mayoral candidate. She hosted an unconventional inaugural celebration, in 2002, that was open to the public with performances that included the hip-hop duo Outkast and the comedian Chris Tucker. Mayor Franklin assumed office as mayor the following Monday, 7 January, and immediately began working to uphold her promises.

During her first term in office Mayor Franklin successfully restored efficiency and accountability to the public sector. She announced the "Clean Water Atlanta" initiative that revamped the city's sewage system, which had been in violation of federal environmental laws. Federal fines incurred by the city council for such lapses had upset Atlanta's budget. Mayor Franklin was praised for making Atlanta one of the nation's most "green" cities notably by increasing the number of buildings certified by Leadership in Energy and Environmental Design (LEED), a U.S. Green Building Council accreditation registration providing a set of standards for environmentally sustainable design, construction, and operation of building and neighborhoods. She also oversaw what was known as the "pothole posse" of city workers who repaired Atlanta's crumbling streets. Also, she established Ethics Legislation as a guideline of standards for city officials to follow. Furthermore, by 2005 she was turned the $82 million deficit she had inherited to a surplus of $18 million, with cuts that included a self-imposed $40,000 decrease in her own salary.

As a result of these achievements, in 2005 Mayor Franklin won over 90 percent of the vote to earn a second term in office. The same year she signed legislation to make panhandling illegal in parts of downtown Atlanta. The following year, in 2006, Mayor Franklin succeeded in securing Dr. Martin Luther King Jr.'s personal papers for his alma mater, Morehouse College in Atlanta, preventing their being sold at auction. As part of her efforts to project Atlanta as a leading international center for business, in September 2006, she was part of an Atlanta Chamber of Commerce delegation to aid Delta Airlines in acquiring a direct route to China. She diligently instituted initiatives to improve Atlanta, including long-range plans for the city's economic development, youth programs for the city's workforce, and commissioned a study of homelessness to eradicate the issue in the city over a period of ten years.

In 2008 Mayor Franklin proposed a city property tax increase to address a budget deficit of between $50 and $60 million. When the Atlanta City Council opposed the measure, Franklin cut 222 public safety jobs to minimize the deficit. Though she claimed the budget shortfall had been caused by poor accounting practices, rather than overspending, Franklin ended her second term with the city once again in deficit.

In 2007 Mayor Franklin openly endorsed Senator Barack Obama when he announced his candidacy for president of the United States. She chose not to endorse any candidate for the 2008 Atlanta mayoral election; however, on the eve of the election in November 2009 she announced her intention to vote for fellow Howard University alum Kasim Reed. On 4 January 2010, Kasim Reed succeeded Franklin as mayor of Atlanta.

Among the awards Mayor Franklin has earned are the Association for Equal Opportunity in Higher Education, Distinguished Alumni Award, 1983; the NAACP Atlanta Chapter 1987 Leadership Award; Big Brothers–Big Sisters of Metro Atlanta 1995 Legacy Award; the 1996 Woman of the Year Award, YWCA; 2002 Honorary Doctor of Laws, Howard University; 2002 Woman of Achievement Award, YWCA; 2005,

John F. Kennedy Profile in Courage Award, John F. Kennedy Library Foundation; and 2009 Pillar Award Honoree, The Council for Quality Growth. In 2009 she earned the first World Chamber of Commerce Visionary Award for International Environmental Stewardship by the World Chamber of Commerce. During her tenure in government Mayor Franklin also served on over thirty civil and cultural organizations; including the National Endowment for the Arts, the Atlanta Symphony Orchestra, National Urban Coalition, Mayors against Illegal Guns Coalition, Delta Sigma Theta Sorority, Democratic National Committee, and Cosby Endowed Professor at Spelman College. In 2005 she was named among the five best big-city mayors by *Time Magazine*.

FURTHER READING

Bayor, Ronald H. *Race and the Shaping of Twentieth Century Atlanta* (2000).

Glanton, Dahleen. "For Atlanta Mayor a Mission to Serve." *Chicago Tribune*, 6 November 2005.

"Atlanta Swears in Shirley Franklin as the City's First Female Mayor." *Jet*, 28 January 2002.

SAFIYA DALILAH HOSKINS

Franks, Gary (9 Feb. 1953–), U.S. Representative, politician, and entrepreneur, was born in Waterbury, Connecticut, the youngest of six children of Richard and Jenary Franks. Richard was a former North Carolina sharecropper with no education beyond the sixth grade. Jenary was a dietary specialist at Waterbury Hospital in Connecticut.

Franks was raised Baptist, but attended Sacred Heart High School, a Catholic school located in the heart of Waterbury. Franks was involved in many extracurricular activities at Sacred Heart. He was an all-New England basketball player and president of his senior class. In 1971 Franks completed high school and then attended Yale University. Uncertain about his political views at the time, Franks registered as a Democrat like many black Americans in the 1970s. Franks continued his involvement in extracurricular activities by joining the Yale basketball team. Although he did not receive much playing time until his senior year, Franks's high score record per game earned him a spot on the weekly Eastern Collegiate Athletic Conference all-star team before graduating with a bachelor of arts degree in 1975.

Shortly after graduation Franks tried out for the NBA's New Orleans Jazz but did not make the team. He then moved back to Connecticut to look for jobs. He would eventually become an industrial and labor relations executive for several

Gary Franks, Republican representative from Connecticut, addresses his supporters in Waterbury, Connecticut, 5 November 1996, after he was defeated in his bid for a fourth term in Congress by Democrat James Maloney. (AP Images.)

Fortune 500 companies Franks landed his first post-college job in 1976 as a management trainee for the Continental Can Company. After only a few months on the job Franks was promoted to top personnel staffer and relocated to Reading, Pennsylvania. In 1978 he began working for Chesebrough-Ponds, a company that specialized in facial care products, as an assistant manager for corporate recruitment before going to work for the candymaker Peter Paul Cadbury. During the latter stages of Franks's business career he started his own real estate firm and bought buildings around Connecticut until he owned over a dozen properties. He eventually developed a reputation as a successful entrepreneur. He also switched political affiliation to the Republican Party. In November 1983 Franks became involved in politics and Connecticut's Republican Party with support from John Rowland, a white Republican politician from Connecticut. He ran for a seat on the Waterbury Republican Town Committee, a local working group that helped Republicans obtain and sustain the majority leadership at the local, state, and federal levels, and won by a slim margin of fewer than a dozen votes. In the mid-1980s Franks ran for one of fifteen seats on the Waterbury board of alderman. After a successful campaign he was sworn in on 1 January 1986. Just six months into his service as alderman Franks ran for the Connecticut state comptroller's post but was unsuccessful, losing by 6 percentage points. Franks's service as alderman concluded in 1990. That same year he married Donna Williams on 10 March. Donna's daughter, Azia, became Franks' stepdaughter once the two married.

Immediately after Franks's marriage he launched a campaign for a seat in the U.S. House of Representatives for the 102nd Congress. Franks campaigned in Connecticut's 5th District which was 90 percent white, mostly blue-collar, and only 4 percent black. Most conservative whites in his district assumed he was a liberal Democrat so he made sure they knew his political affiliation and conservative viewpoints, particularly on issues concerning welfare reform and affirmative action.

His campaign efforts eventually paid off and he defeated the incumbent Toby Moffett, a former local television newscaster. Franks was sworn in to represent Connecticut's 5th District on 3 January 1991. He gained national prominence as the first black congressman elected from the state of Connecticut and the first black Republican to be elected to the U.S. House of Representatives since Oscar Stanton De Priest in 1932. On 11 June 1991 he and his wife gave birth to Jessica Lynn, their first child together.

By itself, the fact that Franks became the first black Republican in Congress in nearly sixty years was monumental for him and for the African American community at large. However, the conservative Franks did not always see eye-to-eye with every member of that community. There were conflicts. One of Franks's most well-publicized debates was with the Congressional Black Caucus (CBC), which did not always welcome his conservative viewpoints. Although the CBC was by design a nonpartisan entity, some of its members persisted in motioning to the effect that the caucus should dissolve into a Democrats-only body. Franks insisted that he be included in all CBC meetings and made his voice heard for the issues he fought for while in Congress.

Franks was adamant about improving the nation's race-relations and was vocal about a number of race-related events that occurred during his term as a congressman. In late April 1992 a jury in Simi Valley, California, acquitted five Los Angeles police officers of beating Rodney King after a high-speed chase. Franks responded to this situation by demanding that the president identify whether any federal civil rights laws were violated and proceed with a federal prosecution. Two officers were eventually convicted as a result of this prosecution.

Franks was also concerned with affirmative action, racial gerrymandering, the leadership within the Nation of Islam, and the Million Man March. Franks's position on these issues led to conflict with other political leaders, especially African American politicians associated with the Democratic Party. He endorsed outreach programs to new pools of minority and women applicants, enforcement of antidiscrimination laws, and flexible goals and timetables to overcome the legacy of the past but opposed quotas, set-asides, race-based election districts, and reverse discrimination.

Despite conflicts with other politicians, Franks remained popular in his home district and was reelected to Congress in 1993. During his second term in the House he introduced a bill to make racially gerrymandered districts illegal. That same year the U.S. Supreme Court ruled the drawing of congressional districts to ensure racial representation was unconstitutional. Franks's disapproval of the Nation of Islam's leadership surfaced in November of 1993 after Khalid Muhammad, one of the Nation's top ministers, made a extremely hostile speech that targeted Catholics, whites, Jews, and gays. During his speech, Muhammad urged all black South Africans to kill all whites who refused to leave the nation within twenty-four hours, including women, children, and disabled people. As a result, Franks did not support the Million Man March led by the group's leader Louis Farrakhan in October 1995. Franks admitted that the Nation of Islam promoted African American issues, but condemned its tactics, which he felt only increased the racial divide.

In May of 1994 Franks first son, Gary Jr., was born. That year, Franks was elected to the House for the third time. However, in 1996, his fourth bid for the House failed when Franks was defeated by James Maloney, a Democratic state senator from Danbury, Connecticut. Two years later, in 1998, Franks ran unsuccessfully for the U.S. Senate against the incumbent Democrat, Christopher Dodd. Franks's popularity apparently did not extend across Connecticut, for he gained only 33 percent of the vote. Thus, his leadership in federal politics came to an end on3

January 1997. Despite this abrupt closure of Franks's political leadership, he will be forever acknowledged as one who expanded African American presence in American politics.

FURTHER READING

Franks, Gary. *Searching for the Promised Land: An African American's Optimistic Odyssey* (1996).

RYAN J. DAVIS

Fraser, Sarah Marinda Loguen. *See* Loguen Fraser, Sarah Marinda.

Fraunces, Samuel (1722–1795), tavern owner and innkeeper in New York City and Philadelphia, was probably born in the French West Indies. There seems to be some controversy regarding his race, as his nickname, "Black Sam," would indicate an African American identity, while some primary sources imply that he was either white or a Mulatto. Historians are generally agreed, however, that Fraunces was African American. Much of what is known about him comes from his 1785 petition for compensation from Congress for services rendered during the American War of Independence, letters from George Washington, and an obituary in the 13 October 1795 issue of the *Gazette of the United States*. He owned an inn in New York City in 1755, and the following year obtained a license to operate an "ordinary," which was a tavern serving meals as well as the usual ales and spirits. At this time he was married to a Mary Carlile, about whom little is known except that she died soon after her husband established himself as a tavern owner. His second wife, Elizabeth Dailey, proved a valuable assistant in his business ventures, and together they raised seven children in a household that included at various times both slaves and indentured servants. From 1759 to 1762 he was the proprietor of the Masons' Arms, the first of several taverns he owned or leased in New York and later in Philadelphia.

In 1762 Fraunces purchased a defunct tavern in Lower Manhattan in the former Delancy mansion for £2,000, refurbished it, and named it the Queen Charlotte's Head. Later known simply as the Queen's Head, Fraunces's second tavern catered to the high-end trade and was noted for its exceptional fare, particularly its high quality wines, thus attracting an elite clientele as well as distinguished visitors, and enjoying the distinction of hosting the first meeting of the New York Chamber of Commerce. In 1765 he left New York City for Philadelphia, renting out the Queen's Head for several years while he operated another tavern until 1768. He returned to New York City in 1770 and resumed proprietorship of the Queen's Head Tavern. Ever keen to expand his business operations, from 1765 to 1774 Fraunces leased from New York City's Trinity Church the Old Bowling Green Gardens fronting the North River, renaming them the Vauxhall Gardens. Like the Queen's Head, this establishment also gained a reputation for fine food, wine, and entertainment, as well as housing a collection of seventy miniature wax statues designed by Fraunces that featured likenesses of famous historical figures, such as the Roman general Publius Scipio.

The Queen's Head served as a focal point for revolutionary activity during the late 1760s and the 1770s, hosting meetings of the New York Sons of Liberty. By the outbreak of the War of Independence the Queen's Head had been renamed Fraunces Tavern, and during the battle for New York in 1775 several Continental army courts-martial were convened there. George Washington frequently dined there, beginning a long association with Fraunces cemented by their shared love of fine wines. In 1776 Fraunces allegedly uncovered a plot among members of the Headquarters Guard to assassinate Washington, though the evidence against Thomas Hickey and other members of the guard is circumstantial, and ultimately unverifiable. When the British seized New York City in the summer of 1776, Fraunces fled with his family to New Jersey, shadowing the Continental army's retreat. However, he was captured by the British in 1778, and returned to New York City to become the household cook for General James Robertson, the military governor of the city. According to Fraunces, he smuggled food and clothing to American prisoners of war and aided them in their escapes. In his petition to Congress, Fraunces recounted these and his other services as an American spy. In a letter to Fraunces written in August 1783 from his headquarters, Washington commended his friend for having, "through the most trying times, maintained a constant friendship and Attention to the Cause of our Country and its Independence and Freedom." He went on to note that "all the good People of these States" should see him "as a warm Friend, and one who has not only suffered in our Cause, but who has deserved well of many Individuals ... One who is deserving the favor and attention of these U States." That same year, after the British evacuation, Fraunces reestablished his New York City tavern, which served as the venue for Washington's famous farewell to his senior officers prior to his departure from the city on 4 December. Washington maintained a regular correspondence

Samuel Fraunces's tavern is the setting for the painting *Washington's Farewell to His Officers.* Engraving by Phillip Brown after Alonzo Chappel. (Library of Congress.)

with Fraunces from Mount Vernon in the years preceding his election to the presidency in 1789. Fraunces, meanwhile, suffered from the unstable postwar economy, and in an attempt to recover his fortunes he unsuccessfully filed suit against the estate of General Charles Lee over an outstanding debt. In 1785 he petitioned Congress, seeking compensation for his wartime services as well as more favorable terms of rental payments owed to him for use of his tavern as executive offices. Congress, influenced doubtless by Washington's support, agreed to compensate Fraunces, as well as to provide early redemption of a loan certificate he owned. Fraunces sold the tavern that year and moved to New Jersey to embark on a career as a farmer, but his failure at this endeavor convinced him to return to Manhattan to resume his former career. Upon Washington's inauguration to the presidency in May 1789, Washington hired Fraunces as a household steward in the temporary capital of New York City. Supervising a large staff, Fraunces became famous again for creating sumptuous banquets. However, such extravagance, which included providing the staff with wine at their meals, forced Washington to dismiss him in February 1790, though he managed to regain his job when the capital was moved to Philadelphia. Fraunces remained with the presidential household until 1794, when he relinquished his position to return to tavern-keeping, this time in Philadelphia.

Fraunces was clearly an exceptional businessman who by the time of his death in 1795 had regained much of the fortune he lost in the Revolution. However, he is buried in an unmarked grave in St. Peter's Episcopal Church cemetery in Philadelphia. In 1904 the Sons of the Revolution in the State of New York purchased Fraunces Tavern and restored it as a public museum.

FURTHER READING

Blockson, Charles L. "Black Samuel Fraunces: Patriot, White House Steward and Restaurateur Par Excellence." Temple University Libraries, Charles L. Blockson Afro-American Collection. Available at http://library.temple.edu/collections/blockson/fraunces.jsp.

Rice, Kym S. *Early American Taverns: For the Entertainment of Friends and Strangers* (1983).

Washington, George. *The Writings of George Washington from the Original Manuscript Sources, 1745–1799*, ed. John C. Fitzpatrick, 39 vols. (1931–1944).

White, Shane. "'We Dwell in Safety and Pursue Our Honest Callings': Free Blacks in New York City, 1783–1810," *Journal of American History* 75 (1988): 445–470.

JOHN HOWARD SMITH

Frazier, E. Franklin (24 Sept. 1894–17 May 1962), sociologist, was born Edward Franklin Frazier in Baltimore, Maryland, the son of James Edward Frazier, a bank messenger, and Mary E. Clark. Frazier's father had taught himself to read and write and until his death in 1904, stressed the usefulness of a formal education as a means of escaping poverty.

Young Frazier's interest in sociology began at an early age. It can be partly traced to James Frazier's attempt to make his children aware of the volatile atmosphere of race relations in Atlanta, Georgia, and Baltimore with daily discussions of articles and editorials from local newspapers. Despite the death of his father when Frazier was eleven years old, it appears that this process had a profound effect on Frazier's intellectual growth. He attended elementary and secondary school in Baltimore, and after graduating from Baltimore Colored High School in 1912, he attended, on scholarship, Howard University in Washington, D.C., graduating with honors in 1916. At Howard he subscribed to a vague socialist philosophy but, more importantly, demonstrated his mastery in languages, literature, and mathematics. He later taught these subjects at successive institutions: mathematics at Tuskegee Institute (1916–1917), English, French, and history at St. Paul's Normal and Industrial School in Lawrenceville, Virginia (1917–1918), and French and mathematics at Baltimore High School (1918–1919).

In 1919 Frazier entered the graduate program in sociology at Clark University (Worcester, Massachusetts), where, under the tutelage of Frank Hankins, he became skilled in the use of sociological methods and theories as objective tools in the examination of racial problems in American society. After receiving his M.A. in 1920, Frazier spent a year as a researcher at the New York School of Social Work (1920–1921) followed by a year at the University of Copenhagen in Denmark (1921–1922), where as a research fellow of the American Scandinavian Foundation, he studied that nation's rural folk high schools.

In 1922, back in the United States, Frazier married Marie Brown. Their union was childless. Earlier that same year he became director of the summer school session at Livingstone College in Salisbury, North Carolina. Until 1927 he also held a combined appointment as director of the Atlanta University School of Social Work and as instructor of sociology at Morehouse College in Atlanta. During these years Frazier published often and widely, more than thirty articles on such topics as the African American family, the activities of black business leaders, and the development of the African American middle class, until the appearance of "The Pathology of Race Prejudice" in the June 1927 issue of *Forum*.

Frazier's analysis of racial discrimination as a social pathology manifested in societal norms was highly controversial. Locals discovered the article with the appearance of several editorials in the *Atlanta Constitution* and the *Atlanta Independent* that condemned the findings revealed in the article. Not only did these editorials criticize Frazier's analysis, but they also questioned his intellectual abilities. Soon thereafter, the Fraziers began to receive harassing phone calls, death threats, and threats of being lynched. As a result of this violent atmosphere, and at the urging of friends, the Fraziers soon left the city.

From Atlanta, Frazier went to the University of Chicago as a graduate student and as a research fellow in the department of sociology. In 1929 he accepted a position as a lecturer in the sociology department at Fisk University in Nashville. After earning a Ph.D. in 1931, Frazier remained at Fisk, where he subsequently became a research professor of sociology in the department of social science. In 1934 he became professor and head of the Department of sociology at Howard University. He retired as professor emeritus of sociology in 1959 but continued to teach through both the African Studies Program at Howard and the School of Advanced International Studies Program at Johns Hopkins University until his death.

The black family—which Frazier viewed as a social unit that helped integrate its members into American society—and race relations in the United States, especially their negative impact on the development of the African American family, as well as the effects of urbanization on black family structure were all explored in Frazier's dissertation, published as *The Negro Family in Chicago* (1932). This pathbreaking book, which has been compared to W. E. B. DuBois's classic study *The Philadelphia Negro* (1899), was followed by his book *The Negro Family in the United States* (1939). This book, which won the Anisfield Award in 1939 for the most significant work in the field of race relations, expanded on Frazier's earlier findings in Chicago and analyzed the various cultural and historical forces that influenced the development of the African American family from the time of slavery until the 1920s.

Frazier's most controversial book was *Black Bourgeoisie* (1957), an examination of the economic, political, and social behavior of the African American middle class as shaped by the experience of slavery and the forces of racial prejudice and discrimination. Frazier argued that the African American middle class had developed as a hybrid group. Lacking a solid economic base and subject to the same social marginality and isolation suffered by the African American population as a whole, the African American middle class tended to adhere to a set of values that differed from that of middle-class whites. More interested in high levels of consumption and status than in production and savings, the black bourgeoisie, Frazier concluded, tended to share the values and mirror the behavior of the white upper class rather than the white middle class. A Guggenheim Fellowship awarded in 1939 enabled Frazier to extend his study of race relations and black family life to Brazil and the Caribbean. An ancillary interest in European and African relations was the focus of his *Race and Culture Contacts in the Modern World* (1957).

Frazier served as president of the District of Columbia Sociological Society and the Eastern Sociology Society and as vice president of the African Studies Association and the American Sociological Society (now the American Sociological Association). His election in 1948 as president of the American Sociological Society marked the first time that an African American had served as chief presiding officer of a national professional association. In 1955 he became an honorary member of the Gamma chapter of Phi Beta Kappa at Howard University. He died in Washington, D.C.

FURTHER READING

Frazier's papers are in the Moorland-Spingarn Research Center, Howard University.

Blackwell, James E., and Morris Janowitz, eds. "E. Franklin Frazier," in *Black Sociologists*.

Edwards, G. Franklin. "E. Franklin Frazier: Race, Education, and Community," in *Sociological Traditions from Generation to Generation*, eds. Robert K. Merton and Matilda White Riley (1980).

Odum, Howard. *American Sociology* (1951).

Platt, Anthony M. *E. Franklin Frazier Reconsidered* (1991).

Vlasek, Dale R. "E. Franklin Frazier and the Problem of Assimilation," in *Ideas in America's Cultures from Republic to Mass Society*, ed. Hamilton Cravens (1982).

Obituary: *New York Times*, 22 May 1962.

This entry is taken from the *American National Biography* and is published here with the permission of the American Council of Learned Societies.

ERIC R. JACKSON

Frazier, Joe (12 Jan. 1944–7 Nov. 2011), boxer and former heavyweight champion of the world, was born Joseph Frazier in Beaufort, South Carolina, the son of Rubin Frazier and Dolly. His father was a sharecropper who supplemented the family's income by making and delivering moonshine liquor. His mother worked a series of jobs in the fields around Beaufort and in some of the small food processing plants.

Frazier's childhood was marked by poverty, hard work, and a growing fascination with boxing. His early hero was Joe Louis, and he spent his teenage years dreaming of becoming a successful and wealthy boxer. He had little interest in school and by age thirteen had officially dropped out. At the age of fifteen, after a run-in with a local white landowner, Frazier decided that his future was not in Beaufort and took a bus to New York, where he lived with one of his brothers for most of the next two years. His scramble for jobs became even more pressing when his girlfriend became pregnant. Frazier then moved to Philadelphia and found work in a slaughterhouse. Finding that he was gaining weight, he decided to visit the local Police Athletic League gym, where he rekindled his love for boxing. His tremendous work ethic, awesome left hook, and ability to absorb terrific punishment while inflicting even more of the same soon brought him to the attention of local trainers and managers. Under their guidance, Frazier quickly developed into one of the top amateur heavyweights in the country.

In 1964 Frazier suffered a loss to Buster Mathis at the Olympic trials. Just before the Olympic Games, held in Tokyo that year, Mathis injured his hand, and Frazier took his place on the U.S. boxing team. Frazier made the most of the opportunity, winning the gold medal by decision. The acclaim following his victory, however, did not translate into the rich endorsement contracts and personal appearance money he might have hoped for. He had married Florence (maiden name not known) in 1962, and by now they had two children. They divorced in 1985. In 1965 Frazier turned professional. During the next year he reeled off eleven straight victories, all by knockout, over a string of journeymen fighters. In September 1966 he moved up in class, facing the world-ranked Oscar Bonavena. The rugged Argentine knocked Frazier to the canvas twice in the first round, but Frazier rallied and earned a unanimous decision win. Over the course of the next year and a half, Frazier fought and beat another half dozen fighters, including George Chuvalo and Doug Jones.

In March 1968 Frazier faced his old nemesis Mathis. Frazier did not leave matters up to the judges this time but steadily ground down the much larger Mathis until the referee stopped the fight in the eleventh round. The victory gave Frazier the New York State heavyweight championship. He defended the title four times over the next two years, including victories over Bonavena and Jerry Quarry. Frazier then met Jimmy Ellis for the vacant World Boxing Association heavyweight championship in 1970 and crushed him in four rounds. Frazier defended the title just once that year, against the aging but still dangerous Bob Foster, whom he dispatched in two rounds.

Then Frazier signed to fight what came to be known as the "fight of the century" and actually lived up to the title. MUHAMMAD ALI had been stripped of his heavyweight title in 1967 after he refused induction into the U.S. military. Ali was not allowed to fight again until 1970. Almost immediately a clamor arose for a match between Frazier and Ali. The fight was set for March 1971 in Madison Square Garden. As the time for the fight approached, it became clear that this was not a mere sporting event. There was no denying, of course, the match's pure sports value: the undefeated Frazier, known for clubbing his opponents into submission, fighting the undefeated Ali, who used unparalleled speed, footwork, and punching accuracy to befuddle and wear down his victims. Yet the fight also carried obvious political overtones. Ali, who joined the Nation of Islam and refused to serve in Vietnam, became a hero to thousands of young African Americans who viewed him as a powerful, influential black man struggling against white domination. Frazier, despite his great accomplishments in the ring, was never able to grab the public's attention as Ali had. Frazier was wounded by the public perception that, while Ali battled the white establishment, Frazier was little more than an "Uncle Tom" who avoided the controversial issues of the day. Ali, training for the fight, kept up an incessant attack on Frazier for being a "sellout" and ridiculed his personal appearance. Yet Frazier had his supporters, many of whom simply hoped he would be the man to finally silence the arrogant Ali.

The fight took place on 8 March 1971. For the first few rounds Ali boxed brilliantly. Frazier, off to his usual slow start, quickly dropped behind. By the fourth round, however, he began to rake Ali with hooks to the body and head, and the fight seemed to swing in his favor. Ali responded late in the fight with a savage attack of his own, and the later rounds seesawed back and forth. Most spectators felt it was too close to call as the fight entered the fifteenth and final round. Both exhausted, Frazier and Ali also knew the round could turn the fight. Frazier mustered one last valiant effort: a perfectly timed and devastating left hook that crashed Ali to the canvas. Although Ali beat the count, the knockdown sealed Frazier's unanimous victory, and he was now proclaimed the undisputed heavyweight champion of the world.

It was Frazier's greatest victory, but it came at a terrible price. He took tremendous physical punishment in the fight and did not defend his title again until 1972, when he fought just two times against lesser opposition. Nevertheless, when he went into the ring against GEORGE FOREMAN in January 1973, Frazier was an overwhelming favorite. In the space of just two rounds, the massive Foreman clubbed Frazier to the floor six times and lifted the championship belt. Stunned by the loss, Frazier regrouped, fought just once more in 1973, and then challenged Ali to a second fight. Ali by this time held the virtually meaningless North American Boxing Federation championship. The fight, held in New York City in January 1974, lacked the drama and action of the first fight, and Ali won by unanimous decision. Again Frazier went on the comeback trail, defeating two old foes, Quarry and

Ellis, in 1974 and 1975, respectively. But the man he wanted more than anyone else was Ali. In October 1974 Ali defeated Foreman to claim the world championship. One year later Frazier and Ali met for the third and final time in Manila, Philippines.

What came to be known as the "Thrilla in Manila" was one of the most brutal and grueling heavyweight fights of all time. By this time both men were moving past their primes as fighters, but their pride and personal animosity guaranteed a competitive fight. It began like their two previous bouts, with Frazier slow to start and Ali sweeping the rounds. In the middle rounds Frazier began an almost inhuman assault, crashing left hooks to Ali's body and head, ignoring the horrific pounding he was accepting to get close enough to land his own blows. In the twelfth round Ali dipped into his own well of willpower and began to chop away at Frazier, and he continued the beating through the next round. The fourteenth round was one of the most brutal poundings ever seen in a championship fight. Ali fired shot after shot, and each landed with frightening results. Frazier's head and face became a mass of welts, bruises, and small cuts, and his eyes were reduced to slits. That Frazier made it through the round at all, to say nothing of staying upright, was a testament to his fighter's heart. His corner, however, decided that the warrior had had enough and signaled surrender, with Frazier loudly protesting. Ali later said that the fight was the closest he had come to death.

Frazier had just one more fight after the battle in Manila, losing by knockout to Foreman in 1976. The three fights with Ali, however, cemented his place in the history of the sport of boxing. He announced his retirement but made an unimpressive comeback in 1981, held to a draw by the mediocre Jumbo Cummings. Frazier finished his career with a record of thirty-two wins, four losses, and one draw. In 1990 he was inducted into the International Boxing Hall of Fame. Frazier died of liver cancer at his home in Philadelphia at the age of 67.

FURTHER READING

Frazier, Joe, with Phil Berger. *Smokin' Joe: The Autobiography of a Heavyweight Champion of the World, Smokin' Joe Frazier* (1996).

Kram, Mark. *Ghosts of Manila: The Fateful Blood Feud between Muhammad Ali and Joe Frazier* (2001).

Obituary: *New York Times*, 8 Nov, 2011. http://www.nytimes.com/2011/11/08/sports/joe-frazier-ex-heavyweight-champ-dies-at-67.html?ref=sports.

MICHAEL L. KRENN

Frazier, Walter (Walt), II (29 Mar. 1945–), Hall of Fame basketball player nicknamed "Clyde" during his professional playing days, was born Walter Frazier Jr. in Atlanta, Georgia, the eldest of nine children of Walter Frazier Sr. At his all-black high school in the racially segregated South of the 1950s, he mastered basketball on a dirt playground, the only facility available to him. Frazier exhibited an athletic brilliance early in his life, becoming a three-sport star at David Howard High School. He quarterbacked the football team, played catcher on the baseball team, and was a versatile player on the basketball team.

After his success at David Howard, Frazier decided to attend Southern Illinois University (SIU) at Carbondale, Illinois. Because of racial segregation, it was not possible for Frazier to attend major colleges in Georgia, such as Georgia Tech and the University of Georgia, or any other major universities in the South. Frazier was actually offered more scholarships for football than basketball, but he decided on basketball. He said, "I was looking hopefully to the day when I could play pro ball, and there were no black quarterbacks on the pro scene then." At Southern Illinois Frazier excelled in his chosen sport. He was named a Division II All-American in 1964 and 1965. In 1965 he led SIU to the NCAA Division II Tournament finals. In 1966 he was academically ineligible for basketball but returned in 1967 to lead his team to the National Invitation Tournament (NIT), beating Marquette University 71-56 for the championship; he was named MVP of the tournament. In his junior year at the University of Southern Illinois, Frazier married Marsha Clark, his college sweetheart. Soon afterward, Walt Frazier III was born, but just after Frazier graduated, the couple filed for divorce. His former wife moved to Chicago with the baby and became a teacher.

Frazier's success in professional basketball was not unexpected. He was named to the NBA All-Rookie Team in 1968 and was an NBA All-Star seven times. He was also named All-Star Game MVP (1975), All-NBA First Team (1970, 1972, 1974, 1975), and All-NBA Second Team (1971, 1973). His ten-year run with the Knicks had him at one point as the team's all-time leader for most games (759), minutes played (28,995), field goals attempted (11,669), field goals made (5,736), free throws attempted (4,017), free throws made (3,145), assists (4,791), and points (14,617). Though Patrick Ewing would eventually break most of those records, Frazier still holds the team's career assists record. Despite the attention he received from the NBA, the most important thing to Frazier was the success of the New York Knicks. The team captured NBA championships in 1970 and 1973, the team's first two and only championships to that point. As he had done earlier in his athletic life, while playing for the Knicks Frazier combined his innate team leadership abilities with exhibitions of individual splendor. This was perhaps exhibited most clearly in the legendary game seven of the 1970 NBA Championship Finals against the Los Angeles Lakers, at that time led by Jerry West and WILT CHAMBERLAIN. The game took its place in sports history because of the inspirational play of the injured center, Willis Reed. But in terms of clutch play, Walt's game that night was extraordinary, and it resulted in a win for the Knicks. He scored 12 of 17 from the field and 12 of 12 from the free throw line to finish with 36 points and 19 assists.

In recognition of Frazier's team and individual performances, the Knicks retired his No. 10 jersey in 1979, and Frazier was inducted into the Naismith Memorial Basketball Hall of Fame in 1987. In 1996 he was elected to the NBA Fiftieth Anniversary All-Time Team, which recognized the top fifty players in the NBA's first fifty years.

While Frazier's athletic success in the country's biggest media market surely contributed to his popularity, it was his off the court "presence" that made him a star in New York and nationally. Perhaps no athlete defined a city and was defined by that city as much as Frazier and New York. They both epitomized cosmopolitanism, style, cool, hard work, and activism. Frazier was known for his fancy clothes, his Rolls-Royce, his cool demeanor, and his overall sense of style off the court. His growth as a cultural icon was captured in the nickname of "Clyde," first given to him by a Knicks trainer. The name came from Clyde Barrow, the bank robber featured in the film *Bonnie and Clyde*, which came out in Frazier's rookie year of 1967. In addition to the wide-brimmed, gangster-style hats he often wore, he could be seen sporting monogrammed, custom-made dress shirts and suits (some made of crushed velvet), fur coats, and even a huge belt buckle, studded CLYDE in rhinestones.

Frazier's contribution to basketball, the Knicks, New York, and fashion continued into the twenty-first century. He began working as a television sports commentator and came to be recognized for his unique commentating during Knicks games by those who watched had him play on the team, as well as by a whole new generation of fans. He was also featured in television commercials.

FURTHER READING

Dodd, Annamarie. "Nothin' But Natty; NBA Hall of Famer and Former New York Knick Walt Frazier Is Still a Clyde-oscope of Style," *Daily News Record* (Dec. 1999).

NBA Encyclopedia. "Walt Frazier." Available online at-http://www.nba.com/history/players/frazier_bio.html.

SARBJIT SINGH

Frederick, Nathaniel Jerome (18 Nov. 1877–7 Sept. 1938), lawyer, entrepreneur, educator, and journalist, was born near Orangeburg, South Carolina, the son of the former slaves Benjamin Frederick and Henrietta Baxter. A Renaissance man among African Americans in South Carolina, Frederick earned a bachelor of arts degree from Orangeburg's Claflin College in 1889 and degrees in history and Latin from the University of Wisconsin in 1901. Shortly after graduating from the latter institution, Frederick moved to Columbia, South Carolina, where he began an eighteen-year career as the principal of the Howard School, one of the first public schools for blacks in that city. He rose to early prominence as an educator and served as president of the South Carolina State Teacher's Association, an organization of that state's black teachers, from 1906 to 1908. He married Corrine Carroll in 1904; they would have four children.

By 1913 Frederick was searching for additional ways to serve his community as conditions for African Americans in South Carolina reached new lows under Governor Coleman L. Blease, who openly endorsed mob violence against blacks and reduced funding for African American schools. Frederick passed the South Carolina bar exam that year and opened his law practice in Columbia in 1914. He also became one of the founding members of South Carolina's charter branch of the National Association for the Advancement of Colored People (NAACP) and an assistant editor of the *Columbia Southern Indicator* newspaper. His business endeavors included partial ownership of Columbia's Victory Savings Bank and Regal Drug Store. By 1921 his reputation among South Carolina's blacks was such that John A. Sexton, a physician of Spartanburg, South Carolina, described Frederick in a 24 July 1921 letter to the *Southern Indicator* as "the coming Negro statesman and lawyer of South Carolina. I have the utmost confidence in him."

In 1925 Frederick decided to venture into editing his own newspaper. Joining the printer and manager George Hampton, Frederick began editing the

Palmetto Leader ("the Palmetto State" being the moniker for South Carolina) on 10 January of that year. Frederick was determined to make this newspaper into a journal far beyond that of black publications of that time and place, which usually centered on church affairs and local gossip but seldom covered topics of major importance among African Americans. From the beginning he was unafraid of frank criticism regardless of the subject matter. He denounced the popular Jamaican leader Marcus Garvey and the religious leader Bishop Charles Emmanuel "Sweet Daddy" Grace as "charlatans" who preyed on what Frederick on 18 September 1926 called "the ignorant colored people" in spite of the large following these men had among his newspaper's readership. He also spoke out against segregationist politicians such as Blease by name and denounced their policies of segregation and lynching.

In a 10 September 1927 editorial in the *Palmetto Leader* titled "Go to School and College," Frederick not only denounced the poor conditions of schools for black South Carolinians, he also criticized parents, whom he referred to as "criminals," for sending "their children out into the cruel world handicapped and an easy victim for the unscrupulous." He encouraged parents who lived near such schools either to demand better places of education from local leaders or to move to places where better schools were provided.

While earning fame as a crusading journalist, Frederick continued to gain renown for his legal career. In 1925 he defended the members of the Lowman family of Aiken, South Carolina. Sheriff H. H. Howard of Aiken entered the Lowmans' property allegedly to investigate allegations of the family manufacturing bootleg liquor. Three of the younger Lowmans were accused of murdering the sheriff, who allegedly pistol-whipped Bertha Lowman. In the midst of the fracas, Annie Lowman was then shot to death by a deputy. A grand jury indicted twenty-one-year-old Demon Lowman, his sister Bertha, and their fifteen-year-old cousin Clarence Lowman for murder. Frederick filed an appeal, and the South Carolina Supreme Court ordered a retrial, in which Demon Lowman was acquitted. Later that same day an Aiken mob took the Lowmans from jail and lynched them. Andrew Simkins, a black Columbian then visiting Aiken, felt Frederick's life was not safe in Aiken and secretly escorted him back to Columbia. Frederick wrote a fiery editorial in the 16 October 1926 *Palmetto Leader* denouncing the events. The South Carolina native and national NAACP leader William Pickens celebrated Frederick in the 20 November 1926 *Palmetto Leader* as "the Bravest Man in South Carolina."

Three years later Frederick tried another dangerous and controversial case. A black man named Ben Bess was convicted of sexual assault against a white woman in 1916, but in 1929 the alleged victim claimed that Bess was actually innocent, and Frederick arranged for South Carolina governor John Richards to issue a pardon. When the alleged victim changed her mind, Governor Richards tried to send Bess back to prison. Frederick took this case to the South Carolina Supreme Court, which ruled that the governor could not revoke pardons under such circumstances. After winning this case, Frederick arranged for Bess to leave South Carolina in safety.

In the midst of his legal career in the 1930s, Frederick continued to editorialize in the pages of the *Palmetto Leader*. Along with his unceasing campaigns against discrimination and racist politicians, Frederick also spoke out on world affairs, such as the League of Nations, the Nazi Holocaust, and the worldwide effects of the Great Depression. He attended the National Republican Conventions during those years and reported on them as well as adding syndicated commentary and wire reports from other newspapers. On 7 May 1938 he wrote his last editorial on the South Carolina Democratic Party's treatment of potential black voters. He died of pneumonia in Columbia. The *Palmetto Leader* survived for another twenty-eight years, and Frederick's ideas and examples led to the beginnings of the modern civil rights movement in South Carolina.

FURTHER READING

Burke, W. Lewis. "Nathaniel Jerome Frederick," in *South Carolina Encyclopedia*, ed. Walter Edgar (2006).

Underwood, James Lowell, and W. Lewis Burke Jr., eds. *Freedom's Lawyers: African American Founding Fathers and Lawyers in Reconstruction South Carolina* (2000).

Obituary: *Columbia Palmetto Leader*, 10 Sept. 1938.

DAMON L. FORDHAM

Frederick, Rivers (25 May 1874–2 Oct. 1954), physician and businessman, was born in New Roads, Louisiana, the second of the seven children of George Frederick and Armantine (maiden name unknown) of Point Coupeé Parish, Louisiana. Frederick received his early education at the plantation school run by the wife of Louis F. Drouillard, the landlord for whom his parents were sharecroppers.

In 1890 Frederick left Point Coupeé for New Orleans, where he enrolled at Straight University. He graduated in 1894, then enrolled at the New Orleans Medical College. Because he would not have been able to study in any of the city's hospitals because of his race, Frederick did not complete his medical education in New Orleans; instead, he left for Chicago in 1896 and enrolled at the College of Physicians and Surgeons. In Chicago he had the benefit of clinical training at Cook County Hospital. Frederick received his M.D. from the College of Physicians and Surgeons in 1897, becoming the school's first African American graduate. He then served a two-year internship at Chicago's John B. Murphy Surgical Clinic before returning to Louisiana in 1899. At that time Louisiana had an African American population of over a half million; but there were fewer than fifty black physicians. Frederick later explained that he decided to return to the South despite the increased racial tensions of the period because of his "growing desire to return to the place of my birth in order to help train young Negroes for adequate service in the growing field of medical practice, badly needed among our people" (Vital, 48).

When Frederick returned to Point Coupeé in 1899, he established himself as the parish physician for both blacks and whites. While he was initially well received by the community and soon developed a racially mixed clientele, his marriage to a poor white woman was too much for the local white community to take, and he was forced out of town. Frederick and his wife moved to Central America, where Frederick became a successful cattle rancher and served as the chief surgeon at the government hospital at El Rio Tan in Honduras. He and his wife had two daughters.

In 1904 Frederick returned to Louisiana, where he was named associate professor of surgery at Flint Medical School in New Orleans. In 1908 he was appointed to the surgical staff at Sarah Goodridge Hospital, later Flint-Goodridge Hospital, the only hospital in the city open to black physicians. He headed the surgery department at Flint-Goodridge until his retirement in 1950, when he was made chief emeritus and consultant in surgery. Despite his position as chief of surgery at Flint-Goodridge, Frederick was repeatedly denied membership to both the American College of Surgeons and the International College of Surgeons by local white physicians because of his race. He was eventually admitted to the International College of Surgeons in 1951. Shunned from white-run medical organizations, Frederick was active in the National Medical Association, the African American counterpart to the American Medical Association, and was one of the organizers of the all-black New Orleans Medical Association.

Frederick was perhaps the single most important figure in improving health care for black Louisianans during the early twentieth century. As chief of surgery at Flint-Goodridge, he instituted free clinics for the indigent black population of New Orleans. By 1935 the Flint-Goodridge clinics attracted over twenty-one thousand patients, 81 percent of whom were treated free of charge. In addition to his practice in New Orleans, Frederick spent time every year traveling throughout rural Louisiana, assisting local physicians in surgery and instructing them in modern techniques. Beginning in 1913 Frederick conducted the Southwestern Council Clinics at the Good Hope Sanitarium in Lafayette, and in 1936, at his prompting, Flint-Goodridge Hospital began an annual series of postgraduate clinics. The first course held at Flint-Goodridge attracted fifty-nine doctors from eight states, and in the program's first five years 206 physicians from ten states attended the program. By 1951 the clinic was six days long and boasted thirty-eight presenters from across the country.

Frederick was also one of Louisiana's most successful black businessmen during the first half of the twentieth century. He became involved in the insurance industry in 1923, when he was appointed to the board of directors of the Louisiana Industrial Life Insurance Company. He eventually became the president and principal stockholder in the company, which by the 1940s was the third largest black-owned enterprise in the state and the largest black insurance agency in the South. It was as an insurance executive, not as a surgeon, that he amassed the bulk of his $1.5 million fortune.

Frederick was also a civic activist. He helped establish the New Orleans Branch of the NAACP in 1915 and was a powerful force in the organization for over thirty-five years. In 1954 he was honored by Thurgood Marshall as someone who "labored valiantly to help bring success to the causes for which we are fighting for." Frederick never served as an officer in the NAACP, although he was on its executive board for a number of years, and he rarely took part in public demonstrations or meetings on behalf of the organization. Instead, he often worked as a liaison with white leaders. New Orleans mayors and Louisiana governors routinely asked for his advice on racial issues, and he sat on numerous interracial councils for the city and state. In recognition of his contributions as both a medical practitioner and a civic leader, in 1954 the Touro Street School in New Orleans, formerly named for Jefferson Davis, was renamed Rivers Frederick Elementary School.

FURTHER READING

Frederick's papers are at the Amistad Research Center, Tulane University, New Orleans, Louisiana.

Vital, Nida Harris. "Dr. Rivers Frederick and the History of Black Medicine in New Orleans." M.A. thesis, University of New Orleans (1978).

Ward, Thomas J., Jr. *Black Physicians in the Jim Crow South* (2003).

TOM J. WARD

Free Frank (Frank McWhorter) (1777–7 Sept. 1854), entrepreneur, pioneer, and town founder, was born near the Pacolet River in Union County, South Carolina, the son of an enslaved woman named Juda. His paternity is a bit murky, but most evidence points to his owner George McWhorter. Little information exists about the West African–born Juda other than that she had been a slave to the McWhorters since 1775. Oral family tradition holds that although George McWhorter sent Juda to the woods with orders to kill the baby at birth, Juda protected Frank, preserved him, and brought him home alive the next morning. The boy who would become Free Frank spent his formative years learning how to farm in the backwoods country of South Carolina. At eighteen Frank moved with his owner to a temporary homestead in Lincoln County, Kentucky. In 1798 George McWhorter bought some farmland in newly formed Pulaski County, Kentucky. In Pulaski, Frank met and fell in love with Lucy Denham, a slave of William Denham. While the Denham and McWhorter farms lay some distance apart, Denham's daughter had married McWhorter's brother in 1795. The family connection no doubt brought Frank and Lucy together. Frank and Lucy married in 1799, but both remained at their respective masters' farms for the time being.

Sometime prior to 1810 George McWhorter moved to Wayne County in southern Kentucky and established a second farm, but he left Frank with the authority to continue to run the Pulaski farm. McWhorter also found it profitable to let Frank hire out his time. While Kentucky's slave codes forbade this, all involved benefited. McWhorter still received the profits from the farms, and he also received an annual payment from Frank out of his wages. Frank kept what was left, giving him extra money to put toward freedom, and the people of labor-starved Pulaski County obtained a well-trained worker.

McWhorter's decision to move south and leave Frank behind benefited the enslaved man in multiple ways. It gave Frank an opportunity to remain close to his growing family, and it also allowed him to build up the savings he needed to purchase his freedom. By the time Frank and Lucy bought their freedom, they already had thirteen slave-born children, although only four of them lived to adulthood. The desire to buy freedom for himself and his family motivated Frank in all his entrepreneurial endeavors.

By 1810 it was apparent that the United States might soon be at war with Great Britain. This combined with the growing need for gunpowder on the ever-expanding western frontier caused sustained price increases for gunpowder and its principal ingredient saltpeter during this era. After finishing his farm work for the day, Frank spent his nights mining crude niter—the natural resource used to make saltpeter—from local limestone caves. He eventually created his own saltpeter manufactory. Manufacturing saltpeter was a laborious but simple process that required few specialized tools. Frank also appropriated a plot of land and sold the produce he grew there alongside that from his master's land, and he may have even dabbled in distilling whiskey and producing salt. Through these endeavors, Frank and Lucy netted over sixteen hundred dollars in approximately ten years. With this money, they bought Lucy's freedom in 1817 (she was expecting again and they wanted the baby to be born free) and Frank's in 1819. Frank valued his freedom so much that he had himself recorded in the 1820 federal census as Free Frank, the name by which he is known to history.

After buying their freedom, Lucy and Free Frank stayed in Kentucky and continued to make saltpeter and participate in other entrepreneurial activities. Free Frank speculated in land, increased his commercial farming activities, and moved his saltpeter works to Danville, Kentucky, to increase trade opportunities. As more white settlers moved into frontier Kentucky during the late 1820s, new legislation made life increasingly harsh for free blacks. Free Frank liquidated his land in Kentucky and acquired 160 acres in Illinois. He also traded his entire saltpeter manufactory for the freedom of Frank, his oldest son. In 1830 Free Frank, his wife Lucy, his manumitted son Frank, and his three surviving freeborn children left Kentucky for Pike County, Illinois.

When Lucy and Free Frank moved to Illinois, they left three children and various grandchildren in slavery. Free Frank geared his activities in Illinois toward the goal of amassing enough money to buy the rest of his children and grandchildren out of slavery. By 1836 Free Frank had acquired six hundred acres of Illinois farmland. To keep his property safe should something happen to him, he petitioned the court to take the legal surname of McWorter. In the same year Free Frank achieved his most notable success by founding New Philadelphia, Illinois. Free Frank sold his first town lots on 28 April 1837, and he continued to sell and develop lots until his death in 1854. New Philadelphia was the earliest town legally founded by a free African American in the United States.

Free Frank dedicated his life to the uplift of his family and those around him. While Free Frank never learned to write, he stressed education to his children and donated the land for the New Philadelphia schoolhouse. Free Frank's family also actively participated in Illinois's Underground Railroad. When Free Frank died in New Philadelphia, he had not quite achieved his dream of freeing his entire family. However, through the settlement of his estate, Free Frank's children bought Free Frank's last five grandchildren and two great grandchildren still held in slavery. From 1817 to 1857 Free Frank and Lucy paid approximately fifteen thousand dollars to buy themselves and over a dozen family members from slavery.

FURTHER READING

Walker, Juliet E. K. *Free Frank: A Black Pioneer on the Antebellum Frontier* (1983).

Walker, Juliet E. K. "Legal Processes and Judicial Challenges: Black Land Ownership on the Western Illinois Frontier," in *Race and Law before Emancipation*, ed. Paul Finkelman (1991).

Walker, Juliet E. K. "Pioneer Slave Entrepreneurship on the Kentucky Pennyroyal Frontier," *Journal of Negro History* 68.2 (Summer 1983): 289–308.

DONOVAN S. WEIGHT

Freedom, British (fl. 1784–1800), free black loyalist in Preston Township, Halifax, Nova Scotia, Canada, and one of the founders of Freetown, Sierra Leone, is a person about whom little early information is known. He may have begun life as a slave in one of the former British colonies before the war, and his name may have been a "freedom name"; that is, one that he chose for himself when his personal liberty came. Probably he was the same British Freedome granted land in the Merigumish Township, Pictou County, Nova Scotia, Canada, for service as a private in the 82nd Regiment of Foot (S. Patterson, *History of County of Pictou*, 460). Some members of that regiment served at the Battle of Yorktown with the British General Cornwallis. Freedom's name is not in the "Book of Negroes" (the list of black Americans freed after the American Revolution and who left with the British from New York in 1783). However, his name may have been overlooked during this mass evacuation from New York in 1783 when thousands of loyalists, both black and white (3,500 blacks and 14,000 whites), left for Nova Scotia. Probably he traveled with the regiment that disbanded from Halifax, Nova Scotia, late in 1783. After the war, the British evacuated free black loyalists and white loyalists with their slaves. Some free blacks moved to London (between 400 and 1,000) while others, like Freedom, sailed to Canada. Many unfortunate southern slaves, seized from their patriot owners, were reenslaved in the Caribbean with new loyalist owners.

In Nova Scotia, black loyalists were supposed to receive land to live on and free food for three years. The British government promised an allotment of one hundred acres for each head of household, plus fifty acres per person for every member of that household (spouse, children, and servants). In reality, about 8 percent received that land, and they had to work for Nova Scotian officials or their designees for necessary food and supplies. Others did what they could to survive. People with skills (blacksmiths, carpenters, shipbuilders, and coopers [barrel makers]) used them. This arrangement left little time for blacks to work for themselves. Some black loyalists who received no land were homeless, lived in the streets, and begged for food to stay alive. Others indentured themselves to white loyalists to survive, and many died. In 1791 British Freedom was among the fifty to one hundred families trying to survive in Preston Township, Halifax County, Nova Scotia, Canada.

By Preston standards, Freedom was very well off. He owned forty acres of land outside of town, granted by the British government in 1784, where he built a small cabin. Freedom also owned one and a half "town lots" in Preston Township itself. In neighboring Pictou County, he may have still held the one hundred acres awarded him in 1785 for his British army service. Perhaps because Merigumish was predominantly white and Scottish, Freedom stayed in Preston and sold the Merigumish land to better himself. Many of his neighbors were granted less land and no tools to work it. Work was hard to get in Nova Scotia, and even those black loyalists who received land often lived in tents or "lean-tos" in a state of near starvation.

Freedom was a God-fearing man. He probably followed the Baptist faith. DAVID GEORGE may have been his pastor. There is an account that in 1785, Freedom attended the preaching of "Black David" (a.k.a. David George), the black itinerant Baptist missionary, formerly a Virginia slave, licensed by Governor Carleton to preach the Gospel only to blacks in Nova Scotia. It was winter, and George almost died of frostbite on the journey home. Many whites disliked George because he preached "all men were equal in God's sight" (Schama, 242–243). Such a man was certainly an inspiration to the African American community in Nova Scotia and beyond.

Crops failed in Nova Scotia in 1789, and famine struck. More than a thousand white loyalists returned to the United States, and hundreds moved to England. However, blacks were reluctant to return to the States, where they would quite likely face reenslavement. The Sierra Leone Company (the British company incorporated in 1799 to form a government for, and attract settlers to, a newly acquired section of the West African country Sierra Leone) offered to relocate the black loyalists to Sierra Leone. In August 1791 recruiting began for blacks willing to be relocated to a new settlement in Sierra Leone, called Granville Town. Their new home promised "a guaranteed plot of land to cultivate (twenty acres per man, ten for his wife and five for each child)" (Schama, 277), a justice system that included black juries, guaranteed equal rights and responsibilities for blacks and whites, and, finally, a zero tolerance for holding slaves or participating in the slave trade. The response to recruitment efforts was overwhelming and too much for Granville Town. The overflow would go to Freetown. When the abolitionist Lieutenant John Clarkson came to Preston to recruit Sierra Leonean emigrants, he was impressed with what they had done under great adversity, by improving their land and selling legumes, corn, and poultry at market. So impressed was he that British Freedom and his Preston neighbors received the contract to supply sitting hens (chickens used for their eggs) for the voyage to Freetown. On 15 January 1792, 1,196 black loyalists—whom Lieutenant Clarkson called "the flower of the Black people"—left Halifax aboard fifteen ships bound for their new home in Sierra Leone (Blakeney, 355). They represented 33 percent of those who came to Nova Scotia nine years earlier in 1783. Freedom and his fellow Prestonians sailed aboard the ship *Eleanor*.

In November 1800, Freedom was one of twenty-four men convicted of treason and banished to Granville Town. They sided with the rebelling Jamaican Maroons. All twenty-four lost their land, which in turn was given to the loyal Maroons. This is apparently the last time history recorded the name British Freedom. Perhaps he remained in Granville Town, changed his name, and eked out a meager existence; failing that, maybe he worked as a laborer on another's farm. Thus, we know neither the beginning nor the end of British Freedom's life, but we do know that he left the new United States as a free black loyalist, settled for a time in Preston, Halifax, Nova Scotia, Canada, and apparently died in Sierra Leone, Africa.

FURTHER READING

Blakeney, Phyllis R. "Boston King: A Negro Loyalist Who Sought Refuge in Nova Scotia," *Dalhousie Review* (Autumn 1968).

Frey, Sylvia. *Water from the Rock: Black Resistance in a Revolutionary Age* (1991).

Pulis, John W., ed. *Moving On: Black Loyalists in the Afro-Atlantic World* (1999).

Schama, Simon. *Rough Crossings: Britain, the Slaves, and the American Revolution* (2006).

Walker, James W. St. G. *The Black Loyalists: The Search for a Promised Land in Nova Scotia and Sierra Leone, 1783–1870* (1976).

Wilson, Ellen Gibson. *The Loyal Blacks* (1976).

KAREN E. SUTTON

Freeman, Al, Jr. (21 Mar. 1934–), actor, director, and educator, was born Albert Cornelius Freeman Jr. in San Antonio, Texas, to Albert Cornelius Freeman and Lottie Brisette Coleman Freeman. His parents divorced when Freeman was nine, leaving him to shuttle between his mother in San Antonio and his father, a jazz pianist, in Columbus, Ohio. Freeman later said that he regretted never getting to know his father, who died in 1968.

Freeman entered Los Angeles City College in 1951, served in the U.S. Air Force from 1951 to 1954, and returned to college in 1954, studying theater, broadcasting, and speech. He made his stage debut in a 1954 Ebony Showcase Theatre production of Sidney Kingsley's *Detective Story*. Freeman also studied acting in Los Angeles with Harold Clifton, Jeff Corey, and the legendary black actor Frank Silvera. In an interview with *Ebony*, he joked that he played so many angry young men in his early days that the poet-playwright Langston Hughes claimed to become sick at his stomach just at the sight of Freeman's name.

Freeman moved to New York in 1959 and made his Broadway debut in a 1960 adaptation of Richard Wright's *The Long Dream*, which ran for only five performances. He married Savara Clemon in January 1960. Because of his subsequent stage work Freeman was acclaimed as one of America's finest actors by Joseph Papp, founder of the New York Shakespeare Festival. For this theater company Freeman appeared in productions of William Shakespeare's *Troilus and Cressida*, with James Earl Jones and Roscoe Lee Brown, in 1965; Eugene O'Neill's *Long Day's Journey into Night*, with Gloria Foster and Earle Hyman, in 1981; and *Measure for Measure*, with Moses Gunn and Christopher Walken, in 1996.

Freeman was inspired by hearing Malcolm X speak in Harlem in 1963, particularly moved by Malcolm's exhortation to his audience to stand up and be men. Many years later the producer Marvin Worth asked him to direct a film about Malcolm X, but Freeman turned down the offer because he did not think the available screenplay did justice to Malcolm's life. Shortly afterward he played Malcolm in the 1979 television miniseries *Roots: The Next Generations*, for which he was nominated for an Emmy.

Freeman's best known stage role came in James Baldwin's *Blues for Mr. Charlie* in 1964. The Broadway play was inspired by the 1955 lynching of Emmett Till in Mississippi. During this time, Freeman also appeared off-Broadway in *Dutchman* (1964) and *The Slave* (1964) by LeRoi Jones (later Amiri Baraka). In 1970 Freeman starred in *Look to the Lilies*, a Broadway musical version of the 1963 Sidney Poitier film *Lilies of the Field* that closed after three weeks.

Freeman's most notable early film role came opposite Shirley Knight in the film adaptation of *Dutchman* (1967). The film historian Donald Bogle praised the intensity of Freeman's performance as a civilized black man who turns the other cheek until finally exploding at the injustices experienced by African Americans. During the 1960s, and perhaps inspired by Malcolm X's 1963 speech, Freeman played spokesmen for a more proactive form of black politics in films like *Black Like Me* (1964), *The Troublemaker* (1964), *Finian's Rainbow* (1968), *The Detective* (1969), and *The Lost Man* (1969), with Sidney Poitier. During this period he embodied on screen the pent-up anger felt by much of black America.

One of the highlights of Freeman's film career was his performance as Elijah Muhammad in Spike Lee's *Malcolm X* (1992). At the cast's first read-through of the script, Freeman reportedly dazzled his fellow actors by already having mastered his character's speech pattern and mannerisms. Paul Lee, the film's historical consultant, told *Ebony* that it was extraordinary how the actor conveyed the complex personality of the Nation of Islam leader. Though many, including the film critic Roger Ebert, expected Freeman to be nominated for an Academy Award, this honor was not forthcoming, though he was named best supporting actor by the NAACP's Image Awards.

Freeman's film career continued in Tim Reid's much-acclaimed *Once Upon a Time ... When We Were Colored* (1995), in which the actor played the dignified patriarch of a Mississippi family confronting the racial polarities of the 1940s and 1950s. He gave another exceptional performance in Maya Angelou's *Down in the Delta* (1998), a more contemporary look at family life and race politics in Mississippi.

Freeman worked frequently in television, appearing in such series as *The Defenders* (1965), *The F.B.I.* (1968), *The Mod Squad* (1972), *Maude* (1974), *Kojack* (1976), *The Cosby Show* (1985), *Homicide: Life on the Street* (1995–1996), and *Law and Order* (1990 and 2004). In 1970 Freeman co-starred with Patty Duke in *My Sweet Charlie*, one of the first made-for-television movies, about an unwed, pregnant white woman and a black New York lawyer on the run in rural Texas after being falsely accused of a crime. He was nominated for an Emmy for this performance. He also starred in a 1972 public television adaptation of Lorraine Hansberry's *To Be Young, Gifted, and Black* and played a supporting role in *King*, a 1978 miniseries with Paul Winfield as Martin Luther King Jr.

Freeman's best known television work, however, was his seventeen years, beginning in 1972, as police detective Ed Hall on the daytime drama *One Life to Live*, for which he won a Daytime Emmy as outstanding actor in a daytime drama series in 1979 and was nominated for the supporting actor Daytime Emmy in 1983 and 1986. Freeman directed several episodes of *One Life to Live*, becoming the first African American to direct a soap opera. He also directed the 1971 film *A Fable*, based on Baraka's *The Slave*, and co-wrote, with the director and star Ossie Davis, the African revolution film *Countdown at Kusini* (1976).

Freeman and his wife separated in 1985. Beginning in 1988 he taught acting at Howard University, serving as acting chair of the theater arts department for a time. Freeman said that teaching helped fill the gap in his life created by never being a father. Until his appearance in *Malcolm X* many Howard students did not know who Freeman was, but after the film's release they began to treat him as a star.

FURTHER READING

Bogle, Donald. *Toms, Coons, Mulattoes, Mammies, and Bucks: An Interpretive History of Blacks in American Films* (1973).

Randolph, Laura B. "Al Freeman Jr.'s Triumphant Return," *Ebony* (Mar. 1993).

MICHAEL ADAMS

Freeman, Amos Noë (Nov. 1809–28 July 1893), evangelical abolitionist, educator, minister, and "conductor" in the Underground Railroad, was born in Rahway, New Jersey.

A towering figure in nineteenth-century black civil rights circles on the East Coast and beyond, Amos Noë Freeman's words and deeds as a civic leader for nearly seventy years were rivaled only by the exemplary company he kept. His closest colleagues in the abolitionist movement included FREDERICK DOUGLASS, John Brown, Theodore Dwight Weld, Henry Ward Beecher, Beriah Green, Gerrit Smith, THEODORE SEDGWICK WRIGHT, Simeon Jocelyn, Archibald Grimké, Arthur and Lewis Tappan, and former Oneida Institute classmates HENRY HIGHLAND GARNET, ALEXANDER CRUMMELL, AMOS G. BEMAN, and J. W. C. PENNINGTON.

Little is known about Freeman's parentage or childhood, including whether he was ever enslaved or indentured, having been born in a state where the gradual abolition of slavery began five years before his birth and full emancipation of its enslaved residents became law in 1845, the last state to do so in the North. It also remains a mystery why Freeman's life and contributions are so sparsely documented by historians in light of his many achievements regarding the uplift of African Americans,. Freeman was, nevertheless, a respected and active member of the abolitionist and temperance movements.

By his own account, Freeman left his home state of New Jersey for New York City while still a youth and became involved there in the black Presbyterian church. He was mentored from an early age by Rev. Theodore Sedgwick Wright, himself an abolitionist, educator, and Presbyterian minister who attended Princeton to become the nation's first black graduate of a theological seminary in 1828. While a student at the African Free School in Manhattan, Freeman was inspired to further his education and pursue the vocation of ministry.

Returning to his native Rahway, Freeman entered high school for just eighteen months under the tutelage of Henry Cornelius Edgar, a white Princeton-educated teacher who would later publish several of his sermons as an ordained minister.

From Rahway, Freeman entered Oneida Institute in Whitesboro, New York, an avant-garde but highly controversial institution of higher education founded by the Oneida Presbytery circa 1828 on a 114-acre farm that fused manual labor with a liberal arts curriculum and religious instruction within a larger context of radical abolitionism. Later funded by the white progressive philanthropist Gerrit Smith, a cousin and mentor to author, abolitionist, and women's rights activist Elizabeth Cady Stanton, Oneida operated in a political climate where Northern anti-abolitionist sentiment was high, resulting in the dissolution of other integrated educational institutions such as the Noyes Academy in New Hampshire, which was burned down by a riotous white mob in 1835.

The Oneida Institute was under the leadership of radical Presbyterian minister Rev. Beriah Green, who, in his role as president, ensured that each incoming class was racially integrated and inculcated with principles of social justice that were so ahead of their time that the school's bold mission would ensure its own demise within just eleven years of its founding.

In 1835, around the same time that the Noyes Academy was destroyed, Freeman arrived at Oneida where he was one of four black students in a freshman class of thirty-three men of various ethnic and socioeconomic backgrounds and nationalities. There, he studied, among other courses, Hebrew and Greek, in addition to performing three hours of manual labor every day.

After graduating from Oneida, Freeman returned to New Jersey where he taught black youth in New Brunswick. Little is known about his short time in this capacity. But as a consequence of his work there, Freeman was recruited to take charge of the black school system of Newark, which he did for two years.

On Christmas Eve of 1839, Freeman married Christiana Taylor Livingston Williams of New York City, daughter of Barbara Williams, an enslaved West Indian concubine of Philip Henry Livingston, who was the wealthy white Jamaican-born grandson of Philip Livingston—a noted signer of the Declaration of Independence. Amos and Christiana had four children, three of whom lived to adulthood, including daughter Mary Christiana Freeman Wheeler, the mother of LAURA WHEELER WARING, the celebrated early twentieth-century portrait artist.

In May of 1841, Freeman was licensed by the Manhattan Association of New York as an ordained Presbyterian minister, and shortly thereafter, moved to Portland, Maine, to be installed at the Abyssinian Congregational Church as its first full-time pastor. He led this small but active congregation, composed largely of black fishermen and their families, for about eleven years, holding church services that were occasionally integrated by white Portland residents as well as captains of vessels lying in port who were drawn to his evangelical services and singing prowess. While in Portland, he taught school for eight years, sang at the local prison, and eventually purchased a home for his family where, as a "conductor" in the Underground Railroad, he sheltered fugitives from slavery in well-orchestrated efforts to resettle them to Canada and other places. His work as an agent in this secret, integrated network of antislavery activists began in earnest after the Fugitive Slave Law of 1850 which practically extended slavery to free states and encouraged the proliferation of slave catchers, who threatened the safety of fugitives and free people of color alike.

In 1852, Freeman accepted a call to pastor Siloam Presbyterian Church in Brooklyn, New York. He pastored this black church until 1860 when he accepted a call from the colored Talcott Street Congregational Church in Hartford, Connecticut. He stayed there until 1864 before returning to the pastorate of Siloam in Brooklyn where he remained until his retirement in 1885.

Freeman's most well-known act of heroism was documented in a letter to his long time friend, the wealthy merchant and progressive philanthropist Lewis Tappan; he detailed how he personally transported a young girl, Ann Maria Weems, who was disguised as a boy, over 500 miles from New York City to Niagara Falls to the town of Dresden in Ontario, Canada, where she was reunited with her incredulous and overjoyed aunt and uncle. This account, later published in the acclaimed book, *The Underground Railroad: Authentic Narratives and First-Hand Accounts*, by fellow black abolitionist WILLIAM STILL, described the perils Freeman faced for his beliefs and shed light on the harrowing lengths to which black fugitives went to escape slavery and the unrelenting kidnappers who pursued them in the Northern states.

In over a half-century of public service as a pastor, abolitionist, educator, and civic leader, Rev. Freeman took on many different leadership positions in a host of religious and civic organizations locally and nationally, including affiliations with the Brooklyn Presbytery, the Vigilance Committee of New York, the Union Missionary Society, the American Missionary Committee, and the African Civilization Society, which by 1868, according to *The New York Times*, hired 127 teachers and taught 8,000 black students in the Reconstruction South.

Rev. Freeman died in his Brooklyn home at 33 Fleet Street at age 83. He was interred at Evergreen Cemetery in Brooklyn.

FURTHER READING

Green, Beriah. *The Miscellaneous Writings of Beriah Green*. (1841).

Sernett, Milton C. *Abolition's Axe: Beriah Green, Oneida Institute, and the Black Freedom Struggle*. (2004).

Sorin, Gerald. *The New York Abolitionists: A Case Study of Political Radicalism*. (1970).

Still, William J. *The Underground Railroad: Authentic Narratives and First-Hand Accounts*. (1879).

Obituary: *New York Times*, 31 July 1893, online at http://www.genealogy.com/users/d/u/f/Joseph-Hairston-Duff/FILE/0003text.txt.

CHRISTOPHER M. RABB

Freeman, Daniel (1868–1947), artist, photographer, and entrepreneur, was born in Alexandria, Virginia, to Thomas Freeman and Sarah Freeman. Following his father's death, in 1877 he and his sister Delilah moved with their mother to Washington, where Freeman attended Washington, D.C., public schools and excelled in drawing and painting. It is not known if he finished high school. He held a variety of jobs, including laborer and waiter, to help support the family.

In 1885, at the age of seventeen, Freeman started to advertise his services as a painter in addition to art framer and bicycle repairman. Gradually he began to pursue a career as an artist and photographer. His early work consisted of pastel drawings of Washington's elite African American community. His most famous portraits were of the Washington lawyer JOHN MERCER LANGSTON, completed in 1893, and of the abolitionist FREDERICK DOUGLASS in 1895. That same year Freeman was chosen to develop and install the art exhibit in the Negro Building at the Atlanta Exposition, where both portraits were displayed.

At the exposition, BOOKER T. WASHINGTON delivered his Atlanta Compromise speech on racial progress, and Freeman may have been influenced by Washington's business philosophy. Freeman observed gaps in the services available to black Washingtonians at the turn of the century and developed skills in those areas. In addition to conducting his business, he organized the Washington Amateur Art Society for African Americans near the turn of the century and was also active in local benevolent organizations. From 1898 to 1899 he was president of the Social Temperance Assembly, which raised money and provided food and clothing for the Children's Home.

At some point between 1885 and 1893, Freeman apprenticed under the white photographer E. J. Pullman and learned photography and darkroom work. Freeman began advertising his services as an artist and photographer, as well as an art framer, painter, and bicycle repairman, around 1885, when he was seventeen years old. He used his painting skills to paint his own backdrops in photographed portraits. Business advertisements indicated that he taught drawing and painting as well as photography and photo retouching. His clientele included prominent local residents, Masonic lodges, and local schools.

The Union League of the District of Columbia, established in 1892, was organized to unite the city's African American residents and to promote and develop their economic status. In the same year it was founded, the League canvassed the city and produced a directory of black-owned businesses and organizations. Advertising his services as a portrait artist, sign painter, art instructor, and photographer, Freeman was the only African American photographer listed in this city directory, although not the first. Washington had had a succession of black photographers offering commercial photographic services. Among them was daguerreotypist John B. Washington, who began operating some time before 1860. Freeman advertised the same services in the 1894 directory, but at a new address. He focused exclusively on photography after 1900.

In 1900 Andrew Hilyer, the founder and president of the Union League, presented a paper titled "The Colored American in Business" at the National Negro Business League convention in Boston. Hilyer was so impressed with the successes of black businesses around the country that in 1901 he produced a third directory of Washington businesses and included a history of entrepreneurship which profiled some of the city's more prominent businessmen, including Freeman. The directory included two separate advertisements for Freeman's businesses: one for his bicycle repair services and related sundries and the other strictly for photographic services. Three other African American photographers had begun operating in Washington at the turn of the century: Edward M. Johnson, Jerome O'Hagan, and ADDISON SCURLOCK. Although Scurlock began listing his photographic services in the 1901 city directories, his Scurlock Studios, ultimately Washington's most successful and longest continuously operating black-owned photography business, did not officially open until 1911.

Both Scurlock and Freeman participated in the Jamestown Exposition of 1909; Scurlock won a gold medal for his portraiture, and Freeman received a bronze medal for his photographs of D.C. African American school buildings and classes. Both photographers had lucrative businesses and dominated the industry during their lifetimes. While it is not clear if there was serious competition between the two studios, records indicated that they received the majority patronage from Washington's growing African American population.

Around 1914 Freeman was elected president of the Washington, D.C., chapter of Booker T. Washington's National Business League. At the league's national meeting held in Baltimore, Maryland, in 1915, Freeman described the business atmosphere in the city and his current studio, indicating that the four successful African American-owned photographic studios in the city listed in the 1901 business directory were the only ones in operation.

In an early 1920s survey of advertisements in the *Washington Tribune* 125 black-owned offices and businesses were identified in the nine blocks of U Street between Fifth Street and Fourteenth Street, including three photography studios: the Scurlock Studio, Daniel Freeman Studios, and the studio of Jerome O'Hagan. Known affectionately as the "Black Broadway," the U Street corridor was the leading business district for black city residents. In the 1930s Freeman began teaching photography and art at Frelinghuysen University, under the direction of the renowned educator ANNA JULIA COOPER. The school offered evening classes to working adults. He continued to operate his studio while teaching. Freeman was killed in an automobile accident in 1947.

Throughout his career, Freeman specialized in portraiture, but a small body of his photographs recorded early Masonic activities, local businesses, and school groups as well, all reminiscent of the photographs by Frances Benjamin Johnston of students at Hampton University taken around the same time. Freeman's known body of portrait work was not extensive, but what survived revealed a highly skilled mastery of portraiture and an understanding of the lighting, posing, and other studio techniques that compliment the skin tones and texture of persons of color.

FURTHER READING

Hilyer, Andrew F. *The Twentieth Century Union League Directory* (1901).

Willis-Thomas, Deborah. *Black Photographers 1840–1940: An Illustrated Bio-bibliography* (1985).

DONNA M. WELLS

Freeman, Elizabeth (c. 1744–28 Dec. 1829), civil rights litigant, known as Mum Bett, was born a slave in Claverack, New York, most likely to African parents. Mum Bett and her sister were owned by the Dutch Hogeboom family in Claverack. At an uncertain date, the sisters were sold to the family of John Ashley, a judge in the Massachusetts Court of Common Pleas and a prominent citizen of Sheffield, Massachusetts. Little is known about Mum Bett's life with the Ashleys, but it probably resembled the life of many northern slaves during the eighteenth century. Most slaves lived in small households in proximity to their owners and performed a wide range of tasks to support the North's diversified economy.

Mum Bett's decision to sue for freedom was sparked by an incident of cruelty that is prominent in accounts of her life. When her mistress, Hannah Ashley, struck Mum Bett's sister "in a fit of passion" with a heated shovel, Mum Bett interposed and was struck instead. She "received the blow; and bore the honorable scar it left to the day of her death" (Swan, 52). After the incident, Mum Bett left the Ashleys and refused to return. John Ashley—who had, ironically, chaired the committee that drafted the 1773 Sheffield Declaration, which resolved that "Mankind in a State of Nature are equal, free and independent of each other, and have a right to the undisturbed Enjoyment of their lives, their Liberty and Property"—appealed to the law for the return of his slave, Mum Bett. Instead of returning to the Ashleys, Mum Bett approached Theodore Sedgwick Sr., a lawyer she may have first met when he was working with Ashley on the Sheffield Declaration. Mum Bett convinced Sedgwick to represent her in suing for her freedom. Massachusetts's newly enacted 1780 state constitution had declared all men born free and equal, Mum Bett reasoned, and so her bondage must be illegal. Sedgwick agreed to take the case, which was joined by a man named Brom, another of Ashley's slaves. When curious interviewers subsequently asked her how she had arrived at that premise, perhaps presuming wrongly that an illiterate slave would not have any legal knowledge, she is reported to have said, "By keepin' still and mindin' things." By this she meant "when she was waiting at table, she heard gentlemen talking over the Bill of Rights and the new constitution of Massachusetts; and in all they said she never heard but that all people were born free and equal, and she thought long about it, and resolved she would try whether she did not come in among them" (Kaplan, 244). In this way Mum Bett, like many African Americans, was capitalizing on the hard-won knowledge she acquired as an exploited worker. On her own initiative, this northern workingwoman tested Massachusetts's state constitution by claiming that its theory of men's equality made slavery illegal.

Sedgwick won the case, *Brom and Bett v. J. Ashley Esq.*, in 1781. A state court granted Mum Bett and Brom their freedom and required Ashley to pay them thirty shillings in damages. The case was subsequently hailed as a precedent-setting, landmark civil rights decision that helped diminish the practice and effects of slavery in Massachusetts, though scholars are quick to point out that technically speaking, slavery was not abolished in the state until 1866. At the time of the suit, Mum Bett is believed to have been the widow of a Revolutionary War veteran and the mother of one daughter, called Little Bett. After gaining her freedom, Mum Bett gave herself the surname "Freeman." The case brought Freeman and Sedgwick, who later became a judge and a senator, notoriety in their day and linked their names for posterity.

After the ruling, Freeman went to work for the Sedgwicks. Consequently, the most documented period of her life is the time she worked for this prominent New England family. Freeman was remembered fondly, if somewhat paternalistically, by the Sedgwick children, Theodore Sedgwick Jr. and his sister, the writer Catherine Maria Sedgwick, for her skilled nursing, her long tenure as the family's loyal and faithful servant, and her spirited defense of the family's property during Shays's Rebellion in 1786. Freeman is buried in the Sedgwick family plot. Her tombstone reads, "She was born a slave and remained a slave for nearly thirty years. She could neither read nor write yet in her own sphere she had no superior or equal. She neither wasted time nor property. She never violated a trust nor failed to perform a duty. In every situation of domestic trial, she was the most efficient helper, and the tenderest friend. Good mother, farewell." Freeman inspired admiration from the family for her independent spirit. As Theodore Sedgwick Jr. related during an 1831 abolitionist speech in which he invoked Freeman's experience, "If there could be a practical refutation of the imagined superiority of our race to hers, the life and character of this woman would afford that refutation.... She had nothing of the submissive or subdued character, which succumbs to superior force.... On the contrary, ... she uniformly ... obtained an ascendancy over all those with whom she was associated in service" (Kaplan, 246).

Freeman is one of the most visible exemplars of often invisible, illiterate African Americans who contributed to black communities' challenges to racial inequality in the early republic. Their courageous efforts occurred well before the more famous ones of nineteenth-century black abolitionists such as FREDERICK DOUGLASS and SOJOURNER TRUTH. Though relatively little is known about Elizabeth Freeman, parallels exist between her life and that of Truth, another northern black workingwoman. As an impecunious former slave, before becoming renowned as an abolitionist, Truth did not hesitate to appeal to the courts for the return of her illegally sold son, despite her unlettered and lowly social status. In this way, Truth followed in Freeman's footsteps, both of them exemplifying a tradition of overlooked African American women who fearlessly claimed their inheritance of liberty as civic participants and contributors to national life.

Freeman eventually left the Sedgwicks' employ and became a sought-after nurse and midwife. She lived with her daughter in a house next door to the Revolutionary War veteran Agrippa Hull. Elizabeth Freeman died a freewoman in 1829. Nearly forty years after Freeman's death, W. E. B. DUBOIS was born in Great Barrington, Massachusetts, the town where Mum Bett's historic case was argued. Indeed, Mum Bett was the the second wife of DuBois's great-grandfather, Jacob Burghardt. DuBois's direct line of descent was through Jacob's first wife Violet.

FURTHER READING

The Sedgwick family papers are available in a special collection at the Stockbridge Public Library, Stockbridge, Massachusetts.

Kaplan, Sidney. *The Black Presence in the Era of the American Revolution, 1770–1800* (1973).

Martineau, Harriet. *Retrospect of Western Travel 2* (1838).

Nell, William C. *The Colored Patriots of the American Revolution* (1855, repr. 1968).

Sedgwick, Theodore. *The Practicability of the Abolition of Slavery* (1831).

Swan, Jon. "The Slave Who Sued for Freedom," *American Heritage* 41 (Mar. 1990).

XIOMARA SANTAMARINA

Freeman, Frankie Muse (24 Nov. 1916–), civil rights lawyer, U.S. civil rights commissioner, was born Marie Frankie Muse in Danville, Virginia, the oldest of eight children of William Brown Muse, a railroad postal clerk, and Maud Beatrice Smith Muse. Maud Muse, a 1911 graduate of the historically black Hampton University, and her husband, William, who was one of the first African Americans employed as a railroad postal clerk in Danville, exemplified for their children lives of dignity despite the indignities of Jim Crow life around them. The Muse family and other black Danville residents had to travel forty-eight miles to the nearest black movie theater. Danville blacks also attended segregated schools and faced racial discrimination in public accommodations. Frankie Muse learned at an early age to overcome these obstacles through self-discipline and perseverance. These were lessons that she and her siblings gleaned from their parents, who taught them that moral character and personal dignity sometimes meant walking instead of riding in segregated transportation.

In the black community of Danville, the Muse family was well-off—they were one of the few families in the community with a home telephone. Muse recalled that many nationally renowned African Americans would lodge with black families in her neighborhood because local hotels refused to accommodate black guests.

The African American Danville that Muse knew was like a village, where adults taught children to be self-disciplined and self-reliant. The young Muse played piano and excelled in school. She attended Westmoreland High School (later John M. Langston High School), graduating as the valedictorian of the class of 1933. At age sixteen Muse headed to Hampton University in Virginia, alma mater not only to her mother but also to several of her siblings, nieces, and nephews. At Hampton, Muse majored in mathematics, graduating in 1937.

New York City beckoned Muse in 1936, and there she met Shelby Freeman, a Lincoln University (Missouri) graduate and Columbia University Teachers College graduate student from St. Louis. Frankie and Shelby were married on 15 December

1938, and the following year Frankie Muse Freeman gave birth to a daughter, Shelbe Patricia Freeman.

Frankie Freeman worked as a clerk in the Department of the Treasury and the Office of Price Administration. In 1944 she entered Howard University's Law School, one of the prestigious historically black colleges and universities and well known for its distinguished faculty and alumni. At Howard, Freeman drew upon those lessons of perseverance she learned as a young girl. As one of only a few female law students at Howard, she learned to balance her studies with the demands of motherhood and marriage. Her efforts paid off, for she was one of only two female students to pass the District of Columbia bar exam after graduating in 1947.

Upon graduating from law school, Freeman joined her husband in Sampson, New York, where he taught finance at the Associated Colleges of Upper New York (later the College Center of the Finger Lakes). She taught business law at the college until 1948, when the family relocated to St. Louis, Shelby's hometown. At that time, St. Louis was segregated. There was, however, a well-established African American population in the city, and in June 1949 Freeman opened her own law firm. In her autobiography Freeman noted:

> In those days, the law was an absolutely male-dominated profession—and the fact that I wanted to try cases made it all the worse.... People sometimes ask "Ms. Freeman, have you been discriminated against more because of your race or your sex?" I say, "I don't know. I have scar tissue from both (Freeman, 42–43).

Freeman joined the St. Louis NAACP and soon took on its next big civil rights case, involving two segregated high schools. She and her team fought for three African American students attending the all-black school who wanted to enroll in an aviation course that was offered only at the all-white school. The curriculum was eventually removed at the all-white school. In 1952 Freeman and the NAACP attorney Constance Baker Motley took on the St. Louis Land Clearance and Housing Authority, arguing that the housing authority violated the equal protection clause of the Fourteenth Amendment and citing other federal cases that involved integration. This case ended racial discrimination and segregation in low-income public housing. After her legal victory against the St. Louis Land Clearance and Housing Authority, in 1956 she became the associate general counsel for the housing authority, where she was responsible for housing policy, litigation, and contract resolution.

During this period Freeman positioned herself to lead policy changes on a regional and national level. In 1950 she joined Delta Sigma Theta Sorority, Inc., a national public service organization comprising college-educated African American women, later becoming its president in 1967. In 1958 Freeman joined the Missouri State Advisory Committee of the Civil Rights Commission, formed in response to the 1957 federal Civil Rights Act. She continued to champion causes of women and people of color when she became vice president of the National Council of Negro Women, and in 1964 she was the only woman appointed by President Lyndon Johnson to serve on the U.S. Commission on Civil Rights. As a commissioner, Freeman researched and wrote opinions concerning school segregation. In the same year, she became the general counsel over housing when the St. Louis Land Clearance and Housing Authority became the St. Louis Housing Authority. She was abruptly terminated from the Housing Authority in 1970, allegedly based on her views concerning affirmative action. Subsequently she served as a consultant to a St. Louis radio station until President Jimmy Carter appointed her an inspector general for the Community Services Administration, a federal anti-poverty agency. She resigned from her duties on the U.S. Commission on Civil Rights in 1980, after serving sixteen years and through the administration of four presidents. Soon after President Ronald Reagan was elected, he dismissed the inspector generals appointed by President Carter, including Freeman.

Back in St. Louis, Freeman took up teaching and became a counsel to a black St. Louis law firm. She remained active in local, regional, and national organizations. She was a member of the board of directors for the National Council on the Aging and for her two alma maters, Hampton University and Howard University, from which she received honorary degrees. In 1991 her fifty-two-year marriage ended when her husband died. She shared her life story in her 2003 autobiography, *A Song of Faith and Hope: The Life of Frankie Muse Freeman*. Freeman received numerous awards for her lifetime achievements, including induction into the National Bar Association's Hall of Fame (1990). In 2011 Freeman was honored by the NAACP as its 95th Spingarn Medalist.

FURTHER READING

Freeman, Frankie. *A Song of Faith and Hope: The Life of Frankie Muse Freeman* (2003).

Wesley, Dorothy. *Lift Every Voice and Sing: St. Louis African Americans in the Twentieth Century* (1999).

LANESHA NEGALE DEBARDELABEN

Freeman, Harry Lawrence (9 Oct. 1869–21 Mar. 1954), composer and conductor, was born in Cleveland, Ohio, the son of Agnes Sims (father's name unknown). Freeman studied piano as a child with Edwin Schonert and later with Carlos Sobrino. He engaged in the study of theory, composition, and orchestration with Johann Beck, founder and first conductor of the Cleveland Symphony Orchestra. By age ten Freeman had organized a boys' quartet, for which he arranged most of the music, was accompanying pianist, and sang soprano. By age twelve he was assistant organist and later became organist for his family church. While in his early twenties Freeman moved to Denver, Colorado, where he began composing salon pieces, dances, and marches.

The motivation behind his attraction to composition on a larger scale was his attendance of a performance of Richard Wagner's opera *Tannhäuser* by the Emma Juch grand opera company. For nearly the next six months an inspired Freeman produced a new composition almost every day. An avid student of "history, the great poets, romances, and the tragic dramas" (Hipsher, p. 190), his first large work was an opera, *The Martyr*, composed in 1893, about Platonus, an Egyptian nobleman who is condemned to death for accepting the faith of Jehovah instead of that of his ancestors. He formed the Freeman Grand Opera Company, which presented *The Martyr* at the Deutsches Theater in Denver and, later, in Chicago, Cleveland, and Wilberforce, Ohio. The performance at Wilberforce is explained by his membership on the Wilberforce University faculty (1902–1904). Under the leadership of Beck the Cleveland Symphony performed scenes from *Zuluki* (1898), Freeman's second opera (originally known as *Nada*), in 1900.

Around Freeman's composing of "serious" larger works he spent several years composing (either individually or collectively) and conducting works in a lighter vein. His most notable activities in this area took place in the first decade of the twentieth century, during which he served for a brief period as music director of Chicago's Pekin Theater and was also music director of the road show John Larkins Musical Comedy. Freeman was music director for the noted entertainer Ernest Hogan's *Rufus Rastus* company (1906), composed the music for *Captain Rufus* (1907), and with James "Tim" Brymn composed the music for *Panama* (1908).

Freeman married the singer and actress Carlotta Thomas from Charleston, South Carolina (year unknown). They had one child, Valdo Lee. Both mother and son starred in several of Freeman's operas, and Valdo produced and directed many of them.

As the second decade of the twentieth century approached, Freeman and his family moved to New York City. There Freeman worked with the Bob Cole/Johnson Brothers' (John Rosamond Johnson and James Weldon Johnson) *Red Moon* company. When *Red Moon* closed in 1910 Freeman moved on to other activities. He established the Freeman School of Music and the Freeman School of Grand Opera, served as choral conductor with the Negro Choral Society, organized the Negro Grand Opera Company, engaged in music criticism, and taught at the Salem School of Music.

Freeman received a William E. Harmon Foundation first-place award in 1930, resulting in a gold medal and $400 as "the composer of the first Negro grand opera." (The musicologist Eileen Southern, however, points out that this distinction belongs to John Thomas Douglass for *Virginia's Ball* in the 1860s.) Also in 1930 excerpts from nine of Freeman's fourteen operas were presented in concert at Steinway Hall in New York City.

Freeman himself was the librettist for most of his operas. Synopses of several of these appeared in the historian Benjamin Brawley's essay "A Composer of Fourteen Operas," published in *Southern Workman* (July 1933). Brawley wrote, "Anyone who has opportunity to study his work at close range is amazed at his achievement and overwhelmed by the sheer power exhibited. His creative faculty is just now at its height. What he may yet produce in the years to come is beyond all estimate." Although the number of operas remained at fourteen, Freeman did many revisions of earlier ones.

Much of his recognition stemmed from the 1928 production of his opera *Voodoo* (1923), produced by Freeman himself at the Palm Garden in New York City, though he did not attain financial success from it or any of his other compositions. Performed by an "all-Negro cast of thirty" and an all-black orchestra, the presentation was reviewed by the *New York Times* (11 Sept. 1928). The reviewer said of the musical character of the work: "The composer utilizes themes from spirituals, Southern melodies and jazz rhythms which, combined with traditional Italian operatic forms, produces a curiously naive mélange of varied styles." An abridged version of *Voodoo* was presented on WCBS radio. In her 1936 publication *Negro Musicians and Their Music*, the music historian Maud Cuney-Hare reported that

Paramount Film Company "purchased 'Voodoo,' to be presented on the screen in a condensed version." There is no evidence that filming took place or that a film was released.

Other titles of Freeman's known operas are *An African Kraal* (1903), *The Octoroon* (1904), *Valdo* (1905), *The Tryst* (1909), *The Plantation* (1915), *Athalia* (1916), and *Vendetta* (1924). Brawley indicated that at the time of his *Southern Workman* article, Freeman was working on his fourteenth opera, *Uzziah*. Other works by Freeman include ballet music, a symphonic poem for chorus and orchestra, two cantatas, songs, and instrumental pieces. Freeman was guest conductor and music director of the pageant *O Sing a New Song* at the Chicago World's Fair in 1934. *The Martyr* was presented in concert at Carnegie Hall in 1947. Freeman died in his home in New York City.

Not only is Freeman important to the history of African American music but his work also demands recognition in the annals of American music. As the first African American to attain any type of recognition and respectability as a composer of operatic compositions, he was an American pioneer. That he had but little formal instruction makes his accomplishments all the more remarkable. To stage his productions it was necessary to establish his own opera companies and schools; to finance the productions it was necessary for him to teach and engage in less demanding theatrical activities. But Freeman never lost faith in himself and his abilities, nor did he lose faith in the eventual eradication of a segregated system.

FURTHER READING

Hipsher, Edward Ellsworth. *American Opera and Its Composers* (1927).

Sampson, Henry. *Blacks in Blackface: A Source Book on Early Black Musical Shows* (1980).

Southern, Eileen. *The Music of Black Americans: A History* (1983).

Obituary: *New York Times*, 26 Mar. 1954.

This entry is taken from the *American National Biography* and is published here with the permission of the American Council of Learned Societies.

ANTOINETTE HANDY

Freeman, Jordan (?–6 Sept. 1781), a soldier in the American Revolution, was the personal servant of Lieutenant Colonel William Ledyard. Freeman served primarily as an orderly while Ledyard was in command of Fort Griswold at New London, Connecticut. A British force under the command of Brigadier General Benedict Arnold on 6 September 1781 besieged the fort. Freeman demonstrated an exceptional degree of courage during the fighting of what came to be known as the Battle of Groton Heights.

The operations undertaken by Arnold were part of a larger British strategy to impede George Washington's efforts to encircle Cornwallis at Yorktown by using diversionary forces to draw Americans out. Arnold's immediate objective was to seize the port of New London. The British force succeeded in burning New London, and a defensive force from the town drew back to Fort Griswold on the Groton side of the Thames River. The small American force numbered approximately one hundred and fifty men and was eventually overrun by the superior British numbers. Ledyard held the fort only under the understanding that the local Groton militia would reinforce him, yet the militia failed to appear. A general court-martial convened after the battle with some militia officers acquitted and others convicted over their failure to reinforce Fort Griswold

The British force suffered heavy casualties in their attack on the entrenched position of the Americans. When the British at last began to make their way through openings in the walls of the fort, the Americans switched from using firearms to using pikes or spears of approximately fifteen feet in length. It was with one of these spears that Freeman killed the leader of the British assaulting force, Major Montgomery, who had succeeded to the command after Colonel Eyre was wounded. The reports of Montgomery's death at the hands of Freeman are based on reports from the battle, one the account from a witness, George Middleton. In some versions Montgomery was killed in hand-to-hand combat. Other sources, however, attribute Montgomery's death to Freeman and Captain Adam Shapley, and still others attribute it to Freeman and Lieutenant Henry Williams. Freeman remains the common thread in versions of Montgomery's death, however, whether by his efforts alone or in combination with some other American.

The British suffered heavy losses in taking the fort, which may explain their failure to show clemency when the Americans finally laid down their arms. The assault cost Arnold 163 men, including many officers. Ledyard surrendered to Major Stephen Bromfield, who asked who commanded the fort. Ledyard replied, "I did sir, but you do now," while handing over his sword. After the exchange Bromfield killed Ledyard with the same sword. Accounts of Ledyard's death, like those of Montgomery's, differ, with some tracing the murder to a Captain George Beckwith and others tracing it to Lieutenant Colonel Buskirk of the New Jersey Volunteers, an American Loyalist officer. In later accounts another African American, a slave, Lambert Latham, was credited with bayoneting the officer who killed Ledyard. Latham had come to the fort, following his master into danger though he was instructed to stay with the stock. The killing of Ledyard initiated a more general massacre of the Americans who had surrendered in the fort. Freeman himself was killed either in combat or in the massacre of the Americans that occurred after the surrender of the fort. Freeman was buried in a Ledyard family cemetery plot.

In 1830 the state of Connecticut erected a monument to the patriots at the site of the Battle of Groton Heights. The names of those Americans who died at the battle are listed, starting with Ledyard's name at the top; Jordan Freeman and Lambert Latham are listed at the bottom of the tablet on the monument under the description "colored men." Latham's first name was listed as Sambo, which derived from the shortening of Lambert to Lambo and then to Sambo. The courage demonstrated by Freeman and Latham at the battle of Groton Heights became an oft-cited example of multiracial support for the American cause, but it also served as an example for future advocates of African American participation in the armed forces of the United States.

FURTHER READING

Harris, William W. *The Battle of Groton Heights: A Collection of Narrative, Official Reports, Records, etc. of the Storming of Fort Griswold* (1882).

Johnson, Edward A. *A School History of the Negro Race in America from 1619 to 1890* (1911).

Kaplan, Sidney, and Emma Nogrady Kaplan. *The Black Presence in the Era of the American Revolution* (1989).

National Society Daughters of the American Revolution. *Minority Military Service Connecticut, 1775–1783* (1988).

Nell, William C. *Services of Colored Americans in the Wars of 1776 and 1812* (1851).

Quarles, Benjamin. *The Negro in the Era of the American Revolution* (1961).

Rathbun, Jonathan. *The Narrative of Jonathan Rathbun* (1840).

White, David. *Connecticut's Black Soldiers, 1775–1783* (1973).

M. KELLY BEAUCHAMP

Freeman, Martin Henry (11 Sept. 1826–13 Mar. 1889), educator and emigrationist, was born in bucolic Rutland, Vermont. Freeman's life can be divided into two periods: his thirty-seven-year residence in America and his twenty-five-year stay in Liberia, Africa. In Rutland, he attended the predominantly white East Parish Congregational Church, whose pastor recognized Freeman's precocity and volunteered to prepare him for college. Freeman was accepted into Middlebury College and graduated class salutatorian in 1849. He taught briefly in Boston before accepting an invitation to join the faculty of the newly established Allegheny Institute and Mission Church (later Avery College) in Pittsburgh, Pennsylvania, in 1850. Freeman's appointment at the first state-chartered degree-granting institution for blacks distinguished him as the first college-educated black professor in America. In recognition of his advanced study in mathematics and natural philosophy, Middlebury College voted to award him an M.A. degree in 1852. In 1856, when Avery College's first white president resigned, Freeman was elected president.

The decade of the 1850s proved chilling to free blacks, most notably because of the Fugitive Slave Act of 1850, which put all persons of color, even in the free North, at risk of enslavement. Such legislation prompted serious-minded free blacks to act decisively in defense of their interests. Freeman was counted among the leading thinkers within Pittsburgh's African American community addressing these issues and formulating policy and thought around black emigration ideology. Of all the people in Freeman's circle of friends, he was influenced most by the writings and force of personality of MARTIN R. DELANY. It was during this time that Freeman came to fully grasp the ubiquity and depth of American racism, since his early years in Rutland had ill-prepared him to handle the reality of physical assaults and other racial insults. His occupational status was no buffer from such harsh treatments.

Additional accomplishments of Freeman during this time period included his membership on the National Board of Commissioners and his service as Special Foreign Secretary of the National Emigration Convention of 1854. He was a forceful contributor to *Frederick Douglass's Paper* and *The Anglo-American Magazine*, a short-lived publication inspired by the emigration movement.

On 11 September 1857, Freeman married Louisa Eleanor Peck, a graduate of Oberlin College. This was the same month the Supreme Court issued its decision in *Dred Scott*, a ruling that instantly made life in America much more perilous for free blacks. With a wife and the prospect of children, Freeman was convinced America would never accept free blacks as coequal citizens and so looked to build a new life in Africa.

Consequently, Freeman resigned the presidency of Avery College in 1863 to accept an appointment as Professor of Mathematics and Natural Philosophy at Liberia College. The faculty of Liberia College, notably ALEXANDER CRUMMELL and EDWARD BLYDEN, consisted of men much like his comrades in Pittsburgh. Within Liberia College, Freeman was among men who placed pride of race at the center of their pedagogy, philosophy, and action. Blyden, Crummell, and Freeman shared something else. They were each dark skinned men in an Americo-Liberian society that placed a premium on light skin. Contending with the existential quandary of Liberian life placed upon him, Freeman came to terms with his predicament and lamented, "I am not a Liberian, I am simply a Negro at-large on this planet, stopping just now in the Mulatto Republic of Liberia solely because life is more tolerable here than in the Anglo-Saxon Republic across the Atlantic." The skirmishes on skin color not only framed the politics of Liberia but soon brought dissension within Liberia College as well.

Freeman was a reticent man who did not seek prominence at Liberia College. Yet, when called on, he never shrank from what he regarded as his duty to Liberia College. After the death of the college's first president, responsibilities fell increasingly on Freeman, which he found extremely onerous. Experiencing failing health Freeman visited the United States in 1887 seeking medical assistance. While he was in America the governing board of Liberia College bestowed upon Freeman an honorary Doctor of Laws degree. Shortly after his return to Liberia, he was elected the third president of Liberia College. Freeman relished being a professor of mathematics and science on two continents but found the visibility of being a college president on the same less attractive. Freeman died on 13 March 1889 and was buried in Monrovia, Liberia.

FURTHER READING

Irvine, Russell W. "Martin H. Freeman of Rutland, America's First Black College Professor and Pioneering Black Social Activist," *Rutland Historical Society Quarterly* 26, no. 3 (1996): 71–99.

Irvine, Russell W. *Nation Building: The Origins and Development of Liberia College, 1849–1868* (2010).

RUSSELL W. IRVINE

Freeman, Morgan (1 June 1937–), actor, producer, director, nightclub owner, and restaurateur, was born in Memphis, Tennessee, to Mayme Edna Revere Freeman and Morgan Porterfield Freeman. When he was two years old, Morgan's parents, like many others at the time, went north to look for work and to escape the Jim Crow conditions of the Deep South. Morgan and his sister, Iris, went to Mississippi to live with their paternal grandmother until her death four years later. Morgan and his sister then rejoined his parents in Chicago. A few months later, Morgan's mother and father separated and for a few years Morgan and his sister moved back and forth between Mississippi and Chicago.

After graduating in 1955 from Greenwood High School in Mississippi, Morgan joined the air force, where he served as a radar mechanic between 1955 and 1959. After he was discharged, Morgan went to Los Angeles where he worked at Los Angeles City College. While there, he also took acting, diction, and voice classes. For a few years after that he traveled back and forth between the East and West Coasts looking for his big break. In 1967 while working at a local travel agency, Freeman met and then married Jeanette Bradshaw. Freeman adopted Bradshaw's daughter, Deena, and in 1971 Freeman's own daughter Morgana was born. But Freeman and Bradshaw's marriage ended in 1979. Freeman also had two sons from previous relationships: Alfonso, born in 1959, and Saifoulaye, born in 1960. In 1967, Freeman landed a role in an Off-Broadway production of George Tabori's *The Niggerlovers* at the Orpheum Theatre in New York. After that role, his acting career took off and until 1970 he acted in theatre productions in Boston, Philadelphia, and New York. In 1970 he got his first television role as Easy Reader in the popular children's show *The Electric Company*. Freeman continued to appear in theater productions during his five-year stint on the *Electric Company*. In 1972 he played Nate in Richard Wesley's play *Gettin' It Together*, and in 1978 he starred in another Wesley production, *The Mighty Gents*, in which he played the wino Zeke. That role earned him a Tony nomination, a Drama Desk Award for Outstanding Actor, and a Clarence Derwent Award for Best Newcomer. The following year, Freeman landed a supporting role in Shakespeare's *Julius Caesar* for the New York Shakespeare Festival. His performance was so captivating he was given the starring role in their next Shakespeare production, *Coriolanus*, for which Freeman was nominated for an Obie Award.

Morgan Freeman poses at the Park Hyatt Hotel in Los Angeles, 7 March 2003. (AP Images.)

In 1980 Freeman landed his first film role in *Brubaker*, directed by Robert Redford, and from 1982 to 1984 he played Roy Bingham on the daytime soap opera *Another World*. But it wasn't until 1984 that Freeman returned to film when the actor Paul Newman hired him to appear in *Harry and Son*. That same year, on 16 June, Freeman married Myrna Colley-Lee, a costume designer and art director. Shortly after, Freeman finally won an Obie Award for his starring role in the 1988 Broadway production of *The Gospel at Colonus*. Freeman's acting career, and his star status, were solidified when he took the role of Fast Black in the 1987 thriller *Street Smart*. His riveting performance earned him his first Oscar and Golden Globe nominations for Best Supporting Actor. He won the New York Film Critics Circle award, the Los Angeles Film Critics award, and the National Society of Film Critics award. One year later, he landed his first starring role in a film as the high school principal Joe Clark in *Lean on Me*, for which he won an NAACP Image Award.

By this time Freeman was a well-known actor, and avoided taking demeaning or stereotyped roles and instead returned to the theater until something more substantial came along. In 1986 Freeman took the part of the chauffeur Hoke Colburn in the off-Broadway hit *Driving Miss Daisy*. Though some critics felt the role reinforced the black "servant" stereotype, Freeman's stunning performance demonstrated his mesmerizing ability to create a complex multi-dimensional character who, though in a subservient role, rejects the confines of the chauffeur stereotype. In 1989 Freeman reprised his role in the film version of *Driving Miss Daisy*, winning a Golden Globe award for Best Actor, an Image Award for Best Actor, and an Oscar nomination for Best Actor.

With his career on solid ground, Freeman began to choose a broader range of roles. In 1992 he played a cowboy in Clint Eastwood's Oscar-winning film *Unforgiven*. In 1993 he directed his first film, *Bohpa!*, and in 1994 Freeman's portrayal of Red in *The Shawshank Redemption* earned him another Oscar nomination. In 1996 Freeman and Lori McCreary, his co-producer on *Bopha!*, created Revelations Entertainment, a production company. In 1997 Freeman's role as a freed slave in *Amistad*, the story of a group of Africans who challenged American slavery and won, earned him an Image Award for Outstanding Supporting Actor. In 2005 the actor finally won an Oscar for Best Supporting Actor in Clint Eastwood's *Million Dollar Baby*. He also won the Screen Actors Guild Award for Best Supporting Actor for the same film. Freeman was again nominated for a Best Actor in a Leading Role Oscar in 2010, for his performance as South African president, Nelson Mandela, in *Invictus* (2009).

In 1997 Freeman won the ALFS award for Actor of the Year from the London Critics Circle Film Awards, and in 2000 he earned the Hollywood Film Award for Outstanding Achievement in Acting. In 2003 Freeman was awarded the Special Prize for Outstanding Contribution to World Cinema by the Karlovy Vary International Film Festival. That same year he earned a Career Achievement Award by the National Board of Review, USA. In 2001 Freeman and the attorney Bill Luckett opened an upscale restaurant, Madidi, in Clarksdale, Mississippi. That same year, Freeman, Luckett, and Howard Stovall, a Memphis entertainment executive, opened the Ground Zero Blues Club, featuring local Mississippi Delta blues, reflecting two of Freeman's lifelong loves: food and the blues. In 2005 Freeman's Revelations Entertainment combined forces with Intel Corp. and created Clickstar, a service to deliver movies digitally over the internet.

FURTHER READING

Angelis, Gina De. *Morgan Freeman* (2000).

Tracy, Kathleen. *Morgan Freeman: A Biography* (2006)

DEBBIE CLARE OLSON

Freeman, Robert Tanner (1846?–10 June 1873), dentist, was born in Washington, D.C., the son of Waller Freeman. His mother's name is not known. His father, a carpenter in Raleigh, North Carolina, purchased his freedom from slavery in 1830. After purchasing his wife's freedom, he moved with her to Washington, D.C., where Robert T. Freeman was born, raised, and educated.

Freeman's early interest in medicine after high school led him to apply for a position as a dental assistant in the office of Dr. Henry Bliss Noble on Pennsylvania Avenue. Impressed by Freeman's determination and earnestness, Noble hired him and tutored him privately in the "art and science of the practice of dentistry." In light of strained race relations and rigid segregation in the nation's capital following the Civil War, it was unusual to have a "person of color" working so close to white patients in a dental office. Noble nevertheless encouraged Freeman to pursue a dental career through formal training.

When Harvard University established its School of Dental Medicine in 1867—the country's first nonproprietary dental school attached to a university—Freeman applied. He entered with the initial class of sixteen matriculants in 1868. In early March 1869 he was one of only six students who passed the first examination. On 10 March 1869 Freeman received the DDM degree. Speaking later of the school's first group of graduates, Dean Henry M. S. Miner noted, "Robert Tanner Freeman, a colored man who has been rejected by two other dental schools on account of his race, was another successful candidate. The dental faculty maintained that right and justice should be placed above expediency and insisted that intolerance must not be permitted. Dr. Freeman was the first of his race to receive in America a dental school education and dental degree."

After graduating from Harvard, Dr. Freeman moved back to Washington, D.C., and started his own dental practice on Pennsylvania Avenue. He developed a thriving practice, which lasted until his early death some fourteen years later.

The first dental society composed of African Americans, the Washington Society of Colored Dentists, was founded in 1900. In 1909 this society changed its name to honor America's first African American in dentistry. The Robert Tanner Freeman Dental Society attained a membership of more than six hundred dentists in the metropolitan Washington, D.C., area and became an active chapter of the National Dental Association established by African Americans in dentistry in 1913—forty years after the death of Robert Tanner Freeman.

FURTHER READING

Dummett, Clifton O. "Courage and Grace in Dentistry: The Noble, Freeman Connection," *Journal of the Massachusetts Dental Society* 44.3 (Fall 1995): 23–26, 31.

Dummett, Clifton O. *The Growth and Development of the Negro in Dentistry in the United States* (1952)

ROBERT C. HAYDEN

Freeman, Von (3 Oct. 1922–), jazz tenor saxophonist, innovator, mentor, and one of the founders of the Chicago jazz lexicon, was born Earl Lavon Freeman in Chicago, the second of three sons of George Thomas Freeman Sr. from Savannah, Georgia, and Earle Kree Granberry from Tennessee. Freeman Sr. became one of the first African Americans to serve as a Chicago police officer, and ultimately he was killed in the line of duty. Von's mother spent many of her younger years traveling the black church circuit as a professional gospel singer, but she eventually settled into a life of raising her sons, which included the eldest, Eldridge "Bruz" Freeman, and the youngest, George Freeman Jr. All three boys developed into world-renowned jazz musicians. The family first laid roots in the rougher and more street-savvy West Side of Chicago, a section that cradled many of the city's blues musicians. Freeman Sr. soon moved his family to the black middle-class South Side of Chicago before Von was a year old.

At an early age Von showed an astute aptitude for understanding basic concepts in music. He was captivated by the sounds coming out of his father's Victrola. Freeman recounted on many occasions that he would immerse himself in the sounds of ragtime and Dixieland music, which he said are the foundations on which all genres of modern-day jazz are built. His enthusiasm for music prompted his parents to purchase a piano when he was only one. By age five Freeman had taken the tube off of the Victrola, punched holes in it, and made a crude version of what would be his first saxophone. At age seven Freeman's father felt that his son was ready to receive a real C-melody tenor saxophone. A good friend of Freeman's father also saw promise in the young boy's eagerness and offered guidance. This friend was the jazz great LOUIS ARMSTRONG.

In the mid-1930s Freeman attended DuSable High School in Chicago. The South Side high school would prove over time to be an incubator for some of the greatest jazz musicians to come out of the Windy City. It was there that Freeman learned to hone his craft on the tenor saxophone, alongside such notable musicians as the saxophonists GENE AMMONS and Johnny Griffin and the trombonist Bennie Green. Although Freeman's high school music instructor insisted that his students learn to play various instruments, Von continued to follow the beckoning of the tenor saxophone. He would pattern his sound around his heroes, the lush tones of LESTER YOUNG and the powerful aggressive blowing of COLEMAN HAWKINS.

"Coleman Hawkins was a friend of my father. Daddy wanted me to meet this man who played the tenor sax. I finally met him and played at the Bee-Hive with him once, and it was a wonderful experience," Freeman said, explaining how he became acquainted with the two jazz icons. "I knew Lester Young personally. When I was a kid I used to watch him play baseball with COUNT BASIE in Washington Park. Every week they had a big band at the Regal Theater" (quoted by John Litweller in *The Great Divide*, Premonition Records).

In the late-1930s, big-band jazz was the popular music sweeping the nation. Freeman got his first taste as an actual professional working jazz musician in the Horace Henderson Band in 1939. Although the young Freeman was initially impressed with himself in being chosen to play in the band, the experience quickly taught him that he had much to learn. In 1941 Freeman joined the U.S. Navy and was stationed in Hawaii. There several great musicians, such as the trumpeter CLARK TERRY, took a liking to the young tenor saxophonist and gave him tips on how to develop and hone in his craft. Although never a formal educator himself, Freeman applied those same principles in instructing future young musicians.

Freeman met and married Ruby Gorens shortly after his four-year stint in the navy. The couple had four children. The eldest child, Earl Lavon Freeman Jr., followed in his father's footsteps in becoming a famous jazz musician, under the name Chico Freeman. It was also during the 1940s and 1950s that Von Freeman began to perform with his two brothers, guitarist George and drummer Eldridge. The trio of brothers played as a backing band for such jazz greats as CHARLIE PARKER, DIZZY GILLESPIE, and EARL "FATHA" HINES.

Although the now highly developed and skillful musician was offered work in New York, Freeman opted to stay in Chicago to raise his family. While there he continued to develop a distinctive sound on the tenor saxophone and helped give crucial exposure to such younger jazz stars such as the pianists AHMAD JAMAL and ANDREW HILL. In 1948 Freeman became a founding member of the Arkestra, a groundbreaking group of musicians led by the pianist SUN RA that ushered in the avant-garde movement in jazz. Ironically Freeman did not record under his own name until 1972, although he had appeared on countless other artists' albums.

Freeman may have borrowed elements of technique introduced by the likes of Lester Young, Colman Hawkins, and eventually Charlie Parker, but he mixed those elements into a sound distinctly his own. Some critics refer to Freeman's sound as brash and a bit harsh, but many of his compositions are characterized by bluesy, lush, and lyrical tones. Chico Freeman noted that his father's style of playing comes close to the human voice.

What is so striking about Freeman's contributions to jazz is that he never aligned himself with any one school of jazz. Many musicians consider him a trailblazer in innovations ranging from swing to bebop to avant-garde. "Each genre is on the tree of jazz," Freeman once explained. "You can play anything if you find that constant beat and motion that goes through all music. I mean you only have so many chords. They are the same chords no matter if you play country, church music, or even rock and roll" (personal interview). In 2002 the city of Chicago honored Freeman with an eightieth birthday celebration that culminated with a street being renamed after the jazz legend.

FURTHER READING

Grant, Jeremy. *Financial Times*, 20 Aug. 2004.

Yanow, Scott. *All Music Guide to Jazz*, ed. Michael Erlewine, 3rd ed. (1998).

DEMETRIUS PATTERSON

French, George Tony, Jr. (17 Nov. 1961–), college president and ordained Christian Methodist Episcopal minister, was born in Louisville, Kentucky, one of five children and the only son of Dorothy Jewell Duffy and George Tony French, Sr. Residing in Louisville's West End, his mother worked as a file clerk and his father was an employee for the Department of Defense Mapping Agency. When George was seven his father sat him down and foretold that someday his only son would become President of the United States. French, Sr., explained, as young George listened closely, that 95 percent of the U.S. Presidents had been attorneys, then members of Congress before attaining the White House. French, Jr., was thus set on his path. With his eye on politics, eleven-year-old French, Jr., sat intently with a tape recorder and microphone directed at his family's television set as the 1973 Senate hearings on the Watergate Scandal and subsequent Nixon resignation were broadcast.

In 1980 French, Jr., was enrolled at the University of Louisville. During his tenure there, his knowledge of the classics flourished. Rapidly emerging as a socialite, French, Jr., was a force on campus, serving as student representative to the Board of Trustees and Student Government Association representative in addition to other activities. Following in the steps of his role model, civil rights activist Dr. MARTIN LUTHER KING, JR., in 1982, French, Jr., joined the university's Alpha Pi Chapter of Alpha Phi Alpha Fraternity Inc., the nation's first intercollegiate African American fraternity. In 1986 French, Jr., graduated from the University of Louisville with a bachelor of arts in political science and went to work as a campaign manager, holding sales positions in between elections. Three years later he married Joyce Parker of Louisville, Kentucky; they had three children: Lashelle, George III, and Jasmine.

Abiding by his father's calculations and his own long held aspirations, French, Jr., moved to Virginia and entered law school at the University of Richmond in 1988. An aunt who lived in Richmond consistently invited him to attend her Christian Methodist Episcopal (CME) church, but he declined on the basis of his Baptist affiliation. After finally being persuaded to visit the Broomfield CME Church, French, Jr., found himself attending services regularly; the pastor encouraged him to join but he remained resistant due to his Baptist upbringing. Ultimately he would acquiesce to being taken under "watch-care" by the church. French, Jr., began to assist the pastor, accompanying him to CME functions and engaging in concentrated study of the CME doctrine. One evening the pastor revealed to him that there was no such thing as watch-care and that he saw a natural leader in the poised and charismatic 27-year-old and had been grooming him for CME ministry all along. French, Jr., was ordained as a CME minister in 1991.

In July 1991 French, Jr., was sent to pastor the flagging Ebenezer CME Church in South Boston, Virginia, and within three years had tripled the congregation and its coffers. In 1994, Bishop Joseph C. Coles, presiding elder of Ebenezer, died and CME notables from across the nation gathered in Richmond to pay tribute. It was at Bishop Cole's funeral that French, Jr., was introduced to ALBERT J. H. SLOAN II, thirteenth President of Miles College, a historically black college (HBCU) established in 1905. President Sloan was impressed by the gentlemanly scholar and after discussing professional pursuits and various topics, invited French, Jr., to work at Miles. Two years later, on 3 July 1996, French, Jr., relocated to Birmingham, Alabama, to assume his appointment as Director of Sponsored Programs and Title III.

In 1999, as Director of Institutional Research and Development, French, Jr., led Miles's most successful capital campaign, raising over $12 million. During the same year he completed his Juris Doctorate at Miles Law School. President Sloan was pleased with French, Jr.'s seemingly natural ability and commitment to Miles, and earnestly began to mentor his chosen successor. In October 2005 President Sloan became seriously ill and French, Jr., was appointed interim president. President Sloan passed away in November 2005.

Inaugurated on 13 October 2006, 44-year-old French, Jr., became the fourteenth president of Miles College, and the nation's youngest HBCU president. Within months, President French realized his first goal of doubling the size of the college's 35-acre campus with the purchase of the neighboring 41-acre HealthSouth Metro West Hospital complex, dubbed the North Campus. In January 2007, President French set another record-breaking capital campaign goal at Miles by raising $30 million. President French became board member to the United Negro College Fund and Birmingham Civil Rights Institute. He joined the National Bar Association, among other academic and professional organizations.

In 2009, President French earned a Doctor of Philosophy in Urban Higher Education from Jackson State University in Jackson, Mississippi, an HBCU established in 1877.

FURTHER READING

"George French Named as Miles College President," *Jet*, 10 July 2006.

Miles College Centennial History Committee. *Miles College: The First Hundred Years*. (July 2005).

Mitchell, Sybil C. "Historical Black Colleges and Universities Featuring Miles College: A 20th Century Southern Gem," *Tri-State Defender*, Dec. 2005.

Smith, Barry Wise. "Minutes Away, Miles Ahead: President George T. French Is Poised to Lead Historic Miles College into the Future," *Portico*, Feb. 2007.

SAFIYA DALILAH HOSKINS

French, Robert "Bob" (27 Dec. 1937–), drummer, bandleader, was born in New Orleans, Louisiana, the second son of musician and bandleader Albert "Papa" French and Claudia Samuel French. He was raised in New Orleans and in Jefferson Parish, mostly in houses built by his carpenter father. "My daddy built a grocery with a house and after we lived there, he rented it out to a Cajun family. They were the only white family in the neighborhood so ... there was integration before there was integration. The only thing that segregated us children was school" (Bob French personal interview with author).

Eventually Albert French Sr. shed carpentry for full-time musician duties. "There were two things always around my house," Bob said. "Music and musicians." The camaraderie was strong and Bob referred to all of the elder musicians as "uncle this or uncle that." At fifteen he got his driving license and started driving The Original Tuxedo Jazz Band (established 1910) to gigs in bandleader OSCAR "PAPA" CELESTIN's school bus. Dissuaded from playing drums by his father, who argued that drummers were "always the first to arrive and the last to leave a gig," Bob persisted, gave up the trumpet, and, accompanied by LOUIS BARBARIN, made his foray into the rhythm section with a $110 set of Premiere's bought at a pawnshop.

French attended St. Augustine High School ("for $7.00 a month") where he met Charles Neville, and in 1951 started playing R & B in his first band, The Turquoise (with James Booker, Art Neville, Charles Neville, J. C. Goodes, Donald Russo, and Cyrus Cagnolatti). Their first professional gig was on Mardi Gras, performing on a flatbed truck at a Creole party. "They had their parties and we had ours," French said. "Once I went to a Creole party and felt like I was on the outside lookin' in. I never went again." St. Augustine was 85 percent Creole, with very few Uptowners in attendance, but Bob French went "because Catholic school was a mandate." He claimed that he excelled at nothing but music. In his senior year, The Turquoise fell apart, so he started playing with James "Sugarboy" Crawford, six days a week, while still a high school student. For a whole year French led the double life of high school student and professional musician, often getting only four hours of sleep a night. They frequently played The Joy Lounge, a segregated club on New Orleans's west bank, to which Bob took the Jackson Street ferry. "The Italians treated you with respect. Sure, we had to go in the back door but there was always a fifth a liquor on the table and a made to order meal."

Meanwhile, Oscar "Papa" Celestin's Original Tuxedo Jazz Band achieved success and status; they even played President Eisenhower's inauguration. Oscar "Papa" Celestin died in 1954 and Bob's father took over as bandleader—retaining the nickname "Papa"—until his death in 1977.

Bob attended Grambling University, returning to New Orleans after two years to play music professionally. He had a new incarnation of The Turquoise, including James Rivers, George Davis, and Alvin "Shine" Robinson. He claimed, "If you heard Alvin sing, then you heard Ray Charles." In 1956 Bob and his girlfriend Gloria Lambert had a daughter, Joycelyn Lambert.

Segregation was "worse in the country than in New Orleans." French remembered a club in Thibodeaux, Louisiana, where a policeman stood at the bottom of the bandstand. He was there in case a girl passed a request along to the band. "He read it first, to make sure it wasn't a phone number, then he'd hand it to us."

By the 1950s Bob was a notable and regular drummer on the New Orleans circuit. He recorded with Dave Bartholomew at the legendary Cosimo Matassa's studio, playing on countless records including those by FATS DOMINO, Earl King, The Spiders, and many for Imperial Records. Fats Domino offered Bob a generous touring gig afterward but French turned it down after being told that, "Fats would give me $450 a week but a thousand dollars worth of trouble."

In 1961 French was drafted and served as an E-5 sergeant in the U.S. Army from 1961–1965, mostly in Augusta, Georgia. He married Dolores Porche in 1962. They had a son, Robert "Bob" Jr. the same year. Their daughter Diedre was born in 1964. The couple divorced in 1970. In 1973 a son, Albert Jr. was born to Bob and Muriel Joyner.

After the Army, French lived in New Orleans, playing R & B almost every night with Frogman Henry at the (integrated) 544 Club on Bourbon Street. He also played traditional jazz with The Storyville Jazz Band (including brother George French, Ellis Marsalis, Freddy Lonzo, and Teddy Riley) at Crazy Shirley's for six years, and drummed for Frank Assunto & The Dukes of Dixieland. Bob and his father opened up their own club, Tradition Hall, in the French Quarter where eight-year-old Harry Connick Jr. used to come every Saturday, "climbing the light poles and playing two or three little tunes." Bob also played a gig for King Hussein in the French Quarter. He closed Tradition Hall soon after the elder French died.

French took over bandleader duties for The Original Tuxedo Jazz Band in 1977. In the late 1980s, French started touring Europe with Danny Barker, Jim Robinson, Chester Zarders, and Percy Humphrey. The drummer recalls The Original Tuxedo Jazz Band 1995 Paris tour (sponsored by New Orleans music lover and billionaire Sir Peter Goldsmith) as among the "most hospitable."

Despite hurricane Katrina's impact on New Orleans—French swore "it ruined everything"—the bandleader continued to play in the city and elsewhere, in addition to his award-winning radio show on New Orleans's WWOZ. According to French, The Original Tuxedo Jazz Band is the oldest continuously operating jazz band in the world. Bob French continues to invite onto his bandstand young and upcoming musicians, carrying on The Original Tuxedo Jazz Band tradition of intergenerational performance. When asked what he will do in the next chapter of his life, French said, "New Orleans musicians don't retire. They just die."

FURTHER READING

Bob French personal interview with author, 6 November 2008.

Aiges, Scott. "Musical Family Trees to Entwine at Show," *New Orleans Times-Picayune*, 25 October 1990, B-1, B-2.

Down Beat (Vol. 73, no. 9, September 2006), 30–35.

Grady, Bill. "Slice of Life: Drummer Shucks the Jive from Dixie—Son Takes Up Torch of Papa's Old Groove," *New Orleans Times-Picayune*, 17 September 2000, B-1, B-2.

Kunian, David. "Fest Focus: Bob French," *OffBeat*, May 2001, 130, 154.

Rawls, Lou. "Back Talk with Lou Rawls," *OffBeat: Louisiana Music & Culture Magazine*, vol. 20, no. 4, April 2007.

DISCOGRAPHY

Live At Tradition Hall, Vol. III (Tuxedo Records 2006; original LP 1978).

Live at Jazz Fest (Tuxedo Records 2004).

Livin' The Legacy (Tuxedo Records 2003).

Marsalis Music Honors Series Presents Bob French (Rounder 2007).

The Legacy Lives On (Royal Tuxedo Records 2001).

Three Generations (2003).

WENDI BERMAN GARY

Frierson, Andrew Bennie (29 Mar. 1929–), opera singer, college and music conservatory professor, composer, activist, and genealogist, the youngest of seven children, was born in Columbia, Tennessee, and reared in Louisville, Kentucky, where his family moved in search of suitable employment and better schools. Andrew's mother, Lue Vergia Esters Frierson, was a homemaker. His father, Robert Clinton Frierson, was a laborer.

At age three Frierson first dramatically showcased his musical talent. One afternoon he accompanied his mother to the home of an old family friend where there was a piano. Frierson saw the instrument, went to it, and instinctively began to play recognizable songs. Frierson's mother and her friends were astounded because he had never even seen a piano. By the age of five Frierson was playing all over the town.

After four years of piano study with William King, and graduation from high school, Frierson went to Fisk University in Nashville, Tennessee, as a music major. There Frierson studied piano with William Duncan Allen. Two years after he became a student at Fisk, Pearl Harbor and World War II took center stage. Frierson served two and one half years in the U.S. Army. During this time he began to sing, and was encouraged by a special service officer to pursue singing as a career. Frierson sang at many base affairs throughout the South Pacific where he was stationed.

After his discharge from the armed forces, Frierson entered Juilliard School of Music, where as a voice major he studied with Belle Julie Soudant and worked alongside classmates VIRGINIA CAPERS, GLORIA DAVY, and LEONTYNE PRICE. In 1949, before graduating, Frierson made a formal debut at Carnegie Recital Hall, to the delight of New York metropolitan music critics. This was the beginning of his professional music career, and was followed by a number of other concerts. After graduation from Julliard in 1950 with a bachelor of science degree in Voice, he worked for a year at Southern University in Baton Rouge, Louisiana, where he taught and directed the university choir. One of Frierson's colleagues in the music department at Southern University was the musicologist Eileen Southern.

After his Southern University tenure, Frierson returned to New York. While fulfilling professional engagements and pursuing a master of arts degree in Voice at New York's Manhattan School of Music with voice teacher Earnest McChesney, Frierson was invited to join the New York City Opera. During eight seasons with the company, he sang the roles of Cal in Marc Blitzstein's *Regina*; Henry Davis in Kurt Weill's *Street Scene*; Yamadori in Giacomo Puccini's *Madama Butterfly*; Mandarin in Giacomo Puccini's *Turandot*; Messenger in Igor Stravinsky's *Oedipus Rex*; Ramfis in Giuseppe Verdi's *Aida*; Monterone in Giuseppe Verdi's *Rigoletto*; Judge Bell in Carlisle Floyd's *Passion of Jonathan Wade*; Caronte in Claudio Montreverdi's *Orfeo*, conducted by Leopold Stokowski; Porgy in George Gershwin's *Porgy and Bess*; and toured as Joe in Oscar Hammerstein and Jerome Kern's Show Boat.

In addition to the New York City Opera, Frierson performed operatic roles with other companies and in other settings: Don Alfonso in Wolfgang Amadeus Mozart's *Cosi fan tutte* at the Bermuda Festival, Marymount College, and with the Los Angeles Opera conducted by Wilfred Pelletier; Dr. Dulcamar in Gaetano Denizetti's *L'elisir d'amore* in New York; King Melchior in Gian Carlo Menotti's *Amahl and the Night Visitors*; Hermann and Schlemil in Jacques Offenbach's *Les contes d'Hoffman* (performed at Lewishon Stadium); baritone soloist in Carl Orff's *Carmina Burana* (performed at New York State Theater); and extensive tours in Gershwin's *Porgy and Bess*. He appeared in many concert tours that included oratorio performances and Ludwig van Beethoven's Ninth Symphony.

After Frierson's tenure at New York City Opera and his graduation from Manhattan School of Music in 1970, he served as director of New York's Henry Street Settlement Music School (1970–72) and professor of voice at Oberlin College Conservatory in Oberlin, Ohio (1973–75). At Oberlin, in addition to teaching voice, he directed the Oberlin black ensemble, a performance group that specialized in works by African American composers. Wendell Logan, a professor at Oberlin, composed *Ice and Fire*, a cycle of five songs set to poems by Mari Evans, for Frierson and his late wife, the soprano Billie Lynn Daniel. The cycle premiered on 3 February 1975 at Oberlin in Warner Concert Hall. Two of the songs from this cycle were published in *Anthology of Art Songs by Black American Composers*.

Frierson developed an involved interest in genealogy and became a member of the African American Historical and Genealogical Society. An exciting and historic result of this interest occurred in 2003, when descendents of the slave master Thomas James Frierson and his African American slaves gathered in a Tennessee community to learn about their shared past.

Frierson was an activist. Not only did he speak out about racism in opera and how black opera singers must become responsible for improving their own plight within the lyric theater but he also founded the Independent Black Opera Singers, Inc. The Independent Black Opera Singers was founded with a threefold purpose: to let the world know that there were black male opera singers; to create opportunities for black male opera singers; and to serve as a clearinghouse for information about black male opera singers. A concert arranged by the group was held on 6 June 1982 at Alice Tully Hall.

Frierson maintained a career as a performing artist during his tenure as administrator at Henry Street Settlement Music School and professor of voice at Oberlin. His career as a singer took him back to New York from Oberlin, where he maintained a voice studio. Frierson's honors include the Concert Artist Guild Award, a Rockefeller Foundation Grant for music, a National Opera Legacy Award, a Harlem Opera Award, and a Symphony Saintpaulia Lifetime Achievement Award.

In a professional career that spanned more than six decades, Andrew Frierson continued to grow as an artist, thinker, and personality. His convictions were born, shaped, and nurtured by living, exploring, and understanding the African American experience from musical, activist, and genealogical perspectives. Frierson articulated his views on racism and other issues in *Dialogues on Opera and the African American Experience*. Andrew Frierson served as an authoritative, powerful, and sobering voice within the communities of performing arts, criticism, and philosophy.

FURTHER READING

Cheatham, Wallace McClain. *Dialogues on Opera and the African American Experience* (1997).
Gray, John. *Blacks in Classical Music* (1988)
Sokel, Martin L. *The New York City Opera* (1981)
Southern, Eileen. *Biographical Dictionary of Afro-American and African Musicians* (1962)
Smith, Eric Ledell. *Blacks in Opera* (1995).
McClure, Sue. "Reunion Brings Common Ground," *Tennessean*, 9 Oct. 2003.

WALLACE MCCLAIN CHEATHAM

Frisby, Herbert (6 Mar. 1886–26 July 1983), Arctic explorer, science teacher, and newspaper correspondent, was born Herbert Milton Frisby in South Baltimore, the oldest of the seven children of Ida Frisby (née Henry) and Joseph S. Frisby, a keeper of grain tallies in the port of Baltimore. Born into poverty, young Herbert Frisby worked his way through school by selling peanuts, working as a butler, and playing jazz piano. He graduated from Baltimore Colored High School in 1908 and earned his B.A. in Liberal Arts from Howard University in 1912. He received an M.A. in Education from Columbia University in 1936. Frisby married Annie Russell in 1919; they had one son, H. Russell Frisby Sr.

As a sixth-grader Frisby was inspired by the accomplishments of the explorer MATTHEW HENSON, the first African American to reach the North Pole in 1909 with Admiral Robert E. Peary. When Henson was denigrated by a white teacher, young Frisby insisted that he would be the second person of color to reach the pole. His passion for Arctic study shaped his life's ambition to challenge the notion that "a Negro isn't expected to be interested in such things," as he explained in 1971 (Maryland History Society oral history).

Frisby began teaching science in the segregated Baltimore elementary schools in 1912. In 1919 he moved to Douglass High School, rising to principal of its evening school in 1928 and head of its science department in 1935, a position that he held until his retirement. He also taught briefly at Coppin State Teachers' College (later Coppin State University).

In 1943 Frisby enlisted in the U.S. Army as a captain and requested assignment to the Alaskan and Northwest service commands, which encompassed Alaska, Arctic Canada, and the Aleutian Islands. On 11 February 1942 President Franklin D. Roosevelt authorized construction of a land road linking the lower forty-eight states with Alaska, after the far north had become a strategic concern. Approximately one-third of the soldiers sent to work on the Alaskan Highway were African American, a circumstance that helped convince the skeptical *Baltimore Afro-American* to provide Frisby with accreditation as a reporter. The only African American correspondent in Alaska during World War II, Frisby was so immediately popular that the *Afro-American* paid him for regular columns in 1943 and 1944, some of which were later collected in *This Is Our War* (1945). He reported on the progress of the highway, on the lives of African American troops in Alaska, and on Eskimo life, always emphasizing the potential for cross-cultural understanding. He was promoted to the rank of major in 1944 and continued reporting from Alaska for the *Afro-American* until 1949.

Frisby returned to teaching in Baltimore in 1945, making annual summer trips to the Arctic. His foray into Alaskan reporting quickened his determination to pursue studies in anthropology to enhance his understanding of Arctic life. Maryland's institutions of higher education remained segregated, however, and he found the courses at the Negro colleges inadequate. In May 1951 he filed suit against the Maryland Commission for Scholarships for Negroes, requesting reimbursement for tuition and living expenses at University of Alaska. The commission provided him a grant of $376 but denied his full request on the grounds that the University of Alaska was not a U.S. institution. (Alaska gained statehood in 1959.) Frisby ultimately took graduate courses at the University of Pennsylvania, New York University, and the University of Chicago, among others. Morgan State University awarded him an honorary doctorate in 1964.

While teaching, Frisby made more than twenty research missions to Alaska, Arctic Canada, Labrador, Greenland, and Siberia. He missed becoming the first African American to visit both poles when a premonition prevented him from joining an ill-fated Antarctic expedition in 1972. On many of his missions he lived with Eskimos, documenting their beliefs, folktales, songs, and traditional dances. He collected a wealth of ethnological artifacts that he stored in his Baltimore home, dubbed The Igloo. All of these he incorporated into lectures and articles, as well as classroom science lessons. In 1955 he was cited by both the Drexel Institute of Technology and the American Chemical Society for his contributions to science education. During the 1957–1958 International Geophysical Year, Frisby was the only American on an international team exploring the Svalbard Islands.

Perhaps Frisby's most significant historical contribution was his determination to ensure that Matthew Henson's accomplishment would be recognized by history. Frisby learned that Henson arrived at the North Pole forty-five minutes before Admiral Peary, who was disabled by frostbitten toes; Peary later confirmed Henson's calculations. Acknowledging Henson as the inspiration for his own scientific passion, Frisby tirelessly lobbied government officials to secure Henson's recognition as codiscoverer of the North Pole. Frisby's efforts resulted in a Defense Department citation for Henson in 1949 and a 1954 White House invitation from President Dwight D. Eisenhower.

On 12 August 1956 Herbert Frisby realized his own lifelong aim of becoming the second African American to the pole when he used a U.S. Air Force special flyover to drop a bronze plaque memorializing Henson's achievement. On 18 November 1961 Frisby witnessed the placement of the Matthew A. Henson Memorial Tablet in the State House in Annapolis, Maryland. Frisby also spearheaded efforts to move Henson's remains to a place of honor next to Admiral Peary at the U.S. National Cemetery at Arlington, Virginia. This was accomplished on 6 April 1988, five years after Frisby's own death in 1983.

FURTHER READING

Herbert M. Frisby's correspondence, clipping files, research mission notes, and audiotapes are housed in the collection of the Banneker-Douglass Museum, Annapolis, Maryland. The Maryland Historical Society in Baltimore holds an oral history taken in 1971.

Frisby, Herbert. *This Is Our War* (1945)

Dreyfuss, Joel. "On Top of the World," *Washington Post*, 10 Apr. 1976.

Fleming, Paul. "Baltimore Student of Arctic Peoples," *Sunday Baltimore Sun Magazine*, 9 Jan. 1966.

Stevens, John D. "Black Correspondents of World War II Cover the Supply Routes," *Journal of Negro History* 57 (Oct. 1972).

"Student Sues in Tuition Case," *Baltimore Sun*, 11 May 1951.

ELIZABETH P. STEWART

Fry, Windsor (1759–1 Feb. 1823), a soldier in the American Revolution, was born in East Greenwich, Kent County, Rhode Island. Little is known of his parents. In 1781 Fry was recorded as twenty-two years old, about five feet ten and a half inches tall, with black hair and "mustee complexion," a description that in his time implied that he was of mixed black and Indian parentage. He worked as a laborer, and in March 1775 he enlisted in the army. The war had not yet begun. He was probably in the Kentish Guard as a private in Captain Thomas Holden's company. The Kentish Guard was formed in 1774 with members like James Varnum, Christopher Green, Nathanael Green, and Samuel Ward Jr. The Kentish Guard was with Captain James Varnum as Rhode Islanders prepared for war. On 3 April 1775 a general muster was held. Fifteen hundred men reported for duty in Kent County, and two thousand reported in Providence. Fry was there and thus would have witnessed Nathanael Green's promotion from private with the regiment from Rhode Island to general of the Continental Line.

The Rhode Island General Assembly decided to raise 1,500 men to be "properly armed and disciplined." This battalion was labeled the Army of Observation. They offered a cash bounty of four dollars for six months' service. For a man with his own gun, bayonet, and other accoutrements, the bounty was forty shillings. The monthly salary was one pound sixteen shillings. Fry went to Massachusetts as a soldier in Captain Thomas Holden's company of Varnum's regiment for the Siege of Boston (each regiment comprised several companies).

On 2 July 1775 General George Washington from Virginia arrived and took charge of the army. At the time Washington was not in favor of African American soldiers. The rules of the Continental Congress and the state of Rhode Island did not allow recruiting or enlisting of Africans, free or slave, even though they had fought at Lexington and Concord in April. The young Fry was not alone in his situation. African American men like William Flora of Virginia, Pompey Blackman of Rhode Island, and Cuff Whitmore, Prince Estabrook, Peter Salem, and Salem Poor of Massachusetts fought from the first shots of the war but were barred by the policy of mid-1775.

On 10 July 1775 the adjutant general of the American army, Horatio Gates, instructed his recruiters not to enlist "Deserters from the Minstrel army, nor any stroller, negro, or vagabond." In Philadelphia at the Continental Congress and across the colonies, policies were against black men who wanted to serve in the army. Edward Rutledge of South Carolina resolved that all blacks be discharged from service in the army. The Continental Congress rejected this proposal on 26 September 1775. General Washington held a meeting of his generals at Cambridge, Massachusetts. The officers voted that black men should be excluded. By 31 October 1775 headquarters was directed to supply clothes to all but blacks, and recruiting officers were forbidden to enlist "Negroes, boys unable to bear arms nor old men unfit to endure the fatigues of Campaign." This would put Fry out of the army on two counts: his youth and his color.

The men began to reenlist in November, and four other African Americans joined the Rhode Island regiments: John Brooks, Abraham Cook, Simeon Cook, and Prince Redwood. The attitude of the white American army was changed by Lord Dunmore's proclamation of 7 November 1775, which encouraged southern slaves and indentured servants belonging to Patriots to join the British and be immediately freed. Partly in reaction to this British policy, the colonies changed their own. Washington changed the army's policy on reenlisting blacks on 30 December 1775.

In January 1776 Washington reorganized the army; the Rhode Islanders were put in the Ninth and Eleventh Continental regiments. Men began to reenlist in December for one year. Fry's captain, Thomas Holden, left the service, and Fry joined in Lieutenant Colonel Archibald Crary's command of Colonel Varnum's Ninth Continental Regiment of Foot. On 17 March 1776 the British abandoned Boston, and Washington's forces came into the city to a joyous welcome. On 31 March Colonel Varnum's Ninth Continental Regiment was ordered to move to New York. They marched from Boston to New London, Connecticut, where they boarded schooners and sloops and sailed into New York City on 22 April. They were sent across the East River to Long Island to watch for signs of a British invasion. Fry fought in the defense of New York in August. He crossed the Delaware River with General Hand in December 1776 and participated in the battles of Second Trenton and Princeton, New Jersey, in 1777. After a short stop at Morristown, New Jersey, Fry went home.

On 11 March 1777 Fry joined Captain John Garzia's company of artillery in Colonel Robert Elliott's Militia Regiment. On 20 July 1777 Fry enlisted as a private to serve in Colonel Christopher Green's First Rhode Island Regiment and Captain Ebenezer Flagg's company. The men were inoculated for smallpox (an endemic disease that was spreading rapidly in wartime) at Peekskill, New York, and took part in local operations with New York regiments while waiting to respond to the vaccination. The regiment marched from Peekskill, New York, to Red Bank, New Jersey. Fry fought at Fort Mercer in the Battle of Red Bank on 22 October 1777. His regiment wintered and retrained at Valley Forge, Pennsylvania, from December 1777 to June 1778. On 1 June 1778 he was detached to Captain Thomas Arnold and fought at the Battle of Monmouth, New Jersey, on 28 June 1778. On 1 July he moved to Captain Jonathan Wallen's company. At this point the First Rhode Island came to be known as the "black regiment"; more than 130 blacks, along with many Indians, served in Green's regiment. The regiment returned to Rhode Island to participate in the Battle of Rhode Island on 29 August 1778.

In November 1778 Fry was in Captain Thomas Coles's company, serving during the capture of the sloop *George* in September 1779. He deserted on 5 February 1780 but returned 1 September 1780. In October the First and Second Rhode Island regiments were ordered to be consolidated. On 6 December 1780 Fry was issued a new uniform in East Greenwich. Fry was in Stephen Olney's company at the attack at Pines Bridge, New York, on 14 May 1781 and at the Siege of Yorktown in October. Olney's company was the first to capture the redoubt. Fry thus marched from New York to Virginia and back. In 1782 he was in Captain Z. Brown's company, in February 1783 he was on the march to Oswego, New York, and on 15 June 1783 he was discharged.

On 31 December 1789 Fry received a land grant of one hundred acres. In 1790 he was working again as a laborer and was living in North Kingstown, Rhode Island, as head of a household of seven free blacks. On 25 September 1818 he was living in East Greenwich, Rhode Island, and was awarded a pension of eight dollars a month and back pay of $88.53. Fry died in East Greenwich on 1 February 1823, sixty-four years old.

FURTHER READING

Information about Windsor Fry can be found in the Military Service and Pension records at the National Archives in Philadelphia, Pennsylvania; in the Valley Forge Muster List 1777–1778, Valley Forge National Historic Park, Valley Forge, Pennsylvania; and in the folder "Minorities in the Revolution" at the Rhode Island State Archives in Providence, Rhode Island.

Kaplan, Sidney, and Emma Nogrady Kaplan. *The Black Presence in the Era of the American Revolution, 1770–1800* (1973).
Lanning, Michael Lee. *Defenders of Liberty* (2000).
Quarles, Benjamin. *The Negro in the American Revolution* (1961).

JOSEPH W. BECTON

Frye, Henry E. (1 Aug. 1931–), lawyer, educator, and first black chief justice of the North Carolina Supreme Court, was born in Ellerbe, North Carolina, the eighth of the twelve children of Walter Frye and Pearl Motley, farmers. In the late 1920s his father sought to ensure financial security for his family by purchasing a forty-six-acre tobacco and cotton farm with the assistance of a loan from a local bank, which made him one of only a handful of blacks who owned land in Ellerbe. Later his father purchased a small sawmill from white owners. Frye attended the segregated Mineral Springs School in Ellerbe and graduated as valedictorian in 1949. In June 1953 he earned a B.S. in biology with highest honors from North Carolina Agricultural and Technical College (later North Carolina Agricultural and Technical State University). He was commissioned a second lieutenant in the U.S. Air Force and served for two years in Japan and Korea.

Upon his return to the United States, in 1955 he married his college classmate Shirley E. Taylor; they had two sons. In 1956 Frye enrolled at the University of North Carolina at Chapel Hill School of Law. In 1959 he received his jurist doctorate degree with honors, becoming one of the earliest African Americans to graduate from the university. Shortly thereafter he was admitted to the North Carolina bar and the federal court. He held certification in commercial arbitration and mediation in the American Arbitration Association.

Frye practiced law in Greensboro, North Carolina, from 1959 to 1962 and handled a variety of cases. Robert F. Kennedy appointed Frye assistant U.S. attorney, Middle District of North Carolina, a position he held from 1963 to 1965. From 1965 to 1967 he was a professor at the North Carolina Central University Law School.

Henry Frye, North Carolina Supreme Court Chief Justice, surrounded by his granddaughters Whitney Frye (left), Jordan Frye (middle), and Endya Frye on 2 August 1998 in Raleigh. (AP Images.)

In 1968 Frye became the first African American elected to the North Carolina House of Representatives in the twentieth century. He served in that body for twelve years and was then elected to a two-year term in the North Carolina Senate. From 1971 to 1983 he was the organizer and president of the Greensboro National Bank and served on its board of directors. He continued to practice law and remembered the early lessons of his parents, who taught him thrift and financial uplift as an avenue to personal success and racial empowerment. In his role as president of the bank, which later became the Mutual Community Savings Bank, he helped provide social mobility to low- and moderate-income blacks who could not borrow from mainstream banks. In 1983 North Carolina governor Jim Hunt appointed Frye to the North Carolina Supreme Court, making him the first black to serve on that court. Frye, a Democrat, successfully ran for the position in 1984 and subsequently won seven more terms, becoming North Carolina's longest serving supreme court justice. In 1999 Frye became the first black chief justice of the North Carolina Supreme Court. He was responsible for the scope and direction not only of the state supreme court but also of the state's lower court system. As chief justice he oversaw and set policy for over three hundred courts and directly managed five thousand employees with a budget of $360 million. He is credited with many policy improvements, such as making court information more accessible to the media, advocating for the use of arbitration to resolve lawsuits, and launching a five-year plan to improve the court's information technology infrastructure.

In 2000 Frye lost his bid for reelection to a conservative Republican, I. Beverly Lake Jr., an associate justice on the court. After leaving the supreme court on 1 January 2001, Frye became a counsel with Brooks, Pierce, McLendon, Humphrey, and Leonard in Greensboro, North Carolina. His practice specialized in appellate advocacy, mediation, and commercial arbitration. In addition he was a visiting professor of political science and justice at North Carolina Agricultural and Technical State University. His numerous awards and honors included the first North Carolina Agricultural and Technical State University Alumni Excellence Award (1971), the Carolina Peacemaker Award (1983), the Richard R. Wright Award of the National Bankers Association (1983), the Charles McIver Award of the University of North Carolina at Greensboro (1986), the Outstanding Alumnus Award of the University of North Carolina at Chapel Hill (1995), the W. E. B. DuBois Award of the Association of Social and Behavioral Sciences (2002), the Laurel Wreath Award of Kappa Alpha Psi Fraternity (2003), the Liberty Bell Award of the North Carolina Bar Association (2004), and the William Hastie Award for Excellence in Legal Scholarship of the Judicial Counsel of the National Bar Association (2004).

Frye was a recognized business leader and community advocate. He served in leadership roles in many nonprofit, academic, professional, and civic organizations. He was a member of the North Carolina Bar Association; the American Bar Association; the National Bar Association; the American Judicature Society, which he served as vice president from 1991 to 1993 and chair of the board of directors from 1995 to 1996; the North Carolina Association of Black Lawyers; and the Fourth Circuit Judicial Conference (permanent member). In 2002–2003 he served on the Planning Committee of the National Conference on Preventing the Conviction of Innocent Persons. Frye's civic involvement was a testament to his belief that public service and civic mindedness go hand in hand. He served on the boards of the Moses Cone Health System; the Community Foundation of Greater Greensboro; the North Carolina Mutual Life Insurance Company; the University of North Carolina Law Alumni Association; Leadership North Carolina; the North Carolina Community Foundation; and Kappa Alpha Psi Fraternity.

FURTHER READING

Center for Urban Affairs, North Carolina State University. "Henry E. Frye," in *Paths toward Freedom*, ed. Frank Emory (1976).

Crow, Jeffrey J., Paul D. Escott, and Flora J. Hatley. *A History of African Americans in North Carolina* (2002).

Scanzoni, David. "Henry E. Frye," in *The North Carolina Century: Tar Heels Who Made a Difference, 1900–2000*, eds. Howard E. Covington Jr. and Marion A. Ellis (2002).

Smith, Jessie Carney. *Black Firsts* (1994).

ANDRE D. VANN

Fudge, Ann Marie (1 Apr. 1951–), business executive and leader, was born Ann Marie Brown in Washington, D.C., the daughter of Malcolm R. Brown, a U.S. Postal Service employee, and Bettye Lewis, a manager at the National Security Agency. Fudge attended a series of Catholic schools before matriculating at Simmons College in Boston in 1969. She recalls the riots after the assassination of MARTIN LUTHER KING JR. in 1968 as a "hurtful but

Ann Marie Fudge, of Young and Rubicam, has risen to the top ranks of corporate America. (Austin/Thompson Collection.)

formative experience … they made me incredibly determined. I wanted to do something that black people hadn't done before" (Dobrzynski). She became involved in student government and civil rights activism at Simmons. During her sophomore year she met Richard Fudge, a graduate student at Harvard's Graduate School of Education. They married in 1971 and had two children. Fudge graduated from Simmons in 1973 with a degree in management. Two of her Simmons professors, Margaret Hennig and Charles Coverdale, encouraged her to apply to Harvard Business School. Fudge applied and was accepted, but she deferred her acceptance for two years to work at General Electric in the human resources department. She started her MBA in 1975.

After graduating with her MBA in 1977, Fudge chose not to apply for prestigious consulting and banking jobs that would require long hours. Instead, she took a job as a marketing assistant with General Mills and relocated to the Midwest with her family. Her first manager was skeptical as to whether she could successfully meet the demands of her job while also raising two children. Fudge proved that she was more than capable of juggling the demands of her schedule and was a successful member of the marketing teams that introduced many popular products, including Honey Nut Cheerios and Bisquik. During her first six years at General Mills, she was steadily given increasing responsibility, and in 1986 she became a marketing director. Her management style was marked by her bright personality, affable nature, rigorous work ethic, and ability to connect with her employees. As she advanced in her career, Fudge was guided by her own definition of success. "I truly believe that most successful people—and let me clearly state that I don't define success as monetary success or celebrity, but rather as full realization of life's potential—most truly successful people are authentic, they are credible" (Clarke). In 1986 Fudge was recruited by Philip Morris to head General Foods, where she steadily climbed the corporate ladder, becoming president of the flagship division, Maxwell House, in 1994. In addition to managing Maxwell House's $1.4 billion coffee business, she also oversaw the $1.3 billion

Post Cereals unit. In 1997 Fudge became president of a $5 billion division that included the brands Kool-Aid, Altoids, and Jell-O.

When Fudge was at the apex of her career, she took the corporate world by surprise and decided to retire in 1999. She was fifty years old and ready for a change. She and her husband traveled around the world, visiting Morocco, Thailand, and Bali. Fudge also learned how to ride a bicycle, planned her son's wedding, and worked on a book titled *The Artist's Way at Work*, aimed at spurring creativity and innovation in the workplace. She was still active in the nonprofit sector and continued her involvement on corporate boards. In partnership with the Boys and Girls Clubs of America and Harvard Business School, she started a literacy program for children that she oversaw full time.

Fudge had worked with Sir Martin Sorrell at Kraft Foods, who subsequently became chief executive of WPP Group, a British media conglomerate. Sorrell approached Fudge in early 2003 to come out of retirement and head one of WPP's companies, Young and Rubicam, which was in financial trouble. Young and Rubicam was a media giant with offices in 80 countries that managed marketing for high-profile companies. Fudge accepted and returned to work full time as chief executive and chairman of Young and Rubicam in May 2003. Her return to a powerful position in the corporate world received significant media attention. Most women found it difficult to secure jobs after taking time off, and if they did find jobs, they lost significant earning power and influence in their re-entry positions.

Fudge held several board appointments, including at General Electric, Honeywell International, and Marriott International. She was a governor for the Boys and Girls Clubs of America; a director for Catalyst, an organization that aims to improve opportunities and work conditions for women; a trustee of the Brookings Institution; and a member of the Committee of 200, the Council on Foreign Relations, the Advertising Council, and the Advertising Educational Foundation. Her numerous awards include the 1998 Harvard Business School Alumni Achievement Award, the 2004 Matrix Award for Advertising, and leadership awards from the Executive Leadership Council, the YMCA, and the Corporate Women's Network. *Fortune* magazine named Fudge one of the 50 most powerful women in American business in 1998 and 2003. Fudge cites values as the guiding ethos in her business and personal life:

> My core beliefs are honesty, integrity, and dealing with people as I want to be dealt with. I use that as a basis for the things I stand for, and for deciding when to make a compromise. Sometimes people have different ways of reaching an end goal. As long as I get there, I am willing to compromise on the approach. But I don't compromise on credibility and integrity or on treating people fairly (*Black Enterprise*).

FURTHER READING

Alleyne, Sonia. "A Commercial Success: Ann Fudge Takes the Helm as the First African American to Head a Major Advertising Agency," *Black Enterprise* (July 2003).

Brady, Diane. "Act II: Ann Fudge's Two Year Break from Work Changed Her Life; Will Those Lessons Help Her Fix Young and Rubicam?" *BusinessWeek*, 29 Mar. 2004.

Clarke, Caroline V. "Memos from the CEOs: Marked Urgent; Richard Parsons, Ann Fudge, and Ken Chenault Offer Powerful Lessons in Leadership," *Black Enterprise* (1 Feb. 2005).

Dobrzynski, J. H. "Maxwell House Finds a Coffee Achiever: Ann Fudge Is a Corporate Pioneer," *New York Times*, 3 June 1995.

AYESHA KANJI

Fudge, Marcia (29 Oct. 1952–), United States congresswoman, was born in Cleveland, Ohio, the daughter of single mother Marian Saffold, a union organizer for the American Federation of State, County, and Municipal Employees. Growing up, Marcia was active in various civic and service activities throughout the community. Her mother and aunt were active volunteers with political campaigns, which fostered Marcia's interest in politics and improving the community. In the sixth grade, Fudge moved from Cleveland to Shaker Heights, Ohio, where she lived until she graduated from Shaker Heights High School in 1971. During her high school days, she was a prominent athlete, participating in field hockey and volleyball. Even with her physical talents, Fudge found it more important to focus her attention on her education. After high school, she attended Ohio State University and earned her Bachelor of Science degree in Business Administration in 1975. In the summer of 1983 Fudge earned her Juris Doctor from the Marshall College of Law at Cleveland State University.

While pursing her advanced degrees, Fudge became interested in working with numbers and specialized in finance. She used these skills to hold jobs in many areas of both the public and private sector of law. Early in her career, Fudge worked as a law clerk and legal researcher. This work was influential in her later position as a visiting judge. In addition, Fudge held jobs as director of the personal property tax department, deputy county auditor of the estate tax department, director of the Cuyahoga County (Cleveland) budget commission, and director of budget & finance in the Cuyahoga county prosecutor's office. On top of her job responsibilities, Fudge still found time to serve as the twenty-first national president of Delta Sigma Theta Sorority (1913) during the years 1996–2000. This public service organization of mostly black, college-educated women consists of over 200,000 members across the world.

Fudge served under the future U.S. Congresswoman STEPHANIE TUBBS JONES as chief administrator during her term as Cuyahoga County prosecutor, and Tubbs Jones took a personal interest in getting Fudge more involved in politics. In 1998, when Tubbs Jones was elected to represent the 11th congressional district in the U.S. House of Representatives, she convinced Fudge to serve as her chief of staff, although Fudge would only commit to the position for a year. When Fudge returned home, residents convinced her to run for the office of mayor of Warrensville Heights, Ohio. In 2000, she was elected into the position, where she remained for nine years. The first back and first female mayor of the town, Fudge made economic development a priority. During her time in office, the city built over two hundred homes for residents, and improved the retail industry. Even after her success in local office, Fudge still was could not be convinced to pursue higher political positions. This changed in August 2008, when Congresswoman Tubbs Jones unexpectedly died of a brain aneurism. Encouraged by local mayors, friends of Tubbs Jones, and local residents, Fudge agreed to run for Tubbs Jones's unexpired term in the House of Representatives. She was nominated by the Democratic Party for the congressional seat and overwhelmingly beat Republican Thomas Pekarek in the November 2008 general election, making her the 11th congressional district representative for the 111th congress. She ran unopposed in a special election two weeks later to serve the remaining two months of Tubbs Jones's unexpired term.

Sworn into the 110th Congress on 19 November 2008, Fudge became the second African American female from Ohio in the House. During her time first term in Congress, Fudge served on various committees including: the Education and Labor committee; the subcommittee on Higher Education; the Lifelong Learning and Competitiveness Committee; the Science and Technology Committee; the subcommittee on Health Employment, Labor and Pensions; the subcommittee on Space and Aeronautics; and the subcommittee on Research and Science Education (vice chair). In addition to these accomplishments Fudge has remained active in many prominent civic organizations. She has been a cochair of the national social action committee for Delta Sigma Theta, an active member of the Congressional Black Caucus, a board member for the Cleveland Public Library, and a member of Zion Chapel Baptist Church.

FURTHER READING

Bernardo, Joseph. *Marcia Fudge*. www.blackpast.org.

U.S. House of Representatives. Marcia L. Fudge. http://fudge.house.gov.

MACKENZIE JORDAN

Fuhr, Grant Scott (28 Sept. 1962–), hockey player, was born to an interracial couple and adopted by white parents, Robert Fuhr, an insurance salesman, and Betty of Spruce Grove, Alberta, Canada. Robert Fuhr, an avid recreational golfer and hockey player, encouraged his son's boundless energy and athleticism at an early age. Grant received his first skates at age four, and soon he flooded the family basement, creating an improvised ice rink. His athletic abilities developed rapidly. As a sixteen-year-old student at Composite High School in Spruce Grove he received an offer to join a minor league affiliate of the Pittsburgh Pirates baseball team, an offer he summarily rejected to pursue his dream of being a National Hockey League (NHL) goaltender.

With athletics both his primary interest and a potentially lucrative career path, Fuhr quit school at sixteen. His talents as a goaltender earned him a starting spot on the junior A team of the Western Hockey League (WHL) Victoria Cougars. His star rose quickly; he was named to the WHL All-Star Team in each of the two seasons he spent with the Cougars. In the 1980–1981 season Victoria won the league title on the shoulders of Fuhr's breakout performance.

Canada had an extremely small black population, less than 0.5 percent of the total at the time, and hockey was not a diverse environment. Because Fuhr played under the mask and padding of a goaltender, many fans and opponents were unaware of his race. A Montreal coach commented that Fuhr likely would have been steered away from hockey had he entered the sport in the more populous eastern portion of Canada and noted that the mask that concealed his race enabled his career. If playing in Victoria molded Fuhr into a dynamic goaltender, it also exposed him to the racial insensitivity inherent in the hockey establishment and the larger society. Nevertheless, his outstanding performance drew the attention of the Edmonton Oilers, who made him their first pick in the 1981 NHL draft.

While most rookies spend years in the minor leagues preparing for NHL competition, Fuhr wowed the Oilers immediately with his poise and skill. He played in forty-eight games as a rookie, forty-three of which were victories, and earned a spot on the NHL second team all-star list. However, Fuhr's second season was one of growing pains. His fellow goaltender and future all-star Andy Moog supplanted Fuhr, earning Fuhr a brief stint in the minor leagues in an effort to recapture his confidence. In the following season the Oilers gelled into a team that stands among the finest in NHL history. Superstars like Wayne Gretzky, Mark Messier, Paul Coffey, and the goalie tandem of Moog and Fuhr ran roughshod over the league. In the playoffs Fuhr carried the team to a victory in the 1983 Stanley Cup finals over the New York Islanders.

The success was not short-lived. With a cadre of future Hall of Fame players, the Oilers won four Stanley Cup championships in the 1980s. Numerous honors were feted on Fuhr and his teammates during those years. Fuhr became a regular at the all-star game and won the prestigious Vezina Trophy, awarded to the league's best goaltender, in 1988. The Oilers were both a local and a national sensation. With their new celebrity status, Fuhr, a small-town young man who was rather naive, was soon introduced to a lifestyle of partying, free spending, and drugs.

Fuhr became a casual cocaine user, and the high living took a toll on his playing career and personal life, contributing to the dissolution of his first marriage to Corrine, with whom he had two daughters. When the 1988–1989 season concluded, an exhausted Fuhr rashly retired. Canada was stunned to hear of a twenty-seven-year-old superstar retiring in his prime. However, the Oilers management was aware of his drug use. Along with his agent, the managers convinced Fuhr to enter two rehabilitation programs, and he successfully put his life back in order. He married for a second time and planned to resume his playing career. Unfortunately, although he had put drug use behind him, the *Edmonton Journal* ran a highly publicized exposé of his past in 1990. The NHL suspended Fuhr for one season, later reducing his punishment to sixty games in recognition of his rehabilitation. The glory days in Edmonton ended. Fuhr was traded to Toronto in 1991 and then to Buffalo and Los Angeles in rapid succession. Plagued by injuries, his career was presumed over.

What followed was one of the great comebacks in hockey history. Fuhr convinced the Saint Louis Blues to give him another chance. Aging and playing on two surgically reconstructed knees, Fuhr somehow found his old form, recording four star-studded years with the Blues between 1995 and 1999. Defying his age, he started an unheard of seventy-three games in 1996. Confident that his career would end on a well-deserved high note, the thirty-eight-year-old accepted a trade to the Calgary Flames in 1999 to mentor a promising young black goalie who considered Fuhr his idol. After appearing in only twenty-three games for Calgary, Fuhr retired. In 2003 he was elected to the Hockey Hall of Fame, the first black player so honored. In retirement he tutored goaltenders for Calgary and became a coach for the Phoenix Coyotes. He lived in Edmonton with his third wife Candace and his four children.

Fuhr was perhaps the finest goaltender of his era, but more importantly he was the first black superstar in a racially homogeneous sport. Like all celebrities, his mistakes became fodder for public consumption, but he persevered and resurrected his career long after he was considered washed-up. As the first black player to have his name engraved on the Stanley Cup and enter the Hall of Fame, Fuhr created a legacy for the growing group of black players in the NHL who cite him as an influence and an inspiration.

FURTHER READING

Diamond, Dan, ed. *Total Hockey: The Official Encyclopedia of the National Hockey League* (2000).

Kram, Mark. "Grant Fuhr," in *Contemporary Black Biography*, vol. 1 (2005).

EDWARD M. BURMILA

Fulani, Lenora Branch (25 Apr. 1950–), developmental psychologist, educator, and national independent political leader, was born Lenora Branch in Chester, Pennsylvania. A youth leader in the black Baptist Church, Fulani grew up in a working-class black community; her mother, Pearl, was a nurse, and her father, Charles Lee, was a baggage carrier on the Pennsylvania Railroad. As a child, Fulani briefly participated in the public school desegregation process following *Brown v. Board of Education*

Lenora Fulani, independent presidential candidate, 1988. (AP Images.)

(1954). While still in her early teens she decided to become a psychologist to help her immediate community; during the 1970s, reflecting her pride in being of African descent, she changed her surname to Fulani, the name of various West African nomadic groupings of people.

Fulani won a scholarship to Hofstra University on Long Island, New York, where she majored in psychology. Divorced when her two children, Ainka and Amani, were still very young, she brought them up as a single parent while working toward her doctorate in Developmental Psychology at the City University of New York, where she received her Ph.D. in 1984. While still at Hofstra, Fulani had begun to be influenced by the writings of Frantz Fanon, the revolutionary black psychiatrist from Martinique, and other black and feminist psychologists. Over the next few years she became increasingly critical of traditional psychology. Her dissertation, "Children's Understanding of Number Symbols in Formal and Informal Contexts," an exploration of the ways in which poor black children learn mathematics inside and outside school, reflected her growing interest in the discoveries of the early Soviet methodologist Lev Vygotsky.

From 1973 to 1977 Fulani worked as a guest researcher at Rockefeller University, where she specialized in the interplay between social environment and learning, with a particular focus on the black community. During this time Fulani began to question the value of efforts to reform traditional psychology—including black, feminist, and gay psychology—when these very reform efforts perpetuated key features of it, such as labeling. In 1978 Dr. Lois Holzman, a colleague at Rockefeller, introduced Fulani to Dr. Fred Newman, the Stanford-trained philosopher of science who became her mentor and her closest collaborator in the work of creating political and educational alternatives for the black community. Fulani's most significant contributions—and the source of her controversialism—derive from this work, which has engendered opposition and outright hostility from black leaders and others associated with conventional solutions to poverty, disenfranchisement, underachievement, and other problems affecting the African American community. Since the late 1970s Fulani worked with Newman, Holzman, and others to create social therapy, a radically humanistic, performance-based clinical approach to curing emotional pain that is grounded in the writings of Karl Marx, Vygotsky, and the philosopher Ludwig Wittgenstein. The social-therapeutic approach informs the All Stars Talent Show Network, an internationally recognized and award-winning supplementary education program for inner-city youth co-founded in the early 1980s by Newman and Fulani. Fulani also helped to found the All Stars' sister program, the Joseph A. Forgione Development School for Youth, a leadership training school for young people. The programs—both projects of the nonprofit All Stars Project, Inc.—do not rely on government funding but are entirely supported by individual and corporate donors.

Fulani, who became a leader of the independent New Alliance Party (NAP) shortly after it was founded in 1979, was a tireless organizer of the independent political movement that emerged in the United States through the late twentieth and early twenty-first centuries. In 1988, running on the NAP line, Fulani became the first woman and the first African American presidential candidate in history to be on the ballot in all fifty states. Campaigning under the slogan "Two Roads Are Better than One," she encouraged voters to support the Reverend Jesse Jackson in the Democratic primaries and to support her in the general election should he not receive his party's nomination.

Fulani was again an independent candidate in 1990 when she ran for governor of New York on the New Alliance Party line and was endorsed by the Reverend AL SHARPTON and Minister LOUIS FARRAKHAN.

In 1989 Fulani and Sharpton, who at her urging soon entered electoral politics but rejected running as an independent, led a series of marches through the Bensonhurst section of Brooklyn to protest the murder of a black teenager, Yusuf Hawkins. Fulani's constant presence in the black community encouraged black and Latino families to call on Fulani for support in subsequent cases of police brutality; in 1991 she played an instrumental role in preventing the escalation of violence in the Crown Heights section of Brooklyn when she placed herself between the police and young African American men rioting in response to the hit-and-run death of a black child there.

Fulani's relentless efforts to build an independent political movement that could liberate the black community from its dependence on the Democratic Party have entailed making unconventional alliances with other political forces in the form of left-center-right coalitions. In 1993 Fulani, along with political activists who supported H. Ross Perot for president in 1992, launched a nationwide effort to create an independent, pro-reform populist party that would include African American leadership and provide African Americans with an electoral alternative to the two major parties; in 1995 she became one of the founders of the national Reform Party. A year earlier she had co-founded the Committee for a Unified Independent Party, Inc., a nonpartisan think tank designed to pursue strategies for empowering independent voters.

During these years Fulani worked to build New York's Independence Party, which has since become the third largest party in the state, while she became one of its most prominent leaders. In 2001 the Independence Party provided the margin of victory for Michael Bloomberg in his campaign for mayor of New York City. For more than two decades Fulani spearheaded numerous legislative and legal reforms, including nonpartisan municipal elections, initiative and referendum, and open primaries—all designed to empower voters.

In 2004 Fulani was featured in *America behind the Color Line*, a PBS/ BBC documentary by Harvard University's HENRY LOUIS GATES JR. that showcased her innovative educational work. Over the years she appeared as a guest on hundreds of television and radio programs, and her social commentaries have appeared in major daily newspapers. She was the author of a political autobiography, *The Making of A Fringe Candidate* (1992), was the editor of *The Psychopathology of Everyday Racism and Sexism* (1988), and was a contributing author to *Postmodern Psychologies, Societal Practice, and Political Life* (2000).

FURTHER READING

Fulani, Lenora B. *The Making of a Fringe Candidate* (1992).

Ali, Omar. "The Perot Movement," in *History in Dispute: American Social and Political Movements, 1945–2000*, ed. Robert J. Allison (2000).

Gates, Henry Louis, Jr. *America behind the Color Line: Dialogues with Africans Americans* (2004).

OMAR H. ALI

Fuller, Blind Boy (10 July 1907?–13 Feb. 1941), blues singer and guitarist, was born Fulton Allen in Wadesboro, North Carolina, the son of Calvin Allen and Mary Jane Walker. The exact date of his birth remains debatable because two different years are listed on official documents. Little is known of his early life except that he attended school through the fourth grade in Wadesboro and began learning to play guitar in his teens. After his mother's death in the mid-1920s he moved with his father and the rest of his family to Rockingham, North Carolina; there he met Cora Mae Martin, whom he married around 1926. They married in Bennettsville, South Carolina, possibly for legal reasons—she was only fourteen, and he was either nineteen or seventeen (depending on his actual birth date). It is believed that they raised one adopted child.

By the time of his marriage Allen was developing vision problems and was diagnosed as having ulcers behind his eyes. In 1927 he and his wife moved to Winston-Salem, North Carolina. He worked in a coal yard for a short time, but his failing vision caused him to quit, and by 1928 he was totally blind. At this point he turned to music to make a living. He and Cora Mae settled in Durham, North Carolina, and by the early 1930s he was an established street musician. It was during the 1930s that he also picked up the name Blind Boy Fuller—possibly a street corruption of his real first name or, in some accounts, a name he was given after he started recording.

Although Fuller's repertoire and guitar technique was derived mainly from phonograph records, he also learned from GARY DAVIS, a blind street singer and gifted guitarist who had come to

Durham from Greenville, South Carolina. He also kept company with the washboard player George Washington, better known as Bull City Red, who doubled as Fuller's guide. In 1935 Fuller encountered James Baxter "J.-B." Long, a scout for ARC records and manager of the Durham United Dollar Store. After writing to ARC in New York, Long used his family's 1935 summer vacation to drive Fuller, Davis, and Bull City Red to ARC's New York studio. The resulting sessions—presided over by Art Satherly, a veteran of race records (as recordings by black musicians were then known)—took place over four days, beginning 23 July. Fuller recorded a dozen issued sides, playing solo on some and accompanied by Davis and Red on others. The session produced a substantial hit, "Rag, Mama, Rag," a typical Piedmont ragtime dance blues.

Nine months later, in April 1936, Long again used his vacation time to record Fuller in New York. Apparently Long had had a falling-out with Davis, so Fuller recorded ten solo sides, including another classic Piedmont dance piece, "Truckin' My Blues Away." By this time his recordings had made him something of a celebrity, and other musicians, including the blues guitarists Richard and Willie Trice, who lived outside Durham, sought him out. Fuller used his connections with the recording studio to act as a scout, supposedly charging a ten-dollar fee to musicians he helped record.

Willie Trice later told the biographer Bruce Bastin that Fuller was an ardent poker player, using a sighted person to tell him what cards he was holding. Hot-tempered and suspicious, he always carried a pistol and would brandish it to discourage cheating. "People didn't know what to do when a blind man began waving a pistol in their faces," Trice told Bastin.

In 1937, by far Fuller's most productive recording year, he cut an astonishing forty-nine titles. His first session in February was a three-day affair, yielding fourteen sides. Reunited with Bull City Red, he also brought along a new protégé, Floyd "Dipper Boy" Council, a truck driver from Chapel Hill, North Carolina, who played guitar. The session produced more dance tunes, a fine version of the traditional Piedmont blues "Mamie," and a tune called "Boots and Shoes," a reprise of Amon Easton's hit "Meet Me in the Bottom."

Along with artistic success, 1937 also brought difficulties—first a contract squabble, then a criminal charge. The contract matter started after Fuller went to New York and recorded a dozen sides for Decca. When Decca released two of the tunes, Long bluffed Decca into withdrawing the releases and issuing no further sides by implying that he had an exclusive recording contract with Fuller, when in fact he did not. Long and Fuller then came to terms on an exclusive lifetime contract.

The criminal charge stemmed from a shooting in which Fuller's wife was wounded in the leg. The shooting might have been an accident but Cora Mae's uncle swore out a warrant, and Fuller was jailed. When his wife did not press charges, the case was dropped. Fuller later commemorated his experience in the song "Big House Bound."

Taking advantage of his new contract, Long set up two more ARC sessions in 1937, one in September and one in December. The sessions produced thirty sides. The December session paired Fuller with SONNY TERRY, a harmonica player who had come to Durham from Georgia and who had worked the streets with Fuller as early as 1930.

An October 1938 session in Columbia, South Carolina, included Terry and Bull City Red and produced the expected dozen sides. The same group was in Memphis, Tennessee, on 12 July 1939 for a two-day session. Fuller recorded a dozen solo cuts, and the others joined him for an additional six religious sides, issued as performed by Brother George and His Sanctified Singers. In March 1940 another two-day session with Terry and Red yielded Fuller's best seller, a two-sided hit: "Step It Up and Go," supposedly written by Long, and "Little Woman You're So Sweet," a tune influenced by traditional field hollers. Four of the dozen issued sides from this session were "Brother George" gospel tunes.

Although Fuller's health was beginning to decline, he traveled to Chicago in July 1940 for what would be his last session, accompanied by the guitarist BROWNIE MCGHEE as well as Terry and Red. A month later he underwent an operation related to kidney problems. He was in and out of the hospital several times in subsequent months and finally went home to die. He died in Durham of a bladder infection and blood poisoning.

By any measure, Blind Boy Fuller was one of the most popular and prolific blues artists of his time, recording 135 titles in a mere six years. A highly versatile guitarist, he was at ease with several styles—bottleneck, ragtime, dance tunes, and deep blues—and had a gift for reworking the hits of other artists. In this sense he was a synthesizer of styles, parallel in many ways to Mississippi's ROBERT JOHNSON, his contemporary. Like Johnson, Fuller died young.

Much of Fuller's output was good-time house-party music, often with risqué double-entendre lyrics. But his more serious music, such as "Lost Lover

Blues," "Mamie," and "Big House Bound," was as emotionally charged as any ever recorded.

According to Richard Trice, quoted in Bastin's biography of Fuller, Fuller renounced the blues on his deathbed—an act also attributed to Robert Johnson. However, his influence and many of his songs lived on in the styles and repertoires of blues and country musicians who followed him, including John Jackson, John Cephas, and Merle Travis. In sum, Fuller was probably the Southeast's most important and influential blues artist.

FURTHER READING

Bastin, Bruce. *Crying for the Carolines* (1971).

Bastin, Bruce. *Red River Blues* (1986).

DISCOGRAPHY

Blind Boy Fuller. East Coast Piedmont Style (Columbia Legacy CK 46777).

Blind Boy Fuller. Truckin' My Blues Away (Yazoo 1060).

Dixon, Robert M. W., and John Godrich. *Blues and Gospel Records: 1902–1943* (1982).

Oliver, Paul, ed. *The Blackwell Guide to Blues Records* (1989).

This entry is taken from the *American National Biography* and is published here with the permission of the American Council of Learned Societies.

BARRY LEE PEARSON AND BILL MCCULLOCH

Fuller, Charles Henry, Jr. (5 Mar. 1939–), Pulitzer Prize-winning playwright, director, educator, and screenwriter, was born in Philadelphia, Pennsylvania, one of the three children of Lillian (Anderson) and Charles H. Fuller Sr., a printer who instilled in his son the love for words. Fuller was raised in northern Philadelphia in an integrated neighborhood. When he was thirteen he saw his first theatre performance at the Walnut Street Theatre in Philadelphia. The experience made a lasting impression on him. Later, he became a voracious reader. His readings made him aware of the cultural and racial biases he made his life's mission to correct.

Success did not come easy to him, though. After graduating high school in 1956, Fuller attended Villanova University in hopes of becoming a writer. There he was confronted with racism for the first time as a student, being told by his professors that writing was not a good profession for a black person. His attempts to publish in the school's magazine were not received well either.

Such obstacles only made him more determined. In 1959 he joined the army and was stationed in Virginia, Japan, and South Korea, never forgetting his dream. He tried to improve as a writer, supporting himself by working at a bank, as a counselor for minority students at Templeton University (where he returned in 1988 as professor of African American studies), and as a housing inspector. He drew upon these various experiences in his plays to explore the different facets of racism. During this time, he met and, in 1962, married Miriam A. Nesbitt, a nurse and teacher. The couple had two sons, Charles III and David.

In 1968 Fuller earned a degree in fine arts from La Salle College. During the same year he wrote *The Village: A Party* for the McCarter Theater in Princeton, New Jersey. In 1969 it ran for twenty-one performances off-Broadway at Tambellini's Gate Theater as *The Perfect Party*. Although later in his career he would not think much of this play, at the time it gave him the confidence to move to New York to become a playwright. In 1974 the Negro Ensemble Company at the St. Mark's Playhouse produced *In the Deepest Part of Sleep*. It played for over a decade and was the first in a series of his plays produced by the company. Next, Fuller wrote a historical play about the Brownsville affair (an altercation between black soldiers and the residents of Brownsville, Texas). *The Brownsville Raid*, which anticipated the later *A Soldier's Play*, was staged off-Broadway at Theater de Lys and received solid reviews. But it was his next play *Zooman and the Sign*, a social drama, that established Fuller's reputation as a playwright. Although not a box-office success, the production received two Obie Awards and an Audelco Award for best playwright in 1980.

Considered by the *New York Times* to be "one of the contemporary American theatre's most forceful and original voices," Fuller made his major contribution to the development of African American theatre in 1982 when he won the Pulitzer Prize for his drama *A Soldier's Play*, the story of a black army sergeant murdered on a military base in Louisiana. He was the second African American playwright to receive the prestigious award. The play also won the Audelco and Theater Club awards for best play, the Outer Circle Critics Award for best Off-Broadway play, and the New York Drama Critics Award for best American play. The movie adaptation of the play, called *A Soldier's Story*, for which Fuller wrote the screenplay, was nominated for two Academy Awards in 1984.

Throughout the 1980s, Fuller continued writing and producing. His works include *Eliot's Coming* (1988), *Sally and the Prince Under the Umbrella*, and *We* (both 1989). *Sally and the Prince Under the Umbrella* was staged at Theater Four in New York City. The following year, Fuller completed another drama, *Jonquil*, which was performed by the Negro Ensemble Company. The production received mixed reviews: praise for the playwright's vision to open up the genre and innovative approach to playwriting, but disappointment with the final effect.

Faithful to his teenage resolution to change cultural and racial biases, Fuller tackled black history and cultural and racial stereotypes with originality, complexity, and talent. The open-mindedness of his scrutiny of social issues, including internalized racism within the African American community, often made his work uncomfortable for audiences, black and white alike. His works' ingenuity and sophistication contributed to his considerable legacy in American theater.

Besides his successful career as a playwright Fuller also wrote scripts for television, a Philadelphia radio show, as well as short stories and nonfiction. His short stories were published in anthologies and periodicals such as *Black Dialogue* and *Liberator*.

Besides his Obie and Pulitzer, Fuller received a number of fellowships and other awards, including the Creative Artist Public Service Award in 1974, a Rockefeller Foundation fellowship in 1975, a National Endowment for the Arts fellowship in 1976, a Guggenheim fellowship in 1977–1978, and the Hazelitt Award from the Pennsylvania State Council on the Artsin 1984. He was also the recipient of a number of honorary degrees from several institutions, including Villanova University (1983), his first college.

FURTHER READING

Harriott, Esther. *American Voices: Five Contemporary Playwrights in Essays and Interviews* (1988).

Malinowski, Sharon, ed. *Black Writers. A Selection of Sketches from Contemporary Authors* (1994).

Savran, David. *In Their Own Words: Contemporary American Playwrights* (1988).

MARIA ORBAN

Fuller, Howard (14 Jan. 1941–), educator, civil rights activist, and community organizer, was born in Shreveport, Louisiana, the only child of Tom and Juanita Fuller. Fuller's maternal grandmother, Pearl Wagner, raised him until 1948, at which time Fuller and his mother moved to Milwaukee, Wisconsin, in search of better opportunities in the North. Fuller attended St. Boniface Catholic School through the seventh grade, where he was the only black student in his early years at the school. Fuller attended North Division High School, serving as senior class and student council presidents, and he excelled as center for the school's Blue Devils basketball team. Following graduation from North Division in 1958, Fuller received a scholarship to and graduated from predominantly white Carroll College in Waukesha, Wisconsin, where he served as president of the student senate and became the record-holding rebounder for the Pioneer basketball team. Fuller earned an M.A. in social administration (1964) from Western Reserve (later Case Western Reserve) in Cleveland, Ohio, which he attended on an Urban League scholarship.

While at Western Reserve, Fuller participated in the Congress of Racial Equality's (CORE) effort to integrate Cleveland's public schools. He was jailed briefly during a school board demonstration, and he was involved in an effort to block construction of a new all-black school, during which a white minister, Bruce Klunder, was accidentally killed when a bulldozer crushed him. Fuller spent 1964 and 1965 as an employment specialist for the Urban League in Chicago, fulfilling what had been a stipulation of his scholarship at Western Reserve.

In spring 1965 Fuller took a job in Durham, North Carolina. Working for the federally funded Operation Breakthrough, Fuller put his energy into local antipoverty programs. Operation Breakthrough's white leadership expected that since Fuller had worked for the moderate Urban League, he would be a moderate community worker, but over time Operation Breakthrough's board became increasingly wary of Fuller, who did not fit their expectations of a moderate—or even passive—black employee. Fuller focused his tireless energy on improving the substandard housing he found in Hayti, the black section of Durham. From the start, Fuller did not try to alleviate the residents' problems; rather he nurtured leadership from within the community to empower black citizens to force landlords—both white and black—to provide more livable conditions at fairer rents.

When Fuller's activism backfired and a newly christened housing organizer, Joyce Thorpe, was evicted, Fuller worked to empower residents in other ways. He was able to convince fewer than a dozen tenants—they, too, were afraid of reprisals—to picket the landlord of Thorpe's building, but he recruited fifty students from North Carolina College to join the protests, giving the appearance of greater community outrage and activism. He also secured legal assistance for Thorpe, whose case against the landlord eventually resulted in a Supreme Court decision (*Joyce C. Thorpe v. Housing Authority of the City of Durham*, 1966) prohibiting landlords from evicting public housing residents without cause.

Fuller raised greater anxiety among Durham's leadership and Operation Breakthrough's board at a 1966 gathering at Woodland, North Carolina. Even though Fuller did not speak at the gathering as a representative of Operation Breakthrough, his call for "black power" frightened many whites, causing Breakthrough's board and Durham's white power structure to look for ways to neutralize Fuller's growing popularity and effectiveness. Because Breakthrough received federal funding, the group was restricted from overt political activism; the board used this limitation to try to curtail Fuller's organizing activities. Another incident, this one in 1968, illustrates how white leaders in Durham tried to limit Fuller's leadership. Students at South Carolina State College in Orangeburg had recently protested a segregated bowling alley in town; after a number of days of demonstrations, state and local police—believing that demonstrators had shot a fellow officer—opened fire on the demonstrators, killing three and wounding more than thirty. When black residents of Durham held a memorial for the students who had been killed in the massacre, Fuller was arrested for assault and resisting arrest when he intervened between Durham police and black demonstrators. (Fuller was acquitted of assault; his conviction for resisting arrest was overturned on appeal.)

While in Durham, Fuller and other local leaders founded MALCOLM X Liberation University (1969) to create an atmosphere in which students could learn black history and culture and be trained in practical arts and community activism. Fuller traveled to southern Africa in 1971 to speak about black education; he stayed for a month, spending time with Marxist guerrillas in Mozambique, who had invited him to witness their efforts to liberate the country. The experience was transforming, both because it informed his Pan-Africanist thinking and because it impelled him to help organize African Liberation Day, in which thirty thousand people marched in Washington, D.C., on 25 May 1972, to support African liberation. In addition to directing and trying to raise money for Malcolm X Liberation University, as well as frequently making speeches, around 1975 Fuller attempted to organize Duke University's black hospital workers. His efforts were unsuccessful, and the activist and organizer found himself mentally and physically exhausted.

Fuller returned to Milwaukee in 1976 and sold insurance before becoming associate director of the Educational Opportunity Program at Marquette University in 1979. That year also saw the nexus of Fuller as educator and activist in the controversy over North Division High School in Milwaukee. Milwaukee Public Schools planned to change North Division from a traditional neighborhood school—albeit an overwhelmingly black one—to a magnet school that would attract a large minority of white students. Fuller and the Coalition to Save North Division argued that blacks again were being forced to bear the brunt of integration, since many black students already at North Division would be bused away from North Division to accommodate large numbers of white students. Fuller reshaped *Brown v. Board* for Milwaukee, arguing that North Division as an all-black school was not inherently unequal; rather, features of the larger Milwaukee society—housing patterns, employment opportunities, property taxes—created barriers to equal opportunities in education. In the end, Fuller and the coalition saved North Division as a neighborhood school—and one whose enrollment would be at least 60 percent African American.

In 1985 Fuller earned his Ph.D. in the sociological foundations of education from Marquette University, and he held a number of positions in the 1980s. He served as secretary of the Wisconsin Department of Employment Relations in Democratic Governor Tony Earl's administration (1983–1986), he was dean of general education at Milwaukee Area Technical College (1986–1988), and he was director of Milwaukee County Health and Human Services (1988–1991). In light of Milwaukee's failure to provide greater educational opportunities for blacks, in 1987 Fuller proposed to the state legislature the New North Division School District, a district independent of—but an island within—Milwaukee public schools. Fuller envisioned his proposed district as an island of exceptionalism, an all-black school district within the city of Milwaukee, a haven where black students could excel. The legislature defeated Fuller's proposal, on the grounds that creating the district would be impractical and too costly.

Fuller was hired as superintendent of Milwaukee Public Schools in 1991, and he oversaw the opening of two schools that would immerse students in African American history and culture, MARTIN LUTHER KING JR. Elementary and Malcolm X Academy. In 1993 Fuller devoted his personal and professional energies to a failed referendum that would have required Milwaukee property owners to pay more for Milwaukee public schools. The failure of the referendum, the election of a majority of school board members not in sympathy with Fuller's goals, and flagging energy led Fuller to resign as superintendent in 1995.

In 1995 Fuller was appointed the director of the Institute for the Transformation of Learning at Marquette University. An outspoken and tireless advocate of school choice, he argued that black students have greater opportunities to realize self-determination if parents can use public dollars to choose successful private schools.

FURTHER READING

Coleman, Jonathan. *Long Way to Go: Black and White in America* (1997).

Davidson, Osha Gray. *The Best of Enemies: Race and Redemption in the New South* (1996).

Dougherty, Jack. *More Than One Struggle: The Evolution of Black School Reform in Milwaukee* (2004).

Greene, Christina. *Our Separate Ways: Women and the Black Freedom Movement in Durham, North Carolina* (2005).

DAVID SCHROEDER

Fuller, Hoyt William (10 Sept. 1927–11 May 1981), editor and literary critic, was born in Atlanta, Georgia, the son of Thomas Fuller and Lillie Beatrice Ellafair Thomas. A member of the African American middle class, Fuller was raised in Detroit, Michigan, and came of age against the backdrop of the violent race riots in that city in 1943.

Fuller attended Wayne State University in Detroit, where he received his B.A. in 1950. As a student, he was deeply influenced by Fred Hart Williams, a historian who specialized in the experiences of blacks in the Michigan-Ontario area and who founded what would later be known as the Hackley Memorial Collection of Black Arts at the Detroit Public Library. Williams introduced Fuller to regional black history and to African history, beginning Fuller's deep and abiding commitment to African affairs.

Fuller worked as a reporter for the *Detroit Tribune* from 1949 to 1951 and as feature editor for the *Michigan Chronicle* from 1951 to 1954. In 1954 he became associate editor of *Ebony* magazine, a position he held until 1957. In that year he left the United States, choosing—like an earlier generation of black writers and intellectuals—voluntary exile in Europe. As he later commented in *Journey to Africa* (1971): "I had quit *Ebony* magazine, for the magazine did not seem to be moving in any direction that it seemed important for me to go. ... I had left the United States in 1957 because, quite literally, I could not live there. That was the year of Little Rock." For the next three years, Fuller lived on the Spanish island of Mallorca, supporting himself by working as the West African correspondent for the Amsterdam *Haagse Post*. During that time he traveled to North Africa and West Africa and spent three months in Guinea shortly after Sékou Touré proclaimed its independence in 1958. His experiences in Africa became the basis of *Journey to Africa*. In 1960 he returned to the United States, where he worked as assistant editor at *Collier's Encyclopedia* before joining *Negro Digest* as managing editor in 1961.

Created in 1942 by the Chicago-based publisher John Johnson (1918–2005), *Negro Digest* was initially closely modeled after *Reader's Digest*, but instead of focusing primarily on white America it reprinted generally upbeat articles about African American life. The original *Negro Digest* ceased publication in 1951; Fuller's appointment represented an attempt to resurrect the magazine after a ten-year hiatus. To this task, he brought a sensibility shaped and nurtured by years of experience as a journalist and a passionate commitment to the cause of black freedom in the United States. During the next fifteen years, he turned *Negro Digest* into the most influential journal of its kind in the country.

Initially, the revived *Negro Digest* continued the practices and policies of its predecessor, reprinting articles from other magazines and journals and expressing a generally optimistic outlook in its editorial column. Beginning in August 1962, however, when Fuller assumed sole authorship of the editorial column, he charted a course that steered *Negro Digest* from the ethos of the civil rights movement through the Black Power/Black Arts movements into its Pan-Africanist position as *Black World* magazine (1970–1976). In a broad sense, the shifts and turns of Fuller's ideological perspective corresponded to shifts in the mood and outlook of black activists in the United States, which Fuller helped to shape by his uncompromising editorial positions. Beginning with his June 1964 essay "Ivory Towerist vs. Activist: The Role of the Negro Writer in an Era of Struggle" Fuller insisted that there was an inextricable connection between politics and literature and that the black writer had a critical role to play in shaping the social and political consciousness of the black community. By the mid-1960s he was directing his verbal attacks at two targets: white literary critics and anthologists, such as David Littlejohn, whom he saw as cultural interlopers lacking the requisite understanding to interpret black literature, and African American writers—most notably Ralph Ellison—who emphasized craft and technique over political commitment.

After another trip to the African continent on a John Hay Whitney Opportunity Fellowship in 1965–1966, Fuller became even more outspoken in his views. He spurred on the debate about the "black aesthetic," an attempt to define the fundamental characteristics of African American cultural expression, establishing himself as one of the key spokesmen for the Black Arts Movement. By the late 1960s *Negro Digest* had become the national forum for established and emerging black writers and intellectuals, the key arena in which many of the debates about black literature, culture, and politics occurred. LeRoi Jones/Amiri Baraka, Larry Neal, Carolyn Gerald, Sonia Sanchez, Addison Gayle Jr., Harold Cruse, Mari Evans, Gwendolyn Brooks, and Ishmael Reed were among the writers who appeared in its pages.

Fuller's role as an editor was complemented by his organizational efforts in other arenas. Although he later became sharply critical of the organization, he was actively involved in the American Society for African Culture and participated in the first World Festival of Negro Arts in Dakar, Senegal, in 1966. In 1967 he was a founding member of the influential Organization of Black American Culture in Chicago, where he conducted a weekly writer's workshop. He taught African American literature at Northwestern University in 1969–1970, at Indiana University in 1970–1971, and at Wayne State University in 1974. Having moved to Atlanta in 1976, he taught at Emory University and traveled back and forth to Ithaca, New York, to teach in the Africana Studies Program at Cornell University. A tireless speaker, Fuller was a frequent participant in the black writers' conferences and gatherings that flourished, nationally and internationally, from the late 1960s through the mid-1970s. In 1977 he served as the North American vice chair of the second World Black and African Festival of Arts and Culture in Lagos, Nigeria.

In April 1976 John Johnson ceased publication of *Black World*, a decision that signaled a radical shift in the cultural, economic, and political climate within which the magazine had flourished. In a post–civil rights, post–Black Power era, many of the issues with which Fuller and *Black World* had been identified seemed out of step with the mood of the times. Fuller returned to his native Atlanta where, with a number of supporters, he launched a new journal, *First World*, which he edited until his death in Atlanta. At the time of his death he was working on a novel, "An Hour of Breath," and two literary histories, "History and Analysis of the Black Arts Movement" and "The New Black Renaissance." He never married.

Hoyt Fuller's significance rests primarily in the central role that he played as an editor during a historical moment when the relationships between blacks and whites in the United States were being sharply contested and actively renegotiated. Through the pages of *Negro Digest*, *Black World*, and *First World*, his influential essays and editorials, and his public statements, Fuller helped to shape the context in which many of these cultural and political issues were raised and debated.

FURTHER READING

The Hoyt W. Fuller Papers are in the Atlanta University Library.

Parks, Carole A., ed. *Nommo: A Literary Legacy of Black Chicago, 1967–1987* (1987).

Obituary: *New York Times*, 13 May 1981.

This entry is taken from the *American National Biography* and is published here with the permission of the American Council of Learned Societies.

JAMES A. MILLER

Fuller, Jesse (12 Mar. 1896–29 Jan. 1976), songster and one-man band, was born in Jonesboro, Georgia, near Atlanta. Raised by a succession of foster families, he never knew his father and barely knew his mother. "My mother used to give me away to different people and they were so darn mean to me I used to run away," Fuller told interviewer Richard Noblett many years later. Fuller showed an early aptitude for making musical instruments, constructing a mouth bow at age seven or eight. He was eight and still being cared for by a foster family when his mother died. He dropped out of third grade and spent the next year or two working various jobs, including tending cattle outside Atlanta and carrying water at a grading camp. At age ten he ran away from foster care for good, staying briefly with his sister and her husband in the Atlanta area, where he learned to play banjo and harmonica. Fuller then spent the next ten years moving from job to job, mostly in northern Georgia.

In his early teens, Fuller heard guitarists around the town of McDonough and was inspired to make a guitar. Later, around the age of eighteen, he was taught to play guitar by Debbie Fletcher, a woman who lived in Stockbridge. He studied with her until her husband put an end to the lessons. Having absorbed local musical traditions from the house-party circuit and from traveling shows, as well as from his teacher, Fuller began to play square dances, earning twenty cents a set. In 1916 he married Curley Mae (maiden name unknown), but the couple soon separated.

While working for a junk dealer during World War I, Fuller was arrested and accused of receiving stolen goods, but he supposedly escaped from jail. Around 1918 he moved to Cincinnati, where he worked for a streetcar company. Still footloose, Fuller joined the Hagenbeck Wallace Circus, traveling with it for six to eight months as a tent stretcher and roustabout. In Big Rapids, Michigan, he played music for a group of soldiers and, by his own account, earned a substantial sum of money. From there he hoboed around the country, supporting himself by playing in stores or on streets and taking odd jobs. In the early 1920s he slowly made his way to California, where he lived for the rest of his life.

In Los Angeles around 1923 Fuller carved wooden snakes and sold them on the streets; he later shined shoes across from United Artists Studios. There he met various film personalities, including the actor Douglas Fairbanks and the director Raoul Walsh, who helped him set up a hot dog stand on the studio lot and get work as a film extra. In 1927 Fuller also tried to reconcile with Curley Mae, but not long after they moved to Bakersfield, California, around 1928, the marriage ended for good. She later committed suicide.

In the early 1930s Fuller worked as a yard hand with the Southern Pacific Railroad. Using his railroad pass—good for "self and wife"—he traveled to Atlanta in search of a bride, and in 1935 he married Gertrude Johnson, a much younger woman who had known his sister.

By 1938 Fuller and his wife were living in Oakland. As the country mobilized for war, Fuller left the railroad for more lucrative work as a shipyard welder, earning enough to buy a house for his family. He and Gertrude eventually had three daughters. Following the war, Fuller resumed work as a laborer, sometimes playing his twelve-string guitar at parties or clubs to earn extra money.

In 1944 Fuller met his fellow songster and twelve-string guitar player LEAD BELLY. They played together several times, doubtless inspiring Fuller to become a more active performer, but it wasn't until 1951 that he dreamed up the one-man-band format that became his trademark. He put together an ensemble that, at various times, included amplified twelve-string guitar, harmonica, kazoo, vocal microphone, foot cymbal, washboard, and an instrument of his own invention: a double bass that was played with a foot pedal. His wife referred to the creation as a "foot diller," a term later dignified to "fotdella."

Playing as a one-man band, Fuller worked local clubs and made several television appearances in the early 1950s. In 1954 he recorded for World Song, the label's only release. The record included his "San Francisco Bay Blues," which would go on to become one of the anthems of the folk revival in the 1960s. Through the 1950s into the 1960s Fuller recorded several more times in the San Francisco area and also picked up bookings at festivals and clubs, mostly working jazz venues in the 1950s and folk clubs in the 1960s. He toured England and Europe in 1960–1961 and helped spark a fleeting interest in American skiffle—a term for music played by small street ensembles employing washboards, jugs, or other unorthodox instruments. Admired and promoted by such folk revival stars as Jack Elliott and Bob Dylan, he did well on the folk circuit in the 1960s. He recorded for Folk-Lyric, Prestige, and Fontana; worked top folk clubs like Gerdes Folk City in New York; and appeared at Newport and other major festivals. In 1968 Fuller appeared in a short film, *Jesse "Lone Cat" Fuller*, and also was heard on the soundtrack of the film *The Great White Hope* (1970), about the boxer JACK JOHNSON, starring JAMES EARL JONES.

Despite health problems in the early 1970s, Fuller continued to perform, although less frequently, finding yet another comfortable venue: blues festivals. In 1976 he entered Dowling Convalescent Hospital, where he died.

Nicknamed "Lone Cat" because of his one-man-band format, Fuller was a songster with an electric repertoire and a singular style. As a guitarist he employed a northern Georgia/Piedmont picking style and could play in open-tuned slide style as well. While there were other songsters, from Lead Belly to HENRY THOMAS, and other one-man bands, from Joe Hill Louis to Doctor Ross, Fuller was an original. His music, heavily flavored by years of rambling and street playing, combined traditions of the Old South with those of the San Francisco Bay area. His material was drawn from blues, ragtime, religious songs, folk ballads, work songs, novelty tunes, pop tunes, and jazz.

One of the few traditional African American artists who began playing mostly to white audiences as early as the mid-1950s, Fuller reached the peak of his influence during the folk revival. His accessible, good-time sound, combined with his wit, charm, hustling ability, and penchant for philosophizing, endeared him to revival audiences and musicians alike.

FURTHER READING

Dane, Barbara. "Lone Cat Jesse Fuller," *Sing Out* 16, no. 1 (Feb.–Mar. 1966).

Harris, Sheldon. *Blues Who's Who: A Biographical Dictionary of Blues Singers* (1989).

Noblett, Richard, and John Offord. "I Got a Mind to Ramble and I Don't Want to Settle Down," *Blues World* 25 (Oct. 1969) and 26 (June 1970).

This entry is taken from the *American National Biography* and is published here with the permission of the American Council of Learned Societies.

BARRY LEE PEARSON AND BILL MCCULLOCH

Fuller, Meta Warrick (9 June 1877–Mar. 1968), sculptor, was born Meta Vaux Warrick in Philadelphia, Pennsylvania, the daughter of William H. Warrick and Emma Jones. Meta's great grandmother, according to family lore, was an Ethiopian princess brought to the American colonies as a slave. Emma owned and operated several hairdressing parlors that catered to a white clientele. William owned a chain of barbershops and dabbled in real estate. Meta was ten years younger than her two siblings, William and Blanche. Through lessons and field trips to museums and concerts, the Warricks introduced their children to art and encouraged their creative endeavors. Meta, who played the guitar, took dancing lessons, and sang in the church choir, exhibited an early talent for drawing.

After graduation from public high school in 1894, Warrick won a three-year scholarship to the Pennsylvania Museum and School for Industrial Arts (now the Philadelphia College of Art). In 1897 her stay was extended when she was awarded a postgraduate scholarship to study sculpture. She graduated in 1899 with honors and took home first prize for best general work in modeling.

In 1899, following a generation of American artists who made pilgrimages to perfect their training and elevate their stature, Warrick left for Paris, which by the late nineteenth century had become the center of fine arts in the Western world. Paris later became the preferred destination for African American artists like WILLIAM H. JOHNSON, HALE WOODRUFF, and

Ethiopia Awakening. Made in 1914, this bronze is one of Meta Warrick Fuller's first sculptures embodying the struggles and aspirations of African Americans. (Schomburg Center.)

LOÏS MAILOU JONES, who were weary of America's racist and segregationist policies. The African American painter HENRY OSSAWA TANNER, a friend of Warrick's uncle, had moved to Paris in 1891 and acted as her guardian during her stay in France. She studied at the École des Beaux-Arts, the epicenter of academic art instruction, and, from 1900 to 1902, at the Academie Colarossi, where she met the American sculptor Augustus Saint-Gaudens.

In the summer of 1900 Warrick met W. E. B. DUBOIS, who was in Paris for the Universal Exposition. DuBois took the young artist under his wing, escorting her to social events, introducing her to the city's literati, and encouraging her to adopt African American themes in her work. The next summer Warrick arrived at the house of sculptor Auguste Rodin with her sculpture *Secret Sorrow (The Man Eating His Heart)* under her arm. "Mademoiselle," Rodin is said to have exclaimed, "you are a sculptor. You have the sense of flow in your fingers." Encouraged by Saint-Gaudens and Rodin, Warrick began holding private exhibitions at her studio. In 1902 S. Bing mounted a one-woman show of her work at his prestigious gallery, L'Art Nouveau. Warrick's Parisian period culminated in 1903 when the Salon d'Automne exhibited *The Wretched*, a sculpture depicting seven figures in varying forms of human anguish. Traditionally trained in the academic style, Warrick was one of only a few women to study in Paris at the turn of the century. Emotional, expressive, and imbued with themes of death and sorrow, her Parisian work owes a great deal to Rodin and to the Romantic realist sculptural style popular in late nineteenth-century France.

Upon her return to the United States in 1902, Warrick enrolled at the Pennsylvania Academy of Fine Arts, where she won the school's top award in ceramics. Encouraged by her success in Paris, she set up a studio in Philadelphia. Local dealers, however, failed to buy her work. Certain that her race was the reason behind their disinterest, Warrick turned to clients in Philadelphia's black community. Her reengagement with the African American community resulted in an increase in black subjects in her work. In 1907 she became the first African American woman to receive a federal art commission when she was selected to produce a sculpture for the Negro Pavilion at the Jamestown Tercentennial Exposition. A depiction of the history of African Americans since settling in Jamestown in 1607, the tableau was composed of fifteen pieces and 150 figures. In 1909 Warrick married SOLOMON FULLER, a neuropathologist and psychiatrist from Monrovia, Liberia, whose father was a repatriated former American slave. The newlyweds moved to Framingham, Massachusetts, over the objections of racist neighbors who organized a petition attempting to stop the Fullers from integrating the predominantly white suburb of Boston. A year later most of Fuller's work was destroyed in a fire that razed the Philadelphia warehouse where she was storing the contents of her studio. Devastated by her loss, which included almost all of her Parisian sculptures, Fuller shifted her focus to starting a family. Between 1910 and 1916 she gave birth to three sons: Solomon Jr., Perry James, and William Thomas. Fuller eventually returned to sculpting, and she thrived in the Boston-area art scene. Critics have argued that Fuller's focus on domestic life, which was encouraged by her husband, kept her from becoming an internationally recognized artist.

It was DuBois who both reignited Fuller's career and prompted her serious adoption of African American subject matter. In 1913, while editor of the *Crisis*, he commissioned a sculpture commemorating the fiftieth anniversary of the Emancipation Proclamation. In the resulting work, *Spirit of Emancipation*, an eight-foot-tall figural grouping, Fuller eschewed images of victimization and paternalism common to representations of slavery and featured instead a boy and girl with distinctly African features. The work exhibited a quieter, more stoic, and less emotionally wrought quality than her Parisian pieces. Inspired by DuBois's Pan-African philosophy, Fuller emphasized the commonality of black Americans' heritage by mining African and African American themes and forms.

Fuller's sculpture *Ethiopia Awakening* marks a shift in African American representation. While Fuller's twelve-inch plaster prototype was produced as early as 1914, the final, lifesize bronze sculpture was unveiled in 1922 at the Making of America exhibit in New York City. Drawing from African and especially Egyptian sculptural forms, Fuller's figure, a standing female wearing the headdress of ancient Egyptian royalty, emerges from mummy wrappings. The figure adopts the stillness, formality, and highly symbolic nature of Egyptian sculpture. Fuller departed, however, from traditional Egyptian sculptural imagery in insisting on frontality and by adding movement by turning her figure's head. As a statement of racial pride and anticolonialist protest, Fuller's image differs significantly from the work of contemporaries like Picasso, who appropriated African sculpture for its "primitivist" quality but removed it from its aesthetic and political contexts. Fuller, conversely, uses her image to connect black America to Africa, to the beauty of African women, and to the optimism of a new "awakening."

One of the first African American artists to draw heavily on African sculpture and themes, Fuller predated ALAIN LOCKE's call for artists to fashion a black aesthetic by turning to Africa, an idea codified in his 1925 essay "The Legacy of the Ancestral Arts." An important precursor to the Harlem Renaissance, Fuller led the way in style and content for the next generation of black artists. Although Fuller never lived in Harlem, she exhibited with and served as a juror for the Harmon Foundation. Fuller showed regularly at the Philadelphia Academy of Art and focused on themes relating to war, violence, and the search for peace. She received second prize for *Peace Halting the Ruthlessness of War* in a competition sponsored by the Women's Peace Party in 1915. Fuller's most significant works confronted the political and social climate of her time. Her 1919 sculpture, *Mary Turner (A Silent Protest against Mob Violence)*, memorialized both the 1917 brutal lynching of MARY TURNER, who was eight months' pregnant, and the subsequent silent protest march organized by the NAACP in Harlem.

In 1929 Fuller built a studio near her home, which served as a salon where she entertained, taught classes, and mounted annual exhibitions. She celebrated the places and people that were important to her by creating sculptures for a host of local organizations, as well as busts of family, friends, and people she admired, including CHARLOTTE HAWKINS BROWN and Samuel Coleridge-Taylor. She exhibited extensively in the Boston area, as well as at the 1936 Texas Centennial Exposition in Dallas, the AUGUSTA SAVAGE Studios in New York, the 1940 Exposition of the Art of the American Negro 1851–1940 in Chicago, and the seventy-fifth anniversary of the Emancipation Proclamation exhibition held at the Library of Congress in Washington, D.C., in 1940.

In 1950, when her husband became blind as a result of diabetes, Fuller gave up her studio to care for him. Shortly after his death in 1953, she contracted tuberculosis and remained in a sanatorium for two years. Following her recovery she resumed work, donating the proceeds from her art to the civil rights movement and producing a series of sculptures of ten famous black women for the Afro-American Women's Council in Washington, D.C., in 1957. She continued honoring African American lives with works like *The Crucifixion* (1963), which eulogizes the four girls murdered in the 1963 Birmingham, Alabama, church bombing, and *Good Shepherd* (1965), dedicated to the clergymen who marched with MARTIN LUTHER KING JR.

Fuller died in 1968, and her ashes were dispersed off the coast of Martha's Vineyard, Massachusetts. Although she remained artistically active until her death at age ninety, a retrospective of her work was not mounted until 1984. The posthumous exhibition An Independent Woman: The Life and Art of Meta Warrick Fuller was held at the Danforth Museum of Art in her adopted city of Framingham.

FURTHER READING

Fuller's papers and photograph collection are held at the New York Public Library's Schomburg Center for Research in Black Culture.

Brawley, Benjamin Griffith. *The Negro in Literature and Art in the United States* (1929).

Driskell, David, ed. *Harlem Renaissance: Art of Black America* (1987).

LISA E. RIVO

Fuller, S. B. (4 June 1905–24 Oct. 1988), businessman, publisher, and self-help advocate, was born Samuel Bacon Fuller in Monroe, Louisiana, the son of William Fuller, a sharecropper and commercial fisherman, and Ethel Johnson Fuller, a domestic servant. His formal education ended after the sixth grade, and the young Fuller took up door-to-door sales. In 1920 the Fuller family moved to Memphis, Tennessee. When his mother died in 1922, Fuller's father abandoned the family, leaving S. B. in charge of six siblings; they refused charity and worked various jobs to survive. In 1923 Fuller married Lorena Whitfield; they had six children before they divorced in 1945. One year later Fuller married Lestine Thornton, a long time assistant. In 1928 Fuller moved to Chicago, joining the Great Migration of African Americans from the South to northern cities. There he worked for seven years, first as a coal deliverer, then as a life insurance salesman and manager for the black-owned Commonwealth Burial Association.

Fuller's entrepreneurial career began in 1935, when he established Fuller Products Company with only $25. He began by selling soap door to door on the South Side of Chicago, an area where other black migrants had settled. Sales grew rapidly and Fuller hired salespeople to peddle soap and other beauty products door-to-door. During this time he gave many inspirational speeches to salesman and business associations. In later years he put his oratorical ability to use by speaking to audiences of black and white businesspeople. He served as president of Chicago's Negro Chamber of Commerce. Following in the tradition of BOOKER T. WASHINGTON, Fuller was a staunch advocate of free enterprise and an opponent of government assistance in any form.

In 1947 Fuller expanded his manufacturing capability by purchasing the white-owned Boyer International Laboratories. Reflecting his commitment to integration, he kept the white employees on the payroll. The Boyer Company extended Fuller's reach into the South, where the firm sold men's hairdressing products, women's cosmetics, and beauty shop supplies. Also during the 1940s and 1950s he trained or influenced many future icons of black business: George Johnson, who founded Johnson Products Company, a competing hair-product firm; JOHN JOHNSON (1918–2005), the publisher of *Ebony*; Joe Dudley of Dudley Products; Mary Ellen Schadd Strong, founder of *Black Family Magazine*, and Rick McGuire of Seaway Furniture.

By the early 1960s Fuller had become perhaps the richest black man in the United States. His company (not to be confused with the Fuller Brush Company) grossed ten million dollars annually, sold three hundred products, and employed five thousand salespersons in thirty-eight states. He further diversified by purchasing real estate, a large Chicago department store, and two major newspapers, the influential *New York Age* and the nationally distributed *Pittsburgh Courier*. He was the first black businessperson admitted to the National Association of Manufacturers (NAM) and the National Association of Direct Sellers. His goal was to create a self-sustaining $100 million enterprise that would outlive him; he feared small "black businesses die when the founder dies" (Casey, 72).

Politically Fuller was a conservative Republican who believed in small government. Yet, he was also a member of the National Association for the Advancement of Colored People (NAACP), supporting its legal efforts for equality, while downplaying the need for direct confrontation or demonstrations in the streets. During the Montgomery bus boycott, for example, he tried unsuccessfully to purchase the bus company, reasoning that there would be no discrimination if blacks owned the money-losing enterprise. Eventually, however, Fuller's conservative philosophy of self-help and color blindness damaged his enterprise. In 1963 he gave an address to a NAM convention that sparked a backlash in the African American community. In his NAM address Fuller stated that blacks created a "racial barrier" against themselves by failing to start businesses in their communities. The *Amsterdam News*, a New York City black newspaper, published an article in which civil rights leaders blasted Fuller for his seeming indifference to the plight of other African Americans. His critics included the NAACP, the National Urban League, the Southern Christian Leadership Conference, the Congress of Racial Equality, and even JACKIE ROBINSON. Soon there were boycotts of Fuller products in the North, while white citizens councils in the South boycotted his company when they discovered he owned the formerly white-owned Boyer Company.

Trying to bail out his struggling company, Fuller issued unregistered promissory notes, which led the Securities and Exchange Commission to investigate and fine the company. In 1968 Fuller Products Company filed for bankruptcy. After reorganizing and selling off its subsidiaries, the company enjoyed a modest recovery in the 1970s before finally selling out to Dudley Products, a firm started by a former Fuller employee.

During his years of success, Fuller gave to many church and charitable causes. In his final years the man who always rejected charity received it in the form of testimonial contributions from successful "Fullerites" who had learned from "the Dean of Black Entrepreneurs." One of these contributors, Johnson, said of Fuller, "If there had been no you, there would be no us" (Casey, 140).

Fuller advocated the Washingtonian philosophy of self-help and epitomized an early generation of black businesspeople who achieved success through determination, talented selling, and inspiring his employees with uplifting rhetoric rather than formal education or political influence. Tragically, Fuller's success led to backlash from resentful whites and militant blacks. Nevertheless, his legacy lived on in the careers of other black entrepreneurs and he is still revered by many in the black business community.

FURTHER READING

Casey, Mary Fuller. *S. B. Fuller: Pioneer in Black Economic Development* (2003).

Fuller, S. B. "A Negro Businessman Speaks His Mind," *U.S. News and World Report*, 19 Aug. 1963.

Ingham, John, and Lynne B. Feldman. "Fuller, S. B.," in *African-American Business Leaders: A Biographical Dictionary* (1994).

"S. B. Fuller: A Man and His Products," *Black Enterprise* 6.1 (Aug. 1975): 47–50.

Obituary: *Chicago Tribune*, 26 Oct. 1988.

JONATHAN J. BEAN

Fuller, Solomon Carter (11 Aug. 1872–16 Jan. 1953), neuropathologist and psychiatrist, was born in Monrovia, Liberia, the son of Solomon Carter Fuller, a coffee planter and Liberian government official, and Anna Ursala James. His father, the son of a repatriated former American slave, was able to provide a private education for his children at a school he established on his prosperous plantation. In the summer of 1889 young Solomon Fuller left home to return to the country where his grandfather had once been held in bondage. He sought higher education at Livingstone College in

Salisbury, North Carolina, a college for black students founded ten years earlier.

Fuller graduated from Livingstone in 1893 with an AB and proceeded to pursue a medical degree at Long Island College Hospital in Brooklyn, New York. After one year he transferred to Boston University School of Medicine, where he received an M.D. in 1897. Although he was deeply disturbed by the racism he found in America, Fuller decided that he would not return to Liberia. Shortly after graduating he accepted an appointment as an intern at the Westborough State Hospital for the Insane, west of Boston. Two years later he was promoted to become the institution's chief pathologist, beginning a forty-five-year tenure at Westborough—twenty-two years as a pathologist and twenty-three as a consultant. In 1899 he also accepted a part-time instructorship in pathology at Boston University, where he quickly established a reputation as a talented teacher.

During these early years as a pathologist, Fuller took his room and board on the grounds of the Westborough State Hospital, which allowed him to spend long hours in the laboratory he directed. He concentrated on photography of extremely thin sections of brain tissue, employing great technical skill with microtome, microscope, and camera to search for connections between mental disorder and organic disease.

During the 1904–1905 academic year Fuller took a leave from his positions at Westborough and Boston and traveled overseas. At the University of Munich he studied under several prominent German medical scientists, including Alois Alzheimer, who would soon identify Alzheimer's disease. On a sightseeing trip to Berlin in 1905, Fuller worked up the courage to introduce himself to the famed immunologist Paul Ehrlich. Much to Fuller's surprise, Ehrlich was happy to have the company of the young American pathologist for the afternoon, and the two continued their friendship by correspondence for years.

A few years after Fuller's return to Massachusetts, he had another brush with greatness. In 1909 Sigmund Freud was invited to give a series of five lectures at Clark University in Worcester, Massachusetts, not far from Westborough. Those lectures stand as a landmark in the history of American psychiatry, and Fuller was among the invited members of the audience. In the same year Fuller married Meta Vaux Warrick (META WARRICK FULLER), a woman of exceptional artistic talent whom he met when she happened to visit Westborough State Hospital. Meta Fuller's special gift was sculpture, and her works were often dramatic renderings of the black experience in America. In the years immediately surrounding the turn of the century, she had spent time in Paris and emerged briefly as an artistic sensation in the French capital when she won the admiration of Auguste Rodin, who said to her on their initial meeting, "My child, you are a sculptor; you have the sense of form in your fingers" (Velma J. Hoover, "Meta Vaux Fuller: Her Life and Art," *Negro History Bulletin* 40 (Mar.–Apr. 1977): 678). However, after returning home to Philadelphia, racial discrimination—and the traditional expectations of her upper-class black family—sapped much of the energy from Meta's artistic rise. When she met and married Fuller, Meta continued with her sculpture as an avocation and found some significant but limited success; she gave up the pursuit of her art as an all-consuming passion.

The newlyweds bought a house in Framingham, Massachusetts, roughly halfway between Boston University and Westborough State Hospital. Their initial welcome was not warm in the predominantly white community: some of the citizens circulated a petition in an unsuccessful attempt to prevent the black doctor and his wife from purchasing a house there. The Fullers managed to overcome—or at least to ignore—this insult and less overt manifestations of racism and went on to establish a comfortable home in Framingham, where they would raise three children and live out their days. Soon after their arrival in Framingham, Solomon Fuller began a private psychotherapy practice out of an office in his home, which added another layer of responsibility. Fuller's practice became large and included both white and black patients. His son recalled: "My father had great spiritual qualities. People came to him for a spiritual communion that was a refreshing, inspiring, and motivating experience.... My father had such a gracious, loving, radiant, and quieting personality that it had a great calming effect on his patients' problems" (Hayden and Harris, 27).

Although Fuller's private practice focused on psychiatric counseling, his research and teaching continued to center on neurology. He published a number of papers, including several on the disease named for his German mentor Alzheimer (Fuller is credited as having identified the ninth case of Alzheimer's disease in a 1911 publication). He also served for many years as the editor of the *Westborough State Hospital Papers*, an outlet for the publication of scientific work carried out by members of the hospital staff.

After twenty years of service at Boston University, in 1919 Fuller was named an associate professor of neuropathology; in 1921 his title was revised to associate professor of neurology. From 1928 until 1933 he functioned as the effective chair of the university's department of neurology. He retired in 1933, when a white assistant professor was promoted over him to a full professorship and officially named head of the department. Through his long years as a popular and respected teacher at Boston University, Fuller had never been placed officially on the school's payroll, although he had been paid for his services. The promotion of the junior colleague over him in 1933 was the final blow in a series of institutional indignities. On the occasion of his resignation, he stated with characteristic grace: "I regard life as a battle in which we win or lose. As far as I am concerned, to be vanquished, if not ingloriously, is not so bad after all." But he added, with understatement, "With the sort of work that I have done, I might have gone farther and reached a higher plane had it not been for the color of my skin" (Hayden and Harris, 22).

Soon after his retirement from Boston University, Fuller began to suffer increasingly from diabetes. By 1944 his eyesight had failed entirely as a result of the disease, and he was forced to end his long association with Westborough State Hospital. Although he lived his final decade in darkness, he continued to meet with a limited number of patients in his private psychiatric practice nearly until the time of his death in Framingham.

Fuller had returned to the country where his grandfather had begun life as a slave, and there he had won a high degree of professional success. His attainments might have been greater if his skin had been white, but in the place of some unrealized aspirations we are left with an impressive legacy of patience and perseverance.

FURTHER READING

Cobb, W. Montague. *Journal of the National Medical Association* 46 (1954): 370–72.

Hayden, Robert C., and Jacqueline Harris. *Nine Black American Doctors* (1976).

JON M. HARKNESS

Fuller, Thomas (1710–1790), calculator, was born in West Africa. Nothing is known of his parents or other relatives. At the age of fourteen he was brought as a slave to colonial America and apparently lived the remainder of his life in Virginia. In his old age he was owned by Elizabeth Coxe of Alexandria.

Fuller led the typical life of a slave and never learned to read or write, but he was widely noted late in his life for his extraordinary ability to perform rapid and complicated mathematical calculations in his head. He was often visited by travelers wanting to witness his skill. One of them was Benjamin Rush of Philadelphia, the noted physician and educator. Rush quizzed him and verified the accuracy of his answers. Among other feats, Fuller could multiply nine figures by nine, give the number of seconds in a year, calculate how many seconds anyone had lived, and determine the number of yards, feet, and inches in any distance. His legendary abilities earned him the sobriquet "the Virginia Calculator." Told that it was regrettable that he had not had a formal education commensurate with his abilities, Fuller replied, "It is best I got no learning; for many learned men be great fools."

Although it is impossible to determine the source of Fuller's talent from a medical or psychological point of view, there is no doubt that in the area of arithmetic calculations he was a prodigy. He seems to have been otherwise normal and displayed none of the idiot savant symptoms of mental retardation accompanied by extraordinary skill in one particular area.

FURTHER READING

Grégoire, Henri. *An Enquiry Concerning the Intellectual and Moral Faculties and Literature of Negroes* (1810; repr. 1967).

Sammons, Vivian. *Blacks in Science and Medicine* (1990).

Williams, George Washington. *History of the Negro Race in America*, vol. 1 (1883).

Obituary: *Columbia Centinel*, 29 Dec. 1790.

WILLIAM F. MUGLESTON

Fuller, Thomas Oscar (25 Oct. 1867–21 June 1942), educator, clergyman, and politician, was born in Franklinton, North Carolina, the son of J. Henderson Fuller and Mary Elizabeth (maiden name unknown). Fuller's father was a former slave who had purchased his freedom and later his wife's with money earned as a skilled wheelwright and carpenter. As a slave, the elder Fuller taught himself to read, and after the Civil War he became active in Republican politics. During Reconstruction he served as a delegate to the 1868 state Republican convention and as a local magistrate.

Fuller completed his primary education in local schools and subsequently attended the Franklinton Normal School, an institution founded to educate black teachers. He graduated from Shaw University in 1890 and received a Master of Arts from the same institution in 1893. After graduation, Fuller simultaneously pursued careers in education and the ministry. Raised in a devoutly religious family, he was ordained as a Baptist minister, and in 1893 he was called to the pulpit of Benton Creek Church in Oxford, North Carolina. Inasmuch as the church paid Fuller only fifty dollars per year, the young minister earned most of his livelihood by teaching public school in Granville County. In 1892 he returned to Franklinton to organize a primary school for local black women, called the Girls' Training School, and in 1895 he was appointed principal of the Shiloh Institute in Warrenton.

Fuller served in this position for three years and became a respected leader of the black community. He was also active in local Republican politics. In 1898 he reluctantly accepted the party nomination for the state legislature, representing the Eleventh District, comprising Vance and Warren counties. He won election easily.

Fuller, the last black to serve in the North Carolina legislature until 1968, was one of several black North Carolinians elected to state and national offices between 1894 and 1901 as a result of a shaky political alliance between Republicans and Populists. When this alliance provoked a campaign of violence from white supremacists, first in Wilmington and later throughout the state, Fuller called on blacks to avoid confrontation and suppress the temptation to riot. Nevertheless, he could not escape the prevailing racial sentiments of the day. Reflecting in his memoirs on his reception as a newly elected state senator, Fuller recalled that he was seated last, after white senators who were seated alphabetically. Furthermore, such prejudice prevented him from being appointed to any senate committee. However, he lobbied for legislation that benefited both races in North Carolina. His belief in temperance, derived undoubtedly from his staunch Baptist faith, led Fuller to lobby for a law that closed an open bar in Warrenton. He also introduced a bill to allow the criminal court to meet every four months and to give the state superior court concurrent jurisdiction with county courts, a measure that decreased docket loads and led to speedier trials. Two of his legislative triumphs directly aided blacks. One act incorporated the North Carolina Mutual and Provident Association, forerunner to the North Carolina Mutual Life Insurance Company, a model for black businesses of the period. He also sponsored a bill to allow outside labor agents to recruit black workers in North Carolina, a practice previously forbidden by law and custom. In 1899 the legislature began debating measures to disfranchise blacks through literacy tests, a poll tax, and a grandfather clause. Fuller was in the center of these debates, arguing that whites had nothing to fear from a black electorate. Despite his eloquent oratory, the resolution passed, and the constitutional amendment took effect in 1900.

Fuller's passionate defense of black voting rights was his last shining moment in the legislature. In 1900 he went to Memphis to pastor the First Baptist Church, a post he held until 1941. In 1902 he also became principal of the Howe Institute, a coeducational normal school, where he taught theology and law, among other subjects. He served as president of the institute until 1912, when it merged with Roger Williams College.

Fuller's abilities and character were widely recognized in the black community. He remained active in the National Baptist Convention, serving as a secretary for twenty-five years. President Theodore Roosevelt briefly considered appointing Fuller ambassador to Liberia in 1906, but much to Fuller's relief, the appointment never materialized.

An author of note, Fuller wrote on a variety of subjects, but race was an important theme in most of his works. His memoir, *Twenty Years in Public Life: 1890–1910, North Carolina-Tennessee* (1910), provides an excellent overview of his political, educational, and ministerial careers. Furthermore, it is an excellent case study of the triumphs and tribulations of a black leader in the Jim Crow South. In *Banks and Banking* (1920) Fuller outlined the steps necessary to organize and manage a bank as an attempt to stimulate the growth of a black financial community. *Pictorial History of the American Negro* (1933), *Negro Baptists in Tennessee* (1936), and *Story of Church Life among Negroes* (1938) contain useful biographical information about black leaders and insight into the social life of blacks in the early twentieth century. Other works include *Flashes and Gems of Thought and Eloquence* (1920), *Bridging the Racial Chasms: A Brief Survey of Inter-Racial Attitudes and Relations* (1937), and *Notes on Parliamentary Law* (1940).

Although Fuller married four times, little is known of his spouses or the dates of his marriages. His first wife was Lucy G. Davis. With his second wife, Laura Faulkner, he had two sons, only one of whom survived childhood. Little is known of his third wife, Rosa, and his fourth wife, Dixie Williams. His first three marriages ended with the death of each wife.

After his death in Memphis, Fuller was eulogized as a great minister, teacher, and leader of the black community. Through his educational, religious, and political efforts, he attempted to better the lives of his fellow blacks during a tumultuous time in American history. Although he is not as well known as many of his contemporaries, Fuller's drive, eloquence, and example helped pave the way for future black leaders in the quest for civil rights.

FURTHER READING

Fuller, Thomas Oscar. *Twenty Years in Public Life: 1890–1910, North Carolina-Tennessee* (1910).

Edmonds, Helen G. *The Negro and Fusion Politics in North Carolina, 1894–1901* (1951).

Obituary: *National Baptist Voice*, 15 July 1942.

This entry is taken from the *American National Biography* and is published here with the permission of the American Council of Learned Societies.

RICHARD D. STARNES

Fuller, William Edward, Sr. (29 Jan. 1875–20 Jan. 1958), preacher, bishop of the Fire-Baptized Holiness Church of God of the Americas, and Pentecostal leader, was born in Mountville, South Carolina, to sharecroppers, George and Martha Fuller. His father died when he was still a boy, and he was raised largely by his aunt, Ida Fuller Vance, and his grandparents, Richard and Mahulda Fuller. Like many other African American youths in the post–Civil War South, he hungered for a full education, and he walked five miles to his log cabin schoolhouse where he learned to read and write. The young Fuller developed a deep religious faith and became a devoted member of New Hope Methodist Church in Mountville, where he was converted under the ministry of the Reverend W. Burgess. New Hope was one of the many Methodist churches that entered the region after the war and drew black members from Southern, white-dominated denominations. Fuller served as a class leader and a steward before receiving a ministerial license while still in his teens. Often penniless and poorly attired, he preached in small churches, homes, and on street corners to anyone who would listen.

Fuller's search for religious power and righteousness drew him to the holiness movement, which, like Northern-based Methodist denominations, gained ground in the American South following the Civil War. Holiness converts found inspiration in the words of Paul in Romans 12:1–2 [AV]. The new movement, coupled with the institutionalization of Jim Crow laws, divided black and white churches and pitted evangelicals in the region against one another. Perfectionists like Fuller denounced the many ordinary pleasures and conveniences that helped characterize the New South: Sunday newspapers, Coca-Cola, theater attendance, pew rentals in churches, and whatever else they deemed wicked. Mainline officials in traditional Protestant churches decried the "holy rollers" and religious "cranks" who poisoned their churches, and in turn, holiness and later Pentecostal folk railed against dead churches and "whisky-drinking backsliders."

In 1895 Fuller claimed to have experienced sanctification, or being made sinless, in a cornfield, not in a church. In December of that year he married his first wife, Martha Fuller. Fuller married two other times, and with his third wife, Emma Clare Fuller, he had seven children. To support his growing family, he supplemented his preaching income by laboring for the Seaboard Railroad Company, doing odd jobs on farms, and working for the Vanderbilt Estate in Asheville, North Carolina.

Fuller, like many other blacks and whites in the region who embraced holiness and Pentecostalism, was a zealous religious adventurer, always seeking what initiates called "greater works of the Spirit." So, in 1897 when the young preacher heard of a new, radical holiness group called the Fire-Baptized Holiness Association, he enthusiastically joined it. The white Fire-Baptized leader from Iowa, B. H. Irwin, preached a "baptism of fire," as described in Matthew 3:11, and proclaimed the second coming of Jesus. Fuller read of Irwin's mystical fire experience in the pages of *The Way of Faith*, a perfectionist newspaper in South Carolina. After seeing that testimony, Fuller "went down before God and got the wonderful experience of fire, which filled my entire being." He subsequently broke ties with the sedate Methodists of Mountville.

In 1898 Fuller took a mule he borrowed from his brother and made a forty-mile journey from Mountville to Anderson, South Carolina, where he attended the national convention of the Fire-Baptized Holiness Association. On his way to the meeting, he later recalled, he unloosed his necktie and tossed it into a ditch, never to wear one again. Fire-Baptized Holiness believers were strict, austere perfectionists. The faithful could not wear ties, drink coffee, or eat pork, and in these early years, some declared that they would rather hang a snake around their neck than wear a tie.

The only African American present at the Anderson meeting, Fuller was invited into the egalitarian fellowship and elected as a member of the church's executive board. Joseph H. King and other Fire-Baptized leaders then sent Fuller out to set up churches in African American communities. He preached to whites and blacks across the former Confederacy in these years and succeeded where white stalwarts failed. A 1904 report on Fuller's work showed five hundred conversions and a host of new Fire-Baptized churches set up in South Carolina, North Carolina, and Georgia. By 1908 the new church had caved to the forces of Jim Crow, and members of the fellowship agreed to separate along racial lines. That same year in Greer, South Carolina, Fuller gathered 988 members into an independent, Colored Fire-Baptized Holiness Church. That body changed its name in 1922 to the Fire Baptized Holiness Church of God. In 1926 the church's greater emphasis on missions led to its current name, the Fire-Baptized Holiness Church of God of the Americas (FBHCGA).

Under Fuller's leadership, the new church began to publish a periodical in 1909 called *The True Witness*. Through that organ and from pulpits across the South, the denomination distinguished itself on doctrine: sanctification as a second definite work of grace, baptism with the Holy Ghost and fire, tongues speaking, divine healing, and an emphasis on the premillennial second coming of Jesus. Members who joined the exodus of the Great Migration would plant Fire-Baptized churches in Philadelphia, New York, Chicago, Detroit, and Cincinnati. Although the denomination is still centered in Georgia and South Carolina (headquarters and a church-sponsored school are in Greenville), FBHCGA churches can be found all over the United States, as well as Jamaica, the Virgin Islands, and England. In 1994 the church Fuller organized reported a membership of 24,406 in 1,003 churches and missions. When Fuller died in 1958, his son, W. E. Fuller Jr., became bishop of the FBHCGA. The elder Fuller was a leading force in the spread of the black holiness and Pentecostal movement. His rousing oratory and successful church organization prepared the ground for larger denominations in the region, such as the Church of God in Christ and the United Holy Church.

FURTHER READING

Synan, Vinson. *Old Time Power: The Centennial History of the International Pentecostal Holiness Church* (1998).

RANDALL J. STEPHENS

Fulson, Lowell (31 Mar. 1921–6 Mar. 1999), blues guitarist, vocalist, and recording artist, was born of African American and Choctaw parents on a reservation in Tulsa, Oklahoma. Lowell was the first of four children. Little is known of Fulson's early years in Tulsa except that he was heavily exposed to the musical styles that later served as the two major formative influences on his long career: Western swing, exemplified by the recordings of Bob Wills, and classic gospel music. Fulson's was a highly musical family: his grandfather played violin, and his two uncles played guitar. It was from these two uncles that Lowell and his younger brother Martin learned to play. Lowell Fulson began his career in 1939–1940 under the veteran country bluesman Alger "Texas" Alexander—Fulson replaced an as-yet-unknown guitarist named Chester Burnett—touring Oklahoma and Texas with Alexander's band.

Fulson was drafted by the United States Navy in 1943 and was stationed in Oakland, California. Upon completion of his tour of duty in 1945, Fulson

Lowell Fulson, blues singer famous for his 1954 hit "Reconsider Baby," holding a Gretsch guitar. (AP Images.)

remained in California, one of several notable exceptions to the larger trend of African American blues musicians migrating from the South to Chicago at the war's end. By 1948 Fulson was part of the burgeoning "West Coast jump blues" scene, which included such notables as ROY MILTON, Roy Brown, and Johnny Otis. Fulson formed his first band—which featured his brother Martin on rhythm guitar and RAY CHARLES on piano—in 1946, and he recorded his first 78s for Big Time Records in that year as well.

However, 1948 was Fulson's first great year. His first smash hit, "3 O'Clock Blues" (later covered by B. B. KING, among others), was recorded, and he was quickly signed by the impresario Jack Lauderdale of Swing Time Records. Under this label Fulson churned out a series of hits, the most memorable of which were "Every Day I Have the Blues," "Lonesome Christmas," and "Low Society Blues." Fulson augmented his reputation as one of the most popular and influential blues guitarists of the 1950s not only through his records but also through his relentless touring. Fulson's reputation brought him to the attention of Chess Records, which at that time sought to broaden its appeal beyond Chicago and the Mississippi Delta; it signed Fulson to a long-term recording contract in 1954.

Moving to Chess's "Checker" label brought Fulson immediate rewards: it earned him the biggest hit of his career, "Reconsider Baby" (1954), whose massive popularity can be gauged not only in terms of record sales but also in terms of the numerous cover versions that it spawned (Elvis Presley's, for one). However, after "Reconsider" Fulson's career went into the doldrums for a full decade; this was odd considering that his recorded material boasted the same driving combination of guitar and piano and the same robust lyrical stylings found in "Reconsider."

Fulson remained within the Chess fold until 1962 when he joined the Los Angeles–based Kent Records. The change of label once again produced immediate results: "Black Nights" (1965) represented a commercial return to form, even as it and "Tramp" (1967) represented a slight departure from the familiar West Coast jump style in favor of the funk and rhythm and blues sound coming out of Philadelphia and Memphis at that time. As with "3 O'Clock Blues" and "Reconsider Baby," "Tramp" spawned cover versions whose popularity soon eclipsed that of the original—in this case, the cover versions by OTIS REDDING and Carla Thomas, released within a few months of Fulson's version.

"Black Nights" and "Tramp" were followed up by some lesser-known hits, such as "I'm a Drifter" (1967) and "Let's Go Get Stoned" (1968), but these were not enough to prevent Fulson from jumping labels yet again—this time to Jewel Records, owned by his old friend Stan Lewis, who was busily stockpiling authentic blues talent in an ambitious attempt to replace Chess Records. This migration ushered in two quieter decades for Fulson, who never stopped touring or recording but who failed to crack the high end of the charts, though his ill-advised cover of the Beatles' "Why Don't We Do It in the Road?" (1970) did gain him some notoriety.

Nevertheless Fulson maintained a well-deserved status as a blues "old master" into the early 1990s—a status that was confirmed in 1993 when he was inducted into both the Rhythm and Blues Hall of Fame and the Blues Foundation's National Hall of Fame. Fulson garnered further acclaim that year when he won five W. C. HANDY awards, given annually by the national recording industry for excellence within the idiom. Fulson's last studio album, *Them Update Blues*, was nominated for a Grammy in 1995 under the category of Best Traditional Blues Album. Arguably at the height of his critical acclaim Fulson went back on the road, where until this latest spate of awards he had always enjoyed his greatest popularity. However, arguably as the result of four decades of almost tireless touring, his health began to deteriorate, and in 1997 a combination of kidney disease, diabetes, and congestive heart failure forced Fulson reluctantly to retire from touring. In the last two years of his life Fulson remained active in the studio, contributing guitar tracks to the albums of old friends like Jimmy Rogers. On 6 March 1999, Lowell Fulson died of congestive heart failure in Long Beach, California, his home for fifteen years. He was survived by his longtime girlfriend, Tina Mayfield, with whom he had two sons, Lowell Jr. and Richard, and two daughters, Yvonne and Edna.

Lowell Fulson never quite achieved the widespread fame that many on the blues scene felt that he so richly deserved. One commentator has labeled him "the most famous bluesman nobody ever heard of." However, his influence on the blues genre is not to be underestimated. His legacy first and foremost was as a performer who consistently pleased crowds all across the country for more than five decades with a guitar style that was simultaneously contemporary and steeped in the great country blues of Fulson's youth. In addition Fulson must be credited with a central role, along with T-BONE

WALKER, Roy Milton, and Johnny Otis, in fusing West Coast jump with Texas-style swing to create a dynamic alternative to the Mississippi–Chicago matrix in African American musical culture.

FURTHER READING

Center for the Study of Southern Culture, University of Mississippi. *Living Blues Blues Directory* (1989–).

Cohn, Lawrence. *Nothing but the Blues: The Music and the Musicians* (1993).

Obituary: *New York Times*, 8 Mar. 1999.

DISCOGRAPHY

Lowell Fulson (Chess Records CH2-92504).

Sinner's Prayer (Night Train Records 7011).

Them Update Blues (Bullseye Blues 9558).

ANDREW JAMES KELLETT

Fulwood, Sam (28 Aug. 1956–), journalist, lecturer, and educator, was born Samuel Fulwood III in Charlotte, North Carolina, the eldest son of Hallie Massey, a schoolteacher, and the Reverend Samuel L. Fulwood Jr. Fulwood and his younger brother George were raised in McCrorey Heights, a middle-class black community in Charlotte. Despite his parents' efforts to shelter their children from the evils of racism, racial issues eventually invaded the Fulwood refuge. Fulwood's earliest recollection of racial injustice occurred in the early 1960s when he and his brother George begged their parents to ride the donkeys in the parking lot of Clark's Department Store in downtown Charlotte. Young Samuel could not understand why his skin color prohibited him from riding the donkeys. "I was not prepared for any of this. It was the first time I was made aware of the fact that white people had any power to deny my wishes" (Fulwood, *Waking from the Dream*, 17).

While in sixth grade Fulwood was one of a half-dozen black students from his elementary school selected to integrate the previously all-white Ranson Junior High. The elementary school principal, Gwen Cunningham, assured him that he could do his "best, even if white children are in the same classroom" (Fulwood, *Waking from the Dream*, 25). Though his application was rejected without reasonable explanation, Fulwood felt empowered. "Mrs. Cunningham had set my life on a new mission, one I accepted because she made me feel special, needed and chosen. I could not refuse. I could not fail" (Fulwood, *Waking from the Dream*, 26).

Court-ordered busing went into effect in Charlotte in 1971 when Fulwood entered the ninth grade. He continued, despite being surrounded by racial tension, to excel in school and won the East Mecklenburg Optimist Club Oratorical Contest in 1971. Fulwood, the only black student in the competition, won the next round.

His high school involvement with *The Rambler*, the school newspaper that he coedited his senior year, sparked his interest in journalism. Fulwood's mother was not happy when he chose to major in journalism at the University of North Carolina at Chapel Hill, hoping that he would choose a more secure future as an education major at Johnson C. Smith University, a historically black college in Charlotte. Fulwood came into his own at Chapel Hill, finding a supportive community of black students, who were outnumbered by white students twenty to one.

An active member of the Black Student movement and Alpha Phi Alpha fraternity, Fulwood became a reporter for the student newspaper, the *Daily Tar Heel*, "because it served two purposes—it got me involved in a campus activity and it helped advance my career in journalism" (Fulwood, *Waking from the Dream*, 62). His involvement with the paper aided him when he began his job search after college, particularly since the publisher of the *Charlotte Observer* was a former *Daily Tar Heel* editor.

After earning his B.A. in journalism in 1978 Fulwood entered the *Charlotte Observer*'s newsroom as a police beat reporter and later became a sports reporter. While at the *Charlotte Observer* he met Cynthia Bell, a receptionist at the *Charlotte News*. A huge sports fan and more knowledgeable about football than was Fulwood, Bell accompanied him on some of his assignments. Their relationship grew and in 1984 they were married.

Having honed his journalistic skills, Fulwood was approached by the *Charlotte Observer*'s business editor to join his staff. A year later, as the paper launched its new "Business Monday" section, Fulwood was offered a promotion. In 1983 Fulwood's front-page coverage of the NAACP Convention garnered national attention. Soon after, Fulwood joined the staff of the *Baltimore Sun* as business writer.

Racial controversy exploded throughout Baltimore when the *Evening Sun* published a series of stories in December 1984 depicting the lifestyles of an overwhelming number of black families headed by young women. The black community in Baltimore felt that the paper was "mean-spirited" and "one-sided" in its coverage, and the local NAACP chapter met to organize a protest against the newspaper's treatment of blacks in Baltimore. Resolution talks resulted in the newspaper's hosting a series of community gatherings where concerned black Baltimoreans could meet the editors. Fulwood's attempt to clarify the argument for each side led to his becoming an editorial writer at the *Sun*.

A stint as a foreign correspondent in Johannesburg, South Africa, the following year awakened Fulwood from his ideal vision of the American dream. During the height of apartheid, his foreign status allowed him access to restaurants, theaters, clubs, and other places that black South Africans were prohibited by law from visiting. After witnessing firsthand the undisguised discrimination of apartheid, Fulwood vowed never to visit any place where black South Africans were prohibited. "Being there was like living within a Picasso, surreal and disjointed, yet exciting and colorful" (Fulwood, *Waking from the Dream*, 163).

Fulwood was a Livingston Award finalist for international reporting in 1986. In 1987 he accepted a position as assistant business editor at the *Atlanta Constitution*, just weeks after his daughter, Katherine Amanda, was born. A 1988 first-place recipient of Unity Awards in Media for economic reporting, he became a Washington correspondent for the *Los Angeles Times* in 1989 and created a race relations beat. A contributor to the 1992 Pulitzer Prize Spot News reporting coverage for the Los Angeles riots, Fulwood received several honors, including a 1993–1994 Nieman Fellowship at Harvard, a 2000 Institute of Politics fellowship at Harvard, and the 2001 National Association of Black Journalists' Salute to Excellence for newspaper commentary. In 2000 Fulwood joined the staff of the *Cleveland Plain Dealer* as a columnist. He co-hosted the PBS show *The Calling* and was a frequent keynote speaker and panelist on issues of race relations and diversity. In 2004 Fulwood was an inaugural Presidential Fellow in the SAGES program at Case Western Reserve University in Cleveland, where he taught a seminar, Media Literacy: Racial Images, Pop Culture and Public Policy, Private Choices.

FURTHER READING

Fulwood, Sam. *Full of It: Strong Words and Fresh Thinking for Cleveland* (2004).

Fulwood, Sam. *Waking from the Dream: My Life in the Black Middle Class* (1996).

TREVY A. MCDONALD

Funnye, Capers C., Jr. (14 Apr. 1952–), rabbi, educator, and one of America's best-known black Jews, was born Capers Charles Funnye Jr., in Georgetown, South Carolina, to Charles Funnye Sr. and Verdelle, native South Carolinians. Raised in the African Methodist Episcopal (AME) Church, Funnye nearly attended the seminary to become a minister. He grew up on Chicago's South Side, where his parents had moved when he was a child, and he saw the effects of segregation firsthand. After MARTIN LUTHER KING JR. was assassinated, he wanted to do something to change society and fight racism. In his senior year in high school, a pastor he respected suggested that he would make a good minister, and for a time, he seriously considered it. But he had been having doubts about Christianity and embarked on a search for the right spiritual path. Ultimately, he encountered members of a sect called the Hebrew Israelites. They were African Americans who practiced their own unique form of Judaism. In the early 1900s they were usually referred to by the press as the "Commandment Keepers," or "Ethiopian Hebrews," and the headquarters of their movement was in Harlem, although members could be found in cities like Chicago. The founder and leader of the Commandment Keepers was WENTWORTH A. MATTHEW, a self-proclaimed rabbi who believed that Judaism was the true religion of black people and that slave masters had taken this religion away from them. Mainstream denominations of Judaism did not accept the Commandment Keepers as Jews because they had never formally converted. But the group believed such conversion was not necessary. The Commandment Keepers believed that they had originally been Jewish, and now they were once again observing Jewish law, studying Jewish texts, and living in accordance with Jewish custom. They even established their own seminary to train future rabbis. As Funnye began to learn more about Judaism, he found the Jewish teachings so meaningful that by the late 1970s, he had enrolled in the Hebrew Israelite School in New York for further study. He decided to become a rabbi and was ordained by the Israelite Rabbinic Academy in the early 1980s. He took the Hebrew name "Shmuel" (Samuel) in honor of his grandfather on his father's side.

One of the challenges for Rabbi Funnye was combating the stereotypic image of the American Jew as somebody whose ancestors are from Europe. That may have been true at one time, but demographic studies showed that a growing number of Jews in the United States were nonwhite. Some were born into biracial families, some converted to Judaism. Estimates vary, but several studies have found that between fifty thousand to one hundred thousand African Americans practice Judaism. And yet, the rabbi frequently met people, including Jews, who wondered if he was "really Jewish." That was why he felt it was so important for Jews of color to establish relationships with the mainstream, largely white, Jewish establishment, so that meeting a black Jew would no longer be seen as something unusual. While many Commandment Keepers and Ethiopian Hebrews remained outside the mainstream community, Rabbi Funnye did not. He pursued further education, attending Chicago's Spertus College of Judaica (later the Spertus Institute of Jewish Studies), where he received a B.A. in Jewish Studies and an M.S. in Human Service Administration. Then in 1985 he decided to convert to Conservative Judaism. Asked by a reporter why he had done so, he explained that "[a]lthough I felt a distinct connection with the ancient Israelites, the majority of American Jews are Ashkenazi [of European descent] ... So I didn't consider going through conversion to be taking anything away from me. To me, personally, I saw it as adding something. It was saying, I am your brother. I remove every semblance of doubt that any in your quarter might have regarding my sincerity" (Fishkoff, *Jerusalem Post).*

In February 1991 he became the rabbi of a mostly black synagogue in Chicago, Beth Shalom B'Nai Zaken Ethiopian Hebrew Congregation. The congregation grew so much under his leadership that it had to move to a larger building in 2004. Many of the members have been born into the Ethiopian Hebrew movement, while others have chosen to join. Some followed their rabbi's lead and underwent a formal conversion, although Rabbi Funnye preferred to call it a "reversion," because he believed that "blacks who are Jews ... are reverting to their own past" (Beiser, *Jerusalem Report*, Dec. 1996). He has described his synagogue as "Conservadox," referring to rituals and customs that blend Conservative and Orthodox Jewish practice, but the congregation's musical influences are African and Caribbean (Fishkoff, 4B).

Since he was both black and Jewish, Rabbi Funnye was frequently in demand as a guest speaker. He traveled to college campuses and spoke at both Jewish and interfaith conferences, frequently dispelling stereotypes that African Americans and European Jews had about each other. He was known as a passionate spokesperson for Jewish diversity, and at many of his speaking engagements he was the first Jew of color the audience had ever met. Known as someone who could build bridges between communities, he engaged in dialogue with such members of the black community as the outspoken Muslim minister LOUIS FARRAKHAN. Farrakhan had made controversial comments about the Jews and Judaism. In an effort to debunk the stereotypes Minister Farrakhan seemed to believe, Rabbi Funnye participated in a series of meetings with him. Rabbi Funnye was also a member of Brit Tzedek v'Shalom (the Jewish Alliance for Justice and Peace), which worked to bring about a negotiated two-state solution and an end to conflict between Israelis and Palestinians.

In 1995 Rabbi Funnye was one of the founders of the National Alliance of Black Jews. That project was short-lived, but it led to his work with the San Francisco–based Institute for Jewish and Community Research, where he served as a senior research associate. Rabbi Funnye was a delegate and speaker at the 2004 Parliament of the World's Religions held in Barcelona, Spain—a three-day gathering of religious and spiritual leaders from all faiths and traditions. In 2005 he was a participant in a national conference on Jews and Social Justice, where he was cofacilitator of a workshop on building and encouraging Jewish diversity.

Among the many groups to which Rabbi Funnye devoted his time are Chicago's Du Sable Museum of African American History, the Jewish Council on Urban Affairs, and the American Jewish Congress. In 1997 he became the first Jew of color elected to the Chicago Board of Rabbis. He became the vice president of the Israelite Board of Rabbis, and in 2005 he was involved in ordaining two new rabbis at his Chicago synagogue.

He and his wife Mary (Miriam), who were married on 8 May 1976, had four children.

FURTHER READING

Beiser, Vince. "Funnye's Flock," *Jerusalem Report* (Dec. 1996).

Fishkoff, Sue. "Black and Jewish in America," *Jerusalem Post*, 2 Apr. 1999.

Nussbaum Cohen, Debra. "The Color of Inclusion: West Coast Conference Brings Together Jews of Color from Across the Globe to Celebrate Diversity," *The Jewish Week* (Feb. 2005).

Phillips, Aliza. "Black Hebrews Seek to Bridge Gap with White Jews: Claiming Return to Ancestral Religion, 'Soldiers of the Lord' See No Need to Convert," *Forward* (July 2000).

Working, Russell. "A Synagogue Twice Blessed," *Chicago Tribune* (June 2004).

DONNA HALPER

Fuqua, Harvey (27 July 1929–6 July 2010), singer, songwriter, producer, and record executive, was born in Louisville, Kentucky. He was the nephew of Charlie Fuqua, who was the guitarist for the Ink Spots, a popular 1940s vocal group. Harvey Fuqua, at the age of fourteen, began singing songs by the Ink Spots and other artists on street corners with his friends. In 1949, he was a member of a vocal duo, and after moving to Cleveland in the early 1950s, Fuqua was a founder of the Crazy Sounds, the jazz vocal group that evolved into the Moonglows, a major doo-wop group of the 1950s. Among the Moonglows' classic hit recordings are "Sincerely" (1954), written by Fuqua, and "The Ten Commandments of Love" (1958), which was released with the group's new name, Harvey and the Moonglows. Shortly thereafter, the other members of the group quit, and Fuqua transformed the Marquees, a Washington, D.C., group that included nineteen-year-old MARVIN GAYE, into Harvey and the Moonglows. Although the group disbanded by the early 1960s, Fuqua, cognizant of Gaye's talent, continued to mentor Gaye.

Fuqua and Gaye moved to Detroit, where Fuqua worked for Anna Records, which was co-owned by Gwen Gordy. Fuqua and Gordy married, and they established the Tri-Phi and Harvey record labels in 1961. The Spinners, Shorty Long, and Johnny Bristol, as well as Junior Walker and the All Stars were among the artists who recorded on the labels before the Fuquas dissolved the record labels and sold their artists' contracts (including Marvin Gaye's) to Motown Records in 1963. BERRY GORDY JR., Motown's founder and Fuqua's brother-in-law (the Fuquas later divorced), chose Fuqua to head the Artist Development Department, which was created to improve the entertainers' stage presence and refine their public image. Fuqua hired the choreographer Cholly Atkins, musical director Maurice King, and charm school maven Maxine Powell to assist Motown's young artists. During Fuqua's tenure at Motown, he continued to write and produce. After selecting MARY WELLS and Kim Weston to record duets with Marvin Gaye, Fuqua paired Gaye with Tammi Terrell, and they recorded Motown's most popular duets.

Fuqua and Johnny Bristol formed a highly successful songwriting and producing partnership. They wrote hit songs such as Gaye and Terrell's "If I Could Build My Whole World around You"

Harvey Fuqua sits in his home in Concord, North Carolina, in 2000. (AP Images.)

(1967), Edwin Starr's "Twenty-Five Miles" (1969), Junior Walker and the All Stars' "What Does It Take" (1969), David Ruffin's "My Whole World Ended" (1969), and DIANA Ross and the Supremes' "Someday We'll Be Together" (1969). These records, with the exception of the Supremes' hit, were coproduced by Fuqua and Bristol. Their additional production credits include Junior Walker and the All Stars' "How Sweet It Is" (1966); Gaye and Terrell's "Ain't No Mountain High Enough" (1967), "Your Precious Love" (1967), and "If This World Were Mine" (1967).

When Motown relocated to Los Angeles in the early 1970s, Fuqua left the company and signed on as a producer at RCA Records. He produced hit records for New Birth including "I Can Understand It" (1973), "It's Been a Long Time" (1974), "Wildflower" (1974), and "Dream Merchant" (1975). During the disco era, Fuqua discovered Sylvester and Two Tons of Fun (before they became the Weather Girls) and produced hit records for both acts including SYLVESTER's "You Make Me Feel" (1978) and Two Tons of Fun's "Just Us" (1980). In 1982 Fuqua worked with Gaye again in the recording studio as a production advisor for Gaye's "Midnight Love," his last album before his death in 1984. Fuqua was also a background vocalist on "Sexual Healing," the album's mega-hit and Grammy Award–winning single.

The Moonglows were the recipients of the Rhythm and Blues Foundation's Pioneer Award in 1995, and they were inducted into the Vocal Group Hall of Fame in 1999 and the Rock and Roll Hall of Fame in 2000. Also in 2000, Fuqua founded Resurging Artists Records in order to promote his contemporaries who remained active in the music industry.

Harvey Fuqua died on 6 July 2010 in Detroit. He is survived by his third wife, Dr. Carolyn Fuqua, who is the founder of Circles of Light Ministries; children; grandchildren; and other relatives including the film director Antoine Fuqua.

FURTHER READING

Ritz, David. *Divided Soul: The Life of Marvin Gaye* (1985).

Smith, Jessie Carney, ed. "Harvey Fuqua," in *Notable Black American Men Book II* (2006).

Obituaries: *Louisville Courier-Journal*, 7 July 2010. *New York Times*, 7 July 2010. *Washington Post*, 8 July 2010. *Los Angeles Sentinel*, 15 July 2010.

LINDA M. CARTER

Furbush, William Hines (1839–3 Sept. 1902), photographer, politician, sheriff, assayer, barber, and lawyer, was born a slave in Carroll County, Kentucky. William Hines Furbush became a member of the Arkansas General Assembly as well as the first sheriff of Lee County, Arkansas. His Arkansas political career began in the Republican Party at the close of Reconstruction and ended in the Democratic Party just as political disfranchisement began.

Little is known about Furbush's early life, though his literacy suggests a formal childhood education. Around 1860 he operated a photography studio in Delaware, Ohio. In March 1862 he traveled to Union-controlled Helena in Phillips County, Arkansas, on *Kate Adams* and continued to work as a photographer. In Franklin County, Ohio, that December he married Susan Dickey. A few years later, in February 1865, he joined the Forty-second Colored Infantry at Columbus, Ohio. He received an honorable discharge at the rank of commissary sergeant in January 1866. Later that year he departed for Liberia on *Golconda*, an American Colonization Society (ACS) ship. "Willis H. Furbush" was listed in the ACS roll books as a twenty-seven-year-old photographer of the Presbyterian faith, with a "good" education and traveling with no family. He returned to the United States after just eighteen months.

According to the 1870 U.S. Census, Furbush was back in Arkansas, living in Phillips County with Susan Furbush and two young Furbush boys, Edward and Harry, and working as a photographer. He had property and real estate worth $2,500. In 1872 he was elected as a Republican representative to the General Assembly for the Eleventh District (Phillips and Monroe counties), a cotton-producing, black-majority district. While in the legislature Furbush became involved in civil rights issues. In February 1873 he assaulted two waiters after they refused him service in a Little Rock restaurant. He was fined $75. Two months later, following the passage of Arkansas's 1873 Civil Rights Act, he and three other prominent blacks (R. A. Dawson, J. R. Roland, and Lloyd G. Wheeler) were refused service in a saloon. The men filed suit against the bartender. The African American prosecutors Lloyd Wheeler and MIFFLIN WISTAR GIBBS won a verdict of $46.80 for the three plaintiffs—the only known successful prosecution under the 1873 Civil Rights Act.

Furbush's main accomplishment was the establishment of Lee County, Arkansas, with Marianna as the county seat. Strong opposition against the bill emerged from Phillips County, first under the name "Coolidge County" and then "Woodford County." Furbush persisted and finally pushed his bill through when the county's name was changed to honor Robert E. Lee. Following the legislation the Republican governor Elisha Baxter appointed Furbush sheriff.

With his first marriage apparently over, Furbush married Emma S. Owens on 7 April 1874 in Memphis. Owens, an eighteen-year-old schoolteacher from a prominent Memphis family, taught at LeMoyne Normal School in Memphis. From 1873 to 1879 Furbush served as Lee County's sheriff. He won reelection twice through a fusion political system that combined the voting power of black Republicans with the economic power of white Democrats. Ideally, fusion split uncontested political offices between parties to avoid political violence. Violence did emerge in Lee County when Republicans in October 1874, upset by Furbush's apparent manipulation of candidate names on the ballot and his campaign for the fusion ticket, confronted Furbush in the streets of Marianna. Furbush tussled with at least one black Republican before he was attacked with a knife from behind. Reacting to the cuts on his neck and face, Furbush shot and mortally wounded an "innocent" twenty-seven-year-old Tom Wood, the son of Dr. George Wood and brother of the future Democratic politician James E. Wood. Furbush survived, sent runners to rural Lee County to report that he had been attacked, and formed his own posse, composed of black field hands, to reestablish order and capture the "conspirators." The racial tensions escalated, and an African American mob gathered and began marching toward Marianna, reportedly to burn the town. The mob disbanded when James Wood and others confronted and stood the mob down.

Despite the Republican leanings of his constituents Furbush continued to move closer to the Democratic Party. In 1876 he was removed from his position as sheriff by a circuit judge for failure to respond to a writ of habeas corpus and to control a county prisoner. Against some Democrats' wishes the Democratic governor Augustus H. Garland reinstated him. Named the Democratic nominee for representative in late summer 1878, Furbush gave up his position as sheriff for a white candidate. Both the *Marianna Index* and the *Arkansas Gazette* praised his decision. The 1878 election season, notorious in Lee and Phillips counties for intimidation of Republicans and African Americans by Democratic militias, sent Furbush to the General Assembly as a Democrat—perhaps its first African American Democrat.

The 1879 session in the General Assembly was rocked by charges of bribery in the House's election of a U.S. senator. Furbush, a vocal proponent for the formation of an investigative committee, suddenly found his own character questioned. Furbush struck back with a vigorous defense, often clashing with the committee chairman and future governor W. M. Fishback. The investigation concluded with a final report but no criminal charges.

In March 1879, cleared of bribery charges, Furbush left for booming Colorado with plans to return in a month. However, it seems that Lee County's officials no longer favored him, and reports surfaced that claimed he had skipped out on his debts. Following his departure his wife, Emma, died from yellow fever in her native city of Memphis. Their newborn daughter Eve died of dysentery a few days later. In Colorado Furbush worked as an assayer in the mining town of Bonanza and was reportedly a gambler and barber in Denver. In Bonanza, Furbush shot and killed the town's constable and then narrowly escaped a lynch mob. At his trial in Saguache County, Furbush pleaded self-defense. After fifteen witnesses the jury returned with a verdict of not guilty. The Colorado *Saguache Chronicle* agreed that the trial was as "fair and impartial as could have been granted a man of any complexion" (14, 21 Sept. 1883). However, he may have fallen on hard times. In February 1884 the *Arkansas Gazette* reported that Furbush had attempted suicide by overdosing on morphine in Denver.

In November 1886 Furbush was teaching music in Washington Court House, Ohio. Two years later he was back in Little Rock again, inserting himself in Arkansas politics as a Democratic lawyer and activist. In December 1889 he and E. A. Fulton announced the publication of the *National Democrat*, a Democratic paper for "colored citizens of Arkansas." His goal of attracting black voters to the Democratic Party was largely unsuccessful. Nevertheless as the Republican "lily-white" movement gained in Arkansas, his biting rhetorical responses exposed the paradox of racist white Republicans.

Furbush's frustrations quite likely peaked in the early 1890s as Arkansas Democrats passed election and separate-coach laws that legally transformed blacks into second-class citizens. He soon left Little Rock for South Carolina and relocated to Savannah, Georgia, in 1900, living off a federal pension of $12 per month. He made a final move to the National Home for Disabled Veterans in Marion, Indiana, in October 1901.

Furbush's complex role in Arkansas African American history makes it difficult to categorize him. He has been either neglected or misunderstood by historians. Historical assessment of Furbush in Lee County ranges from racism to omission. Sadly there is no public tribute to his role in creating the county. However, in Marianna's town square there is a monument to Robert E. Lee and Confederate soldiers erected in 1910. A positive memory did survive within the black community, at least into the 1930s. A WPA interviewee recalled, "Every slave could vote after freedom. Some colored folks held office. I knew several magistrates and sheriffs. There was one at Helena and one at Marianna. He was a High Sheriff" (Wintory, 156–161).

FURTHER READING

Brown, Robert L. *Ghost Towns of the Colorado Rockies* (1968).

"The Colored Legislators," *Arkansas Gazette*, 1 Feb. 1873.

Dillard, Tom W. "'Golden Prospects and Fraternal Amenities': Mifflin W. Gibbs's Arkansas Years," *Arkansas Historical Quarterly* (1976).

Foner, Eric. *Freedom's Lawmakers: A Directory of Black Officeholders during Reconstruction* (1996).

"Negro Intimidation: Attorney Furbusch Tells What He Knows of the Practices in Pulaski County," *Arkansas Gazette*, 2 Aug. 1889.

Wall, Effie Allision. "Formation of Lee County," *Arkansas Historical Quarterly* (1949).

Wintory, Blake. "William Hines Furbush: African American, Carpetbagger, Republican, Fusionist, and Democrat," *Arkansas Historical Quarterly* (2004).

Obituary: *Marion Daily Leader* (IN), 3 Sept. 1902.

BLAKE WINTORY

Furniss, Henry Watson (14 Feb. 1868–20 Dec. 1955), physician and diplomat, was born in Brooklyn, New York, the older son of William Henry and Mary Elizabeth (Williams) Furniss. As a child he lived in Jackson, Mississippi, where his father served as assistant secretary of state under Secretary of State James R. Lynch, and later on the staff of the new Alcorn University. His sons were educated in the public schools of Indianapolis, Indiana, where William Furniss became superintendent of special delivery for the U.S. Post Office Department after 1877.

Henry Furniss began his professional studies at the medical department of the University of Indianapolis in 1887, transferring in 1890 to Howard University in Washington, DC, where he worked as a clerk for the U.S. Bureau of the Census to finance his studies. In 1891 he graduated from the Howard medical department, and later received a doctoral degree in pharmacy from Howard (1895). He also studied medicine at the postgraduate level at Harvard University in Boston in 1892 and at the New York Post-Graduate School and Hospital in 1894. After a year's internship as an assistant surgeon at Freedmen's Hospital in Washington, DC, Furniss established a private practice in Indianapolis with his younger brother, Sumner A. Furniss, a graduate of Indiana University's medical department, in 1896. There he quickly gained a strong reputation for both academic and professional excellence.

Henry Furniss's earlier census work had involved extensive study of international wealth, debt, and tax policies, leading to frequent correspondence with U.S. consuls abroad to acquire the necessary information. Indiana's Republican congressmen and other local leaders in Indianapolis, impressed with his abilities, endorsed the appointment of Furniss as a U.S. diplomat, and late that year, President William McKinley selected Furniss as the U.S. consul in Bahia, Brazil, a former colonial capital in the country's northeastern region. After passing the State Department's consular examination in early 1898, Furniss proceeded to Bahia, where he remained until 1905, having become fluent in Portuguese, in addition to his language skills in French and Spanish.

In November 1905, President Theodore Roosevelt appointed Dr. Furniss as the U.S. minister to Haiti, with the rank of envoy extraordinaire and minister plenipotentiary, to succeed William F. Powell, the longest-serving minister to Haiti in U.S. history. Now the highest-ranking U.S. black diplomat, Furniss remained envoy to Haiti through the Taft administration and into the first year of the Wilson administration. He resigned in September 1913, after seven years and nine months as minister, second only to Powell's tenure. Furniss was then succeeded as envoy to Haiti by Madison R. Smith, who was appointed by President Woodrow Wilson.

During his tenure in Haiti, Furniss gained a reputation for thoughtful reporting and skillful diplomacy during a particularly tense period for Haitian-American relations, and his dispatches to Washington were often reported in U.S. newspapers. During the political crisis of 1911, during which American bankers sought to force Haiti into receivership, the *New York Times* praised Furniss—described as "the colored man who represents us there"—as "a man of large caliber [who] knows almost every square mile of the country. Minister Furniss appreciates the crisis—a crisis made more acute by the fact that millions of American dollars are now involved" (3 Sept. 1911). For his efforts, however, Furniss was reportedly condemned by National City Bank vice president Roger L. Farnham as "hostile to American interests" (Schmidt, pp. 49–50).

Furniss was a member of a number of professional organizations, including the American Medical Association, the American Microscopical Society, the American Public Health Association, the Indiana Medical Society, and the American Society of International Law. He was also a thirty-third-degree Mason. Following his return from Haiti in 1913, Dr. Furniss and his family briefly returned to Indianapolis, before eventually settling in West Hartford, Connecticut, where he practiced medicine until his retirement in the early 1950s.

Furniss was married to Anna Wichmann of Hamburg, Germany, on 19 October 1904, in London, England. Their children were William R. Furniss, born in Haiti in 1912, and Elizabeth Furniss Prouix, born in Haiti in 1913.

Dr. Furniss died of pneumonia at age eighty-seven in Hartford, Connecticut, in 1955. His wife Anna died a year later.

FURTHER READING

"Furniss, Henry Watson." In *The National Cyclopedia of American Biography, Volume XIV,* (Supplement 1910).

Schmidt, Hans. *The United States Occupation of Haiti, 1915–1934* (1995).

BENJAMIN R. JUSTESEN

Futch, Eddie (9 Aug 1911–10 Oct 2001), boxing trainer who guided twenty-two fighters to championships, was born in Hillsboro, Mississippi, where his father was a sharecropper. His family moved to Detroit while Futch was still a child, and while growing up in the tough Black Bottom neighborhood he became a proficient athlete in boxing and basketball. In 1932 Futch won the lightweight boxing championship of the Detroit Athletic Association, and in 1933 he became the Detroit Golden Gloves lightweight champion. The five foot, seven inch tall, 135 pound fighter became friendly with the Motor City's future heavyweight boxing champion JOE LOUIS, then still an amateur, at the gym in the Brewster Recreation Center. Louis often sparred with the quicker Futch to improve his own speed and reflexes.

On the brink of his own professional career, Futch was forced to quit boxing because of a heart murmur. He began teaching boys to box, enforcing a strict code of behavior and never hesitating to throw out those who misbehaved—one of whom was the future champion SUGAR RAY ROBINSON. Futch showed natural talent as a mentor, but was unable at first to make a living as a coach and had to work various manual labor jobs to make ends meet. By the 1950s he was able to devote himself to training boxers on a full-time basis, and he began to work with professionals. In 1958 Futch became the first trainer to groom a California-born fighter into a champion when he guided welterweight Don Jordan to a world title.

Futch was a master strategist. With Jordan he emphasized the left jab as an effective weapon. When Jordan stepped into the ring to defend his title for the first time, he forgot the jab and sought a knockout with the right hand. After Jordan injured his right hand, Futch instructed him to return to the jab and Jordan won the fight. Futch went on to train leading fighters in several weight classes, including JOE FRAZIER, LARRY HOLMES, Trevor Berbick, Michael Spinks, and RIDDICK BOWE.

Futch developed a reputation for training his fighters to exploit the weaknesses in great opponents, and he played a role in handing MUHAMMAD ALI the first two defeats of his career. The "Fight of the Century" matched undefeated heavyweights Ali and Joe Frazier for the first time at Madison Square Garden on 8 March 1971. Futch, the strategic guru for manager Yank Durham, counseled Frazier to avoid Ali's uppercut and left jab by staying low, bobbing and weaving, and relentlessly pounding Ali's body. He prepared Frazier to wait until Ali's right hand lowered from fatigue, and then to quickly unload with his feared left hook when Ali started to throw his high uppercut. This Frazier did with spectacular success in the eleventh round when he landed a clean hard shot to Ali's face, and again in the fifteenth round when he crossed his left over Ali's uppercut to drop him on the canvas. Ali did get up to finish the fight, but Frazier had won handily.

The second man whom Futch guided to victory over Ali was the ex-Marine KEN NORTON. Futch trained Norton to jab as effectively as Ali, and to crowd Ali to prevent his throwing punches from a comfortable range. In the first of their three fights, Norton broke Ali's jaw early and pressed on to victory. Ali won their second and third fights, but they were narrow decisions and some commentators thought that Norton should have been awarded the third bout.

Ali also came back to beat Frazier twice, but in their third fight (1975), dubbed the "Thrilla in Manila," it was Eddie Futch who gained wide recognition for an act of compassion and wisdom. After fourteen furious rounds in which the momentum of the fight had turned twice, Frazier sat battered in his corner. Ali had come on in the late rounds and pounded Frazier's face until both eyes swelled nearly shut, leaving him effectively blind and a sitting duck for the upcoming final round. Futch acted to save his fighter from the possibility of grievous physical harm, later saying, "I knew Joe was a great father.... He loved those kids and those kids loved him.... I said, 'Now I can't let this man get hurt. All these kids are his life—and he is their life.' I said, 'If he wound up a vegetable, that would be one of the greatest tragedies of all time.... I just can't let this happen.'" Futch signaled to the referee that he would not allow Frazier to continue. Ali was the winner, but Frazier was remembered for his courage and Futch for his decency; nevertheless, Frazier resented the stopping of the fight.

Futch's long career wound on. When heavyweight champion Larry Holmes had a falling-out with his longtime trainer Richie Giachetti in 1983, Holmes brought Futch in to take over, but this ultimately led to a quandary for the trainer. After several victories with Futch in his corner, Holmes signed to fight Michael Spinks—also trained by Futch—on 21 September 1985. Futch elected to give up a big paycheck and withdraw from the fight entirely rather than choose between two of his fighters.

Eddie Futch, universally regarded as a rare man of honesty and integrity in a sport riddled with corruption, remained as tough and fair with his champions and their large egos as he had been with his young amateurs in the 1930s. When fighters slacked off in their training regimens, or ceased to listen to his instruction, Futch sometimes broke with them (though usually he was apologized to and asked back). Late in Futch's career, the 1988 Olympic silver medalist Riddick Bowe asked him to become his trainer. Futch, wary of Bowe's image as a lazy and undisciplined fighter, hesitated. Once on board, he changed Bowe's ways and guided him to the heavyweight title via a splendid upset of EVANDER HOLYFIELD.

Futch received several awards from the Boxing Writers Association of America, including the Al Buck award for Manager of the Year in 1975, Long and Meritorious Service in 1982, Trainer of the Year in both 1991 and 1992, and the James A. Farley Award for honesty and integrity in boxing in 1996. He was inducted into boxing's International Hall of Fame in 1994. In 1999 he served on a panel commissioned by the Associated Press to select the Fighter of the Century and the best fighters in ten weight classes.

Eddie Futch stepped away from active involvement in professional boxing at age eighty-six and died in Las Vegas, where he had long resided, two months after his ninetieth birthday. He was survived by his third wife Eva and three children.

FURTHER READING

Anderson, Dave. *In The Corner: Great Boxing Trainers Talk About Their Art* (1991).

Fried, Ronald K. *Corner Men: The Great Boxing Trainers* (1991).

Kram, Mark. *Ghosts of Manila: The Fateful Blood Feud Between Muhammad Ali and Joe Frazier* (2001).

DAVID BORSVOLD

Futrell, Mary Hatwood (24 May 1940–), educator, was born Mary Alice Franklin Hatwood in Altavista, Virginia. Born into a poor, working-class family, Futrell was raised by her mother, Josephine Austin, a factory worker and domestic. Futrell's parents divorced when she was young. Later, as an adult, she developed a relationship with her father, John Calloway, a construction worker. From the age of twelve, Futrell cleaned churches, homes, and businesses to help support her family.

In 1958, Futrell earned a high school diploma from Dunbar High School in Lynchburg, Virginia, where she was a member of the National Honor Society, Future Business Leaders of America, student government, and cheerleader squad. In 1962, Futrell graduated with a degree in business education from Virginia State College (later Virginia State University), a historically black college/university. While at Virginia State College, she was a member of Delta Sigma Theta Sorority and a cheerleader.

From 1962 to 1964, she was a high school teacher in the segregated schools of Alexandria, Virginia, and taught at the all-black Parker-Gray School. In 1965, she helped to integrate the teaching staff at George Washington High School where she taught business education until 1980.

Shortly after earning her master's degree in Secondary Education from Georgia Washington University, Futrell became chair of the business education department at Parker-Gray School. In 1976, she was elected president of the Virginia Education Association (VEA) and waged many successful battles on behalf of Virginia teachers and children. For example, in 1977 when the Virginia Supreme Court banned collective bargaining for public employees and struck down negotiated agreements that had worked well for Virginia teachers, Futrell took action. She led seven thousand teachers in a "Walk the Walk: We've Heard the Talk" march on Capitol Square in Richmond, Virginia, on 5 February 1977 in a show for education funding and collective bargaining legislation. At that time, the march was the largest ever to take place in Virginia. Similarly, when the retirement system for Virginia teachers was threatened by the General Assembly in 1978 and the grievance system was also under attack, the VEA under Futrell's leadership engaged in the Fair Pay for Teachers campaign for higher salaries to attract highly qualified teachers.

In 1978, during the closing days of her second term as VEA president, Futrell was elected to the board of directors for the National Education Association (NEA), the nation's largest organization of teachers, professors, and allied school employees. Two years later, she was elected to the NEA office of secretary-treasurer and was reelected to that position in 1982. In 1983, Futrell was elected president of the nearly two million-member NEA. Futrell, the third African American woman elected as president of NEA, served an unprecedented six-year term. NEA changed its bylaws to allow Futrell to serve a third term. During her presidency, from 1983 to 1989, she helped the organization expand its civil and human rights agenda and its advocacy of women's rights. As NEA president, Futrell initiated Operation Rescue, a national campaign focused on reducing the national dropout rate. Begun in 1985, the project awarded over $556,000 in grants to twenty-one dropout prevention programs around the country. This program represented but one example of Futrell's deep concern for disadvantaged children, as well as her remarkable resolve to initiate and enact change in underserved schools and communities. In honor of her unparalleled commitment to equal educational opportunity for women and girls and social justice in education, NEA annually bestowed the Mary Hatwood Futrell Award to an individual who best exemplifies Futrell's dedication to these causes.

Futrell joined the faculty at George Washington University in 1989 and earned an Ed.D. in Educational Policy Studies in 1992. From 1995 through the 2000s, she served as dean of the Graduate School of Education and Human Development at George Washington, and she was also a professor of education and director of the university's Institute for Curriculum, Standards, and Technology. A former president of several education and civic organizations, Futrell was noted for her tireless leadership to improve education and further democratic ideals worldwide. As president of ERAmerica, she helped to advance the organization's mission to achieve the passage of the Equal Rights Amendment to the U.S. Constitution and educational and economic parity for women and girls.

Futrell's firm belief in and constant fight for education for women and girls gained her worldwide recognition. From 1993 to 2004 Futrell served as the founding president of Education International, an organization that represents 29 million educators in 165 countries. In 1999, she received the United Nations Global Award for Peace and Education. At the 2004 International Conference on Education in Geneva, Switzerland, Futrell was named U.S. Laureate of the Jan Amos Comenius Medal. The award, created in 1992 by the United Nations Educational, Scientific and Cultural Organization (UNESCO) and the Ministry of National Education, Youth, and Sport of the Czech Republic, recognizes outstanding achievements and innovations in the fields of teaching and educational research. It is one of UNESCO's most prestigious honors. Futrell, one of only two Americans to ever receive the award, was nominated for her advocacy of education for all people (especially women and girls) and her relentless support of universal human rights and respect for diversity. According to Futrell, "Education is a global human right and a critical component of global progress."

Futrell served on the boards of the Institute for Educational Leadership, the Kettering Foundation, and the Carnegie Foundation for the Advancement of Teaching, and she held an appointment as a senior consultant for Quality Education for Minorities Network. She became a member of the editorial board for the prominent education journal, *Phi Delta Kappan*. In 2002, she was the recipient of the National Association for the Advancement of Colored People President's Award. In 2001, she received the David Imig Award for Distinguished Achievement in Teacher Education from the American Association of Colleges for Teacher Education. An international speaker, lecturer, author, and activist, Futrell received more than twenty honorary degrees. For her dedication to the improvement of quality and access in education, she was recognized by *Ebony* magazine as one of the most influential blacks in America and by

Ms. magazine as one of twelve Women of the Year. Her publications include research on education reform, K–12 and higher education policy, teacher leadership, national board certification for teachers, professional development of teachers, and minorities and women in education. Futrell's research and commentary articles appear in numerous scholarly journals including *Phi Delta Kappan*, *Educational Leadership*, *Educational Administration Quarterly*, *Foreign Language Annals*, and *Education Record.*

FURTHER READING

Johnson, Julie. "Retiring Teachers' Leader Calls For Restructuring of School System," *New York Times*, 3 July 1989.

LESLIE T. FENWICK

Gabriel (1776–10 Oct. 1800), slave and revolutionary, was born near Richmond, Virginia, at Brookfield, the Henrico County plantation of Thomas Prosser. The identity of Gabriel's parents is lost to history, but it is known that he had two older brothers, Martin and Solomon. Most likely, Gabriel's father was a blacksmith, the craft chosen for Gabriel and Solomon; in Virginia, the offspring of skilled bondpersons frequently inherited their parent's profession.

Status as an apprentice artisan provided the young craftsman with considerable standing in the slave community, as did his ability to read and write (a skill perhaps taught to him by the plantation mistress Ann Prosser). As Gabriel developed into an unusually tall young man, even older slaves looked to him for leadership. By the mid-1790s, as he approached the age of twenty, Gabriel stood "six feet two or three inches high," and the muscles in his arms and chest betrayed nearly a decade in Brookfield's forge. A long and "bony face, well made," was marred by the loss of two front teeth and "two or three scars on his head." His hair was cut short and was as dark as his complexion. Blacks and whites alike regarded him as "a fellow of courage and intellect above his rank in life."

During these years Gabriel married a young slave named Nanny (Nancy Prosser). Little is known about her, including the identity of her owner and whether she had any children with Gabriel. It is likely that she lived on a nearby farm or tobacco plantation.

In the fall of 1798 Gabriel's old master died, and ownership of Brookfield fell to twenty-two-year-old Thomas Henry Prosser. An ambitious young man with a Richmond townhouse and a lucrative auction business, Prosser increasingly maximized his profits by hiring out his surplus slaves. Even the most efficient planters could not find enough tasks to keep their slave artisans occupied year-round, and many masters routinely hired out their craftsmen to neighboring farms and urban businessmen. Despite all of the work to be done at Brookfield, Gabriel doubtless spent a considerable part of each month smithing in and around Richmond. Though no less a slave under Virginia law, Gabriel enjoyed a rough form of freedom as his ties to young Prosser became ever more tenuous.

Emboldened by this quasi liberty, in September 1799 Gabriel moved toward overt rebellion. Caught in the act of stealing a pig, a delicacy slaves used to supplement their meager diet, Gabriel refused to suffer his white neighbor's verbal abuse. Instead, he wrestled his tormentor to the ground and bit off the better "part of his left Ear." Under Virginia law, slaves were not tried as whites; instead they were prosecuted under a 1692 statute that established special segregated county tribunals known as courts of oyer and terminer composed of five justices of the peace. There was no jury and no route for appeal except to the governor. On 7 October Gabriel was formally charged with attacking a white man, a capital crime in Virginia. Although he was found guilty, Gabriel escaped the gallows through an ancient clause that, ironically, was now denied to white defendants. Slaves possessed the right of "benefit of clergy," which allowed them to escape hanging in favor of being branded on the thumb by a small cross if they were able to recite a verse from the Bible, an option available to Gabriel thanks to the Afro-Baptist faith of his parents. (There is no truth, however, to the Gilded Age myth that Gabriel was a messianic figure who wore his hair long in imitation of his hero Samson.)

Gabriel's branding and incarceration was the final indignity. By the early spring of 1800, his fury began to turn into a carefully considered plan to bring about his freedom—and the end of slavery in Virginia. As he explained it to his brothers Solomon and Martin, slaves from Henrico County would gather at the blacksmith shop at Brookfield on the evening of 30 August. As the small but determined band of insurgents—armed with crude swords fashioned from scythes—neared Richmond, it would split into three groups. The center column planned to swarm into Capitol Square and seize the guns stored in the building. Governor—and later U.S. president—James Monroe, slumbering in the adjacent executive mansion, was to be taken as a hostage but otherwise left unharmed. The other columns would set fire to Rocketts Landing, the warehouse district, as a diversion and then fortify the town. A small number of town leaders were to die, while most would live as hostages in order to force the Virginia elite to grant the rebels' demands, which included their freedom and an equitable division of city property. "Quakers, Methodists and French people," three groups who had earned a sometimes undeserved reputation as foes of slavery, were not to be harmed. The "poor white people," who had no more political power than did the slaves, "would also join" the rebels. If the town leaders agreed to Gabriel's demands, the slave general intended to "hoist a white flag" and drink a toast "with the merchants of the city."

Using their ability to hire their time away from their owners, Gabriel and his chief lieutenants contacted only those slaves whose talents and skills meant they had little contact with their owners. Recruiters moved north into Hanover, Goochland, and Caroline counties, while black mariners ferried word of the uprising down the James River to Petersburg, Norfolk, and Gloucester County.

The uprising, set to begin on the night of Saturday, 30 August, collapsed just before sunset on the appointed day when a severe thunderstorm hit southern Henrico. Creeks rose, washing away fragile wooden bridges and cutting off communications between Brookfield plantation and the city. Perhaps only a dozen slaves reached the blacksmith shop. The chaos of the storm convinced two Henrico house slaves, Tom and Pharaoh, that the revolt could not succeed. They informed their owner of the conspiracy, and he hurried word to Governor Monroe in Richmond. As the militia closed in, Gabriel escaped south by way of-the swampy Chickahominy River. After hiding along the James River for nearly two weeks, Gabriel decided to risk boarding the schooner *Mary*. Captain Richardson Taylor, a former overseer who had recently converted to Methodism, willingly spirited Gabriel downriver to Norfolk. There Gabriel was betrayed by Billy, a slave crewman who had heard of Monroe's three-hundred-dollar reward for Gabriel's capture. Returned to Richmond under heavy guard, Gabriel was found guilty of "conspiracy and insurrection." On 10 October 1800 the slave general died with quiet composure at the town gallows near Fifteenth and Broad. He was twenty-four. In all, twenty-six slaves, including Gabriel, were hanged for their part in the conspiracy. Another bondman allegedly hanged himself while in custody. Eight more rebels were transported to Spanish New Orleans; at least thirty-two others were found not guilty. Reliable sources placed the number of slaves who knew of the plot to be between five and six hundred.

Although the abortive uprising failed in its goals, southern whites were painfully aware that it was the most extensive and carefully planned slave plot yet devised in North America. In the aftermath, Virginia legislators labored to ensure that it would not be repeated. Intent on crushing black autonomy, the general assembly passed a number of laws abolishing black liberties, including the right to congregate on Sunday for religious services. After 1806 all manumitted slaves had twelve months to leave the state or be "apprehended and sold" back into bondage.

FURTHER READING

The trial records for Gabriel and his fellow conspirators are located in the Library of Virginia (Richmond). State newspapers covered the trials in great detail; the (Richmond) *Virginia Argus* and (Fredericksburg) *Virginia Herald* are especially useful. The papers of Thomas Jefferson and James Monroe, both in the Library of Congress, discuss the plot, as do the Tucker-Coleman Papers at the College of William and Mary; see also George Tucker's anonymous pamphlet, *Letter to a Member of the General Assembly of Virginia, on the Subject of the Late Conspiracy of the Slaves* (1801).

Aptheker, Herbert. *American Negro Slave Revolts* (1943).

Egerton, Douglas R. *Gabriel's Rebellion: The Virginia Slave Conspiracies of 1800 and 1802* (1993).
Mullin, Gerald. *Flight and Rebellion: Slave Resistance in Eighteenth-Century Virginia* (1972).
Schwarz, Philip J. *Twice Condemned: Slaves and the Criminal Law of Virginia, 1705–1865* (1988).

This entry is taken from the *American National Biography* and is published here with the permission of the American Council of Learned Societies.

DOUGLAS R. EGERTON

Gaddy, Bea (20 Feb. 1933–3 Oct. 2001), community activist, city councilwoman, and ordained minister, was born Beatrice Frankie Fowler in Wake Forest, North Carolina, to Maude Fowler, a domestic worker, and to a father who left when she was a toddler. In a 1989 *Baltimore Sun Magazine* article, Gaddy recalled "many days" that she and her four siblings (Mottie Fowler, Pete Young, Tony Fowler, and Mabel Beasly) "didn't eat because when my mother didn't work and couldn't bring home leftover food, there was nothing to eat. And, even when there was food, if my stepfather had been drinking, he'd come home and throw our plates out in the back yard or through the window." A high school dropout, Gaddy was divorced twice by her early twenties. As a single mother, she struggled for years to make a living for herself and her children (Cynthia, Sandra, John, Michael, and Pamela), working as a maid and as a nurse's assistant. At times, she relied on welfare.

In 1964, she moved her family to Baltimore, where she met and three years later married her third husband, Lacy Gaddy, a professional cook, who died in 1995. In the East Baltimore neighborhood where they lived, Gaddy developed a reputation as "that beggar lady." She hustled local grocery store owners for food for her family and for others who were poverty-stricken. She even searched garbage cans looking for edible food. She used her kitchen as a storage pantry from which she distributed food to those in need. While working as a crossing guard, she befriended the local attorney Bernard Potts. With his support, she obtained her high school diploma through a correspondence course and in 1977—at age forty-four—graduated from Antioch University's Baltimore division with a degree in Human Services. Potts helped her establish a corporation for the operation of her food center, which officially opened in October 1981. The following month, Gaddy won $290 in the lottery and used the money for a Thanksgiving Day meal for her family and thirty-nine neighbors, eating at tables set up on the sidewalk in front of her row house. That sidewalk became a center for those in need of donated shoes, clothing, household items, furniture, and nonperishable food.

By 1988 Gaddy had opened two shelters for homeless women and children and, with the help of volunteers, gave out donated food and gifts to approximately 3,000 people. The National Council of Negro Women honored her efforts that year with its Humanitarian Award. Her Thanksgiving dinners became an annual event and eventually were moved to a Baltimore city middle school in 1986 and then, in 2000, to a large recreation center in her East Baltimore neighborhood. By the late 1990s over 20,000 Baltimoreans were enjoying "Miss Bea's" full-course meals. A Homiletics Online article in March 2002 described how an "army" of more than 3,500 volunteers prepared and served the food, which included "80 tons of food, 30,000 paper plates, 50 cases of aluminum foil, 2,000 pumpkin pies, and 100 cases of sweet potatoes." She had recruited inmates from a state correctional facility to prepare the turkeys—a tradition that would continue for subsequent Thanksgivings.

In 1992 President George H. W. Bush named Gaddy the 695th member of his Thousand Points of Light—individuals who demonstrate exemplary volunteer service in their communities. That same year, the *Baltimore Sun* honored her as its Marylander of the Year. In 1994 Bea was inducted into the African American Hall of Fame in Atlanta, Georgia, and in 2000 the University of Maryland's board of regents honored her with its FREDERICK DOUGLASS Award. In 1999 she ran for Baltimore's city council and served her local district until her death in 2001 from breast cancer. By then she had begun work on a master's degree, and two months before her death she was ordained as a minister in a ceremony at Mount Pisgah African Methodist Episcopal (AME) Church in Columbia, Maryland.

When Gaddy died, Baltimore's mayor Martin O'Malley ordered city flags to be flown at half-mast. At her funeral service, the former mayor KURT SCHMOKE called her "the Mother Theresa [*sic*] of Baltimore" while the Maryland governor Parris Glendenning remarked that she had been "a beacon of hope for the homeless." The U.S. congressman Elijah Cummings, representing Maryland's Seventh Congressional District, wrote in a 13 October 2001 tribute printed in the *Baltimore AFRO-American* newspaper that Gaddy had inspired him to use what he had learned from his own background of poverty to work to "uplift others."

Soon after Gaddy's passing, the Baltimore City Council, led by its president, Sheila Dixon (later mayor), voted to sponsor an annual Bea Gaddy Day on or near the 3 October anniversary of her death. Every year, major business sponsors, medical institutions, and local police and fire stations in Baltimore join in commemorating Gaddy's service to the poor by helping to gather and distribute clothing and food. Free medical screenings for breast cancer and prostate cancer are offered to needy residents. Gaddy's daughter, Sandra, attributed her mother's accomplishments to one of her favorite Bible verses, Matthew 17:20 (Revised Standard Version): "If you have faith as a grain of mustard seed, you will say to this mountain, 'Move hence to yonder place,' and it will move; and nothing will be impossible to you." Gaddy spent her life moving mountains, cajoling others to donate time, money, and assistance so that the city's neediest could be fed, clothed, and sheltered. Her legacy continued through services provided by the Bea Gaddy Family Center established in 1989. In a fitting tribute, about two months after her death, her family shared Thanksgiving dinner with an estimated 45,000 other Baltimoreans.

A wax figure of Gaddy stands in Baltimore's National Great Blacks in Wax Museum. In November 2006 Gaddy was posthumously elected to the Maryland Woman's Hall of Fame.

FURTHER READING

Sandra Briggs, one of Bea's daughters, was helpful in providing information about her mother for this entry.

Cummings, Elijah E. "Bea Gaddy's Legacy: Seeing Ourselves through the Eyes of a Saint," *Baltimore AFRO American*, 13 Oct. 2001.

Kelly, J., Rasmussen, F. N., and Thompson, M. D., "Advocate 'Was Always on a Mission' for Poor," *Baltimore Sun*, 4 Oct. 2001.

Mikulski, Barbara. Comments regarding Mrs. Gaddy's passing, *Congressional Record*, 10 Oct. 2001.

Tyehimba, Afefe. "Shadow of Her Smile," *City Paper*, 4 Dec. 2002.

SANDRA KELMAN

Gaetjens, Joe (19 Mar. 1924–10 July 1964), soccer player, was born Joseph Nicolas Gaetjens in Port-au-Prince, Haiti, to a Belgian father and a Haitian mother. Some sources give his middle name as Edouard. Little is known about his early life before he immigrated to New York City as a twenty-three-year-old in 1947. There he studied accounting at Columbia University and paid his rent and tuition by washing dishes in a Manhattan restaurant. When the restaurant manager discovered that Gaetjens had played soccer for L'Étoile Haïtienne in Port-au-Prince, he arranged a trial for him with the Brookhattan team of the semiprofessional American Soccer League (ASL), a division composed of teams from New York, New Jersey, Philadelphia, and Baltimore. There was at that time no national American soccer league but only a patchwork of regional leagues populated largely by immigrants from the British Isles, the Caribbean, and southern and eastern Europe. Although most of the teams in the ASL had distinctively ethnic names and origins, Brookhattan, like the Kearney Scots, the Brooklyn Hispanos, and the Brooklyn Hakoah, a Jewish club, welcomed players from all ethnic backgrounds. While there was no African American team, there were several black soccer players in the various regional leagues at that time. Most were immigrants from Haiti, like Gaetjens; Jamaica, like GILES HERON of the Chicago Wolverine; or Cuba.

From his debut in the 1947–1948 season Gaetjens made an immediate impression at Brookhattan. The team had won both the ASL championship and the U.S. Open Cup—the only national soccer competition—in 1945 but had struggled in the two seasons prior to Gaetjens's arrival, finishing second from the bottom of the ASL in 1947. Gaetjens's hat trick early in the 1947–1948 season against Brooklyn Hispano signaled something of a Brookhattan revival. Gaetjens was a wiry, fast, and combative player with an unorthodox style. Walter Bahr, a Philadelphia Nationals midfielder who played with Gaetjens on the U.S. national team, described him as "a little nuts.... But he makes the most uncanny goals you've ever seen in your life" (Douglas, 20). Gaetjens's sartorial style on the field also drew comments. He refused to cooperate with regulations requiring that players wear their socks pulled up, rolling them down to his ankles as soon as the match kicked off. He also played with the ties at the neck of his jersey as loose as possible. Brookhattan fans forgave Gaetjens his eccentricities and unpredictability, however, since he also did what was required of a center forward: score goals. His fourteen goals in his debut season, several of them spectacular and one directly from a corner kick, was the second highest in the ASL. Although the team finished only two places higher than the previous season, Brookhattan made it to the finals of that year's Lewis Cup, a tournament open to all members of the ASL, losing narrowly to the Kearny Scots. The following year Brookhattan improved to a creditable fourth, but it ended in last position in 1949–1950. Gaetjens, however, scored eighteen times that season, netting more than half of Brookhattan's goals. In addition to leading the ASL scoring charts, he earned a call up to the U.S. national squad, which qualified for the 1950 soccer World Cup in Brazil.

When the U.S. team was drawn into a first round group that included Spain, Chile, and England, most commentators expected the Americans to lose all of their games. Only one member of the U.S. team was a full professional. The others, mostly Portuguese, Italian, and Scottish immigrants, played semiprofessionally and included, in addition to Gaetjens, the student-dishwasher, a mechanic and a hearse driver. Prior to the World Cup the United States had lost seven straight matches, scoring only twice while giving up a total of forty-five goals. Gaetjens, one of three noncitizens on the American squad, did not play in those matches and had only played against professional opposition in friendly matches for New York select teams against Besiktas of Turkey, in which he scored a hat trick, Liverpool of England, and Belfast Celtic. Gaetjens made his international debut on 25 June 1950 in the United States' opening match against Spain in Curitiba, which the Americans lost 3 to 1, despite taking a surprise first-half lead. Few expected the United States to do any better in its second match against England, which included the world-class professionals Stanley Mortenson and Tom Finney and which felt secure enough of victory to rest its most famous player, Stanley Matthews. The match took place on 29 June 1950 in Belo Horizonte, a hardscrabble mining town in remote northern Brazil. The locals quickly adopted the "pobres Americanos" (poor Americans) in part because they included several Portuguese-speaking players and the English were Brazil's main rivals for the tournament but also because the large mining company that controlled the town was English.

As expected, the disciplined English side dominated the early stages of the game. The Americans, most of whom, including Gaetjens, were still suffering from hangovers, made few chances. In the thirty-seventh minute, however, an American throw-in ten yards inside the English half landed at the feet of the U.S. midfielder Bahr, who ran with it toward the English goal. Challenged by an English defender, Bahr struck the ball from twenty-five yards to the right of the English goalkeeper Bert Williams, who moved quickly to parry it away from the goal. As the ball approached the goal line, however, Gaetjens sprinted to it, dived fourteen feet to barely clip the ball with his forehead, and redirected the ball to the left of Williams and into the net. One of Gaetjens's teammates described the goal as "goddamn impossible … as though he thought he could fly or something" (Douglas, 44). Despite continued English pressure, the Americans did not collapse as they had against Spain but held onto their lead. Gaetjens indeed almost doubled the American tally with a header that skied three inches over the crossbar. At the final whistle the largely Brazilian crowd stormed the field and carried Gaetjens and the other players aloft on their shoulders in celebration.

Believing that wire reports had mistakenly credited the victory to the United States, some European newspapers initially listed the score as 10 to 1 for England. Few Americans, however, learned of their team's famous victory or Gaetjens's dramatic goal, which the *New York Times* erroneously assigned to his teammate Ed Souza. This was attributable not only to the general lack of interest in soccer in the United States—only one American reporter made the lengthy and expensive trip to Brazil—but also to the fact that the game coincided with the beginning of the Korean War. The U.S. team also failed to capitalize on its famous victory, losing 5 to 2 in its final group match to Chile, thereby exiting the tournament. Gaetjens scored one of the American goals but never played for the U.S. national team again.

Like a handful of American soccer players in the 1950s, notably Heron, who played for Glasgow Celtic in Scotland, Gaetjens sought his fortune in the European leagues. He played for Racing Club of Paris, the leading French club team at that time, but struggled there and at a less famous French club, Troyes, before returning to Haiti in 1953. Despite having represented the United States three years earlier, he played that fall for the Haitian national team against Mexico. Two years later he married Lyliane Defay, with whom he had three sons. They settled in Port-au-Prince, where Gaetjens opened a dry-cleaning business, coached a youth soccer team, and briefly managed the Haitian national team. Unlike his brothers, outspoken opponents of the Haitian dictator François "Papa Doc" Duvalier, Gaetjens showed little interest in politics. Following the exile of his brothers to the Dominican Republic in the early 1960s, however, he was arrested by two members of Duvalier's secret police, the Ton Ton Macoutes, while opening his dry-cleaning business on the morning of 8 July 1964. Taken to the infamous Fort Dimanche prison, Gaetjens was never seen again. His son later discovered that Gaetjens was executed in the prison two days after his arrest, shot by a firing squad that included two of his best friends. Officially, despite a formal investigation of the case begun in 1971 by the Inter-American Commission on Human Rights of the Organization of American States, Gaetjens remains one of thousands of Haitians who "disappeared" during the Duvalier regime.

Gaetjens was inducted into the U.S. Soccer Hall of Fame in 1976 but remains largely unknown in the United States, despite soccer's growing popularity and his role in what is still the nation's most famous victory in that sport. *The Game of Their Lives*, a 2005 Hollywood movie about America's improbable victory over England in Belo Horizonte, and the emergence of a new generation of black American soccer stars, such as Eddie Pope, Tim Howard, and Freddy Adu, might yet rescue Gaetjens from relative obscurity.

FURTHER READING

Information on Gaetjens is in the U.S. Soccer Hall of Fame in Oneonta, N.Y.

Douglas, Geoffrey. *The Game of Their Lives* (1996).

Habib, Hal. "Shot from Nowhere," *Palm Beach (Fla.) Post*, 12 Feb. 2000.

STEVEN J. NIVEN

Gaillard, Slim (3 Jan. 1906, 1911, or 1916–26 Feb. 1991), jazz musician and composer, was born Bulee Gaillard, probably in Santa Clara, Cuba (although a birth certificate shows Claiborne, Alabama), the son of Theophilus Rothschild, a ship's steward, and Mary Gaillard. Apparently he was always known by his mother's maiden name. Any formal education may have come in Pensacola, Florida, which he allegedly left at age twelve to travel the world with his father. Gaillard—a lifelong embellisher of his own legend—later claimed that en route he was accidentally left on Crete and that he lived there for at least four years, taking up various occupations and learning to speak Greek. He subsequently traveled the Mediterranean as a ship's cook, learning languages, including Armenian and Arabic dialects, that he later worked into his compositions and improvisations.

In 1932 Gaillard surfaced in Detroit, where he lived with an Armenian family. During the next few years he worked for morticians, slaughterers, hatters, shoemakers, and gangsters. Crediting his redemption from a life of crime to a resourceful judge and a tough policeman, Gaillard took up boxing and music, learning vibraphone, guitar, and piano, an instrument from which he soon could coax music even with the backs of his hands.

By the mid-1930s Gaillard was playing in small jazz groups in towns as far east as Pennsylvania. His first recording was as a singer with FRANKIE NEWTON's band in New York City in 1937. He met SLAM STEWART, a bassist whose specialty was humming—an octave higher—the tune he was bowing. Gaillard and Stewart became a duo, appearing regularly on radio on the *Original Amateur Hour* (with Slim occasionally tap dancing) and in breakfast shows at the Criterion Theatre, where the master of ceremonies Martin Block christened them Slim and Slam. Soon they were regulars on New York radio station WNEW.

Slim and Slam's eccentric composition "Flat Foot Floogie" (originally either "Flat Fleet Floogie" or "Flat Foot Floosie") became a hit in May 1938, when it was recorded by Benny Goodman's swing band, then America's favorite. Having recorded it themselves that January, Slim and Slam soon became famous. (Their version was buried in the 1939 New York World's Fair time capsule.) The song surpassed contemporary nonsense novelties such as "Hold Tight" ("foodley yacky sacky, want some seafood, Mama") largely because of its authentic jazz underpinning. Gaillard called it "mostly a riff with jive lyrics." These lyrics stemmed from scat singing, the vocal attempt to mimic instrumental music. Gaillard's subsequent variation on scat, a playful, multicultural, and highly personal language he called "vout," became his trademark.

Slim and Slam's partnership, which lasted until 1942, produced memorable odes to food, such as "Tutti Frutti." At the beginning of a nightclub set Gaillard might begin baking a cake in the kitchen and at the end invite everyone to eat it. On one occasion he stopped the music and joined the conversation taking place at a table of Greeks. Turning to the audience, he said, "It's OK. We just talkin' 'bout cheeseburgers."

In 1941 Gaillard and Stewart moved to Hollywood and appeared in the film *Hellzapoppin'*, released the next year. They played with Lee and LESTER YOUNG in shows that were broadcast with Gaillard as the supremely "hip" master of ceremonies. In 1942 Gaillard appeared as a musician in the films *Almost Married* and *Star Spangled Rhythm*.

Drafted in 1942 or 1943, Gaillard served as a pilot in the South Pacific. After being wounded, he suffered a nervous breakdown and was discharged in 1944. He returned to Los Angeles, replaced Stewart with "Bam" Brown, with whom he recorded "Dunkin' Bagels," and opened at Billy Berg's club in Hollywood, where his affably entertaining form of jazz quickly made him popular. In 1945 Dizzy Gillespie and Charlie Parker, proponents of bebop, appeared at Berg's with Gaillard, recording "Slim's Jam" and "Dizzy's Boogie," with Slim introducing the solos.

It was during these years that Los Angeles newspapers, reporting on Gaillard's romantic involvements among the film set, dubbed him "the Dark Gable." He lived with many women in his lifetime and fathered at least four children. In 1946 "Cement Mixer (Put-ti, Put-ti)," another "vout" song, written with Lee Ricks, was the country's most popular song for eight weeks; that same year Gaillard and Brown recorded the lengthy "Opera in Vout," a jam session in jive, Gaillard's *Vout-o-Renee Dictionary* was published, and he appeared in the film *The Sweetheart of Sigma Chi*. He became a radio regular, and his song "Laguna O Vouty" (1947) earned him the key to the city of Laguna Beach.

Between 1947 and 1949 Gaillard was often in New York, playing at Birdland and other clubs. Also in those years he recorded "Yep Roc Heresay," whose lyrics were an Armenian restaurant's menu; "Laughin' in Rhythm" (1951), which had no lyrics, only laughter; "Down by the Station" (1947), a hit children's song that Gaillard later claimed inspired the Reverend W. V. Awdrey to write a series of British children's books about Thomas the Tank Engine (Awdrey firmly denied that there was a connection).

In 1950 Gaillard moved to San Francisco, where he married Nettie Walker; they had one child. In 1952 the Gaillard Trio, which usually included the drummer Zutty Singleton, made two short films. Gaillard appeared at San Francisco's Say When club, where he met the writer Jack Kerouac, a "good listener," friend, and fellow cook. *On the Road*, Kerouac's novel of the outsider "beat generation," was published in 1957, with Gaillard and the pianist George Shearing serving as symbols of the inner freedom that Kerouac believed jazzmen embodied. In the book Gaillard is described as a "tall, thin Negro with big sad eyes who's always saying 'Right-orooni.' ... Great eager crowds of young semi-intellectuals sat at his feet and listened to him on the piano, guitar and bongo drums." Kerouac added, "He'll join *any*body, but he won't guarantee to be there with you in spirit," a comment that seems to have prefigured one of Slim's later reflections: "From time to time I used to get lost."

Gaillard remained popular throughout the jazz boom of the 1950s, playing clubs and concerts throughout the United States and aiding the rise of Afro-Cuban jazz, but in 1959, divorced, he returned to Los Angeles. As rock music ascended, his popularity waned. He moved around the western states, working as a disc jockey, managing clubs, and buying and selling farms and businesses.

After a reunion with Stewart at the 1970 Monterey Jazz Festival, Gaillard dropped out of music, finding his way as an actor in nonmusical films and television series, such as *Roots: The Next Generation* (1978). Then, in 1982, Gaillard's hand clapping was featured in a recording by his son-in-law, Marvin Gaye, and in the same year Gaillard's son Mark (with Frances Miller) persuaded him to perform again in public. That September Gaillard reportedly caused "hysteria in the audience" at a jazz festival in Nice, France. Gaillard moved to London, and for the next nine years the white-bearded performer became, in the words of the jazz critic Paul Bradshaw, a new generation's embodiment of "the hipster and Fifty-second Street, a bebop Santa Claus." In 1985 Gaillard married Angela Mary Gorman in London.

The Gaillard revival was an international phenomenon. His recordings were reissued in Europe and Asia, and he became a clothing model in Japan. British critics likened his humor to that of surreal, anarchic contemporaries such as Peter Sellers. He traveled to the United States, playing in jazz clubs while the BBC prepared a four-part television series about him (1989). A new song, "Very Easy to Assemble but Hard to Take Apart," was recorded by the American rap group the Dream Warriors in 1990, with Gaillard as guest vocalist. At the time of his death in London an autobiography and a screenplay about his Birdland days remained incomplete.

A genuinely able pianist with a mellow, beguiling voice, a natural entertainer who sometimes played the vibraphone with swizzle sticks and coaxed tunes from snare drums, Slim Gaillard carved out a career as a jazz cartoon character; his only rival as a humorous jazzman was Thomas Fats Waller. His verbal fantasies—"How High the Moon" conjured moon potatoes as large as the Hollywood Bowl, diggable only by bulldozers—outweighed his instrumental improvisations. His lyrics were often doggerel, but also (as on the night at Birdland when he created the impromptu "Billie Holiday, I Love You" in order to restore the haggard Billie Holiday's confidence) typically playful, human, and kind.

FURTHER READING
Crow, Bill. *From Birdland to Broadway: Scenes from a Jazz Life* (1992).
Discographical Forum 49 and 50 (1985).
Shaw, Arnold. *The Street That Never Slept: New York's Fabled Fifty-second Street* (1971).
Obituary: *Los Angeles Times*, 27 Feb. 1991.
This entry is taken from the *American National Biography* and is published here with the permission of the American Council of Learned Societies.

JAMES ROSS MOORE

Gaines, Clarence Edward "Big House" (21 May 1923–18 Apr. 2005), basketball coach, was born in Paducah, Kentucky, the only child of Lester Gaines, a cook, and Olivia Bolen, a domestic worker. By the time he entered Lincoln High School in rural Paducah, he was already six feet, five inches tall and weighed 265 pounds. He became a powerhouse on the football team and made All-Conference. In 1941 Gaines graduated third in his class of thirty-five.

Education was very important to his parents, so it was understood that he would go to college. While visiting Morgan State College in Baltimore, where he ultimately enrolled in 1941, the business manager, James "Stump" Carter, spotted Gaines walking across campus and exclaimed, "Man! The only thing I've ever seen bigger than you is a house!" (Gaines, 2004). From that day forward Gaines became known as "Big House."

Gaines excelled in college athletics. He made All-American for two years and All-CIAA (Central Intercollegiate Athletic Association) all four years. Graduating in 1945 with a BS in Chemistry, Gaines intended to go to dental school. He had the grades but not the money. His college coach contacted Howard "Brutus" Wilson, athletic director of Winston-Salem Teachers College (WSTC) in Winston-Salem, North Carolina, and recommended Gaines as an assistant football coach. In 1946 Gaines accepted the position at the school, where he would remain for forty-seven years. When Wilson accepted a position at Shaw University in Raleigh, North Carolina, the following year, Gaines, then only twenty-three years old, became head football coach. Three years later he was named CIAA Football Coach of the Year. After four years he decided to stop coaching football and concentrate on other sports, especially basketball. To enhance his coaching skills, Gaines registered for a basketball coaches' clinic at predominantly white Murray State College. After some initial hesitation on the part of the school, he was permitted to attend the segregated clinic.

Racial segregation permeated the fabric of American life during the 1950s, including college sports. White and black schools had separate athletic associations. The National Collegiate Athletic Association (NCAA) and the National Association of Intercollegiate Athletics (NAIA), whites-only college sports organizations, held tournaments to showcase the talents of their players. The CIAA consisted of historically black colleges located in the southeastern part of the United States. The CIAA established its first basketball tournament in 1946, which was the same year Gaines began coaching.

After developing his basketball coaching skills and establishing himself at WSTC, Gaines embarked on the critical task of recruiting players. He had to compete with such CIAA powerhouse teams as North Carolina Central College in Durham, North Carolina, coached by JOHN MCLENDON. McLendon was the inventor of the "fast-break," which revolutionized college basketball to the point that the rulebook had to be literally rewritten.

Gaines's team also had to face Coach Mark Cardwell's West Virginia State College team, featuring Earl "Big Cat" Lloyd, a six-foot-six, 220-pound forward. The West Virginia State Yellow Jackets won the CIAA basketball tournament in 1948 and 1949. Since Gaines needed to find talent quickly, he set his sights on the Northeast, where outdoor basketball courts were filled with talented black players.

The point-shaving scandal of 1950–1951 rocked the college basketball world. A total of seven schools involving thirty-two players, both black and white, were involved in fixing eighty-five games during the two-year period of investigation. Although it was a black athlete who simply called attention to the crime, it was black players who were blamed for the point-shaving. This incident was said to have delayed the integration of black athletes into the mainstream of college education for at least ten years. White college coaches virtually stopped recruiting black players from inner-city neighborhood courts, and the best black talent flocked to small black colleges as a result.

Gaines developed a successful basketball program at WSTC, which became Winston Salem State University (WSSU), through excellent recruiting. Gaines's first major recruit was six-foot-seven-inch Willie Johnson, who helped him win his first CIAA championship in 1953. He continued to recruit while pursuing a master's degree in Physical Education at Columbia University in New York. During the mid-1960s, with the point-shaving scandal long forgotten and school integration being the important issue of the day, the best black athletes were again being aggressively recruited by the larger, well-known (and mostly white) institutions. This made it difficult for small black schools to fill and retain a pool of black talent. Gaines continued to be a successful recruiter because he looked for good players who put academics ahead of athletics.

Among the talented players Gaines coached at WSSU were Cleo Hill, Vernon Earl "The Pearl" Monroe, and William English. The jump shot, the fast break, and the four corners dominated play in the CIAA during this time. Gaines's 1967 squad, led by Monroe, was his best ever; they ended the season with a 31-1 record. That same year, they became the first predominantly black college team to win an NCAA title, and Gaines became the first black coach to be named NCAA College Division Coach of the Year.

Gaines's awards and accomplishments were many. He was a hall-of-fame inductee in ten different sports, won twelve CIAA championships, and was named Chairman of the NAIA District 26 for six years. Gaines was also named CIAA Basketball Coach of the Year five times, voted CIAA Outstanding Tournament Coach eight times, served as CIAA president for four years, and as CIAA basketball coaches president for ten years. He was also a U.S. Olympic Committee member for three years and a member of the board of directors for the Naismith Memorial Basketball Hall of Fame from 1980 to 1990. An accomplishment attributed to Gaines that was as great as any he ever received was the near 80 percent graduation rate of his student athletes.

Gaines retired as basketball coach and Athletic Director of WSSU after the 1992–1993 basketball season with 828 wins, making him, at that time, the most successful coach in NCAA history behind Adolph Rupp, University of Kentucky's basketball coach from 1930 to 1972. While Gaines's coaching accomplishments were legendary, he was also a community leader, an educator, and a mentor. He was survived by his wife Clara Bolen Gaines and their two children.

FURTHER READING

Gaines, Clarence E., and Clint Johnson. *They Call Me Big House* (2004).

Miller, Patrick B., and David Kenneth Wiggins. *Sport and the Color Line: Black Athletes and Race Relations in Twentieth-Century America* (2004).

EUTHENA M. NEWMAN

Gaines, Ernest J. (15 Jan. 1933–), novelist, short-story writer, and professor, was born in Oscar, Louisiana, to Manuel and Adrienne J. Gaines, sharecroppers. The first of Adrienne's twelve children—seven to Manuel and five to her second husband—Ernest Gaines was raised on River Lake Plantation in Pointe Coupée Parish, Louisiana, and was very much part of the landscape when he was a child, working in the fields like his father. His childhood was marked by his father's absence, his parents having separated when he was eight. Gaines was by most accounts raised by his great-aunt Augusteen Jefferson when his parents worked in the fields and then when his father left and his mother moved to New Orleans in search of work. "Aunt Teen" is a figure who dominated Gaines's childhood memories and literary reconstructions, most notably in the figure of Jane Pittman, the title character of what is arguably Gaines's most recognized novel.

Years later, in 1948, Gaines was separated from his boyhood home when he left Louisiana to attend high school in Vallejo, California, joining his mother and his merchant seaman stepfather, Raphael Norbert Colar Sr. Gaines's memories of the stories that he heard during his childhood increased his longing for Louisiana. At the Vallejo library, looking for those types of stories in print, Gaines instead found a sympathy with nineteenth-century Russian writers such as Dostoyevsky and Tolstoy, who according to Gaines represented a similar struggle. In this sense Gaines's writing from an early age reflected these multiple traditions. At sixteen Gaines wrote his first novel, "A Little Stream," and sent it to a publisher in New York. Although it was not published, and Gaines destroyed it when it was returned to him unopened, the book was a point of origin for his first published novel and for later works.

After Gaines graduated from high school he attended Vallejo Junior College, graduating in 1953, and he spent two years in the U.S. Army (1953–1955) before attending San Francisco State College and earning a B.A. in 1957. During this time Gaines saw his work in print; his story "The Turtles" was published in the San Francisco magazine *Transfer* in 1956. From 1958 to 1959 Gaines did graduate work at Stanford University on a Wallace Stegner Creative Writing Fellowship. While Gaines was writing and publishing short fiction, he also began working on a novel, specifically reworking "A Little Stream." The new novel, *Catherine Carmier* (1964), which was awarded the Joseph Henry Jackson Literary Prize, established the setting of Bayonne, Louisiana, as the site that became the nexus of his works. This

Ernest J. Gaines, novelist, short story writer, and teacher. (Wikimedia Commons.)

first novel is expansive and invested in unraveling the stories of generations living in the plantation community. Critics noted that Gaines's fictive plantation is like William Faulkner's Yoknapatawpha County; it is a site based on his childhood memories, yet transformed.

With the support of a 1966 grant from the National Endowment for the Arts Gaines published a second novel, *Of Love and Dust* (1967), which was followed by *Bloodline* (1968), a short story collection that included many of his early works. In 1971 *A Long Day in November*, a story first published in *Bloodline*, was published as a children's book. But it was Gaines's third novel, *The Autobiography of Miss Jane Pittman* (1971), with its title character based on his great-aunt, that solidified his critical reputation; it was nominated for a Pulitzer Prize and led to Gaines's receiving the Louisiana Library Association Award, the California Gold Medal, and the Black Academy of Arts and Letters Fiction Award in 1972, as well as earning him a Guggenheim Fellowship in 1974. *In My Father's House* (1978), Gaines's fourth novel, like the others, reexamined Gaines's past and reconstructed the Louisiana of his boyhood, but it significantly considered the complex relationship between father and son, a theme that came to dominate much of Gaines's work. *A Gathering of Old Men* (1983) broadened the scope of the gaze by considering the factors that drive a group of old men to stand together as a community and protest racial injustice and violence. Though it was another ten years before Gaines published a new novel, he retained a central role in the literary tradition, receiving an award from the American Academy and Institute of Arts and Letters in 1987. *A Lesson before Dying* (1993) returned to a singular focus—the construction of selfhood in the midst of identity politics in a violent South.

Gaines's influence on twentieth-century African American literature was significant, as evidenced by his critical reception and recognition. Yet as he said in an interview with Scott Jaschik in 1994, "I've been called a Southern writer who happened to live in the West, a California writer who writes about the South, a black writer, a Louisiana writer.... I don't know where I fit in and I don't give a damn" (quoted in Lowe, 287). Valerie Melissa Babb described Gaines as a "regionalist writer in the tradition of Zora Neale Hurston and William Faulkner" who "addresses the social implications of race and class in terms stemming from the rural Louisiana world he depicts in his works" by focusing on "characters' internal desires and passions and how they position themselves in relation to their immediate society and environment" (137). This homecoming, the return to Louisiana and the analysis of "cultural displacement," informed Gaines's work and was an important part of his own narrative. *A Lesson before Dying* was a marker for Gaines's professional achievements: Gaines was again nominated for the Pulitzer Prize and was awarded both a MacArthur Fellowship and the National Book Critics Circle Award for the best American novel.

Also in 1993 Gaines married Dianne Saulney, an assistant district attorney from Florida who grew up in Louisiana. Although the two divided their time among Florida, Louisiana, and San Francisco, Gaines remained committed to completing the arc—returning always to Louisiana, where he was writer-in-residence at the University of Southwestern Louisiana, Lafayette, and his first education. In 2000 Gaines received the National Humanities Medal from the National Endowment for the Humanities, signifying his prominent role in the twentieth- and twenty-first century literary tradition. The publication in 2005 of his new work, *Mozart and Leadbelly: Stories and Essays*, continued this progressive narrative.

FURTHER READING

A collection of Gaines's manuscripts is located at the Dupree Library, University of Southwestern Louisiana, Lafayette.

Babb, Valerie Melissa. *Ernest Gaines* (1991).

Gaudet, Marcia, and Carl Wooton. *Porch Talk with Ernest Gaines: Conversations on the Writer's Craft* (1990).

Lowe, John, ed. *Conversations with Ernest Gaines* (1995).

Simpson, Anne K. *A Gathering of Gaines: The Man and the Writer* (1991)

LISA K. PERDIGAO

Gaines, Irene McCoy (25 Oct. 1892–30 Mar. 1964), social worker and clubwoman, was born in Ocala, Florida, the daughter of Charles McCoy and Mamie Ellis. She grew up in Chicago, where her mother moved after her parents divorced in 1903. Beginning in 1905 she attended the Fisk University Normal School in Nashville, Tennessee, from which she graduated in 1910.

Returning to Chicago after her graduation, McCoy could not find work as a teacher because of racism. She engaged in the kind of drudgework most black women were able to find at that time: laundry and cleaning, earning as little as five dollars per week. In 1914 she married Harris B. Gaines, a Chicago lawyer; they had two sons. She returned to school in 1918, studying social work at the University of Chicago until 1921. She eventually did further study at Loyola University's School of Social Administration from 1935 to 1937.

Gaines's social service career began in 1917, when she was the county organizer for War Camp Community Services, directing the Girls' Work Division. From there she began a fifteen-year career as a social worker with the Cook County Bureau of Public Welfare. She initially worked as a typist in Chicago's Juvenile Court. She was assigned to the complaint department, which exposed her more fully to the problems faced by blacks, particularly women and children. She also worked as a caseworker for the Bureau of Public Welfare, where she started clubs for young people.

Gaines worked with the Urban League, serving as a recruiter and director of its women's division. She was industrial secretary of the first black branch of the YWCA from 1920 to 1922. Her last official position was that of executive director of a recreational program for teenagers at the Parkway Community House, from 1945 until her retirement in 1947.

In 1936 Gaines was one of the founders and president of the Chicago Council of Negro Organizations. This group served as a central coordinating body of nearly one hundred social, civic, labor, educational, and religious organizations in Chicago. She used it to launch attacks against social problems that plagued the black community, such as teenage pregnancy, problems facing domestic workers, and employment discrimination.

Active in Republican Party politics as well, Gaines worked in several campaigns, including that of her husband, who served in the Illinois legislature from 1928 to 1936. She was the Republican state central committeewoman for the First Congressional District of Illinois from 1928 to 1930 and was a member of the Second Ward Republican Organization. In 1940 she ran for public office, the first black woman to seek the position of Illinois state representative. Although unsuccessful in her bid, she was victorious in her run for the Republican nomination for Chicago's representative to the Board of County Commissioners in 1948 and led the ticket of candidates for that position.

Gaines was an outspoken critic of inequality and segregation. In 1941 she led a group of fifty Chicagoans on a march on Washington to protest employment discrimination. She investigated and protested the working conditions for domestics and testified before congressional committees on fair employment practices and legislation.

An active clubwoman whose advocacy for social reform earned her a national reputation, Gaines served as president of the Illinois Federation of Republican Colored Women's Clubs from 1924 to 1935. This was the first federation of Republican clubs in the state. She was also president of the Chicago and Northern District Federation of Colored Women's Clubs and the Illinois Association of Colored Women. Through the Northern District Federation she created a program called Negro in Art Week, designed to promote artistic and cultural development in young black men and women.

From 1952 to 1958 Gaines served as president of the National Association of Colored Women's Clubs (NACW), a position in which she focused on promoting international peace and human rights. She also continued the organization's efforts to restore the home of Frederick Douglass in the Anacostia area of Washington, D.C. She directed the members to heed the organization's motto—"To lift as we climb"—and to focus on solving problems that affected the black community. She felt it was their responsibility to enhance the quality of life for black Americans.

Gaines worked through the NACW and as vice president of the Chicago chapter of the Congress of American Women to address issues of global sisterhood. She spoke before the secretary-general of the United Nations, Trygve Lie, expressing concern over the inferior status of black women in the United States and throughout the world.

Gaines was active in other organizations, including Sigma Gamma Rho Sorority and the African Methodist Episcopal (AME) Church. She was a steward of the Bethel AME Church and often used biblical themes and phrases in her speeches and lectures. For her years of outstanding service, she was named Woman of the Year by Sigma Gamma Rho, the Women's Division of the AME Church, and the Northern District of Colored Women's Clubs. Gaines died in Chicago.

FURTHER READING

Gaines's papers are in the Chicago Historical Society.
Davis, Elizabeth L., ed. *Lifting as They Climb* (1996).
White, Deborah Gray. *Too Heavy a Load: Black Women in Defense of Themselves, 1894–1994* (1999).

This entry is taken from the *American National Biography* and is published here with the permission of the American Council of Learned Societies.

MAMIE E. LOCKE

Gaines, Lloyd L. (1911–disappeared April 1939), symbolic legal figure and civil rights pioneer, was born Lloyd Lionel Gaines to Carrie Gaines in 1911 in northern Mississippi. Little is known of his exact date of birth, nor of that of his father; however, it is known that Gaines was the youngest son of five children, and that his father passed away when Lloyd was still a child. By 1926 the Gaines family (headed by Carrie Gaines) moved from Oxford, Mississippi, to St. Louis, Missouri.

Without a father present in the Gaines household, Gaines's older brothers George and Milton delayed their education and worked to support the family. Gaines entered the all-black Vashon High School in 1928. An honor student, he graduated first in his high school class, earning the school's alumni award designated as the most outstanding graduate and a $250 scholarship (won in an essay contest) toward his college education. He completed his high school education in three years.

In the fall of 1931, Gaines entered Stowe Teacher's College (now Harris-Stowe State University), a public land grant historically black college in St. Louis. Because he was unable to afford tuition, he was forced to drop out of school a year later. A few months after leaving Stowe Teacher's College, Gaines earned a curator's grant from Lincoln University, a historically black college in Jefferson City, Missouri, which enabled him to continue his undergraduate studies. On 4 August 1935, Gaines graduated from Lincoln University with honors in history and sought to pursue legal education at the all-white University of Missouri in Columbia.

In Missouri, like many states that had segregation laws, African Americans who sought graduate and professional school training attended schools in neighboring states (i.e., Kansas, Illinois, Indiana, etc.) paid for by the state of Missouri through a special out-of-state scholarship. By 1935, for example, all of the thirty-six African American lawyers then in Missouri had received their legal training outside the state of Missouri. Knowing that the University of Missouri would not accept African Americans, Gaines applied and submitted a blank application accompanied with his transcripts to its law school. The school's registrar Sy Woodson Canada realized that Gaines (who met the admissions requirements) was an African American and was instructed by his superiors to deny him admission on the account of the state of Missouri's racial segregation laws. The University of Missouri formally rejected Gaines in March 1936.

Instead of applying for the out-of-state scholarship to pursue legal education elsewhere, Gaines decided to challenge Missouri's segregation law. His decision to challenge it was based on the advice of his former high school civics teacher and active National Association for the Advancement of Colored People (NAACP) member, Zaid D. Lenoir. The NAACP Legal Defense Fund, under the direction of Charles Hamilton Houston, St. Louis's NAACP president Sidney Redmond, and St. Louis private attorney Henry Espy, came to the aid of Gaines. On 10 July 1936, Gaines's prospect of being admitted to the University of Missouri looked dismal when Boone County Circuit Judge Dinwiddle agreed with the defendants' (the University of Missouri) arguments citing that "under Missouri law, Lincoln University was supposed to open new schools when the need arose. Until new schools were opened, the practice of granting scholarships to black students for graduate studies outside of Missouri served to equalize educational facilities" (Kelleher, p. 265).

Gaines and the NAACP immediately appealed this decision to the Missouri Supreme Court, which subsequently rejected it. On 9 November 1938,

Gaines and the NAACP appealed to the United States Supreme Court (*Gaines v. Canada*), which rendered a verdict a month later. On a 6-2 decision, the high court agreed with the plaintiffs' argument based on legal precedent set forth by the 1896 *Plessy* decision, in which government services and accommodations could be legally racially separate, but had to be equal. The high court provided the state of Missouri with an ultimatum: admit Gaines or build a separate law school for African Americans at Lincoln University. The state of Missouri chose the latter and would further pass the Taylor Bill, which made it mandatory for the Board of Curators at Lincoln University to establish new academic programs and schools when there was need. The state legislature also appropriated $200,000 to establish a law school for African Americans in Missouri.

While Gaines's case was pending, he attended the University of Michigan, earning a master's degree in Economics in 1937. He also found employment as a WPA (Works Progress Administration) clerk in Lansing, Michigan. When the Supreme Court rendered their decision, Gaines resigned his position in Lansing and returned to St. Louis, hoping to enter the University of Missouri's law school. While awaiting admission, Gaines found employment at a gas station. Lincoln University's officials decided to build the law school in St. Louis rather than Jefferson City. Renting the Poro building in St. Louis, the new law school employed four local lawyers and a dean from Howard University, acquired classroom space and a 10,000-volume library, and enrolled its first-year class of thirty students by 21 September 1939. Gaines, however, was not among the first class to enroll at the new law school.

The following month, the NAACP legal trio (Houston, Redmond, and Espy) sought to challenge the separate but equal doctrine by inspecting the new law school and taking depositions from students and faculty. The process revealed that Gaines had been missing for several months when he failed to report for questioning. His mother and sister reported that they had not heard from him since he left St. Louis en route to Kansas City's Centennial Methodist Church to make a speech for the local branch of the NAACP in late April of 1939. Gaines's photo and story made national news. Appeals were made, with no success. In fact, the Selective Service System was unsuccessful in tracking Gaines's whereabouts. It was determined that after leaving Kansas City, Gaines spent some time in Chicago living at an Alpha Phi Alpha fraternity house. Gaines was last seen by the fraternity house's housekeeper, who reported to police that Gaines left the house to buy stamps, but never returned.

Gaines's deposition for the NAACP was critical for the appeal. On 2 January 1940 the case was dismissed. But all would not be lost for the NAACP. As Gaines became an afterthought, a new civil rights pioneer, Lucile Bluford, emerged on the national stage. Bluford, a fellow Missourian, sought to enter the University of Missouri's School of Journalism. Although Bluford would ultimately attend the newly created journalism school at Lincoln University (under the Taylor Bill), it was the Gaines and Bluford suits that would begin an unprecedented legal effort to challenge racial segregation in graduate and professional schools in states across the South. It must be noted that the Gaines case was the first NAACP educational suit to be heard by the United States Supreme Court and it was this case that set the precedent for the Supreme Court to overturn racial segregation with the *Brown* decision in 1954.

The University of Missouri awarded Gaines posthumously an honorary law degree on 13 May 2006, and the Missouri Bar Association admitted him to the bar on 28 August of the same year. While this gesture appeared to provide some closure to a history marred with racial prejudice and ultimately a mysterious disappearance of the NAACP's poster child, new information has arisen on the whereabouts of Gaines. In the wake of his disappearance, there was speculation that he had been murdered, or even that he had been paid off to simply walk away from the case. However, a 4 April 2007 article in the *Riverfront Times* reported that Professor Lorenzo Greene, a longtime professor at Lincoln University and a former professor of Gaines, claimed (in a late-1970s interview with Sid Reedy, who had an interest in the whereabouts of Gaines) to have communicated with Gaines over the phone during the 1940s. Greene speculated that Gaines was tired of the litigation (Gaines shared this sentiment with his mother in a correspondence dated 3 March 1939) and had left the country for Mexico, where he established a relatively successful business. While Gaines agreed to meet Greene in a Mexico City restaurant, he never showed up.

Although Gaines never entered or completed his legal education at the University of Missouri School of Law, and his whereabouts are unclear, he, like Ada Sipuel, Heman Sweatt, John Wrighten, and others, is remembered by many in the civil rights movement as a courageous figure who broke racial barriers to gain access to a legal education. More importantly, these were trailblazers who openly challenged racial segregation in education at the federal level, which eventually led to the dismantlement of the separate but equal doctrine.

FURTHER READING

Garrison, Chad. "The Mystery of Lloyd Gaines." *Riverfront Times,* April 4, 2007. Available at http://www.riverfronttimes.com/2007-04-04/news/the-mystery-of-lloyd-gaines/ (accessed 23 June 2011).

Grothaus, Larry. "The Inevitable Mr. Gaines: The Long Struggle to Desegregate the University of Missouri 1936–1950." *Arizona and the West* 26, no. 1 (1984): 21–42.

Kelleher, Daniel T. "The Case of Lloyd Lionel Gaines: The Demise of the Separate but Equal Doctrine." *Journal of Negro History* 56, no. 4 (1971): 262–271.

"The Mysterious Case of Lloyd Gaines: Pioneer of University Desegregation." *Journal of Blacks in Higher Education,* no. 9 (1995): 22.

TRAVIS D. BOYCE AND WINSOME CHUNNU

Gaines, Matthew (4 Aug. 1842–11 June 1900), politician and Texas state senator, was born in Alexandria, Louisiana. His parents (names unknown) were slaves on the plantation of Martin G. Despallier, where Gaines learned to read and write. In 1858, after Despallier's death, Gaines was sold to an owner in New Orleans who hired him out to work on a steamboat. He escaped on a trip up the Ouachita River and lived in Camden, Arkansas, for six months. He later went back to New Orleans, where he was captured and returned to his master, who subsequently sold him in 1859 to C. C. Hearne, a planter in Robertson County, Texas.

In 1863 Gaines ran away from the Hearne plantation hoping to escape to Mexico. He was captured by a frontier ranger company near Fort McKavitt in western Texas. The company did not send him back to Hearne but left him in Fredericksburg, where he worked as a blacksmith. He ran away again and worked as a shepherd in nearby Texas hill country until the end of the Civil War.

After the war Gaines moved to Burton in Washington County, Texas, where he farmed and also was the preacher for a local Baptist church. He became involved in politics as a member of the Republican Party and in 1869 was elected to the state senate from Washington County. During the Twelfth Legislature (1870–1871), he was an outspoken advocate of the interests of his black constituents and a strong proponent of measures to secure their civil rights. To those ends Gaines supported most measures of Republican governor Edmund J. Davis, including the organization of a state police, creation of the state militia, providing frontier protection, and legislation to encourage both public and private education. He antagonized many whites with his support of integrated public schools. As a state senator, he gained a reputation as an excellent speaker and a shrewd politician.

During the Thirteenth Legislature, in 1873, Gaines became increasingly radical on racial issues. He introduced legislation to prohibit racial discrimination on the state's railroads. He also sponsored a bill to give farm tenants, primarily blacks, a lien upon their crops to be held against damages by landlords or landowners. Both measures encountered strong opposition from white Democrats and Republicans and were defeated. Gaines had also been increasingly critical of Governor Davis and his party for blocking efforts by blacks to run for public office. In 1871 the senator broke with Davis over the renomination of the white congressman William T. Clark in the state's Third Congressional District. Gaines bolted the regular party to back RICHARD NELSON, a black justice of the peace from Galveston, who lost to Clark.

Thwarted by white leaders, Gaines continued to push for more black recognition and to that end encouraged blacks to take more control over local Republican organizations. In 1872, at his urging, blacks in his senatorial district put forward a slate of black officers and seized control of the party's local machinery. In July 1873 Gaines was prominent in the organization of Texas's first Colored Men's Convention, which sought to give blacks a greater role in state politics. That convention endorsed the national Republican Party and the civil rights bill being considered in the U.S. Senate but refused to endorse the Republican state administration.

Controversial from the beginning of his career, Gaines attracted the hostility of whites, who assaulted his character in efforts to undermine his political strength. In 1871 James G. Tracy, secretary of the Republican State Executive Committee, tried to undercut the senator by promoting rumors that Gaines had been indicted for rape. On 9 December 1871 the district court of Fayette County, Texas, under the control of white Democrats, indicted Gaines for bigamy. He had in fact married Elizabeth Harrison in 1870, after being informed by the minister who had performed his first marriage, to Fanny Sutton in 1867, that this marriage was illegal. After failing in repeated appeals to have his case transferred to federal court, Gaines was found guilty by the court in Fayette County on 15 July 1873, and he was sentenced to one year in prison. Gaines appealed that decision, and on 24 November 1873 the state supreme court reversed the district court. Through such measures, however, his enemies severely hampered his political effectiveness, forcing him to defend himself in the courts for some two years.

In 1874 Gaines again ran for the state senate. He appeared to have been elected, but the results were contested by Seth Shepard, a white Democrat. The legislature, controlled at this time by Democrats, seated his opponent, citing Gaines's conviction for bigamy as a reason.

Gaines never held state office again, but he continued to be active in local politics in Giddings, Texas, and an outspoken advocate of black rights. At Giddings, he was a prominent Baptist preacher until his death there.

FURTHER READING

Brewer, J. Mason. *Negro Legislators and Their Descendants* (1935).

Malone, Ann P. "Matthew Gaines: Reconstruction Politics," in *Negro Legislators of Texas and Their Descendants*, eds. Alwyn Barr and Robert Calvert (1981).

Pitre, Merline. *Through Many Dangers Trials and Snares: Black Leadership in Texas, 1868–1900* (1985).

This entry is taken from the *American National Biography* and is published here with the permission of the American Council of Learned Societies.

CARL H. MONEYHON

Gaines, Patrice Jean (19 May 1949–), journalist, healer, philosopher, motivational speaker, and activist, was born in New Bern, North Carolina, the oldest of seven children of Bill Gaines, a career U.S. Marine, and Eleanor Murrell, a housewife. A military child of the civil rights era, Gaines lived an insulated life as a "colored queen" in Quantico, Virginia (Gaines, p. 7). Living on a military base with everything a community needed including an integrated school, Gaines watched all the drama of school integration on television failing at ten years old to fully understand racism or the fact it wasn't limited to the "south," which she considered nowhere close to Quantico. This would help to foster an identity crisis and feelings of low self-esteem for much of her life.

When she was thirteen, her father received orders for Albany, Georgia. Her parents, deciding Albany might be dangerous, bought a house in a new, black, middle-class Washington suburb where Gaines, her mother, and sisters lived while her father served in Albany. Devastated by her perceived lack of love and support from her emotionally and physically absent father as a teenager, Gaines became rebellious and took up with a young man, Ben, she knew her parents would never accept and was the very antithesis of her father.

Ben gave her syphilis and was the first in a long line of thugs, hustlers, drug addicts, and abusive men with whom she developed relationships. By the time she graduated from high school, Gaines believed "life was meaningless without a man" (Gaines, p. 69). Eventually she met, married, and divorced four unsuitable men.

Upon graduation from high school in 1967 and with no real goals, Gaines entered fashion-merchandising school to become a buyer. She got her first job in a local department store and continued her relationship with Ben. When she became pregnant, they planned to elope, but he was drafted and sent to Vietnam. On 19 November 1968 Gaines's daughter was born. About a month after the birth, Gaines got high for the first time by drinking a bottle of cough syrup.

Alone when Ben returned from Vietnam in April 1969, Gaines went back to him. Her vacillation between men confused her. During this time she began writing poetry and shot up heroin for the first time with Ben. In the fall of 1969, Ben was transferred to Fort Bragg, North Carolina, and she moved to Charlotte with his family. She stopped shooting heroin but met new friends and began taking LSD. "I had learned to do whatever was necessary to make myself lovable and popular, to win new friends in a snap." (Gaines, p. 40).

In June 1970, while attending a concert with Ben and another friend, all three were arrested on drug charges. Since the heroin, needles, and syringe were in Gaines's purse, she was charged with possession with intent to sell and jailed. The only way for Gaines to see her two-year-old daughter, whom her mother had brought to visit, was to peer out of a window. When Gaines realized her daughter could not find her among the sea of windows, she committed to changing her life. It was a difficult task.

After cutting a deal with the prosecution for five years' probation and a $2,000 fine, Gaines attended a community college with the goal of becoming an executive secretary. She got a job at a mental health center after she accepted the advice of the woman who wanted to hire her to check "No" on the felony question.

From 1971 through 1973 Gaines continued attempting to change her life, but lapsed back into several relationships with abusive men, one of which she married and later divorced; and another who beat her so badly she nearly died. It was a turning for the better.

One of these relationships resulted in her leaving the mental health facility. She followed that with several jobs until, she found a secretary-receptionist position with Rainbows, Inc., a business management consultant firm owned by a black woman and her father. That job led her to a job as the only black secretary at the *Charlotte Observer* where her boss eventually gave her a writing position on the company monthly newsletter. That was her introduction to journalism as a career path.

From 1973 to 1985 Gaines progressed from newspaper to newspaper until she was hired by the *Washington Post.* Also during this period, she had poetry published in the Johnson C. Smith University literary magazine. She began writing freelance articles, short stories, and eventually a novel. Even with those accomplishments, Gaines was reluctant to appreciate her efforts. She saw herself at age thirty-six with "three failed marriages and not one published novel." (Gaines, p. 223).

In 1985 Gaines was hired at the *Washington Post*, and as she had done since 1971, checked "No" when asked about felony charges. In 1986 Gaines befriended a gay, black male coworker at the *Post*. She discovered she was more comfortable with gay men. "Gone was the possibility of sex, which always complicated my relationships and kept me feeling ashamed, since I always thought I slept with someone too soon." (Gaines, p. 231).

She started seeing a therapist, which she called, "one of the single most important decisions of my life" (Gaines, p. 237). She gave her first inspirational speech at a job-training site in Washington, D.C. Realizing a reporter might cover the speech, Gaines discussed her drug-related past with the managing editor at the *Post* leaving out any mention of jail. During the same time she was one of several reporters involved in a union suit against the paper because of pay inequities. During a preparation session with a union lawyer, Gaines informed the attorney that the "No" on the felony question was not true. She discussed her past and was advised by the attorney to inform the managing editor. Gaines informed the assistant managing editor the next day when the managing editor and publisher, Ben Bradlee, were unavailable. She was immediately informed the situation was career breaking, that she could be fired. After about five months, a decision was made to keep her. Bradlee informed her "We wavered. But in the end, it was your talent that pushed you. If you weren't so damned talented ..." (Gaines, p. 244).

In 1992 Gaines was part of a team of reporters for the *Post* nominated for a Pulitzer Prize for a series of articles on gun violence in Washington, D.C. That same year, she won an award from the National Association of Black Journalists for her commentary work. She left the *Post* in 2001 to freelance and increase her motivational speaking opportunities. She continued to publish articles in the *Post*, the *New York Times* and such magazines as *Essence*, *Crisis*, and *Black Issues Book Review*. She also wrote a monthly column for *USA Today*.

In 2004, Gaines cofounded the Brown Angel Center in Charlotte, North Carolina with her long-time friend Gaile Burton, a corporate trainer. The purpose of the center was to assist formerly incarcerated women gain the practical life skills needed to embrace the opportunity to change their lives.

FURTHER READING

Gaines, Patrice. *Laughing in the Dark: From Colored Girl to Woman of Color—A Journey from Prison to Power* (1995).

Gaines, Patrice. *Moments of Grace: Meeting the Challenge to Change* (1997).

Peacock, Scot, ed. *Contemporary Authors* (2003).

Williams Page, Yolanda, ed. *Encyclopedia of African American Women Writers* (2007).

CLARANNE PERKINS

Gaines, Wesley John (4 Oct. 1840–12 Jan. 1912), author, bishop, and educator, was born a slave in Wilkes County, Georgia, to parents whose names are unknown. He was owned by a man named Robert Toombs. The seventh of fourteen children, Gaines was a sickly child, but during his bouts of illness he secretly taught himself to read and studied diligently.

Gaines became a member of the Methodist Episcopal Church of the South in 1849, following in his father's footsteps. After the Civil War, he became a preacher in the church, but his tenure there was short-lived as he and numerous other black Americans left the branch of the Methodist Church that had condoned slavery. His brother convinced him to move to the African Methodist Episcopal (AME) Church, where he was quickly ordained as an elder. In the 1880s Gaines became the second pastor of the Bethel African Methodist Episcopal Church in Atlanta, commonly known as "Big Bethel," which was at that time the largest black church in the South. In 1885 he was elected the sixteenth bishop of the AME Church.

That same year Gaines founded Morris Brown College in Atlanta, the first university in Georgia funded exclusively by African American patrons. Morris Brown was founded when a delegation from Clark College asked for a donation from Big Bethel and a church member suggested that the church should instead open a school of its own. Gaines set to work, and by October the school opened its doors. The school was dedicated to both the intellectual and the moral growth of its students and was particularly invested in improving the education of students from underprivileged families. Morris Brown's founding principles also reflect Gaines's support for the ideas of BOOKER T. WASHINGTON and others who promoted a philosophy of economic progress through self-help in the black community. In 1891 Gaines was appointed vice president of the AME Church's Payne Theological Seminary.

Gaines wrote two histories. The first, *African Methodism in the South; or, Twenty-five Years of Freedom* (1890), is an institutional history of the church that draws on his extensive involvement in the denomination after emancipation. Gaines had been present at every meeting of the AME Church in Georgia since its inception in 1866 and was privy to all its documents, elections, finances, and statistics. The volume also highlights the importance of early childhood education to the future of the church and of the African American community generally and addresses the role of the church in sending missions to Christianize Africa.

Gaines's second book, *The Negro and the White Man* (1897), is a more overtly political work. In it he examines the "Negro Question" in all its aspects from what he claims is an unbiased and "conservative" viewpoint. Aimed primarily at white audiences, the work argues that slavery was morally degrading for both the enslaved and the master classes. Gaines employs statistics to document the traffic of the slave trade and the death tolls of the Middle Passage and to condemn both the practice of slavery and its roots in Christian nations. He also discusses the history of abolition, highlighting the importance of William Wilberforce, FREDERICK DOUGLASS, Abraham Lincoln, and John Brown. Gaines's analysis of the Civil War focuses primarily on the role of African Americans in that conflict. After an extensive section on the difficulties of emancipation, Gaines addresses his primary interest: education. He argues, through extensive statistics, that African Americans rose from illiteracy more rapidly than any other group in world history and that education should be a major priority for both the black community and America at large. *The Negro and the White Man* engages with many other issues facing the black community at the end of the nineteenth century, such as property accumulation, interracial marriage, divorce, party politics, emigration, and religion. The work ends with a plea for the equal consideration and treatment of all African American citizens.

Gaines is buried in the "Black Section" of Atlanta's historic Oakland Cemetery, the final resting place for many Georgia slaves before the Civil War, when they were identified by both their own names and their owners' names. Gaines's church work in Georgia not only served the communities in which he preached but also represented the growing ability of the black community to provide for its own social needs and concerns. His written works highlight his commitment to promoting the citizenship rights of all African Americans.

FURTHER READING

Meier, August. *Negro Thought in America 1880–1915: Racial Ideologies in the Age of Booker T. Washington* (1963).

LAURA MURPHY

Galloway, Abraham Hankins (13 Feb. 1837–3 Sept. 1870), fugitive slave, abolitionist, Union spy, and state senator, was born in Smithville (now Southport), Brunswick County, North Carolina, the son of Hester Hankins, a slave, and John Wesley Galloway, the son of a white planter who later became a ship's captain. In 1846 Hester Hankins married Amos Galloway, one of John Wesley Galloway's slaves. Abraham Galloway later recalled that his biological father "recognized me as his son and protected me as far as he was allowed so to do" (Still, 150), but John Wesley Galloway did not own Abraham. Abraham's owner was Marsden Milton Hankins, a wealthy railroad mechanic from nearby Wilmington who may also have owned Hester Hankins. Abraham considered Marsden Hankins a fair master, but he was less forgiving of Hankins's wife, who was overly fond of the whip. Abraham apprenticed as a brick mason, and as was common in Wilmington and the lower Cape Fear region, he began to hire out his own time. This arrangement, which gave him greater freedom of movement than most slaves, was beneficial to Marsden Hankins as long as Abraham continued to pay his master fifteen dollars per month from his earnings.

When Abraham Galloway was twenty, he escaped from Wilmington in part because he could no longer earn fifteen dollars per month. Fearing that his master would sell him to rice or cotton planters, Galloway and a fellow slave named Richard Eden persuaded a schooner captain to hide them among turpentine barrels in the boat's cargo hold. In June 1857 they arrived undetected in Philadelphia, where they met WILLIAM STILL, the renowned conductor of the Underground Railroad, who helped transport Galloway and Eden to Kingston, Ontario, Canada. There Galloway worked as a bricklayer and in the four years before the outbreak of the Civil War became active in the abolitionist movement. He may even have traveled to Ohio to deliver abolitionist speeches, an act that risked his capture under the Fugitive Slave Law.

When the Civil War broke out in 1861, Galloway was recruited by the U.S. Army general Benjamin Butler to serve as a Union spy in the coastal regions of Virginia and North Carolina, which were occupied early in the war by Union forces. Among his duties, Galloway scouted the coast for likely landing sites for the federal forces of General Ambrose Burnside. Once the Union forces captured the strategically important port of New Bern, North Carolina, in 1862, Galloway became the leading black intelligence operative in the eastern Carolinas. He knew the region well from his time as a bricklayer and eventually made contact with hundreds of fugitive slaves who had taken advantage of the military occupation to flee slavery and who were hiding in contraband refugee camps and in hastily erected shantytowns throughout southeastern North Carolina. Galloway's exploits as an abolitionist and a Union spy and his frequent raids into Confederate territory earned him the trust of the fugitives, who appointed him their leader.

When the Union army attempted to recruit a regiment of African American soldiers in New Bern in 1863, they sought Galloway to assist them. He did so, but only after extracting—at gunpoint—a promise from the Union recruiting agent, Edward W. Kinsley, that the pay and conditions of black soldiers would be equal to whites. When Kinsley—who clearly had few other options—swore a personal oath that he would do so, Galloway released him. The next day hundreds of black volunteers enlisted in New Bern, the first of more than five thousand soldiers of the African Brigade, which was later known as the Thirty-fifth, Thirty-sixth, and Thirty-seventh Regiments of the U.S. Colored Troops. Galloway continued to engage in spying missions for the Union, often striking deep into Confederate territory. In November 1863 he even secured his own mother's escape from Wilmington, which was at that time a Confederate stronghold. The following month, with his mother perhaps in attendance, Galloway married the eighteen-year-old Martha Ann Dixon in Beaufort, North Carolina, where he had made his home.

Galloway insisted that African Americans' military service to save the Union qualified them for full citizenship. "If the negro knows how to use the cartridge box," he often remarked, "he knows how to use the ballot box" (Cecelski, 49). Increasingly Galloway became active in the political organizations that emerged from North Carolina's contraband camps, and he was a frequent orator at black churches and at Independence Day and Emancipation Day rallies. He also traveled to Boston and New York City to encourage Northern support for black voting rights, and in May 1864 he was one of five African American leaders who met with Abraham Lincoln in the hope that the president would support the suffrage cause. Later that year Galloway attended the National Convention of Colored Citizens of the United States in Syracuse, New York, which established the National Equal Rights League and demanded equal citizenship rights for African Americans. By end of the Civil War, Galloway had established a state chapter and several branches of the National Equal Rights League in North Carolina. His keynote address at the Equal Rights League's Fourth of July parade in Beaufort was typical in its demand for "all equal rights before the law, and nothing more" (Cecelski, 49).

It soon became apparent to Galloway and other African Americans in North Carolina that whites would not easily give up the privileges they had enjoyed before the war. Throughout the state, blacks complained of beatings and whippings by former masters who demanded their labor for free. Blacks chafed under restrictive black codes, local and state laws that threatened to return them to near slave-like conditions. In response, in September 1865 Galloway presided over a statewide freed people's convention in Raleigh, which demanded full voting rights, public schooling for all, and reasonable working hours. Such demands were bolstered with the passage of Radical Reconstruction legislation by Congress in 1867, which reestablished U.S. military authority over the South and required the former Confederate states to establish universal male suffrage before being readmitted to the Union.

Galloway was one of thirteen African Americans elected to the state constitutional convention that followed in 1868, and later that year he became one of the first three black senators to serve in the North Carolina General Assembly. Although he was illiterate, his powerful oratory earned him the passionate loyalty of his fellow Republicans and the enmity of his white Democratic opponents. Galloway famously wore a pistol tucked into his belt and enjoyed reminding his enemies that he was as much a southern aristocrat as they. When a Democrat insulted him on the senate floor, Galloway threatened to "prove to him the blood of a true Southron" (Cecelski, 56). While in the senate, Galloway supported the passage of the Fourteenth and Fifteenth amendments to the U.S. Constitution (which guaranteed "equal protection" to all citizens and extended to black men the right to vote), advocated increased public spending on education, and vigorously opposed the Ku Klux Klan and other white terrorist groups that roved throughout North Carolina during Reconstruction. Galloway was also an early but unsuccessful advocate of women's rights who twice introduced legislation extending suffrage to women, and he also condemned a state supreme court ruling that allowed husbands to beat their wives.

At the age of thirty-three, Galloway succumbed to a fever and jaundice and died in Wilmington. More than six thousand people—his political supporters, army comrades, militiamen, and masons—attended his funeral at Wilmington's St. Paul's Episcopal Church. One newspaper reported it as the largest funeral in North Carolina's history. The era of black political mobilization that began with Galloway and New Bern's black militias in 1862 ended nearly forty years later, when the New Bern native GEORGE HENRY WHITE left the U.S. Congress and North Carolina enacted legislation to disfranchise all black voters. That black political activism proved more dynamic and durable in North Carolina than elsewhere in the South, however, owed much to the life and example of Galloway.

FURTHER READING

Cecelski, David S. "Abraham H. Galloway: Wilmington's Lost Prophet and the Rise of Black Radicalism in the American South," in *Time Longer Than Rope: A Century of African American Activism, 1850–1950*, eds. Charles M. Payne and Adam Green (2003).

Evans, W. McKee. *Ballots and Fence Rails: Reconstruction on the Lower Cape Fear* (1967).

Still, William. *The Underground Rail Road* (1872).

Obituary: *Raleigh Weekly Standard*, 17 Sept. 1870.

STEVEN J. NIVEN

Galloway, Charley (1869–1921), a guitarist and bandleader, was born in New Orleans to William Galloway, a coachman and driver. Nothing is known of his mother.

No one knows for certain when jazz was born. The first recordings of jazz bands date from 1917, when the genre already was well developed. When researchers much later set out to document the early history of jazz, they had few sources other than the often inconsistent recollections of aging musicians, some of whom seized the opportunity to write themselves into history by claiming parentage of the music. Perhaps more importantly, jazz did not suddenly spring into being. Some New Orleans musicians who played in the 1890s and early 1900s were puzzled by researchers' trying to establish a timeline for the birth of jazz since, from their perspectives, lancers, waltzes, and schottisches, the popular dances of the 1880s, morphed seamlessly across the ragtime era into the music that only later would be labeled "jazz." The guitarist Emile "Stalebread" Lacoume undoubtedly had it right when he shrugged off the suggestion that he and his Razzy Dazzy Spasm Band created the genre: "Nobody invented that music," he told jazz researcher Al Rose.

Though there may be no precise point in time when jazz emerged as something new from New Orleans dance music, the cornet player Charles "BUDDY" BOLDEN (1877–1931) is nonetheless cited in many jazz histories as the musician who, around the turn of the twentieth century, was the first to play a style of music modern listeners might recognize as jazz. While it is unlikely he actually invented the genre, Bolden by all accounts was an innovator. Musicians who heard Bolden play praised the power of his tone, his rhythmic drive, and the emotional content of his blues playing. His pioneering work, however, did not occur in a vacuum.

Bolden was deeply enmeshed in the "Uptown" New Orleans music scene. He was one of a group of musicians who hung out at a barbershop on South Rampart Street owned by Charley "Sweet Lovin'" Galloway, and who played in bands led by Galloway. Galloway gave Bolden his start, probably first using the teenage cornet player in his dance band around 1895. The men that comprised Bolden's famous early-twentieth-century band were drawn substantially from Galloway's inner circle of musicians. If Bolden is indeed the "father" of jazz, then Galloway deserves to be known as its grandfather.

The details of Galloway's life are sketchy. Born in New Orleans in 1869, Galloway reportedly was a polio victim. In 1881 he was living with his father,

William, on St. Andrew Street between Locust and Magnolia. Some of Bolden's relatives lived on the same block, and it is likely that Galloway and Bolden knew one another from an early age.

Early jazz researchers Al Rose and Edmond Souchon report that Galloway and another future Bolden associate, the guitarist Jefferson "Brock" Mumford, were playing together on New Orleans streets as early as 1885. Around the same time he reportedly also played on the streets in what now would be called a skiffle band with the bassist Bob Lyons. Street corner bands, typically composed of a guitar and mandolin, and sometimes a bass player, were a common sight in New Orleans at that time. Soon afterward Galloway formed a string band to perform at parties and dances.

Though Rose and Souchon describe him as an "extraordinarily skilled instrumentalist," music was a sideline for Galloway—he principally made his living as a barber. He opened his first barbershop at 435 South Rampart Street in 1894 or 1895. He moved up the street to 761 South Rampart Street in 1897, and to 1324–26 Lafayette Street in 1899. Galloway's barbershop was a hangout for musicians and, as a result, he became an informal booking agent, assembling groups from his clientele for dances and parties.

String bands, typically composed of guitar, bass, and either mandolin or violin, were the most common type of ensemble for late-nineteenth-century New Orleans parties and smaller dances. We do not know precisely what Galloway's group played, but for most string bands of that era, waltzes, schottisches, mazurkas, and quadrilles, plus popular songs (usually instrumental versions—bands with singers were rare), made up much of the repertoire. As ragtime became popular in the 1890s, commercial ragtime tunes were added. Some bands also played blues numbers—or at least a type of music called "the blues," which was likely an early urban ancestor of the blues style with which we now are familiar. Nonreading musicians "faked" their parts, but the type of improvised solo that later characterized jazz was unknown in these early groups.

The New Orleans string band, which began incorporating brass and woodwind players at least as early as the 1880s, was the immediate precursor of the familiar jazz combo of the 1920s. Galloway played an important role in the transition of the string band (plus an occasional horn) to the familiar jazz band lineup of a brass and woodwind "front line" backed by a rhythm section. Rose and Souchon report that the earliest organized "jazz" band using conventional instruments they had identified was Galloway's 1889 band.

Galloway's early string band was comprised of guitar, violin, and bass. Musicians associated with that group include the bassists Bob Lyons and Albert Glenny and the violinists Tom Adams and Dee Dee Brooks and Brock Mumford, who sometimes played second guitar. The clarinet player Frank Lewis sat in from time to time. By the 1890s Galloway had added cornet, valve trombone, clarinet, and drums to the lineup to form a dance "orchestra." The additional musicians included Willie "Red" Warner on clarinet, Edward Clem on cornet, Tom Landry on valve trombone, and a drummer known as "Barnet." Wallace Collins sometimes played tuba. The lineup was fluid, expanding and contracting according to the type of event and the availability of the musicians. This group occasionally played at Masonic Hall, also known as Odd Fellows Hall, one of the often cited birthplaces of jazz, as well as other leading Uptown venues. Bolden apparently took up the cornet in 1894 when he began taking lessons from a neighbor, Manuel Hall. He probably began playing with Galloway's group the following year.

The origin of jazz centers around two New Orleans ethnic communities—the "Creoles of color," who were mixed-race descendents of early French and Spanish immigrants and their slaves, and non-Creole African Americans, who also may have been of mixed race, but not descended from French or Spanish ancestors. The interaction between these two groups during the 1880s and 1890s was probably greater than some histories of jazz have suggested, but they were nonetheless distinct ethnic communities, divided by language, religion, tradition, and customs. Broadly speaking, "Downtown" prejazz Creole ensembles tended to be reading bands that stuck close to written score. They monopolized the more upscale venues including country clubs and hotel ballrooms. "Uptown" bands, on the other hand, were more likely to "fake" arrangements and improvise their parts (though many more black musicians could read music than generally has been acknowledged by authors of jazz histories). Galloway and the musicians that hung out at his barber shop were part of the Uptown music scene.

Uptown bands were found in the rough saloons and dance halls often associated with the early days of jazz, but the better groups played the full gamut of social events for the different strata of New Orleans black society. Bolden's band, for example, was often hired for dances given by the Blue Ribbon Social Club, a teen organization. Common ground for the Uptown and Downtown bands were amusement parks such as Lincoln Park and Johnson Park, which provided a variety of entertainment options, and sometimes had as many as three bands playing simultaneously at different locations.

Some histories of early jazz describe Bolden and Galloway as rivals, but there is little hard evidence that this was the case. Sometime after 1895, leadership of Galloway's group shifted to Bolden, but the transition seems to have been more an evolutionary process than a struggle for power. Bolden was a dynamic and charismatic performer, and a powerful horn player. It is not surprising that he came to dominate the ensemble. Galloway continued to play guitar with Bolden for a while, but he eventually left and was replaced by his old friend, Brock Mumford. Lorenzo Stultz, a guitarist more renowned for his obscene songs than for his guitar skills, also was one of Bolden's guitarists during this period.

The New Orleans guitarist DANNY BARKER claimed Galloway "just faded from the picture" after leaving Bolden's band, but other musicians on the scene at the time recalled that he continued to perform occasionally with a different group. Trombonist KID ORY remembered him leading a band at a club called La Place. According to Ory, Galloway was playing "Bolden's tunes," perhaps trading on his former role with Bolden's by then very popular ensemble. By the mid-1900s, however, he seemingly had retired from music. Galloway continued to cut hair, and in 1907 he moved his shop from Lafayette Street to Bolivar Street. He died in 1921.

FURTHER READING

Marquis, Donald. *In Search of Buddy Bolden, First Man of Jazz* (2005).

Rose, Al, and Souchon, Edmond. *New Orleans Jazz, A Family Album* (1967).

DAVID K. BRADFORD

Gammon, Reginald (21 Mar. 1921–4 Nov. 2005), painter, printmaker, and educator, was born Reginald Adolphus Gammon Jr. in Philadelphia, Pennsylvania, the son of Reginald Gammon Sr. and Martha Brown, Jamaican émigrés. An academic-track student, Gammon graduated from Benjamin Franklin High School in 1941. The caption under his yearbook portrait states that he is "one of the best artists."

In 1941 Gammon received a scholarship to the Philadelphia Museum School of Industrial Arts (later the Philadelphia Museum College of Art). During the summer of 1942, he worked at the Philadelphia Naval Shipyard refurbishing battleships for the war effort. He lost his scholarship when his job caused him to miss the September registration date, and for the next eighteen months, he worked at the shipyards during the day and went to art school at night. With the arrival of his draft notice, Gammon joined the navy and served from 1944 to 1946 with an all-black unit stationed in Guam. After the war, he returned to Philadelphia. Although he was offered a full scholarship at the Tyler School of Fine Arts, he declined it so he could help support his family.

In 1948, after two years of working and going to school, Gammon left Philadelphia and moved to New York City. To support himself, he sorted mail for the U.S. Post Office, painted lampshades, and designed advertisement copy. He devoted his evenings and weekends to painting. It was during this period that he met Janice (Jonnie) Goldberger, whom he married in 1972. An apartment building fire in 1958 destroyed his studio and all of his personal belongings, and between the emotional stress and the financial loss, Gammon did not paint for more than a year (interview with Jonnie Gammon, Dec. 2005).

In 1963, Gammon and fourteen other African American artists, including ROMARE BEARDEN and RICHARD MAYHEW, founded an artists' club called Spiral. According to Mayhew, the purpose was to stimulate an ongoing exchange of evolving ideas about art and society (interview with Richard Mayhew, Dec. 2005). In 1965, Spiral held its only group exhibition at the Christopher Street Gallery in New York City. Called Black and White, this show was a pointed civil rights movement statement. The exhibit pieces, all in various shades of black and white, included Gammon's painting *Freedom Now* (1965). The group disbanded shortly afterward. In 1969, Gammon and former Spiral members joined the Black Emergency Cultural Coalition, a group that picketed the Metropolitan Museum of Art and the Whitney Museum of American Art to protest the exclusion of black artists and curators at both institutions. This, according to his former student James Watkins, showed Gammon as "a man of his art" (interview with James Watkins, Feb. 2006).

About this time, Gammon landed a teaching job as a resident art expert with the New York public schools. Teaching in the Saturday Academy Program, Gammon established an informal painting studio for children living in Harlem. This experience opened other doors when the painter

HUGHIE LEE-SMITH recommended him for a visiting lectureship at Western Michigan University in Kalamazoo. Realizing the contributions Gammon could make to the university's Arts and Ideas program, its humanities faculty asked the dean to extend the ten-day lectureship to a one-semester teaching contract. Gammon arrived at the university on 1 January 1970, and the position—designed to last four months—ended twenty-one years later with his retirement in 1991.

Dr. Larry ten Harmsel, the dean of the Lee Honors College at Western Michigan University, said that "Gammon brought his intense, sometimes combative, love of the world of ideas into the classroom. He was always looking for beauty and wisdom in the midst of struggle and his students found him unforgettably engaging" (interview with Larry ten Harmsel, Feb. 2006). His former students, describing him as a "walking encyclopedia," also remember the art connections he made for them throughout the country (interviews with his former students James Palmore and James Watkins, Jan. 2006). Gammon, a prolific letter writer, stayed in contact with many students after his retirement.

Although Gammon did not have traditional academic credentials, the Arts and Ideas chair Harvey Overton made sure that Gammon received academic promotions based on his professional achievements. In 1980, Gammon became an associate professor of fine arts and humanities and achieved the rank of full professor a few years later (interview with Harvey Overton, Jan. 2006).

After moving to Albuquerque, New Mexico, in 1992, Gammon joined the New Mexico African American Artists' Guild. He participated in its exhibits and was its treasurer from 1999 until his death. He was artist-in-residence from 1992 to 2005 at the Harwood Art Center, where he painted. Gammon was one of the founding members of New Grounds Print Workshop (1997), where he did monotypes, photogravure, and mezzotints. He developed his last body of work, a collection of monotypes, photogravures, and mezzotints of historically important jazz musicians and gospel singers, at New Grounds. His last prints, photogravures, were the beginnings of a series on voodoo and the mystical arts.

Gammon, a sensitive observer of the human condition, used portraiture to communicate the dignity of everyday lives and quiet heroes. Although *Freedom Now* is probably his most well-known work, many say his SCOTTSBORO BOYS' trial paintings (1969) and his portrait of JACK JOHNSON (1967), the first African American heavyweight boxing champion, are among his most powerful.

Influenced by the Cubist movement, Gammon often used collage and overlays to incorporate multiple points of view. Inspired by the civil right movement and the Scottsboro trials (1931–1950), his paintings are powerful statements of injustice, exclusion, and powerlessness. Gammon often said that "art speaks for those who cannot speak for themselves." In the 1970s, music and musicians became an important theme in his work that he maintained until his death. In the 1980s, his interest in tattooing produced a series of portraits that explored body art and self-adornment. Subtle humor, another important thematic element, was especially evident in some of his later works, depicting health club activities and church services. In describing his own work, Gammon said his images "render the human presence in all its variety, dignity, and sometimes depravity or grandeur" (Regina Held, owner/director New Grounds Print Workshop and Gallery, Jan. 2005).

At a time when abstract impressionism was the style, Gammon documented historical events and the human condition. Watkins said Gammon "had a backbone stronger than steel" and never strayed from the subjects he found personally important (interview with his former student James Watkins, Jan. 2006). Because Gammon had steadfast determination and a well-developed sense of self, his work, never static and always reaching, provided an intimate view of nearly seventy years of African American history.

FURTHER READING

Bearden, Romare, and Harry Henderson. *A History of African-American Artists: From 1792 to the Present* (1993).

Lewis, Samella. *Art: African American* (1978).

JANET YAGODA SHAGAM

Ganaway, King Daniel (27 Oct. 1884–16 Mar. 1944), photographer, was born in Murfreesboro, Tennessee, and attended Howard High School in Chattanooga. His parents were King and Hattie Murfrees Ganaway. Ganaway did not go to college, although his sister, Mamie Egester, graduated from college in Chattanooga. He worked as a butler from 1906 to 1925 for Mary A. Lawrence, the widow of Edward F. Lawrence, a prominent Chicagoan, who lived on Lake Shore Drive, Chicago's "Gold Coast." During these years, he tried to revive a childhood interest in drawing, but frustrated with his efforts, he turned to photography. He was self-taught, spending his off days perfecting his photographic skills.

Ganaway's photo, "Spirit of Transportation"—an image of two sections of a passenger train, the 20th Century Limited, arriving in Chicago on a cold day in February 1918—captivated the media when it won the first prize in the fifteenth annual exhibition of photographs at Wanamaker's Department Store in Philadelphia in March 1921. Ganaway received $100 for this scene, which was chosen from about 900 entries, including ones submitted by Edward Weston, Man Ray, and Paul Strand, all of whom became prominent photographers. "Spirit of Transportation" appeared in the African American newspaper the *Chicago Defender* in April 1921 and the *Fort Dearborn Magazine*, a monthly published by the city's Fort Dearborn Bank, in December 1921. It was reproduced in *National Geographic* in March 1923 and in Lucius Beebe and Charles Clegg's *The Trains We Rode* in 1965. Ganaway used a reproduction of the image at the top of his letterhead, followed by the slogan "Industrial and commercial photographs with the poster effect."

Almost immediately after winning the prize, Ganaway started selling photographs. From 1921 to 1924 the *Fort Dearborn Magazine* featured a wide range of his Chicago subjects. In addition to newspapers such as the *Chicago Daily News* and the *Chicago Herald-Examiner*, industrial magazines and publications issued by railroad companies and the Chicago public school published his photographs. For example, the Illinois Central Railroad used two photos in a travel booklet, *Chicago for the Tourist*.

In a March 1925 article for *American Magazine*, Edith M. Lloyd profiled Ganaway and his photography. Lloyd, of the Chicago advertising agency Rauthraff and Ryan, quoted an unnamed art critic, who described Ganaway's pictures as "the strongest, most masterful studies of commerce and industry ever produced by a camera."

Ganaway told Lloyd that he planned the composition of the "Spirit of Transportation" for two years, first only visualizing the image in his mind. When he finally set out to take the photograph in 1918, Ganaway was suspected of spying; fears of treason and sabotage ran high in the World War I era. He explained to Lloyd:

> Everything seemed just right for the picture. It was a cold, snappy day, and the steam was forming into beautiful clouds: The sun was sending down big shafts of light, and, rarest of all, the two engines took exactly the position I had in mind. Just as I snapped the picture, a detective saw me and came running up, demanding to know what I was doing. I tried to explain to him; but he could not imagine why I wanted a picture of those trains. The more I talked, the more suspicious he became. Every minute I expected him to grab my camera and put me under arrest (Lloyd, *American Magazine article*).

When the *Chicago Bee*, an African American newspaper founded by Anthony Overton, commenced publication in October 1925, Ganaway left his butler's job to become the weekly newspaper's staff photographer and produce its rotogravure section. Although the *Bee*'s building at 3647 South State Street was designated in 1998 a Chicago landmark and a historic site in journalism by the Society for Professional Journalists, copies of Ganaway's work in the paper were not preserved, as only scattered copies of the *Bee* are available, except for some on microfilm for 1943 to 1947.

Ganaway's fame reached Christopher Morley, a columnist for the *Saturday Review of Literature*. In 1927, as the 20th Century Limited was about to celebrate its twenty-fifth anniversary, he wrote: "I hear much of King Ganaway, the Chicago photographer who has done marvelous pictures of engines. I hope he'll do the Century as she pulls out of La Salle Street on the morning of June 15" (2 Apr. 1927, 695).

Beulah Mitchell Hill, the music and society editor of the *Bee*, nominated Ganaway for the William E. Harmon Awards for Distinguished Achievement among Negroes in 1929, writing that his "genius displays itself in the taking of the common, almost sordid pictures of every-day life and making them into works of art" (nomination letter, 29 Aug. 1929). Letters of recommendation also came from Anthony Overton, publisher of the *Bee*; Lloyd; and W. Frank McClure, former editor of the *Fort Dearborn Magazine* and then vice president of Albert Frank & Company, who considered him the "greatest photographer I ever knew" (letter of recommendation, 21 Sept. 1929). Alain Leroy Locke, a Howard University professor, praised Ganaway as a pictorialist and a "most promising and serious craftsman" (Willis). As a result of winning the award, four of Ganaway's photos appeared in the Harmon Foundation's traveling exhibits in 1930 and 1931.

Ganaway also exhibited at the Art Institute of Chicago, 1927; the International Photographic Salon at the 1933 Century of Progress Exposition in Chicago; the Museum of Science and Industry, 1935; the New Jersey State Museum at Trenton, 1935; and the Texas Centennial, 1936. Curiously, his photos disappeared from the pages of the *Bee* in the 1930s.

Ganaway was a member of the Chicago Art League and the Greater Bethel African Methodist Episcopal (AME) Church. At the time of his death, he was a teacher at a local Unity Center. According to U.S. census listings, he was married twice: to Pauline Barrew, born in Sweden (one child, Lucile, was born about 1907); and to Jennie, born in Tennessee, who survived him. A short obituary in the *Sunday Chicago Bee* published on 26 March 1944 noted that "his commercial photography was rated among the finest."

Ganaway appears in *A Century of Black Photographers*, a catalog of an exhibition at the Rhode Island School of Design in 1983. The art historian DEBORAH WILLIS, then curator at the Smithsonian Institution's Center for African American History and Culture, recognized his importance in Chicago in *Reflections in Black* (2000); she wrote that Ganaway "was intrigued with industrial life on the waterfront and equally fascinated with water, massive structures, angles, and elements of mysticism." Willis also included Ganaway in her chapter about photographers in *Against the Odds: African-American Artists and the Harmon Foundation* (1989).

FURTHER READING

"Ganaway Captures Train's Spirit," *Railroad Heritage* (2001).

Lloyd, Edith M. "The Negro Butler Has Become Famous as a Photographer," *American Magazine* (Mar. 1925).

Willis, Deborah. "Photography and the Harmon Foundation," in *Against the Odds: African-American Artists and the Harmon Foundation* (1989).

JOHN GRUBER

Gans, Joe (25 Nov. 1874–10 Aug. 1910), professional boxer, was born in Baltimore, Maryland. He reputedly was the son of an African American baseball player, Joseph Butts. His mother's name is unknown. He was adopted at age four by Maria Gant and her husband. It is not known why he altered his name from Gant to Gans or if in fact previously printed sources had misspelled his adopted mother's surname. Gans began fighting in 1890 in battle royales, brawls in which several African Americans fought each other for money, with the last one standing declared the winner. These free-for-alls taught him to block, dodge, and lead with his punches. His first real fight was for a $2 side bet; in addition, he collected $5.40 in change from the crowd.

A fish market clerk, the five-foot-six, 133-pound Gans turned professional in 1891, fighting almost exclusively in Baltimore. He won all of his early bouts, gaining a reputation for ingenuity in the ring, excellent timing, and knockout ability with either hand. He went undefeated until his thirty-third fight, which he lost to the left-hander Dal Hawkins in fifteen rounds in October 1896. Four years later, on 31 August, Gans evened the score with a third-round knockout of Hawkins in the last legal fight held in New York under the Horton Act.

A deadly puncher and counterpuncher, Gans fought for the lightweight championship on 23 March 1900 in New York City, but he was knocked out by titleholder Frank Erne in the twelfth round. After winning his next several bouts, Gans was matched in December 1900 in Chicago against the featherweight champion Terry McGovern, who outweighed him by ten pounds; the fight was attended by seventeen thousand spectators, a record local crowd. Gans was a 3 to 1 favorite, but he agreed to fix the result. Many fighters in that era were known to prearrange the outcomes of their fights. African American boxers often had to throw fights because they had a difficult time getting matches and needed the money. Prominent African American gamblers were forewarned that Gans was not in top shape, but his loyal fans were left in the dark. Gans hardly defended himself against McGovern and lost by a second-round knockout. The fix was so obvious that disgruntled spectators started a riot that nearly ended prizefighting in Chicago.

Gans won his next nineteen fights, including eleven straight knockouts, and he secured a rematch with lightweight champion Erne in May 1902 in Fort Erie, Canada. With his first and only punch, Gans knocked out the champion, the first time that had happened in a title fight. Gans had a hard time getting fights while he was champion because ranking contenders, who were afraid of losing to him, drew the color line as an excuse. He occasionally fought at higher weights, taking on physically stronger boxers like the middleweight black Canadian SAM LANGFORD, one of the greatest fighters of all time, who defeated him in December 1903 in fifteen rounds, and the welterweight champion JOE WALCOTT from Bermuda, who Gans met in 1904 in a nontitle fight that ended in a draw. Gans fought only twice in 1905, having contracted tuberculosis. Because his manager Al Herford is said to have taken advantage of him, they split up in 1905; Gans also believed that it was a mistake to have a white manager.

Gans married twice. (His wives' maiden names and the dates of the marriages are unknown.) His first marriage was to Madge, a Chicago actress, with whom he had two children before they divorced. His second wife was Margaret, a teacher.

Gans's most memorable defense of his championship occurred on 3 September 1906 in the obscure mining town of Goldfield, Nevada. The match was the first major fight promoted by Tex Rickard, who, working for a saloon and gambling casino, hoped to entertain the miners, boost the town's fame, and make a lot of money. Gans signed for $11,000, although his white challenger O. M. "Battling" Nelson was guaranteed $23,000. A prohibitive 6 to 1 favorite, Gans had to limit himself before the fight to beef tea to make the 133-pound limit at the ringside weigh-in. Seven thousand spectators, including 500 women, attended the contest, nearly $70,000 in total ticket sales. After forty-two rounds of vicious brawling, during which Nelson repeatedly fouled the champion with head butts, referee George Siler halted the bout, disqualifying Nelson for a punch to the champion's groin. Experts of that era regarded it as one of the greatest fights of its time.

Rickard promoted another outdoors lightweight championship fight for Gans four months later, on New Year's Day 1907, at the Tonopah Casino A.C. in Reno, Nevada, pitting him against Kid Herman, who like Nelson was from Chicago. The match took place in zero-degree weather, and the three thousand fans who watched it wore overcoats and gloves. The champion was a 4 to 1 favorite and won an uninteresting eight-rounder. Gans received $12,000 of the $31,000 gate, and Herman got $8,000. On 4 July 1908 Gans defended his crown for the second time against Nelson in Colma, California, outside San Francisco, then the national boxing center. Gans had physically deteriorated from tuberculosis and was further worn down by the dreadful conditions of the Herman fight. He lost the championship, knocked out in the seventeenth round. A rematch was staged on 9 September, and Gans was again knocked out, this time in the twenty-first round.

The "Old Master," as some sportswriters called him, fought just once more, in March 1909, before he retired, moving to Arizona for the benefits of its climate. It was too late to stem his tuberculosis, however, and he died in Baltimore. The *Baltimore Sun* reported that he was worth $70,000, primarily invested in the heavily mortgaged Hotel Goldfield in Baltimore and in two adjoining homes. It is unclear how much he actually had saved during his career because of crooked management and an addiction to dice.

Gans had 156 professional fights, with a record of 120 wins, 8 losses, 10 draws, and 18 no-decisions; nearly half of his victories (55) came from knockouts. Many boxing experts consider him the greatest lightweight fighter of his time. He was elected to the *Ring* magazine Hall of Fame in 1954.

FURTHER READING

Doherty, Bill. "The Old Master," *Ring* 18 (Nov. 1939): 31, 44.

Fleischer, Nat. *Black Dynamite: The Story of the Negro in the Prize Ring*, vol. 3 (1938).

The Ring *Record Book and Boxing Encyclopedia* (1984).

Obituaries: *Baltimore Sun*, *New York Times*, and *Chicago Defender*, 11 Aug. 1910.

This entry is taken from the *American National Biography* and is published here with the permission of the American Council of Learned Societies.

STEVEN A. RIESS

Gans, Panama Joe (14 Nov. 1896– ?), boxer, was born Cyril Quinton Jr. in Barbados, British West Indies. As is the case with many of the good black fighters of the early 1900s who were denied the chance to fight for world titles, little is known about his early life. The names of his father and mother are unknown, although it may be surmised that the father's name was Cyril Quinton Sr.

It is known that while Quinton was young he and his family moved to Panama and that his father passed away soon after. After a run-in with the law and a short stay in a juvenile detention center, Quinton turned to prizefighting as a way of making a living sometime in 1914. It was a good time for black fighters in Panama. There was less racial prejudice there than fighters faced in the United States, and the influx of canal workers, sailors, merchants, gamblers, and less savory types assured plenty of money and gambling. Many of the best black American fighters fought in Panama at one time or another, and Quinton soon had a steady stream of good opponents and decent paydays. Sometime early in his career, he adopted the name of Panama Joe Gans. Like many up and coming black fighters during that time, he took on the name of the original JOE GANS who had died in 1914 and had been the first American-born black to win a world title when he became lightweight champ in 1902. In early 1917 Panama Joe Gans fought nearly every worthy challenger in Panama, amassing a record of twenty-four wins, three defeats, two draws, and one no contest. Along the way he won both the lightweight championship of Panama and the middleweight championships of South and Central America. With this impressive showing, Gans came to the attention of an American boxing promoter, who brought the young fighter to the United States in mid-1917.

The move proved both profitable and frustrating. Gans earned more money fighting in the United States, and the level of opposition increased. However, he quickly encountered two obstacles he had not faced in Panama. The first was the relatively new "no decision" rule that dominated much of American boxing. In an attempt to end possible bribery of judges and referees to buy decisions for fighters, many states adopted a policy that stated that unless a fighter knocked out his opponent or forced his opponent to quit, the bout was declared no decision. Eleven of Gans's first thirteen bouts in the United States ended in no decision, and he eventually amassed thirty no decision fights on his record. Thus unless a fighter was a murderous knockout artist, it was difficult to maintain anything approaching a "winning" streak. Gans, though powerful, was not one of those artists. The more insurmountable problem was that Gans was black. He had the misfortune of moving to the United States just two years after JACK JOHNSON, the first black heavyweight champion of the world, was defeated and the belt returned to, in the view of most white Americans, its proper place—around a white fighter's waist. The fury of white Americans against Johnson was immense and carried over for years into the boxing game. As a result it became extremely hard for black fighters to have meaningful fights or to challenge for a world title. Despite his impressive record, Gans was never allowed to fight in a world championship bout.

During the next three years, Gans fought at least forty-two fights, winning seventeen, losing three, with two draws and twenty no decisions. This record of achievement did nothing to gain Gans a shot at the World Middleweight Championship. Finally, in October 1920 Gans met and defeated George Robinson for what was called the World Colored Middleweight Championship. Although the title was virtually meaningless and the entire "colored championship" idea was a way to sidetrack good black boxers from meeting white champions, Gans had at least secured a championship and looked forward to better paydays and opposition.

Disaster struck in early 1921, however, when Gans contracted pneumonia. A serious ailment in any age, during the early twentieth century pneumonia was a feared illness that killed many and left others debilitated. Even someone in peak physical condition, such as a prizefighter like Gans, could be floored by the sickness. Gans did not fight for nearly five months. Instead of showing the effects of his bout with pneumonia, he came back with a vengeance. Fighting nearly fifty times from mid-1921 through the end of 1923, he was almost perfect, losing only six times (often the result of suspicious decisions in the other fighter's hometown). Along the way he crushed an up-and-coming young black middleweight named TIGER FLOWERS and then fought him to a no decision two years later. He also earned a "newspaper decision" over the future light heavyweight champion Mike McTigue. (Although many states had the no decision rule, this did not stop newspapers from announcing who they thought had won the bouts.)

In late 1923 Gans again contracted pneumonia. This time the illness nearly killed him, and when he decided to return to boxing the following year, it was clear that the disease had taken a terrible toll. In his first defense of the World Colored Middleweight Championship in 1924, he was unmercifully battered by Larry Estridge and lost the title. The two men met less than two months later, and again Gans absorbed a horrific beating. Following the drubbings by Estridge, Gans fought just thirteen more times in the next four years. Most of the bouts took place in Latin America—Panama, Barbados, Cuba, and Puerto Rico. His record during that time was five wins, five losses, two draws, and one no decision. After losing his last fight in June 1928, he retired. With that he disappeared from the limelight and from history. His place and date of death went unnoticed in American newspapers.

Despite a ring record of over ninety wins, Gans never broke through the color line that divided boxing—and the United States—during the early 1900s. Ironically, it was just at the end of his career that the line was broken in the middleweight championship. Flowers, the man Gans had easily defeated in 1921, won the title in 1926.

FURTHER READING

Ashe, Arthur R., Jr. *A Hard Road to Glory: A History of the African-American Athlete, 1919–1945* (1988).

Kaye, Andrew M. *The Pussycat of Prizefighting: Tiger Flowers and the Politics of Black Celebrity* (2004).

MICHAEL L. KRENN

Gantt, Harvey (14 Jan. 1943–), architect, politician, and community leader, was born Harvey Bernard Gantt in Charleston, South Carolina, the first of five children of Wilhelmenia Gordon and Christopher

C. Gantt. His father was a skilled mechanic at the Charleston Naval Shipyard and an active member of the National Association for the Advancement of Colored People, and he encouraged his son to speak out against the segregated society in which they lived. Gantt graduated in 1960 from Burke High School, where he was salutatorian of his class and captain of the football team. Only a month before graduation, he helped twenty-two other student leaders from the all-black school stage a sit-in demonstration at the S. H. Kress lunch counter. In Gantt's later assessment, the action "started a change in the minds of the whole [city]" and "ultimately ended up in a movement that spread throughout all of Charleston" (Haessly, 47).

Gantt attended Iowa State University with a stipend from the state of South Carolina, which refused to admit him to all-white Clemson College (later Clemson University), the only school in the state with an architecture program. When Clemson failed to act on his second application for admission, Gantt filed suit in federal court on 7 July 1962.

In spite of South Carolina's sometimes violent response to demands for black civil rights, the state's political and business establishment vowed not to allow a repetition of the turbulence that characterized James Howard Meredith's entry to the University of Mississippi in September 1962. Clemson quietly acquiesced when a federal court ordered Gantt admitted. On 28 January 1963 Gantt enrolled at Clemson surrounded by elaborate security precautions, an estimated 160 reporters, and a small crowd of protesting students. For his part, Gantt's quiet and dignified response to the situation won praise from many vocal critics of integration, including his future nemesis, Jesse Helms, then a commentator at WRAL-TV in Raleigh, North Carolina. Helms noted that Gantt "has done a great deal—probably more than he himself realizes—to establish respectful communications across sensitive barriers in human relations" (Ellis, 394).

Gantt married Lucinda (Cindy) Brawley, the second African American student to attend Clemson, in 1964 and received a bachelor's degree in Architecture with honors from the college the following year. He then joined the architectural firm of Odell and Associates in Charlotte, North Carolina. In the three years he spent there, he learned firsthand from the principal of the firm the significant influence architects could have—not just on designing buildings but on urban planning. Believing that he needed further education, Gantt entered the Massachusetts Institute of Technology and earned a master's degree in city planning in 1970. He moved back to North Carolina, and for a year he directed physical planning for Soul City, a small town in Warren County that Floyd Bixler McKissick, a civil rights leader, sought to develop as a model biracial community.

Gantt returned to Charlotte in 1971 and opened his own architectural practice with Jeffrey Huberman, who had likewise started his professional career with the Odell firm. He also became associated with Fred Alexander, the first African American member of the Charlotte city council in the twentieth century. When Alexander won election to the North Carolina State Senate and vacated his council seat in 1974, Gantt was appointed to fill the remaining year in his mentor's term. He won reelection on his own in 1975 and 1977, and he missed winning the Democratic Party primary contest for mayor in 1979 by only twelve hundred votes out of nearly fifty-one thousand cast. Two years later, he led all at-large candidates for city council and became mayor pro tem. Gantt ran for mayor again in 1983; and although he faced an electorate that was less than one-fourth black, became Charlotte's first African American mayor. In 1985 he was easily reelected with 61 percent of the total vote.

Journalist Margaret Edds noted that Gantt's "lexicon was that of an urban planner, not a civil rights activist" (207). In a city that was in one of its recurrent growth cycles, he stressed the need for revitalizing the center city and balancing growth in the suburbs. Such issues as the site of a new coliseum, public transportation, disputes over where beltways should be located to move traffic most effectively, and impact fees for developers and payroll taxes for commuters consumed much of Gantt's attention during his two terms. Many of these issues affected African Americans, of course, and Gantt did work for increased black involvement in the awarding of city contracts.

Although his reelection in 1987 seemed certain, Gantt and his supporters, including the city's business and political elite, underestimated his opponent and the negative feelings about growth, especially relating to traffic congestion, that had arisen since his first win. Republican voter registration, resulting in large part from an influx of newcomers more accustomed than natives to voting for Republicans in local races, had increased by 6 percent during 1983; and the Gantt organization failed to turn out the black vote as vigorously as it had in previous campaigns. Gantt's maverick rival,

Sue Myrick, adopted a more aggressive style of campaigning than had traditionally been the custom in relatively reserved Charlotte, and she went on to become the city's first woman mayor. Still, the election was very close, and a shift of only five hundred votes would have resulted in Gantt's winning a third term.

In 1990 Gantt took on the formidable Helms, one of the Republican right's major icons, who was trying for his fourth term in the U.S. Senate. Gantt led the field against three white candidates in the Democratic Party primary and won the nomination in a runoff. As the incumbent, Helms enjoyed a natural advantage, and Gantt was little known outside his home county. Helms portrayed Gantt as a typical "tax and spend liberal" (Ellis, 395), but Gantt fought back by stressing education, environmental issues, and Helms's indifference to the real needs of the state's citizens. As the election neared, Gantt led in some polls, and his advisors had begun to think that race would not be a factor. With less than two weeks remaining, however, the Helms campaign began broadcasting television ads pointedly attacking Gantt's support for affirmative action and blatantly playing on racial fears. In the end, Helms won with 52 percent of the vote to Gantt's 48 percent. Six years later the two men faced each other again, and Helms won by a seven percent margin.

In the years after his second loss to Helms, Gantt concentrated on practicing architecture; and the Gantt Huberman firm grew to include more than forty architects and interior designers. Gantt was recognized as a fellow of the American Institute of Architects in 1987 and received honorary degrees from his alma mater and several other universities. He was a guest lecturer at numerous institutions, including Yale, Cornell, and Hampton, and he served as a member of the accreditation committees at the schools of architecture at Howard University and Southern University and as a member of the visiting committee of the Harvard University Graduate School of Design for 2006–2008. Showing continued commitment to his hometown, in 2005 he cochaired a task force to study the management and governance structure of Charlotte public schools.

Gantt's success as a politician and the respect he enjoyed in Charlotte had roots in his ability to build consensus. According to his partner, Huberman, Gantt "has always worked very hard to lead others with different ideas into a unified point of view or perspective" (Ellis, 396).

FURTHER READING

Gantt's papers as mayor of Charlotte, from 1983 to 1987, are at the Atkins Library, University of North Carolina at Charlotte.

Edds, Margaret. *Free at Last: What Really Happened when Civil Rights Came to Southern Politics* (1987).

Ellis, Marion. "Harvey Gantt" in *The North Carolina Century: Tar Heels Who Made a Difference, 1900–2000* (2002).

Haessly, Lynn. "'We're Becoming the Mayors': An interview with former sit-in leader Harvey Gantt, now Charlotte's mayor," *Southern Exposure* (Mar./Apr. 1986).

McMillan, George. "Integration with Dignity: The Inside Story of How South Carolina Kept the Peace," *Saturday Evening Post*, 16 Mar. 1963.

Strickland, Ruth Ann, and Marcia Lynn Whicker. "Comparing the Wilder and Gantt Campaigns: A Model for Black Candidate Success in Statewide Elections," *PS: Political Science and Politics* (June 1992).

ROBIN BRABHAM

Gardiner, Leon (25 Nov. 1892–5 Mar. 1945), bibliophile, researcher, and photographer, was born in Atlantic City, New Jersey, the son of Jacob Gardiner and Martha (maiden name unknown). In 1902 he and his family moved to Philadelphia, Pennsylvania. From childhood he was interested in reading, cross-country running, hiking, camping, and bicycling. Later he developed an interest in music, choir singing, and photography. Racial discrimination kept him from attending the photography school of his choice in Philadelphia, to his great disappointment. In the early 1900s he began to collect material of various kinds concerning black achievements, black institutions, and the lynching of blacks.

From about 1908 to 1923 Gardiner attended meetings of the Philadelphia Afro-American Historical Society (later the American Negro Historical Society), expressed his ideas, and described his findings in what he called "race literature." He continued to build his collection of black memorabilia, and helped to form a group of bibliophiles. His nighttime job at a post office in Philadelphia left him free during daylight hours to read books and articles on black history, to collect black oral history, to seek the advice of rare-book dealers, and to continue assembling books, memorabilia, and manuscripts pertaining to his absorbing interest. He sought out survivors and descendants of Philadelphia's black families and strenuously urged them to ferret out old correspondence and printed matter from their cellars and attics. He was instrumental in securing the collections of the deceased bibliophiles Jacob C. White and Robert Mara Adger from their separate estates. Materials therein included rare books and pamphlets, brochures, letters, and autographs.

After the American Negro Historical Society became inactive in 1923 or soon thereafter, Gardiner and some other members joined the Association for the Study of Negro Life and History, which had been formed in Chicago in 1915 by CARTER GODWIN WOODSON. Gardiner was later credited as the only member to keep the association's collection intact. Heirs of several other prominent collectors unfortunately did not do so. Gardiner was also a member of the Philadelphia Society for Negro Records and Research, which was active from 1937 until 1952.

In the 1930s and early 1940s Gardiner wrote articles for the *Philadelphia Tribune* and the *Philadelphia Independent*. Some of these pieces were cowritten with his friend ARTHUR HUFF FAUSET, author of *Sojourner Truth, God's Faithful Pilgrim* (1938) and *Black Gods of the Metropolis: Negro Religious Cults of the Urban North* (1944). Gardiner's popular essay "One Hundred Years Have Passed since Garrison Handed This Promise to the World" (*Philadelphia Tribune*, 7 Dec. 1933) advanced his reputation. Over the years Gardiner was frequently called upon to answer queries from fellow African American scholars throughout the United States. His knowledge and experience as a researcher made him a valued resource, and he was well known for cooperating generously. His most enduring work, however, was the result of his fixed belief that individual publications would be insufficient and that permanent, free-standing collections of black historical materials of all sorts should be gathered and maintained. To this end, he acquired and carefully preserved the collection of the Afro-American Historical Society and added other materials that he had been gathering for years. In 1933 he deposited his collections in the Historical Society of Pennsylvania and in the Berean Institute, both in Philadelphia. The collections include books and documents from as early as 1766, much nineteenth-century material, varied correspondence from often highly prominent African Americans, and documents relating to black history, political efforts, charitable organizations, literary organizations, and church, educational, and athletic activities.

Gardiner was married twice. His first wife was Bernice Modeste; the couple had three children. After her death he married another woman named Bernice in 1940; she was the niece of the African American novelist CHARLES WADDELL CHESNUTT. The couple had no children. Each of his wives enthusiastically aided Gardiner in his efforts. He worked so energetically that he severely impaired his health. When he was advised to schedule more time for leisure or rest, he insisted that his desire to accomplish his goals was more important to him than life itself. He died suddenly of a heart attack in Philadelphia.

FURTHER READING

Gardiner's papers and related materials are in the Berean Institute, the Historical Society of Pennsylvania, and the Moorland-Spingarn Research Center, all in Philadelphia.

Blockson, Charles L. *African Americans in Pennsylvania: A History and Guide* (1994).

Spady, James G. "The Afro-American Historical Society: The Nucleus of Black Bibliophiles (1897–1923)," *Negro History Bulletin* 37 (June–July 1974).

This entry is taken from the *American National Biography* and is published here with the permission of the American Council of Learned Societies.

ROBERT L. GALE

Gardiner, Ronnie (25 July 1932–), jazz drummer and medical inventor, was born Ronald Edwin Gardiner in Westerly, Rhode Island, to Maude Hannah Francis, a homemaker, and Ralph Alton Gardiner, a chef. The youngest of four sons, Gardiner was a precocious child. At only three and a half—when he was already tap-dancing—he asked for a toy drum for Christmas. His parents obliged so that he would stop playing on his mother's pots and pans.

After graduating from high school, he remained in Westerly and played at weddings and parties. In 1951 Gardiner moved to New York City to study privately with Charlie Tappin at the Henry Adler Music School. In 1953 during one of his weekend train rides back from Westerly to New York, Gardiner played an impromptu performance with CHARLIE PARKER, one of jazz's most influential saxophonists. Gardiner returned to Westerly after four years of studying to work as Westerly High School's assistant director of music. He also taught privately and continued to perform with local musicians as well as with music legends, such as the prolific African American musical director, dance arranger, and orchestra composer LUTHER HENDERSON.

Gardiner traveled through Europe for five weeks in 1961, visiting five countries. He performed in Holland with Diamond Five at Scheherazade and in Denmark with the double bassist Niels-Henning Orsted Pedersen. Upon his return Gardiner accepted a position at the post office, resumed working at Westerly High School, taught privately, and toured Rhode Island with the Ronnie Gardiner Quartet. But he found jazz's popularity in deep decline, as evidenced by many of America's greatest jazz players' relocation to Scandinavia. According to the historian and documentary filmmaker Ken Burns, there were several contributing factors, including the increased popularity of television and British rock bands. Perhaps the major influence was expressed in the grievances of black musicians: whites controlled nearly every aspect of the jazz player's life, from marketing and distribution to performance venues and compensation.

In 1962, after rejecting the post office's offer of a permanent clerk's position and Dizzy Gillespie's invitation to become an apprentice and permanent band member, Gardiner relocated to Europe. He wanted to take advantage of the continent's longstanding acceptance of black artists and enthusiasm for jazz. He purchased a one-way boat ticket from New York to Sweden and did not return to America for five years.

Gardiner first disembarked in Copenhagen, Denmark, a popular destination for many expatriate jazz musicians, including the multi-instrumentalist Roland Kirk and the tenor saxophonist Dexter Gordon. Gardiner first played with the house band at Jazzhus Montmarte before Gordon hired him to replace his drummer at Billie's Bounce. He played with Gordon until January 1963 when Paul Hansen, the new owner of Adlon, hired Gardiner and his newly formed quartet as the club's house band. That year he went on to open numerous jazz rooms and clubs in Norway and Sweden, where he eventually settled. In 1964 he met Sigbrit Alice Christina Pennemo, the owner of a dry cleaning shop; three years later they visited the United States to share their engagement with the Gardiner family.

After five years with his band, Gardiner retired and became a theater musician, also playing occasional gigs in the small Swedish town where he lived with Pennemo. That summer, in 1969, they vacationed in Spain's Canary Islands, where Gardiner was serendipitously hired to open the Half Note. Between 1969 and 1980 he played every summer season in the Canary Islands. Unfortunately, in the 1980 season, Gardiner and Pennemo's sixteen-year relationship was brought to an abrupt and violent end. On 11 March 1980 Pennemo was brutally murdered with a hammer by a close friend. Gardiner remained in the Canary Islands during the inquest and trial, but the loss led him to attempt suicide. He went to the boardwalk to drown himself, but Mikael Andersson, an armless and legless young man, stopped Gardiner with his broad smile. Though it was nineteen years before the two men spoke, Andersson's positive attitude despite his disability inspired Gardiner to combine his passion for rhythm with his newfound passion for helping people.

Gardiner entered a five-year depression in which he nonetheless studied physiology, cognitive science, and the impact of rhythm on both. The result was a revolutionary therapeutic method to improve the coordination between mind and body. In 1985 Gardiner registered with the U.S. Patent Office his method, the Coordinated Rhythm for Mind and Body Balance Awareness. Eight years passed before he publicly tested the method. Dr. Bertil Nyman, chairman of the Stockholm Stroke Victims Association, invited Gardiner to spend twelve weeks working with patients. Patients' speech, memory, and concentration were improved. Since then more than fifty therapists worldwide have been trained in what is now known as the Ronnie Gardiner Rhythm Method.

Gardiner has been greatly recognized for his artistic and musical contributions. In 1998 Stockholm's legendary club Nalen opened Ronnie's Room, a celebrated venue for jazz and jazz-related music. That same year Gardiner inaugurated the Ronnie Gardiner Scholarship for Swedish Drummers Deserving Wider Recognition. In 2001 he became the first foreigner to win the Medal of St. Erik, Stockholm's highest honor for citizens, and in 2004 he won the Topsy Award for his musical achievements. Over the course of his sixty-year career Gardiner has recorded more than seventy CDs with many international and Swedish jazz greats, such as Albert Ayler and Charlie Norman. His own groups, the Ronnie Gardiner Octet and the Ronnie Gardiner Septet, have recorded three albums, the most recent being *Tivoli Happy Jazz Band: 10th Anniversary Live at Grona Lund* (2002).

Gardiner continued to make his home in Sweden, performing with his band and teaching and promoting the Ronnie Gardiner Rhythm Method. He also began acting for the Swedish educational television program *Go, Yo-Yo, Go!* designed to teach children English.

CRYSTAL AM NELSON

Gardner, Charles W. (1782–6 Apr. 1863), abolitionist and Episcopal minister, was born near Shoemakertown, New Jersey. Nothing else is known about his family background. Eloquent, forceful, and determined, Gardner earned the respect and admiration of his colleagues and congregants. The great black nationalist MARTIN R. DELANY considered him a man of "might and talent" who compelled whites to "recognize and respect" African Americans (*Christian Recorder*, 29 Apr. 1880). Theodore Dwight Weld, a celebrated antislavery lecturer, considered Gardner one of the country's leading black orators, and in 1837 Gardner became the first African American to address an annual meeting of the American Anti-Slavery Society.

He began his ministerial career in 1809 as an itinerant Methodist preacher, visiting churches throughout the Chesapeake region. The experience led him to condemn the institution of slavery and the colonization movement, which aimed at the expatriation of free blacks to Africa. His criticism of Methodist slaveholders, especially Methodist ministers, who he implied bore responsibility for the 1831 NAT TURNER rebellion, brought him into conflict with the region's bishop, who warned him to halt his antislavery preaching or lose his license to preach. Gardner advised the bishop that nothing but the end of slavery would make him stop. His denunciations of colonization included assertions that newly freed slaves should be given the option of settling in western American territories instead of removal to Liberia, and he personally approached President Andrew Jackson in Washington, D.C., to convince him to halt the deportations to Africa. Fearing that Gardner's anticolonization lectures had gained ground among free blacks, the Maryland Colonization Society swore out an arrest warrant against him in 1832, forcing him to flee the state.

Gardner had moved to Philadelphia around 1827 and began preaching for the First African Presbyterian Church, despite his standing as a Methodist minister. In April 1830 he probably withdrew from the church to devote more of his time to the kind of antislavery lecturing that so outraged white Marylanders and to the early Black National Convention movement, where he served as chaplain at its first two meetings. He returned to Philadelphia's First African Church in 1836, a full member of the Philadelphia Presbytery, and began his twelve-year tenure there. A mild-mannered Christian, Gardner emphasized fiscal discipline, social activism, and children's education while at First African. No other black church in the city, according to Gardner's successor William T. Catto, "could compare with the church at this time ... for the number of young intellectuals that were members of it" (McBride, 155).

Not long after Gardner's return to Philadelphia, the state began action to disfranchise African Americans who had enjoyed the right to vote since the formation of the state. He feverishly organized resistance and in 1837 helped found the Pennsylvania Anti-Slavery Society in Harrisburg. A member of the Philadelphia Anti-Slavery Society, Gardner joined with ROBERT PURVIS, James McCrummill, Frederick A. Hinton, and other black leaders to defend the black community. A June 1837 protest meeting at the Bethel African Methodist Episcopal Church in Philadelphia requested that Gardner and Hinton draw up a protest memorial to the state constitutional convention. The memorial, delivered to Harrisburg on 6 January 1838 by James Biddle, a prominent white Philadelphia Whig, asserted that the proposed change created "a distinction among men unknown in the law of God." Moreover, they asserted that the state's African American community represented a people "'more sinned against than sinning'" that had done nothing to merit deprivation "of our rights and" to be "disowned as citizens" (McBride, 160–162). The state constitutional convention rejected the appeal and agreed to put disfranchisement of the state's black citizens to a general vote. To bolster African American protests, Gardner and the white abolitionist Benjamin C. Bacon canvassed the black community on behalf of the Pennsylvania Abolition Society and printed a census of Philadelphia's black population to prove that African Americans were responsible, hard working, and educated, worthy of retaining their voting rights. As Gardner had declared before the American Anti-Slavery Society in 1837, if as slaves blacks could become "skilful [*sic*] mechanics, trusty housekeepers, and safe nurses," as southern slaveholders readily admitted, "would they be less so, if made free[?]" (Ripley, vol. 3, 207). White racists turned this sensible tactic against them by asserting that the wealth generated by Philadelphia blacks would allow them to seize power, control patronage, and invite to resettle in the city hordes of southern free blacks, "a refuse population, ignorant, indolent, and fit to be instruments of evil" (Winch, *A Gentleman of Color*, 299). Blacks lost the right to vote in 1838 and despite eighty-one petition drives did not regain it until 1873.

The defeat led Gardner and many of his colleagues to reconsider black immigration plans. In the fall of 1839 Trinidad sent agents to Philadelphia to recruit settlers. Gardner, who once had favored Canadian resettlement, Hinton, Purvis, and others became interested in the scheme, but negative reports that came trickling back from those who had gone to Trinidad killed interest in the project. Instead, Gardner renewed his antislavery actions and joined the Philadelphia Vigilant Committee, becoming its president in 1844, and also helped form the Union Missionary Society. He left Philadelphia in 1848 and returned to his native New Jersey, where he led efforts among Princeton blacks to petition the state legislature to "grant us the right of elective franchise" (*North Star*, 7 Apr. 1849).

Between 1850 and 1857 Gardner filled pulpits in Hartford, Connecticut, and Newport, Rhode Island, where he established the first Sabbath school at the state's oldest African American congregation. He then moved to Harrisburg, Pennsylvania, where he organized the Elder Street—later known as the Capital Street—Presbyterian Church. He also helped organize First of August parades that included a unit of fully armed Henry Highland Garnet Guards and a Toussaint L'Ouverture Club, reflecting the militancy of Gardner and his new neighbors. As William T. Catto observed in his recollection of Gardner's career (*Liberator*, 24 Apr. 1863), the eighty-one-year-old clergyman had been a fiery abolitionist long before anyone had ever heard of William Lloyd Garrison and remained one to the last day of his life.

FURTHER READING

Battle, Charles A. *Negroes on the Island of Rhode Island* (1932).

McBride, David. "Black Protest against Racial Politics: Gardner, Hinton, and Their Memorial of 1838," *Pennsylvania History* 46 (Apr. 1979): 149–162.

Quarles, Benjamin. *Black Abolitionists* (1969).

Ripley, C. Peter, ed. *The Black Abolitionist Papers*, 5 vols. (1985–1992).

Winch, Julie. *A Gentleman of Color: The Life of James Forten* (2002).

Winch, Julie. *Philadelphia's Black Elite: Activism, Accommodation, and the Struggle for Autonomy, 1787–1848* (1988).

DONALD YACOVONE

Gardner, Edward G. (15 Feb. 1925–), businessman and civic leader, was born in Chicago, Illinois, the son of Frank Gardner, a U.S. federal employee, and Eva. Residing in his parents' West Chesterfield home on Chicago's far South Side, Gardner attended Gillespie Elementary. In elementary school Gardner exhibited his gifts of salesmanship and initiative when he began delivering the *Chicago Defender* newspaper door-to-door in his neighborhood. The community contacts he developed as a newspaper boy continued long after he had given up his paper route. He and his older brother Frank were the only two African American students enrolled in Fenger High School. Edward's high school extracurricular interests were intramural sports, primarily basketball, and creative art. His artistic abilities resulted in summer scholarships to the Ray Vogue Art School. Gardner was drafted into the U.S. military after his high school graduation in 1943. Stationed in Japan and the Pacific islands in World War II, he served as a staff sergeant in the segregated army with the Port Battalion Corps.

After his discharge from the military, Gardner entered Chicago Teachers College (later Chicago State University), where he earned a degree in Elementary Education; soon after, he earned a master of arts degree from the University of Chicago. While attending Chicago Teachers College and working nights at the U.S. Post Office, Gardner met Bettiann Gueno. They married in 1950 and had four children.

The growth of his family motivated the energetic and innovative Gardner to supplement his salary as an elementary classroom teacher and vice principal of young African American students by selling ethnic hair care products after school hours. He discussed with area hairstylists the types of products needed to best service their salon clients. These conversations led Gardner to develop his own line of hair care products. Using a chemist and an at-home lab for product development, Gardner perfected the styling creams, conditioners, and shampoos, and Bettiann Gardner organized the accompanying office business systems. This was the beginning of Soft Sheen Products, Inc. With the success of the emerging business, Gardner left the Chicago Board of Education and became a full-time marketing wizard and enterprising entrepreneur. The company he and his wife cofounded became the fifth largest black-owned and black-operated corporation in the United States, an $81 million enterprise with international scope. Soft Sheen employees totaled four hundred, and each of the young Gardners held executive positions in the company. Soft Sheen had the loyal support of many hairstylists and professional technicians, winning tradeshow trophies and industry-wide recognition. The expansion of the personal care products to include the Carefree Curl and the Optimum hair straightening system in the 1980s skyrocketed the company into ethnic hair care leadership. In the early twenty-first century Soft Sheen-Carson Products came under the umbrella of L'Oreal USA.

Gardner led the industry in the formation of the American Health and Beauty Aids Institute (AHBAI), a cohesive and supportive organization devoted to the unity of competitive African American companies in the beauty aids field. This type of open forum and intercommunication assisted African American business survival. As cofounders and publishers of the ethnic magazine *ShopTalk*, a trade publication, the Gardners presented an opportunity for all manufacturers of ethnic beauty aids to be featured in lead stories and as advertisers along with salon professionals.

An ongoing priority for Gardner was the balancing of his corporate successes with his commitment to the African American community. His projects included major financial backing for the massive voter registration drive that led to the 1983 election of Chicago's first African American mayor HAROLD WASHINGTON. Gardner founded the Black on Black Love campaign against black on black crime and illiteracy. He contributed financially to charities (such as organizations dedicated to fighting sickle cell anemia), causes and groups (such as ex-offenders), and families and individuals.

Gardner served on the boards of the Cook County Commission on Human Rights, the Chicago Urban League, the Beauty and Barber Supply Institute (BBSI), Seaway National Bank, Provident Hospital, the Chicago Capital Fund, Chicago United, and the Board of Trustees of DePaul University. He founded and served as the CEO of Perfect Pinch seasoning company, he became a minority owner of the Chicago Bulls, and he cofounded the New Regal Theatre, Lady Roll Entertainment, and Garden Investment Partners, comprising affordable housing sites and a family entertainment center. In each of his business endeavors he trained and guided young employees toward business excellence. He became a role model, a mentor, and a source of encouragement to many. When presenting Gardner with the 1999 Golden Pyramid Award for business leadership, Jacoby Dickens, chair of the board of Seaway National Bank, stated that Gardner had "a rare combination of qualities; responsible leadership, unselfish generosity and unwavering commitment and is ... one of the great community leaders of our time" (*Jet*, 24 May 1999).

FURTHER READING

Hicks, Jonathan P. "Blacks Fight for Market Niche," *New York Times*, 5 June 1985.

JEAN M. BRANNON

Gardner, Eliza Ann (28 May 1831–4 Jan. 1922), abolitionist and social leader, was born in New York City to free parents, James and Dorothy Gardner. Her father was a shipping contractor who made sails for large vessels. About 1845, while Gardner was in her teens, her family took up residence in Boston, Massachusetts, and opened its own business. Gardner attended the Boston Public School for Colored Children (also known as the Smith School, after the white businessman Abiel Smith, who donated funds). She was educated by leaders in the antislavery movement and developed an appreciation for their cause. The school was also used as a meeting place for the "colored citizens" to discuss issues of concern in their communities. During Gardner's time in Boston's only "colored" grammar school, Boston's African American community was fighting tirelessly to abolish colored schools and end school segregation using the *Roberts v. Boston* case as the catalyst. Gardner was a gifted student with a sharp intellect and exceptional memory, which enabled her to excel as a student and to earn numerous scholarships.

Learning the art of sewing from her mother and business savvy from her father, Eliza Ann Gardner became an accomplished seamstress and tailor, securing contracts for banners and flags for local businesses as well as for ladies' garments. She made the first banner for the Plymouth Rock Odd Fellows Lodge. Known for her embroidery and dressmaking skills, she became a mantua maker. Mantuas were loose gowns worn over ladies' petticoats but were open in the front. Mantua makers began making these garments in the late seventeenth century, and mantua maker was listed as an occupation up to the early twentieth century. The uniqueness of mantuas was in their construction as fitted garments without the use of bones or other restrictive materials. The title of mantua maker brought prestige to a dressmaking shop, and Gardner was sought out for her skills as a mantua maker.

Gardner never forgot the lessons of antislavery and social justice that she learned and witnessed while a student at the Smith School. After she inherited her parents' home upon their death she bravely used it as a stop along the Underground Railroad. She continued her work as a mantua maker but dedicated the rest of her life to the abolitionist movement, the temperance movement, and her religion. She worked alongside the famed abolitionists SOJOURNER TRUTH, HARRIET TUBMAN, FREDRICK DOUGLASS, William Lloyd Garrison, and LEWIS HAYDEN. Hayden was so moved by the commitment and work of the Boston abolitionist community that he and his wife, Harriet, moved to a home in Beacon Hill, which also became a station on the Underground Railroad.

In addition to Gardner's ardent activism in the antislavery movement she was known for her involvement in the temperance movement, championed at the time by a white women's organization, the Woman's Christian Temperance Union (WCTU), founded in 1874. The WCTU was the largest women's organization in the United States, with interests crossing racial, religious, and class lines. However, the ongoing conflict between Frances Willard, who became president of the WCTU in 1879, and IDA B. WELLS-BARNETT, a leader in the antilynching movement, in addition to segregation within the organization, caused friction between the races.

Gardner's religious faith and belief in the ills of alcohol and its negative impact on families and society compelled her to activism, and she founded the Women's Era Club, also known as the Colored Women's Club of Boston. There is some dispute as to who founded the organization, some giving credit to JOSEPHINE ST. PIERRE RUFFIN in 1894 possibly because she was also working in Boston. Ruffin founded the National Federation of Afro-American Women in 1895 and organized, along with MARY CHURCH TERRELL, the National Association of Colored Women (NACW) in 1896, which absorbed many women's clubs, including the Women's Era Club of Boston.

Morality, education, and unity of women for the improvement of quality of life for the African American community were the goals of the NACW. A branch of the NACW worked for the equality of women, including voting rights; however, Gardner's intention and activism around women's suffrage is not clear. Moreover, Gardner was held in high esteem within her church and remained devoted to it throughout her life. She was often referred to as the "Mother of the AME." In 1909 Gardner organized the Butler Club of Zion Church and remained president until her death.

Eliza Ann Gardner was an activist and organizer in Boston well before W. E. B. DUBOIS established the Boston chapter of the NAACP in 1912 or the Boston Urban League was established in 1919. She never married, dedicating her life to the betterment of her race and the empowerment of young girls. Her acknowledged contributions to the antislavery movement and the temperance movement, as well as her lifelong devotion to the church, are her legacies. She died at the age of ninety-one on 4 January 1922.

FURTHER READING

Brown, Hallie Quinn. *Homespun Heroines and Other Women of Distinction* (1926).

Giddings, Paula. *When and Where I Enter: The Impact of Black Women on Race and Sex in America* (1984).

Hine, Darlene Clark, and Kathleen Thompson. *A Shining Thread of Hope: The History of Black Women in America* (1999).

Horton, James Oliver, and Lois E. Horton. *Black Bostonians: Family Life and Community Struggle in the Antebellum North* (1979).

C. Eric Lincoln, and Lawrence H. Mamiya. *The Black Church in the African American Experience* (1990).

Mitchell, Henry H. *Black Church Beginnings: The Long-hidden Realities of the First Years* (2004).

CAROL PARKER TERHUNE

Gardner, James Daniel (16 Sept. 1839–29 Sept. 1905), Civil War soldier and Medal of Honor recipient, was born in Gloucester, Virginia, and was likely a slave prior to the Civil War. When Gardner enlisted for service in the Union army on 15 September 1863, he listed his occupation as that of an oysterman. The service of James Gardner and thousands of other African Americans in the Union army represented a quest to destroy slavery and establish a foundation for postwar demands for full citizenship. For the federal government and most of the North, however, black patriotism was unwillingly accepted only out of sheer necessity—two years of battle and staggering Union casualties compelled Northerners to swallow their opposition to black recruitment (and the measure of racial equality that service implied) in order to fill their depleted army ranks. Indeed, early war-time fever had dissipated and voluntary enlistments faded, making it difficult for states to reach their recruitment quotas. African Americans were ready and willing to join the fight at the war's outset, but were denied the right to serve in any capacity other than that of military laborers. With President Lincoln's call for black troops in the Emancipation Proclamation and the establishment of the Bureau of U.S. Colored Troops (USCT) in mid-1863, however, scores of USCT regiments were established, some initially at the state level.

James Daniel Gardner, c. 1900. Civil War veteran and recipient of the Medal of Honor for his actions at the Battle of Chaffin's Farm. (Library of Congress/Daniel Murray Collection.)

One such regiment was the 2nd North Carolina Colored Infantry, established in the summer of 1863, drawing its men from North Carolina and Virginia. Company officers were sent throughout the area to recruit men, among them James Gardner and Miles James in Virginia. Gardner joined Company I, and service records note that he measured 5'7" inches tall. Among the other enlistees in Company I were fellow oysterman Humphrey Gilley, possibly a friend, as well as Anthony, Henry, and Samuel Fuller, either brothers or former slaves from the same plantation—all farmers hailing from Virginia's Princess Ann County. Gardner, however, was not formally mustered into the 2nd North Carolina until the unit moved north to Virginia on 28 October 1863. When the regiment reached full strength, it was assigned to garrison and training duty. In January 1864 it was redesignated as the 36th USCT regiment. Occasional non-combat losses hit the 36th USCT and Company I. In January 1864, for instance, Private Charles Gorden died of disease in the hospital at Fort Monroe, Virginia. In April 1864, while stationed at the prisoner of war camp at Point Lookout, Maryland, nineteen-year-old Private John Green was killed by the accidental discharge of his gun. Such losses due to disease and accident were common during the Civil War. By July 1864 Gardner and the men of the 36th USCT were on the front lines before the Confederate capitol of Richmond, where fighting had largely evolved into trench and siege warfare. To put an end to the stalemate, General Ulysses Grant developed a two-part plan to breach the enemy lines. With simultaneous attacks on both sides of the James River, the main punch would be delivered by Major General Benjamin Butler's Army and its USCT regiments. Grant hoped to capture four key forts, including Fort Harrison that served as an anchor to the south and located on a bluff known as New Market Heights, which would compel the Confederates to evacuate their capitol. Among those regiments sent in for the attack in the early hours of 29 September 1864 were the 4th, 6th, 36th, and 38th USCT regiments. The fighting in the fortifications around Fort Harrison was fierce, but the men of the USCT prevailed. Among those in the thick of battle that day was Private James Gardner, one of the first men, along with Edward Ratcliff and others, to breach Fort Harrison's defenses. Gardner "rushed in advance of his brigade, shot at a rebel officer, who was on the parapet cheering his men, and then ran him through with his bayonet" (*Official Records*, 168). The battle of New Market Heights would turn out to be a draw, however, with only one Confederate fort captured in two days of fighting. But for the men of the USCT regiments, gallant soldiers like Gardner, Samuel Gilchrist, and Robert Pinn, it was a banner day. No more could the courage and capability of black troops be questioned. Indeed, General Butler would later state that "In the charge of the enemy's works ... better men were never better led, better officers never led better men ... a few more such gallant charges and to command colored troops will be the post of honor in the American Armies" (*Official Records*, 163). For their gallantry at New Market Heights, fourteen black soldiers received the Medal of Honor, including James Daniel Gardner. Many others also received promotions in rank, with Gardner advancing to sergeant.

Gardner and his regiment continued serving through the remainder of the war, stationed in Texas until the end of 1865 and through much of 1866. Despite his promotion, Gardner did not distinguish himself as a model soldier. Indeed, he was demoted back to private on 13 July 1865, and later imprisoned for reasons unknown at Brazos Santiago, Texas on 29 March 1866. On 20 September 1866 Gardner and most of the 36th USCT was mustered out of the service and returned home. With the war over, Gardner returned to Virginia and by 1867 had married a woman named Judith (b. 1845). The couple had two children, Rosana (b. 1867) and William (b. 1873), and resided in New Town Township in King and Queen County, Virginia. While Judith Gardner worked as a domestic servant, Gardner performed farm work but later worked on a railroad gang. Although the pay was lucrative, such work was hard and crews typically traveled and lived in converted box cars that earned the nicknamed "Hell on wheels" for the poor living conditions they afforded.

The 1900 federal census identified Gardner as a railroad laborer, working in the Covington Magisterial District of Virginia. Performing this difficult work at the age of sixty certainly demonstrated Gardner's hardy constitution and a measure of the toughness that he displayed at New Market Heights. The circumstances of Gardner's death in 1905 are unknown. He was buried in Calvary Cemetery in Ottumwa, Iowa. How Gardner ended up so far from home and without his wife, who still resided in New Town Township (and remained a widow as late as 1920), is unknown, but it was likely related to his railroad work. Perhaps he was a worker on the Great Burlington Route Railroad that ran through Ottumwa, and was buried there after an accident or sudden death. One unverified source, however, stated that Gardner died in Clark's Summit, Pennsylvania, in the eastern part of the state, near Scranton. If true, it is puzzling why Gardner would have been buried in Iowa. Whatever the circumstances of his death, Gardner will always be remembered as a Medal of Honor winner that fought with courage and valor in the cause of freedom.

FURTHER READING

United States Government Printing Office. *The War of the Rebellion: Official Records of the Union and Confederate Armies*, Series I, vol. 42, Part III (1893).

GLENN ALLEN KNOBLOCK

Gardner, Matt (18 July 1848–5 June 1943), a former slave, became a respected minister, entrepreneurial landowner, and philanthropic community leader during the years after Civil War. Born on a plantation in Elkton, Giles County, Tennessee, Gardner was the eldest son of the four children of Rachel Vasser Gardner and Martin Gardner, both of whom were slaves. While enslaved, his family was owned by three different families. Little is known about their first owner except that he was an Atlantic slave trader by the name of Franklin; his forename may have been Isaac. Gardner's second slave master was Richard Whitehead Vasser, who owned his own dry goods and mortgage company in Limestone County, Alabama. During this time Gardner's father, Martin, was sold or died, and his mother Rachel took another husband, Tom Gardner, with whom she had three children. The Vassers proved especially cruel. Occasionally, the slave master's son went out and got too drunk to find his way home, and the elder Vasser paid Gardner to bring the young man home. Gardner saved his money and waited for an opportunity to use it when freedom came.

In November 1862 Richard W. Vasser sold Gardner's family and eighty-one other slaves along with some land he owned in Giles County to Dr. Richard C. Gardner, a merchant and partner of Evans, Gardner and Company, a dry goods dealer on Broadway in New York City. Dr. Gardner was also partner in another dry goods business, Evan, Fite and Company, located in Nashville, Tennessee. After the purchase of the slaves, Dr. Gardner moved to Giles County, where Matt and his family became house servants and were allowed to own small articles of property. The Magnussons, a Swedish family who worked for Dr. Gardner in return for their passage to the United States, later recalled fond memories of the two families living together in a log cabin. They remembered the children playing together and Matt teaching the Magnusson boys how to speak English.

The signing of the 1863 Emancipation Proclamation did not apply to Tennessee, although it prompted some slaves to claim their freedom behind Union lines. Slavery was not abolished in Tennessee until 22 February 1865, and by then the seventeen-year-old Matt Gardner had saved a hundred dollars. Now a freeman he continued to work and save his money for what he knew was most valuable—land. Gardner worked for whites as a farm laborer and was paid twenty-five cents a day for his work; at night he plowed and worked his own family's crops by moonlight. At the age of twenty-nine, to prove he was serious about marriage, and to ensure that the woman he married and their children would be taken care of financially, Gardner posted a $1,250 marriage bond to marry Henrietta (Brown) Jenkins, a former slave, and the two wed on 18 January 1877, eventually having eleven children. Four years after his marriage, Gardner received his first opportunity to purchase land, 106 acres in Elkton, Tennessee. Gardner and another man originally purchased the land jointly on a four-year payment plan. It is believed the other man was either bought out or could not pay his share, so Gardner eventually received a deed for all 106 acres. He thus became one of the few independent black farmers in post–Civil War Tennessee.

During the 1890s Gardner's philanthropic spirit and entrepreneurial abilities evolved. In about 1896 he built a two-story "saddlebag-I house"—a dwelling with a central chimney and a simple floor plan that typified the folk architecture of well-to-do farmers on the southeastern agricultural landscape. The home boldly displayed Gardner's prosperity and increasing prominence in the community. Gardner erected outbuildings for his farm products and livestock, and to serve the local black community. These structures included a sorghum gin and a "storehouse" from which Gardner sold food to neighbors for cash, exchange, and credit. At about the same time, Gardner financed and helped build the first school for Elkton's black children. As well as paying the teachers' salaries, he provided them with room and board and supplied the books. Around Gardner's farm grew an African American community that Gardner named Dixontown for John Dixon, the oldest freed black who resided in the area. That community is still in existence in the twenty-first century. In 1922 Gardner paid $3,261.50 in cash to purchase an additional 181.2 acres of land, giving him approximately 300 acres of the most prime land located on and around the banks of the Elk River.

The Ku Klux Klan was organized in the winter of 1865–1866 in Pulaski, Tennessee, just eighteen miles from Matt Gardner's home. Because Gardner owned so much prime land and helped others in the black community, the Klan and other whites threatened him and declared that they could take his land. To ensure this never happened, Gardner and an unidentified white man reportedly traveled three days by horse to register his land in Nashville. In another incident members of the KKK confronted Gardner as he sat on his front porch. The men fired gunshots into his home and threatened him. In reaction to this, Gardner instructed his family to sit only on the back porch and congregate, socialize, and play only at the rear of the property. Refusing to bow to intimidation, Gardner, through the Depression and the New Deal era, made loans to many blacks so they could purchase or keep their own land. He cosigned for black individuals buying land on contract. Gardner also made loans to whites, including members of the Magnusson family, and records show that he appeared in court many times on behalf of both blacks and whites in many situations. On one occasion, for example, Matt ensured a $3,000 bond for a man who was becoming the legal guardian of his father. Gardner also held many recorded trust deeds and chattel mortgages for individuals in Elkton.

Although illiterate, Gardner was a well-known and profound preacher. He traveled around Giles County and Limestone County, Alabama, preaching at several different churches. In 1902 Gardner purchased a gravel island in the middle of the Elk River on which to perform baptisms for his and other church congregations in the community. In 1911 he became the pastor of the New Hope Primitive Church in Elkton, where he stayed until his death.

In 1926 the school in Elkton that Gardner financed burned down, and Gardner spearheaded local efforts to acquire a Rosenwald school. He led the necessary community fund-raising efforts to match the contributions of the Rosenwald Fund and the state government. In January 1930 the Rosenwald Colored School opened in Elkton, with Gardner as the chairman of the African American school board.

Matt Gardner represents an often overlooked generation of rural African Americans who succeeded in the segregated South despite tremendous barriers. He provided crucial leadership to his communities in the areas of education, religion, agriculture, and land ownership. On 25 November 1942 Gardner received a certificate of recognition signed by Governor Prentice Cooper for the Tennessee Home Food Supply Program, for meritorious achievement. The certificate was awarded "for having grown 75% or more of all the food necessary for the family and livestock and in leadership for better living in the community."

Gardner's wife Henrietta died in 1940, and he passed away three years later. Eulogies in the local papers emphasized the many contributions that both Gardners had made to the local community. The *Pulaski Citizen* wrote of him and his wife after her passing:

> Her home was more than a dwelling, it became a shrine. All races went there, that's where Matt and Henrietta stay and everybody knew for what they stood. Some went for information, others for inspiration. Many went to satisfy their appetites. All felt benefited for having gone. Elkton has suffered a great loss, the Negro race the greatest loss.

And of Matt Gardner, the *Pulaski Recorder* wrote: "His influence upon his race was noticeable and he commanded the respect of all the hundreds who knew him while here. So Matt was justly honored in death as he had been all throughout his life." The body was withheld from burial for five days, pending the arrival of relatives and friends. It was estimated that more than one thousand people attended Gardner's funeral. It was said to be the largest number ever assembled for a funeral in the Elkton area.

FURTHER READING

Jones, Carla J. "Matt Gardner," in *The Heritage of Giles County, Tennessee, Vol. 1* (2006).

Jones, Carla J. "The Matt Gardner Story: An African American Treasure among Us, Unknown and Unseen," *Pulaski Free Press*, 18, 20 Nov. 2004; 2 Dec. 2004; *Pulaski Citizen*, 23, 30 Nov. 2004.

Stevenson Gardner, Lisa. "Gardner House Placed on National Registry of Historical Places," *Giles County Historical Society Bulletin* 23 (1996).

Obituaries: *Pulaski Citizen*, 7 Aug. 1940; *Pulaski Recorder*, 16 June 1943.

CARLA J. JONES

Gardner, Newport (1743– ?), community leader and musician, was born Occramer Marycoo in West Africa. Although his country of origin is unknown, a 1757 ship manifest shows that he was brought to America at the age of fourteen. He was on one of that year's seven slaving voyages that brought a total of 831 African slaves to Rhode Island. Gardner was one of the 106,544 slaves brought to Newport, Rhode Island, between 1709 and 1807. Caleb Gardner, a white merchant and member of the principal slave-trading team Briggs & Gardner, bought the teenage Marycoo and baptized him into the Congregational faith as Newport Gardner.

The forced exposure to Christianity aided Gardner's rise to a leadership position in the New World. He quickly learned English from daily Bible studies with his master, who freed Gardner after overhearing him pray for emancipation. Upon gaining his freedom Gardner combined his new religious fervor with his interest in returning to Africa—an interest shared by the considerable African community that developed in Newport as a result of Rhode Island's 60 to 90 percent control over the transatlantic slave trade during the eighteenth century.

In 1780 Gardner and his fellow black Newporters founded the African Union Society, the first black association in America, whose mission was to facilitate the self-improvement of Newport's black community. The society worked with other Northeast abolitionist groups to emancipate the slaves so that they could return to Africa, an initiative that became known as "the colonization struggle" (Armstead, 29). Gardner also collaborated on a plan for an African American Christian settlement that was developed by Dr. Samuel Hopkins, a white pastor of the First Congregational Church and an outspoken antislavery activist. Hopkins considered Gardner to be an exceptional colleague whose religious devotion and commitment to a new, independent African state proved a tremendous asset to the struggle for freedom.

Gardner's devotion and commitment were reflected in his family. After his emancipation Gardner married. He and his wife, Limas, had four children: Abraham, Charles, Salmar, and Silva. Abraham, Charles, and Silva died from unknown causes before reaching the age of five and are buried in God's Little Acre, Rhode Island's famed African burial ground.

Gardner was also a skilled musician who taught as a music instructor after his emancipation. He was the first published African American composer, and musical historians consider him to be among the top black composers of the late eighteenth to the early twentieth centuries. Gardner's most notable work is an anthem titled "Promise," of which no known copies exist today.

On 17 January 1826, at the age of eighty-two, Gardner and his last surviving son, Salmar Nubia, joined a party of sixteen on a voyage to Liberia. After sixty years of working on the colonization struggle he reconciled himself to America's political and social climate that stood in opposition to the autonomous black state that he and the African Union Society advocated. Gardner returned to Africa hoping to set an example for the youth upon whom, he believed, the future elevation of American blacks depended.

FURTHER READING

Armstead, Myra B. Young. *Lord, Please Don't Take Me in August: African Americans in Newport and Saratoga Springs, 1870–1930* (1999).

Coughtry, Jay. *The Notorious Triangle: Rhode Island and the African Slave Trade, 1700–1807* (1981).

"Newport Gardner (1746–1826)." *The Black Perspective in Music*, vol. 4, no. 2, Bicentennial Number (July; 1976), 202–207.

CRYSTAL AM NELSON

Garland, Hazel B. (28 Jan. 1913–5 Apr. 1988), journalist and civic leader, was born Hazel Barbara Maxine

Hill on a farm outside Terre Haute, Indiana, the oldest of sixteen children born to George, a coalminer, and Hazel Hill. In the 1920s the family moved to Pennsylvania, where George Hill worked as a coal miner. Although an avid learner, Garland dropped out of high school to work as a maid and to help her younger brother continue his studies. She completed her education herself, saying that she "lived in libraries" (Collins, 105). She married Percy A. Garland, a photographer and businessman, in 1935 and settled in McKeesport, a suburb of Pittsburgh, where she gave birth to her only child, a daughter named Phyllis.

Garland became active in local organizations and, because she liked to write, frequently served as the club reporter. She was on the publicity committee for the local YWCA when its first black staff worker was hired in 1943. The *Pittsburgh Courier* sent a reporter to cover the tea honoring the first Y in Allegheny County to be integrated, but the reporter got lost on the way there, so Garland was asked to take her notes on the event to the city editor, WENDELL SMITH. Smith was impressed by her writing and offered her a position as a stringer with the *Courier*. As a stringer, she reported on local events and persons and was paid two dollars for each article the *Courier* printed.

Garland liaised with city councils, police stations, and churches, producing so much material that Smith suggested she write a column called "Tri-City News." While working as a stringer, Garland sought to improve her skills in journalism by attending Saturday morning lectures on journalism given by *Courier* editors. One editor, who felt that journalism was a man's world, sent her to cover a murder in a brothel. Young and attractive, Garland feared she might be mistaken for a prostitute, so she paid a male reporter to get the information for her, and then wrote the story.

In 1946 Garland was offered a full-time position at the *Pittsburgh Courier* as a reporter and assistant women's editor. The name of her column was changed to "Things to Talk About." She covered community events, such as weddings, births, promotions, awards, and church activities. Community columns were a staple of black newspapers because mainstream publications covered few African Americans and, when they did, much of that coverage was negative.

At this time, the *Courier* was the most popular black newspaper in the country. It published fourteen editions, including local and national editions, and had branch offices in twelve cities. It attained a circulation of 357,212 in May 1947, a record for audited black newspapers. Garland described the *Courier* in the 1940s as a strong, crusading newspaper: "We were protesting lynching. We were trying to get the poll tax abolished. During World War II, we fought for victory at home as well as victory abroad. We called it the Double V campaign. That meant we were working for racial equality at home as well as victory in the war" (Collins, 110). During this period of time, the *Courier* was also successful at leading efforts to integrate national sports. *Courier* editor Wendell Smith served as the liaison between JACKIE ROBINSON and Branch Rickey, general manager of the Brooklyn Dodgers, resulting in Robinson's joining that team in 1947.

As a full-time staff reporter, Garland was sent all over the country. In 1952, she traveled to a rural area of South Carolina to do a story on a black nurse-midwife who had delivered most of the babies, black and white, in her community. Garland was appalled at the poverty and lack of education she saw in the region, and she wrote a series of articles about it titled "The Three I's: Ignorance, Illiteracy, and Illegitimacy." The *Courier* entered the series in a regional journalism competition judged by writers from the nation's leading newspapers, and Garland's series was awarded the top prize.

In 1955, Garland began writing a weekly television column called "Video Vignettes." She focused on programs featuring African Americans, and she was frequently sent to Hollywood, where she interviewed both black and white stars. In her column, she critiqued the way blacks were portrayed on television and protested when black performers and newscasters were dismissed or programs showcasing blacks were discontinued. She was the first African American journalist to write such a column, which, at her death, was one of the longest-running television columns in newspaper history.

In 1966 John Sengstack bought the *Courier*, renamed it the *New Pittsburgh Courier*, and offered Garland the position of city editor. Garland reorganized the paper into sections, published more features, and had a reporter cover labor news. In 1972, she became editor in chief, the first African American woman to hold this position in a nationally circulated newspaper. In 1974, Garland was named Editor of the Year by the National Newspaper Publisher's Association (NNPA). That year she was also named News Hen of the year by the Women's Press Club of Pittsburgh. In 1975 she received a National Headline Award from Women in Communications, Inc., formerly Theta Sigma Phi.

In 1974 she stepped down as editor in chief because of health problems, but she was named assistant to the publisher by Sengstack. In 1977, Garland retired from full-time work, but she continued to write her two columns, "Things to Talk About" and "Video Vignettes." In 1978 and 1979 she served as a juror for the Pulitzer Prize. In 1988, *Renaissance Too*, a Pittsburgh magazine, established a scholarship fund for journalism students in her name and that of Mal Goode, a former Pittsburgh *Courier* journalist.

Hazel Garland died in McKeesport in 1988 of a heart attack. She is remembered as a pioneering female journalist who was committed to the black press. She believed that "there's still a need for a good black press because we haven't reached a utopia. There still has to be a voice" (Collins, 118).

FURTHER READING

The archives of the *New Pittsburgh Courier* (1966–1988) and the *Pittsburgh Courier* (1943–1966) contain the writings of Hazel B. Garland.

Collins, Jean E. *She Was There: Stories of Pioneering Women Journalists* (1980).

Davis, Marianna W., ed. *Contributions of Black Women to America, Vol. 1* (1982).

Garland, Phyl. "Hazel B. Garland (1913–1988): Journalist, editor," in Jessie Carney Smith, ed. *Notable Black American Women, Book II* (1996).

Garland, Phyl. "Journalism," in Jack Salzman, David L. Smith and Cornel West, eds. *Encyclopedia of African-American Culture and History, Vol. 3* (1996).

Obituaries: *New Pittsburgh Courier*, 6 Apr. 1988; *Jet 74* (25 Apr. 1988).

EUGENIE P. ALMEIDA

Garland, Red (13 May 1923–23 Apr. 1984), jazz pianist, was born William McKinley Garland Jr. in Dallas, Texas, the son of William Garland Sr., an elevator operator. His mother's name is unknown. Garland played clarinet and then alto saxophone in high school during which time he received lessons from the renowned jazz saxophonist Buster Smith, who took a disciplined approach to Garland's learning to read music. Before settling into music Garland had thirty-five fights as a lightweight professional boxer, at one point losing to SUGAR RAY ROBINSON.

While serving in the army Garland switched from alto sax to piano. At Fort Huachuca in Arizona he demonstrated his ability to read music and received informal lessons from the pianist JOHN LEWIS, who cofounded the Modern Jazz Quartet. He later studied with the pianist Lee Barnes. Discharged in 1944 Garland performed in Fort Worth, Texas, in 1945, when visiting trumpeter HOT LIPS PAGE hired him for a tour to New York City. He arrived in New York around March 1946 and during that year joined the singer BILLY ECKSTINE's bop big band for about six weeks.

From 1947 to 1949 Garland performed at the Down Beat Club in Philadelphia as the house pianist. In that capacity he accompanied all-star guest soloists such as the alto saxophonist CHARLIE PARKER and the trumpeters MILES DAVIS and FATS NAVARRO. He toured with the tenor saxophonist COLEMAN HAWKINS and the trumpeter ROY ELDRIDGE at some point early in the 1950s, worked as a soloist, and then rejoined Hawkins. He led a trio in Boston, Massachusetts, and also worked with the tenor saxophonist LESTER YOUNG.

Garland's fame derives from his position as pianist in Miles Davis's hard bop combos. In the summer of 1955 Davis formed a quintet with Garland, the tenor saxophonist Sonny Rollins, the bassist PAUL CHAMBERS, and the drummer Philly Joe Jones for a residency at the Café Bohemia in New York. The group began touring in the fall with JOHN COLTRANE replacing Rollins, and in this form they recorded the acclaimed Columbia album *'Round about Midnight* (1955–1956) and numerous sessions for the Prestige label. Garland also made albums without Davis as a leader on Prestige, introducing in a trio session on the album *Red Garland's Piano* (1956–1957) a version of "If I Were a Bell" that Davis soon made his own. Garland also headed a quintet that included Coltrane and the trumpeter Donald Byrd for *All Mornin' Long* and *Soul Junction* (both 1957). Also in 1957, with Chambers, Jones, and the alto saxophonist ART PEPPER, Garland made the album *Art Pepper Meets the Rhythm Section* for the Contemporary label.

While working with Davis, Garland became addicted to heroin, as did Chambers, Coltrane, and Jones. Despite great success, as measured in the modest world of jazz finance, he was often broke, compelled to spend nearly all his money on drugs. Because of personal problems, Garland was replaced by the pianist Tommy Flanagan in fall 1957. After Davis's solo tour of Europe, Garland rejoined him in December 1957. At the same time, Coltrane, who had been in and out of the group, overcame his addiction and rejoined the group, making Davis the leader of a sextet with the alto saxophonist CANNONBALL ADDERLEY, Chambers, and Jones.

Garland was featured in a swinging trio version of "Billy Boy" on the sextet album *Milestones*, and the fresh, punching, chordal patterns at the opening of that album's title track, "Milestones," contribute to one of the most exhilarating moments in recorded jazz. But Garland was dissatisfied with his lack of opportunity to take solos on *Milestones*, and he quit the sextet in 1958. His replacement was Bill Evans. Garland began to lead his own trio, and he worked with Jones, who left Davis soon thereafter. In late November 1958, after Evans, suffering from exhaustion, resigned, Garland returned to the sextet. He remained until February 1959, when Davis hired the pianist Wynton Kelly.

Garland performed in Philadelphia during the early 1960s. In 1965, when his mother died, he returned to Dallas to live with his father. At some point he married Lillie (maiden name unknown); they had two children. Debilitated by drug addiction and having lost his youthful zeal for the peripatetic jazz life, Garland devoted himself to his family and showed no interest in pursuing a potentially international career. From 1969 onward he usually worked with the saxophonist Marchel Ivery, and they appeared at local clubs such as the Rounders, Wellington's Arandas, and the Texas Magic Asylum.

Garland did leave Dallas to perform in New York in May 1971 at which time he recorded two albums, including *The Quota*, for the German MPS label, and in March 1974 he had a brief stand at the Keystone Korner in San Francisco, leading a trio with local bassist James Leary and the drummer Eddie Marshall. But in 1975–1976 he stopped playing altogether for eighteen months. He resumed his career at the aptly named Recovery Room in Dallas.

After 1977, when he recorded *Red Alert*, and into the early 1980s Garland was once again making records regularly. He returned to the Keystone Korner in May 1977, with Jones in his trio, and again in May 1978 with a quartet featuring the alto saxophonist Leo Wright. He performed briefly with the bassist Bob Cunningham and the drummer Ben Riley at Salt Peanuts in New York in midsummer 1980. Details of a European and a Japanese tour are unknown. In June 1982 he spent a week at Lush Life in New York with the bassist George Mraz, drummer Al Foster, and Ivery as his sidemen. He died of heart disease in Dallas.

According to the jazz educator Jerry Coker, Garland

> omitted the root from the bottom, if not altogether, placing instead a seventh or third (usually) on the bottom, and played the voicings more in the middle and upper rather than the lower portions of the keyboard. Within a very short time, virtually all jazz pianists made a similar change, sometimes modifying Garland's exact voicings. It was plain to see that we were not going to be hearing many root-oriented voicings again, except perhaps in ballads or at important cadence points in faster selections (Chambers, 220).

This innovative musical detail may be evident only to expert listeners. More generally Garland was not an innovator but a keeper of the flame. He is remembered as a soloist for utilizing block chords (two-handed melody and harmony locked in rhythmic unison) after the manner of MILT BUCKNER and George Shearing. As an accompanist he formed, with Chambers and Jones, one of the most swinging and fiery rhythm sections in jazz history.

FURTHER READING

Chambers, J. K. *Milestones: The Music and Times of Miles Davis* (1983).

Lyons, Len. *The Great Jazz Pianists: Speaking of Their Lives and Music* (1983).

Owens, Thomas. *Bebop: The Music and Its Players* (1995).

Ramsey, Douglas K. *Jazz Matters* (1989).

Obituary: *New York Times*, 26 Apr. 1984.

This entry is taken from the *American National Biography* and is published here with the permission of the American Council of Learned Societies.

BARRY KERNFELD

Garland, Samuel (24 Feb. 1847–9 July 1946), buffalo soldier, pioneer settler, and entrepreneur, was born in Lafayette County, Mississippi, to a Native American mother and an African American father. At the age of fourteen he boarded a riverboat on the Mississippi River and became a cabin boy. During the Civil War, Garland served as a Union volunteer. After the war, in 1867, he joined the Tenth U.S. Cavalry and was assigned to Company F at Leavenworth, Kansas. Leavenworth became the first headquarters for the Tenth U.S. Cavalry. In 1866 the U.S. Congress designated the Ninth and Tenth Cavalries and the Twenty-fourth and Twenty-fifth Infantries. These regiments were composed solely of African Americans, except for their white officers, the soldiers of these regiments were the first to officially serve in the military after the Civil War. After training, Company F was assigned to forts in western Kansas, responsible for a number of tasks, including subduing Indians, guarding railroad workers, and building forts.

Garland's first encounter with Indians almost cost him his life. On 1 August 1867 at Campbell's Camp, a railroad camp east of Hays, Kansas, near the town of Victoria, Garland and other troops were guarding railroad workers when they were attacked by Cheyenne warriors. During the battle Garland, who was shot in the head with an arrow, was knocked from his horse and left for dead. He recovered, and a day later the same warriors were tracked down and attacked by Troop F near the Saline River. In the battle of the Saline River the soldier William Christy was killed, the first buffalo soldier to be killed in battle.

In September 1868 Garland, who was stationed at Fort Wallace, Kansas, participated in the rescue of federal troops at the battle of Beecher Island. This battle found a detachment of Indian scouts led by Colonel George A. Forsyth pitted against Chief Roman Nose of the Cheyenne and his warriors at a small island on the Arickaree Fork of the Republican River near the Colorado-Kansas border. The battle lasted for nine days. Eventually surrounded by the Cheyenne, the scouts could not escape the island, and they had to eat horses and a coyote to keep from starving to death. Two scouts finally escaped and made their way to nearby Fort Wallace to secure help. Garland and other buffalo soldiers of the Tenth Cavalry rode off to rescue the remaining scouts stranded on Beecher Island.

In 1872, after six years with the U.S. Calvary, Garland was honorably discharged from the U.S. Army and returned to civilian life. In Leavenworth he met Mary Samuels, and they married on 23 December 1875. They had three children, William, Mary, and Eugenia. Mary Samuels's parents were originally from Georgetown, Kentucky. Her father John Samuels was a former slave of Imogene Pence, the daughter of Vice President Richard M. Johnson. In 1879, at the beginning of the great African American exodus from the South into the West, thousands were making their way to the so-called promised land of Kansas, and some settled in the newly established all-black town of Nicodemus.

Many former slaves, their families and friends being from Georgetown, Kentucky, had established this African American town on the high plains of Kansas. Word spread across the state that "exodusters," as they were called, were being encouraged to settle there. While in Leavenworth, Garland met John Niles, a promoting agent for the town of Nicodemus. Niles was in Leavenworth soliciting private citizens and organizations for aid in the form of food, money, and general household and farm supplies to assist the isolated and struggling settlers of Nicodemus and to lead a group of interested settlers to the town. Garland and his family joined the group of black Kentuckians headed for Nicodemus, arriving in the spring of 1879. Garland and others in the group settled on homestead lands in an area called Keybar, about six miles southwest of Nicodemus.

Most of the Nicodemus settlers did not know how to read and write. Although Garland never attended school, he had learned to read, write, and speak well mostly through his military experience. These were verbal skills that the community of Nicodemus could utilize. He befriended town promoters and organizers and in particular the census taker Abraham Hall and the Graham County clerk Edward P. McCabe. Garland became a real-estate agent and began assisting settlers in filing and settling on their homestead claims. Garland, also an excellent horseman, opened and operated a livery company, providing horses and wagon services—as well as horseshoeing services—to those in the community and travelers in the area. In the spring of 1886 he opened a farm implement company, selling farm equipment to settlers in the area. In August 1887 Garland purchased and operated the Commercial House Hotel in Nicodemus.

Garland was also politically active. A powerful orator on behalf of Republican causes, he in 1887 was elected chairman of the Kansas Republican Central Committee. He campaigned and spoke in support of his friend McCabe, who ran for state auditor of Kansas. Garland then helped organize a colony of family members and friends who moved to southeastern Colorado and established the town of Manzanola. In 1888 Garland and his family moved to Downs, Kansas, about sixty miles east of Nicodemus, where he worked as a high school janitor. His wife died in 1931. Garland spent the last two years of his life with his two daughters, one of whom lived in Kansas City, Kansas, and the other in Bogue, near Nicodemus. His son married in Downs then moved to Nicodemus.

FURTHER READING

Craig, Lula. "Lula Craig Manuscript" (c. 1930), University of Kansas, Spencer Research Library, Kansas Collection.

Lyman, Robert. *The Battle of Beecher Island Annual Reunion* (1904).

Monnett, John H. *The Battle of Beecher Island and the Indian War of 1867–1869* (1992).

U.S. Department of the Interior, National Park Service. *Promises Land on the Solomon: Black Settlement at Nicodemus* (1986).

ANGELA BATES

Garland, William (Will) (30 Dec. 1878–after 1938), singer, musician, and theatrical entertainer, was born in Keokuk, Lee County, Iowa. As a juvenile comedian and singer he was a member of the Ponce de Leon Comedy Four with the Mahara Minstrels. In Mahara's brass band, then directed by the composer W. C. HANDY, he worked in Cuba as a tuba player from 1899 to 1900, and Handy recalled him in his autobiography, *Father of the Blues* (1941). Garland and his trombone playing girl friend, Nettie Geoff, toured with Craine & Garland's Big Alabama Minstrels, followed by engagements with G. W. Washburn's Southern Minstrels (1900), Johnson and Stratter's Colored Minstrel Carnival (1901), and A Holiday in Coontown Company (1901). By 1903 Garland was playing the tuba with Richard & Pringle's Georgia Minstrels.

Garland and Nettie Geoff, now Mrs. Garland, contributed to the success of *In Dahomey*, the black revue that took London by storm in 1903. In 1904, in collaboration with Fred Douglas (sometimes spelled Douglass), PETE HAMPTON, and LAURA BOWMAN, he travelled as "the Quartet from *In Dahomey*," later re-named "the Darktown Entertainers" (the name under which they recorded for the Favorite company of Hanover, Germany). Their repertoire ranged from operatic arias to "Negro lullabies" such as "Mammy's Only Child." Garland provided the piano accompaniment but the *pièce de résistance* for his powerful tenor voice was a rendition of the flower song from Bizet's opera *Carmen*, in which he held a note for over three minutes while the others went down to the audience and passed roses to the women. His composition "Liza," which dates from this period (it was recorded by the Darktown Entertainers in 1906), was not published until years later in Budapest.

Douglas and Garland then organized *A Trip to Coontown* (after 1909 called *The Bogus Prince*) and toured the British Empire Theatre circuit throughout Europe with a cast that also featured Hampton and Bowman. Most of 1907 was spent in Germany, where Garland participated in at least one, but possibly four, short sound movies; they were referred to in the contemporary press as "Neger-Quintett" (Die Douglas Truppe), released as *Deutsche Vitascope Nr.188;* "Cake Walks and Intermezzos" (Garland and Douglas Truppe), released as a *Bioscope Tonbild;* "Flower Song—Blumenlied der Neger" (Die Douglas Truppe), released by Alfred Duskes Filmfabriken as Nr. 606; and "Flower Song—An deinem Herzen treu geborgen" (Die Douglas Truppe), released as *Messter Tonbild MP.655*.

Continental touring took Garland and his troupe, numbering between eighteen and thirty, to Hungary, Austria, France, Russia, and Belgium into 1910. Managing a "coloured" song-and-dance troupe had additional problems when illness or resignation caused recruitment problems. Garland's Negro Operetta Company, which toured from London far into imperial Russia, in 1913 numbered six black Americans, and three black and five white British. At the outbreak of war in 1914 he happened to be on tour in Germany. He returned to the United States on the *Lusitania* in October but found racial and economic conditions at home unsatisfactory and returned to London only a few months later.

Garland travelled with *A Trip to Coontown* in Dublin in May 1915, then in England (now as *In Dahomey*) into 1916. Garland's *Coloured Society* was reported in Britain to 1917. His *All Black* show appeared in 1917 and early 1918. In 1921 *All Black* appeared "with 25 Coloured Performers and A Chorus of Creole Belles" in the south of England (*Portsmouth Evening News*, 12 Dec. 1921). Garland, and the popular success of his *Coloured Society*, angered the Actors Association, which in 1922–1923 unsuccessfully sought a police investigation into the group.

Garland took a new revue, *Down South*, to the Netherlands in 1923. In 1924 in Germany, he recorded two discs, the rare survivor exhibiting spirituals on one side and a camp meeting quintet of genuine African American singing on the other side. In late 1925 he took *Coloured Lights* to the Hammersmith Palais, London; the summer of 1926 was spent in Switzerland, followed by months touring Britain. Garland's continental touring took him far from his base in London, where, with his English second wife, Rosie, he kept in contact with black performers newly arriving in Europe. He knew of shows imported from America, such as *Blackbirds*. Beginning in 1927 his *Brownbirds* toured Britain, presenting a mixture of popular song, the latest American dances, jazzy music, and comedy. For this tour he was joined by his trombone-playing brother Cat Williams, also an old-time minstrel veteran. In spite of its title, his 1929 *Swanee River* had a South Sea element, and the published music of the foxtrot song "Tahiti" from this production featured the drawing of a Tahitian girl in a tropical setting; it also has an inset photo portrait of Will Garland. This is presumably the same show that toured Germany in 1930 as *Südseezauber* (*"Die grosse Hawaian Neger-Revue"*)—*Enchantment of the South Seas (The Great Hawaiian-Negro Revue)*—with an orchestra directed by Arthur Dibbin. The American theme of Garland's song-and-dance shows was again evident in *Dark Doings* (the star was Elisabeth Welch) and *Rhapsody in Black* (both 1933), *Down South* (1936), and *Brownbirds* (1937), which was billed as "all-American."

The files of the BBC contain *Mississippi Nights*, a radio programme broadcast on 8 May 1938, in which Garland led the choir in "My Old Kentucky Home." Colleagues included John C. Payne, Rollin Smith (who had worked with LOUIS ARMSTRONG), and Ida Shepley, the English-born daughter of a West African, whose radio career developed in the 1940s. That this radio programme was preserved when almost all others of the era were not suggests that the show was regarded as valuable. In the summer of 1938 a Garland show was billed at the Empire Theatre, Woolwich (southeast London), but after that nothing further is known of him.

That he was a pioneer in the recording and sound picture business reveal qualities that deserve respect. In an age when people of African birth or descent were widely regarded as inherently inferior and lacking leadership or skills, opportunities provided by Garland from his base in London gave hope to British-born black people. That he earned a living in the entertainment business shows that he was a skilled operator. That major theatrical chains employed him over decades confirm that he had a solidly professional approach.

FURTHER READING

Abbott, Lynn, and Doug Seroff. *Ragged but Right: Black Travelling Shows, "Coon Songs," and the Dark Pathway to Blues* (2007).

Handy, William C. *Father of the Blues* (1941).

Lotz, Rainer E. *Black People: Entertainers of African Descent in Europe and Germany* [with audio CD] (1997).

Lotz, Rainer E. "The Negro Operetta Company and the Foreign Office 1913," *New Community. Journal of the Commission for Racial Equality* 13.2 (Fall 1986).

Lotz, Rainer E., and Ian Pegg, eds. *Under the Imperial Carpet. Essays in Black History 1780–1950* (1986).

RAINER E. LOTZ

Garlic, Delia T. (c. 1837– ?), former slave and narrator, was the youngest of thirteen children born to a slave woman in Powhatan, Virginia, probably in the late 1830s. All that is known about Garlic appears in a 1937 Federal Writers' Project (FWP) interview she gave in Fruithurst, Alabama, when she claimed to be one hundred years old. In that interview Garlic provides one of the most searing indictments of life under slavery in the nearly twenty-five hundred FWP interviews of former slaves. As in many Works Progress Administration narratives, Garlic's interviewer transcribed her speech in a dialect that somewhat exaggerates the rhythm and syntax of southern Black English.

Delia Garlic never knew eleven of her siblings or her father. When Delia was an infant, she, her mother, and her brother William were taken by slave speculators to Richmond, Virginia, where they were kept in a warehouse before being placed on an auction block. Delia and her mother were sold to the highest bidder, a sheriff in Henrico County named Carter; William was sold elsewhere and never saw his mother or sister again. When asked by her white interviewer if children cried during these auctions, Delia Garlic answered indignantly: "Course dey cry; you think dey not cry when dey was sold like cattle? I could tell you 'bout it all day, but even den you couldn't guess the awfulness of it" (Rawick, 129).

As a child, Garlic helped nurse the baby of Carter's daughter. Her experience was fairly typical of young antebellum house slaves, for whom "quick blows and occasional whippings rapidly became an expected feature of daily life" (Fox-Genovese, 154). On one occasion the daughter beat her with a hot poker when the baby in Garlic's care hurt her hand and began crying. A few years later Garlic's master's new wife became enraged when she found that Garlic had blackened her eyebrows with smut in what the mistress viewed as an attempt to mock her own application of eye makeup. For such apparent insolence, the mistress beat Garlic on the head with a stick of stove wood, knocking her unconscious. When Garlic regained consciousness, she ran off, but she returned later that night to find a speculator waiting to take her to Richmond. Sold to a hotelier in McDonough, Georgia, she never saw her mother again but remembered for the rest of her life their final moments together. "She pressed my han' in both of hers an' said: 'Be good an' trus' in de Lawd.'" Garlic recalled in her interview that "trustin' was de only hope of de poor black critters in dem days.... [We] jest prayed for strength to endure it to de end. We didn't expect nothin' but to stay in bondage 'till we died" (Rawick, 131).

When the hotelier's business failed, Garlic was sold first to a businessman in Atlanta and then to a planter named Garlic in Louisiana, where she worked as a field hand, plowing, hoeing, and chopping cotton. Although her narrative mentions neither whippings nor beatings in the field, Garlic recalled that she "didn't know nothing 'cept to work" (Rawick, 131). Rising at 3:00 or 4:00 in the morning, she ate only a piece of cornbread for breakfast—unsalted during the Civil War years because of shortages—and had the same for supper. For dinner she generally ate boiled greens, beans, and peas, "but never knowed nothing bout coffee" (Rawick, 132). The monotony of that diet was fairly typical, although historians have found that other slaves, like TEMPIE HERNDON DURHAM, were able to augment these meager provisions with vegetables from their own gardens. Garlic's owners, however, provided the slaves with "no way to cook, nor nothin' to cook in our cabins" (Rawick, 131). Her clothing was also basic, consisting of a shimmy and a slip for a dress made out of cheap, unbleached but durable cloth.

Sometime before the Civil War, Garlic married a slave named Chatfield who worked on a nearby plantation and was forced into service for the Confederate cause in 1861. Garlic and her fellow slaves knew then that the war was going on but did not pay much attention to it, because they "never dreamed dat freedom would ever come" (Rawick, 131). Not all slaves were so fatalistic, but many probably shared Garlic's schadenfreude on seeing their owners grieve as their sons marched off to war. "It made us glad to see dem cry. Dey made *us* cry so much" (Rawick, 132). When Chatfield failed to return at the end of the war, Delia married Miles Garlic, who worked on the same plantation.

When the war ended and freedom came, Garlic remembered that "everybody wanted to git out" (Rawick, 132). Her husband found work on the railroad in Wetumpka, Alabama, but returned frequently to Louisiana, where Delia Garlic continued to work on the Garlic plantation and live in the former slave quarters. After the birth of her second baby—it is unclear whether her first was with Chatfield or Garlic—she moved to Alabama to raise her family, first to Wetumpka and then, after her husband's death, to Montgomery. Aged one hundred at the depth of the Great Depression in 1937, she declared that she was having the best time of her life and was delighted to be eating white bread rather than cornbread. She nevertheless welcomed death and expected to go to heaven. Speaking of her thirty years in bondage, however, Delia Garlic had only hatred and bitterness, declaring to her white interviewer, "Dem days was hell" (Rawick, 129).

FURTHER READING

Garlic, Delia. "Interview of Delia Garlic," in *The American Slave: A Composite Autobiography*, ed. George P. Rawick, ser. 1, vol. 6: *Alabama and Indiana Narratives* (1973–1976).

Fox-Genovese, Elizabeth. *Within the Plantation Household: Black and White Women of the Old South* (1988).

STEVEN J. NIVEN

Garlick, Charles (1827–4 May 1912), escaped slave and narrator, was born Abel Bogguess to enslaved parents near Shinnston in present-day West Virginia. Richard Bogguess, a white bachelor with a large plantation, claimed Abel Bogguess's family as his property. Abel's mother was in charge of the household, and his father worked on the farm. He was one of eleven children.

Richard Bogguess died in 1843, leaving a will that freed his slaves. Justifiably suspicious that he would not be given his freedom despite the will, Abel ran away with his mother and five siblings. The family hid just a short distance from the farm on which they had lived, and after a couple of days a relative found them, informed them that the will would probably stand, and suggested that Abel's mother and his siblings head back to the farm. He advised Abel, on the other hand, to continue on the road to the North. After bidding his family goodbye, sixteen-year-old Abel set out on the trail of the Underground Railroad.

Abel crossed into the northern states, picking up work where he could, and managed to evade slave catchers when they came near. He eventually ended up at the Ohio home of Anson Kirby Garlick, who offered to educate him if he stayed on. Abel agreed and eventually even changed his name to Garlick to show his appreciation and affiliation with the man who helped change his life. For three years Abel Bogguess, now Charles or Charley Garlick, studied at the local school and worked on Anson Garlick's farm in West Andover, Ohio.

In 1847 Charles Garlick enrolled at Oberlin College, joining a segregated class of sixty or seventy young black men. In the same year, while he was back in Ashtabula County, Ohio, he recognized a group of slave chasers by the style of their hats. At great risk to his own life, he ran through the fields warning other black citizens that they could be caught at any moment. He informed abolitionist friends of the coming danger, and together a black and white alliance ran the slave catchers out of town. They never heard from such a posse again.

After Anson Garlick's death in 1852, fearing that he no longer had a benefactor or protector, Charles Garlick made his way to Canada. He quickly returned to the United States despite his fear of the Fugitive Slave Law and headed back to Ashtabula County. Over the next fifty years he remained in that area and worked for several prominent men in the region, including the famous abolitionist Joshua R. Giddings. Garlick was so much a part of the Giddings family that he lived in their home and is buried near Joshua Giddings in the Oakdale Cemetery in Jefferson, Ohio. Garlick was known in his later years as a fine violinist and was invited regularly to perform for social gatherings near his home.

In 1902 Garlick published his autobiography, *Life, Including His Escape and Struggle for Liberty, of Charles A. Garlick, Born a Slave in Old Virginia, Who Secured His Freedom by Running Away from His Master's Farm in 1843*. Prior to its publication, he contacted many of his old friends from his days in slavery and as a fugitive and collected information from them for the preparation of his pamphlet. What makes Garlick's narrative interesting and different from those published during the time of slavery is that, four decades after emancipation, he can name and express gratitude for abolitionists and members of the Underground Railroad without fear of provoking reprisals against them or endangering the lives of other runaways seeking to use the same routes to freedom.

In addition to his narrative, Garlick published several short autobiographical pieces in local newspapers. He also commented on late-nineteenth-century social problems, denouncing lynching and the passage of Jim Crow laws.

FURTHER READING

Garlick, Charles. *Life, Including His Escape and Struggle for Liberty, of Charles A. Garlick, Born a Slave in Old Virginia, Who Secured His Freedom by Running Away from His Master's Farm in 1843* (1902).

LAURA MURPHY

Garner, Erroll (15 June 1921–2 Jan. 1977), jazz pianist and composer, was born Earl (as "Erroll" was pronounced) Garner in Pittsburgh, Pennsylvania, the son of Louis Ernest Garner, an electrical worker, cook, musician, and dance- and pool-hall entrepreneur, and Estella Darcus, a dressmaker. At around age two he began reproducing on the piano the tunes he heard on the family piano rolls and phonograph. He never learned to read music and could imitate nonmusical sounds on the piano. Fellow musician Eddie Calhoun insisted that Garner could hear sounds "up into an animal range." At age ten Garner became a soloist with the Kan D Kids, an African American children's troupe that performed on radio station KQV. He played for church socials and in neighborhood houses on Friday nights (admission was ten cents). He played tuba for his high school band and tried all the other instruments. Garner later said that he loved big bands so much that he wanted to make his piano sound like an orchestra. By the time he withdrew from Westinghouse High School in 1939, Garner was locally famous. He played for "no money, hour after hour" at clubs such as the Crawford Grill, run by the owner of the Pittsburgh Crawfords, a leading baseball team in the black leagues. Garner made two local recordings at age sixteen, and he joined LeRoy Brown's small band and visited New York. By 1939 he had briefly led a sextet and was working for Brown's big band.

Short but muscular and massive, with long arms and hands that could reach a thirteenth—hands that the jazz critic Whitney Balliett said "moved like thieves on the keyboard"—Garner began to attract wider attention. In 1941 he was an accompanist in New York; he spent the next summer at the Edgewater, a Prohibition-era roadhouse in Wanamassa, near Asbury Park, New Jersey. After another year in Pittsburgh he returned to the Edgewater and was "discovered" by Timme Rosenkrantz, a record producer, who took him to New York.

By this time Garner's distinctive style had emerged. His sister said, "Erroll's hands had complete independence.... It was almost like being able to split your thinking in half." His powerful left hand (an arranger commented that he could probably have played the entire instrument left-handed) provided a swinging beat often likened to that of a guitar, tuba, or drum. His right hand, improvisational and embellishing, often lagged behind the beat as much as an eighth note. The result was nearly contrapuntal and thoroughly orchestral. His third New York date in 1944 was at Tondelayo's; he was invited to play at Times Hall. When the pianist ART TATUM went on vacation in 1945 from his engagement at the Three Deuces on Fifty-second Street, his bassist Leroy "Slam" Stewart recruited

Erroll Garner, performing in New York City, c. 1947. (© William P. Gottlieb; www.jazzphotos.com.)

Garner as a replacement. When Tatum left for good, they became the Slam Stewart Trio.

By late 1946 Garner had moved to Los Angeles and formed his own trio. His early recordings for Signature, Portrait, Savoy, and other small labels marked the direction he would take from then on. Applying his unique manner to familiar popular songs not usually thought of as jazz standards, such as "Laura," "Penthouse Serenade," and "Stairway to the Stars," he opened with a lengthy, fanciful introduction, virtually a separate composition in itself, then swung into the main tune. Unlike many jazz virtuosos, Garner left the main tune easily recognizable.

In 1947 Garner recorded with the bebop saxophonist CHARLIE PARKER. "Playing with Bird," Garner said, "you never felt that you had to play the same thing you had played the night before." That same year he was named Pianist of the Year in an *Esquire* magazine jazz poll. In 1948 Garner made his first Paris appearance. He returned to New York to perform at the Three Deuces and Birdland, and he became a regular at major jazz clubs in Chicago and San Francisco. His audience widened after the release of his 1951 *Piano Moods* album (Columbia), which included "I'm in the Mood for Love," "The Way You Look Tonight," "I Cover the Waterfront," "Body and Soul," and his own lilting "Play, Piano, Play."

Garner's career altered course permanently when his brother Linton, a swing band trumpeter, pianist, and arranger, introduced him to Martha Glaser, who became his manager. After the 1953 Modern American Jazz Festival, he played his first Carnegie Hall concert in 1954 and in 1955 his first Newport Jazz Festival. In the early 1950s Garner was on a plane landing in Denver. Moved by dewdrops on the windows, he composed the impressionistic "Misty," using his knees for a piano keyboard. With lyrics added later, "Misty" was eventually recorded more than three hundred times by a host of performers. After a 1955 date at the Blackhawk in San Francisco that became a duel of trios with the cerebral Dave Brubeck, Garner played in Carmel, California, on 19 September 1955. As his bassist Calhoun recalled, "We were still smokin'." Glaser reluctantly allowed a nearby army radio station to tape the performance and play it for the soldiers. The result was *The Concert by the Sea* (Columbia, 1956), which sold relentlessly, even to people who ordinarily did not buy jazz records.

Garner made his first appearance with a symphony orchestra in Cleveland in 1956. Readily identifiable by his shiny, slick hair, huge mustache, and infectious, rhythmic growling, he became one of the most frequent jazz performers on American television. In 1957 he made his first European tour. The Columbia LP *Other Voices*, adapting Garner's voicings to an entire orchestra, was a best-seller. Such recordings catapulted Garner into mass popularity, although his right-hand embroideries sometimes sounded uncomfortably like the rippling music of "cocktail pianists." Also in 1957 Garner received the Grand Prix du Disque in Paris (where his recording of "Play, Piano, Play" was buried in a time capsule) and the *Down Beat* magazine award as the year's outstanding instrumentalist. He became the first jazz artist to sign with concert impresario Sol Hurok and in 1958 the first jazz artist to sell 1 million copies of a long-playing record: *The Concert by the Sea*. In 1960, when Columbia released without his approval an LP of previously unused tapes that he considered substandard and damaging to his reputation, Garner became the first artist successfully to enjoin a record company from releasing a record. This was a landmark in bolstering artists' control over their recorded performances.

In 1962 Garner made the first of eleven annual European concert tours, and in 1963 he composed part of the score for the Paris-set film *A New Kind of Love*. He appeared at the 1964 New York World's Fair and in 1967 briefly in the German film *Negresco—Eine Tödliche Affaire* (*My Bed Is Not for Sleeping*). His *That's My Kick*, for MGM records in 1967, captured the flow of one of his all-night recording sessions. In 1970 came Garner's first Asian tour. The same year he played at a Syracuse, New York, high school in order to quiet rioting students. In 1971 his portrait appeared on a stamp issued by the Republic of Mali and his star was embedded in the Hollywood Boulevard Walk of Fame. The pianist OSCAR PETERSON recorded "Tribute to Erroll Garner."

Garner's last concert was with the National Symphony Orchestra in Washington, D.C., in 1974. His last public performance was at Mr. Kelly's Club in Chicago in February 1975, the year he was operated on for lung cancer in Los Angeles. Garner died in the elevator of a Los Angeles apartment house of emphysema and fluid in his lungs that resulted from his cancer and subsequent surgery. Although he spawned imitators and helped extend jazz into the concert halls, he exerted no real influence on pianistic jazz. He started and ended as an original—in Balliett's words, "trapped inside his style," like many another unschooled virtuoso. His last bass player called him "a happy musician who could get a smile out of the piano." Garner remained a man who could be told to stop in the middle of a recording because he had made an obvious mistake and yet roll on to the end, explaining, "I just wanted to see how it would come out."

FURTHER READING

Doran, James M. *Erroll Garner: The Most Happy Piano* (1985).

Obituary: *Los Angeles Times*, 3 Jan. 1977.

This entry is taken from the *American National Biography* and is published here with the permission of the American Council of Learned Societies.

JAMES ROSS MOORE

Garner, Margaret (June 4 1833– ?), was born to an enslaved mother on Maplewood Plantation in Boone County, Kentucky. Her mother, Priscilla, worked in the plantation house and helped to raise the children of John P. Gaines, her owner and later a U.S. congressman and governor of the Oregon territory. While Priscilla is listed as "black" in the 1850 census, Margaret Garner is listed as "mulatto" suggesting that John Gaines was perhaps Margaret's father. When Gaines left to govern Oregon, he abruptly sold his plantation and all of the slaves on it to his brother, Archibald James, who thus became Margaret's owner.

On 27 January 1856 Garner and sixteen other slaves escaped from the various Kentucky plantations on which they worked. They stole two horses to which they hitched a sled to carry them to the Ohio River. Leaving Covington, Kentucky, together, they crossed the frozen Ohio River, after which they split up for fear of being caught. Nine of the seventeen escapees made it safely to Canada. But Margaret and her husband, Robert, along with their four children and Robert's parents, headed toward the Cincinnati home of a black freeman named Elijah Kite, who conspired to help them. Kite turned to Levi Coffin, sometimes called the "President" of the Underground Railroad, for help in leading the fugitives to safety.

That very day, however, Kite's house was ambushed by a posse. The Garners were put in a desperate situation, and Margaret Garner chose to decide her own fate. She resolved that she would take her own life and the life of her children rather than return to a life of enslavement. Garner managed to slit the throat of her youngest daughter, nearly decapitating her with a knife, but did not succeed in completing her attempt to kill herself and the other children before the police broke down the door and arrested the entire family.

On 29 January 1856 the *Cincinnati Enquirer* ran a sensational article about the Garners' arrest, which described the angry crowd that gathered to condemn the family as they were being driven from the scene of the crime. The author remarked, on the other hand, that the incident was also producing ample material for abolitionists, who claimed that the crime was a testament to the injustice of slavery.

Following this near massacre, the entire Garner family was arrested and put in prison. The family was put on trial, and their defense argued that, due to a stint of work done in a free state, Margaret was technically free and therefore so were her children. They sought to have her tried for murder instead of for fleeing slavery, and in a free state instead of in the South, in order that she could be tried as a human being and not as chattel. The hope was that she and the children could be at the very least freed from slavery, even if Margaret might face imprisonment or death for her crime. They were denied on the grounds of the property laws of Kentucky, and the family was sent back to the South and slavery. The case brought added attention to the Fugitive Slave Law of 1850, which asserted that any enslaved person found in a free state would be forced by law to return to their owners. In response to this case, the Ohio state legislature officially denounced the Fugitive Slave Law. This law and Garner's trial ran to the heart of the controversy between North and South, which eventually led to the Civil War.

Garner and her family were put on a ship called the *Lewis* and headed to New Orleans to be sold. On the way south, the vessel collided with another one, killing twenty-five people, including Margaret Garner's remaining daughter. Garner is said to have rejoiced to see her daughter die before being returned to slavery and to have announced her own intention to drown as well. Again, she did not succeed in taking her own life, and she was later sold into slavery in Louisiana.

The famous Quaker abolitionist, Levi Coffin, wrote in a passionate article that Margaret Garner's case was one which he remembered with the greatest interest and deepest sympathy. Over the years Garner's story has been the subject of a variety of works of art, including a painting by Thomas Satterwhite Noble, titled *The Modern Medea*. She is also the basis for the character of Sethe in Toni Morrison's novel *Beloved*, as well as Morrison's more recent opera titled *Margaret Garner*.

FURTHER READING

Blockson, Charles L. *The Underground Railroad* (1987).

Campbell, Stanley W. *The Slave Catchers: Enforcement of the Fugitive Slave Law, 1850–1860* (1970).

Coffin, Levi. *Reminiscences* (1876).

Foner, Philip S. *History of Black Americans: From the Compromise of 1850 to the End of the Civil War* (1983).

Weisenburger, Steven. *Modern Medea* (1999).

LAURA MURPHY

Garnet, Henry Highland (23 Dec. 1815–12 Feb. 1882), minister, author, editor, and activist, was born near New Market, Maryland, to an enslaved couple then known as George and Henrietta Trusty. A few weeks after the death of their owner, Henry, his parents, his sister, and seven other relatives escaped to Wilmington, Delaware. Part of the Trusty family went to New Jersey, but George and Henrietta, having changed their surname to Garnet, continued on to New Hope, Pennsylvania, where nine-year-old Henry had his first days of formal education. In 1825 the family moved to New York City. Henry, along with his cousin SAMUEL RINGGOLD WARD (whose family were also fugitive slaves) and his neighbor ALEXANDER CRUMMELL, attended the African Free School. About 1830, while apprenticed to a Quaker farmer on Long Island, Henry was crippled in an accident. The intrepid fifteen-year-old returned to New York City and enrolled at Canal Street High School. In 1835 Garnet, with his school chums Alexander Crummell and Thomas Sidney moved to Canaan, New Hampshire, and enrolled at Noyes Academy. Their stay was brief because a white mob burned the school and fired shots into the boys' sleeping quarters. According to Crummell, Garnet saved their lives because he "quickly replied by a discharge from a double barreled shotgun" (Crummell, 280). The boys had to flee Canaan, but the next year they enrolled at the Oneida Institute in Whitesboro, New York.

As his response to the Noyes attack indicates, Garnet did not conform to ideas of nonviolence and moral suasion as the only means of achieving an end. As a student involved in the abolitionist movement, however, he did try to use reason and persuasion in his letters that appeared frequently in the *Colored American*, sometimes under the pseudonym of "Sidney," in his speeches to groups such as New York City's Phoenix Society, and in his work with the Colored Young Men Organization that circulated petitions for equal rights to the New York state legislature. By 1840, when he graduated from Oneida, Henry Highland Garnet had already achieved a reputation as an impressive communicator and indomitable leader.

Garnet's first years after graduation were a period of intense activity and serious challenges. Between 1840 and 1841 he suffered the amputation of his leg, but this did not stop him from becoming a founding member of the American and Foreign Anti-Slavery Society, serving as pastor of the Liberty Street Presbyterian Church in Troy, New York, and gaining prominence as a leader in both the temperance movement and the Liberty Party. For a brief time he was employed by the American Home Missionary Society to do abolition and temperance work, but he resigned when the society objected to his increasingly radical politics. JAMES MCCUNE SMITH writes that Garnet's marriage in 1841 to Julia Ward Williams was "a most happy wedlock" (Smith, 32). Williams was herself no stranger to racial activism. She, too, had been a student at Noyes and before that had been enrolled at Prudence Crandall's school, which had also been shut down by racist attacks. Garnet admired her "as a good Christian and a scholar" and often acknowledged his wife as the source of ideas in his lectures. During their marriage Julia Garnet generally worked alongside her husband in such capacities as head of the Female Industrial School in Jamaica or as president of the Free Labor Bazaar in London. The couple had four children and adopted a young fugitive slave.

Garnet's radical politics and persuasive rhetoric made him a prominent but controversial leader in the state and national colored conventions of the 1840s. "An Address to the Slaves of the United States," which he offered for the endorsement of the 1843 convention in Buffalo, New York, is a particularly inflammatory example. Its beginning lines convey the tone and tenor of this remarkable document:

> Brethren and Fellow-Citizens: Your brethren of the North, East, and West have been accustomed to meet together in National Conventions, to sympathize with each other, and to weep over your unhappy condition. In these meetings we have addressed all classes of the free, but we have never, until this time, sent a word of consolation and advice to you. We have been contented in sitting still and mourning over your sorrows, earnestly hoping that before this day your sacred liberties would have been restored. But, we have hoped in vain.

Arguing that it was "sinful in the Extreme" to "voluntarily" accept enslavement, Garnet declared it was their "solemn and imperative duty to use every means, both moral, intellectual, and physical" to obtain freedom, and he evoked DENMARK VESEY, NAT TURNER, CINQUÉ, and MADISON WASHINGTON as revolutionary role models. The speech scandalized more conservative delegates such as FREDERICK DOUGLASS, who reportedly delivered an hour-long tirade against advocating physical violence. When all was said and the vote taken, the endorsement failed by one vote.

Many of Garnet's speeches, including "An Address to the Slaves," were published in pamphlet form. He was also an active journalist who contributed articles to the *Colored American*, the *Voice of the Fugitive*, the *North Star*, and other periodicals. He served as agent for the *Palladium of Liberty* and the *Weekly Anglo African*, and he edited two papers, the *Clarion* and the *National Watchman*.

In 1850 Garnet went to Great Britain to campaign on behalf of the Free-Produce movement, a segment of abolitionists who urged a boycott of all slave-made products. Garnet traveled extensively in England, Ireland, Scotland, and France, sometimes in the company of other antislavery lecturers such as JAMES W.-C. PENNINGTON, JOSIAH HENSON, and Alexander Crummell. He was a delegate to the World Peace Congress in Frankfurt, Germany. In 1852 the United Presbyterian Church of Scotland employed Garnet as a missionary to Jamaica, where he served for about three years.

By 1856 Garnet was back in New York City as the pastor of the Shiloh Baptist Church, succeeding his former teacher and mentor, THEODORE S. WRIGHT. He quickly reestablished himself as a leader in African American communities and in some white abolitionist and religious circles. Garnet served on the executive council of the American Missionary Association, helped organize the Evangelical Association of Negro Ministers, and established an African American counterpart of the white Young Men's Christian Association. But it was his involvement with the African Civilization Society that provoked the greatest response before the Civil War.

Garnet's reasons for helping to found the African Civilization Society were quite complex. He had a sincere missionary zeal to convert masses of Africans to Christianity, and his experiences in the freer societies of Europe and Jamaica probably made it more difficult for him to accept the persistence of slavery and racial discrimination in the United States. And he also believed that with selective emigration of skilled and industrious individuals, black people could "establish a grand center of Negro nationality, from which shall flow streams of commercial, intellectual, and political power which shall make colored people respected everywhere" (Schor, 161). At first, leaders such as Frederick Douglass, WILLIAM WELLS BROWN, and GEORGE T. DOWNING vociferously denounced Garnet's project. Others, such as MARTIN R. DELANY, initially considered Garnet's plan competitive to their own emigration proposals. But by 1861 Douglass, Delany, and others had either endorsed Garnet's plan or stopped their public opposition. Then came the Civil War, and Garnet, like most African American leaders, turned his attention to supporting the Union army.

During the Civil War, Garnet recruited African American soldiers and served as a military chaplain. He moved to Washington, D.C., where he became pastor of the Fifteenth Street Presbyterian Church, a church with a congregation of prominent social activists. For example, the Contraband Relief Association, founded by ELIZABETH KECKLY, was based at Fifteenth Avenue Presbyterian. Garnet helped establish the Colored Soldiers Aid Society and various organizations to help the newly freed slaves.

After the war Garnet became the first African American invited to address the United States House of Representatives. He responded on 12 February 1865 with a sermon based upon Matthew 23:4 about the obligations of the advantaged to the disadvantaged. With citations that ranged from Plato, Socrates, Augustine, and Moses to Thomas Jefferson, Pope Leo X, General Lafayette, and William Ellery Channing (who had issued the invitation to speak),

Garnet urged the legislators to "*Emancipate, enfranchise, educate, and give the blessing of the gospel to every American citizen*" [italics his].

In 1868 Garnet served for a year as president of Avery College in Pittsburgh, Pennsylvania, then returned to his earlier position at Shiloh Presbyterian Church in New York. Around 1879, after the death of his first wife, Garnet married Sarah Smith Tompkins. He continued to agitate for equal rights in the United States and to espouse various Pan-Africanist plans, but his health and his political influence had declined precipitously. In 1881 his fondest hope was realized when he was appointed to a diplomatic post in Liberia. Garnet gave his farewell sermon on 6 November 1881 and sailed for Monrovia, where he died of a fever three months later.

Despite the early loss of a leg and countless other challenges, personal, political, and racial, the Reverend Henry Highland Garnet achieved international stature. In an acrostic published on 5 August 1865 in the *Weekly Anglo African*, he is summed up as a man "noble and earnest," "eloquent and faithful," and "a noble hero in the battle's shock."

FURTHER READING

Crummell, Alexander. "Eulogium on Henry Highland Garnet, D.D. Before the Union Literary and Historical Association; Washington, D.C., May 4th, 1882," in *Africa and America* (1969).

Ofari, Earl. *Let Your Motto Be Resistance: The Life and Thought of Henry Highland Garnet* (1972).

Schor, Joel. *Henry Highland Garnet: A Voice of Radicalism in the Nineteenth Century* (1977).

Smith, James McCune. "Sketch of the Life and Labors of Rev. Henry Highland Garnet" (1865).

FRANCES SMITH FOSTER

Garnet, Sarah Smith Tompkins (31 Aug. 1831–17 Sept. 1911), educator and suffragist, was born Minisarah J. Smith in Queens County, New York, the daughter of Sylvanus Smith and Ann Eliza Springsteel, farmers who were of mixed Native American, black, and white descent. Although Garnet's great-grandmother had established a school that her father attended, little is known about Garnet's own early schooling other than that she was taught by her father. However, she was a teacher's assistant at age fourteen with a salary of twenty dollars per year while she studied at various normal schools in the Queens County area. By 1854 Garnet (known as Sarah) was teaching in the private African Free School in the Williamsburg section of Brooklyn. In 1863 she became the first African American principal appointed by the New York Public School System, serving at the all-black P.S. 80 from her appointment until her retirement in 1900.

The annual closing exercises at Garnet's school were well known for the students' various public presentations and performances of excerpts of literature by standard authors. Garnet also founded a night school that taught basic literacy, sewing, homemaking, and vocational skills to adults. Among her school's better-known graduates were the violinist Walter F. Craig and Susan Elizabeth Frazier, the first African American to be assigned in 1896 to a white-staffed New York City school.

In 1883, when the school board discussed closing three of its African American schools, Garnet was active in fighting the proposed change. The compromise reached in 1884 allowed students of both races to attend either the previously all-white or all-black schools, and Garnet may have had white students in her school after that date. The staff of P.S. 80 remained all-black, however. Additionally, in 1883 Garnet opened a seamstress shop, which she operated until her death.

Garnet married an Episcopal priest, Samuel Tompkins, early in life and had two children; the three of them predeceased her. In 1879 she married HENRY HIGHLAND GARNET, an abolitionist and Presbyterian minister, who served as resident minister to Liberia. He died three years later.

Sarah Garnet was consistently active in civic affairs. In the late 1880s, two decades or more before women's suffrage became a popular issue for women in general or in the African American community, she organized the Equal Suffrage League, the only African American suffrage organization in Brooklyn. She was active in the National Association of Colored Women's Clubs (NACWC), serving as the superintendent of its suffrage department. At the NACWC convention following her death she was memorialized as "the most noted suffragist of our race."

When the presses of the journalist IDA B. WELLS-BARNETT's Memphis, Tennessee, newspaper were burned in 1892 because of her antilynching editorials, Garnet and other prominent black women formed a committee to raise the funds to replace them. She also assisted later in the formation of the Brooklyn Home for Aged Colored People.

A few months before her death, Garnet attended the Universal Races Congress in London and brought suffrage literature back home to her suffrage club. Her sister, SUSAN SMITH MCKINNEY STEWARD, one of the nation's first African American female physicians, traveled with her to

Europe. W. E. B. DuBois was a guest at a reception held in Garnet's honor after her return. Garnet died at her Brooklyn home.

Garnet is remembered locally for her groundbreaking role as an African American woman in the New York public school administration and nationally as one of the earliest African American suffragists.

FURTHER READING

Dannett, Sylvia G. L. *Profiles of Negro Womanhood*, vol. 1 (1964).

Lyons, Maritcha R. *Homespun Heroines and Other Women of Distinction*, ed. Hallie Q. Brown (1926; repr. 1992).

Salem, Dorothy. *To Better Our World: Black Women in Organized Reform, 1890–1920* (1990).

Wesley, Charles Harris. *The History of the National Association of Colored Women's Clubs* (1984).

Obituary: *New York Age*, 21 Sept. 1911.

This entry is taken from the *American National Biography* and is published here with the permission of the American Council of Learned Societies.

ELIZABETH L. IHLE

Garrett, Bill (4 Apr. 1929–7 Aug. 1974), basketball player who broke the color line in the Big Ten basketball, was born in Shelbyville, Indiana, the eldest son of Laura and Leon Garrett, a clerk and a laborer, respectively. At the time Indiana was segregated by a patchwork of law and unspoken custom, and Shelbyville had segregated grade schools but an integrated high school.

Garrett grew up playing basketball on the dirt court behind Booker T. Washington, Shelbyville's black elementary school. Fast, agile, and dominant, Garrett was a natural center though only six feet, two inches tall. He honed his skills by competing in pick-up games against grown men, some of them semiprofessionals barnstorming around Indiana.

On 22 March 1947 Garrett led Shelbyville High School's basketball team to the Indiana state championship before a live audience of fifteen thousand and a radio audience of over two million. Garrett's Shelbyville basketball team was the first integrated team in Indiana to have three African American starters (Garrett, Emerson Johnson, and Marshall Murray).

After the championship, sportswriters widely regarded Garrett as the best high school player in Indiana. In May 1947 they elected him the state's "Mr. Basketball." But even as lesser white players, including one of Garrett's teammates, were offered college basketball scholarships, no white university basketball coach recruited Garrett.

In 1947 basketball coaches in the Big Ten (Illinois, Indiana, Iowa, Michigan, Minnesota, Northwestern, Purdue, Ohio State, and Wisconsin, soon to be joined by Michigan State) observed an unwritten "gentleman's agreement," barring blacks from their teams. Only one African American, Dick Culberson, a reserve for Iowa in 1944, had ever worn a Big Ten uniform. Indiana University's basketball coach, Branch McCracken, had pointedly passed over Indiana's 1946 "Mr. Basketball," Johnny Wilson, an African American player from Anderson. Throughout the spring and summer of 1947 McCracken's friend Nate Kaufman, a Shelbyville businessman and college referee, pressed McCracken to recruit Garrett. But McCracken refused, citing the gentleman's agreement and his fear of reactions by fans and alumni.

In late August 1947 Vernon McCain drove Garrett to Nashville to enroll in Tennessee Agricultural and Industrial College (now Tennessee State University), where McCain was the basketball coach. But Faburn DeFrantz, the Executive Director of Indianapolis's Senate Avenue YMCA, the largest African American Y in the country, had been working with Indiana University (IU) president Herman Wells to integrate the Bloomington campus. In early September 1947 DeFrantz met with Wells, demanded that IU let Garrett try out for basketball, and implicitly threatened a lawsuit if the university did not. Wells was concerned about lawsuits and bad publicity. The NAACP Legal Defense Fund's Thurgood Marshall had visited the campus the previous year, and NAACP president Walter White was planning a visit. Persuaded by DeFrantz, Wells struck a bargain with McCracken: if the coach would let Garrett try out, Wells would back McCracken no matter the reactions. Garrett arrived at IU by bus in September 1947, after classes had begun. He made the freshman basketball team as a walk-on and joined the varsity as a sophomore, playing his first varsity game on 4 December 1948.

In the 1940s basketball was the nation's most popular amateur sport. African American newspapers around the country covered Garrett's integration of Big Ten basketball. Many viewed sports as a bellwether for civil rights efforts and hoped that Garrett would do for college basketball what Jackie Robinson was doing for major league baseball.

Garrett became the best player Indiana University had ever had, set scoring and rebounding records, and was named an all-American in the spring of 1951, his senior year. He was the only African American player in the Big Ten during his four years at IU. But Garrett's example on and off the court was so profound that by his junior year basketball coaches throughout the North began explicitly looking for "Bill Garretts." In 1952, the year after Garrett graduated, there were six African Americans on five Big Ten teams. The steady integration of college basketball had begun.

Garrett often faced difficulties on the road and his team had trouble finding hotels and restaurants that would accommodate them as a group. But after initial hesitation by some, his IU teammates, notably Gene Ring, Phil Buck, and Bill Tosheff, consistently supported him, and Garrett became a fan favorite. He left the IU floor for the last time to a memorably sustained and heartfelt standing ovation.

The Boston Celtics drafted Garrett in April 1951, making him the third African American drafted by an NBA team. But that June, Garrett also received draft papers from the Army. Before going overseas, Garrett married his college sweetheart, Betty Guess, with whom he would have four children: Tina, Judith, Laurie, and Bill, Jr. Garrett served for two years, running recreation leagues for the Army Special Services in Japan. Honorably discharged in August 1953, Garrett discovered that the Celtics had released him and the Harlem Globetrotters were offering a contract. He joined the Globetrotters in September 1953 but hated the showmanship and constant travel and left the team after an unhappy eighteen months. Following a year in Toledo, where his wife was teaching, Garrett returned with Betty to Indianapolis where he began teaching and coaching in the newly integrated public high schools. In March 1959 Garrett coached all-black Crispus Attucks High School to the Indiana basketball championship, making him the state's only Mr. Basketball to play on and coach a state championship team.

In 1969 Garrett became Crispus Attucks's athletic director. Two years later he became director of continuing education at Indiana Vocational Technical College. In 1970 and 1971 he ran for the Indiana University Board of Trustees, seeking to become the first African American member, but he lost by a narrow margin both times. Garrett applied for the vacant IU basketball coaching job in 1971 but lost to Bob Knight. In 1973 Garrett became assistant dean of student activities at the newly created Indiana University–Purdue University at Indianapolis. Less than a year later, in August 1974, Garrett died of a heart attack, at the age of forty-five.

FURTHER READING

Graham, Thomas, and Rachel Graham Cody. *Getting Open: The Unknown Story of Bill Garrett and the Integration of College Basketball* (2006).

Gray, Hetty. *Net Prophet: The Bill Garrett Story* (2001).

RACHEL CODY

Garrett, Leroy (26 Nov. 1913–21 July 1980), radio broadcaster, was born in Talladega County, Alabama, the son of Roy and Edna Garrett, tenant farmers. Although Garrett's father was illiterate, his mother could read and write and was concerned that her children be educated. By age five Garrett was literate and attended school with his siblings. He also helped his brothers and father farm the land they rented.

Not much is known about Garrett's childhood. By the 1940s he was living in Birmingham, Alabama, where he owned a dry cleaning business. Garrett also worked as a disc jockey at "soul" station WVOK and used his personal records and turntables. In 1957, motivated by the opportunity to secure a broadcast frequency and determined to establish a radio station, Garrett moved to Huntsville, Alabama. He was denied a building permit by the city government, however, and was arrested when he began construction without one.

Garrett protested the city's discriminatory policy and was allowed to continue with his plans. He converted a house trailer into a radio station on Oakwood Avenue. Garrett was one of the first African Americans to own and operate a radio station in the United States. Previously most radio stations broadcasting black programming were owned by whites who employed both white and black disc jockeys. Broadcasts often presented stereotyped music and programming that station owners and managers mistakenly believed would appeal to black listeners. Radio stations were concerned with attracting advertising and often ignored black businesses and consumers. African Americans expressed "widespread dissatisfaction" at this nominally black-oriented radio.

Atlanta's WERD became the first black-owned radio station in 1950 when J. B. Blayton Jr. purchased it. In the early 1950s Alabama's black population enjoyed the programming of WBIL in Tuskegee and Birmingham's WENN, owned by the BOOKER T. WASHINGTON Broadcasting Company. Garrett was influenced by these stations. Black Birmingham entrepreneur A. G. Gaston, a self-made tycoon, encouraged Garrett in his pioneering radio pursuits.

Garrett applied for a Federal Communications Commission (FCC) license, but the call letters he submitted were rejected. After several failed attempts to secure a call sign, a discouraged Garrett desperately sought a suitable name that would appeal to listeners. He looked through local newspapers and saw an advertisement for 7-Up soda and decided to try WEUP. The FCC accepted these call letters, and WEUP-AM was licensed to Garrett Broadcasting, Inc.

On 20 March 1958 Garrett conducted his first broadcast. His 1,000-watt AM station played at the frequency of 1,600 kilocycles from four in the morning to six at night every day of the week. A variety of gospel and popular music programming was interspersed with news and sermons. The *Huntsville Times* noted, "New Broadcast Station On Air WEUP Is Only Negro Station In Vicinity." The newspaper said that the station would reach listeners within a sixty- to seventy-mile radius. WEUP was the fourth radio station established in Huntsville and the only Alabama station north of Birmingham broadcasting primarily for blacks.

Garrett was community minded and attempted to provide wholesome broadcasts for the African American community. Religious programming dominated WEUP's broadcasts. Hundley Batts Sr. who bought WEUP after Garrett's death, remembered attending gospel singings at WEUP's auditorium, known as the Syler Tabernacle, as a child. Garrett gave gifts to radio listeners, mainly promotional items such as keychains emblazoned with advertising slogans and the WEUP symbol. Batts recalled that everyone who attended the singings was presented with WEUP trinkets to take home, which was important to blacks in Huntsville and helped secure dedicated listeners.

Garrett hoped that listeners would feel a personal connection with WEUP and that the station would entertain and empower individuals and the African American community. He wanted to call the station "Magic 1600," but listeners preferred the motto "WEUP is you." Although some groups and people pressured Garrett to use WEUP to voice racial and political concerns, such as police mistreatment of blacks, he refused to misuse his broadcasting power. Acknowledging that segregationist Huntsville was a difficult environment for blacks, Garrett hoped that his station's programming would aid blacks to gain self-esteem and religious strength to counter social problems.

In addition to choosing carefully what WEUP broadcast, Garrett also selectively hired disc jockeys. He especially was concerned with training minority broadcasters, and WEUP became an educational center for black broadcasters. A "good businessman," Garrett made WEUP profitable. He banked in Huntsville but channeled the bulk of his funds to Birmingham millionaire Gaston, who invested them for him.

Garrett decided that he wanted to improve WEUP by increasing its power and broadcasting twenty-four hours daily. During the 1960s Huntsville had quickly expanded with the arrival of aerospace and military industry. He applied to the FCC for a night broadcast permit in 1968. The FCC denied his request, basing their rejection on technical reasons. Garrett realized that the denial was racially motivated and filed a lawsuit against the FCC, which he believed had been influenced by wealthy white radio competitors. The FCC had waived technical rules for white stations, and Garrett demanded that WEUP be allowed to build facilities for unlimited broadcast time.

The case was argued at the U.S. Court of Appeals, District of Columbia Circuit, on 28 May 1974. Circuit Judge Spottswood W. Robinson III issued his ruling on 2 June 1975, holding that the "fact that radio station in question was owned and operated by blacks was relevant" and questioned the "inconsistent" actions of the FCC. Robinson commented that the FCC had waived restrictions in other cases and labeled their "arbitrary treatment" as "an abuse of discretion."

Robinson insisted that WEUP be allowed to broadcast at night, asserting that "its black oriented programming would surpass that of older area stations." He emphasized that "WEUP was and is one of the infinitesimal number of black-owned and operated broadcasting stations to be found anywhere in the United States." Garrett's landmark case decision has been cited by minorities suing against discrimination in communications.

The decision affected federal law. On 2 November 1978 the Ninety-fifth Congress passed Public Law 95-567, amending the Communications Act of 1934. Section 392 (f) stated that the FCC "shall give special consideration to applications which would increase minority and women's ownership of, operation of, and participation in public telecommunications entities." The FCC was also required to inform minorities of available funds and locations needing radio service.

Garrett expanded WEUP to an eleven-acre complex with a 5,000-watt capacity. He died in the Huntsville hospital. News of his death was reported in the *New York Times* but ignored by most Alabama newspapers. The Talladega *Advance* stated that the Talladega native had "emerged from the cotton fields" to own the "first black owned and operated radio station in Alabama." Garrett's son Arnold and nephews Emanuel and Bruce, whom he had raised, managed the station.

After Garrett's death WEUP expanded to four FM stations in north Alabama and Tennessee. In 1987 his widow, Viola M. Garrett, sold the station to Batts and his wife, Virginia Caples, who continued Garrett's tradition of community service and involvement.

FURTHER READING

Dates, Jannette, and William Barlow, eds. *Split Image: African Americans in the Mass Media*, 2d ed. (1993).

Downing, John. "Ethnic Minority Radio in the USA," *Howard Journal of Communication* 1 (1989).

Obituary: *New York Times*, 23 July 1980.

This entry is taken from the *American National Biography* and is published here with the permission of the American Council of Learned Societies.

ELIZABETH D. SCHAFER

Garrido, Juan (fl. 1508–1536), explorer, Indian fighter, and gold miner, was born in West Africa and traveled to Lisbon, Portugal, in the late fifteenth century. It is not known if he went to Portugal as a slave or as a free man: both were possible. From Lisbon, Garrido went to Seville and joined a Spanish expedition sailing for the island of Hispaniola (modern Haiti and the Dominican Republic). Garrido may have been part of Governor Nicolás de Ovando's expedition of 1503 and he stated he was a free man when he sailed for the Americas. Alongside other free blacks, Garrido took part in the "wars of pacification" against the Taíno Indians, and there he found a patron in Juan Ponce de León. In 1508 Ponce de León received a charter to conquer Puerto Rico, and Garrido went with him, as did several other free and enslaved blacks. Garrido identified himself in Spanish documents as "of black color, free" but never as a slave (cited in Alegría, 9). Once the Indians of Puerto Rico were defeated, Garrido became a gold miner and had several African slaves working for him. By that time native populations in the Caribbean were succumbing in large numbers to epidemic diseases introduced by the Europeans and Africans, and the Europeans needed more laborers to work their new mines, ranches, and sugar plantations. Garrido joined Spanish slave raiders sweeping through the Caribbean islands of Guadalupe, Dominica, and Santa Cruz. In 1512 Ponce de León received a new charter to further explore and conquer, and Garrido was with him when he "discovered" Bimini and claimed La Florida for Spain. Garrido thus became the first African known to have reached what became the United States. Sometime thereafter he went to Cuba, where he joined Hernán Cortés's expedition to conquer the Aztec Empire in Mexico. Several native codices depict Garrido as Cortés's page, holding his horse or standing nearby him when Cortés received Indian emissaries.

In his postconquest petition to the Spanish Crown, Garrido stated that he had helped the Spaniards in the conquest of the Aztec Empire and had buried the bodies of dead Spaniards when the fighting ended. He also claimed to have built a chapel at the site of the burials in 1521 and to have been the first person to plant wheat in Mexico. For these services, Garrido received a plot of land and several government posts, including doorman of the Mexico City council and guardian of the Chapultepec aqueduct. He later took part in expeditions to Michoacán and Zacatula, Mexico, and he returned to the latter to direct another gold mining operation with a gang of black slaves.

In 1533 the experienced explorer, Indian fighter, and gold miner joined Cortés once again to search for black Amazons in Baja California. This final adventure came to naught, and Garrido returned to Mexico in 1536. He died sometime thereafter, leaving behind a wife and children. The name of Garrido's wife is unknown, but she may have been an indigenous women since few African or Spanish women lived in New Spain in the early post-conquest years. Garrido never became wealthy as some of the Spanish expedition leaders did, but he lived an adventurous, free, propertied, and respectable life in the Americas and made his mark on history.

FURTHER READING

Alegría, Ricardo E. *Juan Garrido, el conquistador negro en las Antillas, Florida, México, y California c. 1502–1540* (1990).

Landers, Jane. *Black Society in Spanish Florida* (1999).

Rhestall, Matthew. *Seven Myths of the Spanish Conquest* (2003).

JANE G. LANDERS

Garrison, Memphis Tennessee (4 March 1890 or 1892–25 July 1988), educator, community activist, and NAACP organizer, was born Memphis Tennessee Carter in Hollins, Virginia, to former slaves

Wesley and Cassie Thomas Carter. She was named Memphis Tennessee for an aunt who was named for the town in which she was born. Carter's maternal family was filled with teachers and preachers who heavily influenced her life choices. Her white great-grandfather educated his black daughters, even though they were slaves. Her great-grandmother was an African-born slave whose tales of defiance lived on past her death. Carter's father worked in coalmines and died in a railroad accident when she was young. Her mother, who took in laundry, moved her two children, Memphis and John, into the home of her father, Marshall Thomas in Gary, West Virginia. Carter attended grade school in the nearby Elkhorn public school but was forced to attend high school in Ohio because McDowell County did not have a black high school. In 1917 Carter met William Melvin Garrison, an electrician who worked as United States Steel's only black foreman, operating the Jeffrey coal machines. At that time she was working at her first teaching job. On 5 October 1918 they married. Although she loved children and wanted ten of her own, the couple never had any biological children. Instead, they helped raise several "protégés" and financially supported their niece and others through school.

Supporting children and strengthening her community were key concerns of Garrison's. She first heard of the NAACP after W. E. B. DuBois visited Bluefield, West Virginia, in 1920. He gave a friend of hers a copy of *The Crisis*, the NAACP's journal. Soon afterward Garrison had her students selling subscriptions throughout town. The next year she organized the McDowell County Chapter of the NAACP, West Virginia's third NAACP branch. The chapter's strength was exemplified by its survival through the Depression, even as other chapters collapsed, owing to members' inability to pay dues. She coordinated a local "Freedom Seals" project for legal defense for two Mississippi boys charged with murdering a white boy and initiated an annual Emancipation Day celebration on 9 April, the date that the Confederate general Robert E. Lee surrendered to the Union army general Ulysses S. Grant. Choosing this date rather than the date of the Emancipation Proclamation spurred a controversy, yet Garrison refused to consider the Emancipation Proclamation as the true date of Emancipation. Eventually the celebration was renamed Freedom Day.

The NAACP was not Garrison's only springboard for community activism. In the 1920s Garrison wrote articles for the *Baltimore Afro-American* and a black community column for *Welch Daily News*. She helped develop plays about local black history and began a Negro artist series that brought nationally acclaimed African Americans to the West Virginian coal camps.

Garrison's career in education began in 1917 with her four-month teaching job in McDowell County, West Virginia. The first black high school opened in the early 1920s. Once the school system became countywide in 1932, her school term was extended to nine months, which was the same length of that of the white schools. Although she had originally wanted to be a lawyer, Garrison studied education at West Virginia State College and Ohio University, graduating magna cum laude from segregated Bluefield State College of West Virginia in 1939. She continued taking graduate courses throughout her life, the death of her brother thwarting her entrance into Ohio University's master's program. She could not otherwise afford housing. She obtained a tri-state teacher's certificate and taught for thirty-five years, with five additional years outside the classroom as well as doing substitute teaching in Ohio, Kentucky, and West Virginia.

Garrison was dedicated to her students and to the profession of teaching. She paid particular attention to students who fell behind their classmates, and she struggled to develop teaching practices for them. The result was a slow-readers' program connected with the Horace Mann School, affiliated with Columbia University. She also organized a school breakfast program. Garrison became principal of the elementary school and ran for a position on the school board. In addition, she played piano for the silent-movie theater and kept a dressmaking shop. She was a member of the West Virginia State Teachers Association (WVSTA) and in 1929 began a year's leadership as the association's first female president. The all-black organization occasionally met with the West Virginia Education Association (WVEA), the white statewide meetings. She became the chair of the WVSTA board, and after the WVSTA merged with the WVEA, she protested that blacks were excluded from the panel of past presidents. She was also the Bluefield College Alumni Association's president for four years and, later, the secretary-treasurer.

Garrison lost her job as teacher in the late 1930s, after Democrats won control of Mercer County. She attributed losing her job to her refusal to change her Republican registration to Democratic and her support of a local candidate who lost the election. An ardent, lifelong Republican, Garrison ran for the school board, and from 1932 to 1940 she led her county chapter of the Colored Republican Women.

After her teaching job ended, Garrison worked from 1931 to 1946 as a welfare worker for United States Steel Corporation, where she focused on improvements in domestic hygiene and recreation. She also worked with the Red Cross and helped to open a medical clinic. There, with a Black Artist's Series, she coordinated the creation of a recreation center and arranged entertainment for the African American residents in McDowell County. In 1961 she coordinated the sending of Cabell County public school textbooks to Nigeria. She developed an affinity with the "coal boss," Colonel Edward O'Toole, to whom she reported families who were experiencing domestic difficulties. Garrison's respect was evidently returned, since "the Colonel" agreed to finance most projects she suggested.

Garrison's mother, Cassie, lived with the Garrisons until her death in 1941. Garrison credited her mother's help with the cooking and keeping house for the longevity of her marriage and her participation in local activities. The following year Garrison's husband, William, died.

After a West Virginia state chapter of the NAACP formed, Garrison was the chapter's treasurer from 1945 to 1966. From 1963 to 1966 she served on both the national NAACP board and the West Virginia Human Rights Commission. In 1988 Garrison received the Governor's Living the Dream Award, which annually honors the citizen who best exemplifies the principles and goals of MARTIN LUTHER KING JR. Her life is testimony to the strong presence and contributions of African Americans in Appalachia, a region more commonly thought of as settled exclusively by whites from northern Europe. Garrison died in Cabell County, West Virginia.

FURTHER READING

Marshall University's Oral History of Appalachia Program (OHAP) interviewed Garrison in 1969. The university includes information about Garrison at http://www.marshall.edu/orahist/memphist.html. A published version of this extended oral history is found in Ancella R. Bickley and Lynda Ann Ewen, eds., *Memphis Tennessee Garrison: The Remarkable Story of a Black Appalachian Woman* (2001).

Johnson, D. "Memphis Tennessee Garrison: The Real Gains of a Life, 1890–1988," *West Virginia Beacon Digest*, 30 Aug.–7 Sept. 1988.

Maurer, B. B., ed. *Mountain Heritage* (1980).

Trotter, Joe W., Jr., and Ancella Radford Bickley. *Honoring Our Past: Proceedings of the First Two Conferences on West Virginia's Black History* (1991).

Turner, William H. "Blacks in Appalachia," *Appalachian Heritage: A Magazine of Southern Appalachian Life and Culture* 19.64 (Fall 1991).

Turner, William H., and Edward J. Cabbell, eds. *Blacks in Appalachia* (1985).

KATHRYN L. STALEY

Garrison, Zina Lynna (16 Nov. 1963–), tennis player, was born in Houston, Texas, the youngest of six children, to Ulysses Garrison, a postal worker, and Mary Elizabeth Garrison, a nursing home aide. Though initially diagnosed with a stomach tumor, Garrison's mother discovered she was pregnant at 42 years old, ten years after her previous child. Her parents chose to begin her name with "Z" to emphasize that she would be the last of their children.

Garrison grew up in the working-class African American neighborhood of Sunnyside Gardens in Houston. When she was eleven months old, her father died of a stroke; three months later, her oldest brother Willie, a catcher in the Milwaukee Braves minor league system, was struck by a baseball, developed a tumor, and died two years later.

Garrison was ten years old when her older brother, Rodney, introduced her to a free tennis program at nearby MacGregor Park. Two months after the program's coach, John Wilkerson, let her hit around with an old wooden racket, Garrison entered her first tournament and reached the finals.

As Garrison trained with Wilkerson and began entering regional and international tournaments, her family held fish fries and sponsored dances to raise money for her and fellow future tennis star Lori McNeil to attend the matches. Garrison attended the all-black Ross Sterling High School in Houston, where she was two grades behind the future NBA Hall-of-Famer CLYDE DREXLER.

By 1978 Garrison was ranked among the top five junior girls in the country, and number one in Texas, the first black female to achieve that status. The following year, the fifteen-year-old Garrison became the youngest player to win the American Tennis Association junior championship. In 1981 she won the junior singles titles at Wimbledon and the U.S. Open, became the number-one ranked junior in the world, and was feted in Washington, D.C., when the mayor dubbed 2 January 1982, "Zina Garrison Day." In the spring of 1982, she missed her high school graduation for her first professional tournament—the French Open, where she lost to Martina Navratilova in the quarterfinals.

As Garrison started touring professionally, her mother was diagnosed with acute diabetes. In the spring of 1983, Mary Garrison slipped into a coma; when Zina lost her fourth-round match in the U.S. Open, she flew back to Houston to be with her mother before she died the next morning.

Though Garrison had dealt with eating issues in the past, the death of her mother drove her to bulimia more extensively. As Garrison herself admitted, "I had lost the only person who loved me unconditionally. The pressure of being labeled 'the next Althea Gibson' only made things worse ... Bulimia was my way of coping." Despite her troubles, Garrison continued to have professional success. In 1985 Garrison reached fifth in the WTA rankings, beating Chris Evert in the Sunkist/WTA Championship, and reaching the Wimbledon semifinals and U.S. Open and Australian Open quarterfinals.

Playing in a generation between ALTHEA GIBSON and SERENA AND VENUS WILLIAMS, Garrison had her own issues of race to deal with. During youth USTA tournaments, white parents raised complaints about her size, forcing tournament officials to ask for proof of a birth certificate date. In 1987 the clothing company Pony opted not to renew her sponsorship contract, despite her being ranked seventh in the world. In a May 1987 article on racism, *Sports Illustrated* wrote that "Pony officials say tight budgets, not race, caused them to cut their ties to Garrison. The company is spending its money on a Golden Girl concept featuring a white player, bodysuit-clad Anne White, who is ranked No. 46 in the world." Fittingly, the black doubles team of Garrison and McNeil would reach the Australian Open finals that year.

In 1988 Garrison enjoyed her best professional year, winning the mixed doubles championship at Wimbledon with Sherwood Stewart, taking home the gold medal for doubles and the bronze medal for singles at the Summer Olympics in Seoul, and reaching the U.S. Open semifinals after defeating Navratilova for the first time in twenty-one attempts. That fall, she met her future husband, Willard L. Jackson Jr.; the two were engaged in December, and married 23 September 1989. Garrison divorced Jackson in 1997.

In 1989 Garrison reached fourth in the WTA rankings, defeated Chris Evert in the U.S. Open semifinals, and won the mixed doubles championship at the Australian Open. At Wimbledon in 1990, Garrison became the first black woman to reach a Grand Slam singles final since Althea Gibson in 1958. Though she lost to erstwhile foe Navratilova in the finals, Garrison won the mixed doubles title.

When she retired at the end of the 1996 season, Garrison enjoyed a lifetime record of 587–281, 20 doubles titles, and 15 singles titles. Garrison joined the tennis broadcasting team for HBO, and later became an assistant coach for the Davis Cup team, captain on the U.S. Federation Cup team, and the head of the U.S. Women's team at the 2008 Beijing Games.

Following her playing career, Garrison remained active with her community initiatives, including the Zina Garrison All-Court Tennis Program, which provides tennis opportunities for inner-city children in Houston.

FURTHER READING
Garrison, Zina, with Doug Smith. *Zina: My Life in Women's Tennis* (2001).
Moore, Kenny, and J. E. Vader. "Living a Dream," *Sports Illustrated*, 27 Nov. 1989.
Porter, A. P. *Zina Garrison: Ace* (1992).

ADAM W. GREEN

Garvey, Amy Ashwood (18 Jan. 1897–3 May 1969), Pan-African activist, was born Amy Ashwood in Port Antonio, Jamaica, to relatively prosperous middle-class parents. Her father was a successful caterer in Panama, and shortly after her birth Amy traveled with her brother and mother to live there. She returned to Jamaica in 1907 to be educated at the renowned Westwood Training College for Women, from which she graduated in 1914. It was there that the twelve-year-old first learned that her forebears had been taken forcibly from Africa by British traders and enslaved in Jamaica. Though frightened and angered to learn the horrors of the Middle Passage, Ashwood also became determined to learn more about her African roots. A visit to her elderly grandmother, who had been sold into slavery as a girl on the African Gold Coast, instilled in her a strong sense of pride in her Ashanti ancestors. She determined then that she had a mission "to help Africa and all her sons and daughters" (Martin, [1983], 224–225).

In 1914, at a debating society in Kingston, she met MARCUS GARVEY, a journalist and fellow Jamaican, who had recently returned from England. In Ashwood's account of their meeting, she and Garvey shared a "bond of comradeship" based on their common commitment to improving the conditions

Amy Ashwood Garvey, noted Pan-Africanist and proponent of women's activism, was the first wife of Marcus Garvey. (Schomburg Center for Research in Black Culture, New York Public Library.)

of black people in Jamaica and in the rest of the African diaspora. Toward that end Garvey launched the Universal Negro Improvement Association (UNIA) in Jamaica in July 1914 with Amy Ashwood as cofounder. Over the next two years she traveled extensively with Garvey as he tried to drum up support for the UNIA, which at that time espoused a mildly reformist program influenced by the self-help philosophy of BOOKER T. WASHINGTON. As secretary of the UNIA's Ladies' Division, Ashwood raised funds for the organization even after Garvey left for the United States in 1916. Shortly thereafter, however, Ashwood returned to Panama, in part because her parents disapproved of Garvey, who came from a more humble background than her own. Garvey continued to correspond with Ashwood, however, sending love letters to his "Josephine," which he signed, "your devoted Napoleon, Marcus." When Ashwood reunited with Garvey in New York City in late 1918, the UNIA had adopted a more defiantly Pan-Africanist and anticolonialist philosophy. Garvey's powerful street-corner oratory and his newspaper, the *Negro World*, struck a chord with American blacks living in an era of intense racial violence. Hundreds were killed in race riots between 1917 and 1921. Thousands more returned from a war fought to make the world safe for democracy to find continued disenfranchisement in the South and poverty in the North. An efficient fund-raiser and a powerful speaker in her own right, Amy Ashwood again served as Garvey's partner in the UNIA, which by 1920 had hundreds of chapters worldwide and eventually became the largest international black movement in history. It was Ashwood who ensured that black women enjoyed prominent roles within local UNIA chapters. She also contributed to the *Negro World* and served as a director of the Black Star Line Steamship Corporation, which was intended to transport Garveyites wishing to return to Africa. Ashwood even thwarted an assassination attempt on Garvey in October 1919. On Christmas Day 1919 Ashwood married Garvey, and the couple held an elaborate reception for three thousand invited guests, before leaving for Canada with several UNIA officials, including Ashwood's maid of honor, Amy Jacques (AMY JACQUES GARVEY).

Ashwood's marriage to Garvey was short-lived and stormy. The couple shared their cramped Lenox Avenue apartment with Amy Jacques, Ashwood's brother Claudius, and another man, not an unusual arrangement in Harlem's crowded tenements. The major source of contention in the marriage was Garvey's determination that his new wife withdraw from her public role within the UNIA and that she subordinate her own goals to his more traditionalist view of a woman's proper place. Ashwood, very much an independent "new woman" of the 1920s, refused to alter her ways of public activism, public drinking, and maintenance of friendships with men other than Garvey. In March 1920 Garvey announced that he had separated from Ashwood, and in July he sought an annulment, accusing her of having affairs and of misappropriating UNIA funds. Ashwood denied the charges. Around this time Amy Jacques, already Garvey's private secretary, moved with him to a new apartment. Believing rumors that Garvey and Jacques had also begun an affair, Ashwood sued for divorce that August and moved to Canada. In her view, the relationship between Garvey and Jacques had been a double betrayal, since she had befriended Jacques in Jamaica and had introduced her to the UNIA and Garvey. Jacques, for her part, claimed not to have known Ashwood until 1918. In June 1922 Garvey won a divorce from his wife and married Jacques two months later. Amy Ashwood challenged the divorce in court and refused to sign the divorce decree.

In late 1922 Ashwood moved to London and immediately immersed herself in that city's cosmopolitan literary and political circles. She began working with a group of Nigerian students in the city to "promote African literatures, institutions, self-knowledge, welfare and a sense of duty to 'our country and race'" (Adi, 70). She also collaborated with Trinidadian calypso singer Sam Manning in the musical revues *Hey, Hey!*, *Brown Sugar*, and *Black Magic*, touring England, the United States, and the Caribbean. In the 1930s she and Manning opened a nightclub in London that became a haven for Pan-Africanist intellectuals like C. L. R. James and George Padmore; it was also, James remarked, the only place in London that served good food. When Italy invaded Abyssinia (Ethiopia) in 1935, Ashwood and Padmore formed the International African Friends of Abyssinia (IAFA). Her skills as a public speaker and fund-raiser were also useful in the International African Service Bureau, an anticolonialist organization, in which she served alongside Jomo Kenyatta, later the first prime minister of an independent Kenya.

Ashwood's commitment to Pan-Africanism prompted several trips to Jamaica and the United States. In the early 1940s she attempted to found a school for domestic workers in her native land and also dabbled, unsuccessfully, in party politics. She had greater success assisting the 1944 congressional campaign of Adam Clayton Powell Jr., though her links to Powell and her friendship with Paul Robeson ensured the close attention of the FBI. She returned to London in 1945. That year, along with W. E. B. DuBois, she chaired the opening session of the Fifth Pan-African Congress, held in Manchester, England. Over the next two decades, several of the Congress's participants, notably Kenyatta and Ghana's Kwame Nkrumah, would lead their nations to independence.

Of greater significance to Ashwood herself, however, was her first trip to Africa. From 1946 to 1949 she traveled throughout West Africa, lecturing to women's groups and encouraging women's participation in decolonization efforts in Senegal, Nigeria, and Ghana. While in Ghana, she traveled to the Gold Coast, where she found her grandmother's birthplace and was officially welcomed as a member of the Ashanti people.

Ashwood maintained a hectic schedule in the 1950s. She invested, poorly, in several businesses in Africa and also traveled to the Caribbean to encourage women's activism there. In England she served as a social worker in Handsworth, Birmingham, and in Notting Hill, London. Both districts had large West Indian populations, most of them recent arrivals, who had been recruited in large numbers by British employers seeking cheap labor. When a race riot erupted in Notting Hill in 1958, Ashwood, who ran a community center in the district, led efforts to ease racial tensions and to ensure justice for blacks imprisoned following the riot.

In 1964 Ashwood moved back to Jamaica and arranged to return Marcus Garvey's body for burial as requested by the newly independent Jamaican government. Garvey had died in London in 1940, and the British authorities recognized her claim to be his widow, notwithstanding that Garvey had lived with Amy Jacques Garvey as his wife from 1922 until 1938. That year Jacques Garvey left her husband in London and returned to Jamaica. Ashwood spent her final days in Jamaica but journeyed to Harlem in 1968, where she praised the widespread adoption of the natural "Afro" hairstyle by black women and took great satisfaction in the renewed veneration of the Garveyites and the UNIA. She died, penniless, in Jamaica in May 1969.

Much more than Marcus Garvey's "Wife Number 1," Amy Ashwood enjoys a distinctive place in the history of Pan-Africanism, most notably in encouraging women of the African diaspora to play a significant role in the cause.

FURTHER READING

Amy Ashwood Garvey's papers are scattered in private collections in London, New York, and Kingston, Jamaica. See also the *Marcus Garvey and Universal Negro Improvement Association Papers*, ed. Robert A. Hill (1983–).

Adi, Hakim, and Marika Sherwood. "Amy Ashwood Garvey," in *Pan-African History: Political Figures from Africa and the Diaspora since 1787* (2003).

Martin, Tony. *Amy Ashwood Garvey: Pan-Africanist, Feminist, and Wife No. 1* (1988).

Martin, Tony. *The Pan-African Connection: From Slavery to Garvey and Beyond* (1983).

Stein, Judith. *The World of Marcus Garvey* (1986).

Taylor, Ula. "Intellectual Pan-African Feminists: Amy Ashwood Garvey and Amy Jacques Garvey," in *Time Longer than Rope: A Century of African American Activism, 1850–1950*, eds. Charles Payne and Adam Green (2003).

Yard, Lionel M. *Biography of Amy Ashwood Garvey, 1897–1969: Co-founder of the Universal Negro Improvement Association* (1990).

STEVEN J. NIVEN

Garvey, Amy Euphemia Jacques (31 Dec. 1896–25 July 1973), journalist and Pan-Africanist, was born in Kingston, Jamaica, the daughter of George Samuel Jacques, a cigar manufacturer and landlord, and Charlotte Henrietta, a member of the Jamaican aristocracy. Amy's family traced their ancestry on the island back to John Jacques, a white property owner and the first mayor of Kingston. She grew up as part of the "brown elite," who were considered socially and economically superior to the black majority. After completing her secondary education at the exclusive Wolmer's Girls School, Amy worked in the law office of T. R. MacMillian for four years and had thoughts of becoming a lawyer. However, in April 1917 she left Jamaica for New York, arguing that the cooler climate would mitigate her recurring bouts of malaria.

Amy Jacques arrived in Harlem, the Mecca for ambitious Caribbean immigrants—particularly those animated by the new black nationalist philosophy of MARCUS GARVEY. In the summer of 1919 she attended a meeting of Garvey's Universal Negro Improvement Association (UNIA) at the six-thousand-seat headquarters, Liberty Hall. According to her account, after she peppered Garvey with some difficult questions about his program, he invited her into his office to continue their conversation. Noticing that his office was in a state of disarray, she offered her organizational services and soon become his private secretary, helping to plan, among other things, Garvey's lavish wedding to Amy Ashwood (AMY ASHWOOD GARVEY) on Christmas Day, where she served as the maid of honor. Jacques shared an apartment with Garvey and Amy Ashwood and two other men until Garvey separated from his wife in March 1920. She then moved to the same boardinghouse as Garvey, so that she would be "better protected at nights coming from meetings" (Garvey, 43). In July 1922 Garvey and Amy Jacques were married in Baltimore, shortly after his divorce from Amy Ashwood was granted.

Amy Jacques's prominence in the UNIA grew as Garvey's legal troubles began to mount and as popular and financial support for the organization began to wane. When Garvey was convicted on one count of mail fraud in June 1923, Amy Jacques became his most trusted spokesperson, his unofficial emissary, and the leader of the campaign to win his freedom. She first published a pamphlet about the trial called *Was Justice Defeated?* to demonstrate that Garvey was railroaded for his political beliefs. To correct what she and Garvey thought were distortions of his views, she then published two volumes of Garvey's speeches and articles in *The Philosophy and Opinions of Marcus Garvey* (1923, 1925). She took great liberty in selecting his least militant work and quietly omitted and added text where she thought appropriate. Some of the elected officers of the UNIA resented the influence that her ex officio status as Garvey's wife afforded her, but though she had been loath to assert herself publicly in the past, she now began to claim the mantle of his leadership.

Though never a dynamic speaker, Jacques was a gifted and prolific writer who used the printed word to give voice to issues of Pan-Africanism and the concerns of black women. When she became an associate editor of the *Negro World*, the main organ of the UNIA, in February 1924, she found a platform from which to express her ideas. T. THOMAS FORTUNE recognized her talent and encouraged her to write a new column in the paper, called "Our Women and What They Think." This column consciously avoided stories about women's fashions, celebrity gossip, and recipes in favor of the more serious matters that would "prove that Negro women are great thinkers as well as doers." In articles such as "No Sex in Brains and Ability," Jacques wrote, "Some men declare that women should remain in the homes and leave professions and legislation to men, but this is an antiquated belief, and has been exploded by woman's competency in these new fields and further by the fact that their homes have not suffered by a division of their time and interest" (Taylor, 74).

Jacques advocated expanding women's roles beyond the domestic sphere, but she was not a feminist in the modern sense. Like early black female intellectuals FRANCES ELLEN WATKINS HARPER and MARY CHURCH TERRELL and fellow journalist IDA WELLS-BARNETT, Jacques wanted black women to achieve a social status equal to that of the white, middle-class women of her generation—despite the inherent contradiction posed between that Victorian vision and their simultaneous desire to have careers outside the home. In fact, in her article "Are Negro Women More Easily Satisfied than White Women?" she wrote "black women [would] come out of Miss Ann's kitchen, leave her washtub and preside over their own homes," if their men would "bring home the bacon" (Taylor, 84). By the time the column was discontinued in June 1927, Jacques had contributed nearly two hundred editorials and established an identity that was clearly distinct from her husband's.

In November 1927 Garvey was released from prison and deported to Jamaica. During his incarceration Jacques had come to feel that her role in his life had once again been reduced to that of a personal secretary, important only to carry out his instructions. Reflecting on a love poem that Garvey had sent to her that waxed long about his suffering but hardly acknowledged the tremendous strain she was under, Jacques wrote: "What did he ever give in return? The value of a wife to him was like a gold coin—expendable, to get what he wanted, and hard enough to withstand rough usage in the process" (Garvey, 169).

Despite the fact that she had become a U.S. citizen the year before, she decided to join her husband in Jamaica in hopes of rekindling their relationship. When she arrived, they did not take the vacation he had promised; instead Garvey threw himself into his work, cashed in his life insurance policy to start a newspaper, the *Blackman*, and mortgaged their home and furniture to rent office space for the new UNIA that he intended to run from Jamaica. However, Garvey soon discovered that he had become persona non grata in many countries that either feared his populist rhetoric or yielded to American pressure. Once again Jacques was pressed into service as his representative to countries that barred him, and in 1929, when Garvey's leadership of the People's Political Party got him thrown into a Jamaican jail for three months for judicial contempt, it was Jacques who again came to the aid of her husband, who by then had been diagnosed with diabetes.

In 1930, after seven years of marriage, Jacques delivered their first son at home. Garvey was delighted by the news, rushed home to see them, and then returned to his office. By the time their second son was born in 1933, Jacques had become much more anxious about the family's precarious finances, worsened by the Depression, and she was greatly disappointed by Garvey's detachment as a husband and father. Garvey was singularly devoted to black liberation; "towards that purpose no one will ever stand in my way—no mother, no father, no wife, no sweetheart, no affiliation," he once said (James, 142). Feeling that the island of Jamaica had become his Elba, Garvey moved his family to London in 1935, where Jacques felt increasingly torn between her commitment to the movement and her responsibility to her children. Out of frustration, Jacques returned with the children to Jamaica in 1938 while Garvey was away on a speaking tour, never to see him again.

During their estrangement they communicated indirectly through the letters of their sons until Jacques received notice that Garvey had suffered a stroke in January 1940; this time she made no effort to be by his side. He died in June 1940 and his body remained in London until 1964, when Jacques found herself embroiled in a dispute with Amy Ashwood—who never accepted the legality of the 1922 divorce—over deciding Garvey's final resting place. Both women had competed for recognition as wife, widow, and political heir. Jacques created Garvey's African Communities League and often spoke in strangely spiritual terms of being led by Garvey, of speaking to him in her dreams, and literally declaring that "when I talk, I talk for Garvey" (Taylor, 225). Since Garvey left her no money and the promised pension from the UNIA never materialized, Jacques could rarely afford to travel, but she wrote incessantly to Pan-Africanists all over the world. She wrote a manifesto called *Memorandum Correlative of Africa, the West Indies and the Americas*, sent it to her former adversary W. E. B. DuBois, and hoped to attend the Fifth Pan-African Congress in Manchester, England in 1945. Unfortunately she was unable to attend, so George Padmore read excerpts from her manuscript.

Jacques became a writer for *The African: Journal of African Affairs*, and during the 1960s she traveled to Africa, met with Kwame Nkrumah, spoke out in defense of Patrice Lumumba, and was honored by Martin Luther King Jr. In 1963 she wrote *Garvey and Garveyism*, her memoir of the movement, and though she acknowledged the shortcomings of her personal relationship with Garvey, she remained deeply passionate about preserving his memory and their shared vision of Pan-Africanism until cancer slowed her activity. She died in 1973.

FURTHER READING

The papers of Amy Jacques Garvey are located in the Fisk University Special Collections, Nashville, Tennessee.

Garvey, Amy Jacques. *Garvey and Garveyism* (1963, repr. 1978).

James, Winston. *Holding Aloft the Banner of Ethiopia* (1998).

Taylor, Ula Yvette. *The Veiled Garvey: The Life and Times of Amy Jacques Garvey* (2002).

Obituary: *Jamaica Daily News*, 7 Aug. 1973.

SHOLOMO B. LEVY

Garvey, Marcus (17 Aug. 1887–10 June 1940), black nationalist, was born Marcus Moziah Garvey in St. Ann's Bay, Jamaica, the son of Marcus Moziah Garvey, a stonemason, and Sarah Jane Richards. He attended the local elementary school and read widely on his own. Difficult family finances forced him into employment at age fourteen as a printer's

Marcus Garvey, dressed in a military uniform as the "Provisional President of Africa" during a parade up Lenox Avenue in Harlem, New York, for the opening day exercises of the annual Convention of the Negro Peoples of the World, August 1922. (AP Images.)

apprentice. Three years later he moved to Kingston, found work as a printer, and became involved in local union activities. In 1907 he took part in an unsuccessful printers' strike. These early experiences honed his journalistic skills and raised his consciousness about the bleak conditions of the black working class in his native land.

After brief stints working in Costa Rica on a banana plantation and in Panama as the editor of several short-lived radical newspapers, Garvey moved to London, England, in 1912 and continued to work as a printer. The next two years there would profoundly mold his thoughts on black advancement and racial solidarity. He probably studied at the University of London's Birkbeck College; absorbed BOOKER T. WASHINGTON's philosophy of black self-advancement in his autobiographical *Up from Slavery*; and, perhaps most important, met MOHAMMED ALI DUSE, a Sudanese-Egyptian who was working for African self-rule and Egyptian independence. Duse Mohammed published a small magazine, *Africa Times and Orient Review*. He allowed Garvey to write for the magazine and introduced him to other Africans. Garvey left London convinced that blacks worldwide would have to fend for themselves if they were ever to break the shackles of white racism and free the African continent from European colonial rule.

Back home in Jamaica in 1914, Garvey founded the Universal Negro Improvement and Conservation Association and African Communities League, usually known as the Universal Negro Improvement Association (UNIA). The UNIA would be the vehicle for Garvey's efforts at racial advancement for the rest of his life. His initial undertaking, a trade school in Jamaica, did not succeed, and in 1916 he took his organization and cause to the burgeoning "black mecca" of Harlem in New York City.

Over the next few years Garvey's movement experienced extraordinary growth for a number of reasons. With its slogan "One Aim, One God, One Destiny," the UNIA appealed to black American soldiers who had served abroad in World War I and were unhappy returning to a nation still steeped in racism. Harlem was a fortuitous location for Garvey's headquarters, with its sizable working-class black population, large number of West Indian immigrants, and the cultural explosion of the Harlem Renaissance in the 1920s. A Pan-African movement was already under way by the early 1920s, emphasizing the liberation of the African continent and black racial pride worldwide, and Garvey successfully tapped into this sentiment. Garvey himself was a gifted writer (using his weekly newspaper the *Negro World* as his mouthpiece) and a spellbinding orator in dazzling paramilitary garb.

Garvey's first marriage in 1919, to his secretary AMY ASHWOOD GARVEY, was an unhappy relationship that ended in divorce three years later. The couple was childless. In 1922 he married AMY JACQUES GARVEY, his new secretary. They had two sons.

By the early 1920s the UNIA had probably 65,000 to 75,000 dues-paying members with chapters in some thirty American cities, as well as in the West Indies, Latin America, and Africa. On various occasions Garvey claimed anywhere from 2 to 6 million members. Accurate membership figures are impossible to obtain, but unquestionably millions of other blacks were followers in spirit. Auxiliary organizations included the Universal Black Cross Nurses, the Black Eagle Flying Corps, and the Universal African Legion. The *Negro World* had a circulation of some 50,000. In August 1920 the UNIA hosted a huge monthlong international convention in New York City, with several thousand black delegates from all parts of the world, complete with uniforms, mass meetings, and parades. Garvey was named provisional president of a nonexistent but symbolically powerful "Republic of Africa." This latter move reflected Garvey's interest in the regeneration of Africa. He had already been exploring with the government of Liberia a UNIA construction and development project there and the potential for a back-to-Africa colonization movement for American blacks. Unfortunately, this undertaking foundered as his domestic businesses came into increasing difficulty. Garvey's business enterprises were his proudest achievements and ultimately the source of his undoing. Inspired by Booker T. Washington's support of black businesses, Garvey founded the Negro Factories Corporation to encourage black entrepreneurship in the United States and abroad. The corporation sponsored a number of small businesses in the United States, including a Harlem hotel and a publishing company.

The crown jewel of Garvey's enterprises was the Black Star Line, a steamship company founded in 1919 to carry passengers and trade among Africa, the Caribbean, and the United States. Garvey launched the line with his usual grandiose promises and a stock sale that raised more than $600,000 (at $5 a share) the first year. What followed in the next twenty-four months was a tragic series of mishaps and mismanagement. The Black Star Line consisted of three aging, overpriced vessels that were plagued by mechanical breakdowns, accidents, and incompetent crews. The business side of the operation suffered from sloppy record keeping, inflated claims made to investors, and dishonest and possibly criminal practices on the part of company officers. One of the ships sank; another was auctioned off; the third was abandoned in Cuba.

Some of Garvey's critics, including many blacks, had begun to question his ethics, his business practices, and the whole UNIA operation. Notable among his black opponents was W. E. B. DuBois of the National Association for the Advancement of Colored People. Garvey's insistence on black nationalism ran counter to the NAACP's goal of full integration into American society. When Garvey associated openly with leaders of the white racist Ku Klux Klan and declared that the Klan was a better friend of his race than the NAACP "for telling us what they are, and what they mean, thereby giving us a chance to stir for ourselves," thousands of blacks were outraged.

In 1922 Garvey and three other Black Star Line officials were indicted by the U.S. government for using the mails fraudulently to solicit stock for the defunct steamship line. Ever the showman, Garvey used his trial for a flamboyant defense of himself and the larger cause of black advancement, striking a chord with at least some of his remaining followers, who saw him as a victim of white persecution. Unimpressed, the jury convicted Garvey (though not his codefendants), and he was sentenced to five years' imprisonment. After a failed appeal to the U.S. Supreme Court, Garvey began his term in February 1925. That he was able to continue running the UNIA from his Atlanta jail cell was a tribute to his influence over his followers.

In 1927 President Calvin Coolidge commuted Garvey's sentence, and he was deported to Jamaica. The remainder of his life was a struggle to rebuild his movement. He attempted to rekindle his cause by getting involved in Jamaican politics but to no avail. He presided over UNIA conventions in Kingston in 1929 and Toronto in the late 1930s, but the grim realities of the Great Depression left most blacks with little interest and fewer resources to support movements such as his. He died of a stroke in London, where he had moved in 1935.

Obituaries of Garvey emphasized his business failures and portrayed him as an irrelevant relic from the past. His real achievement, however, was in creating the first genuine black mass movement in the United States and in extending that influence to millions of blacks abroad. He emphasized racial pride and purity, the proud history of his race, self-respect, and self-reliance. For his millions of poor and working-class American followers, Garvey's message of black pride and solidarity in the early 1920s came at a critical nadir of race relations. Such themes drew on the philosophy of Booker T. Washington as well as DuBois, his sworn enemy. He was a harbinger of later black nationalist leaders such as Malcolm X, Stokely Carmichael, and Louis Farrakhan. Garvey thus served as an important link between early twentieth-century black leaders and modern spokesmen. Moreover, he inspired modern African nationalist leaders, such as Kwame Nkrumah of Ghana and Jomo Kenyatta of Kenya, in their struggles against European colonialism.

FURTHER READING

Garvey's papers and materials from the UNIA can be found in the multivolume *Marcus Garvey and Universal Negro Improvement Association Papers*, ed. Robert A. Hill (1983–). Amy Jacques Garvey, ed., *Philosophy and Opinions of Marcus Garvey* (1968), is a collection of his early writings up to 1925.

Cronon, E. David. *Black Moses: The Story of Marcus Garvey and the Universal Negro Improvement Association* (1955).

Davis, Daniel S. *Marcus Garvey* (1972).

Garvey, Amy Jacques. *Garvey and Garveyism* (1963).

Martin, Tony. *Race First: The Ideological and Organizational Struggles of Marcus Garvey and the Universal Negro Improvement Association* (1976).

Stein, Judith. *The World of Marcus Garvey: Race and Class in Modern Society* (1986).

Vincent, Theodore. *Black Power and the Garvey Movement* (1971).

Obituary: *New York Times*, 12 June 1940.

WILLIAM F. MUGLESTON

Garvin, Charles Herbert (27 Oct. 1890–17 July 1968), physician, was born in Jacksonville, Florida, the son of Charles Edward Garvin, a mounted letter carrier, and Theresa De Courcey. He was educated first at Atlanta University and later graduated from Howard University in 1911 and from its medical school in 1915. At Howard, Garvin was recognized as an outstanding student and leader. He served as president of Alpha Phi Alpha fraternity while in the undergraduate chapter and later served as its national president. During his medical school training Garvin was awarded top honors in obstetrics and physical examinations. In 1916 he moved to Cleveland, Ohio, to begin medical practice. He chose Cleveland at the urging of George Crile, a well-known surgeon with whom he became acquainted while working as a dining-car waiter during the summers when he was at Howard. The city at that time had a rapidly growing black population drawn by the labor demands of the war industry.

When the United States entered World War I Garvin enlisted and was among the first black physicians to be commissioned in the armed forces. He served in France as captain and commanding officer of the all-black 368th Ambulance Company, 92nd Division. Later, in a response to negative reports and what he described as "insidious propaganda" from General John J. Pershing, he described the superior performance in the face of adversity of African American soldiers and officers who served in the war. Garvin's letter was published nationally in black newspapers in 1931. In 1943 he expanded on the role of black medical officers in an article titled "The Negro in the Special Services of the U.S. Army World War I and II" (*Journal of Negro Education* 12, no. 3 [Summer 1943]: 335–344).

After completing his service in 1920 Garvin married Rosalind West, a native of Charlottesville, Virginia, and graduate of the Howard University Normal School. He then resumed his practice in Cleveland, where he remained until his death. The couple had two sons.

In Cleveland, as in many cities, black physicians had limited access to hospital privileges, so Garvin's patients were treated primarily in the office and at home. However, he held a succession of courtesy appointments at Lakeside Hospital from 1920 until his retirement in 1968. During his years in practice he was well known and respected both as an expert in urology and as a tireless advocate for increased opportunities for African American physicians.

Garvin's interest in medicine extended beyond the practice to research and writing. He published at least thirty-six articles in medical journals, most of them in the *Journal of the National Medical Association* (an organization of African American physicians), with emphasis on urological diseases and disorders. He also published articles in the *Woman's Voice*, a national women's magazine, and *Opportunity Magazine*, the official publication of the national Urban League. His popular articles dealt with another topic that absorbed much of his attention: the historic contributions of Africans and African Americans in medicine. He completed a manuscript on this subject titled "Africa's Contribution to Medicine: The Negroid Peoples Role in Its Evolution," which, as of 2007, remained unpublished.

Garvin was also an active businessman and civic leader. He was a founder of the Dunbar Life Insurance Company (1943), and he helped to organize the Quincy Savings and Loan Company, where he served as a director and chairman of the board (1954). Both businesses were established to serve the new wave of black migrants who came north for work during and after World War II, and both businesses prospered during his lifetime. Garvin also was appointed as the first African American trustee on Cleveland's public library board in 1939 and served as its president during 1940–1941. Other key civic positions included terms as trustee of the nationally recognized Karamu Settlement House, the Urban League, the National Association for the Advancement of Colored People (NAACP), and Mount Zion Congregational Church. He was a founding member of Tau Boule of Sigma Pi Phi fraternity and an active member of the Fraternal Order of the Elks and the Order of Moose. In addition, he served on the board of trustees of Howard University, as a member of its executive committee and in other capacities, from 1932 until 1964. The university's organization of former interns and residents gave him its William A. Warfield Award in 1963 for his contributions to medicine and to the institution.

The Garvin family was thrust into the national spotlight as pioneers in integrated housing in 1926, when Garvin purchased a lot in an exclusive allotment near Western Reserve University. When neighbors learned that a black family was going to build, they vigorously opposed Garvin's plans. In spite of repeated threats of violence and two bombings after the house was built, the Garvins refused to move. These incidents, which were widely covered by the news media, illuminated some of the problems faced by successful African American families and forecast the continuing racial polarization in housing in Cleveland and other large urban centers during the twentieth century.

Garvin's career as a practicing physician, his contributions to medical research and medical history, and his business and civic activities exemplify the multiple roles that were often required of and assumed by black middle-class leaders during the twentieth century. His experiences as an armed forces officer, a physician, and an African American citizen also serve as models of resistance against the barriers of racism that plagued American society during an era when two world wars were fought for democracy.

FURTHER READING

Garvin's papers, including articles, awards, and citations, are at the Western Reserve Historical Society in Cleveland, Ohio.

Davis, Russell. *Black Americans in Cleveland* (1972).

Tassel, David Van, and John Grabowski. *The Encyclopedia of Cleveland History* (1987).

Obituaries: *Cleveland Press* and the *Plain Dealer*, 18 July 1968; *Cleveland Call and Post*, 27 July 1968.

This entry is taken from the *American National Biography* and is published here with the permission of the American Council of Learned Societies.

ADRIENNE LASH JONES

Gaston, A. G. (4 July 1892–19 Jan. 1996), entrepreneur, was born Arthur George Gaston in Demopolis, Alabama, the son of Tom Gaston, a railroad worker, and Rosa Gaston (maiden name unknown), a cook. He grew up in poverty in rural Alabama before he and his mother moved to Birmingham, Alabama, after his father's death. He attended, and for a good time resided at, Tuggle Institute, where he received a moral and industrial education. In 1910 he graduated from the school with a tenth grade certificate. Before and after graduation he worked at a number of part-time jobs, including selling subscriptions for the *Birmingham Reporter*.

Gaston served in World War I in France as a sergeant in the 317th Ammunition Train of the all-black 92nd Division of the U.S. army. Upon his return to the United States he briefly worked at a dry-cleaning factory for $5 a day before landing a job at the Tennessee Coal and Iron (TCI) plant in Westfield, Alabama, constructing railroad cars. Always searching for a means of making more money, he supplemented his daily wage of $3.10 by selling his mother's homemade sandwiches and loaning money to colleagues who did not share his obsession for saving money.

Gaston early on exhibited signs of ambition and enterprise. As a young man he joined several fraternal organizations, where he gained visibility among members of the black community and nurtured relationships that helped him to develop a large client base when he started his own businesses. Birmingham's budding and segregated economy provided the opportunity for several black entrepreneurs looking for an opening to establish a business. Early in the twentieth century Thomas W. Walker, William R. Pettiford, Oscar Adams, and Thomas C. Windham were all enterprising men who parlayed their energies into successful businesses that catered almost exclusively to Birmingham's black residents. They served as role models for Gaston who combined their business strategies with BOOKER T. WASHINGTON's self-help philosophy to engineer a modest business empire.

Gaston followed in the footsteps of his predecessor and competitor, Charles M. Harris, who founded the venerable Davenport and Harris Funeral Home in 1899 and then the Protective Burial Association in the 1920s. During the 1920s and 1930s numerous black entrepreneurs established burial and insurance companies to ensure members of their own race a respectable funeral. In the early 1920s Gaston married Creola Smith, who died during their first years of marriage. In 1923 he resigned his position at TCI and founded, with his father-in-law, Abraham Lincoln "Dad" Smith, the Booker T. Washington Burial Society and later the Smith and Gaston Funeral Home. In 1932 they incorporated the Booker T. Washington Burial Insurance Company in Fairfield, Alabama, when legal complications forced him to abandon the burial society. Gaston financed all his subsequent business ventures through this corporation. The company not only weathered the Great Depression but also enjoyed a longevity that many of its competitors did not.

Gaston's carefully designed business tactics enabled his companies to survive the ravages of the Depression that felled thousands of businesses throughout the nation. In Birmingham alone, all the black-run newspapers failed, and of the 200 black-owned retail stores in 1929, only 132 remained in 1935. Gaston accurately read the market and created businesses that served the black community's needs. He established diverse businesses that both trained blacks for future employment and provided them with essential services. In 1939 he and his second wife, Minnie Lee Gardner (with whom he had one son), established the Booker T. Washington Business College to teach black students clerical skills. Gaston hired graduates of the college to fill the vacancies in his own companies, positions that were previously held by out-of-state blacks. He filled another void in 1954 when he constructed the Gaston Motel, which served blacks who otherwise were denied access to public accommodations in Alabama. Hailed as "one of the finest in the Southeast" by white hotel owners and praised as a wonderful symbol by blacks, the motel earned for Gaston the respect of representatives from both races. This facility later served as a meeting place during the civil rights movement.

While Gaston was creating his business empire he chose a route that would benefit not only him but also other members of the black community. Wanting to enable black homeownership, he founded the Citizens Federal Savings and Loan Association in 1957, later Citizens Federal Savings Bank. By and large, Birmingham's white-owned banks had discriminatory lending practices that successfully kept blacks out of the housing market. Members of the black community rallied behind Gaston's newest venture and helped the bank realize a steady growth in profits. By 1961 it ranked eleventh among all black-managed savings and loan, with assets totaling $5,120,633.85. By 1968 more than $6 million had been invested in home and church mortgages owned by blacks. In 1989 it was rated the safest savings and loan in Birmingham. Despite the savings and loan controversy that damaged the industry in the 1980s, and the loss of twenty-six of the forty-three black-owned thrifts, Gaston's company weathered the industry's dismantling and experienced growth. In 1991 it declared assets of $72,084,000 and deposits amounting to $65,563,000. Despite a decline in assets by 1995 to $58 million, Citizens Federal Savings Bank maintained its position as the largest black-owned bank in Alabama and the eighth largest in the country. Gaston remained chairman of the bank until his death.

In 1987 Gaston unexpectedly sold his insurance company and almost all of his other investments to his 400 employees for $3.5 million—a nominal sum, given the company's $34 million in assets and $726 million worth of insurance in force. He owned 97 percent controlling interest in Booker T. Washington Insurance (the remaining 3 percent was held by his wife, Minnie Gaston, and his employees). Gaston was determined to give something back to the community that had given him so much. Included in the transaction were his Booker T. Washington Broadcasting, which owned Birmingham-based radio stations WENN and WAGG; the A. G. Gaston Construction Company; Zion Memorial Gardens and New Grace Hill cemeteries; A. G. Gaston Senior Citizens Home; and Vulcan Realty and Investment Corporation. He only retained ownership of Citizens Federal Savings Bank and the Smith and Gaston Funeral Homes.

Gaston also played an important role in the civil rights campaign that rocked Birmingham in 1963, when protests against racial discrimination, led by MARTIN LUTHER KING JR., met with violence from Birmingham's white residents and police. Gaston adopted a low profile during the demonstrations, although he openly criticized the movement's use of children to draw greater sympathy for its cause. But his apparent fence-sitting belied what he was doing behind the scenes. He opened his motel for King and other Southern Christian Leadership Conference (SCLC) officials to plot their strategies, supplied them with the necessary office materials, put up bail, and secretly met with the city's white power structure to "broker for every citizen's basic rights" (*Birmingham News*, 20 Jan. 1996). His motel and home were bombed; yet he continued his effort to make peace with Birmingham's white community and opposed a plan to dispatch troops to the city, believing that local residents could come to terms without federal interference.

Gaston's negotiating with the white power structure and his criticism of King's use of small children in the demonstrations did not win him favor among many blacks. Yet as JOSEPH LOWERY, a longtime civil rights activist declared, "Without A. G. Gaston, we would have been up the creek without a boat or a fishing pole. The motel, and his money for bond, were effective tools in the struggle against segregation in Birmingham" (*Birmingham News*, 20 Jan. 1996). Gaston defended his actions: "I was convinced it was now time to use the conference table instead of the streets to try to settle differences. If wanting to spare children, save lives, bring peace is Uncle Tomism, then I wanted to be a Super Uncle Tom" (Gaston, 125). Following the demonstrations Gaston continued to meet with influential whites to effect change. He was a moving force behind the creation of Operation New Birmingham's Community Affairs Committee, which was credited with promoting cooperation and reconciliation between the races. Although his involvement in these types of organizations drew criticisms from many members of the black community, he moved ahead.

Gaston recognized that he had achieved something that others could not and was willing to share his expertise, time, and philosophy with those less fortunate. In 1966 he founded the A. G. Gaston Boys' Club of America, donating $50,000 as well as the proceeds from the sale of his autobiography, *Green Power*. He declared the Boys' Club "one of the greatest things I've done" (*Birmingham News*, 20 Dec. 1987).

Gaston created a business empire in spite of the prevailing race prejudice, relying on "green power" (the power of money) to seize the opportunities available to him. Inspired by Booker T. Washington, he became a role model for others. In 1992 *Black Enterprise* named him "Entrepreneur of the Century." He died in Birmingham.

FURTHER READING

The University of Alabama at Birmingham holds an oral history of Gaston conducted in 1976 and 1977.

Gaston, A. G. *Green Power: The Successful Way of A. G. Gaston* (1968).

Garrow, David J. *Bearing the Cross: Martin Luther King, Jr., and the Southern Christian Leadership Conference* (1986).

Ingham, John N., and Lynne B. Feldman. *African-American Business Leaders: A Biographical Dictionary* (1994).

Raines, Howell. *My Soul Is Rested: The Story of the Civil Rights Movement in the Deep South* (1977).

Obituaries: *Birmingham News*, 19 and 20 Jan. 1996.

This entry is taken from the *American National Biography* and is published here with the permission of the American Council of Learned Societies.

LYNNE B. FELDMAN

Gaston, Clarence Edwin "Cito" (17 Mar. 1944–), baseball player and manager, was born Clarence Edwin Gaston in San Antonio, Texas, to Sam Gaston, a truck driver, and Gertrude Corley, a waitress. Gaston's mother remarried during his childhood, and he was raised with five sisters. He excelled at baseball, football, and basketball at Holy Cross High in San Antonio and Solomon High School in Corpus Christi. Gaston earned the nickname "Cito" when one of his friends noted his similarity to an obscure Mexican wrestler of the same name.

Following his graduation from Solomon in 1961, Gaston worked as a garage attendant and city sanitation worker in San Antonio while playing for a semiprofessional team, the Cardona Welders. In 1963 a Milwaukee Braves scout aggressively pursued and signed Gaston after watching him play just one game in which he hit a homer and beat out an infield hit. Used to the Jim Crow laws of his hometown—segregated movie theaters and public buses—Gaston saw more of it in his minor league tenure, in smaller towns like Waycross, Georgia, and Leesburg, Florida, where he bunked at different hotels from the white players.

Gaston spent five seasons in the Braves' minor league system before being selected by the San Diego Padres in the 1968 expansion draft and breaking camp with the major league team the following spring. His best year came in 1970, when he hit 29 home runs, batted .317, and was named to the National League All-Star team. Traded back to the Braves in 1974, Gaston was a platoon outfielder and pinch-hitter for the Braves and Pirates through 1978. After a year and a half playing with a short-lived independent minor league team and the Mexican League, Gaston retired as a player in 1980.

Gaston agreed to be a minor-league hitting coach for Atlanta after being courted by his former roommate and then-vice-president for the Braves, HANK AARON. He became the Toronto Blue Jays' hitting coach the following season, and served in the job for seven and a half years. In May 1989, Toronto fired manager Jimy Williams, and turned to Gaston to be their interim manager. Though Gaston at first demurred, he eventually relented, becoming just the fourth African American manager, after

FRANK ROBINSON, LARRY DOBY, and Maury Willis. Initially given the job temporarily, Gaston earned a full-time contract after winning the division and finishing second to Robinson in the Manager of the Year award voting.

Gaston's Blue Jays won the division four out of the next five years, and he became the first black manager to win the World Series when he won back-to-back championships in 1992 and 1993. As the team faltered over the next couple of years, Gaston was let go in September 1997.

Despite Gaston's impressive resume, no other team offered him a major-league managing position. Though famously placid and even-tempered as a manager, he wasn't shy about insinuating that he thought race played a role, even wondering if job interviews he received were because teams were forced to have token interviews with minority candidates. Gaston served Toronto in smaller capacities—as hitting coach in 2000–01 and special assistant to the president in 2002—before being hired once again as the Blue Jays manager in June 2008. Gaston had two daughters, Rochelle and Shawn, with his first wife, Lena Green; adopted his second wife's (Denise's) children, Carly and Adrian; and married his third wife, Lynda, in 2003. He was elected to the Canadian Baseball Hall of Fame in 2002, and won the Jackie Robinson Lifetime Achievement Award from the Negro Leagues Baseball Museum in 2009.

FURTHER READING

Leavy, Walter. "On Top of the Baseball World." *Ebony*, May 1994.

Vecsey, George. "One Baseball Man Who Got His Chance." *New York Times*, 24 Sept. 1989.

ADAM W. GREEN

Gaston, Felecia Gail (1 Dec. 1955–), performing arts educator, was born in the Fort McPherson Army Hospital in Atlanta, Georgia, the daughter of an air force serviceman, George Gaston, and a U.S. Post Office worker, Roberta Lofton. Roberta Lofton Gaston later married and became Roberta Lofton Hayes. The same day Gaston was born, ROSA PARKS made history in Montgomery, Alabama, for refusing to let a white bus rider take her seat. Parks's refusal and subsequent arrest made a crack in the wall of segregation that ultimately caused the inequality barriers to crumble, yet segregation was still very strong in the South when Gaston was a child.

Gaston's parents separated when she was a year old, and she and her mother lived with her grandmother, Estelle Lofton, in Marietta, Georgia. Her mother worked long hours at the U.S. Post Office, and Grandmother Estelle became Gaston's primary caregiver.

In her grandmother's care, Gaston grew up surrounded by the sweet harmonies of the Sacred Hearts, Georgia's first black female gospel group. Estelle was one of the founders and an active singer in the group. Gaston grew up with a strong faith and recited frequently in the Baptist Church Sunday school. These experiences helped her develop the idea that poverty did not have to be ugly and squalid.

Gaston's grandmother instilled in her the belief that she could be a success if she had high hopes and worked hard, but Gaston lived in a society that treated her as a second-class citizen. Discrimination made a lifelong impression on the young Gaston. Her greatest dream was to learn dance at the local ballet school, but that dream was denied her because of her race, and she never forgot it. Later in life, it led her to give children the chance she never had.

When Gaston was fourteen, her mother remarried and the family moved to Los Angeles; her grandmother stayed behind in Georgia. Gaston's life changed dramatically. Los Angeles was a huge, fast-moving city. Moreover, the family moved there on 1 December 1969, and their neighborhood was racked with violence following a brutal incident between the LAPD and one of the neighborhood's African American residents.

Gaston's mother and her new husband provided a good home for Felecia, her two sisters, and her brother. With parents working during the day, the children no longer had their grandmother, family, and childhood friends around them. Gaston's mother enrolled the children in the Wilshire District's charm school to keep them occupied learning valuable social skills. There Gaston learned poise, etiquette, and self-confidence.

While attending Los Angeles City College in 1975 through 1979 Gaston worked for the Los Angeles Police Department as a radio operator. In this position she got a daily dose of the grief and tragedy that engulfed the Watts residents. She saw nothing to inspire the neighborhood children and thought that their lives would be different if they could be exposed to the better things in life. She thought she could make a difference by volunteering in church activities at the Greater Liberty Baptist Church in Los Angeles. She was secretary to the church artistic director, helped make costumes and put on plays to keep children engaged and involved in safe, constructive activities. During this period, Gaston also made time for her childhood dreams. At age twenty-four, she finally began ballet lessons.

Gaston moved to San Francisco in 1980. She majored in geography and environmental studies at the California State Universities at Hayward and San Francisco. In 1982 she also started a public relations firm called Migrations Limited, which coordinated receptions for visiting artists. She volunteered with the San Francisco International Film Festival and organized receptions for visiting filmmakers, including SPIKE LEE's first reception in San Francisco, following the debut of *She's Gotta Have It*. In addition, Gaston volunteered for Women in Film and Television. During this time, she wrote and published a book called *Gaston's Guide* (1985), a listing of more than one hundred San Francisco Bay Area black-owned restaurants.

Next, Gaston moved to Marin City, an unincorporated community in Sausalito, California. From 1984 to 1990, she was an administrative assistant, then a community relations and cultural events coordinator for the Marin City Multi-Service Center, a family service agency designed to strengthen the family. Gaston saw that, despite many caring parents, many young people became high school dropouts, drug users, and teenage mothers and fathers.

In December 1988, Gaston and Phyllis Thelen, Marin Ballet's development director, established a scholarship program for minority children. Gaston directed the program, the Performing Stars, at the Marin City Multi-Service Center. Over time, Performing Stars of Marin grew larger and the scholarships offered by major art organizations increased. These scholarships provided private lessons in the performing arts for low-income children and fostered integration in a mostly white Marin County.

Gaston's Boys to Men program included a young men's drill team, color guard and martial arts group. A Girls to Ladies program included a song and dance variety troupe and a young ladies' marching unit. In addition, Gaston started preschool music classes; a program of storytelling and reading poetry and the classics; and a photography workshop. She also provided field trips and put on a major annual performance of the Performing Stars.

As executive director of Performing Stars of Marin, Gaston took a struggling neighborhood program with no budget and turned it into a successful organization enthusiastically supported by the community. For persistently following through on her belief that all children should have a chance to reach for the stars, Gaston was recognized as a Marin Women's Hall of Fame 1999 Honoree in Education and Social Change. In 2006 she was awarded a Jefferson Award by the American Institute for Public Service for serving her community.

FURTHER READING

Kramer, Jill. *Pacific Sun*, 18 Nov. 2005.

Maddan, Heather. *San Francisco Chronicle*, 16 Apr. 2006.

MARILYN L. GEARY

Gates, Henry Louis "Skip," Jr. (16 Sept. 1950–), educator, literary and cultural critic, and leading scholar in African and African American studies, was born Louis Smith Gates in Keyser, West Virginia. Gates, nicknamed "Skip" by his mother at birth, grew up in nearby Piedmont, the son of Henry Louis Gates Sr., a mill worker and janitor, and Pauline Coleman Gates, a homemaker and seamstress. Born four years before the landmark U.S. Supreme Court decision *Brown v. Board of Education* and encouraged by his parents, he excelled in Piedmont's integrated schools, including the Davis Free School and Piedmont High School, as did his older brother Paul, known as "Rocky," who would become Chief of Oral Surgery at Bronx Lebanon Hospital.

At age fourteen, Gates experienced two cataclysmic events in his young life: the first, a misdiagnosed slipped epithesis, a hip injury that led to three surgeries in a year; and the second, his joining the Episcopal church of his father and leaving the Methodist church of his mother. After attending Peterkin, the Episcopal church camp of the diocese of West Virginia, and meeting prep school students for the first time, he applied to and was accepted at Phillips Exeter Academy in Exeter, New Hampshire. However, he stayed at Exeter only a short while before returning to Piedmont High School, where he continued to excel.

Deeply interested in the civil rights movement as a teenager, Gates delivered a fiery valedictory address upon graduation in 1968 from Piedmont High School. He attended Potomac State University in Keyser, hoping to transfer to the Ivy League in his sophomore year to study medicine. Under the supervision of the literature professor Duke Anthony Whitmore, Gates embarked on a course of study at Potomac State that grounded him firmly in the English and American literature canons, which he continued to study after transferring to Yale University in fall 1969.

At Yale, Gates, one of ninety-six black students admitted to the class of 1973, was accepted to the highly selective Five-Year B.A. Program, funded by the Carnegie Foundation, which sent twelve students to the Third World for a one-year non-academic working experience. Gates spent the academic year 1970 to 1971 working in an Anglican Mission hospital in Kilimatinde, Tanzania. Later, he and another student hitchhiked from the Indian Ocean to the Atlantic Ocean, across the Equator.

Upon returning from Africa, Gates became a history major and a student of the political historian John Morton Blum. Elected to Phi Beta Kappa in his junior year, Gates, along with eleven other students, was selected as "Scholar of the House" for his senior year and completed a book-length study of the unsuccessful West Virginia gubernatorial campaign of John D. Rockefeller IV, titled "The Making of a Governor." As a senior, he also wrote a guest column for the *Yale Daily News* and became a member of the Book and Snake Secret Society. He graduated summa cum laude from Yale with a B.A. in History in 1973.

After Yale, Gates undertook graduate studies in English Language and Literature at the University of Cambridge on a Mellon Fellowship. He studied under John Holloway, George Steiner, Raymond Williams, and Wole Soyinka, the Nigerian playwright and political activist who first encouraged Gates to get a Ph.D. Gates's dissertation was on the place of Africa and Africans in the eighteenth-century Enlightenment. In October 1973, Gates, Soyinka, and KWAME ANTHONY APPIAH, a Cambridge philosophy undergraduate, decided over dinner and drinks to realize the dream of W. E. B. DUBOIS to create an "Encyclopaedia Africana," modeled on the *Encyclopaedia Britannica*. While at Cambridge, Gates also worked as a staff correspondent in the London bureau of *Time* magazine.

In the summer of 1975, prior to returning to New Haven, Gates legally changed his name to Henry Louis Gates Jr. to honor his father. Back at Yale, he enrolled in law school and worked as a secretary for the chair of the Afro-American Studies program, Charles T. Davis. Davis championed the study of black literature as literature, not as social science. Soyinka had introduced Gates to the study of African literature and mythology, and, at Davis's insistence, Gates enrolled in Davis's graduate seminar, "The Afro-American Literary Tradition," Gates's formal introduction to African American literature. During this time, Gates also worked closely with the Yale historian of slavery, John W. Blassingame. The following year, Davis hired Gates as a lecturer in Afro-American studies and English literature, a position he held until 1979, when he completed his dissertation and became the first African American to receive a Ph.D. in English from the University of Cambridge.

That year, Gates married Sharon Adams, whom he had met while working on the Rockefeller campaign and with whom he had two daughters, Maud and Elizabeth. He became Assistant Professor of English and Afro-American Studies at Yale, where he continued his partnership with Davis, serving as co-editor on the Black Periodical Literature Project. The recipient of a MacArthur Foundation "genius grant" in 1981, Gates discovered a copy of *Our Nig: Or, Sketches from the Life of a Free Black*, a novel by the free black HARRIET E. WILSON that had fallen into obscurity almost immediately after its publication in 1859. Through rigorous archival research and biographical detective work, Gates authenticated the novel as the first by an African American woman to be published, and Gates published a new edition in 1983. He had already written several highly regarded scholarly articles, but this feat of literary and historical sleuthing made him a highly visible player in the contemporary debate about canon formation and the future of literary studies.

Yale promoted Gates to associate professor in 1984, the same year that he published the collection *Black Literature and Literary Theory*, the first essay collection to articulate an imperative for a body of theory addressing the formal, linguistic, and social structures of black literature. Gates resigned from Yale to join the faculty of Cornell University. In 1988, on the heels of his editing a special issue of the journal *Critical Inquiry*, published in 1985 as *"Race," Writing, and Difference*, and the 1987 publication of his book *Figures in Black: Words, Signs, and the Racial Self*, Cornell named Gates the W. E. B. DuBois Professor of Literature, making him the first African American to hold an endowed chair at the university.

Gates published the landmark *The Signifying Monkey: A Theory of Afro-American Literary Criticism* in 1988, winning the American Book Award in 1989. In it, Gates argued that African American literature was rooted in a vernacular language consisting of stylistic repetition, verbal dexterity, and parodic double entendres. Gates's identification of these traits of African American literature as well as his claim that they existed outside of the American mainstream and thus were misinterpreted, diminished, or entirely devalued by traditional literary critics and theorists made a dramatic impact on the field of literary studies. Gates left Cornell in 1989 for Duke University. His participation that year in the First Amendment trial of LUTHER CAMPBELL and 2 Live Crew made him a target of conservatives' wrath, both inside and outside the academy.

After two years at Duke, Gates moved to Harvard University to take charge of the floundering Department of Afro-American Studies and become the director of the W. E. B. DuBois Institute for Afro-American Research. Gates assembled what he often referred to as the "Dream Team," hiring the philosophers CORNEL WEST and Kwame Anthony Appiah, and later the historian EVELYN BROOKS HIGGINBOTHAM and the sociologists WILLIAM JULIUS WILSON and Lawrence Bobo, transforming a languishing department into the preeminent center for African and African American studies.

Throughout the 1990s, Gates gained prominence as a public intellectual, with articles and essays appearing in *Time*, the *New Yorker*, and the *New York Times*. His books began to focus less on literary theory and more on cultural criticism, and included *Loose Canons: Notes on the Culture Wars* (1992), *Colored People: A Memoir* (1994), *The Future of the Race* (with Cornel West, 1996), and *Thirteen Ways of Looking at a Black Man* (1997). For his role in shaping a national discussion about literary canon formation, and for introducing African American literature to a broad audience, in 1997 *Time* named him one of their "25 Most Influential Americans." In the 1990s, Gates also edited several influential anthologies, including *The Schomburg Library of Nineteenth-Century Black Women Writers* (1991) and *The Norton Anthology of African American Literature* (1996), as well as editing and publishing numerous slave narratives. He was awarded the National Humanities Medal in 1998 by President Bill Clinton, and was elected to the American Academy of Arts and Letters in 1999.

Also in 1999—twenty-six years after hatching their initial plan with Soyinka to realize DuBois's dream of an encyclopedia of the African diaspora—Gates and Appiah published *Encarta Africana*, an interactive CD-ROM put out by Microsoft, and a companion volume, *Africana*, which was published by Perseus Books. Gates and Appiah, the general editors, and Soyinka, the chair of the editorial board, worked with an international team of hundreds of scholars who drew on the burgeoning study of African and African American literature, art, politics, philosophy, social systems and structures, religion, music, and other disciplines to create a single authoritative text on the culture and history of the African diaspora.

After *Africana*, Gates's long-standing interest in Africa found a new outlet in documentary film. He had already produced three one-hour documentaries, "From Great Zimbabwe to Kilimatinde" in the BBC/PBS series *Great Rail Journeys*, and *The Two Nations of Black America* and *Leaving Eldridge Cleaver* for WGBH in Boston. In 2000, PBS broadcast his six-hour series *Wonders of the African World*. While recovering from a hip replacement in 2001, Gates purchased a handwritten manuscript from the early 1850s by a black woman identified as HANNAH CRAFTS. As he had done a decade earlier with *Our Nig*, he undertook the historical and literary detective work that in 2002 led to the publication of *The Bondwoman's Narrative* by Hannah Crafts, a novel that predates Wilson's and is considered one of the first novels written by an African American woman.

Gates's public profile continued to rise with new forays into mainstream media. In February 2004, PBS aired his four-hour documentary, *America Beyond the Color Line*, a study of race and class within the black community, and in August and September he had a stint as a guest columnist for the *New York Times*. Along with Evelyn Brooks Higginbotham he became the editor in chief of the *African American National Biography* (published in 2008), the largest biographical dictionary of African Americans to that date.

Gates's next major project was the PBS documentary *African American Lives*. Broadcast in February 2006, it featured several African American celebrities, including OPRAH WINFREY and QUINCY JONES. Working with a team of geneticists and genealogists, Gates traced the ancestry of his subjects and of himself back to slavery and then, through their DNA, to their African roots. The series demonstrated that slavery had not rendered African American ancestry untraceable and that advances in DNA science and genealogical research provided African Americans with the opportunity to trace their roots further than had been thought possible. Also that year, after publishing the second much-expanded edition of *Africana* in five volumes, Oxford University Press launched the online Oxford African American Studies Center, which the *Library Journal* named the Best Reference Source of 2006. As editor in chief, Gates oversaw the shaping of the largest scholarly online resource for African and African American studies to date. In 2007 Gates also edited *The Oxford W. E. B. DuBois* for OUP.

Personal and professional changes marked 2006. Gates and Sharon Adams divorced. Through research done on his own family for *African American Lives*, genealogists unearthed three sets of Gates's fourth great-grandparents, who were "Free Negros," and traced the birth of two to the middle of the 1700s. One, JOHN REDMAN, fought in the Continental Army during the Revolutionary War, leading to Gates's induction into the Sons of the American Revolution. Gates stepped down in July from the chairmanship of the department that he had steered for fifteen years, and was named the Alphonse Fletcher University Professor in October. In December, he received the Jay B. Hubbell Award for Lifetime Achievement in American Literary Studies from the Modern Language Association.

After 2006, Gates's output and involvement with literature, history, and the culture at large showed no signs of tapering off. In 2007, he produced the documentary *Oprah's Roots* and the book *Finding Oprah's Roots, Finding Your Own*. In 2008, PBS broadcast "African American Lives 2," featuring the theologian PETER GOMES the poet MAYA ANGELOU, comedian CHRIS ROCK and the singer TINA TURNER, among others. He and EVELYN BROOKS HIGGINBOTHAM co-edited *the African American National Biography* (AANB), an eight-volume biographical dictionary containing more than 4000 entries in its initial print edition published by Oxford University Press in 2008; a further four print volumes of the AANB were to be published in 2012, with 2000 more entries to be added over time to Oxford's online African American Studies Center. Additionally, Gates launched The Root.com, a daily online magazine addressing topics in African American culture and politics, in a joint venture with the Washington Post company, for which he serves as the Editor-in-Chief. Gates has also published several essays and interviews in TheRoot.com. In 2009, he published the book, *In Search of Our Roots: How 19 Extraordinary African Americans Reclaimed Their Past*, which elaborated on the stories told in the two "African American Lives" documentaries for PBS. He also edited, with Donald Yacovone, *Lincoln on Race and Slavery* (2009), and his documentary, "Looking for Lincoln," aired on PBS in February 2009, to mark the bicentennial of Lincoln's birth. In 2010, he published another book on genealogy entitled *Faces of America: How 12 Extraordinary Americans Reclaimed Their Pasts*, as well as *Tradition and the Black Atlantic: Critical Theory in the African Diaspora*. His book, *Black in Latin America*, was published in 2011, and his documentary of the same name aired on PBS in April and May of that year. In November 2011 Knopf published Gates's *Life upon These Shores: Looking at African American History (1513–2008)*. Between 2010 and 2011, Harvard University Press published six of a projected ten books making up *The Image of the Black in Western Art*, co-edited by Gates and David Bindman. The final volumes will be published between 2012 and 2014.

He continued to receive awards for his work both inside and outside the academy, including the German Cultures of Peace Award (2007), the *Wired* magazine Rave award (2007), the Frank E. Taplin, Jr., Public Intellectual Award from the Woodrow Wilson Foundation (2009), the 2008 Ralph Lowell Award from the Corporation for Public Broadcasting (2009, which is the highest award in public television), The Madison Freedom Award (2009), 2009 Empire State Archives and History Award (2009), Distinguished West Virginian Award from The HistoryMakers (2009), NAACP Image Award for a Literary Work, Non-Fiction, for *In Search of Our Roots* (2010), Lifetime Achievement Award in Genealogy and Genetics, New England Historical and Genealogical Society (2010), American Vision Award, Children's Book Press (2010), and the 2011 Media Bridge-Builder Award, Tanenbaum Center (2011). In 2011 Gates was appointed a Walter Channing Cabot Fellow at Harvard. *Booklist* named the *African American National Biography* to the "Top of the List" for Best Reference Source (2009), and "African American Lives 2" won the Gold Award in Television from the Parents' Choice Awards. *Ebony* magazine named Gates to its "Power List" twice: the "Power 100" in 2010, and the "Power 150" in 2009. By 2009 he had received 51 honorary degrees. He served on numerous boards, including the New York Public Library, the Whitney Museum, the Lincoln Center Theater, Jazz at Lincoln Center, the Aspen Institute, the Studio Museum in Harlem, the NAACP Legal Defense Fund, and the Center for Advanced Study in the Behavioral Sciences at Stanford University.

FURTHER READING

Gates, Henry Louis, Jr. *Colored People: A Memoir*. (1994).

Appiah, K. A., and H. L. Gates, eds. Introduction. *Africana: The Encyclopedia of the African and the African American Experience* (1999).

"Conversation with Henry Louis Gates, Jr," Africana Press Release. Available at www.africanaencyclopedia.com/press_release.html.

Gates, Henry Louis, Jr. "Native Sons of Liberty," *New York Times*, 6 August 2006.

Heffernan, Virginia. "Taking Black Family Trees Out of Slavery's Shadow," *New York Times*, 1 February 2006.

Hutner, Gordon. "Citation for the Jay B. Hubbell Medal for Lifetime Achievement," MLA, 28 December 2006. Available at http://als-mla.org/HMGates.htm.

Jefferson Lecturer in the Humanities, Interview, 2002. Available at www.neh.gov/whoweare/gates/interview.html.

ABBY WOLF

Gates, William "Pop" (30 Aug. 1917–1 Dec. 1999), professional basketball player, was born William Penn Gates in Decatur, Alabama. Gates moved to New York City with his family when he was three and grew up playing basketball at the Harlem YMCA. Interestingly he did not owe his nickname to this game but earned it from playing stickball with boys who thought he was older than he was. He attended Benjamin Franklin High School and helped the school's basketball team win the Public Schools Athletic League championship in 1938.

Following his graduation, Gates briefly attended Clark College in Atlanta, Georgia, but quickly went back to New York because he "didn't like the barriers of prejudice down there" (*New York Times*, 19 Feb. 1989). The 6-foot-3-inch forward and guard started playing with the Harlem Yankees. Soon thereafter the all-black Harlem Renaissance, who had seen him practice, bought Gates's contract for $100. He was one of the few athletes who went from a High School championship directly to a world championship. He won the World Professional Basketball Tournament championship with the Harlem Renaissance in his first season in 1939, finishing the season as the team's top scorer. He made $125 a month as a Renaissance rookie. In his second season, Gates claimed the title of World Tournament All-Pro, an honor he earned a total of eight times throughout his career. He stayed with the Renaissance until 1946.

In the same year he became one of the first African American players in the National Basketball League (NBL), playing for the Moline Blackhawks. During one Blackhawks game against the Syracuse Nationals in the 1946/47 season, Nationals fans stormed the court, after a hard foul by Gates against a Syracuse player, trying to get to him. Fistfights broke out across the court. The NBL branded this incident a "race riot" and reacted by returning to an all-white sport the following year. Not surprisingly, black players of that time suffered the usual indignities such as sleeping and eating separately and having to endure racial slurs from the stands. Gates met these with surprising indifference. "They're going to say (racist comments) anyway, so there's no sense getting too terribly upset. It was just something you had to put up with to make a dollar bill at that particular time" (*New York Daily News*, 13 Apr. 1997).

Gates returned to the league in 1948 with the Dayton Rens, the first and only all-black team in a white league in the 1948/49 season, serving as a player and the first black coach in the NBL. The former New York Renaissance had moved to Dayton in the middle of the season to replace the Detroit Vagabond Kings. Fearing competition from the newly formed National Basketball Association (NBA), the NBL had invited the popular Renaissance to join the league in hopes of boosting its image. Unfortunately many good players had retired or signed with other teams and the Rens finished the season in last place and, along with the NBL, ceased to exist. The NBA proved to be too strong a competitor. Gates ended his career in 1955 after serving as player/coach for the Harlem Globetrotters for five years.

Retiring from basketball, he worked as a security supervisor for the New York City Department of Social Services. Toward the end of his life, arthritis along with hip and knee replacements put him in a motorized reclining chair. When he died of heart failure at the age of eighty-two in 1999, he had been married to his wife Cleo Pennington Gates for fifty-eight years and had lived with her for fifty-seven years in the same one-bedroom apartment in Harlem.

Contemporaries called him "a marvelous player." "There was nothing he couldn't do," said Red Holzman, who played against Gates many times and coached the New York Knicks to their 1970 and 1973 titles. "He was the best black player of that time, by far" (*New York Daily News*, 13 Apr. 1997). Gates participated in over two thousand games and averaged 14 points a game "when 14 were a lot of points" (*New York Times*, 5 Dec. 1999). He was the only player to play in all ten World Pro tournaments. Gates was included as a player in the Basketball Hall of Fame in Springfield, Massachusetts, in 1989, and presented with his Harlem Globetrotters "Legends" Ring in 1995 at Madison Square Garden, New York. He continued to follow the NBA's games throughout his lifetime but remained proud of his era's assertiveness.

Marvin Gaye, performing at Radio City Music Hall in New York City, May 1983. (AP Images.)

"When we played, you had to earn your grits," he said (*New York Times*, 5 Dec. 1999).

FURTHER READING

Ashe Jr., Arthur R. *A Hard Road to Glory: A History of the African American Athlete: Basketball* (1993).

Gould, Todd. *Pioneers of the Hardwood: Indiana and the Birth of Professional Basketball* (1998).

Obituary: *New York Times*, 5 Dec. 1999.

GRETA KÖHLER

Gaye, Marvin (2 Apr. 1939–1 Apr. 1984), singer and songwriter, was born Marvin Pentz Gay Jr. in Washington, D.C., the son of Marvin Pentz Gay Sr., a Pentecostal minister, and Alberta (maiden name unknown), a domestic worker. The younger Marvin grew up in Washington, where he began his musical career by singing in the choir and playing organ at his father's church. At Cardozo High School in Washington, he played piano in a doo-wop group called the D.C. Tones. He left school after eleventh grade and enlisted in the U.S. Air Force. After a year of openly rebelling against his commanding officers and feigning mental illness, he was discharged in 1957 for inability to serve.

Gaye (as he later came to spell his name) then returned to Washington and formed a doo-wop group called the Marquees. In 1957 they recorded a single, "Wyatt Earp" and "Hey, Little School Girl," produced by blues singer and songwriter Bo Diddley, which failed commercially, and Gaye supported himself by working as a dishwasher at a whites-only drugstore lunch counter in Washington.

In 1958 Harvey Fuqua, a successful rhythm and blues singer and producer, hired the Marquees to replace his backup singers, the Moonglows. The newly formed Harvey and the Moonglows moved to Chicago in 1959, touring the United States and making several recordings on the Chess Records label.

In 1960 Gaye and Fuqua moved to Detroit in an effort to sing with Berry Gordy Jr., founder of the fledgling Motown Records label. Soon after arriving in Detroit, Gaye was signed to the Motown label as a drummer for the label's star group, the Miracles. In 1961 Gordy agreed to produce an album featuring him as a singer, and *The Soulful Moods of Marvin Gaye*, which marked the official addition of the "e" to his last name, was the result. The album departed from other Motown recordings with its jazz-based sound. It was aimed at the "crossover" white market but failed commercially. Urged on by Gordy, Gaye changed his approach to appeal to the growing black music market. In 1962 he wrote and recorded "Stubborn Kind of Fellow," a rhythm and blues dance song that failed to attract a significant white audience but reached the top ten of the R&B sales chart. "At that point I knew I'd have to travel the same road as all black artists before me—establish a soul audience and then reach beyond that," Gaye said. In 1962 Gaye performed in the first Motortown Revue, a traveling concert featuring Motown's top stars.

Gaye finally broke into the popular music charts in 1963 with "Hitch Hike," which he cowrote and recorded as a Motown single. On Dick Clark's *American Bandstand* television show, he performed a new dance named after the song. His next single, "Pride and Joy," reached the top ten of the pop chart. Later that year Gaye married Anna Gordy, the subject of "Pride and Joy" and Berry Gordy's sister. The couple adopted a son, Marvin Pentz Gaye III, in 1965. Gaye's 1963 live album, *Marvin Gaye: Live on Stage*, cemented his position as a leading rhythm and blues performer.

Gaye scored various hits for Motown in the mid-1960s, including "How Sweet It Is" and "You're a